W9-DFW-274

REFERENCE

Form 178 rev. 01-07

Presents

The World of
Professional Golf

Founded by
Mark H. McCormack

2008

sports · entertainment · media

Editor: Bev Norwood
Contributors: Andy Farrell, Doug Ferguson, Donald (Doc) Giffin, Marino Parascenzo

First published 2008
© IMG Operations, Inc. 2008

Designed and produced by Davis Design

ISBN-13: 978-1-878843-52-4
ISBN-10: 1-878843-52-4

Printed and bound in the United States.

Contents

APPENDIXES

Introduction

Rolex has done so many things over the years that were and are good for golf. Sponsorship of this publication is a prime example. My friends at Rolex, recognizing the historic and research value *The World of Professional Golf* has provided to the game continuously since the middle 1960s, stepped up in 2005 with the support necessary to continue its existence and the service it extends to the world of golf.

I well remember my conversations with my close friend and business manager, the late Mark McCormack, when he outlined his concept of filling a written gap in the game's history with an annual book carrying detailed stories and statistics covering every organized national and international tournament during that particular calendar year. The idea made complete sense to me and I encouraged him to proceed. He did, recruiting a group of talented golf journalists to work with him in producing the first edition that covered the 1966 season worldwide. Its publication has continued and grown in size and scope ever since, keeping pace with the tremendous growth of the game throughout the world.

Mark McCormack passed away in 2003, but his contribution to the historical record of golf did not die. Credit for this goes to IMG executives and others within the organization who considered the book an important continuing tribute to Mark and to Patrick Heiniger and his executive associates at Rolex, whose support has kept the literary chain intact.

Arnold Palmer
Orlando, Florida

Foreword
(Written in 1968)

It has long been my feeling that a sport as compelling as professional golf is deserving of a history, and by history I do not mean an account culled years later from the adjectives and enthusiasms of on-the-spot reports that have then sat in newspaper morgues for decades waiting for some patient drudge to paste them together and call them lore. Such works can be excellent when insight and perspective are added to the research, but this rarely happens. What I am talking about is a running history, a chronology written at the time, which would serve both as a record of the sport and as a commentary upon the sport in any given year—an annual, if you will....

When I embarked on this project two years ago (the first of these annuals was published in Great Britain in 1967), I was repeatedly told that such a compendium of world golf was impossible, that it would be years out of date before it could be assembled and published, that it would be hopelessly expensive to produce and that only the golf fanatic would want a copy anyway. In the last analysis, it was that final stipulation that spurred me on. There must be a lot of golf fanatics, I decided. I can't be the only one. And then one winter day I was sitting in Arnold Palmer's den in Latrobe, Pennsylvania, going through the usual motions of spreading papers around so that Arnold and I could discuss some business project, when Arnold happened to mention that he wanted to collect a copy of each new golf book that was published from now on, in order to build a golf library of his own. "It's really too bad that there isn't a book every year on the pro tour," he said. "Ah," I thought. "Another golf fanatic. That makes two of us." So I decided to do the book. And I have. And I hope you like it. If so, you can join Arnold and me as golf fanatics.

Mark H. McCormack
Cleveland, Ohio
January 1968

Mark H. McCormack
1930 – 2003

In 1960, Mark Hume McCormack shook hands with a young golfer named Arnold Palmer. That historic handshake established a business that would evolve into today's IMG, the world's premier sports and lifestyle marketing and management company —representing hundreds of sports figures, entertainers, models, celebrities, broadcasters, television properties, and prestigious organizations and events around the world. With just a handshake Mark McCormack had invented a global industry.

Sean McManus, President of CBS News and Sports, reflects, "I don't think it's an overstatement to say that like Henry Ford and Bill Gates, Mark McCormack literally created, fostered and led an entirely new worldwide industry. There was no sports marketing before Mark McCormack. Every athlete who's ever appeared in a commercial, or every right holder who sold their rights to anyone, owes a huge debt of gratitude to Mark McCormack."

Mark McCormack's philosophy was simple. "Be the best," he said. "Learn the business and expand by applying what you already know." This philosophy served him well, not only as an entrepreneur and CEO of IMG, but also as an author, a consultant and a confidant to a host of global leaders in the world of business, politics, finance, science, sports and entertainment.

He was among the most-honored entrepreneurs of his time. *Sports Illustrated* recognized him as "The Most Powerful Man in Sports." In 1999, ESPN's Sports Century listed him as one of the century's 10 "Most Influential People in the Business of Sport."

Golf Magazine called McCormack "the most powerful man in golf" and honored him along with Arnold Palmer, Gerald Ford, Dwight D. Eisenhower, Bob Hope and Ben Hogan as one of the 100 all-time "American Heroes of Golf." *Tennis* magazine and *Racquet* magazine named him "the most powerful man in tennis." Tennis legend Billie Jean King believes, "Mark McCormack was the king of sports marketing. He shaped the way all sports are marketed around the world. He was the first in the marketplace, and his influence on the world of sports, particularly his ability to combine athlete representation, property development and television broadcasting, will forever be the standard of the industry."

The London *Sunday Times* listed him as one of the 1000 people who influenced the 20th century. Alastair Cooke on the BBC said simply that "McCormack was the Oracle; the creator of the talent industry, the maker of people famous in their profession famous to the rest of the world and making for them a fortune in the process … He took on as clients people already famous in their profession as golfer, opera singer, author, footballer, racing car driver, violinist—and from time to time if they needed special help, a prime minister, or even the Pope."

McCormack was honored posthumously by the Golf Writers Association of America with the 2004 William D. Richardson Award, the organization's highest honor, "Given to recognize an individual who has consistently made an outstanding contribution to golf."

Among McCormack's other honors were the 2001 PGA Distinguished Service Award, given to those who have helped perpetuate the values and ideals of the PGA of America. He was also named a Commander of the Royal Order of the Polar Star by the King of Sweden (the highest honor for a person living outside of Sweden) for his contribution to the Nobel Foundation.

Journalist Frank Deford states, "There have been what we love to call dynasties in every sport. IMG has been different. What this one brilliant man, Mark McCormack, created is the only dynasty ever over all sport."

Through IMG, Mark McCormack demonstrated the value of sports and lifestyle activities as effective corporate marketing tools, but more importantly, his lifelong dedication to his vocation—begun with just a simple handshake—brought enjoyment to millions of people worldwide who watch and cheer their heroes and heroines. That is his legacy.

ROLEX

Looking back over another exciting year of intense competition on the professional golf circuit, this 42nd edition of *Rolex presents the World of Professional Golf* highlights a number of outstanding events and achievements during 2007.

To celebrate 40 years of association between the brand and the world of golf, Rolex invited Arnold Palmer, Gary Player and Jack Nicklaus in July to a ceremony at its Geneva headquarters. This memorable meeting was the first time that Rolex had had the honour of receiving the "Big Three" together.

Since Arnold Palmer became the first Rolex Testimonee, Rolex has continued to strengthen its relationship to golf, developing partnerships over the years with a number of important tournaments, associations and personalities. The year 2007 saw Lorena Ochoa, a Rolex Testimonee, climb to number one in the Rolex Rankings after winning her first Major at St Andrews, home of the Royal and Ancient.

Rolex is especially proud to be a sponsor of all four Major tournaments in men's golf. As of 2008, it has become an International Partner of the Masters Tournament at Augusta. In addition, the brand has renewed its affiliation with the Ryder Cup until 2014, when the tournament will be held in Europe at Gleneagles, and it continues its association with the Solheim Cup as a Global Partner.

Rolex is proud of the support it lends to this prestigious game and to be associated with promoting the heritage and values of golf around the world. The twenty men and women who are our Testimonees in the sport embody the rigour, precision and the passion in the pursuit of perfection that is a hallmark of the brand.

Golf is Rolex!

Patrick Heiniger
Managing Director
Chief Executive Officer
Rolex SA
March 2008

Rolex and Golf

The late Mark H. McCormack (left) and the late Andre Heiniger were great friends and business associates.

Mark H. McCormack (second from right) with Jack Nicklaus, Gary Player and Arnold Palmer in their prime.

Patrick Heiniger (second from right) welcomed Jack Nicklaus, Gary Player and Arnold Palmer to Geneva in July 2007.

Rolex's Top 10 of Women's Golf

David Cannon/Getty Images

1. Lorena Ochoa (Mexico) 17.63 points

Andy Lyons/Getty Images

2. Suzann Pettersen (Norway) 8.34 points

Ezra Shaw/Getty Images

3. Karrie Webb (Australia) 8.30 points

David Cannon/Getty Images

4. Annika Sorenstam (Sweden) 8.28 points

5. Paula Creamer (USA) 6.93 points

6. Cristie Kerr (USA) 6.88 points

7. Ji-Yai Shin (Korea) 5.54 points

8. Juli Inkster (USA) 5.54 points

9. Mi Hyun Kim (Korea) 5.34 points

10. Se Ri Pak (Korea) 5.27 points

David Cannon/Getty Images

U.S. Open Championship

Warren Little/Getty Images

Chris Turvey

PLAYER
WELL PLAYED
PADRAIG
SEE YOU AT
ROYAL
BIRKDALE
2008

The Open Championship

Rolex and Sport

Since 1927, Rolex has been associated with the quest for excellence in sport, when it placed a Rolex Oyster on the wrist of a young swimmer, Mercedes Gleitze, as she swam across the English Channel. In 1933, Rolex began to sponsor Himalayan and polar expeditions, including the first successful ascent of Everest by Sir Edmund Hillary in 1953.

Today Rolex supports top sporting and cultural events all over the world. It is present at more than 150 events in the realms of golf, yachting, tennis, equestrian events, motor sports, exploration, culture and the arts, as well as philanthropic awards programs. Because of the commitment and continuity of these relationships, Rolex is seen not only as a sponsor ... but as a real partner.

Chris Turvey

Phil Mickelson

Stan Badz/PGA Tour/WireImage

Presidents Cup captains Gary Player and Jack Nicklaus

Chris Turvey

Lorena Ochoa and Annika Sorenstam at the Ricoh Women's British Open at St. Andrews.

Chris Turvey

Evian Masters

Chris Turvey

PGA Championship

Adam Scott

Robert Trent Jones, Jr.

Retief Goosen

Luke Donald

Trevor Immelman

Rolex Rankings

The story of women's professional golf in 2008 was the rise of Lorena Ochoa to the No. 1 position on the Rolex Rankings. The young Mexican, who won eight times, reached the top early in the year then claimed her first major championship in the Ricoh Women's British Open and wrapped up the year with the ADT Championship and its $1 million first prize.

Also rising fast in women's golf was Suzann Pettersen of Norway, whose six victories included a major title at the McDonald's LPGA Championship.

Meanwhile Annika Sorenstam, who was No. 1, had her year wrecked by a ruptured disk in her neck and a bulging disk in her back. The Swede made only 13 starts for 25th place on the LPGA money list. But Sorenstam ended the year on a positive note with her only victory, not on the LPGA Tour but in the Dubai Ladies Classic.

Climbing from No. 2, Ochoa finished the year with a 17.63 points average on the Rolex Rankings, more than double the 8.34 average of the new No. 2, Pettersen, who began the year with the No. 51 world ranking. Karrie Webb, who had two victories, both in Australia, her home country, was No. 3 (the same position as in 2007) with an 8.30 average, Sorenstam was No. 4 with an 8.28 average (down from a 14.42 average), and Paula Creamer, an American with two LPGA victories, rounded out the top five with a 6.93 average.

The top 10 of the Rolex Rankings consisted of three Americans, three South Koreans, and one player each from Mexico, Norway, Australia and Sweden. The last five on that list were No. 6 Cristie Kerr, an American and the U.S. Women's Open champion, No. 7 Ji-Yai Shin of South Korea, No. 8 Juli Inkster of the United States, No. 9 Mi Hyun Kim and No. 10 Se Ri Pak, both of South Korea.

Morgan Pressel, a major winner in the Kraft Nabisco Championship, was ranked No. 12. Michelle Wie dropped 60 positions, from No. 13 to No. 73, in a disastrous year.

The Rolex Rankings—which was developed at the May 2004 World Congress of Women's Golf—is sanctioned by the five major women's professional golf tours: the Ladies Professional Golf Association (LPGA), Ladies European Tour (LET), Ladies Professional Golfers' Association of Japan (JLPGA), Korea Ladies Professional Golf Association (KLPGA), Australian Ladies Professional Golf (ALPG) and the Ladies' Golf Union (LGU).

The five major golf tours and the LGU developed the rankings and the protocol that governs the ranking while R2IT, an independent software development company, was retained to develop the software and to maintain the rankings on a weekly basis. The official events from all of the tours are taken into account and points are awarded according to the strength of the field, with the exception of the four major championships on the LPGA Tour schedule and the Futures Tour events, which have a fixed points distribution. The players' points averages are determined by taking the number of points awarded over a two-year rolling period and dividing that by the number of tournaments played, with a minimum divisor of 35.

The Rolex Rankings are updated and released following the completion of the previous week's tournaments around the world.

Rolex Rankings
(As of December 31, 2007)

Rank	Player	Country	No. of Events	Average Points	Total Points
1	Lorena Ochoa	Mex	51	17.63	899.03
2	Suzann Pettersen	Nor	51	8.34	425.24
3	Karrie Webb	Aus	47	8.30	390.23
4	Annika Sorenstam	Swe	37	8.28	306.49
5	Paula Creamer	USA	56	6.93	388.27
6	Cristie Kerr	USA	51	6.88	350.94
7	Ji-Yai Shin	Kor	43	5.54	238.36
8	Juli Inkster	USA	41	5.54	227.01
9	Mi Hyun Kim	Kor	59	5.34	314.91
10	Se Ri Pak	Kor	46	5.27	242.61
11	Jeong Jang	Kor	57	5.10	290.46
12	Morgan Pressel	USA	50	5.06	252.85
13	Momoko Ueda	Jpn	66	4.91	323.93
14	Jee Young Lee	Kor	54	4.75	256.67
15	Stacy Prammanasudh	USA	50	4.64	232.15
16	Brittany Lincicome	USA	49	4.47	218.89
17	Sakura Yokomine	Jpn	66	4.28	282.68
18	Ai Miyazato	Jpn	54	4.27	230.76
19	Seon Hwa Lee	Kor	57	4.22	240.37
20	Shiho Oyama	Jpn	68	4.19	285.21
21	Yuri Fudoh	Jpn	45	4.17	187.79
22	Natalie Gulbis	USA	51	4.16	211.91
23	Mi-Jeong Jeon	Kor	63	4.12	259.38
24	Sherri Steinhauer	USA	48	3.88	186.31
25	Catriona Matthew	Sco	41	3.76	154.21
26	Na Zhang	Chn	31	3.76	131.49
27	Sophie Gustafson	Swe	51	3.70	188.87
28	Eun Hee Ji	Kor	39	3.68	143.53
29	Angela Park	Bra	46	3.68	169.25
30	Nicole Castrale	USA	49	3.66	179.44
31	Maria Hjorth	Swe	61	3.62	220.99
32	Miki Saiki	Jpn	33	3.40	119.10
33	Angela Stanford	USA	49	3.39	166.12
34	Pat Hurst	USA	46	3.27	150.47
35	Shi Hyun Ahn	Kor	39	3.25	126.57
36	Hee-Won Han	Kor	35	3.23	113.01
37	Sun Ju Ahn	Kor	36	3.20	115.37
38	Laura Davies	Eng	63	3.01	189.62
39	Akiko Fukushima	Jpn	55	2.97	163.36
40	Miho Koga	Jpn	67	2.88	193.23
41	Laura Diaz	USA	47	2.84	133.65
42	Sarah Lee	Kor	53	2.83	149.90
43	Julieta Granada	Par	57	2.69	153.23
44	Hyun-Ju Shin	Kor	63	2.56	160.97
45	Shinobu Moromizato	Jpn	65	2.55	165.91
46	Christina Kim	USA	58	2.43	141.11
47	In-Kyung Kim	Kor	26	2.32	81.06
48	Reilley Rankin	USA	45	2.30	103.64
49	Na Yeon Choi	Kor	38	2.15	81.72
50	Akane Iijima	Jpn	64	2.12	135.66

Rank	Player	Country	No. of Events	Average Points	Total Points
51	Meaghan Francella	USA	46	2.08	95.64
52	Ji-Hee Lee	Kor	57	1.99	113.67
53	Brittany Lang	USA	54	1.98	106.71
54	Jin Joo Hong	Kor	36	1.98	71.10
55	Yuko Mitsuka	Jpn	30	1.93	67.48
56	Rachel Hetherington	Aus	53	1.92	101.72
57	Erina Hara	Jpn	33	1.91	67.00
58	Young Kim	Kor	51	1.88	96.08
59	Hee Young Park	Kor	37	1.86	68.89
60	Chie Arimura	Jpn	48	1.84	88.09
61	Lindsey Wright	Aus	54	1.82	98.25
62	Mie Nakata	Jpn	62	1.81	112.49
63	Na On Min	Kor	21	1.80	63.11
64	Joo Mi Kim	Kor	51	1.79	91.39
65	Gwladys Nocera	Fra	44	1.77	78.03
66	Nikki Campbell	Aus	59	1.76	103.92
67	Meena Lee	Kor	55	1.75	96.46
68	Yun-Jye Wei	Twn	68	1.73	117.33
69	In-Bee Park	Kor	46	1.68	77.50
70	Hyun Hee Moon	Kor	31	1.68	58.78
71	Linda Wessberg	Swe	41	1.67	68.63
72	Hiromi Mogi	Jpn	69	1.67	115.26
73	Michelle Wie	USA	16	1.62	56.85
74	Wendy Ward	USA	46	1.61	74.26
75	Mhairi McKay	Sco	36	1.56	56.17
76	Yui Kawahara	Jpn	67	1.53	102.74
77	Gloria Park	Kor	51	1.53	78.09
78	Bo-Bae Song	Kor	49	1.50	73.69
79	Jimin Kang	Kor	43	1.49	63.93
80	Michele Redman	USA	41	1.41	57.61
81	Midori Yoneyama	Jpn	58	1.38	79.78
82	Becky Brewerton	Wal	34	1.35	47.25
83	Il Mi Chung	Kor	57	1.32	75.49
84	Candie Kung	Twn	42	1.32	55.26
85	Trish Johnson	Eng	36	1.31	47.09
86	Mikiyo Nishizuka	Jpn	66	1.31	86.23
87	Kyeong Bae	Kor	56	1.30	73.01
88	Diana D`Alessio	USA	53	1.30	68.81
89	Namika Omata	Jpn	40	1.29	51.52
90	Eun-A Lim	Kor	33	1.28	44.79
91	Janice Moodie	Sco	35	1.26	44.05
92	Karen Stupples	Eng	32	1.25	43.59
93	Hye Jung Choi	Kor	48	1.24	59.56
94	Birdie Kim	Kor	45	1.23	55.28
95	Amy Hung	Twn	50	1.23	61.26
96	Michiko Hattori	Jpn	61	1.22	74.70
97	Saiki Fujita	Jpn	61	1.21	73.92
98	Rui Kitada	Jpn	59	1.20	70.96
99	Karine Icher	Fra	52	1.17	60.61
100	Kuniko Maeda	Jpn	66	1.16	76.58

Rank	Player	Country	No. of Events	Average Points	Total Points
101	Yukari Baba	Jpn	65	1.16	75.31
102	Kaori Higo	Jpn	57	1.15	65.63
103	Helen Alfredsson	Swe	34	1.14	39.78
104	So-Hee Kim	Kor	44	1.14	50.01
105	Jae-Hee Bae	Kor	62	1.10	68.32
106	Lorie Kane	Can	51	1.09	55.55
107	Alena Sharp	Can	46	1.08	49.56
108	Becky Morgan	Wal	51	1.08	54.84
109	Ayako Uehara	Jpn	72	1.07	77.21
110	Hiroko Yamaguchi	Jpn	69	1.07	73.71
111	Beth Bader	USA	50	1.05	52.68
112	Tamie Durdin	Aus	56	1.05	58.97
113	Silvia Cavalleri	Ita	46	1.05	48.41
114	Heather Young	USA	53	1.01	53.48
115	Nikki Garrett	Aus	38	0.99	37.79
116	Bettina Hauert	Ger	36	0.99	35.75
117	Wendy Doolan	Aus	37	0.99	36.66
118	Sung Ah Yim	Kor	48	0.97	46.72
119	Iben Tinning	Den	28	0.97	34.03
120	Karin Sjodin	Swe	46	0.97	44.68
121	Ji-Yeon Han	Kor	61	0.97	58.87
122	Joanne Mills	Aus	36	0.96	34.70
123	Carin Koch	Swe	46	0.96	44.23
124	Young Jo	Kor	48	0.95	45.63
125	Aree Song	Kor	46	0.94	43.34
126	Michie Ohba	Jpn	52	0.94	48.91
127	Teresa Lu	Twn	43	0.93	40.06
128	Marisa Baena	Col	32	0.92	32.30
129	Nancy Scranton	USA	47	0.91	42.81
130	Mihoko Takahashi	Jpn	60	0.90	54.04
131	Ran Hong	Kor	38	0.90	34.14
132	Giulia Sergas	Ita	44	0.90	39.51
133	Rebecca Hudson	Eng	36	0.90	32.25
134	Sophie Giquel	Fra	36	0.88	31.67
135	Yun-Joo Jeong	Kor	60	0.88	52.59
136	Yuko Saitoh	Jpn	63	0.87	54.72
137	Virginie Lagoutte-Clement	Fra	41	0.86	35.40
138	Nobuko Kizawa	Jpn	68	0.84	56.80
139	Liselotte Neumann	Swe	42	0.83	35.04
140	Young Ran Jo	Kor	31	0.83	29.15
141	Toshimi Kimura	Jpn	56	0.83	46.30
142	Veronica Zorzi	Ita	40	0.83	33.03
143	Sun Young Yoo	Kor	49	0.82	40.42
144	Jeong-Eun Lee	Kor	28	0.82	28.84
145	Ji Na Lim	Kor	33	0.82	28.73
146	Carri Wood	USA	32	0.81	28.49
147	Yuka Shiroto	Jpn	62	0.81	50.46
148	Charlotte Mayorkas	USA	36	0.80	28.93
149	Kim Saiki-Maloney	USA	35	0.80	28.07
150	Beth Daniel	USA	20	0.80	28.03

Rank	Player	Country	No. of Events	Average Points	Total Points
151	Katherine Hull	Aus	50	0.79	39.48
152	Ji-Hyun Lee	Kor	41	0.77	31.65
153	Soo Young Moon	Kor	46	0.77	35.28
154	Kaori Aoyama	Jpn	14	0.77	26.81
155	Dorothy Delasin	USA	45	0.76	34.42
156	Hee Kyung Seo	Kor	30	0.75	26.28
157	Mihoko Iseri	Jpn	46	0.75	34.28
158	Mayumi Shimomura	Jpn	63	0.74	46.81
159	Chieko Amanuma	Jpn	62	0.73	45.31
160	Mayu Hattori	Jpn	16	0.73	25.56
161	Ya Ni Tseng	Twn	9	0.72	25.10
162	Leta Lindley	USA	24	0.71	24.88
163	Hae-Jung Kim	Kor	32	0.70	24.35
164	Ji-Young Oh	Kor	22	0.69	24.25
165	Na-Rr Lee	Kor	63	0.69	43.51
166	Minea Blomqvist	Fin	43	0.69	29.54
167	Kim Hall	USA	32	0.68	23.82
168	Kirsty Taylor	Eng	36	0.68	24.49
169	Grace Park	Kor	31	0.68	23.80
170	Junko Omote	Jpn	59	0.67	39.74
171	Kurumi Dohi	Jpn	40	0.67	26.88
172	Yun-Hee Ku	Kor	68	0.67	45.62
173	Mitsuko Kawasaki	Jpn	66	0.66	43.82
174	Paula Marti	Sp	18	0.66	23.24
175	Louise Stahle	Swe	32	0.66	23.22
176	Kasumi Fujii	Jpn	52	0.66	34.09
177	Amy Yang	Kor	16	0.65	22.87
178	Patricia Meunier-Lebouc	Fra	45	0.65	29.22
179	Marcy Hart	USA	43	0.65	27.92
180	Meg Mallon	USA	26	0.64	22.36
181	Yasuko Satoh	Jpn	62	0.64	39.51
182	Sherri Turner	USA	42	0.64	26.75
183	Yuka Irie	Jpn	59	0.63	37.42
184	Yayoi Arasaki	Jpn	30	0.63	22.12
185	Mikaela Parmlid	Swe	42	0.63	26.36
186	Lisa Hall	Eng	43	0.62	26.73
187	Maiko Wakabayashi	Jpn	21	0.62	21.67
188	Iyoko Wada	Jpn	33	0.61	21.51
189	Julie Lu	Twn	60	0.61	36.85
190	Sarah Kemp	Aus	38	0.61	23.29
191	Brandie Burton	USA	33	0.61	21.21
192	Martina Eberl	Ger	35	0.60	21.15
193	Da Ye Na	Kor	29	0.60	21.06
194	Keiko Sasaki	Jpn	66	0.60	39.41
195	Asuka Tsujimura	Jpn	16	0.59	20.68
196	Yuriko Ohtsuka	Jpn	51	0.58	29.78
197	Eun-Hye Lee	Kor	62	0.58	36.08
198	Hsiu-Feng Tseng	Twn	42	0.58	24.35
199	Bo Kyung Kim	Kor	32	0.58	20.21
200	Ya Huei Lu	Twn	51	0.57	29.04

Official World Golf Ranking

(As of December 31, 2007)

Ranking		Player	Country	Points Average	Total Points	No. of Events	05/06 Points Lost	2007 Points Gained
1	(1)	Tiger Woods	USA	19.62	784.60	40	-756.18	689.60
2	(3)	Phil Mickelson	USA	8.72	383.46	44	-312.38	410.70
3	(2)	Jim Furyk	USA	6.55	327.55	50	-390.84	235.36
4	(5)	Ernie Els	SAf	6.51	377.55	58	-261.23	351.06
5	(63)	Steve Stricker	USA	6.45	257.94	40	-98.05	272.04
6	(51)	Justin Rose	Eng	6.00	311.84	52	-133.04	301.55
7	(4)	Adam Scott	Aus	5.81	284.52	49	-296.71	215.48
8	(8)	Padraig Harrington	Ire	5.57	317.46	57	-244.62	252.80
9	(29)	K.J. Choi	Kor	5.15	298.44	58	-180.13	297.82
10	(7)	Vijay Singh	Fij	5.08	309.88	61	-344.89	326.01
11	(39)	Rory Sabbatini	SAf	4.96	253.10	51	-161.10	284.28
12	(11)	Sergio Garcia	Spn	4.78	243.75	51	-238.11	232.85
13	(10)	Geoff Ogilvy	Aus	4.65	218.47	47	-245.45	194.72
14	(28)	Angel Cabrera	Arg	4.46	227.29	51	-144.41	216.59
15	(54)	Zach Johnson	USA	4.17	208.32	50	-154.68	233.63
16	(12)	Henrik Stenson	Swe	4.06	219.33	54	-242.85	221.74
17	(9)	Luke Donald	Eng	3.95	201.27	51	-237.13	168.93
18	(87)	Aaron Baddeley	Aus	3.94	208.79	53	-109.75	231.13
19	(13)	Trevor Immelman	SAf	3.78	204.26	54	-201.75	156.99
20	(42)	Niclas Fasth	Swe	3.43	178.11	52	-124.89	179.58
21	(15)	Paul Casey	Eng	3.41	173.67	51	-186.56	150.45
22	(34)	Ian Poulter	Eng	3.35	201.27	60	-144.88	164.78
23	(49)	Lee Westwood	Eng	3.27	183.13	56	-109.59	162.49
24	(26)	Stewart Cink	USA	3.21	166.83	52	-144.33	147.80
25	(52)	Scott Verplank	USA	3.21	153.88	48	-128.27	168.17
26	(6)	Retief Goosen	SAf	3.14	191.69	61	-311.53	164.81
27	(80)	Toru Taniguchi	Jpn	3.04	157.82	52	-75.74	135.94
28	(109)	Andres Romero	Arg	2.94	144.30	49	-59.70	144.09
29	(23)	Tim Clark	SAf	2.93	137.60	47	-153.01	119.80
30	(44)	Arron Oberholser	USA	2.78	122.41	44	-102.95	113.86
31	(136)	Woody Austin	USA	2.71	159.99	59	-75.56	163.42
32	(40)	Brett Wetterich	USA	2.70	148.77	55	-125.76	129.43
33	(43)	Stephen Ames	Can	2.68	118.02	44	-113.65	113.96
34	(219)	Hunter Mahan	USA	2.67	152.02	57	-56.53	158.14
35	(45)	Mike Weir	Can	2.66	132.77	50	-105.93	118.68
36	(22)	Stuart Appleby	Aus	2.62	146.86	56	-167.37	139.01
37	(21)	Nick O'Hern	Aus	2.62	138.73	53	-155.75	127.37
38	(73)	Miguel A. Jimenez	Spn	2.59	137.12	53	-100.77	138.43
39	(24)	Shingo Katayama	Jpn	2.59	142.20	55	-129.40	102.69
40	(65)	Richard Green	Aus	2.58	111.01	43	-93.34	102.48
41	(31)	Robert Karlsson	Swe	2.55	145.44	57	-128.65	103.21
42	(82)	Charles Howell	USA	2.54	144.99	57	-135.08	183.64
43	(19)	David Toms	USA	2.51	110.46	44	-165.72	117.45
44	(196)	Richard Sterne	SAf	2.46	118.19	48	-64.60	142.10
45	(204)	Boo Weekley	USA	2.45	132.55	54	-57.28	150.03
46	(157)	Soren Hansen	Den	2.41	125.28	52	-52.45	119.53
47	(243)	Brandt Snedeker	USA	2.37	139.86	59	-46.13	149.42
48	(115)	Nick Dougherty	Eng	2.35	126.87	54	-82.44	132.82
49	(143)	Mark Calcavecchia	USA	2.33	128.28	55	-85.74	152.70
50	(105)	Anders Hansen	Den	2.29	109.97	48	-72.28	114.03

( ) Ranking in brackets indicates position as of December 31, 2006.

Ranking		Player	Country	Points Average	Total Points	No. of Events	05/06 Points Lost	2007 Points Gained
51	(47)	Robert Allenby	Aus	2.28	127.51	56	-163.45	132.09
52	(30)	Rod Pampling	Aus	2.24	123.32	55	-147.91	107.58
53	(50)	Bradley Dredge	Wal	2.10	94.52	45	-88.97	76.14
54	(166)	Peter Hanson	Swe	2.08	103.96	50	-56.44	114.72
55	(68)	John Senden	Aus	2.07	126.22	61	-105.68	113.40
56	(117)	Camilo Villegas	Col	2.02	112.85	56	-84.68	111.02
57	(17)	Colin Montgomerie	Sco	2.01	110.32	55	-185.05	88.83
58	(86)	Peter Lonard	Aus	2.01	112.32	56	-79.19	103.44
59	(263)	Brendan Jones	Aus	2.00	92.21	46	-36.17	95.23
60	(98)	Jonathan Byrd	USA	1.93	82.98	43	-67.19	75.31
61	(36)	Carl Pettersson	Swe	1.93	119.50	62	-160.04	100.24
62	(355)	Mikko Ilonen	Fin	1.93	77.06	40	-28.09	84.33
63	(95)	Jerry Kelly	USA	1.88	112.90	60	-97.24	119.60
64	(88)	Simon Dyson	Eng	1.84	116.06	63	-91.67	104.47
65	(67)	Sean O'Hair	USA	1.83	107.74	59	-102.36	96.16
65	(127)	John Rollins	USA	1.83	104.09	57	-95.91	128.16
67	(16)	Davis Love	USA	1.82	80.24	44	-150.90	58.08
68	(96)	Hideto Tanihara	Jpn	1.77	86.94	49	-56.89	63.08
69	(137)	Soren Kjeldsen	Den	1.76	98.84	56	-56.03	90.33
70	(173)	Pat Perez	USA	1.73	79.35	46	-58.25	92.82
71	(18)	Jose Maria Olazabal	Spn	1.72	74.16	43	-165.09	56.81
72	(156)	Prayad Marksaeng	Tha	1.72	103.10	60	-61.66	95.52
73	(110)	Heath Slocum	USA	1.71	99.24	58	-84.43	106.31
74	(79)	Ryan Moore	USA	1.70	88.43	52	-68.15	84.24
75	(533)	Anthony Kim	USA	1.70	67.99	40	-26.53	82.67
76	(164)	Martin Kaymer	Ger	1.69	67.54	40	-32.56	56.42
77	(37)	Jeev Milkha Singh	Ind	1.67	128.68	77	-124.32	59.79
78	(151)	Bernhard Langer	Ger	1.65	70.97	43	-59.17	79.75
79	(20)	Chris DiMarco	USA	1.64	90.42	55	-157.36	71.66
80	(205)	Steve Webster	Eng	1.63	71.67	44	-32.24	71.20
81	(38)	Lucas Glover	USA	1.63	97.51	60	-137.73	82.81
82	(146)	Fredrik Jacobson	Swe	1.62	64.92	40	-50.41	65.54
83	(55)	Charl Schwartzel	SAf	1.61	93.46	58	-104.76	66.60
84	(287)	Ross Fisher	Eng	1.59	86.05	54	-32.67	85.92
85	(32)	Joe Durant	USA	1.59	89.02	56	-102.30	37.59
86	(140)	Liang Wen-chong	Chi	1.58	88.74	56	-63.48	87.26
87	(84)	Jyoti Randhawa	Ind	1.56	79.57	51	-63.67	65.02
88	(106)	Raphael Jacquelin	Frn	1.55	80.55	52	-72.20	84.54
89	(126)	Justin Leonard	USA	1.55	85.14	55	-58.68	85.55
90	(129)	G. Fernandez-Castano	Spn	1.54	80.02	52	-57.74	72.57
91	(138)	Steve Flesch	USA	1.51	96.91	64	-60.40	83.59
92	(58)	Kenny Perry	USA	1.51	69.64	46	-89.34	70.22
93	(27)	Chad Campbell	USA	1.50	79.45	53	-148.67	72.90
94	(33)	Y.E. Yang	Kor	1.50	70.30	47	-88.58	21.36
95	(78)	Nathan Green	Aus	1.48	99.41	67	-91.45	76.27
96	(75)	Thongchai Jaidee	Tha	1.48	81.37	55	-75.13	64.88
97	(194T)	Markus Brier	Aut	1.47	74.95	51	-46.23	73.80
98	(111)	David Smail	NZl	1.47	76.31	52	-51.39	58.96
99	(69)	Vaughn Taylor	USA	1.47	79.13	54	-109.38	78.92
100	(81)	Troy Matteson	USA	1.46	84.92	58	-73.49	58.50

( ) Ranking in brackets indicates position as of December 31, 2006.

Ranking		Player	Country	Points Average	Total Points	No. of Events	05/06 Points Lost	2007 Points Gained
101	(368)	Oliver Wilson	Eng	1.46	78.88	54	-33.85	88.90
102	(1309T)	Joost Luiten	Hol	1.46	58.34	40	-8.52	66.86
103	(57)	Shaun Micheel	USA	1.45	86.78	60	-94.49	50.72
104	(46)	Thomas Bjorn	Den	1.44	75.09	52	-112.23	59.93
105	(135)	Paul Goydos	USA	1.44	62.03	43	-55.40	70.59
106	(132)	Graeme McDowell	Nir	1.43	79.86	56	-62.35	79.25
107	(168)	Bubba Watson	USA	1.42	76.87	54	-69.62	87.46
108	(207)	Phillip Archer	Eng	1.40	83.95	60	-41.18	78.51
109	(1309T)	Ross McGowan	Eng	1.40	55.82	40	-7.69	63.52
110	(160)	Tomohiro Kondo	Jpn	1.39	69.55	50	-45.63	58.09
111	(92)	Billy Mayfair	USA	1.39	81.80	59	-89.18	82.64
112	(337)	Louis Oosthuizen	SAf	1.38	69.23	50	-36.22	81.68
113	(70)	J.J. Henry	USA	1.38	74.61	54	-99.81	54.64
114	(341)	Rocco Mediate	USA	1.38	55.01	40	-38.39	73.32
115	(1309T)	George McNeill	USA	1.37	54.86	40	-6.87	61.73
116	(170)	Ken Duke	USA	1.35	81.22	60	-50.54	78.86
117	(56)	Tom Lehman	USA	1.35	58.07	43	-83.81	50.55
118	(72)	Dean Wilson	USA	1.35	83.39	62	-98.34	62.63
119	(74)	Ben Curtis	USA	1.34	69.44	52	-81.78	50.03
120	(131)	Daniel Chopra	Swe	1.33	97.24	73	-71.85	81.50
120	(544)	Richard Johnson	Wal	1.33	62.60	47	-10.44	62.54
122	(183)	Craig Parry	Aus	1.32	62.06	47	-35.25	57.63
123	(48)	Johan Edfors	Swe	1.31	64.19	49	-92.08	32.93
124	(270)	Mark Wilson	USA	1.28	63.81	50	-49.53	81.93
125	(197)	Alejandro Canizares	Spn	1.27	50.99	40	-27.76	43.08
126	(104)	Bo Van Pelt	USA	1.26	73.27	58	-86.74	73.11
127	(60)	Brett Quigley	USA	1.26	73.25	58	-100.21	41.01
128	(178)	Hiroyuki Fujita	Jpn	1.25	63.92	51	-40.59	53.00
129	(435T)	Lee Dong-hwan	Kor	1.25	51.32	41	-15.81	52.17
130	(202)	Charley Hoffman	USA	1.24	74.55	60	-54.85	81.55
131	(59)	Anthony Wall	Eng	1.23	67.88	55	-78.45	39.94
132	(327)	Jose Coceres	Arg	1.23	49.20	40	-32.64	61.16
133	(123)	Peter O'Malley	Aus	1.23	66.28	54	-49.91	51.85
134	(53)	Bart Bryant	USA	1.21	61.53	51	-118.08	61.17
135	(351)	Gregory Havret	Frn	1.21	67.56	56	-30.55	73.87
136	(261)	Jeff Quinney	USA	1.19	68.09	57	-47.79	80.81
137	(171)	Nick Watney	USA	1.19	65.66	55	-58.97	65.63
138	(211)	Gregory Bourdy	Frn	1.19	59.33	50	-36.32	53.74
139	(345)	Chapchai Nirat	Tha	1.18	61.26	52	-26.17	67.02
140	(122)	Tetsuji Hiratsuka	Jpn	1.18	62.35	53	-58.22	46.17
141	(657T)	Michael Lorenzo-Vera	Frn	1.18	47.04	40	-9.30	49.37
142	(303)	Robert-Jan Derksen	Hol	1.18	64.65	55	-32.21	70.48
143	(398)	Alastair Forsyth	Sco	1.18	59.94	51	-23.93	63.55
144	(338)	Lu Wen-teh	Twn	1.17	46.67	40	-21.77	48.57
145	(152)	Brett Rumford	Aus	1.16	66.15	57	-47.18	52.73
146	(91)	Taichi Teshima	Jpn	1.16	57.80	50	-61.53	34.18
147	(322)	Simon Yates	Sco	1.16	46.21	40	-21.41	47.30
148	(85)	Fred Funk	USA	1.15	58.65	51	-92.88	53.52
149	(186)	Graeme Storm	Eng	1.15	68.81	60	-51.02	70.13
150	(241)	Kevin Sutherland	USA	1.14	61.41	54	-45.23	68.52

( ) Ranking in brackets indicates position as of December 31, 2006.

Ranking		Player	Country	Points Average	Total Points	No. of Events	05/06 Points Lost	2007 Points Gained
151	(83)	Simon Khan	Eng	1.12	59.32	53	-65.59	40.35
152	(185)	Prom Meesawat	Tha	1.11	60.13	54	-37.72	53.32
153	(120)	Marc Warren	Sco	1.11	61.02	55	-48.80	41.36
154	(61)	Tom Pernice, Jr.	USA	1.11	70.91	64	-115.37	53.55
155	(349)	James Kingston	SAf	1.10	58.09	53	-25.03	57.91
156	(689)	Pelle Edberg	Swe	1.08	44.44	41	-10.39	49.28
157	(284)	Brian Bateman	USA	1.08	47.63	44	-30.33	43.83
158	(128)	Keiichiro Fukabori	Jpn	1.08	54.01	50	-51.70	37.75
159	(614)	F. Andersson Hed	Swe	1.07	53.32	50	-14.54	58.55
160	(119)	John Bickerton	Eng	1.05	54.44	52	-56.85	35.75
161	(264)	Peter Hedblom	Swe	1.05	50.19	48	-37.49	56.79
162	(66)	Tim Herron	USA	1.04	56.29	54	-93.70	44.88
163	(176)	Katsumasa Miyamoto	Jpn	1.04	55.04	53	-41.97	42.53
164	(444)	John Mallinger	USA	1.01	52.62	52	-22.70	60.61
165	(14)	David Howell	Eng	1.01	52.33	52	-173.14	12.76
166	(212)	Frankie Minoza	Phi	1.00	60.20	60	-32.49	57.63
167	(118)	Kevin Stadler	USA	1.00	67.15	67	-70.36	50.44
168	(201)	Stephen Leaney	Aus	1.00	57.91	58	-48.27	57.18
169	(359)	Robert Garrigus	USA	0.98	54.97	56	-26.11	58.63
170	(277)	Felipe Aguilar	Chl	0.98	49.06	50	-19.69	44.22
171	(231)	Lin Wen-tang	Twn	0.98	39.09	40	-20.40	28.95
172	(1030T)	Robert Dinwiddie	Eng	0.97	38.83	40	-3.75	41.15
173	(130)	Jason Gore	USA	0.97	56.19	58	-57.95	53.79
174	(25)	Michael Campbell	NZl	0.96	51.03	53	-137.76	20.70
175	(641)	Jason Day	Aus	0.96	38.49	40	-11.02	42.64
176	(712)	Koumei Oda	Jpn	0.96	45.08	47	-8.28	48.27
177	(147)	Francesco Molinari	Ity	0.96	48.87	51	-52.32	35.97
178	(97)	Jesper Parnevik	Swe	0.95	50.24	53	-61.96	39.84
179	(227)	Juvic Pagunsan	Phi	0.95	37.86	40	-16.83	24.00
180	(181)	Ryuji Imada	Jpn	0.94	62.27	66	-54.36	60.83
181	(358)	Andrew McLardy	SAf	0.94	50.68	54	-30.56	57.94
182	(191)	Charlie Wi	Kor	0.93	54.20	58	-43.61	49.86
183	(245)	Kevin Na	USA	0.93	38.28	41	-29.94	38.51
184	(149)	Joe Ogilvie	USA	0.93	55.62	60	-57.35	50.17
185	(514)	Mads Vibe-Hastrup	Den	0.93	46.28	50	-13.71	44.47
186	(221)	Brian Davis	Eng	0.93	55.52	60	-46.96	56.73
187	(188)	Alexander Noren	Swe	0.92	48.84	53	-28.20	40.95
188	(154)	Mark Hensby	Aus	0.92	43.14	47	-45.38	43.97
189	(607)	Daniel Vancsik	Arg	0.91	50.31	55	-15.62	55.66
190	(64)	Paul Broadhurst	Eng	0.91	45.63	50	-90.04	32.51
191	(124)	Mathew Goggin	Aus	0.91	53.57	59	-61.24	40.84
192	(77)	Jason Bohn	USA	0.91	41.72	46	-85.78	27.97
193	(339)	Nick Flanagan	Aus	0.90	47.60	53	-23.73	52.16
194	(76)	Jose Manuel Lara	Spn	0.90	47.57	53	-68.14	14.88
195	(114)	Frank Lickliter	USA	0.88	52.07	59	-58.46	27.32
196	(155)	Steve Elkington	Aus	0.88	38.79	44	-48.45	45.00
197	(252)	Yusaku Miyazato	Jpn	0.88	44.86	51	-27.06	35.35
198	(292)	Anton Haig	SAf	0.88	48.24	55	-30.77	55.14
199	(163)	Thaworn Wiratchant	Tha	0.88	51.67	59	-50.21	41.18
199	(420T)	Steve Marino	USA	0.88	44.66	51	-20.80	50.00

( ) Ranking in brackets indicates position as of December 31, 2006.

Age Groups of Current Top 100 World Ranked Players

Under 25	25-28	29-32	33-36	37-40	41-44	45 & Over
		Woods				
		Sabbatini	Harrington			
		Ogilvy	Fasth			
		Z. Johnson	Westwood			
	Rose	Stenson	Cink	Mickelson		
	Scott	Donald	Wetterich	Furyk		
	Garcia	Casey	Appleby	Els		
	Baddeley	Poulter	Katayama	Stricker		
	Immelman	T. Clark	O'Hern	K.J. Choi		
	A. Romero	Oberholser	R. Green	Cabrera		
	Mahan	P. Hanson	Weekley	Goosen		
	C. Howell	B. Jones	S. Hansen	Taniguchi		
	Sterne	Byrd	Allenby	Weir	V. Singh	
	Snedeker	Pettersson	Dredge	Karlsson	Verplank	
	Dougherty	Dyson	Senden	Toms	Austin	
	Villegas	Rollins	Slocum	A. Hansen	Ames	
	Ilonen	Tanihara	J.M. Singh	Pampling	Jimenez	
	O'Hair	Kjeldsen	Jacobson	Lonard	Montgomerie	
	Moore	Perez	Randhawa	DiMarco	Kelly	
	Glover	C. Webster	Jacquelin	Flesch	Love	
A. Kim	R. Fisher	Liang Wen-c.	Leonard	Jaidee	Olazabal	Calcavecchia
Kaymer	Fdez-Castano	N. Green	C. Campbell	Brier	Marksaeng	Langer
Schwartzel	Matteson	V. Taylor	Y.E. Yang	Smail	Durant	K. Perry

2007 World Ranking Review

Major Movements

Upward				Downward			
	Net Points	**Position**			**Net Points**	**Position**	
Name	**Gained**	**2006**	**2007**	**Name**	**Lost**	**2006**	**2007**
Steve Stricker	174	63	5	David Howell	160	14	165
Justin Rose	169	51	6	Jim Furyk	155	2	3
Rory Sabbatini	123	39	11	Retief Goosen	147	6	26
Aaron Baddeley	121	87	18	Michael Campbell	117	25	174
K.J. Choi	118	29	9	Jose Maria Olazabal	108	18	71
Brandt Snedeker	103	243	47	Colin Montgomerie	96	17	57
Hunter Mahan	102	219	34	Davis Love	93	16	67
Phil Mickelson	98	3	2	Ben Crane	86	41	205
Boo Weekley	93	204	45	Chris DiMarco	86	20	79
Ernie Els	90	5	4	Adam Scott	81	6	7
Woody Austin	88	136	31	Chad Campbell	76	27	93
Andres Romero	84	109	28	Darren Clarke	75	35	225
Zach Johnson	79	54	15	Fred Couples	70	62	541
Richard Sterne	77	196	44	Luke Donald	68	9	17
Angel Cabrera	72	28	14	Y.E. Yang	67	33	94
Soren Hansen	67	157	46	Joe Durant	65	32	85
Mark Calcavecchia	67	143	49	Jeev Milkha Singh	64	37	77
Toru Taniguchi	60	80	27				
Brendan Jones	59	263	59				
Peter Hanson	58	166	54				
Mikko Ilonen	56	355	62				
Anthony Kim	56	533	75				

Highest-Rated Events of 2007

	Event	Top 5	Top 15	Top 30	Top 50	Top 100	World Rating Points
			No. of World Ranked Players Participating				World Rating Points
1	PGA Championship	5	15	30	49	97	844
2	The Open Championship	5	15	30	47	77	775
3	Masters Tournament	5	15	30	50	72	758
4	U.S. Open Championship	5	15	30	47	73	745
5	The Players Championship	5	15	29	48	78	772
6	WGC - Accenture Match Play	5	15	30	50	64	730
7	WGC - CA Championship	5	15	30	49	67	718
8	WGC - Bridgestone Invitational	4	14	29	49	68	708
9	Wachovia Championship	5	14	27	40	67	687
10	The Barclays	4	14	25	40	71	674
11	Deutsche Bank Champ.	4	14	24	39	67	667
12	Nissan Open	4	11	22	35	63	597
13	Memorial Tournament	5	11	23	30	56	574
14	BMW Championship	4	13	23	35	54	569
15	Arnold Palmer Invitational	3	12	22	33	60	566
16	BMW PGA Championship	1	7	11	15	33	304
17	AT&T National	4	6	15	22	47	452
18	The Tour Championship	5	13	18	24	30	443
19	Sony Open	2	5	11	18	43	366
20	FBR Open	1	4	10	21	47	360
21	Verizon Heritage	2	4	10	19	45	352
22	HSBC Champions	2	7	15	22	34	347
23	EDS Byron Nelson Champ.	1	4	12	20	40	328
24	Crowne Plaza Colonial	1	2	9	20	43	315
25	Dubai Desert Classic	2	6	10	13	32	283
26	Barclays Scottish Open	2	5	8	16	31	285
27	Mercedes-Benz Championship	2	6	12	18	26	279
28	Buick Invitational	2	3	6	14	33	300
29	Honda Classic	1	3	9	15	39	295
30	Stanford St. Jude Champ.	1	6	10	16	34	296
31	AT&T Pebble Beach Pro-Am	1	5	9	14	29	281
32	PODS Championship	0	4	8	15	40	280
33	Alfred Dunhill Links	1	4	9	15	29	240
34	Commercialbank Qatar Masters	1	5	10	14	27	241
35	Travelers Championship	0	3	9	16	30	255
36	Volvo Masters	0	4	9	14	27	219
37	Shell Houston Open	1	2	7	15	28	245
38	Abu Dhabi Championship	0	5	9	13	22	202
39	Johnnie Walker Classic	1	4	6	9	16	169
40	HSBC World Match Play	1	4	9	15	16	190

World Golf Rankings 1968-2007

Year	No. 1	No. 2	No. 3	No. 4	No. 5
1968	Nicklaus	Palmer	Casper	Player	Charles
1969	Nicklaus	Player	Casper	Palmer	Charles
1970	Nicklaus	Player	Casper	Trevino	Charles
1971	Nicklaus	Trevino	Player	Palmer	Casper
1972	Nicklaus	Player	Trevino	Crampton	Palmer
1973	Nicklaus	Weiskopf	Trevino	Player	Crampton
1974	Nicklaus	Miller	Player	Weiskopf	Trevino
1975	Nicklaus	Miller	Weiskopf	Irwin	Player
1976	Nicklaus	Irwin	Miller	Player	Green
1977	Nicklàus	Watson	Green	Irwin	Crenshaw
1978	Watson	Nicklaus	Irwin	Green	Player
1979	Watson	Nicklaus	Irwin	Trevino	Player
1980	Watson	Trevino	Aoki	Crenshaw	Nicklaus
1981	Watson	Rogers	Aoki	Pate	Trevino
1982	Watson	Floyd	Ballesteros	Kite	Stadler
1983	Ballesteros	Watson	Floyd	Norman	Kite
1984	Ballesteros	Watson	Norman	Wadkins	Langer
1985	Ballesteros	Langer	Norman	Watson	Nakajima
1986	Norman	Langer	Ballesteros	Nakajima	Bean
1987	Norman	Ballesteros	Langer	Lyle	Strange
1988	Ballesteros	Norman	Lyle	Faldo	Strange
1989	Norman	Faldo	Ballesteros	Strange	Stewart
1990	Norman	Faldo	Olazabal	Woosnam	Stewart
1991	Woosnam	Faldo	Olazabal	Ballesteros	Norman
1992	Faldo	Couples	Woosnam	Olazabal	Norman
1993	Faldo	Norman	Langer	Price	Couples
1994	Price	Norman	Faldo	Langer	Olazabal
1995	Norman	Price	Langer	Els	Montgomerie
1996	Norman	Lehman	Montgomerie	Els	Couples
1997	Norman	Woods	Price	Els	Love
1998	Woods	O'Meara	Duval	Love	Els
1999	Woods	Duval	Montgomerie	Love	Els
2000	Woods	Els	Duval	Mickelson	Westwood
2001	Woods	Mickelson	Duval	Els	Love
2002	Woods	Mickelson	Els	Garcia	Goosen
2003	Woods	Singh	Els	Love	Furyk
2004	Singh	Woods	Els	Goosen	Mickelson
2005	Woods	Singh	Mickelson	Goosen	Els
2006	Woods	Furyk	Mickelson	Scott	Els
2007	Woods	Mickelson	Furyk	Els	Stricker

(The World of Professional Golf 1968-1985; World Ranking 1986-2007)

Year	No. 6	No. 7	No. 8	No. 9	No. 10
1968	Boros	Coles	Thomson	Beard	Nagle
1969	Beard	Archer	Trevino	Barber	Sikes
1970	Devlin	Coles	Jacklin	Beard	Huggett
1971	Barber	Crampton	Charles	Devlin	Weiskopf
1972	Jacklin	Weiskopf	Oosterhuis	Heard	Devlin
1973	Miller	Oosterhuis	Wadkins	Heard	Brewer
1974	M. Ozaki	Crampton	Irwin	Green	Heard
1975	Green	Trevino	Casper	Crampton	Watson
1976	Watson	Weiskopf	Marsh	Crenshaw	Geiberger
1977	Marsh	Player	Weiskopf	Floyd	Ballesteros
1978	Crenshaw	Marsh	Ballesteros	Trevino	Aoki
1979	Aoki	Green	Crenshaw	Ballesteros	Wadkins
1980	Pate	Ballesteros	Bean	Irwin	Player
1981	Ballesteros	Graham	Crenshaw	Floyd	Lietzke
1982	Pate	Nicklaus	Rogers	Aoki	Strange
1983	Nicklaus	Nakajima	Stadler	Aoki	Wadkins
1984	Faldo	Nakajima	Stadler	Kite	Peete
1985	Wadkins	O'Meara	Strange	Pavin	Sutton
1986	Tway	Sutton	Strange	Stewart	O'Meara
1987	Woosnam	Stewart	Wadkins	McNulty	Crenshaw
1988	Crenshaw	Woosnam	Frost	Azinger	Calcavecchia
1989	Kite	Olazabal	Calcavecchia	Woosnam	Azinger
1990	Azinger	Ballesteros	Kite	McNulty	Calcavecchia
1991	Couples	Langer	Stewart	Azinger	Davis
1992	Langer	Cook	Price	Azinger	Love
1993	Azinger	Woosnam	Kite	Love	Pavin
1994	Els	Couples	Montgomerie	M. Ozaki	Pavin
1995	Pavin	Faldo	Couples	M. Ozaki	Elkington
1996	Faldo	Mickelson	M. Ozaki	Love	O'Meara
1997	Mickelson	Montgomerie	M. Ozaki	Lehman	O'Meara
1998	Price	Montgomerie	Westwood	Singh	Mickelson
1999	Westwood	Singh	Price	Mickelson	O'Meara
2000	Montgomerie	Love	Sutton	Singh	Lehman
2001	Garcia	Toms	Singh	Clarke	Goosen
2002	Toms	Harrington	Singh	Love	Montgomerie
2003	Weir	Goosen	Harrington	Toms	Perry
2004	Harrington	Garcia	Weir	Love	Cink
2005	Garcia	Furyk	Montgomerie	Scott	DiMarco
2006	Goosen	Singh	Harrington	Donald	Ogilvy
2007	Rose	Scott	Harrington	Choi	Singh

World's Winners of 2007

U.S. PGA TOUR

Mercedes-Benz Championship	Vijay Singh
Sony Open in Hawaii	Paul Goydos
Bob Hope Chrysler Classic	Charley Hoffman
Buick Invitational	Tiger Woods
FBR Open	Aaron Baddeley
AT&T Pebble Beach National Pro-Am	Phil Mickelson
Nissan Open	Charles Howell
WGC - Accenture Match Play Championship	Henrik Stenson (2)
Mayakoba Golf Classic at Riviera Maya-Cancun	Fred Funk (2)
Honda Classic	Mark Wilson
PODS Championship	Mark Calcavecchia
Arnold Palmer Invitational	Vijay Singh (2)
WGC - CA Championship	Tiger Woods (2)
Shell Houston Open	Adam Scott
Masters Tournament	Zach Johnson
Verizon Heritage	Boo Weekley
Zurich Classic of New Orleans	Nick Watney
EDS Byron Nelson Championship	Scott Verplank
Wachovia Championship	Tiger Woods (3)
The Players Championship	Phil Mickelson (2)
AT&T Classic	Zach Johnson (2)
Crowne Plaza Invitational at Colonial	Rory Sabbatini
Memorial Tournament	K.J. Choi
Stanford St. Jude Championship	Woody Austin
U.S. Open Championship	Angel Cabrera (2)
Travelers Championship	Hunter Mahan
Buick Open	Brian Bateman
AT&T National	K.J. Choi (2)
John Deere Classic	Jonathan Byrd
U.S. Bank Championship in Milwaukee	Joe Ogilvie
Canadian Open	Jim Furyk
WGC - Bridgestone Invitational	Tiger Woods (4)
Reno-Tahoe Open	Steve Flesch
PGA Championship	Tiger Woods (5)
Wyndham Championship	Brandt Snedeker

PGA TOUR PLAYOFFS FOR THE FEDEX CUP

The Barclays	Steve Stricker
Deutsche Bank Championship	Phil Mickelson (3)
BMW Championship	Tiger Woods (6)
The Tour Championship	Tiger Woods (7)

PGA TOUR FALL SERIES

Turning Stone Resort Championship	Steve Flesch (2)
The Presidents Cup	United States
Viking Classic	Chad Campbell
Valero Texas Open	Justin Leonard
Frys.com Open	George McNeill
Fry's Electronics Open	Mike Weir
Ginn sur Mer Classic at Tesoro	Daniel Chopra
Children's Miracle Network Classic	Stephen Ames

SPECIAL EVENTS

Tavistock Cup	Lake Nona
CVS Caremark Charity Classic	Stewart Cink/J.J. Henry
PGA Grand Slam of Golf	Angel Cabrera (3)
Callaway Golf Pebble Beach Invitational	Tommy Armour

Del Webb Father-Son Challenge — Larry/Josh Nelson
Merrill Lynch Shootout — Woody Austin (2)/
    Mark Calcavecchia (2)

Target World Challenge — Tiger Woods (8)

NATIONWIDE TOUR

Movistar Panama Championship	Miguel Carballo
Chitimacha Louisiana Open	Skip Kendall
Livermore Valley Wine Country Championship	Omar Uresti
South Georgia Classic	John Kimbell
Athens Regional Foundation Classic	Martin Laird
Henrico County Open	Nick Flanagan
Fort Smith Classic	Jay Williamson
BMW Charity Pro-Am at The Cliffs	Nick Flanagan (2)
Melwood Prince George's County Open	Paul Claxton
LaSalle Bank Open	John Riegger
The Rex Hospital Open	Kyle Thompson
Rochester Area Charities Showdown at Somerby	Chris Riley
Knoxville Open	Chez Reavie
Peek'n Peak Classic	Roland Thatcher
Legend Financial Group Classic	Jason Day
Nationwide Children's Hospital Invitational	*Daniel Summerhays
Price Cutter Charity Championship	Tom Scherrer
Cox Classic	Roland Thatcher (2)
Preferred Health Systems Wichita Open	Brad Elder
Northeast Pennsylvania Classic	Justin Bolli
Xerox Classic	Nick Flanagan (3)
National Mining Association Pete Dye Classic	Jimmy Walker
Utah EnergySolutions Championship	Franklin Langham
Oregon Classic	Kyle Thompson (2)
Albertsons Boise Open	Jon Mills
Mark Christopher Charity Classic	Richard Johnson
WNB Golf Classic	Brad Adamonis
Chattanooga Classic	Ron Whittaker
Miccosukee Championship	Marc Turnesa
Nationwide Tour Championship at Barona Creek	Richard Johnson (2)

CANADIAN TOUR

San Jose International Open	Adam Bland
Northern California Classic	Wes Heffernan
Corona Mazatlan Classic	Byron Smith
Ford Culiacan Open	Adam Bland (2)
Riviera Nayarit Classic	Wes Heffernan (2)
Iberostar Riviera Maya Open	Spencer Levin
Times Colonist Open	Spencer Levin (2)
Greataer Vancouver Charity Classic	James Lepp
ATB Financial Classic	Mike Grob
Telus Edmonton Open	Dustin Risdon
Free Press Manitoba Classic	Mike Mezei
Desjardins Montreal Open	Brent Schwarzrock
Jane Rogers Championship of Mississauga	Byron Smith (2)
Canadian Tour Championship	Bret Guetz

TOUR DE LAS AMERICAS (SOUTH AMERICA)

Colombia Masters	Edoardo Molinari
Kai Fieberg Costa Rica Open	Miguel Rodriguez
Guatemala Open	Jamie Donaldson
Abierto Visa del Centro	Angel Cabrera
Canal i Abierto de Venezuela	Jesus Amaya
Torneo de Maestros	Angel Cabrera (4)

Abierto de Chile — Angel Fernandez
Abierto de San Luis — Emilio Dominguez
Abierto de Litoral Personal — Miguel Rodriguez (2)
Abierto Visa de la Republica — Marco Ruiz

EUROPEAN TOUR

Abu Dhabi Golf Championship	Paul Casey
Commercialbank Qatar Masters	Retief Goosen
Dubai Desert Classic	Henrik Stenson
Madeira Islands Open BPI	Daniel Vancsik
Estoril Open de Portugal	*Pablo Martin-Benavides
Open de Espana	Charl Schwartzel
Telecom Italia Open	Gonzalo Fernandez-Castano
Valle Romano Open de Andalucia	Lee Westwood
Irish Open	Padraig Harrington
BMW PGA Championship	Anders Hansen
Celtic Manor Wales Open	Richard Sterne (2)
BA-CA Golf Open	Richard Green
Open de Saint-Omer	Carl Suneson
BMW International Open	Niclas Fasth
Open de France ALSTOM	Graeme Storm
Smurfit Kappa European Open	Colin Montgomerie
Barclays Scottish Open	Gregory Havret
The Open Championship	Padraig Harrington (2)
Deutsche Bank Players' Championship of Europe	Andres Romero
Russian Open Golf Championship	Per-Ulrik Johansson
Scandinavian Masters	Mikko Ilonen (2)
KLM Open	Ross Fisher
Johnnie Walker Championship at Gleneagles	Marc Warren
Omega European Masters	Brett Rumford
Mercedez-Benz Championship	Soren Hansen
Quinn Direct British Masters	Lee Westwood (2)
The Seve Trophy	Great Britain & Ireland
Alfred Dunhill Links Championship	Nick Dougherty
HSBC World Match Play	Ernie Els
Open de Madrid Valle Romano	Mads Vibe-Hastrup
Portugal Masters	Steve Webster
Mallorca Classic	Gregory Bourdy
Volvo Masters	Justin Rose

CHALLENGE TOUR

Tusker Kenya Open	Eduardo Molinari (2)
Tessali-Metaponto Open di Puglia e Basilicata	Michael Hoey
A.G.F. Allianz Golf Open de Toulouse	Joost Luiten
Telenet Trophy	Nicolas Vanhootegem
Open Mahou de Madrid	Ben Mason
Oceanico Developments Pro-Am Challenge	Ross McGowan
Vodafone Challenge	Joost Luiten (2)
Credit Suisse Challenge	Peter Baker
Estoril Challenge de Portugal	Ross McGowan (2)
AGF-Allianz Open des Volcans	Gareth Paddison
MAN NO Open	Anders Schmidt Hansen
FirstPlus Wales Challenge	Colm Moriarty
Challenge of Ireland	Magnus A. Carlsson
Scottish Challenge	Robert Dinwiddie
Rolex Trophy	Robert Dinwiddie (2)
Lexus Open	Martin Wiegele
Postbank Challenge	Felipe Aguilar
ECCO Tour Championship	Iain Pyman
Telia Challenge Waxholm	Iain Pyman (2)
OKI Mahou Challenge de Espana	Felipe Aguilar (2)

Kazakhstan Open	Leif Westerberg
The Dutch Futures	Peter Whiteford
Open AGF-Allianz Cotes d'Armor Bretagne	Peter Baker (2)
doc Salbe PGA European Challenge	Peter Whiteford (2)
Toscana Open Italian Federation Cup	Mikael Lundberg
Apulia San Domenico Grand Final	Michael Lorenzo-Vera

ASIAN TOUR

The Royal Trophy	Europe
Pakistan Open	Airil Rizman Zahari
Philippine Open	Frankie Minoza
Maybank Malaysian Open	Peter Hedblom
Enjoy Jakarta Astro Indonesia Open	Mikko Ilonen
Johnnie Walker Classic	Anton Haig
Clariden Leu Singapore Masters	Liang Wen-chong
TCL Classic	Chapchai Nirat
Motorola International Bintan	Jason Knutzon
Volvo China Open	Markus Brier
BMW Asian Open	Raphael Jacquelin
Pine Valley Beijing Open	Gaurav Ghei
GS Caltex Maekyung Open	Kim Kyung-tae
Macau Open	Lu Wen-teh
SK Telecom Open	Bae Sang-moon
Bangkok Airways Open	Lee Sung
Iskandar Johor Open	Artemio Murakami
Brunei Open	Lin Wen-tang
Midea China Classic	Thaworn Wiratchant
Mercuries Taiwan Masters	Lu Wen-teh (2)
Kolon-Hana Bank Korea Open	Vijay Singh (3)
Hero Honda Indian Open	Jyoti Randhawa
Pertamina Indonesia President Invitational	Juvic Pagunsan
Barclays Singapore Open	Angel Cabrera (5)
HSBC Champions	Phil Mickelson (4)
UBS Hong Kong Open	Miguel Angel Jimenez
Omega Mission Hills World Cup	Colin Montgomerie (2)/ Marc Warren (2)
Hana Bank Vietnam Masters	Chapchai Nirat (2)
Johnnie Walker Cambodian Open	Bryan Saltus
Volvo Masters of Asia	Prayad Marksaeng

OMEGA CHINA TOUR

Sofitel Golf Championship	Wu Kang-chun
Quindao Leg	Zhang Lian-wei
Guangzhou Leg	Zhang Lian-wei (2)
Yanji Golf Championship	Li Chao
Shanghai Leg	Li Chao (2)
Kunming Leg	Zheng Wen-gen
Xiamen Leg	Li Chao (3)
Omega Championship	Zhang Lian-wei (3)

JAPAN TOUR

Token Homemate Cup	Yui Ueda
Tsuruya Open	Brendan Jones
The Crowns	Hirofumi Miyase
Japan PGA Championship	Toshimitsu Izawa
Munsingwear Open KSB Cup	*Ryo Ishikawa
Mitsubishi Diamond Cup	Tetsuji Hiratsuka
JCB Classic	Tomohiro Kondo
Gateway to the Open Mizuno Open	Lee Dong-hwan
UBS Japan Golf Tour Championship	Shingo Katayama

Woodone Open Hiroshima	Toru Taniguchi
Nagashima Shigeo Invitational Sega Sammy Cup	Toru Taniguchi (2)
Sun Chlorella Classic	Jun Kikuchi
KBC Augusta	Katsumasa Miyamoto
Fujisankei Classic	Hideto Tanihara
Suntory Open	Hideto Tanihara (2)
ANA Open	Norio Shinozaki
Coca-Cola Tokai Classic	Camilo Villegas
Japan Open	Toru Taniguchi (3)
Bridgestone Open	Shingo Katayama (2)
ABC Championship	Frankie Minoza (2)
Mitsui Sumitomo Visa Taiheiyo Masters	Brendan Jones (2)
Dunlop Phoenix	Ian Poulter
Casio World Open	Taichi Teshima
Golf Nippon Series JT Cup	Brendan Jones (3)

AUSTRALASIAN TOUR

Jacob's Creek Open	Scott Sterling
HSBC New Zealand PGA Championship	Nicholas Thompson
MasterCard Masters	Aaron Baddeley (2)
Michael Hill New Zealand Open	Richard Finch
Cadbury Schweppes Australian PGA	Peter Lonard
MFS Australian Open	Craig Parry

AFRICAN TOURS

Joburg Open	Ariel Canete
Dimension Data Pro-Am	Louis Oosthuizen
Nashua Masters	Jean Hugo
Vodacom Championship	Richard Sterne
Telkom PGA Championship	Louis Oosthuizen (2)
Mount Edgecombe Trophy	Steve van Vuuren
Finance Bank Zambia Open	Steve Basson
Eskom Power Cup	Chris Swanepoel
Vodacom Origins of Golf Tour at Arabella	Andrew Curlewis
Samsung Royal Swazi Sun Open	Des Terblanche
Vodacom Origins of Golf Tour at Pretoria	Hennie Otto
Suncoast Classic	Adilson da Silva
Lombard Insurance Classic	Peter Karmis
Vodacom Origins of Golf Tour at Selborne	George Coetzee
Nashua Golf Challenge	Warren Abery
Vodacom Origins of Golf Tour at Bloemfontein	Ulrich van den Berg
Vodacom Origins of Golf Tour at Fancourt	Adilson da Silva (2)
Telkom PGA Pro-Am	Michiel Bothma
Seekers Travel Pro-Am	James Kamte
Vodacom Origins of Golf Tour Final	Titch Moore
Bearing Man Highveld Classic	Marc Cayeux
MTC Namibia PGA Championship	Keith Horne
Platinum Classic	Louis Oosthuizen (3)
Hassan II Trophy	Padraig Harrington (3)
Coca-Cola Charity Championship	Titch Moore (2)
Nedbank Affinity Cup	Mark Murless
Nedbank Golf Challenge	Trevor Immelman
Alfred Dunhill Championship	John Bickerton
South African Airways Open	James Kingston

U.S. LPGA TOUR

SBS Open at Turtle Bay	Paula Creamer
Fields Open in Hawaii	Stacy Prammanasudh
MasterCard Classic Honoring Alejo Peralta	Meaghan Francella
Safeway International	Lorena Ochoa
Kraft Nabisco Championship	Morgan Pressel
Ginn Open	Brittany Lincicome

Corona Championship	Silvia Cavalleri
SemGroup Championship	Mi Hyun Kim
Michelob Ultra Open at Kingsmill	Suzann Pettersen
Sybase Classic	Lorena Ochoa (2)
LPGA Corning Classic	Young Kim
Ginn Tribute Hosted by Annika	Nicole Castrale
McDonald's LPGA Championship	Suzann Pettersen (2)
Wegmans LPGA	Lorena Ochoa (3)
U.S. Women's Open	Cristie Kerr
Jamie Farr Owens Corning Classic	Se Ri Pak
HSBC Women's World Match Play	Seon Hwa Lee
CN Canadian Women's Open	Lorena Ochoa (5)
Safeway Classic	Lorena Ochoa (6)
State Farm Classic	Sherri Steinhauer
NW Arkansas Championship	Cancelled
Navistar LPGA Classic	Maria Hjorth
Longs Drugs Challenge	Suzann Pettersen (4)
Samsung World Championship	Lorena Ochoa (7)
Honda LPGA Thailand	Suzann Pettersen (6)
The Mitchell Co. Tournament of Champions	Paula Creamer (2)
ADT Championship	Lorena Ochoa (8)

LADIES EUROPEAN TOUR

Tenerife Ladies Open	Nikki Garrett
Open de Espana Femenino	Nikki Garrett (2)
Deutsche Bank Ladies Swiss Open	Bettina Hauert
BMW Ladies Italian Open	Trish Johnson
Northern Ireland Ladies Open	Lisa Hall
KLM Ladies Open	Gwladys Nocera
Catalonia Ladies Masters	Ashleigh Simon (2)
Vediorbis Open de France	Linda Wessberg
Ladies Open de Portugal	Sophie Giquel
Golf Punk Ladies English Open	Becky Brewerton
Evian Masters	Natalie Gulbis
Ricoh Women's British Open	Lorena Ochoa (4)
Scandinavian TPC Hosted by Annika	Catriona Matthew
S4/C Wales Ladies Championship of Europe	Joanne Mills
SAS Masters	Suzann Pettersen (3)
Finnair Masters	Bettina Hauert (2)
Nykredit Masters	Lisa Hall (2)
The Solheim Cup	United States
De Vere Ladies Scottish Open	Sophie Gustafson
UNIQA Ladies Golf Open	Laura Davies
Madrid Ladies Masters	Martina Eberl
EMAAR-MGF Ladies Masters	Gwladys Nocera (3)
Dubai Ladies Masters	Annika Sorenstam

JAPAN LPGA TOUR

Daikin Orchid Ladies	Midori Yoneyama
Accordia Golf Ladies	Toshimi Kimura
Studio Alice Ladies Open	Jae-Hee Bae
Life Card Ladies	Momoko Ueda
Fujisankei Ladies Classic	Miki Saiki
Yashima Queens	Mi-Jeong Jeon
Salonpas World Ladies	Mi-Jeong Jeon (2)
Vernal Ladies	Mi-Jeong Jeon (3)
Chukyo TV Bridgestone Ladies Open	Sakura Yokomine
Kosaido Ladies Golf Cup	Yuri Fudoh
Resort Trust Ladies	Momoko Ueda (2)
We Love Kobe Suntory Ladies Open	Na Zhang
Nichirei PGM Ladies	Shiho Oyama

Promise Ladies	Saiki Fujita
Belluna Ladies Cup	Akiko Fukushima
Meiji Chocolate Cup	Shiho Oyama (2)
Stanley Ladies	Momoko Ueda (3)
Kracie Philanthropy Players Championship	Na Zhang (2)
AXA Ladies	Na Zhang (3)
Crystal Geyser Ladies	Hiromi Mogi
NEC Karuizawa 72	Akiko Fukushima (2)
Shin Caterpillar Mitsubishi Ladies	Sakura Yokomine (2)
Yonex Ladies	Yuri Fudoh (2)
Golf 5 Ladies	Akane Iijima
Japan LPGA Championship Konica Minolta Cup	Akane Iijima (2)
Munsingwear Ladies Tokai Classic	Na Zhang (4)
Miyagi TV Cup Dunlop Ladies Open	Yuko Mitsuka
Japan Women's Open	Shinobu Moromizato
Sankyo Ladies Open	So-Hee Kim
Fujitsu Ladies	Sakura Yokomine (3)
Masters Golf Club Ladies	Miho Koga
Hisako Higuchi IDC Otsuka Ladies	Mi-Jeong Jeon (4)
Mizuno Classic	Momoko Ueda (4)
Itoen Ladies	Rui Kitada
Daiohseishi Elleair Ladies Open	Momoko Ueda (5)
Japan LPGA Tour Championship Ricoh Cup	Miho Koga (2)
The Kyoraku Cup	Japan

KOREA LPGA TOUR

Asia Miles Binhai Ladies Open	Da Ye Na
KB Star Tour in Busan	Sun Ju Ahn
MBC Tour MC Square Cup Ladies Open	Ji-Yai Shin
Phoenix Park Classic	Eun Hee Ji
KB Star Tour in Hampyung	Eun Hee Ji (2)
Taeyoung Cup Korea Women's Open	Sun Ju Ahn (2)
Hill State SeoKyung Ladies Open	Ji-Yai Shin (2)
MBC Tour BC Card Classic	Ji-Yai Shin (3)
KB Star Tour in Pohang	Ji-Yai Shin (4)
MBC Tour Korea Golf Art Village Open	Sun Ju Ahn (3)
KB Star Tour in Chungcheong	Ji-Yai Shin (5)
SK Energy Invitational	Ji-Yai Shin (6)
Shinsegye Cup KLPGA Championship	Na Yeon Choi
Samsung Finance Ladies Championship	Ji-Yai Shin (7)
Hite Cup Ladies Championship	Hye Jung Choi
Hana Bank-Kolon Championship	Suzann Pettersen (5)
Interburgo Masters	Ji-Yai Shin (8)
KB Star Tour in Seoul	Young Ran Jo
MBC Tour	Ji Na Lim
ADT CAPS Championship	Ji-Yai Shin (9)
Orient China Ladies Open	Ji-Yai Shin (10)

AUSTRALIAN LADIES TOUR

MFS Women's Australian Open	Karrie Webb
ANZ Ladies Masters	Karrie Webb (2)
Lexus Cup	Asia

LADIES AFRICAN TOUR

Women's World Cup of Golf	Julieta Granada/Celeste Troche
Pam Golding Ladies International	Lee-Anne Pace
WPGA Masters	Kaisa Ruuttila
Acer Women's South African Open	*Ashleigh Simon
Telkom Women's Classic	Tania Elosegui
Princess Lalla Meryem Cup	Gwladys Nocera (2)

CHAMPIONS TOUR

MasterCard Championship at Hualalai	Hale Irwin
Turtle Bay Championship	Fred Funk
Allianz Championship	Mark James
Outback Steakhouse Pro-Am	Tom Watson
ACE Group Classic	Bobby Wadkins
Toshiba Classic	Jay Haas
AT&T Champions Classic	Tom Purtzer
Ginn Championship Hammock Beach Resort	Keith Fergus
Liberty Mutual Legends of Golf	Jay Haas (2)
FedEx Kinko's Classic	Scott Hoch
Regions Charity Classic	Brad Bryant
Senior PGA Championship	Denis Watson
Boeing Championship at Sandestin	Loren Roberts
Principal Charity Classic	Jay Haas (3)
Bank of America Championship	Jay Haas (4)
Commerce Bank Championship	Lonnie Nielsen
U.S. Senior Open	Brad Bryant (2)
Dick's Sporting Goods Open	R.W. Eaks
3M Championship	D.A. Weibring
JELD-WEN Tradition	Mark McNulty
Boeing Classic	Denis Watson (2)
Wal-Mart First Tee Open at Pebble Beach	Gil Morgan
Greater Hickory Classic at Rock Barn	R.W. Eaks (2)
SAS Championship	Mark Wiebe
Constellation Energy Senior Players Champ.	Loren Roberts (2)
Administaff Small Business Classic	Bernhard Langer
AT&T Championship	John Cook
Charles Schwab Cup Championship	Jim Thorpe

EUROPEAN SENIORS TOUR

DGM Barbados Open	Gordon J. Brand
The Gloria Classic	Nick Job
Sharp Italian Seniors Open	Simon Owen
AIB Irish Seniors Open	Costantino Rocca
Jersey Seniors Classic	Bobby Lincoln
Ryder Cup Wales Seniors Open	Carl Mason
Bendinat London Seniors Masters	Sam Torrance
Open de France Senior de Divonne	Juan Quiros
The Senior Open Championship	Tom Watson (2)
Wentworth Senior Masters	Des Smyth
Bad Ragaz PGA Seniors Open	Carl Mason (2)
The Midas English Seniors Open	Bill Longmuir
European Senior Masters	Carl Mason (3)
PGA Seniors Championship	Carl Mason (4)
Scandinavian Senior Open	John Chillas
Charles Church Scottish Seniors Open	Jose Rivero
OKI Castellon Open de Espana Senior	Carl Mason (5)
The Kingdom of Bahrain Trophy	Costantino Rocca (2)

JAPAN SENIOR TOUR

Aderans Wellness Open	Katsunari Takahashi
Fancl Classic	Kiyoshi Murota
Big Raisac Senior Open	Masahiro Kuramoto
Japan PGA Senior Championship	Tateo Ozaki
PGA Handa Cup Philanthropy Senior Open	Katsuyoshi Tomori
Komatsu Open	Toyotake Nakao
Japan Senior Open	Isao Aoki
Kinojyo Senior Open	Chip Beck

Multiple Winners of 2007

PLAYER	WINS	PLAYER	WINS
Ji-Yai Shin	10	Nikki Garrett	2
Lorena Ochoa	8	Lisa Hall	2
Tiger Woods	8	Bettina Hauert	2
Suzann Pettersen	6	Wes Heffernan	2
Angel Cabrera	5	Akane Iijima	2
Carl Mason	5	Mikko Ilonen	2
Momoko Ueda	5	Eun Hee Ji	2
Jay Haas	4	Richard Johnson	2
Mi-Jeong Jeon	4	Zach Johnson	2
Phil Mickelson	4	Shingo Katayama	2
Na Zhang	4	Miho Koga	2
Sun Ju Ahn	3	Spencer Levin	2
Nick Flanagan	3	Lu Wen-teh	2
Padraig Harrington	3	Joost Luiten	2
Brendan Jones	3	Ross McGowan	2
Li Chao	3	Frankie Minoza	2
Gwladys Nocera	3	Eduardo Molinari	2
Louis Oosthuizen	3	Colin Montgomerie	2
Vijay Singh	3	Titch Moore	2
Toru Taniguchi	3	Chapchai Nirat	2
Sakura Yokomine	3	Shiho Oyama	2
Zhang Lian-wei	3	Iain Pyman	2
Felipe Aguilar	2	Loren Roberts	2
Woody Austin	2	Costantino Rocca	2
Aaron Baddeley	2	Miguel Rodriguez	2
Peter Baker	2	Ashleigh Simon	2
Adam Bland	2	Byron Smith	2
Brad Bryant	2	Henrik Stenson	2
Mark Calcavecchia	2	Richard Sterne	2
K.J. Choi	2	Hideto Tanihara	2
Paula Creamer	2	Roland Thatcher	2
Adilson da Silva	2	Kyle Thompson	2
Robert Dinwiddie	2	Marc Warren	2
R.W. Eaks	2	Denis Watson	2
Steve Flesch	2	Tom Watson	2
Yuri Fudoh	2	Karrie Webb	2
Akiko Fukushima	2	Lee Westwood	2
Fred Funk	2	Peter Whiteford	2

World Money List

This list of the 350 leading money winners in the world of professional golf in 2007 was compiled from the results of men's (excluding seniors) tournaments carried in the Appendixes of this edition. This list includes tournaments with a minimum of 36 holes and four contestants and does not include such competitions as skins games, pro-ams and shootouts.

In the 42 years during which World Money Lists have been compiled, the earnings of the player in the 200th position have risen from a total of $3,326 in 1966 to $637,018 in 2007. The top 200 players in 1966 earned a total of $4,680,287. In 2007, the comparable total was $482,091,478.

The world money list of the International Federation of PGA Tours was used for the official money list events of the U.S. PGA Tour, PGA European Tour, PGA Tour of Japan, Asian Tour, Southern Africa Tour and PGA Tour of Australasia. The conversion rates used for 2007 for other events and other tours were: Euro = US$1.40; British pound = US$2.04; Japanese yen = US$0.0089; South African rand = US$0.14; Australian dollar = US$0.86; Canadian dollar = US$0.94.

POS.	PLAYER, COUNTRY	TOTAL MONEY
1	Tiger Woods, USA	$12,902,706
2	Phil Mickelson, USA	7,372,685
3	Ernie Els, South Africa	6,790,239
4	Justin Rose, England	6,329,362
5	Vijay Singh, Fiji	6,280,678
6	Rory Sabbatini, South Africa	5,232,836
7	Zach Johnson, USA	5,118,588
8	Jim Furyk, USA	4,974,046
9	Steve Stricker, USA	4,948,077
10	K.J. Choi, Korea	4,877,042
11	Padraig Harrington, Ireland	4,797,016
12	Angel Cabrera, Argentina	4,164,956
13	Adam Scott, Australia	4,057,282
14	Sergio Garcia, Spain	3,951,622
15	Henrik Stenson, Sweden	3,864,830
16	Aaron Baddeley, Australia	3,773,396
17	Mark Calcavecchia, USA	3,583,332
18	Trevor Immelman, South Africa	3,485,514
19	Woody Austin, USA	3,360,233
20	Geoff Ogilvy, Australia	3,279,091
21	Luke Donald, England	3,257,855
22	Niclas Fasth, Sweden	3,194,867
23	Hunter Mahan, USA	3,140,005
24	Scott Verplank, USA	3,114,289
25	Boo Weekley, USA	3,066,651
26	Brandt Snedeker, USA	3,055,134
27	Colin Montgomerie, Scotland	3,050,694
28	Lee Westwood, England	3,022,287
29	Charles Howell, USA	2,997,491
30	Stewart Cink, USA	2,889,278
31	Ian Poulter, England	2,877,681

POS.	PLAYER, COUNTRY	TOTAL MONEY
32	Tim Clark, South Africa	2,681,552
33	Heath Slocum, USA	2,584,379
34	Brett Wetterich, USA	2,507,912
35	Andres Romero, Argentina	2,497,756
36	John Rollins, USA	2,488,891
37	Soren Hansen, Denmark	2,488,697
38	Retief Goosen, South Africa	2,444,083
39	Robert Allenby, Australia	2,326,289
40	Paul Casey, England	2,324,031
41	Steve Flesch, USA	2,288,899
42	Camilo Villegas, Colombia	2,235,713
43	Jerry Kelly, USA	2,195,671
44	Mike Weir, Canada	2,154,535
45	David Toms, USA	2,150,837
46	Justin Leonard, USA	2,147,998
47	Nick Dougherty, England	2,130,378
48	Stuart Appleby, Australia	2,125,885
49	Stephen Ames, Canada	2,103,426
50	Carl Pettersson, Sweden	2,040,938
51	Richard Sterne, South Africa	2,003,409
52	Robert Karlsson, Sweden	1,985,398
53	Sean O'Hair, USA	1,972,476
54	John Senden, Australia	1,966,070
55	Gregory Havret, France	1,945,921
56	Daniel Chopra, Sweden	1,943,593
57	Ken Duke, USA	1,937,702
58	Anders Hansen, Denmark	1,915,700
59	Nick O'Hern, Australia	1,911,413
60	Miguel Angel Jimenez, Spain	1,882,618
61	Bubba Watson, USA	1,881,847
62	Jonathan Byrd, USA	1,854,906
63	Peter Hanson, Sweden	1,848,533
64	Nick Watney, USA	1,844,379
65	Billy Mayfair, USA	1,814,518
66	Charley Hoffman, USA	1,811,106
67	Arron Oberholser, USA	1,797,458
68	Graeme Storm, England	1,777,637
69	Marc Warren, Scotland	1,762,270
70	Raphael Jacquelin, France	1,724,253
71	Rod Pampling, Australia	1,707,577
72	Chad Campbell, USA	1,701,242
73	Simon Dyson, England	1,691,213
74	John Mallinger, USA	1,683,089
75	Pat Perez, Uruguay	1,678,295
76	Lucas Glover, USA	1,664,167
77	Soren Kjeldsen, Denmark	1,652,842
78	Mark Wilson, USA	1,637,112
79	Anthony Kim, USA	1,620,195
80	Bradley Dredge, Wales	1,614,035
81	Jeff Quinney, USA	1,612,056
82	Ryan Moore, USA	1,569,963
83	Bo Van Pelt, USA	1,559,181
84	Oliver Wilson, England	1,556,646
85	Peter Lonard, Australia	1,537,584

POS.	PLAYER, COUNTRY	TOTAL MONEY
86	Nathan Green, Australia	1,531,624
87	Toru Taniguchi, Japan	1,522,842
88	George McNeill, USA	1,504,627
89	Fredrik Jacobson, Sweden	1,469,541
90	Ryuji Imada, Japan	1,444,892
91	Steve Webster, England	1,395,564
92	Philip Archer, England	1,392,187
93	Richard Green, Australia	1,370,821
94	Markus Brier, Austria	1,366,517
95	Ross Fisher, England	1,360,460
96	Kevin Sutherland, USA	1,355,817
97	Mikko Ilonen, Finland	1,346,737
98	Chris DiMarco, USA	1,346,524
99	Joe Ogilvie, USA	1,341,263
100	Graeme McDowell, N. Ireland	1,331,299
101	Vaughn Taylor, USA	1,313,353
102	Brian Davis, England	1,294,796
103	Kenny Perry, USA	1,292,618
104	Jose Coceres, Argentina	1,289,603
105	Troy Matteson, USA	1,282,421
106	Robert Garrigus, USA	1,260,010
107	Dean Wilson, USA	1,258,507
108	Paul Goydos, USA	1,229,355
109	J.J. Henry, USA	1,213,660
110	Robert-Jan Derksen, Netherlands	1,208,430
111	Shingo Katayama, Japan	1,207,263
112	Charl Schwartzel, South Africa	1,206,185
113	Gonzalo Fernandez-Castano, Spain	1,190,754
114	Rocco Mediate, USA	1,190,594
115	Charlie Wi, Korea	1,190,009
116	Steve Marino, USA	1,181,275
117	Bart Bryant, USA	1,167,874
118	Jason Gore, USA	1,152,234
119	Jesper Parnevik, Sweden	1,131,873
120	Will MacKenzie, USA	1,116,507
121	Brian Gay, USA	1,114,571
122	Martin Kaymer, Germany	1,113,354
123	D.J. Trahan, USA	1,107,699
124	Kevin Stadler, USA	1,084,407
125	Thomas Bjorn, Denmark	1,083,835
126	Jyoti Randhawa, India	1,070,718
127	Stephen Leaney, Australia	1,070,179
128	Charles Warren, USA	1,068,440
129	Tim Petrovic, USA	1,052,447
130	Alex Cejka, Germany	1,051,275
131	Brendan Jones, Australia	1,049,445
132	Jeff Overton, USA	1,043,291
133	Shaun Micheel, USA	1,028,813
134	Brian Bateman, USA	1,022,763
135	Michael Allen, Ireland	1,016,952
136	Davis Love, USA	1,016,489
137	Jose Maria Olazabal, Spain	1,013,188
138	Johnson Wagner, USA	1,013,024
139	Steve Elkington, Australia	1,006,875

POS.	PLAYER, COUNTRY	TOTAL MONEY
140	Shigeki Maruyama, Japan	1,005,684
141	Fredrik Andersson Hed, Sweden	1,001,831
142	Mark Hensby, Australia	998,731
143	Gregory Bourdy, France	990,916
144	Jay Williamson, USA	988,764
145	Briny Baird, USA	985,453
146	Jeev Milkha Singh, India	982,395
147	Tommy Armour, USA	979,134
148	Mathew Goggin, Australia	969,488
149	Bill Haas, USA	967,443
150	Alastair Forsyth, Scotland	956,920
151	Tim Herron, USA	951,200
152	Thongchai Jaidee, Thailand	942,906
153	Tom Lehman, USA	937,645
154	Brett Rumford, Australia	932,609
155	Tom Pernice, Jr., USA	927,408
156	Cameron Beckman, USA	902,258
157	J.B. Holmes, USA	901,752
158	Cliff Kresge, USA	901,549
159	J.P. Hayes, USA	890,815
160	Matt Kuchar, USA	886,146
161	Pelle Edberg, Sweden	886,127
162	Bob Estes, USA	878,051
163	Anthony Wall, England	874,194
164	Ben Curtis, USA	872,321
165	Rich Beem, USA	869,983
166	Ryan Armour, USA	866,179
167	Prayad Marksaeng, Thailand	864,721
168	Peter O'Malley, Australia	860,734
169	Mark Foster, England	858,508
170	Kevin Na, Korea	856,669
171	Louis Oosthuizen, South Africa	850,319
172	Jeff Maggert, USA	845,585
173	Simon Khan, England	844,587
174	Peter Hedblom, Sweden	821,139
175	Paul McGinley, Ireland	820,665
176	Mathias Gronberg, Sweden	806,431
177	Andrew McLardy, South Africa	798,091
178	Simon Wakefield, England	797,932
179	Brett Quigley, USA	782,411
180	Ted Purdy, USA	758,734
181	Craig Kanada, USA	743,305
182	Liang Wen-chong, China	734,504
183	Anton Haig, South Africa	727,129
184	Joe Durant, USA	723,599
185	Alexander Noren, Sweden	701,823
186	Harrison Frazar, USA	699,859
187	Robert Gamez, USA	696,445
188	Mads Vibe-Hastrup, Denmark	693,903
189	Hideto Tanihara, Japan	690,078
190	Chris Stroud, USA	689,356
191	Prom Meesawat, Thailand	676,120
192	Johan Edfors, Sweden	673,545
193	John Merrick, USA	663,838

POS.	PLAYER, COUNTRY	TOTAL MONEY
194	James Kingston, South Africa	656,448
195	Parker McLachlin, USA	656,042
196	Francesco Molinari, Italy	654,354
197	Kent Jones, USA	651,108
198	Bob Heintz, USA	649,342
199	Daisuke Maruyama, Japan	645,658
200	Tomohiro Kondo, Japan	637,018
201	Tetsuji Hiratsuka, Japan	629,476
202	Alejandro Canizares, Spain	622,501
203	Daniel Vancsik, Argentina	621,268
204	Doug LaBelle, USA	604,633
205	Frankie Minoza, Philippines	599,238
206	Peter Lawrie, Ireland	594,289
207	Steve Allan, Australia	592,644
208	David Lynn, England	584,811
209	Frank Lickliter, USA	584,084
210	Lee Dong-hwan, Korea	583,630
211	Darren Clarke, N. Ireland	580,510
212	Paul Lawrie, Scotland	576,473
213	Jason Dufner, USA	574,992
214	Ariel Canete, Argentina	570,789
215	Craig Parry, Australia	569,788
216	Bob Tway, USA	564,767
217	Paul Broadhurst, England	564,262
218	Damian McGrane, Ireland	557,661
219	Martin Erlandsson, Sweden	554,501
220	Katsumasa Miyamoto, Japan	554,496
221	Corey Pavin, USA	553,947
222	Hiroyuki Fujita, Japan	551,279
223	Billy Andrade, USA	550,447
224	David Smail, New Zealand	549,535
225	Richard Finch, England	535,900
226	Jeff Gove, USA	533,811
227	Sam Little, England	532,448
228	Chris Riley, USA	527,661
229	Jason Bohn, USA	527,512
230	Marco Dawson, Germany	525,532
231	Ryan Palmer, USA	524,988
232	Gavin Coles, Australia	524,750
233	Michael Sims, Bermuda	514,922
234	John Bickerton, England	514,724
235	Andrew Buckle, Australia	513,630
236	Chapchai Nirat, Thailand	512,527
237	Koumei Oda, Japan	511,085
238	Y.E. Yang, Korea	508,979
239	Nick Flanagan, Australia	507,019
240	Steve Lowery, USA	502,622
241	Christian Cevaer, France	500,321
242	Taichi Teshima, Japan	499,497
243	Joost Luiten, Netherlands	490,881
244	Maarten Lafeber, Netherlands	475,170
245	Thomas Levet, France	473,223
246	Tripp Isenhour, USA	471,980
247	Per-Ulrik Johansson, Sweden	461,216

POS.	PLAYER, COUNTRY	TOTAL MONEY
248	Jean-Francois Lucquin, France	461,086
249	Lee Janzen, USA	459,189
250	Sam Walker, England	454,766
251	Brendon de Jonge, Zimbabwe	448,942
252	Richard Johnson, Wales	445,421
253	Tag Ridings, USA	445,408
254	Eric Axley, USA	443,461
255	Jarrod Lyle, Australia	442,068
256	Keiichiro Fukabori, Japan	437,460
257	Carlos Rodiles, Spain	436,954
258	Ricardo Gonzalez, Argentina	435,656
259	Shiv Kapur, India	435,128
260	Michael Campbell, New Zealand	432,316
261	Gary Murphy, Ireland	429,993
262	Yusaku Miyazato, Japan	427,604
263	Greg Owen, England	426,601
264	Garry Houston, Wales	424,557
265	Michael Putnam, USA	424,429
266	Stephen Gallacher, Scotland	422,648
267	Scott Hend, Australia	422,439
268	Dicky Pride, USA	415,792
269	Roland Thatcher, USA	415,124
270	Simon Yates, Scotland	409,348
271	Rory McIlroy, N. Ireland	408,929
272	Jose-Filipe Lima, Portugal	408,381
273	Toshi Izawa, Japan	406,692
274	Lee Slattery, England	403,064
275	Glen Day, USA	399,370
276	Marcus Fraser, Australia	396,724
277	Hiroshi Iwata, Japan	390,193
278	Jean Baptiste Gonnet, France	388,008
279	Chris Tidland, USA	387,661
280	Benn Barham, England	383,238
281	Zane, Scotland, England	382,640
282	David Frost, South Africa	380,182
283	Richard S. Johnson, Sweden	377,951
284	Barry Lane, England	376,501
285	David Griffiths, England	375,080
286	B.J. Staten, USA	368,596
287	Miles Tunnicliff, England	366,637
288	Jon Mills, Canada	366,244
289	Duffy Waldorf, USA	365,024
290	Chris Couch, USA	355,386
291	Steven Conran, Australia	354,203
292	John Daly, USA	350,632
293	Rich Barcelo, USA	350,494
294	Jose Manuel Lara, Spain	350,474
295	Jean-Francois Remesy, France	347,562
296	Hirofumi Miyase, Japan	347,500
297	Vance Veazey, USA	347,430
298	Garrett Willis, USA	345,622
299	Oliver Fisher, England	343,933
300	Kaname Yokoo, Japan	339,980
301	Thaworn Wiratchant, Thailand	338,735

POS.	PLAYER, COUNTRY	TOTAL MONEY
302	Yui Ueda, Japan	337,835
303	Scott Strange, Australia	336,375
304	Tom Whitehouse, England	335,535
305	Craig Bowden, USA	333,970
306	Nicholas Thompson, USA	333,206
307	Mardan Mamat, Singapore	332,984
308	Azuma Yano, Japan	332,662
309	Jason Day, Australia	331,542
310	Jun Kikuchi, Japan	330,278
311	Emanuele Canonica, Italy	328,681
312	Chawalit Plaphol, Thailand	328,140
313	Kyron Sullivan, Wales	325,824
314	David Branshaw, USA	323,407
315	Jarmo Sandelin, Sweden	319,390
316	Craig Lile, South Africa	318,846
317	Kirk Triplett, USA	317,359
318	Matt Jones, Australia	317,225
319	Lee Seung-ho, Korea	315,331
320	Skip Kendall, USA	312,148
321	Omar Uresti, USA	311,705
322	Phillip Price, Wales	310,976
323	Joey Sindelar, USA	310,717
324	Rafael Echenique, Argentina	308,953
325	Kim Kyung-tae, Korea	308,943
326	Greg Kraft, USA	308,322
327	Gaurav Ghei, India	304,867
328	Olin Browne, USA	304,605
329	Peter Fowler, Australia	303,558
330	Scott Gutschewski, USA	302,849
331	David Howell, England	302,332
332	Michael Jonzon, Sweden	301,017
333	Dudley Hart, USA	299,249
334	Ignacio Garrido, Spain	297,595
335	Henrik Nystrom, Sweden	296,489
336	Kyle Thompson, USA	294,148
337	Justin Bolli, USA	293,834
338	Kiyoshi Miyazato, Japan	292,033
339	Ross McGowan, England	291,154
340	Fred Couples, USA	290,585
341	D.J. Brigman, USA	290,205
342	Yasuharu Imano, Japan	290,183
343	Ian Garbutt, England	288,643
344	Norio Shinozaki, Japan	284,054
345	Stephen Dodd, Wales	283,798
346	Satoru Hirota, Japan	283,678
347	Paul Stankowski, USA	282,389
348	Patrick Sheehan, USA	281,523
349	Kyle Reifers, USA	281,189
350	Lu Wen-teh, Taiwan	280,606

World Money List Leaders

YEAR	PLAYER, COUNTRY	TOTAL MONEY
1966	Jack Nicklaus, USA	$168,088
1967	Jack Nicklaus, USA	276,166
1968	Billy Casper, USA	222,436
1969	Frank Beard, USA	186,993
1970	Jack Nicklaus, USA	222,583
1971	Jack Nicklaus, USA	285,897
1972	Jack Nicklaus, USA	341,792
1973	Tom Weiskopf, USA	349,645
1974	Johnny Miller, USA	400,255
1975	Jack Nicklaus, USA	332,610
1976	Jack Nicklaus, USA	316,086
1977	Tom Watson, USA	358,034
1978	Tom Watson, USA	384,388
1979	Tom Watson, USA	506,912
1980	Tom Watson, USA	651,921
1981	Johnny Miller, USA	704,204
1982	Raymond Floyd, USA	738,699
1983	Seve Ballesteros, Spain	686,088
1984	Seve Ballesteros, Spain	688,047
1985	Bernhard Langer, Germany	860,262
1986	Greg Norman, Australia	1,146,584
1987	Ian Woosnam, Wales	1,793,268
1988	Seve Ballesteros, Spain	1,261,275
1989	David Frost, South Africa	1,650,230
1990	Jose Maria Olazabal, Spain	1,633,640
1991	Bernhard Langer, Germany	2,186,700
1992	Nick Faldo, England	2,748,248
1993	Nick Faldo, England	2,825,280
1994	Ernie Els, South Africa	2,862,854
1995	Corey Pavin, USA	2,746,340
1996	Colin Montgomerie, Scotland	3,071,442
1997	Colin Montgomerie, Scotland	3,366,900
1998	Tiger Woods, USA	2,927,946
1999	Tiger Woods, USA	7,681,625
2000	Tiger Woods, USA	11,034,530
2001	Tiger Woods, USA	7,771,562
2002	Tiger Woods, USA	8,292,188
2003	Vijay Singh, Fiji	8,499,611
2004	Vijay Singh, Fiji	11,638,699
2005	Tiger Woods, USA	12,280,404
2006	Tiger Woods, USA	13,325,949
2007	Tiger Woods, USA	12,902,706

Career World Money List

Here is a list of the 50 leading money winners for their careers through the 2007 season. It includes players active on both the regular and senior tours of the world. The World Money List from this and the 41 previous editions of the annual and a table prepared for a companion book, *The Wonderful World of Professional Golf* (Atheneum, 1973) form the basis for this compilation. Additional figures were taken from official records of major golf associations, although shortcomings in records-keeping outside the United States in the 1950s and 1960s and a few exclusions from U.S. records during those years prevent these figures from being completely accurate, although the careers of virtually all of these top 50 players began after that time. Conversion of foreign currency figures to U.S. dollars is based on average values during the particular years involved.

POS.	PLAYER, COUNTRY	TOTAL MONEY
1	Tiger Woods, USA	$93,961,496
2	Vijay Singh, Fiji	66,066,862
3	Ernie Els, South Africa	63,993,354
4	Phil Mickelson, USA	49,824,642
5	Davis Love, USA	44,447,473
6	Jim Furyk, USA	42,361,932
7	Colin Montgomerie, Scotland	38,985,500
8	Retief Goosen, South Africa	35,574,095
9	Hale Irwin, USA	35,022,801
10	Padraig Harrington, Ireland	32,953,894
11	Sergio Garcia, Spain	31,729,132
12	Nick Price, Zimbabwe	31,618,270
13	Bernhard Langer, Germany	30,844,548
14	David Toms, USA	30,147,653
15	Fred Couples, USA	29,417,847
16	Mark Calcavecchia, USA	27,528,296
17	Tom Kite, USA	26,640,979
18	Jose Maria Olazabal, Spain	26,037,098
19	Darren Clarke, N. Ireland	25,987,498
20	Justin Leonard, USA	25,643,628
21	Tom Lehman, USA	25,334,099
22	Gil Morgan, USA	25,280,425
23	Greg Norman, Australia	24,715,241
24	Scott Hoch, USA	24,576,710
25	Fred Funk, USA	24,132,564
26	Jay Haas, USA	23,970,250
27	Kenny Perry, USA	23,809,921
28	Stuart Appleby, Australia	23,785,243
29	Chris DiMarco, USA	23,642,113
30	Adam Scott, Australia	23,595,051
31	Lee Westwood, England	23,308,316
32	Tom Watson, USA	23,286,851
33	Stuart Cink, USA	23,272,829
34	Mike Weir, Canada	22,966,384
35	Masashi Ozaki, Japan	21,861,349
36	Scott Verplank, USA	21,776,264
37	Mark O'Meara, USA	21,727,866
38	Loren Roberts, USA	21,682,058

POS.	PLAYER, COUNTRY	TOTAL MONEY
39	Robert Allenby, Australia	21,306,693
40	Jeff Sluman, USA	21,287,830
41	Brad Faxon, USA	21,262,412
42	Nick Faldo, England	20,563,137
43	Raymond Floyd, USA	20,460,105
44	Craig Stadler, USA	20,372,038
45	David Duval, USA	20,244,946
46	Larry Nelson, USA	19,957,560
47	Shigeki Maruyama, Japan	19,842,404
48	K.J. Choi, Korea	19,474,696
49	Jesper Parnevik, Sweden	18,591,533
50	Ian Woosnam, Wales	18,317,611

These 50 players have won $1,453,191,497 in their careers.

Women's World Money List

This list includes official earnings on the U.S. LPGA Tour, Ladies European Tour, Japan LPGA Tour and Korea LPGA Tour, along with other winnings in established unofficial events when reliable figures could be obtained.

POS.	PLAYER, COUNTRY	TOTAL MONEY
1	Lorena Ochoa, Mexico	$4,364,994
2	Suzann Pettersen, Norway	1,916,577
3	Momoko Ueda, Japan	1,575,449
4	Paula Creamer, USA	1,507,832
5	Mi Hyun Kim, Korea	1,273,848
6	Ji-Yai Shin, Korea	1,244,091
7	Cristie Kerr, USA	1,204,141
8	Seon Hwa Lee, Korea	1,164,986
9	Jeong Jang, Korea	1,155,718
10	Sakura Yokomine, Japan	1,102,298
11	Maria Hjorth, Sweden	1,035,208
12	Mi-Jeong Jeon, Korea	1,031,201
13	Jee Young Lee, Korea	1,031,044
14	Angela Park, Brazil	1,013,922
15	Morgan Pressel, USA	1,002,452
16	Natalie Gulbis, USA	963,904
17	Brittany Lincicome, USA	945,591
18	Laura Davies, England	900,406
19	Stacy Prammanasudh, USA	893,045
20	Se Ri Pak, Korea	884,917
21	Nicole Castrale, USA	884,292
22	Juli Inkster, USA	869,896
23	Miho Koga, Japan	868,802
24	Karrie Webb, Australia	838,030

POS.	PLAYER, COUNTRY	TOTAL MONEY
25	Yuri Fudoh, Japan	826,296
26	Ai Miyazato, Japan	824,077
27	Na Zhang, China	819,892
28	Shinobu Moromizato, Japan	797,476
29	Sarah Lee, Korea	777,872
30	Angela Stanford, USA	713,880
31	Catriona Matthew, Scotland	704,058
32	Sophie Gustafson, Sweden	691,824
33	Annika Sorenstam, Sweden	687,064
34	Shiho Oyama, Japan	679,971
35	Miki Saiki, Japan	648,103
36	Christina Kim, USA	626,075
37	Laura Diaz, USA	591,554
38	Shi Hyun Ahn, Korea	586,255
39	Sherri Steinhauer, USA	574,270
40	Akane Iijima, Japan	565,906
41	Julieta Granada, Paraguay	532,440
42	Meaghan, Francella, USA	507,292
43	In-Kyung Kim, Korea	504,226
44	Young Kim, Korea	490,696
45	Eun Hee Ji, Korea	484,124
46	Pat Hurst, USA	477,763
47	Akiko Fukushima, Japan	459,586
48	Chie Arimura, Japan	453,624
49	Sun Ju Ahn, Korea	446,535
50	Hyun-Ju Shin, Korea	446,275
51	Yuko Mitsuka, Japan	432,478
52	Nikki Campbell, Australia	409,960
53	Bo-Bae Song, Korea	409,945
54	Lindsey Wright, Australia	408,070
55	Reilley Rankin, USA	408,037
56	In-Bee Park, Korea	405,943
57	Hye Jung Choi, Korea	400,384
58	Rachel Hetherington, Australia	400,351
59	Yui Kawahara, Japan	400,024
60	Hiromi Mogi, Japan	399,990
61	Erina Hara, Japan	383,065
62	Ayako Uehara, Japan	376,122
63	Amy Hung, Taiwan	375,701
64	Brittany Lang, USA	348,148
65	Midori Yoneyama, Japan	343,517
66	Gwladys Nocera, France	340,337
67	Mie Nakata, Japan	338,939
68	Meena Lee, Korea	334,975
69	Kuniko Maeda, Japan	327,245
70	Bettina Hauert, Germany	313,308
71	Linda Wessberg, Sweden	312,608
72	Na On Min, Korea	309,886
73	Mhairi McKay, Scotland	309,739
74	Trish Johnson, England	308,955
75	Mikiyo Nishizuka, Japan	308,411
76	Kyeong Bae, Korea	308,158
77	Birdie Kim, Korea	308,088
78	Jimin Kang, Korea	304,609

POS.	PLAYER, COUNTRY	TOTAL MONEY
79	Hiroko Yamaguchi, Japan	294,764
80	Saiki Fujita, Japan	287,906
81	Beth Bader, USA	286,761
82	Joo Mi Kim, Korea	285,759
83	Yun-Jye Wei, Taiwan	284,680
84	Silvia Cavalleri, Italy	283,493
85	Becky Morgan, Wales	262,594
86	Nobuko Kizawa, Japan	254,233
87	Il Mi Chung, Korea	250,494
88	Yukari Baba, Japan	248,537
89	Janice Moodie, Scotland	246,756
90	So-Hee Kim, Korea	241,903
91	Ji-Yeon Han, Korea	240,688
92	Yun-Joo Jeong, Korea	238,781
93	Na Yeon Choi, Korea	237,881
94	Ji-Hee Lee, Korea	237,356
95	Gloria Park, Korea	237,024
96	Diana D'Alessio, USA	236,528
97	Rui Kitada, Japan	234,881
98	Michiko Hattori, Japan	233,682
99	Jae-Hee Bae, Korea	232,046
100	Becky Brewerton, Wales	226,620
101	Nikki Garrett, Australia	226,111
102	Wendy Ward, USA	224,452
103	Giulia Sergas, Italy	223,737
104	Alena Sharp, Canada	223,258
105	Tamie Durdin, Australia	219,693
106	Virginie Lagoutte-Clement, France	217,672
107	Martina Eberl, Germany	217,663
108	Mihoko Takahashi, Japan	216,048
109	Iben Tinning, Denmark	216,043
110	Joanne Mills, Australia	211,133
111	Lisa Hall, England	209,023
112	Karin Sjodin, Sweden	198,889
113	Young Ran Jo, Korea	198,213
114	Hee Young Park, Korea	198,143
115	Toshimi Kimura, Japan	196,347
116	Katherine Hull, Australia	195,286
117	Mayumi Shimomura, Japan	191,365
118	Jeong-Eun Lee, Korea	190,032
119	Michele Redman, USA	186,462
120	Namika Omata, Japan	186,160
121	Paula Marti, Spain	186,068
122	Mihoko Iseri, Japan	185,579
123	Teresa Lu, Taiwan	181,025
124	Heather Young, USA	178,421
125	Yuko Saitoh, Japan	171,955
126	Candie Kung, Taiwan	171,505
127	Carin Koch, Sweden	165,548
128	Karine Icher, France	165,253
129	Mayu Hattori, Japan	164,538
130	Rebecca Hudson, England	163,676
131	Sophie Giquel, France	163,299
132	Jin Joo Hong, Korea	162,524

POS.	PLAYER, COUNTRY	TOTAL MONEY
133	Kirsty Taylor, England	161,585
134	Carri Wood, USA	155,737
135	Veronica Zorzi, Italy	155,468
136	Charlotte Mayorkas, USA	154,187
137	Yuka Shiroto, Japan	153,376
138	Ji-Hyun Lee, Korea	151,854
139	Wendy Doolan, Australia	151,437
140	Lotta Wahlin, Sweden	148,922
141	Ji-Young Oh, Korea	148,876
142	Hyun Hee Moon, Korea	148,065
143	Yasuko Satoh, Japan	146,117
144	Yuka Irie, Japan	145,792
145	Kaori Higo, Japan	140,287
146	Ya Ni Tseng, Taiwan	139,911
147	Johanna Westerberg, Sweden	139,878
148	Kurumi Dohi, Japan	139,387
149	Dorothy Delasin, USA	138,615
150	Lorie Kane, Canada	138,465

Senior World Money List

This list includes official earnings from the world money list of the International Federation of PGA Tours, U.S. Senior PGA Tour, European Seniors Tour and Japan Senior Tour, along with other winnings in established unofficial events when reliable figures could be obtained.

POS.	PLAYER, COUNTRY	TOTAL MONEY
1	Jay Haas, USA	$2,581,001
2	Fred Funk, USA	2,332,340
3	Loren Roberts, USA	2,183,287
4	Bernhard Langer, Germany	1,954,676
5	Brad Bryant, USA	1,812,099
6	Denis Watson, Zimbabwe	1,658,312
7	D.A. Weibring, USA	1,557,622
8	R.W. Eaks, USA	1,534,098
9	Tom Kite, USA	1,494,441
10	Mark O'Meara, USA	1,466,730
11	Tom Watson, USA	1,429,715
12	Tom Purtzer, USA	1,391,436
13	Hale Irwin, USA	1,314,013
14	Eduardo Romero, Argentina	1,305,530
15	Keith Fergus, USA	1,237,282
16	Gil Morgan, USA	1,175,162
17	Mark McNulty, Zimbabwe	1,078,736
18	Jim Thorpe, USA	1,047,038
19	Naomichi Ozaki, Japan	1,023,560
20	Scott Hoch, USA	997,487
21	Lonnie Nielsen, USA	989,722

POS.	PLAYER, COUNTRY	TOTAL MONEY
22	David Eger, USA	889,560
23	Andy Bean, USA	869,591
24	Ben Crenshaw, USA	859,496
25	Dana Quigley, USA	854,348
26	Scott Simpson, USA	833,338
27	Des Smyth, Ireland	787,435
28	Mark James, England	778,865
29	David Edwards, USA	756,767
30	Bob Gilder, USA	742,894
31	Bobby Wadkins, USA	726,364
32	Craig Stadler, USA	628,414
33	Kiyoshi Murota, Japan	623,802
34	Tom Jenkins, USA	600,959
35	Carl Mason, England	573,203
36	Nick Price, Zimbabwe	568,292
37	Fuzzy Zoeller, USA	542,316
38	Morris Hatalsky, USA	541,195
39	Don Pooley, USA	540,809
40	Jeff Sluman, USA	505,012
41	Curtis Strange, USA	501,638
42	Masahiro Kuramoto, Japan	491,465
43	Wayne Levi, USA	482,250
44	Tim Simpson, USA	482,035
45	Allen Doyle, USA	472,248
46	Mark Wiebe, USA	463,604
47	John Harris, USA	461,207
48	Jerry Pate, USA	442,745
49	John Cook, USA	435,990
50	Bruce Vaughan, USA	434,934
51	Tom McKnight, USA	415,521
52	Chip Beck, USA	401,739
53	Costantino Rocca, Italy	389,931
54	Mike Reid, USA	379,779
55	Katsuyoshi Tomori, Japan	377,591
56	John Jacobs, USA	373,032
57	Bruce Lietzke, USA	369,218
58	Sam Torrance, Scotland	369,210
59	Larry Nelson, USA	355,611
60	Danny Edwards, USA	337,096
61	Juan Quiros, Spain	327,933
62	Rod Spittle, Canada	325,151
63	Stewart Ginn, Australia	324,634
64	Vicente Fernandez, Argentina	318,116
65	Greg Norman, Australia	313,577
66	Bruce Summerhays, USA	264,893
67	Jay Sigel, USA	263,363
68	Hajime Meshiai, Japan	259,934
69	Bruce Fleisher, USA	254,678
70	Bob Cameron, England	248,526
71	Boonchu Ruangkit, Thailand	240,703
72	Ross Drummond, Scotland	239,083
73	Nick Job, England	234,241
74	Peter Jacobsen, USA	233,646
75	Jose Rivero, Spain	227,586

POS.	PLAYER, COUNTRY	TOTAL MONEY
76	Tateo Ozaki, Japan	226,228
77	Dave Eichelberger, USA	226,158
78	Leonard Thompson, USA	221,431
79	John Bland, South Africa	220,274
80	Katsunari Takahashi, Japan	209,915
81	Isao Aoki, Japan	209,823
82	Mitch Adams, USA	208,297
83	James Mason, USA	201,261
84	Raymond Floyd, USA	200,366
85	Donnie Hammond, USA	198,033
86	Gordon J. Brand, England	193,880
87	Tom Wargo, USA	189,006
88	Mark Johnson, USA	185,315
89	Luis Carbonetti, Argentina	182,832
90	Walter Hall, USA	182,119
91	Doug Johnson, USA	181,544
92	Graham Marsh, Australia	181,395
93	Bill Longmuir, Scotland	178,483
94	Mike McCullough, USA	176,061
95	Dick Mast, USA	171,390
96	Tsuneyuki Nakajima, Japan	170,794
97	Tsukasa Watanabe, Japan	169,670
98	John Chillas, Scotland	158,050
99	Dave Stockton, USA	149,232
100	Kenny Knox, USA	148,659
101	Ed Dougherty, USA	147,572
102	Toyotake Nakao, Japan	143,636
103	Hugh Baiocchi, South Africa	143,133
104	Bobby Lincoln, South Africa	142,753
105	Guillermo Encina, Chile	142,043
106	Seiji Ebihara, Japan	138,084
107	John Ross, USA	137,127
108	David Ishii, USA	134,828
109	Giuseppe Cali, Italy	133,565
110	Tony Allen, England	133,416
111	Horacio Carbonetti, Argentina	132,268
112	Tony Johnstone, Zimbabwe	129,333
113	Tim Conley, USA	127,377
114	David Merriman, Australia	126,954
115	Glenn Ralph, England	126,002
116	Noboru Fujiike, Japan	122,025
117	Mitch Adcock, USA	120,735
118	Simon Owen, New Zealand	119,621
119	Kirk Hanefeld, USA	117,558
120	Ron Streck, USA	115,475
121	Jack Ferenz, USA	107,656
122	Bruce Heuchan, Canada	105,201
123	Pete Oakley, USA	104,943
124	Martin Poxon, England	104,197
125	David Good, Australia	103,452

1. The Year in Retrospect

The world's best gathered at Firestone Country Club for the final World Golf Championship of the year, held one week before the final major championship of the year, and the caddie barn was alive with chatter about whom some considered to be the hottest player in golf. They were talking about Hunter Mahan, a 25-year-old who was starting to fulfill his potential. In his last four tournaments, Mahan had won the Travelers Championship, tied for eighth in the AT&T National, tied for sixth in The Open Championship by closing with 65 at Carnoustie, and tied for fifth in the Canadian Open. Strong stuff, for sure, until it was put into proper perspective.

"Put Tiger Woods's name next to that record," one caddie said, "and you'd call it a slump."

Such are the expectations that Woods has created, and perhaps even more amazing is that he continues to live up to them. When he arrived at Firestone, Woods had gone a whopping five tournaments without winning, including another squandered opportunity in a major championship. That's all it takes for the memory to lose track of his victories in the Buick Invitational, WGC-CA Championship and Wachovia Championship, against some of the strongest fields this side of a major. As usual, it didn't take long for Woods to remind anyone who's the boss. He won the Bridgestone Invitational that week with the lone score under par, eight shots clear of the field.

In sweltering heat at Southern Hills the following week, Woods tied a major championship record with 63 on his way to a two-shot victory at the PGA Championship for his 13th career major title, moving within five of the benchmark held by Jack Nicklaus. After a runner-up finish in his first start of the PGA Tour Playoffs, he won the final two playoff events by a combined 10 shots to capture the inaugural FedExCup. After compiling a winning record in the Presidents Cup, the world's No. 1 player picked up his toys and went home, leaving everyone else to ponder just how large the gap has become.

"There's isn't any comparison," Fred Couples said at the end of the year. "Tiger is the best player, by far. By far."

TIGER WOODS

EVENT	POSITION
Buick Invitational	1
Dubai Desert Classic	T-3
WGC-Accenture Match Play	T-9
Arnold Palmer Invitational	T-22
WGC-CA Championship	1
Masters Tournament	T-2
Wachovia Championship	1
The Players Championship	T-37
Memorial Tournament	T-15
U.S. Open Championship	T-2

AT&T National	T-6
The Open Championship	T-12
WGC - Bridgestone Invitational	1
PGA Championship	1
Deutsche Bank Championship	T-2
BMW Championship	1
The Tour Championship	1
Target World Challenge	1

Not that the rest of the best didn't try. Phil Mickelson hired Woods's old swing coach, Butch Harmon, and raised hopes that he would challenge Woods when he won The Players Championship. He also went head-to-head with Woods for three rounds at the Deutsche Bank Championship, including the final round, to win by two shots. But the months in between were a disaster, a lost summer courtesy of an injured left wrist. And after beating Woods outside Beantown, Woods beat him by 18 shots the next time they played.

Rory Sabbatini tried to take on Woods with his mouth, saying he looked "beatable as ever," this right after Woods beat him by two at the Wachovia Championship. The other time they played together in the final group was at the Bridgestone Invitational. Woods closed with 65, Sabbatini shot 74 and was so frustrated that he asked police to remove a fan who asked him at the turn, "Still look beatable?"

Two guys who slowed Woods's pursuit of Nicklaus were not players anyone would have predicted, Zach Johnson at the Masters Tournament and Angel Cabrera at the U.S. Open Championship, yet those glorious weeks did not stack up to an incomparable year.

For Woods, it was an unforgettable year for as many reasons off the course, one in particular.

After failing to make a birdie on the last nine at Oakmont and finishing one shot behind Cabrera in the U.S. Open, there was a tiny crack in his voice as Woods spoke to network television when he finished. It was not the first time Woods had finished second in a major, or even a U.S. Open. But the emotion had little to do with losing.

Woods flew home to Florida that night, and in the morning, his wife Elin gave birth to their first child. They named her Sam Alexis, Sam being the code name that Woods's father, Earl, had used for him. Woods had come full circle since 2006, when he spent most of the year grieving the death of his father. "Something that Elin and I talked about on our first night was, 'How can you love something so much that didn't exist the day before?'" Speculation on the effect it would have on his golfing career was just as rampant as when his father died. How would he respond? Would being a father distract him from his pursuit of Nicklaus's record? Could he still be as driven? By the end of the year, everyone had their answer. No change.

The victories, the trophies, the awards, they are becoming a blur. The record for 2007 will show that Woods won seven times on the PGA Tour, won the money title again with over $10.8 million, tied his PGA Tour record for lowest adjusted scoring average (67.79) and swept all the major awards. It was one victory (and one major) fewer than 2006, although Woods looked dominant as ever.

Each week brought more comfort with Woods's swing, and it reached a point that he stopped going to the practice range after a round at Carnoustie. Perhaps the biggest change was that Woods no longer had to rely on so many dramatic shots. The swashbuckler gave way to a surgeon, cutting apart the field with precision that made winning inevitable. Even as he reviewed his season, Woods could not think of a single shot that would be highlight material for years, such as the chip-in at the Masters that went up the slope, down the slope and paused briefly at the cut; or that six iron out of the bunker and over the water at the Canadian Open. Or holing out for eagle at Pebble Beach.

If anything, Woods figured the most memorable shot was his 15-foot birdie putt that caught three-quarters of the lip before spinning out, denying him 62 in the second round of the PGA Championship. His best shot was his drive on the 16th in the final round at Southern Hills. It wasn't anything dramatic, but darn close to perfection.

An example of his signature shots in 2007 came at his first tournament, the Buick Invitational. Woods found himself in a surprising dogfight with Charles Howell when he came to the 17th hole with a one-shot lead and no room for error. From 145 yards in the fairway, Woods hit a nine iron with a slight draw over the bunker to three feet for a birdie that essentially sealed the victory. It was his third straight victory at Torrey Pines, and his second straight year opening a new season with a victory. And dating to The Open the year before, it was his seventh consecutive victory on the PGA Tour, the second-longest streak in history behind the 11 in a row won by Byron Nelson in 1945.

Even more than Woods's six-tournament winning streak in 1999-2000, catching Lord Byron looked more possible than ever. Some scribes even surmised when Nelson's record would fall. He had twice won the Accenture Match Play Championship, was the two-time defending champion at the WGC-CA Championship at Doral, he had won four straight times at Bay Hill, and he was the favorite every year at the Masters. And he decided to play the EDS Byron Nelson Championship, well, what a place to reach 12 in a row.

The PGA Tour streak ended sooner than imagined. In a third-round match at The Gallery outside Tucson, Arizona, Woods was on the verge of completing a terrific comeback against Nick O'Hern of Australia, a short-hitting southpaw who had beaten Woods in the second round two years earlier. On the 19th hole, Woods only had to make a four-foot birdie putt to reach the quarter-finals. But he failed to notice a spike mark that he said knocked his ball slightly off its path.

One hole later, O'Hern holed from 12 feet for par to become the first player to beat Woods twice in match play. More significant was the fact that for the first time in nearly eight months, Woods left a PGA Tour event without a trophy. "To go basically from July until now without ever finishing out of the top three, that's not bad," Woods said.

Woods added victories at the CA Championship at Doral, making for a rare repeat. It was his third straight victory at Doral, and his third straight victory in this World Golf Championship, which had taken over for the American Express Championship and moved to the Blue Monster. It also was memorable for one quirky statistic that turned a half-hundred players into footnotes. Brett Wetterich became the 50th player to be runner-up to Woods on the PGA Tour. "Guess I had to be some kind of statistic," Wetterich said.

Despite disappointments in the majors, Woods added a victory in his 24th different PGA Tour event at the Wachovia Championship, where the last nine turned into a struggle. Woods made bogey from 74 yards in the fairway on the par-five 10th hole, and his three-putt double bogey on the 13th momentarily cost him the lead. Even so, it was surprising to hear Sabbatini the following week at The Players Championship say that Woods "looked beatable as ever."

"I've seen Tiger when he hits the ball well," Sabbatini said. "And I've seen Tiger when there's not a facet of his game that you're not amazed. But I think Sunday, he struggled out there. He had to battle for that win. And I think that made me realize ... he's as beatable as ever. I've seen him when he figures it out. It's scary. I don't want to see that anymore. I like the new Tiger."

It was the classic case of tugging on Superman's cape, although Woods was more amused than perturbed. He conceded that he wasn't swinging his best in the final round at Quail Hollow, but Woods cares only about trophies, and he was quick to point out that he already had won three times in six starts for the year, equal to the number of tournaments Sabbatini had won in his entire career.

They would not meet again until the final round at Firestone, where Sabbatini again offered some perplexing comments. He referred to the final round as a rubber match, noting that Woods had won at Wachovia, but that Sabbatini had beaten him in the final round of the NCAA finals in 1996. It was pointed out to the South African that Woods won the NCAA title, but Sabbatini noted that he outscored Woods in the last round, and he counted that as a personal victory. It was hard to tell if he was serious.

Whatever the case, the humor was gone the next day when Sabbatini went from one shot ahead to seven shots behind in nine holes. That was part of a closing stretch in which Woods won four of his last five starts, the final two being the most lucrative.

The PGA Tour promoted a "new era in golf" with the advent of the FedExCup, a season-long points race. The points were reset going into four "playoff" events, and Woods made headlines without even hitting a shot. He wanted a rest instead of teeing it up at The Barclays, deflating Commissioner Tim Finchem's hopes that all the stars would compete four weeks in a row. In fact, the only time everyone showed up was for the season-ending Tour Championship.

Even after sitting out the first week and finishing second to Mickelson in the second week, Woods still managed to suck all the excitement out of golf's version of the playoffs. He won the BMW Championship (formerly known as the Western Open) at Cog Hill outside Chicago to regain the FedExCup lead, then pulled away with an eight-shot victory at The Tour Championship, the first time he won the season-ending event since 1999.

Woods seized control with his best stretch of the year in the second round at East Lake, playing a six-hole stretch in seven under par that culminated with a 70-foot eagle putt on the ninth. Woods had to settle for 63, but the tournament was effectively over, and the mystique added another layer. "I played pretty good," Steve Stricker said. "I was two under and I'm five down. You just start thinking, 'Jeepers, what just happened?' He's got a lot of offense, if you know what I mean. You're just waiting for that run of holes, and then he takes off."

The Playoffs were loaded with high-quality golf and good storylines, from Stricker winning The Barclays for the first time in more than six years, to Mickelson winning his duel against Woods, to the world's No. 1 player making sure his name was the first engraved on the new FedExCup.

The only misstep came at the trophy presentation. The Tour built one of its television advertisement campaigns for the series on "Who will be the first to kiss the cup?" A staff member reminded Finchem of the slogan on the 18th green at East Lake, and Finchem made the mistake of telling Woods upon handing him the trophy that it had never been kissed. And it still hasn't, for telling Woods what to do in such a staged moment is the one way to guarantee that he won't do it.

Woods usually saves his lips for trophies they hand out four weeks out of the year, and the FedExCup was not one of those weeks. It was worth $10 million in deferred compensation, which prompted a couple of hypothetical stories about how much money Woods could stash away if he kept winning the cup and drawing interest on the deferred prize. One had him cashing in for $1 billion.

The Tour got edgy about its tax-deferred plan and changed the payout at year's end so that the 2008 winner will get $9 million in cash and $1 million deferred. Money matters aside, the FedExCup was a snapshot of the year. The drama was missing on the final day, which could be attributed to Woods and his superlative, consistent play. And it really didn't change how golf is perceived, another tribute to Woods and the course he has charted. All it did was bring together a strong collection of players for four straight weeks after the majors were over. That wasn't all bad.

Mickelson would have given away $10 million in exchange for a healthy summer. The advertising slogan "What will Phil do next?" never carried more intrigue going into the 2007 season because of what had transpired the year before, specifically in the U.S. Open at Winged Foot. There was the perception, whether right or wrong, that Mickelson was on the cusp of becoming Woods's peer in popularity and performance.

All Mickelson needed was a par on the final hole of the U.S. Open to join Woods as the only players in the last 50 years to win three straight majors. The rest is history. Mickelson made double bogey to lose by one, and he never came close to winning the rest of the year. He disappeared after going 0-4-1 in the Ryder Cup, and his promise to learn from his mistakes rang hollow at the start of the new season when he failed to finish in the top 25 in his first two tournaments, then missed the cut at the FBR Open.

That started to change when Mickelson opened with 65 at Poppy Hills to share the first-round lead of the AT&T Pebble Beach National Pro-Am, and he never let up. He closed with 66 at Pebble Beach for a five-stroke victory, the 30th of his career, and making him the third player in PGA

Tour history to surpass $40 million in career earnings. The jaw-dropping number, though, was that Mickelson only missed one fairway in the final round, showing remarkable control of the club that for so many years got him into big trouble. Anyone worried about a hangover from Winged Foot could rest easy. "Phil's game hasn't gone anywhere," Kevin Sutherland said. "He played tremendous today. And he's going to be a force the rest of the year."

Sutherland sounded prophetic when, one week later, Mickelson again took charge at Riviera in the Nissan Open and was on his way to victory against a strong field. Even though Woods skipped the tournament, it still had 11 of the top 13 players in the world. Mickelson found himself in a battle late Sunday afternoon against Howell, who a month earlier had the misfortune of running into Woods. Mickelson appeared to close out the title with a straight and powerful tee shot on the par-five 17th and a hybrid to 25 feet for a two-putt birdie and a one-shot lead. But his approach from the left rough on the 18th came out heavy, his chip was horrible by his standards, and he missed an 18-foot par putt that forced a playoff.

Howell finally prevailed on the third extra hole when Mickelson again hit a pedestrian chip and missed a six-foot par putt. For Howell, it was only the second victory of his career and his first in nearly five years. Mickelson had no reason to hang his head. He won convincingly at Pebble Beach. He played well enough to win at Riviera, a course he had not played in six years, and he was excited about the rest of the year. A brief encounter the next week at the Accenture Match Play Championship showed how serious he was.

Butch Harmon, famous for working with Greg Norman and Tiger Woods when they rose to No. 1 in the world, ambled down the practice range at The Gallery outside Tucson, Arizona, and took his position behind Mickelson, hands thrust in his pockets, observing the swing, asking a few questions, making a few suggestions. They walked into a tent to get away from a few curious onlookers, shared a private conversation and Harmon went back to work with his other clients.

Mickelson called his swing coach, Rick Smith, to let him know he had Harmon watch him hit a few balls, worried that this would turn out to be big news. It became just that in due time. Mickelson and Smith are longtime friends, as are their families, and insiders said it was difficult for Mickelson to let him go. But change was inevitable after the Masters, where Mickelson failed to break par the entire tournament, the first time in his career at Augusta National he didn't break par over four straight rounds. He announced the change a few weeks later.

The idea of Mickelson hiring Woods's old swing coach was tantalizing in itself, and that was before the results started to pour in. He tied for third at the EDS Byron Nelson Championship. He tied for third at the Wachovia Championship. And at The Players Championship, Mickelson broke through for his second victory of the year and his first in what many regard as the fifth major. His caddie, Jim Mackay, loosened the flag from the 18th pin as he always does when the boss wins, and Mickelson whipped out a marker and wrote a message: "Butch, the 1st of many." He then handed it to his new swing coach, and they walked arm-in-arm up the hill toward the clubhouse to collect their first trophy. At that moment, it looked like many more would follow.

"What's most exciting is I feel like we're just getting started," Mickelson said that day. "You're just seeing the tip of the iceberg," Harmon gushed.

An iceberg isn't what sunk the Mickelson ocean liner, however. After a two-week break, Mickelson headed to Oakmont Country Club for two days of laborious practice for the U.S. Open, when he circles the greens and chips from every imaginable angle to every imaginable hole location. The U.S. Golf Association had let the grass grow, and after hours of practice, Mickelson felt tenderness in his wrist. When he arrived at the Memorial that week, his wrist felt worse. A trainer came onto the fairway on the first nine of his opening round, and when he reached the 12th tee, Mickelson put his glove in his bag, shook hands with J.B. Holmes and Ryan Palmer and withdrew from the tournament.

Mickelson couldn't continue, and he didn't want to jeopardize his wrist any more with the U.S. Open two weeks away. He said the injury came from chipping at Oakmont in the thick grass, although that puzzled some of his peers, who figured it would be his right wrist that was sore. Whatever the case, he showed up at Oakmont looking more suited for the bowling alley than a major championship. He wore a black brace on his left wrist and said he was healthy enough to give it a try.

While he opened with a respectable 74, Mickelson couldn't keep the ball in play, shot 77 in the second round and was eliminated by the 10-shot rule when Cabrera birdied his 36th hole. It left Mickelson frustrated, and no less analytical about his major preparations. "This really was dangerous doing what I did," he said, "because the rough was twice as long, and I thought that they may play it like that, and certainly with this liquid fertilizer and these new machines that make the grass suck straight up, it absolutely is dangerous." It was his first missed cut in a major championship, and he was not eligible for the Purple Heart.

The rest of his summer essentially was wasted. Mickelson later said his wrist was not pain-free until late August, although that didn't keep him from playing, and almost winning, the Barclays Scottish Open at Loch Lomond. A roller-coaster last nine put him into a playoff with unheralded Frenchman Gregory Havret, who wound up beating the world's No. 2 player. Mickelson didn't find any momentum across Scotland at Carnoustie, where he missed the cut in his second straight major at The Open, or at Southern Hills, where he was never a factor at the PGA Championship and tied for 32nd.

It looked as though his season essentially ended during practice at Oakmont, and Mickelson talked about playing after The Tour Championship, which is rare for him. He planned to make two trips overseas, in Singapore and China, because he was healthy enough to resume work with Harmon on his long game and he wanted to test new equipment. As it turned out, Mickelson recovered sooner than some people imagined.

One aspect of the FedExCup that was widely popular was basing the draw for the first two rounds on the standings. That put Woods, Mickelson and Vijay Singh together for two rounds at the Deutsche Bank Championship, the second installment of the PGA Tour Playoffs, and the fourth hole proved to be an omen for the week. Woods and Mickelson drove into the greenside bunker on the par-four fourth. Woods took three shots to get out and took double bogey. They were paired again in the final round, both trailing Wetterich, and Mickelson again won the battle, a rare head-to-head meeting with Woods in the final round when Mickelson had beaten him.

It was his most significant victory this side of a major championship, and Mickelson used the moment for a power play against Finchem. He said in an interview with NBC Sports after the round that he was frustrated over the last year by the Tour not following through on his requests for the FedExCup, and he would not feel bad if he skipped the next week, which he did. Politics aside, the wheels were churning again, and Mickelson again looked capable of making another run at Woods.

"This is what we hoped the summer would be," Harmon said. "And if it hadn't have been for the hand injury, it would have been." Mickelson added one more victory, at the HSBC Champions in China, before calling it a year. And just like the previous season, he left people wondering what the next year had in store, even if no one was bracing for the worst this time.

Stricker knows a thing or two about tough times. He wasn't good long enough for most people to realize how far he had fallen, but rock bottom came at the end of the 2005 season when the Wisconsin native finished outside the top 150 on the money list, failed to turn in his qualifying application and had to rely on limited status as a former champion and whatever sponsor invitations he could get. So it was no surprise that Stricker was voted the PGA Tour comeback player of the year in 2006 after starting with nothing and earning consideration for the Ryder Cup team.

Stricker wound up 34th on the money list without winning, then made it all the way back in 2007. How far? When he arrived at the Presidents Cup — his first team event in 11 years — he was told that he was part of the "Big Four." Stricker smiled as though someone were pulling his leg. It was that hard to believe, that a guy who only 21 months ago didn't even have his PGA Tour card, could be the No. 4 player in the world ranking behind Woods, Mickelson and Jim Furyk.

All that was missing was a trophy, and Stricker must have wondered if that would ever happen. His first great chance came at the Wachovia Championship, when he quietly stayed in contention ahead of the Woods-Sabbatini final pairing. Woods gave up sole possession of the lead with a three-putt double bogey on the 13th hole, but one of the toughest closing stretches on the PGA Tour ate up Stricker. He took double bogey on the 16th hole at Quail Hollow, rebounded with a birdie on the peninsula-green 17th, only to find water with his approach on the 18th to finish second.

Then came two great opportunities in the majors. Stricker, who possesses one of the purest putting strokes in golf, was among those tied for the lead through nine holes Sunday at Oakmont when he pulled his tee shot into a bunker and took double bogey on the 10th and was not heard from the rest of the day. A month later at Carnoustie, he was in the final group with Sergio Garcia and poised to take advantage of the Spaniard's collapse, but he was ghastly with his best club in the bag. Stricker missed three putts inside five feet and again drifted into obscurity. But those heartaches eventually served him well.

He rarely plays Westchester Country Club and had such a tough time the last time he was there that he told wife Nicki, who was caddying for him at the time, "Take a picture because we're not coming back." This being the start of the PGA Tour Playoffs, he showed up, then kept up with K.J. Choi. Everything pointed to another victory for the South Korean, especially when Choi poured in two birdie putts with a combined length of nearly 100 feet. Stricker refused to give in, however. He holed a 12-foot birdie on the 16th to regain a share of the lead, dropped a wedge into four feet on the 17th for another birdie, and made it three in a row with an eight-foot birdie on the final hole.

The tears were inevitable. Stricker is emotional at Open House for his eight-year-old daughter, and this victory was more than six years in the making. "I've been waiting for this day for a long time," Stricker said, still wiping his eyes. It was no accident. Instead of moping, protesting or demanding privilege, Stricker spent his winter months in Wisconsin inside a mobile home with a wall knocked out, allowing him to hit balls to a frozen range. He wound up second to Woods in the FedExCup standings, and he finished No. 4 on the PGA Tour money list with over $4.6 million, a career-best.

"He should be comeback player of the year again," Woods said during the Playoffs. Turns out he wasn't kidding, and Stricker received the award for an unprecedented second straight year. "I was thinking about what I would have to do to win this three years in a row. Usually, you have to have a better year than last year. I don't know if I did that if I would be out of this ballot and maybe on the player of the year ballot," he said.

Choi had a career season in his own right, adding two impressive trophies to his collection. One came at the Memorial Tournament, where he beat a world-class field and had a private audience with Jack Nicklaus. Perhaps it was only fitting that Choi won at Jack's place, since it was an instruction book by Nicklaus that a high school teacher gave him to nudge him toward golf. Choi studied it religiously and credits Nicklaus with getting him started on the right path. His other victory came at the inaugural AT&T National at Congressional, a new tournament hosted by Woods with money going toward building a second Tiger Woods Learning Center. The tournament came together quickly after The International pulled out.

Other two-time winners on the PGA Tour were Vijay Singh (Mercedes-Benz Championship, Arnold Palmer Invitational), Zach Johnson (Masters, AT&T Classic) and Steve Flesch, who won two opposite-field tournaments that were meaningful in other ways. His victory in the Reno-Tahoe Open earned him the final spot in the PGA Championship, and winning the Turning Stone Resort eventually made him eligible for the Masters and U.S. Open for 2008. Jim Furyk finished the season at No. 3 in the world, becoming the first player in 56 years to win the Canadian Open in consecutive years. That kept frustrations to a minimum, as Furyk lost a playoff at the Crowne Plaza Invitational at Colonial and joined Woods as the runner-up at the U.S. Open.

Strangely enough, Furyk only played the Canadian Open because he was defending champion. With a change in the schedule, that meant playing eight times in nine weeks, although an injury forced him to sit out the Bridgestone Invitational, and he nearly missed the PGA Championship.

Frustration belonged instead to Ernie Els. For the third straight year, he failed to win on the PGA Tour, the longest drought since he burst onto the scene as a 24-year-old winner of the U.S. Open at Oakmont in 1994. His last PGA Tour victory was the WGC-American Express Championship in Ireland in 2004, and his last trophy on U.S. soil came at the Memorial in 2004. Els tore ligaments in his knee in 2005 that forced him to miss the last three months of the season, and many felt he tried to come back too soon, which hampered him in 2006.

This was supposed to be the year that Els stepped back to the plate and challenged Woods, and he showed great promise early. Els came third at the Commercialbank Qatar Masters, then second at the Dubai Desert Classic. He made his PGA Tour debut at the Nissan Open, and tied for third behind Howell and Mickelson. But his progress slowed, and after missing the cut at the Masters, he was on the verge of winning the Verizon Heritage at Hilton Head until Boo Weekley beat him with a chip-in for par on the 17th hole of the final round.

Right when it looked as though Els was fading to the background, however, he emerged to contend at the final two majors. He started the final round at Carnoustie with three birdies through six holes, crawling into contention as Garcia faltered. He was one shot behind until failing to save par from a bunker on the 13th hole, and he wound up two shots behind in a tie for fourth. In the PGA Championship at Southern Hills, a course of which the Big Easy has never been fond, he coped with 100-degree heat and was one under for the championship.

Just his luck, that familiar face — Woods — was again in control. Els has never been bashful about giving Woods his due, and this was no exception. He was asked on Saturday, after trailing by five shots, whether the tournament was over. "The statistics will tell you, yes, it is over. But as a competitor, I can't sit there and tell you it's over. I can't ever do that." But what if he were not a competitor, rather someone watching from home? "If I was not a golfer — a fan on the couch — I'd be putting my house on him, yeah," Els said. But he came out swinging and closed to within one shot until he pulled his tee shot into the trees on the 16th hole and took bogey. Els wound up alone in third.

His consolation came on the European Tour, where Els captured the HSBC World Match Play Championship for a record seventh time. That gave him a decent chance at winning the Order of Merit, which soon became no chance at all when Els realized the season-ending Volvo Masters was the same weekend as the Barclays Singapore Open, where Els already had signed a contract to play. He directed his frustration at the European Tour for the scheduling conflict, while Colin Montgomerie in veiled criticism suggested Els was more interested in appearance money than an esteemed award such as the Order of Merit.

To make matters worse, Els missed the cut in Singapore, and more trouble came his way at the Alfred Dunhill Championship in South Africa, where two balls in the water for a triple bogey on the final hole cost him the title, one of the toughest losses Els has had to swallow. And there have been plenty. He was No. 4 in the world at year's end, but the 38-year-old no longer has age on his side as he tries to reach No. 1, the five-year goal he set for himself in 2006. "It seems like I'm a very patient guy, but I'm quite an impatient person when it comes to getting results," Els said. "And I haven't had the results this year go my way, either in Europe or America or wherever I've played."

If it is hard to believe that Els now has gone three straight years without a PGA Tour victory, imagine the odds of Annika Sorenstam going one season on the LPGA Tour without winning. But that's what happened when women's golf crowned a new queen. Perhaps it was only fitting that No. 1 in the Rolex Rankings went to Lorena Ochoa, whose name is pronounced very similar to "La Reina," which means "queen" in Spanish. The young Mexican star already was on the rise, but she hit warp speed when Sorenstam struggled through a year of injury.

Sorenstam was starting to lose her grip in the Rolex Rankings late in 2006. Even though she was still No. 1, Ochoa had ended her five-year reign as the LPGA Tour player of the year and winner of the money title, beating her in a dramatic duel at the Samsung World Championship. When the new season began, although Ochoa won in her fourth start at the Safeway International in Arizona, the buzz in women's golf was Sorenstam.

In her first start of the year, a time for her to make a statement, Sorenstam blew a two-shot lead with three holes to play and lost in a playoff to rookie Meaghan Francella in the MasterCard Classic. She was never in serious contention at her next event, a rarity for the Swede, and with a renewed goal of the calendar Grand Slam, she stalled at the start by tying for 30th at the Kraft Nabisco Championship. She shot 296, her highest 72-hole score in a major in nearly a decade. Such were her standards and level of play that for the first time since 1999, she had gone three tournaments to start her year without winning.

If the prevailing question on the LPGA Tour was "What's wrong with Annika?" the answer came before she could hit another shot in competition. Sorenstam withdrew from the Ginn Open at Reunion Resort, where she was to open her Annika Academy on the Monday after the tournament, saying she discovered a ruptured disk in her neck and a bulging disk in her back. "I've been playing with quite a bit of pain for the past several weeks. I couldn't take it much more and decided it was time to see someone," Sorenstam said. It was her first serious injury in 13 years on the LPGA and it forced her to miss two months of competition.

Ordinary, the LPGA Tour would have suffered losing its star attraction. But the focus had already shifted to Ochoa, who was quickly making up ground on Sorenstam in the Rolex Rankings. It was only a matter of time before Ochoa became No. 1, and how she got there spoke volumes of her season. She had the best year in women's golf, but it wasn't without a few warts.

With Sorenstam on the sidelines, Ochoa needed a victory at the Ginn Open to take over No. 1, and she was poised to do just that until making a double bogey on the 18th hole and losing to Brittany Lincicome. It was a tough day with blustery conditions and the last nine proved difficult for everyone. But collapses had become part of Ochoa's routine, which is rare for someone that good.

She could not escape questions about her three-wood shot that was a mixture of duck-hook and pop-up and found water on the 72nd hole of the 2005 U.S. Women's Open at Cherry Hills. Also creeping into just about every conversation was Ochoa blowing a three-shot lead with four holes to play against Sorenstam in the Safeway International in 2005. And at the Kraft Nabisco Championship in 2006, she squandered a three-shot lead going into the final round, even though she gave herself one last chance with an eagle on the 72nd hole to force a playoff.

There clearly were two sides to Ochoa, both easily described as explosive. She could run off birdies at an alarming rate, and just as quickly implode with the tournament on the line. Perhaps her best attribute was patience and understanding, and she often said after her worst moments that she would learn from her mistakes. Eventually she did in a major way.

Perhaps it was typical that Ochoa became No. 1 in the world during a week the LPGA Tour had no tournament, between the Ginn Open and the Corona Championship in Mexico. The crowds celebrated, serenaded and coroneted the new No. 1, but Ochoa couldn't deliver them a victory parade when she was beaten by unheralded Italian Silvia Cavalleri. It continued the ups and downs of her 2007 season, winning the Sybase Classic one week, making mistakes in crucial moments to lose the Ginn Tribute Hosted by Annika against Nicole Castrale the next. And while Ochoa had the No. 1 ranking without debate, she was still missing a major championship.

At the Kraft Nabisco, everything was going her way until Ochoa took a "siete" on the 17th hole, a quadruple-bogey seven in the third round that took her from the lead to out of contention. She played solidly but far from spectacular at the McDonald's LPGA Championship, never able to make a run at Suzann Pettersen. And at the U.S. Women's Open at Pine Needles, she was tied for the lead with Cristie Kerr with five holes to play. But when Kerr made a long birdie at the 14th, Ochoa never hit a green in regulation the rest of the way. Again, her miss off the tee was to the left, and it was becoming a trend that raised questions whether she had the full package of stardom. Ochoa remained determined to prove her doubters wrong. "I don't need to be frustrated," Ochoa said. "We still have one more major, and I'm going to try to get that one."

For the first time in 147 years of championship golf, the Old Course at St. Andrews hosted a professional tournament for women, the Ricoh's Women's British Open, which became a historic moment even before the first tee shot was struck. The course played to a par 73, as organizers decided the famous Road Hole, No. 17, should be played as a par-five. For many, it was a sign that the women had finally arrived in golf, and the excitement was palpable. Among the most memorable photos from the week was Paula Creamer doing a cartwheel in front of the Swilcan Bridge on the final hole. But the real excitement came with clubs in hand, and Ochoa was the maestro.

Ochoa started with 67 and never trailed, seizing control in the wind-blown third round with an even-par 73 on a day when the average score was 78.5. That stretched her lead to six strokes, and no way she was going to let this one get away. The only heart palpitation came on the Road Hole in the final round when she hit into a pot bunker well short of the green. She had to come out sideways into the rough, but played a marvelous chip toward the green to limit the damage to a double bogey. She won by four and exorcised major demons along the way. The best in women's golf finally had a trophy that defines the best players. "I did it," Ochoa said. "And there's no more to say."

There was much more to do, of course. Ochoa won her next two starts, at the CN Canadian Women's Open and the Safeway Classic, wrapping up the LPGA Rolex Player of the Year, money title and Vare Trophy for the lowest scoring average for the second straight year. All that remained was the ADT Championship, a quirky format in which half the 32-player field is eliminated after two days, the field is cut to eight for the final round, and the scores are reset after each cut. Not that it mattered. Ochoa was always around the top of the leaderboard, and she blew away the competition until a dramatic finish that played like a life story of her career. There was great golf, a big lead, a shocking collapse and a remarkable recovery, all packed into four hours on the Trump International course.

Ochoa built a five-shot lead through nine holes and looked as though she were playing on a different golf course. She still had a four-stroke lead with two holes to play until a couple of muffed chips and a three-putt led to a triple bogey on the 17th hole. Her lead down to one shot over Natalie Gulbis, the Mexican star then hit a tee shot into rough so thick she could only see the top half of her ball, 161 yards from the hole with water between her and the green. Worse yet, Gulbis struck her second shot to about 12 feet, and one of the greatest collapses of all seemed likely. Ochoa buckled down and hit a six iron to 30 inches for birdie. "The best shot of my career," Ochoa said. "Five years, that was the best one." She finished the season with more than $4 million, this coming 11 years after Karrie Webb became the first $1 million player on the LPGA Tour.

There were other historical moments along the way, the most significant coming at the first major of the year on the LPGA Tour. Pettersen is another explosive player who, like Ochoa, had it going the wrong direction. She did just that at Mission Hills, losing a three-shot lead over the final four holes to set the stage for the youngest major champion in golf since the days of Young Tom Morris. The beneficiary was 18-year-old Morgan Pressel, and it was more than a handout. In dry, firm and difficult conditions, Pressel played the final 24 holes without a bogey and made one last birdie on the 18th that she figured would be enough for second place. She was on the practice range when Pettersen left her birdie putt short on the final hole, giving Pressel her first victory and first major. It was an unpredictable day except for the tears that flowed from Pressel, especially remembering her mother, who had died two years earlier of breast cancer.

Pettersen found redemption at the McDonald's LPGA Championship at Bulle Rock Golf Club, where she had a birdie putt on every hole on the last nine and won by one stroke. And with Kerr winning the U.S. Women's Open, it was the first time since 1995 that players who had not previously won a major captured the Grand Slam events. And the Americans made it two in a row at the Solheim Cup, defeating Europe in Sweden, which was another blow to Sorenstam.

The year was not a total loss for the Super Swede. Sorenstam won her final event of the year, in the Dubai Ladies Classic, stretching her streak to 14 years with at least one victory somewhere in the world. She began to branch out in business, launching her own brand, opening a golf and fitness academy outside Orlando, Florida. She got engaged to Mike McGee, a former agent and the son of former Tour player Jerry McGee.

And Sorenstam put Michelle Wie in her place. It was a lost year for the teenager from Hawaii, who tried to play with injuries to both wrists. The low point came at the Ginn Tribute that Sorenstam hosted in South Carolina, a tournament that offered Wie a sponsor's exemption. With her wrists bandaged and her tee shots going everywhere, Wie stood at 14 over par with two holes to play. Someone started doing the math, for two bogeys or one double bogey — or worse — would add to an 88 or higher, violating the LPGA Tour's "Rule 88," in which non-members who shoot 88 or higher are banned from competition for a year. After a quick huddle with her agent, Wie suddenly withdrew on the 17th hole, claiming injury.

That might have been easier to take except that Wie was seen at Bulle Rock two days later hitting balls in advance of the LPGA Championship. Sorenstam was furious and held nothing back when asked about how Wie withdrew from her tournament. "I just feel that there's a little bit of lack of respect and class just to leave a tournament like that and then come out and practice here," Sorenstam said at Bulle Rock. "It's a little funny that you pull out with an injury and then you start grinding. My doctor told me to rest." Her blunt criticism earned Sorenstam respect from her peers, who had grown tired of the attention heaped on Wie and the manners of her entourage.

It never got any better for Wie, who broke par only twice all year and had a record that even made John Daly look like he was trying. She missed five cuts (once on the PGA Tour) and withdrew twice. In the three tournaments where she played 72 holes, she finished a combined 91 shots behind the leaders.

Harrington's victory at The Open was the highlight of a banner year on the European Tour. Despite winning the Ryder Cup three successive times, the last two by record margins, European golf was hounded by the absence of a major championship since Paul Lawrie's stunning victory at Carnoustie in 1999. Only when the playoff began between an Irishman and a Spaniard was Europe sure of ending its drought. But it also claimed a small piece of world supremacy when Henrik Stenson, the big-hitting Swede, captured his first World Golf Championship at the Accenture Match Play Championship against defending champion Geoff Ogilvy.

For the second straight year, the Order of Merit came down to the final tournament, if not the final nine holes, at Valderrama in the Volvo Masters. Els was atop the list, but miles away in Singapore. Harrington was in second place by a small amount over Rose, so a top finish by either one of them would bring with it the coveted Order of Merit. The odds favored Harrington, not only because he was The Open champion and trying to win the Order of Merit for the second straight year, but Rose had a habit of starting strong and fading.

Rose's lone victory on the European Tour had come at the MasterCard Masters in Australia nearly a year ago, while he had squandered opportunities at the Bob Hope Chrysler Classic on the PGA Tour, at the Masters when he was within a shot of the lead on the last nine, and at the BMW Championship at Wentworth, where he lost in a playoff to Anders Hansen. But he was steady in the face of multiple levels of pressure, and he took a four-stroke lead into the final round over Harrington and Simon Dyson, who played in the final pairing with Rose. The young Englishman kept the margin at four shots going to the back nine, and nearly blew it. But he recovered with a two-putt birdie on the par-five 17th, and despite a 74, Rose earned a spot in the playoff with Dyson and Soren Kjeldsen. That assured him the Order of Merit title, and he made it twice as sweet with a 12-foot putt on the second extra hole to win the Volvo Masters.

Rose became the first Englishman since Lee Westwood in 2000 to win the Order of Merit, and it was extra special given his travails. The indelible image is of the 18-year-old Rose with arms in the air and face awash in a boyish smile after holing out a chip on the final hole of the 1998 Open to tie for fourth. He turned professional immediately after The Open, then proceeded to miss the cut in 21 consecutive tournaments. But his improvement was steady, and this was his biggest year. Despite a series of back injuries, he finished among the top 12 in all four majors. "It's been a long road to get here, but I feel great," he said.

Even so, all roads led back to Woods, as it has been for most of his professional career. He so famously said, "Hello, world," when he turned professional at the Greater Milwaukee Open in 1996, and he has been waving goodbye to the competition ever since. In the last two years, Woods has buried his father and watched his wife give birth to their first child. Sam Alexis made her debut at the PGA Championship, without Woods knowing his daughter was at the golf course until he saw her — decked out in Sunday red, of course — in the scoring room at Southern Hills.

"It's a feeling I've never had before," Woods said. "Having Sam there and having Elin there, it feels a lot more special. And it used to be my mom and dad. And now Elin, and now we have our own daughter. So it's evolved, and this one feels so much more special than the other majors." He called his year a "polar opposite" of 2006, and his game was so frighteningly sound that some wonder if Woods might come full circle. No matter how often he wins, how many majors he keeps adding to his record, Woods cannot seem to escape comparisons to 2000, the season to which he has always been compared. But with each year, whether it's eight wins and two majors or seven wins and one major, talk of 2000 seems to give way to what the future holds.

"The reason people still talk about 2000 is because he won the U.S. Open by 15 and the British Open by eight. Those are the two biggest tournaments, and he won by 23 shots," said his caddie, Steve Williams. "So the public's perception of his year is based on two weeks. That will stand in our memories forever. That's why we're still talking about it." But even Williams, who has the best seat in the house, couldn't help but wonder if his boss is just now starting to hit his stride. "No doubt, this is the best he's ever played."

2. Masters Tournament

Four weeks before the Ryder Cup matches last autumn, world No. 1 Tiger Woods took the four United States rookies — Brett Wetterich, Vaughn Taylor, Zach Johnson and J.J. Henry — to a steakhouse for dinner, his way of bonding with them before leaving for Ireland. The American team played poorly, losing the Ryder Cup 18½ points to 9½, but the rookies did not cost them the trophy and the four have since been better for the experience.

"The Ryder Cup was big-time pressure," Taylor said early in the week of the Masters Tournament. "We all felt it and we all dealt with it. It's helped us. It especially helps here in a major where the pressure is big time."

Wetterich was a co-leader for the first two rounds of the Masters, all four made the 36-hole cut and were on the leaderboards at some point in the tournament, and one reached out to take the biggest prize — Johnson, who entered the Masters ranked No. 56 in the world. In a week at Augusta National Golf Club when the players were generally confounded by the course conditions and the weather, Johnson won the highest-scoring Masters in 51 years.

Playing in only his third Masters, the 2007 champion introduced himself: "I'm Zach Johnson from Cedar Rapids, Iowa," he said to the press. "That's about it. I'm a normal guy."

Johnson, 31 years of age, became the first winner in 17 years not to come out of the final pairing, since Nick Faldo in 1990, and the first since Mark O'Meara in 1998 to come from behind to win after 54 holes. His final round was three-under-par 69, one of only eight scores in the 60s for the week, and he won by two strokes over three players: Woods (72) and a couple of South Africans, Retief Goosen (69) and Rory Sabbatini (69).

He entered the last round two strokes off the Australian Stuart Appleby's lead after posting scores of 71, 73 and 76, and finished as one of only five players to have two under-par scores for the tournament. His 289 total, one over par, tied the highest winning score in Masters history, following Sam Snead, in 1954, and Jack Burke, Jr., in 1956.

The totals for the other Ryder Cup rookies were Taylor, 295 (tied for 10th), Wetterich and Henry, both 302 (tied for 37th).

Johnson's victory came on a fast, dry golf course that stretched to 7,445 yards. It came over four days of challenging conditions, warm and windy to start, then chilly and gusting in the third round, then swirling breezes on the final day. Rain had taken the sting out of the course every year since 460 yards were added in increments starting in 2002. Now golf balls were bouncing over mounds and speeding over humps in all directions. The greens were final-round firm and fast, and the wind was generally an unfavorable northwesterly.

"I think I'm mentally tough," said Johnson, whose only previous victory was the 2004 BellSouth Classic, also in Georgia, near Atlanta. "I don't hit it very far, I don't overpower a golf course, but I think I'm a pretty decent putter. At Augusta National, putting is premium."

First Round

It was just 7:45 a.m. but even at that hour a large number of spectators had gathered when Chairman Billy Payne stepped out from the crowd and to rousing cheers announced: "Ladies and gentlemen, on the first tee at Augusta National, where he belongs ... Mr. Arnold Palmer." He made his familiar swing and knocked his drive down the left side into the rough, and the spectators roared again. A staff member recovered the golf ball.

So it was that Palmer, at Payne's invitation, restored a Masters tradition in serving as the honorary starter, the first since 2002, Sam Snead's last year. Palmer was the seventh in a line which began in 1963 with Jock Hutchison and Fred McLeod, who were followed by Byron Nelson, Gene Sarazen, Ken Venturi (for one year) and Snead.

There was sentiment for Palmer, 77 years of age, to be joined by the other two of the Big Three who ruled golf for more than two decades, but Gary Player, 71, was still competing (this year he tied Palmer's record by playing in his 50th Masters) and Jack Nicklaus, a non-competitor at 67, told the press in essence to ask again when he was Palmer's age.

It was good fun nonetheless for Palmer, his fellow Augusta National members and the patrons, as Masters spectators are known. After hitting the shot, and before joining Payne and friends for breakfast in the clubhouse, Palmer went to the press building, where he spoke of the shot with emotion in his voice. "I didn't want to top it," he said. "I hit it pretty good. I've always said that if I hit the shot and it went left, it was okay. If it went right, I was in trouble."

Palmer's shot was the start to a beautiful morning, but it was not a day that was enjoyed by many who followed Palmer to the first tee. Of the 96 starters, 82 shot over-par scores, and there were 12 scores in the 80s. Only two players, the Englishman Justin Rose and Brett Wetterich, broke 70. They were the leaders with three-under-par 69s. Rose was the only player without a bogey on his card, and Wetterich had two bogeys but led the field with five birdies. There were two players with 70s, another Englishman, David Howell, and David Toms.

Five more were under par with 71s, Zach Johnson, J.J. Henry, Augusta-area resident Vaughn Taylor, Rich Beem and Tim Clark of South Africa, the runner-up in 2006. For players like Johnson, who spent six years on smaller tours before reaching the PGA Tour in 2004, this week was all about perspective. "You appreciate it more," Johnson said. "Sometimes on the mini-tours, the greens make it feel like you are putting through rough. Now you're putting on marble."

Defending champion Phil Mickelson started with 76, which equaled the highest score in his 54 previous rounds in the Masters. Mickelson hit only six of Augusta National's 14 fairways and eight of 18 greens, but he blamed poor putting for his score. He missed three putts inside 10 feet while making three bogeys and a double bogey on the first seven holes. Then five over par, Mickelson birdied the par-five No. 8 and scored pars on the last 10 holes.

Mickelson three-putted twice on the second nine, for bogey on the par-three No. 12 and for par at the par-five No. 15. His stroke was more successful towards the end of the round, as he holed a four-footer for birdie on No.

15, a 30-footer for birdie on No. 16 and a 15-footer for par on No. 17.

Looking toward the second round, Mickelson said: "Even par is in the hunt. I go out and shoot 68, and I'm right there. And there's some birdies to be made out there."

Tiger Woods, the winner of the last two major championships of 2006, was one under par through 16 holes, but bogeyed his final two holes for 73. He had put together a steady round despite a few wild tee shots until he missed the fairways on Nos. 17 and 18 for the back-to-back bogeys. "I've got to figure a few things out," he said. "I threw away a good round of golf."

Woods, a four-time Masters champion, has never broken 70 in the first round. He made pars on his first six holes before taking a bogey on the seventh. He jumped on the leaderboard with birdies on the two par-five holes on the second nine, Nos. 13 and 15, only to hit his drives into the pine needles on the last two holes. He hit only seven of the 14 fairways. "I just wasn't driving it well," Woods said. Nevertheless, Woods's score was beaten by only 14 players.

Augusta National was "as hard as I've ever played it," said Chris DiMarco, the runner-up to Woods in a playoff in 2005, and who had 75 in starting this Masters.

Rose and Wetterich were hardly veterans here. This was the third Masters for Rose, age 26, and the first for Wetterich, 33. Rose tied for 39th in his first Masters in 2003, and tied for 22nd the last time he was here in 2004. He was the leader of the first and second rounds in 2004, then was blown out of contention with 81 in the third round before finishing with 71.

"I was proud of the fourth round," Rose said. "I was pleased with the way I came back after that third round and shot 71 in the final round. I felt I played very well that day and could have easily been a few better."

Wetterich, whose first victory came in last year's EDS Byron Nelson Championship, was the first rookie to lead the Masters since DiMarco led in 2001 and went on to tie for 10th place. "It's nice to shoot three under and see your name at the top of the leaderboard," Wetterich said, "but it's only Thursday, and an awful lot can happen in the next day and the next two days after that."

First-Round Leaders: Justin Rose 69, Brett Wetterich 69, David Howell 70, David Toms 70, Rich Beem 71, Tim Clark 71, J.J. Henry 71, Zach Johnson 71, Vaughn Taylor 71, Bart Bryant 72, Tim Herron 72, Davis Love 72, Jeev Milkha Singh 72, Henrik Stenson 72

Second Round

Not only was it hard to make low scores on the dry and breezy golf course, but by the second day another difference was becoming apparent. It was remarkably quiet out there. "You don't hear the roars like you used to," said Tim Herron, after finishing a round of 75. Instead of clapping and shouting for birdies and eagles, the spectators offered polite applause for pars and muffled responses for higher numbers.

Brett Wetterich and Tim Clark shared the lead after two rounds at 142, two under par and one stroke in front of Vaughn Taylor. Wetterich, a co-leader in the first round, shot 73, and Clark, who was second the year before, posted 71. Taylor, who had missed the cut in 2006 in his Masters debut, shot even-par 72.

The local press noted that this was the 20th anniversary of the victory by Augusta's Larry Mize, and that Mize also was one stroke off the pace after 36 holes. Taylor, age 31, said he attended the Masters for the first time that year. "It was pretty special," said Taylor. This year Taylor was paired with three-time Masters winner Gary Player.

"I just said to him: 'You played so well. Just hang in there and believe in yourself. You can go out there with a chance of winning,'" Player said.

The leading scores were the highest since 1982, when 144 led the way. The 36-hole cut fell at 152, the highest since the 154 of 1982. There were 79 over-par scores for the round, three fewer than on the first day. Sixty of the 96 starters would stay for the last two rounds, thanks to the 10-shot rule, which meant that all players within 10 strokes of the lead kept playing. The cut did remove some big-name golfers including Michael Campbell, Chris DiMarco and Colin Montgomerie at 153 and Ernie Els, Sergio Garcia and Darren Clarke at 154.

The low scores of the day, and of the tournament, were the four-under-par 68s by the Irishman Padraig Harrington, who was one of six players at 145, tied for eighth place, and the Englishman Paul Casey, who tied for 15th at 147.

There were no bogey-free rounds on the second day and three players departed the tournament without a birdie, Steve Stricker, Bernhard Langer and amateur Richie Ramsay of Scotland. The 1980 and 1983 Masters winner, Seve Ballesteros, was last at 167.

Player improved from 83 to 77 and finished at 160, completing his 50th Masters, which he won in 1961, 1974 and 1978. Fred Couples, the 1992 Masters champion, in the group of 15 players at 152, made his 23rd consecutive cut to tie the record held by Player. The year before, Couples played in the final group with Phil Mickelson and finished third.

Mickelson improved three strokes to 73 and tied for 27th place at 149. Mickelson was stuck in the trees to the left of No. 11, trying to find his ball after a tee shot that sailed far off the mark. When he found it, he took a one-stroke penalty drop, hit a punch shot onto the fairway, laced an iron to the green and made a 10-footer for a bogey.

"I've got to hit more fairways," said Mickelson, who had four bogeys and three birdies. "First day, I drove it horrible, putted horrible. Second day, I drove it horrible and putted better. So I should be okay."

Tiger Woods looked as if he was on his way out of the tournament before he rallied to tie for 15th place with 74 and a 147 total, still in with a chance for his fifth Masters title. He played the last six holes in two under par with birdies on No. 15 and No. 17.

Woods knocked his ball into Rae's Creek on the par-three No. 12 but still scored a bogey after pitching to the green and holing a 20-footer. On the par-five No. 13, Woods hit into a tributary of the same creek, then chipped to five feet and saved his par. "The whole thing is never make a double (bogey) around here," said Woods, who had avoided the high number so far. "You just try to put the ball in the right spot, if you can. And if you can't, somehow don't have any wrecks out there."

His card featured six bogeys and four birdies, including the pair on the closing holes. On No. 15 Woods took two putts from 30 feet after nailing his second shot past the hole. He holed a 15-footer on No. 17.

Wetterich, who finished second to Woods in the WGC - CA Championship two weeks earlier, seemed to be playing with a quiet confidence as he attempted to become only the fourth player to win the Masters in his first appearance. "You always hear the great players say that pars are great in the majors," said Wetterich, a long hitter who was trying a more conservative approach this week. "I was just going out there to try to make as many as I could."

Clark, who holed a bunker shot with his final Masters stroke of 2006, said: "I've dreamt of coming here and playing this tournament as a child, and I'm here now. I'm going to make the most of it."

Some players complained that the course was playing like a U.S. Open venue. The Englishman Lee Westwood, who was at 152, said he no longer liked the Masters. "Not anymore," Westwood said. "When the course was shorter, more of us had an answer. Now only six or seven people in the field can win. I wouldn't say it's unfair, but it's not fair for everybody."

Vijay Singh, the 2000 Masters winner and one of those whom the course was said to favor, was among the four players who were tied for fourth place, two strokes behind at 144. Singh shot 71 and was the only former champion among the top 14 leaders. Also at 144, Jerry Kelly shot 69, Zach Johnson shot 73, and Justin Rose, the co-leader of the first round, shot 75.

Johnson led for quite a while in the afternoon, but three-putted No. 16 from inside five feet for the start of a bogey-bogey-bogey finish. He and his caddie read the putt on No. 16 to go one way and it went the other way. "That's Augusta for you," Johnson said. "I guess I got Augusta-sized or something. But for the most part, I'm putting well and reading the greens well, so I'm very content where I am."

"It's not an easy golf course, and it's not going to get any easier unless they water the greens more than they are," Singh said. "Even par (as the winning score) is looking very good right now."

Second-Round Leaders: Brett Wetterich 73–142, Tim Clark 71–142, Vaughn Taylor 72–143, Jerry Kelly 69–144, Vijay Singh 71–144, Zach Johnson 73–144, Justin Rose 75–144, David Howell 75–145, Lucas Glover 71–145, Padraig Harrington 68–145, Bradley Dredge 70–145, Stuart Appleby 70–145, Geoff Ogilvy 70–145

Third Round

The temperatures were in the low 50s, the northwesterly winds swept in over 20 miles an hour, and no one escaped without at least a few high scores in the third round of the Masters. The Australian Stuart Appleby saw birdies on three of the first four holes offset by a bogey-five at No. 7 and triple-bogey seven on No. 17, but his 73, one over par, was enough to hold the lead at 218 for the 54 holes.

Tiger Woods scored bogey-fours on the last two holes for the second time in three days, and that left the four-time Masters champion with a round of 73 and a 219 total, tied for second place with the Englishman Justin Rose, who posted a 75.

Three were tied for fourth place at 220, two strokes behind. Vaughn Taylor took bogeys on the last three holes for 77, the Irishman Padraig Harrington shot 75 despite a double-bogey seven on No. 15, and Zach Johnson returned with 76, having two nines of 38 with five bogeys and one birdie.

None of the leaders said the golf course was unfair, just tough. Harrington said he enjoyed the round. "No matter what was happening, I was enjoying the idea and the conditions and the questions that were being asked out there," Harrington said.

It was so cool that by late afternoon Johnson said he could barely feel his hands over the last five or six holes. But he was not complaining. "If you're trying to find the beauty of it, it's that it's a matter of survival, which I don't mind," Johnson said. "I don't mind the grind. That's how I've always been."

Seldom have over-par scores served the contenders here so well. The scoring average was 77.35, the fifth highest for any round in Masters history. There was only one under-par round, a two-under 70 by Retief Goosen that took the South African from a tie for 46th place after 36 holes into a tie for eighth at 222, four strokes behind.

As difficult as the conditions were, Goosen said they could have been tougher. "They had pins out where they've never had before," Goosen said. "If they put them where they normally put them, it would have been impossible. They kind of eased off on the pin placements because of the conditions. They were quite generous. I'm sure they will be tougher tomorrow."

Appleby's two-over total of 218 was the highest for a third-round leader in Masters history by two strokes, breaking the record set by Jack Nicklaus and Tommy Jacobs in 1966. "It was a tough day," Appleby said. "I don't think we've seen scores anything like this at Augusta for a long time."

A par-four at No. 17 would have given Appleby a 70 and a four-stroke lead, but instead he took seven. His tee shot went into a greenside bunker on No. 7. His second shot hit the lip of the bunker and landed in the trees short of the 17th fairway. His third went into a greenside bunker, he came out to 12 feet and took three putts.

"That was a hole that I let a couple of shots slip for sure," Appleby said. "Overall I felt there were plenty of holes where I could have let more slip throughout the day. I just happened to bunch one hole up and have a triple."

The 35-year-old Appleby, who had won eight times on the PGA Tour and was ranked No. 19 in the world, was trying to do what Greg Norman could not and become the first Australian to win the Masters. This was his 10th appearance and his best previous finish was a tie for 19th in 2006. "There's a lot of work left," Appleby said.

Appleby would be paired in the final group with Woods. "He won't even know I'm there," Appleby said. "I for sure will know he is there." It was not as if they were strangers. They both were friends, and residents and members of Isleworth Country Club in Orlando, Florida, and they often played golf together there.

Woods had yet to break par this week. His scores had been 73, 74 and

72, which was only the second time he had gone three consecutive rounds at Augusta National without an under-par number. When Woods finished his round, he was four strokes off the lead and tied for eighth place. Then came a frantic final hour, and no one was left on the leaderboards with red, under-par figures.

Even Brett Wetterich, whose conservative game plan worked for two days, was blown away in the conditions. Wetterich, who shared the first- and second-round leads with scores of 69 and 73, came in with 83, which dropped him into a tie for 23rd place at 225, seven strokes off the lead. Second-round co-leader Tim Clark didn't do much better, posting 80 for a 222 total, four off the lead, tied for eighth in a group including Phil Mickelson.

Third-Round Leaders: Stuart Appleby 73–218, Tiger Woods 72–219, Justin Rose 75–219, Padraig Harrington 75–220, Zach Johnson 76–220, Vaughn Taylor 77–220, Bradley Dredge 76–221, Retief Goosen 70–222, Phil Mickelson 73–222, Rory Sabbatini 73–222, David Toms 74–222, Luke Donald 75–222, Jim Furyk 76–222, Jerry Kelly 78–222, Tim Clark 80–222

Fourth Round

The final pairing of Stuart Appleby and Tiger Woods was of the most interest, and unfortunately for Appleby, his challenge was blocked by a double bogey on the first hole, and he joined the list of Australians who came close in the Masters but left without a green jacket. Appleby posted another double bogey on the par-three No. 12 and, with a 75 and a tie for seventh place at 293, he finished four strokes behind Zach Johnson.

The first hole was costly to many, including Johnson, who started with a bogey. Of the top 12 finishers, four began with bogeys and two with double bogeys. Only Luke Donald, who was six strokes behind, started with a birdie, and the first hole knocked out Phil Mickelson with a triple-bogey seven as he shot 77 and fell to a tie for 24th place.

Many have been unable to post low numbers, given the pressures and distractions of being paired with Woods, but Appleby said that wasn't his problem. "The course was ultimately the beast this week," Appleby said. "It was a tough day, but I enjoyed the day."

Woods birdied the second hole and briefly held the lead after a par on the fourth. He lost it with a bogey on the sixth and another bogey on No. 10, and the lead went to Retief Goosen to Rory Sabbatini to Goosen again before Johnson took hold with a 10-foot birdie putt on No. 13 and never let go. It was the first time Woods had lost the lead in the final round of a major championship and not recovered it.

Four strokes behind, playing the par-five No. 13, Woods curled a three-wood tee shot around the trees and was left with 190 yards to the flagstick. He then struck an iron shot to three feet from the hole and made the putt for eagle to cut Johnson's lead to two. The gallery erupted.

Two holes in front, on the par-five No. 15, Johnson stepped away from his ball. "I backed off of the shot, partially because of the roars," Johnson said. "I figured it was Tiger for an eagle. I didn't really know what was going on. I didn't know where I stood. I was still able to execute. I guess ignorance is bliss sometimes." It wasn't until after Johnson finished No. 15 that he was told by his caddie that he had a two-stroke lead.

Woods seemed to have the momentum, but he could not capitalize on the final five holes, playing all in pars for his even-par 72 and 291 total. "I had a chance," Woods said, "but looking back over the week, I basically blew this tournament with two rounds where I had bogey-bogey finishes. That's four over in two holes. The last two holes. You just can't afford to do that and win major championships."

Two groups behind Appleby and Woods, Johnson was paired with Vaughn Taylor, 2006 Ryder Cup teammates and friends for several years before that. Taylor shot 75 to tie for 10th place at 295, but he was a perfect companion for Johnson on this day. "He's a very mellow guy, and I feel like I'm mellow as well, and that's probably how we click," Johnson said.

"He played really solid," Taylor said of Johnson. "He hit the ball well. He made key putts, big-time putts. That's Zach. He showed it on the Ryder Cup. He's one of the toughest guys I know. He's short in stature. He's not a long hitter. He's just downright tough."

Johnson was one under par on the first nine with birdies on Nos. 2, 3 and 9, and bogeys on Nos. 1 and 5. He birdied three of the last six holes (Nos. 13, 14 and 16), offsetting a bogey on No. 17 for his 69 and 289 total.

For the second straight year, the runner-up position went to South Africa, this time tied with Woods. Following Tim Clark's showing of 2006, Goosen and Sabbatini each shot 69 for shares of second place at 291. Goosen had his chances, but saw his 35-foot birdie putt stop seven feet short on No. 12, and he then missed that for a three-putt bogey. He failed to make a birdie on the last six holes. Sabbatini's eagle at No. 8 and birdie at No. 13 vaulted him into contention, but bogeys at Nos. 14 and 16 proved disastrous.

Since Gary Player won his third Masters in 1978, South Africans have finished in second place six times. Meanwhile a determined young man from Cedar Rapids had given Iowa its biggest golf victory since Jack Fleck, a driving-range pro, defeated Ben Hogan in a playoff for the 1955 U.S. Open.

The Final Leaders: Zach Johnson 69–289, Rory Sabbatini 69–291, Retief Goosen 69–291, Tiger Woods 72–291, Jerry Kelly 70–292, Justin Rose 73–292, Padraig Harrington 73–293, Stuart Appleby 75–293, David Toms 72–294, Paul Casey 71–295, Luke Donald 73–295

3. U.S. Open Championship

This has become an era of foreign success not seen since the earliest years of the United States Open Championship. British-born golfers won the first 16 Opens from 1895 through 1910, until John McDermott became the first American-born champion in 1911. Then, from 1922 through 2003, foreign-born golfers never again won consecutive Opens, never mind four in a row, as the count now stands.

Not only that, but these last four Opens have been won by players out of the southern hemisphere, from South Africa (Retief Goosen), New Zealand (Michael Campbell), Australia (Geoff Ogilvy) and now Argentina, with Angel Cabrera, who won in 2007 at Oakmont Country Club, outside Pittsburgh.

From appearances Cabrera was an unlikely winner. He has a generous midriff, chain-smokes and never exercises, but he is strong enough to hit a golf ball huge distances and, on occasion, he putts brilliantly. He was the only player with two rounds in the 60s, and his final-round score of 69 for a 285 total, five over par, was one stroke better than two American-born past U.S. Open champions, Tiger Woods and Jim Furyk.

Cabrera, age 37, became the first Argentine or any other South American to win the U.S. Open, and just the second to win a major championship. Forty years earlier, Roberto de Vicenzo from Argentina won by two strokes over Jack Nicklaus in the Open Championship at Royal Liverpool.

Silva Bertolaccini, Argentina's leading LPGA player, told *Golf World*: "Roberto beat Jack, and now Angel has beaten Tiger. The difference is that the Latin countries barely knew what Roberto had done, while millions watched Angel. Now that Angel has gained confidence, he has the opportunity to do more, for himself and for Latin America."

Now 84 years old, de Vicenzo watched the championship on television at home and declared Cabrera an Argentine hero. "He's my hero," de Vicenzo said. "I'm very happy for him, because I didn't want to leave this world before I saw something like this."

Recalling that he learned to play golf as a caddie, Cabrera felt his winning the Open reached beyond his own dreams. "I never thought this was possible," he said.

With financial help from Argentine Eduardo Romero, who now plays the Champions Tour, Cabrera became a professional golfer at age 20. He qualified for the European Tour on his third try. He won the Paraguay Open in 1995 and has won 11 other South American titles since.

The World Cup came to Argentina in 2000. Tiger Woods and David Duval were representing the United States, and Cabrera and Romero were Argentine teammates. They battled to the final putt before the Americans won. "For my confidence," Cabrera said, "it was a very big thing." Soon after, Cabrera won the 2001 Open de Argentina, an event sanctioned by the European Tour, then he won the 2002 Benson and Hedges International Open and the 2005 BMW Championship, both in England.

Except for this year's BMW Championship, Cabrera would not have been at Oakmont. He was ranked No. 53 in the world, three positions above the cut-off for a qualifying exemption for the U.S. Open. He had decided that he would take the week off rather than play in a qualifying event. Then, on his last opportunity, Cabrera tied for fifth place at Wentworth in the BMW Championship and shot up to No. 39 in the world.

Cabrera had led late in the final round at Wentworth, but dropped two strokes on the 15th hole. As he warmed up for the final round at Oakmont, Cabrera told Manuel Tagle, his manager and translator: "If I get to the 15th today in the same situation, the same thing will not happen." Indeed Cabrera nearly holed his approach to Oakmont's 15th hole. His birdie-three from three feet widened his lead to three strokes, critical to his victory.

First Round

The question in most observers' minds before the opening round was the condition of Phil Mickelson's left wrist. A month earlier, Mickelson had injured it while playing a practice round at Oakmont and had to withdraw from the Memorial Tournament.

Mickelson had hoped to redeem himself for his loss in the 2006 U.S. Open at Winged Foot, when he lost control of his driver on the 72nd hole, took six strokes on the hole and lost to Geoff Ogilvy. In the following year Mickelson went to Butch Harmon as his swing coach, and he demonstrated the mastery of his driver in a victory in The Players Championship in May.

He had to wear a black brace on the tender wrist, and on the Tuesday before the championship, he played only nine holes and did not go to the practice range. Questioned about his condition, Mickelson said: "Wrist injuries are no fun for golfers. I'll do the best I can."

Mickelson's score for the first round was 74, four over par, which tied him for 57th place. Only two players broke Oakmont's par of 70, only two more were at even-par 70, and 15 were at 71, including Tiger Woods.

Off the No. 10 tee at 1:36 p.m., Mickelson parred the first hole without incident but had a problem on the second hole. On his second shot from high grass, he let go of his club with his left hand at impact, then chipped poorly and scored a bogey. Two more bogeys, and he was three over par for his first nine. He bogeyed again on the first hole of the second nine, then played through with eight pars.

After the first nine, Mickelson removed the wrap but was still wearing a small white bandage on his left wrist. He described the injury as "aggravating" rather than painful and said: "It's annoying. That's probably a better word. ... I believe it will get better as the week goes on."

The leader of the first round was Nick Dougherty, who was at 68, two under par and one stroke better than Angel Cabrera. Dougherty came out of the sectional qualifying in England and was playing in his fourth U.S. Open. He had one professional victory, a European Tour event in Singapore two years ago.

In the fourth group off at 7:33 a.m., Dougherty made it look easy, with birdies on Nos. 11, 13 and 17, and played the second nine in 32 strokes. He knew he needed to avoid a recent pattern to his play. "My golf is in great shape," he said. "But this year has been disappointing in a lot of ways for me. I've led six of the 14 tournaments I've played (in Europe), a few of them near the very end, and I haven't finished one off."

That would be a difficult task for anyone at Oakmont, a course which Dougherty called "barbaric."

Nearly half an inch of rain fell during the evening before play began, softening the fairways and greens, yet only Dougherty and Cabrera bettered Oakmont's par. Cabrera scored birdies on three of the first five holes, but finished with three bogeys and a birdie at the 12th for his score of 69. "The golf course is playing much easier because of the rain yesterday," Cabrera said. "The greens are softer and that's why there are some scores below par."

Bubba Watson and Jose Maria Olazabal tied at even-par 70, then came Woods and 15 other players tied at 71. That group included Ogilvy, the defending champion, Jim Furyk, the 2003 Open champion who would hang on until the end with Woods, and Vijay Singh, who would get no closer than this to the lead. Watson also would hang on, but Olazabal would not.

A favorite to win his third Open, Woods yanked his tee shot into the left rough, missed the green and added two putts to start with a bogey-five. He took that stroke back with a birdie at the second hole and added another birdie at the par-three sixth. He was in and out of trouble the rest of the day, but held his round together with his putter. He took bogeys at the 10th and 12th holes, and he seemed destined to also drop shots at the 13th and 16th, but saved pars with wide-breaking eight-foot putts.

First-Round Leaders: Nick Dougherty 68, Angel Cabrera 69, Bubba Watson 70, Jose Maria Olazabal 70, Olin Browne 71, Pablo Martin 71, Ben Curtis 71, Tiger Woods 71, Geoff Ogilvy 71, Anders Hansen 71, Niclas Fasth 71, Peter Hanson 71, Jason Dufner 71, Brandt Snedeker 71, Vijay Singh 71, Fred Funk 71, Lucas Glover 71, Jim Furyk 71, J.J. Henry 71, Justin Rose 71

Second Round

These were among the highlights of the second round: Paul Casey shot 66 and advanced from a tie for 104th place to seventh, Phil Mickelson missed the 36-hole cut, Nick Dougherty, the first-round leader, faded with 77, and Angel Cabrera followed his opening 69 with a score of 71 and was leading the U.S. Open with an even-par 140 total.

Starting on the second nine, Cabrera dropped strokes on the 10th and 12th holes, but got those back with birdies on the 13th and 16th. He recorded two bogeys and one birdie on his other nine, including a wonderful shot to two feet at the ninth. Asked about his finish, Cabrera said: "Yes, definitely, making a birdie at the last hole gives you a good sensation of what is left ahead."

Bubba Watson followed his opening 70 with 71 and claimed second place at 141, followed by Aaron Baddeley, Justin Rose, Stephen Ames and Niclas Fasth, tied for third place at 142. Thus, the top players on the leaderboard represented six different countries: Argentina, United States, Australia, England, Canada and Sweden.

Tiger Woods shot 74 after his opening 71 and dropped from a tie for fifth to a tie for 13th place. Among others of particular interest, who also started with 71s, defending champion Geoff Ogilvy and 2003 Open champion Jim Furyk posted 75s to tie for 19th and Vijay Singh shot 77 to tie for 33rd place.

Starting from the first tee, Mickelson played the first six holes in two under par. He lost both strokes at the seventh, which is not a terribly difficult par-four hole for those who keep the ball in the fairway. Mickelson's drive was in the rough and his second shot went into a ditch with even higher grass. He bogeyed the par-three eighth and the ninth to be out in 37 strokes, and when he took four putts on the 10th green, his prospects for playing on the weekend had all but vanished. He needed others to play badly, and when not enough did, Mickelson was out by one stroke with his 77 and 151 total.

Casey was off early, at 7:33 a.m. from the 10th tee. He raced through his first nine holes in 32 strokes with four birdies and only one dropped shot, at the 18th hole, his ninth of the day. He finished in 34 with a birdie at the seventh and eight pars.

"This is right up there in terms of my best rounds ever," Casey said. "If I had kept the bogey off the card, without a doubt it would have been. I consider the U.S. Open the toughest test in golf, and this is possibly the toughest golf course I have played." He indeed played inspiring golf. He hit 13 of 14 fairways on driving holes, 12 greens and had 26 putts.

No one was more pleased than Watson, who took over second place with his 71. A left-hander who pounds the ball out of sight, Watson stands 6-foot-3 and weighs 180 pounds, a size which helps explain the power of this man out of the Florida panhandle town of Bagdad, where he still lives. "My home course is as tough as this," Watson said. Then he smiled and said: "No, this is it. This is a test of golf all the way. Just walking through the parking lot is hard enough."

Watson scoffed at the suggestion that he was a Cinderella man. "I've made the cut," Watson said. "You can call it a Cinderella story if I win the tournament."

One of four players sharing third place, Ames posted the second-best score of the day, a 69. He scored a birdie-two on the eighth hole, the par-three with tees at 252 and 288 yards. One player suggested it could qualify for the dual prizes of longest drive and closest-to-the-hole. Ames hit a missile-like three wood that settled five feet from the hole. It was his third birdie of the first nine, along with one bogey. He had one birdie and two bogeys on the second nine.

Meantime, Woods struggled. He started from the 10th tee and began just as he had in the first round, hitting his drive into the rough, but managed to save par. He bogeyed the 11th hole and birdied the 12th, but failed to hold on. He bogeyed both the 15th and 18th holes and played his first nine in 37 strokes.

Moving to the first nine, Woods picked up two quick bogeys, at the second and fourth holes, and this turned out to be not one of his better days.

Cabrera, holding the lead at 140, completed his 71 by hitting a stunning approach to the ninth green, his 18th hole, a shot that not only moved Cabrera into first place, but eliminated everyone with scores of 11 over par or worse, those who were not within 10 strokes of the lead. This included

Mickelson. Cabrera objected to the notion that he had knocked out Mickelson. "I didn't knock out Mickelson," he said. "Mickelson knocked himself out."

True enough.

Second-Round Leaders: Angel Cabrera 71–140, Bubba Watson 71–141, Aaron Baddeley 70–142, Justin Rose 71–142, Stephen Ames 69–142, Niclas Fasth 71–142, Paul Casey 66–143, Brandt Snedeker 73–144, Tom Pernice Jr. 72–144, Carl Pettersson 72–144, David Toms 72–144, Scott Verplank 71–144

Third Round

While Tiger Woods played a superb round of golf, second-round leader Angel Cabrera played something less, and Aaron Baddeley shot his second consecutive even-par 70 and took the lead after the third round with a 212 total, two strokes ahead of Woods. Sixteen players stood within six strokes of one another and four of them — Woods, Jim Furyk, David Toms and Vijay Singh — had major championships on their records.

Paul Casey, who had shot 66 in the second round, returned with 72 to share third place with Stephen Ames and Justin Rose, who shot 73s, and Bubba Watson, who shot 74 with a triple-bogey seven on the ninth hole. Watson never again threatened first place.

Cabrera could not be dismissed, even though he didn't play well. A disappointing 76 dropped Cabrera to a tie for seventh place at 216, along with Furyk and Steve Stricker. Furyk shot 70 and Stricker shot 68, the low round of the day.

Niclas Fasth, who played so well in the first two rounds, struggled in the third round. He parred only seven holes, bogeyed seven, double-bogeyed one, birdied two, eagled the fourth, shot 75 and tied for 10th place at 217 with Toms, who shot 73, and Stuart Appleby, who posted 71.

For the third day, only two players shot in the 60s at Oakmont — Stricker with 68 and Woods with 69. In the third round, it also became clear that defending champion Geoff Ogilvy would not repeat. He went from 71 to 75 to 78 and fell into a tie for 40th place at 224.

Baddeley, the 26-year-old leader, was listed as Australian but, in fact, he was born in New Hampshire. He lived there for only about six months while his father worked as a mechanic for race driver Mario Andretti. After that, the family moved to Australia, where they have lived ever since. Baddeley won his first PGA Tour event at the 2006 Verizon Heritage in Hilton Head Island, South Carolina, and earlier in 2007, he won the FBR Open in Scottsdale, Arizona.

As an amateur at age 19 in 1999, Baddeley won the Australian Open and won the championship again the next year as a professional. He played the Nationwide Tour before moving up to the PGA Tour in 2003. Looking ahead to his final-round pairing with Woods, Baddeley was not in awe. He said: "I'm very comfortable playing with Tiger. If I could pick one golfer to play with, it would be him."

In the third round, Baddeley went out in 37 strokes, then turned his game around by running off three birdies on the first four holes of the second nine. He led the field by three strokes, but just as quickly he bogeyed the

15th and 16th holes and nearly gave away another stroke on the 17th. But Baddeley birdied the 18th to hold the lead with his 212 total, two over par. "That birdie was great to carry over to tomorrow," he said. "Tiger is the best player in the world, but I feel like I'm playing well, my swing is good, and I feel great with the putter."

No one felt better about his day than Stricker, who seemed to have found a knack for playing Open courses. At Winged Foot a year earlier, Stricker led after the second round and tied for sixth place. Here at Oakmont, he started with 75 and improved to 73 in the second round before posting his 68 on Saturday. He and Singh played the third round together and apparently spurred one another on. Singh birdied the 16th and 17th holes to put himself a stroke under par but bogeyed the 18th to finish with 70.

Stricker played an approach shot that was yards short of the 18th green, then holed out with a lob wedge for a birdie on his third shot. He played the second nine in 33 strokes.

As one would expect, Stricker felt ecstatic. "You don't expect to hole it, but I thought I could get up closer to a five- or 10-footer and try for a par," he said. "What a way to finish. It gives me a chance tomorrow. I have a chance. I believe I do."

Then there was Furyk, who never should be overlooked. Tied with Stricker and Cabrera, he made his 70 the hard way. He went out in 35 with two birdies and two bogeys, along with a par-three on the eighth hole. Coming back, he bogeyed the 12th and 16th holes, but took care of his problems by birdieing both the 17th and 18th.

"The finish brightened my day and made me feel I'm back in the thick of things," Furyk said. "It definitely took the sting out of the round by birdieing the last two holes. I'm in a heck of a lot better mood with a lot more positive outlook."

Cabrera felt differently after a bogey-infested round of 76. Playing his worst golf of the week, Cabrera missed 10 of the 14 fairways on driving holes, missed seven greens, and took 36 putts in his 76. He said he had a tough day, especially with his driver. "That was pretty much it," Cabrera said. "I missed a couple of fairways just by a little, then I lost confidence."

Nevertheless, Cabrera had one more day to catch up.

Meantime, Woods played a steady round but had little luck with his putter. He hit 17 consecutive greens, and missed only the 18th, perhaps from frustration. Half a dozen of his putts seemed to take a glance at the hole but did not fall. His approach to the 18th green went into a bunker and cost him a bogey. He shot 69 nonetheless, finishing two strokes behind the leader. Woods said: "I'm right there with a shot at it."

Third-Round Leaders: Aaron Baddeley 70–212, Tiger Woods 69–214, Paul Casey 72–215, Stephen Ames 73–215, Justin Rose 73–215, Bubba Watson 74–215, Steve Stricker 68–216, Jim Furyk 70–216, Angel Cabrera 76–216, Stuart Appleby 71–217, David Toms 73–217, Niclas Fasth 75–217

Fourth Round

Posting a score of 69 in the final round, Angel Cabrera won the championship with a total of 285, five over par and one stroke better than Jim Furyk and Tiger Woods. Furyk closed with 70 following a bogey-five at the short 17th hole, a par-four of just 313 deceptive yards. Woods played the final round in 72, and once again was held back by his putting.

"Finishing second is never fun," said Woods, who also placed second in this year's Masters Tournament. "You play so hard, and it's disappointing. My last four majors I've been one, one, two, two, not terrible, but it could have been a little bit better."

Cabrera was ecstatic after watching on television as four groups finished playing behind him before his victory was confirmed. "It's a great moment for me," said Cabrera, who was asked whether he followed this championship while growing up in Argentina. Yes, I watched all the majors on TV when I was a kid, and I never thought I would be here at this moment.

"It is very difficult to describe this moment. Probably tomorrow when I wake up with this trophy beside me in bed, I will realize that I have won the U.S. Open."

After a third round of 75, Niclas Fasth turned his game around. Fasth ran off six threes, played the second nine in 33 strokes and climbed into fourth place at 287, just two strokes off the lead and two ahead of David Toms and Bubba Watson. Beginning the fourth round in a tie for 10th place, Fasth lost two more strokes on the first nine, then played the final nine holes in two under par for his 70.

Anthony Kim, a 22-year-old PGA Tour rookie, waltzed around Oakmont in 67 strokes, the lowest score of the day. In a streak of astounding scoring, Kim played the fifth through the ninth holes in just 15 strokes. Out in 32, he came back in 35, taking a bogey at the difficult 15th. He climbed from 57th place into a tie for 20th, alongside Mike Weir and Vijay Singh, heady company.

Cabrera began his round with three pars then two birdies, leaving Stuart Appleby teetering behind him. Appleby was grossly off his game. He made the turn in 38 and played worse on the homeward nine, 41, for a total of 79, finishing with bogeys at the 16th and 17th and a double bogey at the 18th, while Cabrera fretted, waiting to play the putts that could decide if he won or lost the Open. All that lay ahead, though.

Woods and Aaron Baddeley were about to tee off, with Baddeley playing last as the championship leader. He pushed his tee shot into the right rough. Standing 225 yards from the hole, Baddeley jerked his next shot into the left rough, his pitch ran off the green, and before he quite realized it, he had played the first hole in seven strokes, three over par, and lost all hope of winning the Open. He eventually shot 80.

By then, Cabrera had birdied the fourth and fifth holes, caught Woods and Stephen Ames and passed Baddeley and Paul Casey. Cabrera hit a nine iron within a foot of the hole at the fifth, but then at the sixth, a par-three, he left his nine iron short, in a bunker, and bogeyed. Still, Cabrera was one under par.

Then Woods ran into trouble at the third hole, taking a double bogey and falling into a tie for fifth place. Steve Stricker birdied the sixth and tied Ames for the lead at four over par. Stricker gave that stroke away with a bogey at the seventh, went out in 34, but had nothing left. He shot 76 for a 292 total.

Shortly after Stricker stepped aside, Ames took seven at the seventh hole, losing three strokes, and six at the ninth, losing two more. Out in 40, he came back in 36, and with 76, tied for 10th place at 291.

Cabrera, meantime, birdied the eighth hole, which on this day was lengthened to 300 yards, the longest par-three in history. His two was matched only by Kim. Cabrera had moved to four over par, leading the field, although he needed an eight-foot putt to save par at the ninth.

Woods struggled in his effort to make up strokes. Recovering from his six at the third, Woods birdied the fourth, but then missed a bunch of greens while one-putting his way to pars on four of the next six holes. He made the turn in 36. By that time, Cabrera had reached the 12th hole and it was clear the championship would be won by Cabrera, Woods or possibly Furyk.

Furyk birdied three consecutive holes — the 13th, 14th and 15th — wiping out his mistakes that cost him strokes at the 11th and 12th. Cabrera by then had played through the 15th hole, where he birdied after a nine-iron shot from 160 yards to three feet, improving to three over par and leading the championship by three strokes. The lead didn't stand. Cabrera bogeyed the 16th on three putts, then misplayed the 17th for another stroke lost. His approach ran off the green into short rough, he stubbed his wedge recovery, and missed the putt. Cabrera's margin was now one stroke.

After a par on the 16th hole, Furyk hit his tee shot into the rough on the 17th. His recovery was short of the green, he pitched on, and his putt hit the hole but did not fall. He made a bogey-five, and Cabrera now had a clear lead.

"I played well all day," Furyk said. "I didn't do all that much wrong. I didn't hit many bad shots. I just wasn't able to dig it out of the rough and get the ball on the green in two on 17, and in the end that's going to be the difference."

With a routine par on the 18th and a 285 total, now Cabrera could only watch on television. Woods came to the 18th one stroke behind Cabrera and without a birdie since the fourth hole, his only birdie of the round. He hit a good drive, but just missed the fairway on the right side. His approach shot ran to the back of the green, and his putt never threatened the hole.

"It was actually a triple-breaking putt," Woods said. "I hit it with good speed. The hard part was judging how much it was going to kick to the right. And it took awhile to start coming to the left, and by then it was past the line I needed to be on."

The Final Leaders: Angel Cabrera 69–285, Jim Furyk 70–286, Tiger Woods 72–286, Niclas Fasth 70–287, David Toms 72–289, Bubba Watson 74–289, Nick Dougherty 71–290, Scott Verplank 72–290, Jerry Kelly 72–290, Justin Rose 76–291, Stephen Ames 76–291, Paul Casey 76–291

4. The Open Championship

This was for Ireland as the U.S. Open was for Argentina.

It had been 60 years since Fred Daly won the Open Championship at Hoylake, which stood as the only Open, or any major championship, ever won by an Irishman until Padraig Harrington came along in 2007 on the Sunday afternoon at Carnoustie, the brutal Scottish links that may be the toughest golf course in the world.

It was here in 1999 that the Frenchman Jean Van de Velde went to the final hole with a three-stroke lead, took seven, a triple bogey, and lost in a playoff that was won by Scotland's Paul Lawrie.

No European had won a major since then, and for most of the week it appeared that the Spaniard Sergio Garcia, not Harrington, would be the one to follow Lawrie. Garcia was in front after each of the first three rounds, lost the lead in the final round, got it back briefly, then was denied at the 72nd hole when his par putt lipped out, demonstrating again that a lead is never safe at Carnoustie.

Andres Romero, the young Argentine, also was stung by the finish, dropping three strokes on the last two holes, and even Harrington almost lost it there, hitting two balls into the Barry Burn on the last hole of regulation. Harrington, scoring 67, and Garcia, 73, tied at 277, seven under par, and Romero was third after his 67 and 278 total. In a four-hole playoff, Harrington won with 15 strokes, even par, to Garcia's 16 strokes.

"I've proved in the past that I am capable of making things difficult for myself and still managing to win," Harrington said. The 35-year-old from Dublin had been runner-up 30 times, including twice in playoffs to Garcia. But Harrington also had 11 victories on the European Tour, two on the U.S. PGA Tour, and one in Japan in 2006, when he overtook Tiger Woods and won in a playoff. He won the Irish Open in May, becoming the first home Open winner in 25 years.

In the Irish PGA the week before the Open, when his competition was mostly club pros and younger players, Harrington scored triple bogey on the 17th hole and needed a playoff to win. "There is nothing like having done it before," he said. "That's the greatest reason I'm here with the Claret Jug."

Still, the victory was a shock. "I don't know what to think," Harrington said of watching his four-foot putt find the bottom of the hole at the last in the playoff. "There were so many things going through my head. It was an unbelievable emotion. Am I the Open champion? What does this mean? I had a foot to watch it going in there, and it was just amazing, incredible to see it drop."

There had never been a year like this for Irish golf, starting the previous September when Ireland was host for the first time to the Ryder Cup and a spectacular European victory at The K Club. Amateur Rory McIlroy finished the Open as the winner of the Silver Medal. Joe Carr was announced this week as the first Irishman to enter the World Golf Hall of Fame, and later, the Walker Cup was played at Royal County Down.

"I convinced myself all week that I was going to win the Open, but I never let myself believe it," Harrington said, while acknowledging the tremendous support which Ireland provides for its golfers and other sporting heroes. "Far more people had the belief in me that I would become an Open champion than I ever had in myself."

First Round

The last time Sergio Garcia played at Carnoustie, he left in tears after two days, finishing last after a first-round score of 89. This time on the opening day, Garcia improved by 24 strokes, reaching the top of the leaderboard with 65. Asked what reward he might receive, if there were such prizes, Garcia playfully responded: "Most improved, I guess."

Garcia, the now 27-year-old Spaniard with 16 worldwide career victories but no majors, said his only thought of the 1999 Open came when he birdied the first hole, after hitting a nine iron to eight feet. When he rolled in the putt, Garcia turned to his caddie and said: "Well, that's four better than last time."

"As I said at the beginning of the week," Garcia explained, "this is not about revenge for me. I just want to play solidly, play like I did today, give myself good looks at birdies, not suffer too much on the course, and put myself in a position to do something on Sunday. This is a good start, definitely what the doctor ordered."

Using a belly putter for only the second tournament, Garcia made seven birdies and only dropped a shot at the par-three 16th hole. His score was two strokes better than the best of the 1999 Open, the 67 by Paul Lawrie in the final round. This time the rough was less, the condition of the course superb and the weather not much of a problem. Rain helped soften the course early in the week. The early groups in the first round played in a drizzle, but for the rest of the day, with light winds, the conditions were fine.

"You still have to hit a lot of good shots," Garcia said, and he did. After making the turn in 34, he had a wonderful run coming in. He holed a 30-foot putt at the 10th hole, hit a five iron to 10 feet at 12th, a seven iron to seven feet for a two at the 13th, and claimed a birdie-four at the 14th. After the bogey at the 16th hole, where he was bunkered, Garcia hit a six iron to 10 feet at the 17th for another birdie to reach six under par, where he finished the day, two strokes ahead of Ireland's Paul McGinley.

Sharing in the accolades was the Irish amateur Rory McIlroy, whose 68 gave him a piece of third place with four others. The 18-year-old from Holywood — Belfast, not Los Angeles — won the 2006 European Amateur to earn an exemption into Carnoustie. He was the only player in the field of 156 not to drop a stroke to par in the first round.

Also scoring 68s were the new U.S. Open champion Angel Cabrera, 2005 U.S. Open champion Michael Campbell, Austria's Markus Brier and America's Boo Weekley, who was playing in his first Open.

The first morning belonged to the featured group of Tiger Woods, the 2005 and 2006 champion, Lawrie and Justin Rose. Hopes were high for Rose, after top-10 finishes in the Masters and U.S. Open, but he ran out of steam on the second nine and finished with 75. Woods looked unbeatable on the early holes, with a birdie on the third and an eagle-three on the sixth after a seven iron from 207 yards to within 18 feet of the flagstick.

Woods was briefly tied for the lead with K.J. Choi then posted three bogeys around the turn, at the par-three eighth, the 12th and the par-three 13th. He birdied the ninth and the 16th, where he holed a putt of over 80 feet. It was one of only three birdies all day on the 16th. Lawrie went Woods one better on the 18th, with one of only two birdies on the day, which got the Scot in with 73. The other birdie on the 18th was by Andres Romero, who had 16 straight pars, then finished bogey-birdie for 71.

Woods finished with 69, two over par, and shared eighth place with Choi, Stewart Cink, Miguel Angel Jimenez and Padraig Harrington.

First-Round Leaders: Sergio Garcia 65, Paul McGinley 67, Michael Campbell 68, Markus Brier 68, Angel Cabrera 68, Rory McIlroy 68, Boo Weekley 68, K.J. Choi 69, Tiger Woods 69, Stewart Cink 69, Padraig Harrington 69, Miguel Angel Jimenez 69

Second Round

As Tiger Woods was starting on the first hole, Sergio Garcia was just yards away, saving par on the 18th green to complete his round of 71, even par, and maintain the lead after 36 holes at 136, six under par. "It is always much sweeter to shoot par for the day rather than one over," Garcia said. "It sounds much better, although a 72 today in the conditions we played wouldn't be a bad score."

Garcia's nearest challenger was now K.J. Choi, who was two strokes behind at 138 after two rounds of 69, four under par.

At the same time, Woods saw his hopes for a third successive Open title diminished in one swing from the first tee. Taking an iron, usually regarded as the safe club, Woods smacked a low duck hook that finished in the Barry Burn. This was a hazard that should not have been in play from the first tee for the top professionals. A smile crossed Woods's face, a smile of embarrassment.

"It was such a poor shot because the commitment wasn't there," Woods said. He looked uncomfortable with his swing all day and signed for 74, finishing at 143, one over par, for a share of 20th place.

It was not raining and the temperatures were warmer than in the first round, but there was more wind and the hole positions were a bit more severe, so scoring was not as good. Mike Weir's 68 was the low round of the day. Weir tied for third place at 139 with Miguel Angel Jimenez, who shot 70. "It was more of a grinder's day," Garcia said.

While he often plays with a flair, Garcia can do the grinding, too, as he demonstrated here. He had a birdie and a bogey on each nine, and parred his way through the devilish last four holes. "There were some tough holes coming in against the wind and I hit a lot of good iron shots," he said.

Like Woods, Garcia got into trouble on the first hole, but unlike Tiger, he managed to save par. Thirty yards right of the green and in thick rough, he floated a shot over a bunker and ran it to 18 inches from the hole. Garcia said: "More than anything it was a really nice shot because it kept me on the right mood."

In the clubhouse at 136, Garcia had improved exactly one shot a hole for 36 holes on his position at Carnoustie in 1999, when he was 19 years old and had just become a professional. An 18-year-old was the center of attention on Friday morning. Rory McIlroy shot 76 and made the cut at two-over 144 to win the Silver Medal. The Silver Medal is awarded to the low amateur who makes the cut. None of the other five amateurs in the field made the cut.

In the same group with McIlroy, Jimenez, at age 43, continues to strike the ball as well as ever. Weir moved alongside Jimenez at three under par on his 68. Despite the wind picking up as he made the turn, Weir's second nine of 32 was flawless, with birdies at the 10th, 14th and 16th holes. "Starting at 10 I found my groove," he said. Just behind Weir and Jimenez were Jim Furyk and Boo Weekley at 140. Angel Cabrera was one of six at 141.

Choi, in second place, was one of only four other players to break 70. Three birdies coming home were spoiled by Choi having to lay up at the last hole and taking a bogey. But Choi was the only player to be under 70 both days with his pair of 69s. Raphael Jacquelin also scored 69 which put him at one over par. Sweden's Niclas Fasth and America's Charlie Hoffman also had 69s to join McIlroy at two over.

Paul McGinley, off late in the day, lost the magic from the day before and shot 75 to fall back to even par. Michael Campbell dropped off the leaderboard with 78, making the 36-cut right on the mark at four over. Phil Mickelson, Colin Montgomerie and Paul Lawrie all missed the cut.

Second-Round Leaders: Sergio Garcia 71–136, K.J. Choi 69–138, Miguel Angel Jimenez 70–139, Mike Weir 68–139, Jim Furyk 70–140, Boo Weekley 72–140, Andres Romero 70–141, Angel Cabrera 73–141, Lee Westwood 70–141, Alastair Forsyth 71–141, Retief Goosen 71–141, J.J. Henry 71–141

Third Round

Carnoustie had never seen a day like Saturday for scoring in the Open. Steve Stricker matched the course record with his 64, and 16 others were under 70. Nearly half the field, 33 of 70 players, was at or below even-par 71. Sergio Garcia did not have a bogey on his scorecard as he shot 68 and moved to 204, nine under par, for a three-stroke lead over Stricker, who climbed from a tie for 20th place to second alone.

Seven players in the chasing pack settled on three-under 210, three behind Stricker and six behind Garcia. Of the seven, only Ernie Els had won a major championship. The others were Padraig Harrington, Paul McGinley, Chris DiMarco, Stewart Cink, Paul Broadhurst and K.J. Choi. All but Choi, who shot 72, had third-round scores in the 60s.

There was a forecast of a storm in mid-afternoon but it never happened. The skies were dark and showery, and the wind had shifted slightly, but there was nothing to prevent the players from attacking the course. Vijay Singh shot 68 and was at 211, sharing 10th place with Miguel Angel Jimenez, Mike Weir, Jim Furyk and Andres Romero. Justin Rose and Pelle Edberg both shot 67s and were at 212 along with three Americans: Tiger Woods, Rich Beem, both of whom had 69s, and J.J. Henry.

Ian Poulter was challenging through 14 holes but dropped four strokes in the next three holes, finishing with 70, tied with three others at 216. On his 30th birthday, Paul Casey shot 69 and was at 214 with Nick Dougherty, who also scored 69, and five others.

DiMarco came through with 66 to hold the clubhouse lead at three under. He made seven birdies and two bogeys. "I learned the strategy of the course the last two days," DiMarco said. "I'm hitting the ball the best I have all year."

Stricker started his round by holing putts on the first three holes from 10 feet, 25 feet and 40 feet. He rolled in a 20-footer at the fifth and hit a seven iron to three feet at the seventh. He was out in 31, five under par. His six iron to 15 feet at the 13th hole set up another birdie and he two-putted for a birdie-four at the 14th. He collected seven birdies, just like DiMarco, but did not have a bogey. Back in 33, Stricker's 64 matched the course-record scores of Alan Tait and Colin Montgomerie.

"I've been working on my putting and today I gave myself a lot of opportunities, and they all seemed to go in," Stricker said. "I played very well from tee to green, especially the first 14 holes, but even after that I didn't play too badly, just couldn't quite get it on the green. It was quite a day, quite an experience. It was a lot of fun and gives me a chance tomorrow."

The way Garcia was playing, that was never going to be easy. He birdied the first hole from 11 feet. A five iron to 12 feet at the par-three eighth moved him to eight under, and a wedge to 18 inches at the 11th put him at nine under.

Garcia's game was rock steady until the 17th, where he pulled his four-iron second shot onto the back on the left of the green and the ball struck a photographer on the neck. After handing over a signed glove and ball, Garcia saved par then hit another superb long-iron shot. Unfortunately, he missed the putt, to the disappointment of the spectators packing the huge grandstands.

"I wanted to make the putt on 18 for them and to hear the roar that would have been just out of this world," Garcia said. "But it broke a little to the right."

It meant the difference between a lead of four strokes and three. "I think everyone chasing is hoping for wind tomorrow," Els said. "Otherwise Sergio is playing solidly, he's not making any mistakes and he's leading by three. It's kind of in his hands now. He is in a great position. But there's a lot of guys chasing. It's a major and there's a lot that can still happen."

Harrington birdied three of the first six holes and played in even par from there on. "If it had been a couple of shots better, then it would have been a really good day, but I will certainly take three under," he said.

"The good thing about having the lead," Garcia said, "is that even if you don't have the best of starts, you're still there. But if you're behind and you don't have a good start, it feels like you are falling way back. You have to attack more. I haven't been in this position in a major, but I'm looking forward to it."

Third-Round Leaders: Sergio Garcia 68–204, Steve Stricker 64–207, Chris DiMarco 66–210, Paul McGinley 68–210, Stewart Cink 68–210, Padraig Harrington 68–210, Ernie Els 68–210, Paul Broadhurst 68–210,

K.J. Choi 72–210, Vijay Singh 68–211, Andres Romero 70–211, Jim Furyk 71–211, Mike Weir 72–211, Miguel Angel Jimenez 72–211

Fourth Round

Whereas the drama at Carnoustie in 1999 had not come until the end, this time it built steadily throughout the day. Ben Curtis, the 2003 champion, and Hunter Mahan showed early that a low score was possible, each posting 65 to get to three under par and four under respectively. Then Richard Green, a left-handed Australian, got to eight under for the round and needed a par on the 18th to tie the Open record of 63. He drove in the left rough, laid up and missed a 15-footer on his try for a par.

"I had my focus on shooting the course record, eight under, and that took my mind off my position in the tournament," Green said. "But I suppose I'm a bit disappointed not to be at six under and in with a better chance." He finished at 279, five under and tied for fourth place, his best result in a major championship.

It also was not to be for Tiger Woods to win for the third year in a row. He shot 70 and tied for 12th place at 282.

Sergio Garcia extended his lead to four strokes over Steve Stricker by birdieing the third hole from four feet. Stricker missed from three feet and twice more missed short putts on the outward nine, and his challenge evaporated as he shot 74.

Just as Green reached the clubhouse, Garcia's troubles began. He bogeyed the fifth hole after his tee shot finished on the edge of a bunker and he could only chip back to the fairway. He missed a birdie try from five feet on the sixth, and poor chip shots on the seventh and eighth holes resulted in bogeys.

Suddenly the whole complexion of the championship had changed. Garcia was tied with Andres Romero, the 26-year-old from Argentina whose career record consisted of one victory on Europe's Challenge Tour, two in Argentina and one in Panama.

Romero had shown his promise in last year's Open at Hoylake, sharing eighth place. Now, playing the round of his life, Romero birdied the third and fourth holes, hitting wedge and pitch shots close. He holed another short putt after a three wood to the sixth green, then a 15-foot putt at the eighth. He was still four strokes behind at that time. He bogeyed the ninth but did not lose ground because Garcia had started to struggle. Birdies at the 10th hole from 25 feet and the 11th, where he holed a bunker shot, put him only two strokes behind. As Romero played the par-four 12th, the deficit became one and then none.

But Romero had problems of his own at the 12th. His second shot kicked right into a bush and an unplayable lie, resulting in a double-bogey six, and Romero was two behind again.

Romero wasn't the only one now challenging. Ernie Els was another, and the 2002 Open champion birdied three of the first six holes to get to six under. Els saved par on the 12th, but faltered on the 13th, taking a bogey after hitting into a bunker. He birdied the 14th after missing a 15-foot putt for eagle, then bogeyed the 15th after a poor drive. He finished with 69 to tie Green in the clubhouse at 279.

"I got to one behind, but then lost a bit of momentum," Els said. A fifth top-four finish in the Open in six years was little consolation. "The tee shot on the 13th is the shot I'm going to look back on and not be happy about."

In the group behind Els, two groups ahead of Garcia, Padraig Harrington made good progress but remained under the radar early on. He pitched to four feet for a birdie at the third hole, got a birdie at the par-five sixth, and holed from 15 feet for a birdie-three at the ninth to go out in 33. He was six under and two strokes behind. He scored par at the 10th and moved one behind. At the 11th, a birdie from four feet put him into a tie for the lead at seven under with Garcia and Romero.

Four consecutive birdies starting with the 13th hole sent Romero to the 17th tee leading by two strokes. He holed from 12 feet for two at the 13th, made four at the 14th by getting up and down beside the green, tying for the lead again, then went ahead with a birdie from 15 feet at the 15th and another from 18 feet at the 16th.

On to the 17th tee, where Romero's drive finished in the rough on mounds to the right of the fairway. He then hit a low, hooking two-iron shot that hit the retaining wall of the Barry Burn as it crossed the 17th fairway and — unluckily — rebounded at such an angle that it shot off right and over the out-of-bounds fence on the other side of the 18th hole. Taking a three wood next, Romero did well to find the green and limit the damage to double-bogey six.

Romero missed the green at the last hole and took a bogey, but he was the new leader in the clubhouse at 278, six under. His round of 67 contained 10 birdies, two bogeys and two double bogeys. "Certainly the pressure caught up with me," he said. "But I'm happy to be playing like this with the best players in the world."

The attention turned again to Garcia and Harrington. The Irishman parred the 12th and 13th holes, then eagled the 14th with a 15-foot putt to go to nine under. Behind him, Garcia birdied the 13th from 10 feet and the 14th with two putts. Ahead, Harrington parred the 15th, 16th and 17th, and stood on the final tee one stroke ahead after Garcia bogeyed the 15th with a poor tee shot.

Harrington made a poor swing on the 18th tee, pushing the ball right and into the Barry Burn. He dropped out and took a five iron, aiming for the bunker on the left of the green, unlike Jean Van de Velde, who in 1999 had headed right towards the grandstand with disastrous consequences. But Harrington had another poor shot and found the water again.

"I didn't want to take seven," Harrington said. "It crossed my mind that (Van de Velde) had made seven to lose the Open and I was slipping down that slippery slope." He had a pitch of 47 yards, an advantage because it was exactly the shot he practiced behind his home every day. His shot checked up five feet past the flagstick, and he holed that for six. Harrington finished with 67 and was at 277, seven under.

"Taking six was my fault. I hit two poor shots," Harrington said. "But I took some comfort in getting up and down, and I was really happy with the way I handled myself from then on. I never let it cross my mind that I'd just thrown away the Open. I was as disciplined and focused as I could be not to brood, no ifs or buts."

With Garcia parring the 17th, he needed another par to win. He hit an iron off the tee, then had a delay while the bunkers were raked after the group in front finished. He pulled his three-iron approach into the bunker on the left, and later was annoyed about the wait. The recovery came out to 10 feet, and the putt hit the left side of the cup and stayed out of the hole. Garcia closed with 73 and was tied at 277.

In the four-hole playoff, on the first hole Garcia hit into the front bunker with his approach shot and took a bogey, while Harrington holed from 10 feet for a birdie. Garcia hit the flagstick at the 16th and the ball spun away to 18 feet, although it might have gone farther without the interference. But Garcia saw it as a misfortune. Harrington was off the green to the left and they both scored pars there and again on the 17th.

Two strokes ahead going to the 18th, Harrington chose the safe route, taking a hybrid off the tee and laying up short of the water. "Let's make five," he was thinking. "It seemed sensible to put the pressure on Sergio and make him make a three. If he does, then I'd slap him on the back, say well done, and we would be going on."

Garcia went with his driver off the tee and found the left rough, but then hit a terrific six iron to 20 feet. Harrington's third shot was barely on the green, and his 30-foot putt rolled on four feet past, farther than he would have liked. Once more Garcia thought he had made his putt on the 18th, but it rolled by the edge of the hole. He made the putt coming back, forcing Harrington to do the same.

So it was Harrington who raised the Claret Jug.

Afterwards, Garcia's disappointment was evident. "It is tough mainly because I don't feel like I did anything wrong," Garcia said. "I didn't miss a shot in the playoff and hit unbelievable putts, but they just didn't want to go in. It just wasn't meant to happen. It seems to me that every time I get in this kind of position, I have no room for error. But the week is over. Padraig played well today and well enough to win."

The Final Leaders: Padraig Harrington 67–277 (15 strokes in playoff), Sergio Garcia 73–277 (16), Andres Romero 67–278, Richard Green 64–279, Ernie Els 69–279, Hunter Mahan 65–280, Stewart Cink 70–280, Ben Curtis 65–281, Mike Weir 70–281, K.J. Choi 71–281, Steve Stricker 74–281

5. PGA Championship

One person at Southern Hills Country Club didn't know what all the fuss was about — aside from the clueless among the media — and that was Sam Alexis Woods. And that's because she was only two months old. So it would be quite some years before she would appreciate what her dad, Tiger Woods, did that hot, humid week in Tulsa, Oklahoma.

The PGA Championship had returned to Southern Hills, the seventh major championship to be held there. The first was the 1958 U.S. Open, won by Tommy Bolt. The U.S. Open was also held there in 1977, won by Hubert Green under a death threat, and in 2001 (Retief Goosen). There were three PGAs: 1970 (Dave Stockton), 1982 (Raymond Floyd) and 1994 (Nick Price).

Southern Hills, playing at par 70, is of average length by modern standards, 7,131 yards. It has 11 doglegs, which dictated the strategy for many golfers — an iron off the tee to avoid running through the fairway and into the heavy Bermuda-grass rough.

They could say this for Southern Hills — at many places, they like to say it isn't the heat, it's the humidity. At Southern Hills, it was both, and both were intense all week. The average temperature was 101, making it the hottest major ever. The heat index — the combination of temperature and humidity rating — ranged from 106 the first two days, to 109 on Saturday, and then Sunday was the most punishing, with a temperature of 102 and a heat index of 110.

For the week, Monday through Sunday, 264 spectators had to be treated for serious heat-related conditions and 37 were hospitalized. The weather was every bit the opponent that the golf course was. Golfers spent the week gulping water and sports drinks, some of them 10 or more bottles each day, trying to stay hydrated. Two players withdrew during the first round because of the heat — Anthony Wall and, significantly, Jyoti Randhawa, an Indian.

If it was the same old story for Tiger Woods, this PGA Championship was refreshingly new in many other ways.

Woody Austin was the best feel-good story of the week. Austin worked as a bank teller and bartender, and was best-known for once whacking himself on the head with the shaft of his putter until it bent. Then he chased Woods all the way, and especially through a high-pressure final round, to finish second, his best placing ever in a major championship. "Like I said all along," Austin said, "I was a pretty good player a long time ago. I didn't just come out of the bank, like everybody thought I did."

There was the return — though he hadn't been that far away — of Ernie Els, finishing third, a high point in what he called his "three-year deal," his program to get to or near the No. 1 ranking owned by Woods. "I just need to keep working on it, grinding it out," Els said.

Southern Hills was not friendly to the other three winners of the 2007 major championships. Ireland's Padraig Harrington (The Open) was never in the running, and Zach Johnson (Masters) and Argentina's Angel Cabrera

(U.S. Open) missed the cut. Cabrera and Spain's Sergio Garcia tied for the PGA's most embarrassing moment. Cabrera shot 81 in the first round, thanks in large part to a 10 at the par-three sixth hole, and Garcia was disqualified for signing an incorrect scorecard in the third round, after playing partner Boo Weekley put him down for a four where he'd made a five.

When the final tabulations were in, they showed these two interesting facts: Els made the most birdies and Austin had the fewest bogeys. Els had 19 birdies, but also 11 bogeys and two double bogeys. Austin had 12 birdies and only six bogeys. Tiger Woods had 17 birdies and nine bogeys, and, of course, he had the most important number of all — eight-under-par 272.

First Round

If you like surprises, then the first round of the PGA Championship was your piece of cake. Not so much that Tiger Woods, defending champion and prohibitive favorite (as always), started with a one-over-par 71, six strokes off the lead. The surprise was the erratic way he got it — four birdies and five bogeys. He charged out of the starting gate (from No. 10) with three birdies over his first six holes, but then he sputtered. He was three under, then bogeyed his ninth hole (No. 18) and came home with four bogeys and one birdie. "I missed a couple shots, and also the wind was hard to gauge," he said. "But I felt like I was hitting the ball better than my score indicates, which is good."

If the rest of his round was un-Woods-like, his birdie at the 653-yard par-five fifth hole was pure Tiger Woods. His tee shot left him 286 yards to the front of the green. "I was just trying to roll the ball in the gap, and I should have been in the right bunker," he conceded. But he got a nice break. The ball kicked to the left instead and ended up 15 feet from the cup. Thank you very much, and he got the birdie on two putts.

For a real surprise, try a player with a pure Hollywood name — England's Graeme Storm, age 29, who four years earlier was washing trays in a cake factory to make ends meet. Storm shot a bogey-free five-under 65 for the first-round lead by two strokes over John Daly.

Storm's hard work paid off in a magical first round. He holed a 20-foot putt for a birdie at No. 10, his first hole, then tapped in for another at the par-three 11th. He two-putted from 15 feet at the par-five 15th, and wrapped up a four-under first nine with an eight-foot birdie putt at the 16th. Then he manufactured another birdie at the par-four No. 2 — a drive into the trees, a lay-up just short of the green and then a chip-in for the birdie and the 65. "Didn't expect it at all," Storm said.

Another surprise hit the PGA Championship when big, smiling John Daly, the grip-it and rip-it hero, didn't show up at Southern Hills until opening day, thereby adding another chapter to the Daly legend.

Said one writer, "If you didn't play a practice round here at Southern Hills, how did you prepare for this tournament?"

"I've been playing the slots over at Cherokee Casino," Daly said. "Did good the first day, didn't do too good the other day."

But he did get some practice in — on the casino's course.

It was all because of Tulsa's stifling heat and humidity. "I couldn't see myself playing golf," Daly said. So he warmed up at a nearby casino, indulging his favorite pastime. And Daly shot 67 on a course he hadn't seen in 13 years, when he missed the cut in the 1997 PGA. The last time he showed up cold at a course for a major championship was the 1991 PGA at Crooked Stick, in Indiana, when he got into the field very late, as the ninth alternate. And then shocked the golf world by winning it.

Phil Mickelson, favored to contend for the title, hurt himself with 73 made up of birdies and errors. He bogeyed the par-five sixth through rough and trees, and then bunkered his prized flop shot at No. 8. "You're not going to be able to go all 18 holes here and go unscathed," he said.

Geoff Ogilvy, the 2006 U.S. Open champion, posted a wild 69 — four fours, a two, seven threes and six fives. Sergio Garcia survived both the heat and the clock for 70 that included a stumbling two-bogey finish. Garcia suffered a bitter disappointment just three weeks earlier, when he let the Open Championship at Carnoustie slip through his hands. He was soon to have another. Angel Cabrera, who won the U.S. Open in June, was a big surprise — for shooting 81. It included a 10 on the par-three No. 6. "A bad shot, I make 10," Cabrera said.

The two players who would put the most heat on Woods at the end were in the picture to start. Ernie Els shot two-over 72. Starting at No. 10 in the morning, Els tripped coming in, going bogey-double bogey after making the turn. Woody Austin, age 43, a journeyman known chiefly for being high-strung, also started at the 10th and had two birdies and a bogey going out and one birdie coming in. "I missed a lot of opportunities that last 10 holes," he said. Then there was the unsettling matter of the time. "You're on the clock — that's pretty much what they said."

Arron Oberholser and Stephen Ames also were at 68. Oberholser was practically a walking hospital case. He had injured his back in January, had tendonitis in both elbows, then discovered he had broken his hand back in April. "I never know when the fracture is going to rear its ugly head," Oberholser said. Ames, who started at the 10th hole, caught fire coming in, getting birdies at his last three holes. The keys were a 35-foot putt at his 16th (No. 7), when he was just trying to make par. Then at his 17th (the 245-yard, par-3 No. 8), he put a five-wood shot eight feet from the hole and made the putt. "I think I was rewarded for the way I played today, which was nice," Ames said. Then he added what was on everyone's mind: "God, it's going to be hot every day."

First-Round Leaders: Graeme Storm 65, John Daly 67, Arron Oberholser 68, Woody Austin 68, Stephen Ames 68, Mark Wilson 69, Camilo Villegas 69, Markus Brier 69, Geoff Ogilvy 69, Lee Westwood 69, Padraig Harrington 69, John Senden 69

Second Round

As one headline put it, Tiger Woods shot a 62½ in the second round. That's a kind of poetic license to describe a ball that defies gravity to take a spin around the hole and still stays out. This was on Southern Hills' 18th hole in the second round, where Woods needed a birdie for 62, which would have broken the record for the lowest score in a major championship. But the ball horseshoed out, and Woods had to be content to tie with 22 others who have shot 63 in majors over the years.

The 63 gave Woods the lead through the halfway point of the PGA, just where everyone thought he would be sooner or later. Woods was two up on Scott Verplank, a favorite son who played college golf at Oklahoma State and who lives in Edmond. "I hit a good putt, and I thought I made it," Woods said. "It would have been nice to have a record and got a three-shot lead going into the weekend."

Woods's 63 included a bogey at the par-four No. 7, where he went from rough to bunker, then blasted out and two-putted from 12 feet. His eight birdies went this way:

No. 1 – two iron, eight iron to eight feet, one putt,
No. 4 – three iron off the tee, nine iron to 20 feet, one putt,
No. 5 – driver, six iron, five wood, eight-foot putt,
No. 9 – four iron, eight iron to one foot,
No. 10 – five iron, nine iron to four feet,
No. 13 – three wood, seven iron, bunkered, blast out to two feet,
No. 14 – five iron to fringe, chip-in,
No. 15 – four iron, seven iron to 20 feet.

Verplank's 66 included four birdies, no bogeys and one thrilling save. He was two under par for the round and he had the par-five 13th hole square in his sights. His drive was long and true, 302 yards down the middle. Then came his next shot. "And I'm kind of licking my chops," Verplank admitted, thinking of a chance at an eagle. But his high three-iron shot nicked the top of a tree and came down in the water. Verplank went back to a spot about 130 yards from the green, and flew in a pitching wedge that ended up four feet from the hole and saved his par. He had birdied Nos. 9, 11, 15 and 17, but the par save at the No. 13 held his round together.

"That was obviously big," said Verplank, who led the tournament for part of the day.

Stephen Ames and Geoff Ogilvy tied for third at three-under 137. Ames shot an up-and-down 69, with four birdies and three bogeys. Ogilvy, who shot 68, got to four under on the second nine, then finished bogey-bogey. "That's what happens if you don't hit the fairways," Ogilvy said.

Woody Austin, whose best finish in a PGA Championship was a tie for 16th, stayed firmly in the chase with a par 70, thanks to what he labeled "a really goofy birdie" at the par-four No. 9. "I flew my wedge in the middle of the green, and it spun all the way off the green and 30 yards down in the fairway," he said. "And then I holed it." Austin three-putted the second hole from 30 feet for a bogey, birdied the fifth from 18 inches, then bogeyed the par-five 13th for 70 and a 138 total, alone in fifth place, four off Woods's lead.

Ernie Els started his climb up the leaderboard with a four-birdie, two-bogey 68 for an even-par 140 total. "At least I got myself back into the tournament," said Els, whose best finish in the PGA was a tie for third in 1995. With Woods leading, Els was not counting himself out at this early point. "We all know he's No. 1 and he's on form," Els said. "But I'm playing pretty well myself."

Elsewhere, the field was reshaping itself.

Sergio Garcia was in contention until he came undone on the second nine. It started with a double bogey at the 173-yard, par-three 11th hole. He bunkered his tee shot, took three to get out, and made the five with a 10-foot putt. Then he bogeyed four straight from the 14th hole for 75 and made the cut right on the number, 145. The flip side of that coin was the great reversal by Darren Clarke, an 11-stroke swing from 77 to 66, which put him safely in at 143.

There was a bittersweet story to the second round. The traffic proved a bit too heavy for England's Graeme Storm, the first-round leader with 65. He made no bogeys in the first round, but he made eight bogeys plus a double bogey for a six-over 76 in the second round. His 141 total easily made the cut figure. "Today, anything that could go wrong did go wrong," he said.

Open champion Padraig Harrington, though not a threat, made the cut, 69-73, and would finish tied for 42nd, a far better fate than that of the other 2007 major champions. Zach Johnson (Masters) shot 74-76, and Angel Cabrera (U.S. Open) 81-70, and both missed the cut. Furyk, he of the sore back, couldn't recover from an opening 75 with his 71. Mark Brooks, the 1996 winner, had the worst time of all of the past PGA champions, shooting 79-76–155, missing the cut by 10 strokes.

Among others who missed the 145 cut figure were Davis Love, the 1997 PGA champion, 72-74; Vijay Singh, the 1998 and 2004 champion, 75-71; Justin Leonard, 75-72; and Mike Weir, 77-72.

At day's end, it seemed Tiger Woods wasn't all that excited about just shooting 63 and taking the lead. "I'm very satisfied," Woods said. "I'm just really hungry. I just want to go home and eat."

Second-Round Leaders: Tiger Woods 63–134, Scott Verplank 66–136, Stephen Ames 69–137, Geoff Ogilvy 68–137, Woody Austin 70–138, John Senden 70–139, Niclas Fasth 68–139, Pat Perez 69–139, Paul McGinley 66–140, Adam Scott 68–140, Camilo Villegas 71–140, Arron Oberholser 72–140, Ernie Els 68–140, John Daly 73–140

Third Round

"I accomplished my goal today," Tiger Woods said. "My goal was to shoot under par and increase my lead." That is, he shot a one-under 69 for a seven-under 293 total and increased his lead to three strokes, this time — with Scott Verplank having slipped back — over Stephen Ames. It was almost a routine round of two birdies and one bogey. "I really kept myself out of trouble today," Woods said. He birdied the fourth, hitting a three iron off the tee, then a nine iron to 12 feet. Then he birdied the 12th, hitting a two iron off the tee and an eight iron to 10 feet. At the par-three 14th, he bunkered his tee shot, came out to 18 feet and two-putted.

"I've put myself in that position," Woods said. "I've always enjoyed being out in front. And hopefully tomorrow I can go ahead and play the way I've been playing the last few days."

On that point, the gods revealed a wry sense of humor. They let Stephen Ames shoot a steady 69 in the third round, and that put him in second place and paired with Woods for the final round. Ames was reminded again of his comment when asked what his chances were against Woods in the

Accenture Match Play, and he answered that "anything could happen in match play ... especially where he's hitting the ball." Woods responded by beating him, 9 and 8. And now they were paired. Ames would not be drawn into any sensitive statements, allowing only that "For me, it's a great opportunity of being in the situation," and adding, "Tiger's looking for his 13th (major), I'm looking for my first."

Woody Austin stayed deep in the chase with an amazing 69 — amazing because he hit only four fairways all day. "The chipping was definitely the key today," he said. "I proved you can't drive the ball in the rough and play this game, except unless your sand wedge is pretty good." Austin birdied the fifth after hitting a fairway bunker off the tee, holing a 10-foot putt. He missed the fairway at the 10th and bogeyed. He hit the fairway at the 15th and 16th and birdied both. Then he missed again at the 18th and bogeyed.

Arron Oberholser (70–210) didn't give himself or anybody else much of a chance. Adam Scott (70–210) agreed that a win by Woods was almost a formality at this point. "But there have been 63s, so someone can go out and play the round of their life, put a little pressure on him," Scott said.

As if Sergio Garcia hadn't been hurt enough by his second-nine collapse in the second round, along came the ultimate self-inflicted doom in the third round. Garcia signed an incorrect scorecard and was disqualified. Boo Weekley, Garcia's playing companion, marked him down for a par-four on the 17th. But Garcia actually had five. Garcia had signed his card for 74 and left. Weekley brushed it all aside. "It's my fault for putting the wrong score in there," he said, "but it's his fault for not checking it, you know. It's his score." Said Garcia, when he learned he was out: "Oh, that puts the icing on the cake."

Weekley, meanwhile, shot 65 and moved up to a tie for sixth place at 210, seven strokes behind Woods. He had a chance to match Woods's 63 at the 18th, but he left his birdie putt six feet short and then missed that for par and took his second bogey.

Verplank's hopes evaporated at Southern Hills' celebrated 12th hole, a par-four of 458 yards. He had started the third round two strokes behind Woods, his playing companion in the final grouping. At the 12th, Verplank drove into the left rough, then bounced his approach off a tree and into the gallery, then hit another tree and double-bogeyed. "I should have played more conservatively, but I did what I thought was right — and it wasn't," Verplank said. The rest of the way, he had three bogeys and one birdie for 74 to fall seven shots behind Woods.

John Daly, the no-practice hero of the first round, bogeyed four of his last seven holes for 73 and tied for 17th at 213. "I've played better than I scored the last two days," Daly said. "It's just frustrating."

As if a general knowledge of Woods's performance over the years wasn't enough to establish him as a near-lock to win this PGA the next day, there were other singular facts. Woods, for example, had a 12-0 record in major championships when having at least a share of the lead going into the final round. Then this rarefied statistic: Woods's career average in the final round when he has held at least a share of the lead going in was 69.25 versus the 72.92 of the 12 players paired with him.

At least one player wasn't conceding anything. Or else he was semi-conceding. That was Ernie Els, trailing by six strokes and trying to explain a contradictory position. "The statistics will tell you, yes, it's over," Els said. "But as a competitor, I can't tell you it's over. I can't ever do that. So, as a competitor, you can't ever think it's over. So I need to shoot something unbelievable and he's gotta make mistakes."

Someone pressed the point: If you were a fan watching at home, would you think it's over? "If I was a fan on the couch," Els said, "I'd be putting my house on him."

Third-Round Leaders: Tiger Woods 69–203, Stephen Ames 69–206, Woody Austin 69–207, John Senden 69–208, Ernie Els 69–209, Scott Verplank 74–210, Adam Scott 70–210, Arron Oberholser 70–210, K.J. Choi 68–210, Kevin Sutherland 68–210, Nathan Green 67–210, Boo Weekley 65–210

Fourth Round

In the final round, there were only four other people in Tiger Woods's world — his wife, Elin, and their new daughter, Sam, and Woody Austin and Ernie Els. The rest of the field for this PGA Championship couldn't make a move or couldn't keep up. There was some movement, of course. Simon Dyson, for example, closed with 64, but that got him a tie for sixth place, eight strokes away from Woods's winning 272 total. Otherwise, it was a three-man chase — or rather, two men chasing Woods on the hottest day — temperature, 102; heat index, 110.

Els was determined to add the PGA to his collection of majors, two U.S. Opens and one Open in Britain. His best finish was a tie for third in 1995, and he also tied for fifth in 2003 and tied for fourth in 2004. So he wanted this one for his own portfolio, and also to beat the World No. 1. Austin had played in only six PGAs since 1995, and his best finish was a tie for 16th place in 2006. So both had plenty to shoot for. But then, so did Woods, and especially after he bogeyed the 14th hole and was hanging to the lead by one shot.

"I just felt like, I got myself into this mess, I need to get myself out," Woods said.

There would be no pressure from Stephen Ames, Woods's playing partner in the final group, who started the day three shots behind and then was out of it early. He bogeyed his first two holes, then bogeyed four straight from the 12th, shot 76 and dropped to a tie for 12th place.

Some of the earlier finishers were asked their views on this final round. Here's what a few had to say:

• Phil Mickelson (69, tied for 32nd place) on whether Woods was catchable: "If the past is any sign, then probably not. But you never know in this game. You just never know."

• Geoff Ogilvy (69, tied for sixth), on Woods not having his best game against pressure by Els: "Be fun watching these guys come in. Only a couple up. (Woods) might have to take a risk here or there."

• John Daly (73, tied for 32nd), on whether Woods could be beaten: "No, he's not beatable today."

But it looked as though Woods might be now and then. The quote of the week, right on point, came from Austin. "I'm glad that Ernie and I didn't let him just coast in," Austin said.

Woods was not having one of his great days, but it wasn't all bad. He opened with that three-stroke lead and built it to as much as six strokes before tailing off on the second nine, and finally shot 69 for his 272 total and won by two strokes over Austin (67) and three over Els (66).

Woods bogeyed No. 2 after driving into the rough. He birdied No. 4 off a wedge to 10 feet, next birdied No. 7 from eight feet and No. 8 from 25 feet. At this point, he was nine under par — his lowest — and was leading Austin (in the group behind him) by six strokes and Els (two groups back) by five. The championship seemed to be over. But Woods bogeyed No. 9 off a tee shot into the rough and two putts from 15 feet. It wasn't quite over.

Els missed birdie putts from less than eight feet at No. 9 and No. 11, and was one stroke behind Woods until he pulled his drive at No. 16 into the trees and bogeyed. It was over for Els.

Austin said the turning point of his round came at the par-four 10th, where he scrambled mightily for a par after a five-iron tee shot into the rough. "It was a six turned into a four, that saved my tournament," Austin said. That launched him into birdies over the next three holes — a 15-foot putt at the 11th, a longish putt at the 12th and two putts from 30 feet at the 13th. When Woods bogeyed the 14th behind him, Austin had got to within one stroke, and that's as close as he would get.

"To come from six back against the world's No. 1 was always going to be tough," Els said. "But I gave it a shot."

Austin suddenly had gone from former bank teller, journeyman professional and resident eccentric to someone with a game to be respected. He won the Stanford St. Jude Championship in June, his third career victory but his first since 2004. He had played in only 13 major championships since joining the PGA Tour in 1995, and his previous best finish was a tie for 16th in the 2006 PGA Championship, so this runner-up finish was a quantum leap.

"There's no question it's a breakthrough for me, because I had never been in this position before," Austin said, and then he added, "I'd like to know exactly how I did it today. What the formula is for me, I have no idea."

As for Woods, it was his fourth PGA Championship victory and his 13th professional major championship, his 59th PGA Tour career victory and his fifth victory of 2007. But it was a kind of a breakthrough for him, too. When he left the 18th green and walked into the scoring trailer, there were his wife, Elin, and his infant daughter. "It's a feeling I've never had before," Woods said. "Having Sam there and having Elin there ... this one feels so much more special than the other majors."

The Final Leaders: Tiger Woods 69–272, Woody Austin 67–274, Ernie Els 66–275, Arron Oberholser 69–279, John Senden 71–279, Simon Dyson 64–280, Trevor Immelman 69–280, Geoff Ogilvy 69–280, Scott Verplank 71–281, Kevin Sutherland 71–281, Boo Weekley 71–281

6. Women's Major Championships

Kraft Nabisco Championship

To Morgan Pressel it seemed she had waited all her life for that first LPGA Tour victory. Now she was the leader in the clubhouse in the final round of the Kraft Nabisco Championship, but she would have to wait at least another hour. She could still be beaten, and Suzann Pettersen, another golfer who knew about disappointment, was the one who could do it. Still, Pressel could dream. She knew all about dreaming, but she couldn't dare dream that all those challengers — and especially Pettersen — would obligingly fade away.

But they did, especially Pettersen, the talented Norwegian. She was leading by four strokes with four holes to play, and squandered all down that demanding closing stretch at the Mission Hills course in Rancho Mirage, California. Pettersen's collapse would have Pressel crying again. But these were happy tears this time. She had just won by one stroke. She not only scored her first LPGA victory, but her first major championship as well, all in one grand gesture. She had become — at age 18 years and 10 months — the youngest ever to win an LPGA major. And she was the first American to win this championship since Dottie Pepper in 1999.

"I got off to a little bit of a rough start with two over on the front the first day," Pressel said. "I just said to myself, stay patient. This golf course is playing tough."

This was a last-minute heartbreak for Pettersen. But Pressel already knew all about last-minute heartbreak. She was about to win the 2005 U.S. Women's Open at Cherry Hills as an amateur, coming up the final fairway, when she saw South Korea's Birdie Kim, up at the 18th green, holing out a bunker shot for a birdie and the victory. So Pressel wasn't counting this one yet. She was nervously waiting it out, busying herself hitting balls at the practice range.

Pressel played Mission Hills in 74-72-70-69 for a 285 total, three under par, to win by one over Pettersen, whose collapse left her with 74, her only over-par round of the tournament, Catriona Matthew (71) and Brittany Lincicome (72).

The dynamic Lorena Ochoa, who won the Safeway International the week before, was trying to overtake the slumping and ailing Annika Sorenstam at No. 1 in the Rolex Rankings. A victory in the Kraft Nabisco Championship would do it. Although South Korea's Shi Hyun Ahn took the first-round lead with a six-birdie, four-under 68, all eyes were on Ochoa as she staked her first claim with 69. There was the pressure of the chase.

"No, I'm feeling good," Ochoa said. "I don't feel that pressure. I'm just trying to enjoy, and it's been working. I think it's a process. Just gets better and better, year by year. My goal is to finish No. 1. I have to make sure that I just keep practicing hard and play good for the rest of the season."

Meanwhile, Sorenstam labored for three-over 75, her worst start in a major in seven years, and she had to birdie the 18th for that. "I felt good — I felt ready," Sorenstam said. "And then I got off to a really terrible start." She started on the second nine, and after making birdie at her second hole and finding the fairway with her tee shot on the third, she chunked her second shot, chipped 20 feet past the hole, and three-putted for a double bogey. "I'd like to forget this day," she said.

Ahn swept into the lead with three consecutive birdies through the turn. She hit a five iron to 12 feet at the par-three eighth, a wedge to eight feet at the ninth and a wedge to 20 feet at the 10th. "I do put pressure on myself," Ahn said, "but it's not to the point where I'm coming down on myself."

Ahn got pushed back to a tie for third place when Ochoa, with 71, and Paula Creamer (67) crowded into a one-stroke lead in the second round at four-under 140.

Ochoa scrambled to a double bogey at the 15th. She put her tee shot into the rough under trees and topped a four-iron escape try. Her third ended up on the grassy lip of a bunker, and she chipped across the green and into more rough. She got a stroke back at the par-five 18th, where she had 192 yards to the green and took her caddie's advice and took a five wood instead of a seven wood to the peninsula green. The ball just carried the water, and she chipped to eight feet and birdied. "He saved me," she said.

Creamer was bogey-free in her 67, and she also listened to her caddie at the dangerous 18th. She had 210 yards left to the green, and a birdie would have given her the outright lead. Her caddie advised her to lay up and she settled for her par. "I'm a pretty aggressive player," Creamer said. "If I need to do it, I would have done it. But it's only Friday." So they headed into the weekend with a one-stroke lead on Ahn (73) and Pettersen (69). Pressel, with a 72, was two over par and six off the lead.

Ochoa played herself all but out of the tournament in the third round with a disastrous quadruple-bogey seven at the 173-yard 17th. "I was one behind," she said, "and suddenly I'm way back." She was three under par coming to the 17th. She nicked a tree with her six-iron tee shot, and she pitched into the deep grass behind the green. In her try at a flop shot, she slid the wedge under the ball without touching it. Her next went down the ridge, about 45 feet from the pin, and she three-putted from there for her seven and shot 77. She then was five strokes off the lead. She salvaged some spirit from the crash. "I'm glad I'll be playing behind now," she said. "I have nothing to lose. Hopefully, I'll put pressure on the leaders."

Pettersen and Se Ri Pak took the lead at four-under 212. Pak rolled in a 35-foot birdie putt at the 18th for 70 and put herself into position to become the seventh woman to win the career Grand Slam. "You can't think about that," she said. Pettersen two-putted from 20 feet to birdie the par-five second, lost the stroke with a bogey from the rough at the 13th, and at the 18th hit a rescue club from 210 yards to 30 feet and two-putted for a birdie and 71. "I'm just glad to be in this position again," she said. "Having reloaded to try to get my energy back, being tired at the beginning of the week, it feels nice and feels like I'm in good shape."

The finale promised to be a free-for-all because, going into the last round, 13 players were separated by five strokes. And so it was. Pressel was barely in that group, at par 216 and four strokes off the lead. The key to Pressel's victory lay in a compelling statistic: She had hit 48 of the 56 driving fairways, best in the field, finding her way safely around Mission Hills' demanding rough — the same rough that set up her win. Pressel had finished and was in the scoring tent and saw on television that Pettersen was in the rough at the 16th.

"You can't really miss the fairway there," Pressel said. "I knew I had a shot (at winning)." She had more than a shot. Pettersen was busy self-destructing. She had started the final round tied for the lead with Pak. Meaghan Francella and Paula Creamer were a stroke behind, Brittany Lincicome two behind, and Pressel was four off. The script had been written for her: Ochoa, the pre-tournament favorite, got out of the way in the third round with a triple bogey at the par-three 17th. Sorenstam and defending champion Karrie Webb were never factors. Sorenstam followed her opening 75 with 76 and fell out of sight. Webb was in the picture briefly with a 70 in the first round, then drifted away with 77 in the second. Paula Creamer, a stroke off the lead going into the final round, blew to 78.

The rest of the script for the final round looked this way:

Pak, leading by three on the first nine, bogeyed five of the last six holes and shot 77. Matthew, playing in only her second event since giving birth three months earlier, three-putted the 18th for a bogey and shot 71, tying for second with Pettersen and Lincicome. Lincicome missed a 10-footer for birdie at the last hole and shot 72. How did it feel to finish second? No tears. "It feels good," Lincicome said. "Feels better after I get that check and I see how much I made. I love money."

Pettersen had built up a good head of steam. After bogeys at the third and fourth holes, where she missed the green both times, she birdied four of the next seven holes. At the par-three fifth, she put a six iron to 12 feet. At the par-three eighth, it was a seven iron to four feet. The next two came at par-fives — a six iron to five feet at the ninth, and a wedge to four feet at the 11th.

And so Pettersen was leading by four strokes with four holes to play, then disaster: She two-putted the 15th from 15 feet for bogey; three-putted from 25 feet and double-bogeyed the 16th, and two-putted the 17th from eight feet for another bogey and 74, tying for second place. It was an ironic and 180-degree shift from the way she had lost the week before in the Safeway International. There, she didn't fold, but Ochoa overran her with three birdies over the last four holes.

"I don't know what to say," said a shocked Pettersen. "I know yesterday I said, whoever made the least amount of mistakes would win. I did a few too many on the back. It's actually different. I am disappointed finishing second, probably my personal best, when I was so happy last week for a second place. But this time I felt like I lost the tournament. Last week I felt like I won the second place."

The decks had been cleared for Pressel, but she did her part. Her card reflected calm and quiet compared to most — three birdies, no bogeys. At the par-five second hole, she flipped a wedge from 70 yards to six feet.

At the par-four 12th, she hit a seven iron to 40 feet for possibly the most electrifying birdie of the day. And at the par-five 18th, she lofted a sand wedge from 108 yards to 10 feet for the 69, the three-under 285 total and the one-stroke victory.

"I knew that I had to make some birdies," she said. "And I missed a few opportunities. But in there I made some great clutch par putts of four, five and six feet. I was two under ... had a pretty good chance. And actually going into 17, I turned to my caddie and I said, 'I'd like to get this three (under par) going into the last two holes. I'd like to be three under.' He said that certainly would give them something to think about. And that was what I did."

Pressel had to fret and fidget for about an hour before the situation resolved itself. If she had any comfort, it was in Mission Hills' tough finish.

"I know the last few holes enjoyed taking their tolls on people," she said, "and lucky it wasn't me today."

And then came the tears.

"You guys usually happen to catch me on a bad day," Pressel said. "But I cry every day."

McDonald's LPGA Championship

Suzann Pettersen's stunning three-hole meltdown in the Kraft Nabisco Championship in April had burned its way so deeply and painfully into her mind that she didn't even want to be asked about it. Fast-forward some eight weeks to the McDonald's LPGA Championship, and Pettersen could smile again. She did what she had to do to exorcise that devil of a lost major title, and that was to win one. And that she did in the McDonald's LPGA Championship, and ironically, by reversing the process and over almost the same stretch of holes — this time with great play under the same kind of intense pressure.

"It's certainly a nice feeling to stand on the green by yourself and lift the trophy," said Pettersen, after a clutch performance down the final stretch for a closing 67 and a one-stroke victory over the veteran Karrie Webb, for her second career title but her first major championship. She also was the first Norwegian to win a major on the LPGA Tour. Leading in the second and fourth rounds, she shot 69-67-71-67 for a 274 total, 14 under par at Bulle Rock in Havre de Grace, Maryland.

"I finally proved to all of you that I can actually put it all together and take a major," Pettersen said. "So now I don't have to get that question again." More to the point, she proved it to herself, remembering the bogey-double bogey-bogey collapse down the homestretch that cost her the Kraft Nabisco Championship. This time, under the same intense pressure, she birdied four of the last nine holes, and more to the point, three of the last six for a five-under-par 67 to win by one stroke over Karrie Webb, who had shot 67 just in front of her and was the leader in the clubhouse.

"I needed to keep putting pressure on her," said Webb, who had put on a great finish of her own and now had to wait and watch as Pettersen, in the last group, came to the 18th. Would Pettersen fold again? No. "She executed very well down the stretch, and she should be very proud of herself," said Webb, who won seven majors, including the 2001 LPGA Championship.

Certainly the ghosts from the Kraft Nabisco Championship had to be crawling through Pettersen's mind, but if they were, she didn't give an outward sign in the form, say, of a blowup. How did she keep them quiet?

"The game is difficult enough as it is," Pettersen said. "So just try to hit the easiest shot out there. I could see all the lines, and it was just a matter of if you got the right pace or not. I mean, it was all very confident, very comfortable, and again, I was really calm. I could feel a bit of tension coming on the back nine, and then the last couple of holes. But I must say, experience — it does help. It felt good."

Webb finished second by one stroke with her 67 and 275 total, and South Korean rookie Na On Min, 18, playing in only her sixth tournament, finished third, one stroke behind Webb and two behind Pettersen.

Min, about as unknown as a professional golfer could be, was the surprise of the tournament and was bidding to be the surprise of the year. In the third round, she bogeyed the second hole, then chalked up eight birdies from there for a seven-under 65, the tournament low, vaulting from five strokes behind to a one-stroke lead on Pettersen. Min didn't begin playing golf until she was 12, and now, at 18, the youngest player on the LPGA Tour, was bidding to become the youngest ever to win an LPGA major.

"I'm just really excited," Min said. "This is my first major. I'll do my best to keep focus on each shot." She did nothing but focus in her third-round charge. She ran off four straight birdies from the 13th on putts of six, 15, 12 and six feet. With both Pettersen and Webb heating up in the final round, Min had a shaky spell, bogeying three straight from the sixth, then rebounding for 70 and a 12-under 276 total.

It was the stuff of fiction that no one had heard of Min before she made her grand emergence here. She went to South Africa alone at age 12 to learn golf and English and stayed there for two years. She went home to South Korea for three years, then moved with her family in the spring of 2006, and won non-exempt status on the LPGA Tour at the qualifying tournament.

Another teenager created a different kind of heat. Michelle Wie had withdrawn abruptly from the Ginn Tribute the week before, complaining of her injured wrist, then showed up two days later at Bulle Rock and was hitting golf balls. Her honesty was, in effect, called into question by many, and most notably by Annika Sorenstam and LPGA Commissioner Carolyn Bivens. To which Wie responded: "I don't think I need to apologize for anything."

So there would be a dark undercurrent running through this championship. Was Wie's wrist injury exaggerated, or perhaps a convenience? Those seemed to be the questions rippling through. At any rate, Wie had her trainer walking with her inside the ropes to massage both wrists. Wie played what she called "Betty Boop golf," meaning she didn't try to play a power game. Just once in the 72 holes did she hit her driver off the tee, and she played in 73-74-83-79 for a 309 total, 21 over par and 84th and last of those who made the cut.

"I was playing it by ear and testing the water," Wie said. "And I felt this week is a lot better than last week. And I hope the U.S. (Women's) Open is going to be a lot better."

Lorena Ochoa, the top-ranked player in the world, and Sorenstam, the woman she replaced, were on the fringe of contention but couldn't get into the chase. Ochoa, who tied for sixth at 280, six behind Pettersen, had to endure the continuing question — when was she going to win a major? "I tried really hard and I gave everything," she said. "There is nothing else I can do. I played really good. Just my putting didn't help me ... and I'm a little upset about it, but there is nothing else I can do."

Sorenstam, the winner of three straight LPGA Championships from 2003 and trying to come back from injuries, tied for 15th at 283. "I must say I felt really good all day," said Sorenstam after her closing 71. "There was something special today. The score might not show it, but I had a pretty good feel with the grip. I'm really looking forward to the (U.S. Women's) Open. It's been awhile since I've looked forward to another tournament."

The championship opened with a small traffic jam, with Birdie Kim, 2001 U.S. Women's Open champion, 18-year-old Angela Park and the veteran Kim Saiki-Maloney tied for the first-round lead at five-under 67. Webb was just one shot behind in a group at 68, and Pettersen was two behind. Almost perversely, the attention was focused on Wie, her wrist and the controversy swirling around her.

As for Wie not using the driver, her swing coach, David Leadbetter, noted: "It's a tough strategy for her. It's like owning a Ferrari and not being allowed to get out of second gear." She started shakily, then recovered with three birdies in a four-hole stretch. But she raised eyebrows when she called for a rules official at her sixth hole, No. 13. But it was to ask permission to have her therapist work on her wrist, after she hit several shots out of deep rough. Her 73 put her six shots off the lead and that would be as close as she would get.

Pettersen had some good fortune for the second round, an early tee time that allowed her to escape the worst of the 90-degree heat that had others carrying umbrellas against the hot sun. "I was lucky, being on this side of the draw," Pettersen said. But she put on some heat of her own, birdieing three of her last four holes for 67 that gave her an eight-under 136 total and a one-stroke lead over Webb. Ochoa sidetracked herself at the fourth, where she hit over the green and double-bogeyed. Her 71 left her six off the lead. "Maybe tomorrow," she said.

Then the third round belonged to Na On Min, the 18-year-old rookie, and her 65. She bogeyed the second, then made eight birdies over the next 14 holes. A two-putt birdie from the fringe at the par-five 15th moved her into a tie for first. Pettersen took a one-shot lead with an eagle from 10 feet at the par-five 11th, but Min caught her with a birdie at the 16th from 10 feet. Pettersen then double-bogeyed the 13th after missing the fairway, and with a birdie from 12 feet at the 17th, she shot 71 and sat a stroke behind Min going into the final round. It seemed like a mismatch.

Said Min: "Maybe tomorrow I'll be nervous. But I'll just do my best and not think about my position. I've never experienced anything like this before."

Pettersen, like everyone else, conceded that she had never heard of Min. "I'll probably know her when I see her on the first tee," she said.

The Na On Min fairy tale faded in a shaky start in the fourth round. That left the chase to Pettersen and Webb. Min rallied spectacularly for four straight birdies from the 13th, holing putts of six, 15, 12 and six feet for 70. But she had lost too much ground to Pettersen. "I thought too much in my head when I'm putting," Min said, explaining how the pressure got to her. "When I get, like 16, my last birdie, I didn't know, just focus."

Webb, playing in front of Pettersen, birdied the fourth hole then bogeyed the next two — No. 5 after hitting two bunkers and missing the green and No. 6 from the rough. Then she birdied six of the next 11 holes, including the 14th, 17th and 18th on putts of 15, 15 and 25 feet for a round of 67.

"I'm disappointed that I lost by one, but I'm pretty happy with my performance," Webb said. "Coming down the stretch, I did a lot of good things, but I didn't execute very well off the tee at 15 and 16 (where she parred). That really was the difference. So, you know, I made Suzann think about it on the last, which is all I could ask for at the end when I was two shots behind playing the last."

Pettersen birdied the fifth and eighth, then bogeyed the ninth, where she missed the green with a wedge from 110 yards. Was the pressure setting in? She answered that with a sizzling finish, with four birdies coming home. At the par-four 10th, she wedged from 120 yards to six feet and holed the birdie. At the par-four 13th, she lofted an eight iron from 140 yards to 10 feet. Then it was a three wood from 230 yards to 35 feet and two putts at the par-five 15th, and finally at the 171-yard par-three 17th, a seven iron to 15 feet. She came to the 18th nursing a one-stroke lead on Webb. Pressure?

"On the back nine, I looked on the leaderboard and I could see a lot of players were playing well," Pettersen said. "So walking off 15 with a birdie, that felt good. I knew I could make one coming in, and I was really relieved when I hit the fairway on 18. Then I knew I could do it.

"I'm starting to feel good coming down and being one of the favorites. Teeing off on the last on the leaderboard, that's where you want to be in every major, in every tournament. You want to be under the pressure. It's a good test. Sometimes you will pass it and sometimes you will fail it. In this game, you will probably fail it more than you win it. So you just have to appreciate the wins when you finally do get them.

Petersen clearly embraced this one. This was more that the McDonald's LPGA Championship. It was a demon slain and a dream restored. "I believe I can be the best player in the world," Petersen said, "but you have to give me time."

U.S. Women's Open

For most, winning the U.S. Women's Open is a dream come true. Not so for Cristie Kerr. For Kerr, it was more. It was a self-fulfilling prophecy. This was the conversation from her caddie, Jason Gilroyed: "We talked about it last year. She said, 'If I'm going to win my first major, it's going to be here.' She knew it all along." And by "here," she meant Pine Needles, the testing par-71 course draped across the gentle sand hills region of North Carolina.

And this came from Kerr herself, when she was entering the final round with a fingertip lead: "I just knew I was going to win. I know that's kind of odd to say, but I just knew it." Was this a case in precognition?

Well, if anyone was surprised, Kerr — age 29 and a 10-time winner on the LPGA Tour — was not when she held off Lorena Ochoa, No. 1 on the Rolex Rankings. Pine Needles was where Kerr came to national attention at age 18 when she finished as low amateur in the 1996 Women's Open and thus where she developed such an affinity for the course that she was convinced she would win there.

And the term "Open" meant really open in this case. For the first time since the Women's Open was first played in 1953, there were more foreign players (84) than American (76), clearly demonstrating the spread of women's golf in the world. Just seven years earlier, Americans outnumbered foreign players by two to one.

The first round was a prime time for a spotlight on youth. There was the surprising Alexis Thompson, at age 12 the youngest qualifier in Women's Open history. She made a good start, just three over par on her first nine — the tougher last nine — and she three-putted the 18th (her ninth) at that. A lightning threat forced a delay of play, letting only 78 players finish the round. (She finished with a credible 76 the next day, but then shot 82 in the second round and missed the cut.)

The youth attracting the most attention early on was Michelle Wie, the 17-year-old whiz who had been misfiring for such a long time. She misfired again, hitting only four fairways and shooting 82, matching her highest score in the Women's Open. "It's just a very fine line between shooting 69 and shooting what I shot today," Wie insisted.

Wie withdrew after hitting her tee shot at her 10th hole of the second round. For 27 holes, she hit only four of 21 fairways, six of 27 greens, made one birdie, 16 bogeys and one double bogey — a 17-over-par performance.

At the other end of the youth spectrum, there was Angela Park, only 18, taking the first-round lead with a three-under-par 68. Park was born in Brazil to South Korean parents and grew up in California. She played in the morning and found the course friendlier after a late-night rain. She led off with three straight birdies and got to four under for much of the way until she bogeyed the 17th after hitting her drive into the trees. Park also tied for the lead in the McDonald's LPGA Championship, but went on to finish fifth. "Maybe this week will be different," she said. She led by one over In-Bee Park and Shiho Oyama, who finished their rounds on Friday.

Karrie Webb, the tough veteran and winner of seven majors — and winner of the Women's Open when it was played at Pine Needles in 2001 — shot 83, her highest score on the LPGA Tour. "I have no excuses," Webb said, after logging 10 bogeys, one double bogey and using 37 putts. "I'm not that kind of player. Do you think I had any idea I would shoot 83? It was a terrible round, one of the worst days of my career." Webb became incensed at the media asking about the round. "Is that enough?" she said. "Do you have another question to ask on that? Because really, you can't really elaborate on that, can you?"

Ochoa, a three-time winner, including the Wegmans LPGA the week before, was pleased with a par-71 that included a sharp high and a sharp low. At the 14th, she hit a five wood from 195 yards out of a fairway bunker. The ball landed on the green and rolled neatly into the hole for an eagle. At the 17th, she hit a seven wood out of the rough that cleared the green and threaded its way through two sets of bleachers and zipped out of bounds. She double bogeyed. "A little bit of bad luck," Ochoa said. "But nothing you can do. Playing in a U.S. Open, it's always good to be around par." And that's where Cristie Kerr was, right with Ochoa, in a group at 71.

Heavy rain continued to be a problem and most of the players had to play the second round on Saturday, the third day. When it was finally in the books, it would be notable not only for Angela Park hanging on to a share of the lead, with 69–137, but for Kerr slipping three more further behind, to six off the lead, with 71–143.

The halfway point also marked the end of a small but interesting bit of history. There was Maria Kostina, who opened with 89, added 87 and finished dead last in the field. More importantly, she was a first — the first Russian ever to play in the Women's Open. Maria and her sister Anastasia played college golf at Washington State and were now on the Duramed Futures Tour, the LPGA's developmental tour. They learned their golf at Moscow Country Club, which has the only 27 holes of golf in Russia.

Park was one of a crowd who didn't even tee off on Friday. "It's not frustrating at all," she said. "I'm just having a good time relaxing at the locker room. I'm very calm and eager to play the next three rounds." When she finally got to her second round, she made it worth the wait. She shot 69 for a 137 total, upping her lead by two, to five under par. Tied for second were Amy Hung, Ji-Yai Shin and Julieta Grenada, who all shot 69s and were three under.

For many, Friday — a day of delays — was a day of frustration. Juli Inkster, the 1999 and 2002 winner, for one, arrived at the course at 5:30 a.m. and was there for more than 12 hours and still hadn't finished her second round. "It's very frustrating to be out here all day, and then you've got to get up at 5 a.m. (Saturday) to play one hole," she said. And that turned out to be costly. She bogeyed her 18th (the ninth), shot 71–149, and missed the cut by a stroke. Also gone, in addition to Webb, were Christina Kim and the fast-rising Norwegian Suzann Pettersen.

Kerr came to the top in the storm-fragmented third round with a tournament-low five-under 66. But more exciting, she said, was "I'm starting to hit it where I want to hit it." It paid off with a 31 on the first nine Saturday, with birdies at Nos. 4, 5, 7 and 9. Coming back out early Sunday, when 63 players had to return to finish the third round, she birdied the 11th, bogeyed the 14th and birdied the 15th for the 66 and a one-stroke lead on Ochoa (68), Shin (71) and Morgan Pressel (69).

Two of Kerr's pursuers fell away in the fourth round. Shin shot 74 to finish sixth. The other, Pressel, played in the final group with Kerr and Ochoa. She hung on, two strokes behind with five holes to go. Then she staggered at the end to 77 and tied for 10th place.

Angela Park, bidding to become the youngest player to win a major championship, was also part of the final chase, but she was a little too erratic. Like Ochoa, she started birdie-bogey-birdie, but then had a rockier road the rest of the way. She finished birdie-bogey-bogey-birdie for a five-birdie, four-bogey 70 to tie Ochoa for second at 281. "I wanted to win, obviously," Park said. "But I had this feeling that (Kerr) was going to win. I wasn't surprised at all that she actually pulled it off."

Kerr got her sternest test — not surprisingly — from Ochoa, the world's No. 1. Ochoa made up that one-stroke deficit in a hurry, starting birdie-bogey-birdie and quickly tying Kerr. Kerr, who had birdied the third to stay one ahead, bogeyed the eighth from a bunker and slipped into a tie with Ochoa. From there, it was a shootout.

They remained tied with pars at the next five holes. Ochoa missed a good birdie chance from eight feet at the par-three 13th. Then Kerr saw her big chance at the 426-yard, par-four 14th, which played as the third toughest hole. She hit the fairway with her tee shot, then fired a four iron from 190 yards to 18 feet and dropped the birdie putt to get to five under and take the lead for good. Kerr was walking confidently toward the cup before the putt even dropped.

"I've been walking putts in all week," Kerr said, "and that was a pretty good one." It gave her a one-shot lead and the lead for good.

Then came the 440-yard, par-four 17th, a dogleg left and the second toughest hole at Pine Needles. Kerr hit a draw around the dogleg and into the fairway. Ochoa tried to cut the dogleg by flying the trees. Her tee shot nicked a tree and dropped into a bunker. She tried to hit a five wood out but moved the ball only some 60 yards.

"I was trying to put the ball on the green and just swung a little bit too fast," Ochoa said. She put her next on the green, about 20 feet from the cup, but two-putted for a bogey. Kerr parred the 17th and also the 18th for a one-under 70, a five-under 279 total and the U.S. Women's Open title by two strokes. "Today was my day," Kerr said. "That birdie at 14 was unbelievable. To hold it together — it's a dream come true."

Ochoa was disappointed, but unfazed. "I don't need to be frustrated," she said. "We still have one more major, and I'm going to try to get that one."

And so ended Kerr's 0-for-41 streak in the majors. And so also went her identity crisis, it would seem. One thing that had particularly irked Kerr was that she was generally ignored when the discussion or the media coverage turned to the subject of rising young American golfers. The names usually were Paula Creamer, Morgan Pressel, Natalie Gulbis and Michelle Wie. Maybe winning the Women's Open would change that now for Kerr. Then again, maybe not. No matter. Kerr could shrug now.

"The media is the media and they'll write what they want to write," Kerr said. "I know in my heart of hearts who I am and how many wins I have and what I've done."

And then there was the matter of the good vibes she had about Pine Needles, the precognition. "Everything has been pointing to this tournament," Kerr said. "I saw it all week, the same scene — and it happened."

Ricoh Women's British Open

It could have been Tiger Woods. There was the world No. 1 with a comfortable lead walking up the 18th fairway taking the acclaim of the gallery at the Home of Golf. Instead, it was Lorena Ochoa, following in the footsteps of Woods, Bobby Jones, Sam Snead, Jack Nicklaus and the rest, in winning an Open Championship on the Old Course at St. Andrews, Scotland. This was always going to be a historic Ricoh Women's British Open, but the 25-year-old Mexican brilliantly made it all her own.

With a final round of 74 and a five-under-par total of 287, Ochoa claimed a four-stroke victory and left her own imprint on the famous scene at the 18th green. After being doused in champagne by her father, Javier, Ochoa said: "This was my time. It's a blessing the whole week. I wanted to win the tournament so badly and I worked so hard. I had the picture in my mind of me lifting the trophy, but I always thought very clearly. I just said to myself, 'I am ready.' It has been a long wait for a major, but now I can see it was for a reason. This is the most special tournament I've ever played."

Ochoa, emphatically putting behind her past major failures, joined Morgan Pressel, Suzann Pettersen and Cristie Kerr in a quartet of first-time major winners in 2007. At the U.S. Women's Open a month earlier, Ochoa chased home Kerr, but the American was just too strong on the final day. But she had taken over from Annika Sorenstam as the No. 1 on the Rolex Rankings, thanks partly to the Swede's neck injury but also to Ochoa's six wins in 2006, three more early in 2007, plus four runner-up finishes.

She arrived at St. Andrews leading the LPGA Tour money list, having won it in 2006 for the first time, with more top-10 finishes, more rounds under par and in the 60s than anyone else for the season. Only one thing was missing, but the Mexican was not worried herself. "I think my family and the media worry more than me," she said. "I really believed that 2007 was going to be my year."

She had one last chance, and what a chance — to make history by winning the first professional tournament for women on the Old Course. Amateur events have been staged there and some of the winners of the St. Rule Trophy were in the field. Scotland's Catriona Matthew won it twice, Sorenstam another time, Maria Hjorth, while a bursary student of the Royal and Ancient Golf Club at Stirling University, won it, and the 2007 winner was Melissa Reid.

Reid, an 19-year-old Englishwoman from Derbyshire, went on to win a fierce battle for the Smyth Silver Salver as the leading amateur in 16th place after eight of them, including Scotland's 16-year-old Sally Watson, made the cut. Although the Curtis Cup was due to be played on the Old Course in 2008, Reid turned professional at the end of the season.

The enthusiasm for playing at such a famous venue had been evident for months prior to the championship. Paula Creamer, who had an extra reason to look forward to the final day as it was her 21st birthday, was one of those who made a transatlantic trip especially to play the Old Course for the first time.

Once everyone had arrived from France after the Evian Masters, the excitement was palpable. It was probably best summed up by the photograph of Creamer doing a cartwheel in front of the Swilken Burn bridge with the R&A clubhouse in the background. The famous building was opened up to all competitors, but walking the course of legends provided most memories. Beth Daniel, the distinguished Hall-of-Famer, decided to end her career here, a la Nicklaus. There was not quite the fanfare on the Swilken Bridge as for Jack, but Daniel's last steps up the 18th on Sunday were just as emotional, and Juli Inkster and LPGA co-founder Louise Suggs met her with hugs as she stepped off the green.

"I am just in awe of the golf course and the city," said Sherri Steinhauer, the three-time winner and defending champion from Royal Lytham in 2006. "Everybody who plays golf should come here. It's always different from watching on television. To be here is magnificent. It's a surreal feeling being out there and knowing you are walking the fairways that all the greats from the past, from Jack Nicklaus to Tom Morris, have walked."

Laura Davies, the 1986 Women's British Open champion, had, amazingly, never played on the Old Course. "Our paths have just never crossed," she said. The opening tee shot of her practice round was not one to remember. She pulled the ball out of bounds across the widest fairway in the world and into the road on the left, just as Ian Baker-Finch did in the 1995 Open. Often Davies has been compared in her style of play to John Daly, the 1995 champion, and hopes sprung eternal for the 43-year-old. Alas she missed the cut, going out of bounds into the hotel at the 17th in the second round when she was battling to hang on to a place for the weekend.

Ochoa had the slight advantage of her coach, Raphael Alarcon, having played in the Dunhill Links Championship. He would often say, while practicing on a course, "This is a shot like St. Andrews." Seeing it in the flesh was another matter, however. "You don't realize how hard it is until you get here. It's like the Masters, you don't see 100 percent until you are playing it," said Ochoa. She added: "Here we are, we need to stand on the first tee with a big smile, appreciate it and enjoy every step and every moment."

Out early in the calm conditions on Thursday morning, Ochoa did exactly that. She did not drop a stroke to par, did not go in any of the 112 bunkers, made six birdies and recorded 67 against a par of 73. The infamous 17th, the Road Hole, was changed from a par four to a five for the week and Ochoa took advantage by hitting the green with a five iron and two-putting from 30 feet for a birdie-four. It immediately became one of the best rounds of her career. "The first at St. Andrews, six under, that's going to be special," she said. "I'm going to keep the ball and the scorecard. It was nice conditions and I'm glad I took advantage."

Ochoa held a two-stroke lead over Sweden's Louise Friberg and In-Bee Park of Korea, with Japan's Ai Miyazato and Rebecca Hudson a further shot back at 70. Hudson, the Englishwoman from Doncaster, had been woken early by the parakeets in an aviary next door to her accommodation. Annika Sorenstam, using the yardage book Tiger Woods used in winning the Open in 2000 and 2005, scored 72, alongside Steinhauer. "He asked me if I'd like it and I said, 'Sure,'" Sorenstam said. "His advice was to stay left and practice my lag putting." Among those at 73, even par, were Creamer, Reid and Michelle Wie.

Wie was still recovering from the wrist injury that plagued her 2007 season and limited her appearances, but a bright outward nine could not be entirely spoiled by a couple of late bogeys. It was a different story the next day when she had a triple-bogey seven at the 13th and even a birdie at the 18th from 10 feet could not save her from failing to break 80. It was the fourth time in 13 competitive rounds she had suffered that horrid fate. Along with Pressel, who had 80 in the first round, she was among the famous names to miss the cut.

The day's best rounds were the 68s of Inkster, who made sure she survived the cut after an opening 79, and Matthew, who was the only player not to drop a stroke on the day. Enthusiastically applauded by the home gallery, Matthew came in at five under par, alongside Wendy Ward, the American who has often worked her way onto the leaderboard at the Women's British Open.

The pair were just one behind Ochoa, whose advantage would have been doubled if she had not three-putted at the last hole. She was safely in at even-par 73, however, and held a three-shot lead over those sharing fourth place, including Sorenstam, Steinhauer and Hudson. Sorenstam and Steinhauer both had 71s and appeared to be moving into threatening positions. For the American, however, it was a bit too early in the week to be making a run at the title. Her past triumphs had mostly been achieved with a strong finish.

After two days of breezy weather, the wind was blowing at a strong 25 miles an hour on Saturday and gusting up to 35. A third of the field failed to break 80, and with Ochoa battling brilliantly at the top of the leaderboard, it was getting to be a problem for the challengers to sustain their efforts. Ochoa had 73, almost as good a round as her 67 on Thursday. Only three players broke par on the day, Hjorth, Linda Wessberg and Stacy Prammanasudh, all with 72s. The average score for the day was 78.5. In the last six pairings, the closest anyone managed to Ochoa's even-par score were the 77s of Sorenstam, Karine Icher and Eun Hee Ji.

Matthew, the home favorite, went into the burn at the first and bogeyed the first two holes. Ward suffered as well, and by the time Ochoa birdied the fourth she was four ahead. She went five ahead when Ward bogeyed the sixth, and a two-shot swing back the other way at the seventh was only a temporary setback for the leader. Ochoa hit a wonderful pitch shot to a foot at the 12th and was six ahead. That was her advantage at the end of the day, with Sweden's Wessberg, a two-time winner on the Ladies European Tour, in second place at even par. Ochoa at six under was the only player left in red figures. Four players were at one over par: Sorenstam, Icher, Hjorth and Jee Young Lee.

There was little breeze on Sunday, but it was wet, with occasionally heavy showers, but Ochoa was unaffected. Birdies at the fifth and the sixth, where she put her approach to two feet, put her briefly seven ahead. Sorenstam made a couple of early birdies, but then fell away to a 76 and four over. A couple of 67s from Mhairi McKay and Se Ri Pak pulled them up the leaderboard, but not far enough. Lee and Hjorth both closed with 71s to reach the clubhouse at one under, while Reilly Rankin, an American whose college career was interrupted for two years by breaking her sternum and back diving off a cliff, also had a 71 to be at even par.

But Ochoa, despite not feeling as comfortable in the cold and wet as she was in the wind, still was untouchable. She three-putted the short eighth but got the shot back at the ninth, then dropped shots at the 11th and 15th. Wessberg, playing with Ochoa, saw her challenge fade with a double bogey at the 14th and two more bogeys as she slipped to 75 and two over.

No round on the Old Course is in the books until the 17th has been played. Ochoa drove well away from the out of bounds on the right and found the left rough. Her second shot with a wood then found the bunker and she was under the lip. It was only the third time she had visited sand all week and she had to play out sideways, but a terrific fourth shot, still from the rough, found the green, and two putts gave her nothing worse than a bogey-six. "It was a great relief," she said. "And after I hit the 18th tee shot, it's a pretty wide fairway, I thought, 'Yes, we did it.'"

7. HSBC World Match Play

When reviewing the career of Ernie Els, two U.S. Open victories and an Open Championship triumph are at the summit of his achievements. And who is to say he will not be scaling more peaks in the majors? But for an illustration of the considerable merits of this wonderful South African golfer, look no further than his seven victories in the HSBC World Match Play Championship at the Wentworth Club in Virginia Water, England. Vardon won six Opens, Nicklaus six Masters, yet seven victories in this head-to-head form of the game, from only 12 appearances in the tournament, stands just as proudly in the history of the game.

By winning the 2007 event at Wentworth, Els increased his individual match record to 26 wins and only five defeats. It is quicker to list the losses: to Vijay Singh in the 1997 final, twice to Lee Westwood and once each to Padraig Harrington and, in the first round in 2006, to Angel Cabrera. Since those defeats, Els has taken revenge every time and did so against Cabrera in the 2007 final by defeating the reigning U.S. Open champion 6 and 4.

This was an important win not just for the history books but for Els's current state of mind. Since his knee injury in the summer of 2005, Els had won twice in South Africa but not on the big stage, either in America or Europe. His last win of a similar standing came at the same tournament in 2006. The near-misses were beginning to mount up and frustrate the man for whom the moniker "Big Easy" is not always apt. "It seems like I'm quite a patient guy, but I'm quite an impatient person when it comes to getting results," Els said. "I've played well for the last two years but results have not gone my way. I've either lost in playoffs or finished second or thereabouts. To get a win and play the way I did, that's really satisfying."

Only the previous Sunday, Els had been one behind the leader, Nick Dougherty, at the Alfred Dunhill Links Championship at St. Andrews when he putted into a bunker at the 16th for a triple-bogey seven. "I don't care how many years you are in this profession, if you ever stuff up like that, it certainly sits on your mind," he said. "You try to downplay it and get on with the next week, but last Sunday night it wasn't a happy plane ride back from Scotland."

Immediately following his victory at Wentworth there were a pair of much more enjoyable plane rides as he went off to Paris that evening to see South Africa beat Argentina — it was the second clash of the two countries that day — in the semi-finals of the Rugby World Cup. Els visited his victorious countrymen in the locker room afterwards and the South African camp stated later how they had been boosted by Els's victory at Wentworth in the afternoon.

Only five men have made more appearances than Els in the World Match Play — whether as an invitational or under the current qualifications it is an achievement just to tee up in the elite event — and of those only Seve Ballesteros has more match victories. Seve's record was 28-15, while Gary Player won 26 matches, like Els, but lost 15. Els left behind the previous record of championship victories of five by Player and Ballesteros long ago.

Not only does Els have a home on the West Course, but he has helped polish the Harry Colt gem in recent years. No one feels more comfortable on the layout, and over 36 holes Els simply does not expect to lose. Other individual records of note include three-time winner Ian Woosnam's 19 wins to 11 losses, while Nick Faldo won 17 and lost 16 times, and Colin Montgomerie also has 17 wins and 13 losses.

Montgomerie's latest defeat was at the hands of Els in the first round here. It was a shame for the two men to meet so early in the week, but it was mostly a shame for the Scot, for whom Els is something of a nemesis. There were the two U.S. Open defeats, and the only time Montgomerie could recall getting the better of the South African came at the Million Dollar Challenge at Sun City, when the presentation ceremony took place to virtual silence as Els's countrymen rapidly departed. The pair had met twice before at Wentworth, in the final in 1994 and in the quarter-finals in 2002, and on each occasion Els had won.

More than that, Montgomerie had never been ahead at any stage and the same ran true again as Els won 6 and 5. From the moment Montgomerie bogeyed the first hole of the morning, he was his flustered old self. He immediately got on even terms by holing from 25 feet at the second, but Els was three up at the turn and won the 17th and 18th to get to five ahead. The South African shot 66 in the morning, and although Montgomerie won the first hole in the afternoon, he then lost three holes in a row to go seven down and there was no way back. "It was tough for both of us to play each other so early in the tournament," said Els. "I'm glad I'm through, but it's sad to see Colin go out in the first round."

Also departing, from a home point of view, were Open champion Padraig Harrington and Justin Rose. Harrington lost 4 and 2 to Anders Hansen, the Dane who, unlike the Irishman, has won twice at Wentworth. Hansen won the BMW PGA Championship for a second time earlier in the summer and played with the confidence that instills. Before the match Harrington said he prefers the West Course in the autumn to the spring, when the PGA is played, but to counteract that he also explained that his match-play prowess appears to have declined as he has become more consistent in stroke play.

As an amateur, the Irishman was every opponent's worst nightmare, since whatever the state of the match, Harrington would conjure up some magic, holing a chip or converting an outrageous number of putts to steal a win. As an increasingly successful professional, such make-it-happen moments have been reserved for winning stroke-play events. As Open champion, he was not complaining.

Once more Harrington struggled back in the match-play format and Hansen's consistent play was good enough to keep him in front after taking the lead. "You could tell Padraig was trying to press to catch up and made mistakes, which helped me," said Hansen. By remarkable co-incidence, when Hansen won the PGA in 2002, his countryman but no relation, Soren Hansen, also won during the season. The same happened in 2007 and Soren also qualified for the World Match Play. Soren's 4-and-3 win over South

African Rory Sabbatini gave Denmark two representatives in the last eight, while Britain had only one.

Paul Casey, the defending champion after his victory in his debut in 2006, continued his winning run with a 3-and-2 victory over America's Jerry Kelly. The Englishman was three up after the opening round, when he played some fine golf and hung on despite suddenly losing his form. "I played all right in the morning, but there was a spell in the afternoon where I was hitting it sideways," said Casey, who found three ditches in seven holes at one point. "I feel very fortunate to get through. Jerry could have taken the match further." By going to the 34th hole, Casey played more golf than any of his four matches in winning the title the year before.

Rose's defeat came at the hands of Hunter Mahan, the young American who came to prominence with a string of fine results in the summer, including his first win on the U.S. PGA Tour. His form was so good he was picked as a wild card for the American team in the Presidents Cup with the phone call from the captain, Jack Nicklaus, doing wonders for Mahan's morale. It was a match of two gifted young players with Rose coming off a season in which he made the cut at each of the four majors for the first time. Returning to a venue where he used to watch the stars as a junior, Rose finished as the runner-up in the BMW PGA when he lost the playoff to Anders Hansen.

Rose's form this time was not at the same level and some poor putting was the reason for a 5-and-4 loss to the American. "The hole looked smaller than the ball today," Rose said. "It was a curious day. I felt I was going to play well, but just didn't." Mahan enjoyed the atmosphere of the match with a large gallery following proceeds, but also reveled in playing his first individual match-play event since finishing runner-up at the U.S. Amateur in 2002.

Fog delayed the start of play on the first day for two hours, so it was a battle to get all the matches finished. There was no problem with Cabrera's 6-and-5 demolition of Retief Goosen. Cabrera shot 65 in the morning against the two-time U.S. Open winner, but only took the lead at the 16th. It was only in the afternoon that things started to get away from Goosen as the 2007 Oakmont champion eased through. Two matches had to be held over to Friday morning, but neither took long to be completed as Argentina's Andres Romero completed a 3-and-2 win over Niclas Fasth and Henrik Stenson beat Woody Austin at the 36th hole.

As dark descended the previous evening, Stenson pulled a shot out of bounds at the 17th, so they were all square playing the last, where they resumed the next morning, essentially as a one-hole shootout. Austin became a bit of a celebrity at the Presidents Cup after splashing into a lake, but was playing in Britain for the first time in 11 years. Stenson was disturbed on the tee as a there was no marshal to stop a car crossing the fairway at the early hour. Both players laid up at the par-five, but it was Stenson who stopped his softly hit wedge shot 12 feet away and holed for the birdie.

Stenson won the WGC - Accenture Match Play in February, the same month he defeated Els and Tiger Woods at the Dubai Desert Classic. His form over the summer was affected by the birth of his daughter and an allergy to summer grasses. Not that the Swede was using it as an excuse given that Woods was also in the same situation on both counts. Back in the head-to-head mode at Wentworth his form was returning, and later in the day he completed a crushing 7-and-6 win over Anders Hansen in the quarter-finals.

Stenson was credited with 64 in the morning round to go four up, and three bogeys on the first nine in the afternoon did the Dane no favors. But there was a moment of joy at the short 10th for Hansen when he holed in one — Stenson had already put his tee shot to six feet. "It comes to something when you have to hole-in-one to win a hole," Hansen said. "But that's how well Henrik was playing today." His was the fourth ace in the history of the World Match Play: Brian Barnes also holed out at the 10th, Isao Aoki made a one at the second, Thomas Bjorn, another Dane, made his at the 14th. Only the fifth remains to be aced in the competition.

Stenson's next opponent would be Els, who cruised through against Romero, the youngster who almost stole the Open from Harrington and Sergio Garcia but then won the following week in Germany. But the Argentinean was not at his best. "It was a weird match," said Els. "There were a few holes given either way." Winning the 11th, 13th and 14th holes in the morning put the South African four up and he ran out a 6-and-5 winner. He admitted to being a little out of sync with his swing, but his short game saved him whenever necessary.

Romero's countryman, Cabrera, was faring better and he put an end to Casey's winning streak in the event. On a day of one-sided affairs, this was the best match. Both players had 67s in the morning, but a birdie at the 17th put Cabrera one up. Cabrera had gone birdie-eagle-birdie from the third to be three up, so Casey was the happier of the pair to keep the match tight for the rest of the morning. After lunch, Cabrera won the first hole with a birdie and then the six holes were halved.

Suddenly the match got away from the Englishman. He three-putted the eighth and drove into a ditch at the ninth to go four down. He looked like getting a hole back at the short 10th, but Cabrera, still not on the green in two, chipped in for a par and a halve. It was a crucial moment that kept the momentum with the big man from Argentina, who then birdied the 11th. The final score was 4 and 3. "I played much better than yesterday, but over 36 holes the best player is going to win," Casey said. "You cannot fluke your way to a win and he flat out played better golf. He's in fine form and is going to be a very tough guy to beat."

The next man to attempt to beat Cabrera would be Mahan, who was always in control of his match against Soren Hansen in the quarter-finals. He was five up after only 13 holes, and although he was pegged back to three up at lunch, the American came away with a 6-and-4 win. "Match play is definitely starting to suit me," said the former U.S. Junior winner. "I felt I carried on from where I left off against Justin and maybe even played a bit better. I'm getting to know the course more and I like it a lot."

In Cabrera, Mahan was facing a semi-final opponent who was not only the reigning U.S. Open champion but a former winner of the PGA at Wentworth. After six rounds of this tournament, Cabrera, loping along like a giant rambling over the Pampas, was 32 under par and looking as comfortable on the West Course as the resident Els. At the 18th at lunchtime Cabrera hit a three wood to five feet and was conceded the eagle to go three up.

A few holes later, at the fourth in the afternoon, he added another eagle by holing from 18 feet and that put him six up. But to the eternal credit of the young American, Mahan was not finished yet and his last 14 holes included eight birdies. He won four of the next six holes, holing from long range for a two at the 10th. The 25-year-old took Cabrera all the way to the 35th hole before losing 2 and 1, but not before winning a lot of new admirers worried that he could become a dangerous opponent at the next Ryder Cup. "He played well and it was not my mistakes," Cabrera said. "It was a tight match, but I knew I had to keep playing as I was."

As predicted, a South African-Argentina final came about after Els beat Stenson. At the Accenture Match Play, all of the matches except the final are over 18 holes, and on that basis the Swede would have won. Els three-putted the second and Stenson was one up for most of the morning, a score he lunched on after his winning birdie at the 18th. But Els, vastly experienced at this format, rarely lets someone get the better of him in two successive rounds at Wentworth. Having putted poorly, he worked on a fix at lunchtime. Holing a 12-footer at the first to square the match turned the momentum his way, but he did not get in front until the seventh. There he two-putted the tricky green, while Stenson three-putted. "It was a relief to finally get my nose in front," Els said.

Birdies followed at the next two holes and he was three up. Stenson won the short 10th and suddenly Els found himself battling for halves to maintain his advantage. He single-putted seven out of eight greens before securing the 3-and-2 win. "I putted awfully this morning, but the putter saved me this afternoon," he said.

Summing up his qualities in this format, Els added: "I can't imagine another sport that tests you mentally like this game. You have to find a way of countering your feelings when things don't go your way. I didn't play better than Henrik today, but I guess it was persistence that got me through."

In keeping with most of the finals since the format was changed to ensure all the players played all four days, even these two giants of the southern hemisphere — Cabrera 38 years of age and Els soon to be so — were beginning to feel the effects of playing eight rounds in quick succession. The third hole in the afternoon, one of glorious autumnal sunshine, proved to be crucial. Els, carving his drive to the right and hitting a tree with his second, should never have won it.

But Els hit an eight iron to 12 feet and holed the putt for an unlikely par, while Cabrera failed to get up and down. He was four down and could not respond. The end came when Els won three holes in a row from the 12th. At the short 14th, Els hit a lovely tee shot to 10 feet and was primed to make his 13th birdie of the day, but after Cabrera overshot the green and chipped past the hole, the match was conceded. "I played my best today but it wasn't enough," Cabrera said. "Ernie played very well, he knows the course so well and he is so comfortable here. He is the king of Wentworth."

8. American Tours

Tiger Woods's year in 2007 was a blockbuster no matter which way you looked at it. You could stick to the standard — victories and money. He made 16 starts and won seven of them. In baseball, that's a dazzling batting average, .438. In golf, that's absurd. He also won $10,867,052 in official PGA Tour earnings, about $5 million more than Phil Mickelson, in second place.

There's more: Woods was No. 1 in scoring average, at 67.79 strokes per round, which was a full 1.50 strokes ahead of the second-place finisher, Ernie Els (69.29). This was the largest gap between the top two since 1950. Woods was first in birdies per round with 4.03, and fourth in putts per greens in regulation, 1.733.

Then here was another way to look at Woods's season. In the 15 stroke-play events he entered, he made an average of $2,589.74 every time he hit a golf ball. He capped his year with his fourth PGA Championship and his 13th professional major championship in 11 full seasons as a pro, and then closed out the year with The Tour Championship (his 61st career win) and the first FedExCup. That meant four wins in his last five starts. The fifth start? He finished second. It's superfluous, but a matter of history to note that he won Player of the Year honors again.

But not everything important in Woods's life was connected to golf. The most important was the arrival of his daughter, Sam Alexis, born shortly after he tied for second in the U.S. Open in June. "I know I've had some nice success on the golf course," Woods said, "but this year, having the birth of our first child has been just truly amazing."

The year 2007 was the year of the FedExCup, a season-long system of golfers piling up performance points in tournaments, leading up to a series of four tournaments that also served as playoffs, the final being The Tour Championship, with its added reward of the deferred FedExCup jackpot. The point of the whole thing was to generate interest in golf at a time when sports fans were turning toward football and other seasonal sports. Tiger Woods sat out the first playoff tournament, then came on to win one playoff and then the big brass ring.

The millennium came to golf, so to speak, when drug-testing arrived. The pressure from the World Anti-Doping Agency and other organizations moved PGA Tour Commissioner Tim Finchem to organize a testing program, much like those in professional baseball and football, to go into practice in 2008. For the Tour itself, the target date was July. The testing was aimed at the full spectrum of the various substances prominent in sports, both "recreational" use of narcotics to performance-enhancing and body-building substances. Leading golf organizations elsewhere in the world agreed to implement testing programs.

There were six multiple winners on the Tour. Two had more than two victories — Woods, with his seven, and Phil Mickelson, with three. The other four had two each — Vijay Singh, K.J. Choi, Steve Flesch and Zach Johnson.

Johnson was one of three to win their first major championship, and all three did it with great finishes, of one kind or another. Johnson took the Masters, locking it up with an exquisite chip shot at the 18th. Argentina's Angel Cabrera, who had won 15 times around the world, took the U.S. Open with a great approach at Oakmont's 18th hole. And Ireland's Padraig Harrington bagged the Open Championship despite hitting into the water twice at Carnoustie's 18th.

Steve Stricker continued to be the warming story on the Tour. After years in oblivion, he rediscovered his game and began to return in 2006. Then in 2007, he topped a solid season of six top-five finishes with a victory in The Barclays, the first of the PGA Tour Playoffs in the FedExCup series, and he made the winning U.S. Presidents Cup team. Stricker won $4.6 million, finishing fourth on the money list, $65,000 behind Singh.

The U.S. ran away with the Presidents Cup, but Canada's Mike Weir, who thrilled the country when he won the 2003 Masters, turned himself into a national hero again by beating Tiger Woods in the singles. After laboring with swing changes early in the year, he finished strong, beating Woods and then winning the Fry's Electronics Open.

And was the long-troubled David Duval rounding back into form? He made the cut in four of his seven tournaments, but under great stress, with his wife having a difficult pregnancy. Duval and Dudley Hart convinced the Tour to accept family crisis as part of the regulations on medical exemptions, and both will be eligible to play in 2008.

The year also was marked by the landmark debut of Brandt Snedeker, 27, former successful Nationwide Tour player. He ground out 29 starts, won the Wyndham Championship and had enough other high finishes to win $2.8 million, 17th on the money list. This was a Rookie of the Year performance if there ever was one.

Life in 2007 wasn't quite so agreeable for a number of others. Davis Love, for one, made just 13 cuts and had just three top-10 finishes in 21 starts, then suffered an injured ankle early in the autumn. He fell out of the top 50 in the World Ranking for the first time in 17 years. John Daly made just eight cuts in 24 starts, withdrew six times, finished 188th on the money list and lost his Tour card for 2008. South Africa's Retief Goosen, two-time U.S. Open champion, started with promise, tying for second in the Masters. Then he just lost the touch. He didn't have another top-20 finish and he dropped out of the top 20 in the world.

Mercedes-Benz Championship
Maui, Hawaii
Winner: Vijay Singh

All work and no play made Vijay Singh a dull golfer, so to speak.

Singh, famed for how long he practices, said that somehow, while trying to get more distance, he became too right-handed with his swing. And that was the main reason, he said, for his labored year with only one victory in 2006. "When I was playing well, it was left-handed," said Singh, who had slipped to No. 7 in the Official World Golf Ranking. And so he went back to the drawing board in the off-season. The payoff was immediate — a victory in the PGA Tour's 2007 season-opening Mercedes-Benz Championship, for 34 winners from 2006, at Kapalua, in Hawaii. Singh took it handily, wire-to-wire, shooting 69-69-70-70, a 14-under-par 278 total.

Singh had company only in the first round, a tie for the lead with Will MacKenzie, K.J. Choi, Stephen Ames and Brett Wetterich. Singh fought off the ripping trade winds for six birdies in his four-under 69, and rolled from there to a two-stroke win over Adam Scott (69–280). Stuart Appleby, bidding to tie the record of winning the same tournament four straight times, never got on track after his opening par 73 and finished tied for 13th.

In the rainy and windy second round, Singh edged into the lead when he rescued his tee shot from the rough and parred the par-five eighth for another four-under 69 and a one-stroke edge over MacKenzie (70) and Trevor Immelman (68). "I just tried to let one go at the last hole and got quick," Singh said. "I hit a good drive yesterday and made par, and a bad drive today and made par," Singh said with a shrug. Big-hitting J.B. Holmes started a move with four straight birdies, ending with one at the 305-yard 14th, where the headwind kept him from driving the green. He shot 68, trailed Singh by three, and never got closer.

Conveniently, challengers went stumbling into trouble in the third round, which was even windier. Love stubbed a couple of chip shots and double-bogeyed No. 5. At No. 9, Holmes was in the weeds twice and three-putted for a double bogey. Meanwhile, Scott birdied three straight in a round of 69 to tie Immelman (72) for second place at eight under. Singh bogeyed the seventh but holed a 50-foot putt for a birdie at the par-three No. 8, and dropped a 12-footer for another at No. 9, shot 70–208, 11 under par, and led by three.

Singh led off the final round with two birdies, on putts of five and eight feet. "And nobody was going to catch me then, I don't think," he said, especially when he had a six-stroke lead after Scott, his playing partner, bogeyed the second. Scott battled back but could only get within two. Singh was home free. "When you don't win for a while, in the back of your head you feel some pressure," Singh said. "This eases the pressure."

Sony Open in Hawaii
Honolulu, Hawaii
Winner: Paul Goydos

The record will show that Paul Goydos, soft-spoken and mild-mannered veteran, age 42, won the Sony Open in Hawaii, the first full-field event of the 2007 season, and that it was his first PGA Tour victory in 11 years. And that this Sony Open, at Waialae Country Club, in Honolulu, was again over-whelmed by a Hawaiian school kid playing on a sponsor's exemption.

This teenager wasn't Michelle Wie. This was Tadd Fujikawa, at five-foot-one and age 16 by a few days, a foot shorter and a year younger than Wie. He became the youngest player in 50 years to make the cut in a PGA Tour event, and he did it with a flourish. To a roaring crowd at the 18th in the second round, he holed a 15-foot putt for an eagle and 71-66–137, three under par, and made the cut by three. "I can't breathe right now," said Fujikawa, who caught his breath and finished 66-72 for a five-under 275 total and tied for 20th among 72 finishers.

Wie, now age 17, again on a sponsor's exemption, tried for the fourth time to become the first female since 1945 to make the cut in a PGA Tour event. She shot 78-76 and missed again, this time by 14 strokes. "I have a lot of game," Wie explained. "It's just not showing now."

The kids stole the show, but Goydos — "I never felt like I was going to win" — had his victory, but not until the closing holes. With a 66-63 start, he trailed Luke Donald by three in the first round and tied with him for the lead in the second. Charles Howell, who started 69-63, emerged with the third-round lead, thanks to two closing birdies for 65, one stroke up on Donald (69) and two up on Goydos (70). "My putter really bailed me out," said Howell, who needed only 25 putts, four of them par saves. Goydos, on the other hand, fought his putter for 70.

Meanwhile, Howell and Donald pulled away from the field. Goydos tagged along, not really waking anyone up until Howell stumbled over his driver on the back nine. At the 12th, Howell pulled his drive and hit a tree with his second and bogeyed, then bogeyed the 13th out of the rough. Then Goydos, after a birdie at the 12th, dropped a 25-footer at the 15th to tie Howell and took the lead at the 16th with a birdie from 15 feet. The tension grew when Goydos bogeyed the 17th, and the issue was settled at the 18th.

Howell needed a birdie at the last to tie, but his eight-iron approach was 50 feet short and his chip shot was 15 feet long and he parred. Donald needed an eagle to tie, but his chip bounced off the pin and he birdied. Goydos's chip shot from 25 feet off the green glanced off the flagstick and stopped a tap-in away. Goydos had his first win since 1996. "I set some goals," Goydos cracked, "and one of them was to win every decade. I'm stunned."

Bob Hope Chrysler Classic
Palm Desert, California
Winner: Charley Hoffman

When Charley Hoffman got through the 16th hole with nothing worse than bogey, after the mess he had got into, he knew it could be his time. Hoffman, age 30, in his second year on the PGA Tour, was just another former Nationwide Tour player in the Bob Hope Chrysler Classic. Despite the punishing winds in the final round, Hoffman had worked his way into contention. Then came the near-disaster at the 16th. His tee shot missed the pond but plugged in a bank. He chipped out, but then plugged his third in a greenside bunker. He blasted out to four feet and dropped the putt into the hole. He had escaped with a bogey.

"After that," said Hoffman's caddie, Miguel Rivera, "we looked at each other and we knew we had a chance. Last year he would really get upset after something like that, but he's started to understand that it's part of the game and you just need to move on."

Hoffman did move on. He finished birdie-eagle for 71 and the clubhouse lead with a 17-under-par 343 total for the five-round tournament. John Rollins, in the final group just behind, birdied the 18th for a 73 to tie. Then Hoffman birdied the first playoff hole for his first PGA Tour victory.

"I survived — definitely a survivor," Hoffman said, and he was talking about the wind battering the field in the final round. Phil Mickelson, who had a distant chance of joining the race, hit shots into the water on three straight holes and overall made two double bogeys and five bogeys and shot 78. The baffled Justin Rose, who led or shared the lead for the middle three rounds, ended up wondering what he had to do to win. He and Lucas Glover were tied with a two-stroke lead going into the final round. Then at the par-five 18th, he bunkered his tee shot, knocked his tying birdie putt too far past and parred for 76, finishing a stroke behind. Rose thought the round should have been called off because of the wind. "When it blows 40 (miles an hour) ... it becomes survival more than anything," Rose said. Glover had two double bogeys and six bogeys, blew to an 80, and plunged to a tie for 13th.

It was from all this thrashing around that Hoffman emerged. After his bogey save at the 16th, he birdied the 17th, and then at the 564-yard, par-five 18th, he hit his second to 11 feet and holed the eagle for his 71. Rollins, with his last chance, birdied the 18th for 73 and tied Hoffman. In the playoff, Rollins hit his tee shot into a fairway bunker, put his third shot 30 feet from the cup and two-putted for a par. Hoffman was on in two, 37 feet away, left his first putt four feet from the hole, then dropped that one for a birdie and his first win. Said a relieved Hoffman: "I didn't think I had a chance with two holes to play."

Buick Invitational
La Jolla, California
Winner: Tiger Woods

Until the final home stretch, it seemed Tiger Woods's winning streak, and the debate, were over. He had won his last six straight PGA Tour starts of 2006, and now, late in January, he was making his first start of 2007 in the Buick Invitational at Torrey Pines. Would this be his seventh straight win, leaving him four shy of Byron Nelson's record 11 in 1945? Or would it simply be the first win of a new year? Woods did nothing but fuel the debate by coming from behind to win.

Woods left some disappointed golfers behind him. Rookie Brandt Snedeker, 26, in his first round of the year, sensed victory with a stunning nine-under outburst on the first nine — "It was a blur" — and an 11-under 61 at the Torrey Pines North Course for a two-shot lead over Charlie Wi. Woods was five behind. Snedeker shot 70 on the tougher South Course in the second round and held the halfway lead by three over Charles Howell, and by seven over Woods. In the third round, Andrew Buckle (68) and Snedeker (74) tied at 11 under, and Woods (69) was two behind. Then came Woods's late surge to lengthen his streak. Or did he?

It wasn't a true streak, Woods said, because he hadn't won in a combined three starts in Europe and Asia. For the moment, there was a more fundamental answer. "To somehow sneak out with a win is a cool feeling," he said. It was his fifth win overall and third in a row in the Buick Invitational, and his 55th career victory.

"Sneak" was the right word. Woods won by two with his scores of 66-72-69-66 for a 273 total, 15 under par, but it took the late outburst and some help from the leaders. Buckle and Jeff Quinney had a share of the lead on the final nine, only to fumble it away. And Howell's late move fell short and he settled for second. Snedeker (71) finished third.

First, though, Buckle had shaken Woods off earlier. Woods had tied him at No. 9 with an eagle from 25 feet. Buckle went back ahead with birdies at the next two holes. But at the 12th, a stray tee shot and an overly strong flop shot cost him a double bogey. He tied for fourth. Quinney's chances evaporated at the 14th, when a flawed bunker shot cost him a double bogey. He tied for seventh.

Howell stepped up with three birdies over four holes from the 12th to draw within a stroke of Woods. But Woods escaped bunkers for pars at the 14th and 15th, and wrapped up the win at the 17th with an approach from 143 yards to 30 inches for a birdie, 66 and a 273 total. Howell had one last chance. He was 50 feet from a tying eagle at the 18th, but he three-putted for a par and a 68 and finished second by two. "I played well down the stretch," Howell said. "He just never flinched."

FBR Open
Scottsdale, Arizona
Winner: Aaron Baddeley

Golf is all about timing, true enough. It couldn't have been better for Aaron Baddeley. As for Jeff Quinney — well, it was strictly the other kind. And for both, it came together as a dramatic last act on golf's rowdiest stage, the FBR Open (formerly the Phoenix Open) at the TPC of Scottsdale, where the galleries are huge and boisterous.

The end was abrupt and astonishing. Baddeley trailed Quinney by three strokes with four holes to play, and so was essentially done for. But as the cliché assures us, it isn't over until it's over. Baddeley exploded for three birdies over the last four holes, and Quinney stumbled home with bogeys on the last two. Although Baddeley trailed all the way, no one could accuse him of backing into the win. After opening 65-70, he shot 64 in the third round to close within two of Quinney, then shot another 64 in the fourth round for a 21-under-par 263 total and a one-stroke win over John Rollins, who slipped past Quinney with a closing 63. Quinney was alone in third place with 68 and a 265 total.

"When I got three back, I was really just thinking, if I can be one back playing the last hole, I've got a chance," Baddeley said. The fact is, Baddeley was one ahead playing the last hole, thanks to a shootout that actually began badly for him back at the par-four 14th. There, Quinney dropped a six-foot birdie putt while Baddeley's string of 35 holes without a bogey ended after he bunkered his tee shot and two-putted from 34 feet. Quinney, who had led since his 63 in the second round, was looking good.

Then at the 15th, Quinney missed a birdie from six feet and Baddeley birdied. Next, at the par-three 16th, ringed by luxury boxes and rowdy fans, Baddeley dropped a 24-foot putt for birdie and Quinney parred again and his lead was down to one. Pressing, the normally straight Quinney used his driver at the short par-four 17th and pulled his tee shot into the water. He took a penalty drop and recovered beautifully, hitting his approach to four feet. Then he missed the putt and bogeyed again while Baddeley sank a tricky 10-footer for his third straight birdie and was one ahead with a hole to play. Rollins tried to head him off, but his wedge to the 18th glanced off the flagstick and bounced off the green.

"I'm sure Jeff is disappointed with the way he finished, but I was just trying to put pressure on him towards the end," Baddeley said. It was the third straight tournament in which Quinney led or shared the lead in the final round but came up short. But he refused to be discouraged. Said Quinney: "You wonder when you're just starting out whether you belong. I finally feel like a complete player."

AT&T Pebble Beach National Pro-Am
Pebble Beach, California
Winner: Phil Mickelson

By the time Phil Mickelson reached the AT&T Pebble Beach National Pro-Am early in February, his debacle in the 2006 U.S. Open at Winged Foot eight months ago was no more of a scar than the scuff he left on that tree at the 18th hole.

This was, for the moment at least, the new Mickelson. The old one at Winged Foot spent more time in the hay than a farmer. This Phil Mickelson hit 45 of 55 driving fairways and also hit 79.2 percent of the greens, and with his putter working nicely, it all translated into a victory. Mickelson tied for the lead in the first three rounds, then ran away to a five-stroke win.

"I didn't think it would take three tournaments to get where I wanted to be," said Mickelson, who so far in 2007 had two so-so finishes and one missed cut. Luckily catching the best of the capricious weather on the Monterey Peninsula, he shot 65-67-70-66 for a 20-under-par 268 total across the tournament's three courses. It went this way:

• In the first round, at Poppy Hills, he closed with an eagle off a four iron from 230 yards to 18 feet for the 65, tying Nick Watney, also at Poppy Hills, and rookie John Mallinger, who caught the worst of the weather at the highly exposed Pebble Beach. Poppy averaged 71.73, Spyglass Hill 73.17 and Pebble 74.98.

• Mickelson shot 67 in the second round at cold, rainy Pebble Beach. He made three straight birdies from the 10th hole and also birdied the 18th to tie Jim Furyk, who shot 65 at Poppy Hills, where he birdied all but one of the par-fives. They led by three over Mallinger and Kevin Sutherland, who shot a 10-birdie, one-bogey 63 at Spyglass. "A 63," Sutherland conceded, "was not the score I was thinking about when I teed off."

• Mickelson came through blustery Spyglass Hill with 70 and a 14-under 202 total in the third round, tying with Sutherland, who shot 67 at Poppy

Hills. Mallinger, also at Poppy Hills, took his first bogey of the tournament at the 15th and shot 68, and was one back going into the final round. Furyk's chances died in the worst of the weather at Pebble Beach. He shot 76 and fell six behind. More bad weather was forecast for Sunday at Pebble Beach, and that didn't bother Mickelson. "I've been driving it better than I think I ever have," he said, "and I'm excited about putting it to the test here."

• The weather was sunny instead on Sunday, and Mickelson more than passed the driver test. He missed only one fairway, shot six-under 66, and that included a lost-ball double bogey at the par-three fifth hole. He rebounded at the sixth with a bunker shot to a foot for a birdie, and birdied the eighth from six feet, the 10th from 15 feet, and he was on his way.

Nissan Open
Pacific Palisades, California
Winner: Charles Howell

It was a most eager Phil Mickelson who packed up his AT&T Pebble Beach National Pro-Am trophy and said, "I can't wait for next week," that being the Nissan Open at Riviera Country Club at Los Angeles. And he had every reason to be excited at the Nissan Open — until the last few holes. That's when long-suffering Charles Howell, a one-time winner but nine times a runner-up, got excited.

Mickelson faced a 10-footer at the third playoff hole, and Howell was telling himself, "It's Phil Mickelson ... I'm giving him the putt. When he missed it, my heart jumped ..."

Then Howell holed his three-footer for his second win, nearly five years after his first, the 2002 Michelob Championship. Since then, he had won nothing. "Not even a game of 'horse,'" Howell said, meaning the basketball game. "This one is definitely a relief."

Not to Mickelson. "I had the tournament under control," said Mickelson, fresh from a five-stroke win at Pebble Beach. "There were a lot of opportunities I let slide."

Actually, Padraig Harrington missed as many, only earlier. Harrington, in his first Nissan Open, started with a blazing eight-under 63 for a three-stroke lead over Mickelson, Briny Baird and Pat Perez. Harrington opened with three straight birdies, then got four in a row after the turn. "I'm feeling invincible," said Harrington, moved by his Irish wit. "I didn't think I was ever not going to make birdie."

Harrington soon thought otherwise. In the second round, he made only two pars in his first 10 holes en route to 68. Mickelson tied him for the lead with 65 that included a stunning eagle at the par-five 17th — a 310-yard tee shot and a 287-yard three wood to 15 feet. They were at 11-under 131, three ahead of Howell (65). With 69 and a 13-under total in the third round, Mickelson was one up on Harrington (70), three up on Howell (69).

Making up three strokes on Mickelson in the final round seemed too much to Howell. "I thought I'd shot my way out of it Saturday," he said. Instead, it was Mickelson who would shoot his way out of it on Sunday.

While Harrington slipped back and Ernie Els's charge ran out of gas, Mickelson built his lead to four ahead of Howell through the 10th hole. Then Howell birdied four of his last five holes, catching Mickelson along the way. Mickelson retook the lead with a birdie at the 17th with a driver, four wood and two putts. Then at the 18th, a short approach, a poor chip and two putts from 18 feet gave him a bogey, 68 and a tie with Howell (65) at 16-under 268.

They parred the first two playoff holes. At the third, the par-three 14th, Mickelson left a putt from the fringe 10 feet from the hole, then missed that one. Howell ran in his three-footer for a par and his second career win, nearly five years after his first. Which meant more to him? "This one," Howell said. "Because ... it's been a long time."

WGC - Accenture Match Play Championship
Marana, Arizona
Winner: Henrik Stenson

At the WGC - Accenture Match Play Championship late in February, two key questions were asked. First, would Tiger Woods win his eighth straight start? The answer was "No," thanks to the gritty Australian, Nick O'Hern. Next, who is Henrik Stenson? Well, Stenson did deliver the winning point for Europe in the 2006 Ryder Cup, but that didn't make him Colin Montgomerie. So the question still stood until Stenson answered — the winner, thank you.

Even so, Stenson, a 30-year-old Swede, was upstaged by the Tiger Woods story at The Gallery in the high desert outside Tucson, Arizona, when O'Hern ended his string of seven straight wins on the second extra hole in the third round. It was still the talk of the tournament, even after the exclusive field had been whittled down to Stenson, the ninth seed, and U.S. Open champion Geoff Ogilvy, the 11th seed. In the end, Stenson was one relieved golfer after his 2-and-1 victory.

"I was struggling, big-time," said Stenson, winning his second in three weeks, after the European Tour's Dubai Desert Classic. "I don't know how I managed to get it all together." Said Ogilvy: "Everybody out here knows he's a good player. People outside the golf world need to see that."

Ogilvy moved convincingly through Steve Stricker, Jose Maria Olazabal, Niclas Fasth, Paul Casey and Chad Campbell. Stenson beat Zach Johnson, K.J. Choi, Aaron Baddeley, O'Hern and Trevor Immelman.

Stenson and Ogilvy were both shaky in the 36-hole final, exchanging the lead five times and losing holes on bogeys. Stenson led two up after the morning round, but Ogilvy reversed him and led by two with 10 holes to play. Stenson took the lead for good at the par-four 12th, blasting from a bunker and holing the six-footer. Ogilvy stayed afloat with fine par saves, on a 12-footer at the 13th and an 18-footer at the 14th.

Stenson then closed him out with back-to-back birdies. He lofted an eight iron to two feet at the par-three 16th, and two-putted from 60 feet at the par-five 17th. "I couldn't say I was floating around thinking how great I was playing," Stenson said. "I was happy I could hang around all day."

It was Stenson's win, but O'Hern's headline. Woods had turned erratic in the third round. He missed a four-foot putt at the third hole, then double-bogeyed the fourth from the water, double-bogeyed the sixth from cactus and bogeyed the seventh from more cactus, and was four down. "I just didn't have control of my swing," Woods said. He battled back to square the match, but at the 19th, he missed a winning four-foot birdie putt. And at the 20th, he missed the green, chipped 15 feet short and missed the putt. O'Hern rolled in his 12-footer for a par and the win, becoming the first to beat Woods twice in professional match play. "To beat him once was an amazing thrill," O'Hern said. "I just know if I played well and played solidly, I could do it again."

Mayakoba Golf Classic at Riviera Maya-Cancun
Riviera Maya, Mexico
Winner: Fred Funk

Fred Funk, age 50, had come to a fork in the road that last week of February. He could play in either the Champions Tour's ACE Group Classic or in the Mayakoba Classic, the PGA Tour's first event ever in Mexico. The three-round Champions tournament would give him a chance to work on his game, but he had already committed to the Mayakoba. Then he learned that the Mayakoba people were using him to promote the tournament, which was playing opposite the limited-field WGC - Accenture Match Play Championship.

"So I had to honor my first commitment," Funk said. "I think it turned out to be a really good decision, based on the first round."

The first round? Just a course-record, eight-under-par 62 for a two-stroke lead. Come Sunday, Funk could be saying the same thing for the entire week. He led or shared the lead all the way, then beat Jose Coceres in a playoff for his eighth PGA Tour victory, and in the process became the second player — after Craig Stadler in 2003 — to win a PGA Tour event after winning on the Champions Tour. Funk had won the Turtle Bay Championship by 11 strokes on the Champions Tour a month earlier.

Funk birdied five of his first seven holes en route to that opening 62, and led a group at 64, including Cameron Beckman, who birdied six out of seven holes and noted, "It's a very playable course."

Funk shot 69–131 in the second round and was tied by Beckman (67) and Boo Weekley, a down-home character who explained his 67 thus: "Some holes I hit it pretty close, and some holes I didn't."

Then things got downright scary for Funk. In the third round, he was face-down in pain behind the 13th tee, with a trainer working on a back so sore he wondered whether he would be able to swing the club. "I just had to get through the round," Funk insisted. That he did — for 64 and a two-stroke lead on Coceres (65).

Funk, still needing massages on the course in the fourth round, bogeyed twice on the first nine, and was tied at the turn. Struggling just to finish, he found a way to stretch to ease his pain. He birdied the 13th and bogeyed the 14th, and Coceres holed a 10-foot birdie putt at the 15th to keep the tie. Coceres just missed birdie tries at the 17th and 18th. Funk finished with one-over 71 to tie Coceres (69) at 14-under 266. Funk then dropped a six-footer for birdie at the second extra hole for the win. He forgot his sore back long enough to throw a jubilant punch into the air.

Honda Classic
Palm Beach Gardens, Florida
Winner: Mark Wilson

For Mark Wilson, a math major in his college days, the numbers at the Honda Classic were punishing — two, 10, 110, 265.

The two was the two-stroke penalty he called on himself after his caddie violated the advice rule in the second round. The 10 was the number of times he had to go through the qualifying school. The 110 was the number of tournaments he had played without winning, and the 265 was his distant World Ranking. They were all wiped out early in March when Wilson survived a four-way playoff in the Honda Classic at PGA National in Florida.

"I'd love to win," Wilson said Sunday evening, after darkness bumped the rest of the playoff over into Monday, "but worst I can do is second, so that's not too bad." But that was analysis, not a concession speech, as Wilson proved the next day. Camilo Villegas and Boo Weekley, who had joined that four-way tie at five-under 275, bowed out with bogeys at the second playoff hole.

At the third extra hole, the par-three 17th, Wilson holed a 10-foot putt for a birdie. Then up stepped Coceres. His putt was a tad shorter and on about the same line. But it lipped out, and Wilson had his win. "After the putts went in on 16, 18, and then in the playoff yesterday (Sunday) at 18," Wilson said, "I just had a feeling someone wanted me to win."

Maybe there was something supernatural about it. Wilson shot 72-66-66-71 over the par-70 course and would have won outright except for the foolish gaffe by his caddie, Chris Jones, in the second round. At the fifth hole, he told Villegas' caddie which club Wilson had hit, a violation of the rule against giving advice. Wilson reported this to a rules official and was penalized two strokes. It gave him 66, but left him three shots instead of one behind going into the third round.

After Charlie Wi and Robert Allenby faded from the top of the leaderboard in the first two rounds, Wilson took the top spot with 66 in the third round, one stroke ahead of Weekley (66). Weekley is another who would have won outright but for a fundamental error. He "hammered" a three-foot par putt past the cup at the 72nd hole. He said it was a case of nerves. "That's golf, man," he said.

What's also golf is what got Wilson his win. In the final round, he holed a 45-foot putt for par at the 16th. At the 18th, he holed an eight-footer to save par. And on the first playoff hole, he made a 30-footer, again for par. As he said — maybe someone wanted him to win.

PODS Championship
Tampa Bay, Florida
Winner: Mark Calcavecchia

There's nothing like beating the traffic, and so Mark Calcavecchia, after opening the PODS Championship with 75, packed his bags that night so that he could get off to a fast start when he missed the cut the next day. Good planning, but a tad premature.

Enter now the tale of the least-ugly putter, and Calcavecchia, at age 46, had his 13th career victory and his first since 2005.

The week before, in the Honda Classic, Calcavecchia had missed the cut, the victim of poor putting. Disgusted, he stopped in at a retail store and bought a new putter for $256.18. And what is the mysterious process by which a professional chooses such a delicate instrument? "I just kind of look at it," Calcavecchia said, "and see which one looks less ugly to me. Or which one I really wouldn't mind breaking."

Calcavecchia used 36 putts with his old putter in that first-round 75, then shot 67-62-70 with the new ugly putter the rest of the way for a 10-under 274 total and a one-stroke victory over Heath Slocum and John Senden at Innisbrook's Copperhead Course in Florida. He averaged just 23 putts through the two middle rounds.

Calcavecchia never lost the lead in the final round, but it wasn't a walkthrough, either. He birdied the second hole from two feet, and went three ahead with a 10-footer for birdie at the sixth. Then he was in a jam. He bogeyed the eighth and 10th holes, missing both greens. And Senden and Lucas Glover caught him at nine under. Then Calcavecchia retook the lead with his new putter — a birdie from three feet at the 11th, another with a 30-footer at the 13th and yet another on a 20-footer at the 14th. But Calcavecchia, a streaky player, missed a four-footer for birdie at the 15th.

Glover, one of five who had tied for the lead at some point, charged for a birdie at the 18th to stay alive, but three-putted for a 69 and tied for fourth. Slocum, meanwhile, after a double bogey at the second hole, was four behind going into the final nine. Then he notched four birdies in five holes from the 10th and was within a stroke when Calcavecchia bogeyed the 16th.

Calcavecchia led by a stroke at the 18th, then nearly lost it all. He was short with his eight-iron approach, then chipped to seven feet and two-putted for a bogey and was ripe for picking. Slocum was on the green, 25 feet from a birdie and needed only a par to tie and force a playoff. But he left the birdie putt four feet short, then missed the par and left Calcavecchia with a welcome packing problem — how to get that trophy home?

Arnold Palmer Invitational
Orlando, Florida
Winner: Vijay Singh

This was the Arnold Palmer Invitational, newly named in 2007, but before that the Bay Hill Invitational, which Tiger Woods had won four straight times from 2000 and which cost Vijay Singh nothing but frustration in 14 trips since 1993, including three runner-up finishes. Woods had this one almost within reach, then suffered a most un-Tiger-like collapse on the final nine. Singh, on the other hand, hit a hot streak on the final front nine and posted a two-stroke victory over resurging Rocco Mediate.

"I love this place," Singh said. "I hate the 18th hole, but I love the rest of it."

Palmer would understand. Bay Hill's mighty 18th had cost Singh two victories. In 1994 he finished bogey-bogey, and in 2005 he hit his seven-iron approach shot into the water and double-bogeyed. He tied for second both times. This time he played the par-four hole in four, four, three, four.

Singh, coming from six strokes behind in the first round and seven in the second, shot 70-68-67-67–272, eight under par on a Bay Hill course cut from par 72 to 70. He won by two over Mediate, whose chronically sore back was calm. Mediate opened with 66 and 65 to take the halfway lead at nine under, seven strokes up on Singh. Mediate bounced back from a third-round 76, in which he needed 33 putts, tied for the lead at the final turn, but bogeyed the 18th. But for someone playing on medical exemptions and sponsors' invitations, the second place was a godsend. The $594,000 secured his PGA Tour card. "This," Mediate said, "is huge."

Singh shot 67 in the third round, when only nine of the 79 in the field broke par. That carried him from a tie for 46th to a tie for third place. Then he broke away in the fourth round. After a birdie-bogey exchange from No. 2, he birdied four of the next five holes, then locked it up coming home. At the par-five 12th, he hit driver-driver, dumping his second shot behind a tree, then hit a brilliant wedge through a six-foot gap to 20 feet and holed the birdie putt. At the 15th, he cut the corner, then flipped a sand wedge to two feet for another birdie and enough margin to absorb bogeys at the 16th and 17th. And, of course, he parred the 18th.

Woods birdied his first two holes and got to within a stroke of the lead at the turn, then crashed. He three-putted the 11th for a double bogey. At the par-three 17th, he hit his tee shot into the water and double-bogeyed. And at the 18th, he chipped out of the rough, hit his third into the water and triple-bogeyed for 76 and a tie for 22nd place.

Said Singh: "I wanted to win this one after so many misses."

WGC - CA Championship
Miami, Florida
Winner: Tiger Woods

Tiger Woods is often a man of few words, as in describing his first round of the WGC - CA Championship. "Pathetic," he said.

In the exclusive field of 73, 15 players had broken par at Doral's Blue Monster, and Woods was one of them — with a one-under-par 71. He handled the strong winds, but not the greens. He needed 32 putts. So he started the tournament four strokes behind Sweden's Henrik Stenson, winner of the WGC - Accenture Match Play a month earlier, and Australia's Robert Allenby, tied at five-under 67. Others had tougher times — Vijay Singh, 74, and Phil Mickelson, 77.

Actually, Woods was just getting settled in. He was at home at Doral. He had won there the last two years when the tournament was the Ford Championship. But he wasn't happy about needing 32 putts. He headed for the practice green and drilled for nearly an hour. It worked.

Woods rode that obedient putter to a six-under 66 and a two-stroke lead in the second round. He figured it was a par-saving putt, a 10-footer at the par-three ninth hole that kept his round going. Then there was the 10-footer for par at the 18th that kept his lead at two strokes. "Any time you make big par putts," Woods said, "I think it's more important to make those than birdie putts." It didn't hurt that he also birdied from three, three, eight, six, 10 and six feet. He was atop the leaderboard to stay.

If anyone thought Woods might ease up in the third round, he caught their attention with an electrifying eagle at the par-five first — a daring four-iron approach into a stiff wind to 10 feet. He bogeyed No. 6, then made three birdies the rest of the way for 68 and a four-stroke lead over Brett Wetterich (67). Wetterich, a big hitter, said he would continue firing at the pins, chasing Woods. "You can't sit back and be happy with making pars," he said.

In the final round, Woods led by four strokes much of the way despite playing rocky golf. Wetterich got within three with a birdie at the 16th. Woods, meanwhile, bogeyed the 11th and 13th, and at the 18th, he teed off with an iron, laid up, hit a wedge 50 feet past the pin, and two-putted for another bogey and a one-over 73. He finished at 10-under 278 for a two-stroke win over Wetterich. Said the man of few words: "Very pleased."

Shell Houston Open
Humble, Texas
Winner: Adam Scott

The Shell Houston Open had become practically a point of entry for Australian golfers, and the 2007 edition became part of that interesting phenomenon when, though in a clumsy finish, Adam Scott, a young Australian, legged it home past fellow Aussie Stuart Appleby. Scott thus became the sixth Australian — including Appleby, the 2006 champion — to win the tournament.

"It was relief along with elation," Scott said. "I was pretty happy for it to be all over with because it was looking a bit messy." Messy it was. At the final hole, Scott and Appleby kicked the title back and forth. But Scott survived the 18th to post his first victory since the 2006 Tour Championship.

Playing together in the final round, they came to the 488-yard, par-four 18th hole with Scott leading Appleby by one stroke. First, Scott gave the tournament to Appleby by pulling his drive into the lake along the left side. Then Appleby gave it back, driving into a fairway bunker and hitting his second shot into the water.

Scott took his penalty drop and hit to the green, but 50 feet from the flag. While Appleby was busy wrapping up a double bogey, Scott rolled in that 50-footer for the most unlikely of pars and 66 at the par-72 Redstone Tournament Course and a three-stroke victory over Appleby (69) and Bubba Watson (72) on a 17-under 271 total.

"Kind of a gift from Stuart," Scott said. And also an echo from the past. In the 2004 Players Championship, Scott led by two playing the 18th and pulled his approach into the water. He survived, winning despite a bogey. "I've gotten away with it twice," Scott said. "Maybe the third time won't be too lucky."

The tournament was a leapfrog contest from the start. Appleby was in a three-way tie at 66 in the first round, then was in a six-way jam in the second. Bubba Watson took a three-stroke lead with 64 in the third round over a crowd that included Scott and Appleby. Then it was Watson's turn to oblige. He faded on his way to 72 and a tie for second. Scott and Appleby wiped out Watson's three-stroke edge with birdies on three of their first five holes. They traded punches until the par-three 14th, where Appleby gave up the lead for good with a bogey.

Scott got to 17 under at the 608-yard 15th with two three-wood shots and two putts for a birdie. Appleby bogeyed the 16th, then birdied the 17th, and they went to the 18th tee with Scott up by one.

"We were solid all day, and all of a sudden, funny shots happened," Scott said.

Appleby swallowed the loss, but acknowledged that at least a fellow Aussie had won, which made it easier. "Marginally," Appleby added.

Masters Tournament
Augusta, Georgia
Winner: Zach Johnson

See Chapter 2.

Verizon Heritage
Hilton Head Island, South Carolina
Winner: Boo Weekley

It looked like a bad case of instant replay for Boo Weekley at the Verizon Heritage. Six weeks earlier, Weekley, down-home guy from the Florida panhandle, blew a short putt at the final hole and his first PGA Tour victory along with it. Now, in mid-April, his three-stroke lead was leaking away down the final stretch. Talk about miracle finishes: How about two long chip-ins at the last two holes to save par and his first victory, a one-stroke win over Ernie Els.

"Unreal. This is unreal," Weekley sputtered. And so it was. Weekley, finally emerging in the fourth round, shot scores of 67-69-66-68–270, 14 under at the par-71 Harbour Town course.

For the first three rounds, it was Els and Jerry Kelly batting the lead back and forth. Kelly, after approaching 60, opened with eight-under 63 and a two-stroke lead on Els. Weekley was four strokes off the lead. Four birdies in five holes on his second nine gave Els another 65, a 130 total and a three-stroke lead after two rounds on Kelly, who — as he put it — turned 75 into 70. Weekley then was six behind.

Then it was Kelly again in the third round, with 67 and a 200 total ignited by a hole-in-one, a four-iron shot at the 200-yard fourth hole. "That was like a little dagger," said Els, who battled through trees for 71 to tie Kevin Na (66) at 201. And Weekley sneaked into the picture with 66 and a 202 total.

The final round spilled over into Monday because of high winds, and there stood a new threat. Stephen Leaney had made up a four-stroke deficit with an outward 30. Coming home, two bogeys and an out-of-bounds double bogey at the 16th cooled him to 68 and solo third place.

Els's chances sputtered at the 17th, where he put his tee shot into the hazard behind the green. He shot 70 and was second by one stroke. Kelly, after an eagle at the par-five second hole, drove into the water at the 10th and blew to 77 and a tie for eighth.

Weekley was making his way uncertainly through this scramble. He took the lead with an eagle at the fifth and a birdie at the sixth, lost it, and retook it at the 15th, scrambling to a par after misjudging the wind. He bogeyed the 16th, against Leaney's double bogey there. Then came the two spectacular chip shots.

At the 136-yard 17th, Weekley's six iron into the wind went over the green. He muffed a high flop shot, leaving it 40 feet short — "Flops ain't my favorite" — then chipped that in to save par. At the 18th, he ran his first chip off the front, 36 feet from the pin, then holed that one coming back for his par and the win. It was time to celebrate. "If there's one thing I can do good," Weekley said, "it's party."

Zurich Classic of New Orleans
Avondale, Louisiana
Winner: Nick Watney

Nick Watney, age 25 and in his third year of frustration on the PGA Tour, finally broke through in the Zurich Classic of New Orleans — a town that translates easily to good times. So this called for a celebration. Said Watney, whose previous best were two ties for fifth in 2006: "I'm pretty much low-key. I probably won't live it up too much. I'll definitely call my parents." So much for the Walter Hagen approach to golf.

Watney made his move in the third round with a clutch of birdies after the turn. He holed an 18-foot putt at the 10th; at the par-five 11th, he scrambled from a bunkered drive and dropped a five-footer, and at the 13th, he sank a 13-footer. He shot 68–204 and led by two over Ken Duke, a 38-year-old rookie who shot a day's-best 66, giving him a boost toward his first victory.

It might have been a good thing that Watney didn't take the lead until the third round. Until the Zurich Classic, he never had the lead going into the final round. He had never had to sleep on a lead — and he didn't sleep on this one, either. He was walking around at 5:30 a.m. "I was definitely nervous to start out," Watney conceded, and it showed. He lost that two-stroke lead in a hurry with bogeys at the third and fourth. But he got well immediately at the par-four fifth hole with an approach from 132 yards that dropped for an eagle that got him back to tied for the lead. That's when he knew, he said, "it was definitely my week."

But not before Watney lost the lead again to Duke, this time when he missed a three-footer for par at No. 10. He bounced right back at the par-five 11th with a birdie. And then came the two-stroke swing that set him up for the win. At the par-three 14th, Duke was short with his tee shot, chipped seven feet past and bogeyed. Watney put his tee shot eight feet from the pin and birdied. Watney parred in the rest of the way for 69 and a 15-under 273 total, and took his first win by three strokes.

"I'm living in a dream right now," Watney said. "But it's definitely more fun to actually do it."

The Zurich Classic introduced Kyle Reifers to the golf world. Reifers, a rookie in only his eighth PGA Tour start, ran off to a course-record, eight-under 64 and a two-stroke lead. "I'm more happy than nervous," Reifers said. He slipped to 73 in the second round, and Mark Calcavecchia, just six weeks after winning the PODS Championship, took over by a stroke with 69. "It's a miracle I don't have any bogeys yet, considering the places I hit it today," Calcavecchia said. Calcavecchia would finish tied for fifth, and Reifers tied for 24th.

EDS Byron Nelson Championship
Irving, Texas
Winner: Scott Verplank

Time was when young Scott Verplank would carry a scoring standard in the EDS Byron Nelson Championship. This time, Verplank was carrying the championship trophy.

This was one of golf's finest feel-good stories — Verplank, age 42, a native son of Dallas, who had idolized the great Lord Byron since he was a kid, finally winning his tournament. Verplank, who considered this tournament his own fifth major, had come close before, only to be turned away. He finally made it on his 21st try.

Verplank missed his idol and old friend, who died on September 26, 2006, at age 94. Nelson, for whom the tournament was named in 1968, was honored with a moment of silence and a jet fighter fly-by in the third round. "Byron meant so much to me," Verplank said. "To be from Dallas and win this is unbelievable."

It was also improbable until the end. Verplank trailed from the start and was three strokes behind Luke Donald through No. 5 in the final round, then birdied five of the next eight holes and — with a big boost from Donald — went on to win by a stroke. It was Verplank's fifth victory in a career of injuries, and his first since 2001.

The tournament was something of a dream for Donald, too. He had shot 10 consecutive rounds in the 60s and never led. But he did this time. In the second round, Donald took the guesswork out of the inconsistent greens at the TPC Las Colinas with chip-in birdies from 25 feet at the par-four 12th and 43 feet at the par-three 17th for a four-under 66 and a one-stroke lead at 133 over Brett Wetterich (68 at Cottonwood Valley) and Fredrik

Jacobson (67) and first-round leader Sean O'Hair (69), both at Las Colinas. Then it turned into a Verplank-Donald shootout. With 67 in the third round, Donald kept the one-stroke lead, this time over Verplank (66), and the script was about to take some strange twists.

In the final round, Donald, starting with a one-shot lead, moved three ahead of Verplank with birdies at the third and fourth holes. They both birdied the sixth, Donald with a 12-foot putt, Verplank with a five-footer. Then Verplank birdied the next two, the par-five seventh after a chip to two feet and the par-four eighth from 12, to close the gap to one. Verplank then leapfrogged into the lead — and for good — when Donald double-bogeyed the par-four ninth after driving into the trees, missing the green and hitting over it. Verplank then birdied the 11th from 13 feet and the 13th from 23 feet. Donald bogeyed the 12th, then rebounded with birdies at the 13th and 16th. Verplank's lead shrank to one when he bogeyed the 15th, but he parred in — including a clutch save out of a bunker at the 17th — for the precious one-stroke victory with 66 and a 13-under 267 total.

Wachovia Championship
Charlotte, North Carolina
Winner: Tiger Woods

On winning the Wachovia Championship, Tiger Woods offered that he didn't have his "best stuff." If so, then maybe this was a good thing. If he'd had his best all the way, he might have turned a very worthy tournament on a very fine course — Quail Hollow Club in Charlotte, North Carolina — into a burlesque, even against a prime field that included 27 of the top 30 players.

So put his performance down as a part-brilliant, part-not 70-68-68-69–275, 13 under par, as Woods beat Steve Stricker by two strokes. It was his 57th PGA Tour career victory, his third of the year (it was only mid-May) and his ninth in 12 starts, and he said it was special.

"Over the course of my career, I've won a few tournaments here and there and it's been nice," Woods said. "This one, considering the field, the golf course and the conditions, I'm ecstatic to have won here."

Apart from Woods's heroics and pratfalls, the climax of the tournament came on Saturday. Rory Sabbatini had shot 64 to take the third-round lead at 11 under par, one stroke ahead of Woods. They would be paired in the final round, and Sabbatini said he welcomed the chance finally to clear the stain off his win in the 2006 Nissan Open, which critics said wasn't valid because Woods had withdrawn from the field with an illness. "He's here this week," Sabbatini said. "Best opportunity I've had to put any of that criticism or doubt aside." Some in the media took this to mean he was predicting he would beat Woods, and so the final round took on the air of fireworks day.

Woods had already been setting off fireworks. One was a bogey at the 18th hole in the first round, when he didn't outguess the wind and flew the green with an eight iron. His 70 left him four strokes behind Padraig Harrington (66). In the second round, Woods, with three birdies through five holes plus five par saves in seven holes, shot 68 and tied for the halfway lead with Vijay Singh (71) and Arron Oberholser (69) at six under.

When it came to fireworks, the third round was like the Fourth of July. Sabbatini launched his 64 with a hole-out eagle at No. 1. Oberholser also had a hole-out eagle, Carl Pettersson and Phil Mickelson chipped in for eagles, and Vijay Singh's wedge shot at the par-four 12th plunged into the cup, came out and spun around the rim, and dropped back in for yet another eagle.

The fourth round was not a Sabbatini-Woods shootout. Sabbatini struggled to 74 and tied for third place. "He got the job done today, I didn't," Sabbatini said. Stricker missed his best chance since 2001 with a double bogey-birdie-bogey finish for 69. Woods labored, but had his moments. At the par-five seventh hole, he just missed water from the tee, then powered an eight iron from 193 yards to 60 feet and rolled in the eagle putt, then birdied the eighth and ninth holes. Then he double-bogeyed the 13th, birdied the 15th and bogeyed the 17th. As he said, this one was special.

The Players Championship
Ponte Vedra Beach, Florida
Winner: Phil Mickelson

The Players Championship was a spring melodrama in four acts, with three principal characters — Phil Mickelson, the hero, scoring his first Players title and his second victory of the season; Sean O'Hair, the innocent fall guy, and Devil's Island, the notorious little par-three 17th that has claimed more victims than the Bermuda Triangle, again the foul villain.

The 17th measures about 137 or so yards, depending on where the tee is set. The hole is most dangerous when the wind is up. There's no margin for error — either hit the island green or hit the water. For a quick thumbnail description, note that in the windy first round a record 50 balls were hit into the water. The last two of the tournament sealed O'Hair's fate and cleared the way for Mickelson.

And Mickelson scribbled a note to his new coach, Butch Harmon: "Butch, the 1st of many." And later, Mickelson said: "What's most exciting is I feel like we're just getting started."

There were a number of subplots. The much anticipated Mickelson-Tiger Woods duel never materialized because Woods, who won the Wachovia Championship the previous week, didn't bring his game. He tied for 71st in fairways hit (29-for-56), tied for 61st in putting and tied for 37th at even-par 288. Peter Lonard's hopes shriveled with two double bogeys on the last nine in the second round. Also in the second round, Jim Furyk, just one shot out of the lead, pulled his approach badly into the lake at No. 7 and double-bogeyed. In the third round, Jose Coceres, one of five who had at least a share of the lead, hit his tee shot into the water and double-bogeyed the 17th. "I let the pressure of 17 get to me," he conceded.

Mickelson tied for the first-round lead with Rory Sabbatini at 67, and was the solo leader by one (72–139) through the second round. In the third round, O'Hair hit a "good, solid" nine iron at the 17th, and then the wind died, and he watched to see his ball drop into the water. Instead, it stopped five feet from the hole. It was the jewel of a birdie-birdie-birdie finish for 66 and a 207 total, and a one-stroke lead over Mickelson (69). Mickelson re-took the lead in the final round, and a frustrated O'Hair just couldn't quite close the two-stroke gap. Then O'Hair wrote an inspiring chapter on the spirit of the game. The 17th was his last best chance to gain ground, so he ignored the safe tee shot to the center of the green, and instead went right at the pin in a do-or-die try. Then his heart sank. His nine-iron shot sailed over the green and into the water. He was dead. He watered another from the drop area, and finally made seven. Mickelson was home free.

"You've got to make something happen," O'Hair said. "I didn't bust my butt for four rounds to get second place." He shot 76, and dropped from a sure second place to 11th, a fall that cost him $747,000.

For the record, Mickelson played the 17th in 3-3-3-3, O'Hair in 5-3-2-7.

The big question on the eve of the Players was whether Mickelson had indeed recovered from the crash that cost him the 2006 U.S. Open. True, he had won at Pebble Beach in February, but now it was May, three months after some indifferent golf and three weeks after he took on Harmon as his new coach.

And so four days after teeing it up at a refurbished TPC at Sawgrass in the flagship tournament of the PGA Tour, Mickelson delivered the answer: It would seem so. A card of 67-72-69-69, 11-under-par 277 — and with O'Hair's help — carried Mickelson to his first Players title by two strokes, his second victory of the year and 31st of his career.

AT&T Classic
Duluth, Georgia
Winner: Zach Johnson

Zach Johnson, native son of Iowa and resident of Florida, was beginning to feel very much at home in Georgia.

On a fine May day near Atlanta, Johnson birdied the first playoff hole against Ryuji Imada to win the AT&T Classic at TPC Sugarloaf. Just six weeks earlier, Johnson won the Masters, just up the road in Augusta. And in 2004, he scored his first PGA Tour victory in the BellSouth Classic (forerunner of this AT&T Classic), also at TPC Sugarloaf. That's three victories, all in Georgia.

This one was late-blooming. While Imada was on the leaderboard from the start and tied for the lead through the middle rounds (67-67-69), Johnson trailed by six, three and three strokes (71-66-69) along the way. Imada hit a bump in the second round, a double bogey at the par-five No. 4, but bounced back for four straight birdies and 67 to tie at 10 under par with Troy Matteson (64). They stayed tied in the third round, both shooting 69 for 13-under 203 totals. Imada was an escape artist. He hit just six fairways, but saved five times out of six bunkers and needed just 26 putts.

Matteson was a contender for the two middle rounds (64-69), and took a two-stroke lead in the final round with birdies at the second and third holes. But he cancelled them out with two quick bogeys. He finally got done in at the par-four 17th, where a pulled tee shot and a plugged second shot cost him a double bogey. A 73 dropped him into a tie for third with Camilo Villegas (71) and Matt Kuchar (70).

Johnson surfaced in the final round with a 42-foot birdie putt at the first hole. Then he ran off three straight birdies from the eighth, and tied Imada with a 15-foot birdie putt at the par-four 15th. And then a two-putt birdie at the 18th gave him the lead. Now Imada had to catch him, which he did at the 18th with a pitch from behind the green setting up a tap-in birdie for a four-birdie, two-bogey 70 and the tie.

They returned to the par-five 18th for the playoff. Johnson drove into the fairway, but Imada hit into the left rough. Certain Johnson would birdie, Imada opted to try for the green from 252 yards. "I knew I had to gamble, even though I was in the rough," he said. But his bold three-wood shot came down short into the fronting pond. That was the decisive shot. Johnson hit a four iron to the back of the green and got down in two for the birdie and his third victory in Georgia. "I guess," Johnson said, "I need to find some property here somewhere."

Crowne Plaza Invitational at Colonial
Fort Worth, Texas
Winner: Rory Sabbatini

Rory Sabbatini got his victory. It wasn't over Tiger Woods, but Jim Furyk and Bernhard Langer put together would do. Sabbatini rolled in a 15-foot birdie putt on the first playoff hole to beat both in the storm-battered Crowne Plaza Invitational at Colonial. Later, Sabbatini was ribbed again about Woods. It will be recalled that at the Wachovia Championship a few weeks earlier he had said that he wanted to beat Woods, and thought he could. Woods won, and Sabbatini was thoroughly ridiculed for his audacity.

He explained his big skull-and-wings belt buckle, the one he wore at the Wachovia Championship. "I got all the jinx off that week," he said, chuckling. So it seemed. Sabbatini wrapped up a third round of 62 on Sunday. At the par-five 11th hole, a great bunker shot left him a tap-in birdie, and he got to 14 under par at the 13th hole with a 28-foot birdie putt. His bid to win in regulation at the 18th died when his 19-foot birdie putt curled off at the last instant.

In the playoff at the 18th, all three were on the green in two strokes. Furyk, putting first, missed from 34 feet. Next, Sabbatini knocked in his 15-footer. Then Langer missed from eight feet.

The storms sent the rounds tumbling one into the other, but they weren't without their interesting moments:

First round: Anthony Kim had quite a talk with himself. "Probably stuff I shouldn't be saying," the 21-year-old rookie said. Whatever he said must have worked. He birdied the last six holes, the longest birdie streak of the season so far, and shot seven-under 63, his lowest as a professional. He finished before another storm forced 57 players, half the field of 114, to finish their round the next day.

Second round: With Tim Clark, it wasn't a personal chat, it was a stiff neck. Nursing himself with anti-inflammatory medicine, he finished the final nine of his first round Friday morning, then shot a bogey-free 64 in the second round for an 11-under 129 total. He made 11 birdies and only one bogey in his 27 holes Friday. Darkness stranded 27 players.

Third round: Scott Verplank, the EDS Byron Nelson winner, had the chance to become the first since Ben Hogan in 1946 to win the Nelson and the Colonial in the same year. Verplank made five birdies in 13 holes Saturday before rain stopped play. At the 14th, unwilling to drop in the rough, he opted to hit from a fairway puddle, caught a greenside bunker, and would have a 10-foot par putt when play resumed. Said Verplank: "I wish we had quit a hole earlier."

But this one was Sabbatini's, and the South African took the opportunity to state his goal without mentioning Tiger Woods. "I told my wife, by the end of the year I'm going to be top 10 in the world rankings," he said. "My goal next year is to probably try to get to No. 1."

Memorial Tournament
Dublin, Ohio
Winner: K.J. Choi

South Korea's mild-mannered K.J. Choi speaks halting English, but he came through soft and clear at the Memorial Tournament: "Thank you, Jack."

This was Choi after plucking the Memorial title and thanking Nicklaus for getting him started in golf — with a book. Back in Choi's school days, a physical education teacher suggested that he pursue a career in professional golf, and he gave the lad a Nicklaus instruction book. And Choi was on his way. He had won four times since joining the PGA Tour full-time in 2000, but was hardly a favorite coming to Nicklaus's Muirfield Village Golf Club in Ohio, not with such as Tiger Woods, Phil Mickelson and Jim Furyk in the field. But Choi brushed past the lot and even broke up an Australian party, and came from the pack in the final round to edge Ryan Moore by one.

The cast of favorites fell on unhappy times. Mickelson withdrew after 11 holes due to the wrist he hurt practicing at Oakmont for the U.S. Open two weeks away. Woods, Furyk, Sergio Garcia, Ernie Els and Vijay Singh were not factors.

There were 11 Australians in the field, taking turns crowding the leaderboard. Rod Pampling and Nick O'Hern shared the first-round lead with American outsider Sean O'Hair at 65. Then Adam Scott torched the soft and agreeable course for a 10-under-par 62 and led Pampling by one stroke and Aussie Aaron Baddeley by two at the halfway point. Pampling re-took the lead with 68 in the third round and led by three over Scott and O'Hair going into the finale. Choi was hardly a candidate to this point. Shooting 69-70-67, he trailed by four, seven and five strokes.

Then in the final round, Choi woke up. At the par-five No. 5, he hit his approach shot into the water, but somehow scratched out a par. Then he reeled off four straight birdies — at No. 6, a 10-foot putt, then two putts from 30 feet at No. 7, a 12-footer at No. 8 and an eight-footer at No. 9 after a sensational seven iron curved around the trees. "A cut shot, Jack-style," Choi said, chuckling.

"It seemed like he was birdieing every hole there for a while," Moore said, "and I thought, what course is he playing?"

Choi was out in 30, and coming home he added two more birdies, took his only bogey of the last 36 holes at the 13th, and scratched out one-putt pars over the last three holes, from seven, 15 and five feet. A 65 gave him a 17-under 271 total and a one-stroke win over Moore (66). Pampling, the best of four Aussies in the top 10, shot 72 and tied for third, two behind Choi.

"I just feel very honored and very happy to be living in the same time as Jack, and to win his tournament is so meaningful to me," Choi said. "I can only think that this was meant to be."

Stanford St. Jude Championship
Memphis, Tennessee
Winner: Woody Austin

Adam Scott, the Australian prodigy-in-waiting, was all set to become a wire-to-wire winner at the Stanford St. Jude Championship, having run off three rounds in the 60s for a tidy three-stroke lead going into the final round at the stubborn TPC Southwind course in Memphis. Then along came free-spirited Woody Austin.

The capricious Austin, always welcome but never tagged "most likely to succeed," broke loose for an eight-under-par 62 and a whopping five-stroke victory over Brian Davis (66) and six strokes over David Toms (69), who hadn't finished worse than 10th at Southwind since 2001.

"That was a true round of golf and was one of those surprises that we all get every once in a while," Austin said. "I'm just happy it happened to me on a Sunday, when it really mattered."

If Austin was a surprise, Scott — ranked No. 4 in the world — was a bigger one. Scott shared the first-round lead and was the solo leader through the next two rounds, shooting 67-66-68. Then, on the par-70 course, he closed with 75 and finished seventh. "I played a lot of good holes this week — 70 good holes and a couple bad ones," Scott said. By which he meant, principally, a tee shot in the water and a three-putt six at the par-three 14th.

But Scott had started well. In the first round, he and Fredrik Jacobson, co-leaders at 67, were two of only seven who broke par on a hot, windy day. Scott had a curious mix — a double bogey, a bogey, four birdies and an eagle.

Austin did not win against a weak field. He won against the tournament's strongest field in years, with six of the top 12 players in the world in it. They had come to sharpen their games in competition for the U.S. Open the following week at Oakmont.

Austin was hardly noticeable along the way with his 72-66-67, trailing by five strokes in the first round, then five and four. There was no hint he had

62 in him. But he was playing some wonderful golf. He made six bogeys in the tournament, but none in the last 49 holes. In his 62, he birdied the second and eagled the third, then had five birdies on the second nine — the 10th, 12th, 14th, 16th and 17th.

Austin's self-help stint paid off in time. This was his first PGA Tour victory since 2004 and his third overall, and at age 43 he was beginning to worry that he was running out of time. So at the Crowne Plaza Invitational two weeks earlier, Austin, a self-taught golfer, took to the practice tee to see if he could solve his swing problems. "I just kept working on the range this week," Austin said, "and it clicked."

U.S. Open Championship
Oakmont, Pennsylvania
Winner: Angel Cabrera

See Chapter 3.

Travelers Championship
Cromwell, Connecticut
Winner: Hunter Mahan

The PGA Tour returned to Hartford, not as the Greater Hartford Open, as it was for some 55 years, but as the Travelers Championship, after a quick and odd schedule shuffle that ended the 84 Lumber Classic. It was also the setting of two silent careers passing at TPC River Highlands, and both came away highly satisfied.

The much celebrated Hunter Mahan, quiet since his outstanding amateur and collegiate careers ended in 2003, opened with a dazzling eight-under-par 62, then dueled the rest of the way with the highly uncelebrated Jay Williamson, a 40-year-old journeyman who had labored on the PGA and Nationwide Tours, then beat him in a playoff.

Mahan opened with 31 on his first nine, then birdied four straight from the 11th and added another at the 17th for the 62 and said the course was comfortable. "There's not really a shot here that I worry about," Mahan said. Williamson was back in the pack with 66, and surfaced in the second round with another 66 to tie for the lead with David Toms (65) at eight-under 132, a stroke up on Mahan (71). Toms bogeyed after a rain delay, but Williamson birdied the 17th and 18th in winds that topped 35 miles an hour. He credited his round to his driving. "You can't play a day like today out of the rough," he said.

Williamson kept the lead in the third round with 67, staying one stroke ahead of Mahan (67), and the duel continued in the fourth round. Mahan made four straight birdies from the 10th and led by two coming down the stretch. Williamson birdied the 15th, and then they were tied again when Mahan bogeyed the par-three 16th. But he bogeyed the 17th and Williamson took the lead with a par. At the 18th, Mahan fired a 144-yard approach to seven feet and holed it for 65 to tie Williamson, who two-putted from

12 feet. They were at 15-under 265, four strokes clear of the field. In the playoff, Mahan lifted his approach from 134 yards to two feet, and Williamson put his to seven feet. Williamson missed, and Mahan tapped in for the win.

Far from being crushed, Williamson was elated with his best finish in 280 PGA Tour starts. "I really feel if I was a great putter, I would have won by a lot," he said. "I know what I need to work on to get to that next level. And I learned that I'm going to be a golfer for a while."

Said Mahan: "After you play out here for a little bit, you realize this is hard."

Buick Open
Grand Blanc, Michigan
Winner: Brian Bateman

Talk about brief conversations and total shock value. It's a wonder Brian Bateman didn't lose his jaw on this one. Bateman, a journeyman professional still stalking his first PGA Tour victory after all these years, insisted that in the hectic final round of the Buick Open, he looked at the leaderboard only once after the ninth hole. It gets better. "I didn't ask my caddie at all how I stood, until I stood in the last fairway and I asked him what we needed," Bateman said. "And he said, 'Birdie to win.'"

Talk about the old lump in the throat. Bateman had never been in this predicament before. At age 34, six years on the tour and 150 starts without a win, this was hardly something he might want to hear. But Bateman braced himself in the fairway and delivered an approach to 12 feet at the 18th green. Then came the crucial putt. "It seemed like it took forever to get to the hole," Bateman said. "Then I just went blank and threw my hands up and said, 'Man, I finally did it.'"

And so he had. That closing birdie gave Bateman cards of 65-70-69-69 for a 273 total, 15 under par at Warwick Hills in Grand Blanc, Michigan. He won by a shot over Jason Gore (67), Justin Leonard (67) and Woody Austin (69). And he survived a huge chase in the process. Fifteen players finished within three stroke of him.

Bateman was the fourth to score his first tour win in the Buick Open, following Austin (1995), Justin Leonard (1996) and Tom Pernice (1999), and he was the eighth first-time winner of 2007.

Rocco Mediate, with new-found relief for his various hip and back problems, opened with 64 and a one-stroke lead, and announced, "I'm ecstatic." He was speaking of his physical condition. "The last three years, I was dead," he said. Bateman was a stroke behind.

Brett Quigley squandered a chance at the lead in the second round when he tried "to force the issue" from a bad lie at the 13th and settled for 69 and a share of the halfway lead with Jim Furyk (68) and Kenny Perry (63). Then it was Tom Pernice in the third round, running off an eagle at the 13th followed by four straight birdies for 66 and a one-stroke lead. The outburst took him by surprise. "The way I was going along," Pernice said, "I never dreamed I would get to six under."

The ever-changing face of the Buick Open would change one final time. Up stepped Bateman, to the 12-footer at the final hole.

"Every player, from Tiger Woods to Brian Bateman," he said, "has to win their first one." And so he did.

AT&T National
Bethesda, Maryland
Winner: K.J. Choi

K.J. Choi, the greatest South Korean golfer, speaks mostly through an interpreter. But the message at the AT&T National was clear: The trophy he had just accepted from Tiger Woods was heavier than the one handed to him by Jack Nicklaus just five weeks earlier at the Memorial Tournament.

The solemn-faced Choi rarely cracks a smile, but he was wearing a huge grin when Woods, host at his inaugural AT&T National at Congressional Country Club near Washington, D.C., handed him a silver-colored model of the U.S. Capitol and said, "Here's your trophy, big guy." Just five weeks earlier, Nicklaus had presented him with a crystal trophy, as the Memorial champion.

Woods, however, was not a factor in his own tournament, and was stung by his putter. In the first round alone he had three three-putts and needed 34 putts overall. He lifted his putter. "I'm about ready to break this thing," he said. He shot 73-66-69-70—278 and tied for sixth place.

Choi, tied for the lead through the first two rounds, trailed by two through the third round, then swept through the fourth for a three-stroke win over Steve Stricker. But first Choi got a huge gift. Stuart Appleby, leading by two over Choi going into the final round, crashed horribly on the first nine. He lost six shots over the first seven holes. His troubles started at the par-three No. 2, where he put his tee shot over the green and two-putted from four feet for a double bogey. That led to 40 on the first nine, a six-over 76 and a tie for third.

But Choi's win didn't come without its "iffy" moments. He suffered three bogeys early on the second nine, but stopped the fall with a birdie at the 12th, sinking a 15-foot putt for a two-stroke lead. Then he holed a bunker shot at the 17th that triggered an outburst of emotion. He threw the ball into the gallery.

Stricker, meanwhile, was frustrated by the bumpy greens, having putts roll away. "You end up just tapping it down there," he said, "and it goes any which way it wants." He had three bogeys on the back nine and shot 70.

Other challengers also stumbled on the back. Jim Furyk had two bogeys after the turn and shot 69, and Mike Weir (74) made three straight bogeys. And so Choi was home free. "It's never looking back, don't look back, just move forward like a tank," Choi said. "It's how I felt when I first came over to the U.S., starting out."

John Deere Classic
Silvis, Illinois
Winner: Jonathan Byrd

The John Deere Classic, in Silvis, Illinois, was a kind of homecoming for Zach Johnson, who grew up in Cedar Rapids, Iowa, just over an hour away. He became a hero to the region when he won the Masters in April. And now, in July at the John Deere Classic, he was the hero come home to conquer the local tournament. But golf doesn't work that easily, and Johnson missed the cut. "I don't have the feel," he said simply.

Johnson, ranked 15th in the world, was the only top-45 player in the tournament, and with his departure, everything was up for grabs.

It was Jonathan Byrd who grabbed last and grabbed best. But he had come to the tournament with one eye on occult forces. He had deliberately left his passport at home. He knew, of course, that if he were to win, it would qualify him for the Open Championship the following week. He wanted that very badly, but he didn't want to tempt the fates by seeming presumptuous enough to bring the passport.

"I haven't been playing well," he said, "and maybe I thought that it would be a jinx or something." In addition, drawing on his recent performances, he had little reason to be confident. Byrd had won twice on the PGA Tour, the last in 2004, but on his way to the John Deere Classic, he missed four straight cuts.

At least he made the cut this time, shooting 67-69—135, but he was back in the pack, trailing Neal Lancaster by three in the first round and Nathan Green by five in the second round. Byrd got on the leaderboard in the third round with a 65 that put him two behind Green. Then Tim Clark, the ever-present South African, stormed into the lead with four birdies on the first nine holes of the final round. He was 18 under par and leading by three. Then it became a Byrd-Clark duel.

Byrd almost put himself out at the 14th hole when he hit his tee shot wide to the right. But he recovered and birdied the hole, and he was on his way. He birdied the 16th and 17th, and went up by one when Clark bogeyed the 17th from a plugged lie in the bunker. Byrd parred the 18th for 66, leaving Clark to birdie to tie him. But Clark didn't, and Byrd had his third victory, a one-stroke win on a 266 total, 18 under par.

So once Byrd had completed the presentation formalities, he had one more important piece of business: To get home to Georgia, pull out that passport and book a flight to Scotland. "I haven't played in the British Open," Byrd said, "and every time I watch it on TV, I just can't wait to get over there."

The Open Championship
Carnoustie, Scotland
Winner: Padraig Harrington

See Chapter 4.

U.S. Bank Championship in Milwaukee
Milwaukee, Wisconsin
Winner: Joe Ogilvie

The topic du jour at the 19th hole was which is the bigger win, the U.S. Bank Championship in Milwaukee or the Open Championship at Carnoustie? To paraphrase Joe Ogilvie, the PGA Tour's resident stock market guru, the answer is: The size of the victory is in the eye of the beholder.

"If Tiger Woods wins the British Open and I win the U.S. Bank Championship, I certainly think it would be a bigger win for me than for him," Ogilvie said. "Your first win is your first major." This was Ogilvie speaking after taking a two-stroke lead in the second round. Two days later, while Padraig Harrington was winning his first major at the Open Championship, Ogilvie was winning his first major — and his career-first victory after 230 starts — at the U.S. Bank Championship. Ogilvie, age 33, had made seven straight cuts, but with lukewarm golf after the halfway point, he hadn't touched a top-10 finish. He chalked up this one on cards of 67-63-69-67 for a 14-under 266 total at the par-70 Brown Deer Park, winning by four strokes over Charlie Wi (68), Tim Herron (72) and Tim Clark (71).

Ogilvie trailed by four strokes in the first round and led by two through the second round after birdieing three of the last four holes for 63. And he acknowledged that he hadn't "played great since I've made the cut." So now, how would he do after this cut? Well, in the third round, after two bogeys on the first nine, he bounced back with an eagle at the 15th and a birdie at the 16th, getting back to 11 under, tied with Clark a stroke off Herron's lead.

Ogilvie, Herron and Clark battled it out through the fourth round, and Wi joined in for good measure. Ogilvie fell two behind with a bogey at the 10th, but birdied the 13th hole from 24 feet. Clark wasted his two-stroke lead with bogeys at the 10th and 16th. Then came Ogilvie's lightning at the par-four 16th. His wedge shot from 119 yards over water hit about 30 feet past the pin, then spun all the way back and dropped for an eagle. He added a birdie at the 18th for the 67 and that first victory.

Ironically, Ogilvie was scoring his first win at the time when his son Patrick, age 10 months, was taking his first steps. Said Ogilvie: "I think maybe Dad took his first steps to maybe a little bit bigger and better things."

Canadian Open
Markham, Ontario, Canada
Winner: Jim Furyk

It's not often — and perhaps not statistically defensible — that you could point to one hole and say that's where a golf tournament was decided. But there was an interesting temptation in the Canadian Open. The hole was the 209-yard, par-three No. 4 at the Angus Glen Golf Club at Markham, Ontario. Jim Furyk played the hole in three birdies and a hole-in-one — a total of seven strokes, five under par. Vijay Singh, on the other hand, played it in three bogeys and a par — 15 strokes, three over.

Furyk won this Canadian Open, his first victory since he won it in 2006, and Singh finished second by a stroke. It was pretty clear where Singh lost the tournament. "Eight strokes — that's a huge turnaround on one hole," said Furyk. But Furyk had to sweat this one out. He had already wrapped up a seven-under-par 64 that included the ace for a 16-under 268 total. Singh (68) needed a birdie at the final hole to tie him, but his 20-footer ran five feet past the cup, leaving Furyk the first to repeat in the Canadian Open since Jim Ferrier in 1951.

Furyk started the first round seven strokes behind leader Hunter Mahan, who shot a 62 that included a remarkable three eagles — a 10-foot putt at the par-five 11th (his second hole) and hole-outs at two par-fours, a six iron from 189 yards at his ninth and a wedge from 81 yards at his 18th. Furyk's 66 in the second round brought him to within three of Steve Allan (68) and John Mallinger (66), tied at 132. The final round became a duel between the only two top-10 players in the field. Furyk was still three off the lead, but the man in front of him now was Singh (68–201).

Furyk barged his way into the lead abruptly. He birdied the par-five No. 1 from 35 feet, birdied the par-four No. 3, then aced the 209-yard No. 4 with a five-iron tee shot that carried a big bunker, hit in the fringe 30 feet short and rolled into the cup. "You dream of a start like that," Furyk said. He parred the next five holes, then birdied three straight from the 10th on a five-footer, two putts from 30 feet and an eight-footer, for a three-shot lead. But he wasn't home free. Then came the suspense at the par-four 18th. Furyk, leading by two, three-putted for a bogey and his 64. Singh, playing two groups behind, hit his 165-yard approach to 20 feet past the flag, and two-putted for 68 and second place.

"I've had a lot of close calls and a lot of ones that stung and a lot of ones that hurt," Furyk said. "But it makes getting over the hump and winning a tournament like today that much more special."

WGC - Bridgestone Invitational
Akron, Ohio
Winner: Tiger Woods

Really, this is getting a little silly. Tiger Woods won at Firestone again, taking the WGC - Bridgestone Invitational in a walk. Actually, he turned it into a carnival, a shambles, a charade. Competition it was for about three rounds, perhaps, and then competition it wasn't. It was another chapter of Golf Monopoly. To reduce it to the absurd minimum, Woods trailed by one stroke going into the final round and won by eight strokes. "This," Woods said, "might just give me a little more confidence."

It was hard to tell what he might mean by that. Woods has had a variety of problems over the years, if in small measure, but a shortage of confidence never seemed to be one of them.

This was also another chapter in the Rory Sabbatini-Tiger Woods soap opera, a tale that began at the Wachovia Championship in May when Sabbatini (to condense things) said that he could beat Woods. He didn't, of course. Then here it came again. Sabbatini was leading Woods by a stroke going into the final round at Firestone. It was over before they reached the turn.

This was Woods's sixth win in nine Bridgestone (and NEC before that) tournaments at Firestone.

Sabbatini's game began to unravel early. At the par-five No. 2, Firestone's easiest hole, he had to play up the No. 3 fairway to save par. He had to save par again at No. 3 after having to lay up short of the fronting pond. Then real trouble hit at the par-four No. 4. He drove into deep rough, failed to get back to the fairway, then failed to clear a bunker, and bogeyed. Woods, playing alongside, holed an 18-foot putt for birdie, and the two-shot swing gave him the outright lead. Woods picked up five shots in a five-hole stretch, and he refused to let up. "I played so hard all day, and the whole idea was not to drop a shot, put the heat on the guys ... for them to come and get me," Woods said.

Woods showed what he meant at the par-four ninth hole. He was wild. He hooked his tee shot into the rough at the 10th fairway. He tried to slice his approach around some trees, caught a branch, and his ball ended up in the crook of a spectator's arm. After a free drop, he pitched over the green, and then chipped in for par.

Sabbatini, on the other hand, took five to reach the green and double-bogeyed. As he headed for the 10th tee, a spectator said, "Hey Rory — still think Tiger is beatable?" Sabbatini summoned a security officer and had the fan removed. It was a low point for Sabbatini, and more so for the PGA Tour, for having a spectator ejected for that. Up ahead of them, Justin Rose had taken some hope. He had made four birdies through eight holes and thought he had a chance. Then he saw a leaderboard. "I thought, 'Oh, well, we're playing for second.'" And so they were.

Woods rolled from there and shot 68-70-69-65 for a 272 total, eight under par, and won by eight over Sabbatini (74) and Justin Rose (68). "This one felt good," Woods said.

Reno-Tahoe Open
Reno, Nevada
Winner: Steve Flesch

It was about 2,000 miles and $5 million from Reno to Akron, as the golf ball flies. But Steve Flesch, frustrated 40-year-old journeyman, couldn't have cared less that the world's top 84 players were at the $8 million WGC - Bridgestone Invitational, at Firestone in Akron, Ohio, while he and all the rest were at the $3 million Reno-Tahoe Open at Montreux Golf and Country Club in Reno, Nevada, that first week of August.

"It really doesn't matter to me," Flesch said. "I haven't won in a couple of years, so that's all I'm concentrating on." Indeed, he was. Two rounds later, he completed a wire-to-wire victory, taking the Reno-Tahoe Open by five strokes. It was his third win on the PGA Tour and his first in two years, and if anyone was happier, it was his eight-year-old son Griffin. Flesch had missed a cut a little while earlier, and Griffin looked at his scorecard and said, "Dad, you're really not playing very well, are you?"

The first round was the toughest for Flesch. He got two eagles, on an 18-foot putt at No. 4 and a 10-footer at No. 11. Add five birdies and no bogeys and he had a nine-under-par 63 to lead by one over Argentina's Jose Coceres. But he had to share the spotlight with Tadd Fujikawa, the 16-year-old Hawaiian prodigy making his professional debut after the big stir he created in the Sony Open in January. This result was different — a six-over 78. (He would miss the cut with 71 the next day.)

The winds came up in the second round and cost Flesch a double bogey, but he logged six birdies for 69, a 132 total and a two-stroke lead on Charles Warren (69). Then he all but wrapped up the Reno title in the third round with 69 that carried him to a five-stroke lead at 201. Accuracy did it. Despite the wind, he led the tournament in greens hit in regulation through the first three rounds, hitting 44 out of 54, an 81.48 percent average.

The winds were gusting to 30 miles an hour in the final round, giving Flesch a big edge if he could keep his head. And this he did, and he produced an unchallenged three-birdie, three-bogey 72 for a 15-under 273 total and a five-stroke win over Warren (71) and Kevin Stadler (70). He had two bogeys in a first-nine 37. He bogeyed the 10th out of a bunker, then birdied two par-fives — the 11th on a 95-yard approach to tap-in range, and at the 636-yard 17th he hit a wind-aided drive of 364 yards, then bunkered his approach, came out to 28 feet and holed it.

The win paid off big for Flesch — the $540,000 first prize, a two-year exemption on the PGA Tour and a berth in the Mercedes Championship in Maui next January. And then there's his son. Said Flesch: "Griffin, that's all he keeps saying — when are we going to go back to Hawaii?" Now Flesch can answer that question, too.

PGA Championship
Tulsa, Oklahoma
Winner: Tiger Woods

See Chapter 5.

Wyndham Championship
Greensboro, North Carolina
Winner: Brandt Snedeker

This is one party Brandt Snedeker wasn't about to miss. This was the Wyndham Championship in mid-August, the week before the start of the FedExCup Playoffs and the final chance to stack up points. For some reason, a bunch of players didn't come, and this didn't bother Snedeker.

Snedeker, a PGA Tour rookie, had come to the tournament in Greensboro, North Carolina, with two goals in mind: One, getting his first PGA Tour victory, and two, on the graduated FedExCup scale, cracking the top 15 leaders in points.

"Everything the Tour has been telling us — you have a legitimate chance to win the FedExCup, (but) you've got to be in the top 15," Snedeker said.

"That's why I came here." But even Snedeker was surprised at how hard it was to get those ambitions to blossom. How about the final two holes?

Snedeker wasn't a prime candidate for success from the start. In the first round, when 64 of the 86 who would finish shot in the 60s, Snedeker opened with a lackluster two-under 70. He was six shots behind the leader, the free-spirited Will MacKenzie (64). A 67 in the second round left Snedeker five behind Jeff Overton (67), John Huston (66) and Steve Marino (67). And in the third round, as though some movie director were setting the stage for the rousing finish, Snedeker (66) was five behind Overton, whose 66 included seven birdies in an 11-hole stretch.

It was in the fourth round that Snedeker's immediate future took shape. First, playing a half-hour ahead of the leaders, he broke free of a pile-up of six players who either led or shared the lead coming down the stretch. Snedeker had started five shots off the lead and bolted into the race with a six-under-par 30 on the front nine, with birdies at Nos. 1, 2, 5, 6, 7 and 9. He bogeyed the 12th and birdied the next three, setting up the dramatic finish.

Tim Petrovic, playing two groups behind, was tied with Snedeker at 21 under par coming to the last two holes. Snedeker, playing first at the 235-yard, par-three 17th, slashed a three iron to 32 feet. "Under the circumstances, probably the best shot of my life," he said. He got his 10th birdie, and a par at the 18th gave him 63 and a 22-under 266 total. Petrovic was still a threat. But at the 17th, he put his tee shot 70 feet from the pin and two-putted for par, then bogeyed the 18th for 67 and slipped into a tie at 268 with Overton (70) and Billy Mayfair (67).

"A guy shoots 63, you've got to take your hat off to him," Petrovic said. "He won it, I didn't lose it."

PGA Tour Playoffs for the FedExCup

The Barclays
Harrison, New York
Winner: Steve Stricker

All those hours of hitting balls from a remodeled trailer out onto a frozen driving range in wintry Wisconsin finally paid off. Steve Stricker, after all those frustrating and barren years, pulled his slipping game back together to win The Barclays, the first of the new PGA Tour Playoffs for the FedExCup.

"I've been waiting for this day for a long time," a tearful Stricker said. To be precise, six years and 146 tournaments. Stricker, who won twice in 1996, last won in the 2001 WGC - Accenture Match Play Championship in Australia, which explained his emotions. Stricker, voted the Comeback Player of the Year in 2006, was having an encouraging but frustrating 2007. His record included four close calls, which were rewarding but which also fell short of victory. And now it seemed he might have a fifth in The Barclays. Coming down the final stretch, he was in a group of 10 players — five of them winners of majors — all within three strokes.

It seemed like the old Stricker for a while in the final round. He bogeyed the second hole, birdied the seventh, then bogeyed the 10th and 13th. But he wasn't discouraged. "I thought I was hitting well enough to maybe make a few birdies coming in," Stricker said, then added with a grin, "Obviously, not four out of the last five holes. But I tried to stay positive and upbeat, just waiting for my time."

And Stricker's time came, dramatically enough, down the homestretch. He birdied the 14th, parred the 15th, and birdied the last three holes for a two-under-par 69 that pulled him from a stroke behind to a two-stroke victory over K.J. Choi. Stricker finished with 268, 16 under par at Westchester Country Club in New York, and took the FedExCup lead, 2,050 points ahead of Choi (70). Rory Sabbatini birdied the last hole for 68 and finished third.

Of the top stars, Phil Mickelson tied for seventh and Tiger Woods opted not to play.

Choi gave Stricker some anxious moments with a bit of uncanny putting. Choi holed a 45-footer for birdie at the 12th and a 50-footer for another at the 15th. Stricker regained a share of the lead with his 12-foot birdie at the par-three 16th, then wedged to four feet for a birdie at the 17th.

"It was hard, but it was fun," Stricker said. "I never knew if I was going to win again." Stricker had come a long way. After his two wins in 1996, his game mysteriously began unraveling. He lost his PGA Tour playing card in 2005.

The playoffs are a series of three tournaments providing points leading up to the final field for The Tour Championship and its $10 million deferred bonus prize. The field was reduced to 120 for the next stop, the Deutsche Bank Championship the following week.

Deutsche Bank Championship
Norton, Massachusetts
Winner: Phil Mickelson

This was the Labor Day Weekend, and fittingly, the Deutsche Bank Championship was a labor of love for Phil Mickelson. "For 10 years I've struggled against Tiger," Mickelson said. "This sure feels great, to go head-to-head … and over the last five or six holes, when he's making a run, it was fun to match him with birdies." Mickelson beat Woods down the final round — even with a needless double bogey in the stretch — closing with a five-under-par 66 and a 16-under 268 total to win by two strokes. Woods shot 67, tying for second with Arron Oberholser (69) and Brett Wetterich (70).

Woods missed a variety of chances to close in on Mickelson. All told, he had four cracks at eagles and could only pick up three strokes. At the par-five second hole, he missed an eagle putt from 15 feet and settled for birdie, and Mickelson matched him off an elegant pitch. At the 298-yard par-four No. 4, Woods drove the green but three-putted from 65 feet for par while Mickelson birdied from 15 feet. Then Mickelson stretched his lead to three with a birdie at No. 5. At the par-five No. 7, Woods missed the eagle and birdied, and Mickelson matched him off a bunker shot to six feet.

Mickelson made one big error that could have been nearly fatal. He came to the par-three 12th leading by three over Oberholser and by five over Woods. Despite these comfortable margins, he was unable to resist the tough and tempting pin, and went for it. His tee shot fell short, into the hazard. He chipped up to within five feet of the cup, but missed the putt and made a double-bogey five. Woods had a great chance for a three-stroke swing, but he missed his 15-footer for birdie. That was two straight chances Woods let slip. Moments earlier, at the 11th, he missed a birdie from eight feet.

Wetterich began the final round leading by a stroke but went lukewarm and didn't post a birdie until the 16th. He also birdied the 18th and picked up enough points to climb 29 spots to No. 22. This put him in with a good chance to get into the field for The Tour Championship. Oberholser saw his chance to win fizzle when he missed a possible eagle on the last hole. He stayed within a stroke of Mickelson for most of the back nine and needed an eagle at the 18th to force a playoff. He missed the eagle, then missed a 10-footer for birdie.

The victory, in early September, was Mickelson's first since The Players Championship in May. He seemed primed to make a good run at Woods, but got sidetracked by injury. Getting in some advance practice for the U.S. Open, he hurt his wrist hitting shots out of deep rough at Oakmont. What seemed at first like a simple injury bothered him for most of the summer. It was only just before the playoffs that Mickelson could swing without obvious pain.

BMW Championship
Lemont, Illinois
Winner: Tiger Woods

Tiger Woods skipped the first of the PGA Tour Playoffs for the FedExCup, tied for second in the second, then rewrote the record book to win the third, the BMW Championship at Cog Hill, near Chicago. This was his fourth victory there, but it didn't come easy.

This one might have gotten away. Woods started hot in the final round and birdied three straight from No. 7 for an outward 31. Meantime, Steve Stricker and Aaron Baddeley were just waiting around. The battle between them got hotter. Stricker birdied Nos. 7, 8, 9 and 10, getting to 19 under par and leading Baddeley by one stroke. But Baddeley tied him instantly at the 11th, flying a long bunker shot to six feet and making birdie.

At the same time, Woods, in the group just ahead, was laboring. At the 10th, he had to work just for a par, and at the par-five 11th, uncharacteristically, he ran a chip shot 15 feet from the flag and had to settle for par. He came to the tee at the par-three 12th and things weren't getting any better.

He put his tee shot fully 50 feet from the cup. And just when things were starting to look gloomy, they brightened. Woods ran in that 50-footer for a birdie and tied for the lead with Stricker and Baddeley. Humming now, Woods birdied the 13th from 20 feet and also birdied the 15th and 16th, and when Baddeley couldn't cash in an eagle from 20 feet at the 15th, Woods was just about home.

Woods finished with eight-under 63, and his 22-under 262 total broke his own course record by five strokes. He won by two over Baddeley (66) and four over Stricker (68). It was the fourth time in 2007 that Woods came from behind in the final round to win. He was sitting pretty in the chase for the FedExCup, the tournament within a tournament. The win gave him a commanding 3,133-point FedExCup lead over Stricker. He also led by 4,120 points over Mickelson, who sat out the BMW.

Mickelson, the winner of the previous week's Deutsche Bank Championship, would have to win The Tour Championship in order to win the FedExCup and its deferred $10 million bonus as well. If Stricker didn't win The Tour Championship, Woods could win the FedExCup by finishing second. Rory Sabbatini and K.J. Choi were the only others with a mathematical chance of winning the FedExCup.

The BMW Championship completed the field of 30 for The Tour Championship the following week. Stewart Cink, Tim Clark and Camilo Villegas finished in the top 10 and won enough points to make the field. Padraig Harrington took the 30th and last spot, but Luke Donald couldn't recover from his opening 76, despite 65 in the final round, and just missed.

Woods knew what the difference was here. He needed just 25 putts, and it was a revelation. "That's what's been missing all week," he said. "Today, I finally felt comfortable."

The Tour Championship
Atlanta, Georgia
Winner: Tiger Woods

"I hit it good this week," Tiger Woods was saying. "It's been a phenomenal week."

This was Woods's statement right after he won the season-ending Tour Championship and its $1.26 million first prize plus the PGA Tour Playoffs for the FedExCup and its $10 million deferred bonus. With 29 other top point leaders in the FedExCup standings in the field, Woods ran off and hid by eight strokes from Zach Johnson and Mark Calcavecchia. Thus there were two things wrong with Woods's statement. First, he didn't hit it "good." He hit it a lot better than good. And second, it wasn't just a phenomenal week. It was more phenomenal than that.

Which is to say that in the rich season climax at East Lake Golf Club at Atlanta, those were Woods's only real errors. It was Woods's seventh victory in 16 PGA Tour starts this season. That's a .438 success rate. In baseball, that's a stunning batting average. In golf, it's absurd.

Woods played the par-70 course in 64-63-64-66 for a 257 total, 23 under par, but he did not win wire-to-wire. In the weather-interrupted first round,

Tim Clark, the diminutive South African, tied the course record with 62 and was one of only 10 players to finish. He led by one over Padraig Harrington. Woods finished his first round the next day with 64. It was the last time he would trail.

Woods reduced the tournament to a picking-over of statistics. He tied for first in putting, needing only an average of 27 per round. He tied for first in hitting greens in regulation, 58. He missed only five of 68 putts from 10 feet or less. The 257 total was his best, and he tied his career-best of 28 birdies.

To keep things in perspective, it should be noted that East Lake was especially vulnerable after record heat nearly killed the greens, and desperate efforts to save them left the surfaces slow and bumpy, and reduced the number of pin placements. The result was generally lower scores. From the 30 players, there were 20 rounds ranging from 60 through 65. Only three players failed to break the total par of 280 — Charles Howell at 281, and Brandt Snedeker and Brett Wetterich at 282.

It can be argued that Woods's only real misplay of the tournament came at the par-five No. 9 in the fourth round, when — thinking he couldn't reach — he opted to hit a five wood out of the rough from 286 yards. The ball went through the green as Sergio Garcia and Zach Johnson were putting. Woods apologized, and he also birdied the hole.

The only real suspense came in the third round, when Zach Johnson, the Masters champion, was at the 223-yard, par-three 18th needing a birdie for 59. "My hands were shaking and my heart was pounding," he said. He bunkered his two-iron tee shot, then nearly holed his bunker shot, and tapped in for a 10-under 60. But there went the 59. "It would have been awesome," Johnson said.

Too late, anyway. Tiger Woods already had awesome all wrapped up.

PGA Tour Fall Series

Turning Stone Resort Championship
Verona, New York
Winner: Steve Flesch

Steve Flesch was sounding more like an America's Cup skipper than a golfer. "I'll be aggressive when I can," Flesch was saying. "Depends on the wind. The conditions are going to dictate how aggressively we're going to play."

But this wasn't the high seas. This was the Atunyote Golf Club in Verona, New York, where Flesch was the best at weathering the brisk September winds and won the inaugural Turning Stone Resort Championship. It was Flesch's second win of the season, just under two months after he took the Reno-Tahoe Open, and his fourth career victory.

Flesch handled the breezes all week long and was superb in the third round. "My iron game has been good, so I don't expect to change," Flesch said. "You know, it boils down to putting — hopefully to make some birdies early on, then relax a bit." Which is not to say complacent, of course.

Case in point: In the third round, he birdied No. 2 on a 17-foot putt. He birdied No. 5, chipping stiff. And he birdied the par-three No. 6 with a tee shot to seven feet. Then, even with Carl Pettersson tying for the lead briefly with back-to-back birdies, and with the field battling the stiffening winds, Flesch birdied four of the last five holes — the 18th with a 20-foot downhill putt — to run up a four-stroke lead with 66.

"I've always said my iron game is the strength of my game," Flesch said. "And when you give us generous fairways like these, I usually find the pins with my irons." Case in point: Over the first 36 holes, he hit 34 greens in regulation. "And if I can get that putter going, I'll make some birdies," he said. And he did.

Flesch was his own worst enemy early in the final round, when he threatened to blow a four-shot lead. He was especially clumsy at the first hole. He drove into a fairway bunker, came out 40 yards short of the green and, despite a perfect lie, he dumped his third into a greenside bunker, came out to 40 feet and two-putted for a bogey-five. At No. 2, he turned a perfect drive into another bogey when he hit his second shot over the green and into the rough and chipped too strong.

Then came some good news. At the par-three No. 3, Flesch hit his tee shot to four feet and birdied. At No. 4, Flesch hit out of a fairway bunker to nine feet and birdied, while Pettersson hooked his shot and bogeyed. And at the par-five No. 5, Pettersson hooked a fairway wood into deep rough and had to take a penalty drop. Flesch was so at ease that he ran off seven pars from No. 9 and even bogeyed two of his last three holes. He shot 73, an 18-under 270 total, and won by two over Michael Allen (68), while Pettersson (73) dropped to a tie for fifth.

The Presidents Cup
Ile Bizard, Montreal, Quebec, Canada
Winner: United States

The Presidents Cup was just another walk in the park for captain Jack Nicklaus's United States team, 19½ points to 14½ over Gary Player's Internationals, but it was a dip in the lake for Woody Austin — literally — and a complete transformation. He stumbled and went face down into a water hazard and emerged a hero.

Austin, age 43 and a rookie in team play, was best known as the nervous, high-strung guy who once punished his putter by banging the shaft on his head until it bent. And so he was a questionable commodity when he made the team. Then a storybook finish. Austin won once and halved three times in team matches, and lost in the singles to U.S. Open champion Angel Cabrera for a 1-1-3 record, and became a kind of rallying point for the team at they upped the U.S. edge to 5-1-1 in the series. Austin took his plunge in the Day 2 better ball at Royal Montreal's 14th hole, where he lost his footing while trying to hit out of a greenside lake.

"By the time I got my head out of the water, I was laughing," Austin said. "That's when I realized I was an idiot. I've always been a crazy guy and this just adds to my legacy."

Austin became everybody's instant hero for taking televised humiliation with such good nature. He and David Toms went on to finish with three birdies for a halve against South Africa's Trevor Immelman and Rory Sabbatini, stalling a run by the Internationals.

The odd thing about this Presidents Cup was that the U.S. team went 10½ to 1½ in alternate-shot matches, raising their performance to 31½ to 11½ in the last four President Cups, while many of the same players were about the reverse when playing in the Ryder Cup. Nicklaus had the explanation: "The game of golf is so strange," he said. "You never know."

While Austin provided the comic-heroic relief, Mike Weir was all hero to his fellow Canadians, beating Tiger Woods, 1 up, in the singles on Sunday. "He had the weight of an entire country on his shoulders," said Woods, who had a 3-2 record. "Not many players can go out and play as well as he did with all the things that were expected of him." Weir did more than beat Woods. Pairing with Vijay Singh and Ernie Els twice each in team play, he was the star of the Internationals with a 3-1-1 record. Els was the next closest at 3-2. "When I look back later in my career, it might be more special than the Masters," Weir said.

The Internationals needed to win 10 of the 12 singles, won seven, but suffered two surprisingly decisive defeats. Phil Mickelson walloped Vijay Singh, 5 and 4, and Stewart Cink thumped Nick O'Hern, 6 and 4. The U.S. was led by David Toms, the top point earner with a 4-0-1 record. Scott Verplank came from behind with two late birdies to beat Sabbatini in singles for a 4-0 record. They were the only unbeaten players on either team.

Viking Classic
Madison, Mississippi
Winner: Chad Campbell

The numbers didn't fit the name. This was Chad Campbell, acclaimed for years as a major talent waiting to happen. He'd had a win a year for three years, but he had slipped into a slump in 2007. Coming into the Viking Classic late in September, he'd had just one top-10 finish, a fourth place and four top-25s — hardly the work of a top performer. Sometimes it's just a matter of a man meeting the right circumstances at the right time, and so it was for Campbell in the Viking at Annadale Golf Club in Madison, Mississippi.

Campbell moved up the scoreboard on three solid rounds of 70-72-64, trailing by seven, eight and then three strokes. Then opportunity arrived. David Branshaw, who led through the second and third rounds, was bumped out of the way by a double bogey at the par-five No. 7. Campbell worked his way from there to a three-under 69 and a one-stroke win over PGA Tour rookie Johnson Wagner. The win didn't answer all of Campbell's questions, but it quieted them.

"I don't know what I got into doing," Campbell said. "I just wanted to get back into what I was doing well — whatever it was." He had run the gamut of taking advice from all comers. But, of course, nothing worked.

Whatever suddenly went right, Campbell leaped into the lead in the final round with two quick birdies after the turn. At the 10th, he dropped a 22-foot putt, and at the par-five 11th, he fired his approach to three feet and dropped the putt to get to 13 under. Another birdie at the 17th got him to 14 under, but he bogeyed the 18th for the 69 and his 13-under 275 total and the one-shot win.

Wagner, a former Nationwide Tour standout seeking his first win, led briefly but bogeyed the 17th. A birdie at the 18th got him to 12 under, a stroke off, and he wasn't quite as disappointed as he might have been. Earlier, he had gone through a tough stretch. He missed 13 cuts in 14 starts. Then starting early in August, he made five straight and had four top-20 finishes. "I finally started believing that I deserve to be out here, and I'm playing like it, so it's nice."

Campbell, too, knew the downside. He said he'd sunk so low that even a clubhouse worker at one tournament wished him luck. And now came the win. "I think it's the first step," Campbell said. "There's still a lot of work to do."

Valero Texas Open
San Antonio, Texas
Winner: Justin Leonard

Jesper Parnevik, so cold for the past six years, was running hot in the Valero Texas Open. He had started with a sizzling 61, then added 65 and 66, and going into the final round, he was leading by three over fellow Swede Mathias Gronberg and by four over native Texan Justin Leonard. Asked to consider his chances, Leonard paused a moment, then delivered his verdict. "His lead," Leonard said, "is not insurmountable."

Of course, everyone could concede that mathematical point to anyone in any tournament, but this message had the heavy weight of experience behind it. Leonard knew what he was talking about. He could recall the 1997 Open at Troon, when Parnevik was leading him by five strokes going into the final round. Leonard won.

Leonard won this one, too, dropping a 10-foot birdie putt on the third playoff hole. That made him the first three-time winner of the Texas Open since Arnold Palmer in 1960-62. It was Leonard's 11th PGA Tour victory and his first since 2005. And it had to be especially bitter stuff for Parnevik. Now age 42, and winless for six years, he had shot four rounds in the 60s (61-65-66-69) and it still wasn't enough to win. But it wasn't totally painful. "It's tough to get into position to win," Parnevik said. "But I'm happy I got to feel it again. It had been awhile."

Parnevik had struck fast with that opening 61 — his career-low — nine under par at the LaCantera golf course in San Antonio. He led by four over a crowd at 65, including Leonard. Then Parnevik added 65-66, and Leonard stuck close with 67-64. Then a crack appeared in Parnevik's game in the fourth round. He started getting wild off the tee. In fact, he hit only six fairways and made three bogeys, and only some superb recoveries kept the damage that low.

At the 15th hole, Parnevik pulled his tee shot into the trees on the left, but from 165 yards found an opening and put his next on the green, 16 feet from the pin, and birdied. Not so at the 16th. He was wide again and had to hit a provisional, which hit a spectator on the head. Then he found his first ball and punched it out and eventually bogeyed. He saved himself from defeat in regulation with a birdie at the par-three 17th off a seven iron to three feet. Leonard missed a win in regulation when his 14-foot birdie putt at the 18th slid by the cup, and he finished with 65-67-64-65, tying Parnevik at 19-under 261.

On the first extra hole, Parnevik made a spectacular save. He had to take a penalty drop from an unplayable tee shot, then hit a 153-yard approach to three feet. Leonard got up-and-down after missing the green. Both parred the second, and on the third, both were putting for birdie. Parnevik missed from 28 feet, but Leonard didn't from 10.

Frys.com Open
Las Vegas, Nevada
Winner: George McNeill

Inspiration can come from anywhere. Classically, from a beautiful sunset, a great painting, enchanting music. For George McNeill, 32, it came from folding shirts in a pro shop. "I know now I really don't want to do that ever again," said McNeill, after finishing as medalist at the 2006 PGA Tour qualifying tournament (on his ninth try), discussing how he felt about being an assistant pro at a country club.

He won't have to go behind the counter again — not unless something goes badly wrong for him — after scoring his first win in the Frys.com Open in Las Vegas in October. He was the 11th first-time winner of the season and the second rookie to win, after Brandt Snedeker, who won the Wyndham Championship. Then McNeill noted that he had already sent in his entry for the 2007 qualifying tournament. That precaution was inspired by a rough stretch a little while earlier in which he missed six cuts and withdrew once in the stretch of eight tournaments.

"In a sense, I know I have a job for the next two years, and it takes the pressure off," said McNeill, referring to the two-year exemption from qualifying that goes with winning. McNeill, who held the solo lead from the third round, shot 66-64-67-67 for a combined 23-under-par 264 total across the tournament's two courses, the TPC Summerlin and the TPC The Canyons for a four-stroke win over D.J. Trahan. And it seemed easy.

"I just kind of ho-hummed it around," McNeill said. "It felt like I didn't do anything that special. So you know, it's nice to kind of buzz around and win by four and not feel like you're doing anything at all great."

It sounded as though McNeill had entered the well-known "zone" that golfers speak of. It carried him from a tie for the lead at the halfway point to a five-stroke lead over Trahan (72) and Robert Garrigus (68) going into the final round. Trahan launched a real threat, birdieing the first four holes and then the ninth to pull within three. But McNeill birdied the 11th, holing a 15-foot putt, then added birdies at the 13th and 14th, closing with 67 to Trahan's 66. Garrigus shot 70 and Cameron Beckman 68 to tie for third.

Interestingly, McNeill had an affinity for No. 9 on both courses, and made up ground on them fast, playing them in five under for the tournament. He eagled Summerlin's, a par-five, in the first round and birdied it in the third, and eagled the Canyons' ninth, a par-four, in the second.

McNeill had his win, but it was John Daly who had the round of the week. Daly, who tied for 44th, posted an amazing 63 in the second round at Summerlin, including 28 on the back nine. He bogeyed three of his first six holes, and then had eight birdies and an eagle. Said Daly, "It was a shock to me."

Fry's Electronics Open
Scottsdale, Arizona
Winner: Mike Weir

It seems a win over Tiger Woods is a gift that just keeps on giving. Mike Weir, the gritty left-hander, suggests that's the case. Consider that Weir, winner of the 2003 Masters and the 2004 Nissan Open, slipped into the doldrums and didn't resurface until the 2007 Presidents Cup, in September, when all he did was the nearly un-doable. He beat Woods head-to-head in singles. Then three weeks later — though this had nothing to do with Woods — Weir took the lead late and hung on to win the Fry's Electronics Open for his first PGA Tour victory in three years and 87 starts. Was he still riding high after beating Woods?

"There are still some good feelings going, that I've taken from there, no question," Weir said. "There's definitely some spillover into this week, I would say."

Weir needed some help from other sources as well. Carl Pettersson, who led after the second and third rounds, opened the final round with a one-stroke edge on Weir and Mark Hensby. The three were all tied after No. 2, and then Pettersson began to drift as brisk winds hit the par-70 Grayhawk Golf Club in Scottsdale, Arizona. Pettersson bogeyed the fifth, then fell out of the chase with three straight bogeys from the 10th and shot 74, tying for fourth. Sean O'Hair inadvertently helped, too. A birdie at the 16th got him a share of the lead, and then he finished double bogey-bogey for 69 and joined Pettersson in fourth place.

Weir opened the tournament with 69, six shots behind Michael Allen's seven-under 63 on a day of some interesting fireworks. Nick Watney, the Zurich Classic winner, had the round of the tournament, an amazing 65. He made only four pars. He had 11 birdies, but also two bogeys and a quadruple bogey. Phil Mickelson (71) went without a three-putt, stretching his string of no three-putts to 225 holes. (Mickelson would go on to miss the cut, and Allen would finish with 78 and plunge to a tie for 56th.)

Weir, who stayed in the hunt with rounds of 69-64-65, battled Hensby through the final round. Weir finally edged in front at the par-four 15th, chipping to a foot for a birdie, and he hung on from there. At the 17th, Weir missed the green left and was on a slope. But Hensby missed his chance to tie when he put his second past the green. Both saved par. Hensby got one more chance at the 18th. Weir bunkered his second, and again Hensby missed the green. Worse, his ball was hanging on the bank, just above the water hazard. Hensby nearly holed his chip and tapped in for his par for 69 and second place. Weir blasted out to six feet and made the putt for his par and 68 for a 14-under 266 total and his eighth career victory.

Ginn sur Mer Classic at Tesoro
Port St. Lucie, Florida
Winner: Daniel Chopra

At first, there was doubt that the tournament would even be played. Then, there was doubt that it could finish. That about sums up the most awkward story of the year on the PGA Tour.

The tournament started out as the Running Horse Championship in Fresno, California, and when the real estate development of the same name went bankrupt, the Tour transferred the fledgling event across the continent, making it the inaugural Ginn sur Mer Classic at Tesoro in Port St. Lucie, Florida. Then there were the terrific cloudbursts delaying play and the shrinking daylight of late October, forcing the finish into Monday morning. By that time all of this meant nothing to Daniel Chopra. The part-Swede, part-Indian noted for his frosted blond hair, had to play his last three holes on Monday morning and inched out of a three-way tie to become the 12th first-time winner of the season. Then he reflected on the words of his coach, Kel Llewellyn.

"It's not meant to be easy," Chopra said. "It's meant to be hard, meant to be tough. And I didn't realize it was going to be that tough." He made it look easy, though. For starters, he went the first 40 holes without a bogey. He played the par-73 Tesoro Club in 67-66-69-71 for a 273 total, 19 under par.

The delays were such that every round had to be carried over to the next day. Bob Estes and Tommy Armour shared the first-round lead on 64s, and then added 68s for 132 totals at the halfway point. (Estes slid to a tie for 12th on his 72-77 finish, and Armour was tied for 16th on 78-72.) Thanks to another storm delay, the third round had to be completed on Sunday morning, and this left Chopra, with 69, at the head of the class, two up on Estes (72) and Briny Baird (65). They slipped soon after the final round started in the afternoon. Baird hit out of bounds at No. 1, on his way to 78, and Estes bogeyed three of the first five and shot 77.

Chopra led by four going into the final round, birdied the first three holes, then saw his lead melt away. Then between his shaky play and a surge by Shigeki Maruyama and Fredrik Jacobson, they were tied at 18 under when darkness stopped play. When they came out Monday to finish, Maruyama and Jacobson parred the last two holes, both for 69s. Chopra was at the par-five 16th, the easiest hole on the course, which he'd already birdied three times. His three-wood tee shot found the rough, but he came out with a nine wood, then put a wedge shot to nine feet and birdied for a one-stroke lead. He parred in for 71 and the victory.

Children's Miracle Network Classic
Lake Buena Vista, Florida
Winner: Stephen Ames

In the best tradition of a visit to Walt Disney World, there had to be that one last ride, that one last thrill. Accordingly, there was something for everyone at the Children's Miracle Network Classic, the final event on the 2007 PGA Tour. For Stephen Ames, it meant the ol' brass ring. "I came down here to work on my golf swing," said Ames, flashing that huge grin, "and here I am, winning an event — which is awesome."

Ames moved into the lead in the third round, tying with Scott Verplank, then stayed ahead of the pack for a one-stroke victory over the ever-challenging Tim Clark, thanks to a terrific bunker shot on the final hole. Ames made his big move with three straight birdies from the 13th, then parred in for the win, his first since the 2006 Players Championship. It was the final par that did the trick.

Ames had pulled his approach shot into a bunker at the Magnolia Course's 492-yard 18th, then lifted a 60-foot bunker shot to two feet to hold off Clark. Ames, who trailed by five in the first round, thus wrapped up a card of 70-63-70-68 for a combined 17-under-par 271 total on the Magnolia and Palm courses (both par-72s). Clark birdied six of the last 10 holes for a 66 and his fifth runner-up finish in three years and third in less than four months.

Ames had been visiting an instructor to rebuild his swing because of a sore back, and was giving it a test run at Disney. He rendered his verdict: "Parts of my swing held up, and parts didn't," Ames said. Clearly, though, more of the former.

Others enjoyed their rewards:

• Kevin Stadler, son of Craig, admitted he grew complacent after he thought he had his 2008 Tour card locked up, then he suddenly needed a good finish at Disney. "I finally got my wake-up call," he said. He tied for 15th, won $73,600 and jumped three spots on the money list to 124th, safe by one spot for 2008.

• Sweden's Mathias Gronberg was fighting to hang onto his card. He started the week at 124th, closed with 71, tied for 37th and won $21,160 to finish right on the edge, at 125th place.

• Bryce Molder, age 28, a former collegiate can't-miss fallen on tough times, enjoyed his best finish of the year. "When you miss 10 or 12 cuts in a row — or 20 or 30, or whatever it was — you start questioning whether you can play out here," he said. He started from 216th on the money list, so he needed a win. But a tie for sixth, his first top-10 finish since 2002, won him $154,100. Now he could head for the qualifying tournament convinced he had the game to make it. "I know I've got it in me," Molder said.

Special Events

Tavistock Cup
Orlando, Florida
Winner: Lake Nona

Tiger Woods, fresh from winning the WGC - CA Championship late in March, went off on one of his streaks, scoring seven straight birdies for a winning 64 in his singles match. That was the only bright spot for Isleworth in the Tavistock Cup, the two-day competition against Lake Nona, the crosstown Orlando golf community rival, both homes to PGA Tour professionals. The 22-to-8 romp was Lake Nona's first win in the four-year series. Isleworth leads the series, 2-1-1.

Woods got off to a rocky start the first day. He and John Cook were walloped, 57-65, in better-ball by Henrik Stenson and Chris DiMarco as Lake Nona buried Isleworth, 10-0. Woods rebounded in singles the next day, beating Justin Rose, 64-66, for his third straight individual title. As to those seven straight birdies: "I have no idea," Woods said. "I just know I got to eight (under par) somehow."

But that was Isleworth's first and last hurrah for the two days. Lake Nona captain Ernie Els teamed with Mark McNulty to breeze past Charles Howell and Mark O'Meara, 62-66, in another standout better-ball match. The closest outgunned Isleworth came was by one stroke in two matches — when Stuart Appleby and Nick O'Hern lost to Retief Goosen and Trevor Immelman, 64-65, and Lee Janzen and Scott Hoch lost to Ben Curtis and Graeme McDowell, 63-64. Isleworth got all eight of its points in singles the next day. Woods and Rose finished first and second. O'Meara, Goosen and Graeme McDowell tied for third with 67s.

CVS Caremark Charity Classic
Barrington, Rhode Island
Winners: Stewart Cink and J.J. Henry

The story was getting very old for Brad Faxon — robbed again in his own event. Faxon and fellow Rhode Islander Billy Andrade founded the CVS Caremark Charity Classic in 1999, and in the 2007 edition, Faxon finished second for the fifth time. This time, Stewart Cink and J.J. Henry exploded on the second nine to rush past Faxon and Masters champion Zach Johnson and pluck the two-day better-ball tournament by one stroke.

Cink and Henry ran off six consecutive birdies on the second nine to snatch away the tournament with 62 and a 20-under-par 122 total at Rhode Island Country Club. Faxon and Johnson, who tied Cink and Henry at 60 in the first round, led by two at the turn in the second round. Then came the explosion. Cink birdied Nos. 11, 13, 15 and 16, and it was his 18-footer at the 15th that gave them the lead for good. Both Faxon and

Johnson were within a stroke of tying. Both had makeable birdie putts on the 18th. But Johnson's 20-footer missed by three inches to the right and Faxon's 15-footer burned the left side of the cup.

The tournament had its first all-female team. Juli Inkster and Natalie Gulbis shot 66-67–133 and finished ninth in the 10-team field, three strokes ahead of K.J. Choi and Jesper Parnevik.

PGA Grand Slam of Golf
Tucker's Town, Bermuda
Winner: Angel Cabrera

Angel Cabrera was saying he wasn't at 100 percent when he shot two-under-par 68 in the first round of the PGA Grand Slam of Golf, so when would he be? "Tomorrow," he said. He didn't get there, but he did catch Padraig Harrington, then beat him with a birdie on the third extra hole of the two-day shootout of the winners of the four major championships — Cabrera, the U.S. Open; Harrington, British Open; Zach Johnson, Masters, and Jim Furyk, sitting in for PGA champion Tiger Woods, who sat this one out. They met at the Mid-Ocean Club in Bermuda, which replaced Poipu Bay in Hawaii, the venue for 13 years.

Harrington struggled in the first round for 67 and a one-stroke lead. "Every shot, I was a bit worried," he said. Cabrera's bid to tie him ended when his 15-foot eagle putt at the 18th stopped short. He birdied for a 68, and Johnson and Furyk shot 71s.

Cabrera made a disastrous start to the second and final round, triple-bogeying No. 1 out of the trees. Then he missed a short par put and bogeyed the 16th and trailed by two strokes. But he made a dazzling finish for 68. He birdied the par-three 17th on a 10-foot putt and eagled the 18th, firing his four-iron second shot to four feet for 68 to tie Harrington (69) at 136. They tied on the first two playoff holes. At the third, the par-five 18th, Cabrera hit a four-iron approach to 18 feet and two-putted for a birdie while Harrington had bunkered his tee shot. Furyk birdied four of the last five holes for 67 for third place at 138, and Johnson made up five shots in five holes for 68 and finished last at 139.

Said Cabrera: "I wouldn't have liked to be second here."

And Johnson: "I just didn't want to finish fifth."

Callaway Golf Pebble Beach Invitational
Pebble Beach, California
Winner: Tommy Armour

The way Kevin Sutherland broke from the starting gate, it seemed there might not be room for anyone else in the Callaway Golf Pebble Beach Invitational. Sutherland took a four-stroke lead with 10-under-par 62, with eight birdies and an eagle on the Del Monte golf course, one of three used for the field of players from the PGA Tour, LPGA, Champions and Nationwide tours, along with mini-tour players and amateurs.

"I drove the ball well, I hit my wedges well and I putted well," said Sutherland. The touch left the next day and he shot 74 at Spyglass (with Pebble Beach rounding out the three used for the mid-November tournament). The largely inactive Ronnie Black, age 49, shot 66 at Del Monte for a one-stroke lead at the halfway point. He would fade later, explaining, "I've only played five or six rounds in the last few years, and I wasn't able to focus on a couple of holes like I should have."

Up jumped Tommy Armour, age 48, in the third round, taking the lead with 65 at Del Monte. "I've played well all three days, so I'm really looking forward to the final round at Pebble Beach," said Armour, who came from three strokes behind with six birdies, an eagle and a bogey for his 65 and a two-stroke lead over Nick Watney.

Once in the driver's seat, Armour, a two-time winner on the PGA Tour, rolled on to the title, shooting two-under 70 in the final round for a 16-under total of 272 and a two-stroke win over Rocco Mediate (67) and Black (68). "I just played well all week and never had a three-putt," Armour said. "I told myself this morning that I had to shoot 70 to win. I shot 70." And won with a stroke to spare.

Del Webb Father-Son Challenge
Orlando, Florida
Winners: Larry and Josh Nelson

Larry Nelson, the guy with the interchangeable sons — he won with Drew in 2004 — teamed up with Josh this time to win the Del Webb Father-Son Challenge on a late eagle-par-birdie stretch that left onrushing Bob and Kevin Tway two strokes to the rear.

"He just doesn't fold under pressure," said a beaming Josh Nelson, recounting dad's heroics. "He rises to the occasion. That's why he's a three-time major champion." At the 220-yard 14th, Larry hit a two-iron hybrid to five feet for a birdie. He hit it at the par-five 16th to 18 feet and rolled in the putt for an eagle. That carried the Nelsons to a 60-60–120 total, 24 under par at ChampionsGate, in Orlando, Florida.

"We just dug ourselves too deep a hole," said Tway, a closing 59 not enough to pull them back from the opening 63. "I think we were trying too hard." It was close, though. Son Kevin, a former U.S. Junior Amateur champion, hit his approach at the 16th to 12 feet. But both narrowly missed the eagle putt.

The tournament had some interesting moments that had nothing to do with the scoreboard. For one, the long-suffering David Duval was in the field with his stepson, Deano Karavites. They tied for ninth. Gary Nicklaus, who recently reverted to amateur status, paired with Jack and tied for 11th. Gretchen Zoeller, the only daughter to have played in the tournament, returned and joined dad Fuzzy, and they tied for 15th. And Lee Trevino, who finished 18th and last with son Daniel, turned 68, and was the third oldest in the field, behind Arnold Palmer, 78, who played with grandson Sam Saunders (tied for sixth) and Billy Casper, 76, who finished 17th with son Bob.

Merrill Lynch Shootout
Naples, Florida
Winners: Woody Austin and Mark Calcavecchia

Woody Austin, unexpected folk hero with the winning American team in the Presidents Cup in September, more or less rose to the same role in the Merrill Lynch Shootout at Tiburon Golf Course in Naples, Florida. Austin holed a 35-foot birdie putt on the final hole to give him and teammate Mark Calcavecchia a wire-to-wire victory by one stroke over host Greg Norman and Bubba Watson.

It was Calcavecchia's second Shootout victory, while Austin became the seventh to win it in his first try.

The birdie gave Austin and Calcavecchia a nine-under-par 63 in the scramble format and a 29-under 187 total. "I had a good vibe for him on that last putt," said Calcavecchia, who putted first and gave Austin a good read. Norman and Watson still had a chance to tie after Austin got his birdie, but both missed birdie tries from 25 feet.

"Am I disappointed for myself? Yeah — but more for Bubba," Norman said. "I would love for him to get a victory." Norman hadn't won since the 2001 LG Skins Game, and Watson hadn't won as a professional.

Austin and Mark Calcavecchia shot 64 in modified alternate-shot play to tie Fred Funk and Jeff Sluman in the first round. In better-ball in the second round, Calcavecchia holed a five-foot eagle putt at the par-five 17th to give him and Austin 60 and a 20-under 124 total.

Target World Challenge
Thousand Oaks, California
Winner: Tiger Woods

This was the Target World Challenge, Tiger Woods's unofficial, pre-Christmas frolic for a field of 16 players, and this time it was Woods again filling two roles. He was both the host and his own special guest, winning the event for the fourth time in its nine playings. Woods, who hadn't played competitively in 10 weeks, took the lead for good in the second round with a 10-under-par 62, the course record at Sherwood Country Club in Thousand Oaks, California. Jim Furyk made it interesting briefly in the final round, but one little mistake and Woods was breezing to a seven-stroke win, tying the tournament record of 22-under 266, shooting scores of 69-62-67-68. Masters champion Zach Johnson closed with 68 to take second place ahead of a stumbling Furyk.

Furyk cut Woods's six-stroke cushion to two at the turn and seemed set to get closer at the 10th hole. Woods put his approach shot 12 feet beneath the hole, and Furyk put his four feet above. Most golfers would prefer the longer uphill putt, and Furyk surely felt the same. Woods holed his uphiller for a birdie, and Furyk saw his short downhiller get away, and he ended up three-putting for a bogey. "Jimmy put a ton of heat on me the front nine," Woods said. "The whole tournament switched on the 10th. That was a big two-shot swing there." It put Woods's lead back to four strokes.

The only suspense for the week came from South African Rory Sabbatini, who had irked Woods with some confident talk earlier in the season. This time, Sabbatini, after shooting 69-81-76, withdrew. The PGA Tour said Sabbatini said he was leaving for personal reasons. Later, his agent said Sabbatini told him he had shin splints.

Nationwide Tour

Back in the summer of 2003, Nick Flanagan, then age 19, and some of his Australian mates went "golf-bumming" in the United States. Short on money, they booked the lowliest of motels, rotated three to a bed and one or maybe two on the floor, and became connoisseurs of American fast food.

As part of that trip, Flanagan decided he might as well take a crack at the U.S. Amateur Championship at Oakmont, and — he won it. He said he hoped to come back to the U.S. and play on the PGA Tour. But first came the Nationwide Tour, whose top 25 money winners each year graduate to the big tour.

But Flanagan did it the exciting way. He got the Nationwide Tour's "battlefield promotion," the automatic pass to the PGA Tour for winning three Nationwide tournaments in the same year. He was the only three-time winner in 2007, and only the eighth in tour history to do so.

There were three other multiple winners on the Nationwide — Richard Johnson, Roland Thatcher and Kyle Thompson.

Flanagan got his three victories spectacularly. After winning the Henrico County Open in April, a month later he took the BMW Charity Pro-Am at The Cliffs, coming from behind in the last round and birdieing the last three holes for 65.

Then he got that precious No. 3 in the Xerox Classic in mid-August, making up a seven-shot deficit in the final round with a flawless 63. He made an eagle and five birdies, the last birdie a 30-footer at the final hole that he needed to edge James Driscoll by a stroke. "I can't believe I won today, that's for sure," Flanagan said. "I didn't think I could quite get there from seven back. Things just went right for me."

Then Flanagan headed for the PGA Tour and the Fall Finish. "I may play the rest of the year for some Christmas money," he said. Some Christmas money. He played in four events and won $122,029, bringing his total to nearly $500,000 for the year.

Flanagan's leap up the Nationwide Tour list was nearly fatal to the slumping Driscoll, who had missed five cuts in his previous seven starts. Happily for Driscoll, second-place money, $64,800, gave him a big leg up on 24th place on the money list, next-to-last on the graduation list.

Richard Johnson, 35, a Welshman who once managed a Waffle House near Augusta National, had won the Mark Christopher Charity Classic and already had his PGA Tour card locked up when he took the season-ending Nationwide Tour Championship with a tournament-record 20-under-par 264 total. The victory carried him from sixth to first with $445,421 for the season, over Thatcher, who had led since July.

Johnson was planning on a January start at the season-opener, the Sony Open in Hawaii. "I've got to get my body in shape," he cracked. "I'm too old for this."

Thatcher, winner of the Peek'n Peak Classic and the Cox Classic, was second with $415,124. Flanagan was third with $369,951.

Kyle Thompson, age 28, had the strangest season. Thompson, had been bumped off the graduation list in 2003 and 2004 and was in dire straits this time. He won the Rex Hospital Open, but had made just nine cuts in 25 events when he took the Oregon Classic in September. "I either miss the cut or I finish top 25," Thompson said. "It drives you crazy." He made only 16 cuts in 28 starts, and had only four top-10 finishes — but two of them were wins.

Dead last at 25th, nearly a quarter-million dollars away from No. 1 Richard Johnson — and immeasurably happier — was Jimmy Walker. Walker was the 2004 Player of the Year but suffered a neck injury on the practice range at his debut in 2005, the season-opening Sony Open, and spent two years making a comeback. And he came back in great style, making up a seven-stroke deficit in the final round to win the National Mining Association Pete Dye Classic. "It has been tough on me and my family," he said. "This win is for all of them." And the $108,000 first prize lifted him to a $195,802 total, and he made that 25th spot by a mere $1,094.

Daniel Summerhays, All-American at Brigham Young University, made history. He was the first amateur ever to win a Nationwide Tour event. Summerhays was one of 10 All-Americans invited to play in the Nationwide Children's Hospital Invitational and ended up winning by two shots with a six-under 278 total. He wasn't able to take the money because of his amateur status, but he did jump at his opportunity to turn professional. "The course of my life completely changed," he said. He went on to make 12 more starts, made 10 cuts and won $46,000.

Elsewhere, there were various and sundry highlights to the 2007 Nationwide Tour:

• Thatcher was the only American in the top five. Johnson (1) is from Wales; Flanagan (3), Australia; Jon Mills (4), Canada, and Jason Day (5), Australia.

• Johnson was the first foreign player to lead the tour in winnings.

• Day, winning the Legend Financial Group Classic, became the youngest winner in tour history — 19 years, 7 months and 16 days.

• Paul Claxton and Tom Scherrer became the first two to top $1 million in winnings on the Nationwide Tour. Claxton finished 10th with $274,004, and Scherrer 20th with $220,138.

• Mills led the tour in top-10 finishes, with three. Johnson and Patrick Sheehan tied with eight each, and Jason Day, Michael Letzig and Nicholas Thompson had seven each. Mills also led in rounds in the 60s with 50.

• The 2007 Nationwide class sent 11 rookies to the PGA Tour: Johnson, Flanagan, Day, Matthew Jones, Michael Letzig, Martin Laird, Kyle Thompson, Marc Turnesa, Chez Reavie, Scott Sterling and Chad Collins.

• Nicholas Thompson and Keith Nolan played in 31 of the tour's 32 tournaments. Thompson made the top 25, Nolan didn't.

• Brad Adamonis didn't make the top 25, but in the WNB Golf Classic in October, he got his first victory and had the distinction of winning a four-way playoff that went eight holes, matching the second-longest in tour history. Ron Whittaker was knocked out on the first hole, Vance Veazey on the second, and Tjaart van der Walt on the eighth. Adamonis went through the playoff with eight straight pars. "I don't care," Adamonis said. "Any way I can get a win is great."

• It was a fine year for foreign players. In addition to taking four of the top five spots, they also had seven in the top 25 and 20 of the top 60.

Canadian Tour

One week, Byron Smith was getting knocked flat by 62 and a 40-foot birdie. The next week, he was punching his way right to the top of the money list. Which is to say that, if you like storybook finishes, 2007 was your year on the Canadian Tour.

The tour started in April with a trio of firsts. Namely, Australian rookie Adam Bland was making his first start in the tour's first event, the San Jose International Open, and he scored, of course, his first win. Now, that is some start. The tale ended up with Byron Smith, a 26-year-old American, not only a first-time winner but a double winner, bouncing back from a demoralizing finish one week to a victory the next to take the Order of Merit with C$91,202. When the season had run its course, you had four double-winners, seven first-time winners.

Back to Bland in the San Jose International at Boulder Creek in California in April. Bret Guetz, a 29-year-old American, was on the verge of doing what his brother Brian did last season — scoring his first Canadian Tour victory. Bret entered the final round with a three-stroke lead, then stumbled to two double bogeys and four bogeys and shot 42 on the final nine for 78. "You've really got to feel bad for Bret," said Bland. "To play so well all week, and have it come apart like that is tough to take."

That opened the door, and who should step through but Bland. He closed with five-under-par 67 to tie Scott Gibson, John Ellis and Spencer Levin, then holed an 18-foot birdie putt on the first playoff hole to win. Bland went on to win the Ford Culiacan at Culiacan (Mexico) Country Club three weeks later.

Byron Smith surfaced at the Corona Mazatlan Classic in Mazatlan, Mexico, late in April. In the final round, Smith had two birdies on the first nine, then got hot on the back with birdies at the 10th, 13th and 14th holes, and after a bogey at the 16th, then a final birdie at the 17th on a 25-foot putt. "Once I made that, I said to myself, 'I think you just won a golf tournament,'" Smith said. And he was right. His closing 67 gave him a 19-under 269 total and a three-stroke victory — his first Canadian win. The rest of the Smith story spun out late in the season. In the Desjardins Montreal Open late in August, Smith closed with 63 and was about to win. But hefty Brent Schwarzrock, age 35, a Nationwide Tour player, came crashing in with a 10-under-par 62 to tie him at 264, eight strokes ahead of the field. The 62 was just the first blow. Schwarzrock then delivered the next one on the first playoff hole, a 40-foot putt for a birdie and his own first tour win.

"These guys weren't going to give me anything — I had to work for it," Smith was to say with a grin. This was the following week at the Jane Rogers Championship of Mississauga at Lakeview Golf Club in Ontario. Smith birdied three of the first six holes, and after seven straight pars he ran off four birdies in a row from the 14th. Smith wrapped up a seven-under 63 for a one-stroke win over Derek Gillespie, his second victory of the season.

Spencer Levin, 23, who lost in the playoff at the season-opening San Jose International, more than made up for that disappointment with his first and second tour wins. The first came in the Iberostar Riviera Maya Open in Mexico late in May. In the final round, he enjoyed a comfortable stroll with one birdie and eight pars at the Iberostar Playa Paraiso Golf Club. Then Levin went on a tear on the second nine. He birdied three straight from the 11th hole, eagled the par-five 14th, then drained a 20-footer for birdie at the 18th for a seven-under 65 and a 21-under 267 total to win his first by one. "I've been playing very well, and to finally seal the deal is a wonderful feeling," Levin said. "It sure felt good to make that final putt."

Levin felt even better at the tour's next stop, the Times Colonist Open at Gorge Vale in Victoria two weeks later. He solved the winds in the final round, shooting 71 for an 11-under 277 total and his second victory, this by three strokes. "I'm very happy with my play this year," Levin said. "You need to push yourself every week and go out there and get it."

Canadian Wes Heffernan overcame an old enemy, Brookside Country Club in Stockton, in the Northern California Classic. "I was chasing pretty well all day long," said Heffernan, who trailed several players in the final round. "This was my nemesis course, but it worked out well this time." Heffernan made two birdies and seven pars on the first nine to turn at 17 under, then birdied the 14th and 15th holes, and finally dropped a four-footer at the 18th for 67 and a 20-under 268 total to win by one.

He found Mexico to his liking as well in May, where he won the Riviera Nayarit Classic at the Club de Golf El Tigre. This one was easy. Heffernan led by five entering the final round, bogeyed the first hole, but closed the door with birdies at Nos. 3 and 4. He birdied two more on the first nine, then three of the first six after the turn, and it took a triple-bogey at the par-four 16th to cut his winning margin to five, the biggest of the season. "It was a weird feeling having that lead," Heffernan said. "It's not as comfortable as you would think."

Tour de las Americas (South America)

An Argentine topped the Order of Merit of the 2007 Tour de las Americas, but not the one most people would have expected. No, not Angel Cabrera, who burst into international fame by winning the U.S. Open, but he certainly did all right for himself. This time, it was Miguel Rodriguez, who parlayed two victories and all-around good play into a season's-best US$60,180.

So there's another name to be reckoned with from what used to be known as the South American Tour, which is sending more players onto the world scene. The tour held 11 tournaments in seven different nations around South America and the Caribbean in 2007, and five of them were co-sanctioned with the European Tour's Challenge Tour, which gave the Tour de las Americas even more of an international presence. That presence was further enhanced when the tour joined the International Federation of PGA Tours as an associate member.

Rodriguez, an Argentine, started his big year by sparing the Kai Fieberg Costa Rica Open its sixth playoff, escaping with a one-stroke victory despite a disastrous bogey triple-bogey finish. He was leading by five strokes through No. 16, so the bogey at the 17th barely hurt him. Then, at the 18th, his tee shot ended up behind a tree. "With the lead I was enjoying (four strokes), I decided to take a chance and try to pass the water hazard," he said. But his shot nicked a tree and ended up in the water. The triple bogey gave him a 72 for a nine-under-par 275 total and the narrow victory. Rodriguez's second win, in the Abierto del Litoral Personal in Argentina, was just as traumatic. Rodriguez led by one starting the final round and stumbled late, then holed a 30-footer for a birdie at the 17th to tie Andres Romero, the defending champion, who had almost won the Open Championship at Carnoustie in July. Romero's eight-iron approach at the final hole got away and cost him a bogey. "I can't deny I felt the pressure," Rodriguez said, "but the putt on 17 was crucial."

Cabrera was certainly heard from, of course. He was the only other double winner on the tour, taking two of the four official TLA events he played in his native Argentina. The first was the Abierto Visa del Centro in April. "I played great golf today," Cabrera said. "I found the good rhythm I had over the first two days." The separation was abrupt. Rodolfo Gonzalez, the overnight leader by five strokes, bogeyed the first three holes. And Cabrera birdied three straight from No. 2, passing Gonzalez, who was on his way to 79. Cabrera shot 65 and won by two over Paraguay's Raul Fretes, taking the title for the third straight time and the seventh time in his career. His next was the Torneo de Maestros (Argentina Masters) in October, another tournament he owned. He won it for the fourth time in the past five tries. It was Cabrera's first competition since winning the U.S. Open in June, when he became the first Latin to win a major championship in 40 years, since Argentina's Roberto de Vicenzo took the 1967 Open in Britain.

Cabrera, despite the long layoff, was plenty sharp enough to hit a six-iron approach from 205 yards to two feet, setting up an easy eagle at the par-five 18th, tying Ricardo Gonzalez. In the playoff at the 18th, both hit the green in two. Gonzalez, putting first from 20 feet, knocked the eagle putt two feet past and then hurriedly stabbed at the birdie putt and missed. Cabrera two-putted for the winning birdie.

The tour started the first week of February, and it was a great start to the year and a career for Italy's Eduardo Molinari. The 2005 U.S. Amateur champion, Molinari scored his first professional victory in the Colombia Masters' inaugural playing. Molinari just missed a winning 14-footer for birdie at the last hole, then beat Colombian Gustavo Mendoza on the second playoff hole.

Understandably, Cabrera was the favorite to win the season-ending Abierto Visa de la Republica (Argentina Open). Instead, it was Paraguay's Marco Ruiz who came through in the clutch. Ruiz closed with birdies at the 15th and 16th, shooting 69 and a five-under 275 total to win by two over Argentina's Daniel Vancsik.

In a season top-heavy with Argentine heroics, Emilio Dominguez, age 21, made his mark as Rookie of the Year. He had made headlines earlier with a runner-up finish in the Guatemala Open, co-sanctioned by the TLA and the Challenge Tour. He shot 61-67 in the last two rounds and finished just a stroke behind the winner, Jamie Donaldson of Wales. Then in November, Dominguez completed his move to win his first career title at Argentina's Abierto de San Luis. He did it in style, getting birdies at three of the last five holes on his way to a four-under 67. "It was quite an unexpected way to finish," said a delighted Dominguez. The victory vaulted him into the second place of the Order of Merit, ahead of experienced players such as Gustavo Acosta, Rafael Gomez and Marco Ruiz.

Wherever this success would carry Dominguez, it was clear that TLA golfers were on the rise. Andres Romero, for example, the 2003 TLA Rookie of the year. After challenging at Carnoustie, he finished third, and then bounced back to win the European Tour's Deutsche Bank Players' Championship a week later in Germany. In addition to Romero, three other Argentines began their international careers on the TLA. Ariel Canete won the European Tour's Joburg Open in January; Miguel Carballo claimed the Nationwide Tour's Movistar Panama Championship in February; and Vancsik won the European Tour's Madeira Islands Open BPI in March.

9. European Tours

As has been noted in recent previous editions of *The World of Professional Golf*, Ryder Cup victories for Europe — the last three in a row — have not been accompanied by any major championship victories. The question of who would follow Open champion Paul Lawrie from Carnoustie in 1999 was becoming tedious and yet unavoidable. The players are good enough, it just needs one to win and then the rest will follow. If there was someone to play the role of Seve from the early 1980s, then another group of major winners would emerge to sit alongside the likes of Faldo and Langer.

Still the uncomfortable debate continued, right up to the return of the Open to Carnoustie. Ballesteros started the week with the announcement of his retirement. Injury and loss of form made it inevitable but no less sad. Something was needed to lighten the spirit. "This might be the week," mouthed the optimists. By the time the dramatic conclusion of yet another Open Championship on the banks of the Barry Burn had reached the stage of a playoff, Europe was indeed assured of a new major champion.

Who it would be was decided by who was the more resilient under the excruciating circumstances. It was to be Padraig Harrington and not Sergio Garcia, but then the Irishman has made a career out of being resilient and persevering no matter what. Being in the dreaded Barry Burn — not once but twice on the 72nd hole — might have finished a lesser mortal, but Harrington fought for his six and survived to reach the playoff. For Garcia, after leading for the first three days, it was the most bitter disappointment of his life, yet an experience that may one day be beneficial if the Spaniard can persuade more putts to drop on a consistent basis.

Harrington almost made a career out of finishing as a runner-up. Even then it would have been a step up from his initial ambition on turning professional, with his accountancy exams behind him just in case, of becoming a journeyman on the tour. Yet by sheer hard work, often for hours on the practice ground at Largs under the eye of Bob Torrance, Harrington built a career stone by stone. The wins did not arrive as regularly as the second places, but they eventually accumulated. Multiple victories in Europe and Asia were followed by two wins on the U.S. PGA Tour in 2005. In 2006 he clinched the European Tour Order of Merit and was in the thick of things as an Irishman in helping to win the Ryder Cup for Europe again at The K Club.

In 2007, in May, he won what he describes as his "fifth major," the Irish Open. It was not easy; it never has been. Then he was the man in front but was caught and again won in a playoff. Skipping the Scottish Open at Loch Lomond, Harrington won the Irish PGA, a non-tour event, at the European Club, a links course, ideal preparation for Carnoustie.

Harrington is thoughtful and articulate in public, and when his veteran coach, Torrance, was honored with a lifetime achievement award on the eve of the Open, he never hesitated in turning up to the presentation dinner and giving his own tribute. It was not the last fine speech he would give that week, the next one coming as he held the Claret Jug. Yet he is not a man of particular airs and graces. Moments after the presentation ceremony, his son Patrick asked if they could use the old trophy as a receptacle for ladybirds. "Indeed we can," came the reply. "We'll put ladybirds in it."

By the end of the year, his wife Caroline had given birth to another boy, Ciaran, just as accolades were coming his way. He was the European Tour's Golfer of the Year and was also awarded the Golf Writers' Trophy. He did not retain his Order of Merit title, despite being involved late into the denouement of the season at the Volvo Masters.

It was a victory at Valderrama, also in dramatic circumstances, by Justin Rose that assured the 27-year-old Englishman the top spot on the money list. He had won late in 2006 at the Australian Masters, but needed a win to top off a season of remarkable consistency, especially as he had to cut his schedule down due to a back injury. On the list of those who made the cut in all four major championships, Rose was second only to Tiger Woods. The young man with an already long career was beginning to fulfill his potential.

Harrington was not the only member of the European Tour to win a major, as Angel Cabrera, of Argentina, completed a mid-summer double by stealing the U.S. Open away from Woods and Jim Furyk at Oakmont. Never before have European Tour members won both the U.S. and British Opens in the same season. It was an audacious performance from Cabrera, the fourth U.S. Open champion in a row from the southern hemisphere.

Ernie Els won his seventh HSBC World Match Play at Wentworth, but then caused a controversy when, as leader of the Order of Merit, he did not go to Valderrama, instead playing in another tournament in Asia.

Scheduling was a significant topic all year as tours around the world found themselves adapting to the new calendar in America. With The Players Championship moving to May and the new FedExCup Playoffs in September, traditionally strong months for the European Tour were affected. The European Tour's response was to announce a new season-ending tournament in Dubai to start in 2009 with a staggering purse of $10 million. The winner of the Race to Dubai — the Order of Merit — will receive a bonus of $2 million, while the season will revert to January through November, rather than year-round. It is nothing new for the European Tour to look outside its geographical borders, but at times in 2007 relations with the Asian Tour were not always cordial as arguments over co-sanctioning continued.

But if saluting a reigning major champion was a new sensation again, admiring the talent of young players coming out of Europe is definitely not. Once again the season proved that more youngsters were ready to play. While Germany's Martin Kaymer won the Sir Henry Cotton Rookie of the Year award, Spain's Pablo Martin-Benavides became the first amateur ever to win on the modern European Tour at the Estoril Open de Portugal. Northern Ireland's Rory McIlroy also astonished. After winning the amateur medal at the Open Championship, he later in the year earned his tour card for 2008 from only four starts, which included a third place at the Alfred Dunhill Links Championship.

Joburg Open
Johannesburg, South Africa
Winner: Ariel Canete

See African Tours chapter.

The Royal Trophy
Bangkok, Thailand
Winner: Europe

See Asia/Japan Tours chapter.

Abu Dhabi Golf Championship
Abu Dhabi, United Arab Emirates
Winner: Paul Casey

On their first appearances of 2007 after only a few weeks' break — particularly so for Padraig Harrington, who in the past took a couple of months off — there was another grand duel between Harrington and Paul Casey, this time with Casey coming out on top. Harrington was the third-round leader in the Abu Dhabi Golf Championship, but Casey produced what he considered as his finest last-day performance with eight birdies in his 65 at the Abu Dhabi Golf Club to win by one over Miguel Angel Jimenez and Peter Hanson.

It would have been a more comfortable margin of victory except for a three-putt bogey at the last which left the 29-year-old Englishman at 271, 17 under par. But only Jimenez could catch him at the 18th and the Spaniard's 25-foot putt to tie came up short. Defending champion Chris DiMarco finished fourth after a closing 66, while Harrington, who made three birdies in four holes at the end of the first nine but then stumbled coming home, tied for fifth place with Retief Goosen and Jean-Francois Lucquin after a 71.

After rounds of 71, 68 and 67, Casey started the final round three behind Harrington, but the daily improvement continued as he made five birdies going out. He then birdied the 10th and 11th before adding a final birdie at the 16th. He credited the work he did in the short off-season with his American coach, Peter Kostis, for helping him win.

"I had a good holiday and then two weeks working very, very hard with Peter," Casey said. "I am very happy I put in all that hard work, as I would not have won today without it. I hit some shots today which I don't think I could have done had I not put in that work, both in fitness — strength training that I've done in the gym — and on the swing."

Harrington said: "I suffered with my focus and bogeyed two holes on the back nine with a wedge for my approach, which doesn't happen too often. Such is the game. It's always disappointing when you have a chance, but I still feel I am well ahead of expectations for this time of year."

Commercialbank Qatar Masters
Doha, Qatar
Winner: Retief Goosen

What was a brilliant last-gasp victory for Retief Goosen was a devastating defeat for Nick O'Hern at the Commercialbank Qatar Masters. Goosen trailed the Australian left-hander by two strokes with two holes to play, but finished with a birdie at the short 17th and then eagled the 18th to win by one. O'Hern left Doha with his seventh runner-up finish on the European Tour rather than a first win.

"Obviously, you feel for the guy," Goosen said. "But what can you say but 'sorry' and 'well played.'" For the South African it was a fine way to start the year. In 2006 he had won only once, at the Volkswagen Masters in China on the Asian Tour. No wins came in Europe or America and his last victory on the European Tour was the South African Open in December 2005.

For the first time in many years, the two-time U.S. Open champion employed a coach, turning to Gregor Jamieson at Lake Nona in Orlando, Florida. They worked principally on a change to his backswing, but at Doha it was still a work in progress and Goosen was still missing more fairways than usual. At the prize-giving ceremony he thanked the volunteers who helped search for his ball on numerous occasions.

After rounds of 65, 68 and 71, Goosen closed with 69 to finish with a 15-under-par 273 total. He spent the weekend playing in a group alongside two left-handers from Australia in O'Hern and Richard Green. Green came back to the pack when he took a double-bogey seven at the last on Saturday. Ernie Els set the clubhouse target at 13 under, but after O'Hern got up and down for a par at the 15th and for a birdie-three at the 16th, he seemed to be in charge.

After a bogey at the 15th, Goosen fell back to 12 under and remarked to his caddie that they somehow needed to get to 15 under. He almost holed in one at the 17th, and then hit two glorious shots, with a driver and three wood, to reach the back of the final green.

O'Hern drove into the rough at the last and could only reach in three at the par-five. Having putted down to four feet, he could not respond when Goosen holed for his eagle.

Dubai Desert Classic
Dubai, United Arab Emirates
Winner: Henrik Stenson

Henrik Stenson enhanced his growing reputation with the biggest victory of his career at the Dubai Desert Classic. Stenson birdied the last hole to beat three-time winner Ernie Els by one stroke and leave Tiger Woods outside the top two at a stroke-play tournament for the first time since he missed the cut at the 2006 U.S. Open.

Woods arrived in Dubai to defend his title after winning for the seventh time in a row on the U.S. PGA Tour in his first event of the year the week before at the Buick Invitational. It was Stenson's fifth win on the European

Tour and his third in just over a year. It came in the city where he has a residence and on a course, at the Emirates, where he is a member.

For once the conditions were not ideal, with the final round played in a Shamaal, the desert sand storm. Els began the day with a two-stroke lead, but dropped three strokes in the first six holes. Stenson's only dropped shot of a closing 68 came at the ninth, where his second shot finished on top of a hospitality building. He had to scale the roof to identify the ball, but on the way home made four birdies, first at the 11th and then two more at the 13th and 14th holes. Els made three birdies on the second nine, including at the 14th where he holed from sand, and by getting up and down at the 18th he forced Stenson to birdie as well. Stenson decided to lay up in front of the water, then hit a superb wedge shot to eight feet and holed the putt.

"Being based down here, this is my second home tournament, so to be able to win in front of family and friends is just unbelievable," Stenson said. "It's always nice to beat Tiger. It's the first tournament I have won that he's been in. He is a great player, so of course that gives you extra satisfaction to beat him. To play four rounds with Ernie and to beat him by a shot coming down the stretch is pretty much the same satisfaction."

Woods blamed his putting, but not the immaculate Emirates greens, and could not match Stenson's 92 percent greens in regulation. He recorded rounds of 68, 64, 69 and 68 for a 19-under-par total of 269. Els closed with a 71 and Woods a 69 to tie for third place with another Swede, Niclas Fasth. England's Ross Fisher finished fifth, a superb result for the 26-year-old from Wentworth who before the final round had only met Woods while working as a ball collector on the range at the 1998 World Match Play.

Maybank Malaysian Open
Kuala Lumpur, Malaysia
Winner: Peter Hedblom

See Asia/Japan Tours chapter.

Enjoy Jakarta Astro Indonesia Open
Jakarta, Indonesia
Winner: Mikko Ilonen

See Asia/Japan Tours chapter.

Johnnie Walker Classic
Phuket, Thailand
Winner: Anton Haig

See Asia/Japan Tours chapter.

Clariden Leu Singapore Masters
Singapore
Winner: Liang Wen-chong

See Asia/Japan Tours chapter.

TCL Classic
Sanya, Hainen Island, China
Winner: Chapchai Nirat

See Asia/Japan Tours chapter.

Madeira Islands Open BPI
Madeira, Portugal
Winner: Daniel Vancsik

As Tiger Woods was winning the WGC - CA Championship at Doral, Daniel Vancsik was proving for himself that controlling his mind was just as important as controlling his golf ball. Vancsik gained his first victory on the European Tour at the Madeira Island Open by an overwhelming seven strokes, the biggest margin of victory of the season to date, only two months after committing to a new regime with his coach and his sports psychologist. Draped in the flag of Argentina and soaked in champagne after the winning putt, the 30-year-old from Buenos Aires reflected on his new success.

"This is amazing," said Vancsik. "I have changed so much of my swing in the last two months and worked so hard to earn this victory. My coach, Jose Cantero, worked with me a lot on my short game, and my psychologist, Paulo Pecora, helped me a lot with my concentration. Before that, anytime I hit a couple of bad shots I would lose my mind completely, but he helped me to stay patient and realize that you do not always hit the ball great in this sport. If you can't control your mind then you will not succeed."

Vancsik, who graduated from the Challenge Tour in 2005 but had to go back to the qualifying tournament after his rookie season in 2006, did not particularly hit the ball well in the final round, which he started with a four-stroke cushion. But he found a way of getting the ball into the hole with impressive regularity. He birdied the first two holes, took a bogey at the third in his stride, and then he effectively ended the tournament with birdies at the seventh, eighth and ninth.

He came home in even par, with two birdies and two bogeys, for a closing round of 68. After opening with 68 at Santo da Serra, a round of 66 had given Vancsik the halfway lead, and then he had another 68 in the third round. It all added up to an 18-under-par score of 270, equaling the tournament record.

"I didn't hit the ball well today," he said after the final round, "but my sand wedge was perfect and I made three great birdie putts on the seventh, eighth and ninth. After that I knew that I could relax and put the ball on the fairways and greens."

Santiago Luna, the 1995 champion, and David Frost, the veteran South African, shared second place at 11 under after rounds of 69 and 68 respectively. Euan Little, Christian Cevaer and Mads Vibe-Hastrup finished tied for fourth place two shots further back.

Estoril Open de Portugal
Estoril, Portugal
Winner: Pablo Martin-Benavides

Pablo Martin-Benavides gave up €208,330 but created history by becoming the first amateur to win in 36 years of the modern European Tour. Martin-Benavides, still a student at Oklahoma State University, won the Estoril Open de Portugal at Oitavos by a stroke over Raphael Jacquelin, who took the first-prize check instead. It was a performance of great maturity from the 20-year-old from Malaga. He came home in 29 on Saturday and returned a bogey-free 68 on the final day. Earlier in the season Martin-Benavides made the cut in a PGA Tour event in Mexico, but this was only his fifth start on the European Tour. In 2003, as a 17-year-old, he led going into the last round of the Spanish Open in Tenerife but, understandably at the time, slipped back to finish 22nd.

"The last time I had a chance to win I was shaking in my shoes. This time it was not so bad," said Pablo, who birdied the 10th to get to seven under and then parred home. A former winner of the Jack Nicklaus Award as the leading college player in the United States, Martin-Benavides stated that he had no intention of turning professional immediately and taking up his exemption on the European Tour. "It doesn't even cross my mind to turn pro," he said. "I've already thought about it. I've got to play with Oklahoma State. They've been giving me so many things and it does not enter my mind right now." Martin-Benavides had a two-week window to take up his exemption, but he was still able to take up a two-year exemption at the end of the season. Before then he would be limited to only five invitations.

It was the 1,145th event in the history of the European Tour and the previous best result by an amateur was the third place of Nick Flanagan at the 2004 ANZ Championship. The last amateur to win a professional tournament in Europe was Dr. David Sheehan at the 1962 Jeyes Tournament at Royal Dublin. Martin-Benavides said he was helped by playing in the final round alongside Alex Noren, a Swede whom he played with at Oklahoma State, and Ross McGowan, the 2006 English Amateur champion. Both men led overnight but fell out of contention with a pair of 76s.

Scott Verplank also won a professional tournament while at Oklahoma State. "My coaches have been giving me stick about that for the last three years," Pablo said. "They kept telling that I was no good if I couldn't win a pro event as an amateur! But it actually helped me a little bit; even though it was a joke it helped me."

Volvo China Open
Shanghai, China
Winner: Markus Brier

See Asia/Japan Tours chapter.

BMW Asian Open
Shanghai, China
Winner: Raphael Jacquelin

See Asia/Japan Tours chapter.

Open de Espana
Madrid, Spain
Winner: Charl Schwartzel

After completing a hat trick of South African Order of Merit titles during the winter, Charl Schwartzel arrived in Europe aiming for a first victory in the northern hemisphere. It arrived at the Open de Espana after an impressive display of stamina on the long final day by the 22-year-old from Johannesburg. Storms had battered the new Centro Nacional course all week and Sunday the leaders had to play all but a few holes of their third round before completing the fourth and final round.

Schwartzel hardly had thoughts of victory at the short lunch break after he had double-bogeyed the 18th hole in the third round to fall three behind 54-hole leader Carlos Rodiles. "Up until then I had had only one bogey all week, so I was really steaming," Schwartzel said. "It was a good thing I could have some lunch and I cooled down again."

The youngster was also helped by his veteran caddie, Ricci Roberts, and his years of experience with Ernie Els. "Having Ricci on the bag is just superb. He had caddied for Ernie for about 16 years and they both fancied a change, and when I asked if he wanted to caddie for me, I was very happy when he said yes. He has so much experience and has seen it all and done it all with something like 50 wins alongside Ernie, so I just felt that experience helped give me an advantage. I had been playing well, but I was just lacking that edge and I think Ricci gave me that, maybe gave me that one shot edge I had been lacking."

Rodiles never felt comfortable in the final round despite being cheered on by his countrymen in the Spanish capital. Instead it was India's Jyoti Randhawa who made a charge with a 67 that set the clubhouse target at 273, 15 under par. It quite an effort from Randhawa, who had been in danger of missing the cut at four over par after four holes of his second round.

Schwartzel utilized his tremendous length to good advantage on the back nine. He drove the green at the 360-yard 13th and made a birdie, and then at the par-five 16th he hit a three iron from 235 yards, a superb shot, to 15 feet and holed the putt for an eagle. He could afford a bogey at the last as rounds of 69, 68, 68 and 67 left him at 272, 16 under and one clear of Randhawa, with Rodiles a further shot back. It was Schwartzel's second victory on the European Tour after he won the 2004 Dunhill Championship in South Africa.

Telecom Italia Open
Milan, Italy
Winner: Gonzalo Fernandez-Castano

As if he was not wet enough after a week of storms and floods in Milan, Gonzalo Fernandez-Castano ended up being thrown in a swimming pool. He did not mind since he was holding the Telecom Italia Open trophy at the time. Only three rounds were possible at Castello di Tolcinasco, but 54 holes were not enough to determine the result. Fernandez-Castano won at the second extra hole with a birdie from five feet which defeated Markus Brier. The Austrian had won his second European Tour title at the Volvo China Open the previous month and he birdied two of the last three holes to gain a place in the playoff after shooting 68.

It was Fernandez-Castano who had set the mark at 16-under-par 200 after coming home in 30. The 26-year-old Spaniard started the third and final round five strokes off the lead and had drifted to six back at the turn. He then produced an eagle and five birdies, as well as a bogey at the 13th, for a closing 65. England's Nick Dougherty had been the frontrunner, but he came home in 39 to waste a three-stroke lead with nine to play.

Five shots are "a lot to make up on a course where everybody can make birdies," Gonzalo said. "I haven't been playing well, but my attitude changed this week, probably because I love coming to Italy, great food, great course, great people," he added. It was his third victory on the European Tour in three years. He won the KLM Open in 2005 during his rookie of the year season and then the BMW Asian Open in 2006, after which he proposed to his girlfriend Alicia. Though inconsistent at times, the winning knack is a good one to have picked up.

For Dougherty this was another near-miss since his first title in 2005. He had to settle for a share of third place alongside defending champion Francesco Molinari, who scored a 65 in the final round, Fredrik Andersson Hed and Henrik Nystrom.

Valle Romano Open de Andalucia
Marbella, Andalucia, Spain
Winner: Lee Westwood

Once Lee Westwood started winning on the European Tour, in Sweden in 1996, he could hardly stop. He acquired the winning habit and indulged it to exhaustion. In 2000 he won seven times around the world and topped the European Order of Merit. Inevitably, a drought followed and two victories in 2003 were only followed up three and a half years later with his 17th European Tour title at the Valle Romano Open de Andalucia.

"I never really thought about going so long without a win," Westwood said. "I knew that winning is fickle. I won so often in the late '90s that if I had a spell where I didn't win, people were always going to highlight it and get on my case about it. But I was never going to get on my own case."

This was a new tournament at the Aloha course in Marbella promoted jointly by Miguel Angel Jimenez, who is from nearby Malaga, and Italian Open winner Gonzalo Fernandez-Castano, who played his first golf shots on the course during his summer holidays. The event filled the gap in the schedule opposite The Players Championship in America, an event Westwood became ineligible for by slipping out of the world's top 50. Victory here put him back in the top 50 and in line for an exemption for the U.S. Open.

Westwood's failing of late had been on the greens and he had toyed with using a long-putter. After a first-round 72, he switched back to a conventional putter and tried the left-hand-below-right method. It worked. He set a course record of 64 and only two bogeys at the last two holes in Saturday's 65 stopped him lowering it further. Six birdies in the first 10 holes on Sunday and he was five shots clear of the field.

But the putting woes had not entirely disappeared. He three-putted for a par-five at the fifth and then dropped shots at the 11th, 13th and 15th holes. Phillip Archer and Fredrik Andersson Hed both eagled the 16th to cut Westwood's lead to one, but he birdied the 16th, and despite finding a greenside bunker at the last, made par by holing a 40-footer. At 20 under par after a 67, he won by two over Archer and Andersson Hed, who was third the week before, and by four over Louis Oosthuizen and Michael Jonzon.

"Winning was very important," Westwood admitted, "and to get the feeling of winning under the pressure. It wouldn't have felt good coming off with second or third after getting in such a good position."

Irish Open
Co. Limerick, Ireland
Winner: Padraig Harrington

John O'Leary was as delighted as any of the 23,000 gallery at Adare Manor as Padraig Harrington became the first home player to win the Irish Open in 25 years. O'Leary was the last to achieve the feat and the wait had appeared to weigh increasingly heavily on the shoulders of the country generation of Irish players. "I am personally delighted Padraig won," O'Leary said. "It is appropriate that this great championship should be won by Europe's No. 1 player as our first home winner after so long."

It was never easy. In the first place Harrington was only one of two players to make the long trip back from The Players Championship at Sawgrass to Limerick. The conditions were typically wet and windy, but the course was flanked by the thickest of "U.S. Open" rough and stretched to 7,400 yards, although some tees were moved up as the week progressed. Harrington opened with 73 to be five strokes off the lead, but went to the top of the leaderboard with 68 on the second day and led by three after 71 in the third round.

A birdie-birdie-eagle finish to the first nine, the three at the ninth coming from seven feet, gave Harrington a four-stroke lead, but it was not to be a rapturous coronation on the second nine. Two dropped shots gave him an inward 38 and a final round of 71 to be five under par. Suddenly it turned into a nervous duel with playing partner Bradley Dredge, who chipped in at the 14th for a birdie, birdied the 15th, bogeyed the 16th, but then hit a brilliant second shot from rough at the 17th for a birdie and a two-shot swing as Harrington bogeyed. Now tied, they both parred the 18th as Dredge added a 68 to his third-round 69 for the best weekend performance.

With the River Maigue running down the left-hand side of the par-five 18th, both went right from the tee in the playoff, but their lay-ups both finished close to the river bank. With the river to be crossed on the approach to the green, Dredge only just made it over and took two chips to find the back of the green. Harrington's third safely found the green and he two-putted for the title.

"I have always said that after the four majors this is the next event I've wanted to win," said Harrington. "The crowd were fantastic and I'm very emotional. I felt the pressure. It was probably the most nervous I've been for many a tournament."

BMW PGA Championship
Virginia Water, Surrey, England
Winner: Anders Hansen

With the attraction of one of the European Tour's most prestigious titles — with "PGA" inserted back into the name after two years' absence — a strong field gathered at Wentworth with five of the world's top-10 players present and a number having returned from America. Fittingly, one of them won, but not Justin Rose, whose return was perhaps most welcome of all. Rose had not played in Britain for three years, during which time he had been establishing himself in America and returning to the world's top-50 list.

Due to a back injury, Rose's only previous start in three months had been at the Masters, where he challenged for the green jacket before pushing his tee shot at the 17th onto the 15th fairway. At Wentworth, an old stamping ground in his early days, a hot putter let him contend again, even overcoming a pulled drive onto the railway tracks at the ninth for a double bogey in the final round. But it was a vile last day of bank holiday rain and wind, and conditions played their part. Paul Broadhurst, the veteran Englishman, had an 80, and his co-leader overnight, the young Ross Fisher, a former scholarship student at Wentworth, found his fairy-tale week turn into a nightmare with an 84.

Angel Cabrera, the winner in 2005, topped the leaderboard until a scuffed drive at the 15th, and for a while Vijay Singh's early 66 for a clubhouse total of 281, seven under par, looked like a winning contribution. But he was finally beaten by Anders Hansen, who got up and down at the last hole for a birdie. The Dane had bogeyed two of the first three holes but also had three birdies in the first five to turn in 34 and then hit a fine four-iron shot at the par-three 14th for the first of two birdies on the back nine. A 69 after rounds of 74, 70 and 67 put him at 280, eight under.

Rose was the only other player who could catch him, and a superb wedge shot for his third at the 18th spun back to six inches for the tying birdie after a final round of 71. In the playoff at the 18th, both men laid up and were pitching for their thirds. Hansen put his to 20 feet while Rose, from seven yards farther back, hit his to 17 feet. It was a case of the first one to hole out wins, and Hansen holed his as Rose missed.

This was Hansen's second win at the PGA, his only other victory coming five years earlier at Wentworth. After earning a card for the U.S. PGA Tour, Hansen spent the early part of the season in America, finishing only once in the top 25 in nine events. He returned to Europe at the Italian Open and then had two weeks practicing at home, also playing in a club match in Denmark. "I think it means a lot more to me this time than the first time I won it," said Hansen. "It's just a fantastic feeling because I have put in so much hard work and effort recently. What means most to me is how I feel about myself and how I feel about my game and what I do, and right now it feels pretty good."

Celtic Manor Wales Open
Newport, Wales
Winner: Richard Sterne

With history repeating itself seemingly from week to week, Bradley Dredge found himself in the same position as Padraig Harrington two weeks earlier and Justin Rose at Wentworth. To great celebration Harrington won his national Open, while Rose could not quite take the PGA title. Dredge had been in the position of pursuing Harrington at the Irish Open, but at Celtic Manor the roles were reversed. This was the eighth playing of the Wales Open, but a Welshman has yet to take the title after Dredge was denied by South Africa's Richard Sterne.

Dredge forced Harrington to a playoff, but ironically could not force extra time on this occasion. Although tied for the lead, Dredge, 33, from Tredegar, looked out of contention at four strokes back in mid-round. But a stunning rally, including birdies at the 15th, 16th and 17th holes, put Dredge one ahead on the last tee. Up ahead on the 18th green, however, Sterne made a six-foot putt for his sixth birdie on the back nine of the short Roman Road course. He came home in 29 for 65 to get to 263, 13 under par. Dredge now needed a par to tie, but drove into a fairway bunker. The day before he had done the same thing and still made a par, but this time he ended up missing a seven-footer to tie.

Sterne, 25, realized he was not the most popular man in Newport. "It's not what the crowd wanted, but it is a special win for me," he said. Following four top-five finishes in his previous five events, including a third place at the BMW PGA Championship, a second European Tour title was a fitting reward for the diminutive South African. "It is always difficult when you are knocking on the door and you don't win, but I was playing well again this week and to get the breakthrough means a lot. I knew I needed to birdie the 18th, but I thought it would only get me a playoff. I didn't expect him to bogey the last."

Dredge, understandably, was left disappointed with a second runner-up finish in three weeks. "I really feel this is a kick in the nuts," he said. "When I holed on 17 I thought that might be enough. It's a bit frustrating, isn't it?" To add to his frustrations, a win would have put Dredge in the world's top 50 and given him exemptions to the U.S. Open and the Open Championship.

BA-CA Golf Open
Vienna, Austria
Winner: Richard Green

Richard Green admitted nerves led to him making a hash of the putting on the 72nd green to win the BA-CA Golf Open. Having waited 10 years and 100 days since his last victory on the European Tour, plus a two-hour delay for thunder and lightning in mid-afternoon, Green only had to endure one extra hole in the playoff to claim the title at Fontana Golf Club, near Vienna.

Green had two putts from 12 feet for the title at the 18th hole in regulation, but raced his first putt four feet past. The next one then lipped out and the 36-year-old Australian had to compose himself before holing out to tie with France's Jean-Francois Remesy. The Frenchman made a great charge with a 64, after starting with a one-over-par 72 and then adding rounds of 67 and 65, to set the target at 16-under 268. A year before, the left-handed Green had closed with 63 at Fontana to finish fourth behind Markus Brier.

He started this year's event in similar fashion with rounds of 66, 65 and 67, but closed with 70 to tie Remesy. Going to the playoff at the 18th, Remesy's approach over the water cleared the wet stuff but finished on the rocks by the edge of the pond. Green chipped to within inches of the hole and the result was assured. Although Green lost a playoff at the KLM Open in 2006, he had won the Australian Masters in extra time in 2004 and also achieved his famous win over Greg Norman and Ian Woosnam at the 1997 Dubai Classic in a playoff.

"I feel very drained and relieved," Green said. "I was very nervous on the 18th green. I suppose it was a bit of adrenaline when I raced it four feet past. I certainly wasn't expecting to hit it that hard, and the second one lipped out. I then had to get the ball into the hole to be sure of being in the playoff. I am relieved now."

After a double bogey at the third hole, Miguel Angel Jimenez took the lead, but the Spaniard was disturbed by a camera click on the 18th tee and finished third alongside Sweden's Michael Jonzon and England's Chris Gane, another left-hander.

Open de Saint-Omer
Lumbres, France
Winner: Carl Suneson

At the end of 2006 Carl Suneson made his way through qualifying for the fifth time. It was his ninth visit and that does not include his four unsuccessful attempts at pre-qualifying for the six-round Finals nor the two occasions when he qualified for the main circuit from the Challenge Tour. His career included five victories on the Challenge Tour, but keeping his card on the main circuit had always been a problem. Not, however, after winning the Open de Saint-Omer. The long road traveled included being diagnosed with diabetes in 1995 and switching to Spanish citizenship in 1996, after playing amateur golf for England.

Suneson was born in Gran Canaria, where his Swedish father and English mother had relocated to escape the northern European winters. A final round of 69 gave the 39-year-old a two-stroke victory over Peter Fowler, the veteran Australian warming up for the seniors circuits, England's Marcus Higley and France's Francois Calmels.

Birdies at the 12th, 14th and 17th holes allowed Suneson to bogey the 18th and still embark on a joyful celebration for his maiden victory in his 256th European Tour start. He dedicated the win to his 94-year-old grandfather, Cyril Jewsbury. "My grandfather introduced my family to this game and he always said he wanted me to win on Tour before he died," explained Suneson with a tear in his eye. "I want to dedicate this to him.

"I am delighted to win. To have led going into the last round and to get through it is amazing. I played well today and I couldn't believe how I felt. I don't know who was helping me out there, because I felt very calm.

"I was also lucky that no one was attacking me. I was leading by one and Higley made bogey on the first and I just told myself to wait for the birdie to come because I don't have to force any situation. They have to come for me, so that's what I did, and no one came for me, so it was kind of relaxing and I just tried to miss on the right side if I was going to miss."

BMW International Open
Munich, Germany
Winner: Niclas Fasth

As Niclas Fasth contemplated a 15-foot putt for par on the 15th green at the BMW International Open, he looked up at the scoreboard for the first time in a while. Usually the Swede pays close attention to the leaderboards, but not today, and it came as something of a shock to see Bernhard Langer's name quite so high up. This, of course, is only to be expected in Germany, where the home country's greatest player can never be discounted. Not even after an opening round of 76 in which he had to have treatment on the course for a neck injury. Free from pain the following day, Langer made the cut on the mark with 66. Still, he started the final round at Eichenreid five strokes behind, but then put on a superb charge as he pulled a number of monster putts, once from 40 feet, twice from 25 feet and twice from 15 feet.

Fasth, however, once more displayed his ability to seize victory when in contention and holed his par putt on the 15th to retain a one-stroke lead. Langer, who could only par the 18th after driving into the rough, settled for 67 and set the target at 11 under par. Fasth had been cruising when he was three ahead at the turn, but a double bogey at the 10th hole made for a tense afternoon. At the 17th he holed from seven feet for a birdie to go two ahead and then he parred the 18th to clinch a two-stroke victory. Portugal's Jose-Filipe Lima, who shared the third-round lead with Fasth, claimed a birdie-four at the last to tie Langer for second place.

Fasth continued his form, but also had to overcome his fatigue, from finishing fourth in the U.S. Open the week before. This was his sixth win on the European Tour and his fifth in just over two years. "All in all I played some amazing golf," said Fasth. "I've improved some things for this year and the biggest difference is my driving. I felt like it was my tournament to win or lose from the start of the final round, and to come through the way I did feels fantastic."

For Langer, two months short of his 50th birthday, it was a second runner-up finish of the season after he lost a playoff to Rory Sabbatini at the Colonial. He was also deprived of a first win in the only German event he has never won. "Every once in a while the old swing shows up, the old talent shows, but unfortunately not often enough," Langer said.

Open de France ALSTOM
Paris, France
Winner: Graeme Storm

Eight years after winning the British Amateur, Graeme Storm completed his first victory on the European Tour by claiming the Open de France ALSTOM at Le Golf National in Paris. Storm lived up to his name by coming from five strokes behind overnight leader Soren Hansen with a brilliant final round of 66, five under par. Having set the target at seven-under-par 277, no one could match it, with Hansen taking second place, one stroke adrift, and a four-way tie for third place at five under involving Colin Montgomerie, Thomas Bjorn, Simon Khan and Damien McGrane, who set the early pace with 65.

Montgomerie, searching for a first victory since 2005, twice got to seven under par, but dropped three shots in the last seven holes. Storm, who did not drop a shot in the final round, birdied the 13th hole and then the par-five 14th to reach seven under. He then parred home, no easy feat over the closing holes at Golf National, where water comes into play on three of the final four holes.

After a bogey at the 12th, Montgomerie got back to seven under with a four at the 14th, but then missed short putts at both the 15th, where he three-putted, and the 16th, where he failed to get up and down from the bank at the back of the green. Hansen had endured two double bogeys in the first six holes, but fought back, and a birdie-two at the short 16th got him within one of Storm, but he could not make either of his long birdie attempts at the last two holes.

Storm qualified for the Open Championship at Carnoustie, where he played as the Amateur champion in 1999. He turned professional after playing in the Masters in 2000, where he earned a footnote in history by becoming the first player to have his mother caddie for him at Augusta. It was only after winning twice on the Challenge Tour in 2004 that Storm managed to retain his card on the main circuit the following year. Early in his career he had taken a winter job in a cream cake factory, washing baking trays outside in the cold, to earn enough to buy Christmas presents. In Paris he collected €666,660, which came in handy as he and wife Sara were just moving house.

"Working in a cake factory was a bit of a come-down for me," Storm said. "But in a way it helped me, because it showed me the other side of life and how hard you have to work. This win has now changed my life."

Smurfit Kappa European Open
Straffan, Co. Kildare, Ireland
Winner: Colin Montgomerie

A week after missing out in France, Colin Montgomerie secured his first win in 19 months at the Smurfit Kappa European Open. "This is not an important win — it's a very, very important win," he said. "You wonder if it's ever going to happen, of course you do. You have self-doubts and I'm so glad. I'm thrilled with the success. I've never made a winner's speech and said I was unlucky and I was fortunate at the last two today." Twice Montgomerie flirted with the water at the last two holes, but then twice the final round had been interrupted by the threat of lightning.

This was the European Tour's first return to The K Club following the Ryder Cup victory the previous September. But this event, as in 2006, was played on the Smurfit course instead of the more famous Palmer course, where the Ryder Cup was staged. Due to rain every day for over three weeks, the course was saturated and the par-five 18th had to be turned into a par-three, making the par for the course 70. That made both the last two holes par-threes over water, and Montgomerie only just made it on each occasion but then saved par.

As in France, Soren Hansen took the third-round lead with Montgomerie four behind, but the Scot stormed to the front with three birdies in the first six holes and two more at the 10th and 11th. But a bogey at the 12th while Niclas Fasth was birdieing the 10th meant the Swede held the lead when the first delay came. After the resumption Montgomerie holed from 15 feet at the 15th and completed a 65 to reach the clubhouse at 11 under par. Fasth dropped shots at the 12th and 13th, but birdied the 15th and just missed an eight-footer for birdie at the 17th when there was another interruption.

Fasth, trying to win his second successive event after victory in Munich, had to wait for 80 minutes before playing the 18th and again missed for birdie from 14 feet to leave Montgomerie victorious. It was the 44-year-old

Scot's 31st victory on the European Tour, taking him one ahead of Nick Faldo and behind only Seve Ballesteros and Bernhard Langer. "I've looked up to Nick Faldo for a long time and now to be one win ahead is great," Montgomerie said.

Barclays Scottish Open
Glasgow, Scotland
Winner Gregory Havret

Phil Mickelson came agonizingly close to winning his first important tournament outside America, but a late stutter allowed Gregory Havret to take advantage in brilliant fashion to capture the biggest victory of his career. Mickelson was the overnight leader at Loch Lomond, but Havret added to his Italian Open victory in 2001 by claiming the Barclays Scottish Open and the £500,000 first prize.

Mickelson won the Perrier tournament at EuroDisney in Paris in 1993 at a time when the event attracted a number of American players. But that was on the Challenge Tour, and a full victory on the European Tour awaited as he led throughout most of the final day. After his victory at The Players Championship, Mickelson injured his wrist in preparation for the U.S. Open and had not made a cut since, but his game appeared to be coming together again. He was particularly pleased with his driving in the third round when he hit 13 of 14 fairways on a day of high winds. But he did not par the last six holes — the last seven including the playoff — as he came home with birdie-bogey golf.

Credit Havret with clinging to Mickelson's tail and being tied with two to play. The 30-year-old Frenchman fell one behind again when Mickelson holed a long putt at the 17th, but the American then failed to get up and down for a par at the last. At the 18th in the playoff, Mickelson almost cut his drive into the loch, could only play out of the reeds since he is a lefty, and saw Havret get up and down from a greenside bunker for the surprise victory. "He played very solid golf and I played very erratic golf," admitted Mickelson.

Havret reveled in both the bagpipes that sounded in celebration and being drowned in champagne by Thomas Levet, the winner of the event in 2004, and Raphael Jacquelin. It also got him in the Open for the first time. "It feels awesome to have won," said Havret. "It's a dream come true."

Havret closed with a 68 to Mickelson's 69, both finishing at 270. Ernie Els finished off with a 65 to take third place at 13 under par, one outside the playoff, while Luke Donald was in fine form with a 64 to share fourth place with Pelle Edberg, Richard Sterne and Louis Oosthuizen.

The Open Championship
Carnoustie, Scotland
Winner: Padraig Harrington

See Chapter 4.

Deutsche Bank Players' Championship of Europe
Hamburg, Germany
Winner: Andres Romero

A week after coming so close to winning the Open Championship, Argentina's Andres Romero claimed his first title on the European Tour by winning the Deutsche Bank Players' Championship of Europe at Gut Kaden. At Carnoustie, the 26-year-old was leading by two strokes standing on the 17th tee. But his second shot from the rough ricocheted off the wall of the Barry Burn and went out of bounds the other side of the 18th hole. He took a double bogey and a bogey at the last and missed out on the playoff by one stroke.

It might have been an experience many players would have needed time to recover from, but in Germany Romero was immediately back in the thick of the action. He was leading by two strokes after the third round, when he produced a superb 63, and birdied three of the first four holes in the final round to extend his lead. He was five ahead playing the ninth, but there found a pond and took a double bogey. It was the wake-up call he needed and he then cruised to a three-stroke victory.

At the 18th he had three putts for it, but rolled in a long one to spark the celebrations despite the sodden conditions. A final round of 69 gave Romero a 19-under-par total of 269. Soren Hansen, of Denmark, closed with 64 to share second place with England's Oliver Wilson, who had a final round of 66.

Romero, who is no relation of Eduardo Romero, admitted he owed much to his illustrious compatriots, including the new U.S. Open champion Angel Cabrera. "I love the way Angel Cabrera plays, and after his win in the U.S. Open he opened all the doors for the Argentineans, and I was thinking I have to do my share now," said Romero. "That helped me a lot, and I'm very grateful to Angel. Because he won the U.S. Open, I have even more confidence for me to play good golf.

"It feels great to win my first tournament," he added. "I didn't expect the win to come this quick, but the last tournament I had a great result and was playing great at the Open. I was thinking this was the time for me. The Open has changed my life."

Russian Open Golf Championship
Moscow, Russia
Winner: Per-Ulrik Johansson

Playing only his third event on the European Tour in 2007, Per-Ulrik Johansson regained his card by winning the Russian Open Golf Championship at Le Meridien Moscow Country Club. It was his sixth victory on the European Tour, but his first for 10 years since the 1997 European Open. The two-time Ryder Cup player, who appeared in Europe's winning teams of 1995 and 1997, went to play on the U.S. PGA Tour in 2001, but lost his card there two years later and played a collection of main circuit and Nationwide Tour events.

He was 15th at the European Open in July, but his lack of competitive play hardly showed as he shot 62 in the second round. The score would have tied the course record but for the wet weather meaning preferred lies were allowed. The 40-year-old Swede led by four strokes at the halfway stage and maintained that advantage with 67 in the third round.

Another 67 on the final day, when play was moved forward to early in the morning to avoid further weather interruptions, brought Johansson a six-stroke win over Holland's Robert-Jan Derksen, whose 69 pipped the 68 of Canadian-based Scot Alan McLean for second place. Johansson made four birdies going out and then added another at the 11th before making important par saves at the 14th and 15th. Then it was a cruise to the finish line.

"I feel great," said Johansson, "not having won since 1997. I have played some good golf since then, but I haven't played this well, so I am very, very pleased. It is tough when you haven't won for that long, but the most important thing is that you still have to play when you get into a position.

"You can't think about winning because you can't control the other people, so I am very pleased with the way I did that. I focused on every shot and the only time my mind wandered away a little bit was in the middle of the round and I was thinking about speeches and stuff, but I kicked myself and said, no, no, think only about the present, and it really worked."

Scandinavian Masters
Stockholm, Sweden
Winner: Mikko Ilonen

Having won his first tournament in Indonesia earlier in the year, Mikko Ilonen claimed his second closer to home at the Scandinavian Masters. Though the event is held in Sweden, this year at the Arlandastad course in Stockholm, the title involves the wider region and Ilonen became the first player from Finland to add his name to the roll of champions. The 27-year-old from Vanajanlinna, who now lives in Switzerland, survived a remarkable turnaround on the closing two par-threes to win by two strokes ahead of a group of five players including Germany's Martin Kaymer.

Ilonen, after a birdie on the 15th hole, led by one, but then found the water at the short 16th and took a double-bogey five. He then missed a short birdie chance at the 17th and so came to the last hole a stroke behind Kaymer, a two-time winner on the Challenge Tour in 2006 but still looking for his first title on the main tour. Ilonen hit a four iron at the 18th, another tough par-three in the closing stretch, and it was a superb shot, finishing five feet away.

With Kaymer watching from the tee, Ilonen holed the putt to join the German at six under par. Now the pressure was on Kaymer and the 22-year-old missed the green and chipped poorly, the ball rolling back down the slope by the green. He ended up taking a double bogey and handing the title to Ilonen. The Finn had started the day three behind Kaymer and South Africa's James Kingston, but closed with 68, for a total of 274, as against Kaymer's 73. Local favorite Peter Hedblom shared second place with the German at four under, along with Nick Dougherty and Frenchmen Christian Cevaer and Jean-Baptiste Gonnet. Kingston slipped to seventh place with Paul Broadhurst and America's Corey Pavin.

"It's an unbelievable feeling," said Ilonen, who first surprised the golfing establishment by winning the 2000 British Amateur. "If I had to pick one tournament to win, alongside the majors, it would be this one. You all saw the support we get from the crowds, it's something we don't get every week and I hope some other tournaments can learn from this. It's unbelievable for the players to be out there."

He added: "It's the first time I've hit the 18th green all week, including a couple of attempts in the practice rounds. My playing partner Paul Broadhurst hit his three iron a little fat and it still ran through the green, so I knew it was a perfect four iron for me."

KLM Open
Zandvoort, Netherlands
Winner: Ross Fisher

Ross Fisher, in his second full season on the European Tour, had been building towards a first title, but he was left with a harrowing wait before the moment arrived at the KLM Open at Kennemer. The 26-year-old from the Wentworth Club in England had played alongside Tiger Woods and not been disgraced as he challenged for the Dubai Desert Classic earlier in the year. He had also been in the running for a fairy-tale maiden win in the BMW PGA Championship at his home club before a disastrous final round. In Holland, Fisher emerged from a three-way tie after 54 holes with David Carter and New Zealand's Steve Alker to lead by four strokes with five holes to play.

With young Dutchman Joost Luiten, who was enjoying a successful season on the Challenge Tour, pressing hard, Fisher's three-putts at the 16th and 17th holes meant his lead had evaporated. But the Englishman confidently holed from eight feet at the last for a one-stroke victory at 12-under 272, his closing 67 just edging out Luiten's final effort of 66. But the drama was not over for Fisher as he was taken back to the 12th hole by a referee and the tournament director to examine a possible rules violation. Fisher had started to move a bramble but immediately stopped after realizing it was attached and not loose. After visiting the spot and watching video footage, the official deemed Fisher was not guilty of improving his lie and Fisher was able to celebrate at last. "It was a thin strand and I went to move it because I thought it was a loose impediment, but when I realized it was attached I literally left it alone," Fisher explained. "They deemed it didn't improve my stance or my swing. I feel very fortunate."

Bernhard Langer, in his first event since having gallstones removed and a day before his 50th birthday, finished tied for third place four strokes behind Fisher, alongside Alker, Thomas Levet, Alex Noren and Alastair Forsyth. The following week Langer made his debut on the Champions Tour in America. At Kennemer, however, he was also keeping a paternal eye on his son Stefan, a 17-year-old amateur making his debut on the European Tour. Unfortunately the tough course was too much for the youngster and he scored rounds of 98 and 91 to be 49 over par.

Johnnie Walker Championship at Gleneagles
Perthshire, Scotland
Winner: Marc Warren

Marc Warren started the week in the beautiful Perthshire hills of the Gleneagles Hotel with a row with his coach Bob Torrance, but finished it as the first Scottish winner of the Johnnie Walker Championship. Frustrated at his recent performances, Warren started to take it out on Torrance on the practice range when the septuagenarian coach told the 26-year-old Scot that if his attitude did not improve then there was nothing more he could do for the player. Later that day the pair made up after a heart-to-heart in which Torrance admitted that the only player not to have given him any grief was Open champion Padraig Harrington.

The next day Torrance changed a couple of things in Warren's stance and in the opening round he scored a flawless eight-under 65. It was England's Simon Wakefield who came through to lead going into the final round, but Warren was only a stroke behind and the pair put on quite a show on the last day in front of record numbers of spectators. Warren was the home favorite, but a bogey at the 17th meant he needed to hole from eight feet at the 18th for a birdie to force the playoff. Warren closed with a 69 to Wakefield's 70 as the pair tied at 280, 12 under, with Soren Hansen and Martin Erlandsson sharing third place a stroke back.

After the first extra hole was halved in par-fives, Warren took the advantage the second time around, also at the 18th, when he found the green in two. But he was 30 yards from the hole and it took a wonderful lag putt, followed by a nerveless three-footer, to seal the victory as Wakefield could do no better than a five. Warren, who holed the winning putt at the 2001 Walker Cup, had won his two Challenge Tour victories in 2005 in playoffs and also his first European Tour title at the Scandinavian Masters in 2006, when he defeated the home favorite Robert Karlsson. This time he was the winner the crowd wanted and he was brought onto the green for the presentation ceremony to wild applause. "It doesn't get any better," he said. "It's a dream come true. To win in Scotland is overwhelming. Victories don't sink in very quickly and I think this one will take a bit of time to register."

Omega European Masters
Crans Montana, Switzerland
Winner: Brett Rumford

When both Brett Rumford and Phillip Archer missed the green at the 18th hole at Crans-sur-Sierre, the first extra hole of their playoff, two up-and-downs for par seemed to be the best they could aim. But Rumford is something of a short game expert and when he chipped in from 30 feet it suddenly left Archer having to follow the Australian in from the back fringe to secure the half. He could not and it was a dramatic way for Rumford to secure his third win on the European Tour at the Omega European Masters. His two previous victories came at the 2003 Aa St. Omer Open and the 2004 Irish Open. The latest triumph could not have come at a better time for the 30-year-old as he was 106th on the Order of Merit going into the last couple of months of the season.

It was Archer, a runner-up at the Open de Andalucia earlier in the season, who made the biggest move on the final day high up in the Alps. His closing 65 took the 35-year-old Englishman to 16 under par, where he tied with Rumford after a 68. The Australian's challenge got serious when he birdied the 11th and 12th holes and then saved par from 35 feet at the 13th. Both Archer and Rumford bogeyed the 17th hole and missed birdie chances of 15 feet at the 18th. Defending champion Bradley Dredge, who was the leader overnight, also had a chance to make the playoff but missed from 12 feet at the last. His 69 left the Welshman one behind in third place but one ahead of compatriot Sion Bebb, who closed with 68 in what he thought would be his last event of the season. His fourth-place finish, however, earned the 38-year-old rookie another start at the Quinn Direct British Masters in order to try to retain his card.

Rumford said: "It's been a pretty tough year. This has proved very emotional and I had to have five minutes in a back room when it all hit me. I've been trying hard, grinding week in week out for not much, but at last it's all come together this week." About the winning chip-in, he added: "You are just suspended there for that brief second in anticipation and there is nothing going through your mind but get in. It was tracking all the way and I thought it was coming up short, but the breeze took it in. My short game has pulled me through this week."

Mercedes-Benz Championship
Cologne, Germany
Winner: Soren Hansen

Soren Hansen survived an all-Danish battle with Thomas Bjorn in the final pairing of the last round to win the Mercedes-Benz Championship at Gut Larchenhof. It was the 33-year-old's second win on the European Tour after winning the Irish Open in 2002. His two wins have followed in the same season that Anders Hansen, no relation, won the PGA Championship.

Hansen broke clear of not just Bjorn but the rest of the field with two eagles in the last six holes as a closing 67 for 17 under par gave him a four-stroke victory over Alastair Forsyth and Phillip Archer, a runner-up for the second week running. Bjorn and Bradley Dredge shared fourth place a further stroke back in the elite field of 78 gathered by host Bernhard Langer.

Hansen played with Langer in the first two rounds and was tipped for the title by the host. "Throughout this week I just played tremendous — the best I have ever played. I had a really good feeling coming into the event.

I've been knocking on the door this summer and I just felt this might be the week for me," said the delighted Hansen.

Hansen chipped in for an eagle-three at the 13th and then two holes later hit a superb three wood from 265 yards to 15 feet to set up another eagle at the 15th. He dropped a shot at the 17th, but his advantage was already established. He said: "Thomas Bjorn in form is a dangerous man and in the past I have looked a little bit too much over my shoulder at what the others were doing, but today I just stuck with what I had and I hit some really good shots to stay on top all the time.

"I never really got into that much trouble today. I stayed really patient and I think that was the key. It was nice to have a few in the bank over the last few holes. I beat 77 other players, all the best players of the year, and I feel really proud about that."

Bjorn was full of praise for his friend, saying: "It's fantastic for Soren. He played brilliant today — but the chip shot on 18 yesterday showed how well he can handle pressure and a difficult situation. He's been knocking on the door for a long time this year and he's that kind of talent who just needs to do this more often."

Quinn Direct British Masters
Sutton Coldfield, West Midlands, England
Winner: Lee Westwood

After three top-10 finishes in the previous three weeks, Lee Westwood knew it was time he capitalized on his good form. There were many reasons to do so at the Quinn Direct British Masters. The tournament is promoted by his manager, Andrew "Chubby" Chandler. The event is played at The Belfry, where he always felt he should play well but had not managed to when the tournament was in the spring. With the switch to September, Westwood felt as comfortable on the Brabazon course as he did in gaining three wins during the 2002 Ryder Cup. The venue is also only an hour away from his home in Worksop, so he was supported by many friends and family.

"The last few weeks I've put too much pressure on myself," he said. "I would be lying in bed on the Saturday night expecting to win. This time I just went out to play well." With the help of a short game tip from Mark Roe, the former player turned media pundit, he played remarkably well. A flawless final round of 65 took him from two behind his Worksop friend Mark Foster to a five-stroke victory over Ian Poulter. A couple of early birdies, leading ahead of the final groups, put Westwood even with Foster.

After an up-and-down start, Foster chipped in at the ninth to stay tied with Westwood, but on the back nine it was no contest. At the 13th Westwood hit in close for a birdie, while at the same hole later on Foster drove out of bounds to take a double bogey and fall out of contention. It was at the 16th that Westwood holed from 40 feet for a vital birdie. He had holed a similar putt on the same green to go one up with two to play in the 2002 Ryder Cup and ended up losing the match, a thought that kept him focused to the end. At the 17th he holed from 35 feet for an eagle, but he thought his best two shots were the drive and three iron at the 18th for a safe par.

"The British Masters is one of our most prestigious events," Westwood said. "I've been building up to doing something like this. What gives me most satisfaction is hitting some great knockdown shots in the wind and doing it when it mattered, whereas a couple of years ago I was not comfortable playing those shots."

The week was also notable for the professional debuts of Walker Cup players Lloyd Saltman and Rory McIlroy. Saltman missed the cut, but McIlroy finished 42nd. "I'd give myself a B-minus for the week," said the 18-year-old.

The Seve Trophy
Killenard, Co. Laois, Ireland
Winner: Great Britain and Ireland

Nick Faldo's first experience of captaincy turned out to be a winning one as Great Britain and Ireland retained The Seve Trophy at the Heritage in Ireland. For the first time there were non-playing captains, with Seve Ballesteros, the man who inspired the event, leading the Continental Europeans as he did in the first three matches, and Faldo, the Ryder Cup captain for Valhalla in 2008, skippering the GBI team, which won for the fourth successive match. A point behind going into the final day, an 8-to-2 rout in the singles, with Sweden's Peter Hanson winning Europe's only full point, led to a comfortable 16½-to-11½ victory.

Not everything went smoothly as one of Faldo's vice-captains for the Ryder Cup, Paul McGinley, choose the week to announce his resignation, and it was disappointing there were no Irishmen involved, with Open champion Padraig Harrington, pleading exhaustion, withdrawing along with 10 other players.

Though the atmosphere was a far cry from that of the Ryder Cup, it was an ideal opportunity for many new players to gain experience of international team competition. Although for Marc Warren the event took an unlikely turn when, on the first evening, he was practicing with a five iron in his hotel room and smashed a glass lamp shade and had to go to the hospital for stitches.

Some of the scoring was extremely good. After the two days of fourballs ended tied, the greensomes on Saturday morning sparkled as Europe took a three-point lead. GBI fought back in the afternoon foursomes to trail by just a point and then won the first three matches in the singles, thanks to Colin Montgomerie, avoiding the embarrassment of scoreless week, Paul Casey and Warren. The three had been spurred on by Sky Sports pundits on Saturday night saying they would not win any of those matches. Casey had struggled with his form earlier in the week but was helped by Faldo's novel on-course coaching. "He has a great eye for the swing and he certainly helped me," said Casey. "I wouldn't normally be receptive to someone offering me advice on the golf course, but it shows that he cares. You could see that he really wanted to win this."

Bradley Dredge won four and a half points out of five, and his partner,

Phil Archer, was also unbeaten, claiming the crucial half against Markus Brier that won the match.

Faldo said: "I've really enjoyed the new role. I've learnt things every day and made lots of notes, though I'm not going to give anything away that I believe will make a difference. But I have learned a lot about the players. I think everybody's impressed me in some area, they really have."

Alfred Dunhill Links Championship
St. Andrews, Scotland
Winner: Nick Dougherty

At 25 years old Nick Dougherty was one of Britain's young hopefuls, but his first win in Singapore in 2005 had yet to be followed up. It was not for the lack of trying and a number of chances came and went, including in Singapore and Italy in 2007. A fine performance at the U.S. Open added to the Liverpool man's confidence and it was an assured display he put on to claim that long-awaited second victory at the Alfred Dunhill Links Championship.

Dougherty survived an event that is played over three courses — albeit in benign conditions of glorious Scottish autumnal sunshine that encouraged bathers in St. Andrews Bay — and the pro-am format to secure a two-stroke victory over Justin Rose. Dougherty started his campaign with a 67 at Kingsbarns, then added rounds of 66 at both Carnoustie, in less forbidding mode than for the Open Championship earlier in the summer, and over the Old Course at St. Andrews. Everyone gathered on the Old Course for the final round, which Dougherty started with a three-stroke lead. It was soon whittled away as he bogeyed the first two holes, but three birdies in a row from the fifth steadied the ship, and it was with terrific maturity that he plowed remorselessly onto victory over the last nine.

Dougherty was tied during the round, but he never lost the lead. Ernie Els, who has never won the event, got within one stroke after 15 holes, but then at the next inexplicably took a triple-bogey seven when he putted into a bunker. Rose, who closed with 69, finished two strokes behind Dougherty's 18-under-par 280 total, but it was a result that kept him in contention for the Order of Merit title. Northern Ireland's Rory McIlroy, at the age of 18, birdied the last two holes to finish third in only his second event as a professional and virtually assure his card for 2008, a remarkable rate of progress since switching from the amateur ranks.

HSBC World Match Play
Virginia Water, Surrey, England
Winner: Ernie Els

See Chapter 7.

Open de Madrid Valle Romano
Madrid, Spain
Winner: Mads Vibe-Hastrup

The production line of winners from Denmark just shows no sign of slowing down. With both Anders and Soren Hansen winning in 2007, to go with the past victories of Thomas Bjorn and Soren Kjeldsen, there can now be added the name of Mads Vibe-Hastrup, who won the Open de Madrid Valle Romano by three strokes at the Real Sociedad Hipica Espanola Club de Campo.

A closing 67 for a 16-under-par total of 272 left Vibe-Hastrup three ahead of home favorite Alejandro Canizares, who scored a final-round 68. Argentina's Daniel Vancsik, the leader for the first three rounds, lost his chance of victory with a quintuple-bogey nine on the fifth hole. Vancsik was two shots ahead of the field at the time, but never recovered from his mishap and had to settle for third place at 12 under with 73. Northern Irish teenager Rory McIlroy's attempt to be the youngest European Tour winner was put on hold again, but by finishing fourth alongside Frenchman Gregory Bourdy the 18-year-old not only ended any doubt about gaining his card for 2008, but proved he is ready to contend for titles.

After Vancsik perished on the fifth by tangling with heavy rough in a gulley, the 29-year-old Vibe-Hastrup took a firm hold of proceedings with three birdies in four holes from the eighth. Canizares stayed in touch with him until missing a short putt to bogey the par-three 17th, shortly after Vibe-Hastrup produced a gem of an approach to three feet to birdie the 16th and effectively end the contest.

Vibe-Hastrup agreed that Vancsik's misfortune at the fifth opened the way to his victory, but by no means meant his job was done. "I still had to play a lot of golf from there," said the Dane. "I was just trying to play my own game. It was the same when we started the round. He made a big number, but I just thought, okay, that's his problem and I don't have to worry about that, just about myself. There was still a lot of golf to play at that point, but it was obviously good for me to take the lead at that point. But my mantra of the day was to play my own game."

Portugal Masters
Vilamoura, Portugal
Winner: Steve Webster

An emotional Steve Webster clinched his second victory on the European Tour and then dissolved into tears in the arms of his father beside the final green. Webster's mother died five months earlier and the 32-year-old Englishman was so concerned about his form that he thought he would lose his card. Instead, he added to his win at the 2005 Italian Open by taking the inaugural Portugal Masters at Oceanico Victoria on the Algarve. Webster produced a brilliant final round of 64 to be 25 under par.

"I was thinking about her all the way round," said Webster. "Losing my mum really knocked me about. I didn't even think I'd get my card because it was quite tough. It was so hard to keep my mind on my golf. I knew she was watching out for me and it's an amazing feeling to play that well down the stretch."

Webster's nearest challenger turned out to be playing partner Robert Karlsson, who finished second, two strokes behind after a 65 of his own. "It was a good effort by me, but I was beaten by a better player," said Karlsson. "He is a worthy winner and especially after what he has gone through this year, it is great to see." Four players shared third place six behind Webster: Fredrik Andersson Hed, Peter Hanson, Lee Westwood and Argentina's Daniel Vancsik.

One behind Vancsik at the start of the day, Webster tied for the lead with an outward 32, then took command with a nine-foot eagle putt on the 12th. Adding three more birdies in the next five holes put him well clear and his only dropped shot came at the last. For the second week running Vancsik took the lead into the final round. At the Madrid Open, he suffered a nine at the fifth hole, but in Portugal he had two trips to the water on the two par-fives on the second nine — the 12th and 17th — which cost him a bogey-six on each occasion.

Mallorca Classic
Mallorca, Spain
Winner: Gregory Bourdy

Gregory Bourdy continued his recent fine form to win his first European Tour title in the Mallorca Classic. The 25-year-old from Bordeaux finished two ahead of England's Sam Little, who had the consolation of securing his playing privileges for the 2008 season in the last full-field event on the 2007 circuit. It is always a nerve-racking weekend for those trying to secure their status, but Bourdy was able to concentrate on winning the tournament. A closing 67 gave him a total of 268, 12 under par, and meant he was greeted on the 18th green in familiar fashion with his French colleagues Thomas Levet and Christian Cevaer dousing Bourdy in champagne.

"To get my first win on Tour feels absolutely fantastic," said the Frenchman, whose previous best had been victory in the 2006 South African PGA Championship on the Sunshine Tour. "I had a great day out there and this is just unbelievable." Bourdy became the 18th first-time winner of the season, a new record number of maiden winners on the European Tour.

Having started the final round in a share of the lead with Robert-Jan Derksen, who ended up in third place, Bourdy did not drop a shot all day, his only departures from par coming with birdies at the sixth, ninth and 10th holes. But he did receive one moment of good fortune at the 16th, where he pulled his drive into the rough. With his club turning over in the long grass, his second shot only just managed to get over the water in front of the green. On dry land by a foot, he chipped and putted for a crucial par. "I did think it was in the water at the 16th, so I was very relieved when I saw it bounce in the rough in front of the green," admitted Bourdy. "It was a bit lucky, but sometimes these little things go your way and perhaps that signifies that it is your day."

Little also closed with 67, a superb effort with his card on the line. Three weeks earlier, when his twin daughters were born, the 32-year-old from London was outside the top 117 on the Order of Merit. After finishing seventh in Madrid and 34th in Portugal he was up to 136th place, and the runner-up finish here took him to 76th place. Richard Finch and Jarmo Sandelin also jumped into the top 117 on the Order of Merit to retain their cards, but Lee Slattery, after missing the cut, slipped to 118th place, just £53.50 behind Sandelin.

Volvo Masters
Sotegrande, Cadiz, Spain
Winner: Justin Rose

Justin Rose finally got the victory he had been looking for all year and his timing was perfect. By winning the Volvo Masters at Valderrama, the 27-year-old Englishman also won the European Tour Order of Merit. Consistent, especially in the majors, but playing a limited schedule due to a back injury and his time in America, Rose was third on the list entering the week. Ernie Els was top, but playing in the Singapore Open instead. Both Open champion Padraig Harrington, in second place, and Rose had to finish in the top three to pass Els and then ahead of each other.

Rose suffered from food poisoning on Thursday morning, but though deathly pale in appearance, a hole-in-one with a six iron at the third hole was a welcome boost. Harrington started poorly, but gritted his teeth as the persistent Irish does in a crisis and came home in four under. The windy conditions that lasted all week made life treacherous. The pair ascended to the top of the leaderboard on day two, Rose leading by four, and he kept the same advantage over Harrington and Simon Dyson going into the last round.

Still four ahead with seven to play on Sunday and it almost all disappeared, however. Bunkered twice at the 11th he took a double-bogey seven. Dropped shots at the 13th and 14th followed. Suddenly, the drama was at its peak. Soren Kjeldsen had birdied four of the first seven holes. Graeme McDowell holed a seven iron from 176 yards for a double eagle at the 17th. Harrington could not find the birdies he needed at the 17th and 18th and was locked out in fourth place with McDowell. Simon Dyson almost holed his second shot at the 16th and his eagle-chip at the 17th and was right there.

Rose's two-putt from 50 feet at the 16th settled him down. Then he drove it down the middle at the 17th and a birdie was the result. Kjeldsen, Rose and Dyson all bogeyed the 18th and it was a three-way playoff at one under par, Rose closing with a 74. They all parred the 18th in the playoff, Rose missing the best chance, but all had birdie chances at the 10th. Rose was the one to hole, from 12 feet, and the relief flooded out of the Englishman. "There must be an easy way to do these things, but that wasn't it," he admitted.

On coming home in 40 he said: "It was terrible, there were too many mental errors. I could feel it all slipping away." Yet there can be no giving up at Valderrama, just as at any major championship. "I just kept grinding away as I've done all week. This place forces you do to that. To be Europe's No. 1 is awesome. The best thing is I hoped to do it this way, as a champion."

HSBC Champions
Shanghai, China
Winner: Phil Mickelson

See Asia/Japan Tours chapter.

UBS Hong Kong Open
Hong Kong
Winner: Miguel Angel Jimenez

See Asia/Japan Tours chapter.

MasterCard Masters
Melbourne, Victoria
Winner: Aaron Baddeley

See Australasian Tour chapter.

Michael Hill New Zealand Open
Queenstown, New Zealand
Winner: Richard Finch

See Australasian Tour chapter.

Alfred Dunhill Championship
Mpumalanga, South Africa
Winner: John Bickerton

See African Tours chapter.

South African Airways Open
Paarl, Western Cape, South Africa
Winner: James Kingston

See African Tours chapter.

Challenge Tour

Michael Lorenzo-Vera, a 22-year-old who got into golf because of Tiger Woods but hates flying, became the first Frenchman to top the Challenge Tour standings by winning the Apulia San Domenico Grand Final in Italy. It was his first victory of the season, but his performances were so consistent that he jumped from seventh place on the rankings to first, ahead of eight players who each won twice on the circuit.

Lorenzo-Vera grew up in Biarritz, surfing and helping out at his parents' food shop in town. His brother Frank, six years older, got him into golf and is now his coach and caddie. But it was watching Woods blow away both opponents and history by winning the Masters in 1997 that got the 12-year-old Michael really interested in golf.

"I could not believe what Tiger did at the 1997 Masters," Lorenzo-Vera recalled. "I didn't think that golf could be like that — people were going crazy, very crazy, because this guy was so good and I just thought: 'I want to do that.' He made it cool to play golf."

Lorenzo-Vera had nine top-10 finishes in 2007, and as well as his win, lost a playoff to Ross McGowan at the Oceanico Developments Pro-Am Challenge in Manchester, tied for second at the Challenge of Ireland and third at the Rolex Trophy. He produced three rounds of nine under par, two of them course records and one of them coming in the opening round of the Grand Final at San Domenico. Yet going into the last round he trailed Jamie Donaldson by two strokes and fell four behind early on the front nine. But coming home it was a different matter.

The Frenchman birdied the 14th, 16th and 17th holes and got up and down from a bunker at the 18th, recovering to just a few inches from the hole for a par. His closing 66 was good enough for a one-stroke win over Donaldson, Dutchman Joost Luiten, Welshman Stuart Manley and Scotland's Eric Ramsay. On an exciting final afternoon of the season, Lorenzo-Vera just edged McGowan at the top of the rankings.

Each of Donaldson, Luiten and Manley also ensured their cards for the 2008 European Tour by finishing in the top 20 on the rankings. McGowan was one of those eight players to win twice during the season, the others being former U.S. Amateur champion Edoardo Molinari from Italy, Luiten, Robert Dinwiddie, Iain Pyman, Felipe Aguilar of Chile, who finished third on the rankings, Scotland's Peter Whiteford and former Ryder Cup player Peter Baker.

After struggling to stay on the main circuit for a number of years, Baker dropped down to the Challenge Tour and recorded his first victories since he won twice on the European Tour in 1993. Veteran Australian Peter Fowler, age 48, earned his card for 2008 after deciding to play on the Challenge Tour as preparation for joining the Seniors Tour. He snuck into the top 20 on the last day of the season along with France's Francois Delamontagne.

The other players to earn their cards were: Leif Westerberg, Magnus A. Carlsson, Mikael Lundberg, Fabrizio Zanotti, Julio Zapata, Alvaro Velasco and Jan-Are Larsen.

10. Asia/Japan Tours

Toru Taniguchi surely would never seriously complain about the excellent season he had on the Japan Tour, but he could be excused if he reflected openly about how dominant it might have been. Taniguchi landed his second money title, leading through the latter half of the season after scoring two of his three 2007 victories back to back in July. His third and last win of the season was the big one — his second Japan Open Championship.

Consider, though, that in at least five other tournaments Taniguchi had single bad scores in late rounds that cost him likely victories. As it was, he finished second three times during the season, which saw the schedule further reduced to 24 tournaments, four fewer than in 2006. His money total was ¥171,744,498, some ¥30 million better than Shingo Katayama, who slipped to second place after leading the race the three previous seasons.

Katayama won the Tour Championship and just one other event during the season, missing several tournaments while playing in major and World Golf Championship events abroad. Still, he had an outside shot at a fourth straight No. 1 title well into the season-ending Nippon Series.

Australian Brendan Jones and Hideto Tanihara were the only other multiple winners. Jones, who missed two months to be with his wife and newborn child, still enjoyed his best of six years in Japan, picking up three victories, including the Visa Taiheiyo Masters and Nippon Series in the late fall, and finishing third on the money list. Tanihara, the 2006 runner-up, was next in the standings, but a distant fourth, after back-to-back wins in September.

The story of the year, though, was the almost unbelievable victory of 15-year-old high school freshman Ryo Ishikawa, a special invitee in the Munsingwear Open KSB Cup. He is by far the youngest player ever to win a tournament on one of the world's recognized tours.

Six other players also won for the first time in Japan, including international stars Camilo Villegas (Coca-Cola Tokai Classic) and Ian Poulter (Dunlop Phoenix). The most promising of the other new winners is Lee Dong-hwan, a 20-year-old South Korean who finished sixth on the money list. Veteran Toshimitsu Izawa took the Japan PGA Championship, his 16th tour title.

Meanwhile, history was made on the Asian Tour when Liang Wen-chong, 29, became the first Chinese golfer to take the UBS Order of Merit title, an accomplishment that underlined China's quick and continuing rise in world golf. Liang won the Clariden Leu Singapore Masters and locked up the money race when he tied for 28th in the season-ending Volvo Masters of Asia to lift his winnings to US$532,590 from 19 starts. He also topped $1 million in career winnings.

The title also will make Liang the first Chinese to play in the Open Championship in Britain and the first Chinese to play in the WGC - CA Championship. There he will be joined by two other Asian Tour breakthrough winners, Thailand's Chapchai Nirat, who won his first Asian event in March, the TCL Classic, and added the Hana Bank Vietnam Masters, and Australia's Anton Haig, the Johnnie Walker Classic winner. Taiwan's Lu Wen-teh was also a double winner, taking the Macau Open and the Mercuries Taiwan Masters.

The Asian Tour was pumping more star power into its fields. Vijay Singh took the Kolon-Hana Bank Korea Open. Then Argentina's Angel Cabrera outlasted Singh down the stretch to take the Barclays Singapore Open in November. Phil Mickelson was back in the pack for that one, but got his first Asian win the following week in the HSBC Champions in Shanghai. The Asian Tour enjoyed unprecedented diversity, thanks of course to the co-sanctioned events, to wit: Finland's Mikko Ilonen won the Indonesia Open, Austria's Marcus Brier the Volvo China Open, and France's Raphael Jacquelin the BMW Asian Open. Ilonen and Brier were the first from their countries to win on the Asian and European tours.

The Royal Trophy
Bangkok, Thailand
Winner: Europe

First came the counting, then came the condolences.

This was The Royal Trophy, a Europe versus Asia match held in Bangkok in January, and while the competition was spirited, the outcome was predicable. Europe took the lead in the opening-day alternate-shot format, built on it in the second-day better-ball, then locked it up comfortably in the singles, and the counting added up to a huge 12½-to-3½ victory.

"That was fantastic golf from the European side," said captain Seve Ballesteros. "These are Ryder Cup champions. They beat the Americans very badly, so this was not a surprise. I think a couple of things made the difference. The Asian team did not have quite the experience that the Europeans had and our side played unbelievable golf."

Asian captain Naomichi Ozaki, of Japan, blamed himself. "I expected that the game would be much closer, but this is my first experience of being a captain," he said, "and I want to take full responsibility for this loss."

It was a noble gesture, but as everyone knows, golf doesn't work that way. Five of Ballesteros's eight-man team were from the European side that beat the Americans in the 2006 Ryder Cup. The Asians' only win was the 2-and-1 victory by Thongchai Jaidee over Niclas Fasth in the final singles match. Otherwise, the Asians' only other points came from five halves.

"There is no getting away from the fact that this was a tough defeat for Asia. But what really matters is how they react to it," said Lee Westwood, who scored 2½ points. "These things can be turned around, and that is something the Asian players must tell themselves — and then go out and make it happen."

Pakistan Open
Karachi, Pakistan
Winner: Airil Rizman Zahari

Happy New Year indeed. Victory itself was nothing new to Malaysia's Airil Rizman Zahari. He had seven wins on the Malaysian domestic circuit. Taking the Pakistan Open was something else — his first win on the Asian

Tour, and a great way to start the new season. "I can't believe I did it," Airil said, maybe as surprised as anyone. "It hasn't sunk in yet."

Rizman Zahari was unexpected, but there was nothing questionable about his performance at the par-72 Karachi Golf Club. He started 67-68 and first trailed Pakistan's Muhammad Shabbir (66) by one stroke, then trailed England's Simon Hurd (68-65) by two. Then with a brilliant 64 in the third round, Airil took the lead and stayed there. But not comfortably.

First Airil had to shake off the ankle injury he suffered Saturday night. Then came the pressure from Australian rookie Scott Hend, making his debut, who more than offset a lone bogey with four birdies for 69. But he had to settle for second place by two strokes against Airil's solid play.

Airil was on and off in the final round, but he was on when he needed it most. He went birdie-bogey at the third and fourth holes, then birdied the sixth. He notched his third birdie at the 14th, then gave the stroke back with a bogey at the 16th. Then came more pressure than he had ever faced in golf. At the 18th, he faced a 25-foot birdie putt to lock up the win. And he dropped it for 70 and a 19-under-par 269 and the two-stroke victory. Then he confessed: He was trying to lag that 25-footer. "But to see the ball rolling slowly to the pin for a birdie ... it was out of this world," he said.

Philippine Open
Manila, Philippines
Winner: Frankie Minoza

The Philippine Open was anyone's tournament from the start. The first-round leaderboard told the tale. China's Liang Wen-chong and five others led at 68, and five others tied at 69, including Thai veteran Prayad Marksaeng. Thus things didn't look promising for Frankie Minoza in the group of 19 players tied for 45th place at 73. Being five strokes behind wasn't a big problem, but climbing over that huge crowd would be. But Minoza, age 47, did not become the Philippines' best golfer by hanging back.

Minoza made up all that ground with 67s in the next two rounds. He was three strokes behind Liang after two rounds, and led him by one in the third round. The next day, Minoza was lifting his second Philippine Open crown and his 15th title in Asia. He made it look easy. "I was looking at the leaderboard, just to see where I stood," Minoza said. "I knew Liang was close at one point, but I wasn't too affected."

Except by the weather. Under tough conditions, Minoza bogeyed the first two holes. He birdied the third but bogeyed the fifth. Birdies at Nos. 6 and 9 extended his lead. But the pressure now was coming from Filipino Gerald Rosales, who was working on his best round ever at Wack Wack Golf Club. Rosales had six birdies, one bogey and an eagle from 10 feet at the par-five 14th for 65.

Minoza was unfazed. He did bogey the 11th, but bounced right back with birdies at the 13th and 14th. At the 18th, he calmly holed a seven-foot par putt for 71, a 10-under-par 278 total and a two-stroke margin over Rosales. "My two bogeys at the opening stages didn't bother me," Minoza said, "because I knew I could handle it."

Maybank Malaysian Open
Kuala Lumpur, Malaysia
Winner: Peter Hedblom

Peter Hedblom had just birdied the 17th hole and fans were congratulating him on winning. There being one hole to play, he refused to let the victory waiting for him be drained away by false confidence.

"I'm focused on making four or five (at the last)," the Swede said. It turned out that he three-putted for a bogey-six, but it was enough for a one-stroke victory over France's Jean-Francois Lucquin in the Maybank Malaysian Open, the co-sponsored Asian and European Tour event at the Saujana Golf and Country Club in Kuala Lumpur early in February. Hedblom was 37 years old, and this was only his second career victory — after the 1996 Moroccan Open — and his first on the Asian Tour. Hedblom did not lack for pressure from marquee names such as Thomas Bjorn, Lee Westwood, Michael Campbell and Darren Clarke.

By any measure, Hedblom's victory was remarkable. In playing the par-72 Saujana course in 73-71-68-68 for an eight-under-par 280 total, Hedblom climbed from a tie for 49th place in the first round, then a tie for 32nd, and then he entered the final round three strokes behind Argentina's Ricardo Gonzalez and England's Marcus Higley.

Hedblom broke out of a traffic jam with birdies on the 13th, 16th and 17th holes. At the 18th, his second shot ended up in a dangerous lie on the edge of a bunker. "If I hit it fat, I would still be in the bunker, if I hit it thin I would be over the green," Hedblom said. "But I hit a great shot to where it was. After that, I was shaking. I couldn't even put my club down on that putt."

And so he three-putted for the bogey, but fortunately, Lucquin (67) had three-putted the 18th ahead of him, also for a bogey. Now Hedblom was accepting the back-slapping.

Enjoy Jakarta Astro Indonesia Open
Jakarta, Indonesia
Winner: Mikko Ilonen

Who's the most likely to succeed in the heat of Indonesia — someone from Southeast Asia or someone from near the Arctic? Enter Mikko Ilonen, winner of the co-sanctioned Enjoy Jakarta Astro Indonesia Open, the first golfer from Finland ever to win on the Asian and European Tours. And the secret was his lunch during a rain delay in the final round. "I always feel like I am swinging really softly after I've just eaten," Ilonen said.

Actually, Ilonen got a leg up on the tournament with some excellent play before the storm, and then was solid afterward to take a one-stroke victory over the Philippines' Frankie Minoza, India's Shiv Kapur and Australia's Andrew Tampion.

Ilonen, who tied for seventh in the Malaysian Open the week before, opened with 66 at Jakarta's par-71 Damai Golf Club. It was the only time he trailed. He shot 68 in the second round and tied with Tampion (66) at eight under par. In the final round, Ilonen birdied the fifth and seventh holes and bogeyed the eighth, then birdied the 13th. Minoza, who won the Philippine Open two weeks earlier, was tied with Ilonen after the 13th, then double-bogeyed the 14th after a poor drive. "But I never gave up, and I kept fighting," Minoza said.

Ilonen parred the 14th, and then came the storm delay and his lunch. He came back and finished off the round for a one-under 70 and a nine-under 275 total for the victory. Ilonen figured his win would help golf in Finland. As for himself: "Now that I have won," Ilonen said, "I feel like I can win again."

Johnnie Walker Classic
Phuket, Thailand
Winner: Anton Haig

It wasn't a surprise that a South African won the Johnnie Walker Classic. The surprise was that it wasn't Ernie Els. It was Anton Haig, only 20 years of age, known but to his countrymen, and he did it in a playoff for his first victory. Haig emerged in the third round, then slugged his way through a field thick with world-class players in the Asian and European Tour co-sanctioned event to beat South African Richard Sterne and England's Oliver Wilson.

"If I could only explain this in words," Haig said, getting his biggest prize ever, $405,000, and a two-year exemption on the European Tour. He was just a face in the crowd until he rocketed into contention in the second round with an eight-under 64, tying the course record at Blue Canyon in Phuket, Thailand. Earlier, Sterne had made the biggest move. He opened with 75, then packed his bags, certain he would miss the cut. He shot 64 in the second round, and then another 64 in the third, and headed into the fourth leading Wilson (70) by one and Haig (70) by two.

Haig trailed Wilson and Sterne by a stroke going to the final hole, and got the lead — or at least a share of it — at that 72nd hole when he rescued a stray drive with a 98-yard wedge shot to three feet and holed the birdie for 70 and a tie at 13-under 275. All three had birdie chances at the first extra hole. Wilson missed from 25 feet, and Sterne from 12 feet. Then Haig dropped his 10-footer for the victory. "Absolutely amazing," Haig said. "At the start of the week, I didn't think this was actually possible."

Clariden Leu Singapore Masters
Singapore
Winner: Liang Wen-chong

There were two big surprises in the Clariden Leu Singapore Masters. First, the man who won, and that was China's top golfer, Liang Wen-chong, with his first victory. And second, who missed the cut in the Asian-European Tour co-sponsored tournament, notably European stars Ian Woosnam, Lee Westwood, David Howell and Darren Clarke. So the closest any European would come to winning the title was England's Simon Dyson, finishing in third place.

Liang had said it in the first round, when he tied Marcus Fraser for the lead at eight-under-par 64. "I don't want the pressure to get to me," he said. "I'm still learning."

He had already had a great day at school, Laguna National. In a bogey-free round, he piled up eight birdies, including four straight from the 12th hole. Frazer made eight birdies, including a chip-in at the 18th. Liang slipped to 72 in the second round, and Jyoti Randhawa took over with 68–133, leading Scotland's Barry Hume (69) by one stroke, and Liang was three behind. England's Gary Lockerbie stepped up in the third round with 69 for a 12-under 204 total, tying Liang, who landed six more birdies, crowned by a 20-foot putt at the 18th for 68.

In the final round, Indian standout Randhawa was another surprise. He dropped four strokes in seven holes coming home, shot 75 and drifted back. Meanwhile, Liang (73) and Iain Steel (71) tied at 277 in an exchange of nerves. Liang double-bogeyed the par-five 15th but birdied the par-four 16th. Steel squandered his chance with a double bogey at the 16th. In the playoff, at the par-four 18th, Liang hit a good drive, wedged to 12 feet and two-putted for par. Steel hit a stray drive, watered his second, and double-bogeyed. "When Iain hit his shot in the water, I knew I had a chance," said Liang, a man who was learning fast.

TCL Classic
Sanya, Hainen Island, China
Winner: Chapchai Nirat

Chapchai Nirat, big-hitting Thai, was discussing the Yalong Bay course after the first round of the TCL Classic. "It looks easy," he was saying. "But it's not that easy when you're playing on it."

Sorry, but a golfer who opens with 61 isn't very convincing when he talks like that. He's even less so after going wire-to-wire, shooting 61-66-68-71 for a 266 total, 22 under par at the resort course at Sanya, China, for a three-stroke win over Argentina's Rafael Echenique, who only got that close because of a closing rush for 68.

The victory made Chapchai only the third Thai, after Thongchai Jaidee and Thaworn Wiratchant, to win a co-sanctioned Asian-European Tour event. Chapchai, age 23, who turned professional at 15, forged that first-round 61 off some sharp iron play. He started on the second nine with birdies at the 10th, 12th and 13th holes, and added two more birdies at the 16th and 18th. Coming home, he birdied the first, fourth, fifth, sixth and seventh holes and then the ninth for the 11-under-par day. "It was good that I managed to hit it straight," he said.

A 66 put him six strokes ahead at the halfway point, and in the third round, fighting his driver, he logged three birdies on the front and three straight from the 11th for a 68 and led by a comfortable five strokes going into the final round. "If I can reach 25 under tomorrow," Chapchai said, "that should be enough to win."

Echenique made a run at him, shooting 68, but Chapchai had the shots when he needed them. He had a two-putt birdie at the par-five ninth, and after bogeying the 10th, he holed a 20-footer for a birdie at the 240-yard, par-three 15th for a four-stroke lead. "I knew it was getting close," Chapchai said, "but I knew I could do it."

Motorola International Bintan
Bintan, Indonesia
Winner: Jason Knutzon

The shot of the week — at least as far American Jason Knutzon was concerned — was his 25-foot birdie putt at the par-five fourth hole in the final round. When the ball dropped, Knutzon, who had little to celebrate recently, was tied for the lead. And then he knew the inaugural Motorola International Bintan was within reach. It would be his second Asian Tour victory, his first since 2004.

The tournament, played at the Ria Bintan Golf Club in Indonesia, was a come-from-nowhere story. Knutzon, shooting the first three rounds in 69-71-68, trailed Mike Cunning and Mark Brown by three strokes in the first round; trailed Cunning and Adam Blyth by five in the second, and then he and Australia's Peter Fowler were two behind Canadian Rick Gibson through the third round. With Gibson stalling out to a three-birdie, three-bogey 72 in the final round, it became a Knutzon-Fowler shootout.

Knutzon made hay with birdies on all four par-fives, the last of them at the 16th, where Fowler missed his chance. After birdies at the seventh and eighth holes, Fowler took his only bogey at the ninth, then birdied the 10th, 12th, 15th, but fatally missed his big chance at the par-five 16th. Knutzon birdied it, but Fowler hit a stray drive and had to settle for a par.

"I knew I probably needed two birdies in the last three holes to have a chance," Fowler said. He got one of them, that at the 17th, to pull within a stroke of Knutzon. Then he got renewed hope at the par-three 18th, when Knutzon, leading by one, put his eight-iron tee shot 12 feet above the pin, then ran his first putt a dangerous three feet past. But Knutzon regrouped and saved his par, a bogey-free 66 and a one-stroke victory at 14-under 274.

"I played pretty good, and putted great," Knutzon said. "It's just a great feeling to win again."

Volvo China Open
Shanghai, China
Winner: Markus Brier

Austrians as a professional golfer are hard to find. So meet the winner of the Volvo China Open in Shanghai, Markus Brier, of Vienna — a city better known for Mozart and waltzes.

"I dreamt about winning yesterday," said Brier, and the dream came true in a breezy five-stroke victory in the Asia-European Tour co-sanctioned event at Shanghai Silport Golf Club in mid-April.

Brier, age 38, turned professional in 1995 at age 27, went through the European Tour qualifying five times, and won the BA-CA Golf Open on the European Tour in 2006, and in 2002 and 2004 when it was on the European Challenge Tour. He came from behind to win this one, and against a field that included Denmark's Thomas Bjorn and Northern Ireland's Graeme McDowell.

Brier was out of sight in the first two rounds. An opening 72 left him four behind China's Huang Ming-je and France's Raphael Jacquelin, and 68 put him five behind Jacquelin (67) in the second round. He broke through in the third round. He bogeyed the first, "but after that I didn't hit many bad shots," Brier said. In fact, he birdied his last three holes for a 67–207 and a one-stroke lead on Australia's Scott Hend (70).

The final was almost a breeze. "I was fortunate not to be too nervous on the last three or four holes," Brier said. "That was the key. I didn't hit it really close but holed a lot of putts." He birdied the second and third, and wrapped it up in style with a five-foot birdie putt at the 18th for 67, a 10-under 274 total, and a five-shot win over Hend.

Brier's formula: "I tried not to think too much about winning," he said.

BMW Asian Open
Shanghai, China
Winner: Raphael Jacquelin

First came the heavy rains over the closing holes, then came the champagne at the 18th, and a drenched Raphael Jacquelin enjoyed both along with the sweet taste of victory in the BMW Asian Open.

Jacquelin, a little-known Frenchman, took the best the Asian and European tours and China Golf Association could throw at him in the co-sanctioned event, and led wire-to-wire at Tomson Shanghai Pudong Golf Club. Threats such as Ernie Els, Retief Goosen and Miguel Angel Jimenez just never got the heat turned up. Jacquelin shot 66-69-70-73 for a 10-under-par 278 total, winning by two strokes over Denmark's Soren Kjeldsen. It was Jacquelin's second win and second wire-to-wire performance, after the 2005 Madrid Open, but he was under hot pursuit most of the way.

"In Madrid, I had a seven-shot lead," Jacquelin said. "But this is a different story." He led by one stroke in the first round, three in the second and one in the third. Jacquelin's closing 73 was stronger than it looked. He started the final round a stroke ahead of Australia's Scott Hend, and under calm conditions raced to a four-stroke lead with an outward 33.

"Then the wind picked up, and the rain," Jacquelin said, "and it was tough from the 12th to the 18th." He struggled to four bogeys coming home, but most golfers had trouble. Hend's chances sank when he hit his tee shot at the par-three 14th into the water and double-bogeyed. He shot 75 and tied for third, leaving second to Kjeldsen on his 73.

Jacquelin set the tone for himself with his opening 66. "I'm going to play exactly the same tomorrow," he said, and that would be his theme. Els, who won the event by 13 strokes in 2005, had a different theme. Never a factor, he tied for fifth. "My putter let me down most of the week," Els said.

Pine Valley Beijing Open
Beijing, China
Winner: Gaurav Ghei

India's Gaurav Ghei had to prove something to his most skeptical critic — himself. He got the opportunity in the inaugural Pine Valley Beijing Open, and he made the most of it. A rally in the third round and an impressive finish in the fourth round, and there it was, his third win on the Asian Tour.

Ghei was out of the lead only in the second round when the Thai duo of Panuwat Muenlek (70) and Chapchai Nirat (67) edged ahead at eight-under-par 136. They led by a stroke over Ghei, who had his worst round, a par 72, and Australia's Scott Strange (68). John Daly, visiting from the U.S. PGA Tour, was two off the lead with 71.

Daly was one of Ghei's major concerns from the start. "It's a course which suits long hitters because the fairways are generous," Ghei said, "and we have guys like John Daly in the field ... it's going to be a tough week." Ghei eased his fears from the start with an eagle at the par-five No. 2, along with seven birdies and two bogeys for a 65 and a one-stroke lead in the first round. He erased that second-round deficit with 68 in the third to tie at 11 under with Muenlek (67), Strange (68) and Adam Blyth (67).

If Ghei still doubted himself, it didn't show in the final round. He birdied the fifth, eighth and 13th holes for a flawless 69 and a 14-under 274 total and a two-stroke win. "Last year was a great win because it ended an 11-year drought," Ghei said. "But I wanted to win another tournament to prove to myself that my win last year was no fluke."

GS Caltex Maekyung Open
Seoul, Korea
Winner: Kim Kyung-tae

Anyone who thinks Korean golf consists of K.J. Choi on the PGA Tour and a battalion of women on the LPGA Tour had better keep an eye on Kim Kyung-tae, age 20, a recent amateur star and a professional of five months by the time the GS Caltex Maekyung Open rolled around early in May.

The first tip-off as to how highly Kim was regarded came when the South Korean government exempted him from military service to let him play golf. The second was his first victory on the Asian Tour, a five-stroke decision that wasn't quite the lark it seemed. He had to hang on like a crusty veteran for three rounds before charging over the last nine holes against Liang Wen-chong, China's top golfer and winner of the Singapore Masters in March.

"This is unexpected," said Kim, and someone could tell him he was speaking for the rest of the golf world, as well.

Kim played the first three rounds in 70-66-67, chasing Liang, who led all three with 64-71-67 at the par-72 Nam Seoul Country Club in South Korea. Both made the final turn in 35, with Liang still leading by a stroke. Then Kim turned the tournament on its ear. Heading for home, Kim squared the battle with a birdie at the 10th. Then he took the lead for the first time with a birdie at the par-three 11th against Liang's bogey. Kim then birdied the 15th and 16th, and after a bogey at the 17th, he polished off his victory with a birdie at the 18th for 67 and an 18-under 270 total and the five-stroke margin over Liang (73–275).

Then Kim revealed his secret. "People said it would be harder in the pro ranks," he said. "But I kept my amateur mindset and kept playing aggressively."

Macau Open
Macau
Winner: Lu Wen-teh

If ever a golfer wanted to take a golf hole home and put it in his trophy case, it would be Taiwan's Lu Wen-teh, and the hole would be the par-five 18th at Macau Golf and Country Club. All he did was birdie it four straight times in the same day — the first time in regulation to tie for the lead, and then three times in the playoff, the last one to beat Australia's Richard Moir in the Macau Open. It was Lu's third victory and, ironically, the third by playoff.

And it was a test of patience and endurance as much as golf. The tournament, battered by heavy storms, was forced into carryover rounds and finally cut to 54 holes.

Lu, 44, had the best combination of game and guts. He opened with 65 and 71 and started the third — and final — round four strokes behind Moir (66-66). Lu finished his second round Sunday morning for 71, then took the lead in the third with birdies at the 13th, 16th and 18th holes. Moir responded with birdies at the last two holes for 69 to tie Lu at 201.

The 18th was the playoff hole. The first time, Moir hit the green in two and Lu was 40 yards short. But Lu chipped to six feet and they matched birdies. They birdied it again the second time. The third time, Moir chipped short and parred, but Lu chipped close again and tapped in for a birdie and the victory. Said Moir, "I thought I had the win on the first playoff hole, but all credit to Lu. He played great. Especially that up-and-down in the first playoff hole was fantastic."

Said Lu: "I birdied the 18th four times today because I just went out there and tried my best."

SK Telecom Open
Seoul, Korea
Winner: Bae Sang-moon

When Bae Sang-moon needed golf advice, he turned to his caddie. When he needed a little boost to his spirits, he turned to his mother. At the SK Telecom Open, he could do both at the same time. Mom was his caddie, and the arrangement worked to perfection, bringing the 20-year-old Korean his first victory — wire-to-wire and by six strokes, no less.

"I was nervous when I got up this morning, thinking about that final round," Bae said. "But my mother told me to picture how I felt during the first round. She knows my game really well. I guess that's why I have been calm and collected."

Then he dedicated the victory to her.

Bae took up the game at age nine, turned professional in 2004, and played the Korean PGA Tour, where he won once. Taking the SK Telecom title achieved his goal for him — a spot on the Asian Tour. He ran away with it at BA Vista Country Club in Seoul, getting stronger with each round.

"I'm confident I will make the cut," Bae said after opening with 64 and a one-stroke lead. He had missed the cut in his last two SK Telecom Opens. A 69 in the second round kept him a stroke ahead and not discouraged. "I know there are two rounds to go," he said. "But I am confident." A three-birdie, two-bogey 71 lifted him to a four-stroke lead over a sagging field. A closing 67 easily turned back Aaron Baddeley (68) and Kim Hyung-tae (69) and gave Bae a 17-under 271 total and the six-stroke victory.

Then it was time to cut the apron strings. "My mother is 51 now," Bae said, "so this is the last time she will caddie for me."

Bangkok Airways Open
Koh Samui, Thailand
Winner: Lee Sung

What does a golfer do after shooting a course record and taking a seven-stroke lead? Some go fishing. Some go to dinner with friends. Maybe some take a walk. Not Lee Sung, at the Bangkok Airways Open. "I will head straight back to the hotel and watch a couple of movies in my room to relax my mind," said Lee, who was born deaf and who communicates through his brother. "Things have been working right for me, and I want to be calm and collected when I tee off on Sunday."

That was Lee after scorching Santiburi Samui Country Club, near Bangkok, with a course-record, nine-under-par 62 in the third round to boost his lead to seven strokes. And when he did tee off on Sunday, he turned in a calm and collected par 71 for a three-stroke victory, his first on the Asian Tour. Lee, a promising South Korean, led wire-to-wire, shooting 66-69-62-71 for a 268 total, 16 under par, beating Thai veteran Prayad Marksaeng (66) by three strokes.

Lee, who turned professional in 2000 and joined the Asian Tour in 2004, broke into the lead in the first round with five birdies and an eagle, that at the par-five ninth off a 213-yard four-iron shot to nine feet. He led by two strokes. He led by only one after the second round, then ran away in the third round. The 62 included three straight birdies from the fifth and a two-footer at the 18th, going seven ahead of Singapore's Mardan Mamat. In the last round, Lee had a shaky spell, a double bogey at the 14th and a bogey at the 15th, but he wasn't in real trouble.

"I was really nervous when Prayad started to close the gap," Lee said. "But I came back with the birdie on the 17th. That was nice."

Iskandar Johor Open
Johor, Malaysia
Winner: Artemio Murakami

You might say this one was phoned in.

Artemio Murakami, a promising young Filipino, was one deflated 24-year-old on the Saturday night of the Iskandar Johor Open at Royal Johor, in Malaysia. He was about to tie for the third-round lead, then he stumbled and ended up two strokes off the lead. He phoned his friend and idol, Frankie Minoza, the famed Filipino golf star.

"I double-bogeyed the final hole and I told Frankie over the phone that this was not going to be my week," Murakami said. "He said that there are 18 more holes to go and I should never give up. He told me that if I gave up, he would not talk to me." Happily, Murakami would remain on speaking terms with Minoza.

Murakami was no threat early on. A one-under-par 70 left him three strokes behind Taiwan's Lin Chien-bing in the first round. He shot 72 in the weather-delayed second round, four behind American Jason Knutzon (67) and Australia's Unho Park (69). In the third round, a par at the 18th would have tied him for the lead with India's Gaurav Ghei (70–209), but he double-bogeyed for 69 and a 211 total. That sent him to call Minoza.

With Ghei, Knutzon, the Philippines' Tony Lascuna and Australia's Adam Le Vesconte all fading, Murakami made up his two-stroke deficit and led by two going into the last two holes. He faced a three-foot putt for par at the 18th to seal the win. With Minoza's words fresh in mind, he dropped it for a bogey-free 68, a five-under 279 total and a one-stroke victory over Lascuna (70) and Scotland's Simon Yates (67).

"I really don't know what to say," Murakami said. "I would like to dedicate this win to Frankie." Which, of course, said it all.

Brunei Open
Bandar Seri Begawan, Brunei
Winner: Lin Wen-tang

The Brunei Open was the tale of two men having the time of their careers. For Australian Adam Le Vesconte, that was for 64 holes. For Taiwan's Lin Wen-tang, it was only 18 holes — the last 18. He had started the final round six strokes behind Le Vesconte, and he went from there to his second Asian Tour victory. "I was feeling very nervous but I told myself to stay focused and maintain my composure," Lin said. And he did.

Le Vesconte and Lin opened in a five-way tie for the lead at 65, six under par at the Empire Hotel course. Then Le Vesconte birdied four of his last five holes of the second round for another 65 and the lead by three over Lin (68), who missed three three-foot putts. Le Vesconte looked catchable in the third round when he parred his first 10 holes. Then he birdied the 11th, the 16th from 25 feet and the 18th from eight feet for 68 and a four-stroke lead. Lin fought for 71 and was six behind going into the final round.

Le Vesconte was still all right in the final round until he triple-bogeyed the par-three fourth hole from a plugged lie in a bunker. He fell into a tie with a bogey at the 10th, and Lin took the lead at the 12th, holing an eight-foot birdie putt. Lin went up by two strokes on a six-footer at the 13th, and a par save at the 17th completed his run for a closing 65 for a 15-under 269 total and the two-shot victory. "I did not have a game plan," Lin said. "I told myself that every shot I hit had to be a very good one."

Midea China Classic
Guangzhou, China
Winner: Thaworn Wiratchant

In a week when the Royal Orchid Golf Club, at Guangzhou, China, was being picked like a common weed, it was Thai veteran Thaworn Wiratchant who plucked the flower, the Midea China Classic. But he had to survive a three-man playoff.

In this tournament, anyone not shooting in the low- to mid-60s need not apply. Thaworn opened with 65-63, young Thai whiz Chinarat Phadungsil had middle rounds of 62-64 and Scotsman Simon Yates had a 64-62 middle, all tying at 21-under-par 263.

Thaworn tied with four others in the first round, a stroke behind South Korean Lee Sung (64). A 63 in the second round put Thaworn one ahead of American Edward Michaels. "I was striking it well," Thaworn said, "but my putting was exceptional today." Chinarat rocketed into third place on a course-record 62.

Eagles flew in the third round. Yates got two, one at the 10th, the other at the 18th to tie Chinarat's fresh record of 62. Chinarat also eagled the 18th for 64 to tie Yates at 194, two ahead of Thaworn (68). It was a scramble in the final round. Yates led by a shot going into the par-five 18th, but could only par for a 69 that dropped him into a tie when Chinarat birdied from two feet for 69 and Thaworn holed a 15-footer for 67. The three tied at 263 and headed into a playoff.

Yates bowed out with a bogey on the first extra hole. Thaworn and Chinarat tied on the next two holes. Then on the fourth hole, at the par-five No. 9, Thaworn lifted his approach from the rough to two feet. Chinarat missed his birdie try from 18 feet, and Thaworn tapped in for his ninth victory, an Asian Tour record. He was as surprised as he was happy. "I didn't expect to win coming into the final round," Thaworn confessed.

Mercuries Taiwan Masters
Tamsui, Chinese Taipei
Winner: Lu Wen-teh

In golf, local knowledge mostly means understanding the greens. For Taiwan's Lu Wen-teh, it meant understanding the winds at his home course, the Taiwan Golf and Country Club, and it paid off in the Mercuries Taiwan Masters. "I have been playing this course for the past 33 years, since I was a kid," said Lu, age 43. "I could adapt well to the windy conditions, which was a huge advantage for me over Ted."

South Korea's Ted Oh, age 31, saw that first win get away again. Oh led Lu by four strokes in the second round, by one in the third round, then stumbled through the fourth round, handing Lu a three-stroke victory. It was Lu's second win of the year and his third Taiwan Masters.

Lu, after trailing on rounds of 72-71-69, cobbled together a curious par 72 against the collapsing Oh. Lu took a two-stroke edge with an eagle at the 480-yard, par-five seventh hole, hitting a three-wood second shot from 240 yards to two feet. He double-bogeyed the 11th, then birdied the 13th and 15th holes, and bogeyed the 16th for a four-under 284 total.

Oh had his moments. He took the lead in the second round, coming out after a second storm delay to drop a 30-foot birdie putt at the 17th, then also birdied the 18th for 68 and a four-stroke lead on Lu. In the third round, Oh birdied the 18th from five feet for 72 to cling to a one-stroke lead. The final round did him in. He went two over on the first nine and had three bogeys and a lone birdie on the second nine for a four-over 76 and a 287 total. "I blew it," Oh said. "I was missing a lot of short putts, and I didn't get up-and-down from anywhere."

Kolon-Hana Bank Korea Open
Cheonan, Korea
Winner: Vijay Singh

Things had become so "iffy" for Vijay Singh coming down the home stretch that his proudest moment — the turning point, he called it — was the par-four he extracted at the 17th hole. After the rough ride he just had getting there, the par kept his head above water, and he took the Kolon-Hana Bank Korea Open by two strokes.

"The pin positions today were the toughest I've played so far," Singh said. It seems the par-71 Woo Jeong Hills Country Club, near Seoul, was loaded with various problems. Singh, ranked No. 12 in the world and the biggest name in the field, took the lead in the second round and stayed there. He was up by three strokes going into the third round, and then by a commanding four strokes going into the fourth round. And there, he authored some very un-Singh-like golf.

By the 16th hole he had two birdies, but five bogeys, and his lead was down to one. And so the par at the 17th was something of a lifesaver. He had a good drive, then hit a nine iron to the right of the pin, just where he wanted it, and two-putted for the par.

Singh added a birdie at the 18th hole, wrapping up rounds of 66-69-70-73 for a six-under 278 total to win by a deceptive two strokes over home favorites Kim Kyung-tae (67) and Y.E. Yang (68). Korea's Kang Kyung-nam was in the thick of it, right behind Singh, but back-to-back bogeys at the 16th and 17th holes knocked him back to a tie for fourth place.

Singh, who last won in South Korea in 1995, was impressed by the progress of Korean golf. "There are a lot more players picking up the game, and a lot more talent," Singh said. "The depth of the game has improved here."

Hero Honda Indian Open
New Delhi, India
Winner: Jyoti Randhawa

Indian star Jyoti Randhawa, who had made a bit of history in his illustrious career, made a big piece of it at the Hero Honda Indian Open. But it was the present that interested him most, and that meant winning the tournament.

After trailing by four strokes in the first round and six in the second, Randhawa, the defending champion, outran the field for a three-stroke victory with a 13-under-par 275 total. It was his third Indian Open win, tying him with the legendary Peter Thomson with a record three victories at Delhi Golf Club.

"Anytime you equal a legendary name like Peter Thomson, you know you've done something good in life," Randhawa said. He moved into the picture in the third round with a seven-birdie 67 for a 10-under 206 total, catching the overnight leader, Thailand's Chapchai Nirat, who cooled to 73 after cautiously turning to using irons off the tees at the tight course.

Randhawa was comfortable but not cautious at the start of the fourth round and made the turn leading by two. Then Taiwan's Chang Tse-peng turned up the heat with a birdie at the 17th hole, getting within one. Randhawa fired back with a sensational eagle at the par-four 16th, holing out an eight iron from 171 yards, and closed with 69 to stay three strokes ahead of Chang.

"I didn't want to go into the 18th with a one-shot lead," Randhawa said. "I wanted to get a birdie somewhere. I was playing easy early on, but on the 16th, I got aggressive. Boy — what a way to get aggressive."

Pertamina Indonesia President Invitational
Jakarta, Indonesia
Winner: Juvic Pagunsan

If the Rookie of the Year Award comes loaded with expectations, then the Philippines' Juvic Pagunsan, the winner of 2006, lived up to them with a crash-bang finish for his first victory in the Pertamina Indonesia President Invitational. Pagunsan, who trailed all the way, vaulted over the unfortunate Gaganjeet Bhullar, a 19-year-old Indian rookie, with a birdie-eagle finish to pick off the title by one stroke. He shot the Damai Indah course in 66-67-71-65 for a 269 total.

Pagunsan trailed by one in the first round when Thai comer Prom Meesawat and Korean rookie Hur In-hoi opened with 65s. He was still a stroke off in the second round behind Lu Wei-chih, Nevin Basic and Anthony Kang. Then Kang moved three ahead of him with 69 in the third round, setting up Pagunsan's theatrics.

"I'm speechless," said Pagunsan. And possibly breathless from that stunning finish. "This is what I've been waiting for in my career." Bhullar was equally breathless, but for a different reason. He had wrapped up 69 and was the leader in the clubhouse about the time Pagunsan birdied the 17th to close the gap to one. Then Bhullar saw his first victory slip away when Pagunsan, playing the par-five 18th, hit a good drive, then fired a six iron from 205 yards to seven feet and holed the eagle putt.

Pagunsan's finish was a fitting bookend to the start of his round. He nailed four birdies over the first nine holes. He got the fifth birdie at the 13th, then bogeyed the 15th. That meant that with only three holes left to play, Pagunsan was trailing by two strokes. That's a tall order for a second-year man, even for a Rookie of the Year, one year removed. But Pagunsan found a way to fill it.

Barclays Singapore Open
Singapore
Winner: Angel Cabrera

The handwriting wasn't on the wall for Vijay Singh, it was on the green — the final green.

"I looked back and saw Angel hit it 400 yards down the middle," Singh said. "He was going in with a medium or short iron, so I knew he would make at least a birdie." And so Singh knew it was over.

Angel Cabrera, the big-hitting Argentine who came to international fame by winning the U.S. Open in June, did follow that booming drive with an iron just where he wanted it on the green, setting up a two-putt birdie-four and a one-stroke win over Singh in a strong international field at the Barclays Singapore Open. Cabrera played Sentosa's Serapong course in 71-63-70-72 for a 276 total, eight under par.

Singh gave it a great try. He started the final round six strokes behind, and with three birdies and an eagle, closed to within two by the turn, and then to one when Cabrera bogeyed the 10th hole. Singh, in the group ahead, figured he had to eagle the 18th to force a playoff. He reached the green in two, but missed his eagle try from 20 feet. He birdied for a course-record 67. But Cabrera reached the 18th himself and birdied for the one-stroke win.

"It was very tough, very windy," Cabrera said. "I knew that Vijay was putting together a good round. It was up to me to play well on the last two holes, and I did that." And Cabrera did it against a tough field. In addition to Singh, there was Adam Scott, two-time defending champion, finishing third at 281, and back in the pack were K.J. Choi tied for 14th, and Darren Clarke and Phil Mickelson, tied for 23rd, while Ernie Els missed the cut.

HSBC Champions
Shanghai, China
Winner: Phil Mickelson

"This," Phil Mickelson was saying, "was a very funny day. I can't believe I'm here as the champion right now."

Mickelson wasn't the only one. How he won the HSBC Champions title had to come right out of Houdini's Book of Illusions — wild play in the final round, blowing a healthy lead, taking a whopping six strokes in penalties, and finally having to go two extra holes before he could pick up his first Asian Tour trophy.

By the third round, Mickelson was having a great time on the Sheshan International course in Shanghai, outrunning a strong field that included Vijay Singh, Padraig Harrington, Ernie Els, Retief Goosen and Angel Cabrera. Rounds of 68-66-68 gave him a two-stroke lead over England's Ross Fisher going into the final round.

The finish was bizarre. Mickelson was leading Fisher by three strokes heading to the 12th hole. Then Mickelson dropped four shots at the 12th, 13th and 15th, and Fisher birdied the 15th and jumped into the lead. Mickelson then birdied the 16th. Westwood, after trailing by nine at the start, rang up six birdies on the last nine for 67.

Fisher led Mickelson by one going to the par-five 18th. Both hit the fairway. Then Fisher caught the deep right rough, then bounced his chip off the green and into the water. He double-bogeyed for 74. Mickelson missed a winning par putt from 10 feet and bogeyed for 76. All three were at 278.

Back to the 18th. They tied on the first playoff hole. On the second, Westwood put two shots into the water and was gone. Fisher came out of a bunker to 10 feet and missed the birdie try. Mickelson chipped to four feet and didn't miss. "I don't know how the day finished like this," Mickelson said. "And I guess it really doesn't matter now."

UBS Hong Kong Open
Fanling, Hong Kong
Winner: Miguel Angel Jimenez

It wasn't pretty but it was effective. Spain's Miguel Angel Jimenez three-putted the par-five 18th hole for a bogey and still won the UBS Hong Kong Open by one stroke. That was because Sweden's Robert Karlsson double-bogeyed. "It's very nice to win again here, it's great," said Jimenez, who won the event in 2004. "The only down part is I feel, I have to say, for Robert, the way it finished as he played so good the whole week."

Jimenez trailed Karlsson by four strokes going into the fourth round and built up momentum on the second nine with two birdies and an eagle at the par-five 13th. Plus, of course, the clinching bogey at the 18th. "I hit my first putt and thought it was going to be very fast, downgrain and downhill," Jimenez said. "And I left it too short, and the same distance that he (Karlsson) had for his bogey. And then I putted first and missed, and he missed his, and that's it."

Karlsson still had the four-stroke lead after three birdies and three bogeys through No. 15. Then came the fatal finish. He went from bunker into the rough, then two-putted for the double bogey that made Jimenez the winner. "I did what I could, but I don't know what I could have done differently," Karlsson said. "End of the day, he beat me fair and square."

Jimenez played the Hong Kong Golf Club in 65-67-66-67 for a 265 total,

15 under par. Karlsson closed with a two-over 72 and tied for second with K.J. Choi and Thongchai Jaidee at 266. Back in the pack were former Masters champion Mike Weir at 271 and Asian Tour Order of Merit leader Liang Wen-chong of China at 272.

Omega Mission Hills World Cup
Shenzhen, China
Winners: Scotland (Colin Montgomerie and Marc Warren)

No matter the competition, just put the name "Cup" on it, and Colin Montgomerie goes out and beats the Americans. And so it was with the Omega Mission Hills World Cup in China in November. Montgomerie, age 44, paired with Marc Warren, 26, to deliver the late heroics that gave Scotland a par on the third playoff hole for the win over Americans Boo Weekley and Heath Slocum, who had led from the first day.

"Fantastic," said Montgomerie, the European team hero in so many Ryder Cup matches. "It's been a long time for Scotland to win the World Cup."

The Scots, after starting 63-68-66, combined in the final-round alternate-shot play for 66 and a 25-under 263 total and were tied by Weekley and Slocum (61-69-66-67), topping the field of 28 two-man teams from around the world at the Olazabal Course at the Mission Hills resort near Shenzhen.

Montgomerie was quick to credit his partner. "The fella sitting on my right — what a putt he holed in the first hole of the playoff," Monty said. "We were out. I hit a terrible drive and a terrible bunker shot, and it's amazing what a good putt can do." Monty was speaking about Warren's 12-foot par save that kept them alive in the playoff. And it was Warren's eight-footer for eagle at the 15th in regulation that put them into the lead.

Slocum holed a six-footer for birdie at the 18th to pull the Americans into a tie in regulation. On the first playoff hole, after Warren's save from 12 feet, Slocum just missed a winning birdie from 10. They tied on the second hole in pars. On the third hole, Weekley's poor chip left Slocum with a 20-footer for par. When Slocum missed, the Scots two-putted for a par and the win.

Hana Bank Vietnam Masters
Hanoi, Vietnam
Winner: Chapchai Nirat

Thailand's Chapchai Nirat certainly did his part to win the inaugural Hana Bank Vietnam Masters at the Hanoi Phoenix Golf Resort. But he would need some help from the other challengers, in the form of misfires and the like. And that's just what he got. "Everything just went well for me today," Chapchai said. "I told myself at the start of the day to just go out there, play my normal game and not get distracted by the scores of the players around me."

Chapchai, who won the TCL Classic in March, was tied for third place to start the final round and announced his intentions with birdies on the first two holes. Then he raced home with three birdies over the last four holes for a five-under 67 and a 12-under 276 total for a two-stroke victory over fellow Thai Chawalit Plaphol (73) and England's Simon Griffiths (72).

Chawalit, the overnight leader, was stung by a short game that turned sour after working so well for three rounds. "My putting really let me down today," Chawalit said. Most notably in a double bogey at the 11th and then a missed birdie at the 17th.

Griffiths, who started the final round in second place behind Chawalit, bogeyed No. 4 when he missed "a silly putt." He hit a poor tee shot at No. 9 and missed the green at No. 12. Griffiths had birdie chances at nearly every hole from the 13th in, but missed them all. "I count myself lucky to finish second, considering that I was fifth at one point," Griffiths said. Irish Ryder Cup player Paul McGinley also was in the late hunt, but stumbled at the 14th, 15th and 16th holes and slipped to a tie for fifth. "I was a little bit impatient at the end," he said.

Johnnie Walker Cambodian Open
Siem Reap, Cambodia
Winner: Bryan Saltus

If this wasn't a first in the history of golf, then history had been curiously silent: A tournament victory dedicated to a rock-and-roll music group. But there it was.

"This is awesome," said American Bryan Saltus, after his come-from-behind, three-stroke victory in the Johnnie Walker Cambodian Open. "I would like to dedicate this win to the Grateful Dead, as they have inspired me all the way." It turned out Saltus was a fierce Greatful Dead fan. He had been to 153 of their concerts. The inspiration really worked in the final round.

"I had a good start with three birdies, and my confidence carried on after that," said Saltus, who came from behind with a five-under-par 67 for a 17-under 271 total at Phokeethra Country Club at Siem Reap.

Australia's Adam Groom, who led going into the final round, had an erratic 71, with five birdies and four bogeys, to finish second at 274. Groom was disappointed, but not badly hurt. "It's been a good week for me," Groom said. "I've shot four rounds under par, which was something I couldn't do all year."

The pressure was intense, what with Saltus birdieing the first three holes, then adding birdies at the 10th and 17th. His secret? "My putting has been the winning formula this week," Saltus said. He wasn't the only winner. Said Saltus: "I told my caddie (Phal Savern) that if I won, I would buy her a motorbike, and now that I've done it, I will get her a brand-new motorbike."

Volvo Masters of Asia
Bangkok, Thailand
Winner: Prayad Marksaeng

The story of the Volvo Masters of Asia, the final event of the 2007 Asian Tour, was the story of the Thai Country Club's 18th hole — who could handle it and who could not.

The answer to who could was Thai native son Prayad Marksaeng. He birdied it in the final round to filch the championship by a stroke from the Philippines' Juvic Pagunsan and England's Chris Rodgers. They both bogeyed it. "I knew if I made par on 17, I could have a chance for birdie on 18," Prayad said. "I was confident of par (at the 17th) even though I hit the water with my second shot. On the last, I knew I could make birdie if I was on the green."

That's confidence talking. Prayad had already shown plenty of it. He saved par out of the water at the 10th, and saved again out of the water at the 17th, both with six-foot putts. Then came the 18th in the final round — a bold six iron to six feet. He birdied for 69, a 13-under 275 total (67-71-68-69) and a one-stroke win.

Pagunsan, who led by four starting the final round, stumbled to a 40 on the first nine and was tied with Prayad at the 18th. But Pagunsan bunkered his eight-iron approach, came out 12 feet past the pin and bogeyed the hole, amazingly, for the fourth straight day for 75. "That is golf," Pagunsan said. Rodgers charged into the chase with five birdies through the 16th hole. Then at the 18th, he hooked his drive into a fairway bunker, came out nicely, but left his chip shot 12 feet short and bogeyed for 68. "All day long," he said, "I thought it was going to be my day."

The season ended on a history note. Liang Wen-chong tied for 28th and pushed his season winnings to $532,590 to become the first Chinese player to win the Order of Merit.

Omega China Tour

The young Omega China Tour is the nation's domestic and developmental tour. It began with four events in 2005, grew to six in 2006, and then to eight in 2007 as the game continued to grow and spread.

The season opened with the Sofitel Championship in May at Zhongshan International Golf Club in Nanjing, and the man of the hour was Wu Kang-chun, age 25, a former amateur standout making his professional debut. He caught fire in the final round and birdied the 10th hole, eagled the 11th and birdied the 13th. After dropping a shot at the 15th, he birdied the 16th for a three-under-par 69 and a nine-under 279 total, scoring his first victory by four over Zhang Lian-wei, the top name in Chinese golf.

Wu was a glimpse into the immediate future, so what were we to make of Ye Jian-fen? Ye was not only an amateur, but he was only age 15. Ye led at the halfway point, then closed with two 73s and finished fourth, the best finish by an amateur since the tour started in 2005. That's not conclusive proof of the growth of Chinese golf, but it's at least an indicator.

It was none other than Zhang Lian-wei, already venerable at age 42, scoring the tour's first back-to-back victories ever. The first came in the Qingdao Leg early in June. Things were really tough at the Qingdao Huashan course. Zhang struggled to a closing 78 for a six-over-par 294 total and still won by two over Li Chao, Wu Wei-huang and Chen Xiao-ma. Zhang got the second win at the next stop, the Guangzhou Leg at Dragon Lake, a comfortable five-stroke win over Yuan Hao. Yuan got within two of Zhang at the final turn, but double-bogeyed the 17th and bogeyed the 18th for 71. Zhang closed with 69 for a nine-under 279 total for his second win of the year and his third win on the tour. He also has five victories on the Asian Tour.

Li Chao wasted no time in giving the tour its second back-to-back winner. First, he won by four strokes in the Yanji Championship at the Yanji Harangang Golf Resort. "It's a relief to finally win again," said Li, who won twice in 2006. "I have been slowly getting back to my best form, step-by-step." Li started the final round one stroke off the lead, then had five birdies and four bogeys for 71 and a one-over-par 289 total. His second win came in the Shanghai Leg at Grand Shanghai International early in August, and with a bit more drama. Li came to the 18th hole leading by one over his playing companion, Taiwan's Tsai Chi-huang. He watched as Tsai rolled in a 20-foot putt for a birdie to tie him. Then Li, just as coolly, rolled in a 15-footer for his own birdie to win by a stroke with 68 and a six-under 282 total.

The reward was late coming for Zheng Wen-gen, but it finally arrived at the Kunming Leg late in August. Zheng, age 41, was one of the first to turn professional in China, this in 1994. He had been a consistent performer, but apart from taking a small domestic event in 2002, he hadn't won. Zheng started the final round ahead by four strokes, and with five birdies, three of them coming in, shot 67 to win by six on a 15-under-par 273 total. "It has been such a long time since I won," Zheng said. "It's been driving me nuts."

The final two tournaments were left to the two dominant figures to divvy up.

Li Chao notched his third victory of the year in the Xiamen Leg at the Orient Golf and Country Club in September. This was a stunning win. Li started the final round seven strokes behind the leader, Wu Kang-chun. While Wu was stumbling to a closing 77, Li was climbing fast on birdies at the first, fifth, 12th and 13th holes. He and Shang Lei were tied with two holes to play. Li birdied the 17th and Shang bogeyed, and the two-stroke swing gave Li the luxury of bogeying the 18th for 66 and 278 total for the one-stroke victory. "I was a bit lucky today because the strong winds helped me catch up with the leaders," said Li, who also wrapped up the Order of Merit with one event left to play.

Zhang Lian-wei saved the best for last. He ran away with the season-ending Omega Championship by seven shots, firing a tournament-low 67 at Tianan Golf Club in Beijing. He started the day three ahead of Li and raced on with a four-under 32 on the first nine. He finished with a five-under 283 total. "I was disappointed to finish third here last year," Zhang said. "However, I am really happy for Li Chao. This tour is really about the young players. It is good to see so many of them coming through. The game has developed so quickly since it started out."

Japan Tour

Token Homemate Cup
Kuwana, Mie
Winner: Yui Ueda

Yui Ueda had not really enjoyed much success in his first six years on the Japan Tour, his best showing a second-place finish in the 2006 Token Homemate Cup tournament. Perhaps a hint of things to come. Although at a different venue when he teed it up in the season-opening 2007 Homemate Cup, Ueda had his game in top form and never trailed as he rolled to his first circuit victory — a one-stroke triumph with an eight-under-par 276. It was the third time in four years that the tournament produced a first-time winner.

Ueda and three others — senior Tateo Ozaki, Hiroyuki Fujita and Mitsuhiro Tateyama — opened with five-under-par 66s on the Nagoya course of Token Tado Country Club in Kuwana, Mie Prefecture. Then Ueda surged into a four-stroke lead with a 65 for 131 in Friday's round as the other three men faded. Keiichiro Fukabori and Katsuya Nakagawa (68-67s) took over second place.

Ueda preserved most of his margin despite a 74 on a wind-blown Saturday. He birdied two of the last three holes to finish with 205 and a three-shot lead over Toshinori Muto, whose 69 was the day's low round. But it was 20-year-old Lee Dong-hwan who put the pressure on Ueda Sunday. The young South Korean produced a 68, falling just a stroke behind Ueda, whose eagle at the 12th hole was critical to the victory.

Tsuruya Open
Kawanishi, Hyogo
Winner: Brendan Jones

Wonder what would have happened if Brendan Jones had not elected to skip the Tsuruya Open in favor of the U.S. PGA Tour in 2005? Four in a row, perhaps? The Australian's dominance of the tournament at Yamanohara Golf Club in Hyogo Prefecture continued in 2007, as he successfully defended the title that he also won in 2004, when his two wins and 11th-place finish on the money list led him to opt for America the next season.

The 32-year-old Canberra native played catch-up the first two days of the Tsuruya as Hirofumi Miyase fired a brilliant, seven-under-par 64 to stake out a two-stroke lead over Australian Scott Laycock, Hiroyuki Fujita and Masahiro (Massy) Kuramoto, the 51-year-old tour star in earlier years who is now campaigning on the senior Champions Tour in the U.S. Miyase, 36, a six-time career victor without a win since the 2003 Munsingwear KSB Cup, followed with a 67–131 Friday as Jones tacked a fine 65 onto his opening 67 and moved into second place.

When Miyase struggled to a 74 Saturday, the Aussie took over the lead with 68–200, three ahead of Takuya Taniguchi. By the 12th hole Sunday, though, Miyase, rebounding on his way to a day's best 65, had cut the gap to a stroke. Jones then birdied the 15th and 17th and, even though missing a three-footer for another at the last hole, again posted 68 for a 16-under-par 268. With a late flurry of birdies, Kuramoto (66) and Taniguchi (67) tied Miyase for second at 270.

The Crowns
Togo, Aichi
Winner: Hirofumi Miyase

Hirofumi Miyase had his hands full, but didn't let another win escape him in the prestigious Crowns tournament. A single weak round had cost Miyase a victory and the end of a lengthy dry spell the previous week in the Tsuruya Open. In The Crowns, Miyase was never more than a stroke out of the lead throughout, but still had to defeat the talented Toru Taniguchi in a playoff to capture his seventh career triumph. He hadn't won on the Japan Tour since a two-victory 2003 season.

The 36-year-old Miyase, who had shot 65 on the Tsuruya's last day in his vain bid, maintained the momentum at Aichi Prefecture's Nagoya Country Club in The Crowns. He shot 67 and shared the first-round lead with Keiichiro Fukabori. Enter Taniguchi the second day when he slipped a shot in front of Miyase with a second 68 as Miyase shot 70–137 and Fukabori 71–138.

Taniguchi had a lone bad round this time, shooting 75 Saturday to drop four shots off the lead. Miyase scored another 70, and Fukabori, seeking his ninth career victory, joined him at the top with 69–207. Back came Taniguchi Sunday. As Fukabori was fading from contention, eventually shooting 74, Taniguchi overtook Miyase with a front-nine 31. Two bogeys, coupled with a birdie, brought Miyase to the final hole needing a par and 71 to tie Taniguchi, already finished with 67 for 278. Miyase made that par and another on the first playoff hole to land the title and first place on the money list.

Japan PGA Championship
Nago, Okinawa
Winner: Toshimitsu Izawa

His two Japan Tour Championship victories were impressive entries among the 15 titles on the impressive record of Toshimitsu Izawa, but the long-time majors were missing — until this season's Japan PGA Championship. The veteran, perhaps at 39 having cause to be concerned about the absences, nailed the PGA title when the championship was staged at Okinawa's Kise Country Club in Nago.

Izawa was never behind through the 72 holes, but couldn't breathe easily until the final putts were holed and his five-under-par 283 was good enough for a one-stroke victory over Satoru Hirota.

The tournament began with a jumble at the top. Izawa's 68 thrust him into a first-place deadlock with Toru Taniguchi, Hiroyuki Fujita, South Korean Kim Jong-duk and 53-year-old Kiyoshi Murota, a four-time winner on the Japan Senior Tour. Then Izawa, the leading money winner in 2001 and 2003, inched a stroke in front Friday with 70–138. Closest to him then were little-known Shoichi Ideguchi at 71-68–139 and Jun Kikuchi and Okinawa's own Yusaku Miyazato at 141.

Little changed Saturday except that the scores were generally higher. Izawa shot 72 and at 210 led Ideguchi (73) by two and Kikuchi (72), Miyazato (72) and Hirota (71) by three. Only Hirota threatened Izawa Sunday and he couldn't take advantage when Izawa bogeyed the final hole for 73–283. It was Izawa's first victory since the 2005 KBC Augusta and just his second since his second money title year of 2003. He has 16 wins overall.

Munsingwear Open KSB Cup
Tamano, Okayama
Winner: Ryo Ishikawa

A bountiful number of phenomenal young golfers like Michele Wie, Tadd Fujikawa and Ai Miyazato have been making headlines around the world in recent years, but their achievements pall when compared to what occurred on May 20 on the Japan Tour. On a day when bad weather brought about a 36-hole finish, the Munsingwear Open KSB Cup tournament produced the youngest (by far) winner ever on any of the world's organized tours.

This historic golfer is Ryo Ishikawa, a 15-year-old high school freshman from Tokyo, who was invited to play in the tournament as a former national junior champion. To put his one-stroke, 12-under-par 276 victory in perspective, these are the record-holders on other major tours:

U.S. PGA Tour: Johnny McDermott, 1911 U.S. Open, 19 years, 11 months.
European Tour: Dale Hayes, 1971 Spanish Open, 18 years, 290 days.
Japan Tour: Seve Ballesteros, 1977 Japan Open, 20 years, seven months.
U.S. LPGA Tour: Marlene Hagge, 1952 Sarasota Open, 18 years, 14 days.
Japan LPGA Tour: Ai Miyazato, 2003 Miyagi TV Cup Dunlop, 18 years, 101 days.

Ishikawa's record feat came out of the blue after high winds battered Tojigaoka Marine Hills Golf Club in Okayama Prefecture and set back the start of the tournament by a day. He made the cut with a quiet 72-69–141 while Toru Taniguchi was unleashing a brilliant, eight-under-par 64 in the delayed opening round, then shot 73 on Saturday and yielded the lead to Thailand's Prayad Marksaeng (68-66–134).

Ishikawa duplicated his 69 on the first 18 holes Sunday to stand four shots behind leader Koumei Oda (69-70-67–206), then turned in a remarkable round under the circumstances of 66, which he called "a dream round," to secure the astonishing triumph. Runner-up Katsumasa Miyamoto received the first-place prize money of ¥20 million.

Mitsubishi Diamond Cup
Oarai, Ibaraki
Winner: Tetsuji Hiratsuka

Tetsuji Hiratsuka took advantage of the surprisingly erratic early-season play of proven winner Toru Taniguchi to tack up his fourth victory in the last five seasons. In the Mitsubishi Diamond Cup tournament, Taniguchi, one of the circuit's leading lights and money leaders during the last decade, failed for the fourth time in 2007 to avoid a bad round and convert a lead into a win as Hiratsuka overcame a four-stroke deficit in the final round and picked off a one-shot victory over Satoru Hirota and Kiyoshi Miyazato.

Taniguchi was the 36- and 54-hole leader, taking over first place Friday from veteran Katsunori Kuwabara (70), the opening day leader who hadn't won on the circuit since 1998. Taniguchi, who hadn't won since the previous July, had rounds of 72-69 and rested a stroke ahead of South Korean Kim Jong-duk at the mid-point of the tournament. Taniguchi added a one-under-par 70 Saturday for 211 total to move two strokes ahead of Hiroyuki Fujita and Thailand's Prayad Marksaeng. At that point, Hiratsuka, at 215 after rounds of 71-73-71, was tied for fifth place with Kim.

Hiratsuka never was in front until the very end, as Taniguchi fell back to his eventual 74–285. Three front-nine birdies established Hiratsuka's run and he offset his lone bogey with a birdie at 10th hole before securing the triumph with a 15-foot birdie putt on the final hole. His 67 gave him a winning 282 total. Hirota and Miyazato also shot 67 for their 283s.

JCB Classic
Ohira, Miyagi
Winner: Tomohiro Kondo

Virtually the same pattern that set up his victory the week before in the Mitsubishi Diamond Cup led Tetsuji Hiratsuka to defeat in his quest for a back-to-back win the first week of June and led Tomohiro Kondo to his third career victory in the JCB Classic at Hananomori Golf Club in Miyagi Prefecture.

Just like Toru Taniguchi a week earlier, Hiratsuka occupied first place after the second and third rounds, only to shoot a 74 Sunday and drop into a seventh-place tie at the finish, yielding to Kondo, whose closing 69 for 271 gave him a one-stroke victory over four other players — Lee Seung-ho (66), Mamoru Osanai and Azuma Yano (68s) and Koumei Oda (69).

Scores were particularly low in the opening round Thursday, Masaya Tomida's 64 giving him just a one-shot margin over Oda, Toshiyuki Miyama and Yusaku Miyazato. Hiratsuka and Kondo were respectable with 67 and 68, respectively. A day later, those two shared the lead, Hiratsuka shooting 67 and Kondo 66. Hiratsuka jumped two strokes ahead with a 66 Saturday as Kondo slipped into a second-place tie with Tomida, the first-round leader, who bounced back from a 72 with 66.

While Hiratsuka was struggling to his 74, Kondo took charge late in

Sunday's final round with a run of three birdies, then nearly gave it back with bogeys on the last two holes.

Gateway to the Open Mizuno Open Yomiuri Classic
Nishinomiya, Hyogo
Winner: Lee Dong-hwan

Exceptional players continue to emerge from South Korea onto the international scene. Lee Dong-hwan, just 20 years old, joined the ranks of winners from his country on the world stage when, not surprisingly in fact, he scored an impressive, four-stroke victory in the weather-abbreviated Gateway to the Open Mizuno Open Yomiuri Classic in late June.

One could see the win coming. Playing in just his second season on the Japan Tour, Lee had opened the year with a second-place showing in the Token Homemate Cup and finished no worse than 30th in the next six events before capturing his first title at Yomiuri Golf Club in Hyogo Prefecture by shooting three successive 68s

The young South Korean seized the lead from seasoned winner Brendan Jones the second day, his 136 giving him a one-shot margin over Masaya Tomida. Jones, who won the Tsuruya Open in April, ballooned from his opening 65 to 74 on the rainy Friday, while Lee ran off four birdies in a six-hole stretch en route to his 68–136. His third 68 expanded his lead to four shots over six other players — Tomida, Hideto Tanihara, who shot 64, Toshinori Muto, Achi Sato, Lin Keng-chi and Lee Seung-ho.

That was all they wrote, as the weather worsened Sunday and forced a cancellation of the round after the leaders had played just five holes.

UBS Japan Golf Tour Championship
Kasama, Ibaraki
Winner: Shingo Katayama

Perhaps all Shingo Katayama needed was an emotional push to get his first victory of 2007 into the books. Japan's most successful active player had been relatively quiet in his previous six starts at home and had mediocre showings in the U.S. in the Masters and Open, but a visit to his late father's grave and being in his home surroundings in Ibaraki Prefecture seemed to inspire the colorful star in the UBS Japan Golf Tour Championship. He wrung out a one-stroke triumph that was the 22nd of his fine career.

The win completed Katayama's sweep of the Japan Tour's major titles, complementing his previous triumphs in the Japan Open (2005) and PGA Championship (2003) and embellishing his four money titles.

Katayama got off to a slow start at Shishido Hills Country Club, finding himself six strokes off the lead when Naoya Takemoto, an unheralded pro, opened with a dazzling 63. Not unexpectedly, Takemoto shot 74 Friday, and Toru Taniguchi and Frankie Minoza, the Philippines veteran, swept by him with 136s. Katayama, with 68, moved into a tie at 137 with Takemoto, Kaname Yokoo and Toshinori Muto.

When Taniguchi (74) and Minoza (73) faltered Saturday, Katayama jumped into the lead with a seven-birdie, four-bogey 67 that gave him a six-under-par 204 and a two-shot lead on Takemoto and Muto, who both shot 69s. Katayama was never seriously challenged Sunday after he eagled the par-four first hole, although Takemoto completed his best tournament in five years with 66–272 to finish just a stroke behind Katayama's 67–271. Lee Dong-hwan, the previous week's winner, also shot 66, finished third and strengthened his hold on the money lead.

Woodone Open Hiroshima
Higashihiroshima, Hiroshima
Winner: Toru Taniguchi

Enough of those near-misses! After an early season burdened with missed victory opportunities, Toru Taniguchi refused to let another one get away, although it still had some of the fingerprints of his previous troubles. Despite having a four-stroke lead disappear in the final round, Taniguchi prevailed in the subsequent playoff in the Woodone Open Hiroshima tournament against Thailand's Prayad Marksaeng. It was his first victory of 2007 and 12th of a career that includes the money title in 2002.

Taniguchi put together four consecutive sub-par rounds on the Hachihom-matsu course of Hiroshima Country Club, riding the lead most of the way. He did trail by three the first day when one-time-winner Makato Inoue, who had been ineffective thus far in 2007, blistered the par-71 course with 64. Taniguchi came up with a 64 of his own Friday, going without a bogey for a second straight round, and vaulted into a four-stroke lead at 131. Marksaeng and Yoichi Shimizu were the runners-up.

Little changed Saturday as Taniguchi retained his four-shot margin with a two-bogey 68 for 199 total and the Thai pro matched it for 203. On Sunday, as had happened before in 2007, Taniguchi failed to hold the lead, which was as much as five strokes after two opening birdies. Prayad not only erased that margin, but was two shots ahead after 16 holes in his bid for his first win on the Japan Tour, which he has played with considerable success since 2001. However, Taniguchi birdied the 17th and Prayad bogeyed the 18th to post 66 against Taniguchi's 70 for their 269 totals. Taniguchi then birdied the first extra hole to score his first win in nearly a year.

Nagashima Shigeo Invitational Sega Sammy Cup
Chitose, Hokkaido
Winner: Toru Taniguchi

Invigorated by the way he avoided disaster with a brave finish in his Wood-one victory the previous Sunday, Toru Taniguchi stayed on a roll when the Japan Tour moved on to Hokkaido and the Nagashima Shigeo Invitational Sega Sammy Cup. The 39-year-old veteran won easily at North Country Club, became the first multiple winner of 2007 and moved into the No. 1 position on the money list.

This time Taniguchi never was out of first place. The first day he had three birdies and a bogey and shared the top spot with Koumei Oda and Prom Meesawat of Thailand at 70. While he remained in the lead with another 70, he was joined at 140 by Australian Wayne Perske, whose lone win in Japan came in the 2006 Token Homemate Cup. Perske matched the day's best score with a 68, after opening with 72.

Taniguchi broke loose from the field with a 68 Saturday, his 208 giving him a three-shot margin over Oda (69) and Perske (71). Another 68 Sunday preserved the three-stroke edge and brought Taniguchi his 13th tour victory. Prom produced the day's best round with 65 and climbed into second place, his best finish ever in Japan. Oda and Perske shot 69s and tied for third place.

Sun Chlorella Classic
Otaru, Hokkaido
Winner: Jun Kikuchi

Victory was a long time in coming for Jun Kikuchi, a 33-year-old journey-man on the Japan Tour, and it came the hard way — in an extended playoff against a proven veteran in the rain-plagued Sun Chlorella Classic, the circuit's only event between mid-July and late August. Kikuchi surged from a three-stroke deficit in the final round to tie Toru Suzuki at five-under-par 283 and became the season's fourth first-time winner with a routine par as Suzuki struggled to a bogey at the third extra hole.

Kikuchi had started the week with a 69 and a one-shot advantage over eight other men, including Suzuki, who then took the second-round lead with 70-68, two ahead of Kazuhiko Hosokawa (70-70) and Tateo (Jet) Ozaki (73-67). The 41-year-old Suzuki, who has won seven times in his 14 seasons, most recently in the 2004 Acom International, still was on top Saturday after the rain-delayed second round was completed and the third round was in the books. He managed only a 74 for 212 and led Mamoru Osanai (68) and Tetsuya Haraguchi (69) by a stroke.

Trailing by three after his second straight 73, Kikuchi leveled a fast finish at Suzuki Sunday. He ran off four consecutive birdies starting at the 11th hole and took over first place with a chip-in birdie at the 16th. However, he missed the 18th green in regulation and a par-saving eight-footer to drop into a tie with Suzuki with 68 to Toru's 71.

Kikuchi's winning playoff par came after the two players parred the first extra hole and bogeyed the second.

KBC Augusta
Shima, Fukuoka
Winner: Katsumasa Miyamoto

The veterans continued to hold sway when play resumed after a two-week hiatus in mid-August with the KBC Augusta tournament in Fukuoka Prefec-ture. Following the back-to-back victories of Toru Taniguchi and the playoff duel between two other pros in their 30s — winner Jun Kikuchi and Toru Suzuki — 34-year-old Katsumasa Miyamoto took his turn.

Leading from his potent 64-64 start on the par-71 Keya Golf Club course at Shima, Miyamoto went wire-to-wire to a shaky, one-stroke victory with a 15-under-par 269 total. It was his sixth tour title, first since the NST Niigata Open in 2003, and moved him into second place on the money list.

Miyamoto's 128 after 36 holes, the year's lowest two-round start, staked him to a four-stroke lead over Australian Steven Conran. He had an eagle and 16 birdies in that sensational stretch. But Conran gave him a run for his money the rest of the way. The Aussie shot 67 Saturday to Miyamoto's 70 and closed to within a shot. However, he was the only player within four shots at that point.

Koumei Oda entered the picture Sunday after starting the final round seven shots off the lead, and those three waged a tight battle down the stretch. Conran tied Katsumasa for the lead momentarily after making the final birdie among the three at the 14th hole, but he followed with bogeys at the next two holes. Miyamoto also had a bogey but hung on for 71 and the one-stroke victory over Conran and Oda.

Fujisankei Classic
Fujikawaguchiko, Yamanashi
Winner: Hideto Tanihara

Hideto Tanihara finally regained the touch that he had in 2006 when he fought his way to victory in the Fujisankei Classic the first weekend of September. Better things had been expected of Tanihara after his banner 2006 season when he won twice and finished second to Shingo Katayama on the money list. Instead, after starting the season at May's Japan PGA Championship, he missed two cuts, was disqualified at another event and tied for 55th in his fourth outing. Three top-10s, including a tie-for-second in the Mizuno Open, put him on track toward the triumph in the venerable Fujisankei tournament, which bad weather reduced to a 54-hole event.

The 28-year-old Tanihara, who took an unsuccessful shot at the U.S. PGA Tour in 2005, broke from a three-way tie when 36 holes were finally in the books Saturday to a three-stroke victory when the third round was over and the fourth cancelled Sunday. He was part of a four-way tie for the lead at 67 with Naoya Takemoto, Masaya Tomida and Yoshikazu Haku the first day and shared the 36-hole lead at 138 with Tomohiro Kondo (69-69), the JCB Classic victor, and Thailand's Prayad Marksaeng (68-70), making another run at a win in Japan.

Tanihara clinched his victory in spectacular fashion. Just two under for the round, with Prayad on his heels, he holed from a bunker for an eagle at Fujizakura Country Club's 17th hole, then parred the 18th for 67 and an eight-under-par 205 total, picking up his fifth tour title. Prayad finished second with 70–208. Fifteen-year-old Ryo Ishikawa, making his first tour appearance since his shockingly brilliant victory in May's Munsingwear Open, had a very respectable showing, contending in the top 10 until a final-round 73 dropped him to 15th place.

Suntory Open
Inzai, Chiba
Winner: Hideto Tanihara

It may be unprecedented — maybe, because such records are not kept — what happened on the Japan Tour in early September. For a second consecutive week, horrid weather dictated the shortening of a tournament to 54 holes and the same player — Hideto Tanihara — was the beneficiary. Typhoon No. 9 raked Chiba Prefecture early on the second day of the Suntory Open at Inzai, leaving the Sobu Country Club course so swamped and debris-laden that the round had to be cancelled.

That meant that Tanihara, coming off his three-shot victory in the Fujisankei Classic, and Toru Taniguchi carried their leading, five-under-par 65s into the delayed second round on Saturday. Taniguchi, looking to fatten his lead in the money race, shot 68 for 133 on the soggy course and established a three-stroke lead over Tanihara (71), Tatsuya Mitsuhashi (68) and Shigeki Maruyama (68), back home after another season on the U.S. PGA Tour.

As occurred more often earlier in the season than he would like to remember, Taniguchi failed to finish things off with a win Sunday. Australia's Brendan Jones, who had only been back in Japan a week after spending nearly two months at home with his wife and first-born child, mounted a challenge on the front nine Sunday, coming from five strokes off the pace to overtake Taniguchi at the turn with Tanihara close behind. However, Jones's charge fizzled on the back nine and, after trading bogeys with Taniguchi, Tanihara went on a birdie run, nailing five on the next six holes around a bogey at No. 16 for a 66–202 and a two-stroke victory over Taniguchi, who finished with a one-over 71. Jones wound up third with 68–206.

ANA Open
Kitahiroshima, Hokkaido
Winner: Norio Shinozaki

Norio Shinozaki's first victory was a long time in coming in more ways than just the fruitless years he had spent on the Japan Tour. The unexpected winner had to battle through five extra holes to annex the ANA Open title in mid-September, the longest playoff of the six that dotted the 2007 schedule.

Shinozaki received little attention the first two days at Sapporo Country Club's Wattsu course, the focus instead on Hideto Tanihara and his bid for three consecutive victories. After posting a modest, one-under-par 70 in a first round that abounded with low scores, starting with Michio Matsumura's 63, Tanihara fired a 66 Friday and moved within a stroke of the lead. Keiichiro Fukabori (66-69) and Tatsuhiko Takahashi (67-68) showed the way with their 135s.

Shinozaki appeared on the leaderboard Saturday when his 68-70-70 put him in a five-way tie for second behind Sushi Ishigaki and Yasuharu Imano, who took over first place with their 207s. Tanihara remained in contention two off the pace despite a 73, but fell short Sunday with 71, tying for 10th.

The playoff developed when Shinozaki and Chawalit Plaphol shot 69s and Imano 70 for 277 totals. After Imano was eliminated on the second playoff hole, Shinozaki won when Chawalit, the first tour winner from Thailand when he captured the ANA in 2004, bogeyed the fifth hole.

Coca-Cola Tokai Classic
Miyoshi, Aichi
Winner: Camilo Villegas

The promising future of colorful Colombian Camilo Villegas got brighter when his second visit to Japan for the Coca-Cola Tokai Classic paid off with the initial professional victory that had been tantalizingly close on several occasions during his first two seasons on the U.S. PGA Tour. Encouraged by a third-place finish there in 2006, Villegas returned for another crack at Miyoshi Country Club's West course and secured the coveted maiden triumph in a two-hole playoff against another winless player, little-known Toyokazu Fujishima.

Both men were contenders from the start in a tournament that yielded very little low scoring. The fancy-dressing Colombian shared the first-round lead with Yudai Maeda at three-under-par 68. Then Villegas joined Fujishima and four others, including ANA victor Norio Shinozaki, at 140, tied for second two shots behind pacesetting Yusaku Miyazato, yet another player trying for a first win.

The 26-year-old Fujishima posted his third straight 70 Saturday and edged a stroke ahead of Makoto Inoue (70), Villegas (71) and the ever-dangerous Shingo Katayama. Villegas, 25, who came to the Tokai Classic on the heels of three consecutive top-10 finishes in the PGA Tour's heralded, season-climaxing FedExCup series, repeated his 71 Sunday, but dropped into the playoff with Fujishima when he bogeyed the 72nd hole. Villegas claimed the victory when he dropped a 20-foot putt for birdie on the second extra hole and Fujishima couldn't match it.

Japan Open
Sagamihara, Kanagawa
Winner: Toru Taniguchi

It's not often that you get a tour's two biggest stars finishing one-two in its most important championship, as happened in mid-October in the 72nd staging of the Japan Open. Toru Taniguchi and Shingo Katayama, the leading lights of the current Japan Tour, wound up that way on the testing East course of Sagamihara Golf Club in Kanagawa Prefecture to the delight of the galleries.

Taniguchi, who enhanced his hold on the money lead with his second win of the year, worked a different pattern in the final round than the one that cost him several times earlier in the season. He couldn't let a third-round lead slip away this time because, instead of leading as he was on past occasions, he was six strokes behind going into the final 18 holes. This time he battered the course with a 66 and beat Katayama by two strokes with his 283 total. Katayama shot 72 Sunday.

It seemed unlikely that Taniguchi would be a factor at Sagamihara after struggling to a 75 in the opening round. Veteran Kaname Yokoo birdied the last three holes for 68 that day and took a two-shot lead over Katayama, Kiyoshi Miyazato, Keiichiro Fukabori and Hidemasa Hoshino. He retained that margin over Katayama with a 71 for 139 Friday. Koumei Oda, winless on the tour but having a fairly strong season, surged into the lead Saturday as Yokoo slumped to 76. Oda birdied four of his first five holes en route to a 69–211, gaining his two-stroke lead over Katayama (72) when Katayama bogeyed the 17th and Oda birdied the 18th.

Oda couldn't handle the stratospheric position of leading the Open after 54 holes and dissolved with an 80 Sunday. Taniguchi, out in 31, raced through that open door and held off Katayama and the other contenders to score the 14th victory of his career and move up to fifth place on the tour's all-time money list. Fukabori shot 71–286 to take third place.

Bridgestone Open
Chiba
Winner: Shingo Katayama

A leader or close contender can't win tournaments with even-par final rounds very often. Shingo Katayama had it illustrated personally in the Japan Open the week before when it happened to him. The Japanese star made sure it didn't occur again when, as co-leader, he played the final 18 holes of the Bridgestone Open. He put up a four-under-par 68 and held off three challengers to win his second tournament of the season and 23rd of his career.

The victory enabled the 34-year-old Katayama to make up ground in his pursuit of leader Toru Taniguchi and his fourth straight (fifth overall) money title. Taniguchi had a quiet, tie-for-18th week after his Japan Open victory.

Tomohiro Kondo, 30, eying his fourth title in the last two seasons, opened the week at Chiba's Sodegaura Country Club with a seven-under-par 65 and a two-stroke lead over six other players, including Keiichiro Fukabori, the third-place finisher in the Open. Katayama was at 68, and when he followed with a 67 Friday, he was just a stroke behind leaders Fukabori (67-67) and Thailand's impressive Prayad Marksaeng (68-66).

Another 67 Saturday forged Katayama's first-place tie with Yasuharu Imano, a three-time winner, who registered a 66 for his 202. Katayama put together a solid 68 Sunday for 270 total, capping the round with a vital birdie at the last hole after Fukabori bogeyed the 17th, Kondo the 18th and the third 271-shooter, Australia's Steven Conran, couldn't match the birdie at the final green.

Ryo Ishikawa, the 15-year-old winner of the Munsingwear Open, missed his second cut in a row. He was ousted by one stroke at the Open, but in the Bridgestone the bottom fell out after he opened nicely with 69 then skied to 80.

ABC Championship
Kato, Hyogo
Winner: Frankie Minoza

It looked like a father-son pairing on the 18th tee of the ABC Golf Club. The "father" was Frankie Minoza, the 47-year-old veteran winner from the Philippines who has victories sprinkled all over Asia. The "son" was Lee Dong-hwan, the up-and-coming 20-year-old from South Korea who won his first title earlier in the year at the Mizuno Open. It was serious business. The two were playing off for the ABC Championship. Experience prevailed as Minoza birdied that first extra hole to land his seventh title on the Japan Tour to go with a half dozen or more in the 1980s and 1990s on the widespread Asian Circuit.

Weather again marred a tournament after Toshimitsu Izawa, the reigning Japan PGA champion, shot 66 to lead Toru Taniguchi, Katsumasa Miyamoto and Hiroyuki Fujita by a shot and the first round was completed without interference. Before a thunderstorm hit Friday, Minoza drilled a 64 for 133 and a tenuous lead when darkness prevented the completion of the round. The next morning Fujita completed a 66 of his own to tie Minoza, and before the day ended had the 54-hole lead to himself. After Minoza bogeyed the 17th, Fujita birdied the 18th for 70–203. Minoza shot 71 for 204.

Lee, who started the third day just a shot off the lead, managed only a 74. However, he rebounded Sunday with 66, and his 274 total put him into the deadlock with Minoza (70) as Fujita tumbled into a tie for fourth place when he shot 73. Shingo Katayama came up a stroke short in his bid for back-to-back victories, but gained a little more ground on Taniguchi (tied for 12th) in the money race.

Mitsui Sumitomo Visa Taiheiyo Masters
Gotemba, Shizuoka
Winner: Brendan Jones

Two of the world's leading players from Australia — Adam Scott and Geoff Ogilvy — graced the field as the Japan Tour began its late-fall trifecta of big-money tournaments with the Mitsui Sumitomo Visa Taiheiyo Masters. But when all was said and done, they played second (actually third and fourth) fiddle to another Aussie, circuit regular Brendan Jones.

Jones squeezed out a one-stroke victory with his 14-under-par 274 on the Taiheiyo Club's Gotemba course in Shizuoka Prefecture and made it clear that he doesn't plan to join those countrymen on the international scene. "I love playing in Japan and hope to play in Japan many, many years," he chortled after scoring his second win of the season and his seventh in six years in Japan.

Money leader Toru Taniguchi continued his consistent, week-to-week competitiveness at Gotemba, sharing the early lead and making the final challenge to Jones Sunday. He, Jones and Scott, along with Koumei Oda and Tatsuhiko Takahashi, started with 67s Thursday, then Taniguchi moved two strokes ahead of Jones Friday with a 66 to Jones's 68.

While Jones was posting a 69, his third round in the 60s, for 204 total and the lead, Taniguchi was experiencing one of the occasional poor rounds that have prevented him from having a truly magnificent season. He fell three back with 74 as Scott, with 70, was the runner-up at 206.

It all came down to the 72nd hole Sunday. Taniguchi made up the three strokes and went to the final hole tied with Jones, but Jones salted away the victory on the par-five 18th when he knocked his second shot onto the edge of the green and holed a 30-foot eagle putt. Taniguchi two-putted for a birdie and second place. His 275 was two better than Scott and three ahead of Ogilvy, who tied for fourth with yet another Aussie, Chris Campbell.

Dunlop Phoenix
Miyazaki
Winner: Ian Poulter

Ian Poulter took a big step toward establishing himself as a top-level international player when he captured the Dunlop Phoenix tournament in mid-November. Already considered one of Europe's brightest stars — in more way than one — Poulter had failed in his six seasons to score a victory outside his seven on the European Tour.

In winning on the par-70 Phoenix Country Club course, the 31-year-old Englishman with a penchant for flashy attire and unorthodox hair styles extended the string of victories by non-Japanese players to five as he joined many of the game's leading players on the winners' list. Only Kaname Yokoo (2002) and Shingo Katayama (2000) have kept the title at home since 1997.

Poulter, who finished fifth in his first visit to the Phoenix in 2006, never trailed this time. The run started Thursday when he, Toshinori Muto and Kim Kyung-tae shot 65s. On Friday, Padraig Harrington, the defending champion, eagled the final hole for a 65 of his own and joined Poulter (68) at the top with 133s. It was back-to-back Englishmen after 54 holes as Poulter scored a 67 for 200 and a two-stroke advantage over Luke Donald, who also came in with a 67 for his 202. Poulter chipped in for one of his four birdies and holed a six-footer at the last hole.

A 69 in tough scoring conditions Sunday established Poulter's final three-stroke margin with his 11-under-par 269 total. Spain's Gonzalo Fernandez-Castano jumped into second place with 68–272, a shot ahead of Donald (71) and Katayama (68). Harrington tied for fifth with American tour rookie Brandt Snedeker.

Casio World Open
Geisei, Kochi
Winner: Taichi Teshima

Taichi Teshima almost ran out of time to salvage something out the 2007 season. After winning twice on the Japan Tour and finishing fifth on the money list in 2006, the 38-year-old veteran took a shot at the European Tour this year and had meager success (only one top-10). Teshima was playing in just his fifth event back home when he rode a final-round spurt to victory in the Casio World Open, the final open event on the 2007 circuit in late November at Geisei's Kochi Kuroshio Country Club.

The 2001 Japan Open champion started the week in a four-way tie for first place with the ever-present Toru Taniguchi, senior Tateo Ozaki and South Korea's Chang Ik-je at 69, then settled a stroke off the lead behind Chang with 68–137. Australia's Chris Campbell, coming off a third-place finish in the Dunlop Phoenix and a fourth in the Visa Taiheiyo Masters the two previous weeks, charged into first place Saturday. Campbell, who has won once in his three years in Japan, birdied his first five holes and eight in all for a tournament-record 64 that jumped him a stroke in front of Taniguchi (70) and Chang (72).

Teshima eclipsed Campbell Sunday when he birdied the last two holes for 65 and 275 total as Campbell shot 69–276. Chang finished third at 277, and leading money winner Taniguchi had another weak finish, his 74 dropping him into a tie for 10th. The victory was Teshima's sixth in a career dating back to 1992.

Golf Nippon Series JT Cup
Tokyo
Winner: Brendan Jones

Brendan Jones capped the finest year of his career at the season-ending Golf Nippon Series JT Cup. He carved out a scintillating, come-from-behind victory at Tokyo's Yomiuri Country Club for his third victory of the season, pairing him with Toru Taniguchi as the most frequent winners of the Japan Tour season. The first prize advanced him to third on the final money list as Taniguchi wrapped up his second title, dethroning Shingo Katayama, who had been No. 1 for the previous three years.

Katayama had a slim chance off overtaking Taniguchi at the Nippon Series, needing a victory and a poor showing by Taniguchi. He kept that possibility alive for two days, shooting 66 on Thursday to lead Liang Wen-chong by a stroke, Taniguchi and seven others by three; then repeated the four-under 66 Friday to sweep five shots ahead of Prayad Marksaeng, Hirofumi Miyase and Jeev Milkha Singh. Taniguchi was then six back (69-69) and Jones lingered at 70-70–140.

Katayama's bid came a-cropper when he shot 75 Saturday. The reshuffled leaderboard showed Hiroshi Iwata and Singh on top with 203s; Taniguchi, Liang, Marksaeng, Miyase and Hiroyuki Fujita next at 205. A 68 left the 32-year-old Jones five strokes off the pace prior to his unheralded fireworks the next day.

Jones turned at three under Sunday, then exploded with six birdies for a back-nine 29 and a 61. With his 11-under 269 total in the bank, he looked on as the final four groups came in. Singh and Liang were also at 11 under when they reached the tough par-three 18th, but both men double-bogeyed the hole and dropped into a five-way tie for third behind Jones and Taniguchi, who shot 65 and came up one shy of the Aussie. Katayama wound up tied for 15th and took second place on the final money list.

11. Australasian Tour

Led by Adam Scott, 11 Australian golfers finished the year in the top 60 of the Official World Golf Ranking. Only America had more representatives — yet another indication of the depth of talent emerging from down under. But while there was major championship success in both 2005 and 2006 for golfers from Australasia — New Zealand's Michael Campbell and then Australia's Geoff Ogilvy winning the U.S. Open — none followed in 2007.

It was not for lack of opportunities. At the Masters, Stuart Appleby led after three rounds but fell back to seventh place after losing his lead with a double bogey at the first hole. No Australian has ever won at Augusta National and the curse seems not just directed at Greg Norman. It was a similar story at Oakmont in the U.S. Open where Aaron Baddeley held the lead with a round to play. But, just like Appleby, Baddeley was playing alongside Tiger Woods and yet neither of them won. Baddeley's demise started with a triple bogey at the opening hole and concluded with a final round of 80 to fall back to 13th place. Richard Green almost reversed the trend at the Open Championship at Carnoustie, posting a brilliant 64 early on the final day but ending up two strokes outside the playoff. As for the U.S. PGA Championship at Southern Hills, John Senden finished fourth and Ogilvy sixth, but Woods, this time, was out of sight.

With increasing numbers on the PGA Tour in America and lots of recent successes, only two victories in 2007 could be classed as a slight disappointment. Baddeley won the FBR Open in Phoenix, while Scott took the Shell Houston Open. Overall, and by his own highest standards, it was something of a quiet year for Scott and he will be expecting to make more noise in 2008 in order to maintain his top-10 ranking. In Europe, Richard Green claimed his first title for 10 years in the northern hemisphere when he won the BA-CA Open in Austria. Brett Rumford used his short game to remarkable effect to win the Omega European Masters in Crans-sur-Sierre. On his debut season on the Asian PGA Tour, Scott Hend finished fourth on the money list with two runner-up finishes. Meanwhile, in Japan, Brendan Jones had another strong year, winning three times, including the Visa Taiheiyo Masters and the Golf Nippon Series JT Cup, to be third on the money list.

The main part of the Australasian Tour is now restricted to just a month at the end of the year. While England's Richard Finch claimed his first win at the Michael Hill New Zealand Open — notable for Sir Bob Charles making the cut at the age of 71 — the three main Australian events all had home winners. Baddeley completed a fine year by winning the MasterCard Masters at Huntingdale, while Peter Lonard claimed the Australian PGA Championship title and Craig Parry, at the age of 41, finally secured the Stonehaven Cup with victory at the MFS Australian Open. An emotional Parry said: "Only winning a major could be better than this." An anomaly remains in that neither Scott nor Ogilvy, for all their successes elsewhere in the world, has won on home soil.

Jacob's Creek Open
Lockleys, South Australia
Winner: Scott Sterling

Scott Sterling gained his first win on the Nationwide Tour at the co-sanctioned Jacob's Creek Open. The 36-year-old American held off a pack of locals, including a member of the host Kooyonga club outside Adelaide. Sterling was tied for the lead playing the final hole with 21-year-old David Lutterus, the favorite of the gallery, which contained many of his family and friends. The 18th is a 370-yard dogleg left, and Sterling, continuing his conservative approach, played a four iron down the middle of the fairway.

Lutterus, however, played his driver but blocked it to the right, into a sandy waste area. A promotional display car had to be moved, but then his second shot went over the green and Lutterus finished with a bogey. Sterling's approach shot was knocked down by the breeze but he two-putted from 55 feet, holing a three-footer for the victory. "I've never hit anything but driver on that hole," Lutterus said. "I always seem to make three or four. Besides, I don't even know what the second shot is like from way back there."

Sterling, who birdied the 12th, 13th and 14th holes to break a five-way tie for the lead, closed with 71 to finish at 12-under-par 276, one ahead of Lutterus, who opened with 64 but finished with a 72. Marc Leishman and Brendan Jones were a further shot behind, with Craig Parry, Peter Senior and Brett Rumford at nine-under 278.

Sterling's putting was superb all week, especially from long range. "My touch was pretty good," he said. "I don't think I've ever holed as many long putts. I was pretty calm, except over the short one at the last. You always have some doubts when it's your first win."

HSBC New Zealand PGA Championship
Christchurch, New Zealand
Winner: Nicholas Thompson

Nicholas Thompson, a member of the victorious American Walker Cup team in 2005, claimed his first professional victory at the HSBC New Zealand PGA Championship, an event co-sanctioned by the Australasian and Nationwide tours. The 24-year-old American won at the first extra hole of a playoff, beating Canadian David Morland at Clearwater in Christchurch.

Morland set the clubhouse target at eight-under-par 280, with no bogeys and four birdies, the last at the 17th, in a closing 68. Thompson matched him with his own 68 after conjuring up two birdies at the last two holes. At the 17th he hit a wedge to six feet and then at the last hit an eight iron to four feet. In the playoff back at the 18th, Morland drove into a fairway bunker, then found a greenside bunker and took a bogey. Thompson was never in trouble on the hole and tapped in for par to win.

"I wasn't nervous at all today," Thompson said. "I was swinging good and I played so well on the last 11 holes. I had a look (for birdie) on every one of them. One of the big keys to this golf course is that you've got to hit a lot of fairways and a lot of greens. I drove it exceptionally well this week. I played a lot of good golf."

Thompson, who lost his card on the PGA Tour in 2006 after getting through the qualifying tournament on his first attempt in 2005, rushed to the airport to get back to Florida and try to qualify for the Honda Classic, his hometown event.

Lee Williamson, a late entrant and one whose clubs only arrived on Tuesday, and fellow American Michael Letzig shared third place at 281, one shot outside the playoff, with Australian James Nitties alone in fifth place.

Johnnie Walker Classic
Phuket, Thailand
Winner: Anton Haig

See Asia/Japan Tours chapter.

MasterCard Masters
Melbourne, Victoria
Winner: Aaron Baddeley

Aaron Baddeley learned to play golf at the famous Huntingdale course in Melbourne that annually hosts the MasterCard Masters. After a four-hole playoff with Daniel Chopra, Baddeley donned the gold jacket awarded to the winner. Chopra was the third-round leader, but Baddeley caught the Swede at 13-under-par 275 with a closing 70, while Chopra had 71. Stuart Appleby had a double bogey at the last hole to fall to third place two strokes behind. Chopra birdied the 15th and 16th holes but bogeyed the 17th, while Baddeley birdied the 17th.

All four holes of the playoff were at the 18th and it was Chopra who was always fighting for his life. Baddeley missed a birdie chance at the first attempt. Both had long birdie attempts the second time around. At the third time of asking, Chopra had to hole a good par putt to carry on. Fourth time around, Baddeley drove deep into the trees, but a brilliant recovery finished just off the green. He chipped to eight feet and rolled in the putt for his par, while Chopra missed from five feet.

It was Baddeley's first win on home soil since the two-time former Australian Open champion won the Greg Norman Holden International in 2001. "In the playoff I felt like I was swinging the club really well. I just kept hitting the same shots and felt that I'd wear him down," said Baddeley. "Every playoff hole I had the chance to win and it was Dan who was saving it to keep it going, but I really had to scrap to win that final playoff hole. But it really feels great to win at home. It's fantastic."

Peter O'Malley took fourth place in the European Tour co-sanctioned event. England's Dave Horsey had the final day's best round, shooting a seven-under-par 65 with eight birdies and a bogey to jump from 30th place to a share of fifth at nine-under-par 279 with Peter Lonard and Rod Pampling.

Michael Hill New Zealand Open
Queenstown, New Zealand
Winner: Richard Finch

England's Richard Finch produced a performance to match the grandeur of his surroundings at The Hills Golf Club in Queenstown to claim his first professional title in the Michael Hill New Zealand Open. Just a few weeks earlier Finch had been battling to save his European Tour card and left it until his final event of the 2007 season before climbing into the all-important top 115 by tying for seventh in the Mallorca Classic. Here, in an event co-sanctioned on the 2008 European Tour, Finch put all that behind him with a commanding three-stroke victory over the Australian pair of Steven Bowditch and Paul Sheehan.

Finch led by three strokes going into the final round and by the turn had extended that advantage to six shots. He finally got his breakthrough when he holed a 12-foot par putt on the 18th for even-par 72, following rounds of 73, 65 and 64 for a total of 14-under-par 274. On Friday his 65 set a new course record before Peter Fowler lowered the mark to 62 the next day. "Going into today, I felt it was in my hands, and if I played well, played as I had been all week, this would be the outcome," Finch said. "I stumbled a bit on the back nine when I started thinking too much about what I was doing. It's the first time I've been in this position and it was difficult to know how to do it."

But stealing the show at The Hills was 71-year-old Sir Bob Charles, who was persuaded to accept a special invitation to play in the centenary edition of the tournament. Charles won the event as an amateur in 1954 and went on to win three more times. After an opening 75, Charles scored 68 on Friday to make the cut — and become the oldest player to play all four rounds on a major non-seniors tour. He matched his age with a 71 on Saturday and then broke his age again with 70 on Sunday and received a stunning ovation at the final hole.

Cadbury Schweppes Australian PGA Championship
Coolum Beach, Queensland
Winner: Peter Lonard

Peter Lonard came from one behind American-based South African Rory Sabbatini to win the Joe Kirkwood Cup for the third time at the Cadbury Schweppes Australian PGA Championship at Coolum. Lonard immediately took the lead in the final round, and a closing 65 put the 40-year-old three clear of New Zealand's David Smail at 20-under-par 268 total. Smail signed off with a 68 to finish two ahead of Greg Chalmers, Scott Laycock and Michael Sim. Adam Scott was a shot further back, while Sabbatini limped in with a 74 to tie for 10th place.

After a punishing schedule on the U.S. PGA Tour, Lonard took eight weeks off to restore his appetite for the game. He admitted spending most of that time on the couch watching television, but also visited Egypt. After returning to Australia for the MasterCard Masters in Melbourne, Lonard was ready to peak again and claimed his ninth Australasian Tour title, and his first on home soil since winning his second PGA Championship in 2004.

"I think today was really good. Today was good for me, not just the way I played, but when I got on the range I had a fire in my belly to play which I haven't had for a long time," said Lonard. "I was shaking the whole day today. Everything irritated me, everyone talking to me irritated me. I just wanted to be left alone and go and play. I was nervous on the first tee and nervous on a lot of shots and that's when you know you are fully focused. So the whole day just the feeling I had before I played was something I hadn't had for a long time, so I think that was the best part. By the end of the year in the States I had been ready to pull my hair out and needed the break."

MFS Australian Open
Sydney, New South Wales
Winner: Craig Parry

At the age of 41, and 20 years after his first win in the NSW Open, also at the Australian Club in Sydney, Craig Parry won the MFS Australian Open for the first time. Parry lifted the famous Stonehaven Cup after a closing 69 put him at 11-under-par 277 and one ahead of fellow Australians Lee Won-joon and Nick O'Hern and American Brandt Snedeker. The victory completed the triple crown for Parry, who had previously won the Australian PGA and Masters titles. It also brought a third Australasian Tour Order of Merit title.

Lee, in his first year as a professional, changed his putter on the advice of his non-golfing mother and had only 24 putts in a final round of 66. He set the target at 10-under-par 278 just as Parry was playing the 10th hole. A birdie there put Parry one behind, and then he holed a long putt at the 13th before a four at the par-five 14th put him one in front. At the 17th Parry needed to get up and down from 90 yards for his par and then he safely parred the 18th. James Nitties could have tied at the 18th, but his chip failed to escape the thick rough. He finished fifth while the other overnight leader, Robert Allenby, fell away with a 75.

"To win the Australian Open has been a longtime dream of mine," Parry said. "I was leading amateur in 1984 when Tom Watson won. I was 17 years of age and I thought this is what I want to do, be the best. I got close a few times, lost a playoff, finished second once, third about eight times. I never thought I'd actually get here and it's an amazing feeling."

12. African Tours

Of all the international achievements of South African players in 2007, James Kamte earning his European Tour card at the qualifying tournament may not appear the most high-profile. It may, however, turn out to be a significant moment. Earlier in the year, Kamte won the Seekers Travel Pro-Am, making the 25-year-old from Queenstown in the Eastern Cape the third black South African to win on the Sunshine Tour after John Mashego in 1991 and Linani Nwandwe in 2001. Kamte also gained experience on the Challenge Tour in Europe, and by earning his tour card hopes to follow in the international footsteps of Vincent Tshabalala, who won the French Open in 1976.

Kamte, a former caddie, came through the Ernie Els Foundation and among others to offer advice have been Tshabalala and Gary Player. "When I met James, I told him he had the ability to go all the way," said Player. "James has the temperament, the personality and determination of a champion. He will be a wonderful ambassador for South Africa. His achievements will open a floodgate of talent among the next generation."

Coached by Gavan Levenson, Kamte has been a professional for four years and recognizes he still has much to learn. "I know I can shoot low rounds, I've learned when to hold back and not get ahead of myself, and I am learning how to handle the pressure when I get into contention," he said. "And I believe I have what it takes to spring a surprise on the guys dominating the local and international scene — maybe in the not-too-distant future."

Dominating early in the year on the Sunshine Tour was Charl Schwartzel, who claimed the Order of Merit title for the third year running. But with the money list reverting to the calendar year, there was a second Order of Merit winner by the end of the year, with James Kingston just beating out Louis Oosthuizen. Kingston won the South African Airways Open, not just the biggest title of his career but his first win on the European Tour as well. Oosthuizen won three times in all during the year, including the Telkom PGA Championship. Both Titch Moore and Adilson da Silva posted two victories.

On the international scene, Rory Sabbatini won the Crowne Plaza Invitational at Colonial on the U.S. PGA Tour, while Els continued his dominance at his home-from-home at Wentworth by winning the HSBC World Match Play Championship for a remarkable seventh time. It was his biggest win for three years, but his year ended on a sour note when he threw away the Alfred Dunhill Championship with a triple-bogey eight at the final hole. Retief Goosen had a quiet year except for winning the Qatar Masters, while other winners on the European Tour were Schwartzel at the Open de Espana, the ever-improving Richard Sterne at the Celtic Manor Wales Open and newcomer Anton Haig, an exciting youngster and a huge hitter of the ball, at the Johnnie Walker Classic in Thailand.

Joburg Open
Johannesburg, South Africa
Winner: Ariel Canete

Ariel Canete, a 31-year-old from Argentina, turned his golfing career around by winning the inaugural Joburg Open at Royal Johannesburg and Kensington Golf Club. Canete lost his playing privileges on the European Tour after finishing 146th on the Order of Merit in 2006 and failed to get his card back at the qualifying tournament. Instead, he had returned to the Challenge Tour, from where he had qualified for the main tour in 2005.

By using both the East and West courses at Royal Johannesburg and Kensington, the tournament was able to offer 200 starting places and Canete had no hesitation in ending his Christmas and New Year holiday early to take part. It was a wise decision, as four rounds in the 60s gave him a three-year exemption on the European Tour. He opened with rounds of 66 and 68 across both courses, and when play switched to just the East course for the weekend, he scored 65 in the third round to take the lead by one over Andrew McLardy.

Canete suffered an early bogey at the par-three second hole, but two birdies on the first nine and then three coming home left him at 19 under par. A brilliant up-and-down from a greenside bunker at the 18th gave him the last of those birdies and a two-stroke win over McLardy, who closed with 68 to Canete's 67. Hennie Otto took third place, one behind McLardy, with Alex Haindl and Mark Murless sharing fourth place.

Dimension Data Pro-Am
Sun City, South Africa
Winner: Louis Oosthuizen

Louis Oosthuizen claimed his first title on the summer swing of the Sunshine Tour just in time to fulfill one of the conditions laid down by his future father-in-law. The 24-year-old was due to marry his fiancée Nel-Mare Alberts four weeks later. "My dad said we could get married when I graduate and Louis wins an event," said Nel-Mare. "Well, we are one down and one to go, but I only graduate in May, so perhaps he'll go a little easier on us now."

As if there was not enough pressure on Oosthuizen. He came to the 18th at the Gary Player Country Club — where the nines were switched so this was the par-five ninth as played at the Nedbank Golf Challenge — needing a birdie to win and he holed a testing 15-footer, downhill and very quick, to beat Omar Sandys by one stroke.

Sandys roared into contention on the final day by posting 65 and setting the clubhouse target at 278, 10 under par. After scores of 66, 71 and 71, Oosthuizen started the final round one behind Michiel Bothma, but went on a brilliant run of five birdies in a row from the second hole. But on the second nine he got too aggressive on the greens, three-putting for a bogey at the 13th and a double bogey at the 14th. At the 18th he drove into the trees and had to lay up before pitching on and holing the winning putt.

"It got tight towards the end," Oosthuizen said. "At the last I was quite pleased it wasn't on the fairway, because it took away the risky option of going for the green. The putt was a lot longer than I'd bargained, but I just committed and gave it some muscle. It was a real beauty." Bothma finished in third place, three behind Oosthuizen's score of 11-under-par 277 after 73 to the winner's 69.

Nashua Masters
Port Edward, Natal
Winner: Jean Hugo

Jean Hugo claimed his first summer victory on the Sunshine Tour for eight years by leading the Nashua Masters from start to finish at the Wild Coast Sun Country Club. But he only won at the first hole of a playoff after a dramatic final-day duel with Titch Moore.

After a two-hour delay due to stormy weather, Hugo began the final round with a two-stroke lead, but by going out in one over was caught by Moore. One ahead again playing the 12th, Hugo took a triple-bogey eight at the par-five on the side of the cliff. With the rain returning, he got back to even with Moore before claiming an eagle to his opponent's birdie at the 16th, but Moore responded again by birdieing the 17th.

The final hole was halved in pars, but when they played the hole again in the playoff, Moore three-putted to allow Hugo to tap in for the victory.

"This wasn't the best finish by a long shot," said Hugo. "I knew I was in for a tough challenge against Titch today. We're the best of friends. We practice together, travel together, and I've lost a few playoffs, so I know how it feels. Personally, I am really proud of myself how I came back up through 16, 17 and 18. After the eight at the 12th, I would have been happy to settle for second alone. The last time I won on the summer tour was the Zimbabwe Open in 1999, so that's a long time."

Hugo had taken the lead with an opening 64 before adding rounds of 67, 68 and 70 for an 11-under-par total of 269. Moore caught him with a final-round 68, having scored 66s on days two and three. Andre Cruse finished in third place, three strokes behind, after a hole-in-one at the fourth hole, while Scot Euan Little and Englishman Justin Waters shared fourth place.

Vodacom Championship
Pretoria, South Africa
Winner: Richard Sterne

Richard Sterne ended a playoff against Louis Oosthuizen by pulling off the "best shot I have ever hit." Sterne won the Vodacom Championship for his second title on the Sunshine Tour at the second extra hole. His closing round of 65 at the Pretoria Country Club set the target at 274, 14 under par, only for Oosthuizen to tie him with an eagle-birdie finish.

Both players birdied the 18th on the first playoff hole, but then Sterne drove deep into the trees when playing the 18th again. He had 210 yards to the green but only a narrow gap in the timber at which to aim. With Oosthuizen safely on the fairway, Sterne took a gamble and smashed the ball onto the green. He then two-putted for a birdie which Oosthuizen could not match.

"I had two options," said Sterne, "I either chip it out or have a go at it. There was a small gap and I had to really get it up. Yes, that's possibly the best shot I've ever hit." In the steamy heat of the final afternoon, the packed leaderboard only slowly thinned out. Sterne, who won R348,700, and Oosthuizen, after a closing 67, tied at 274, with Titch Moore and Marc Cayeux only a shot behind. Hennie Otto, Euan Little and rookie Neil Schietekat shared fifth place, two shots outside the playoff. Adilson da Silva earned a R100,000 bonus from the sponsors for being the most consistent player on the Vodacom Origins of Golf series on the winter circuit combined with the Vodacom Championship, where the Brazilian finished 23rd. He recorded five top-seven finishes in the six Origins of Golf events in 2006.

Telkom PGA Championship
Johannesburg, South Africa
Winner: Louis Oosthuizen

A week after their duel at the Vodacom Championship, Louis Oosthuizen reversed the result to win the Telkom PGA Championship by a stroke over Richard Sterne. It was Oosthuizen's second victory in five weeks and was achieved with a closing round of 65 at Country Club Johannesburg and a 22-under-par total of 266. He birdied the final hole to set the target, but Sterne had to eagle to tie and could only get up and down from the front of the green for a birdie and a final round of 71.

"Over the last three weeks my game has really changed," said Oosthuizen, who recorded his maiden win on the summer leg of the Sunshine Tour in the Dimension Data Pro-Am. "It's changed the way I think on the course and the way I approach a tournament. Pulling that one off really made the difference. I'm looking forward to Europe. Now I know I can really go out and win tournaments." Before getting to the European Tour, Oosthuizen was due to get married the following week to fiancée Nel-Mare, with the bachelor party becoming a double celebration.

Oosthuizen earned R356,625 and second place on the Sunshine Tour's Order of Merit, which was won for the third year running by Charl Schwartzel. The 22-year-old matched Mark McNulty's achievement by closing with his own 65 to share third place with Marc Cayeux. "I've had to dig really deep this week," said Schwartzel, who turned down a trip to the lucrative Accenture World Match Play in America to make his dominance on the South African money list safe. "I said to myself before I went out this morning that I had so many 65s in my life and this was the time to shoot another. I'm happy with my decision to stay on. I've achieved what I wanted."

Mount Edgecombe Trophy
Kwazulu Natal, South Africa
Winner: Steve van Vuuren

Steve van Vuuren, a 47-year-old farmer from Mpumalanga who has never lost his playing privileges on the Sunshine Tour over 26 years, won for the first time in two years at the Mount Edgecombe Trophy, the first event on the 2007-2008 schedule. Having converted to the claw putting grip just three months before, van Vuuren proved he could still play alongside the young guns and he erupted into a huge smile on holing a six-footer at the last.

Van Vuuren, following rounds of 68, 66 and 72, closed with 70 for a total of 276, 12 under par, and a one-stroke win over Des Terblanche, Desvonde Botes and Tjaart van der Walt. It was van der Walt who set the target at 11 under after a brilliant final round of 66. As overnight leader Ross Wellington fell away, van Vuuren found himself playing the 18th with Terblanche in the lead at 12 under.

Van Vuuren was in a fairway bunker off the tee but found the green 60 feet from the hole and managed to two-putt. Terblanche had been in the trees off the tee, missed the green for three, and took a bogey which dropped him back to second place. Behind them, Botes had the chance to tie with a birdie at the 18th, but did well to save par and share second place.

"This gives me a lot of confidence, put it that way," van Vuuren said. "It gives me the feeling that if I can get into contention, I can finish it off. When you are not that long off the tee anymore, just getting into contention is a big thing out here. It also sends a message out there, I think, once people see your name among the young guns; they realize that golf really is a sport with no age limit. You just have to stay fit and keep grinding."

Finance Bank Zambia Open
Ndola, Zambia
Winner: Steve Basson

South Africa's Steve Basson became the first player to win the Finance Bank Zambia Open in successive years. The 28-year-old secured his third Sunshine Tour victory with a final round of 69 to finish at 206, 13 under par, and one stroke ahead of Lindani Ndwandwe. The year before Basson had won by three shots, but this time he was under constant pressure throughout the final round.

Basson shared the lead with rookie Neil Schietekat going into the final 18 holes, while Ndwandwe was two strokes behind. Basson chipped in at the short par-four 10th for an eagle to lead by three, but Ndwandwe then clawed his way into a tie with birdies at the 14th, 15th and, thanks to a eight-footer, the 17th. Basson teed off at the 18th knowing he was now only sharing the lead, but in the group in front Ndwandwe dropped a shot and Basson made sure of his par for the victory. Schietekat, in only his seventh start as a professional, finished alone in third place.

"I have definitely turned a corner since winning last year," said Basson. "I experienced one of my worst seasons last year, especially over the summer, and lost a lot of confidence. But coming here this week, I didn't expect all the pressure from the officials, the crowds and the Zambian press. I think it was the kick up the mental butt I needed. Today I played like a thinking golfer. In my previous wins, I had little pressure, but today I had to plan and execute with precision. And I stuck to that."

Eskom Power Cup
Hartbeespoortdam, South Africa
Winner: Chris Swanepoel

Chris Swanepoel, who had opportunities to win in 2006 but failed to convert his chances, finally claimed his first Sunshine Tour victory with a dominant display at the Eskom Power Cup at Pecanwood. Swanepoel closed with a 66 that included an eagle at the fifth hole, five birdies and a brilliant par save at the 17th after he was plugged in a greenside bunker.

With a 17-under-par total of 199, Swanepoel cruised to a comfortable four-stroke victory over Warren Abery, with James Kamte a further shot behind. It was a day of spectacular scoring. Abery put on an impressive charge with five successive birdies on the second nine in his 64. Kamte closed with 67, while Jakobus Roos was fourth after a 66 in which he briefly tied for the lead with eagles at the 10th and 12th followed by birdies at the 13th and 15th before he finished with three bogeys in a row.

Swanepoel, a 22-year-old from Warmbaths, also sparkled on the second nine as he required only eight putts on the homeward stretch. "I had six top-10 finishes last year and was in contention a few times, but I threw it away," said Swanepoel. "When I got to 10 and saw that James had closed the gap, I told myself to settle and just focus at the job at hand. Hit it, find it, hit it, putt it. Simple."

Swanepoel said he would be celebrating by sharing a bottle of Johnnie Walker Blue Label with his father. He had given the bottle to his father a few months earlier. "He said we would open it when I won a tournament or my sisters finish university, whichever came first. Guess they will have to buy their own bottle now."

Vodacom Origins of Golf Tour at Arabella
Hermanus, South Africa
Winner: Andrew Curlewis

Andrew Curlewis came through a dramatic three-hole playoff to claim his first victory as a professional at the Vodacom Origins of Golf Tour at Arabella Golf Club near Hermanus. The 23-year-old, who had to qualify for the tournament, went on to take the lead after 36 holes with a hole-in-one in his second round, survived determined charges from the rest of the field on the final day, and then beat the experienced Alan Michell in a tense playoff for the title. "It was nerve-racking, to say the least," said Curlewis, who was afforded a two-putt for birdie from four feet to beat Michell's par on the third playoff hole.

Doug McGuigan came from two behind on the final day to lead by three at the turn before an eight at the 13th after he drove into a water hazard. Michell then took over the lead, but despite birdieing the final hole, he was caught by Curlewis's eagle. The playoff remained at the 18th and the first time it was halved in pars after Curlewis got up and down from a greenside bunker. On the second extra hole, Curlewis drove into a fairway bunker on the right, but then hit a five iron from 220 yards just short of the green as the pair halved in birdies.

"That five iron on the second playoff hole was easily the shot of the tournament for me," said Curlewis. "It's so easy to hit those shots fat and I also couldn't see the flag." The win earned Curlewis a two-year exemption on the Sunshine Tour. "That's priceless. The qualifying days are over and I'm one of the big boys now. A lot of hard work has really paid off," he said.

Samsung Royal Swazi Sun Open
Mbabane, Swaziland
Winner: Des Terblanche

Des Terblanche claimed his first victory since taking the same title in 2004 by winning the Samsung Royal Swazi Sun Open under the modified-Stableford scoring system. Terblanche, 41, had a couple of lackluster years after his previous win and recommitted himself to the game in May 2006. His reward was his 17th career victory on the Sunshine Tour.

Terblanche had rounds of 66, 67, 66 and 68. But the scoring system was two points for a birdie, five for an eagle, minus one for a bogey and minus two for a double bogey or worse. His final round scored him 12 points for a total of 50 and a two-point winning margin over James Kamte, 18 years the winner's junior. Kamte, with a 63 that netted him 19 points, had the best score on the final day.

Terblanche eagled the 12th and chipped in for a birdie at the 14th to take the lead away from overnight leader George Coetzee. The 20-year-old rookie responded with birdies at the 12th and 13th, but after watching Terblanche find the water at the par-five 17th for a bogey, Coetzee's hopes of a first win disappeared with a rules infraction.

Coetzee overshot the green and his ball finished in the rough next to a hollow cement boulder. He picked up a broken piece of the boulder that was lying on top in order to put his foot inside, but was penalized two shots because the entire concrete structure was designated an immoveable obstruction. Coetzee three-putted the 18th to fall to third place with 46 points.

"This gives me a lot of confidence," said Terblanche. "It gives me belief that I can still win out here with the best of them, and not only once. I can keep winning. I think that's a belief you want."

Vodacom Origins of Golf Tour at Pretoria
Pretoria, South Africa
Winner: Hennie Otto

An eagle at the 18th hole at Pretoria was the icing on the cake for Hennie Otto as he claimed his seventh victory on the Sunshine Tour at the Vodacom Origins of Golf Tour at Pretoria. Otto, with a closing 69 for a 15-under-par total of 201, won by three strokes over James Kamte, who was second for the second successive week. Des Terblanche, the winner of the Samsung Royal Swazi Sun Open, finished alone in third at 10 under with a final-round 68.

Otto opened with 67, but set the rest of the field the tough task of catching him after a nearly flawless 65 in the second round. The 30-year-old took a four-stroke lead into the final round and ground out a winning score for his first victory in two years. "It got a little frustrating out there," Otto said. "I think the lead was too big and I didn't have to get aggressive or go for birdies, so I made a few mistakes.

"I was five clear of the field through 13 holes and I told Attie, Charl Schwartzel's brother who caddied for me, that I could probably bogey a few and still win by one. It was a new experience for me, not to fight for victory at every hole."

Coming down the stretch, Otto was unaware that Kamte, playing in the group ahead, had birdied the 17th and eagled the 18th in his closing 66. "I had enough time during the round to watch James and he was playing some exceptional golf. If I knew how he finished, I probably wouldn't have gone for the flag at 18," said Otto, who hit his approach 10 feet past the hole for the eagle. "It's only a matter of time before James wins, the way he is playing and his level of consistency."

Suncoast Classic
Durban, South Africa
Winner: Adilson da Silva

Adilson da Silva secured his first victory for almost a decade when he won the Suncoast Classic at Durban Country Club in his adopted home state of Kwazulu Natal. The 34-year-old Brazilian, who was a prolific winner in Zimbabwean golf earlier in his career, had not won on the Sunshine Tour since taking the Leopard Rock Classic in 1998. His third victory came with a closing round of 71 for a winning score of 208, eight under par. He won by a stroke over Doug McGuigan, who closed with 69.

Da Silva opened with 71 and then charged into contention with a 66 in the second round. With a round to go he was three behind Alan Michell, who took the 36-hole lead with two rounds of 67 but then crashed to a 78 on the final day. McGuigan started six behind Michell, but played brilliantly before dropping a shot in the final round to fall back to seven under. Da Silva reached the 17th on the same score, but hit a sand wedge shot stone dead for a birdie to break the deadlock and parred the 18th for the win. Dean Lambert, with 72, and Hendrik Buhrmann, 71, shared third place at five under, while defending champion Alex Haindl was fifth with local player Bradley Davison, who closed with 67.

Da Silva said his victory was the culmination of 12 months of hard work with coach John Dixon and sport psychologist Tim Hartness. "We worked hard and we saw the rewards," said da Silva, who had 11 top-10 finishes in 2006, including three runner-up finishes. "Today I am especially proud. I've waited long for this and it means the world to me that I could win here at home, in front of my friends and fans."

Lombard Insurance Classic
Mbabane, Swaziland
Winner: Peter Karmis

Peter Karmis gave himself the perfect 26th birthday present by winning his first title at the inaugural Lombard Insurance Classic in Swaziland. Karmis, who had led after a first round of 64, fell back with 72 in the second round, but another 64 on the final day, in which he did not drop a shot, gave him a one-stroke victory over Zimbabwe's Tongoona Charamba at the Royal Swazi Sun Country Club.

Charamba, who closed with 67, kept the pressure on Karmis, but when he failed to get up and down for a birdie at the 17th, his chance was effectively lost. Karmis parred the 18th to finish with a 16-under-par total of 200. He was able to hold up the specially designed glass trophy alongside his caddie and soon-to-be brother-in-law, James Mostert. Bradley Davison also scored a 64 to finish in third place, while Warren Abery, Alex Haindl, Bradford Vaughan and Omar Sandys all shared fourth place.

"It's quite unbelievable. I am so drained that it hasn't quite hit me just yet," said Karmis. "I have been in the lead before, but somehow I always messed it up for myself. I just couldn't make a mistake and that's a new thing for me. To apply routines to every shot on 18 holes calls for a lot of concentration, but I pulled it off. No wonder Tiger always looks so drained after winning."

Vodacom Origins of Golf Tour at Selborne
Kwazulu Natal, South Africa
Winner: George Coetzee

Just four months after turning professional, 20-year old George Coetzee won his first title in only his ninth start, claiming success at the third event in the Vodacom Origins of Golf Tour at Selborne. The rookie, who was up and down in the first two rounds, was the model of consistency in the third. Coetzee made 10 pars and seven birdies against a lone bogey in a solid showing for 66 at Selborne Golf Club to win by two over Ulrich van den Berg, who signed for 71. Hennie Otto, already a winner in the series at Pretoria Country Club, holed a sublime bunker shot at the 18th for a 70 to tie veteran Chris Williams for third place.

Coetzee started the day at three under, four shots behind leader van den

Berg. The four-time Sunshine Tour winner remained in the driving seat until the 10th, where Coetzee made a birdie to tie van den Berg for the lead. A birdie at the 12th saw Coetzee nudge ahead and the gap widened when van den Berg bogeyed the 13th. Coetzee dropped a shot at the 16th, but again flirted with the out of bounds at the 17th before sealing victory with an up-and-down from a bunker. "These were the most nervous and luckiest moments of my life," said Coetzee. "Before this weekend my parents were saying I'm spending too much time with my girlfriend. I'm elated to have proved them wrong."

Coetzee won the Kwazulu Natal Open at Selborne in his last event as an amateur earlier in the year and this was his fourth top-10 as a professional.

Nashua Golf Challenge
Sun City, South Africa
Winner: Warren Abery

Warren Abery recorded his first win of the season and his fifth on the Sunshine Tour with a wire-to-wire victory at the Nashua Golf Challenge. Abery finished at nine under par with a total of 207 at the Gary Player Country Club at Sun City. His closing 71 left the 34-year-old four ahead of Brazil's Adilson da Silva and five shots clear of Keith Horne. Da Silva, who carded a final round of 72, avoided sharing the runner-up spot with back-to-back birdies at the 17th and 18th, while Horne had 71 to finish alone in third at four under.

Abery was three ahead at the start of the round and went to the turn in even par to extend his lead to four strokes. "It's always a little difficult when you start the final round so far ahead of the pack, especially on a course like the Gary Player where birdies are hard to come by," said Abery. "You can get complacent, lose your concentration. I tried to keep to the game plan — fairways and greens — but came a little unstuck in the middle of the round. My caddie, Lucky, said we should get a little more aggressive, try to make some birdies and let the other guys catch me. I think he might have gotten a little bored; maybe I did too. But it did snap me out of it."

Vodacom Origins of Golf Tour at Bloemfontein
Bloemfontein, South Africa
Winner: Ulrich van den Berg

Ulrich van den Berg led from start to finish to secure the Vodacom Origins of Golf Tour victory at Bloemfontein. After winning a pro-am event the week before, the 32-year-old from Johannesburg claimed his fifth title on the Sunshine Tour. But it was his first since a dispiriting loss to Ernie Els at the Alfred Dunhill Championship in 2005, which prompted him to think about quitting the game. A final round of 69 for a 14-under-par total gave him a three-stroke win over Bradford Vaughan, who closed with 68.

Two bogeys around the turn, at the ninth and 11th, combined with birdies from Vaughan at the 10th and 11th brought van den Berg's advantage down from five strokes to one. But van den Berg responded with a birdie at the 14th followed by Vaughan's bogeys at the 15th and 16th holes.

"It feels great. The Alfred Dunhill defeat did hurt me, but it taught me a lot of life's lessons," said van den Berg. "It's not as easy as people think to win a tournament. There's immense pressure and players coming at you on the final day. But I feel I'm better equipped for it now. It's been so difficult and so hard for me to come back, and I'm glad it culminated in this victory."

Vodacom Origins of Golf Tour at Fancourt
George, South Africa
Winner: Adilson da Silva

Adilson da Silva secured his second title of the season thanks to a couple of mighty putts on the 18th green at The Links at Fancourt to win the Eastern Cape stop on the Vodacom Origins of Golf Tour. The 35-year-old Brazilian got into trouble in the rough on the par-five finishing hole in regulation play but holed from 25 feet for a par. His closing 70, three under par, gave da Silva a total of two under for the 54-hole tournament. He then watched as Warren Abery, who had been breathing down his back all day, also parred the 18th for 73 to force a playoff.

Playing the 18th again, both players faced putts for birdie of over 30 feet on a similar line. Da Silva was the first away, three feet farther out, and he hit a firm putt from 35 feet that found the cup. Proving the "first in wins" motto, Abery was unable to follow suit to continue the playoff, his effort tailing off to the right.

"Winning in Durban a few weeks ago was great, but this proves to me and everyone else that it was no fluke," said da Silva, who won the Suncoast Classic in May. "It has been a hard couple of months working on swing changes and it's great to see it pay off, to keep the momentum going before the summer." Ulrich van den Berg and Grant Veenstra both signed for 72s to tie for third at even par with overnight leader George Coetzee, who closed with 76.

Telkom PGA Pro-Am
Pretoria, South Africa
Winner: Michiel Bothma

Returning home from a northern hemisphere summer on the European Challenge Tour in order to celebrate the birthdays of his parents, both of which were this week, Michiel Bothma made it a triple celebration and an extra special party by winning the Telkom PGA Pro-Am. The former winner of the Telkom PGA Championship in 2002, for his only other Sunshine Tour victory, had led overnight and was in charge all day at the Centurion Country Club, at least until the very last hole. Bothma drove into the water to give Jaco Van Zyl a hint of victory. But the rookie missed his 12-footer for a birdie and then Bothma holed out for a bogey that was still good enough for a one-stroke victory.

Bothma had not made a mistake all day until then. But his 68 gave him a 12-under-par 204 score and the title, with Hennie Otto in third after also bogeying the 18th.

"I've been struggling a bit recently, trying to play it safe and relying on my putter," said Bothma. "Today I tried not to attack too much. With the long shots I played it safe, because the winner is not the guy who shoots the most birdies, but rather the one who makes the least mistakes. Today that guy was me."

Seekers Travel Pro-Am
Johannesburg, South Africa
Winner: James Kamte

James Kamte confirmed himself as one of the brightest prospects in South African golf by claiming his maiden professional title at the Seekers Travel Pro-Am at Dainfern. Kamte closed with a five-under 67 to post a total of 203, 13 under par for 54 holes, and win by one over Albert Pistorius, who put in a terrific effort on the final day with a 65. But seven birdies from Kamte, including at the 14th and 15th, were good enough for the 25-year-old from Queenstown to become the third black South African to win on the Sunshine Tour after John Mashego in 1991 and Linani Nwandwe in 2001.

"I hope my win inspires other black players to have confidence to know that any one of them can also do it," said Kamte, a member of the Ernie Els Foundation. "It is a great boost for the development initiative of the Sunshine Tour. You see what Tiger did for golf? I hope my win can change the image of the sport a bit. I'll be so happy if I can see the government getting involved in golf. Because we have so many great players, but they need the financial support.

"I don't know what to say," Kamte added. "I'm over the moon right now. I can just thank God for making me believe I can make it. I didn't want to make a mistake today and finally I won. I've been playing well, but seem to always have trouble on the last day." Warren Abery and defending champion Desvonde Botes shared third place, with George Coetzee finishing fifth.

Vodacom Origins of Golf Tour Final
St. Francis Bay, South Africa
Winner: Titch Moore

Port Elizabeth's Titch Moore claimed an Eastern Cape home victory over East London's Ulrich van den Berg to take the Vodacom Origins of Golf Tour Final at St. Francis Links. Moore, at 209, seven under par, won by three strokes after both players closed with rounds of 70. Moore's sixth Sunshine Tour victory was greeted by rapturous applause from the home gallery.

Major Champions

Andrew Redington/Getty Images

Padraig Harrington was the first Open champion from Ireland in 60 years.

Streeter Lecka/Getty Images

Tiger Woods, PGA Championship

Harry How/Getty Images

Zach Johnson, Masters Tournament

Chris McGrath/Getty Images

Angel Cabrera, U.S. Open

With a final round of 69, Zach Johnson tied a Masters record at 289 for the highest winning score.

Rory Sabbatini bogeyed Nos. 14 and 16.

Two bogey-bogey finishes cost Tiger Woods.

Retief Goosen had his chances.

Stuart Appleby led through three rounds.

U.S. Open

Angel Cabrera was the second from Argentina to win a major title, following Roberto de Vicenzo.

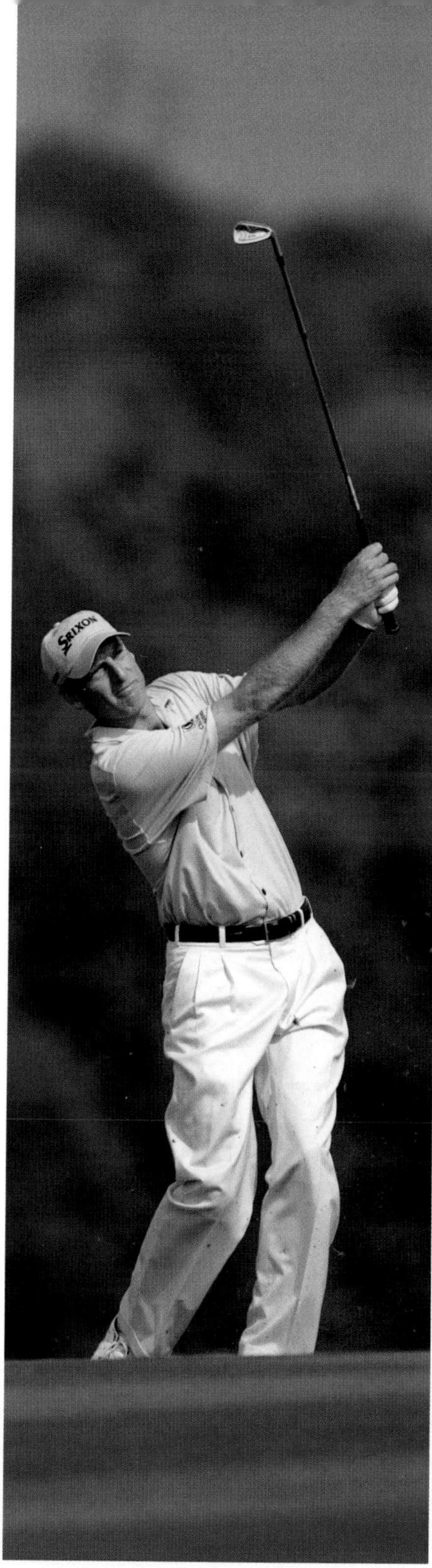

Chris McGrath/Getty Images

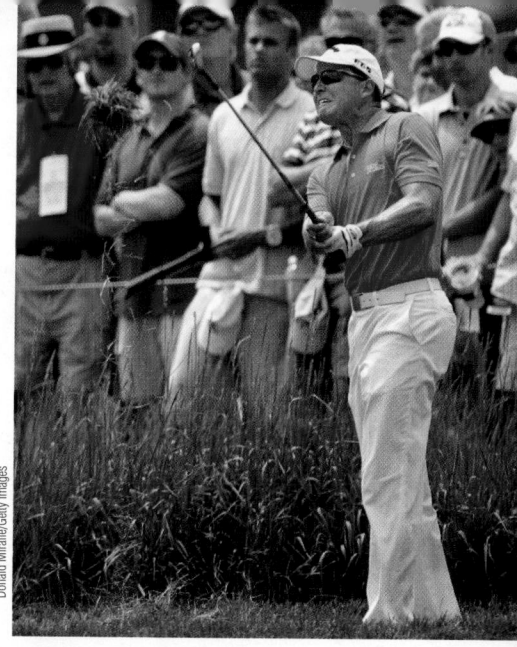

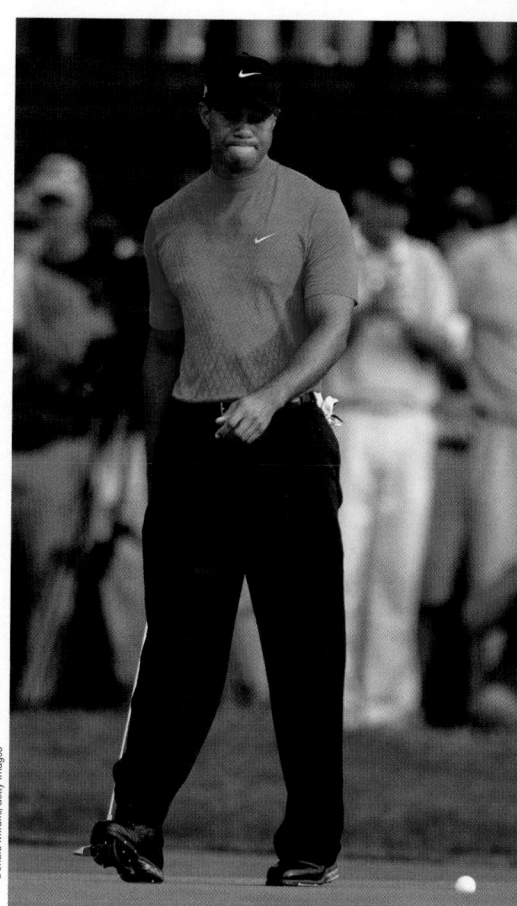

Jim Furyk shot a final-round 70.

Donald Miralle/Getty Images

Niclas Fasth was fourth, two strokes back.

Donald Miralle/Getty Images

Tiger Woods missed a putt to tie on No. 18.

The Open Championship

Before Padraig Harrington, a European had not won a major championship since 1999.

Andy Lyons/Getty Images

Andrew Redington/Getty Images

Andres Romero dropped three shots late.

Sergio Garcia couldn't believe his fate.

Ross Kinnaird/Getty Images

Andrew Redington/Getty Images

Steve Stricker dropped with a disappointing 74.

Ernie Els's 69 left him two behind.

PGA Championship

The PGA Championship was Tiger Woods's 13th career professional major victory.

Jamie Squire/Getty Images

Ernie Els finished third with his 66.

Jeff Gross/Getty Images

Woody Austin took second place.

Jamie Squire/Getty Images

Stephen Ames crashed in the last round.

David Cannon/Getty Images

Arron Oberholser tied for fourth.

Phil Mickelson won three tournaments, starting with the AT&T Pebble Beach National Pro-Am.

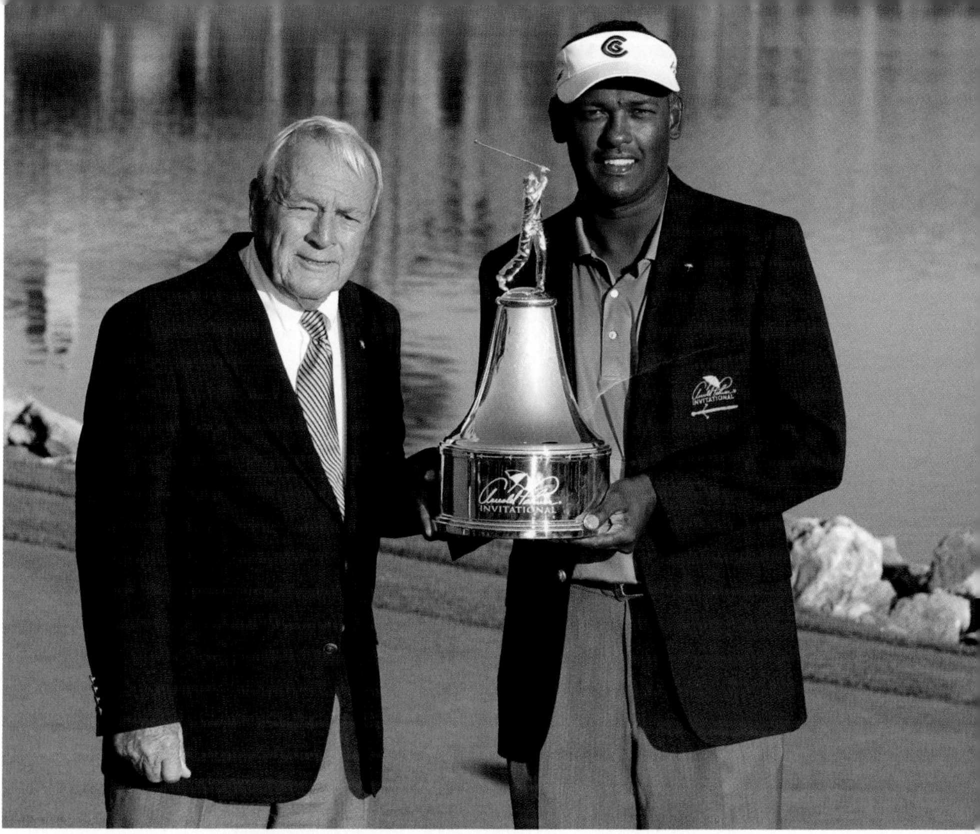

David Cannon/Getty Images

The host presented Vijay Singh with the first Arnold Palmer Invitational trophy.

Hunter Martin/Getty Images

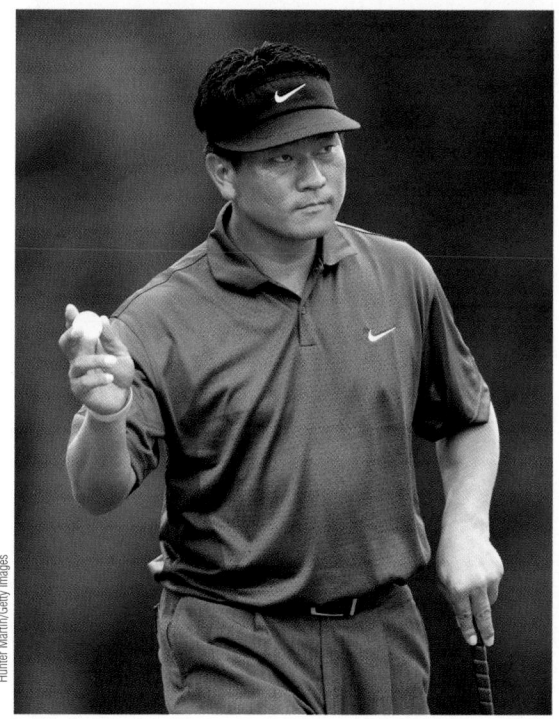

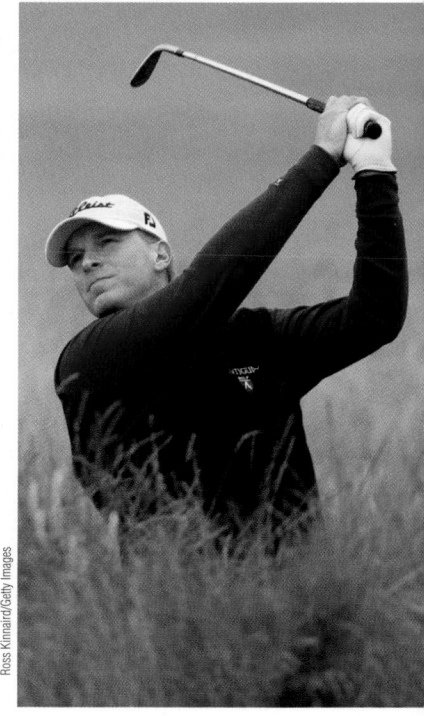

K.J. Choi won events hosted by Nicklaus and Woods.

Ross Kinnaird/Getty Images

Steve Stricker rose to world No. 5.

Stephen Dunn/Getty Images

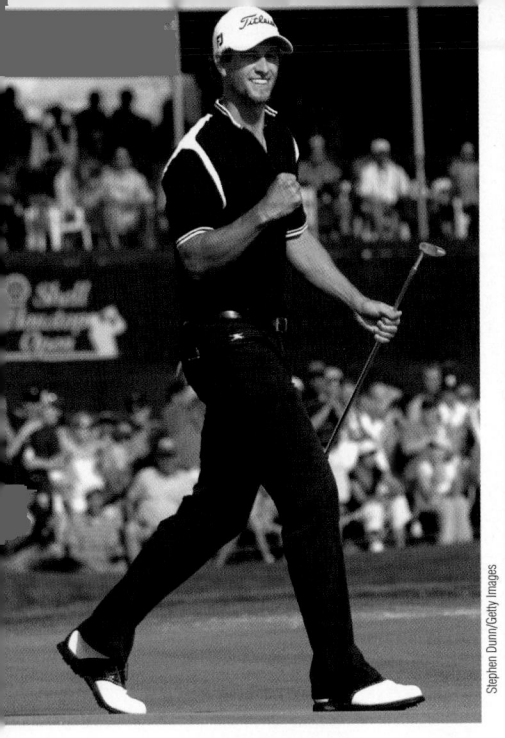

Adam Scott won the Shell Houston Open.

Marc Serota/Getty Images

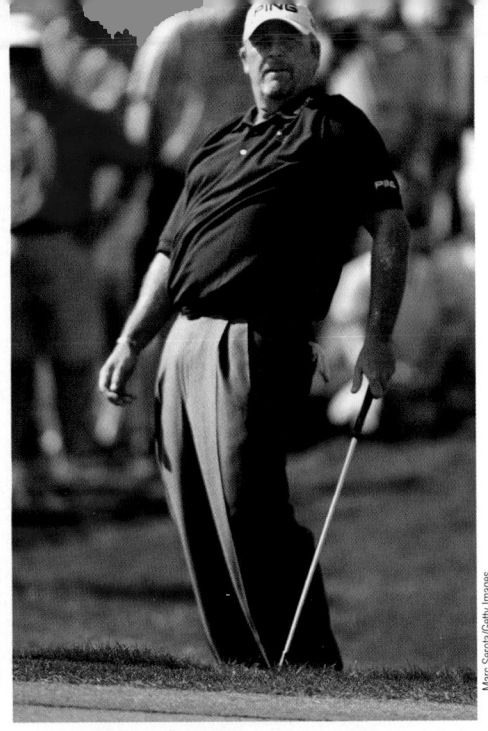

Mark Calcavecchia took the PODS title.

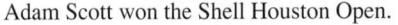

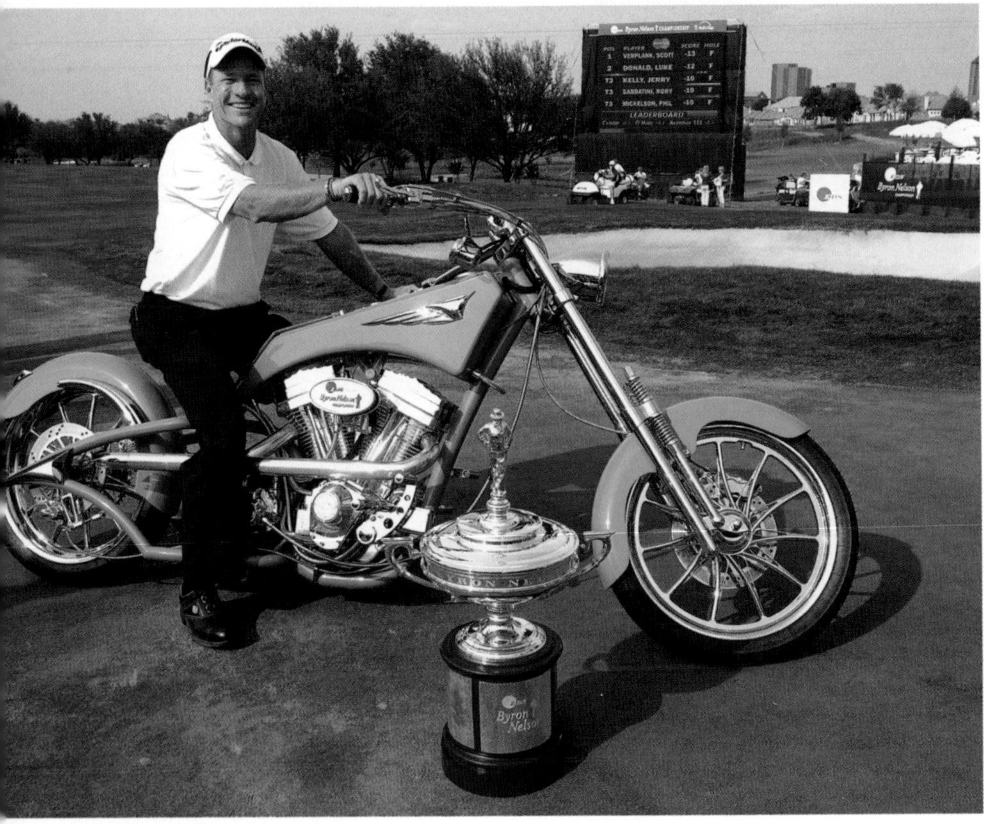

Stephen Dunn/Getty Images

For Scott Verplank, the spoils of victory were to his liking in the EDS Byron Nelson event.

Andy Lyons/Getty Images

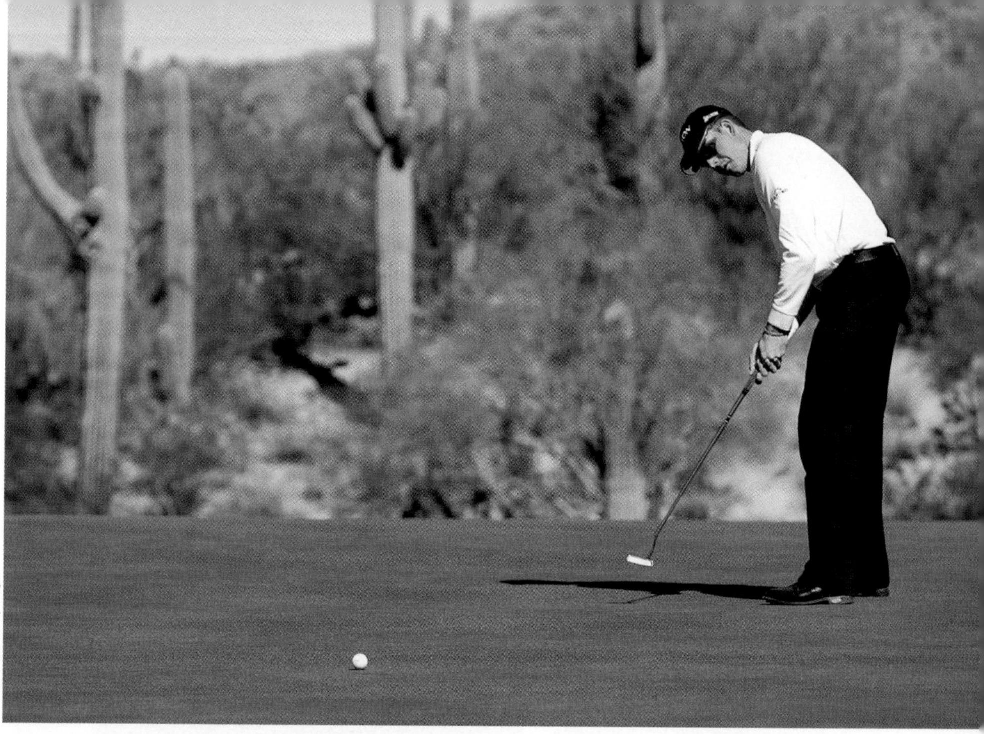

Henrik Stenson claimed a World Golf Championship title at the Accenture Match Play.

Kyle Auclair/Getty Images

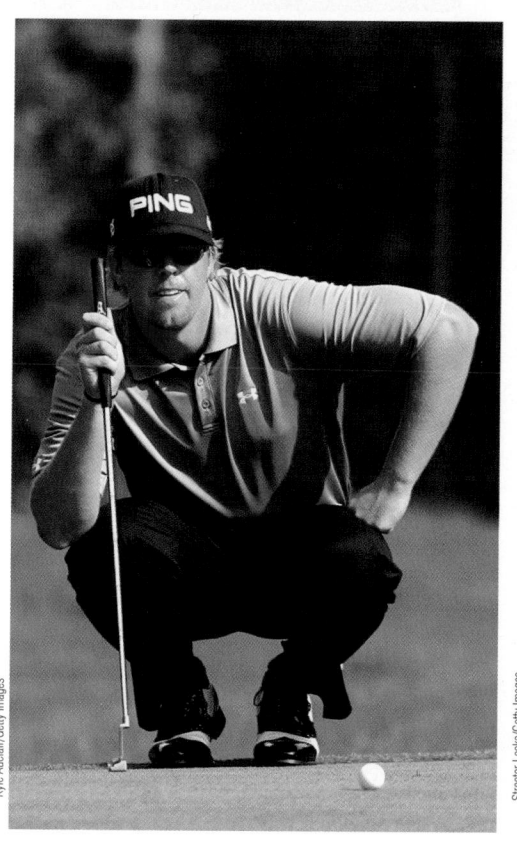

Hunter Mahan climbed to No. 34 in the world.

Streeter Lecka/Getty Images

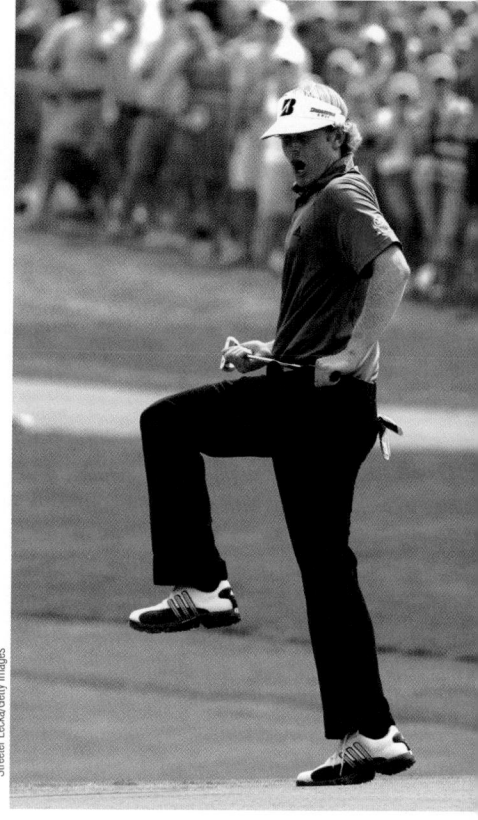

Brandt Snedeker was the Wyndham winner.

Ernie Els won his seventh HSBC World Match Play.

Justin Rose took the Volvo Masters.

Tim Clark earned $2.6 million.   Geoff Ogilvy was runner-up in the Accenture Match Play.

Charles Howell triumphed in the Nissan Open.

Boo Weekley became a popular figure.

Lee Westwood claimed two victories.

Luke Donald had two second-place finishes.

Soren Hansen was a top-10 money winner.

Trevor Immelman was the Nedbank winner.

Colin Montgomerie won the European Open.

Niclas Fasth reached No. 20 in the world.

Moore's final round got off to the worst possible start with a double bogey at the first hole. Three birdies to the turn put him two ahead, but then van den Berg birdied the 10th, 12th and 14th to go two ahead as Moore bogeyed the 11th. Both men birdied the 15th, but then Moore started to turn the tide back in his favor with a birdie at the par-five 16th. Moore made it three in a row at the short 17th, while van den Berg bogeyed to fall one behind. With his opponent in trouble in the rough at the 18th, there was another two-shot swing as Moore eased home, with the scores making it look far more comfortable than it was.

"I had probably the worst start I could've had," said Moore, the only golfer in the field to shoot three rounds under par on a difficult links. "When I dropped two behind Ulrich, I just said to my caddie we need to hang in there and be patient. Anything can happen over the last few holes, and it did. But Uli really gave me a run for it. He is probably playing the best golf of his career and he made me work every step of the way. To win on a links course here before playing three of the finest links courses in the world next week at the Dunhill Links is certainly the best preparation I could've asked for."

Bearing Man Highveld Classic
Witbank, South Africa
Winner: Marc Cayeux

Proving his earlier triumph in 2005 was no fluke, Marc Cayeux again produced an amazing charge in the final round to win the Bearing Man Highveld Classic at Witbank. Had his putt at the 18th not lipped out, the Zimbabwean would have matched his closing 61 from two years previously. As it was, Cayeux could not match his own course record, but a 10-under 62 gave him a three-stroke victory over Ulrich van den Berg.

Cayeux, winning for the eighth time on the Sunshine Tour, finished at 202, 14 under par, while van den Berg, who closed with a 69, was a stroke ahead of George Coetzee and Jbe' Kruger. Cayeux birdied the first two holes, then made three in a row from the fifth. On the back nine he added further birdies at the 10th, 12th, 13th, 15th and 17th holes.

At the 13th the result of the tournament became fairly obvious, given Cayeux's miraculous escape from the trees through a tiny gap and over a water hazard and onto the green. "I played as aggressively as I could today and it paid off," Cayeux said. "I wanted to shoot 61, because the last time I won back in 2005 I shot 61, but it didn't quite happen."

MTC Namibia PGA Championship
Windhoek, Namibia
Winner: Keith Horne

Durban's Keith Horne blasted to an eight-under-par 63 to take the MTC Namibia PGA Championship and leave the field to battle it out for second place at Windhoek Country Club on Saturday. The Asian Tour regular was imperious as he ended a nine-year title drought, nailing eight birdies in his third consecutive blemish-free round for a winning total of 18-under-par 195. Horne, who previously won the 1998 Vodacom Series at Kwazulu Natal, walked away with the top prize of R110,950 and finished five strokes ahead of compatriots Hennie Otto, Ulrich van den Berg and Doug McGuigan, who shared second at 13 under. Otto and McGuigan made up ground on the leader with a 66 and 67 respectively, while co-overnight leader van den Berg claimed his third second in as many starts with a final-round 68.

Thanks to lots of work with fellow pro Hendrik Buhrmann on perfecting his swing, Horne arrived in Windhoek on the back of a tie for 13th at the Hero Honda Indian Open. After negotiating the par-71 layout in earlier rounds of 67 and 65, Horne birdied four of the first seven holes. Van den Berg narrowed the gap from three to two with three birdies in the last five holes before the turn, but while both Horne and van den Berg birdied the 10th and 11th, van den Berg dropped a shot at the 15th. Horne remained majestic as he collected another two shots at the 14th and 18th on his way to the podium.

Winning was sweet for Horne, who tied for second in 2005 and 10th last year. "It has been nine years since I won, so this will take awhile to sink in," said Horne. "The way I played in the last three days, not dropping a shot, is just fantastic. I have to acknowledge Hendrik's coaching in Asia. He certainly put me on track with this new swing."

Platinum Classic
Rustenburg, South Africa
Winner: Louis Oosthuizen

Louis Oosthuizen claimed his third victory of the year after a thrilling playoff finale to the Platinum Classic at Mooinooi. After leading since the first day, Oosthuizen moved up to second in the Order of Merit after tying in regulation with Adilson da Silva and Marc Cayeux at 205, 11 under par. Cayeux, with confidence high after his win three weeks earlier, posted the lowest round of the final day with 64, while Oosthuizen and da Silva closed with 68s. Da Silva had taken an early lead at the second hole, but had to hole a pressure putt at the 18th to make the playoff.

The Brazilian bogeyed the 18th on the first extra hole to fall out of the playoff. Both Oosthuizen and Cayeux drove into the trees at the same hole for the second extra hole, but while the South African was able to find the green, the Zimbabwean could only advance his ball 10 yards. He had an eight-footer to stay alive, but it stopped agonizingly an inch short of the hole.

Oosthuizen, who won the Dimension Data and Telkom PGA titles, became the first player to post three wins in a season since Thomas Aitken in 2005. "I'm obviously delighted with this victory, which is even more special since it's the first time I have played at this incredible nine-hole course," he said. "But I won't lie and tell you it wasn't very tough out there today. I couldn't get anything going, but it was a case of staying patient."

Hassan II Trophy
Rabat, Morocco
Winner: Padraig Harrington

Padraig Harrington completed his first victory on the African continent when the 2007 Open champion won the unofficial Hassan II Trophy at Royal Dar-Es-Salam in Rabat, Morocco. It was Harrington's fourth win of the year after victories in the Irish Open, the Irish PGA and at Carnoustie, and gave the Irishman the perfect boost prior his attempt to regain his European Order of Merit title at the Volvo Masters the following week.

Harrington collected the first prize of US$150,000 and was presented with a ceremonial gold dagger. He had led by six strokes prior to the final round, but stumbled to 74 and, with a total of 280, a three-stroke win over Northern Ireland's Darren Clarke. Harrington struggled with his focus early in the round and Clarke, picking up confidence after a miserable season on the course, got within two shots at the 11th. At the next hole Harrington hit a five wood to 10 feet and never looked back after that.

"When I dropped to only two ahead, that's when I was spurred on, because I played a great shot into 12, and apart from a poor shot at 16, I managed to play good golf for those last seven holes," Harrington said. "That tends to be the story of my golf, because when I'm pushed into things, I tend to play a whole lot better. It's nice to be added to the Hassan roll of honor and I'm really pleased to win on the African continent, as I haven't done that before."

Former winners of the event that dates back to 1971 include Billy Casper, who was watching at the 18th green, Lee Trevino, Vijay Singh, Payne Stewart, Nick Price and David Toms. Clarke closed with 71 to finish two ahead of Simon Dyson, with David Howell two further back.

Coca-Cola Charity Championship
Hermanus, South Africa
Winner: Titch Moore

Titch Moore collected his second title in two months by winning the Coca-Cola Charity Championship hosted by Gary Player at Arabella. Moore teed up in the first round just hours after flying back from Spain, where he failed to earn his card in the European Tour qualifying. But he shot an opening round of 67 and then two 72s for a five-under-par total of 211. The man from Port Elizabeth, who triumphed at the Vodacom Origins of Golf Tour Final, claimed this victory by four strokes over James Kingston, Steve Basson and Louis Oosthuizen.

Moore started the day three ahead of Kingston and had developed a sizeable advantage when he went out of bounds at the 10th hole. The error cost him a double bogey and he also bogeyed the 12th, but then responded with birdies at the next two holes. Kingston put some pressure on with birdies at the 11th and 13th, but came to the par-five 18th trailing by two. Attempting to give himself an opportunity for an eagle, Kingston went out of bounds with his second shot and finished with a seven. He signed off with a 73, while Basson and Oosthuizen both closed with 71s.

"This is fantastic," said the 31-year-old Moore. "I mean, I got here from Tour School with three hours to spare after a 17-hour flight and got into contention right away. Obviously I would have taken a European Tour card, but nothing takes away from a victory. This is really good, coming off the disappointment after last week and going into the co-sanctioned events with another win."

Nedbank Affinity Cup
Sun City, South Africa
Winner: Mark Murless

Mark Murless was the beneficiary of the new Sunshine Tour event staged as a precursor to the Nedbank Golf Challenge. The Nedbank Affinity Cup was played on the Lost City course on the Monday to Wednesday ahead of the traditional elite event at Sun City. Murless claimed his third tour title with a brilliant finish in which he came from five behind to leave James Kingston as a runner-up for the second week running.

Kingston closed with a 71 to tie for second place with Zimbabwe's Tongo Charamba, who finished with 68, but neither could live with the brilliance of Murless, who shot a seven-under-par 65 for 202 total to win by one stroke. After two delays for lightning, Murless missed his eagle attempt from 12 feet at the 18th, but still made his birdie. Then he had to wait to see if Kingston could match his total of 14 under par, but Kingston could only make a par.

"I won't lie," said the 31-year-old Murless. "I was really hoping to win and it was a relief when James missed that final putt and made par. It's great to be in the winner's circle again. It's been a long three years since I last won. I had some chances this year, but just couldn't pull it off. I struggled with my swing most of the season, but overall, kept it going. I owe a huge debt of gratitude to Ulrich van den Berg, though, because he gave me very good advice a couple of days ago that has given me a more consistent, dependable swing."

Nedbank Golf Challenge
Sun City, South Africa
Winner: Trevor Immelman

Trevor Immelman survived a nightmare finish to win the Nedbank Golf Challenge in a thrilling duel with his fellow 27-year-old, the South African-born Englishman Justin Rose. The pair took apart the Gary Player Country Club on the first three days to share the lead at 16 under par. But on the final day, with the pins tucked away, the course fought back. Rose had an early two-shot lead, but Immelman tied him at the ninth. In an extraordinary duel on the back nine, Immelman then chipped in twice, first at the par-five 10th for a birdie where Rose also got his four, secondly at the par-five 14th for another birdie-four. This time Rose, who dropped a shot at the 13th after he missed the green on the left, failed to match the birdie to fall two strokes behind.

Both parred the 15th, but at the short 16th Rose made his par from a bunker while Immelman bogeyed after a weak chip. At the 17th, Rose could only chip out of the rough for his second shot, but then hit a brilliant approach to save par again, while Immelman again chipped poorly to drop another shot. Tied playing the 18th, Immelman again bogeyed but Rose had a double bogey. In the rough again off the tee, Rose had to lay up, then went over the green and took three to get down. Immelman had missed the green and then fluffed his first chip, but the next was better and he had only a short putt for the victory and a check for $1.2 million. Immelman had closed with 72 to finish at 16-under-par 272, while Rose shot 73 for 273, and Ernie Els took third place, five behind the winner, after a 72.

"I don't think I have ever choked like I did then," said Immelman, the seventh southern African winner of "Africa's major." "I wasn't too concerned about going through the green with my approach shot, but that chip! Phew! I felt like jumping in the lake. Fortunately my second chip was a good one, and when Justin missed the putt that could have tied up the match, I had no trouble with the two- or three-footer to win.

"Ever since I was a kid I've watched this event on television. I dreamed of playing it one day, and then I dreamed of winning it. Today that dream has come true and it is a very special moment for me."

Alfred Dunhill Championship
Mpumalanga, South Africa
Winner: John Bickerton

John Bickerton admitted to being "shocked" at winning the Alfred Dunhill Championship at Leopard Creek, but that was nothing to how Ernie Els must have been feeling at missing out on his fourth title in the event. Els, two ahead playing the par-five 18th, suffered one of the worst collapses of his career and finished with a triple-bogey eight. The sorry conclusion led to a sober silence around the 18th green, and Bickerton did not even know he had won as he packed away his things in the clubhouse.

Bickerton started the day four strokes behind Els. An eagle at the second, holing from 30 feet, was a nice start, but he missed a couple of four-footers around the turn. However, his last dropped shot came at the 10th and he birdied the 14th and 17th, from 20 feet, to post the target of 13-under-par 275 after a closing 68. "I was thinking second place was a good week," said the winner of two previous European Tour titles at the Canaries Open in 2005 and the French Open in 2006.

As Els's nearest challenger, England's Lee Slattery, faltered on the back nine, the South African appeared to be in control with birdies at the 14th and 15th. He dropped a shot at the short 16th and missed a birdie chance at the 17th, but split the fairway with his drive at the 18th. He then decided to attack the island green with a six iron for his second shot, but came up short in the water. Dropping about 100 yards from the hole, Els then pitched over the green and into the water again. His sixth shot finished five feet away, which he needed to hole to make a playoff. He missed.

Slattery also missed a birdie chance to tie Bickerton, while Holland's 21-year-old Joost Luiten finished fourth at 277 after weekend scores of 64, including a hole-in-one at the 12th, and 67.

"I have to be honest, disbelief is the main thing I feel right now," Bickerton said. "But that is golf isn't it. Sometimes it jumps up and bites you, and sometimes it goes for you as it did for me today, which obviously I'm delighted about, but I have to say I feel very sorry for Ernie. I really didn't know what was happening at the end. I was packing up my things. I thought I might have a chance of second on my own, which would have been a pretty good week. Then someone came and told me I'd won and, to be honest, I was in shock."

South African Airways Open
Paarl, Western Cape, South Africa
Winner: James Kingston

Reversing the pattern from the previous week, a South African held off the challenge of an Englishman to become the eighth home winner in a row at the South African Airways Open. It was an emotional victory for the 42-year-old James Kingston as he claimed the biggest title of his career after 20 years as a professional. It was his ninth win on the Sunshine Tour but his first in a co-sanctioned event with the European Tour, a circuit where he has suffered a number of disappointments. A closing 71 for a four-under-par total of 284 at Pearl Valley gave Kingston a one-stroke victory over Oliver Wilson, the overnight leader, who finished with 73.

Kingston suffered a double bogey at the fourth hole but responded with birdies at the next two. Wilson's three bogeys on the front nine proved his downfall, and although he tried to challenge again with birdies at the 10th and 11th, he came to the 18th one behind. Wilson had a birdie putt from 15 feet but it came up short, and Kingston made his putt from 10 feet for the victory.

"That was the toughest day I have ever had," said Kingston. "I have had chances before and not made the most of those chances, but today, for once, I clinched it. I couldn't have chosen a better tournament to win in the world than this one. This is the South African Open, my National Open. I have waited 20 years for this and that is a long time. I am so happy to have won such a prestigious title and join such an elite club."

Darren Clarke, finding some form at the end of a season with few highlights, shared third place at 287 with Louis Oosthuizen, Garth Mulroy and Kyron Sullivan. Greg Norman, in a rare appearance and just days after announcing his engagement to former tennis star Chris Event, finished tied for seventh.

Kingston's victory meant he had just beaten Oosthuizen for the Order of Merit title on the Sunshine Tour.

13. Women's Tours

It would be easy to say that the year 2007 was when the guard changed on the LPGA Tour. There was plenty of evidence. Just for openers, the relentless rise of Mexico's Lorena Ochoa, a runaway Rolex Player of the Year, and the emergence of Norway's Suzann Pettersen. Who would argue against this? On the other hand, to say this was really the changing of the guard, one must also concede that Annika Sorenstam, the dominator for years, was through. Who is ready to argue that point?

So if there's been a changing of the guard, it's wearing an asterisk: *Depending on whether Sorenstam recovers from her back and neck problems to regain her form. She made only 13 starts, made 12 cuts, and won only $532,718, 25th on the LPGA's money list, both far below her standards. It was clear she was serious about regaining her No. 1 ranking from Ochoa in 2008. She postponed her wedding until the spring of 2009 and told her associates that she would be cutting back on her off-course activities. It will take some doing.

Ochoa grabbed the No. 1 ranking early in 2007, won her first major championship, the Ricoh Women's British Open, and ended the season with the $1 million first prize in the ADT Championship in November. "It's all about breaking records," Ochoa said, after the ADT victory gave her nearly $4.4 million for the year, making her the first in LPGA history to top $3 million in one season. "It was not only about the money list but also winning eight tournaments this season," she added. "It's been amazing from the start to the end."

Ochoa was just a steamroller that kept building up steam, but Pettersen was the big surprise of 2007. Pettersen hadn't done much in her first four years on the tour, and she didn't look much better in the Kraft Nabisco Championship. She was leading by four strokes with four holes to play and blew it all, letting Morgan Pressel, just age 18, get her first victory and her first major. Pettersen bounced back and won five times, including her own first major, the McDonald's LPGA. She finished second on the money list with $1.8 million.

Elsewhere in the highlights of the 2007 season:

• Cristie Kerr won only once in 2007, but that victory came at the U.S. Women's Open and marked her long-overdue first career major championship. She finished sixth on the money list with nearly $1.1 million in earnings.

• Paula Creamer won twice — her first victories since her rookie season in 2005 — and finished third on the money list with nearly $1.4 million. She was the highest-ranking American on the list, and one of only three in the top 10.

• Mi Hyun Kim had an impressively solid season. She had one win, the SemGroup Championship, two seconds, seven top-fives and overall 10 top-10s, finishing fourth on the list with $1.2 million.

• From any viewpoint, Michelle Wie's 2007 was a disaster. Still trying to make the cut against men, she took a sponsor's exemption into the Sony

Open in January, in the first full-field event on the PGA Tour, and missed the cut by 14 strokes. That was the start of a bad year. At the end, she finished next-to-last at the LPGA's Samsung World Championship.

At the Ginn Tribute Hosted by Annika, Wie withdrew — suspiciously in the minds of many — late in the first round. She said she had a sore wrist, but others noted she was in danger of shooting 88, which would have disqualified her from the LPGA the rest of the year. Two days later she was practicing at the site of the coming McDonald's LPGA. By October, her agent resigned. It was just a year earlier that her first agent resigned.

Women's World Cup of Golf
Sun City, South Africa
Winners: Paraguay (Julieta Granada and Celeste Troche)

See Ladies African Tour section.

SBS Open at Turtle Bay
Oahu, Hawaii
Winner: Paula Creamer

Paula Creamer, 20, one of the young guns on the LPGA Tour, was Rolex Rookie of the Year in 2005, then went winless in 2006 and kept hearing "Why?" So she pre-empted the question in 2007 by winning the season-opening SBS Open, and with authority. She shared the lead in the first two rounds, then held off young Paraguayan sensation Julieta Granada for a one-stroke victory at the Palmer Course at Turtle Bay in Hawaii. "It was one of those years where expectations were incredibly high, and I put pressure on myself," Creamer said, explaining the winless 2006. "I worked really hard this off-season," she added. "I want to win."

Creamer got a jump on the SBS Open in the first round with a bogey-free 67, five under par, highlighted by a 15-foot birdie putt at the 17th, tying veteran Sherri Steinhauer, age 44, the 2006 Weetabix Women's British Open champion, and rookie Paige Mackenzie, age 24. Creamer and Steinhauer shot 70s for seven-under 137 totals in the second round and were tied by another young gun, Morgan Pressel (68), seeking her first LPGA Tour win. "It's going to be exciting, it's going to be fun," Pressel said. Creamer's game plan? "Just take it like I have been — real patient," she said.

In the end, the pressure came from Granada. She sparkled with a hole-out eagle from 150 yards at the par-four seventh, then holed a 15-footer for a birdie at the par-four 18th for 69 and a 208 total, tying Creamer, who was still on the course.

Creamer had birdied four straight from No. 4. But at the 11th, she sliced her drive into the marsh and double-bogeyed, and missed a three-footer for par at the 13th. But with the tournament about to slip away, she dropped a 40-foot birdie putt with a double break at the 17th to re-take the lead. A two-putt par at the par-five 18th gave her 70 and a 207 total for a one-stroke win.

Fields Open in Hawaii
Kapolei, Hawaii
Winner: Stacy Prammanasudh

Stacy Prammanasudh seems to have perfected an element of golf not likely to be found on the practice tee — breathing. "I mean," she explained, "when anybody gets excited, your breathing changes. As long as you can regulate your heartbeat out there, I'm not freaking out or anything." The grammar was labored but the message was clear. This self-control was her way of calming the surge of excitement after those two opening birdies in the final round that sparked her victory in the Fields Open in Hawaii late in February.

"There's still 16 other difficult holes out there, and you just can't get ahead of yourself," Prammanasudh said. "So I just tried to keep breathing and go about my business."

And Prammanasudh's business, in this case, was winning her second LPGA title. Prammanasudh, who shared the lead with rookie Angela Park through the first two rounds (66-68 at the par-72 Ko Olina Golf Club in Hawaii), led the challengers a good chase in the last one, never breaking away but never getting caught, either.

She rushed into the solo lead with the two quick birdies, a wedge to five feet at the par-five No. 1 and a four iron to eight feet at No. 2. She missed the green at No. 3 and it cost her lone bogey. Then she was solid, getting three more birdies from there. She went after the par-five fifth hole, hitting a five iron over the water to 40 feet and two-putting. She hit a wedge to six feet at the 11th, and at the par-five 13th, she knocked a three wood to the edge and two-putted from 30 feet for another 68 and a 14-under-par 202 total, a stroke ahead of South Korea's Jee Young Lee (68).

Lee had two last-gasp birdie chances to tie or even win, but she missed a seven-footer at the 17th, and didn't make the near-miracle 50-footer she needed at the 18th. It was then that Prammanasudh could finally breathe easier.

MasterCard Classic Honoring Alejo Peralta
Mexico City, Mexico
Winner: Meaghan Francella

If you're a rookie in only your sixth tournament and you're not only beating World No. 1 Annika Sorenstam but beating her in a playoff, you might be in a dream. But when the officials handed Meaghan Francella the trophy, she pretty well got the idea that she didn't need to pinch herself.

This was the LPGA's weather-beaten MasterCard Classic early in March at the Bosque Real Country Club outside Mexico City. This was also Sorenstam's first LPGA start of 2007, and she was looking for her third straight title in the event. And she seemed rust-free. She opened with a three-under 69, two behind Stacy Prammanasudh. Francella, a year removed from winning on the developmental Duramed Futures Tour, opened with 68, then was thrust onto the big stage with a second 68 that put her one ahead of Prammanasudh and three ahead of Sorenstam. Francella had started on the second nine and birdied Nos. 11, 15, 8 and 1 to get to eight under, and she shook off the nagging mid-March storms. "It's not a big deal," she said. "Patience is a key factor."

Patience or whatever, the inexperienced Francella held up admirably in the third round in the face of the growing pressure from the formidable Sorenstam. Pressure was hardly the word for it. Sorenstam, three behind Francella at the start, roared to seven birdies in 11 holes and took a two-stroke lead. But Sorenstam bogeyed the 16th and shot 66, letting Francella back in. Francella followed with a birdie at the 16th, then parred in for 69 and tied Sorenstam with an 11-under 205 total.

In the playoff at the 18th, they tied three times in a birdie and two pars. Said Francella, "I was on the third tee with her and I thought, 'Man am I really doing this?' I thought I was dreaming." Then reality set in on the fourth trip. Sorenstam missed her seven-foot birdie putt, but Francella holed from four feet for the victory. "I wasn't expecting Annika to miss that putt," Francella said. "I just stayed in my moment and made that putt. I had nothing to lose out there today."

Safeway International
Superstition Mountain, Arizona
Winner: Lorena Ochoa

The place certainly had the right name — Superstition Mountain, supposed site of the mysterious Lost Dutchman Mine outside Phoenix. What better place than Superstition Mountain Golf and Country Club for a ghost to pop up in front of Lorena Ochoa. In the 2005 Safeway International, Ochoa blew a four-stroke lead with three holes to play and lost to Annika Sorenstam in a playoff. And now, in the 2007 Safeway International, Ochoa led by four strokes going into the final round, and lost it all in five holes. Was it the ghost of 2005? "I never think about what happened in 2005," Ochoa said. "This is a new year, a new tournament."

Accordingly, Ochoa rolled on from there to her first victory of the year and the 10th of her career. But it was a close call. Suzann Pettersen erased Ochoa's four-shot lead with a furious start, but Ochoa charged coming in for a two-stroke victory. "I think she raises the bar for all of us to chase her," said Pettersen.

In a storm-ridden tournament, Ochoa trailed only in the first round, by one stroke, then erupted for 64 sparked by two eagles — on a six-iron hole-out at the par-four No. 6, and a chip-in at the par-five No. 13. She closed with 69-68 for an 18-under 270 total and the two-stroke victory.

It had looked like anything but. In the final round, Pettersen wiped out Ochoa's four-shot lead with four straight birdies from No. 2 on putts of two, 20, 25 and two feet. Ochoa bogeyed the second from a bunker, chipped in for birdie at the third, and when she bogeyed the sixth, Pettersen had the lead. Peterson cooled to two birdies the rest of the way, the last at the 14th, from one foot, where Ochoa matched her, also from a foot. Ochoa then birdied the 15th from one foot, the 17th from 10 feet and the 18th on a chip to two feet for the 68 and the victory.

"I was trying too hard," Ochoa said. "You just have to let it happen and let it come to you."

Kraft Nabisco Championship
Rancho Mirage, California
Winner: Morgan Pressel

See Chapter 6.

Ginn Open
Orlando, Florida
Winner: Brittany Lincicome

When they're sitting around the 19th hole telling tales, maybe someone would be good enough to hoist a glass to the Ginn Open. It's a tale of how Lorena Ochoa, the young Mexican powerhouse, and England's struggling Laura Davies marched in lockstep through the first three rounds, and then how Brittany Lincicome, a promising young American, weathered the tough weather in the final round and climbed over their wreckage to win on the last hole.

The Florida winds whipping the Reunion Resort near Orlando were the key. "My caddie had already said it — just take your par and stay patient," said Lincicome, after winning in a wild finish.

Ochoa and Davies led through the first three rounds on matched scores — 66-66-70. Lincicome (67-72-67) trailed by one, seven and four. The three were in the final grouping, but when they headed out into 40 mile-an-hour winds on Sunday, the tournament still was an Ochoa-Davies duel. Ochoa got two quick birdies to go up by two strokes. Then the fun started. She sprinkled three bogeys and a double bogey through the 16th hole, and Davies had two bogeys and a double through the 17th. The stage was set for the carnival at the 18th.

Lincicome, barely in the picture, bogeyed the seventh hole, then birdied the ninth from a foot and the 10th from seven feet. An unplayable lie cost her a bogey at the 13th, but she birdied the 14th from 15 feet and was one shot off the lead.

The par-four 18th was wild. Davies hit two bunkers and three-putted from 30 feet for a triple-bogey seven and 79. Ochoa went from rough to bunker to rough, and two-putted from 10 feet for six and 77. And Lincicome two-putted from 10 feet for five, par 72, a 10-under 278 total, and a win she never expected. "Oh, yeah," Lincicome said, thinking back, "third place was going to be great."

Corona Championship
Morelia, Michoacan, Mexico
Winner: Silvia Cavalleri

This was the Corona Championship in Morelia, Mexico, and native daughter Lorena Ochoa, three weeks after winning the Safeway International, came home as No. 1 in the Rolex Rankings. Even Mexican President Felipe Calderon was on hand for the celebration. But Italy's Silvia Cavalleri rained on Ochoa's parade.

Beating the World's No. 1 would be terrific, Cavalleri had agreed. But getting that first LPGA Tour win? "That would be much better," said Cavalleri, who became the first Italian to win on the LPGA Tour.

Cavalleri, shooting the par-73 course in 69-68-69, trailed Stacy Prammanasudh (67) by two in the first round, tied in the second with Angela Park (65) and Yu Ping Lin (65), then tied with Ochoa (64) and Julieta Granada (67) in the third. Ochoa sent her partisan fans into orbit with an eagle and eight birdies in that nine-under 64 that surprised even her.

There were two women on the hot seat in the final round. Said Granada: "Everyone will be rooting against me." Said Cavalleri: "I want to play well."

Cavalleri shot a bogey-free 66 in the final round, and she sure didn't play like an underdog. She took the lead on a run of three birdies from the fifth hole. "The first birdie gave me confidence," she said. "After that, I was hot to win."

And with that, she was on her way. She also birdied the ninth, 10th and 13th, and the clincher came at the 17th, with her seventh. "When the ball went in," she said, "I thought, 'I can win now.'" And she did, with a 20-under 272 total, by two over Ochoa (68) and Granada (68).

"I would have loved to have won," Ochoa said, through tears.

For Cavalleri, it was a case of dealing with pressure. She had an interesting way. "Lorena is the favorite, I know," Cavalleri had said, "but the ball is round."

SemGroup Championship
Broken Arrow, Oklahoma
Winner: Mi Hyun Kim

It's not often a woman gets a second chance against the formidable Juli Inkster, but South Korea's Mi Hyun Kim did, and she made the most of it in the SemGroup Championship.

Kim had come from four strokes behind in the first round and from one behind in the second round — indeed, Inkster likewise had come from behind — and needed to hole a five-foot putt on the final hole for the victory. This was some heavy pressure. To miss meant going up against Inkster in a playoff. And she missed, slightly to the right. Kim shot 71-68-71 and Inkster 71-70-69, and they tied at three-under 210 at Cedar Ridge Country Club in Oklahoma.

The playoff went back to the 18th. Inkster outdrove Kim but fired her six-iron approach over the green. "I don't know if it was adrenaline or what, but I just hit it too far," Inkster said. Kim hit a hybrid club to the back fringe. Inkster chipped to six feet but missed the par putt, while Kim tapped her first putt to four feet, then sank that one for her first win of the year and the eighth of her career. "I didn't know even-par two days can get a win today," Kim said. "So a little bit of lucky."

Lorena Ochoa, in her first week as No. 1 on the Rolex Rankings, was a presence but not a threat. She tied for fifth place, two shots off the lead.

The final round began as a toss-up, in a four-way tie with Nicole Castrale, Stephanie Louden, Karin Sjodin and Reilley Rankin all at four-under 138. Not one would be around at the finish line.

Kim took the lead in regulation with a birdie at the 16th, and saved par at the 17th. At the 18th, Inkster holed an 18-footer for a birdie and her 69, and when Kim missed the five-footer, they were tied. "My hands were shaking," Kim said. "That's why I missed the putt." But she got another chance in the playoff. She didn't miss that time.

Michelob Ultra Open at Kingsmill
Williamsburg, Virginia
Winner: Suzann Pettersen

Suzann Pettersen knew how it felt to fail — letting one tournament get away from her and having another plucked from her hands. Now she knew how the other half lives.

"I was like — Wow! It happened!" said Pettersen, after taking the Michelob Ultra Open at the Kingsmill Resort in Virginia. Pettersen trailed all the way and finally caught South Korea's Jee Young Lee and beat her on the third hole of a playoff. For Pettersen, age 26, who joined the LPGA Tour in 2003, it wasn't merely her own first victory, but the first by a Norwegian.

Just six weeks earlier, Pettersen was leading the Kraft Nabisco Championship by three strokes with four to play, but finished bogey-double bogey-bogey-par, clearing the way for Morgan Pressel. The week before that, Lorena Ochoa birdied four of the last five holes to beat her in the Safeway International.

Jee Young Lee took the lead with a course-record, eight-under 63 in the third round, with four of her eight birdies in the 12-to-15-foot range. She had edged one ahead of Sarah Lee, the leader through the first two rounds. In the final round, capricious winds lifted scores and Jee Young had a rocky ride, posting three birdies and four bogeys for 72. Pettersen was the only one able to deal with the breezes. "The wind was good for me — made it a little difficult for the other ones," she said.

Pettersen shot the only no-bogey round of the day, 68 on birdies at the second hole from seven feet, the third from six feet and the 11th with a clutch 25-footer after wedging past the hole, to tie Lee at 10-under 274. In the playoff at the 18th, they parred on the first two visits. On the third, Lee put a seven-iron approach to 12 feet and Pettersen wedged 20 feet past the cup, onto the fringe. Pettersen's first putt was within a foot of the hole.

Lee rolled her winning birdie try two feet past, then impatiently tapped the return — and missed. "I just wanted to putt it and not have to wait," Lee said. And Pettersen dropped her one-footer for the par and the victory.

"I didn't expect to win," Pettersen had said. "Probably the experience from the Kraft Nabisco did come in."

Sybase Classic
Clifton, New Jersey
Winner: Lorena Ochoa

Not that Lorena Ochoa lacked for resolve. That's what got her atop the Rolex Rankings just a few weeks earlier. But she hadn't won since, and she was telling herself: You're No. 1 in the world. Now, go out and play like it.

And so she did, in the Sybase Classic at the Upper Montclair Country Club in New Jersey. Ochoa and Sarah Lee — formerly Jung Yeon Lee — turned the tournament into a two-woman race. And then Ochoa turned it into a solo performance and a three-stroke victory. It was her first victory as No. 1, her second of the year, in addition to two seconds, a fourth and a fifth.

Lee led the first round with 66, two up on Ochoa and four others. Then it was Ochoa and Lee, head-to-head from there. But it looked like Lee early in the second round. She shot an early 69 and left with the clubhouse lead. Ochoa came along later and birdied five of her last eight holes for 67 and a share of the lead at 135.

Lee went two ahead on a third-round 65 to Ochoa's 67, but lost the edge in the first five holes in the last round. At the second hole, her approach hit the pin and ended up 25 feet away in the fringe. She bogeyed. Ochoa tied her with a short birdie putt at the fifth. All told, Lee missed six greens on the front nine and failed to convert on six straight birdie chances on the last nine. At the 18th, she hit her third shot into the water and finished with 73.

Ochoa birdied the eighth from 18 feet, the ninth from 10 feet and the par-five 11th on two putts, on her way to 68 and an 18-under 270 total. How does a new No. 1 feel? "It feels good to get that first time since being named No. 1," Ochoa said, "and I'm going home to celebrate with my family."

LPGA Corning Classic
Corning, New York
Winner: Young Kim

In adding the 72 holes of the LPGA Corning Classic, the number-crunchers could conclude that the tournament came down to the closing stretch, not once but twice, and the second time delivered South Korea's Young Kim her first LPGA Tour victory in 103 starts.

"I cannot believe it," said Young. "Too much good."

The English was spotty but the meaning was clear. Not only was it Kim's first win, it was a three-stroke victory over fellow Korean Mi Hyun Kim and rising star Paula Creamer on rounds of 68-64-68-68 for a total of 268, 20 under par.

It was a scoring carnival that week late in May at the Corning (New York) Country Club. In the first round, more than half of the 144 starters broke par. Overall, an amazing 66 of the 72 finishers had broken the 72-hole par of 288.

In the third round, Creamer, after climbing from three strokes off the lead, chipped to three feet and birdied the 17th, then birdied the 18th from 10 feet for 66 and a tie at 16 under par with Beth Bader (69) and Young Kim (68). They led by one going into the final round.

The next episode belonged to Young in the final round. But first a stumble. Young had gone three strokes ahead with a 24-foot birdie putt at the seventh hole, then bogeyed the eighth from a bunker and bogeyed the ninth from over the green and fell into a tie with Creamer.

"I tried to keep calm," Young said. "If I get two more birdies, maybe I have a chance to win." That chance emerged when Creamer, leading by one, three-putted the 14th hole for a bogey. Young put her third shot within a foot and birdied to take a one-stroke lead on Creamer, Beth Bader and Mi Hyun Kim. Creamer missed a seven-footer for birdie at the par-three 15th, and Young got up-and-down from a bunker for par. Then Young locked it up, going two ahead with a tap-in birdie at the 17th.

"I tried," said Creamer, who hit only six of 14 fairways. "Nothing really clicked."

Ginn Tribute Hosted by Annika
Mt. Pleasant, South Carolina
Winner: Nicole Castrale

The inaugural and rain-soaked Ginn Tribute Hosted by Annika, at River-Towne Country Club in South Carolina, would go down as the tournament in which Nicole Castrale beat top-ranked Lorena Ochoa in a playoff for her first LPGA Tour victory; in which former No. 1 Annika Sorenstam returned after nearly two months off with a back disk injury, and in which Michelle Wie, fading as a teen sensation, wrote a puzzling chapter to her struggling career.

Wie, age 17, left the tournament under a pall of suspicion, having withdrawn with two holes left in the first round as she was verging on shooting 88 or worse, a number for which the LPGA Tour bans non-members from further competition. Wie had just bogeyed her 16th hole and was 14 over par and headed for the next tee when her manager stopped her for a chat. Then she withdrew, citing a sore wrist. Had the Tour sent a warning to her, hoping to keep her drawing power through sponsor exemptions the rest of the year? That was the question in the media.

Back at the tournament, Sorenstam opened with an even-par 72 and overall was pleased. "It's a very long break," said Sorenstam, who would tie for 36th place, "and I have to be patient."

Ochoa opened with 68 and trailed first-round leader Angela Park by two strokes. Then Ochoa came to the top with 67 and a 135 total for a three-stroke lead after 36 holes. Castrale (71–140) was five behind. Ochoa was running wild in the third round when a hole-out eagle at the par-five ninth and a chip-in birdie at the 12th put her six strokes ahead. Three bogeys brought her back to 70–205, within three strokes of Castrale (68–208).

The end was as bizarre as it was exciting. Cristie Kerr came to the 17th hole tied with Castrale at eight under and two behind Ochoa. Kerr double-bogeyed the 17th, shot 73 and finished third.

Ochoa, a two-time winner this year, missed a five-foot par putt at the 11th, and Castrale birdied from nine feet for a two-stroke swing. Ochoa birdied the 15th. Then at the par-three 17th, Castrale put her nine-iron tee shot to 12 feet and birdied, and Ochoa three-putted from the fringe for a bogey and tied. They parred the 18th, Ochoa for 74, Castrale for 71, and they tied at nine-under 279 and headed into the fourth playoff of the year. In the playoff, back at the 18th, Ochoa drove into the marsh and bogeyed. Castrale hit fairway and green and two-putted for a par and the victory.

"I need to improve my playoff percentages," said Ochoa, now 0-4 in playoffs.

"I had an eerie calmness about me all week, and it paid off," Castrale said.

McDonald's LPGA Championship
Havre de Grace, Maryland
Winner: Suzann Pettersen

See Chapter 6.

Wegmans LPGA
Pittsford, New York
Winner: Lorena Ochoa

Lorena Ochoa definitely falls into the legendary category of "It's not bragging if you can do it." Take her statement at the Wegmans LPGA: "I know I can win anytime I play."

This was after she took her only solo lead in the third round. Then she proceeded to botch up the fourth round, lipping out three putts, missing three other makeables on the first nine, powering a sand shot 35 feet past the hole at the 10th. Then she missed a five-foot par putt at the 14th and was trailing by three strokes with two holes to play. Which she made up with an eagle-par finish to tie South Korean rookie In-Kyung Kim, then beat her on the second extra hole for her third victory of the season.

"I will remember that day for the rest of my life," Ochoa said. It was, by the way, her first extra-hole victory, giving her a 1-4 record in playoffs. Ochoa played the Locust Hill course, near Rochester, New York, in 69-71-67-73 for a 280 total, eight under par, to Kim's 70-67-71-72.

Ochoa trailed by three strokes coming to the par-five 17th. There, she hit a four-iron approach from 205 yards to 20 feet and made the eagle against Kim's par. Ochoa still trailed by one shot. At the 18th, Kim hit an eight iron from 112 yards into the rough behind the green, then chipped to seven feet and two-putted for a bogey. Ochoa two-putted for her par and the tie. They tied in pars at the first playoff hole, No. 18. At the second, No. 10, both drove into the right rough. Kim's nine-iron approach was short and she chipped 15 feet past the hole and two-putted for a bogey. Ochoa's second was also short, but she chipped to two feet for a par and the victory.

"I can cry right now, but not for this," said Kim. "I played pretty tight with the No. 1 player."

Said Ochoa about the playoff: "I never had a doubt."

U.S. Women's Open
Southern Pines, North Carolina
Winner: Cristie Kerr

See Chapter 6.

Jamie Farr Owens Corning Classic
Sylvania, Ohio
Winner: Se Ri Pak

Jamie Farr, of Toledo, Ohio, parlayed a large nose and great comic touch into a career as the outrageous Corporal Klinger in television's long-running M*A*S*H, set during the Korean War. Now South Korean Se Ri Pak has turned Toledo's Jamie Farr Owens Corning Classic into a long-running show of her own.

In a burst to the finish, Pak turned the 2007 edition into a runaway for her fifth title in this tournament. It was also her 24th career victory. Pak led all the way, shooting 63-68-69-67 for a 17-under-par 267 total at Highland Meadows. She was three strokes ahead of runner-up Morgan Pressel and nine strokes ahead of a group tied for third place.

It was a contest only briefly in the final round. Pak started the day leading Pressel by two strokes, and a few holes later Pressel was leading. Pressel tied her at the fourth hole, dropping a 12-foot birdie putt to Pak's bogey. Then at the par-three sixth, Pressel hit a seven iron and got her first hole-in-one on the LPGA Tour. Said Pressel: "I thought, 'well, that's a nice time to get a lucky bounce.' I tried to keep hanging in there."

Pak put her tee shot to 18 feet and holed it for a birdie. "As soon as she made ace, it woke me up right away," Pak said. She tied Pressel with birdies on the eighth and ninth holes on putts of six and eight feet. They parred the next five holes. Then Pak holed a two-footer for a birdie at the 15th, a six-footer at the 17th and a tap-in on the par-five 18th for the 67 and the three-stroke victory.

Pak joined Mickey Wright and Annika Sorenstam as LPGA players to win the same tournament five times. "Wow!" Pak said. "First, winning is always great, and whenever you make history, that's pretty special."

HSBC Women's World Match Play
New Rochelle, New York
Winner: Seon Hwa Lee

The HSBC Women's World Match Play was the classic "dream come true" for South Korea's Seon Hwa Lee, who came from nowhere to win it, and also to some extent for Japan's Ai Miyazato, the runner-up. But it was a sponsor's nightmare. Nine of the top 10 seeds, including top-seeded Lorena Ochoa, were knocked out in the first two rounds. And 10th-seeded Mi Hyun Kim was ousted in the semifinals. All of which meant that star attractions at Wykagyl Country Club near New York City weren't in the show any more.

Lee, the No. 22 seed, and Miyazato (No. 12) did their part, and also got great help from the rest of the field. The bouncing of high seeds was so thorough that except for Lee ousting Mi Hyun Kim, neither finalist met a higher seed.

Lee made her way through Diana D'Alessio (No. 43), Janice Moodie (54), Laura Davies (27), Lindsey Wright (35), and Mi Hyun Kim (10). Miyazato beat Becky Morgan (53), Christina Kim (37), Amy Hung (61) and Maria Hjorth (40). This left the tournament up to Lee, the LPGA's Rolex Rookie of the Year in 2006, winner of the ShopRite Classic, and Miyazato, who won 14 times on the Japan LPGA Tour but was winless in 43 starts in the United States.

In the final, Lee took the lead with a par at the third hole and stayed there. She slipped back to one up when she missed the 14th green and bogeyed, but she went back to two up with a birdie at the 15th on a five-foot putt. They halved the next two holes in birdies, and Lee had her victory. "I tried to play aggressive, but she played well, too," said Miyazato. "The experience will lead to a better finish next time around."

Lee thanked her first-round match for setting the tone for the week. Three down with four holes to play against D'Alessio, she won the last four holes — three on birdies — to win one up. "Winning that first match gave me a lot of confidence," Lee said. That and an obedient putter. "Even when I missed a couple of fairways or greens," she said, "I got up-and-down putting."

Evian Masters
Evians-les-Bains, France
Winner: Natalie Gulbis

See Ladies European Tour section.

Ricoh Women's British Open
St. Andrews, Scotland
Winner: Lorena Ochoa

See Ladies European Tour section.

CN Canadian Women's Open
Edmonton, Alberta, Canada
Winner: Lorena Ochoa

"It was just one of those weeks where everything was good from tee to green," Lorena Ochoa was saying. She should have added: "Another one of those weeks." She had just won the CN Canadian Women's Open, her second straight victory — after the Ricoh Women's British Open — and her fifth of the season.

"She's on fire," Juli Inkster said. "She's kind of like the way Annika (Sorenstam) was three or four years ago."

At Royal Mayfair in Edmonton, Ochoa simply wouldn't be denied. She played the par-71 course in 70-65-64-69, trailed through the first two rounds, led the third round by four strokes, then wrapped up a 16-under-par 268 total for a comfortable three-stroke win over Paula Creamer.

Ochoa had to come from behind. Laura Diaz opened with a bogey-free 65 for a one-stroke lead on Kelli Kuehne and Kyeong Bae. Ochoa was five behind with a 70. In the second round, Inkster shot 66 and South Korea's Shi Hyun Ahn 67 to tie for the halfway lead at eight-under 134. Ochoa raced to within one with 65. Then Ochoa took charge in the third. She had five birdies in a front-nine 30 and added two more on the back for a flawless 64 that tied the course record set by Karrie Webb on Friday. She had a three-stroke cushion on Paula Creamer to carry into the final round.

It was almost anti-climatic from there. Creamer made a quick bid with two birdies in the first three holes, but she bogeyed the par-three eighth and then the par-five 14th. Ochoa was cruising along, but of course noticed that Creamer had closed the gap a bit. "I wasn't in rhythm on the front nine," Ochoa said. "And then we made the turn and I started feeling strong. I made a good birdie at No. 12, and I think from there, things kind of changed in my way." As the scoreboard suggested.

Safeway Classic
Portland, Oregon
Winner: Lorena Ochoa

"They keep saying, 'You should play — you can do four in a row,'" Lorena Ochoa was saying. "But it's time for me to go home. I'm happy with my three wins." And so Ochoa, No. 1 on the Rolex Rankings, packed up the Safeway Classic, her third straight victory (and her sixth of the season), and left to take a month off. Not even the chance to match Annika Sorenstam's four in a row in 2001 was enough to lure her back.

Ochoa didn't merely win this one, she cruised by five strokes on a card of 67-66-71 for a 12-under 204 total at Columbia Edgewater in Portland, Oregon. She trailed only in the first round, with a 67, one behind co-leaders Sophie Gustafson and 19-year-old Ji-Young Oh, who had a great putting day. She estimated one of her seven birdie putts at three feet. "It was seven," said her caddie, Doug Wilbur. "That's how well she's putting. Everything looks so close."

Ochoa's runaway started in the second round, though bogeys at the 17th and 18th cooled her to 66 and a one-stroke lead over Gustafson (68). "I was just trying to hang on," Gustafson said. It seemed everyone was hanging on in the final round, and that Ochoa hung on best. Gustafson double-bogeyed the 17th and shot 75. Mhairi McKay (72) moved up but also doubled the 17th and tied for second along with fast-closing Christina Kim (69) and South Korean rookie In-Bee Park, who had a day's-best 64.

Ochoa started with two bogeys in the first three holes, then rebounded with four big birdies — a seven iron to a foot at No. 4, a 15-footer at No. 5, two putts from 45 feet at No. 7, and two from 25 feet at the 10th. A two-putt bogey at the 17th gave her 71 and cut her margin to five. So Ochoa left on vacation with three straight wins, and the LPGA Tour's oldest story got a week older. Teenager Michelle Wie, playing on a sponsor's exemption, shot 79-75 and missed the cut again.

State Farm Classic
Springfield, Illinois
Winner: Sherri Steinhauer

Sherri Steinhauer, age 44, came to the State Farm Classic in a new frame of mind and came away with her career eighth victory and her first since the 2006 Weetabix Women's British Open. Shooting rounds of 67-66-71-67, she led wire-to-wire, and it took all she could muster to hold off hard-charging Christina Kim by one stroke.

Not that Steinhauer was riding a big cushion. She led the first round by one, the second round by two and the third round by one against a strong field at Panther Creek Golf Club in Springfield, Illinois. This is where her new guide star — staying in the present — saw her through. She equated hope with fear. "And I kept telling myself that I'm going to have no hope and no fear, and I'm going to stay in the present," she said.

She logged five birdies in a bogey-free 67 in the first round with some great putting — two 20-footers, a 25-footer and a 30-footer. Then the pressure started to mount in the second round. Kim shot 66 and closed within two, and here came Annika Sorenstam with 65, just three behind. "I thought I played flawless today," Sorenstam said. Said Steinhauer, "When you have Annika behind you, it's not always easy." But Steinhauer made it look easy. She holed three 20-footers in her seven-birdie 66. And in the third round, she birdied three of her last six holes for a 71 and maintained her two-stroke edge, this time over Kim (71) and Michele Redman (64).

Then came the furious finale. Kim shot a no-bogey 66, closing with three straight birdies — a three-footer at the 16th, then a chip-in, then a 28-footer for a 272 total. Steinhauer birded from 10, eight and 20 feet on the first nine, then bogeyed the eighth and 11th holes. Then she got two great birdies of her own — a 30-footer at the 16th, and then a 25-footer at the 17th — and then trying to two-putt for a bogey at the 18th to force a playoff, she dropped a 23-footer from the fringe for the winning par.

"Thank goodness for my putter," Steinhauer said, "or I wouldn't be here."

NW Arkansas Championship
Rogers, Arkansas

This was really one for the books. Questions: When is a tournament not a tournament? And when is a winner not a winner?

LPGA Tour officials were sent digging through records and regulations when heavy early September rains hit the Pinnacle Country Club at Rogers, Arkansas, and forced the inaugural NW Arkansas Championship to be reduced from 54 holes to 18. This left amateur Stacy Lewis, golf star of the University of Arkansas, atop the leaderboard with a bogey-free, seven-under-par 65. But she wasn't the winner.

The reason: No tournament, no winner.

"From the LPGA standpoint," said LPGA Tour official Doug Brecht, explaining that 36 holes had to be finished to make an event official, "this is not a tournament. This is a non-event." Apparently a non-event is one in which prize money and statistics were not official, which was the case here. The professionals would receive unofficial prize money, but Brecht declined to say how much.

As for Lewis? She won admiration, a great experience and an invitation — as a professional or amateur — to the next inaugural 2008 NW Arkansas Championship.

The Solheim Cup
Halmstad, Sweden
Winner: United States

See Ladies European Tour section.

Navistar LPGA Classic
Prattville, Alabama
Winner: Maria Hjorth

Lorena Ochoa, the Rolex world No. 1, had the stage to herself, the chance of a lifetime and the odds in her favor. A six-time winner this season, she had won her last three starts and was driving for the fourth. The trouble was, she also had Maria Hjorth coming to life after years of hibernation.

"It's been awhile, so it's just amazing right now," Hjorth said, after ducking through to win by one over Stacy Prammanasudh and two over Ochoa in the inaugural Navistar LPGA Classic at the Capitol Hills Senator Course in Alabama late in September. But it was the 70th of the 72 holes before anyone noticed that Hjorth was really there.

Hjorth had won twice in her 10 years on the tour, both times in 1999, but in 2004 had to return to the qualifying tournament to get her playing card back.

Her rise in the Navistar event was as unobtrusive as it was eventually impressive. Stacy Prammanasudh led through the first two rounds with 63-68, and Hjorth, on 70-67, trailed by seven, then four. Ochoa (69) took the third-round lead and led Prammanasudh (73) by one and Hjorth (70) by four going into the final round. Ochoa took five of her six wins when leading going into the final round, so the outlook for Hjorth was not promising.

Then Ochoa's game turned erratic. "I just couldn't hit anything close," she said. That translated into a three-birdie, four-bogey 73 for a 12-under-par 276 total and a tie for third. Prammanasudh shot 71 and finished second by a stroke.

In a bogey-free final round, Hjorth owned the par-fives. She eagled No. 5 on a 30-footer and birdied the other three — the eighth on two putts from 15 feet, the 10th after just missing an eagle from six feet and the 17th with a 25-footer from the fringe. The last one, on the 70th hole, gave her the lead for the first time. She wrapped up a tidy 67, a 14-under 274 total and her first win since 1999.

Longs Drugs Challenge
Danville, California
Winner: Suzann Pettersen

Suzann Pettersen, the demonstrative Norwegian, was checking her scorecard after the last round of the Longs Drugs Challenge. It was enough to lift her eyebrows.

"I can't believe I won," Pettersen said. She was referring to a whopping five bogeys on that final card, including a demoralizing three straight from No. 9. But Pettersen bounced back, made three birdies coming in for a total of four, and her closing one-over-par 73 tied her with world No. 1 Lorena Ochoa. Then Pettersen won with an eight-foot birdie putt on the second playoff hole. It was her third victory of the year, and denied Ochoa her seventh and what would have been her fourth in her last five starts.

Pettersen set a tournament record along the way at Blackhawk Country Club, near San Francisco. She opened with 75, then went 65 and 64 for the record low for two rounds. The 65, for a 142 total, got her within four of halfway leaders Karrie Webb (69) and Lorie Kane (69), tied at 138.

Then came Pettersen's remarkable third-round 64 — one bogey, five birdies and two eagles, the second a chip-in at No. 9. "That (chip-in) got me a little upset," Ochoa said. "But it's much better seeing that on Saturday than Sunday."

"Golf is a weird game," said a grinning Pettersen.

And as weird as ever in the final round, an exercise in leapfrog golf. Pettersen started one up on Kane, two on Ochoa, and promptly bogeyed the first and third holes. She birdied the fifth, then bogeyed Nos. 9, 10 and 11. And Ochoa, after bogeying the 11th, four-putted the 12th for a double bogey. When everything settled, Pettersen had a one-over 73, Ochoa a one-under 71, and they tied with 11-under 277 totals. They both birdied the first playoff hole. Then at the second, Ochoa missed a birdie from 20 feet, and Pettersen rolled in her eight-footer for the win.

"You know, you've got to play your heart out," Pettersen said. "There's not a nicer person out there you want to beat."

Samsung World Championship
Palm Desert, California
Winner: Lorena Ochoa

Lorena Ochoa was wearing a big, warm smile made especially for — and by — the occasion. "After what happened in 2006," she said, meaning winning six times last year, "I thought it would be hard to improve — but here I am."

The occasion was the Samsung World Championship, with a fairly exclusive field of 19 other LPGA Tour players that she had just run away from. A handful flirted with the lead along the way, among them Suzann Pettersen, the rampaging Norwegian, and Angela Park, 19, who had already locked up the Rolex Rookie of the Year Award. But Ochoa, the defending champion, exploded from a third-round tie and raced off with the Samsung by four strokes. Six wins in 2006? This was No. 7 in 2007. That's improvement. It also meant her second straight Rolex Player of the Year Award.

The mid-October invitational at Big Horn Golf Club in Palm Desert, California, found fading whiz kid Michelle Wie at about her worst. In the field for marquee value, she shot 79-79-77-71 for a 306 total, 36 strokes behind Ochoa and one stroke out of dead last.

At the other end of the youth spectrum, Angela Park and Paula Creamer shared the first-round lead at 67. Ochoa, after 68, moved to the top of the leaderboard and stayed. A second-round 67 gave her a one-stroke lead on Park (69), Creamer (69) and Angela Stanford (66). In the third round, a solid 69 was only enough to tie with a hot Pettersen, who came charging in with a tournament-low 64.

Ochoa took the lead in the final round with a birdie from five feet at No. 1, but Jeong Jang holed a bunker shot for birdie at No. 9 to tie her at 15 under. Then Ochoa regained the lead with a birdie from four feet at the 10th, and birdied the 14th, 15th and 17th for a 66 and an 18-under-par 270 total. Only runner-up Mi Hyun Kim's two closing birdies kept her from winning by six.

Hana Bank-Kolon Championship
Kyeongbook, South Korea
Winner: Suzann Pettersen

See Korea LPGA Tour section.

Honda LPGA Thailand
Pattaya City, Thailand
Winner: Suzann Pettersen

It seems absurd in the telling, but Suzann Pettersen had opened a seven-stroke lead going into the final round of the Honda LPGA Thailand, at the Siam Country Club, and then noted: "Tomorrow I have to shoot a low round and play aggressive."

But with Laura Davies and Paula Creamer chasing and Pettersen herself stumbling, she had to save herself at the final hole. She hit a good drive, and a three wood from 225 yards, and faced a 15-foot eagle putt. "It was like — Drop! Drop! Drop! Please drop!" Pettersen said. And it dropped. "I think that was the best putt of my life," she said. And Pettersen had her second straight victory, her third in four starts and fifth of the year.

Pettersen, on scores of 65 and 68, led by two strokes through each of the first two rounds, then in the third round birdied Nos. 12, 13, 15, 17 and 18 for 63 and a seven-stroke lead. But Pettersen knew what she was talking about — she would have to shoot low. And she didn't.

In the fourth round, Pettersen had two birdies and one bogey over the first nine, while Davies eagled No. 1 with a six-foot putt, and had two birdies. Creamer birdied Nos. 1, 4, 7, 8 and 9, but double-bogeyed No. 3. Coming in, Creamer eagled the 10th from a paltry two feet and birdied the 15th for 66 and a 270 total.

Pettersen was erratic. She birdied the 15th from five feet, but bogeyed the 16th and 17th. So it came down to Pettersen and Davies. Davies birdied the 14th from 10 feet, but bogeyed the 16th out of a bunker, then birdied the 17th from five feet and tied Pettersen. She reached the 18th in two and two-putted from 25 feet for 65 and a one-stroke lead.

Pettersen stumbled to two straight bogeys, two-putting the 16th from six feet and three-putting the 17th, missing her par from three feet. It was her tournament for 71 holes, but now it was about to slip away. Then came Pettersen's heroic eagle. It would seem that Pettersen and her game had matured. "This victory," she said, "is a sweet one."

Mizuno Classic
Shima-Shi, Mie, Japan
Winner: Momoko Ueda

See Japan LPGA Tour section.

The Mitchell Company Tournament of Champions
Mobile, Alabama
Winner: Paula Creamer

This was The Mitchell Company Tournament of Champions, the grand free-for-all for 2007 winners and Hall of Famers, played at the Crossings Course in Alabama. But Paula Creamer made a shambles of it. The closest anyone got to her was when she and Meg Mallon tied for the first-round lead at five-under-par 67. Then it was all over. Creamer had her career fourth victory by eight strokes. It went this way:

First Round: Creamer and Mallon tied for the lead at 67. Creamer made the turn at two over par, then shot 29 on the second nine, with seven straight birdies from the 12th on putts of two, 15, five and eight feet, two putts from 35 feet, then eight and eight. Her caddie had mentioned finding someone's club in the woods. "Yeah," said Creamer. "That's where I wanted to throw my putter."

Second Round: Creamer was still on fire. She made three birdies on the first nine, then four more on the second nine at the 10th, 15th, 16th (another two-putt) and a 35-footer at the 18th for 65 and a 12-under 132 total. "I'm rolling the ball really well," Creamer said. She led Jin Joo Hong (67) by five strokes, an encouraging sign. All three of her victories came after she led through 36 holes.

Third Round: Sometimes, nothing can go wrong. Creamer missed the 18th green from just 105 yards out and faced a chip shot. "Honestly, when I looked at it," she said, "I thought it was definitely makeable." It was, and she did, for 68, a 16-under 200 total and a six-stroke lead on Pat Hurst (68).

Fourth Round: "I gave myself a lot of chances," Creamer said. "I stayed really confident with myself, and I believed I could do it." She bogeyed the 18th after bunkering her tee shot. It was only her third bogey of the tournament, and the first after 62 holes. She shot another 68 for a 20-under 268 total and won by eight strokes. If anyone wonders who was second, it was Birdie Kim (68). Creamer's 268 was a stroke off Lorena Ochoa's tournament record. "It's a bummer that I didn't get it," Creamer said. "But I'll take it."

ADT Championship
West Palm Beach, Florida
Winner: Lorena Ochoa

There's the old show business adage, "Leave 'em laughing." Lorena Ochoa, No. 1 in the world, carried that a bit further on the very last hole of the LPGA's season-ending ADT Championship: "Leave 'em gasping."

First, in the best show business tradition, Ochoa set up the audience for the rousing finale. This she did at the 17th hole by blowing a four-stroke lead with a double bogey. And then at the 18th, with the hard-pressing Natalie Gulbis already on the green just 15 feet from the pin, and with $1 million at stake, Ochoa hit the shot of her life, a clutch six iron 161 yards out of the rough to a mere 30 inches, and she birdied from there to win.

"I had a horrible lie," Ochoa said. "Because of the conditions and because I was leading by only one shot, I think it was my best shot so far in my career." The birdie gave Ochoa a four-under-par 68 and a two-stroke win over Gulbis (70). It was the end of a dominating year for Ochoa — eight victories and a record $4,364,994 in winnings.

The oddly formatted ADT Championship was an elimination derby that drew 32 top players to the par-72 Trump International in West Palm Beach, Florida. The first cut came at 36 holes and swept out 16 players, including Annika Sorenstam and Brittany Lincicome. With the scores set back to zero for each of the last two rounds, the 54-hole cut ousted eight more players, including Juli Inkster and Morgan Pressel, leaving eight.

Ochoa was turning the final round into a runaway. She shot 31 on the first nine and was leading by five strokes. At the 16th, she passed her first test easily, hitting a seven iron from a bunker across water to about 14 feet and saving par.

She had blown a couple of tournaments with late collapses, and so it was clear what she meant when she said she wanted a three- or four-stroke lead at the par-three 17th, "just in case something happened."

Something did happen. Ochoa's eight-iron tee shot was in the back fringe, and by the time she finished putting, she had a double-bogey five and — with Gulbis making a birdie from seven feet — her lead was down to one stroke. On to the 18th and the shot of her life. And she did leave 'em gasping.

Ladies European Tour

Women's World Cup of Golf
Sun City, South Africa
Winners: Paraguay (Julieta Granada and Celeste Troche)

See Ladies African Tour section.

MFS Women's Australian Open
Sydney, New South Wales
Winner: Karrie Webb

See Australian Ladies Tour section.

ANZ Ladies Masters
Ashmore, Queensland
Winner: Karrie Webb

See Australian Ladies Tour section.

Tenerife Ladies Open
San Miguel de Abona, Tenerife, Spain
Winner: Nikki Garrett

After securing European Rookie of the Year honors in 2006, Nikki Garrett wasted no time in fulfilling her next goal by winning the Tenerife Ladies Open at Golf del Sur. The 23-year-old Australian was the only player to finish under par as she won by two strokes over Trish Johnson and Spain's Tania Elosegui, who was a runner-up in the event for the second year running.

The windy conditions in the Canary Islands did not deter a player who grew up playing a cliff-top course in New South Wales. Nor did she let a numerologist's less than encouraging prediction for her year put her off, and after collecting the first prize of €41,250, Garrett had the last laugh.

Following rounds of 69, 75 and 71, Garrett closed with 72 for a one-under-par total of 287. Johnson had 71 on a day when no one broke 70 and Elosegui shot 72 to be one over. "I'll be honest with you, I came here hitting it really badly," Garrett admitted.

"On the way over here from Australia we stopped at Los Angeles and I met a numerologist who said it wasn't going to be a very good year for me, so I was a bit worried. I thought this year would be a lot harder than last year because I had more expectations on myself. My main goal this year was to win and now I've done it so early I don't know what I'm going to do. I'll have to sit down and re-assess the situation."

Open de Espana Femenino
Castellon, Spain
Winner: Nikki Garrett

Nikki Garrett, just a week after winning her first professional title, repeated the feat of her more illustrious compatriot Karrie Webb from earlier in the season of winning back-to-back and continued the Australian domination of the start of the Ladies European Tour with four wins in four events. Garrett defeated England's Rebecca Hudson by one stroke in the Open de Espana Femenino after an engrossing four-day duel between the two at Club de Campo Mediterraneo in Castellon.

Hudson opened with a course-record 65 to Garrett's 68, but the 23-year-old Australian took the halfway lead with her own 65 to Hudson's 69. The Yorkshirewoman recorded another 69 in the third round to go two ahead again as Garrett shot 72. But on the final day Garrett turned the tables again with a 70 to Hudson's 73.

Garrett did not drop a shot on the final day and birdies at the fourth and eighth holes kept her just one behind Hudson. But Garrett's parring of the entire last nine finally put the pressure on Hudson, who came to grief at the 16th hole, a 154-yard par-three redesigned by club member Sergio Garcia four years ago. Her six-iron shot found the water at the front of the green and she took a double-bogey five. Garrett's seven iron hit the left side of the green and she two-putted for a one-shot lead.

"I wasn't even thinking about winning. The way Rebecca was playing I thought there is no way she is not going to shoot under par today," said Garrett. "I never thought I'd win one tournament, let alone two in a row."

Deutsche Bank Ladies Swiss Open
Ticino, Switzerland
Winner: Bettina Hauert

Bettina Hauert achieved the feat of making seven birdies in a row to win the Deutsche Bank Ladies Swiss Open at Golf Gerre Losone. Germany's Hauert birdied the last three holes of regulation and then the 18th hole four more times to win a three-way playoff against Paula Marti and Anna Rawson. Hauert, 24 from Hagen, won for the first time in her fourth season on the Ladies European Tour, having never previously finished better than seventh.

Hauert shared the lead after every round. Rawson, one of three other players to share the lead with a round to play, looked as if she would continue the run of Australian winners on the Tour. Rawson led by four shots at the turn, but then dropped four in the next seven holes. She birdied the final two holes, as Marti did, to join the playoff at 285, three under par. Marti closed with 70 to set the target, while Rawson and Hauert had 72s.

They returned to the par-five 18th hole and all three birdied it on the first occasion, but Rawson failed to do so the second time to fall out of contention. On the third extra hole, Hauert holed from 12 feet to stay alive, but on the fourth occasion Marti was in trouble off the tee and missed from five feet for her birdie, while Hauert two-putted for victory.

"It was a fight from the first to the last, but it's been great," said Hauert. "I have been in playoffs as an amateur, but never in my professional life. I live for this feeling. This is what we practice for and this is what we live for. Holding the check and holding the trophy is just amazing."

BMW Ladies Italian Open
Rome, Italy
Winner: Trish Johnson

Although Justin Rose did not win the BMW PGA Championship, an English winner was celebrated at Wentworth. With the BMW Ladies Italian Open finishing on a Saturday, champion Trish Johnson was flown to London to share the spotlight with Anders Hansen. It was Johnson's 18th victory, but her first for three years, and came after an extraordinary finish at the Sheraton Parco de Medici in Rome.

Johnson scored 66 and birdied the last three holes to post the winning score of 273, 15 under par. She began the final round two shots behind Italy's own Stefania Croce, who fell back with 73, as Bettina Hauert became the main danger. The German was looking to continue the trend of back-to-back winners on the LET, and after starting in 24th place produced a brilliant 62, lowering her personal best by four shots.

She then came home in 29, eight under par with two eagles and four birdies, to tie the lowest nine holes ever on the European Tour. Hauert led by three when she finished, but Johnson, who had gone out in 33, birdied the 12th and 14th to get within one. A dropped shot at the 15th was recovered with a birdie at the 16th. Another followed at the 17th and then she pitched from 105 yards to three feet at the 18th for the winning birdie-four.

"I was feeling quite sick actually at that stage. I tried not to think about anything and to just breathe," said the 41-year-old Johnson. "I had a dreadful year last year and I don't enjoy that. I just wanted to win again. I've never thought about quitting. I don't think age has anything to do with it."

Northern Ireland Ladies Open
Belfast, Northern Ireland
Winner: Lisa Hall

Lisa Hall quit golf in 2005, but a year after returning to the game the 39-year-old Englishwoman claimed her first victory in 11 years. Having won the Indonesian Open in 1995, Hall's first European Tour win came at the Welsh Open in 1996. The following year the two-time Solheim Cup player was the Rookie of the Year on the LPGA tour, but her career in America never took off. With the help of her coach, husband Martin, Hall returned to the European Tour in 2006 and success arrived at the Northern Ireland Ladies Open at Hilton Templepatrick.

But it did not arrive until after eight holes of a playoff as Hall tied with France's Gwladys Nocera at two under par after both women closed with rounds of 71. Six times the par-five 18th was halved as the rain poured down. They then halved the first before returning to the 18th again. This time Nocera hit her second shot into the water hazard on the left of the fairway. Electing to play the ball, Nocera left her third shot in the hazard and took three more to get down. Hall rolled in a four-foot birdie putt for the victory.

"I'm absolutely delighted. This is the first tournament where Martin has seen me win and that means everything to me," said Hall. "This has been our journey together for 25 years and for him to be here to see me win is an absolutely fantastic feeling."

KLM Ladies Open
Valkenswaard, Holland
Winner: Gwladys Nocera

France's Gwladys Nocera overcame the disappointment of losing an eight-hole playoff the previous week to claim her fourth Ladies European Tour title with a comprehensive seven-stroke victory at the KLM Ladies Open in Holland. Having set a course-record eight-under 64 in the first round, the 32-year-old from Moulins went on to win wire-to-wire. She carded a two-under-par 70 in the second round and closed with a five-under 67. Nocera finished with a total of 201, 15 under par at Eindhovensche Golf, leaving compatriot Virginie Lagoutte-Clement in second place after 69, with England's Georgina Simpson third at seven under after a 73.

"I guess this has shown me that I can win if I'm leading from the first round, so it's one more experience," said Nocera, a three-time winner in 2006. "I was getting a little bit frustrated this season because I was playing well but I couldn't score well. This is a good time to win, but I guess it is always a good time to win."

Nocera held a two-stroke lead over Simpson going into the final round and went out in a steady 35 before leaving the field behind with an inward 32. She birdied the 12th and 14th, eagled the 15th, and birdied the 16th before dropping an inconsequential shot at the 17th. "When I made the putt on the par-five for eagle I guess that was it," she said. "I started to smile, which was a sign, and I just tried to play my best for the rest of the round."

Catalonia Ladies Masters
Barcelona, Spain
Winner: Ashleigh Simon

Playing in her fourth start as a professional, just a month after her 18th birthday, South African prodigy Ashleigh Simon became one of the youngest players ever to win on the Ladies European Tour by claiming the Catalonia Ladies Masters at Masia Bach near Barcelona. Simon had already won four professional titles in her homeland as an amateur, including the South African Open twice. Only 16-year-old amateur Amy Yang was younger when winning the 2006 ANZ Masters in Australia.

With rounds of 70, 68 and 70 for an eight-under-par total of 208, Simon came from one stroke behind Kirsty Taylor to win by two over Taylor and Becky Brewerton, with Trish Johnson a further stroke behind. "This opens so many doors for me," said Simon, who earned a three-year exemption and an invitation to the Evian Masters.

"I don't have to go to qualifying school now, I can play in tournaments and organize my life better. I knew how to win from back home and I'm lucky to have played in so many events already as an amateur."

Simon had been sick throughout the night prior to the final round due to food poisoning. "I was throwing up from about half-past two to about four o'clock," she said. "It was something I ate. I couldn't believe it was happening." Simon made three birdies on the first nine to take the lead, and despite a bogey at the 12th, her sand-save at the 18th preserved a one-stroke lead. Brewerton had a chance to tie at the last before dropping a shot.

Vediorbis Open de France
Anzin St. Aubin, Arras, France
Winner: Linda Wessberg

Returning to Europe proved the perfect tonic for Linda Wessberg as she posted her second career victory at the Vediorbis Open de France at Arras. Wessberg, a 27-year-old from Gothenburg, won her first title at the Wales Open in 2006. She then played the first two LET events of 2007 in Australia before heading for America where she had a conditional card on the LPGA circuit.

With ninth her best result, Wessberg decided to come back to Europe, and a last round of 65 put her one ahead of Trish Johnson. With earlier rounds of 70, 68 and 74, Wessberg came from four behind overnight leader Rebecca Hudson to finish at 11-under 277. The Swede had the perfect start with birdies at the first two holes, added another at the fourth, then three in a row from the sixth — including holing a 40-footer at the seventh — to be out in 30.

Now ahead of the field, Wessberg dropped a shot at the 11th, but birdied the 13th and holed a 20-footer for a birdie-four at the 18th. Johnson's chip to tie came up just two inches short. Stefania Croce and Gwladys Nocera shared third place, while Hudson dropped back to sixth.

"It's nice to be able to show that winning last year wasn't a one-off," said Wessberg. "It was a little frustrating yesterday because I didn't feel like I was playing badly, but no putts went in. I got off to a good start and then all of a sudden I was six under after nine."

Ladies Open de Portugal
Algarve, Portugal
Winner: Sophie Giquel

Sophie Giquel won the Ladies Open de Portugal at Gramacho on the Algarve for her first professional victory in her fourth season on the LET. As the wind approached its strongest at the conclusion of the tournament, Giquel handled the conditions brilliantly with three birdies in the last seven holes to take a two-stroke win over Sweden's Louise Stahle.

Giquel, a 24-year-old Frenchwoman from Lyons, closed with 69 for a wining total of 206, 10 under par. She was tied at seven under after two rounds alongside Stahle, Joanne Mills and compatriot Jade Schaeffer. She was part of a three-way tie at seven under at the turn, but then found herself two behind Stahle, the two-time British Amateur champion in her rookie season on the European tour following a year in America after turning professional.

Stahle birdied the 10th and 11th and also the par-five 12th, where Giquel also birdied to stay two back. However, bogeys from Stahle at the 13th and 16th let Giquel back in, and she capitalized by holing from 38 feet for a birdie at the 17th and then birdieing the 18th. Schaeffer, another rookie, took third place, three behind Stahle, thanks to the help of her sister Fany caddieing for her after missing the cut.

Giquel moved up to fourth in the European Solheim Cup standings, but revealed on the first day of the match she had booked a church ceremony to celebrate her marriage to Axel Batten at the end of 2006. "We will see what happens. I will try to do my best on the golf course, and if I am in, then I will go," she said.

Golf Punk Ladies English Open
Biddenden, Kent, England
Winner: Becky Brewerton

With Karen Stupples and Becky Brewerton tied for the lead with nine holes to play at Chart Hills, there was sure to be a popular winner of the Golf Punk Ladies English Open. Stupples, in her home county of Kent, was playing her first competitive rounds since November and walked a complete 18 holes for the first time since giving birth 10 weeks earlier to her first child, a son Logan. Remarkably steady for the first 45 holes, Stupples admitted lacking a touch of mental sharpness as the pressure mounted on the back nine.

Brewerton proved the stronger finisher as the popular 24-year-old Welsh player claimed her first title in her fourth season on the Tour. She had recorded 16 top-10 finishes in her career, including four runners-up finishes, two as an amateur in 2003. Both players picked up their fourth birdies of the day at the 12th, but Stupples then bogeyed the 13th and drove out of bounds at the 15th for a double bogey. Brewerton settled it with two tremendous blows up the hill at the par-five 16th for another birdie and a four-shot lead. A poor drive at the 18th, which cost a penalty drop and a bogey, still gave her 68 and a three-stroke win at seven-under 209 over Stupples, Kirsty Taylor and Linda Wessberg. Laura Davies and Gwladys Nocera tied for fifth place.

"It means so much to me. I've been trying for so long. To finally do it is just unbelievable, unbelievable," said an emotional Brewerton, who was being watched by her parents. "I can't believe it. I'm just in shock. To have had such a cushion coming up the last was just massive."

Evian Masters
Evians-les-Bains, France
Winner: Natalie Gulbis

Natalie Gulbis claimed her first professional title by winning the Evian Masters in a playoff over Jeong Jang. The 24-year-old Gulbis had joined the LPGA Tour at the age of 18, but it proved a six-year wait to translate her undoubted talent into a victory. While Gulbis is known for her glamorous calendars, proving herself on the course was always her chief motivation. "This is my sixth year on tour and, obviously, in the U.S. there has been quite a bit of hype on if I would ever win a tournament," she admitted.

It was a back problem earlier in the season that, ironically, put Gulbis on the track to victory. What was shaping up as her least successful season forced her to work on her posture, and once she was fully fit her game suddenly came together. Five strokes behind leader Juli Inkster, Gulbis closed with a round of 70 to set the clubhouse target at 284, four under par. Only Jang, the 2005 Weetabix Women's British Open champion, managed to tie that score after the Korean came in with 72. Inkster fell behind on the final nine, but still had a chance to win at the 18th but faced a long birdie putt. She ran it by and ended up three-putting to miss out on the playoff. The veteran American shared third place with Ji-Yai Shin and world No. 1 Lorena Ochoa, who came in early with 68.

In the playoff at the par-five 18th, Jang went over the green for her second shot and could not get up and down. Gulbis two-putted for a birdie and the win. She had lost her only previous playoff in 2006. Parachute jumpers landed on the 18th green at the presentation ceremony and draped Gulbis in the Stars and Stripes, while she celebrated with champagne with Cristie Kerr, a friend who had kept Gulbis calm during the wait for the playoff.

"I lost in the first round of the Match Play last week, but I just tried to stay positive and worked really hard on my game," said Gulbis, who earned €341,145 for the victory. "I got hurt two months ago with a lower back injury and had to take about a month off. It was a blessing in disguise. I worked on my posture and I kept hitting it farther and all the things I wanted to happen on my golf swing started happening."

Ricoh Women's British Open
St. Andrews, Scotland
Winner: Lorena Ochoa

See Chapter 6.

Scandinavian TPC Hosted by Annika
Malmo, Sweden
Winner: Catriona Matthew

Scotland's Catriona Matthew won for the first time since giving birth to daughter Katie eight months earlier in December 2006. The 37-year-old from North Berwick also put behind her a disappointing weekend at the Ricoh Women's British Open at St. Andrews by claiming the Scandinavian TPC Hosted by Annika at Barseback, where Matthew holed the winning putt for Europe in the 2003 Solheim Cup.

It was Matthew's fifth victory but only her second in Europe, the first coming back in 1998. It was also three years since the second of her victories in America and in only her 14th tournament since coming back from maternity leave in March.

After 66 in the third round, when she had two eagles, one only just short of a double eagle, Matthew shared the lead with American Brittany Lincicome. But four birdies in the first five holes gave the Scot a five-stroke lead. Laura Diaz briefly got within one, but Matthew birdied the 12th and 13th to pull away again. She closed with 68 for a total of nine-under-par 279 and a three-stroke win over Diaz and Sweden's Sophie Gustafson, who both had final rounds of 68.

"I have some happy memories here," Matthew said. "I love the greens, I have never holed so many putts. It just about felt like I was playing in Scotland, I had so much support. Obviously, I played really well and it's just fantastic. I haven't won in a couple of years, and there's a great field here this week, so I'm just thankful to have won."

S4/C Wales Ladies Championship of Europe
Llanelli, Carmarthenshire, Wales
Winner: Joanne Mills

What appeared to be inevitable after a number of close finishes during the season finally became reality when Joanne Mills won the S4/C Wales Ladies Championship of Europe. It was only the second LET win for the 37-year-old Australian from Sydney and it had been a long wait, exactly 10 years, since she won the German Open in 1997.

Tied for the lead starting the final round with Rebecca Hudson and Georgina Simpson, both from Yorkshire, Mills survived the wind and drizzle at the Machynys Peninsula Golf Club in Llanelli and won with a closing 73. She finished at six-under-par 282 and one ahead of Simpson, who slipped to a 74, and Germany's Bettina Hauert, whose 71 also confirmed her place on the Solheim Cup team.

But Mills was not interested in the Solheim Cup permutations and just battled her way to a precious win. "I can't believe it. It's taken me 10 years to have another win on the LET. I never thought it would take this long, but it has," said Mills. "I've played well all year and came close in Northern Ireland. I had a good chance in Portugal, but I'm just so pleased to finally get it under my belt again. To tell you the truth, I was nervous from the first tee shot to the last putt. I tried to grind my pars out and fortunately everyone was falling away."

SAS Masters
Oslo, Norway
Winner: Suzann Pettersen

After winning her first major championship, Suzann Pettersen returned home to Norway as the local favorite and added to her heroine status with a resounding nine-stroke victory at the SAS Masters at Losby, a course in an attractive forested valley outside her hometown of Oslo. The 26-year-old moved into the world's top 10 by winning twice in the United States earlier in the season, including the McDonald's LPGA Championship. Here she added not just a third win of the summer but only her second in Europe, the first coming in her rookie season of 2001.

Pettersen was on fire from the very start as she posted a course-record 64 in the opening round to lead by four strokes. In very windy conditions on the second day her even-par 72 extended the lead to five strokes. The Norwegian closed with 68 to finish at 204, 12 under par. Only three other players finished under par for the week. Australian Nikki Garrett won the battle for second place at three-under 213, with Italy's Diana Luna and Germany's Anja Monke sharing third place at one under par.

"It's been a fantastic year, and my third win coming at home, I couldn't ask for more. It feels great and it was nice to actually play well today and shoot my numbers," Pettersen said. "I've been in my own bubble all week and it's been working well. Coming home, you can give something back to Norwegian golf."

Finnair Masters
Tali, Finland
Winner: Bettina Hauert

With one Solheim Cup player winning in Norway, Bettina Hauert, a rookie on the European team, followed Suzann Pettersen's example at the Finnair Masters by also claiming victory in the run-up to the match against the Americans. Like Pettersen the previous week, Hauert started the final round with a comfortable lead, but it was not plain sailing for the 25-year-old German. Hauert, whose first victory in Switzerland earlier in the season set up her Solheim Cup qualification, hit her opening tee shot out of bounds and then three-putted for a quadruple-bogey eight to see her four-shot overnight advantage wiped out.

On a day of difficult winds and heavy showers at Helsinki Golf Club, a 23-year-old Finnish rookie, Kaisa Ruutila then took over the lead, much to the delight of the local gallery, but she dropped four shots in three holes from the fifth to fall out of contention. Sweden's Johanna Westerburg went one ahead of Hauert with birdies at the seventh and ninth, but then triple-bogeyed the 12th. The German's three birdies in a row starting at the same hole claimed her the title. Her closing 72, after rounds of 68 and 67, left Hauert at six-under-par 207 and three ahead of Westerburg, with Lotta Wahlin in third and Asa Gottmo and English teenager Kiran Matharu sharing fourth place.

"A rollercoaster is the best word to describe it," said Hauert, who took over at the top of the money list. "I started very bad, the eight was a shock when everyone said it would be easy to win, and I was fighting my way all the time. Finally I found my rhythm and was calm."

Nykredit Masters
Helsingor, Denmark
Winner: Lisa Hall

A three-way British battle all day long finally went the way of Lisa Hall at the first hole of a playoff. Hall won the Nykredit Masters at Helsingor in Denmark after a par-four at the 18th hole to defeat Kirsty Taylor and Kiran Matharu. It was Hall's second win of a season which had proved a wonderful renaissance for the 39-year-old from Stoke. Hall had won the Northern Ireland Open after an eight-hole playoff, but this time settled the issue much sooner.

But it had taken a whole day to get in a position to win. Hall started the final round a stroke behind 36-year-old Taylor and 18-year-old Matharu. While that pair disputed the lead, Hall kept in touch with a birdie at the last hole, matched by Matharu, who made the playoff when Taylor's second at the 18th hit a tree and went only 10 yards. Her bogey meant all three were tied at nine under, Hall after a closing 67 and Taylor and Matharu after 68s. Matharu clinched the Cross Country Challenge for performances in the four Scandinavian events and won a Volvo car, but said she would have to learn how to drive before enjoying it.

Hall said: "I'm jumping out of my skin right now. I was behind all day, but I knew if I stayed patient I would have a big chance come the end. Everybody could have won it and it made it really exciting."

The Solheim Cup
Halmstad, Sweden
Winner: United States

The United States retained The Solheim Cup and won for only the second time on European soil with a comfortable 16-to-12 victory at Halmstad in Sweden. It was a commanding performance in the singles, similar to the victory at St. Pierre in Wales in 1996, that allowed the Americans to keep the cup and not let Europe repeat their triumph in Sweden at Barseback four years earlier. Betsy King's team played fine golf throughout the three days of often wet and windy weather, although in the fourballs and the foursomes Europe kept fighting back, so much so that going into the singles the home side were a point ahead.

America got the opening foursomes by a point, but then the next two sessions were halved despite the scoreboard often showing red on the board. In the Friday afternoon fourballs, both Annika Sorenstam, with a par at the last, and Laura Davies, with a miracle par at the 16th after hacking out of a bush and then chipping in, fought back to earn halves in their respective matches when it appeared they might both lose twice in the same day for the first time in their Solheim Cup careers.

Twice on Saturday in the foursomes European pairings won the 18th hole to snatch halves. This led to American commentator, and feisty former Solheim Cup player, Dottie Pepper to remark, thinking she was off air, that they were "choking freaking dogs." The comment swept back to Halmstad where nine times on the first two days Americans failed to either win the 18th or a match at the 18th. But, after the final fourballs were completed on Sunday morning due to earlier weather delays, with Europe having edged a point in front, the Americans rarely needed to go as far as the last in the singles.

Catriona Matthew won the top singles to finish with three points for Europe, but only Davies followed her lead while the match was alive. Stacy Prammanasudh, in the match of the day, defeated Suzann Pettersen by two holes to join Pat Hurst, Juli Inkster and Angela Stanford with full points, while Sherri Steinhauer grabbed a halve from Becky Brewerton at the last. Any hope for Europe disappeared with Morgan Pressel's victory over Sorenstam, and wins for Nicole Castrale and Paula Creamer confirmed the victory. Linda Wessberg claimed a win over Cristie Kerr, but Natalie Gulbis's point in the bottom match gave America the singles 8½-to-3½.

Creamer, at the age of 21, was the leading point scorer with three and a half out of five, the same record as on her debut in 2005. "I've always said that winning the Solheim is better than winning a tournament, and I say it again," said Creamer. "I was pretty excited at Crooked Stick as a rookie and this was even better because it was a win overseas."

"I don't think our team played badly, the Americans just played better," said Helen Alfredsson, Europe's captain. "It was absolutely an amazing week to see these girls fight so hard on every single shot. There was a lot of heart and soul out there."

De Vere Ladies Scottish Open
Loch Lomond, Scotland
Winner: Sophie Gustafson

Just six days after being part of the losing European Solheim Cup team in Sweden, Sophie Gustafson braved similar wet and windy weather to win the De Vere Ladies Scottish Open at the Carrick course, a new layout on the banks of Loch Lomond. Six of the European team members were in action, but it was Gustafson who ran away with a five-stroke victory. The 33-year-old Swede said she would celebrate with a couple of beers, but she also admitted there was no making up for the previous week's defeat. "It's two different things. I don't think anything can fix the disappointment from last week," she said after claiming the 22nd victory of her career.

Gustafson had to complete the last six holes of her second round, which gave her a one-stroke lead, before playing the third and final round in torrential rain. Eight pars to start the round extended her lead to four as others fell back. A double bogey and a bogey briefly unsettled her in the middle of the second nine, but the sun emerged as she holed a 30-foot birdie putt at the 18th. A final round of 71 left Gustafson as the only player under par at three-under 210, with England's Danielle Masters and Kirsty Taylor and Sweden's Sofia Renell all sharing second place at two over. Janice Moodie and Lynn Kenny were the leading Scots among those sharing fifth place, while teenage amateurs Carly Booth and Sally Watson both finished in the top 20.

UNIQA Ladies Golf Open
Wiener Neustadt, Austria
Winner: Laura Davies

When Laura Davies missed the cut at the De Vere Scottish Open, it was the first time she had done so in a regular, non–co-sanctioned Ladies European Tour event for 21 years. She called it a "weird week" but added: "It's just one tournament, you have got to forget about that and get on with it." Davies, 43, did just that and the very next week won the UNIQA Ladies Golf Open at Wiener Neustadt in Austria. A course-record 65 in the second round gave her the lead, and then the Englishwoman held off the challenge of defending champion Sophie Gustafson to win by four strokes.

A closing 66 gave Davies a 16-under-par 200 total and her 36th LET win, the 68th of her career, including a win in 22 of her 23 seasons as a professional. Davies prides herself on winning every year. "It was getting a bit late in the year," Davies admitted. "I just love winning trophies. It still wrangles with me that I didn't win a tournament in 2005.

"I couldn't have played much better this week. Last week in Scotland was a bit of a one-off. But being paired with Sophie was the worst news I could have had today. If there was one person I didn't want to be paired with, it was her. She hits it as far as anyone. I was nervous, no question."

Davies started one ahead but was five clear at the turn due to a double bogey from Gustafson at the fifth and an eagle from Davies at the ninth.

Madrid Ladies Masters
Madrid, Spain
Winner: Martina Eberl

Martina Eberl, who had previously finished as a runner-up twice in her five-year career, won for the first time as a professional at the Madrid Ladies Masters by defeating Sophie Gustafson in a thrilling duel at Retamares. Eberl, a 26-year-old from Munich, started the final round five strokes behind Gustafson, who was looking for her second title in three events. But Eberl finished ahead by one after a closing four-under 69, following earlier rounds of 68 and 69, to win at 206, 13 under par.

Eberl's charge began on the first nine with four birdies and then she added another at the 10th. Gustafson was just one ahead, but then bogeyed the 12th to fall back into a tie with Eberl. The German missed a short putt at the 15th to drop one behind, but then Gustafson's par save at the next hole lipped out. At the 18th it was the more experienced Swede who succumbed to the pressure when she hit her second shot into the water on the left and took a bogey-six.

"I didn't know throughout the day how my score was or how Sophie's score was. I think I'm just overwhelmed at the moment," said Eberl. "I'm just so happy. I was hitting the ball well, putting well, good short game, and it all came together today."

Denmark's Iben Tinning took third place in the tournament at 11 under par after 70, while Spain's Tania Elosegui was fourth a stroke further back.

Eberl actually won two titles on the same day as she also claimed victory in the 18 Finest competition sponsored by Banque Baring Brothers, an event featuring 18 holes from nine different tournaments across the season. Eberl collected a check for €56,500 to add to her first prize of €100,000.

EMAAR-MGF Ladies Masters
Bidadi, Bangalore, India
Winner: Gwladys Nocera

A tournament led from the second day by France's Gwladys Nocera turned into an exciting conclusion as the 32-year-old sneaked home by only one stroke at the EMAAR-MGF Ladies Masters, the first Ladies European Tour event in India.

Nocera was five strokes ahead at the halfway stage after two rounds of 69 at the Eagleton course in Bangalore. But a 72 in the third round let her compatriot Virginie Lagoutte-Clement draw within three after shooting 66. On the final day Nocera always stayed in front, leading by three at the turn and four after 12 holes, but could never quite shake off her opponent. At the 13th there was a two-shot swing, with Nocera making a bogey and Lagoutte-Clement a birdie. With just the two in it now, the next three holes were parred, but Lagoutte-Clement drove over the trees at the 345-yard 17th to give herself a 30-foot eagle putt. She had to settle for a birdie, but was now just one stroke behind. However, at the 18th both drove into the left rough and two-putted from long range for their pars.

Nocera, with seven-under-par 281 total, closed with a 71 to Lagoutte-Clement's 69 to claim her second official win of the season, not including the Princess Lalla Meryem Cup in Morocco. "I feel happy to win," said Nocera. "I knew it was going to be tough. I knew Virginie was going to go for the green on 17 and I was hoping that she wouldn't make the putt for eagle because I knew that would be a struggle. I still have a few things to fix. I need to reach more greens and my concentration was a bit on and off throughout the week, so I need to make sure everything is alright for next week."

Dubai Ladies Masters
Dubai, United Arab Emirates
Winner: Annika Sorenstam

At the last chance of asking Annika Sorenstam gained her only win of 2007 when she successfully defended her title at the Dubai Ladies Masters over the Majlis course at the Emirates Golf Club. After a season plagued by neck and back injuries, the 37-year-old Swede announced her intention to try to regain her No. 1 status. A stroke behind Denmark's Iben Tinning with one round to play, Sorenstam closed with 70 to finish at 10-under-par 278 total, two clear of Tinning, who shot 73, and Laura Davies, with 72.

In a closely fought encounter all day, all three players shared the lead at the turn in the final round. Tinning went ahead again and was still one clear with two holes to play. But at the 17th Sorenstam rolled in a vital birdie putt from 20 feet and then Tinning missed from slightly nearer the hole. Tied going to the par-five 18th, both players laid up, but Tinning's third shot did not carry far enough onto the green and spun back into the pond. Sorenstam sealed the victory with a par, while Tinning suffered a double bogey.

"It's been kind of a tough year for me inside the ropes, and to come here and defend a title, and to play so consistent and bring the trophy home, it's just a wonderful feeling," Sorenstam said. "I've missed the feeling. I've missed being in contention. I've missed coming down the stretch and having a chance to win. To get the job done means a lot and it's going to carry on for next year. This is a special win in many ways."

Fellow Swede Sophie Gustafson claimed the New Star money list for the third time, overtaking Bettina Hauert in Dubai. But the German was voted as the Players' Player of the Year after her two wins, two runner-up spots and a debut appearance in the Solheim Cup. Sweden's Louise Stahle won the Bill Johnson Trophy as the Ryder Cup Wales Rookie of the Year.

Japan LPGA Tour

Daikin Orchid Ladies
Nanjo, Okinawa
Winner: Midori Yoneyama

Midori Yoneyama wins her tournaments the hard way these days. Just as she experienced in her previous two victories on the Japan LPGA Tour in 2005, Yoneyama had to go extra holes to extract her seventh career win in the 2007 season-opening Daikin Orchid tournament in March. This time she got help from her playoff opponent as little-known Asuka Tsujimura failed to par the first overtime hole after the two women finished tied at six-under-par 210 at the Ryukyu Golf Club at Nanjo, Okinawa.

The surprise was the presence of Tsujimura in the playoff, because Yoneyama had gone into the final round tied at 138 with Yuri Fudoh, the tour's No. 1 player of the last decade. Fudoh collapsed in the Sunday round, shooting 79, as Tsujimura had a 71 to force the playoff.

Yoneyama had seized a share of the lead Saturday, adding a bogey-free, six-under-par 66 for the 138 that deadlocked her with Fudoh, who had opened with 69, a shot behind leader Tamie Durdin of Australia.

Yoneyama had fallen two behind Tsujimura Sunday through 16 holes, but made a long par-saving putt while Tsujimura was bogeying the 17th, then birdied the 18th to force the extra effort. Okinawa's own Ai Miyazato, back from the LPGA circuit in America, started weakly with 73 and tied for fourth with 213.

Accordia Golf Ladies
Miyazaki
Winner: Toshimi Kimura

Toshimi Kimura flashed the form at the Accordia Golf Ladies tournament that brought her nine victories during her 21 seasons. The 38-year-old veteran eased in front in the opening round at Aoshima Golf Club in Miyazaki with 69 and, never threatened, rolled to a six-stroke victory with a nine-under-par 207.

Kimura had four birdies and a bogey Friday to start a stroke in front of Mayumi Shimomura and Yuri Fudoh, the defending champion who was coming off a disappointing finish the week before in the Daikin Orchid tournament. Kimura retained a cautionary tone Saturday even after surging five strokes ahead of Shiho Oyama, the No. 1 player on the 2006 tour. Kimura had five birdies and a bogey, noted that she hadn't three-putted a green, and said: "A five-shot lead is surmountable. You never know. I might shoot an 80 tomorrow."

That was not the case. She put together a fashionable 70 and widened the final margin to the six strokes as Oyama shot 71 for 213 to finish second, two strokes ahead of Kuniko Maeda.

Studio Alice Ladies Open
Miki, Hyogo
Winner: Jae-Hee Bae

Another South Korean was heard from in the Studio Alice Ladies Open as Jae-Hee Bae scored a two-stroke victory on the Yokawa course at Hanaya-shika Golf Club at Miki, Hyogo Prefecture. She led from start to finish to become the Japan LPGA Tour's initial first-time winner of 2007. It was the second straight tournament with a wire-to-wire winner.

An opening 69 gave Bae a one-stroke lead Friday over Momoko Ueda and Tomomi Hirose and two over veteran winner Michiko Hattori, Ayako Uehara and Yayoi Arasaki. When she repeated the 69 — five birdies, two bogeys — Saturday, the South Korean moved three shots in front of Ueda (70-71), her nearest pursuer. Nobuko Kizawa, Maiko Wakabayashi and Australia's Nikki Campbell were another shot back at 142.

Bae polished off her first tour win with a steady, two-under-par 70 for 208 total. Yui Kawahara mounted a challenge Sunday and jumped into second place with a fine 66 for 210, two strokes ahead of Hyun-Ju Shin and Rui Kitada. Ueda finished at 213 with a closing 72.

Life Card Ladies
Kikuyo, Kumamoto
Winner: Momoko Ueda

Momoko Ueda lived up to the promise she showed in 2006 as a 19-year-old rookie, rolling to a six-stroke victory in the Life Card Ladies at Kumamoto Kuko Country Club. Ueda, who had 11 top-10 showings in 2006, followed the wire-to-wire-winner pattern of the previous two tournaments in claiming her first title on the Japan LPGA Tour and launching her spectacular season.

"I'm happy that I broke par in all three rounds and won in my hometown," said Ueda, who posted a five-under-par 211 for the distance. "My putting was pretty good." It was a chip-in, though, that sparked her game the first day. It gave her an eagle on the final hole and the 70 that put her in front by two strokes over Kaori Aoyama.

Ueda followed with 71 — four birdies, three bogeys — Saturday to retain the two-shot lead, then over South Korea's Hyun-Ju Shin (73-70), a two-time winner over the two previous seasons. Ueda had four more birdies and closed with 70 Sunday to clinch the victory. Yet another young player on the circuit — 19-year-old Erina Hara — shot 73–217 to snatch second place away from Shin by a stroke.

Fujisankei Ladies Classic
Ito, Shizuoka
Winner: Miki Saiki

Miki Saiki wasted no time becoming a winner; in fact, the third consecutive first-time victor on the circuit. Just 112 days after the 22-year-old turned professional, Saiki won the venerable Fujisankei Ladies Classic on the Kawana Hotel Golf Course at Ito, Shizuoka Prefecture, becoming the fastest winner ever on that tour. Ai Miyazato, one of Japan's brightest stars the last three years, had held the record — 146 days in early 2004.

Saiki came from two strokes off the pace Sunday to score the victory, shooting a three-under-par 69 for 210 total and a one-shot margin over Midori Yoneyama (68) and Ayako Uehara (72), who carried the 36-hole lead into the final round with her 69-70–139. Yoneyama had won the season-opening Daikin Orchid tournament. Saiki shared second place after 36 holes with Saiki Fujita, Akane Iijima and China's Na Zhang as veteran Akiko Fukushima, the first-round leader with 68, blew from contention with 78 in her second start of the season.

Three consecutive birdies starting at the 13th hole keyed Saiki's triumph Sunday, prompting her to remark: "I wonder if God was smiling at me. I never thought I could win this early."

Yashima Queens
Takamatsu, Kagawa
Winner: Mi-Jeong Jeon

Mi-Jeong Jeon launched a Japan LPGA record spurt with her come-from-behind victory in the new Yashima Queens tournament. The South Korean, a three-time winner in 2006, produced a final-round 69 at Yashima Country Club to snatch a one-stroke victory with her three-under-par 213.

Veteran Toshimi Kimura was eying her second win of the season as she shared the lead with Australian Nikki Campbell at 143 after 36 holes. As she was after an opening 71 that put her a stroke behind leaders Yui Kawahara and Eun-Hye Lee, Jeon was just one back of Kimura, the Accordia victor in March, and Campbell, whose lone win came in the 2006 Suntory.

Jeon, who had tasted international competition in the Kraft Nabisco Championship earlier in the year in America, utilized two key back-nine birdies Sunday to fashion the 69, barely fending off Chiharu Yamaguchi, who closed with a 68 for 214 total. Campbell shot 72 for 215 and Kimura 73 for 216.

Salonpas World Ladies
Tokyo
Winner: Mi-Jeong Jeon

Mi-Jeong Jeon took the second step toward history on the Japan LPGA Tour in the year's first 72-hole tournament, getting the best of Hall-of-

Famer Karrie Webb in the process of winning the Salonpas World Ladies tournament at Tokyo's noted Yomiuri Country Club. She put the title back to back with her triumph the previous week in the Yashima Queens.

The South Korean had matched strokes with Webb through 54 holes before jumping away to a three-shot victory with a 71 in Sunday's final round and a six-under-par 282 total. It was her fifth win in Japan.

Jeon never made the leaderboard the first day, shooting 72 to trail leader Akane Iijima by five strokes. Webb, a two-time winner of the tournament in 2000 and 2001, was much worse off, opening with 76, but she rebounded with a nine-birdie 65 Friday that was just a shot short of her own course record. That vaulted her into a first-place tie at 141 with young stars Sakura Yokomine and Momoko Ueda, veteran Akiko Fukushima and Iijima.

Jeon joined Webb atop the standings at 211 Saturday, shooting 69 to Webb's 70, then salted away the victory with 71 Sunday. The Australian star slipped to 75, yielding second place to Ueda, who finished with 72.

Vernal Ladies
Asakura, Fukuoka
Winner: Mi-Jeong Jeon

Mi-Jeong Jeon completed her record run in the Vernal Ladies. When she outlasted Yuri Fudoh in a marathon playoff for the title, Jeon became the first player in the history of the organized (1988) Japan LPGA Tour to win three consecutive tournaments.

After 36 holes, Fudoh, with the brilliant record of 40 wins and six money titles, had the upper hand in the Vernal Ladies tournament at Fukuoka Century Golf Club. With rounds of 71-65, she took a three-stroke lead over Jeon (70-69) into the final day and was rolling toward victory with a four-stroke margin after 14 holes when the South Korean caught fire. Sparked by a birdie at the 15th, Jeon sailed home with a 69 to Fudoh's 72, the 208 totals forcing extra holes.

The playoff ended at the sixth hole when the 24-year-old, in her third season in Japan, dropped an eight-foot birdie putt. It was the third-longest playoff in tour history. "I never thought I would end up as the winner of this tournament, particularly when I was so far behind a great player like Fudoh-san," Jeon remarked afterward. "It's really a great honor to put my name in the history books."

Chukyo TV Bridgestone Ladies Open
Toyota, Aichi
Winner: Sakura Yokomine

After the first two rounds of the Chukyo TV Bridgestone Ladies Open, Mi-Jeong Jeon's hopes for a fourth straight victory were very much alive. With the day's best round of 67, Jeon posted 139, two strokes behind co-leaders Yukari Baba and Momoko Ueda. She shared that position with Sakura Yokomine, the bright, 21-year-old Japanese star.

The two went in opposite directions Sunday at Chukyo Golf Club's Ishino course in Toyota, Aichi Prefecture. The South Korean stumbled to a 74–213 and a tie for 10th place in the final standings, but Yokomine proceeded to score her first victory of the year and sixth of her brief career. Yokomine, in just her third season, birdied the final hole for 70–209 and a one-stroke win over Baba, rookie Yuko Mitsuka and Mie Nakata, who fell out of a tie with Yokomine when she bogeyed the 53rd hole.

Like Jeon, Ueda finished badly, plunging to 20th place with a 78. Australian Tamie Durdin, the first-round leader with a sparkling 65, wound up in a five-way tie for fifth place at 211, just two off the winner's pace.

Kosaido Ladies Golf Cup
Ichihara, Chiba
Winner: Yuri Fudoh

Yuri Fudoh was not about to let another victory get away from her. Still smarting from her playoff loss to Mi-Jeong Jeon two weeks earlier when she blew a four-stroke lead on the last four holes, Fudoh broke from a 36-hole tie for the lead with a closing 68–206 and bolted to a five-shot triumph in the Kosaido Ladies Golf Cup tournament. It was the 30-year-old star's first win of 2007 and the 41st of her brilliant nine-year career. Ironically, Jeon, she of the record three wins in a row, was one of four players who finished second with 211s at the Chiba Kosaido Country Club in the late May event.

Bad weather was a problem earlier in the week. Heavy rains forced cancellation of play before any players finished the opening round Friday. Nobody was better than three under par when the overnight suspension came. However, officials did manage to get the complete first two rounds into the books Saturday.

At the end of that long day, Fudoh, with rounds of 70-68, and Noriko Aso, with a pair of 69s, had the lead at 138, a stroke ahead of Sakura Yokomine, the previous week's winner. Fudoh won her second Kosaido Golf Cup with relative ease Sunday, racking up seven birdies to offset a double bogey and a bogey for the 68 and 206 total.

Resort Trust Ladies
Nishigo, Fukushima
Winner: Momoko Ueda

Momoko Ueda survived perhaps the toughest competitive test of her young career in scoring her second victory of the season in the Resort Trust Ladies tournament. The 20-year-old budding star had forged a two-stroke lead — 69-68-137 — after 36 holes at Grande Nasu Shirakawa Golf Club in Nishigo, but was looking over her shoulder at three of Japan's most talented players — Sakura Yokomine two back, Yuri Fudoh three back and Shiho Oyama, the 2006 money leader, among five players four off the lead.

The Sunday challenge came from Fudoh, who was fresh from a five-stroke victory the previous Sunday in the Kosaido Golf Cup. Fudoh, the No. 1 player on the circuit since the turn of the century, generated a stellar, seven-under-par 65 that forced Ueda to put together a 68 to create a tie at 205 and bring on a playoff. Nobody else finished within six strokes of the leaders; Yokomine was at 211.

Fudoh ran out of steam and lost her second playoff of 2007 on the first extra hole. She bogeyed after bungling an approach from the rough from 50 yards and Ueda picked up her second win of the season with a regulation par.

We Love Kobe Suntory Ladies Open
Kobe, Hyogo
Winner: Na Zhang

Another historical event occurred on the 2007 Japan LPGA Tour when Na Zhang captured the We Love Kobe Suntory Ladies Open. Zhang is the first player from the Chinese mainland ever to win on the circuit and she did so in most convincing fashion. She led from the start and finished three strokes in front with a 10-under-par 278 total despite a closing 73.

The 25-year-old from Beijing, playing in Japan for the first season, didn't falter until that final round even though being pursued by several of the leading players. She opened the tournament at Kobe's Rokko Kokusai Golf Club with a 67, one stroke ahead of five players, including Yuri Fudoh, Shiho Oyama and Shinobu Moromizato.

Zhang edged two strokes in front of Moromizato with an erratic but successful round Friday, shooting 69 for 136 with seven birdies, two bogeys and a double bogey. Then, on Saturday, another 69 produced a surprising and overwhelming eight-stroke lead over Moromizato (75) and Fudoh (72). As it turned out Sunday, Oyama (67) and Erina Hara (65) made the best unsuccessful runs at Zhang, Oyama finishing second with 281 and Hara third with 282.

Nichirei PGM Ladies
Miho, Ibaraki
Winner: Shiho Oyama

Shiho Oyama had fallen on diminished times since her commanding 2006 season when she ended Yuri Fudoh's run of six consecutive Japan LPGA money titles. In fact, she scored all five of her victories that season before September and went almost a year before winning again in the Nichirei PGM Ladies in mid-June.

Coming off a runner-up finish the week before in Kobe, Oyama took advantage when Shinobu Moromizato and Miki Saiki, the only two players ahead of her after 36 holes, faltered in the final round. She shot 71 for 207 total to score a one-stroke victory at Miho Golf Club in Ibaraki Prefecture. It was the 30-year-old's ninth tour victory.

Moromizato, the 21-year-old who won her first tournament in the late-season Sankyo tournament in 2006, had things going well for two rounds. She opened Friday with a six-under-par 66, sharing the lead with Akane Iijima, who also was a first-time victor in 2006. Moromizato added a 68 Saturday to take a solo lead with 134, one shot ahead of Saiki (67-68) and two in front of Oyama, who posted her second straight 68. Then on Sunday, Moromizato and Saiki unintentionally paved the way for Oyama's victory when they struggled to 75 and 74 respectively. Kaori Aoyama was the runner-up at 208.

Promise Ladies
Kato, Hyogo
Winner: Saiki Fujita

Saiki Fujita, one of the Japan LPGA Tour's bevy of young standouts, scored her first victory in 2006 in the Promise Ladies. A year later, Fujita, now 21, staged a nearly identical performance in the same tournament to register her second career victory, just as in the first via a one-hole playoff. In accomplishing the unusual feat, she became the first successful title defender of the season.

Fujita reached the playoff in virtually the same circumstances this time, again blowing a lead. The second-round pacesetter by two strokes in 2006, she carried a four-shot margin into the final round a year later. Fujita had started with a four-under-par 68 and a two-stroke lead and doubled the margin Saturday with 69–137 over Miki Saiki (70-71), Akiko Fukushima (73-68) and Momoko Ueda (72-69).

Ueda turned into the lone challenger Sunday on a very wet Madame J Golf Club course at Kato, Hyogo Prefecture. Fujita not only lost her entire lead but had to birdie the final hole for 73 to bring about the playoff, as Ueda finished with 69 and her 210. A par ended the overtime in Fujita's favor when Ueda three-putted for bogey and settled for her second runner-up finish of the year.

Belluna Ladies Cup
Kanra, Gunma
Winner: Akiko Fukushima

Advancing years have had minimal effect on the game of Akiko Fukushima. At 34 the eldest member of the top echelon of mostly young players on the Japan LPGA Tour, Fukushima continues to contend and win on the circuit. Since her banner six-victory season in 1997, Fukushima has failed to notch at least one win in just three years. She added No. 20 the first of July with a two-stroke triumph in the Belluna Ladies Cup tournament to go with the two wins she scored while playing on the LPGA Tour in America in earlier years.

Fukushima's six-under-par 66 in the second round was the springboard to her victory at Kanra's Obatago Golf Club. The six-birdie round came a day after a brilliant performance by 17-year-old Kumiko Kaneda, who has been winning national and world junior and amateur titles since she was eight and tied for fourth in the 2006 Nichirei Ladies. Kaneda fired a flawless, nine-birdie 63 to seize a three-stroke lead over Na Zhang and Mayumi Ishii.

Then came Fukushima's 66 for 135 that gave her a one-stroke advantage over Young-Me Lee and two over Kaneda, who slipped to 74 Saturday. Fukushima was a bit shaky Sunday, but her four-birdie, three-bogey 71 and 206 total gave her the two-shot victory over South Korea's Eun-Hye Lee (69) and veteran Michiko Hattori (70). Kaneda (72) tied for fourth at 209.

Meiji Chocolate Cup
Kitahiroshima, Hokkaido
Winner: Shiho Oyama

None the worse for wear after a quick trip to America and a very respectable 14th-place finish in the U.S. Women's Open, Shiho Oyama further enhanced her mid-season spurt in defense of her money title. She grabbed her second victory in three weeks, going wire to wire in a two-stroke triumph in the Meiji Chocolate Cup tournament.

Showing no signs of jet lag after flying into Hokkaido from the U.S. for the tournament on the Shimamatsu course of Sapporo International Country Club, Oyama began her march to victory with a fine, six-under-par 66, taking a two-stroke lead over Yukari Baba. She remained two in front Saturday with 72 in an erratic round that included five birdies and five bogeys. Mikiyo Nishizuka moved into second place with 69–140 as Baba shot 74 for 142.

Oyama had a scare Sunday when she double-bogeyed the third hole, but recovered with two quick birdies, nursed a one-shot lead in the stretch before extending the margin to two with a birdie at the par-five 18th for 71 and 209 total. Nishizuka also closed with 71 and tied for second at 211 with Shinobu Moromizato (67). The win was Oyama's 10th in her seven years on tour.

Stanley Ladies
Susono, Shizuoka
Winner: Momoko Ueda

With the kind of season Momoko Ueda had in 2007, she seems certain to sport a very gaudy record when her playing days are over. Certainly the strangest entry of her career will be her win in the water-soaked Stanley Ladies in mid-July amid a typhoon that raked Shizuoka Prefecture. Her winning score was 106 and she had to come out on top in a three-way makeshift playoff to get that 27-hole victory.

The tournament was in trouble from the start. It rained steadily all day Friday, but not enough water accumulated to delay or postpone play. When the damp round ended, six players shared the lead at 69 — Sakura Yokomine, Miho Koga, Hiromi Mogi, Junko Omote, Mai Arai and Shiho Oyama, coming off her Meiji Chocolate Cup win the previous Sunday. Four others shot 70 and Ueda had a 71.

The weather worsened Saturday and tournament officials decided to have the entire field play nine holes on the back nine of Tomei Country Club. Ueda and Chie Arimura had 35s and Yokomine 37 for 106 totals to lead, and when normal play proved impossible, a three-hole playoff among the three leaders was staged. Yokomine was eliminated, then Ueda won her third 2007 title with a birdie on the sudden-death hole that followed.

Kracie Philanthropy Japan LPGA Players Championship
Inzai, Chiba
Winner: Na Zhang

Na Zhang passed another test in the Kracie Philanthropy Japan LPGA Players Championship. Zhang, China's first female professional golfer to win in Japan, further embellished her playing reputation when she survived adversity and pulled out her second victory in the season's first major championship.

Armed with a five-stroke lead entering the final round and breezing toward victory, Zhang tripped at the 15th hole, four-putting for a triple bogey. She limped home to a 75 and 286 total, dropping into a tie with Sakura Yokomine, who finished with 70 for her 286. "I was very, very nervous today," admitted the Chinese player. "But somehow I managed to calm down for the playoff." She holed a 15-foot birdie putt on the par-five 18th for the win as Yokomine lost in a playoff for the second straight week.

Zhang kept herself within range during the first two rounds at Narashino Country Club's par-73 King/Queen course as a tour rookie and then a long-suffering veteran held the leads. Kaori Aoyama, fresh from the college ranks (Kyushu Tokia University), shot 67 Thursday to lead five players including Na by one, then gave way to 38-year-old Yuka Irie (71-69–140), who is winless since 1998. Then Zhang, sitting at 143, leaped to her five-stroke margin over Yokomine and three others Saturday with 68–211 before the eventful final round.

AXA Ladies
Tomakomai, Hokkaido
Winner: Na Zhang

Na Zhang became the season's third three-time winner when she won for the second straight week in the AXA Ladies tournament. The Chinese player, who won the previous week's LPGA Players Championship, squeezed out a one-stroke victory in a tight finish on the South course of Tomakomai Golf Resort 72 Emina Golf Club. She joined Mi-Jeong Jeon and Momoko Ueda, who also had three victories on their 2007 record.

For the second week in a row, a tour rookie essayed the first-round lead. South Korea's Bo-Bae Song shot 67 Friday and led Zhang and Yuka Tonsho by a stroke, then yielded first place to Zhang Saturday as the Chinese pro had a birdie on each nine and posted a 70–138 while Song was registering 72–139.

Mayumi Shimomura, who was in a five-player group three shots off the pace, gave Zhang a run for her money Sunday, but her 69–210 left her a stroke short, and Zhang shot 71 for the winning 209. "I went on the course going for par on every hole," she said, and it paid off — barely.

Crystal Geyser Ladies
Chiba
Winner: Hiromi Mogi

Hiromi Mogi ended a three-year dry spell in early August when she captured the Crystal Geyser Ladies title at Chiba's Keiyo Country Club. A strong finish on the final holes gave Mogi a seven-under-par 65 and a four-stroke victory. Her two previous wins came in the Resort Trust and Munsingwear Tokai tournaments in 2004. It was the only time in an eight-tournament stretch that a player scored her first win of 2007.

The lead bounced around throughout the weekend. Akane Iijima, whose lone tour win came in her sophomore 2006 season, shared the lead at 67 with South Korean Eun-Hye Lee the first day. In contrast, both shot 77s Saturday to disappear from contention. Instead, first place wound up in the joint hands of Mie Nakata, Taiwan's Hsiu-Feng Tseng, Hiroko Yamaguchi and Mogi, all at 141. Na Zhang, trying to match Mi-Jeong Jeon's three-in-a-row record feat earlier in the year, was just a stroke off the lead after a pair of 71s.

It was not to be for the streaking Zhang. She faded to 73 as Mogi picked up the victory, gaining four shots on three holes of the final nine. Australian Nikki Campbell (67) and Nakata (69) tied for the runner-up slot at 210.

NEC Karuizawa 72
Karuizawa, Nagano
Winner: Akiko Fukushima

If there truly are "horses for courses," Akiko Fukushima is a steed indeed when the Japan LPGA Tour reaches Nagano Prefecture for its annual event on Karuizawa 72 Golf's North course. Three of the 20 victories on her impressive record on the circuit came on that course — in 1996, 2002 and 2003 — and she added a fourth in 2007 in runaway fashion.

Fukushima was never out of the lead this time around as she added No. 21, her second win of the season. The victor in the Belluna Cup six weeks earlier, she started the NEC event with a six-under-par 66 and shared the first-round lead with Mihoko Takahashi. The second round was decisive. Missing only one green and cranking out six birdies, Fukushima put together another 66 and opened a four-stroke lead over Akane Iijima, Momoko Ueda and American star Paula Creamer, who won the tournament in 2005 when she was 19 and only months out of high school.

Fukushima finished with a flourish Sunday. Her 67, one of the day's two lowest rounds, established her 17-under-par 199 winning score, the lowest 54-hole total of the season, and a seven-shot margin over Namika Omata (68) as Ueda (71) tied for third, Creamer (72) finished fifth and Iijima faded to 74–210.

Shin Caterpillar Mitsubishi Ladies
Hakone, Kanagawa
Winner: Sakura Yokomine

The list of multiple winners continued to grow at the Shin Caterpillar Mitsubishi Ladies tournament as Sakura Yokomine, the brilliant 21-year-old, became the sixth player with more than a single victory during the season.

Yokomine, enjoying much the same kind of early career that Ai Miyazato fashioned before electing to further her fortunes in America, never trailed on the par-73 Daihakone Country Club course, but had to fend off a late charge by Shiho Oyama to preserve a two-stroke victory. Yokomine had won her sixth title in May in the Chukyo TV Bridgestone, and with this win registered her eighth top-five finish in 14 starts.

After co-leading the tournament with Akane Iijima at 67 the first day, Yokomine jumped four strokes in front Saturday with another 67. Miki Saiki, the Fujisankei winner, was at 68-70–138. Iijima, with 72, dropped five off the pace, and Oyama was then seven back at 68-73–141. Yokomine managed just a one-under-par 72 Sunday, but that was good enough for the two-shot final margin over Oyama and her 67–208. Akiko Fukushima, fresh from her NEC win the previous Sunday, took third with 210.

Yonex Ladies
Nagaoka, Niigata
Winner: Yuri Fudoh

What better place for Yuri Fudoh to try to make it clear that she was determined to regain the No. 1 ranking on the Japan LPGA Tour that she held for six straight years before being dethroned in 2006 by Shiho Oyama? Twice earlier in her storied career Fudoh had won the Yonex Ladies tournament, so a third victory at Yonex Country Club in Niigata Prefecture seemed very doable.

And it did prove so, although it required a brave birdie on the 54th hole for Fudoh to stay ahead of Momoko Ueda and capture her second win of the season and 42nd in her brilliant 12-year career.

Fudoh led from the start, opening the tournament with an eight-birdie, seven-under-par 65 to stake a two-stroke lead over Hiromi Sato and amateur Mika Miyazato. Despite a so-so 70 on Saturday, Fudoh extended her margin to three strokes over Ueda and Miki Saiki, who both had 70-68 rounds. Ueda, with a playoff win over Fudoh among her three 2007 victories, seemed the bigger threat — and was.

Fudoh saw her three-stroke edge dwindle precipitously to one at the 53rd hole Sunday when a ball in the water cost her a double bogey. But she responded with the birdie at the 18th hole to preserve her one-stroke margin and win the title with 69 for 204 total. Ueda shot 67 for her 205.

Golf 5 Ladies
Bibai, Hokkaido
Winner: Akane Iijima

An early-season victory in just her second year on tour in 2006 showed the promise of Akane Iijima, but it took well over another season before she verified her credentials with another triumph. That second victory came the hard way in the Golf 5 Ladies tournament on the Bibai course of Alpen Golf Club on Hokkaido as the talented Sakura Yokomine, the first-round leader, took Iijima to overtime before suffering her third playoff loss of the season.

Those two players sat only a stroke off the lead after 36 holes, their 137s leaving them a shot behind South Korea's Bo-Bae Song, who shot 69-67–136. Yokomine had rounds of 67 (as the first-round leader) and 70, while Iijima bounced back from an opening 72 with a sparkling 65.

They both managed 69s Sunday and their 206 totals meant a playoff as Song struggled to a 73 and dropped into a tie for fourth place with Hiroko Yamaguchi. Shinobu Moromizato shot 70 for 208 to take third place. The playoff ended at the fourth extra hole when Yokomine failed to save par.

Japan LPGA Championship Konica Minolta Cup
Akitakata, Hiroshima
Winner: Akane Iijima

Akane Iijima picked a fine time to come up with a hot hand. Riding the momentum of her playoff victory in the Golf 5 Ladies, Iijima followed with another win the next week, this one the major Japan LPGA Championship Konica Minolta Cup, just the fourth 72-hole event on the schedule.

Again, she forced Sakura Yokomine to settle for second place, but this runner-up finish was not as suspenseful as was the four-hole Golf 5 playoff. Iijima won the LPGA Championship by four strokes, shooting a final-round 68 for her 14-under-par 274 as she became the tour's eighth multiple winner of the season.

Ayako Uehara held the lead for two rounds, sharing the top spot with Erina Hara and Yuriko Ohtsuka at 68 the first day, then moving a stroke in front by herself Friday with 70–138. Iijima (71-68) and Yokomine (69-70) were a shot back with Michie Ohba (70-69). Iijima then went in front to stay Saturday. Sparked by a string of three birdies on the front nine, she produced a 67 for 206 and a two-stroke lead over Yokomine (69), with Yuri Fudoh and Miki Saiki another two back. Sunday proved a breeze. Hyun-Ju Shin was next behind runner-up Yokomine, but a 67 only put her seven shots shy of the winner.

Munsingwear Ladies Tokai Classic
Mihama, Aichi
Winner: Na Zhang

Na Zhang's sensational season in Japan continued in the Munsingwear Ladies Tokai Classic in mid-September as she stormed from six strokes off the lead to capture her fourth victory of the season, just three months after landing her first title. The Chinese pro, the first-ever winner from her country in Japan, was the first four-time victor of the season.

After 36 holes, the focus on the Mihama course of Minami Aichi Country Club was on Akane Iijima, who was well on her way to a third consecutive win. Iijima, who took the Golf 5 and Japan LPGA Championship the two previous weeks, had executed a seven-shot swing in the second round. She was four strokes behind the first-round leader, winless veteran Nobuko Kizawa's 65, but shot 67 Saturday and bolted three strokes in front with her 136.

The bubble burst for Iijima Sunday. Her game unraveled to a 78, opening the door in particular to Momoko Ueda and Kizawa, who were at 139 and the only ones within five shots of the leader. Ueda led by two after she birdied the 14th hole, but bogeyed two holes on the way home. Zhang, who had charged into contention with three early birdies, racked up two more on the 15th and 18th holes to acquire the title.

Miyagi TV Cup Dunlop Ladies Open
Rifu, Miyagi
Winner: Yuko Mitsuka

It had been a long dry spell for non-winners. Three months after China's Na Zhang began her run of victories, rookie Yuko Mitsuka broke the ice and became the fifth new face in the winner's circle at the Miyagi TV Cup Dunlop Ladies Open.

Mitsuka carried a one-stroke lead into the final round and admitted afterward to be somewhat of a basket case through those last 18 holes. "I have been too nervous to sleep and eat well since last night and I can't even remember how I played all day," she confessed after posting a one-stroke victory over Tomoko Kusakabe with her eight-under-par 208 total at Rifu Golf Club in Miyagi Prefecture.

What happened was that she maintained her lead with two birdies and a bogey on the front nine and held off Kusakabe, the only real challenger, with nine pars on the back nine for a 71. Kusakabe shot 70 for 209. Sakura Yokomine made another of her many strong showings, finishing third with 72–211. She and money leader Momoko Ueda had been poised to test the untried Mitsuka Sunday, Ueda just one back at 138 and Yokomine two behind with Kusakabe at 139 after Mitsuka seized first place from Yun-Joo Jeong (67) Saturday. Ueda had an uncharacteristic 76 Sunday.

Japan Women's Open
Tomakomai, Hokkaido
Winner: Shinobu Moromizato

Things had been looking up for Shinobu Moromizato since she returned from an unsuccessful foray on the U.S. LPGA Tour in 2006. The now 21-year-old won her first tournament, the Sankyo Open, shortly thereafter in the fall, was in the top 10 with two seconds in her first 24 starts in 2007, and capped it all with her triumph in the prestige-laden Japan Women's Open.

The tiny (5-ft-2) Moromizato had the lead through the final three rounds of the Open, but had to contend with the likes of Yuri Fudoh on the final holes at Tarumae Country Club in Hokkaido before posting a one-stroke victory with her six-under-par 282 total.

Moromizato took first place away from first-round leader Akane Iijima with her second straight 69 Friday, jumping to a four-shot lead over Fudoh and Miho Koga. Fudoh, seeking her second Women's Open title, trimmed a stroke off the margin with a 70 to Moromizato's 71–209 Saturday, with defending champion Jeong Jang sitting another shot back with Miki Saiki.

It all came down to the last two holes. Moromizato got some breathing room when Fudoh bogeyed the 17th and dropped two behind. But an errant tee shot led to a Moromizato bogey at the par-five 18th, where Fudoh missed her birdie putt for a tie. The winner shot 73, the runner-up 71. Australia's Nikki Campbell made a run with 68 and finished third at 284.

Sankyo Ladies Open
Kiryu, Gunma
Winner: So-Hee Kim

It would be hard to imagine a more spectacular way to win one's first tournament than the way it happened in the Sankyo Ladies Open in early October. So-Hee Kim acquired her first title on the Japan LPGA Tour by coming from four strokes off the pace in the final round with a fine 68 to become a part of a three-way deadlock, then holed a 50-foot birdie putt on the first extra hole.

The 24-year-old South Korean, playing in Japan in her initial season, became the sixth first-time winner of the year and the second from her country to join those ranks in 2007.

Chie Arimura, another winless rookie whose seven top-10 finishes included her playoff loss to Momoko Ueda in the Stanley Ladies, started well in the Sankyo at Akagi Country Club in Gunma Prefecture, shooting 68 to join veterans Midori Yoneyama and Michie Ohba. Erina Hara, another first-season player, took over in the second round, her 70-67 giving her a one-shot lead on Ohba (70) and Mi-Jeong Jeon, the three-time winner earlier in the year.

None of them were around at the finish. Mihoko Takahashi shot 69 for her tying 209, and the ever-present Ueda made it a threesome with her

70–209. Ueda ruined her chances in the playoff with a ball in a pond, and Takahashi missed a shorter birdie putt after Kim's monster dropped.

Fujitsu Ladies
Chiba
Winner: Sakura Yokomine

As brilliant as she was during her second season on the Japan LPGA Tour, Momoko Ueda will not be without regrets when she reflects on how much more spectacular it would have been had she been a better playoff performer. After defeating Yuri Fudoh in an early-season overtime duel, Ueda fell the next three times she went extra holes. The third playoff loss came in the Fujitsu Ladies after she wound up in a 54-hole deadlock with Sakura Yokomine, her closest pursuer in the race for the year's money title and No. 1 ranking. Just the week before in the Sankyo playoff, Ueda sank her chances with a ball in the water.

Ueda had a piece of first place from the first round of the Fujitsu Ladies until Yokomine prevailed on the second hole of the playoff. She shared the lead with Akane Iijima and Ji-Hee Lee at 68 the first day when the big noise was Lee's three-under-par albatross on the par-five seventh hole at the Tokyu Seven Hundred Club course, where she holed a 203-yard five-wood shot for the two. It was just the seventh recorded albatross in tour history. Lee remained neck and neck with Ueda Saturday when both shot 69s for 137. Yokomine, who had opened with 72, moved close with a 66, joining Yun-Joo Jeong at 138.

Then, on Sunday, Yokomine overtook Ueda, shooting 69 to Ueda's 70 for nine-under-par 207 totals to force the playoff.

Masters Golf Club Ladies
Miki, Hyogo
Winner: Miho Koga

American star Paula Creamer and Japan's Miho Koga seem to have a particular affinity for the fairways and greens of the Masters Golf Club in Miki. The two exchanged victories in 2005 and 2006, then finished one-two in 2007 when Koga pulled away in the final round to a four-stroke victory in defense of her title. It was the second repeat of the season, Saiki Fujita having won her second straight Promise Ladies crown in June.

Bouncing back from her playoff loss the previous Sunday, the ever-present Momoko Ueda was in the mix again. She fired a 68 in the first round, matching Creamer's start, then inched a stroke in front of Creamer and Koga Saturday, though shooting a mere par 72. Creamer shot 73 and Koga 69 for their 141s.

The 25-year-old Koga sewed up her first win of the season with a blazing, final-round 66 that consisted of seven birdies and a lone bogey at the ninth hole. That gave her a final nine-under-par 207 and the four-stroke margin over Creamer, who closed with a 70–211. Rookie Mayu Hattori was another shot back after a 68, and Sakura Yokomine took fourth with 71–213. Ueda fell into a sixth-place tie when she shot 76 Sunday.

Hisako Higuchi IDC Otsuka Ladies
Hanno, Saitama
Winner: Mi-Jeong Jeon

Mi-Jeong Jeon embellished the reputation she has built over two seasons as the No. 1 South Korean on the Japan LPGA Tour when she added the Hisako Higuchi IDC Otsuka Ladies, her fourth title of the 2007 season, to the three victories that spurred her to the runner-up position on the 2006 money list. Jeon joined Na Zhang as a four-time winner of the year, but both still trailed rankings leader Momoko Ueda, who took a rare week off.

The 24-year-old South Korean hovered just off the lead through the first two rounds at the Musashigaoka golf course in Hanno, Saitama Prefecture. Compatriot Ji-Hyun Lee topped the field with 68 the first day, as Jeon, Miho Koga and Australians Tamie Durdin and Nikki Campbell shot 69. Heavy rains spawned by a neighboring typhoon hiked the scores Saturday, and Koga's two-under-par 70 for 139 before the worst of the weather gave her a two-stroke lead over Jeon, Lee and Yun-Joo Jeong.

Jeon moved in front early Sunday with a chip-in eagle at the first hole and a birdie at the sixth, built the lead to two with another birdie at the 11th, and offset a bogey at the 16th with a birdie at the 18th for 69 and the winning 210 total. She finished one shot ahead of Koga (72), who was gunning for her second straight victory.

Mizuno Classic
Shima, Mie
Winner: Momoko Ueda

Momoko Ueda made the strongest statement of her young career in early November when the Japan LPGA blended with the U.S. LPGA Tour for the Mizuno Classic, the richest women's event in the country. Competing in a tournament that Annika Sorenstam won five straight times, that Karrie Webb won in 2006 and that a Japanese player had not won in a decade, Ueda fired a sparkling final-round 66 to score a two-stroke victory over LPGA regulars Reilley Rankin and Maria Hjorth, the 1999 Mizuno victor.

The triumph, Ueda's fourth of the season, and its ¥23 million prize solidified Ueda's bid for the money title.

England's veteran star Laura Davies had her game going through much of the first two rounds. She rolled in seven birdie putts the first day for 65, leading Rankin and Chie Arimura by a stroke, and seemed likely to retain first place in the second round until a mental mistake cost her a two-stroke penalty at the 14th hole. Davies putted from the wrong spot after moving her marker out of another player's line. Instead of at worst a 70, she posted a 72 and was tied for the lead with Ueda at 137 after Ueda shot 67.

The season's second albatross — a two at the par-five seventh hole

— actually made the difference for Ueda, although her battle with Hjorth and Rankin remained until Ueda birdied the 16th and Hjorth bogeyed the 18th to establish the final margin.

Itoen Ladies
Chonan, Chiba
Winner: Rui Kitada

It took a young Rui Kitada three years to become a winner on the Japan LPGA Tour and in that 2004 season she did it in style with three victories. Yet almost three years passed before Kitada, now 25, came out on top again. She achieved that fourth career win the hard way — in a three-player playoff in the Itoen Ladies at Great Island Club at Chonan, Chiba Prefecture.

Kitada had the lead after 36 holes with rounds of 69 and 70, slipping ahead of Hiromi Mogi (72-68) and Australian Tamie Durdin (67-73) by a stroke. Durdin was in front after the first 18, her 67 giving her a one-stroke lead over veterans Akiko Fukushima, a two-time winner in 2007, and Laura Davies, rebounding from a failed title shot the previous week in the Mizuno Classic.

Miki Saiki, the 22-year-old tour rookie who won the early-season Fuji-sankei Classic, surged in front in the early going Sunday, but let a win get away from her when she bogeyed the last two holes for 69. She dropped into the three-way tie with Kitada, who managed only a par 72 for her 211, and Mogi, who shot 71. Saiki dropped out of the playoff when she bogeyed the first extra hole, and Kitada won with a par when Mogi missed her par putt at the next hole.

Daioseishi Elleair Ladies Open
Mitoyo, Kagawa
Winner: Momoko Ueda

The splendid season of Momoko Ueda climaxed in impressive fashion at the Daioseishi Elleair Ladies Open in mid-November. Ueda clinched the money title with a wire-to-wire victory that was her fifth of the season. The ¥16.2 million prize put her out of reach as the No. 1 winner of the year, and at age 21, she was the youngest in the history of the tour in its current form.

Ueda showed her strong game right from the start at the Elleair Golf Club in Kagawa Prefecture. She birdied four of the first five holes en route to a 66 and a two-stroke lead over four-time winner Na Zhang of China and Ayako Uehara. She gave a stroke back Saturday, her 71–137 leaving her just a shot ahead of Hiromi Mogi and Erina Hara.

High winds raked the course Sunday, and in the end only runner-up Yui Kawahara broke 70, but her 69 merely lodged her in a four-way tie for second place at 212 with Mikiyo Nishizuka, Shinobu Moromizato and Hara. Ueda settled for a par 72 and her seven-under-par 209 total gave her a three-shot final margin. Hara shot 74 and Mogi 75. Yokomine, the nearest challenger to Ueda on the money list, wound up in a six-way tie for sixth place as her slim hopes to catch Ueda died.

Japan LPGA Tour Championship Ricoh Cup
Sadohara, Miyazaki
Winner: Miho Koga

Like everybody else on the Japan LPGA Tour, Miho Koga has great respect for the talents of Yuri Fudoh. "The five-stroke deficit at the start (of the fourth round of the Japan LPGA Tour Championship Ricoh Cup) felt more like 10 strokes," she said of what she faced in the season finale at Miyazaki Country Club. But, as was illustrated a couple of times earlier in what was still a good season for her by most standards, Fudoh is no longer a sure thing when she has a lead or is in strong contention.

This time, the 30-year-old winner of 42 events on the tour let another victory escape her as Koga overcame Fudoh's five-stroke advantage and scored a two-shot triumph, her second of the season and seventh of her career. She shot a 67–275 to Fudoh's 74–277.

Fudoh seemingly had everything going for her for three days. On opening day, she ran off an eagle and five birdies for 65 and a four-stroke lead over Shiho Oyama and Midori Yoneyama. Then it became six on Friday over Momoko Ueda, her successor once removed as No. 1 on the money list. Both shot 69s. Then another 69 gave Fudoh 203 and her five-shot margin over Koga, who blazed a 66 that day and the winning 67 Sunday. Koga caught up quickly with a string of three early birdies while Fudoh was struggling with two bogeys. The two outdistanced the rest of the field, so much so that Bo-Bae Song finished third although six behind Fudoh at the end.

Ueda finished fifth at 285, 10 strokes behind the winner.

The Kyoraku Cup
Asakura, Fukuoka
Winner: Japan

Japan brought The Kyoraku Cup post-season series record close to even with a narrow victory over South Korea in the annual inter-nation event in September, thanks primarily to solid singles play of the country's young stars. The victory at Fukuoka Century Golf Club was Japan's third against four losses and a tie.

The South Koreans produced a 13-11 record in the second and final round to even the competition at 24. Miho Koga then picked up the winning points in the subsequent playoff against Jeong Jang. Her par at the third extra hole proved the winner when Jang missed a par-saving putt.

Sakura Yokomine, Shinobu Moromizato and Miki Saiki, all relative youngsters, scored vital wins for Japan, while Hyun-Ju Shin and Mi Hyun Kim contributed victories for South Korea in Sunday's final round.

Korea LPGA Tour

Although little noticed on the world scene, the most extensive success story of 2007 was played out on the Korea LPGA Tour. Nineteen-year-old Ji-Yai Shin, in just her second professional season, overwhelmed the opposition with nine victories and two second-place finishes in her 18 starts on the circuit's 20-event schedule. Shin had signaled her talent with two wins, five seconds and a third in her initial 15-tournament 2006 season in Korea. Actually, her career win total is 13, since she twice captured the Orient China Ladies Open against an international field in Xiamen, China. She rolled to an easy, five-stroke win there in December with a closing 67.

Her 2007 victories on the KLPGA Tour ranged from a playoff against Jenny Lee in the MC Square Cup to other five-shot breezes in the SK Energy Invitational and the Interburgo Masters. In the playoff in the third event of the season, Shin came from seven shots back with a 67 to catch Lee (74), then birdied the first extra hole. That win launched this subsequent run of victories:

Hill State SeoKyung — Final-round 66 overcame a three-stroke 36-hole deficit for a one-stroke victory (204) over Eun Hee Ji.

BC Card Classic — Final-round 67 made up two shots in the final round for one-stroke victory (204) over Ji Yeon Woo.

KB Star Tour in Pohang — Another closing 66 brought a two-stroke win with 16-under-par 200. Eun Hee Ji again finished second.

KB Star Tour in Chungcheong — Scores of 69-65 led to another two-shot triumph when the tour resumed action after a two-month summer hiatus. Na Yeo Choi was the runner-up in the weather-shortened 36-hole tournament.

SK Energy Invitational — Twelve-under-par 204 provided a five-stroke victory over Hee Young Park and Jin Joo Hong.

Samsung Finance Championship — Final-round 65–210 of Hyun Hee Moon came up two shots short of Shin's 71-67-70–208.

Interburgo Masters — Shin broke away to her five-stroke win with a final-round 67–210. Na Yeo Choi was again second.

ADT CAPS Championship — Shin opened with 74, six strokes off the pace, and won by three with subsequent rounds of 69 and 68 for 211. Sun Wook Lim, the leader by four after 36 holes, shot 75 in the last round to finish in second place.

Shin's huge season overshadowed the performances of Sun Ju Ahn and Eun Hee Ji, the year's two other multiple winners. In fact, though, those three players won all but one of the first 12 tournaments through late September.

Ahn, just 20, scored three victories, highlighted by her four-stroke, four-under-par 212 triumph in the Taeyoung Cup Korea Women's Open. She also posted one-shot wins in the KB Star in Busan and Art Village Open. American star Cristie Kerr again played in the Women's Open and was a runner-up for a second year in a row, tied for second with Ji and Jae Eun Chung.

Ji had a fine season that could have been even better. Besides her back-to-back, early-year victories in the Phoenix Park Classic and KB Star Tour in Hampyung, she finished second eight times during the year. Hee Young Park lost twice to Ji, by one in the Phoenix Park and in a playoff at Hampyung.

One of Ji's second-place finishes came in the Hana Bank-Kolon Championship when the U.S. LPGA Tour began its three-week visit to Asia at Gyeongju. She was sitting just a stroke off the lead when high winds created unplayable conditions at the Mauna Ocean Resort Sunday, forcing cancellation of the final round. The beneficiary was Norway's Suzann Pettersen, who was the leader with 69-72–141 after 36 holes. It was the fourth LPGA victory for the Solheim Cup player, the first non-Korean winner in the six-year history of the Kolon Championship. Lorena Ochoa, the female golfer of the year, placed 16th.

The Korea circuit's other 2007 winners were:

Asia Miles Binhai Ladies Open — Da Ye Na, by two over four others.

Shinsegye Cup KLPGA Championship — Na Yeon Choi, by three over Ji. She led by one after 36 holes and shot a final-round 68.

Hite Cup Ladies Championship — Hye Jung Choi, by one over Ji.

KB Star Tour in Seoul — Young Ran Jo, by one despite a final-round 74 in the only 72-hole tournament of the season.

MBC Tour — Ji Na Lim, by five over Shin on the strength of an opening 65.

What makes Shin's success so heartwarming is how, a humble, self-effacing young lady, she overcame tragedy in her teen years. The daughter of a lay preacher, she lost her mother in an auto accident and nursed her brother and sister back to health from serious injuries.

She has high ambitions, too. After winning her second China Open, she said her goal was to qualify for the LPGA Tour in America and follow in the footsteps of Se Ri Pak and other Korean women who have enjoyed success internationally.

Australian Ladies Tour

MFS Women's Australian Open
Sydney, New South Wales
Winner: Karrie Webb

After winning five times in 2006 and moving back up to No. 3 in the Rolex Rankings, Karrie Webb made the perfect start to her new season. With the MFS Women's Australian Open back on the schedule for the first time since 2004, Webb wasted no time in claiming her first win of the year and collected the Patricia Bridges Bowl for the third time after her victories in 1999 and 2000.

It was the 45th victory of Webb's career and she cruised to a six-stroke winning margin with a final round of 72 for 278 total. A 67 on the first day left her one behind leader Sarah Kemp, but then Webb went in front with 71, before extending her advantage to four shots after a third round of 68. Webb finished at 10 under par after two late dropped shots. Taiwan's Yun-Jye Wei was her closest pursuer over the weekend, but slipped further back coming home for a closing 74. Spain's Paula Marti and Finland's Minea Blomqvist shared third place at two under, while the only other players to finish under par at Royal Sydney were America's Brittany Lincicome and South Korea's Ji-Yai Shin.

ANZ Ladies Masters
Ashmore, Queensland
Winner: Karrie Webb

Karrie Webb completed her second victory in successive weeks with an inspired performance over the weekend at Royal Pines. Webb broke her own course record by one stroke with a 10-under-par 62 in the third round, and then the following day sealed her sixth victory in the ANZ Ladies Masters. She had previously won the event on Queensland's Gold Coast four times in a row from 1998 and also in 2005. It was the third time she had completed the double of winning the Australian Open and the Masters.

Webb was seven shots behind halfway leader Sun Ju Ahn when she peeled off 10 birdies in the third round, including at the 16th and 17th holes, before saving par from a greenside bunker at the 18th. "It was one of those days where it felt as though the hole was as big as a bucket," said Webb. "I think I could have putted with my eyes shut and it would have gone in."

Webb, sharing the lead after three rounds with Michelle Ellis, went to the turn on Sunday in 31 to gain a four-shot advantage. Her last nine was not without incident. She was given a one-shot penalty for marking her hole on the fringe at the 10th hole and missed short putts for par at the last two holes. A closing 68 gave her a total of 269, 19 under par, and a three-stroke win over South Korea's Ji-Yai Shin.

Lexus Cup
Perth, Western Australia
Winner: Asia

Team Asia rode a first-round shutout to an easy victory of 15-to-9 and successful defense of the Lexus Cup against a strong Team International as the women's event was staged for the first time in Perth, Australia, the second week of December, after its initial two were played in Singapore. The Internationals won the inaugural event in 2005.

Three players from South Korea among the nine on the team. Jee Young Lee, In-Kyung Kim and Seon Hwa Lee won all three of their matches to lead the way for Team Asia at The Vines Resort and Country Club. Although all six foursomes matches reached at least the 16th hole, Asia swept all of them in Friday's first round. The Internationals fared better Saturday in the fourball competition, but slipped farther behind in getting only two-and-a-half of the six points. Facing the daunting task of needing to win nine of the 11 singles matches Sunday, each team got a pre-determined half point when Suzann Pettersen couldn't play because of a back injury. The Internationals got early wins from captain Annika Sorenstam and Angela Park. The Asians then closed it out by winning the next three matches.

Ladies African Tour

Women's World Cup of Golf
Sun City, South Africa
Winners: Paraguay (Julieta Granada and Celeste Troche)

Paraguay, not of one the game's biggest nations, won the Women's World Cup of Golf at their first attempt thanks to the superb partnership of Julieta Granada and Celeste Troche. It was a comprehensive victory, leading from the first day and winning by seven strokes ahead of the American combination of Juli Inkster and Pat Hurst.

Paraguay led by four strokes after the first day when both players' scores counted, Granada scoring 70 at the Gary Player Country Club and Troche matching the best round of the day with 69. They maintained their advantage despite a foursome score of 75 on the second day, but closed superbly with a fourball better-ball score of 65.

They did not get off to the best start on the final day as both players made a bogey at the first hole, but then they added eight birdies, including at the last two holes. Troche chipped in at the 17th and then made a four at the 18th as Paraguay finished at nine-under-par 279 total, although by then they were out of sight of the competition.

The United States, 10 strokes behind after the first day, rallied with a better-ball score of 67 to finish second at two-under-par 286, one stroke ahead of South Korea, whose Young Kim and Ji-Yai Shin also closed with 67. The Italian pair of Veronica Zorzi and Giulia Sergas slipped back to a tie for fourth place with Scots Janice Moodie and Mhairi McKay.

Despite finishing second in 2006, Scotland was not automatically exempt, because both Moodie and Catriona Matthew took time out during the year to have babies. But they got in when the Philippines dropped out the week before, with Moodie playing her first event since September.

For Granada this was a second huge win in a row, as the 20-year-old had finished the 2006 season by winning $1 million at the ADT Championship. "I like winning," she said. Granada had spent her rookie season trying to improve her ranking to make sure Paraguay qualified for the World Cup.

Her partner, the 25-year-old Troche, failed to earn full status on the LPGA Tour and was considering her future. "To win this is a great feeling because I have been struggling. I've been wondering what I should do with my life and whether I should continue playing golf, and this week gave me the answer," she said.

Pam Golding Ladies International
Johannesburg, South Africa
Winner: Lee-Anne Pace

Lee-Anne Pace won the Pam Golding Ladies International, the inaugural event on the renamed Ladies African Tour, for her first victory as a professional. The 26-year-old South African turned professional in 2005 and played on the Duramed Futures Tour in America in 2006, finishing 30th on the money list, before earning her card on the European Tour and non-exempt status on the LPGA circuit for 2007.

Her win at Dainfern Country Club in Johannesburg was the perfect start to the season. She took the lead with rounds of 69 and 67 and closed with a one-under 72 for an 11-under-par 208 total. Pace won by a stroke over Denmark's Julie Tvede, who finished with 71, and by three shots over Eleanor Pilgrim of Wales, who rose to third place with a closing 69. Stacy Bregman had a disappointing final round of 75 to tie for fourth place with England's Rebecca Hudson and Kiran Matharu.

"It feels great. But it had to take a second or two to actually sink in," Pace said. "I wanted to win a tournament, especially in South Africa. Coming back here you almost have to prove yourself, so I'm very happy." Pace said her goal was to force her way into the South African World Cup team for 2008.

WPGA Masters
Pretoria, South Africa
Winner: Kaisa Ruuttila

Finland's Kaisa Ruuttila, ninth the previous week at Dainfern, triumphed in only her second tournament as a professional when she won the WPGA Masters at Waterkloof Golf Club in Pretoria. The 23-year-old from Turku, on a brief fly-in holiday from her studies, finished impressively with a final round of 69 to win by three strokes over Julie Tvede, who had to settle for runner-up honors for the second week running after her 74.

Two behind at the start of the day, Ruuttila went three ahead with four to play before she three-putted for a bogey at the short 15th, where Tvede made a birdie for a two-shot swing. Ruuttila, who only turned professional at the end of 2006, missed a short birdie putt at the 16th, but then closed out the victory with birdies at the last two holes to finish at seven-under-par 209 total. Lee-Anne Pace finished six shots adrift in third place alongside Eleanor Pilgrim, Hanna-Leena Salonen, another Finnish rookie, and two South African amateurs, Ashleigh Simon and Kelli Shean.

"I am very happy to have won so early in my career," said Ruuttila. "I'm heading back to Finland now to resume my studies as a sports instructor, and then I'm hoping to join the Ladies European Tour in May, where I should get quite a few starts."

Acer Women's South African Open
Durban, South Africa
Winner: Ashleigh Simon

Ashleigh Simon, the youngest ever winner at the age of 14 in 2004, became the first amateur to win the Acer Women's South African Open twice with a five-stroke victory at Durban Country Club. The 17-year-old also took her fourth professional title in as many seasons. The victory was set up by a brilliant nine-under-par 64 in the second round which gave her a seven-stroke advantage over the field. On a layout utilizing many of the men's tees at the historic Durban Country Club, Simon compiled eight birdies, an eagle and only one bogey.

In the final round Simon cruised to 72 and a 14-under-par total of 205. Stacy Bregman closed with 69 to take second place, one ahead of Laurette Maritz, with another amateur, Kelli Shean, eight behind Simon, and defending champion Rebecca Hudson alone in fifth place. Bregman, in her rookie season as a professional, had joined Simon and Shean in securing the World Amateur Team Championship for South Africa for the first time in 2006.

"I haven't taken it all in yet," Simon said. "At the moment it's just another win on the Ladies African Tour for me and I'm very happy about that. Ever since I won the S.A. Open in 2004, it's been my goal to do so again. It's only now, three years later, when I look back and think that I won it the first time at the age of 14. Then I look around at what other 14-year-olds have achieved and I am quite proud of myself for that."

Telkom Women's Classic
Johannesburg, South Africa
Winner: Tania Elosegui

Tania Elosegui earned her first professional victory at the Telkom Women's Classic at Benoni Lakes. Elosegui was the runner-up in the Rookie of the Year stakes on the European Tour in 2006, and the 25-year-old Spaniard showed she could be a threat in 2007 by claiming a one-stroke win over Stacey Bregman and Rebecca Hudson.

Bregman led after a first round of 65, but Elosegui took the lead by adding her own 65 to an opening 67. Both players closed with 72s as Elosegui posted a total of 12-under-par 204. Hudson gave the leader a scare in the final round with yet another 65, but the Spaniard kept in front due to a run of pars on the back nine and could afford a bogey at the final hole.

"I was very nervous over my last putt," a relieved Elosegui explained. "I was shaking. I put my putter up and my hand was really shaking, but I managed to hold it, so I'm very happy."

Bregman, 20, won the Ladies African Tour Order of Merit after the second runner-up finish of her rookie season. Ashleigh Simon finished fourth and topped the points list that includes the performances of amateurs.

Princess Lalla Meryem Cup
Rabat, Morocco
Winner: Gwladys Nocera

Gwladys Nocera confirmed her status as the favorite for the title by winning the unofficial Princess Lalla Meryem Cup at Royal Dar-Es-Salam in Rabat, Morocco. The event was contested alongside the men's Hassan II Trophy won by Open champion Padraig Harrington.

Nocera, who won her fourth title on the Ladies European Tour at the KLM Open earlier in the season, closed with a two-under-par 71 to finish at 10-under 209 total and win by seven strokes over Spain's Paula Marti Zambrano, who signed off with 74. Sweden's Johanna Westerburg was third, a stroke further back, with Australia's Anna Rawson in fourth place, while the single Moroccan player in the competition, Mounya Amalou Sayeh, finished in 10th place. Sophie Sandolo, the winner in 2006, was forced to withdraw on the last day due to a neck injury.

"I am very proud to have won this tournament and satisfying the expectations of those who said I was the favorite for the event," Nocera said. "After playing as a pro-am in the first two rounds, it was different to be back to playing with my competitors today. I lost concentration after a stupid bogey at the eighth, but got back with a birdie at the 11th."

14. Senior Tours

Jay Haas won four times and topped the money list and Denis Watson won only twice, but they shared the billing as the big stories of the 2007 Champions Tour season. The low-keyed Haas did it on the strength of sheer numbers. No one else won more than twice. With Watson, it wasn't merely a matter of winning, it was a kind of resurrection. Plagued by an intimidating series of health problems, Watson had gone 23 years without winning and, in fact, with limited play. Then he broke through for the Senior PGA Championship and later added the Boeing Classic.

Haas wrapped up a tidy year, topping the money list with $2.5 million off his four wins. He started with the Toshiba Classic in March, the sixth tournament on the schedule, and set a tournament record of 20 under par. In the Liberty Mutual Legends of Golf, Haas was surprised he was the one to survive a late scramble. "I certainly didn't think I would be sitting here at this time," Haas said. "I thought I would be in the car about a hundred miles down the road by now."

In a way, the soft-spoken Haas surprised even himself. "I thought I'd be competitive when I came out here on this tour," Haas said, after taking the Principal Charity Classic. "If somebody would have said I was going to win nine times — no, I wouldn't have said that." And sometimes, when he didn't win, someone handed it to him. Such as the Bank of America Championship, which his good friend Tom Purtzer let get away in the final round. "You can't feel sorry for anybody out here when you're doing it," Haas said. "But I wish he would have had a better day."

Watson, a 51-year-old Zimbabwean, jumped to his opportunity at the Senior PGA Championship when Argentina's Eduardo Romero stumbled late in the final round. "Words cannot describe the feelings," said Watson, who last won in 1984. Watson then won the Boeing Classic. Or rather, survived it, making eagle on the second extra hole to end the first seven-man playoff in the history of big-time professional golf.

There were three other two-time winners — Brad Bryant, Loren Roberts and R.W. Eaks.

Tom Watson was about to win his first U.S. Senior Open, then shot 43 on the last nine and 78 for the final round, pretty much handing the title to Bryant. Bryant paled at the thought that he had joined the company of Palmer, Nicklaus, Trevino and the rest. "Let's face it — I'm not in their league. I wasn't, and I never will be," Bryant said. The victory made Bryant one of five multiple winners of the season. Earlier, he won the Regions Charity Classic in a playoff against Eaks.

Eaks was also a two-time winner, starting with his career-first win in the Dick's Sporting Goods Open. Said Eaks: "Man, this is great! I want to do it again." And so he did, some six weeks later, in the Greater Hickory Classic, where he led by six with nine holes to play, but needed a birdie at the final hole to stay afloat and win by two.

Roberts also won twice, but the first, the Boeing Championship, took him by surprise. "I made it a point not to look (at a leaderboard) until I walked off the 17th hole," Roberts said. By then, he was leading by four. Roberts got No. 2 for the season in the Constellation Energy Senior Players Championship, going wire-to-wire and winning by six.

Carl Mason dominated the senior scene in Europe. The English star racked up five victories on the European Seniors Tour, including the PGA Championship, and was the only man with multiple wins in the season until Italian Costantino Rocca won the season-ending Tour Championship for the second victory of his rookie senior year. The powerhouse year gave Mason the Order of Merit (money) title for a third time and moved him into second place on the all-time victory list with 19. Fellow Englishman Tommy Horton collected 23 wins during his 16 active years on the circuit. Mason's record €412,376 made him the leader on the career money list with €1,642,960.

MasterCard Championship at Hualalai
Ka'upulehu-Kona, Hawaii
Winner: Hale Irwin

It festered in Hale Irwin that for the first time in his 12 seasons on the Champions Tour, he had gone winless in 2006. So when the 2007 season dawned the second week of January, he was taking no chances. Irwin, age 61, just up and ran away with the MasterCard Championship. There was a lot of futile golf going on behind him in the exclusive field of 41 players.

For perspective, take that moment after the second round. "How would you like to shoot 13 under par and be three behind?" Irwin said, referring to Brad Bryant and Tom Kite, who were at those figures. Irwin had just taken command with a 10-under-par 62. And shooting 66-62-65 for a 193 total, 23 under at the Hualalai Resort in Hawaii, Irwin breezed by five strokes to his tour-record 45th victory.

Irwin was three behind Brad Bryant in the first round, then erupted in the second round. He birdied four straight holes going out and four straight coming home in that bogey-free 62, led by three, and promised not to let up. "If you just try to sit on a lead ... you get too careful," Irwin said. "You'll get too anxious and not succeed."

Kite, whose 64 included a 39-footer for eagle at the par-five 10th, knew the task that lay ahead — heading off a hungry Irwin. "He's not the only one hungry, though," Kite said. Jim Thorpe, after a dazzling 63 in which he needed only 22 putts, was four behind Irwin.

In the final round, Irwin birdied three of his first four holes and had seven one-putts on the front nine and made the turn in 32. He had one scary moment, when his tee shot at the par-four 13th stopped about a foot from the lava fields. He saved his par, and birdied the 14th and 15th, and was leading by six. At the 18th, he missed a two-footer for par. The bogey merely cut his lead to five. "I can still do this," Irwin said. "It's not like I've lost it and it's gone. It's back."

Turtle Bay Championship
Oahu, Hawaii
Winner: Fred Funk

Fred Funk is an outgoing man, bubbly at times. He must have been beside himself at the Turtle Bay Championship. It takes a lot to hold a man down when he makes not a solitary bogey in 54 holes and wins by a record 11 strokes.

"All of a sudden," Funk said, "my putter got smoking hot." And it stayed that way. He averaged only 1.533 putts per hole, tops for the tournament, and a mere 25.3 putts per round. He had the rest of the game, as well. He tied for third in driving accuracy (85.7 percent) and tied for second in hitting greens in regulation (83.3).

Add it all up and you get scores of 65-64-64 at the par-72 Palmer Course of the Turtle Bay Resort in Hawaii. Funk's 23-under-par 193 total was a tournament record, and his 11-shot winning margin was a Champions Tour record for a 54-hole event. And it must be some kind of record that he birdied the same five holes in all three rounds — Nos. 3, 5, 7, 14 and 18.

Funk took the outright lead in the first round with a 15-foot birdie putt at the par-four 14th, and he got to seven-under 65 with a birdie at the 18th for a two-stroke lead. In the second round, he turned back early threats with a first-nine 32 that included a 35-foot downhiller at the fifth and a 10-footer at the par-five ninth. In the final round, Funk pretty much locked it up with six birdies on the first nine. A two-putt birdie from 40 feet at the 18th then wrapped up his walk in the park and brightened his outlook as a two-tour player.

"I've always been an underdog, I've always been a journeyman," Funk said. "But that just drives me. I want to stay driven. I'll just see how long I can last."

Allianz Championship
Boca Raton, Florida
Winner: Mark James

Maybe Mark James had discovered another secret to golf — start cold. "I came out here fairly cold from the winter off, and only starting practicing this week," said James, after closing fast to win the Allianz Championship. James, a former European Tour standout, had just arrived in Florida after skiing in the French Alps for three weeks, and goodness knows one doesn't get to hit many shots on the slopes in February.

James played the Old Course at Broken Sound, at Boca Raton, in 64-69-68 for a 201 total, 15 under par, for his third Champions Tour victory, winning by two over Jay Haas, the defending champion and the 2006 Champions Tour Player of the Year.

James was tied for the lead with Haas and Craig Stadler at the start of the final round, then raced to six birdies in the first 12 holes. He bogeyed the 14th, then parred in for his 68. James looked to be in big trouble at the ninth, when he tried to hit his ball out of shallow water and moved it only two feet. He escaped that one with only a bogey, his first of the tournament. But Haas and Stadler also bogeyed, and remained a stroke behind.

Haas, who took a share of the second-round lead with a 65, finished with 70, and had to birdie the last hole to take second alone at 13 under. "As well as I played yesterday was as poorly as I played today," Haas said. "I had been bragging about how good my driver was, but I maybe hit three or four fairways today." Stadler, who opened the tournament with a bogey-free 63, stumbled coming home in the finale. He double-bogeyed the 14th and the 16th for a 74–207.

Nick Price, making his Champions Tour debut, shot 71-71-68–210, six under par, and tied for 20th. "My game left a little to be desired," Price said. "But it's been great, and it's nice to feel wanted again."

Outback Steakhouse Pro-Am
Lutz, Florida
Winner: Tom Watson

Finally — Tom Watson cleared up one of the most intriguing mysteries in golf. How could a person win 39 tournaments — including five British Opens, two Masters and one U.S. Open — but go winless in 93 tries in Florida? "I guess it's just never been cold enough," Watson said. "It took Kansas City weather to make it happen."

The Florida weather in the Outback Steakhouse Pro-Am at the TPC of Tampa Bay got a strong touch of Kansas City in mid-February, especially in the final round, with temperatures in the 40s and winds reaching 30 miles an hour. But Watson flourished and broke his Florida drought with a one-stroke victory over struggling Andy Bean and surging Jay Haas.

Watson hung close for the first two rounds with 70-69. Then in the third round, chasing Bean, Watson parred the first seven holes but slipped three behind with bogeys at the eighth and ninth. Not dead by a long shot, Watson then birdied the 10th, 12th and 13th, and tied Bean. Then came Bean's fatal crash at the par-five 14th. His third shot, an easy pitch from 91 yards, was short, and he shanked his fourth and finally double-bogeyed. "I was in perfect position, and that's what cost me," Bean said.

Watson clutched the lead, and crucial up-and-downs at the 15th and 17th got him home for the one-stroke victory. It was an unlikely trip, as was Mark O'Meara's Champions debut. He shot 74-66-82 and tied for 38th place.

David Eger leaped into the first-round lead with a 67. But Eger slipped, and Bean (67) and Wayne Levi, who finished in near-darkness with a 69, tied for the second-round lead. Watson was three behind in the first round, and one behind in the second. Then came Bean's crash, and Watson closed with a one-under 70 — one of only six under-par rounds that chilling final day — for a four-under 209 total. Bean (72) and Haas (69) tied at 210. And so the Florida mystery was solved. "Now I'm on a streak," Watson said. "I'm 1-for-94."

ACE Group Classic
Naples, Florida
Winner: Bobby Wadkins

The grand old saw says you can't win a tournament in the first round, but Bobby Wadkins sure put up a good argument to the contrary with a pair of eagles and five birdies for an opening 64 in the ACE Group Classic. "I did a good job staying out of my own way," said Wadkins, who then leapfrogged Allen Doyle to win by one stroke. Wadkins shot 64-69-68 for a 201 total, 15 under par at the Quail West Golf and Country Club in Naples, Florida. Doyle, winner of the last two U.S. Senior Opens, shot 65-67-70. Wadkins led the first round, and Doyle jumped ahead in the second. Then Doyle stumbled to the finish line and Wadkins birdied the 18th for his fourth victory.

In the first round, Wadkins eagled the par-five No. 1 and No. 13, and birdied home from the 15th on putts of 20, 12, six and 15 feet. "I just kept myself relaxed and played well today," Wadkins said. Doyle tied at 65 with Gil Morgan and Mark O'Meara. O'Meara, making his second Champions Tour start, pulled out the putter that won him the 1998 Masters and British Open. He would tie for fourth.

Doyle took the second-round lead by one, then in the final round went up by three at the electrifying par-five ninth, where he holed out from the fairway for an eagle and Wadkins came within a whisker of matching him, leaving himself just a tap-in for a birdie. Wadkins went birdie-bogey-birdie, finishing that stretch with a chip-in birdie from behind the 16th to get to 14 under and trailing Doyle by one. Then Doyle took a three-putt bogey at the 17th and they were tied.

It was settled at the par-five 18th. Doyle laid up beautifully, about 90 yards short of the green, but was wide to the right with his pitch and two-putted for his par-five. Wadkins's three-wood second shot was short and right, and having to stand in a bunker, he chipped from a sidehill lie to 13 feet and holed the putt for the birdie and the win.

Toshiba Classic
Newport Beach, California
Winner: Jay Haas

When a birdie putt hangs forever, then finally drops just in time, a man rather gets a hint this might be his week. So it was for Jay Haas in the Toshiba Classic early in March, but he had already got the idea at the start, when he led the field in beating up on defenseless Newport Beach Country Club, where a dry spring left the California course with little rough.

Consider that in the first round Haas and five others led with six-under-par 65s and that the average score for the field of 78 was 69.76. "We enjoy playing this course," said Ben Crenshaw (65). "It's not a killer course." Overall, Haas enjoyed it most, shooting 65-64-65 for a 194 total, 19 under par, for his first victory of the season after three top-five finishes.

"I felt every hole was a birdie hole," said Haas, who posted 20 birdies in the 54 holes and broke Hale Irwin's tournament record of 17 under par. He had just one bogey in the tournament, that at No. 8 in the final round after he chipped badly and missed a 20-footer for his par.

Haas edged into the lead with 64 for a 129 total in the second round, up by one on Peter Jacobsen. He birdied three of his first four holes, and finished the day with seven golfers within four shots of him. "I may have to shoot 61 to beat him," Jacobsen said.

Jacobsen's number was about right, but the pressure came from elsewhere. Naomichi Ozaki got within a stroke with birdies on the first two holes. But Haas went two up with a birdie at the fourth, then by three when he holed a seven-footer for birdie at the seventh. Finally, it was R.W. Eaks who put on what little pressure there was, shooting 65 to finish second by two strokes.

"I got a lot of breaks," Haas said, and the biggest, he agreed, came at No. 11. His birdie putt hung on the edge. The rules allow, oh, maybe 10 seconds. It dropped in eight seconds.

AT&T Champions Classic
Valencia, California
Winner: Tom Purtzer

People who keep track of such things say that Tom Purtzer has the prettiest swing in golf. Maybe so, but it was his putting stroke that did the trick in the AT&T Champions Classic — a putting stroke he credited to Dave Stockton. "I have to thank Dave," Purtzer said. "He gave me a lesson and I putted better."

The key to Stockton's tip? Focus on a spot in front of the ball and roll the putt over that spot.

Stockton gave him the lesson on Wednesday, and the payoff came at a critical time on Sunday. Purtzer sank a 10-foot birdie putt at the 18th hole to tie Loren Roberts at 10-under-par 206 at Valencia (California) Country Club. Then Purtzer beat him on the fourth extra hole.

Purtzer had to come from back in the pack. Hale Irwin started with an eight-under 64 and a two-stroke lead, and still led by one stroke in the second round with 71–135. Then Irwin faded to 73. The final round was a free-for-all. At one point, six players were tied for the lead, including Irwin. "Hale rarely comes back to the field," Purtzer said. The record bears this out. Irwin won 33 times out of the 47 that he led going into the final round.

"I haven't made too many crunch-time putts in my career," Purtzer said. He did this time. At the final hole, Roberts missed a 19-foot putt that would have won, and Purtzer tied him with a 10-footer for birdie. In the playoff — four trips up the 18th — they parred the first three times, and Purtzer had to hole a 15-footer for par to stay alive that third time. Finally, the fourth time, Purtzer birdied from 17 feet, and Roberts missed from 12 feet.

Ginn Championship Hammock Beach Resort
Palm Coast, Florida
Winner: Keith Fergus

Most golfers would rather get the yips than admit they choked. But Keith Fergus readily conceded the point in the inaugural Ginn Championship Hammock Beach Resort in Palm Coast, Florida. Of course, that was after he had his first Champions Tour title safely in his bag. "I had that choke factor going in," Fergus said, explaining his wobbly final round after leading through the first two rounds without a bogey. "But I was after that trophy," he said. "It's why we work and leave our families — for moments like this."

Fergus didn't dominate the tournament, but he led from the start. He tied for the lead in the first round with Brad Bryant at 67, then shot another 67 and led by one over Bryant (68) and Tom Purtzer (66). The wobbles hit in the final round. Fergus hit his tee shot in the water on the par-three fourth hole, but chipped in for par. He also hit his tee shot in the water at the fifth and suffered his first bogey in 41 holes. Then he got hot at the par-fives. He birdied the sixth hole, eagled the 10th on a bunker shot, and with a two-putt birdie at the 14th he was leading by two strokes.

Then more wobbling. He bogeyed the 16th out of the rough and needed a seven-foot putt to save par at the par-three 17th. Then he bogeyed the par-four 18th, driving into a bunker, pitching into the fairway, and finally two-putting from 13 feet for 70, a 12-under 204 total and a one-stroke win over Mark O'Meara and Hale Irwin, becoming only the second man to have won on the PGA Tour, the Nationwide Tour and the Champions Tour.

The week seemed destined to be Fergus's from the start. Fergus survived a blast from Bryant in the first round — an eagle and four birdies in a six-hole stretch to tie him at 67. In the windy second round, Irwin took the lead but bogeyed the last three holes, and Fergus responded by birdieing all four par-fives and parring the last four holes. And in the final round, with a chance to catch a sagging Fergus, Irwin bogeyed the 18th and shared second place with O'Meara.

Liberty Mutual Legends of Golf
Savannah, Georgia
Winner: Jay Haas

It was a legendary finish, a perfect fit for the Liberty Mutual Legends of Golf. "Any number of guys could have won," said playoff runner-up Tom Kite.

Said Jay Haas, the defending champion and again the winner: "I certainly didn't think I would be sitting here at this time. I thought I would be in the car about a hundred miles down the road by now."

As for Brad Bryant, Mark James, Wayne Levi and Gil Morgan — they ended up talking to themselves.

James, who won the Allianz Championship earlier, led the first round with five-under-par 67 that included an eagle from six feet at the 11th, but also three-putt bogeys at the 16th and 17th. Haas took a one-shot lead into the final round with a 69–137 total, and offered, "I've got to be sharper. There are too many good players right behind me."

Haas led Bryant, Levi and James by one stroke, Kite by two. Kite birdied Nos. 3, 6, 8 and 11, bogeyed the 12th, then birdied the 16th for his 68. The other three shot 70s. James fizzled with three-putt bogeys at the last two holes. Levi stumbled to a double bogey at the sixth and two bogeys down the stretch. Bryant spoiled a four-birdie surge with a bogey at the 15th. Gil Morgan eagled the 11th and shot 67 to tie them for third place at 208.

Haas, after his only bogey at the third hole, birdied the 11th, 13th and 14th, and tapped in for par at the 18th after a sensational 90-foot bunker shot, and shot 68 to tie the waiting Kite at nine-under 207. In the playoff at the tough 457-yard par-four 18th, Kite was on the green in two, but three-putted from 56 feet and bogeyed. Haas was over the green in two, chipped back to three feet, and holed it for his second win of the young season and his eighth on the Champions Tour.

FedEx Kinko's Classic
Austin, Texas
Winner: Scott Hoch

Scott Hoch, an 11-time winner on the PGA Tour, was beginning to wonder whether he would ever win on the Champions Tour. He reached age 50 in 2006, still trying to come back from wrist surgery for two severed tendons in late 2005. Finally his patience paid off in the FedEx Kinko's Classic early in May.

Hoch seized the lead in the second round and took a two-stroke victory over D.A. Weibring at The Hills Country Club outside Austin, Texas. "I hung on to win, but it feels good," Hoch said. He was second to first-round leader Leonard Thompson (64) and led the rest of the way, shooting 67-66-68 for a 201 total, 15 under par.

"I haven't been healthy since I came out here or I think I would have done better," Hoch said. He did all right this time. He went through the first two rounds without a bogey — the only player in the field to do so — and didn't make a bogey until the ninth hole in the final round.

Hoch took control with four birdies in his first eight holes in the second round, then added to it with birdies at the 14th and 15th. "The whole key to this course is to hit it in the fairways," Hoch said, "and that's why I'm here today, because I haven't wasted many good shots."

He was in command throughout the final round, starting with birdies at Nos. 3, 6 and 8. After his first bogey of the tournament at the ninth, he had four straight pars and birdied the 14th and 15th to open a three-stroke lead on Weibring. At the par-three 16th it seemed his tee shot might not clear the water, but it did, and he played his way home safely. "It always feels good to win when you've been tested," Hoch said.

Regions Charity Classic
Birmingham, Alabama
Winner: Brad Bryant

It was a time for celebrating for Brad Bryant. For Seve Ballesteros, it was a time for anything but celebrating.

Bryant, coming of age on the Champions Tour, won his second straight Regions Charity Classic — at Ross Bridge, near Birmingham, Alabama — and his third victory overall, this in a playoff against R.W. Eaks. Ballesteros was making his Champions Tour debut and it was a debut he would rather forget.

Ballesteros, whose brilliant career was shortened by chronic back problems, had played in just two tournaments in the last two years — The Open in 2006 and the Masters just a month previously, about the time he reached age 50 in April. It was a tough start. Ballesteros opened with 78, six over par and 13 strokes behind first-round leader Scott Hoch (65). Ballesteros went on to shoot 81-73 and finish 78th and last with a 16-over 216 total. "My game is not there," Ballesteros said. "I'm very disappointed, but I did the best I could."

It turned out to be the one and only venture on the Champions Tour for Ballesteros, who announced his retirement from competitive golf at Carnoustie, where he had played his first major championship in 1975.

Hoch ran off four straight birdies from the 12th and bogeyed the 18th hole for his opening 65. Bob Gilder, a nine-time career winner, got a quick back adjustment for the second round, eagled the 16th and birdied the 17th for a 66–134 total and a two-stroke lead on Hoch.

Bryant and Eaks started the final round five behind Gilder — who would fall away with 73 — and shot 65s to tie with 12-under 204 totals. Eaks just missed winning in regulation when his 15-foot birdie putt at the 18th slipped by. Bryant figured his key was a wedge shot out of a fairway bunker to eight feet at the 17th. He made the birdie. "That wedge shot and that putt on that hole was where I won," Bryant said. Except there was the matter of a playoff. They tied on the first two extra holes in pars, and then Bryant holed a 13-footer for birdie on the third for his third career seniors victory, his second at Ross Bridge.

Senior PGA Championship
Kiawah Island, South Carolina
Winner: Denis Watson

Few golfers have ever had to come from so far behind to win. For Denis Watson, it was only two strokes, but 23 years.

Watson, the Zimbabwean whose promising career was derailed by medical problems, came into the Senior PGA Championship with expectations not much more than simple hope. But Argentina's Eduardo Romero, after leading through three rounds, stumbled down the final homestretch, and Watson broke through for the victory. It was his first in 23 years and came on a strong showing of 71-71-69-68 for a 279 total, nine under par against the heavy winds at Kiawah Island's Ocean Course in South Carolina.

"Words cannot describe the feelings," Watson said.

Watson, age 51, had last won in 1984 — three times on the PGA Tour. Then in 1985, at a tournament in South Africa, he hit a stump he couldn't see. The damage to his neck, wrist, back and shoulders required eight or nine operations — he wasn't sure which — and months of rehabilitation. He had played only 30 times in 14 years.

Romero had the championship all but in his bag. He opened with 68 and a one-stroke lead on Naomichi Ozaki on a day when only seven out of the 156 starters could break par. Was the wind strong? Romero birdied the par-four 10th off a downwind drive of 360 yards and a wedge to three feet. A 70 in the second round put him two up on Ozaki. Watson, meantime, trailed by three in the first round, then slipped to four behind in the second round, burning up all four by double-bogeying the last two holes.

It was Romero's turn in the third round for a tough finish, bogey-bogey for 71 that left him two ahead of Watson (69) and Nick Price (70). The development served to show how little attention other golfers paid to Watson. Said Romero, contemplating the final round, "Tomorrow it's a different day because the guy behind me is Nick — one of the toughest guys in the world." He said nothing of Watson.

Watson straightened that all out in the fourth round. He closed within one with two birdies on the first nine, then birdied the 11th, but Romero went back up by two with birdies at the 11th and 12th. Next, the fall: Romero bogeyed the 13th and double-bogeyed the par-three 14th from a bunker. Watson birdied the 14th from 10 feet, bogeyed the 15th, but birdied the 16th and parred in for the two-stroke victory. After 23 dark years, he knew what winning felt like again. "Just to believe in my ability again," he said.

Boeing Championship at Sandestin
Destin, Florida
Winner: Loren Roberts

It was a kind of working vacation for the Roberts family at Destin, Florida, early in June. Kimberly and the girls, Alexandria and Addison, went sightseeing while Loren went to work at the Boeing Championship at the Raven Golf Club. Mom and the girls came home with tourist stuff and Dad came home with his first championship of the season and the sixth in his three seasons on the Champions Tour.

"We had great quality time together — I probably was more relaxed," said Roberts, who always looks relaxed.

But the finish in this one would test anyone's nerves. Roberts, shooting 65-67, trailed by three strokes — behind Tom Purtzer and Eduardo Romero, tied at 62 in the first round, and Jay Haas (64-65–129) in the second round. Then it was a dogfight. The four were tied through the ninth hole and then held or shared the lead at least twice through the 11th. Then Roberts broke free with a birdie at the 12th to Haas's par and bogeys by Purtzer and Romero. But Roberts preferred to remain oblivious to it all and didn't check the leaderboards.

"I made it a point not to look until I walked off the 17th hole," Roberts said. By then, he was on a cakewalk, leading by four. He had seven birdies and he could well afford his lone bogey of the day, that at the 18th. His 65, for a 16-under 197 total, gave him a three-stroke win over Romero (69), who was second the week before in the Senior PGA Championship. "My time is coming — I can smell it," the Argentine said.

Haas wished he could say the same when it comes to Florida. He shot 73 and fell to a tie for fifth place. He was now a career 0-for-108 in Florida.

Principal Charity Classic
West Des Moines, Iowa
Winner: Jay Haas

Jay Haas was saying there most likely wouldn't be another Hale Irwin ravaging the Champions Tour. Maybe not, but Haas himself was doing a pretty fair imitation, what with his wire-to-wire romp in the Principal Charity Classic early in June for his third victory of the year and the ninth of his career.

"That might be out of reach," Haas said, speaking of Irwin's 45 career victories, "but I just don't want to be hot for a while and fade away." Haas showed no signs of fading away in this tournament in West Des Moines, Iowa.

Haas ran away with it, playing the par-71 Glen Oaks Country Club in 65-67-69–201, 12 under par. He led by one stroke in the first round, by three in the second round, and his lead got up to six strokes during the third and final round and shrank back to a final three after he coasted home over R.W. Eaks (64) and Brad Bryant (67). "I knew I had no chance of catching him," said Eaks. "I was just hoping for a top-five (finish)." He and Bryant tied for second at nine under.

Haas needed just 27 putts in the first round, shooting 65 when only 23 of the 76 starters could break par. He closed with a seven iron that left him a putt that broke five feet, then dropped. Haas broke away in the second round. After a double bogey at the eighth, he birdied six of the next seven holes. The centerpiece was a 44-foot birdie putt at the 13th. "That was pretty lucky," Haas conceded. David Edwards faded after hitting his approach shot into the water at the 17th and bogeying.

In the third round, Haas stretched his three-stroke lead with birdies at the second and fourth and led by six at the 10th. He went conservative the rest of the way, birdied the 15th, and bogeyed the last two holes. "I thought I'd be competitive when I came out here on this tour," Haas said. "If somebody would have said I was going to win nine times — no, I wouldn't have said that."

Bank of America Championship
Concord, Massachusetts
Winner: Jay Haas

Not that Jay Haas didn't want to win, but the Bank of America Championship was shaping up into a second-place finish for him, and that was fine because it meant his good friend, Tom Purtzer, was about to win. But Purtzer went about the business of self-destruction in the final round, and there it was: Haas's second consecutive victory, his fourth of the season and his 10th in 49 starts on the Champions Tour.

"You can't feel sorry for anybody out here when you're doing it," Haas said. "But I wish he would have had a better day."

It was history repeating itself at Nashawtuc Country Club, near Boston. Twice before Purtzer led going into the final round. But Craig Stadler overran him with 64 in 2004 and Mark McNulty beat him in a playoff in 2005.

Purtzer opened with six-under-par 66, one stroke behind Tom Watson's amazing bogey-free 65 in foul weather. The Spirit of Nashawtuc descended on Purtzer again in the second round. He birdied the first, third and fifth holes, then bogeyed three of the next seven, then birdied the 13th from six feet, the 15th from seven feet and the 18th from nine feet for 68 and a three-stroke lead over a crowd, including Haas (66).

Then the Curse of Nashawtuc struck again. In the final round, Purtzer was leading Haas by one stroke through the turn. Haas sprinted to four birdies in the first seven holes and still wasn't thinking about winning. "It looked like we were all playing for second place," Haas said. In the final round, Purtzer bogeyed three straight and double-bogeyed the par-three 17th. "I self-destructed more than anything," Purtzer said. But before that, Haas birdied the 14th and 17th for a bogey-free 66, a 13-under 203 total and a three-stroke win over Leonard Thompson (68).

Purtzer shot 73, finished fourth, and now was 0-for-3 leading going into the final round. Did he still like Nashawtuc? "There's nothing wrong with the course," Purtzer said. "It was self-induced."

Commerce Bank Championship
East Meadow, New York
Winner: Lonnie Nielsen

It's all in how you look at it, Lonnie Nielsen was saying. He was talking about his record on the Champions Tour, just after winning the Commerce Bank Championship. "One-for-92, huh?" he said. "That's better than 0-for-92." And so it was that Nielsen put into proper statistical context his first victory after 91 Champions events and 124 PGA Tour events before that: One win isn't much, but it's better than none. And it's a start.

It looked like another day in the office at first. Nielsen opened with 66, five under par at Eisenhower Park at East Meadow, New York, two strokes behind leader Loren Roberts. Nielsen took over from there, leading the rest of the way with 64-69 for a 14-under 199 total and a two-stroke win over Roberts.

Nielsen started his decisive second round in unconvincing fashion — with a bogey at the par-three second hole. He rebounded with three birdies on the first nine, including a 40-foot putt at the par-four sixth. He started his second-nine assault at the 11th, on a putt from 15 feet. Then he birdied the 12th, 14th, 15th and par-five 17th, with two putts from the fringe. Nielsen later said it was this string of birdies that let him dare to think he could win. Nielsen was reasonably solid with a three-stroke lead on Tom McKnight (66). It was the first time he was the solo leader going into the final round on the Champions Tour.

Nielsen got to 14 under and a five-stroke lead with a birdie at the par-three fifth. He bogeyed the sixth, then went four up on Roberts with a two-putt birdie at the par-five 12th. Roberts closed to within two with birdies at the 14th and 18th, and that was it. "If I couldn't win, I was sure happy to see Lonnie win," Roberts said.

Nielsen admitted that emotion gripped him as he walked up the 18th fairway. "I had to get the tears out of my eyes and two-putt from 10 feet, and I did," Nielsen said. "I've worked my whole life for this. I don't know how it can be more special than that."

U.S. Senior Open
Kohler, Wisconsin
Winner: Brad Bryant

It was Satchel Paige, philosopher of baseball, who offered this secret to a happy life: "Don't look back. Someone might be gaining on you."

It would have been the other way around for Brad Bryant. If he had looked back coming home at the U.S. Senior Open, at hot and windy Whistling Straits, he would have been stunned to discover that he was pulling away from everyone. Behind him was Tom Watson, who had finished second in three of the previous five Senior Opens and who seemed ready to win his first — until the final nine, when he nosed-over into a horrendous crash. He made three double bogeys and two bogeys for a second-nine 43 and a 78 total. And Bryant didn't know a thing until the 18th.

"I was blissfully unaware of what was going on behind me," Bryant said. Then at the 18th, he gave in and asked his caddie to check the leaderboard. Imagine the Christmas feeling. Bryant, trailing by five at the turn, found himself leading by three. Bryant wrapped up rounds of 71-72-71-68 for a 282 total, six under par, for a three-stroke win over Ben Crenshaw (70). Watson (70-66-73-78), who led for two-plus rounds, finished fourth, five shots back.

"I hit my ball in the rough too many times," Watson said, "and today I got my just reward." There was a lot of that going on at the Pete Dye creation in Wisconsin on the shores of Lake Michigan.

Argentina's Eduardo Romero shot 66 for the first-round lead, then blew to 77. Watson shot 66 for a three-stroke lead in the second round, and said he wasn't comfortable with the course. Watson battled for 73 in the third round and still led by three, as no one could make much headway in the heavier winds. Bryant trailed by five strokes in the first round, seven in the second and five in the third. In the final round, even with stiffer winds and 90-degree heat, Watson seemed to have a lock on the tournament. He shot one under on the first nine and birdied the 10th and was nine under. Then came his stunning collapse.

Bryant plowed away. He bogeyed the 12th and 14th holes, and though he didn't know it at the time, when he birdied the par-five 16th from five feet, he had the lead for good. And then he was told that he was in the book alongside Arnold Palmer, Jack Nicklaus and Lee Trevino. "What an honor," Bryant said. "Let's face it — I'm not in their league. I wasn't, and I never will be. I'm a journeyman who happened to have a really great week."

Dick's Sporting Goods Open
Endicott, New York
Winner: R.W. Eaks

Golfers say that trees are 90 percent air. Okay, but it's the other 10 percent that kills you. Except for R.W. Eaks. By the time he had finished bouncing balls off trees at the En-Joie Golf Club, he had his career-first victory, the inaugural Dick's Sporting Goods Open, the Champions Tour event that replaced the B.C. Open, which was dropped from the PGA Tour. He had gone six years and 90 tournaments on the Champions Tour and 12 years and 77 tournaments on the PGA Tour without winning. Few have waited so long or worked so hard for that first one.

"I honestly didn't know if I could win a tournament," Eaks said.

He could thank the trees. Eaks opened with a one-under-par 71, two strokes behind the leaders, Craig Stadler, Scott Hoch and Rod Spittle, all at 69. He wouldn't trail again. In the second round, Eaks shot an amazing career-low 62 that included a chip-in eagle from 45 feet at the par-five third hole, a hole-in-one with a five iron at the 193-yard seventh, and five hit trees. At 11-under 133, he led rookie Bruce Vaughan (64) by one and Scott Hoch (66) by two going into the final round.

Eaks wrapped it up handily in the final round, with 66 for a 17-under 199 total, beating a frustrated Vaughan (68) by three strokes. And Eaks remained aggressive to the end, and even hit another tree — at the first hole — and got away with it. "I just go ahead and hit it," Eaks said, "and if it hits trees, hopefully it'll bounce back in the fairway." Eaks saved par at the seventh with a brilliant bunker shot to three feet, and birdied the par-five eighth after reaching the green in two. When Vaughan missed a seven-footer for par at the 16th, Eaks pretty much had it clinched.

"Man, this is great!" Eaks said. "I want to do it again."

The Senior Open Championship
East Lothian, Scotland
Winner: Tom Watson

See European Seniors Tour section.

3M Championship
Blaine, Minnesota
Winner: D.A. Weibring

The 3M Championship opened with a duck shoot, as Jim Thorpe put it. He would know. He and Tom Jenkins shot eight-under-par 64s, leading a charge across the TPC Twin Cities, near Minneapolis, that ended up with the field averaging 69.83, the lowest first-round figure in the tournament's 15 years. And piled up behind them was a five-way tie at 65, including D.A. Weibring, who hadn't won since 2005. He would end that dry spell forthwith, thanks to hot streaks late in the last two rounds.

Weibring birdied four of his last six holes in the second round for 66 and a tournament record 13-under 131 total for 36 holes, and led by one over Jim Thorpe (68), who was among the double-bogey victims of the pivotal par-four 16th, scary with bunkers left and water right. Weibring had one of the few birdies there. "My caddie didn't think I could get to the bunker, so I just wanted to make a good, solid swing," Weibring said. Great choice. He hit driver, then a nine iron to 20 feet, and made the putt.

In the final round, Weibring needed that second burst of birdies down the stretch. Jay Haas, starting from behind, shot 63 and was already in at 17 under par. Weibring was 15 under coming to the 16th. He birdied it again, this time off a five-iron approach, then birdied the par-three 17th from three feet. Now, at the par-five 18th, just one more birdie to win. But he couldn't go for the green in two. He had an iffy lie and some mud on his ball. So he played safely to the left of the water, pitched to 10 feet, and got his birdie and the win.

Said Weibring: "It's great to be back in the winner's circle."

JELD-WEN Tradition
Sunriver, Oregon
Winner: Mark McNulty

When it comes to the margin of victory, Gary Player had the definitive answer for Mark McNulty. "Mark," Player was saying, "as long as you win by one, you've won."

McNulty, who hadn't finished in the top 10 in 13 starts this season, must have been kicking himself at the JELD-WEN Tradition. He double-bogeyed the final hole — and only won by five strokes. Well, it wasn't the reduced margin that concerned him. It was the little lapse in concentration that cost him the double bogey. But it was understandable. A guy leading by seven strokes with one hole to play might tend to daydream.

McNulty, who was out of the lead only in the second round, played the Crosswater Golf Club in Oregon in 66-68-70-68 for a 16-under-par 272 total and a comfortable win over David Edwards. It was McNulty's sixth Champions victory but the first since 2005. And it was just in time. He needed a top-30 finish on the money list to be fully exempt in 2008.

He tied for the first-round lead with Mike Reid at six-under 66 for a one-stroke edge on Edwards. Reid birdied four of the last six holes, capped off by a 14-foot birdie putt at the 18th. "The birdies were great," Reid said, "but what really kept me going were a couple of key par saves." McNulty birdied his last four holes. "Anytime you shoot 66," McNulty said, "you've got to make the four-footers, the 20-footers, the 30-footers." Tom Watson was making birdies, too. He racked up eight of them, but also four bogeys and shot 68, two off the lead. He plotted his strategy for the rest of the tournament. "Try to keep the eight birdies every day," Watson said, "and get rid of the bogeys."

McNulty trailed only in the second round, when 68 left him two behind Edwards (65), who refused to get excited about his position. "If I've finished in the top 10, I've played well," Edwards said. "If I win, great." Edwards's fatalistic attitude served him well in the third round. He spoke of avoiding the "emotional roller coaster." Case in point: He holed out from 146 yards for an eagle at the par-five 12th, but he double-bogeyed the par-three 17th for 72. That dropped him into a share of the lead with McNulty (70) at 204.

The fourth round, obviously, belonged to McNulty. He birdied Nos. 2, 3, 5 and 7 to charge into a three-stroke lead over Edwards. McNulty mentioned "bonuses" — a 30-foot putt at the third hole and a 24-footer at the fifth. "Those putts set the tone and enabled me to keep my concentration," he said.

McNulty, long troubled by a sore back, finally allowed himself to think he could win when he birdied the par-four 11th, which had bedeviled him all week. He also birdied the 15th and was in clover until the 18th, when he two-putted from four feet for the double bogey. The five-stroke cushion eased the pain. "People ask me, 'What's your best win,'" McNulty said. "I say my last one, because you never know when the next one is going to come.

Boeing Classic
Snoqualmie, Washington
Winner: Denis Watson

For a moment, it looked liked the grounds crew coming down the fairway — seven of them, marching along. But they didn't have rakes and shovels. Those were golf clubs they were swinging. This was a sevensome, the first seven-man playoff in the history of major professional golf. Such an unprecedented situation deserved a fitting finish, and Denis Watson provided it with an eagle on the second extra hole.

"The only thing you like about being in that playoff is when you come out on top," said Watson, taking his second Champions Tour victory of the season, shooting three 69s at the par-72 TPC Snoqualmie Ridge course near Seattle.

It was Watson himself who triggered the traffic jam. He hit his tee shot in the water on the par-three 17th hole, and there went his chance to win in regulation. He finished with a nine-under-par 207 total, and the others piled up behind him in a variety of ways, most notably: David Eger with 69, Craig Stadler (68) with birdies at the last two holes, and Naomichi Ozaki (67), with a birdie at the 18th.

All seven trooped to the tee at the par-five 18th for the playoff.

R.W. Eaks seemed the most likely to succeed when he flipped his third shot to 18 inches. But it soon turned into a clutch putt he would need to stay alive. Watson had put his third into the fringe at the edge of the green, 23 feet from the pin. He chipped in for the first birdie. Stadler had hit the green and was 22 feet away. He holed that to tie Watson. That left Eaks having to hole his 18-incher to keep pace, which he did. Eger, Ozaki, Gil Morgan and Dana Quigley were ousted by pars on the first visit.

On the second visit, all three survivors hit the green in two. Stadler's long eagle putt was just short. Watson then rolled in his 18-footer for an eagle. When Eaks missed his own eagle from 12 feet, Watson had the victory. "It's tough to win," Watson said. "The emotions that grab hold of you — people who haven't done it don't understand it."

Wal-Mart First Tee Open at Pebble Beach
Pebble Beach, California
Winner: Gil Morgan

Maybe Gil Morgan was a champion just for being able to step out on the first tee at Pebble Beach. Who could forget that meltdown in the 1992 U.S. Open? That was in the third round, when he became the first ever to get to 10 under par in the U.S. Open, and then even got to 12 under with a birdie at No. 7. Then Morgan played the next seven holes in nine over par and ended up tying for 13th. "I was thinking maybe Pebble Beach is feeling sorry enough for me to let me survive another day here," Morgan said. "Maybe they gave me a reprieve this time at Pebble."

Whatever it was, Morgan outlasted Hale Irwin to take the Wal-Mart First Tee Open, the Champions Tour event which pairs First Tee juniors and amateurs with the professionals.

Morris Hatalsky and Bruce Vaughan led the first round on seven-under-par 65s at Pebble, then the big show started. In the second round, at neighboring Del Monte, Morgan logged eight birdies, including three-footers on the last two holes, for 65, and Irwin made nine birdies for 65 to tie at nine-under 135. Des Smyth joined them with 64, including a seven-birdie 29 on the second nine.

The final act, fittingly, came at Pebble Beach. Irwin double-bogeyed the first hole, but came charging back with a birdie at the second, an eagle at the sixth and a birdie at the 13th, and shot 69. It wasn't enough. Morgan got off and running with four birdies in the first six holes and shot a bogey-free 67 for a 14-under 202 total and a two-stroke victory over Irwin.

"I felt it was mine to lose or win coming down the stretch," Morgan said. "It's always fun to win because, as you get older, you wonder whether you can win again."

It didn't make up for 1992, but it helped.

Greater Hickory Classic at Rock Barn
Conover, North Carolina
Winner: R.W. Eaks

The Greater Hickory Classic at Rock Barn came down to this: R.W. Eaks was embarrassed by his embarrassment of riches. First, he had a golfer's dream — a six-shot lead with nine holes to play. Then it was a golfer's worst nightmare. Suddenly, he was fighting to stay afloat.

"I just started playing too safe," Eaks admitted. "I didn't think anyone could catch me. I probably did a couple things out there that I normally wouldn't do." Breaking tournament records along the way, Eaks played Rock Barn, in North Carolina, in 63-66-70 — a 17-under-par 199 total, getting his second Champions Tour win of the season and his career, winning by two over Jay Haas and Rod Spittle.

Storms halted the first round, forcing Eaks and others to play two rounds on Saturday. This Eaks did in 63 (tying the tournament record) and 66 for a 129 total that broke the tournament record by three strokes. He led Spittle by three going into the final round.

Eaks stretched that margin to a mesmerizing six strokes with three birdies on the first nine. Then he down-shifted his game. Oops. He began straying off the tee. He bogeyed the 11th and 15th holes and had to scramble for pars at Nos. 14, 16 and 17. Haas, a four-time winner already, rushed home with 66 and a 15-under 201 total. "I figured I needed something really special to catch R.W.," Haas said. "Still, it was nice to give him a little bit of a push."

Eaks regained control of his game at the par-five 18th, reaching in two and two-putting for a birdie and the 70 for the two-stroke win, and wiped his brow. "I always told myself that if I ever had that kind of lead, it'd be the easiest thing to do, to keep it," Eaks said. "I'll never do that again."

SAS Championship
Cary, North Carolina
Winner: Mark Wiebe

Mark Wiebe, wrapping up the SAS Championship as the 12th player to win his first start on the Champions Tour, put things in a different perspective. "It's been 21 years," he said. "That's three kids' worth."

So it was a big celebration that September night in the Wiebe household when he went wire-to-wire in a record-setting victory at Prestonwood Country Club in Cary, North Carolina. Wiebe, a two-time winner on the PGA Tour, shooting 65-66-67, rang up a tournament-record 18-under-par 198 total, beating Dana Quigley by three strokes. And at age 50 years and 10 months, he matched Bobby Wadkins as the Champions Tour's youngest winners.

Wiebe stayed a jump ahead in the first two rounds. He birdied his first two holes and two of the last three in a seven-under-par 65, tying Thailand's Boonchu Ruangkit, a late addition to the field. Boonchu missed just one fairway and hit all the greens. "I just tried to do my best," he said. But he was to fade to a tie for 29th. In the second round, Wiebe was four under par on the first nine, including a 30-foot birdie putt at the par-four No. 5. He also dropped a long putt for birdie at the 16th for a 13-under 131 total. "I'm not surprised at how I'm playing," he said. "I'm surprised at how low the scoring is." Dick Mast had two birdies and an eagle in his last four holes for 65, and Dana Quigley birdied the par-four 18th for 66, both closing to within one of Wiebe.

Wiebe started the third and final round with a bogey at No. 1, his first in 38 holes and only his second of the tournament. He snapped back with a birdie at the par-three third hole, rolling in a 25-foot putt. Quigley gave chase, but a bogey at the fourth sidetracked him, and Wiebe rolled on to a three-stroke win that didn't surprise him as much as his scoring did. "I've been hitting the ball well," Wiebe said, "but I didn't think I'd shoot 18 under."

Constellation Energy Senior Players Championship
Timonium, Maryland
Winner: Loren Roberts

This was more than just winning a golf tournament to Loren Roberts. This was an act of revenge — on himself. At the 2006 Senior Players (then under Ford sponsorship), Roberts blew the lead with two double bogeys down the final nine. This time it was the Constellation Energy Senior Players Championship, and Roberts went wire-to-wire, sharing the lead in the first round, then going solo the rest of the way and winning by six strokes over Tom Watson.

"I really exorcised some demons today," Roberts said. Said Watson, his playing companion: "The ball was right in the middle of the clubface. I could see the handwriting on the wall early in the round."

The tournament, after 15 years at the TPC of Michigan, now was at the par-70 Baltimore Country Club, which was baffling the field. Only 19 players broke par in the first round. Gil Morgan had a lock on the first-round lead until he triple-bogeyed the par-four 18th hole. He didn't challenge the rest of the way.

Roberts started in a five-way tie for the lead at 67, then pulled away in the second round, dropping a two-footer for birdie at the tough 18th for 66 to lead Scott Hoch (68) by two. He opened the third round bogey-birdie-bogey, then caught fire on the second nine with birdies at the 10th, 11th and 13th holes from eight, eight and 10 feet, fueling a score of 67 for a three-stroke lead over Fred Funk (66).

It wasn't long into the final round that Watson began seeing the handwriting on the wall. Roberts ran off four straight birdies from No. 2 — a tap-in and putts of seven, eight (after a bunker shot) and six feet, and then a tap-in at No. 9. Roberts wrapped it up with 67 for a 13-under 267 total and the six-stroke win. It was his second win of the season and the sixth on the Champions Tour, but maybe it was his biggest. "This one might be the sweetest for me," Roberts said, "because of what happened last year."

Administaff Small Business Classic
Spring, Texas
Winner: Bernhard Langer

Bernhard Langer is a gentle man with an easy smile, but there was nothing gentle about the way he took his first Champions Tour victory. This was the Administaff Small Business Classic, his fourth Champions Tour start since reaching age 50 in August, and all he did was start off with 62, lead all the way, set a number of records, and win by a dominating eight shots over Mark O'Meara. "We all got hammered," said Tom Kite, finishing third. "Bernhard did some awesome things out there."

Kite and a whole bunch of others shot six-under-par 66 in the first round and were a distant four strokes behind Langer, and that's the closest anyone got the rest of the week. Augusta Pines Golf Club, at Spring, Texas, was Langer's private playground. The 62 — he started birdie-eagle — was merely the first of his records.

Langer bogeyed No. 2 in the second round, his only bogey of the tournament, then was on his way, notching eight birdies, three consecutively, for 65 for a 17-under 127 total — another record for 36 holes — to keep his four-stroke lead, this time over Kite and O'Meara. Langer had a tournament-record 30 on the first nine and offered, "If I could putt like this, I'd be happy the rest of my life." Indeed. He had a tournament-best 76 putts, an average of 1.535 per green hit in regulation.

The final round was an anti-climax. He birdied the last three holes of the final round, shot 64, and finished with a 25-under 191 total, tying Tour records for a 54-hole event. The eight-stroke win was posted, then came the ultimate compliment. Said Langer: "Some of the guys in the locker room kidded me and said, 'Why don't you find somewhere else to play.'"

AT&T Championship
San Antonio, Texas
Winner: John Cook

Tom Kite was 0-for-119 in his native Texas coming into the AT&T Championship at San Antonio. He saw the light at the end of the tunnel this time, being tied for the lead going into the final round. He even edged into the lead at the last turn, then stumbled. And John Cook, in only his second start on the Champions Tour, slipped ahead and kept on going for his first victory. And Kite went to 0-for-120.

Cook, an 11-time winner on the PGA Tour, shot 65-68-65–198, 15 under par at Oak Hills, to win by two strokes and make Mark O'Meara, also a rookie, a runner-up for the fourth time. "I was 30 under par for the last two weeks and I didn't win," said O'Meara, who had the first-round lead with a 63. "I guess I'd better play better." As for Kite, thwarted again: "A frustrating day. I missed four putts on the backside that I haven't been missing."

Cook, who tied for 36th place in his senior debut in the Administaff Classic the week before, was two behind O'Meara with 65 in the first round. He was still two behind in the second, when Kite shot 65 and tied O'Meara (68) at 131. Then came the tense finale. Cook bogeyed the third hole and fell three behind, but he recovered with birdies at the fourth and fifth. Kite took the lead with a birdie from 10 feet at the ninth. But at the 14th, he put his 130-yard approach into a front bunker and bogeyed. Then he bunkered his second shot at the par-five 15th and missed a chance to birdie.

O'Meara had four birdies but also three bogeys on the last nine, and thus the door had been thrown open. Cook birdied three straight holes from No. 9, added birdies at the 15th and 16th, and saved par on a seven-foot putt after bunkering his tee shot at the par-three 18th for a 65 and his first victory. "Thrilled?" Cook said. "I guess I would be thrilled."

Charles Schwab Cup Championship
Sonoma, California
Winner: Jim Thorpe

"I've been in a major funk on the golf course — you know what I mean?" Jim Thorpe was saying. The figures showed what he meant. The Charles Schwab Cup Championship late in October, ending the Champions Tour season, was his last chance to make his mark. Thorpe, now age 58, hadn't won since the 2006 Schwab event (he also won it in 2003) and he hadn't had a top-10 finish since early August. And he had just barely qualified for this championship, taking the 30th and last spot by just $4,000.

"I'm just happy to be here," said Thorpe, making himself right at home at Sonoma (California) Country Club, where he won his previous Schwab tournaments. An eight-under-par 64 tied him for the first-round lead with Argentina's Eduardo Romero, who needed just 23 putts. "If I could do that every round, I'd always shoot 62, 63 or 64," he said.

Thorpe slipped a stroke behind Romero in the second round with 69, tying with the resurrected Denis Watson (64). In the third, Thorpe was bogey-free until the par-four 18th, where he turned cautious, laid up, and double-bogeyed for 69. "If I had taken another look at that pin, I wouldn't have laid up," said Thorpe, finishing a stroke behind Watson (68).

In the final round, five of the last six players were within two shots of each other with four holes to play until Thorpe broke out and birdied all four. He birdied the 15th from 17 feet, the 16th from six feet, the par-three 17th from five feet, and this time he went right at the pin at the 18th and ended up within six feet. He dropped that putt for 66 and a 20-under 268 total and a three-stroke victory over Watson (70) and Fred Funk (66). Then Thorpe reflected on his career and the Champions Tour. "I know I'm on the downswing," Thorpe said. "But I don't think anybody has enjoyed himself as much as I have. This mulligan was sent from the Big Guy up top."

European Seniors Tour

DGM Barbados Open
St. James, Barbados
Winner: Gordon J. Brand

In circumstances identical to those experienced by Carl Mason two years earlier, Gordon J. Brand launched the 2007 European Seniors Tour season with a victory in the DGM Barbados Open. Duplicating Mason's 2004-2005 feat, Brand posted multiple wins at the end of the 2006 and the season-opening triumph on March 2 in the isolated tournament in the Caribbean more than two months before the regular season got underway in earnest back in Europe.

"It's amazing to win again," said Brand, starting his third season on the over-50 circuit after landing two of the final three titles in 2006. "To be honest, I hadn't expected it, although I always seem to play better in hot weather. I hadn't played much golf before coming here."

His 72-70 start at Royal Westmoreland Resort didn't excite him very much until he realized that it put him in a six-way, fourth-place tie, five strokes behind leader Giuseppe Cali. The Italian, a two-time winner on the tour, had stormed into a three-stroke lead Saturday with 69–137, sailing past Nick Job, the first-round leader who had tuned up for Barbados by playing in some mini-tour events in the United States.

Job followed his opening-round 67 with a 75 to join Brand, Ross Drummond, Doug Johnson, Ian Mosey and Juan Quiros at 142. Englishman Bob Cameron (70-70) and Delroy Cambridge, the Jamaican (71-70), were Brand's closest pursuers entering the final round.

Brand birdied the first two holes Sunday, but the turning point didn't come until the middle of the round as Cali turned in 35 and clung to the lead. Brand then poured in four birdie putts around a bogey at the 11th hole to take the lead, saved par from a bunker at the 15th and parred in for his eight-under-par 208 total. Cali bogeyed the 17th and dropped into third place with his 73–210, a shot behind Johnson. The American birdied three of the last five holes for 67–209.

The Gloria Classic
Belek, Turkey
Winner: Nick Job

Nick Job was standing in the middle of the 18th fairway when he won The Gloria Classic as the European Seniors Tour resumed action in early May in Turkey. Fellow Englishman Martin Poxon had just plunked a second ball in the water as he faced Job at the start of a playoff and, with Job's ball at the edge of the green in two, walked over and shook hands with Job, conceding to him his fourth victory in his eighth season at age 57.

"Poor old Poxy," said Job sympathetically of his six-years-younger opponent, but pointed out, "It is very important to get a win in the bank so early in the season and secure another two-year exemption." His last win had been in the 2005 Charles Church Scottish Open. On the other hand, Poxon remained without a victory in his careers on the regular and senior tours in Europe.

Poxon's decision that discretion was the better part of valor one hole earlier may have cost him that elusive win. Playing that same par-five hole as his 54th, he elected to lay up rather than risk a long, fading second shot and settled for a par and a 70 that tied him with Job at 10-under-par 206. Job, who began the final round at 138, two shots behind leaders Poxon and American Doug Johnson, finished birdie-eagle for 68 and his 206. Poxon drove into the water hazard along the left side of the fairway in the play-off and, facing a difficult third shot across the water at the green, had to gamble with Job safely across, but failed.

Stewart Ginn, who shared the first-round lead at 67 with Delroy Cambridge and Tony Johnstone, had the lead early in the final round, but finished a shot out of the playoff in third place with Cambridge and Luis Carbonetti.

Sharp Italian Seniors Open
Venice, Italy
Winner: Simon Owen

The situation was right down Simon Owen's alley — a playoff for the Sharp Italian Seniors Open title. Owen sized things up this way when he wound up in a four-man deadlock after the regulation 54 holes at the Circolo Golf Venezia: "When you go into a playoff situation, you don't know what is going to happen, but it was always in the back of my mind that I have a great playoff record."

Having scored his two most recent victories via the overtime route, the 56-year-old New Zealander did it again in Italy when he wedged to two feet for an easy birdie to beat Englishmen Carl Mason and Tony Allen and American John Benda. It was Owen's first win since his initial senior victory at Tunisia in 2001.

Mason, the tour's leading performer since 2003, put the other three to the test on the final Sunday. Benda, winless in Europe, had taken the lead Saturday with a scintillating 63 for 134 with nine birdies, all from inside 12 feet. He was one ahead of Owen (70-65), two in front of Allen (71-66) and, believe it, nine shots ahead of Mason at the start of the day. While the other three were struggling, Mason, first or second on the Order of Merit in his four seasons on tour, raced up the standings with 65 and posted the eight-under 208 target score.

When the other three players reached the 18th green, Benda had the best chance for the title, but missed from six feet. He also was the only other player besides Owen to hit the green in the playoff, but couldn't hole the birdie putt to extend the playoff. It was Mason's seventh runner-up finish to go with his 14 victories. Bob Cameron, who led by three after the first round, finished sixth at 211.

AIB Irish Seniors Open
Co. Kildare, Ireland
Winner: Costantino Rocca

It took only three starts for Costantino Rocca to become a winner on the European Seniors Tour. Italy's most successful professional missed doing it two weeks earlier in his home country, but instead won in Ireland, where he had landed his last previous victory in 1999 on the regular European Tour. He shot a one-under-par 71 in the final round of the AIB Irish Seniors Open for a two-stroke triumph at Palmerstown House's PGA National Ireland course.

It was a disappointing outcome for Australia's Stewart Ginn, the leader the first two days. Ginn, who turned 58 Saturday, has played most of his senior golf in America, where he won the Senior Players Championship in 2002, but is winless in Europe. He came close three times in 2006, the first season he played an extensive European schedule, losing the Irish Open to Sam Torrance in a four-man playoff.

Ginn birdied four of his last five holes in Friday's opening round for 67 and a one-stroke lead over South African Gavan Levenson. Rocca was just another shot back and remained two off Ginn's pace when Ginn followed with 71 of his own Saturday, bouncing back from bogeys on two of the first three holes. American Doug Johnson shared the 140 spot with Rocca.

The Italian's victory on a rainy Sunday revolved around the 11th hole, where he holed a spectacular chip shot for his first of three par saves on the back nine to salvage the winning 71 for 211 total. He two-putted from 50 feet off the front edge of the last green, reminiscent of the huge putt he holed on the final hole of the 1995 Open Championship to force the playoff he then lost to John Daly. An early double bogey and a three-putt from six feet at the 17th dropped Ginn to 76–214, tied for fourth with Johnson (74), a shot behind runners-up Juan Quiros and Kevin Spurgeon, who both had 72s.

Jersey Seniors Classic
Jersey, Channel Isles
Winner: Bobby Lincoln

When South African Bobby Lincoln won for the first time on the European Seniors Tour in the Jersey Seniors Classic, he came to this conclusion: "Now I feel that I belong out here." Lincoln broke from a three-man tie after 36 holes with Carl Mason and Bill Longmuir and rolled to a two-stroke victory, shooting a final-round 67 for 11-under-par 205 at La Moye Golf Club.

Lincoln polished off the victory with a flourish, even though he admitted "I was very nervous when I went out." Early birdies at the second and fourth holes settled him down and he was never seriously challenged after that, although Longmuir stayed within range and shot 69 to finish second. Uncharacteristically, Mason faded with 75 and dropped into a five-way tie for third at 213.

The 53-year-old South African had two more birdies on the outgoing stretch after dropping a shot at the fifth, the latter birdie at No. 8 with a pitch from "an impossible lie," then played the back nine in two under with three birdies and a bogey.

Longmuir, winless for two years on the circuit, jumped off in front Friday with a six-under 66, "the best round I've played all year." That staked him to a two-stroke lead over Mason and fellow Englishman Bob Larratt. Five others, including defending champion Guillermo Encina, were at 69 and Lincoln sat in a 12th-place deadlock at 71.

A chip-in eagle at the 16th following five birdies and a pair of bogeys hoisted Lincoln into the tie at 138 Saturday. Longmuir shot par 72. Mason shot 70 despite hitting a five iron out of bounds early in the round.

Ryder Cup Wales Seniors Open
Conwy (Caenarvonshire), Wales
Winner: Carl Mason

Sooner or later, it seemed certain that Carl Mason would register his first victory of 2007. When he teed off in the Ryder Cup Wales Seniors Open, Mason already had two top-three finishes in his first four starts as the European Seniors Tour's leading player sought his 15th victory.

The win did come at Conwy Golf Club in Wales, but not easily. The 54-year-old Mason sprinted from four strokes off the pace with just 10 holes to play, carved out a four-under-par 68 and won the tournament by two strokes over Spain's Juan Quiros and winless Scot Ross Drummond with his 210 total. He collected the season's second largest check — €110,358 — in landing his second Wales Seniors Open title in three years.

A so-so 73 left him four strokes behind Chile's Guillermo Encina the first day. Encina's 69 on a windy Friday gave him a one-stroke lead over Maurice Bembridge, the Ryder Cup veteran; fellow Englishman Tony Allen and Costantino Rocca, the Irish Seniors Open winner two weeks earlier.

Calm weather prevailed Saturday and Quiros took advantage, blazing a 64 that shot him from a tie for 34th place (75) into a two-stroke lead over Rocca and three over Mason (69) and Argentina's Horacio Carbonetti (70). Quiros had a remarkable mid-round run of five birdies and an eagle starting at the seventh hole as he tied the course record.

The 430-yard 16th was the pivotal hole Sunday. Mason's 35-foot birdie putt there gave him control of the lead. Rocca bogeyed there, as did Quiros and Drummond at the 17th, and Mason closed it out with pars on the final two holes.

Bendinat London Seniors Masters
Ash, Kent, England
Winner: Sam Torrance

A week after Carl Mason made a statement regarding a third Order of Merit title with his initial victory, Sam Torrance showed his intention to match that distinction. The Scot made a brave bogey on the 54nd hole of the Bendinat London Seniors Masters to secure his first win of 2007 and ninth of his part-time five-year career that saw him lead the Order of Merit money list in 2005 and 2006.

Winning the London Masters for the second time in its three-season history, Torrance shot 70 for 16-under-par 206, finishing a shot ahead of Spanish ex-Ryder Cupper Jose Rivero and two in front of Mason and Ireland's Eamonn Darcy. After winning at the London Golf Club in 2005, Torrance let a three-stroke lead slip away there in 2006 or it would have been three in a row.

Torrance and Mason posted four-under-par 68s and formed a powerhouse leadership duo the first day. Each with five birdies and a bogey on their cards, they led by a stroke over Rivero, Tony Allen of England and Jerry Bruner of the United States.

The eventual winner forged two shots ahead Saturday with another 68 for 136, as Mason settled for 70 and a share of second place with Ross Drummond (70-68), in contention for his first tour victory for a second consecutive week. Four birdies in five holes on the back nine spurred Torrance to the 68 and sole possession of first place.

The Scot was in command all day Sunday. He went out in 32 and had a four-stroke lead until taking bogeys at the 13th and 16th holes. Then, at the 18th, he drove into the water and missed the green after taking his drop. But he pitched 30 yards across the green to within inches of the cup to salvage a bogey, and that stood up for the win.

Open de France Senior de Divonne
Divonne les Bains, France
Winner: Juan Quiros

There's something about the Alps that inspires Juan Quiros. In 2006, the Spaniard won the Bad Ragaz PGA Seniors Open in the mountains in Switzerland, his first European Seniors Tour title. In mid-July in 2007, he won again in Mount Blanc country in the Open de France Senior de Divonne at Divonne les Bains, France, easing home with a one-stroke victory over England's Tony Allen.

The win off a closing 70 for eight-under-par 208 total gave Quiros some solace for the one that got away two events earlier when he blew a two-shot lead in the final round of the Wales Open after shooting a brilliant 64 on the second day.

Allen, enjoying his best of six seasons on the tour, made things interesting for Quiros Sunday. The Englishman, who was one of the playoff losers to Simon Owen in the Italian Senior Open in May, closed with four threes and put his 68–209 on the board before Quiros finished. Quiros had rallied from a poor start and took a one-stroke lead with a birdie at the 17th hole. Then, after missing the green at the par-three 18th, he chipped to tap-in range for the victory.

Quiros had trailed by a shot after 36 holes following a pair of 69s as South Africa's Tony Johnstone, Chile's Guillermo Encina and Australia's

David Good held the lead at 137. Countryman Emilio Rodriguez and Japan's Seiji Ebihara, a six-time winner on the circuit, joined Quiros at 138 and, acknowledging the presence of Divonne's prominent gambling casino with 20 players within five shots of the lead, Good observed: "You'll need to toss the dice to decide the winner."

Things didn't look promising for Quiros in the early going Sunday. He double-bogeyed the fourth hole and bogeyed the fifth, but he recovered with a birdie at the seventh and an eagle off a seven iron to a foot at the eighth. Another birdie at the 12th got him thinking ahead to the 17th — "a very easy hole for me." He was right and insured the victory with that final birdie.

The Senior Open Championship
Gullane, East Lothian, Scotland
Winner: Tom Watson

Tom Watson's remarkable reign of success in the British Isles lives on. Thirty-two years after capturing his first of five Open Championships, the brilliant American landed his third Senior Open Championship — a feat tying Gary Player's tournament victory record — when the championship was staged for the first time at storied Muirfield. Watson has won eight major championships on six of the most testing courses in Scotland and England.

Watson had also prevailed at Muirfield in the 1980 Open Championship and drew upon that experience in 2007. "I had a good feeling all day," he remarked after surviving an adventurous final hole and hanging up a 73 that let him escape with an even-par 284 total for a one-stroke victory over fellow American Mark O'Meara and Stewart Ginn of Australia. It provided some consolation for his closing collapse three weeks earlier in the U.S. Senior Open, when he blew a three-shot lead over the final eight holes and finished fourth.

The Hall of Famer, at home in the typical cold and blustery Scottish weather, was a challenger from the start, although the attention the first day was on the surprising start of Nick Faldo, the great English star making his first start as a senior on the course where he twice won the Open Championship. Faldo shared the first-round lead at 68 with fellow Englishmen Nick Job and Gordon J. Brand.

Watson shot 70, then 71 on a gusty Friday when his bogey at the last hole dropped him a stroke behind leader Des Smyth, whose 70 for 140 early in the day matched the low scores of the round. Ginn, also at 141, produced a fine 69 on another tough weather day Saturday and edged a stroke ahead of Watson (70–211) and three in front of O'Meara (70–213).

Watson took the lead for the first time at the sixth hole Sunday, fended off challenges from Ginn, O'Meara and Eduardo Romero of Argentina, and reached the 18th tee with a three-shot lead. His finish wasn't pretty. He drove into a fairway bunker, took two shots to clear the sand and, after Ginn and O'Meara missed birdie tries, two-putted from the fringe for the double bogey and the win, the 49th of his brilliant career, 10th as a senior and second of the year. Faldo finished eight shots behind Watson in 14th place.

Wentworth Senior Masters
Virginia Water, Surrey, England
Winner: Des Smyth

Irishman Des Smyth has been a full-timer of some success on the Champions Tour in America since turning 50 in 2003, but every now and then he pops back to Europe to play a few events on the European Seniors Tour. It paid off for a second time when he took home a two-stroke victory in the Wentworth Senior Masters at the historic Wentworth Club outside of London in early August.

The win came as a bit of a surprise to Smyth. "I have struggled all year (in America) with my game," he noted, glossing over his top-10 finishes in his two earlier starts in 2007 in Europe. It was unlike 2005 when he won the season-ending Arcapita Tour Championship in Bahrain on the heels of two wins on the Champions Tour.

His strongest challenger this year at Wentworth was the remarkable Bob Charles. Still competitive at age 71, the New Zealand left-hander undershot his age Sunday with a two-under-par 70 after two earlier rounds of 71 and picked off second place with his 212 total. Smyth closed with 69, the day's lowest round, for his victorious 210 and observed that "this makes up for the playoff I lost here to Rodger Davis in the PGA Championship in 1986."

Smyth shadowed the leaders the first two days on Wentworth's Edinburgh course. Japan's globe-trotting Katsuyoshi Tomori led the first day with his five-under-par 67, one stroke better than England's David J. Russell. Smyth was three back in a five-way tie at 70. Eduardo Romero, hoping to follow in the successful 2007 footsteps of fellow Argentines Angel Cabrera, the U.S. Open champion, and Andres Romero, the recent winner of the Deutsche Bank Players' Championship, improved two shots on his opening 71 and took the lead Saturday at 140, a stroke in front of Smyth (71) and Tomori (74).

Smyth's putting played the major role in his Sunday finish. He got the lead with birdies at the third and fifth holes after Romero started the round by driving into a gorse bush and taking a double bogey. While Romero was struggling on the final holes and failing to make up ground on playing partner Smyth, Charles slipped past him into second place when he birdied the 15th, 16th and 17th holes.

Bad Ragaz PGA Seniors Open
Zurich, Switzerland
Winner: Carl Mason

The long run of different winners on the European Seniors Tour came to an end in the Bad Ragaz PGA Seniors Open in Switzerland, not surprisingly through the handiwork of Carl Mason, currently the circuit's most successful player. Eleven players championed the first 11 events on the 2007 schedule before Mason's domineering six-stroke victory at Golf Club Bad Ragaz, his second win of the year.

With the victory, Mason moved into second place on the tour's all-time list. It was his 16th win in just his fifth senior season, jumping him one ahead of Neil Coles. Tommy Horton leads the list with 23.

The tournament was Mason at his finest. He tacked together rounds of 65, 64 and 65 in posting the season's lowest total in a 54-hole event. His 16-under-par 194 was just a shot off the all-time-record 193 shot by Bob Cameron in the Sanremo Masters on a par-69 course.

Yet, it was not a wire-to-wire triumph. Argentina's Horacio Carbonetti and Scot Steve Martin shot 64 in the opening round to stand one ahead of Mason and Jimmy Heggarty. Fireworks erupted Saturday as Costantino Rocca scorched the course with 62 and Tony Johnstone had a hole-in-one as he shot 65, but Mason moved in front to stay with his 129. Rocca was at 130 and Carbonetti and Martin, the first-day leaders, matched 67s for 131.

Those three and David J. Russell remained close through the front nine Sunday as Mason went out with an even-par 35. But then Mason poured on the gas with birdies at Nos. 10 and 11 and wrapped up the easy victory with consecutive birdies at the 14th, 15th and 16th before parring in for the 65 and 194 total. Carbonetti, Rocca and Russell tied for second place with 200s.

The Midas English Seniors Open
St. Mellion, Cornwall, England
Winner: Bill Longmuir

It was an unlikely victory for Bill Longmuir. His game had tailed off a bit since his last win nearly two years earlier and old rival Carl Mason, with his game razor sharp, was going after his fourth straight Midas English Seniors Open title.

Longmuir had not mustered much of a challenge to Mason since finishing second to him on the 2003 Order of Merit and remarked after his victory at St. Mellion Hotel, Golf and Country Club: "What made it harder was that I was up against Carl. He won last week and has had four great years in this event, so I'm really proud that I held him off."

Actually, Longmuir had to overtake him. Mason grabbed the lead the first day and was in front of him by a stroke going into the final round. Trying to extend his English Open streak and win for the second week in a row, Mason posted a three-under-par 69 Friday to sit one stroke ahead of eight other players, including Longmuir.

He followed with another 69 in the weather-extended second round when heavy rains forced a nearly six-hour suspension at midday, taking 33 strokes over nine holes Saturday before dark and 36 strokes early Sunday morning. Longmuir also shot 69 in the interrupted round and went into the final round alone in second place, with Northern Ireland's Jimmy Heggarty two behind Mason in third place.

Strong winds replaced the rain Sunday and the final round became a duel between Mason and Longmuir early. In fact, the Scot started to run away on the front nine, spurting three strokes in front with three birdies on the first seven holes. His putter failing him, Mason never got closer that two shots the rest of the way, and Longmuir had plenty of room for his three-putt bogey on the 18th for 69–208 and the two-stroke win, his sixth as a senior.

European Senior Masters
Milton Keynes, England
Winner: Carl Mason

Carl Mason picked up a special plum when he squeezed out his third win of the season — a successful defense of the European Senior Masters. The first-place money from his hard-earned overtime victory over Costantino Rocca elevated Mason past Tommy Horton to become the all-time leading money winner on the European Seniors Tour.

When he zeroed in a wedge shot to two feet on the first playoff hole for the winning birdie, Mason was rewarded with a €49,713 check, setting a new career record total of €1,521,836. The victory came on the heels of a win in Switzerland and a runner-up finish in the Midas English Open as the Englishman reasserted his dominance with his 17th victory on the circuit.

Rocca had cause for disappointment when it was over. The Italian, seeking his second senior win in his rookie season, led the first day on the Dukes Course at Woburn Golf Club, where he was the special guest of the Duke of Bedford. He fell one behind Mason the second day but had the lead until the last hole Sunday. He shot 69 Friday, one in front of John Chillas, Adam Sowa, Manuel Pinero and David Good. Mason had a 71, then took over the top spot with a sparkling 66 as Rocca posted another 69.

The two men, though clear of the rest of the field, played somewhat erratically through 14 holes Sunday. Then Mason, one ahead, faltered badly with bogeys on the next three holes to fall two strokes behind Rocca. At the dramatic final hole, Mason holed a 35-foot birdie putt for 73 and Rocca bogeyed from a greenside bunker for 72 and the tie at six-under-par 210. Rocca missed an 18-foot birdie putt before Mason tapped in the winner in the playoff.

PGA Seniors Championship
Colchester, Suffolk, England
Winner: Carl Mason

What a month for Carl Mason! It started at Bad Ragaz in Switzerland on August 10 and ended on September 9, when he played his most impressive of four consecutive tournaments. Posting his third win in four starts with a runner-up finish in the other, Mason overpowered the field and rolled to a six-stroke victory in the major PGA Seniors Championship at the Stoke-by-Nayland Club in Suffolk, England.

In the remarkable performance, Mason carved out four consecutive rounds of five-under-par 67, never trailing as he posted the 20-under-par 268 on the Gainsborough course for his fourth win of the European Seniors Tour season and 18th of his career.

"I have to admit that my win here was special," he said afterward. "It feels wonderful to win the PGA Championship for the second time in my career. I'm very pleased with my consistency. It's not easy to lead for all four days. I don't think I've ever shot four 67s in a tournament."

Little-known Canadian Bruce Heuchan, who led the pre-season qualifier to get his playing privileges, hung in with Mason, matching his 67s to share the lead with him through the first two rounds. Mason had seven birdies and an eagle the first day and a bogey-free round the second day. At that point, he and Heuchan led Luis Carbonetti and Costantino Rocca, Mason's playoff victim in the preceding tournament, by a stroke.

Mason broke away to a four-shot margin with his third 67 Saturday. John Bland, the long-time South African senior, moved into second place with 69–205, a shot in front of Heuchan (72) and Rocca (71). Mason was never in trouble Sunday, going out in 33 and finishing it off with birdies at the 16th and 17th and a one-putt par from the sand at the par-three 18th. Rocca finished a runner-up for the second straight tournament with 68–274, joined in that spot by Frenchman Philippe Dugeny, who closed with 63, the week's best round.

Scandinavian Senior Open
Copenhagen, Denmark
Winner: John Chillas

John Chillas emerged from the menacing shadow cast by the domineering Carl Mason to end a three-year victory drought in a soggy Scandinavian Senior Open in Copenhagen, Denmark. At the end, the 56-year-old Scot had to go four extra holes before claiming his third European Seniors Tour title in a playoff battle with Englishman Glenn Ralph.

For two days at Royal Copenhagen Golf Club, it seemed likely that Mason was headed for his fourth victory in his last five starts. Mason posted 68 at the rain-drenched, par-71 course to stake out a one-stroke lead over the foursome of American Doug Johnson, Englishman Tim Rastall, South African Bertus Smit and Spaniard Juan Quiros.

Even though he yielded the top spot to Frenchman Philippe Dugeny, who shot 66 for 136 Saturday, Mason loomed large as he shared second place at 69–137 with Bobby Lincoln (71-66) and Chillas, who tacked a 67 onto his opening 70.

Contrary to recent form, though, Mason never challenged Sunday, even though Dugeny faded away quickly. Chillas and Johnson took up the chase and Chillas moved ahead at seven under par with a birdie at the 11th. Johnson slipped toward a third-place finish with a bogey at the 12th, but Ralph entered the picture ahead of them with three late birdies to finish with a 65 and an eight-under 205 total. A birdie at the 16th and a par from the sand at the 18th gave Chillas his tying 68.

After holing a 30-foot birdie putt to save the third extra hole, the Scot took the title with a par on the next hole when the winless Ralph bunkered his tee shot and couldn't match it.

Charles Church Scottish Seniors Open
Edinburgh, Scotland
Winner: Jose Rivero

With the season drawing to a close, Jose Rivero became the second Spanish winner at the end of September. Rivero joined Juan Quiros (French Open) in the winner's circle when he held off native son Ross Drummond on the final holes of the Charles Church Scottish Seniors Open. The one-stroke victory for the two-time Ryder Cupper at the Marriott Dalmahoy Hotel and Country Club in Edinburgh complemented two wins in his first full season in 2006.

A sizzling six-under-par 66 in Saturday's second round set up Rivero's victory. Three off the first-round pace of Costantino Rocca with 70, Rivero surged three strokes ahead of Drummond and Bobby Lincoln the second day. Rocca, whose opening 67 was sparked by a hole-in-one at the 17th hole, struggled to a 73 Saturday after injuring his hip on his second shot to the 14th.

Drummond, seeking his first senior victory, mounted his Sunday challenge on Dalmahoy's back nine. He holed a 117-yard wedge shot for an eagle at the 12th and was tied for the lead when Rivero bogeyed the 14th. However, Drummond promptly bogeyed the next hole, and fell two back when Rivero birdied the par-five 16th and parred in. Drummond's birdie at the last hole merely cut the final margin in half.

It was four strokes back to Bob Cameron and Nick Job in third place. Carl Mason's momentum finally ran out. The four-time winner was never a factor and tied for 43rd with 222.

OKI Castellon Open de Espana Senior
Castellon, Spain
Winner: Carl Mason

Carl Mason had one regret as he reflected on the fifth victory of his remarkable season. There he was after rolling to an easy victory in the OKI Castellon Open de Espana Senior, the year's No. 1 spot already wrapped up with another tournament to go. He had clinched the Order of Merit for a third time in five years on the strength of record seasonal earnings. So, what was the problem?

"I just wish I'd felt this confident and comfortable on the golf course when I was on the main tour," said the 54-year-old Englishman, who scored just two victories during his 25 years on the European Tour and three others in slim-field African events. "It's having confidence to win that makes all the difference."

Only the scorching 64 of Argentina's Luis Carbonetti in the second round prevented Mason from making it a wire-to-wire triumph in mid-October at Club de Campo del Mediterraneo, the home course of international star Sergio Garcia and his father, Victor. The elder Garcia played in the tournament with his famous son on the bag.

Mason shot 66 the first day to lead native son Emilio Rodriguez and Chile's Guillermo Encina by a stroke. Carbonetti's 64 on Saturday — nine birdies and a bogey — jumped him a stroke in front of Mason, who had two late bogeys and 68 for 134. There were then 10 players within six strokes of the lead, but, as Carbonetti put it, "Carl is always the man to beat."

Nobody even came close Sunday. Mason conjured up a seven-under-par 65 to finish 17 under par at 199 and register his 19th victory on the circuit. He finished with a four-shot margin over runner-up Carbonetti (70) and six over David Good (68) in third place.

The Kingdom of Bahrain Trophy - Seniors Tour Championship
Denham, England
Winner: Costantino Rocca

When Carl Mason was unable to apply the coup de grace by topping off his sensational season with a victory in the year-ending Senior Tour Championship, it was appropriate that Costantino Rocca stepped up to win the tournament and collect not only the event's Kingdom of Bahrain Trophy but also the Hardy's Rookie of the Year award of the European Seniors Tour.

Rocca, the only Italian to have ever played in the Ryder Cup, had already distinguished himself in his first year with a victory in the Irish Open and three runner-up finishes to Mason, one in a playoff. The one-stroke win in the Tour Championship at Buckinghamshire Golf Club in England solidified his claim to the Hardy's award and to second place in the final Order of Merit standings. Rocca was the only multiple winner besides Mason for the season.

Mason, who didn't get on track until a final-round 66 jumped him into a tie for eighth place, had already clinched his third Order of Merit title. His five victories, a pair of second-place postings and 13 top-10 finishes in 17 starts helped him pile up €412,376. A single-season record, that moved him past Tommy Horton into first place on the career money list with €1,642,960. His previous Order of Merit titles came in 2003 and 2004.

Like Mason, Rocca fired a six-under-par 66 Sunday, racing from a four-stroke deficit to score the winning 206 total. He and Englishman Nick Job were at 140 Saturday, both with pairs of 70s. They trailed Adan Sowa of Argentina, who solved blustery conditions at Buckinghamshire with rounds of 67 and 69 to move a stroke ahead of first-round co-leader John Chillas.

Job matched scores with Rocca until the very end Sunday, blowing a playoff opportunity when he three-putted from 25 feet on the final green for 67–207.

Thrilled with his victory, Rocca quipped about the freshman award: "I am 'Rocca of the Year.' I wanted to win this week to finish second behind 'Carletto.' He has been fantastic."

Japan Senior Tour

Aderans Wellness Open
Nakajo, Niigata
Winner: Katsunari Takahashi

Katsunari Takahashi continued his consistent and relentless pace of success on the Japan Senior Tour at the season-opening Aderans Wellness Open. With his playoff win in the Aderans tournament in June, the 56-year-old Takahashi became the career victory leader with his 12th title since joining the circuit in 2000. Winless only in the 2006 season, he had been tied with Fujio Kobayashi with 11 titles apiece.

Takahashi's victory at Nakajo Golf Club, Niigata Prefecture, came at the expense of Kiyoshi Murota, the runaway money leader in 2006, who shared the top spot the first two days. He shot 67 Friday, a score matched by Seiji Ebihara and Minoru Hatsumi, and 68 Saturday for 135. Takahashi (68-67) joined him and Ebihara at the top with Tsuneyuki (Tommy) Nakajima just a stroke back.

Their 69s for 204 totals Sunday sent Takahashi and Murota to the playoff, where Takahashi holed a 26-foot birdie putt on the first extra hole.

Fancl Classic
Shizuoka
Winner: Kiyoshi Murota

Kiyoshi Murota evened the score two months later when the seniors gathered again for the Fancl Classic, the season's second event. Murota successfully defended that title, picking up his fourth senior win with a one-stroke triumph over Motomasa Aoki, who just missed an eagle putt for a tie on the final green. Murota closed with 68 for 204 total, Aoki with 69–205.

Those two players had entered the final round at Susono Country Club in Shizuoka Prefecture with 136s — Murota off 66-70 and Aoki off 70-66. They were a stroke behind Tsuneyuki Nakajima, who lost the 2006 Fancl Classic in a playoff against Murota.

Nakajima had shot 65 for 135 Saturday and was nip and tuck with Murota again through the first 12 holes Sunday. However, as Nakajima faded to a back-nine 40 for 74 and a fifth-place finish, Murota completed his four-birdies, no-bogeys 68 for the victory.

Big Raisac Senior Open
Miyagi
Winner: Masahiro Kuramoto

Perhaps the experience of playing a full schedule on the Champions Tour in America helped when Masahiro (Massy) Kuramoto made a brief return to Japan and captured his first senior victory in the Big Raisac Senior Open in early September. Medalist in the tough Champions Tour qualifier, the 52-year-old Kuramoto had four finishes of 13th or better prior to the quick trip home and his four-stroke triumph at Big Raisac Country Club in Miyagi Prefecture.

It was a lead-sharing wire-to-wire win at that for Kuramoto, who was a popular star during his years on the Japan Tour, where he registered 34 victories and shot the circuit's only 59.

Kuramoto's opening, two-under-par 70 gave him a three-way piece of first place with Yoshio Fumiyama and Hawaiian David Ishii, a former No. 1 on the Japan Tour. Kuramoto and Fumiyama followed Saturday with 69s to remain in front at 139, one ahead of Minoru Hatsumi, who had a day's-best 67. Kuramoto then finished it off in style with 68 for 207 total, Hatsumi taking second place with 71–211 as Fumiyama shot 73 and slipped into a third-place tie with Takashi Miyoshi.

Japan PGA Senior Championship
Hitachiomiya, Ibaraki
Winner: Tateo Ozaki

Tateo (Jet) Ozaki, the only one of the three famous golfing brothers to have ventured into the senior golf realm, has a major championship to show for it. The 53-year-old Ozaki came from a stroke off the lead to capture the Japan PGA Senior Championship, his second victory in the over-50 arena.

The middle brother, whose competent career on the Japan Tour was overshadowed by the exploits of the older Masashi and younger Naomichi, had four solid, unspectacular rounds in winning the championship at Shizu Hills Country Club in Ibaraki Prefecture.

Ozaki started four behind Masami Ito, the little-known first-round leader, who carved out a five-under-par 67, then bounced into a tie for second place Friday with his 71-69–140, deadlocked with Ito, who slumped to 73 on his way to a 13th-place finish. Tsuneyuki Nakajima seized the lead with 67–137.

Another victory duel between Nakajima and Kiyoshi Murota seemed likely when Murota shot 68 to Nakajima's 72 Saturday and they shared the lead at 209 heading into the final round, with Ozaki (70) and Yoshio Fumiyama (68) trailing by one. Instead, they both crumbled surprisingly with 77s and Ozaki posted another 70 for 280 total and won by two strokes over Seiji Ebihara (70), Hajime Meshiai (71) and Katsuyoshi Tomori (71).

PGA Handa Cup Philanthropy Senior Open
Ibaraki
Winner: Katsuyoshi Tomori

Money talked for Katsuyoshi Tomori. The 52-year-old player, one of the limited number of Japanese who have played extensively on the world scene, hadn't won in more than two years on the Japan Senior Tour. He did, though, when the PGA Handa Cup Philanthropy Senior Open, the richest event in the circuit's history, came up on the schedule at the end of September.

Coming off a tie-for-second finish in the PGA Senior Championship, Tomori raced from a stroke off the lead to a three-stroke victory, a second win to go with his 2005 Aderans Wellness title. His victim was Tsukasa Watanabe, a tour rookie who held first place through the first two rounds. The first day it was with a 66 to 67s of Tomori, Hajime Meshiai and Kiyoshi Murota. On the second day Noboru Fujiike bolted into the picture with an eight-under-par 64 on Ibaraki Golf Club's West course. He joined Tomori at 138, one behind Watanabe.

Watanabe shot a respectable 70 Sunday, but that was no match for the 66 scored by Tomori as he finished with a 12-under-par 204 total and the three-shot margin over Watanabe.

Komatsu Open
Ishikawa
Winner: Toyotake Nakao

Toyotake Nakao produced the first true wire-to-wire victory of the season in the Komatsu Open, the final tournament of a three-event early-fall stretch. Unlike his earlier victory in the 2004 Aderans Wellness Open when he exploded from behind with a closing 64, Nakao opened his final margin to three with a comfortable 67 to shake off threatening Kiyoshi Murota, who already had a win and a playoff loss earlier in the year.

Nakao carried a one-stroke lead through the first two rounds. With 68 Friday, he took a one-stroke advantage over Teruo Nakamura and Kimpachi Yoshimura. On Saturday, Nakao managed just a par 72 for 140, keeping his one-shot lead, then over Murota (71-70) and Nakamura (69-72). While Nakao was opening his winning margin, Murota was shooting 69, edging Nakamura (70) for the runner-up spot.

Japan Senior Open
Kikuchi, Kumamoto
Winner: Isao Aoki

Isao Aoki resurrected his old magic to make history in the Japan Senior Open. Japan's greatest international star ever provided yet another gem of evidence of that fact by shooting his age — 65 — in the final round and becoming the oldest Senior Open champion in history.

With the remarkable climatic 18 holes, Aoki demolished Kiyoshi Murota's six-stroke lead and won his fifth Senior Open by a stroke with his 12-under-par 276 at Kumamoto Chuo Country Club. His four earlier Open victories came in a row in the middle 1990s. He also won the senior N. Cup Open in 2002.

Murota, with a win and two seconds already posted for 2007, sailed along atop the leaderboard for three rounds. He struck early with 66 and led Hajime Meshiai by two the first day. He doubled that margin with 68–134 Friday, then over Katsunari Takahashi, who had a pair of 69s. Takahashi cut the lead back to two with his third straight 69 Saturday as Murota settled for 71. Although six back at that point, Aoki (72-69-70) had only four players to pass, which he did Sunday with his eight-birdie, single-bogey flourish to victory.

Kinojyo Senior Open
Okayama
Winner: Chip Beck

In a different sense, Chip Beck's victory in the Kinojyo Senior Open was as unlikely as was that of Isao Aoki in the Japan Senior Open two weeks earlier. In the middle 1990s, Beck's playing career seemed to be over. The game had suddenly disappeared along with the playing privileges on the U.S. PGA Tour of a player who had four wins, once shot 59 and made the 1993 Ryder Cup team.

Although Beck revived his game, he had done little earlier in 2007 in his first full season on the Champions Tour before getting a spot in the field of the Japan Senior Tour's final event in mid-November. The first round at Kinojyo Golf Club in Okayama Prefecture gave no hint of what was to happen as Beck shot 72 and was tied for 37th place, seven strokes behind leader Yoshio Fumiyama.

Beck entered the fray the second day. His 66 moved him within three strokes of co-leaders Minoru Hatsumi (70-65) and Tsukasa Watanabe (66-69). Only two players — Beck (69) and Katsunari Takahashi (67) — broke 70 Sunday and they wound up tied for first place at 207. Beck then picked up the victory on the first playoff hole when Takahashi three-putted for a bogey.

APPENDIXES

American Tours

Mercedes-Benz Championship

Plantation Course at Kapalua, Maui, Hawaii
Par 36-37–73; 7,411 yards

January 4-7
purse, $5,500,000

	SCORES				TOTAL	MONEY
Vijay Singh	69	69	70	70	278	$1,100,000
Adam Scott	73	69	69	69	280	630,000
Trevor Immelman	71	68	72	72	283	410,000
J.B. Holmes	73	68	71	72	284	260,000
Davis Love	70	71	75	68	284	260,000
Will MacKenzie	69	70	73	72	284	260,000
Luke Donald	72	71	71	71	285	193,000
K.J. Choi	69	77	71	69	286	170,000
J.J. Henry	74	73	68	71	286	170,000
David Toms	75	72	72	67	286	170,000
Stephen Ames	69	74	74	70	287	145,000
Troy Matteson	73	70	70	74	287	145,000
Stuart Appleby	73	72	72	71	288	120,000
Chris Couch	71	70	77	70	288	120,000
Rory Sabbatini	71	78	68	71	288	120,000
Joe Durant	73	73	72	71	289	95,000
Kirk Triplett	75	73	69	72	289	95,000
Jim Furyk	71	74	76	71	292	80,000
John Senden	73	74	75	71	293	71,333.34
Tim Herron	75	72	72	74	293	71,333.33
Geoff Ogilvy	74	72	74	73	293	71,333.33
Rod Pampling	74	80	71	69	294	65,000
Carl Pettersson	72	75	77	70	294	65,000
Brett Wetterich	69	79	73	73	294	65,000
John Rollins	77	74	70	74	295	61,000
Eric Axley	78	75	74	69	296	59,000
Aaron Baddeley	77	72	78	70	297	57,000
Corey Pavin	75	75	74	77	301	56,000
Dean Wilson	80	78	72	72	302	55,000
Jeff Maggert	76	74	74	79	303	54,000
Chad Campbell	77	75	78	75	305	53,000
D.J. Trahan	79	77	75	75	306	52,000
Ben Curtis	81	78	77	76	312	51,000
Arron Oberholser	73				WD	

Sony Open in Hawaii

Waialae Country Club, Honolulu, Hawaii
Par 35-35–70; 7,060 yards

January 11-14
purse, $5,200,000

	SCORES				TOTAL	MONEY
Paul Goydos	66	63	70	67	266	$936,000
Luke Donald	63	66	69	69	267	457,600
Charles Howell	69	63	65	70	267	457,600
K.J. Choi	64	71	68	68	271	204,750
Jim Furyk	65	68	69	69	271	204,750
Doug LaBelle	69	71	66	65	271	204,750
Steve Stricker	67	67	67	70	271	204,750

	SCORES			TOTAL	MONEY
Robert Allenby	67	66	70	69	272	156,000
Geoff Ogilvy	67	72	69	64	272	156,000
Craig Kanada	72	65	66	70	273	130,000
Steve Lowery	72	67	67	67	273	130,000
Pat Perez	68	70	69	66	273	130,000
Jason Dufner	67	68	70	69	274	89,142.86
Jerry Kelly	69	65	71	69	274	89,142.86
George McNeill	70	66	70	68	274	89,142.86
David Toms	70	68	68	68	274	89,142.86
Bo Van Pelt	69	70	66	69	274	89,142.86
Paul Azinger	68	66	68	72	274	89,142.85
Bart Bryant	69	69	66	70	274	89,142.85
John Rollins	66	70	72	67	275	54,228.58
Ryuji Imada	66	70	68	71	275	54,228.57
Jeff Maggert	73	65	67	70	275	54,228.57
Ted Purdy	67	68	66	74	275	54,228.57
John Senden	69	67	68	71	275	54,228.57
Heath Slocum	66	68	71	70	275	54,228.57
Boo Weekley	69	67	71	68	275	54,228.57
*Tadd Fujikawa	71	66	66	72	275	
Andrew Buckle	70	66	70	70	276	36,140
Daniel Chopra	68	72	70	66	276	36,140
John Daly	69	68	71	68	276	36,140
Robert Garrigus	68	72	67	69	276	36,140
Troy Matteson	69	68	69	70	276	36,140
Jesper Parnevik	69	67	68	72	276	36,140
Harrison Frazar	71	67	69	70	277	26,325
Nathan Green	67	71	70	69	277	26,325
Craig Lile	70	67	71	69	277	26,325
Stephen Marino	68	71	66	72	277	26,325
Daisuke Maruyama	66	72	69	70	277	26,325
Rory Sabbatini	69	71	70	67	277	26,325
Vijay Singh	71	67	70	69	277	26,325
Johnson Wagner	70	67	70	70	277	26,325
Shane Bertsch	66	70	71	71	278	19,760
Trevor Immelman	67	70	68	73	278	19,760
Jarrod Lyle	68	71	71	68	278	19,760
Will MacKenzie	65	68	74	71	278	19,760
Chad Campbell	66	65	75	73	279	16,640
Kaname Yokoo	69	70	70	70	279	16,640
Eric Axley	72	67	75	66	280	13,537.34
Jeff Sluman	66	72	75	67	280	13,537.34
David Branshaw	67	69	76	68	280	13,537.33
Yusaku Miyazato	69	70	71	70	280	13,537.33
Rod Pampling	71	66	71	72	280	13,537.33
Bubba Watson	71	66	72	71	280	13,537.33
Rich Beem	69	66	71	75	281	11,980.80
Glen Day	71	69	72	69	281	11,980.80
Brian Gay	68	69	70	74	281	11,980.80
J.P. Hayes	70	70	71	70	281	11,980.80
Kenny Perry	71	66	70	74	281	11,980.80
Briny Baird	67	72	72	71	282	11,492
Cliff Kresge	71	67	71	73	282	11,492
Tim Petrovic	70	68	74	70	282	11,492
Brett Quigley	70	70	73	69	282	11,492
Gavin Coles	71	67	69	76	283	11,180
Ken Duke	69	69	71	74	283	11,180
Cameron Beckman	69	70	70	75	284	10,920
Joe Daley	70	69	74	71	284	10,920
Azuma Yano	73	66	74	71	284	10,920
J.J. Henry	68	72	70	75	285	10,608
Davis Love	70	70	71	74	285	10,608
Michael Putnam	71	69	70	75	285	10,608

	SCORES				TOTAL	MONEY
Jeff Quinney	69	71	73	74	287	10,400
Tom Lehman	68	72	76	75	291	10,296

Bob Hope Chrysler Classic

The Classic Club: Par 36-36–72; 7,305 yards
Bermuda Dunes CC: Par 36-36–72; 6,927 yards
La Quinta CC: Par 36-36–72; 7,060 yards
PGA West, Palmer Course: Par 36-36–72; 6,950 yards
Palm Desert, California

January 17-21
purse, $5,000,000

	SCORES					TOTAL	MONEY
Charley Hoffman	66	70	68	68	71	343	$900,000
John Rollins	67	67	69	67	73	343	540,000
(Hoffman defeated Rollins on first playoff hole.)							
Justin Rose	67	65	66	70	76	344	340,000
Jeff Quinney	68	69	69	66	73	345	220,000
Heath Slocum	68	68	69	68	72	345	220,000
Cliff Kresge	72	68	68	66	72	346	173,750
Charles Warren	71	67	67	69	72	346	173,750
Robert Allenby	63	70	70	70	74	347	135,000
Mark Calcavecchia	65	70	75	68	69	347	135,000
Harrison Frazar	68	71	68	69	71	347	135,000
Dudley Hart	66	70	70	67	74	347	135,000
Scott Verplank	66	66	68	74	73	347	135,000
Lucas Glover	69	68	66	65	80	348	91,000
Bernhard Langer	70	73	63	69	73	348	91,000
Ted Purdy	70	65	71	70	72	348	91,000
Johnson Wagner	66	67	74	67	74	348	91,000
Nick Watney	71	68	71	68	70	348	91,000
Tommy Armour	69	69	71	68	72	349	56,666.67
Andrew Buckle	67	73	66	69	74	349	56,666.67
Nathan Green	70	68	68	68	75	349	56,666.67
Mark Hensby	71	71	67	68	72	349	56,666.67
Tom Johnson	70	68	68	71	72	349	56,666.67
Will MacKenzie	70	71	67	71	70	349	56,666.67
Joe Durant	68	68	69	68	76	349	56,666.66
Joe Ogilvie	71	72	67	71	68	349	56,666.66
Duffy Waldorf	71	71	65	66	76	349	56,666.66
Jonathan Byrd	70	69	70	67	74	350	34,750
Steve Flesch	68	70	70	69	73	350	34,750
Bill Haas	68	73	67	70	72	350	34,750
Craig Kanada	65	73	68	69	75	350	34,750
Matt Kuchar	66	68	71	68	77	350	34,750
Paul Stankowski	71	71	67	69	72	350	34,750
Cameron Beckman	70	69	69	68	75	351	26,416.67
Anders Hansen	67	70	69	72	73	351	26,416.67
George McNeill	71	68	68	72	72	351	26,416.67
John Senden	73	64	68	72	74	351	26,416.67
Vaughn Taylor	69	70	69	65	78	351	26,416.66
Mark Wilson	70	72	71	69	69	351	26,416.66
Shane Bertsch	67	68	71	70	76	352	20,000
David Duval	67	71	72	68	74	352	20,000
Lee Janzen	71	66	71	71	73	352	20,000
Richard S. Johnson	71	71	67	70	73	352	20,000
Peter Lonard	72	69	72	67	72	352	20,000
Bob Tway	70	70	69	68	75	352	20,000
Daniel Chopra	69	67	71	68	78	353	15,500
Anthony Kim	72	72	70	67	72	353	15,500
Phil Mickelson	70	70	69	66	78	353	15,500

		SCORES			TOTAL	MONEY
Ryan Armour	70	66	72 74	73	355	12,720
Paul Gow	68	73	70 69	75	355	12,720
Paul Goydos	68	71	75 68	73	355	12,720
Shaun Micheel	69	69	75 68	74	355	12,720
Mike Weir	72	68	69 70	76	355	12,720
Woody Austin	69	70	73 64	80	356	11,414.29
Paul Azinger	75	69	68 68	76	356	11,414.29
Jason Dufner	74	66	74 66	76	356	11,414.29
Ken Duke	69	74	68 68	77	356	11,414.29
Craig Barlow	69	73	72 68	74	356	11,414.28
Brian Gay	71	70	69 72	74	356	11,414.28
Corey Pavin	67	70	73 70	76	356	11,414.28
Stephen Marino	75	69	67 68	78	357	10,800
Ian Poulter	68	72	74 67	76	357	10,800
Brandt Snedeker	70	73	69 69	76	357	10,800
Kevin Stadler	69	70	71 71	76	357	10,800
Kevin Sutherland	69	69	74 68	77	357	10,800
Robert Gamez	70	73	69 70	76	358	10,250
Jason Gore	66	75	67 72	78	358	10,250
Bob Heintz	66	71	69 74	78	358	10,250
Charles Howell	70	71	72 69	76	358	10,250
Kenny Perry	69	67	71 73	78	358	10,250
Dean Wilson	70	68	67 69	84	358	10,250
Rich Barcelo	72	70	74 66	77	359	9,850
Tripp Isenhour	66	70	73 71	79	359	9,850
Kevin Na	68	71	75 66	80	360	9,700
Briny Baird	71	69	68 74	79	361	9,600
Hunter Mahan	71	71	70 70	80	362	9,500
Steve Lowery	71	70	74 67	81	363	9,400

Buick Invitational

Torrey Pines Golf Course, La Jolla, California
South Course: Par 36-36–72; 7,208 yards
North Course: Par 36-36–72; 6,874 yards

January 25-28
purse, $5,200,000

	SCORES				TOTAL	MONEY
Tiger Woods	66	72	69	66	273	$936,000
Charles Howell	70	64	73	68	275	561,600
Brandt Snedeker	61	70	74	71	276	353,600
Bubba Watson	67	74	69	67	277	214,933.34
Andrew Buckle	66	71	68	72	277	214,933.33
Mark Calcavecchia	66	74	68	69	277	214,933.33
Bart Bryant	66	73	70	69	278	167,700
Jeff Quinney	64	74	70	70	278	167,700
Robert Allenby	70	70	71	68	279	130,000
Rich Beem	67	68	73	71	279	130,000
Ian Poulter	72	68	71	68	279	130,000
Nick Watney	69	69	70	71	279	130,000
Charlie Wi	63	72	73	71	279	130,000
Stewart Cink	68	71	71	70	280	96,200
Kevin Sutherland	65	71	70	74	280	96,200
Ryuji Imada	68	71	69	73	281	80,600
Lee Janzen	72	66	74	69	281	80,600
Ryan Moore	70	69	73	69	281	80,600
Michael Putnam	71	66	74	70	281	80,600
Craig Kanada	66	75	72	69	282	62,746.67
Stephen Marino	65	74	71	72	282	62,746.67
Bill Haas	69	66	72	75	282	62,746.66
Gavin Coles	65	75	71	72	283	42,770

	SCORES				TOTAL	MONEY
Bob Estes	70	71	71	71	283	42,770
Robert Garrigus	65	73	72	73	283	42,770
Dudley Hart	71	68	72	72	283	42,770
Troy Matteson	71	67	69	76	283	42,770
Parker McLachlin	70	67	76	70	283	42,770
Kevin Stadler	68	72	69	74	283	42,770
Brett Wetterich	70	71	70	72	283	42,770
Steve Allan	67	73	71	73	284	28,860
Cameron Beckman	70	68	72	74	284	28,860
Charley Hoffman	72	67	73	72	284	28,860
Tripp Isenhour	71	70	73	70	284	28,860
Cliff Kresge	65	72	71	76	284	28,860
John Senden	64	75	75	70	284	28,860
Johnson Wagner	65	74	70	75	284	28,860
Mark Wilson	73	68	71	72	284	28,860
Rich Barcelo	70	68	71	76	285	21,320
D.J. Brigman	66	70	77	72	285	21,320
Tom Johnson	74	67	69	75	285	21,320
Mark O'Meara	70	69	74	72	285	21,320
Vijay Singh	75	66	74	70	285	21,320
*Jamie Lovemark	66	74	73	72	285	
Zach Johnson	72	69	73	72	286	15,721.34
Jarrod Lyle	70	68	73	75	286	15,721.34
David Duval	66	75	75	70	286	15,721.33
Ted Purdy	74	67	73	72	286	15,721.33
Chris Riley	70	71	74	71	286	15,721.33
Darron Stiles	65	73	71	77	286	15,721.33
Glen Day	73	65	76	73	287	12,542.40
Paul Gow	71	70	73	73	287	12,542.40
Phil Mickelson	74	66	73	74	287	12,542.40
Rod Pampling	72	69	70	76	287	12,542.40
Justin Rose	68	73	73	73	287	12,542.40
Michael Allen	66	75	72	75	288	11,804
Craig Barlow	75	66	75	72	288	11,804
Tom Byrum	71	70	72	75	288	11,804
Hunter Mahan	75	65	75	73	288	11,804
Matt Hendrix	70	70	74	75	289	11,388
Stephen Leaney	71	70	73	75	289	11,388
John Merrick	72	68	76	73	289	11,388
Bob Tway	72	66	76	75	289	11,388
Tommy Armour	68	73	76	73	290	11,024
Harrison Frazar	74	67	74	75	290	11,024
Doug LaBelle	67	74	77	72	290	11,024
Jason Bohn	71	69	77	74	291	10,660
Mathias Gronberg	70	70	76	75	291	10,660
John Mallinger	70	70	73	78	291	10,660
Brett Quigley	67	71	78	75	291	10,660
Jeff Gove	73	68	75	77	293	10,400
Todd Hamilton	71	67	80	76	294	10,296
Michael Bradley	72	68	80	75	295	10,192

FBR Open

TPC of Scottsdale, Scottsdale, Arizona
Par 35-36–71; 7,216 yards

February 1-4
purse, $6,000,000

	SCORES				TOTAL	MONEY
Aaron Baddeley	65	70	64	64	263	$1,080,000
John Rollins	65	68	68	63	264	648,000
Jeff Quinney	66	63	68	68	265	408,000

	SCORES				TOTAL	MONEY
Bart Bryant	66	66	68	66	266	288,000
Billy Mayfair	66	66	70	65	267	240,000
Heath Slocum	67	68	67	66	268	216,000
Vijay Singh	71	67	67	64	269	201,000
David Toms	65	69	68	68	270	174,000
Bubba Watson	66	67	69	68	270	174,000
Dean Wilson	70	69	65	66	270	174,000
Jason Bohn	70	66	67	68	271	138,000
Robert Garrigus	66	67	68	70	271	138,000
Vaughn Taylor	67	67	67	70	271	138,000
Ryuji Imada	68	67	68	69	272	105,000
Peter Lonard	69	68	66	69	272	105,000
Troy Matteson	71	68	64	69	272	105,000
Brett Quigley	67	67	66	72	272	105,000
Fred Funk	70	69	67	67	273	87,000
Charles Warren	71	68	66	68	273	87,000
Lucas Glover	71	67	67	69	274	72,400
Dudley Hart	64	71	69	70	274	72,400
Cliff Kresge	70	68	68	68	274	72,400
Alejandro Canizares	68	68	70	69	275	48,200
Brian Gay	65	71	70	69	275	48,200
Charles Howell	67	66	72	70	275	48,200
Parker McLachlin	70	70	70	65	275	48,200
John Merrick	71	68	69	67	275	48,200
Tom Pernice, Jr.	65	71	68	71	275	48,200
Tim Petrovic	67	71	69	68	275	48,200
Ted Purdy	69	70	67	69	275	48,200
Brandt Snedeker	71	68	68	68	275	48,200
Woody Austin	69	67	69	71	276	32,485.72
Joe Ogilvie	68	67	71	70	276	32,485.72
Nick Watney	68	68	71	69	276	32,485.72
Briny Baird	69	67	73	67	276	32,485.71
Kenny Perry	69	67	68	72	276	32,485.71
Mike Weir	70	69	70	67	276	32,485.71
Charlie Wi	68	70	67	71	276	32,485.71
Lee Janzen	72	67	69	69	277	24,600
Will MacKenzie	70	68	70	69	277	24,600
George McNeill	67	68	70	72	277	24,600
Justin Rose	70	70	66	71	277	24,600
Bo Van Pelt	69	71	68	69	277	24,600
Paul Azinger	65	71	73	69	278	16,728
Craig Bowden	69	68	72	69	278	16,728
Brian Davis	70	69	67	72	278	16,728
Steve Elkington	69	69	67	73	278	16,728
Bob Estes	71	69	66	72	278	16,728
Mathias Gronberg	71	68	70	69	278	16,728
Davis Love	71	69	73	65	278	16,728
Hunter Mahan	71	68	72	67	278	16,728
Steve Stricker	68	68	69	73	278	16,728
Brett Wetterich	70	70	69	69	278	16,728
Eric Axley	69	71	73	66	279	13,680
Steve Flesch	68	69	73	69	279	13,680
Nathan Green	70	70	70	69	279	13,680
Rod Pampling	69	71	70	69	279	13,680
Boo Weekley	71	69	70	69	279	13,680
Chris DiMarco	68	68	71	73	280	13,200
Jose Maria Olazabal	71	69	68	72	280	13,200
Rory Sabbatini	68	71	75	66	280	13,200
Ben Curtis	67	72	69	73	281	12,780
Jason Dufner	69	71	68	73	281	12,780
Jeff Gove	68	72	68	73	281	12,780
Steve Wheatcroft	70	70	70	71	281	12,780
Daniel Chopra	66	71	74	71	282	12,480

	SCORES				TOTAL	MONEY
Richard S. Johnson	70	70	71	72	283	12,300
Kevin Na	72	68	71	72	283	12,300
Stewart Cink	70	70	72	72	284	12,060
Kent Jones	70	69	72	73	284	12,060
J.P. Hayes	69	69	72	76	286	11,820
Tripp Isenhour	71	69	73	73	286	11,820
Mark Hensby	69	68	76	74	287	11,640

AT&T Pebble Beach National Pro-Am

Pebble Beach GL: Par 36-36–72; 6,799 yards
Poppy Hills GC: Par 36-36–72; 6,833 yards
Spyglass Hill GC: Par 36-36–72; 6,858 yards
Pebble Beach, California

February 8-11
purse, $5,500,000

	SCORES				TOTAL	MONEY
Phil Mickelson	65	67	70	66	268	$990,000
Kevin Sutherland	72	63	67	71	273	594,000
John Mallinger	65	70	68	71	274	374,000
Davis Love	70	67	70	69	276	242,000
Greg Owen	68	70	71	67	276	242,000
Jim Furyk	67	65	76	69	277	184,250
Matt Kuchar	72	69	70	66	277	184,250
Corey Pavin	68	72	67	70	277	184,250
Ryan Armour	68	71	72	67	278	154,000
Ted Purdy	73	70	68	67	278	154,000
Daniel Chopra	71	70	68	70	279	116,600
Steve Flesch	70	70	68	71	279	116,600
Vijay Singh	73	66	71	69	279	116,600
Bo Van Pelt	72	68	71	68	279	116,600
Camilo Villegas	73	70	69	67	279	116,600
Glen Day	74	69	69	68	280	88,000
J.B. Holmes	76	66	68	70	280	88,000
Hunter Mahan	69	72	70	69	280	88,000
Aaron Baddeley	68	71	71	71	281	64,350
Craig Kanada	68	69	71	73	281	64,350
Ryan Moore	69	76	70	66	281	64,350
Jeff Overton	70	69	69	73	281	64,350
Omar Uresti	70	68	71	72	281	64,350
Tom Watson	70	68	72	71	281	64,350
Tim Petrovic	71	73	69	69	282	42,900
Brett Quigley	70	72	70	70	282	42,900
Kyle Thompson	68	71	73	70	282	42,900
Garrett Willis	72	68	72	70	282	42,900
Mark Wilson	70	71	72	69	282	42,900
Alex Cejka	75	67	73	68	283	33,412.50
Paul Goydos	68	74	71	70	283	33,412.50
Padraig Harrington	74	72	68	69	283	33,412.50
Bob Heintz	72	71	71	69	283	33,412.50
Doug LaBelle	70	73	70	70	283	33,412.50
Dean Wilson	68	72	73	70	283	33,412.50
Arjun Atwal	67	75	71	71	284	25,345.84
David Duval	72	68	72	72	284	25,345.84
Tom Lehman	69	72	74	69	284	25,345.83
Michael Putnam	72	70	73	69	284	25,345.83
Brandt Snedeker	71	69	74	70	284	25,345.83
Johnson Wagner	74	72	68	70	284	25,345.83
Jose Maria Olazabal	71	70	69	75	285	20,900
Nick Watney	65	75	72	73	285	20,900
Craig Barlow	69	73	71	73	286	16,628.34

	SCORES				TOTAL	MONEY
Jose Coceres	72	69	72	73	286	16,628.34
Tommy Armour	73	67	74	72	286	16,628.33
Brendon de Jonge	68	71	74	73	286	16,628.33
Tom Pernice, Jr.	74	71	70	71	286	16,628.33
Bubba Watson	70	70	75	71	286	16,628.33
Mark Hensby	69	68	77	73	287	13,163.34
Tim Herron	73	74	66	74	287	13,163.34
Charley Hoffman	70	69	75	73	287	13,163.33
Tom Johnson	71	71	73	72	287	13,163.33
Paul McGinley	69	73	73	72	287	13,163.33
Duffy Waldorf	74	72	69	72	287	13,163.33
Ricky Barnes	72	74	69	73	288	12,540
Pat Perez	72	69	73	75	289	12,375
Charles Warren	68	76	71	74	289	12,375
Michael Allen	72	70	72	76	290	12,155
Jim McGovern	75	67	73	75	290	12,155

Nissan Open

Riviera Country Club, Pacific Palisades, California
Par 35-36–71; 6,987 yards

February 15-18
purse, $5,200,000

	SCORES				TOTAL	MONEY
Charles Howell	69	65	69	65	268	$936,000
Phil Mickelson	66	65	69	68	268	561,600
(Howell defeated Mickelson on third playoff hole.)						
Robert Allenby	69	66	68	68	271	270,400
Ernie Els	69	68	67	67	271	270,400
Jim Furyk	67	70	67	67	271	270,400
Sergio Garcia	67	68	69	69	273	187,200
Padraig Harrington	63	68	70	73	274	174,200
Pat Perez	66	69	75	65	275	161,200
Anthony Kim	72	69	71	64	276	135,200
Rocco Mediate	71	66	71	68	276	135,200
Jeff Quinney	70	70	67	69	276	135,200
Rory Sabbatini	69	70	67	70	276	135,200
Aaron Baddeley	68	69	70	70	277	94,640
Rich Beem	69	68	65	75	277	94,640
Harrison Frazar	70	72	67	68	277	94,640
Jose Maria Olazabal	70	70	68	69	277	94,640
Carl Pettersson	72	69	68	68	277	94,640
Bart Bryant	72	68	70	68	278	70,200
Steve Elkington	69	69	69	71	278	70,200
Cliff Kresge	70	69	71	68	278	70,200
John Rollins	70	69	67	72	278	70,200
John Daly	70	72	68	69	279	46,874.29
Bill Haas	71	68	69	71	279	46,874.29
J.J. Henry	70	71	70	68	279	46,874.29
Johnson Wagner	71	66	72	70	279	46,874.29
Cameron Beckman	67	71	69	72	279	46,874.28
K.J. Choi	72	67	66	74	279	46,874.28
Mike Weir	74	69	70	66	279	46,874.28
David Howell	67	68	73	72	280	34,580
Richard S. Johnson	70	71	71	68	280	34,580
Vijay Singh	68	71	69	72	280	34,580
Kevin Stadler	67	75	70	68	280	34,580
Stewart Cink	70	71	69	71	281	28,730
Lucas Glover	69	72	71	69	281	28,730
Zach Johnson	69	73	70	69	281	28,730
Kevin Na	70	69	69	73	281	28,730
Briny Baird	66	73	67	76	282	22,360

	SCORES				TOTAL	MONEY
Ben Curtis	69	69	69	75	282	22,360
Paul McGinley	70	71	69	72	282	22,360
Corey Pavin	72	66	73	71	282	22,360
Kenny Perry	70	73	68	71	282	22,360
Ted Purdy	69	71	72	70	282	22,360
David Toms	69	70	70	73	282	22,360
Jason Bohn	71	69	70	73	283	15,347.43
Trevor Immelman	70	72	72	69	283	15,347.43
George McNeill	71	70	67	75	283	15,347.43
Rod Pampling	68	71	75	69	283	15,347.43
Tim Petrovic	74	68	70	71	283	15,347.43
Scott Verplank	70	72	72	69	283	15,347.43
Heath Slocum	69	74	72	68	283	15,347.42
Retief Goosen	71	70	72	71	284	12,313.60
Geoff Ogilvy	68	70	67	79	284	12,313.60
John Senden	71	70	71	72	284	12,313.60
Vaughn Taylor	71	71	68	74	284	12,313.60
Bo Van Pelt	69	73	71	71	284	12,313.60
Matt Kuchar	71	72	71	71	285	11,596
Tom Lehman	73	66	72	74	285	11,596
Peter Lonard	71	70	70	74	285	11,596
Sean O'Hair	72	71	69	73	285	11,596
Tom Pernice, Jr.	70	69	71	75	285	11,596
Kirk Triplett	70	70	73	72	285	11,596
Craig Barlow	71	71	68	76	286	11,128
Justin Rose	72	70	72	72	286	11,128
Kevin Sutherland	76	67	71	72	286	11,128
Ryuji Imada	71	70	72	74	287	10,868
Shaun Micheel	70	69	71	77	287	10,868
Ken Duke	71	72	74	71	288	10,660
Nick O'Hern	71	70	72	75	288	10,660
Billy Andrade	71	72	73	73	289	10,296
Stuart Appleby	70	73	73	73	289	10,296
Charley Hoffman	69	72	75	73	289	10,296
Robert Karlsson	69	74	71	75	289	10,296
Adam Scott	72	70	75	72	289	10,296
Daisuke Maruyama	72	71	70	77	290	9,984
Eric Axley	68	73	75	75	291	9,828
Tripp Isenhour	70	71	77	73	291	9,828
Chad Campbell	74	67	75	76	292	9,620
Shigeki Maruyama	71	70	75	76	292	9,620
Mathew Goggin	71	72	78	74	295	9,464

WGC - Accenture Match Play Championship

The Gallery at Dove Mountain, South Course, Marana, Arizona February 21-25
Par 36-36–72; 7,446 yards purse, $8,000,000

FIRST ROUND

Tiger Woods defeated J.J. Henry, 3 and 2.
Tim Clark defeated Robert Allenby, 2 and 1.
Nick O'Hern defeated Lucas Glover, 4 and 3.
Rory Sabbatini defeated David Howell, 2 up.
Luke Donald defeated Miguel Angel Jimenez, 3 and 1.
Aaron Baddeley defeated Shingo Katayama, 1 up.
Henrik Stenson defeated Zach Johnson, 1 up.
K.J. Choi defeated Carl Pettersson, 2 and 1.
Phil Mickelson defeated Richard Green, 1 up.
Justin Rose defeated Michael Campbell, 6 and 5.
Sergio Garcia defeated Darren Clarke, 19 holes.
Charles Howell defeated Stuart Appleby, 4 and 3.

Bradley Dredge defeated Ernie Els, 4 and 2.
Ian Poulter defeated Bart Bryant, 5 and 4.
Trevor Immelman defeated Thomas Bjorn, 6 and 5.
Chris DiMarco defeated Brett Wetterich, 4 and 3.
Jim Furyk defeated Brett Quigley, 2 and 1.
Chad Campbell defeated Angel Cabrera, 1 up.
Ben Crane defeated Davis Love, 3 and 1.
David Toms defeated Arron Oberholser, 5 and 4.
Vijay Singh defeated John Rollins, 4 and 3.
Stephen Ames defeated Robert Karlsson, 8 and 7.
Padraig Harrington defeated Lee Westwood, 19 holes.
Stewart Cink defeated Jeev Milkha Singh, 3 and 2.
Shaun Micheel defeated Adam Scott, 21 holes.
Rod Pampling defeated Y.E. Yang, 5 and 4.
Paul Casey defeated Mike Weir, 1 up.
Colin Montgomerie defeated Johan Edfors, 2 and 1.
Retief Goosen defeated Scott Verplank, 5 and 4.
Niclas Fasth defeated Joe Durant, 1 up.
Geoff Ogilvy defeated Steve Stricker, 4 and 3.
Jose Maria Olazabal defeated Paul Goydos, 19 holes.

(Each losing player received $40,000.)

SECOND ROUND

Woods defeated Clark, 5 and 4.
O'Hern defeated Sabbatini, 2 and 1.
Baddeley defeated Donald, 1 up.
Stenson defeated Choi, 2 up.
Rose defeated Mickelson, 3 and 1.
Howell defeated Garcia, 4 and 3.
Poulter defeated Dredge, 3 and 1.
Immelman defeated DiMarco, 3 and 1.
Chad Campbell defeated Furyk, 19 holes.
Toms defeated Crane, 3 and 2.
Ames defeated Vijay Singh, 19 holes.
Cink defeated Harrington, 1 up.
Micheel defeated Pampling, 1 up.
Casey defeated Montgomerie, 4 and 3.
Fasth defeated Goosen, 1 up.
Ogilvy defeated Olazabal, 2 and 1.

(Each losing player received $90,000.)

THIRD ROUND

O'Hern defeated Woods, 20 holes.
Stenson defeated Baddeley, 4 and 3.
Rose defeated Howell, 3 and 2.
Immelman defeated Poulter, 2 and 1.
Chad Campbell defeated Toms, 1 up.
Ames defeated Cink, 3 and 1.
Casey defeated Micheel, 2 up.
Ogilvy defeated Fasth, 2 and 1.

(Each losing player received $130,000.)

QUARTER-FINALS

Stenson defeated O'Hern, 1 up.
Immelman defeated Rose, 5 and 4.
Chad Campbell defeated Ames, 1 up.
Ogilvy defeated Casey, 5 and 4.

(Each losing player received $260,000.)

SEMI-FINALS

Ogilvy defeated Chad Campbell, 3 and 2.
Stenson defeated Immelman, 3 and 2.

PLAYOFF FOR THIRD-FOURTH PLACE

Immelman defeated Chad Campbell, 4 and 2.

(Immelman earned $575,000; Campbell earned $475,000.)

FINAL

Stenson defeated Ogilvy, 2 and 1.

(Stenson earned $1,350,000; Ogilvy earned $800,000.)

Mayakoba Golf Classic at Riviera Maya-Cancun

El Camaleon, Riviera Maya, Mexico
Par 35-35–70; 7,060 yards

February 22-25
purse, $3,500,000

	SCORES				TOTAL	MONEY
Fred Funk	62	69	64	71	266	$630,000
Jose Coceres	67	65	65	69	266	378,000
(Funk defeated Coceres on second playoff hole.)						
Peter Lonard	65	68	67	67	267	238,000
Ryan Armour	68	65	69	66	268	168,000
Bill Haas	66	66	70	67	269	140,000
Boo Weekley	64	67	70	69	270	126,000
Cameron Beckman	64	67	69	71	271	117,250
Stephen Marino	68	68	69	67	272	108,500
Gavin Coles	69	66	70	68	273	91,000
Brendon de Jonge	69	71	68	65	273	91,000
Skip Kendall	69	69	63	72	273	91,000
Larry Mize	71	66	71	65	273	91,000
Mark Brooks	69	65	68	72	274	63,700
Alejandro Canizares	68	68	69	69	274	63,700
Pat Perez	71	69	65	69	274	63,700
Jeff Sluman	67	70	69	68	274	63,700
Kevin Stadler	66	69	71	68	274	63,700
Steve Elkington	69	71	69	66	275	41,125
Paul Gow	68	68	72	67	275	41,125
Matt Kuchar	71	68	70	66	275	41,125
Parker McLachlin	69	68	69	69	275	41,125
Joe Ogilvie	72	66	68	69	275	41,125
Chris Riley	69	66	71	69	275	41,125
Paul Stankowski	70	68	68	69	275	41,125
Bob Tway	71	63	69	72	275	41,125
John Cook	68	66	73	69	276	25,900
Craig Kanada	67	68	71	70	276	25,900
Jerry Kelly	68	69	71	68	276	25,900
Doug LaBelle	70	67	67	72	276	25,900
Fabrizio Zanotti	71	63	70	72	276	25,900
Brian Bateman	71	67	67	72	277	21,218.75
Tim Herron	70	68	69	70	277	21,218.75
Ryuji Imada	70	66	72	69	277	21,218.75
Jim Rutledge	69	71	67	70	277	21,218.75
Tommy Armour	69	66	73	70	278	16,887.50
Brent Geiberger	73	62	70	73	278	16,887.50
Jarrod Lyle	72	65	71	70	278	16,887.50
Daisuke Maruyama	71	67	70	70	278	16,887.50

	SCORES				TOTAL	MONEY
Jesper Parnevik	69	67	73	69	278	16,887.50
Michael Putnam	66	68	72	72	278	16,887.50
Mark Calcavecchia	70	69	74	66	279	12,250
Danny Ellis	72	67	74	66	279	12,250
Brian Gay	65	67	70	77	279	12,250
Nathan Green	72	65	70	72	279	12,250
Scott Gutschewski	66	69	72	72	279	12,250
Darron Stiles	70	67	66	76	279	12,250
Esteban Toledo	66	70	72	71	279	12,250
Bubba Dickerson	68	67	70	75	280	8,700
Anders Hansen	69	71	68	72	280	8,700
Dudley Hart	68	69	72	71	280	8,700
Tripp Isenhour	68	70	70	72	280	8,700
John Merrick	64	69	73	74	280	8,700
Ted Purdy	67	71	71	71	280	8,700
Brandt Snedeker	72	68	69	71	280	8,700
Steve Allan	72	67	72	70	281	7,805
Michael Boyd	67	72	69	73	281	7,805
Scott Gump	71	69	69	72	281	7,805
Dicky Pride	69	71	68	73	281	7,805
Jason Schultz	69	70	69	73	281	7,805
B.J. Staten	70	68	72	71	281	7,805
Vaughn Taylor	65	71	73	72	281	7,805
Steve Wheatcroft	68	68	71	74	281	7,805
Briny Baird	70	67	71	74	282	7,455
Graeme McDowell	67	70	72	73	282	7,455
*Pablo Martin	70	69	70	73	282	
D.J. Brigman	67	69	71	76	283	7,245
Robert Gamez	69	69	70	75	283	7,245
Bob Heintz	70	67	73	73	283	7,245
Mark Wilson	74	66	69	74	283	7,245
Glen Day	67	69	77	71	284	7,035
Vance Veazey	71	69	70	74	284	7,035
John Huston	67	69	71	78	285	6,860
Neal Lancaster	69	68	74	74	285	6,860
George McNeill	64	70	75	76	285	6,860
Chris Tidland	72	67	72	75	286	6,720
Steve Jones	68	68	72	79	287	6,650
Grant Waite	71	69	72	76	288	6,580
Michael Allen	71	69	73	76	289	6,510

Honda Classic

PGA National Resort & Spa, Champion Course,
Palm Beach Gardens, Florida
Par 35-35—70; 7,048 yards
(Event concluded on Monday—darkness.)

March 1-5
purse, $5,500,000

	SCORES				TOTAL	MONEY
Mark Wilson	72	66	66	71	275	$990,000
Jose Coceres	69	71	69	66	275	410,666.67
Boo Weekley	71	68	66	70	275	410,666.67
Camilo Villegas	70	68	71	66	275	410,666.66
(Wilson defeated Weekley and Villegas on second and Coceres on third playoff hole.)						
Robert Allenby	67	68	73	68	276	200,750
Tripp Isenhour	71	70	68	67	276	200,750
Steve Stricker	68	69	70	69	276	200,750
Daniel Chopra	70	68	68	71	277	165,000
Brett Wetterich	68	71	71	67	277	165,000
J.P. Hayes	71	73	67	68	279	137,500

	SCORES				TOTAL	MONEY
Bernhard Langer	66	75	70	68	279	137,500
Arron Oberholser	68	73	69	69	279	137,500
Bill Haas	76	67	69	68	280	94,285.72
Doug LaBelle	72	70	72	66	280	94,285.72
Davis Love	68	74	70	68	280	94,285.72
Jason Dufner	71	70	68	71	280	94,285.71
Padraig Harrington	68	71	70	71	280	94,285.71
Frank Lickliter	73	69	68	70	280	94,285.71
Charlie Wi	65	70	72	73	280	94,285.71
Stephen Marino	70	71	68	72	281	68,750
David Toms	72	68	70	71	281	68,750
Rich Barcelo	73	68	74	67	282	47,055.56
Rich Beem	73	67	73	69	282	47,055.56
Mathias Gronberg	72	66	75	69	282	47,055.56
Anders Hansen	68	72	73	69	282	47,055.56
Carl Pettersson	73	71	69	69	282	47,055.56
Glen Day	69	70	71	72	282	47,055.55
J.J. Henry	70	73	68	71	282	47,055.55
Will MacKenzie	68	69	74	71	282	47,055.55
Billy Mayfair	73	71	69	69	282	47,055.55
Jason Bohn	72	72	69	70	283	30,525
Chris DiMarco	69	74	72	68	283	30,525
Jim Furyk	69	71	73	70	283	30,525
Bob Heintz	73	70	70	70	283	30,525
Tim Herron	75	67	71	70	283	30,525
John Merrick	74	69	70	70	283	30,525
Joe Ogilvie	67	71	73	72	283	30,525
Charles Warren	68	73	71	71	283	30,525
Steve Allan	75	69	70	70	284	21,450
Marco Dawson	67	74	74	69	284	21,450
Matt Kuchar	72	68	76	68	284	21,450
Jarrod Lyle	70	70	75	69	284	21,450
Rocco Mediate	71	72	74	67	284	21,450
John Senden	74	69	71	70	284	21,450
Brandt Snedeker	68	72	72	72	284	21,450
Luke Donald	77	67	72	69	285	14,708.58
Brian Davis	68	73	73	71	285	14,708.57
Jeff Gove	72	69	70	74	285	14,708.57
Anthony Kim	70	73	67	75	285	14,708.57
Jesper Parnevik	70	69	71	75	285	14,708.57
Ian Poulter	70	73	72	70	285	14,708.57
Wes Short, Jr.	70	74	71	70	285	14,708.57
Woody Austin	72	68	76	70	286	12,555.72
Gavin Coles	70	72	78	66	286	12,555.72
Cliff Kresge	67	74	74	71	286	12,555.72
Ryan Armour	71	73	69	73	286	12,555.71
Ben Curtis	71	73	70	72	286	12,555.71
Tom Pernice, Jr.	71	73	69	73	286	12,555.71
Kevin Stadler	71	71	72	72	286	12,555.71
Chris Couch	72	70	75	70	287	12,045
Mathew Goggin	70	72	77	68	287	12,045
Lucas Glover	70	72	72	74	288	11,715
Peter Lonard	71	69	74	74	288	11,715
George McNeill	70	73	75	70	288	11,715
Jeff Quinney	70	74	70	74	288	11,715
Billy Andrade	74	68	75	72	289	11,440
Dicky Pride	71	71	73	75	290	11,330
Richard S. Johnson	73	70	78	70	291	11,165
Johnson Wagner	70	74	67	80	291	11,165
Alan Morin	71	73	75	74	293	11,000
Kyle Reifers	71	71	81	73	296	10,890
Michael Putnam	70	74	81	72	297	10,780
Robert Garrigus	73	70	71	84	298	10,670

PODS Championship

Innisbrook Resort & Golf Club, Copperhead Course,
Tampa Bay, Florida
Par 36-35–71; 7,230 yards

March 8-11
purse, $5,300,000

	SCORES				TOTAL	MONEY
Mark Calcavecchia	75	67	62	70	274	$954,000
John Senden	69	71	69	66	275	466,400
Heath Slocum	68	69	67	71	275	466,400
Brian Gay	69	72	66	69	276	233,200
Lucas Glover	72	68	67	69	276	233,200
K.J. Choi	69	69	67	72	277	184,175
Charles Howell	70	74	68	65	277	184,175
Jonathan Byrd	69	69	72	68	278	148,400
J.B. Holmes	72	68	69	69	278	148,400
Stephen Leaney	69	67	72	70	278	148,400
Ryan Moore	69	71	68	70	278	148,400
Bart Bryant	71	69	69	70	279	116,600
Nathan Green	70	72	70	67	279	116,600
Billy Andrade	69	70	69	72	280	90,100
Jason Bohn	69	70	70	71	280	90,100
Zach Johnson	71	71	66	72	280	90,100
Anthony Kim	67	73	68	72	280	90,100
Pat Perez	68	70	69	73	280	90,100
Eric Axley	71	72	69	69	281	57,637.50
Chris DiMarco	69	69	69	74	281	57,637.50
Frank Lickliter	70	73	68	70	281	57,637.50
Kenny Perry	73	69	72	67	281	57,637.50
John Rollins	74	68	70	69	281	57,637.50
Vijay Singh	70	70	72	69	281	57,637.50
Bubba Watson	71	71	69	70	281	57,637.50
Dean Wilson	72	70	68	71	281	57,637.50
Daniel Chopra	67	71	73	71	282	36,040
Jeff Gove	70	70	71	71	282	36,040
Paul Goydos	71	69	69	73	282	36,040
Charley Hoffman	72	69	67	74	282	36,040
Peter Lonard	71	72	71	68	282	36,040
Will MacKenzie	71	72	70	69	282	36,040
Bo Van Pelt	71	72	73	66	282	36,040
Rich Beem	73	69	67	74	283	27,957.50
Cliff Kresge	65	74	71	73	283	27,957.50
Arron Oberholser	67	72	75	69	283	27,957.50
Ryan Palmer	72	70	73	68	283	27,957.50
Ken Duke	71	72	71	70	284	22,790
Tim Herron	73	71	68	72	284	22,790
Doug LaBelle	67	71	74	72	284	22,790
Jeff Quinney	69	71	71	73	284	22,790
Mark Wilson	69	71	70	74	284	22,790
Cameron Beckman	71	69	72	73	285	17,490
Chris Couch	70	71	70	74	285	17,490
Trevor Immelman	69	72	71	73	285	17,490
Tom Lehman	69	73	73	70	285	17,490
Charlie Wi	72	69	70	74	285	17,490
Briny Baird	71	71	68	76	286	13,051.25
Brian Davis	72	68	72	74	286	13,051.25
Brad Faxon	70	74	73	69	286	13,051.25
George McNeill	70	70	76	70	286	13,051.25
Jesper Parnevik	68	75	71	72	286	13,051.25
Brandt Snedeker	69	75	68	74	286	13,051.25
Vaughn Taylor	70	68	71	77	286	13,051.25
Nick Watney	71	71	70	74	286	13,051.25
David Branshaw	71	73	72	71	287	11,978

	SCORES				TOTAL	MONEY
J.J. Henry	72	68	75	72	287	11,978
Johnson Wagner	72	70	69	76	287	11,978
Sergio Garcia	70	71	74	73	288	11,607
Joe Ogilvie	70	72	75	71	288	11,607
Joey Sindelar	68	75	73	72	288	11,607
Kirk Triplett	74	67	76	71	288	11,607
Woody Austin	70	73	71	75	289	11,289
D.J. Trahan	73	71	73	72	289	11,289
Gavin Coles	70	71	72	77	290	11,024
Shaun Micheel	72	71	73	74	290	11,024
Michael Putnam	70	73	72	75	290	11,024
Glen Day	71	73	74	73	291	10,600
Bob Heintz	75	69	73	74	291	10,600
Shigeki Maruyama	73	71	74	73	291	10,600
Troy Matteson	70	73	74	74	291	10,600
Camilo Villegas	68	73	75	75	291	10,600
Richard S. Johnson	73	71	76	72	292	10,282
Ryan Armour	69	73	75	76	293	10,070
Dudley Hart	71	73	77	72	293	10,070
Mark Hensby	72	71	77	73	293	10,070

Arnold Palmer Invitational

Bay Hill Club & Lodge, Orlando, Florida
Par 35-35–70; 7,137 yards

March 15-18
purse, $5,500,000

	SCORES				TOTAL	MONEY
Vijay Singh	70	68	67	67	272	$990,000
Rocco Mediate	66	65	76	67	274	594,000
Vaughn Taylor	64	71	67	73	275	374,000
Ben Curtis	68	67	69	72	276	264,000
Sergio Garcia	66	69	71	71	277	200,750
Tom Lehman	67	69	69	72	277	200,750
John Rollins	69	65	72	71	277	200,750
Luke Donald	68	71	70	69	278	170,500
Stephen Ames	68	67	72	72	279	148,500
Trevor Immelman	66	70	70	73	279	148,500
Jerry Kelly	67	69	70	73	279	148,500
Shaun Micheel	67	68	71	74	280	121,000
Kyle Reifers	70	68	72	70	280	121,000
Paul Casey	64	70	73	74	281	96,250
Sean O'Hair	66	70	72	73	281	96,250
Geoff Ogilvy	69	70	70	72	281	96,250
Boo Weekley	68	72	69	72	281	96,250
Bart Bryant	70	68	70	74	282	74,250
Ernie Els	69	70	71	72	282	74,250
Retief Goosen	69	68	70	75	282	74,250
Scott Verplank	67	73	70	72	282	74,250
Brandt Snedeker	70	70	69	74	283	51,058.34
Henrik Stenson	68	71	72	72	283	51,058.34
Chad Campbell	71	69	68	75	283	51,058.33
Chris Couch	68	70	69	76	283	51,058.33
Bo Van Pelt	67	70	70	76	283	51,058.33
Tiger Woods	64	73	70	76	283	51,058.33
Mark Calcavecchia	67	73	72	72	284	38,225
Johan Edfors	72	67	71	74	284	38,225
Robert Gamez	69	73	70	72	284	38,225
Pat Perez	67	72	76	69	284	38,225
Robert Allenby	70	73	71	71	285	31,831.25
Stewart Cink	70	69	69	77	285	31,831.25

	SCORES				TOTAL	MONEY
Jason Dufner	67	70	72	76	285	31,831.25
Tom Pernice, Jr.	70	71	74	70	285	31,831.25
Skip Kendall	72	68	73	73	286	25,345.84
Mark Wilson	68	71	76	71	286	25,345.84
Jason Bohn	69	71	72	74	286	25,345.83
Frank Lickliter	69	68	73	76	286	25,345.83
Phil Mickelson	72	68	72	74	286	25,345.83
D.J. Trahan	70	68	73	75	286	25,345.83
Woody Austin	67	74	73	73	287	20,350
Zach Johnson	71	72	71	73	287	20,350
Carl Pettersson	66	73	71	77	287	20,350
Stuart Appleby	70	70	73	75	288	15,138.75
Ryan Armour	71	70	77	70	288	15,138.75
Aaron Baddeley	72	70	75	71	288	15,138.75
Brian Gay	68	70	73	77	288	15,138.75
Paul Goydos	70	70	75	73	288	15,138.75
Mark Hensby	72	69	74	73	288	15,138.75
Peter Lonard	68	71	74	75	288	15,138.75
Colin Montgomerie	70	73	73	72	288	15,138.75
Paul Azinger	73	65	76	75	289	12,796.67
Steve Elkington	70	73	73	73	289	12,796.67
Charles Warren	68	73	73	75	289	12,796.66
Bob Estes	73	68	71	78	290	12,320
Brad Faxon	71	69	78	72	290	12,320
Charles Howell	71	71	72	76	290	12,320
Craig Kanada	69	70	73	78	290	12,320
Cliff Kresge	69	70	75	76	290	12,320
Camilo Villegas	70	69	75	77	291	11,990
Stephen Marino	67	70	76	79	292	11,880
Tim Herron	70	72	76	75	293	11,715
Heath Slocum	72	70	74	77	293	11,715
Richard S. Johnson	70	71	76	77	294	11,440
Brett Quigley	72	71	72	79	294	11,440
Joey Sindelar	68	75	72	79	294	11,440
Troy Matteson	70	73	77	75	295	11,220
Steve Flesch	68	72	75	81	296	11,110
Tom Johnson	71	69	79	78	297	10,945
John Mallinger	70	72	73	82	297	10,945
Eric Axley	71	72	78	77	298	10,670
Jeff Quinney	72	69	76	81	298	10,670
Mike Weir	70	72	79	77	298	10,670
Justin Leonard	70	73	79	78	300	10,395
Y.E. Yang	72	69	79	80	300	10,395
J.B. Holmes	71	72	77	83	303	10,175
Robert Karlsson	70	72	77	84	303	10,175

WGC - CA Championship

Doral Golf Resort & Spa, Blue Course, Miami, Florida　　　　　　March 22-25
Par 36-36–72; 7,266 yards　　　　　　　　　　　　　　purse, $8,000,000

	SCORES				TOTAL	MONEY
Tiger Woods	71	66	68	73	278	$1,350,000
Brett Wetterich	72	70	67	71	280	800,000
Robert Allenby	67	74	74	67	282	378,333.34
Sergio Garcia	71	70	71	70	282	378,333.33
Geoff Ogilvy	72	69	71	70	282	378,333.33
Aaron Baddeley	69	71	71	72	283	212,500
Niclas Fasth	72	70	70	71	283	212,500
Nick O'Hern	72	72	66	73	283	212,500

	SCORES				TOTAL	MONEY
Paul Casey	76	70	66	72	284	157,500
Zach Johnson	72	68	73	71	284	157,500
Thomas Bjorn	68	72	71	74	285	111,000
Ernie Els	70	70	71	74	285	111,000
Robert Karlsson	74	74	68	69	285	111,000
Tom Pernice, Jr.	71	70	70	74	285	111,000
Vijay Singh	74	68	69	74	285	111,000
Ian Poulter	73	68	75	70	286	87,333.34
Charles Howell	69	71	71	75	286	87,333.33
Dean Wilson	73	75	66	72	286	87,333.33
Angel Cabrera	72	70	75	70	287	80,000
K.J. Choi	71	73	71	72	287	80,000
Padraig Harrington	73	70	73	71	287	80,000
Henrik Stenson	67	73	72	75	287	80,000
Thongchai Jaidee	72	74	70	72	288	74,000
Phil Mickelson	77	72	70	69	288	74,000
Mark Wilson	74	72	72	71	289	71,000
Luke Donald	74	70	75	71	290	69,500
Lucas Glover	73	73	72	72	290	69,500
Stephen Ames	74	70	74	73	291	66,500
Rod Pampling	70	69	74	78	291	66,500
John Rollins	73	70	70	78	291	66,500
Jeev Milkha Singh	74	70	70	77	291	66,500
Mark Calcavecchia	74	71	70	77	292	63,000
Chris DiMarco	76	72	69	75	292	63,000
Anton Haig	75	69	74	74	292	63,000
Stuart Appleby	79	72	71	71	293	56,500
Bart Bryant	71	73	75	74	293	56,500
Chad Campbell	75	74	72	72	293	56,500
Jim Furyk	70	73	72	78	293	56,500
Trevor Immelman	72	68	74	79	293	56,500
Jose Maria Olazabal	69	80	72	72	293	56,500
Carl Pettersson	72	72	74	75	293	56,500
Rory Sabbatini	71	75	73	74	293	56,500
Charl Schwartzel	75	74	70	74	293	56,500
Steve Stricker	74	69	73	77	293	56,500
Paul Broadhurst	73	71	73	77	294	49,000
Stewart Cink	74	68	73	79	294	49,000
Johan Edfors	74	73	74	73	294	49,000
Arron Oberholser	74	76	71	73	294	49,000
David Toms	72	72	76	74	294	49,000
John Bickerton	77	72	74	72	295	45,000
Paul Goydos	74	75	70	76	295	45,000
Louis Oosthuizen	74	75	77	69	295	45,000
Brett Quigley	73	72	73	77	295	45,000
Mike Weir	73	75	73	74	295	45,000
J.J. Henry	73	74	78	71	296	43,000
David Howell	74	73	73	76	296	43,000
Colin Montgomerie	76	72	73	75	296	43,000
Ben Curtis	76	75	69	77	297	41,500
Retief Goosen	77	70	78	72	297	41,500
Nathan Green	72	71	76	78	297	41,500
Charley Hoffman	75	75	77	72	299	40,250
Adam Scott	76	71	72	80	299	40,250
Tim Clark	76	78	71	75	300	39,250
Hennie Otto	74	73	74	79	300	39,250
Joe Durant	73	73	77	78	301	38,000
Anthony Wall	80	73	75	73	301	38,000
Y.E. Yang	76	77	73	75	301	38,000
Prom Meesawat	74	71	82	77	304	36,750
Kevin Stadler	73	71	78	82	304	36,750
Hideto Tanihara	80	75	73	77	305	36,000
Michael Campbell	77	76	78	75	306	35,750

	SCORES			TOTAL	MONEY
Shingo Katayama	81	78	74	75	308	35,500
Davis Love	74	73	77		WD	

Shell Houston Open

Redstone Golf Club, Tournament Course, Humble, Texas
Par 36-36–72; 7,457 yards

March 29-April 1
purse, $5,500,000

	SCORES				TOTAL	MONEY
Adam Scott	69	71	65	66	271	$990,000
Stuart Appleby	66	72	67	69	274	484,000
Bubba Watson	71	67	64	72	274	484,000
Tommy Armour	68	71	70	66	275	264,000
Robert Garrigus	69	72	70	65	276	200,750
Anthony Kim	70	73	66	67	276	200,750
Hunter Mahan	68	71	68	69	276	200,750
D.J. Trahan	71	72	66	68	277	170,500
Bob Estes	67	71	69	71	278	137,500
Bernhard Langer	71	70	67	70	278	137,500
Arron Oberholser	70	71	69	68	278	137,500
Steve Stricker	68	73	68	69	278	137,500
Johnson Wagner	66	75	64	73	278	137,500
Tom Byrum	71	68	71	69	279	93,500
Jeff Maggert	67	71	67	74	279	93,500
Sean O'Hair	70	71	69	69	279	93,500
Paul Stankowski	69	71	65	74	279	93,500
Bo Van Pelt	71	70	68	70	279	93,500
Jonathan Byrd	69	72	68	71	280	66,660
Angel Cabrera	74	70	69	67	280	66,660
K.J. Choi	70	70	71	69	280	66,660
Jason Gore	70	68	70	72	280	66,660
Stephen Leaney	70	71	69	70	280	66,660
Ryan Armour	71	70	74	66	281	48,400
Daniel Chopra	68	72	68	73	281	48,400
Padraig Harrington	71	72	66	72	281	48,400
John Cook	72	70	68	72	282	39,875
Jeff Gove	76	69	65	72	282	39,875
Vaughn Taylor	67	74	68	73	282	39,875
David Toms	73	71	68	70	282	39,875
Matt Hendrix	67	78	69	69	283	34,100
Charley Hoffman	73	69	67	74	283	34,100
John Senden	71	72	72	68	283	34,100
Craig Kanada	71	73	69	71	284	30,387.50
Dicky Pride	74	69	72	69	284	30,387.50
Briny Baird	73	70	71	71	285	25,345.84
Justin Leonard	67	73	73	72	285	25,345.84
Gavin Coles	74	69	73	69	285	25,345.83
Marco Dawson	71	72	69	73	285	25,345.83
John Mallinger	69	72	69	75	285	25,345.83
Chris Riley	69	75	72	69	285	25,345.83
Woody Austin	69	75	71	71	286	18,181.43
Craig Bowden	69	74	70	73	286	18,181.43
D.J. Brigman	70	68	72	76	286	18,181.43
Alex Cejka	72	69	72	73	286	18,181.43
George McNeill	71	71	72	72	286	18,181.43
Nick Watney	74	71	71	70	286	18,181.43
Chris Couch	71	74	72	69	286	18,181.42
Ken Duke	69	73	72	73	287	13,325.72
David Howell	70	73	71	73	287	13,325.72
Kyle Reifers	67	75	71	74	287	13,325.72

	SCORES				TOTAL	MONEY
Steve Flesch	74	70	70	73	287	13,325.71
Mathew Goggin	74	70	75	68	287	13,325.71
Anders Hansen	74	69	68	76	287	13,325.71
Parker McLachlin	74	70	73	70	287	13,325.71
Billy Mayfair	73	71	72	72	288	12,265
Greg Owen	74	70	73	71	288	12,265
Michael Putnam	72	72	74	70	288	12,265
Joey Sindelar	70	71	75	72	288	12,265
Kevin Sutherland	66	75	71	76	288	12,265
Lee Westwood	68	75	72	73	288	12,265
Tim Clark	70	70	77	72	289	11,715
Dudley Hart	71	71	74	73	289	11,715
Shaun Micheel	71	74	72	72	289	11,715
Jim Rutledge	72	73	73	71	289	11,715
Rich Barcelo	73	71	73	73	290	11,330
Blaine McCallister	72	72	74	72	290	11,330
Charles Warren	73	69	74	74	290	11,330
David Branshaw	70	71	74	76	291	10,890
Ryuji Imada	71	70	77	73	291	10,890
Stephen Marino	73	70	75	73	291	10,890
Wes Short, Jr.	69	74	69	79	291	10,890
Bob Tway	72	72	73	74	291	10,890
Steve Allan	73	72	70	77	292	10,505
Michael Boyd	75	70	76	71	292	10,505
Brian Gay	72	73	77	73	295	10,285
John Merrick	72	73	74	76	295	10,285
Jeev Milkha Singh	73	72	72	79	296	10,120

Masters Tournament

Augusta National Golf Club, Augusta, Georgia
Par 36-36–72; 7,445 yards

April 5-8
purse, $7,000,000

	SCORES				TOTAL	MONEY
Zach Johnson	71	73	76	69	289	$1,305,000
Tiger Woods	73	74	72	72	291	541,333
Retief Goosen	76	76	70	69	291	541,333
Rory Sabbatini	73	76	73	69	291	541,333
Justin Rose	69	75	75	73	292	275,500
Jerry Kelly	75	69	78	70	292	275,500
Stuart Appleby	75	70	73	75	293	233,812
Padraig Harrington	77	68	75	73	293	233,812
David Toms	70	78	74	72	294	210,250
Vaughn Taylor	71	72	77	75	295	181,250
Luke Donald	73	74	75	73	295	181,250
Paul Casey	79	68	77	71	295	181,250
Jim Furyk	75	71	76	74	296	135,937
Tim Clark	71	71	80	74	296	135,937
Vijay Singh	73	71	79	73	296	135,937
Ian Poulter	75	75	76	70	296	135,937
Henrik Stenson	72	76	77	72	297	108,750
Tom Pernice, Jr.	75	72	79	71	297	108,750
Stewart Cink	77	75	75	70	297	108,750
Lucas Glover	74	71	79	74	298	84,462
Mark Calcavecchia	76	71	78	73	298	84,462
John Rollins	77	74	76	71	298	84,462
Mike Weir	75	72	80	71	298	84,462
Phil Mickelson	76	73	73	77	299	63,800
Geoff Ogilvy	75	70	81	73	299	63,800
Stephen Ames	76	74	77	72	299	63,000

	SCORES				TOTAL	MONEY
K.J. Choi	75	75	74	76	300	53,650
Davis Love	72	77	77	74	300	53,650
Adam Scott	74	78	76	72	300	53,650
Dean Wilson	75	72	76	78	301	43,085
Lee Westwood	79	73	72	77	301	43,085
Scott Verplank	73	77	76	75	301	43,085
Charles Howell	75	77	75	74	301	43,085
Y.E. Yang	75	74	78	74	301	43,085
Fred Couples	76	76	78	71	301	43,085
Jeev Milkha Singh	72	75	76	79	302	31,900
Rod Pampling	77	75	74	76	302	31,900
Brett Wetterich	69	73	83	77	302	31,900
J.J. Henry	71	78	77	76	302	31,900
Tim Herron	72	75	83	72	302	31,900
Angel Cabrera	77	75	79	71	302	31,900
Sandy Lyle	79	73	80	71	303	26,825
Bradley Dredge	75	70	76	83	304	22,533
Jose Maria Olazabal	74	75	78	77	304	22,533
David Howell	70	75	82	77	304	22,533
Miguel Angel Jimenez	79	73	76	76	304	22,533
Shingo Katayama	79	72	80	73	304	22,533
Craig Stadler	74	73	79	79	305	18,560
Jeff Sluman	76	75	79	75	305	18,560
Brett Quigley	76	76	79	75	306	17,835
Aaron Baddeley	79	72	76	80	307	17,255
Carl Pettersson	76	76	79	76	307	17,255
Rich Beem	71	81	75	81	308	16,820
Niclas Fasth	77	75	77	80	309	16,530
Trevor Immelman	74	77	81	77	309	16,530
Ben Crenshaw	76	74	84	75	309	16,530
Arron Oberholser	74	76	84	76	310	16,240
Billy Mayfair	76	75	83	77	311	16,095
Fuzzy Zoeller	74	78	79	82	313	15,950

Out of Final 36 Holes

Michael Campbell	76	77	153	*Richie Ramsay	76	80	156
Chris DiMarco	75	78	153	Raymond Floyd	77	80	157
Tom Watson	75	78	153	Ben Crane	79	78	157
Mark O'Meara	77	76	153	John Edfors	78	79	157
Colin Montgomerie	76	77	153	Paul Goydos	79	79	158
Todd Hamilton	74	80	154	Troy Matteson	79	79	158
Darren Clarke	83	71	154	Kenneth Ferrie	75	83	158
Thomas Bjorn	77	77	154	Robert Allenby	79	80	159
*John Kelly	77	77	154	Shaun Micheel	82	77	159
Chad Campbell	77	77	154	Gary Player	83	77	160
Ernie Els	78	76	154	Larry Mize	83	78	161
Sergio Garcia	76	78	154	Hideto Tanihara	85	79	164
Bart Bryant	72	82	154	*Julien Guerrier	83	81	164
Joe Durant	80	75	155	Camilo Villegas	80	85	165
Fred Funk	82	73	155	*Casey Watabu	87	78	165
Bernhard Langer	78	77	155	*Dave Womack	84	81	165
Ben Curtis	76	80	156	Seve Ballesteros	86	80	166
Nick O'Hern	76	80	156	Ian Woosnam			WD
Steve Stricker	77	79	156				

(Professionals who did not complete 72 holes received $5,000.)

Verizon Heritage

Harbour Town Golf Links, Hilton Head Island, South Carolina   April 12-16
Par 35-36—71; 6,973 yards   purse, $5,400,000
(Event completed on Monday—high winds.)

	SCORES				TOTAL	MONEY
Boo Weekley	67	69	66	68	270	$972,000
Ernie Els	65	65	71	70	271	583,200
Stephen Leaney	66	68	70	68	272	367,200
Kevin Na	67	68	66	73	274	237,600
Vaughn Taylor	71	66	67	70	274	237,600
Zach Johnson	70	68	66	71	275	194,400
Sean O'Hair	69	66	69	72	276	180,900
Jerry Kelly	63	70	67	77	277	162,000
Carl Pettersson	71	68	67	71	277	162,000
Aaron Baddeley	70	66	70	72	278	124,200
Ken Duke	71	67	67	73	278	124,200
Tom Pernice, Jr.	74	67	65	72	278	124,200
Bo Van Pelt	71	67	70	70	278	124,200
Dean Wilson	69	68	68	73	278	124,200
Jesper Parnevik	71	67	69	72	279	97,200
Jason Bohn	70	68	68	74	280	81,000
Brian Gay	70	70	67	73	280	81,000
Justin Leonard	69	72	70	69	280	81,000
Rod Pampling	69	67	69	75	280	81,000
Brandt Snedeker	71	67	69	73	280	81,000
Stephen Ames	72	68	64	77	281	62,640
Fred Funk	67	67	72	75	281	62,640
Mark Calcavecchia	69	71	70	72	282	49,680
Ben Crane	71	67	68	76	282	49,680
Joe Durant	72	69	66	75	282	49,680
Nick O'Hern	69	71	66	76	282	49,680
Jonathan Byrd	76	67	68	72	283	40,770
Robert Garrigus	74	69	68	72	283	40,770
Jose Coceres	66	72	72	74	284	33,595.72
Mathew Goggin	76	67	68	73	284	33,595.72
Mark Hensby	71	70	70	73	284	33,595.72
Briny Baird	72	69	69	74	284	33,595.71
Glen Day	71	72	69	72	284	33,595.71
J.P. Hayes	67	72	66	79	284	33,595.71
Camilo Villegas	74	67	67	76	284	33,595.71
John Daly	73	70	70	72	285	23,793.75
Steve Elkington	71	71	69	74	285	23,793.75
J.B. Holmes	70	73	68	74	285	23,793.75
Anthony Kim	69	72	70	74	285	23,793.75
Peter Lonard	70	70	70	75	285	23,793.75
Davis Love	74	69	73	69	285	23,793.75
Ryan Palmer	73	67	71	74	285	23,793.75
Mark Wilson	72	70	69	74	285	23,793.75
Jeff Gove	71	71	70	74	286	16,326
Nathan Green	71	66	71	78	286	16,326
Kent Jones	73	65	72	76	286	16,326
Hunter Mahan	72	70	69	75	286	16,326
Kelly Mitchum	72	70	68	76	286	16,326
Charles Warren	70	72	73	71	286	16,326
Stewart Cink	67	75	71	74	287	12,924
Jason Gore	70	72	72	73	287	12,924
Tim Herron	69	73	72	73	287	12,924
Will MacKenzie	72	70	71	74	287	12,924
Jeff Maggert	72	70	71	74	287	12,924
Geoff Ogilvy	70	73	70	74	287	12,924
Ryan Moore	69	73	73	73	288	12,258

	SCORES				TOTAL	MONEY
D.J. Trahan	70	70	71	77	288	12,258
Doug LaBelle	70	70	74	75	289	12,096
Greg Owen	70	71	74	75	290	11,934
Scott Verplank	71	72	73	74	290	11,934
Ben Curtis	72	70	74	75	291	11,664
Matt Kuchar	74	69	74	74	291	11,664
Heath Slocum	74	68	74	75	291	11,664
Eric Axley	71	69	78	74	292	11,394
Kirk Triplett	72	70	79	71	292	11,394
Ryan Armour	69	71	72	81	293	11,232
David Branshaw	70	72	75	77	294	11,124
Brandt Jobe	70	72	74	79	295	11,016
Brian Bateman	72	70	73	82	297	10,908
Tim Petrovic	72	71	76	79	298	10,800

Zurich Classic of New Orleans

TPC Louisiana, Avondale, Louisiana
Par 36-36–72; 7,341 yards

April 19-22
purse, $6,100,000

	SCORES				TOTAL	MONEY
Nick Watney	69	67	68	69	273	$1,098,000
Ken Duke	69	71	66	70	276	658,800
Anthony Kim	71	72	69	65	277	353,800
John Mallinger	69	70	71	67	277	353,800
Mark Calcavecchia	66	69	72	71	278	222,650
Chris Stroud	68	70	71	69	278	222,650
Bubba Watson	72	67	70	69	278	222,650
Alex Cejka	70	72	69	68	279	176,900
Bob Estes	69	71	70	69	279	176,900
Lucas Glover	67	69	74	69	279	176,900
Mathias Gronberg	72	70	71	67	280	134,200
Jeff Maggert	72	69	68	71	280	134,200
Ryan Moore	70	72	70	68	280	134,200
Steve Stricker	71	72	70	67	280	134,200
Daniel Chopra	70	68	75	68	281	103,700
Harrison Frazar	71	69	71	70	281	103,700
Sean O'Hair	71	70	69	71	281	103,700
Woody Austin	70	73	70	69	282	76,860
Frank Lickliter	72	70	69	71	282	76,860
John Merrick	69	70	72	71	282	76,860
Shaun Micheel	71	72	69	70	282	76,860
Michael Sim	71	69	70	72	282	76,860
Duffy Waldorf	68	71	71	72	282	76,860
Scott Gutschewski	70	70	67	76	283	52,002.50
Lee Janzen	69	74	73	67	283	52,002.50
Tim Petrovic	67	72	74	70	283	52,002.50
Kyle Reifers	64	73	71	75	283	52,002.50
Michael Allen	69	70	75	70	284	37,210
Steve Elkington	70	72	72	70	284	37,210
Mathew Goggin	70	72	71	71	284	37,210
Jarrod Lyle	71	69	71	73	284	37,210
Will MacKenzie	72	69	70	73	284	37,210
Jesper Parnevik	70	73	69	72	284	37,210
Michael Putnam	73	69	71	71	284	37,210
Jason Schultz	67	71	72	74	284	37,210
Darron Stiles	68	74	71	71	284	37,210
Bo Van Pelt	70	71	71	72	284	37,210
Craig Bowden	71	70	72	72	285	25,620
John Huston	70	70	73	72	285	25,620

	SCORES				TOTAL	MONEY
Doug LaBelle	69	73	73	70	285	25,620
Peter Lonard	71	68	74	72	285	25,620
Ryan Palmer	70	69	71	75	285	25,620
Jerry Smith	70	71	75	69	285	25,620
Jay Delsing	73	70	70	73	286	16,520.84
Jason Dufner	74	69	70	73	286	16,520.84
Danny Ellis	69	72	72	73	286	16,520.84
Shigeki Maruyama	72	71	70	73	286	16,520.84
Ryan Armour	72	69	75	70	286	16,520.83
Briny Baird	71	70	73	72	286	16,520.83
Carlos Franco	68	74	73	71	286	16,520.83
Tom Johnson	67	76	70	73	286	16,520.83
George McNeill	69	72	74	71	286	16,520.83
Wes Short, Jr.	69	69	71	77	286	16,520.83
David Toms	69	71	74	72	286	16,520.83
Charlie Wi	71	69	72	74	286	16,520.83
Steve Allan	72	71	72	72	287	13,481
Brian Bateman	70	73	67	77	287	13,481
Nathan Green	71	71	74	71	287	13,481
Fredrik Jacobson	69	73	72	73	287	13,481
Matt Kuchar	72	69	71	75	287	13,481
Chris Smith	72	71	73	71	287	13,481
Paul Stankowski	69	69	71	78	287	13,481
Vance Veazey	71	72	75	69	287	13,481
Ted Purdy	69	71	72	76	288	12,871
Steve Wheatcroft	68	70	74	76	288	12,871
John Cook	74	69	73	73	289	12,261
Dan Forsman	71	71	74	73	289	12,261
Mark Hensby	72	69	72	76	289	12,261
Charley Hoffman	68	69	73	79	289	12,261
Ryuji Imada	71	72	74	72	289	12,261
Craig Kanada	71	70	73	75	289	12,261
Kenny Perry	70	73	72	74	289	12,261
Kirk Triplett	72	71	74	72	289	12,261
Brian Gay	73	69	77	71	290	11,529
Troy Matteson	73	70	72	75	290	11,529
Rocco Mediate	71	70	73	76	290	11,529
Kevin Stadler	71	71	72	76	290	11,529
Craig Lile	77	65	76	73	291	11,163
Martin Rominger	73	68	76	74	291	11,163
Rich Barcelo	72	71	76	73	292	10,736
Chris Couch	72	71	75	74	292	10,736
Chris DiMarco	71	70	80	71	292	10,736
Joe Ogilvie	69	73	78	72	292	10,736
Kevin Sutherland	68	73	76	75	292	10,736
Tommy Armour	70	73	71	80	294	10,370

EDS Byron Nelson Championship

TPC Four Seasons Resort at Las Colinas:
Par 35-35–70; 7,022 yards
Cottonwood Valley Course: Par 34-36–70; 6,847 yards
Irving, Texas

April 26-29
purse, $6,300,000

	SCORES				TOTAL	MONEY
Scott Verplank	67	68	66	66	267	$1,134,000
Luke Donald	67	66	67	68	268	680,400
Jerry Kelly	69	70	67	64	270	302,400
Phil Mickelson	69	70	66	65	270	302,400
Ian Poulter	70	69	65	66	270	302,400

	SCORES				TOTAL	MONEY
Rory Sabbatini	70	69	67	64	270	302,400
Ken Duke	68	73	64	66	271	203,175
Fredrik Jacobson	67	67	71	66	271	203,175
Ryuji Imada	70	68	67	67	272	182,700
Stephen Marino	69	67	70	67	273	157,500
Rod Pampling	68	70	69	66	273	157,500
Brett Wetterich	66	68	72	67	273	157,500
Chad Campbell	73	65	69	67	274	111,300
J.J. Henry	72	69	67	66	274	111,300
John Merrick	68	69	70	67	274	111,300
Vijay Singh	69	67	69	69	274	111,300
Bob Tway	71	67	69	67	274	111,300
Bo Van Pelt	68	72	68	66	274	111,300
Steve Allan	69	68	71	67	275	73,710
Michael Allen	69	69	64	73	275	73,710
Shaun Micheel	69	71	67	68	275	73,710
Carl Pettersson	73	68	67	67	275	73,710
John Rollins	70	71	66	68	275	73,710
Mike Weir	70	68	69	68	275	73,710
Tommy Armour	72	69	67	68	276	50,242.50
Jonathan Byrd	69	69	68	70	276	50,242.50
Ben Crane	70	68	73	65	276	50,242.50
Sean O'Hair	65	69	74	68	276	50,242.50
Craig Bowden	70	70	70	67	277	36,729
Kris Cox	70	71	69	67	277	36,729
Nathan Green	67	70	73	67	277	36,729
Kent Jones	69	66	71	71	277	36,729
Doug LaBelle	68	71	71	67	277	36,729
Stephen Leaney	70	68	70	69	277	36,729
Troy Matteson	69	72	71	65	277	36,729
Arron Oberholser	71	69	69	68	277	36,729
Darron Stiles	70	70	70	67	277	36,729
Kevin Sutherland	75	65	69	68	277	36,729
Robert Allenby	68	70	69	71	278	25,830
Daniel Chopra	73	66	72	67	278	25,830
Matt Kuchar	72	68	69	69	278	25,830
Billy Mayfair	72	67	70	69	278	25,830
John Senden	67	69	71	71	278	25,830
Gavin Coles	70	69	71	69	279	18,594
Steve Elkington	70	70	70	69	279	18,594
Jason Gore	71	66	73	69	279	18,594
Anders Hansen	66	73	69	71	279	18,594
Dudley Hart	71	70	70	68	279	18,594
Robert Karlsson	70	70	68	71	279	18,594
Shigeki Maruyama	71	66	70	72	279	18,594
Brendon de Jonge	70	69	69	72	280	15,025.50
Jeff Gove	70	68	71	71	280	15,025.50
Anthony Kim	70	66	77	67	280	15,025.50
Justin Leonard	71	70	71	68	280	15,025.50
Mathias Gronberg	71	70	69	71	281	14,238
Craig Kanada	69	70	73	69	281	14,238
Tim Petrovic	69	72	66	74	281	14,238
Jason Schultz	71	70	67	73	281	14,238
D.J. Trahan	73	67	69	72	281	14,238
Rich Barcelo	73	67	72	70	282	13,797
Brandt Snedeker	69	71	74	68	282	13,797
Robert Garrigus	72	67	70	74	283	13,419
Cliff Kresge	68	71	70	74	283	13,419
Bernhard Langer	70	69	72	72	283	13,419
Joe Ogilvie	69	72	70	72	283	13,419
Glen Day	69	67	71	77	284	13,104
J.L. Lewis	71	70	75	70	286	12,915
Pat Perez	68	73	70	75	286	12,915

	SCORES				TOTAL	MONEY
*Colt Knost	74	64	74	74	286	
Sergio Garcia	71	70	71	75	287	12,726
Charlie Wi	69	68	79	72	288	12,600
Marco Dawson	70	69	77	74	290	12,411
Parker McLachlin	71	69	73	77	290	12,411

Wachovia Championship

Quail Hollow Club, Charlotte, North Carolina
Par 36-36–72; 7,438 yards

May 3-6
purse, $6,300,000

	SCORES				TOTAL	MONEY
Tiger Woods	70	68	68	69	275	$1,134,000
Steve Stricker	72	70	66	69	277	680,400
Phil Mickelson	70	71	68	70	279	365,400
Rory Sabbatini	70	71	64	74	279	365,400
Stewart Cink	70	71	69	70	280	239,400
Anthony Kim	72	69	69	70	280	239,400
Ken Duke	70	70	68	73	281	196,350
Arron Oberholser	69	69	69	74	281	196,350
Vijay Singh	67	71	69	74	281	196,350
Bernhard Langer	70	73	71	69	283	151,200
Billy Mayfair	73	71	67	72	283	151,200
Brett Quigley	70	74	69	70	283	151,200
John Senden	72	70	69	72	283	151,200
Sergio Garcia	71	71	70	72	284	116,550
Trevor Immelman	68	74	68	74	284	116,550
Briny Baird	72	73	70	70	285	91,350
Robert Garrigus	72	73	67	73	285	91,350
J.J. Henry	72	73	69	71	285	91,350
Fredrik Jacobson	70	73	71	71	285	91,350
Jose Maria Olazabal	70	72	71	72	285	91,350
Rod Pampling	71	70	71	73	285	91,350
Carl Pettersson	68	73	71	74	286	68,040
Joey Sindelar	69	72	70	75	286	68,040
K.J. Choi	70	74	69	74	287	46,620
J.P. Hayes	75	72	69	71	287	46,620
Robert Karlsson	71	72	72	72	287	46,620
Geoff Ogilvy	72	73	69	73	287	46,620
Ted Purdy	70	69	74	74	287	46,620
Adam Scott	73	69	73	72	287	46,620
Heath Slocum	68	77	71	71	287	46,620
Kevin Sutherland	75	69	71	72	287	46,620
Nick Watney	72	71	74	70	287	46,620
Mike Weir	73	71	70	73	287	46,620
Robert Allenby	70	76	69	73	288	29,820
Ernie Els	71	74	73	70	288	29,820
Lucas Glover	75	72	68	73	288	29,820
Mathew Goggin	70	73	72	73	288	29,820
Nathan Green	70	76	71	71	288	29,820
J.B. Holmes	69	74	71	74	288	29,820
Stephen Marino	74	71	70	73	288	29,820
Parker McLachlin	71	75	69	73	288	29,820
Nick O'Hern	75	69	69	75	288	29,820
Woody Austin	71	74	72	72	289	18,774
Aaron Baddeley	71	75	71	72	289	18,774
Ben Curtis	70	75	74	70	289	18,774
Retief Goosen	72	74	72	71	289	18,774
Padraig Harrington	66	75	79	69	289	18,774
Jerry Kelly	69	73	70	77	289	18,774

	SCORES				TOTAL	MONEY
Davis Love	74	72	67	76	289	18,774
Camilo Villegas	69	76	72	72	289	18,774
Boo Weekley	72	75	69	73	289	18,774
Jason Bohn	67	72	73	78	290	14,773.50
Charles Howell	78	69	74	69	290	14,773.50
Ryuji Imada	70	73	75	72	290	14,773.50
Jeff Maggert	68	74	77	71	290	14,773.50
Cameron Beckman	75	72	72	72	291	14,112
Michael Putnam	72	70	76	73	291	14,112
John Rollins	70	76	73	72	291	14,112
Charlie Wi	74	68	75	74	291	14,112
Dean Wilson	72	75	72	72	291	14,112
Stephen Ames	69	73	74	76	292	13,419
Jeff Gove	74	69	72	77	292	13,419
Bo Van Pelt	77	70	75	70	292	13,419
Charles Warren	70	73	76	73	292	13,419
Lee Westwood	72	74	74	72	292	13,419
Mark Wilson	76	70	71	75	292	13,419
Steve Flesch	70	74	71	78	293	12,915
Jeff Sluman	71	76	73	73	293	12,915
Billy Andrade	73	74	72	75	294	12,411
Brian Davis	72	75	72	75	294	12,411
Todd Demsey	72	75	72	75	294	12,411
Chris DiMarco	74	71	73	76	294	12,411
Robert Gamez	75	71	73	75	294	12,411
Henrik Stenson	72	74	72	76	294	12,411
Ryan Moore	74	72	74	75	295	11,907
Bob Tway	72	75	71	77	295	11,907
Gavin Coles	76	71	72	77	296	11,655
Cliff Kresge	75	72	77	72	296	11,655
Tripp Isenhour	75	72	77	73	297	11,340
Craig Kanada	73	73	77	74	297	11,340
Stephen Leaney	75	70	75	77	297	11,340
David Berganio, Jr.	69	76	71	83	299	11,025
Shigeki Maruyama	73	74	78	74	299	11,025
Zach Johnson	71	75	75	80	301	10,836

The Players Championship

TPC at Sawgrass, Stadium Course, Ponte Vedra Beach, Florida
Par 36-36–72; 7,093 yards

May 10-13
purse, $9,000,000

	SCORES				TOTAL	MONEY
Phil Mickelson	67	72	69	69	277	$1,620,000
Sergio Garcia	73	73	67	66	279	972,000
Stewart Cink	74	69	71	66	280	522,000
Jose Maria Olazabal	78	66	69	67	280	522,000
Jose Coceres	73	70	68	70	281	360,000
J.P. Hayes	71	73	68	70	282	281,700
Robert Karlsson	77	68	71	66	282	281,700
Peter Lonard	69	72	68	73	282	281,700
Jeff Quinney	71	74	64	73	282	281,700
Adam Scott	74	71	70	67	282	281,700
Sean O'Hair	72	69	66	76	283	225,000
Chris DiMarco	68	74	69	73	284	182,250
Steve Elkington	73	71	70	70	284	182,250
Mathew Goggin	72	71	71	70	284	182,250
Brandt Snedeker	72	74	68	70	284	182,250
Jonathan Byrd	74	71	71	69	285	126,257.15
J.B. Holmes	76	72	69	68	285	126,257.15

	SCORES				TOTAL	MONEY
Stuart Appleby	74	71	71	69	285	126,257.14
Luke Donald	74	72	65	74	285	126,257.14
Nathan Green	71	69	74	71	285	126,257.14
Zach Johnson	73	73	70	69	285	126,257.14
Ted Purdy	74	73	67	71	285	126,257.14
K.J. Choi	71	74	70	71	286	80,100
Jason Gore	70	74	72	70	286	80,100
Tom Lehman	70	73	73	70	286	80,100
Henrik Stenson	72	76	66	72	286	80,100
Kirk Triplett	75	68	73	70	286	80,100
Joe Durant	76	71	69	71	287	56,100
Jim Furyk	71	72	74	70	287	56,100
Retief Goosen	71	74	71	71	287	56,100
Jerry Kelly	73	73	69	72	287	56,100
Cliff Kresge	72	72	69	74	287	56,100
Steve Lowery	78	66	71	72	287	56,100
Tom Pernice, Jr.	74	68	72	73	287	56,100
Carl Pettersson	70	71	70	76	287	56,100
Ian Poulter	75	71	72	69	287	56,100
Aaron Baddeley	72	72	67	77	288	38,700
Ken Duke	76	72	70	70	288	38,700
Ernie Els	73	73	72	70	288	38,700
Frank Lickliter	77	72	69	70	288	38,700
Geoff Ogilvy	74	71	67	76	288	38,700
Mike Weir	75	72	72	69	288	38,700
Tiger Woods	75	73	73	67	288	38,700
Daniel Chopra	74	71	76	68	289	26,010
Rocco Mediate	72	71	77	69	289	26,010
Rod Pampling	70	71	80	68	289	26,010
Rory Sabbatini	67	79	71	72	289	26,010
Vijay Singh	74	71	70	74	289	26,010
Heath Slocum	78	71	69	71	289	26,010
Scott Verplank	72	77	68	72	289	26,010
Boo Weekley	74	73	71	71	289	26,010
Harrison Frazar	74	71	73	72	290	20,880
Padraig Harrington	76	70	74	70	290	20,880
Tim Herron	77	71	73	69	290	20,880
John Senden	73	74	71	72	290	20,880
Steve Stricker	72	75	70	73	290	20,880
Brett Wetterich	74	75	71	70	290	20,880
Rich Beem	71	73	74	73	291	19,710
Bernhard Langer	72	77	73	69	291	19,710
Kenny Perry	73	75	73	70	291	19,710
John Rollins	76	71	68	76	291	19,710
Charl Schwartzel	74	75	69	73	291	19,710
Kevin Sutherland	73	71	74	73	291	19,710
Paul Azinger	78	71	70	73	292	18,810
John Mallinger	73	74	72	73	292	18,810
Arron Oberholser	73	73	79	67	292	18,810
David Toms	77	72	73	70	292	18,810
Tim Clark	73	72	67	81	293	18,090
Ryuji Imada	77	71	75	70	293	18,090
Ryan Moore	78	69	75	71	293	18,090
Joey Sindelar	74	75	72	72	293	18,090
Mathias Gronberg	75	73	74	72	294	17,460
Bill Haas	76	73	73	72	294	17,460
Corey Pavin	75	72	71	76	294	17,460
Todd Hamilton	75	73	76	71	295	16,830
Charley Hoffman	75	69	76	75	295	16,830
Davis Love	77	71	73	74	295	16,830
Ryan Palmer	77	72	71	75	295	16,830
Charles Howell	73	74	75	76	298	16,380

AT&T Classic

TPC Sugarloaf, Duluth, Georgia
Par 36-36–72; 7,293 yards

May 17-20
purse, $5,400,000

	SCORES			TOTAL	MONEY
Zach Johnson	71	66	69	67	273	$972,000
Ryuji Imada	67	67	69	70	273	583,200
(Johnson defeated Imada on first playoff hole.)						
Matt Kuchar	70	72	64	70	276	280,800
Troy Matteson	70	64	69	73	276	280,800
Camilo Villegas	70	67	68	71	276	280,800
Bob Estes	71	69	67	70	277	180,900
Stephen Marino	67	71	69	70	277	180,900
Chris Tidland	71	67	71	68	277	180,900
Briny Baird	69	71	70	68	278	135,000
Olin Browne	69	69	74	66	278	135,000
Jonathan Byrd	69	72	68	69	278	135,000
Robert Gamez	70	69	71	68	278	135,000
Henrik Stenson	70	69	71	68	278	135,000
Gavin Coles	74	68	69	68	279	99,900
Joe Ogilvie	68	70	69	72	279	99,900
Billy Andrade	70	68	72	70	280	81,000
Steve Elkington	70	70	67	73	280	81,000
Lee Janzen	69	70	67	74	280	81,000
Parker McLachlin	70	72	72	66	280	81,000
Kevin Sutherland	65	71	71	73	280	81,000
Tommy Armour	67	71	70	73	281	60,480
Brian Davis	69	74	68	70	281	60,480
Craig Kanada	67	70	73	71	281	60,480
Stewart Cink	70	73	71	68	282	43,740
Mathias Gronberg	72	70	72	68	282	43,740
Neal Lancaster	72	71	70	69	282	43,740
John Merrick	70	73	73	66	282	43,740
Rory Sabbatini	69	70	70	73	282	43,740
Darron Stiles	71	67	73	71	282	43,740
D.J. Brigman	68	67	73	75	283	30,720
John Cook	71	70	70	72	283	30,720
Bill Haas	69	72	72	70	283	30,720
J.P. Hayes	72	70	72	69	283	30,720
Bob Heintz	73	67	74	69	283	30,720
Franklin Langham	71	70	68	74	283	30,720
Tag Ridings	69	71	70	73	283	30,720
David Toms	71	68	74	70	283	30,720
Charles Warren	73	67	70	73	283	30,720
Jason Bohn	69	72	69	74	284	22,680
Kevin Na	70	73	70	71	284	22,680
Tim Petrovic	73	68	71	72	284	22,680
Garrett Willis	71	71	72	70	284	22,680
Richard S. Johnson	71	72	73	69	285	17,820
Kent Jones	70	73	71	71	285	17,820
Daisuke Maruyama	71	71	74	69	285	17,820
Dicky Pride	68	73	74	70	285	17,820
D.J. Trahan	70	71	70	74	285	17,820
Michael Allen	74	67	74	71	286	13,297.50
Paul Azinger	71	70	76	69	286	13,297.50
Glen Day	72	71	70	73	286	13,297.50
Bob May	67	73	70	76	286	13,297.50
Shaun Micheel	72	70	71	73	286	13,297.50
Jerry Smith	71	72	68	75	286	13,297.50
Paul Stankowski	70	72	76	68	286	13,297.50
Jaco Van Zyl	72	69	70	75	286	13,297.50
Dan Forsman	72	69	77	69	287	12,096

	SCORES				TOTAL	MONEY
Brian Gay	70	72	73	72	287	12,096
J.J. Henry	74	69	73	71	287	12,096
Tom Johnson	73	70	74	70	287	12,096
Michael Putnam	75	66	74	72	287	12,096
Steve Jones	71	70	70	77	288	11,772
Marco Dawson	72	70	76	71	289	11,556
Mark Hensby	71	70	74	74	289	11,556
Steve Lowery	71	72	76	70	289	11,556
Ryan Armour	70	73	77	72	292	11,232
Grant Waite	69	74	77	72	292	11,232
Duffy Waldorf	72	71	75	74	292	11,232
Craig Bowden	71	72	78	73	294	10,908
Bob Burns	75	68	78	73	294	10,908
Hunter Mahan	74	69	78	73	294	10,908
Eric Axley	72	69	75	79	295	10,692

Crowne Plaza Invitational at Colonial

Colonial Country Club, Fort Worth, Texas
Par 35-35–70; 7,054 yards

May 24-27
purse, $6,000,000

	SCORES				TOTAL	MONEY
Rory Sabbatini	70	67	62	67	266	$1,080,000
Jim Furyk	65	66	68	67	266	528,000
Bernhard Langer	65	68	66	67	266	528,000
(Sabbatini defeated Furyk and Langer on first playoff hole.)						
Pat Perez	66	67	69	66	268	288,000
Nathan Green	65	66	72	66	269	228,000
Tom Lehman	66	67	68	68	269	228,000
Harrison Frazar	68	67	69	66	270	174,600
Jerry Kelly	70	64	69	67	270	174,600
Kevin Na	63	69	70	68	270	174,600
D.J. Trahan	67	67	69	67	270	174,600
Scott Verplank	70	66	63	71	270	174,600
Tim Clark	65	64	74	68	271	114,000
Mark Hensby	69	67	68	67	271	114,000
Jeff Maggert	64	69	68	70	271	114,000
Nick O'Hern	70	66	68	67	271	114,000
Rod Pampling	67	69	70	65	271	114,000
Tim Petrovic	70	68	67	66	271	114,000
Jason Bohn	68	66	70	68	272	75,600
Stewart Cink	67	69	66	70	272	75,600
Anthony Kim	63	69	73	67	272	75,600
Justin Leonard	69	70	66	67	272	75,600
Peter Lonard	65	69	67	71	272	75,600
David Toms	70	68	68	66	272	75,600
Eric Axley	68	67	69	69	273	49,800
K.J. Choi	67	70	69	67	273	49,800
Steve Marino	69	68	71	65	273	49,800
John Rollins	69	68	67	69	273	49,800
Steve Stricker	67	71	68	67	273	49,800
Ben Curtis	64	67	74	69	274	37,328.58
Lucas Glover	67	68	68	71	274	37,328.57
Cliff Kresge	69	67	70	68	274	37,328.57
Ryan Moore	71	66	66	71	274	37,328.57
Arron Oberholser	64	66	73	71	274	37,328.57
Brandt Snedeker	66	70	67	71	274	37,328.57
Dean Wilson	68	67	71	68	274	37,328.57
Mark Brooks	67	71	70	67	275	25,230
Chad Campbell	67	68	68	72	275	25,230

	SCORES				TOTAL	MONEY
Alex Cejka	67	65	72	71	275	25,230
Matt Kuchar	68	70	70	67	275	25,230
Doug LaBelle	67	70	69	69	275	25,230
Stephen Leaney	68	68	70	69	275	25,230
Frank Lickliter	65	71	69	70	275	25,230
Ted Purdy	64	71	72	68	275	25,230
Michael Putnam	69	65	70	71	275	25,230
Jeff Quinney	65	72	68	70	275	25,230
Joe Durant	67	72	68	69	276	16,320
Tim Herron	67	68	70	71	276	16,320
Billy Mayfair	71	67	71	67	276	16,320
Heath Slocum	70	65	72	69	276	16,320
Bob Tway	73	64	70	69	276	16,320
Bo Van Pelt	68	71	67	70	276	16,320
Stephen Ames	69	67	70	71	277	13,920
Steve Elkington	67	69	71	70	277	13,920
J.J. Henry	68	67	72	70	277	13,920
Will MacKenzie	67	71	70	69	277	13,920
Carl Pettersson	74	65	70	68	277	13,920
Brett Wetterich	66	69	71	71	277	13,920
Mathew Goggin	70	69	70	69	278	13,320
Davis Love	69	68	72	69	278	13,320
Charles Warren	69	68	69	72	278	13,320
Tommy Armour	71	68	71	70	280	12,960
Steve Flesch	70	69	69	72	280	12,960
Mark Wilson	68	71	70	71	280	12,960
Ryan Armour	67	72	74	70	283	12,420
Matthew Every	69	66	75	73	283	12,420
Richard S. Johnson	70	68	76	69	283	12,420
Rocco Mediate	70	68	70	75	283	12,420
Brett Quigley	67	72	70	74	283	12,420
Duffy Waldorf	70	69	72	72	283	12,420
Ryan Palmer	70	69	73	73	285	12,000

Memorial Tournament

Muirfield Village Golf Club, Dublin, Ohio
Par 36-36–72; 7,300 yards

May 31-June 3
purse, $6,000,000

	SCORES				TOTAL	MONEY
K.J. Choi	69	70	67	65	271	$1,080,000
Ryan Moore	66	69	71	66	272	648,000
Rod Pampling	65	68	68	72	273	348,000
Kenny Perry	69	74	67	63	273	348,000
Stewart Cink	69	71	65	69	274	210,750
Fredrik Jacobson	68	68	70	68	274	210,750
Sean O'Hair	65	70	69	70	274	210,750
Adam Scott	70	62	72	70	274	210,750
Aaron Baddeley	66	68	71	71	276	168,000
Geoff Ogilvy	70	67	69	70	276	168,000
Will MacKenzie	67	73	65	72	277	144,000
Brett Quigley	70	69	71	67	277	144,000
Matt Kuchar	68	73	69	68	278	120,000
Billy Mayfair	68	71	71	68	278	120,000
Ernie Els	66	75	71	67	279	93,000
Jason Gore	70	70	71	68	279	93,000
Tim Herron	66	73	69	71	279	93,000
Rocco Mediate	69	73	72	65	279	93,000
Vijay Singh	69	72	71	67	279	93,000
Tiger Woods	70	72	70	67	279	93,000

	SCORES				TOTAL	MONEY
Alex Cejka	71	72	68	69	280	69,600
Richard S. Johnson	73	69	68	70	280	69,600
Jim Furyk	70	69	71	71	281	51,900
Sergio Garcia	69	73	69	70	281	51,900
Nick O'Hern	65	74	69	73	281	51,900
Ted Purdy	68	69	72	72	281	51,900
Bo Van Pelt	74	72	70	65	281	51,900
Bubba Watson	66	68	73	74	281	51,900
Steve Marino	73	71	66	72	282	41,700
Boo Weekley	69	69	72	72	282	41,700
Paul Casey	72	69	70	72	283	36,375
Trevor Immelman	72	67	70	74	283	36,375
Carl Pettersson	68	75	70	70	283	36,375
Camilo Villegas	69	71	72	71	283	36,375
Mark Calcavecchia	70	70	72	72	284	28,950
Luke Donald	73	70	71	70	284	28,950
Robert Garrigus	69	74	70	71	284	28,950
Craig Kanada	70	70	70	74	284	28,950
Anthony Kim	74	72	71	67	284	28,950
D.J. Trahan	69	71	71	73	284	28,950
Ben Curtis	70	72	69	74	285	22,800
Nathan Green	73	70	71	71	285	22,800
Tom Pernice, Jr.	71	74	70	70	285	22,800
Nick Watney	68	69	73	75	285	22,800
Woody Austin	71	72	70	73	286	17,160
Jerry Kelly	73	72	69	72	286	17,160
Tom Lehman	71	71	71	73	286	17,160
Ryan Palmer	70	74	72	70	286	17,160
John Senden	71	72	73	70	286	17,160
Bob Tway	69	72	68	77	286	17,160
Stuart Appleby	70	74	71	72	287	14,310
Ken Duke	73	72	73	69	287	14,310
Ryuji Imada	69	75	74	69	287	14,310
Jeff Quinney	74	72	71	70	287	14,310
Daniel Chopra	71	72	74	71	288	13,620
Charley Hoffman	72	73	72	71	288	13,620
Justin Leonard	70	71	73	74	288	13,620
Jeff Sluman	72	71	75	70	288	13,620
Jose Coceres	74	72	69	74	289	13,200
Steve Lowery	68	75	73	73	289	13,200
Mark Wilson	71	75	68	75	289	13,200
Bart Bryant	73	72	75	70	290	12,780
Johan Edfors	70	72	76	72	290	12,780
Corey Pavin	70	73	75	72	290	12,780
Charl Schwartzel	70	74	72	74	290	12,780
Todd Hamilton	75	71	75	70	291	12,480
Mark Hensby	71	71	73	77	292	12,360
Shaun Micheel	74	69	77	73	293	12,240
Frank Lickliter	75	70	72	77	294	12,120
Billy Andrade	74	69	78	75	296	12,000
Paul Azinger	74	71	76	77	298	11,880

Stanford St. Jude Championship

TPC at Southwind, Memphis, Tennessee
Par 35-35–70; 7,244 yards

June 7-10
purse, $6,000,000

	SCORES				TOTAL	MONEY
Woody Austin	72	66	67	62	267	$1,080,000
Brian Davis	70	68	68	66	272	648,000

	SCORES				TOTAL	MONEY
David Toms	70	68	66	69	273	408,000
Brian Gay	68	66	70	70	274	288,000
Brandt Snedeker	70	68	69	68	275	228,000
Dean Wilson	70	71	66	68	275	228,000
Adam Scott	67	66	68	75	276	201,000
Will MacKenzie	71	69	67	70	277	180,000
Scott Verplank	69	69	70	69	277	180,000
Jeff Overton	71	71	70	66	278	156,000
Vance Veazey	73	71	67	67	278	156,000
Robert Allenby	70	69	70	70	279	117,600
Steve Lowery	71	69	68	71	279	117,600
Shaun Micheel	72	69	69	69	279	117,600
Heath Slocum	72	69	71	67	279	117,600
Duffy Waldorf	69	69	71	70	279	117,600
Tim Herron	73	68	71	68	280	87,000
Fredrik Jacobson	67	70	70	73	280	87,000
Hunter Mahan	74	68	70	68	280	87,000
Troy Matteson	75	68	70	67	280	87,000
Eric Axley	71	69	70	71	281	64,800
Scott Gutschewski	72	71	70	68	281	64,800
Richard S. Johnson	70	72	68	71	281	64,800
Stephen Leaney	74	70	69	68	281	64,800
Andrew Buckle	70	66	75	71	282	46,800
Joe Durant	73	66	68	75	282	46,800
Anthony Kim	72	73	69	68	282	46,800
Daisuke Maruyama	74	68	66	74	282	46,800
Joe Ogilvie	72	68	74	68	282	46,800
Jason Schultz	72	73	68	70	283	34,133.34
Vijay Singh	72	69	71	71	283	34,133.34
Bob Tway	72	68	72	71	283	34,133.34
Stephen Ames	71	68	70	74	283	34,133.33
Billy Andrade	74	68	70	71	283	34,133.33
Marco Dawson	77	65	70	71	283	34,133.33
Retief Goosen	68	74	69	72	283	34,133.33
Cliff Kresge	72	67	70	74	283	34,133.33
D.J. Trahan	75	67	70	71	283	34,133.33
Ryan Armour	72	71	72	69	284	23,400
Gavin Coles	69	72	72	71	284	23,400
Jeff Gove	73	69	72	70	284	23,400
Craig Lile	74	68	72	70	284	23,400
Michael Putnam	73	67	71	73	284	23,400
Darron Stiles	70	73	72	69	284	23,400
Mike Weir	75	68	71	70	284	23,400
Steve Elkington	71	69	72	73	285	15,600
Steve Flesch	74	69	72	70	285	15,600
Fred Funk	73	70	71	71	285	15,600
Matt Kuchar	75	69	71	70	285	15,600
Justin Leonard	70	74	68	73	285	15,600
Bob May	71	72	71	71	285	15,600
Sean O'Hair	72	73	68	72	285	15,600
Vaughn Taylor	74	71	70	70	285	15,600
Camilo Villegas	74	69	69	73	285	15,600
D.J. Brigman	74	69	69	74	286	13,380
Bart Bryant	75	68	69	74	286	13,380
Glen Day	73	72	70	71	286	13,380
Ken Duke	76	66	70	74	286	13,380
Jim Gallagher, Jr.	74	69	71	72	286	13,380
Sergio Garcia	74	70	72	70	286	13,380
Tim Petrovic	74	68	70	74	286	13,380
Charles Warren	71	74	71	70	286	13,380
Briny Baird	71	72	71	73	287	12,660
Paul Goydos	78	67	71	71	287	12,660
Loren Roberts	74	69	73	71	287	12,660

	SCORES				TOTAL	MONEY
Chris Stroud	72	71	74	70	287	12,660
Jose Maria Olazabal	73	66	76	73	288	12,360
Bob Heintz	73	70	74	72	289	12,180
Parker McLachlin	73	70	72	74	289	12,180
Steve Allan	75	69	71	75	290	11,940
Chris DiMarco	73	72	77	68	290	11,940
Nathan Green	75	70	73	73	291	11,700
B.J. Staten	72	71	77	71	291	11,700
Michael Boyd	73	70	75	74	292	11,520
John Mallinger	72	73	79	69	293	11,340
Charlie Wi	73	71	77	72	293	11,340
Brian Bateman	74	70	73	77	294	11,100
Robert Gamez	76	69	75	74	294	11,100
John Daly	70	74	75	79	298	10,920
Rich Barcelo	75	70	79	78	302	10,800

U.S. Open Championship

Oakmont Country Club, Oakmont, Pennsylvania
Par 35-35–70; 7,230 yards

June 14-17
purse, $7,000,000

	SCORES				TOTAL	MONEY
Angel Cabrera	69	71	76	69	285	$1,260,000
Jim Furyk	71	75	70	70	286	611,336
Tiger Woods	71	74	69	72	286	611,336
Niclas Fasth	71	71	75	70	287	325,923
David Toms	72	72	73	72	289	248,948
Bubba Watson	70	71	74	74	289	248,948
Nick Dougherty	68	77	74	71	290	194,245
Scott Verplank	73	71	74	72	290	194,245
Jerry Kelly	74	71	73	72	290	194,245
Justin Rose	71	71	73	76	291	154,093
Stephen Ames	73	69	73	76	291	154,093
Paul Casey	77	66	72	76	291	154,093
Lee Janzen	73	73	73	73	292	124,706
Hunter Mahan	73	74	72	73	292	124,706
Steve Stricker	75	73	68	76	292	124,706
Aaron Baddeley	72	70	70	80	292	124,706
Carl Pettersson	72	72	75	74	293	102,536
Tim Clark	72	76	71	74	293	102,536
Jeff Brehaut	73	75	70	75	293	102,536
Anthony Kim	74	73	80	67	294	86,200
Mike Weir	74	72	73	75	294	86,200
Vijay Singh	71	77	70	76	294	86,200
Ken Duke	74	75	73	73	295	71,905
Brandt Snedeker	71	73	77	74	295	71,905
Nick O'Hern	76	74	71	74	295	71,905
Camilo Villegas	73	77	75	71	296	57,026
Boo Weekley	72	75	77	72	296	57,026
J.J. Henry	71	78	75	72	296	57,026
Stuart Appleby	74	72	71	79	296	57,026
Pablo Martin	71	76	77	73	297	45,313
Peter Hanson	71	74	78	74	297	45,313
Fred Funk	71	78	74	74	297	45,313
D.J. Brigman	74	74	74	75	297	45,313
Charles Schwartzel	75	73	73	76	297	45,313
Graeme McDowell	73	72	75	77	297	45,313
Lee Westwood	72	75	79	72	298	37,159
Shingo Katayama	72	74	79	73	298	37,159
Mathew Goggin	77	73	74	74	298	37,159

	SCORES				TOTAL	MONEY
Jeev Milkha Singh	75	75	73	75	298	37,159
Ian Poulter	72	77	72	77	298	37,159
Tom Pernice, Jr.	72	72	75	79	298	37,159
Kenneth Ferrie	74	76	77	72	299	31,084
Geoff Ogilvy	71	75	78	75	299	31,084
John Rollins	75	74	74	76	299	31,084
Marcus Fraser	72	78	77	73	300	25,016
Olin Browne	71	75	80	74	300	25,016
Ben Curtis	71	77	78	74	300	25,016
Jose Maria Olazabal	70	78	78	74	300	25,016
Zach Johnson	76	74	76	74	300	25,016
Chris DiMarco	76	73	73	78	300	25,016
Rory Sabbatini	73	77	78	73	301	20,282
Charles Howell	76	73	77	75	301	20,282
Dean Wilson	76	74	76	75	301	20,282
Ernie Els	73	76	74	78	301	20,282
Anders Hansen	71	79	79	73	302	18,829
Michael Putnam	73	74	72	83	302	18,829
Chad Campbell	73	72	77	81	303	18,184
Kevin Sutherland	74	76	79	75	304	17,371
Bob Estes	75	75	77	77	304	17,371
Michael Campbell	73	77	75	79	304	17,371
Harrison Frazar	74	74	74	82	304	17,371
Jason Dufner	71	75	79	80	305	16,647
George McNeill	72	76	77	81	306	16,343

Out of Final 36 Holes

Shaun Micheel	78	73	151	Tom Gillis	77	78	155
Joe Durant	75	76	151	Ricky Barnes	76	79	155
Joey Sindelar	73	78	151	Kyle Dobbs	77	78	155
Paul Goydos	78	73	151	Darren Fichardt	75	81	156
Ryan Moore	78	73	151	Luke List	77	79	156
Phil Mickelson	74	77	151	Rod Pampling	81	75	156
Lucas Glover	71	80	151	Adam Speirs	78	78	156
Tripp Isenhour	74	77	151	Nathan Green	74	82	156
Soren Kjeldsen	76	75	151	Geoffrey Sisk	77	79	156
Eric Axley	79	72	151	Michael Block	79	77	156
*Mark Harrell	75	76	151	Michael Berg	81	75	156
Jon Mills	73	78	151	*Jason Kokrak	76	80	156
Kirk Triplett	73	78	151	Steve Marino	79	78	157
Thomas Bjorn	75	76	151	Tim Petrovic	78	79	157
Justin Leonard	75	76	151	*Rhys Davies	74	83	157
Luke Donald	74	77	151	Craig Kanada	72	85	157
Johan Edfors	75	76	151	Todd Fischer	79	79	158
Nick Watney	79	72	151	Robert Karlsson	77	81	158
Woody Austin	74	77	151	Adam Scott	76	82	158
Brett Wetterich	77	75	152	Rich Beem	73	85	158
Trevor Immelman	73	79	152	Frank Bensel	79	79	158
Stewart Cink	72	80	152	Lee Williams	80	78	158
Jeff Sluman	74	78	152	*John Kelly	74	84	158
Tom Byrum	73	79	152	Colin Montgomerie	76	82	158
Ryuji Imada	74	78	152	Todd Hamilton	81	77	158
Vaughn Taylor	74	78	152	John Koskinen	78	80	158
K.J. Choi	77	75	152	*Trip Kuehne	79	80	159
*Richard Ramsay	78	74	152	Miguel Rodriguez	84	76	160
Kaname Yokoo	78	75	153	Johnson Wagner	77	83	160
Toru Taniguchi	78	75	153	Andy Matthews	79	81	160
Sean O'Hair	73	80	153	*Jeff Golden	82	78	160
Joe Daley	77	76	153	Jason Allen	80	81	161
Nobuhiro Masuda	76	77	153	*Chris Condello	79	83	162
Padraig Harrington	73	80	153	Christian Cevaer	78	85	163
Retief Goosen	76	77	153	*Alex Prugh	82	81	163

Andrew Buckle	73	81	154
Darron Stiles	74	80	154
Anthony Wall	73	81	154
Sergio Garcia	79	75	154
Robert Allenby	75	79	154
Arron Oberholser	73	81	154
Pat Perez	76	78	154
Warren Pineo	82	72	154
Chris Stroud	80	75	155
Martin Laird	76	79	155
Davis Love	75	80	155
Henrik Stenson	79	76	155

Steve Elkington	84	79	163
*Martin Ureta	80	83	163
*Philip Pettitt, Jr.	81	82	163
Mike Small	86	77	163
Brett Quigley	78	86	164
Todd Rossetti	78	87	165
Sam Walker	78	89	167
Allen Doyle	81	86	167
Jacob Rogers	85	83	168
Ryan Palmer	84	84	168
*Richard Lee	79		WD

(Professionals who did not complete 72 holes received $2,000.)

Travelers Championship

TPC at River Highlands, Cromwell, Connecticut
Par 35-35–70; 6,844 yards

June 21-24
purse, $6,000,000

	SCORES				TOTAL	MONEY
Hunter Mahan	62	71	67	65	265	$1,080,000
Jay Williamson	66	66	67	66	265	648,000
(Mahan defeated Williamson on first playoff hole.)						
Nick O'Hern	67	70	66	66	269	408,000
Vijay Singh	68	71	66	65	270	288,000
Fred Funk	70	65	67	69	271	240,000
Tom Lehman	67	68	70	67	272	201,000
David Toms	67	65	69	71	272	201,000
Bo Van Pelt	73	68	67	64	272	201,000
Billy Mayfair	67	72	66	68	273	156,000
Kevin Na	70	67	69	67	273	156,000
Justin Rose	69	68	68	68	273	156,000
B.J. Staten	67	71	69	66	273	156,000
J.J. Henry	68	73	69	64	274	120,000
Steve Marino	68	67	71	68	274	120,000
Steve Allan	66	75	67	67	275	90,000
Chad Campbell	69	70	70	66	275	90,000
Mathew Goggin	69	71	67	68	275	90,000
Jerry Kelly	69	68	68	70	275	90,000
Shigeki Maruyama	67	69	73	66	275	90,000
Kenny Perry	65	71	70	69	275	90,000
Carl Pettersson	65	72	72	66	275	90,000
Billy Andrade	66	71	71	68	276	54,085.72
Joe Ogilvie	71	68	69	68	276	54,085.72
Charles Warren	67	67	73	69	276	54,085.72
Eric Axley	67	70	69	70	276	54,085.71
Olin Browne	67	67	72	70	276	54,085.71
Tom Pernice, Jr.	68	70	68	70	276	54,085.71
Heath Slocum	68	68	70	70	276	54,085.71
Arjun Atwal	68	71	74	64	277	39,900
Bill Haas	72	68	68	69	277	39,900
Peter Lonard	68	69	73	67	277	39,900
Kevin Sutherland	68	71	73	65	277	39,900
Brad Faxon	65	74	70	69	278	33,900
Ryan Moore	66	71	69	72	278	33,900
Tim Petrovic	71	68	68	71	278	33,900
Craig Bowden	71	69	71	68	279	27,042.86
Rod Pampling	66	71	72	70	279	27,042.86
Corey Pavin	70	66	77	66	279	27,042.86
Michael Sim	65	70	78	66	279	27,042.86
Bob Tway	71	70	69	69	279	27,042.86

	SCORES				TOTAL	MONEY
Pat Perez	69	68	66	76	279	27,042.85
Joey Sindelar	66	70	72	71	279	27,042.85
Woody Austin	66	73	71	70	280	21,000
Brian Davis	71	69	74	66	280	21,000
Doug LaBelle	68	73	71	68	280	21,000
Michael Allen	66	69	76	70	281	15,810
Andrew Buckle	71	70	72	68	281	15,810
Chris DiMarco	64	70	74	73	281	15,810
Brent Geiberger	73	68	70	70	281	15,810
Jason Gore	68	70	72	71	281	15,810
J.B. Holmes	72	69	71	69	281	15,810
Cliff Kresge	71	70	69	71	281	15,810
Steve Wheatcroft	68	71	74	68	281	15,810
Ryan Armour	67	74	68	73	282	13,560
Mark Calcavecchia	71	70	71	70	282	13,560
Ben Curtis	69	71	73	69	282	13,560
Padraig Harrington	71	68	74	69	282	13,560
Tim Herron	71	70	74	67	282	13,560
Jeff Overton	69	71	72	70	282	13,560
Kevin Stadler	68	70	75	69	282	13,560
Cameron Beckman	75	65	74	69	283	12,900
Bob Heintz	65	72	76	70	283	12,900
Frank Lickliter	69	71	75	68	283	12,900
Daisuke Maruyama	68	72	75	68	283	12,900
David Branshaw	70	71	69	74	284	12,540
Jesper Parnevik	72	69	78	65	284	12,540
Jason Dufner	71	70	70	74	285	12,180
Steve Flesch	71	69	72	73	285	12,180
Robert Gamez	70	69	73	73	285	12,180
Brett Wetterich	70	70	80	65	285	12,180
Alex Cejka	68	71	77	70	286	11,880
Glen Day	69	70	76	73	288	11,640
Will MacKenzie	67	74	75	72	288	11,640
John Mallinger	71	69	75	73	288	11,640
Stewart Cink	68	70	75	76	289	11,340
Craig Kanada	68	71	75	75	289	11,340
Tripp Isenhour	72	68	73	77	290	11,160
Mark Brooks	70	70	78	73	291	11,040
Scott Gutschewski	72	69	77	78	296	10,920

Buick Open

Warwick Hills Golf & Country Club, Grand Blanc, Michigan
Par 36-36–72; 7,127 yards

June 28-July 1
purse, $4,900,000

	SCORES				TOTAL	MONEY
Brian Bateman	65	70	69	69	273	$882,000
Jason Gore	71	66	70	67	274	365,866.67
Justin Leonard	69	72	66	67	274	365,866.67
Woody Austin	65	71	69	69	274	365,866.66
Marco Dawson	68	71	68	68	275	166,110
Steve Elkington	66	70	71	68	275	166,110
Jim Furyk	66	68	71	70	275	166,110
John Rollins	70	71	67	67	275	166,110
Scott Verplank	66	69	69	71	275	166,110
Gavin Coles	68	70	68	70	276	108,616.67
Lucas Glover	68	68	70	70	276	108,616.67
Steve Marino	69	70	68	69	276	108,616.67
Brandt Snedeker	71	69	66	70	276	108,616.67
Fredrik Jacobson	68	70	67	71	276	108,616.66

	SCORES				TOTAL	MONEY
Kenny Perry	71	63	71	71	276	108,616.66
Briny Baird	70	69	71	67	277	75,950
John Daly	69	70	69	69	277	75,950
Jesper Parnevik	72	68	64	73	277	75,950
Charlie Wi	68	70	70	69	277	75,950
Brian Davis	70	69	70	69	278	51,100
Fred Funk	70	70	68	70	278	51,100
Stephen Leaney	69	69	69	71	278	51,100
Tom Lehman	71	70	68	69	278	51,100
Tom Pernice, Jr.	70	67	66	75	278	51,100
Michael Putnam	70	67	69	72	278	51,100
Jay Williamson	71	67	71	69	278	51,100
Michael Boyd	70	68	71	70	279	33,320
Bubba Dickerson	68	69	69	73	279	33,320
Bob Estes	69	70	70	70	279	33,320
Craig Kanada	67	70	74	68	279	33,320
Sean O'Hair	71	70	68	70	279	33,320
Kevin Stadler	71	68	68	72	279	33,320
Bob Tway	70	71	72	66	279	33,320
Glen Day	71	70	70	69	280	23,193.34
Robert Gamez	70	68	73	69	280	23,193.34
Jeff Sluman	70	71	71	68	280	23,193.34
Ken Duke	71	68	71	70	280	23,193.33
Mathias Gronberg	71	70	68	71	280	23,193.33
Mark Hensby	67	70	71	72	280	23,193.33
Tripp Isenhour	69	70	66	75	280	23,193.33
Kent Jones	71	69	70	70	280	23,193.33
Kevin Na	70	71	67	72	280	23,193.33
D.J. Brigman	70	70	70	71	281	15,712.67
Alex Cejka	68	70	72	71	281	15,712.67
Brett Quigley	65	69	75	72	281	15,712.67
Tag Ridings	71	70	71	69	281	15,712.67
Joe Ogilvie	69	72	67	73	281	15,712.66
Dicky Pride	70	69	69	73	281	15,712.66
Billy Andrade	68	69	73	72	282	12,380.67
Darren Clarke	73	68	70	71	282	12,380.67
Daniel Chopra	70	68	72	72	282	12,380.66
Rich Barcelo	72	65	75	71	283	11,152.40
Jeff Brehaut	72	65	70	76	283	11,152.40
Steve Flesch	70	70	71	72	283	11,152.40
Brent Geiberger	70	71	71	71	283	11,152.40
Tom Gillis	71	70	69	73	283	11,152.40
Scott Gutschewski	71	70	71	71	283	11,152.40
Greg Owen	70	70	72	71	283	11,152.40
Andrew Ruthkoski	69	70	73	71	283	11,152.40
Joey Sindelar	69	68	70	76	283	11,152.40
Lee Williams	69	72	71	71	283	11,152.40
Rocco Mediate	64	71	76	73	284	10,535
Corey Pavin	68	73	69	74	284	10,535
Robert Allenby	69	70	72	74	285	10,143
Craig Bowden	69	72	70	74	285	10,143
Brian Gay	69	72	72	72	285	10,143
Jeff Quinney	67	72	75	71	285	10,143
Paul Sheehan	72	68	73	72	285	10,143
Johnson Wagner	71	68	72	74	285	10,143
Arjun Atwal	70	71	73	72	286	9,751
Chris DiMarco	72	67	73	74	286	9,751
Cameron Beckman	66	73	75	73	287	9,604
Jeff Gove	71	68	76	73	288	9,408
Steve Lowery	70	70	75	73	288	9,408
Michael Sim	72	68	75	73	288	9,408
Daisuke Maruyama	69	71	74	78	292	9,212
Robert Garrigus	68	73	75	77	293	9,114

AT&T National

Congressional Country Club, Bethesda, Maryland
Par 35-35–70; 7,255 yards

July 5-8
purse, $6,000,000

	SCORES				TOTAL	MONEY
K.J. Choi	66	67	70	68	271	$1,080,000
Steve Stricker	67	70	67	70	274	648,000
Stuart Appleby	66	67	68	76	277	312,000
Jim Furyk	66	74	68	69	277	312,000
Pat Perez	71	70	69	67	277	312,000
Robert Allenby	70	71	69	68	278	208,500
Tiger Woods	73	66	69	70	278	208,500
Hunter Mahan	70	74	70	65	279	168,000
Rocco Mediate	75	68	70	66	279	168,000
Brandt Snedeker	69	72	70	68	279	168,000
Mike Weir	72	66	67	74	279	168,000
Mathew Goggin	73	69	67	71	280	110,571.43
Craig Kanada	69	67	74	70	280	110,571.43
Geoff Ogilvy	69	75	68	68	280	110,571.43
Jeff Quinney	67	75	69	69	280	110,571.43
Vijay Singh	66	71	73	70	280	110,571.43
Boo Weekley	70	72	67	71	280	110,571.43
Lucas Glover	71	69	66	74	280	110,571.42
Billy Andrade	68	68	73	72	281	70,200
Charley Hoffman	71	69	67	74	281	70,200
Shigeki Maruyama	72	70	65	74	281	70,200
Rod Pampling	70	70	69	72	281	70,200
Jesper Parnevik	70	68	73	70	281	70,200
Chris Riley	70	71	70	70	281	70,200
Anthony Kim	71	69	69	73	282	46,800
Justin Leonard	73	70	71	68	282	46,800
Ryan Moore	74	70	66	72	282	46,800
Sean O'Hair	71	70	73	68	282	46,800
Corey Pavin	67	73	75	67	282	46,800
Briny Baird	70	73	68	72	283	33,420
Olin Browne	70	73	70	70	283	33,420
Brian Davis	69	70	70	74	283	33,420
Robert Garrigus	69	67	73	74	283	33,420
Brian Gay	71	70	69	73	283	33,420
Bill Haas	69	72	71	71	283	33,420
Kent Jones	71	70	70	72	283	33,420
Stephen Leaney	71	71	70	71	283	33,420
Justin Rose	69	69	70	75	283	33,420
D.J. Trahan	71	72	71	69	283	33,420
Chris DiMarco	72	72	70	70	284	23,400
Fredrik Jacobson	68	69	76	71	284	23,400
Brett Quigley	72	70	70	72	284	23,400
John Senden	70	74	73	67	284	23,400
Kevin Stadler	69	70	69	76	284	23,400
Rich Beem	67	77	70	71	285	16,515
Mathias Gronberg	71	72	68	74	285	16,515
Jerry Kelly	71	68	73	73	285	16,515
Cliff Kresge	69	70	70	76	285	16,515
Frank Lickliter	71	72	72	70	285	16,515
Arron Oberholser	74	68	69	74	285	16,515
Joe Ogilvie	66	77	72	70	285	16,515
Charles Warren	68	73	68	76	285	16,515
*Jamie Lovemark	67	74	73	71	285	
Craig Barlow	70	74	69	73	286	13,635
Notah Begay	73	70	71	72	286	13,635
Tim Herron	71	73	72	70	286	13,635
Peter Lonard	75	69	70	72	286	13,635

	SCORES				TOTAL	MONEY
Will MacKenzie	72	70	75	69	286	13,635
Billy Mayfair	72	71	71	72	286	13,635
Michael Putnam	69	75	75	67	286	13,635
Bo Van Pelt	70	71	72	73	286	13,635
Chris Couch	68	72	77	70	287	12,900
Fred Funk	67	77	74	69	287	12,900
Greg Owen	67	74	75	71	287	12,900
Mark Wilson	71	72	72	72	287	12,900
Tommy Armour	70	72	74	73	289	12,480
Jason Bohn	73	69	71	76	289	12,480
Jason Gore	71	73	73	72	289	12,480
Aaron Baddeley	74	69	68	79	290	12,120
Joe Durant	73	71	71	75	290	12,120
Ryuji Imada	73	71	78	68	290	12,120
Vaughn Taylor	72	68	78	73	291	11,880
Todd Hamilton	69	70	77	76	292	11,760
Brad Faxon	69	74	73	77	293	11,640

John Deere Classic

TPC at Deere Run, Silvis, Illinois
Par 35-36–71; 7,257 yards

July 12-15
purse, $4,100,000

	SCORES				TOTAL	MONEY
Jonathan Byrd	67	68	65	66	266	$738,000
Tim Clark	68	65	66	68	267	442,800
Nathan Green	67	63	68	71	269	237,800
Troy Matteson	69	67	67	66	269	237,800
Carl Pettersson	67	64	71	68	270	164,000
Jason Dufner	65	66	72	68	271	128,330
Jeff Gove	69	68	66	68	271	128,330
Neal Lancaster	64	68	70	69	271	128,330
Heath Slocum	70	69	67	65	271	128,330
Kevin Sutherland	66	67	70	68	271	128,330
Lucas Glover	71	69	65	67	272	90,200
Billy Mayfair	69	66	67	70	272	90,200
Kenny Perry	65	68	68	71	272	90,200
Michael Sim	69	67	68	68	272	90,200
Briny Baird	67	70	68	68	273	69,700
J.P. Hayes	70	65	69	69	273	69,700
Stephen Leaney	69	69	67	68	273	69,700
Tommy Armour	69	70	68	67	274	55,350
Marco Dawson	68	72	69	65	274	55,350
Brian Gay	72	63	66	73	274	55,350
Greg Kraft	69	71	68	66	274	55,350
Cameron Beckman	67	70	68	70	275	34,235
Chris Couch	68	69	72	66	275	34,235
George McNeill	71	69	70	65	275	34,235
Jesper Parnevik	69	68	71	67	275	34,235
Tim Petrovic	68	68	72	67	275	34,235
Dicky Pride	70	69	67	69	275	34,235
Ted Purdy	70	70	69	66	275	34,235
Paul Stankowski	65	70	69	71	275	34,235
Darron Stiles	70	70	71	64	275	34,235
Chris Stroud	71	67	68	69	275	34,235
Harrison Frazar	69	68	73	66	276	21,274.45
Tim Herron	69	69	71	67	276	21,274.45
Kevin Na	68	69	72	67	276	21,274.45
Brandt Snedeker	69	68	73	66	276	21,274.45
Steve Allan	71	66	70	69	276	21,274.44

	SCORES				TOTAL	MONEY
Scott Gutschewski	65	71	72	68	276	21,274.44
Bernhard Langer	72	68	69	67	276	21,274.44
Craig Lile	67	71	69	69	276	21,274.44
D.J. Trahan	67	68	71	70	276	21,274.44
Tom Byrum	69	70	71	67	277	13,593.78
Bob Heintz	67	70	71	69	277	13,593.78
John Huston	70	68	72	67	277	13,593.78
Richard S. Johnson	71	68	70	68	277	13,593.78
Jeff Overton	70	66	69	72	277	13,593.78
Kirk Triplett	67	72	69	69	277	13,593.78
Charles Warren	68	71	71	67	277	13,593.78
Mark Brooks	70	68	66	73	277	13,593.77
Bob May	66	67	71	73	277	13,593.77
Woody Austin	72	67	69	70	278	9,983.50
Paul Goydos	67	71	74	66	278	9,983.50
Chris Tidland	69	69	69	71	278	9,983.50
Duffy Waldorf	65	68	73	72	278	9,983.50
Gavin Coles	72	68	68	71	279	9,430
John Merrick	72	67	70	70	279	9,430
Chris Riley	72	67	72	68	279	9,430
Paul Gow	69	68	72	71	280	9,102
Tom Johnson	68	68	72	72	280	9,102
Joe Ogilvie	71	68	72	69	280	9,102
Brady Schnell	70	68	73	69	280	9,102
Phil Tataurangi	68	71	73	68	280	9,102
Brendon de Jonge	67	68	74	72	281	8,692
Jason Gore	69	68	78	66	281	8,692
Kent Jones	67	72	72	70	281	8,692
Bronson Lacassie	71	66	74	70	281	8,692
Vance Veazey	69	69	73	70	281	8,692
Doug LaBelle	70	68	69	75	282	8,405
Jay Williamson	70	70	69	73	282	8,405
Jose Coceres	71	69	71	74	285	8,282
Grant Waite	71	69	75	73	288	8,200
Jim Rutledge	72	68	73	76	289	8,077
Jerry Smith	70	69	74	76	289	8,077

The Open Championship

See European Tours chapter.

U.S. Bank Championship in Milwaukee

Brown Deer Park Golf Course, Milwaukee, Wisconsin
Par 34-36–70; 6,759 yards

July 19-22
purse, $4,000,000

	SCORES				TOTAL	MONEY
Joe Ogilvie	67	63	69	67	266	$720,000
Tim Herron	66	67	65	72	270	298,666.67
Charlie Wi	70	66	66	68	270	298,666.67
Tim Clark	68	65	66	71	270	298,666.66
Steve Flesch	69	64	71	68	272	140,500
Bob Heintz	69	64	71	68	272	140,500
Jeff Maggert	63	69	71	69	272	140,500
Kenny Perry	69	65	67	71	272	140,500
Craig Bowden	66	67	71	69	273	104,000
Billy Mayfair	69	64	70	70	273	104,000
Jeff Sluman	71	67	65	70	273	104,000
Mark Wilson	67	70	67	69	273	104,000

	SCORES				TOTAL	MONEY
Steve Allan	68	66	69	71	274	72,800
Tom Byrum	68	68	70	68	274	72,800
Chris Couch	70	67	70	67	274	72,800
Jay Delsing	72	65	68	69	274	72,800
John Mallinger	68	66	70	70	274	72,800
Tommy Armour	70	66	70	69	275	54,000
Kent Jones	72	66	67	70	275	54,000
Bernhard Langer	72	65	69	69	275	54,000
Steve Wheatcroft	68	69	68	70	275	54,000
Olin Browne	71	69	70	66	276	37,133.34
Heath Slocum	69	69	69	69	276	37,133.34
Michael Allen	71	67	68	70	276	37,133.33
Jeff Brehaut	71	66	65	74	276	37,133.33
J.P. Hayes	67	71	69	69	276	37,133.33
Chris Riley	70	68	66	72	276	37,133.33
Mathew Goggin	70	67	70	70	277	24,933.34
Dicky Pride	68	72	68	69	277	24,933.34
Jay Williamson	65	72	71	69	277	24,933.34
Briny Baird	68	71	67	71	277	24,933.33
Brendon de Jonge	63	74	67	73	277	24,933.33
Tom Johnson	66	69	71	71	277	24,933.33
Jesper Parnevik	66	69	68	74	277	24,933.33
D.J. Trahan	71	68	68	70	277	24,933.33
Camilo Villegas	67	67	71	72	277	24,933.33
Rich Barcelo	71	67	70	70	278	16,400
Bubba Dickerson	68	69	68	73	278	16,400
Ryuji Imada	70	66	70	72	278	16,400
Anthony Kim	72	68	69	69	278	16,400
Cliff Kresge	67	69	68	74	278	16,400
Jarrod Lyle	68	69	73	68	278	16,400
Will MacKenzie	70	64	73	71	278	16,400
George McNeill	69	69	68	72	278	16,400
Chris Smith	69	70	69	70	278	16,400
Ryan Palmer	72	68	71	68	279	10,697.15
Bob Tway	75	65	71	68	279	10,697.15
Michael Bradley	71	69	67	72	279	10,697.14
Steve Elkington	66	73	71	69	279	10,697.14
Bob Estes	68	72	70	69	279	10,697.14
Jeff Gove	70	68	69	72	279	10,697.14
Garrett Willis	64	68	75	72	279	10,697.14
Alex Cejka	68	71	68	73	280	9,260
Matt Hendrix	74	66	69	71	280	9,260
Jeff Overton	68	71	72	69	280	9,260
Kirk Triplett	70	69	71	70	280	9,260
Mark Brooks	71	69	71	70	281	8,880
Nathan Green	71	69	74	67	281	8,880
Mathias Gronberg	74	65	68	74	281	8,880
Craig Kanada	70	70	69	72	281	8,880
Joey Sindelar	73	66	73	69	281	8,880
Chris Tidland	68	72	75	67	282	8,640
Marco Dawson	70	69	74	71	284	8,440
Jason Dufner	70	70	73	71	284	8,440
Robert Gamez	65	72	74	73	284	8,440
Daisuke Maruyama	73	67	74	70	284	8,440
Stephen Leaney	69	70	74	72	285	8,200
Larry Mize	68	72	74	71	285	8,200
Richard S. Johnson	69	71	77	70	287	8,080
Tony Finau	75	65	76	72	288	7,960
Andrew Ruthkoski	74	64	74	76	288	7,960

Canadian Open

Angus Glen Golf Club, North Course,
Markham, Ontario, Canada
Par 35-36–71; 7,320 yards

July 26-29
purse, $5,000,000

	SCORES				TOTAL	MONEY
Jim Furyk	69	66	69	64	268	$900,000
Vijay Singh	68	65	68	68	269	540,000
George McNeill	70	69	66	66	271	290,000
Ryan Palmer	67	67	71	66	271	290,000
Bob Heintz	69	69	67	67	272	190,000
Hunter Mahan	62	74	67	69	272	190,000
Brandt Snedeker	67	68	70	68	273	155,833.34
Steve Allan	64	68	70	71	273	155,833.33
John Mallinger	66	66	70	71	273	155,833.33
Alex Cejka	69	70	71	64	274	115,000
Paul Gow	70	69	67	68	274	115,000
Pat Perez	68	70	66	70	274	115,000
Tom Pernice, Jr.	68	68	69	69	274	115,000
Camilo Villegas	68	68	72	66	274	115,000
Glen Day	67	70	68	70	275	75,000
Tripp Isenhour	65	68	73	69	275	75,000
Cliff Kresge	70	65	71	69	275	75,000
Stephen Leaney	70	67	72	66	275	75,000
Steve Marino	70	66	70	69	275	75,000
Tim Petrovic	72	69	68	66	275	75,000
Bo Van Pelt	66	70	69	70	275	75,000
Billy Andrade	69	67	74	66	276	48,000
Steve Elkington	72	69	69	66	276	48,000
Shigeki Maruyama	69	69	68	70	276	48,000
Dicky Pride	68	68	70	70	276	48,000
Charlie Wi	66	71	70	69	276	48,000
Stephen Ames	70	69	69	69	277	36,250
Briny Baird	69	69	70	69	277	36,250
Brian Davis	70	70	68	69	277	36,250
Bill Haas	68	71	71	67	277	36,250
Bart Bryant	68	71	71	68	278	31,000
Frank Lickliter	69	69	73	67	278	31,000
Bob Tway	69	71	66	72	278	31,000
Michael Allen	73	67	73	66	279	23,666.67
Robert Garrigus	67	71	73	68	279	23,666.67
Corey Pavin	69	72	70	68	279	23,666.67
Michael Sim	69	67	73	70	279	23,666.67
Jeff Sluman	72	65	72	70	279	23,666.67
Mike Weir	71	70	67	71	279	23,666.67
Mathew Goggin	68	70	69	72	279	23,666.66
Michael Putnam	66	68	72	73	279	23,666.66
Brett Quigley	68	68	71	72	279	23,666.66
Charles Warren	71	70	68	71	280	18,500
Carlos Franco	69	69	72	71	281	16,500
Steve Jones	68	69	72	72	281	16,500
Craig Lile	72	69	71	69	281	16,500
Bob May	74	64	75	69	282	13,733.34
Brad Faxon	70	69	71	72	282	13,733.33
Jarrod Lyle	75	65	72	70	282	13,733.33
Craig Bowden	72	68	69	74	283	11,812.50
Mark Calcavecchia	67	71	74	71	283	11,812.50
Bob Estes	71	70	71	71	283	11,812.50
Steve Flesch	72	69	70	72	283	11,812.50
Doug LaBelle	67	68	74	74	283	11,812.50
John Merrick	69	71	73	70	283	11,812.50
Sean O'Hair	68	70	75	70	283	11,812.50

	SCORES				TOTAL	MONEY
Tag Ridings	67	71	75	70	283	11,812.50
Olin Browne	66	74	71	73	284	10,850
Ken Duke	73	68	71	72	284	10,850
Jeff Gove	74	67	68	75	284	10,850
David Hearn	65	73	73	73	284	10,850
Kent Jones	69	71	74	70	284	10,850
Justin Leonard	69	72	69	74	284	10,850
Bryce Molder	68	70	71	75	284	10,850
Ted Purdy	68	69	71	76	284	10,850
David Branshaw	73	68	68	76	285	10,200
Mike Grob	71	69	75	70	285	10,200
Scott Gutschewski	71	69	75	70	285	10,200
Daisuke Maruyama	68	69	70	78	285	10,200
Troy Matteson	67	71	68	79	285	10,200
Chris Baryla	74	66	74	72	286	9,800
Chris DiMarco	71	70	70	75	286	9,800
Jerry Smith	69	71	74	72	286	9,800
Parker McLachlin	72	67	72	76	287	9,600
Chris Smith	68	71	77	72	288	9,500
Bubba Watson	74	66	73	76	289	9,400
Joey Sindelar	69	71	72	78	290	9,300
Steve Lowery	72	69	74	78	293	9,200

WGC - Bridgestone Invitational

Firestone Country Club, South Course, Akron, Ohio
Par 35-35–70; 7,360 yards

August 2-5
purse, $8,000,000

	SCORES				TOTAL	MONEY
Tiger Woods	68	70	69	65	272	$1,350,000
Justin Rose	69	72	71	68	280	635,000
Rory Sabbatini	67	67	72	74	280	635,000
Chris DiMarco	69	70	72	70	281	310,000
Peter Lonard	70	70	73	68	281	310,000
Tim Clark	71	70	72	69	282	202,000
Davis Love	74	65	74	69	282	202,000
Andres Romero	71	71	69	71	282	202,000
Justin Leonard	73	67	71	72	283	147,500
Scott Verplank	70	68	73	72	283	147,500
Zach Johnson	71	65	76	72	284	115,333.34
K.J. Choi	71	73	69	71	284	115,333.33
Kenny Perry	69	69	71	75	284	115,333.33
Mark Calcavecchia	68	72	76	69	285	86,583.34
Rod Pampling	71	73	74	67	285	86,583.34
Stuart Appleby	68	74	69	74	285	86,583.33
Joe Durant	74	67	71	73	285	86,583.33
Padraig Harrington	72	69	72	72	285	86,583.33
Arron Oberholser	68	74	72	71	285	86,583.33
Aaron Baddeley	70	74	67	75	286	75,500
Sergio Garcia	71	77	71	67	286	75,500
Stephen Ames	71	73	71	72	287	66,250
Luke Donald	75	75	67	70	287	66,250
Ernie Els	70	77	72	68	287	66,250
Niclas Fasth	75	73	70	69	287	66,250
Anders Hansen	71	72	71	73	287	66,250
Charley Hoffman	71	73	74	69	287	66,250
Hunter Mahan	67	73	71	76	287	66,250
Lee Westwood	68	71	79	69	287	66,250
Richard Green	73	73	68	74	288	58,000
Carl Pettersson	70	79	68	71	288	58,000

	SCORES				TOTAL	MONEY
Ian Poulter	71	73	74	70	288	58,000
John Rollins	73	75	68	72	288	58,000
Boo Weekley	68	78	70	72	288	58,000
Brett Wetterich	74	75	70	69	288	58,000
Trevor Immelman	73	76	69	71	289	53,500
Adam Scott	75	76	70	68	289	53,500
Mark Wilson	76	75	68	70	289	53,500
Charles Howell	72	76	70	72	290	51,000
Paul McGinley	72	74	73	71	290	51,000
J.J. Henry	73	69	74	75	291	48,000
Colin Montgomerie	71	72	73	75	291	48,000
Henrik Stenson	72	74	72	73	291	48,000
Steve Stricker	70	73	76	72	291	48,000
John Senden	71	69	78	74	292	46,000
Michael Campbell	71	74	72	76	293	44,500
Thongchai Jaidee	73	76	73	71	293	44,500
Shingo Katayama	71	73	75	74	293	44,500
Jerry Kelly	73	71	74	75	293	44,500
Phil Mickelson	74	72	74	73	293	44,500
Paul Casey	67	73	76	78	294	42,000
Troy Matteson	71	74	73	76	294	42,000
Geoff Ogilvy	73	71	72	78	294	42,000
Jeev Milkha Singh	72	74	72	76	294	42,000
Richard Sterne	77	72	74	71	294	42,000
Woody Austin	74	77	68	76	295	39,500
Stewart Cink	79	67	76	73	295	39,500
Nick O'Hern	72	72	75	76	295	39,500
Vijay Singh	74	72	75	74	295	39,500
Y.E. Yang	73	74	70	78	295	39,500
Retief Goosen	74	73	72	77	296	36,750
David Howell	74	77	75	70	296	36,750
Liang Wen-chong	75	74	72	75	296	36,750
Vaughn Taylor	72	77	71	76	296	36,750
David Toms	76	74	71	75	296	36,750
Nick Watney	72	72	76	76	296	36,750
Darren Clarke	70	76	76	75	297	34,750
Mark Hensby	73	71	79	74	297	34,750
Angel Cabrera	73	76	74	75	298	33,500
Fred Funk	75	74	74	75	298	33,500
Gregory Havret	73	73	76	76	298	33,500
Robert Karlsson	76	72	72	78	298	33,500
Graeme Storm	75	72	76	75	298	33,500
Brian Bateman	77	75	72	75	299	32,625
Paul Goydos	69	76	73	81	299	32,625
Jose Manuel Lara	71	77	77	75	300	32,250
Chad Campbell	73	73	77	79	302	31,750
Anton Haig	77	75	71	79	302	31,750
Raphael Jacquelin	71	77	73	81	302	31,750
Ben Curtis	74	79	77	73	303	31,250
Robert Allenby	76	74	82	80	312	31,000
Jose Maria Olazabal	77	80	78	79	314	30,750

Reno-Tahoe Open

Montreux Golf & Country Club, Reno, Nevada
Par 36-36–72; 7,472 yards

August 2-5
purse, $3,000,000

	SCORES				TOTAL	MONEY
Steve Flesch	63	69	69	72	273	$540,000
Kevin Stadler	74	67	67	70	278	264,000
Charles Warren	71	63	73	71	278	264,000
Rich Barcelo	71	72	69	68	280	132,000
John Merrick	65	73	68	74	280	132,000
Brendon de Jonge	67	70	72	72	281	100,500
Steve Elkington	69	70	69	73	281	100,500
Shaun Micheel	68	70	71	72	281	100,500
Michael Allen	70	72	70	70	282	81,000
Brian Davis	68	73	71	70	282	81,000
Todd Fischer	69	68	69	76	282	81,000
Steve Allan	65	72	69	77	283	52,000
Alex Cejka	70	74	69	70	283	52,000
Jose Coceres	64	72	72	75	283	52,000
Ken Duke	74	66	72	71	283	52,000
Lucas Glover	67	72	74	70	283	52,000
Jarrod Lyle	67	71	75	70	283	52,000
Paul Stankowski	74	69	71	69	283	52,000
Johnson Wagner	68	69	74	72	283	52,000
Dean Wilson	71	71	69	72	283	52,000
Carlos Franco	72	68	73	71	284	32,400
Brian Gay	69	70	76	69	284	32,400
Kent Jones	67	73	72	72	284	32,400
Corey Pavin	67	71	72	74	284	32,400
Craig Barlow	68	73	70	74	285	23,400
Cameron Beckman	69	70	73	73	285	23,400
Greg Kraft	69	69	72	75	285	23,400
Kevin Na	71	69	71	74	285	23,400
Grant Waite	68	72	70	75	285	23,400
Will MacKenzie	66	73	73	74	286	17,828.58
Daniel Chopra	71	69	70	76	286	17,828.57
Gavin Coles	71	69	75	71	286	17,828.57
Jeff Maggert	70	72	67	77	286	17,828.57
John Mallinger	68	71	72	75	286	17,828.57
Chris Riley	70	70	70	76	286	17,828.57
D.J. Trahan	70	71	71	74	286	17,828.57
Craig Bowden	74	68	69	76	287	12,600
Jason Gore	66	72	75	74	287	12,600
Mathias Gronberg	67	72	74	74	287	12,600
Todd Hamilton	75	68	71	73	287	12,600
John Huston	70	70	72	75	287	12,600
Parker McLachlin	72	72	72	71	287	12,600
Bryce Molder	70	74	70	73	287	12,600
Jay Williamson	68	72	73	74	287	12,600
Jeff Gove	70	73	72	73	288	9,030
J.P. Hayes	69	71	74	74	288	9,030
Anthony Kim	70	72	70	76	288	9,030
Bob Tway	69	72	70	77	288	9,030
Ted Purdy	70	73	71	75	289	7,268.58
Ryan Armour	70	73	73	73	289	7,268.57
Guy Boros	72	71	72	74	289	7,268.57
Jeff Brehaut	75	69	75	70	289	7,268.57
Tom Johnson	73	68	74	74	289	7,268.57
Tim Petrovic	76	66	75	72	289	7,268.57
Jason Schultz	74	70	71	74	289	7,268.57
Tom Pernice, Jr.	71	72	74	73	290	6,840
Andrew Buckle	71	73	76	71	291	6,540

	SCORES				TOTAL	MONEY
Jason Dufner	67	70	72	82	291	6,540
Bob Heintz	73	70	73	75	291	6,540
Neal Lancaster	69	73	73	76	291	6,540
Craig Lile	69	74	72	76	291	6,540
Bob May	72	72	72	75	291	6,540
Jim McGovern	74	69	72	76	291	6,540
Larry Mize	71	71	75	74	291	6,540
Jerry Smith	73	71	70	77	291	6,540
Jay Delsing	70	74	78	70	292	6,180
Tripp Isenhour	74	68	74	76	292	6,180
Tag Ridings	68	71	73	80	292	6,180
Brent Geiberger	71	68	72	82	293	6,030
Charlie Wi	66	74	75	78	293	6,030
Chris Couch	71	71	76	76	294	5,940
Jaco Van Zyl	71	73	74	78	296	5,880
Eric Axley	68	75	75	79	297	5,760
Bill Haas	71	69	78	79	297	5,760
Kyle Reifers	70	69	77	81	297	5,760
Notah Begay	68	74	75	81	298	5,610
Steve Marino	69	75	75	79	298	5,610
Richard S. Johnson	70	71	76	82	299	5,520

PGA Championship

Southern Hills Country Club, Tulsa, Oklahoma
Par 35-35–70; 7,131 yards

August 9-12
purse, $7,000,000

	SCORES				TOTAL	MONEY
Tiger Woods	71	63	69	69	272	$1,260,000
Woody Austin	68	70	69	67	274	756,000
Ernie Els	72	68	69	66	275	476,000
Arron Oberholser	68	72	70	69	279	308,000
John Senden	69	70	69	71	279	308,000
Simon Dyson	73	71	72	64	280	227,500
Trevor Immelman	75	70	66	69	280	227,500
Geoff Ogilvy	69	68	74	69	280	227,500
Scott Verplank	70	66	74	71	281	170,333.34
Kevin Sutherland	73	69	68	71	281	170,333.33
Boo Weekley	76	69	65	71	281	170,333.33
Stuart Appleby	73	68	72	69	282	119,833.34
Anders Hansen	71	71	71	69	282	119,833.34
Stephen Ames	68	69	69	76	282	119,833.33
K.J. Choi	71	71	68	72	282	119,833.33
Justin Rose	70	73	70	69	282	119,833.33
Adam Scott	72	68	70	72	282	119,833.33
Ken Duke	73	71	69	71	284	81,600
Joe Durant	71	73	70	70	284	81,600
Hunter Mahan	71	73	72	68	284	81,600
Pat Perez	70	69	77	68	284	81,600
Brandt Snedeker	74	71	69	70	284	81,600
Steve Flesch	72	73	68	72	285	51,000
Retief Goosen	70	71	74	70	285	51,000
Nathan Green	75	68	67	75	285	51,000
Peter Hanson	72	71	69	73	285	51,000
Kenny Perry	72	72	71	70	285	51,000
Ian Poulter	71	73	70	71	285	51,000
Heath Slocum	72	70	72	71	285	51,000
Steve Stricker	77	68	69	71	285	51,000
Camilo Villegas	69	71	74	71	285	51,000
Bart Bryant	74	70	72	70	286	34,750

		SCORES			TOTAL	MONEY
Stewart Cink	72	70	72	72	286	34,750
John Daly	67	73	73	73	286	34,750
Luke Donald	72	71	70	73	286	34,750
Shaun Micheel	73	71	70	72	286	34,750
Phil Mickelson	73	69	75	69	286	34,750
Lee Westwood	69	74	75	68	286	34,750
Brett Wetterich	74	71	70	71	286	34,750
Paul Casey	72	70	74	71	287	27,350
Richard Green	72	73	70	72	287	27,350
Darren Clarke	77	66	71	74	288	20,850
Niclas Fasth	71	68	79	70	288	20,850
Padraig Harrington	69	73	72	74	288	20,850
Charles Howell	75	70	72	71	288	20,850
Colin Montgomerie	72	73	73	70	288	20,850
Sean O'Hair	70	72	70	76	288	20,850
Rod Pampling	70	74	72	72	288	20,850
David Toms	71	74	71	72	288	20,850
Brian Bateman	71	74	76	68	289	15,235.72
Lucas Glover	70	75	74	70	289	15,235.72
Frank Lickliter	70	75	75	69	289	15,235.72
Shingo Katayama	76	67	72	74	289	15,235.71
Anthony Kim	73	72	71	73	289	15,235.71
Nick O'Hern	72	72	72	73	289	15,235.71
Bob Tway	71	72	71	75	289	15,235.71
Chad Campbell	77	68	73	72	290	14,400
Robert Karlsson	73	71	75	71	290	14,400
Will MacKenzie	72	70	74	74	290	14,400
Billy Mayfair	76	69	75	71	291	14,025
Paul McGinley	74	66	76	75	291	14,025
Thomas Bjorn	73	71	76	73	293	13,650
Corey Pavin	74	68	72	79	293	13,650
Brett Quigley	76	67	73	77	293	13,650
Graeme Storm	65	76	74	78	293	13,650
Todd Hamilton	73	72	74	75	294	13,300
Tim Herron	75	68	71	80	294	13,300
Troy Matteson	72	69	73	80	294	13,300
Tom Lehman	73	71	74	78	296	13,050
Mike Small	73	70	78	75	296	13,050
Ryan Benzel	71	72	80	74	297	12,900

Out of Final 36 Holes

Robert Allenby	74	72	146	Charley Hoffman	75	76	151
Rich Beem	76	70	146	Bo Van Pelt	77	74	151
Markus Brier	69	77	146	Eric Axley	75	77	152
Jonathan Byrd	74	72	146	Chris DiMarco	79	73	152
Ben Curtis	75	71	146	Fred Funk	76	76	152
Jim Furyk	75	71	146	John O'Leary	75	77	152
J.J. Henry	71	75	146	Ted Purdy	76	76	152
Brad Lardon	70	76	146	Jeff Quinney	78	74	152
Davis Love	72	74	146	Nick Dougherty	79	74	153
Vijay Singh	75	71	146	Steve Elkington	75	78	153
D.J. Trahan	72	74	146	Soren Hansen	74	79	153
Mark Wilson	69	77	146	Thongchai Jaidee	80	73	153
Aaron Baddeley	73	74	147	Ryan Moore	79	74	153
Bradley Dredge	73	74	147	Andres Romero	81	72	153
David Howell	75	72	147	Charl Schwartzel	77	76	153
Justin Leonard	75	72	147	Nick Watney	78	75	153
Liang Wen-chong	73	74	147	Tim Clark	82	72	154
Joe Ogilvie	77	70	147	Robert Gaus	78	76	154
Tom Pernice, Jr.	73	74	147	Mark Brooks	79	76	155
Phil Schmitt	79	68	147	Kevin Burton	79	76	155
Jeff Sluman	74	73	147	Johan Edfors	79	76	155

Jose Coceres	71	77	148
Paul Goydos	75	73	148
John Rollins	73	75	148
Dean Wilson	75	73	148
Michael Campbell	74	75	149
Daniel Chopra	76	73	149
Gregory Havret	75	74	149
Ryuji Imada	78	71	149
Raphael Jacquelin	76	73	149
Kelly Mitchum	77	72	149
Henrik Stenson	75	74	149
Toru Taniguchi	77	72	149
Tim Thelen	74	75	149
Mike Weir	77	72	149
Miguel Angel Jimenez	78	72	150
Zach Johnson	74	76	150
Rory Sabbatini	74	76	150
Jeev Milkha Singh	76	74	150
Vaughn Taylor	76	74	150
Y.E. Yang	74	76	150
Angel Cabrera	81	70	151
Mark Calcavecchia	79	72	151

Scott Hebert	79	76	155
Stephen Leaney	77	78	155
Jose Maria Olazabal	75	80	155
Jerry Kelly	79	77	156
Butch Sheehan	82	74	156
William Amundsen	76	81	157
Matthew Call	81	76	157
Bob McGrath	80	78	158
Chip Sullivan	78	80	158
Bubba Watson	79	79	158
Denis Watson	74	84	158
Don Yrene	80	78	158
Micah Rudosky	83	76	159
Erik Wolf	83	77	160
Gregory Bisconti	82	79	161
Matt Seitz	83	81	164
Sergio Garcia	70	75	DQ
Rocco Mediate	72		WD
Richard Sterne	76		WD
Jyoti Randhawa			WD
Anthony Wall			WD

Wyndham Championship

Forest Oaks Country Club, Greensboro, North Carolina
Par 36-36–72; 7,311 yards

August 16-19
purse, $5,000,000

	SCORES				TOTAL	MONEY
Brandt Snedeker	70	67	66	63	266	$900,000
Tim Petrovic	68	65	68	67	268	373,333.34
Billy Mayfair	69	68	64	67	268	373,333.33
Jeff Overton	65	67	66	70	268	373,333.33
Carl Pettersson	66	67	68	68	269	200,000
Greg Kraft	66	67	71	66	270	180,000
Jason Gore	67	68	69	67	271	150,625
Will MacKenzie	64	71	68	68	271	150,625
Shigeki Maruyama	66	69	67	69	271	150,625
Kevin Stadler	68	67	70	66	271	150,625
Anders Hansen	69	64	68	71	272	120,000
Jeff Maggert	67	70	69	66	272	120,000
Jonathan Byrd	69	66	73	65	273	85,714.29
Frank Lickliter	68	70	68	67	273	85,714.29
Charles Warren	68	67	70	68	273	85,714.29
Dean Wilson	70	68	70	65	273	85,714.29
Brian Gay	69	67	69	68	273	85,714.28
Nathan Green	68	66	70	69	273	85,714.28
Joey Sindelar	69	67	68	69	273	85,714.28
Andy Bare	70	66	68	70	274	52,142.86
John Huston	66	66	72	70	274	52,142.86
Tripp Isenhour	69	70	65	70	274	52,142.86
Peter Lonard	70	69	67	68	274	52,142.86
Johnson Wagner	68	68	69	69	274	52,142.86
Lucas Glover	65	71	66	72	274	52,142.85
John Merrick	66	69	69	70	274	52,142.85
Eric Axley	68	70	69	68	275	34,750
Bob Estes	69	69	68	69	275	34,750
Brent Geiberger	68	68	70	69	275	34,750
J.J. Henry	70	69	67	69	275	34,750
Kent Jones	67	70	69	69	275	34,750
Vaughn Taylor	67	70	69	69	275	34,750
Craig Bowden	70	69	68	69	276	27,625

	SCORES				TOTAL	MONEY
Craig Kanada	68	65	70	73	276	27,625
Ryan Palmer	68	70	70	68	276	27,625
Jaco Van Zyl	70	69	69	68	276	27,625
Cameron Beckman	68	68	69	72	277	19,016.67
Rich Beem	69	69	69	70	277	19,016.67
Alex Cejka	68	67	72	70	277	19,016.67
Brian Davis	65	73	68	71	277	19,016.67
Mark Hensby	67	70	72	68	277	19,016.67
Jason Schultz	69	67	70	71	277	19,016.67
Bob Tway	67	69	73	68	277	19,016.67
Jay Williamson	70	68	70	69	277	19,016.67
Jeff Brehaut	71	66	67	73	277	19,016.66
Steve Marino	65	67	71	74	277	19,016.66
Kevin Na	69	70	70	68	277	19,016.66
Chris Tidland	68	71	71	67	277	19,016.66
Tommy Armour	72	64	69	73	278	12,025
Mathew Goggin	69	70	70	69	278	12,025
Scott Gutschewski	68	70	70	70	278	12,025
Fredrik Jacobson	70	66	70	72	278	12,025
Jarrod Lyle	69	69	70	70	278	12,025
D.J. Trahan	68	70	71	69	278	12,025
Steve Wheatcroft	68	66	71	73	278	12,025
Charlie Wi	68	67	70	73	278	12,025
Billy Andrade	68	71	70	70	279	11,000
Craig Barlow	68	71	72	68	279	11,000
Michael Bradley	69	70	68	72	279	11,000
Todd Fischer	66	72	71	70	279	11,000
Michael Putnam	67	68	73	71	279	11,000
Tag Ridings	70	66	72	71	279	11,000
John Senden	67	70	70	72	279	11,000
Daniel Chopra	68	71	70	71	280	10,500
Mathias Gronberg	72	67	71	70	280	10,500
George McNeill	70	68	68	74	280	10,500
Chad Campbell	69	68	72	72	281	10,000
Jay Delsing	68	69	68	76	281	10,000
Joe Durant	67	69	72	73	281	10,000
Robert Garrigus	69	69	73	70	281	10,000
Cliff Kresge	67	69	69	76	281	10,000
Spike McRoy	71	66	73	71	281	10,000
Kirk Triplett	67	69	72	73	281	10,000
Paul Gow	68	70	73	72	283	9,500
Todd Hamilton	66	69	77	71	283	9,500
Stephen Leaney	69	70	70	74	283	9,500
Briny Baird	70	69	73	72	284	9,100
Olin Browne	70	68	75	71	284	9,100
Tom Johnson	70	69	73	72	284	9,100
Craig Lile	70	69	70	75	284	9,100
Chris Riley	70	68	74	72	284	9,100
Ryan Blaum	71	68	72	74	285	8,800
Willie Wood	71	68	71	76	286	8,700
Neal Lancaster	69	69	77	73	288	8,600
Jim Gallagher, Jr.	69	70	71	81	291	8,500
Steve Allan	67	72	74	79	292	8,400

PGA Tour Playoffs for the FedExCup

The Barclays

Westchester Country Club, West Course, Harrison, New York
Par 36-35–71; 6,839 yards

August 23-26
purse, $7,000,000

	SCORES				TOTAL	MONEY
Steve Stricker	67	67	65	69	268	$1,260,000
K.J. Choi	64	66	70	70	270	756,000
Rory Sabbatini	63	71	69	68	271	476,000
Mark Calcavecchia	67	75	65	65	272	289,333.34
Ernie Els	65	71	68	68	272	289,333.33
Geoff Ogilvy	68	66	69	69	272	289,333.33
Rich Beem	64	68	69	72	273	225,750
Phil Mickelson	67	70	69	67	273	225,750
Robert Garrigus	70	70	68	66	274	189,000
Jerry Kelly	67	70	69	68	274	189,000
Ian Poulter	70	67	70	67	274	189,000
Woody Austin	69	68	66	72	275	154,000
Steve Flesch	65	72	67	71	275	154,000
Justin Rose	70	68	70	68	276	126,000
Adam Scott	67	69	72	68	276	126,000
Heath Slocum	66	73	67	70	276	126,000
Tim Clark	69	68	72	68	277	101,500
Bob Heintz	69	73	70	65	277	101,500
Anthony Kim	68	68	71	70	277	101,500
Hunter Mahan	70	69	62	76	277	101,500
Ryan Armour	72	67	70	69	278	75,600
Arron Oberholser	67	70	68	73	278	75,600
Tim Petrovic	69	69	68	72	278	75,600
Camilo Villegas	68	70	73	67	278	75,600
Aaron Baddeley	71	67	70	71	279	49,035
Stewart Cink	72	67	73	67	279	49,035
Jason Dufner	73	69	68	69	279	49,035
Jim Furyk	70	69	71	69	279	49,035
Sergio Garcia	69	67	70	73	279	49,035
Zach Johnson	68	71	70	70	279	49,035
Sean O'Hair	73	69	69	68	279	49,035
Kenny Perry	69	67	68	75	279	49,035
Brett Quigley	67	73	72	67	279	49,035
Nick Watney	70	72	68	69	279	49,035
Padraig Harrington	71	68	70	71	280	33,775
Matt Kuchar	69	68	69	74	280	33,775
Nick O'Hern	71	66	70	73	280	33,775
Rod Pampling	69	72	69	70	280	33,775
Scott Verplank	68	71	69	72	280	33,775
Boo Weekley	71	67	72	70	280	33,775
Briny Baird	66	75	71	69	281	24,500
Brian Gay	65	73	72	71	281	24,500
J.B. Holmes	76	66	65	74	281	24,500
Doug LaBelle	69	73	71	68	281	24,500
Frank Lickliter	71	69	70	71	281	24,500
Davis Love	69	69	72	71	281	24,500
Mike Weir	69	73	72	67	281	24,500
Fred Funk	71	69	73	69	282	17,593.34
Tim Herron	71	70	71	70	282	17,593.34
Paul Goydos	71	69	66	76	282	17,593.33
Bill Haas	68	68	72	74	282	17,593.33
Charley Hoffman	69	72	70	71	282	17,593.33
Troy Matteson	70	71	70	71	282	17,593.33

	SCORES				TOTAL	MONEY
Brian Davis	68	71	70	74	283	15,890
J.P. Hayes	75	67	71	70	283	15,890
Fredrik Jacobson	70	67	77	69	283	15,890
Cliff Kresge	69	70	72	72	283	15,890
Corey Pavin	68	73	72	70	283	15,890
John Rollins	71	71	70	71	283	15,890
Joe Durant	71	69	72	72	284	15,120
Retief Goosen	68	68	74	74	284	15,120
Vaughn Taylor	71	71	77	65	284	15,120
D.J. Trahan	73	68	70	73	284	15,120
Dean Wilson	74	68	68	74	284	15,120
Bart Bryant	72	70	70	73	285	14,490
Andrew Buckle	71	69	71	74	285	14,490
Bob Estes	70	72	71	72	285	14,490
Johnson Wagner	73	69	76	67	285	14,490
Nathan Green	72	70	74	70	286	14,070
Steve Marino	72	69	74	71	286	14,070
Jason Gore	72	67	75	73	287	13,860
Jeff Maggert	66	73	73	76	288	13,580
John Mallinger	68	72	74	74	288	13,580
Carl Pettersson	65	72	74	77	288	13,580
Rocco Mediate	69	73	74	74	290	13,300

Deutsche Bank Championship

TPC of Boston, Norton, Massachusetts
Par 36-35–71; 7,415 yards

August 31-September 3
purse, $7,000,000

	SCORES				TOTAL	MONEY
Phil Mickelson	70	64	68	66	268	$1,260,000
Brett Wetterich	66	68	66	70	270	522,666.67
Tiger Woods	72	64	67	67	270	522,666.67
Arron Oberholser	69	66	66	69	270	522,666.66
Aaron Baddeley	67	66	70	70	273	280,000
Geoff Ogilvy	70	70	67	67	274	243,250
Rory Sabbatini	68	67	70	69	274	243,250
Robert Allenby	69	69	70	67	275	217,000
Fredrik Jacobson	66	72	70	68	276	175,000
Troy Matteson	71	66	69	70	276	175,000
Sean O'Hair	68	66	74	68	276	175,000
Steve Stricker	67	69	69	71	276	175,000
Camilo Villegas	63	72	69	72	276	175,000
Lucas Glover	69	70	66	72	277	126,000
John Mallinger	73	69	67	68	277	126,000
Charlie Wi	67	72	69	69	277	126,000
Nathan Green	72	70	67	69	278	94,733.34
George McNeill	71	69	70	68	278	94,733.34
Sergio Garcia	67	71	68	72	278	94,733.33
Ryuji Imada	69	66	72	71	278	94,733.33
Cliff Kresge	69	71	67	71	278	94,733.33
Adam Scott	68	72	66	72	278	94,733.33
Jonathan Byrd	69	70	70	70	279	59,000
Angel Cabrera	70	69	65	75	279	59,000
Steve Elkington	66	70	70	73	279	59,000
Jason Gore	70	71	64	74	279	59,000
Trevor Immelman	67	74	68	70	279	59,000
John Senden	67	71	67	74	279	59,000
Heath Slocum	66	70	72	71	279	59,000
Woody Austin	71	68	70	71	280	38,181.82
Rich Beem	67	66	73	74	280	38,181.82

	SCORES				TOTAL	MONEY
Paul Goydos	75	67	71	67	280	38,181.82
Charles Howell	69	69	72	70	280	38,181.82
Zach Johnson	68	72	68	72	280	38,181.82
Will MacKenzie	70	72	65	73	280	38,181.82
Mike Weir	65	68	74	73	280	38,181.82
Dean Wilson	70	71	71	68	280	38,181.82
Mark Wilson	73	68	72	67	280	38,181.82
Briny Baird	71	68	67	74	280	38,181.81
Bo Van Pelt	68	69	69	74	280	38,181.81
Bart Bryant	72	67	66	76	281	25,200
Matt Kuchar	68	72	68	73	281	25,200
Ryan Moore	65	69	77	70	281	25,200
Rod Pampling	74	67	68	72	281	25,200
Vaughn Taylor	68	73	68	72	281	25,200
Boo Weekley	73	69	66	73	281	25,200
Brian Bateman	69	72	70	71	282	18,508
Doug LaBelle	73	69	69	71	282	18,508
Kenny Perry	68	71	73	70	282	18,508
John Rollins	70	69	72	71	282	18,508
Brandt Snedeker	71	72	73	66	282	18,508
Rocco Mediate	71	72	66	74	283	16,520
Joe Ogilvie	70	69	72	72	283	16,520
Tom Pernice, Jr.	75	65	67	76	283	16,520
Stephen Ames	68	73	69	74	284	15,820
Jim Furyk	68	73	69	74	284	15,820
Craig Kanada	67	68	72	77	284	15,820
Justin Leonard	72	70	75	67	284	15,820
Henrik Stenson	66	73	75	70	284	15,820
Tommy Armour	68	70	72	75	285	15,120
Chad Campbell	70	70	71	74	285	15,120
Luke Donald	72	66	73	74	285	15,120
Tim Herron	71	72	74	68	285	15,120
Vijay Singh	74	66	73	72	285	15,120
Ken Duke	70	72	69	75	286	14,490
Robert Garrigus	69	72	72	73	286	14,490
Jerry Kelly	71	72	73	70	286	14,490
Jeff Maggert	69	73	70	74	286	14,490
Kevin Na	71	71	69	76	287	14,140
Daniel Chopra	70	70	74	74	288	13,930
Brian Gay	74	69	72	73	288	13,930
Mark Calcavecchia	72	70	77	71	290	13,580
Brian Davis	68	71	75	76	290	13,580
Charles Warren	69	74	73	74	290	13,580
Steve Flesch	71	72	71	78	292	13,300

BMW Championship

Cog Hill Golf & Country Club, Lemont, Illinois
Par 35-36–71; 7,326 yards

September 6-9
purse, $7,000,000

	SCORES				TOTAL	MONEY
Tiger Woods	67	67	65	63	262	$1,260,000
Aaron Baddeley	68	65	65	66	264	756,000
Steve Stricker	68	66	64	68	266	480,000
Adam Scott	69	69	67	65	270	340,000
Tim Clark	68	69	67	67	271	270,000
Justin Rose	65	69	69	68	271	270,000
Stewart Cink	66	73	68	65	272	229,000
Camilo Villegas	65	69	71	67	272	229,000
Sergio Garcia	68	70	69	67	274	206,000

	SCORES				TOTAL	MONEY
Jonathan Byrd	64	69	71	71	275	171,000
Carl Pettersson	71	68	69	67	275	171,000
Ian Poulter	68	72	69	66	275	171,000
Rory Sabbatini	69	72	68	66	275	171,000
Jim Furyk	70	69	67	70	276	123,625
Lucas Glover	70	71	67	68	276	123,625
Nathan Green	67	71	67	71	276	123,625
Brandt Snedeker	70	71	65	70	276	123,625
Ernie Els	73	67	68	69	277	85,260
Charles Howell	68	73	67	69	277	85,260
Ryan Moore	69	70	68	70	277	85,260
Pat Perez	66	69	70	72	277	85,260
David Toms	72	70	68	67	277	85,260
Bo Van Pelt	69	71	68	69	277	85,260
Bubba Watson	71	69	69	68	277	85,260
Stuart Appleby	68	68	71	71	278	54,600
Charley Hoffman	68	70	72	68	278	54,600
Ryuji Imada	67	70	71	70	278	54,600
Kevin Sutherland	70	73	69	66	278	54,600
Mark Wilson	76	69	68	65	278	54,600
Angel Cabrera	72	69	71	67	279	40,687.50
Luke Donald	76	70	68	65	279	40,687.50
Hunter Mahan	69	68	71	71	279	40,687.50
John Mallinger	74	68	69	68	279	40,687.50
Rocco Mediate	70	70	68	71	279	40,687.50
Vaughn Taylor	73	68	69	69	279	40,687.50
Scott Verplank	69	70	70	70	279	40,687.50
Brett Wetterich	68	72	71	68	279	40,687.50
Robert Allenby	75	68	69	68	280	28,000
Stephen Ames	71	68	69	72	280	28,000
Woody Austin	67	73	71	69	280	28,000
K.J. Choi	68	70	71	71	280	28,000
Trevor Immelman	70	70	69	71	280	28,000
Zach Johnson	72	71	70	67	280	28,000
Billy Mayfair	72	69	67	72	280	28,000
Rod Pampling	73	72	66	69	280	28,000
Heath Slocum	71	68	72	70	281	21,700
Troy Matteson	66	77	68	71	282	19,740
Kenny Perry	71	71	66	74	282	19,740
Brian Bateman	70	72	72	69	283	17,686.67
Jerry Kelly	74	72	68	69	283	17,686.67
Steve Marino	73	70	69	71	283	17,686.66
Ken Duke	67	73	71	73	284	16,415
Anthony Kim	74	70	70	70	284	16,415
John Senden	71	75	71	67	284	16,415
Henrik Stenson	75	71	68	70	284	16,415
John Rollins	69	71	74	71	285	15,960
Sean O'Hair	74	72	71	69	286	15,750
Boo Weekley	75	72	72	67	286	15,750
Jose Coceres	70	69	70	78	287	15,470
Nick Watney	72	73	72	70	287	15,470
Nick O'Hern	70	73	74	71	288	15,190
Geoff Ogilvy	78	73	68	69	288	15,190
Jeff Quinney	72	73	70	74	289	14,980
Vijay Singh	74	69	77	70	290	14,840
Mark Calcavecchia	77	71	75	74	297	14,700

The Tour Championship

East Lake Golf Club, Atlanta, Georgia
Par 35-35–70; 7,154 yards

September 13-16
purse, $7,000,000

		SCORES			TOTAL	MONEY
Tiger Woods	64	63	64	66	257	$1,260,000
Mark Calcavecchia	65	66	63	71	265	619,500
Zach Johnson	71	66	60	68	265	619,500
Sergio Garcia	68	64	64	70	266	336,000
Hunter Mahan	65	68	65	71	269	266,000
Scott Verplank	66	68	67	68	269	266,000
Tim Clark	62	69	70	69	270	231,000
Vijay Singh	68	68	65	69	270	231,000
Rory Sabbatini	68	68	67	68	271	204,400
Camilo Villegas	67	68	70	66	271	204,400
Robert Allenby	68	71	68	66	273	167,300
Woody Austin	65	65	69	74	273	167,300
Stewart Cink	67	66	71	69	273	167,300
Jim Furyk	71	69	67	66	273	167,300
Padraig Harrington	63	70	67	73	273	167,300
Justin Rose	69	71	66	67	273	167,300
Geoff Ogilvy	68	70	62	74	274	140,000
Heath Slocum	71	64	69	70	274	140,000
Steve Stricker	69	67	71	67	274	140,000
Phil Mickelson	68	66	70	71	275	134,400
K.J. Choi	67	65	75	69	276	130,200
Boo Weekley	70	67	68	71	276	130,200
Jonathan Byrd	71	70	65	71	277	126,000
Aaron Baddeley	69	70	68	71	278	123,200
John Rollins	64	69	73	73	279	120,400
Ernie Els	69	69	73	69	280	116,900
Adam Scott	65	66	71	78	280	116,900
Charles Howell	68	71	68	74	281	114,800
Brandt Snedeker	71	72	68	71	282	112,700
Brett Wetterich	68	69	70	75	282	112,700

Final Standings – PGA Tour Playoffs for the FedExCup

RANK	NAME	FEDEXCUP POINTS	BONUS MONEY
1	Tiger Woods	123,033	$10,000,000
2	Steve Stricker	110,455	3,000,000
3	Phil Mickelson	109,358	2,000,000
4	Rory Sabbatini	105,193	1,500,000
5	K.J. Choi	103,765	1,000,000
6	Aaron Baddeley	103,350	800,000
7	Zach Johnson	102,873	700,000
8	Mark Calcavecchia	102,069	600,000
9	Sergio Garcia	101,077	550,000
10	Vijay Singh	101,064	500,000
11	Jim Furyk	101,022	300,000
12	Adam Scott	100,684	290,000
13	Geoff Ogilvy	98,918	280,000
14	Scott Verplank	98,812	270,000
15	Hunter Mahan	98,696	250,000
16	Justin Rose	98,434	245,000
17	Woody Austin	98,407	240,000
18	Charles Howell	98,051	235,000
19	Ernie Els	98,033	230,000
20	Brandt Snedeker	97,907	225,000
21	Tim Clark	97,275	220,000

RANK	NAME	FEDEXCUP POINTS	BONUS MONEY
22	Stewart Cink	96,697	215,000
23	Robert Allenby	96,634	210,000
24	Camilo Villegas	96,608	205,000
25	Boo Weekley	96,399	200,000
26	John Rollins	96,220	195,000
27	Brett Wetterich	96,174	190,000
28	Jonathan Byrd	96,061	185,000
29	Padraig Harrington	96,025	180,000
30	Heath Slocum	95,731	175,000

PGA Tour Fall Series

Turning Stone Resort Championship

Atunyote Golf Club, Verona, New York
Par 36-36–72; 7,482 yards

September 20-23
purse, $6,000,000

	SCORES				TOTAL	MONEY
Steve Flesch	66	65	66	73	270	$1,080,000
Michael Allen	69	67	68	68	272	648,000
John Mallinger	67	70	68	68	273	348,000
John Senden	66	70	70	67	273	348,000
Tommy Armour	70	68	68	68	274	203,400
Mathew Goggin	66	69	70	69	274	203,400
Charley Hoffman	69	65	71	69	274	203,400
Parker McLachlin	70	68	65	71	274	203,400
Carl Pettersson	69	66	66	73	274	203,400
Bill Haas	69	66	69	71	275	156,000
Charles Warren	68	65	68	74	275	156,000
Jeff Overton	70	65	72	69	276	138,000
David Branshaw	68	71	70	68	277	109,200
Brendon de Jonge	66	66	75	70	277	109,200
Justin Leonard	68	71	66	72	277	109,200
Sean O'Hair	71	68	66	72	277	109,200
Johnson Wagner	69	67	69	72	277	109,200
Charlie Wi	69	68	73	68	278	73,028.58
Stuart Appleby	70	67	72	69	278	73,028.57
Briny Baird	69	66	71	72	278	73,028.57
Nick Flanagan	72	68	70	68	278	73,028.57
John Rollins	67	69	73	69	278	73,028.57
Vaughn Taylor	71	66	70	71	278	73,028.57
Chris Tidland	69	71	67	71	278	73,028.57
Robert Allenby	67	70	69	73	279	42,030
Ryan Armour	70	70	67	72	279	42,030
Bart Bryant	68	68	69	74	279	42,030
Andrew Buckle	69	71	67	72	279	42,030
Cliff Kresge	69	70	71	69	279	42,030
Craig Lile	69	67	71	72	279	42,030
Jarrod Lyle	73	64	68	74	279	42,030
Jeff Maggert	71	64	71	73	279	42,030
Jeff Quinney	69	71	69	70	279	42,030
Kirk Triplett	70	68	68	73	279	42,030
Scott Gutschewski	72	68	70	70	280	30,225
Shaun Micheel	69	70	71	70	280	30,225
Nick O'Hern	71	68	69	72	280	30,225
Chris Stroud	69	65	74	72	280	30,225

	SCORES				TOTAL	MONEY
Cameron Beckman	69	71	70	71	281	24,000
Robert Garrigus	73	67	68	73	281	24,000
Matt Hendrix	67	67	75	72	281	24,000
Tim Herron	69	70	68	74	281	24,000
Daisuke Maruyama	71	69	70	71	281	24,000
Joe Ogilvie	70	67	68	76	281	24,000
Bob Estes	70	70	69	73	282	17,160
J.B. Holmes	72	67	67	76	282	17,160
Tim Petrovic	69	70	70	73	282	17,160
Kyle Reifers	69	69	70	74	282	17,160
Tag Ridings	67	69	70	76	282	17,160
Joey Sindelar	68	68	73	73	282	17,160
Craig Bowden	70	65	70	78	283	14,580
Rocco Mediate	70	70	70	73	283	14,580
Alex Cejka	71	68	72	73	284	14,160
Chad Campbell	65	72	72	76	285	13,800
Kent Jones	70	70	72	73	285	13,800
Steve Lowery	68	72	69	76	285	13,800
Billy Andrade	70	68	77	71	286	13,320
Robert Gamez	68	68	76	74	286	13,320
Jeff Gove	65	67	76	78	286	13,320
Mark Hensby	68	69	76	73	286	13,320
Corey Pavin	70	68	73	75	286	13,320
Jerry Kelly	68	71	75	73	287	12,960
Eric Axley	69	66	76	77	288	12,660
Brian Davis	69	71	73	75	288	12,660
Bubba Dickerson	69	70	71	78	288	12,660
Todd Hamilton	70	70	74	74	288	12,660
Nathan Green	70	68	74	77	289	12,360
Fred Funk	70	69	74	77	290	12,180
Jay Williamson	70	70	69	81	290	12,180
D.J. Brigman	69	67	78	77	291	12,000

The Presidents Cup

Royal Montreal Golf Club, Blue Course,　　　　　　　　　　　September 27-30
Ile Bizard, Montreal, Quebec, Canada
Par 35-35–70; 7,171 yards

FIRST DAY
Foursomes

Steve Stricker and Hunter Mahan (US) defeated Adam Scott and Geoff Ogilvy, 3 and 2.
Phil Mickelson and Woody Austin (US) halved with Vijay Singh and Mike Weir.
Stewart Cink and Zach Johnson (US) defeated Rory Sabbatini and Trevor Immelman, 1 up.
David Toms and Jim Furyk (US) defeated Ernie Els and Angel Cabrera, 1 up.
Lucas Glover and Scott Verplank (US) defeated Stuart Appleby and Retief Goosen, 2 up.
Tiger Woods and Charles Howell (US) defeated K.J. Choi and Nick O'Hern, 3 and 1.

POINTS: U.S. 5½, International ½

SECOND DAY
Fourball

Cabrera and Goosen (Int'l) defeated Mickelson and Mahan, 1 up.
Singh and Appleby (Int'l) defeated Woods and Furyk, 5 and 4.
Els and Weir (Int'l) defeated Johnson and Howell, 3 and 1.
Stricker and Verplank (US) defeated Scott and Choi, 2 and 1.
Ogilvy and O'Hern (Int'l) defeated Cink and Glover, 1 up.
Austin and Toms (US) halved with Immelman and Sabbatini.

POINTS: U.S. 7, International 5

THIRD DAY
Morning Foursomes

Stricker and Mahan (US) defeated Immelman and Sabbatini, 2 up.
Mickelson and Austin (US) defeated Goosen and Appleby, 5 and 4.
Woods and Furyk (US) defeated Scott and Els, 4 and 3.
Glover and Verplank (US) defeated Singh and Weir, 2 and 1.
Johnson and Toms (US) defeated O'Hern and Ogilvy, 2 and 1.

POINTS: U.S. 12, International 5

THIRD DAY
Afternoon Fourball

Furyk and Cink (US) defeated Cabrera and Choi, 1 up.
Mickelson and Austin (US) halved with Scott and Goosen.
Weir and Els (Int'l) defeated Glover and Howell, 4 and 2.
Singh and Appleby (Int'l) defeated Stricker and Mahan, 1 up.
Woods and Toms (US), defeated O'Hern and Ogilvy, 5 and 3.

POINTS: U.S. 14½, International 7½

FINAL DAY
Singles

Verplank (US) defeated Sabbatini, 2 and 1.
Els (Int'l) defeated Glover, 2 up.
Mickelson (US) defeated Singh, 5 and 4.
Weir (Int'l) defeated Woods, 1 up.
Cabrera (Int'l) defeated Austin, 2 and 1.
Scott (Int'l) defeated Johnson, 2 and 1.
Toms (US) defeated Immelman, 2 up.
Cink (US) defeated O'Hern, 6 and 4.
Ogilvy (Int'l) defeated Stricker, 1 up.
Choi (Int'l) defeated Mahan, 3 and 2.
Howell (US) defeated Appleby, 2 and 1.
Goosen (Int'l) defeated Furyk, 2 and 1.

TOTAL POINTS: U.S. 19½, International 14½

Viking Classic

Annandale Golf Club, Madison, Mississippi
Par 36-36–72; 7,199 yards

September 27-30
purse, $3,500,000

	SCORES				TOTAL	MONEY
Chad Campbell	70	72	64	69	275	$630,000
Johnson Wagner	73	65	68	70	276	378,000
Bill Haas	68	67	70	72	277	203,000
Boo Weekley	68	69	70	70	277	203,000
David Branshaw	66	68	69	75	278	127,750
Shaun Micheel	70	68	68	72	278	127,750
John Senden	68	69	71	70	278	127,750
Alex Cejka	69	72	68	70	279	101,500
Kent Jones	71	70	67	71	279	101,500
Bo Van Pelt	70	71	68	70	279	101,500
Ken Duke	74	70	71	65	280	84,000
Harrison Frazar	71	67	70	72	280	84,000
Jay Delsing	72	65	70	74	281	65,625
J.P. Hayes	68	68	73	72	281	65,625
Daisuke Maruyama	73	70	65	73	281	65,625
Heath Slocum	70	71	70	70	281	65,625

	SCORES				TOTAL	MONEY
Joe Durant	72	69	72	69	282	49,000
Nick Flanagan	68	69	73	72	282	49,000
Mark Hensby	73	70	69	70	282	49,000
Steve Lowery	66	77	69	70	282	49,000
Jesper Parnevik	68	73	72	69	282	49,000
Jason Dufner	69	71	70	73	283	31,550
Fred Funk	69	69	69	76	283	31,550
Charley Hoffman	69	68	71	75	283	31,550
Craig Lile	70	68	73	72	283	31,550
John Merrick	73	69	69	72	283	31,550
Michael Sim	68	75	69	71	283	31,550
Jay Williamson	72	72	69	70	283	31,550
Billy Andrade	69	71	71	73	284	22,750
Cameron Beckman	65	70	74	75	284	22,750
Brendon de Jonge	70	73	70	71	284	22,750
Jeff Overton	68	69	76	71	284	22,750
Jason Schultz	68	71	75	70	284	22,750
Craig Barlow	66	72	76	71	285	18,060
Robert Damron	73	68	71	73	285	18,060
George McNeill	69	70	73	73	285	18,060
Kevin Na	68	73	70	74	285	18,060
Duffy Waldorf	70	70	70	75	285	18,060
Arjun Atwal	70	70	71	75	286	14,350
Rich Barcelo	72	70	72	72	286	14,350
Andrew Buckle	71	73	68	74	286	14,350
Steve Elkington	69	72	67	78	286	14,350
Richard S. Johnson	69	74	73	70	286	14,350
Briny Baird	63	78	72	74	287	10,878
David Duval	72	69	72	74	287	10,878
Matt Hendrix	71	73	71	72	287	10,878
Ryan Palmer	72	71	69	75	287	10,878
Steve Wheatcroft	70	71	75	71	287	10,878
Michael Boyd	71	70	73	74	288	8,638
Jim McGovern	72	69	73	74	288	8,638
Greg Owen	71	72	69	76	288	8,638
Chris Riley	70	70	72	76	288	8,638
D.J. Trahan	66	74	74	74	288	8,638
Michael Allen	68	74	74	73	289	7,980
John Daly	68	72	76	73	289	7,980
Bubba Dickerson	71	73	73	72	289	7,980
Scott Gutschewski	72	72	72	73	289	7,980
Tag Ridings	70	73	73	73	289	7,980
Eric Axley	68	70	75	77	290	7,630
Gavin Coles	67	76	73	74	290	7,630
Carl Pettersson	73	71	72	74	290	7,630
Kevin Stadler	69	71	73	77	290	7,630
Oliver Thomson	69	75	73	73	290	7,630
Daniel Chopra	71	72	74	74	291	7,385
Mathew Goggin	69	75	73	74	291	7,385
Bob Burns	71	73	74	74	292	7,245
Jim Rutledge	72	70	75	75	292	7,245
Marco Dawson	69	75	73	76	293	7,140
Jim Gallagher, Jr.	74	69	77	75	295	7,035
Fredrik Jacobson	73	71	74	77	295	7,035
Bryce Molder	71	71	75	81	298	6,930

Valero Texas Open

LaCantera Golf Club, Resort Course, San Antonio, Texas
Par 35-35–70; 6,896 yards

October 4-7
purse, $4,500,000

	SCORES				TOTAL	MONEY
Justin Leonard	65	67	64	65	261	$810,000
Jesper Parnevik	61	65	66	69	261	486,000
(Leonard defeated Parnevik on third playoff hole.)						
Daniel Chopra	65	69	64	66	264	261,000
Mathias Gronberg	65	65	65	69	264	261,000
Heath Slocum	69	65	70	62	266	180,000
Ryan Armour	67	67	64	69	267	140,850
Dan Forsman	65	68	67	67	267	140,850
J.J. Henry	71	65	67	64	267	140,850
Chris Stroud	69	65	64	69	267	140,850
Dean Wilson	68	67	66	66	267	140,850
Charley Hoffman	67	68	66	67	268	99,000
Shigeki Maruyama	65	68	65	70	268	99,000
Chris Riley	66	68	67	67	268	99,000
Bo Van Pelt	69	67	65	67	268	99,000
Chad Campbell	66	68	65	70	269	72,000
Ken Duke	69	66	68	66	269	72,000
Richard S. Johnson	65	66	73	65	269	72,000
John Mallinger	68	70	65	66	269	72,000
Nick Watney	67	70	66	66	269	72,000
Tim Petrovic	70	65	67	68	270	58,500
Robert Gamez	65	71	67	68	271	50,400
Fredrik Jacobson	66	65	71	69	271	50,400
John Merrick	67	71	66	67	271	50,400
D.J. Brigman	69	66	66	71	272	41,400
Marco Dawson	66	73	68	65	272	41,400
Cameron Beckman	67	68	69	69	273	31,950
Andrew Buckle	69	69	70	65	273	31,950
Alex Cejka	72	65	68	68	273	31,950
Mathew Goggin	69	69	69	66	273	31,950
Greg Owen	70	68	67	68	273	31,950
Tom Pernice, Jr.	70	69	66	68	273	31,950
Kyle Reifers	69	66	70	68	273	31,950
Bart Bryant	66	70	74	64	274	24,862.50
Neal Lancaster	65	71	69	69	274	24,862.50
Daisuke Maruyama	71	66	69	68	274	24,862.50
Ryan Palmer	67	71	69	67	274	24,862.50
Bob Estes	70	66	67	72	275	19,350
Carlos Franco	68	66	71	70	275	19,350
Scott Gutschewski	68	67	71	69	275	19,350
Bob Heintz	66	69	67	73	275	19,350
Steve Lowery	68	70	71	66	275	19,350
Ted Purdy	68	70	66	71	275	19,350
Bob Tway	65	72	70	68	275	19,350
Stephen Ames	72	66	66	72	276	13,986
Eric Axley	67	70	67	72	276	13,986
Glen Day	67	72	67	70	276	13,986
Anthony Kim	72	65	69	70	276	13,986
Jim Rutledge	68	70	70	68	276	13,986
Briny Baird	71	66	74	66	277	10,683
Michael Boyd	70	69	67	71	277	10,683
Gavin Coles	66	69	69	73	277	10,683
Brian Davis	72	65	68	72	277	10,683
Jay Delsing	69	70	67	71	277	10,683
Matt Hendrix	65	71	73	68	277	10,683
Colt Knost	71	68	68	70	277	10,683
Craig Lile	69	70	69	69	277	10,683

	SCORES				TOTAL	MONEY
Jeff Overton	68	70	68	71	277	10,683
Corey Pavin	66	71	73	67	277	10,683
Tom Byrum	66	70	70	72	278	9,810
Paul Gow	70	68	69	71	278	9,810
Tom Johnson	68	71	67	72	278	9,810
Charlie Wi	72	66	69	71	278	9,810
Jay Williamson	70	67	71	70	278	9,810
Jeff Gove	69	66	73	71	279	9,405
Jarrod Lyle	68	70	69	72	279	9,405
Bob May	72	67	67	73	279	9,405
Garrett Willis	69	68	69	73	279	9,405
Arjun Atwal	67	71	72	70	280	9,135
Doug LaBelle	68	68	72	72	280	9,135
Michael Sim	68	71	69	73	281	9,000
Rich Beem	68	71	71	72	282	8,820
Jeff Brehaut	68	70	72	72	282	8,820
Bryce Molder	69	68	72	73	282	8,820
Tripp Isenhour	66	73	74	70	283	8,595
Frank Lickliter	68	69	75	71	283	8,595
David Branshaw	70	69	78	70	287	8,460
Bubba Dickerson	66	70	74	78	288	8,370
Spike McRoy	72	67	72	79	290	8,280

Frys.com Open

TPC at Summerlin: Par 36-36–72; 7,243 yards
TPC at The Canyons: Par 36-35–71; 7,019 yards
Las Vegas, Nevada

October 11-14
purse, $4,000,000

	SCORES				TOTAL	MONEY
George McNeill	66	64	67	67	264	$720,000
D.J. Trahan	65	65	72	66	268	432,000
Cameron Beckman	65	71	68	68	272	232,000
Robert Garrigus	71	63	68	70	272	232,000
Bob May	63	70	71	69	273	152,000
Bo Van Pelt	66	69	68	70	273	152,000
Jason Gore	63	68	73	70	274	124,666.67
Mathias Gronberg	69	64	71	70	274	124,666.67
Garrett Willis	68	62	73	71	274	124,666.66
Kent Jones	68	67	68	72	275	96,000
Joe Ogilvie	71	65	71	68	275	96,000
Mike Weir	69	67	69	70	275	96,000
Mark Wilson	66	67	71	71	275	96,000
Mark Calcavecchia	69	67	72	68	276	68,000
Tim Herron	70	64	76	66	276	68,000
Jesper Parnevik	68	69	70	69	276	68,000
Phil Tataurangi	67	70	68	71	276	68,000
Bubba Watson	69	67	72	68	276	68,000
Kevin Na	67	70	69	71	277	54,000
Jeff Overton	65	71	71	70	277	54,000
Arjun Atwal	68	69	72	69	278	36,533.34
Marco Dawson	65	70	74	69	278	36,533.34
Mathew Goggin	68	67	76	67	278	36,533.34
Jeff Gove	67	67	70	74	278	36,533.33
Bill Haas	67	67	74	70	278	36,533.33
John Huston	66	65	72	75	278	36,533.33
Stephen Leaney	67	68	69	74	278	36,533.33
Billy Mayfair	69	64	72	73	278	36,533.33
Jeff Quinney	69	67	72	70	278	36,533.33
Alex Cejka	68	70	75	66	279	23,250

		SCORES			TOTAL	MONEY
Brian Davis	70	68	73	68	279	23,250
Carlos Franco	68	71	69	71	279	23,250
Steve Lowery	66	67	73	73	279	23,250
Greg Owen	72	66	72	69	279	23,250
Pat Perez	71	65	73	70	279	23,250
Tom Pernice, Jr.	69	65	73	72	279	23,250
Duffy Waldorf	66	68	73	72	279	23,250
Rich Beem	64	71	74	71	280	16,800
Michael Boyd	66	68	80	66	280	16,800
Ben Crane	66	67	73	74	280	16,800
Colt Knost	67	69	69	75	280	16,800
Chris Stroud	71	64	74	71	280	16,800
Grant Waite	66	69	75	70	280	16,800
Daniel Chopra	66	70	73	72	281	12,093.34
Bryce Molder	70	69	72	70	281	12,093.34
John Daly	74	63	77	67	281	12,093.33
Craig Lile	66	72	75	68	281	12,093.33
Bill Lunde	69	68	71	73	281	12,093.33
Darron Stiles	72	67	74	68	281	12,093.33
Gavin Coles	69	65	79	69	282	9,740
Jason Dufner	66	70	73	73	282	9,740
Ken Duke	70	65	73	74	282	9,740
Frank Lickliter	69	69	73	71	282	9,740
Mark Brooks	69	68	73	73	283	9,120
Ryuji Imada	67	71	74	71	283	9,120
Jarrod Lyle	70	66	76	71	283	9,120
Ryan Moore	68	69	76	70	283	9,120
Kevin Sutherland	71	67	72	73	283	9,120
Brian Gay	68	70	75	71	284	8,800
Nick Watney	67	65	76	76	284	8,800
Steve Wheatcroft	68	71	76	69	284	8,800
Glen Day	69	70	76	70	285	8,520
Will MacKenzie	67	71	78	69	285	8,520
Shigeki Maruyama	69	68	75	73	285	8,520
Kirk Triplett	68	71	69	77	285	8,520
Ryan Armour	68	68	79	71	286	8,200
Bart Bryant	70	69	80	67	286	8,200
J.P. Hayes	69	69	75	73	286	8,200
Jay Williamson	69	70	76	71	286	8,200
Matt Hendrix	69	66	76	76	287	7,960
Ted Purdy	69	69	74	75	287	7,960
Billy Andrade	73	65	74	76	288	7,800
Brendon de Jonge	66	73	74	75	288	7,800
Chad Campbell	75	63	77	74	289	7,640
Paul Trittler	67	71	78	73	289	7,640
Michael Allen	67	70	80	73	290	7,400
Jeff Brehaut	66	73	79	72	290	7,400
Richard Green	71	66	79	74	290	7,400
Daisuke Maruyama	67	67	76	80	290	7,400
Brent Geiberger	69	70	76	76	291	7,120
Andres Gonzales	68	71	77	75	291	7,120
Kevin Stadler	69	70	73	79	291	7,120
Jaco Van Zyl	70	69	80	73	292	6,960

Fry's Electronics Open

Grayhawk Golf Club, Raptor Course, Scottsdale, Arizona
Par 35-35–70; 7,125 yards

October 18-21
purse, $5,000,000

	SCORES				TOTAL	MONEY
Mike Weir	69	64	65	68	266	$900,000
Mark Hensby	71	61	66	69	267	540,000
Billy Mayfair	68	66	68	68	270	340,000
Sean O'Hair	68	66	68	69	271	220,000
Carl Pettersson	67	66	64	74	271	220,000
Alex Cejka	68	67	68	69	272	151,250
Brian Davis	70	67	66	69	272	151,250
Justin Leonard	68	68	65	71	272	151,250
Daisuke Maruyama	67	65	69	71	272	151,250
Ryan Moore	66	63	71	72	272	151,250
Pat Perez	66	71	67	68	272	151,250
Jarrod Lyle	69	67	64	73	273	110,000
Chris Stroud	69	65	69	70	273	110,000
Briny Baird	70	65	69	70	274	92,500
Marco Dawson	67	67	70	70	274	92,500
Kent Jones	68	66	68	73	275	82,500
George McNeill	69	68	65	73	275	82,500
Bob Estes	72	64	69	71	276	60,857.15
Chris Riley	70	69	66	71	276	60,857.15
Tim Clark	71	67	66	72	276	60,857.14
Ben Crane	66	66	69	75	276	60,857.14
Jason Gore	67	67	70	72	276	60,857.14
Fredrik Jacobson	68	66	69	73	276	60,857.14
Arron Oberholser	67	68	68	73	276	60,857.14
Ryan Armour	67	68	72	70	277	42,000
Dean Wilson	70	68	70	69	277	42,000
Stephen Ames	70	68	72	68	278	33,281.25
Steve Flesch	68	68	71	71	278	33,281.25
Jeff Gove	69	69	70	70	278	33,281.25
Tim Herron	67	72	70	69	278	33,281.25
Ryuji Imada	68	68	67	75	278	33,281.25
Joe Ogilvie	70	69	69	70	278	33,281.25
Tom Pernice, Jr.	66	69	71	72	278	33,281.25
Chris Tidland	68	71	67	72	278	33,281.25
Craig Barlow	70	70	66	73	279	22,583.34
Joe Durant	68	67	71	73	279	22,583.34
Jeff Quinney	68	69	70	72	279	22,583.34
Rich Barcelo	67	67	69	76	279	22,583.33
Cameron Beckman	73	67	65	74	279	22,583.33
Mathias Gronberg	68	68	68	75	279	22,583.33
Shigeki Maruyama	70	69	71	69	279	22,583.33
Shaun Micheel	69	69	73	68	279	22,583.33
Nick Watney	65	68	69	77	279	22,583.33
Rich Beem	65	70	74	71	280	16,000
Craig Lile	71	66	70	73	280	16,000
Ryan Palmer	67	71	71	71	280	16,000
Bo Van Pelt	70	68	68	74	280	16,000
D.J. Brigman	68	70	68	75	281	13,100
Will MacKenzie	68	69	67	77	281	13,100
Kevin Sutherland	69	69	70	73	281	13,100
Bill Haas	70	70	68	74	282	12,150
John Merrick	67	68	74	73	282	12,150
J.P. Hayes	71	67	73	72	283	11,700
Michael Putnam	68	71	71	73	283	11,700
Michael Allen	63	71	72	78	284	11,250
Paul Gow	70	69	70	75	284	11,250
Jeff Maggert	72	68	70	74	284	11,250

	SCORES				TOTAL	MONEY
Greg Owen	68	71	73	72	284	11,250
Tim Petrovic	71	69	74	70	284	11,250
Ted Purdy	69	70	74	71	284	11,250
Andrew Buckle	67	73	71	74	285	10,700
Jason Dufner	68	70	71	76	285	10,700
J.B. Holmes	72	68	72	73	285	10,700
Jerry Kelly	67	69	79	70	285	10,700
Kevin Na	72	67	74	72	285	10,700
Todd Hamilton	70	70	74	72	286	10,350
Charles Warren	69	69	69	79	286	10,350
Frank Lickliter	65	69	80	73	287	10,150
Jason Schultz	68	72	73	74	287	10,150
Brendon de Jonge	71	68	74	75	288	9,800
Cliff Kresge	70	67	76	75	288	9,800
John Mallinger	71	66	72	79	288	9,800
Bob May	69	71	73	75	288	9,800
John Rollins	71	66	74	77	288	9,800

Ginn sur Mer Classic at Tesoro

Tesoro Club, Port St. Lucie, Florida
Par 37-36–73; 7,381 yards
(Event completed on Monday — darkness.)

October 25-29
purse, $4,500,000

	SCORES				TOTAL	MONEY
Daniel Chopra	67	66	69	71	273	$810,000
Fredrik Jacobson	71	67	67	69	274	396,000
Shigeki Maruyama	69	68	68	69	274	396,000
Dicky Pride	73	70	69	64	276	216,000
Cameron Beckman	70	70	67	72	279	158,062.50
Ken Duke	72	67	70	70	279	158,062.50
Sean O'Hair	68	68	69	74	279	158,062.50
Charlie Wi	69	71	68	71	279	158,062.50
Robert Gamez	72	71	71	66	280	121,500
Robert Garrigus	72	70	67	71	280	121,500
Michael Sim	69	67	72	72	280	121,500
Bob Estes	64	68	72	77	281	91,125
Jerry Kelly	72	72	68	69	281	91,125
Parker McLachlin	71	68	70	72	281	91,125
Chris Stroud	70	69	70	72	281	91,125
Tommy Armour	64	68	78	72	282	67,500
Briny Baird	69	70	65	78	282	67,500
Kent Jones	69	71	73	69	282	67,500
Daisuke Maruyama	71	66	71	74	282	67,500
Jeff Quinney	73	64	72	73	282	67,500
Bryce Molder	67	71	72	73	283	52,200
Greg Owen	70	71	68	74	283	52,200
Rich Beem	71	72	71	70	284	43,200
Lucas Glover	71	68	73	72	284	43,200
Cliff Kresge	74	70	70	70	284	43,200
Mark Brooks	69	72	71	73	285	31,275
Russ Cochran	73	69	72	71	285	31,275
Brendon de Jonge	74	70	68	73	285	31,275
Paul Gow	70	70	70	75	285	31,275
Matt Kuchar	72	70	69	74	285	31,275
Justin Leonard	73	69	68	75	285	31,275
Frank Lickliter	68	72	74	71	285	31,275
Kevin Na	68	70	73	74	285	31,275
Ryan Armour	72	72	72	70	286	23,220
Andrew Buckle	72	72	71	71	286	23,220

	SCORES				TOTAL	MONEY
Brian Gay	70	70	75	71	286	23,220
John Huston	70	69	76	71	286	23,220
Garrett Willis	73	71	70	72	286	23,220
Craig Bowden	71	70	70	76	287	18,000
Michael Boyd	73	68	72	74	287	18,000
Joe Durant	71	71	75	70	287	18,000
Lee Janzen	75	68	73	71	287	18,000
Craig Kanada	67	71	76	73	287	18,000
Johnson Wagner	73	71	71	72	287	18,000
Rich Barcelo	74	68	73	73	288	12,870
Ben Curtis	75	66	73	74	288	12,870
Jason Dufner	71	70	72	75	288	12,870
Ryuji Imada	68	71	70	79	288	12,870
Ryan Palmer	71	71	71	75	288	12,870
Michael Putnam	68	70	73	77	288	12,870
Steve Flesch	68	73	71	77	289	10,732.50
Steve Lowery	70	66	76	77	289	10,732.50
Ted Purdy	69	68	77	75	289	10,732.50
Steve Wheatcroft	72	72	72	73	289	10,732.50
Brian Davis	73	71	73	73	290	10,215
Jeff Gove	73	70	73	74	290	10,215
Bob Tway	70	70	73	77	290	10,215
Duffy Waldorf	71	72	74	73	290	10,215
Harrison Frazar	75	68	73	75	291	9,720
Jim Gallagher, Jr.	70	74	72	75	291	9,720
Greg Kraft	72	70	73	76	291	9,720
Craig Lile	73	70	71	77	291	9,720
Steve Marino	73	71	74	73	291	9,720
Kyle Reifers	73	68	73	77	291	9,720
Jay Williamson	69	75	72	75	291	9,720
Dan Forsman	70	72	73	77	292	9,315
Doug LaBelle	75	69	73	75	292	9,315
Jesper Parnevik	72	72	70	79	293	9,135
Grant Waite	72	72	72	77	293	9,135
Bart Bryant	72	72	73	77	294	8,955
John Merrick	72	70	73	79	294	8,955
Chris Riley	70	74	72	82	298	8,820

Children's Miracle Network Classic

Walt Disney World Resort, Lake Buena Vista, Florida
Magnolia Course: Par 36-36–72; 7,516 yards
Palm Course: Par 36-36–72; 6,957 yards

November 1-4
purse, $4,600,000

	SCORES				TOTAL	MONEY
Stephen Ames	70	63	70	68	271	$828,000
Tim Clark	67	69	70	66	272	496,800
Robert Gamez	70	69	67	68	274	239,200
Tag Ridings	67	66	71	70	274	239,200
Scott Verplank	66	66	71	71	274	239,200
Justin Leonard	67	67	70	71	275	154,100
Bryce Molder	68	69	70	68	275	154,100
Jeff Overton	67	68	69	71	275	154,100
J.P. Hayes	65	69	72	70	276	119,600
J.B. Holmes	70	66	70	70	276	119,600
Heath Slocum	68	68	69	71	276	119,600
Nick Watney	68	68	73	67	276	119,600
Stewart Cink	69	67	70	71	277	92,000
Brian Gay	70	69	69	69	277	92,000
Jeff Gove	72	67	68	71	278	73,600

	SCORES				TOTAL	MONEY
Ryuji Imada	66	71	69	72	278	73,600
Sean O'Hair	68	66	76	68	278	73,600
Kevin Stadler	69	69	69	71	278	73,600
Brett Wetterich	69	65	72	72	278	73,600
Cameron Beckman	66	68	72	73	279	49,833.34
Bart Bryant	69	65	75	70	279	49,833.34
Rich Beem	70	66	70	73	279	49,833.33
D.J. Brigman	70	65	71	73	279	49,833.33
Mathew Goggin	68	67	69	75	279	49,833.33
Steve Marino	68	66	72	73	279	49,833.33
Michael Allen	69	68	73	70	280	30,025.46
Jesper Parnevik	70	68	72	70	280	30,025.46
Carl Pettersson	68	70	73	69	280	30,025.46
Joey Sindelar	69	69	73	69	280	30,025.46
Vaughn Taylor	67	67	75	71	280	30,025.46
Joe Durant	68	72	69	71	280	30,025.45
Bob Heintz	69	67	72	72	280	30,025.45
Craig Kanada	70	67	71	72	280	30,025.45
Steve Lowery	71	65	71	73	280	30,025.45
Billy Mayfair	70	67	71	72	280	30,025.45
Parker McLachlin	68	69	72	71	280	30,025.45
Jason Dufner	74	64	70	73	281	21,160
Mathias Gronberg	70	71	69	71	281	21,160
Tim Petrovic	68	68	68	77	281	21,160
Charles Warren	69	69	71	72	281	21,160
Ken Duke	69	71	70	72	282	14,561.10
Ryan Armour	69	64	76	73	282	14,561.09
Craig Barlow	70	69	72	71	282	14,561.09
Glen Day	74	67	73	68	282	14,561.09
Tripp Isenhour	71	67	69	75	282	14,561.09
Fredrik Jacobson	71	70	71	70	282	14,561.09
Jarrod Lyle	69	69	73	71	282	14,561.09
Ryan Moore	70	67	72	73	282	14,561.09
Tom Pernice, Jr.	72	69	70	71	282	14,561.09
Kyle Reifers	72	67	72	71	282	14,561.09
Chris Stroud	70	68	75	69	282	14,561.09
Daniel Chopra	72	68	71	72	283	10,672
Ben Crane	70	68	73	72	283	10,672
Joe Ogilvie	70	68	77	68	283	10,672
Jason Schultz	67	72	72	72	283	10,672
Michael Sim	71	69	68	75	283	10,672
Kirk Triplett	70	67	72	74	283	10,672
Brian Davis	73	67	72	72	284	10,120
Greg Kraft	73	68	71	72	284	10,120
Matt Kuchar	71	70	73	70	284	10,120
Doug LaBelle	70	68	73	73	284	10,120
Neal Lancaster	69	72	71	72	284	10,120
Michael Boyd	73	68	73	71	285	9,568
Brendon de Jonge	70	69	76	70	285	9,568
Lucas Glover	68	73	72	72	285	9,568
Kent Jones	73	68	71	73	285	9,568
Dicky Pride	67	70	74	74	285	9,568
Duffy Waldorf	72	69	71	73	285	9,568
Charlie Wi	70	71	70	74	285	9,568
Jeff Brehaut	71	68	76	71	286	9,062
Marco Dawson	71	70	74	71	286	9,062
Rocco Mediate	72	67	76	71	286	9,062
Greg Owen	71	69	76	70	286	9,062
Woody Austin	67	74	71	75	287	8,694
John Mallinger	68	73	71	75	287	8,694
Ryan Palmer	74	67	74	72	287	8,694
Boo Weekley	73	67	72	75	287	8,694
Billy Andrade	72	69	73	74	288	8,280

	SCORES				TOTAL	MONEY
Lee Janzen	74	67	71	76	288	8,280
Frank Lickliter	69	72	73	74	288	8,280
Craig Lile	70	71	74	73	288	8,280
Jeff Maggert	69	68	75	76	288	8,280
Briny Baird	73	67	75	74	289	7,912
Chris Tidland	71	67	71	80	289	7,912
Bubba Watson	70	69	71	79	289	7,912
David Branshaw	71	70	77	74	292	7,728
Bob Tway	70	70	78	76	294	7,636
Steve Wheatcroft	73	68	78	77	296	7,544

Omega Mission Hills World Cup

See Asia/Japan Tours chapter.

Special Events

Tavistock Cup

Lake Nona Golf & Country Club, Orlando, Florida
Par 36-36–72; 7,016 yards

March 26-27
purse, $2,600,000

FIRST DAY
(Team better ball; 2 points for win, 1 point for tie)

Henrik Stenson and Chris DiMarco (Lake Nona) defeated Tiger Woods and John Cook (Isleworth), 57-65.
Retief Goosen and Trevor Immelman (LN) defeated Stuart Appleby and Nick O'Hern (Isle), 64-65.
Justin Rose and Ian Poulter (LN) defeated Robert Allenby and Craig Parry (Isle), 61-67.
Ben Curtis and Graeme McDowell (LN) defeated Lee Janzen and Scott Hoch (Isle), 63-64.
Ernie Els and Mark McNulty (LN) defeated Charles Howell and Mark O'Meara (Isle) 62-66.

POINTS: Lake Nona 10, Isleworth 0

SECOND DAY
(Singles versus both players on other team; 1 point for win, 1/2 point for tie)

O'Meara 67 and Cook 71 (Isle) versus Curtis 68 and McNulty 71 (LN).
Janzen 70 and Hoch 78 (Isle) versus McDowell 67 and DiMarco 70 (LN).
Allenby 76 and O'Hern 71 (Isle) versus Immelman 68 and Rose 66 (LN).
Appleby 69 and Parry 70 (Isle) versus Stenson 69 and Poulter 71 (LN).
Woods 64 and Howell 68 (Isle) versus Els 68 and Goosen 67 (LN).

POINTS: Lake Nona 12, Isleworth 8
TWO-DAY TOTAL: Lake Nona 22, Isleworth 8

(Each member of the Lake Nona team received $100,000; each member of the Isleworth team received $50,000. Woods received $500,000, Rose received $300,000, and Goosen, McDowell and O'Meara received $66,667 each for the lowest scores on the second day. Els received $100,000 for winning the long drive challenge.)

CVS Caremark Charity Classic

Rhode Island Country Club, Barrington, Rhode Island
Par 35-36–71; 6,688 yards

June 17-19
purse $1,350,000

	SCORES		TOTAL	MONEY (Team)
Stewart Cink/J.J. Henry	60	62	122	$250,000
Brad Faxon/Zach Johnson	60	63	123	175,000
Chris DiMarco/Camilo Villegas	61	64	125	130,000
Dana Quigley/Brett Quigley	63	62	125	130,000
Nick Price/Tim Clark	63	64	127	115,000
David Toms/Trevor Immelman	65	63	128	110,000
Peter Jacobsen/Sean O'Hair	67	63	130	102,500
Billy Andrade/Lee Trevino	66	64	130	102,500
Natalie Gulbis/Juli Inkster	66	67	133	95,000
K.J. Choi/Jesper Parnevik	68	68	136	90,000

PGA Grand Slam of Golf

Mid-Ocean Club, Tucker's Town, Bermuda
Par 34-36–70; 6,666 yards

October 16-17
purse, $1,250,000

	SCORES		TOTAL	MONEY
Angel Cabrera	68	68	136	$600,000
Padraig Harrington	67	69	136	300,000
(Cabrera defeated Harrington on third playoff hole.)				
Jim Furyk	71	67	138	250,000
Zach Johnson	71	68	139	200,000

Callaway Golf Pebble Beach Invitational

Pebble Beach GL: Par 36-36–72; 6,828 yards
Spyglass Hills GC: Par 36-36–72; 6,953 yards
Del Monte GC: Par 36-36–72; 6,365 yards
Pebble Beach, California

November 15-18
purse, $300,000

	SCORES				TOTAL	MONEY
Tommy Armour	68	69	65	70	272	$60,000
Ronnie Black	68	66	72	68	274	24,300
Rocco Mediate	66	74	67	67	274	24,300
Ken Duke	70	68	71	67	276	10,600
Tommy Purtzer	68	69	70	70	277	9,000
Jason Gore	72	68	67	71	278	7,166.66
Joel Kribel	66	69	72	71	278	7,166.66
Jeff Gove	69	68	71	70	278	7,166.66
Nick Watney	72	65	67	75	279	5,750
Steve Allan	69	72	66	72	279	5,750
Isaac Weintraub	70	67	72	71	280	5,200
Jeff Overton	73	69	68	71	281	4,750
Alex Aragon	75	70	66	70	281	4,750
Kevin Sutherland	62	74	75	71	282	3,875
Mark Wiebe	73	65	73	71	282	3,875
Gary Hallberg	72	74	67	69	282	3,875
Leta Lindley	68	71	74	69	282	3,875
D.A. Points	71	71	70	71	283	3,200
Curt Byrum	67	73	72	72	284	2,850
John Cook	70	72	72	70	284	2,850

	SCORES				TOTAL	MONEY
James McLean	72	72	66	75	285	2,550
Craig Barlow	67	70	75	73	285	2,550
Michael Wilson	69	70	73	73	285	2,550
David Duval	70	71	73	71	285	2,550
Marc Turnesa	72	66	72	76	286	2,250
Eric Axley	74	66	71	75	286	2,250
Kyle Thompson	71	71	71	73	286	2,250
Charley Hoffman	74	71	67	76	288	2,110
Ryan Armour	75	72	66	75	288	2,110
Stephen Marino	72	73	68	75	288	2,110
Joe Ogilvie	74	68	71	75	288	2,110
Parker McLachlin	70	73	70	76	289	2,060
Bubba Watson	75	67	71	78	291	2,040
Bruce Fleisher	71	70	73	214	WD	2,020

Del Webb Father-Son Challenge

ChampionsGate Golf Resort, Orlando, Florida
Par 37-35–72; 7,139 yards

December 1-2
purse, $1,085,000

	SCORES		TOTAL	MONEY (Won by professional)
Larry/Josh Nelson	60	60	120	$200,000
Bob/Kevin Tway	63	59	122	108,000
Mark/Shaun O'Meara	62	62	124	80,000
Raymond/Robert Floyd	62	63	125	60,000
Curtis/Thomas Strange	62	63	125	60,000
Vijay/Qass Singh	64	62	126	49,000
Arnold Palmer/Sam Saunders	62	64	126	49,000
Greg/Gregory Norman	63	63	126	49,000
David Duval/Deano Karavites	61	66	127	46,500
Bernhard/Stefan Langer	64	63	127	46,500
Hale/Steve Irwin	67	61	128	44,500
Jack/Gary Nicklaus	66	62	128	44,500
Tom/Thomas Lehman	66	63	129	42,500
Tom/David Kite	66	63	129	42,500
Craig/Chris Stadler	66	64	130	41,250
Fuzzy/Gretchen Zoeller	65	65	130	41,250
Billy/Bob Casper	69	71	140	40,500
Lee/Daniel Trevino	71	73	144	40,000

Merrill Lynch Shootout

Tiburon Golf Course, Naples, Florida
Par 36-36–72; 7,288 yards

December 7-9
purse, $2,800,000

	SCORES			TOTAL	MONEY (Each)
Woody Austin/Mark Calcavecchia	64	60	63	187	$350,000
Greg Norman/Bubba Watson	65	61	62	188	225,000
Chris DiMarco/Camilo Villegas	68	65	59	192	95,000
Fred Funk/Jeff Sluman	64	67	61	192	95,000
Steve Elkington/Scott McCarron	68	62	62	192	95,000
Jerry Kelly/Rod Pampling	66	64	62	192	95,000
Scott Hoch/Kenny Perry	68	62	62	192	95,000
Anthony Kim/Mark O'Meara	68	63	62	193	75,000
Fred Couples/John Daly	70	64	60	194	72,500
Brad Faxon/Justin Leonard	68	65	64	197	68,750
Stewart Cink/Zach Johnson	69	65	63	197	68,750
Charles Howell/Nick Price	68	65	66	199	65,000

Target World Challenge

Sherwood Country Club, Thousand Oaks, California
Par 36-36–72; 7,085 yards

December 13-16
purse, $5,750,000

	SCORES				TOTAL	MONEY
Tiger Woods	69	62	67	68	266	$1,350,000
Zach Johnson	69	67	69	68	273	840,000
Jim Furyk	68	67	69	71	275	570,000
Lee Westwood	72	71	68	66	277	420,000
Henrik Stenson	69	72	65	73	279	285,000
Steve Stricker	72	69	68	70	279	285,000
Mark Calcavecchia	71	71	70	69	281	240,000
Colin Montgomerie	80	67	69	66	282	225,000
Vijay Singh	72	68	69	73	282	225,000
Padraig Harrington	71	67	75	73	286	210,000
Luke Donald	74	67	75	71	287	195,000
Paul Casey	72	67	72	76	287	195,000
Niclas Fasth	72	72	73	71	288	185,000
Brett Wetterich	73	73	75	69	290	180,000
Fred Couples	74	69	76	72	291	175,000
Rory Sabbatini	69	81	76		WD	170,000

Nationwide Tour

Movistar Panama Championship

Panama Golf Club, Panama City, Panama
Par 35-35–70; 7,042 yards

January 25-28
purse, US$550,000

	SCORES				TOTAL	MONEY
Miguel Carballo	69	67	73	65	274	US$99,000
Hunter Haas	67	68	71	70	276	41,066.67
Jim McGovern	71	68	71	66	276	41,066.67
Patrick Sheehan	69	64	72	71	276	41,066.66
Camilo Benedetti	70	70	72	65	277	20,900
Marc Turnesa	73	66	65	73	277	20,900
Jeremy Anderson	71	67	73	67	278	16,005
Gary Christian	70	68	68	72	278	16,005
Richard Johnson	70	72	66	70	278	16,005
Chris Nallen	71	71	68	68	278	16,005
Tim Wilkinson	73	66	69	70	278	16,005
Tim O'Neal	69	68	73	69	279	11,550
Ted Potter, Jr.	70	67	69	73	279	11,550
Omar Uresti	69	70	72	68	279	11,550
Justin Bolli	74	66	71	69	280	9,900
Rick Price	69	69	72	71	281	9,075
Adam Riddering	70	65	74	72	281	9,075
Ryan Blaum	73	67	70	72	282	7,425

	SCORES				TOTAL	MONEY
John Kimbell	72	69	71	70	282	7,425
Garth Mulroy	67	70	74	71	282	7,425
Steve Pate	70	72	70	70	282	7,425
Danny Briggs	73	70	73	67	283	5,324
Bob Burns	68	73	71	71	283	5,324
Jason Caron	71	71	69	72	283	5,324
Kevin Gessino-Kraft	74	68	71	70	283	5,324
Chris Smith	71	71	72	69	283	5,324

Jacob's Creek Open

See Australasian Tour chapter.

HSBC New Zealand PGA Championship

See Australasian Tour chapter.

Chitimacha Louisiana Open

Le Triomphe Country Club, Broussard, Louisiana
Par 36-35–71; 7,004 yards

March 22-25
purse, $500,000

	SCORES				TOTAL	MONEY
Skip Kendall	66	66	66	70	268	$90,000
Paul Claxton	71	68	64	65	268	54,000
(Kendall defeated Claxton on third playoff hole.)						
Jarrod Lyle	68	70	63	68	269	34,000
D.J. Brigman	68	70	67	66	271	22,000
Tom Byrum	67	67	67	70	271	22,000
Tag Ridings	67	70	64	71	272	17,375
Chris Tidland	68	71	66	67	272	17,375
John Cook	68	68	70	67	273	14,000
Jess Daley	68	70	70	65	273	14,000
Greg Sonnier	70	71	62	70	273	14,000
Aaron Watkins	66	68	71	68	273	14,000
Ryan Blaum	69	67	70	68	274	11,000
Brenden Pappas	60	74	71	69	274	11,000
Scott Dunlap	70	67	69	69	275	8,500
Matt Hendrix	69	70	67	69	275	8,500
David McKenzie	69	72	67	67	275	8,500
Jeff Overton	68	69	70	68	275	8,500
Jason Schultz	69	68	69	69	275	8,500
Steven Bowditch	70	71	68	67	276	5,642.86
Chad Collins	70	69	67	70	276	5,642.86
Matt Hansen	66	70	72	68	276	5,642.86
Hank Kuehne	68	67	71	70	276	5,642.86
Tim Wilkinson	69	72	69	66	276	5,642.86
Peter Tomasulo	72	66	67	71	276	5,642.85
Jay Williamson	69	70	66	71	276	5,642.85

Livermore Valley Wine Country Championship

The Course at Wente Vineyards, Livermore, California
Par 36-36–72; 7,185 yards

March 29-April 1
purse, $625,000

	SCORES				TOTAL	MONEY
Omar Uresti	69	69	74	76	288	$112,500
Skip Kendall	72	72	72	74	290	55,000
Aron Price	70	74	73	73	290	55,000
Gary Christian	73	71	72	75	291	27,500
Danny Ellis	75	71	73	72	291	27,500
Arjun Atwal	74	74	68	76	292	20,937.50
Todd Demsey	73	70	75	74	292	20,937.50
Brian Smock	71	73	73	75	292	20,937.50
Henrik Bjornstad	68	78	71	76	293	16,250
Brad Elder	73	70	75	75	293	16,250
Steve Friesen	77	71	70	75	293	16,250
Chez Reavie	73	74	72	74	293	16,250
John Kimbell	73	72	76	73	294	10,714.29
Martin Laird	73	71	78	72	294	10,714.29
Roland Thatcher	71	73	80	70	294	10,714.29
Esteban Toledo	75	73	75	71	294	10,714.29
John Riegger	76	70	73	75	294	10,714.28
B.J. Staten	77	71	71	75	294	10,714.28
Mario Tiziani	71	75	70	78	294	10,714.28
Jason Caron	72	76	73	74	295	6,770.84
Peter Tomasulo	73	72	78	72	295	6,770.84
Ricky Barnes	74	72	74	75	295	6,770.83
Dan Forsman	75	73	71	76	295	6,770.83
Brock Mackenzie	73	71	74	77	295	6,770.83
David Morland	71	77	71	76	295	6,770.83

South Georgia Classic

Kinderlou Forest Golf Club, Valdosta, Georgia
Par 36-36–72; 7,781 yards

April 12-15
purse, $600,000

	SCORES				TOTAL	MONEY
John Kimbell	68	70	71	69	278	$108,000
Matthew Jones	71	67	70	71	279	64,800
Jeff Klauk	70	74	68	71	283	34,800
Chez Reavie	71	69	71	72	283	34,800
Carlos Franco	72	67	72	73	284	24,000
Jason Allred	72	69	74	70	285	18,780
Tom Byrum	71	72	69	73	285	18,780
Paul Claxton	71	72	70	72	285	18,780
Scott Gutschewski	73	71	68	73	285	18,780
Ron Whittaker	69	72	72	72	285	18,780
Tee McCabe	68	73	73	72	286	14,400
John Merrick	69	74	72	71	286	14,400
Steven Bowditch	69	67	77	74	287	10,285.72
Tag Ridings	70	70	74	73	287	10,285.72
Chris Tidland	70	72	72	73	287	10,285.72
Steve Allan	75	67	70	75	287	10,285.71
Paul Dickinson	64	71	73	79	287	10,285.71
Brenden Pappas	71	71	71	74	287	10,285.71
Aron Price	70	70	71	76	287	10,285.71
Chris Baryla	70	75	72	71	288	6,500
Justin Bolli	68	75	67	78	288	6,500
Greg Chalmers	71	73	72	72	288	6,500

	SCORES				TOTAL	MONEY
Todd Demsey	73	69	73	73	288	6,500
David McKenzie	68	73	74	73	288	6,500
Roland Thatcher	72	72	74	70	288	6,500

Athens Regional Foundation Classic

Jennings Mill Country Club, Athens, Georgia   April 19-22
Par 36-36–72; 7,004 yards   purse, $500,000

	SCORES				TOTAL	MONEY
Martin Laird	66	67	70	69	272	$90,000
Jeremy Anderson	68	73	66	66	273	44,000
Justin Bolli	74	68	65	66	273	44,000
Michael Letzig	68	71	69	66	274	24,000
Robert Damron	68	75	68	64	275	20,000
Hunter Haas	69	69	71	67	276	16,750
David Hearn	72	69	68	67	276	16,750
Nicholas Thompson	71	66	67	72	276	16,750
John Riegger	70	69	72	66	277	14,500
Greg Chalmers	71	71	66	70	278	12,000
Kim Felton	70	72	68	68	278	12,000
Tom Scherrer	69	69	72	68	278	12,000
Omar Uresti	69	70	69	70	278	12,000
Paul Claxton	69	70	69	71	279	8,000
Scott Dunlap	69	72	68	70	279	8,000
Kevin Johnson	73	68	69	69	279	8,000
Steve Jones	67	71	71	70	279	8,000
Brian Quackenbush	70	68	72	69	279	8,000
Peter Tomasulo	69	72	68	70	279	8,000
Matt Weibring	70	71	69	69	279	8,000
Miguel Carballo	71	66	76	67	280	5,600
Skip Kendall	70	68	70	72	280	5,600
Jim McGovern	67	72	71	70	280	5,600
Chris Baryla	68	73	71	69	281	4,240
Henrik Bjornstad	71	70	68	72	281	4,240
Elliot Gealy	70	73	70	68	281	4,240
Fran Quinn	69	73	73	66	281	4,240
Roland Thatcher	72	70	69	70	281	4,240

Henrico County Open

The Dominion Club, Richmond, Virginia   April 26-29
Par 36-36–72; 7,089 yards   purse, $450,000

	SCORES				TOTAL	MONEY
Nick Flanagan	70	66	69	70	275	$81,000
Chris Baryla	69	68	68	70	275	33,600
Bryn Parry	69	70	65	71	275	33,600
Roland Thatcher	70	68	66	71	275	33,600
(Flanagan defeated Parry on first, Thatcher on second and Baryla on third playoff hole.)						
Greg Chalmers	70	68	69	69	276	16,425
Brad Elder	70	69	67	70	276	16,425
Chris Smith	68	74	66	68	276	16,425
Bob Burns	70	67	67	74	278	12,150
Rick Price	72	67	72	67	278	12,150
David Sanchez	72	66	67	73	278	12,150
Nicholas Thompson	70	69	69	70	278	12,150
Omar Uresti	70	68	69	71	278	12,150

	SCORES				TOTAL	MONEY
Camilo Benedetti	73	69	69	68	279	8,190
Chad Collins	69	68	74	68	279	8,190
Michael Letzig	70	66	69	74	279	8,190
Brad Ott	71	71	67	70	279	8,190
Jeff Overton	68	70	70	71	279	8,190
Henrik Bjornstad	70	65	71	74	280	5,868
Miguel Carballo	70	69	71	70	280	5,868
Gary Christian	72	70	70	68	280	5,868
Roger Tambellini	75	65	71	69	280	5,868
Jay Williamson	70	72	67	71	280	5,868
Arjun Atwal	70	71	69	71	281	4,320
Todd Demsey	71	65	72	73	281	4,320
Jon Mills	74	66	69	72	281	4,320

Fort Smith Classic

Hardscrabble Country Club, Fort Smith, Arkansas   May 3-6
Par 35-35–70; 6,783 yards   purse, $525,000

	SCORES				TOTAL	MONEY
Jay Williamson	69	66	66	63	264	$94,500
Justin Bolli	69	63	63	70	265	46,200
Garrett Willis	66	69	64	66	265	46,200
Jason Day	68	67	69	62	266	23,100
Tee McCabe	67	70	65	64	266	23,100
Brad Elder	64	71	65	67	267	18,243.75
Craig Lile	65	64	70	68	267	18,243.75
Michael Boyd	65	66	68	69	268	14,700
Andrew Johnson	66	68	66	68	268	14,700
Adam Riddering	68	69	65	66	268	14,700
Patrick Sheehan	68	65	69	66	268	14,700
Todd Fischer	65	70	69	65	269	10,290
Scott Gutschewski	63	67	69	70	269	10,290
Matt Hendrix	67	67	65	70	269	10,290
Chris Smith	68	66	68	67	269	10,290
Ron Whittaker	64	70	64	71	269	10,290
Scott Dunlap	67	67	65	71	270	6,870
Richard Johnson	65	71	67	67	270	6,870
Matthew Jones	69	68	66	67	270	6,870
Jon Mills	65	66	67	72	270	6,870
David Morland	70	64	65	71	270	6,870
Dave Rummells	70	64	67	69	270	6,870
Roland Thatcher	70	67	69	64	270	6,870
Chris Baryla	70	66	64	71	271	4,690
Nicholas Thompson	66	70	70	65	271	4,690
Omar Uresti	70	66	66	69	271	4,690

BMW Charity Pro-Am at The Cliffs

The Cliffs Golf & Country Club, Greenville, South Carolina   May 17-20
Cliffs Valley: Par 36-36–72; 7,023 yards   purse, $650,000
Keowee Vineyards: Par 36-35–71; 7,006 yards
Cliffs at Walnut Grove: Par 36-35–71; 7,000 yards

	SCORES				TOTAL	MONEY
Nick Flanagan	68	72	66	65	271	$117,000
Nicholas Thompson	72	68	68	64	272	70,200

	SCORES				TOTAL	MONEY
Richard Johnson	66	69	68	70	273	37,700
Marc Turnesa	70	70	67	66	273	37,700
Todd Fischer	67	70	69	68	274	24,700
Peter Tomasulo	67	69	69	69	274	24,700
Patrick Sheehan	70	72	66	67	275	20,258.34
Andrew Johnson	68	73	65	69	275	20,258.33
Roger Tambellini	68	72	67	68	275	20,258.33
David Hearn	63	74	68	71	276	16,250
Skip Kendall	70	68	68	70	276	16,250
Chez Reavie	67	69	71	69	276	16,250
David Mathis	74	69	62	72	277	12,187.50
Tim O'Neal	70	71	67	69	277	12,187.50
Ron Whittaker	71	70	68	68	277	12,187.50
Zoran Zorkic	68	69	69	71	277	12,187.50
Kevin Gessino-Kraft	69	70	71	68	278	9,750
Greg Kraft	71	70	68	69	278	9,750
Rick Price	73	68	69	68	278	9,750
Jason Allred	69	66	74	70	279	7,572.50
Josh Broadaway	69	72	68	70	279	7,572.50
Martin Laird	67	72	71	69	279	7,572.50
Jimmy Walker	66	73	73	67	279	7,572.50
Joseph Alfieri	68	70	73	69	280	5,373.34
Brent Delahoussaye	68	73	69	70	280	5,373.34
Gary Christian	71	70	69	70	280	5,373.33
Joe Daley	69	69	71	71	280	5,373.33
David McKenzie	73	66	69	72	280	5,373.33
Omar Uresti	77	65	70	68	280	5,373.33

Melwood Prince George's County Open

The Country Club at Woodmore, Mitchellville, Maryland
Par 36-36–72; 7,059 yards

May 24-27
purse $600,000

	SCORES				TOTAL	MONEY
Paul Claxton	70	66	67	67	270	$108,000
James Driscoll	71	66	68	66	271	52,800
Jaco Van Zyl	70	65	68	68	271	52,800
Jon Mills	66	71	67	69	273	28,800
Nick Flanagan	67	70	71	66	274	20,340
Matthew Jones	70	70	67	67	274	20,340
Kyle Thompson	69	68	67	70	274	20,340
Esteban Toledo	71	65	68	70	274	20,340
Matt Weibring	69	69	68	68	274	20,340
Brenden Pappas	72	67	69	67	275	15,600
Omar Uresti	69	67	71	68	275	15,600
Todd Fischer	72	68	68	68	276	13,200
Peter Tomasulo	68	67	72	69	276	13,200
Arjun Atwal	72	69	68	68	277	10,200
Patrick Sheehan	69	66	68	74	277	10,200
Michael Sim	72	70	69	66	277	10,200
Marc Turnesa	67	71	68	71	277	10,200
Garrett Willis	68	71	69	69	277	10,200
Jason Caron	67	70	73	68	278	8,400
Scott Dunlap	67	73	71	68	279	6,744
Kevin Gessino-Kraft	74	66	69	70	279	6,744
Matt Hansen	67	71	72	69	279	6,744
B.J. Staten	73	67	67	72	279	6,744
Chris Thompson	68	72	66	73	279	6,744
Kris Blanks	74	66	72	68	280	4,680
Bob Burns	72	68	71	69	280	4,680

	SCORES				TOTAL	MONEY
Danny Ellis	72	70	65	73	280	4,680
Ryan Howison	68	69	72	71	280	4,680
Roland Thatcher	68	72	68	72	280	4,680
Jay Williamson	66	74	73	67	280	4,680

LaSalle Bank Open

The Glen Club, Glenview, Illinois
Par 36-36–72; 7,263 yards

May 31-June 3
purse, $750,000

	SCORES				TOTAL	MONEY
John Riegger	70	65	68	68	271	$135,000
B.J. Staten	66	69	69	68	272	81,000
Kris Blanks	68	71	67	67	273	43,500
Roland Thatcher	72	65	67	69	273	43,500
Tag Ridings	71	64	68	71	274	28,500
Jay Williamson	71	67	68	68	274	28,500
Chris Smith	71	67	70	67	275	24,187.50
Omar Uresti	70	63	71	71	275	24,187.50
Rich Barcelo	68	73	67	68	276	16,250
Dustin Bray	68	68	70	70	276	16,250
Bob Burns	70	68	69	69	276	16,250
Jason Day	66	69	68	73	276	16,250
James Driscoll	69	66	71	70	276	16,250
Jeff Klauk	73	66	69	68	276	16,250
Michael Long	71	69	71	65	276	16,250
Tee McCabe	71	70	69	66	276	16,250
Chris Stroud	72	69	66	69	276	16,250
Arjun Atwal	71	66	72	68	277	8,533.34
Tom Carter	70	67	72	68	277	8,533.34
Garrett Willis	72	69	68	68	277	8,533.34
Paul Claxton	69	69	68	71	277	8,533.33
Keoke Cotner	67	70	71	69	277	8,533.33
Neal Lancaster	70	70	71	66	277	8,533.33
Jeff Overton	71	67	70	69	277	8,533.33
Patrick Sheehan	70	70	71	66	277	8,533.33
Kevin Stadler	71	67	71	68	277	8,533.33

The Rex Hospital Open

TPC at Wakefield Plantation, Raleigh, North Carolina
Par 35-36–71; 6,724 yards

June 7-10
purse, $450,000

	SCORES				TOTAL	MONEY
Kyle Thompson	64	65	69	70	268	$81,000
Bob Burns	69	63	70	68	270	48,600
Rick Price	65	68	72	67	272	30,600
Garrett Willis	69	70	70	64	273	21,600
Tommy Biershenk	69	65	71	69	274	16,425
D.A. Points	69	70	68	67	274	16,425
Marc Turnesa	67	71	69	67	274	16,425
Matt Weibring	70	69	68	68	275	13,950
Tee McCabe	65	71	70	70	276	10,414.29
Rich Morris	69	71	68	68	276	10,414.29
Garth Mulroy	70	66	70	70	276	10,414.29
Mario Tiziani	67	69	70	70	276	10,414.29
David McKenzie	70	70	64	72	276	10,414.28

	SCORES				TOTAL	MONEY
Keith Nolan	72	66	68	70	276	10,414.28
Aron Price	68	70	67	71	276	10,414.28
Keoke Cotner	68	68	70	71	277	7,425
David Hearn	72	67	70	68	277	7,425
Kris Cox	68	68	73	69	278	5,868
James Driscoll	73	67	70	68	278	5,868
Elliot Gealy	66	72	71	69	278	5,868
Jeff Klauk	69	69	70	70	278	5,868
Lee Williams	69	68	70	71	278	5,868
Kris Blanks	67	70	76	66	279	3,857.15
Jeff Wood	68	70	73	68	279	3,857.15
Dustin Bray	72	68	69	70	279	3,857.14
Scott Dunlap	73	65	68	73	279	3,857.14
Matt Hansen	71	64	75	69	279	3,857.14
Michael Letzig	64	71	74	70	279	3,857.14
Phil Tataurangi	67	68	73	71	279	3,857.14

Rochester Area Charities Showdown at Somerby

Somerby Golf Club, Byron, Minnesota   June 14-17
Par 36-36–72; 7,209 yards   purse, $500,000

	SCORES				TOTAL	MONEY
Chris Riley	67	68	67	70	272	$90,000
*Jamie Lovemark	68	68	71	65	272	
(Riley defeated Lovemark on second playoff hole.)						
Greg Chalmers	70	65	67	72	274	44,000
Esteban Toledo	67	68	66	73	274	44,000
Jeremy Anderson	68	66	69	72	275	18,125
Gary Christian	69	69	66	71	275	18,125
Jay Delsing	65	68	68	74	275	18,125
Richard Johnson	67	68	68	72	275	18,125
Patrick Sheehan	72	65	66	72	275	18,125
Lee Williamson	70	64	69	72	275	18,125
Josh Broadaway	72	67	69	68	276	11,083.34
Fabian Gomez	70	69	69	68	276	11,083.34
Chris Anderson	66	69	69	72	276	11,083.33
Jason Enloe	68	68	66	74	276	11,083.33
Chez Reavie	69	71	67	69	276	11,083.33
Tommy Tolles	66	70	68	72	276	11,083.33
Chris Nallen	75	65	70	67	277	8,250
Scott Sterling	71	68	70	68	277	8,250
Emlyn Aubrey	68	70	68	72	278	6,520
Brad Elder	66	70	67	75	278	6,520
Deane Pappas	70	69	67	72	278	6,520
Jay Williamson	71	69	68	70	278	6,520
Jeff Wood	65	74	71	68	278	6,520
Tommy Biershenk	69	68	68	74	279	4,650
Chris Thompson	73	67	71	68	279	4,650
Omar Uresti	68	72	69	70	279	4,650
Tim Weinhart	69	68	69	73	279	4,650

Knoxville Open

Fox Den Country Club, Knoxville, Tennessee
Par 36-36–72; 7,110 yards

June 21-24
purse, $475,000

	SCORES				TOTAL	MONEY
Chez Reavie	68	70	65	68	271	$85,500
Kyle McCarthy	64	70	70	70	274	51,300
Michael Letzig	69	69	71	66	275	32,300
Deane Pappas	67	68	74	67	276	22,800
Tommy Biershenk	71	70	65	71	277	17,337.50
Scott Gardiner	69	70	68	70	277	17,337.50
Jon Mills	68	69	68	72	277	17,337.50
Esteban Toledo	71	68	69	70	278	14,725
Joe Daley	73	68	70	68	279	11,875
Roland Thatcher	71	66	73	69	279	11,875
Nicholas Thompson	75	68	66	70	279	11,875
Tim Wilkinson	70	73	70	66	279	11,875
Jeff Wood	74	68	67	70	279	11,875
Pat Bates	74	69	70	67	280	6,916
Camilo Benedetti	72	70	66	72	280	6,916
Danny Briggs	72	71	66	71	280	6,916
Jason Caron	72	69	69	70	280	6,916
Kevin Gessino-Kraft	71	67	69	73	280	6,916
Brenden Pappas	72	70	66	72	280	6,916
Brian Quackenbush	70	72	66	72	280	6,916
Michael Sims	68	71	71	70	280	6,916
Garrett Willis	72	70	68	70	280	6,916
Willie Wood	72	68	69	71	280	6,916
Brent Delahoussaye	72	69	70	70	281	4,028
Stephen Gangluff	71	72	69	69	281	4,028
Boyd Summerhays	68	73	71	69	281	4,028
Jimmy Walker	69	72	69	71	281	4,028
Lee Williams	70	72	68	71	281	4,028

Peek'n Peak Classic

Peek'n Peak Resort, Upper Course, Findley Lake, New York
Par 36-36–72; 6,888 yards

June 28-July 1
purse, $600,000

	SCORES				TOTAL	MONEY
Roland Thatcher	69	67	69	68	273	$108,000
Paul Claxton	66	66	74	70	276	64,800
Brock Mackenzie	73	70	70	65	278	40,800
Scott Gardiner	72	67	70	71	280	28,800
Brenden Pappas	74	69	65	73	281	24,000
Kelly Grunewald	69	70	69	74	282	20,850
Tjaart van der Walt	68	71	70	73	282	20,850
Danny Briggs	68	72	73	70	283	15,000
Joe Daley	68	70	70	75	283	15,000
Todd Demsey	70	70	75	68	283	15,000
Jon Mills	68	68	74	73	283	15,000
Andrew Pratt	70	70	71	72	283	15,000
Jon Turcott	73	70	68	72	283	15,000
Jimmy Walker	68	72	71	72	283	15,000
Chad Collins	70	70	70	74	284	9,900
Jason Day	69	73	70	72	284	9,900
James Driscoll	73	69	72	70	284	9,900
Sal Spallone	71	70	71	72	284	9,900
Justin Bolli	73	67	70	75	285	7,530

	SCORES				TOTAL	MONEY
David Mathis	70	69	73	73	285	7,530
Mario Tiziani	73	69	73	70	285	7,530
Tim Wilkinson	70	73	70	72	285	7,530
Michael Letzig	66	73	70	77	286	5,424
Tom Scherrer	72	70	73	71	286	5,424
Phil Tataurangi	70	73	70	73	286	5,424
Chris Thompson	70	72	72	72	286	5,424
Esteban Toledo	71	72	68	75	286	5,424

Legend Financial Group Classic

StoneWater Golf Club, Highland Heights, Ohio
Par 35-36–71; 7,045 yards

July 5-8
purse, $525,000

	SCORES				TOTAL	MONEY
Jason Day	68	66	67	67	268	$94,500
Scott Gardiner	66	66	70	67	269	56,700
Arjun Atwal	70	68	66	66	270	35,700
Joe Daley	67	67	68	70	272	25,200
Chad Collins	70	70	66	67	273	18,440.63
Martin Laird	67	68	72	66	273	18,440.63
David McKenzie	66	69	66	72	273	18,440.62
John Riegger	70	67	68	68	273	18,440.62
Todd Fischer	69	69	67	69	274	14,700
Brock Mackenzie	68	67	68	71	274	14,700
James Driscoll	65	68	70	72	275	12,075
Garth Mulroy	68	68	69	70	275	12,075
Marc Turnesa	68	68	69	70	275	12,075
Chris Anderson	72	65	70	69	276	9,187.50
Keith Nolan	68	65	71	72	276	9,187.50
Kenneth Staton	66	73	67	70	276	9,187.50
Kyle Thompson	66	74	67	69	276	9,187.50
Kris Cox	69	65	69	74	277	6,390
David Hearn	70	69	71	67	277	6,390
Tee McCabe	67	70	69	71	277	6,390
Jim Rutledge	69	68	69	71	277	6,390
Roland Thatcher	65	71	71	70	277	6,390
Jimmy Walker	67	69	72	69	277	6,390
Tim Wilkinson	69	70	70	68	277	6,390
Josh Broadaway	68	72	71	67	278	4,515
Jeff Klauk	68	66	74	70	278	4,515

Nationwide Children's Hospital Invitational

The OSU Golf Club, Scarlet Course, Columbus, Ohio
Par 36-35–71; 7,141 yards

July 12-15
purse, $700,000

	SCORES				TOTAL	MONEY
*Daniel Summerhays	68	69	72	69	278	
Chad Collins	69	72	70	69	280	$100,800
Chris Nallen	67	72	70	71	280	100,800
Tjaart van der Walt	72	71	69	69	281	47,600
Steven Bowditch	72	73	71	66	282	26,390
Jason Day	74	70	71	67	282	26,390
Brenden Pappas	72	72	71	67	282	26,390
Tom Scherrer	72	71	72	67	282	26,390
Patrick Sheehan	73	67	76	66	282	26,390

	SCORES				TOTAL	MONEY
Danny Ellis	75	70	69	69	283	18,200
David McKenzie	73	70	71	69	283	18,200
Jon Mills	72	69	75	67	283	18,200
Michael Sims	74	69	72	68	283	18,200
Brad Adamonis	70	70	72	72	284	14,000
Kelly Grunewald	68	71	76	69	284	14,000
Joe Daley	71	71	73	70	285	11,550
Todd Demsey	74	70	72	69	285	11,550
Scott Gardiner	72	68	73	72	285	11,550
Jimmy Walker	72	73	71	69	285	11,550
Jess Daley	71	75	71	69	286	8,785
Brock Mackenzie	76	70	72	68	286	8,785
Rick Price	70	72	77	67	286	8,785
Kyle Thompson	76	68	68	74	286	8,785
Brian Smock	73	72	72	70	287	6,720
Esteban Toledo	72	71	71	73	287	6,720
Marc Turnesa	75	70	73	69	287	6,720

Price Cutter Charity Championship

Highland Springs Country Club, Springfield, Missouri
Par 36-36–72; 7,060 yards

July 19-22
purse, $556,000

	SCORES				TOTAL	MONEY
Tom Scherrer	66	63	66	67	262	$100,080
Franklin Langham	68	64	66	68	266	60,048
Justin Bolli	65	66	69	70	270	37,808
Michael Letzig	66	70	68	67	271	24,464
Zoran Zorkic	71	67	67	66	271	24,464
Scott Sterling	67	71	67	67	272	20,016
Scott Parel	68	70	68	67	273	17,931
Ron Whittaker	71	68	66	68	273	17,931
Chad Collins	67	67	68	73	275	14,456
Keoke Cotner	71	70	67	67	275	14,456
Kelly Grunewald	72	67	69	67	275	14,456
Andrew Pratt	67	68	68	72	275	14,456
Thomas Aiken	69	72	66	69	276	8,957.78
Ricky Barnes	72	69	67	68	276	8,957.78
Jess Daley	69	70	69	68	276	8,957.78
Mike Heinen	70	67	70	69	276	8,957.78
Steve Pate	69	69	73	65	276	8,957.78
Vance Veazey	67	71	68	70	276	8,957.78
Tim Wilkinson	68	74	66	68	276	8,957.78
Hunter Haas	66	71	68	71	276	8,957.77
John Kimbell	69	70	64	73	276	8,957.77
Guy Boros	73	67	69	68	277	4,948.40
Brian Guetz	68	70	66	73	277	4,948.40
Matt Hansen	70	68	70	69	277	4,948.40
Jeff Hart	71	70	66	70	277	4,948.40
Ryan Hietala	69	70	67	71	277	4,948.40
Edward Loar	69	69	67	72	277	4,948.40
Brian Smock	69	69	70	69	277	4,948.40
Mark Walker	66	70	70	71	277	4,948.40

Cox Classic

Champions Run, Omaha, Nebraska
Par 35-36–71; 7,145 yards

July 26-29
purse, $650,000

		SCORES			TOTAL	MONEY
Roland Thatcher	64	63	68	65	260	$117,000
Jason Day	66	70	62	63	261	70,200
Vance Veazey	66	68	66	64	264	44,200
Jason Enloe	66	67	66	66	265	25,593.75
Martin Laird	68	65	66	66	265	25,593.75
Richard Swift	70	64	66	65	265	25,593.75
Ron Whittaker	69	66	63	67	265	25,593.75
Tommy Gainey	68	66	67	65	266	17,550
Kelly Grunewald	63	70	65	68	266	17,550
Jin Park	67	67	66	66	266	17,550
Scott Sterling	61	68	69	68	266	17,550
Chris Thompson	60	71	69	66	266	17,550
Blake Adams	69	65	66	67	267	12,187.50
Greg Chalmers	65	71	66	65	267	12,187.50
B.J. Staten	67	66	64	70	267	12,187.50
Roger Tambellini	69	68	66	64	267	12,187.50
Brad Adamonis	66	70	63	69	268	9,100
Chad Collins	65	70	65	68	268	9,100
Matthew Jones	66	71	66	65	268	9,100
Jon Mills	65	69	69	65	268	9,100
Patrick Sheehan	67	68	66	67	268	9,100
Wil Collins	66	67	69	67	269	7,280
Steven Bowditch	68	69	65	68	270	5,571.43
Chez Reavie	67	65	68	70	270	5,571.43
Tom Scherrer	65	69	67	69	270	5,571.43
Michael Walton	67	64	69	70	270	5,571.43
Scott Weatherly	69	67	67	67	270	5,571.43
Tim Wilkinson	66	68	68	68	270	5,571.43
Kris Blanks	69	64	72	65	270	5,571.42

Preferred Health Systems Wichita Open

Crestview Country Club, Wichita, Kansas
Par 35-36–71; 6,913 yards

August 2-5
purse, $500,000

		SCORES			TOTAL	MONEY
Brad Elder	65	64	71	65	265	$90,000
Fabian Gomez	71	66	67	65	269	54,000
Miguel Carballo	70	65	68	67	270	24,000
Stephen Gangluff	66	70	67	67	270	24,000
David Hearn	68	65	70	67	270	24,000
Vance Veazey	66	66	68	70	270	24,000
Kris Blanks	67	70	67	67	271	14,041.67
Keoke Cotner	70	67	66	68	271	14,041.67
Jeff Klauk	67	64	71	69	271	14,041.67
Martin Laird	65	68	69	69	271	14,041.67
Bradley Hughes	67	62	71	71	271	14,041.66
David McKenzie	65	67	68	71	271	14,041.66
Andrew Dresser	69	66	71	66	272	8,833.34
Justin Hicks	67	69	69	67	272	8,833.34
Jason Day	66	68	69	69	272	8,833.33
Rich Morris	70	67	64	71	272	8,833.33
Michael Walton	67	66	66	73	272	8,833.33
Aaron Watkins	69	68	66	69	272	8,833.33

	SCORES				TOTAL	MONEY
Chris Baryla	69	65	71	68	273	5,850
Jason Enloe	65	68	70	70	273	5,850
Scott Gardiner	67	66	67	73	273	5,850
Garth Mulroy	68	65	71	69	273	5,850
Deane Pappas	68	68	68	69	273	5,850
Justin Smith	66	65	72	70	273	5,850
Erik Compton	67	68	72	67	274	4,000
Pete Jordan	70	64	70	70	274	4,000
Troy Kelly	65	71	71	67	274	4,000
Marc Leishman	70	63	68	73	274	4,000
Andy Morse	68	69	69	68	274	4,000

Northeast Pennsylvania Classic

Glenmaura National Golf Club, Scranton, Pennsylvania   August 9-12
Par 35-36–71; 6,990 yards   purse, $500,000

	SCORES				TOTAL	MONEY
Justin Bolli	68	67	69	66	270	$90,000
Richard Johnson	68	64	67	72	271	44,000
Patrick Sheehan	70	69	64	68	271	44,000
Jason Allred	69	67	67	71	274	19,687.50
Jim McGovern	64	67	74	69	274	19,687.50
Garth Mulroy	69	69	69	67	274	19,687.50
D.A. Points	67	65	68	74	274	19,687.50
Chad Collins	62	69	72	72	275	15,000
Kevin Gessino-Kraft	68	65	68	74	275	15,000
Michael Letzig	69	64	72	71	276	11,500
Rick Price	69	64	71	72	276	11,500
Daniel Summerhays	71	67	67	71	276	11,500
Nicholas Thompson	70	68	69	69	276	11,500
Lee Williams	67	71	68	70	276	11,500
Ricky Barnes	65	70	71	71	277	8,500
Brad Elder	67	70	70	70	277	8,500
Tee McCabe	72	68	65	72	277	8,500
Marc Leishman	71	68	72	67	278	7,000
David McKenzie	66	72	69	71	278	7,000
Omar Uresti	71	64	70	73	278	7,000
Arjun Atwal	70	68	73	68	279	4,622.23
Phil Tataurangi	72	68	71	68	279	4,622.23
Chris Baryla	68	71	69	71	279	4,622.22
Greg Chalmers	69	68	72	70	279	4,622.22
Jeff Curl	64	72	70	73	279	4,622.22
Andrew Dresser	66	71	68	74	279	4,622.22
B.J. Staten	67	68	73	71	279	4,622.22
Scott Sterling	66	69	72	72	279	4,622.22
Ron Whittaker	67	67	73	72	279	4,622.22

Xerox Classic

Irondequoit Country Club, Rochester, New York   August 16-19
Par 35-35–70; 6,720 yards   purse, $600,000

	SCORES				TOTAL	MONEY
Nick Flanagan	69	68	70	63	270	$108,000
James Driscoll	64	66	70	71	271	64,800
Jason Day	70	66	68	69	273	40,800

	SCORES				TOTAL	MONEY
Justin Bolli	71	64	69	70	274	24,800
David McKenzie	73	65	69	67	274	24,800
Scott Parel	68	65	71	70	274	24,800
David Mathis	67	69	67	72	275	20,100
Fran Quinn	69	67	73	67	276	18,600
Jon Mills	71	67	70	69	277	16,200
Dennis Paulson	70	70	68	69	277	16,200
Omar Uresti	69	70	69	69	277	16,200
Ricky Barnes	71	71	69	67	278	12,600
Roland Thatcher	72	69	64	73	278	12,600
Tim Wilkinson	70	71	70	67	278	12,600
Tom Carter	68	73	66	72	279	9,600
Todd Demsey	67	70	74	68	279	9,600
Andrew Dresser	72	67	74	66	279	9,600
Chez Reavie	68	72	70	69	279	9,600
Mark Wiebe	67	69	71	72	279	9,600
Kevin Gessino-Kraft	69	72	72	67	280	6,744
David Hearn	67	69	74	70	280	6,744
Tim O'Neal	72	69	71	68	280	6,744
Brenden Pappas	73	67	70	70	280	6,744
Chris Thompson	73	69	69	69	280	6,744
Jason Allred	67	73	72	69	281	4,320
Jess Daley	67	75	72	67	281	4,320
Joe Daley	70	67	73	71	281	4,320
Hunter Haas	64	74	71	72	281	4,320
Jeff Klauk	70	70	73	68	281	4,320
Martin Laird	70	70	72	69	281	4,320
Keith Nolan	70	72	69	70	281	4,320
Daniel Summerhays	71	71	73	66	281	4,320
Jon Turcott	71	69	71	70	281	4,320
Lee Williamson	71	71	67	72	281	4,320

National Mining Association Pete Dye Classic

Pete Dye Golf Club, Bridgeport, West Virginia
Par 36-36–72; 7,309 yards

August 23-26
purse, $600,000

	SCORES				TOTAL	MONEY
Jimmy Walker	68	70	68	67	273	$108,000
Justin Hicks	71	66	71	66	274	52,800
Matthew Jones	68	67	71	68	274	52,800
Tom Carter	68	70	71	67	276	26,400
Parker McLachlin	63	68	68	77	276	26,400
Scott Gutschewski	69	73	67	68	277	21,600
Ian Leggatt	67	70	70	71	278	17,460
Scott Parel	65	71	70	72	278	17,460
Kyle Thompson	67	71	70	70	278	17,460
Tommy Tolles	72	71	67	68	278	17,460
Lee Williams	70	70	70	68	278	17,460
Kris Blanks	71	68	67	73	279	12,150
Bubba Dickerson	72	70	67	70	279	12,150
Scott Dunlap	71	66	70	72	279	12,150
Edward Loar	70	64	74	71	279	12,150
Arjun Atwal	72	66	69	73	280	8,145
Mike Capone	70	69	71	70	280	8,145
Kevin Gessino-Kraft	67	70	75	68	280	8,145
Michael Maness	73	68	69	70	280	8,145
Jon Mills	72	71	68	69	280	8,145
Garth Mulroy	70	69	74	67	280	8,145
Jason Schultz	71	70	67	72	280	8,145

	SCORES				TOTAL	MONEY
Garrett Willis	71	70	73	66	280	8,145
Henrik Bjornstad	71	72	70	68	281	5,220
Brad Elder	72	67	73	69	281	5,220
Franklin Langham	70	69	71	71	281	5,220
Brenden Pappas	72	67	70	72	281	5,220

Utah EnergySolutions Championship

Willow Creek Country Club, Sandy, Utah
Par 35-36–71; 7,104 yards

September 6-9
purse, $500,000

	SCORES				TOTAL	MONEY
Franklin Langham	63	67	66	68	264	$90,000
Richard Johnson	67	64	67	68	266	54,000
Mark Hensby	67	66	67	67	267	29,000
Edward Loar	65	66	69	67	267	29,000
Fabian Gomez	72	65	65	66	268	18,250
Chris Tidland	68	67	67	66	268	18,250
Ron Whittaker	66	66	68	68	268	18,250
Jeremy Anderson	67	66	66	70	269	14,000
Adam Meyer	68	68	66	67	269	14,000
D.A. Points	68	70	64	67	269	14,000
Vance Veazey	66	66	68	69	269	14,000
Chris Baryla	66	67	68	69	270	9,800
Craig Lile	63	68	68	71	270	9,800
David Mathis	67	70	66	67	270	9,800
Jon Mills	71	66	67	66	270	9,800
Matt Weibring	68	70	63	69	270	9,800
Bob Burns	70	67	70	64	271	7,500
Todd Demsey	64	74	64	69	271	7,500
Patrick Sheehan	67	69	67	68	271	7,500
Chris Anderson	66	67	70	69	272	5,620
Brock Mackenzie	70	65	66	71	272	5,620
Aron Price	68	68	66	70	272	5,620
Tom Scherrer	65	68	70	69	272	5,620
Tim Wilkinson	66	67	70	69	272	5,620
Ricky Barnes	69	69	68	67	273	4,000
Kevin Gessino-Kraft	67	68	70	68	273	4,000
Chris Nallen	70	67	67	69	273	4,000
Tag Ridings	71	67	66	69	273	4,000
John Riegger	66	68	72	67	273	4,000

Oregon Classic

Shadow Hills Country Club, Junction City, Oregon
Par 36-36–72; 7,007 yards

September 13-16
purse, $475,000

	SCORES				TOTAL	MONEY
Kyle Thompson	72	65	67	67	271	$85,500
Matthew Jones	66	71	68	66	271	41,800
Jon Turcott	68	66	68	69	271	41,800
(Thompson defeated Turcott on first and Jones on second playoff hole.)						
Brad Elder	67	69	66	71	273	20,900
Brenden Pappas	71	68	66	68	273	20,900
Mike Heinen	66	69	70	69	274	15,378.13
Peter Tomasulo	72	70	67	65	274	15,378.13
Richard Johnson	68	64	69	73	274	15,378.12

	SCORES				TOTAL	MONEY
Roland Thatcher	66	71	67	70	274	15,378.12
Chad Collins	69	70	69	67	275	11,400
Rick Price	73	67	68	67	275	11,400
B.J. Staten	74	62	69	70	275	11,400
Matt Weibring	68	71	70	66	275	11,400
Jason Day	66	67	69	74	276	8,550
Jon Mills	72	69	70	65	276	8,550
Kenneth Staton	74	64	71	67	276	8,550
Todd Fischer	66	73	66	72	277	7,125
Kelly Grunewald	66	69	73	69	277	7,125
Scott Parel	69	72	68	68	277	7,125
Brock Mackenzie	68	69	71	70	278	5,937.50
Tom Scherrer	71	71	66	70	278	5,937.50
Henrik Bjornstad	67	69	71	72	279	4,465
Jeff Klauk	68	70	70	71	279	4,465
Jim McGovern	69	70	71	69	279	4,465
Chris Nallen	72	67	69	71	279	4,465
John Riegger	69	72	68	70	279	4,465
Patrick Sheehan	72	69	69	69	279	4,465

Albertsons Boise Open

Hillcrest Country Club, Boise, Idaho
Par 36-35–71; 6,698 yards

September 20-23
purse, $675,000

	SCORES				TOTAL	MONEY
Jon Mills	65	68	66	64	263	$121,500
D.A. Points	64	69	63	70	266	72,900
Garth Mulroy	64	68	68	67	267	39,150
Nicholas Thompson	63	68	70	66	267	39,150
Matthew Jones	67	65	67	69	268	25,650
Jim McGovern	63	65	68	72	268	25,650
Jeremy Anderson	65	69	69	66	269	21,037.50
Aron Price	66	67	65	71	269	21,037.50
Peter Tomasulo	69	66	64	70	269	21,037.50
Brenden Pappas	63	67	68	72	270	18,225
Ben Bates	67	71	65	68	271	14,850
Henrik Bjornstad	69	63	69	70	271	14,850
Todd Demsey	65	66	68	72	271	14,850
Brock Mackenzie	68	67	65	71	271	14,850
James Driscoll	69	65	68	70	272	11,475
Boyd Summerhays	67	67	65	73	272	11,475
Vance Veazey	65	70	66	71	272	11,475
Brad Adamonis	65	69	67	72	273	8,802
Jeff Klauk	63	71	69	70	273	8,802
Bryn Parry	68	70	67	68	273	8,802
Omar Uresti	68	68	70	67	273	8,802
Tim Wilkinson	68	66	69	70	273	8,802
David Mathis	67	70	67	70	274	6,750
Esteban Toledo	69	68	67	70	274	6,750
Andy Bare	70	66	67	72	275	5,670
Jason Caron	69	69	68	69	275	5,670
Scott Dunlap	70	66	69	70	275	5,670

Mark Christopher Charity Classic

Empire Lakes Golf Club, Rancho Cucamonga, California
Par 35-36–71; 7,017 yards

October 4-7
purse, $525,000

	SCORES				TOTAL	MONEY
Richard Johnson	65	72	69	67	273	$94,500
Jeremy Anderson	68	68	71	66	273	46,200
Matthew Jones	70	68	69	66	273	46,200
(Johnson defeated Anderson and Jones on first playoff hole.)						
Tommy Tolles	70	73	65	66	274	25,200
Brad Adamonis	74	68	67	66	275	18,440.63
Brian Smock	70	70	68	67	275	18,440.63
Keoke Cotner	66	69	72	68	275	18,440.62
Tom Gillis	70	68	67	70	275	18,440.62
Ricky Barnes	69	69	70	68	276	14,175
Jon Mills	65	68	75	68	276	14,175
B.J. Staten	66	72	69	69	276	14,175
Bob Burns	70	66	71	70	277	12,075
Ronnie Black	68	73	69	68	278	9,843.75
Keith Nolan	66	76	67	69	278	9,843.75
Brenden Pappas	65	70	74	69	278	9,843.75
Daniel Summerhays	66	72	72	68	278	9,843.75
Jeff Klauk	68	70	71	70	279	7,105
Tee McCabe	66	73	69	71	279	7,105
Chez Reavie	71	68	71	69	279	7,105
Jon Turcott	71	67	73	68	279	7,105
Marc Turnesa	71	69	69	70	279	7,105
Ron Whittaker	73	70	69	67	279	7,105
Chris Baryla	67	66	77	70	280	4,620
Scott Dunlap	74	68	67	71	280	4,620
Todd Fischer	73	70	69	68	280	4,620
Bryn Parry	73	69	71	67	280	4,620
Aron Price	70	69	72	69	280	4,620
Jimmy Walker	72	68	73	67	280	4,620

WNB Golf Classic

Midland Country Club, Odessa, Texas
Par 36-36–72; 7,354 yards

October 11-14
purse, $475,000

	SCORES				TOTAL	MONEY
Brad Adamonis	68	68	72	70	278	$85,500
Vance Veazey	70	67	73	68	278	35,466.67
Ron Whittaker	67	70	70	71	278	35,466.67
Tjaart van der Walt	71	69	70	68	278	35,466.66
(Adamonis defeated Whittaker on first, Veazey on second, and van der Walt on eighth playoff hole.)						
Brian Guetz	63	71	70	75	279	16,102.50
Jim McGovern	70	70	72	67	279	16,102.50
Jon Mills	67	71	70	71	279	16,102.50
Garth Mulroy	66	71	73	69	279	16,102.50
B.J. Staten	68	69	71	71	279	16,102.50
Jason Allred	67	70	71	72	280	10,925
Miguel Carballo	73	66	71	70	280	10,925
Tom Gillis	71	67	68	74	280	10,925
Michael Letzig	65	71	76	68	280	10,925
Esteban Toledo	64	73	72	71	280	10,925
Greg Chalmers	68	65	71	77	281	7,600
Matthew Jones	71	70	67	73	281	7,600

	SCORES				TOTAL	MONEY
Adam Meyer	67	75	67	72	281	7,600
Brenden Pappas	68	67	75	71	281	7,600
John Riegger	68	68	69	76	281	7,600
Todd Demsey	72	69	72	69	282	4,980.72
Brad Ott	70	67	76	69	282	4,980.72
Jimmy Walker	71	70	72	69	282	4,980.72
Jeremy Anderson	67	67	73	75	282	4,980.71
Jeff Klauk	70	68	71	73	282	4,980.71
Deane Pappas	68	73	69	72	282	4,980.71
Bryn Parry	68	69	72	73	282	4,980.71

Chattanooga Classic

Black Creek Club, Chattanooga, Tennessee
Par 36-36–72; 7,040 yards

October 18-21
purse, $475,000

	SCORES				TOTAL	MONEY
Ron Whittaker	66	67	68	70	271	$85,500
David McKenzie	67	68	69	68	272	51,300
Tag Ridings	62	69	74	68	273	24,700
Patrick Sheehan	72	65	67	69	273	24,700
Tommy Tolles	66	71	68	68	273	24,700
Henrik Bjornstad	69	66	67	72	274	16,506.25
Brad Elder	68	69	68	69	274	16,506.25
Camilo Benedetti	66	74	67	68	275	13,775
Scott Sterling	64	67	73	71	275	13,775
Zoran Zorkic	67	69	69	70	275	13,775
Justin Bolli	68	67	72	69	276	9,737.50
Martin Laird	64	75	65	72	276	9,737.50
David Lutterus	68	71	70	67	276	9,737.50
Aron Price	68	65	70	73	276	9,737.50
Fran Quinn	69	71	68	68	276	9,737.50
Marc Turnesa	69	67	73	67	276	9,737.50
Tommy Biershenk	69	69	69	70	277	5,805.56
David Mathis	69	70	68	70	277	5,805.56
Justin Smith	67	71	72	67	277	5,805.56
Chris Thompson	71	69	70	67	277	5,805.56
Jon Turcott	66	70	70	71	277	5,805.56
Scott Gardiner	66	71	68	72	277	5,805.55
Brenden Pappas	67	69	70	71	277	5,805.55
Bryn Parry	70	63	72	72	277	5,805.55
Nicholas Thompson	66	67	69	75	277	5,805.55

Miccosukee Championship

Miccosukee Golf & Country Club, Miami, Florida
Par 36-35–71; 7,200 yards

October 25-28
purse, $575,000

	SCORES				TOTAL	MONEY
Marc Turnesa	67	63	69	70	269	$103,500
David Mathis	73	66	67	64	270	50,600
Jon Mills	67	67	66	70	270	50,600
Kelly Grunewald	68	67	72	67	274	25,300
Jeff Klauk	71	67	69	67	274	25,300
David Hearn	71	66	67	71	275	19,981.25
Patrick Sheehan	71	67	70	67	275	19,981.25
Kevin Johnson	72	66	69	69	276	17,250

	SCORES				TOTAL	MONEY
Roger Tambellini	69	69	69	69	276	17,250
Deane Pappas	69	70	67	71	277	12,745.84
Scott Weatherly	67	73	69	68	277	12,745.84
Dustin Bray	65	70	72	70	277	12,745.83
Jeff Corr	71	65	69	72	277	12,745.83
John Kimbell	68	69	72	68	277	12,745.83
Jon Turcott	68	66	72	71	277	12,745.83
Stephen Gangluff	69	70	68	71	278	8,066.43
Fabian Gomez	67	68	70	73	278	8,066.43
Ryan Hietala	69	69	71	69	278	8,066.43
David McKenzie	72	68	71	67	278	8,066.43
Nicholas Thompson	68	72	69	69	278	8,066.43
Vance Veazey	75	63	70	70	278	8,066.43
Roland Thatcher	67	68	69	74	278	8,066.42
Jason Caron	72	68	69	70	279	5,347.50
Daniel Summerhays	71	64	71	73	279	5,347.50
Esteban Toledo	71	67	69	72	279	5,347.50
Tim Wilkinson	69	69	73	68	279	5,347.50

Nationwide Tour Championship at Barona Creek

Barona Creek Golf Club, Lakeside, California
Par 35-36–71; 7,088 yards

November 1-4
purse, $775,000

	SCORES				TOTAL	MONEY
Richard Johnson	66	64	67	67	264	$139,500
Michael Letzig	60	66	73	66	265	83,700
Martin Laird	65	68	67	66	266	44,950
Tom Scherrer	66	65	67	68	266	44,950
Scott Gardiner	71	67	63	66	267	29,450
Brenden Pappas	66	66	68	67	267	29,450
David Hearn	70	66	67	65	268	25,962.50
James Driscoll	64	71	67	67	269	21,700
Kelly Grunewald	67	65	67	70	269	21,700
Garth Mulroy	69	70	65	65	269	21,700
B.J. Staten	65	66	69	69	269	21,700
Jeremy Anderson	71	68	66	65	270	17,050
Ron Whittaker	69	66	66	69	270	17,050
Gary Christian	63	69	69	70	271	13,950
Chez Reavie	67	67	68	69	271	13,950
Kyle Thompson	68	69	66	68	271	13,950
Jeff Klauk	66	71	68	67	272	11,237.50
Jim McGovern	65	66	68	73	272	11,237.50
Scott Sterling	69	67	68	68	272	11,237.50
Tjaart van der Walt	63	68	71	70	272	11,237.50
Brad Adamonis	66	70	68	69	273	7,410.94
Fabian Gomez	66	69	70	68	273	7,410.94
Skip Kendall	68	67	69	69	273	7,410.94
David Mathis	69	67	70	67	273	7,410.94
David McKenzie	67	68	69	69	273	7,410.94
Nicholas Thompson	69	67	71	66	273	7,410.94
Brock Mackenzie	67	68	68	70	273	7,410.93

Canadian Tour

San Jose International Open

Golf Club at Boulder Ridge, San Jose, California
Par 36-36–72; 6,923 yards

April 12-15
purse, US$100,000

		SCORES			TOTAL	MONEY
Adam Bland	74	67	71	67	279	US$16,000
Spencer Levin	68	70	69	72	279	6,800
Scott Gibson	69	70	71	69	279	6,800
John Ellis	73	64	70	72	279	6,800
(Bland defeated Levin, Gibson and Ellis on first playoff hole.)						
Marc Lawless	70	67	71	73	281	3,800
Michael Harris	74	71	65	71	281	3,800
Michael Walton	77	69	67	69	282	3,100
Wes Heffernan	76	69	69	68	282	3,100
Bret Guetz	73	62	69	78	282	3,100
Brendan Steele	69	67	74	74	284	2,700
Luke Hickmott	71	72	72	70	285	2,500
Jason Hartwick	73	69	72	72	286	2,200
Brian Guetz	75	70	68	73	286	2,200
Byron Smith	71	68	71	77	287	1,850
Stuart Anderson	71	70	71	75	287	1,850
Ryan Vallely	73	68	74	73	288	1,500
Eugene Smith	78	68	72	70	288	1,500
Jim Seki	77	68	72	71	288	1,500
James Love	71	72	72	73	288	1,500
Dong Yi	75	66	74	73	288	1,500
Michael Nicoletti	73	71	70	75	289	1,200
Seann Harlingten	77	68	72	72	289	1,200
Christopher Botsford	79	68	68	74	289	1,200
Madalitso Muthiya	76	71	69	74	290	1,028
Jim Lemon	75	65	77	73	290	1,028
Richard Gilkey	71	73	71	75	290	1,028
Dirk Ayers	69	70	70	81	290	1,028

Northern California Classic

Brookside Golf & Country Club, Stockton, California
Par 36-36–72; 6,720 yards

April 19-22
purse, US$100,000

		SCORES			TOTAL	MONEY
Wes Heffernan	70	66	65	67	268	US$16,000
John Ellis	70	65	67	67	269	7,800
Joseph Lanza	67	71	64	67	269	7,800
Stephen Gangluff	66	65	70	69	270	4,133
Spencer Levin	69	68	66	67	270	4,133
Adam Speirs	70	65	65	70	270	4,133
Eugene Smith	68	64	71	68	271	3,300
Matt Bettencourt	68	68	68	68	272	3,000
Bret Guetz	68	65	69	70	272	3,000
Graham DeLaet	68	67	67	71	273	2,700
James Love	67	71	71	65	274	2,400
David Walker	71	63	70	70	274	2,400

	SCORES				TOTAL	MONEY
Scott Ford	67	70	71	67	275	1,617
Scott Gibson	68	67	75	65	275	1,617
Christo Greyling	72	64	70	69	275	1,617
Darren Griff	70	69	68	68	275	1,617
Andrew Johnson	69	70	70	66	275	1,617
Hoyt McGarity	69	65	68	73	275	1,617
Kevin Pom Arleau	68	64	74	69	275	1,617
Conner Robbins	67	68	69	71	275	1,617
Jim Seki	70	69	67	69	275	1,617
Derek Gillespie	69	66	71	70	276	1,077
Scott Hawley	72	67	68	69	276	1,077
Kristoffer Marshall	72	67	64	73	276	1,077
Byron Smith	70	68	70	68	276	1,077
Todd Tanner	70	70	66	70	276	1,077
Lee Williamson	68	70	70	68	276	1,077

Corona Mazatlan Classic

El Cid Resort, Mazatlan, Mexico
Par 36-36–72; 6,470 yards

April 26-29
purse, US$125,000

	SCORES				TOTAL	MONEY
Byron Smith	66	70	66	67	269	US$20,000
Scott Hawley	65	75	63	69	272	12,000
Spencer Levin	71	68	69	66	274	7,500
Jose Trauwitz	69	68	68	71	276	5,500
Taylor Wood	70	69	69	68	276	5,500
Adam Bland	70	67	69	71	277	3,900
Graham DeLaet	74	68	68	67	277	3,900
Steve Friesen	71	66	69	71	277	3,900
Mike Mezei	70	71	70	66	277	3,900
Paulo Pinto	70	67	69	71	277	3,900
Wil Collins	69	69	70	70	278	2,750
Josh Habig	71	67	69	71	278	2,750
Kevin Kim	68	71	67	72	278	2,750
Jim Lemon	71	69	67	71	278	2,750
Bret Guetz	67	72	71	69	279	2,250
Ryan Vallely	69	73	68	70	280	2,125
Derek Gillespie	66	75	69	71	281	1,719
Ben Hayes	66	71	69	75	281	1,719
Liam Kendregan	74	71	70	66	281	1,719
Jose Antonio Maldonado	68	71	70	72	281	1,719
Anthony Rodriguez	69	69	74	69	281	1,719
Eric Wang	71	67	73	70	281	1,719
Octavio Gonzalez	74	66	71	71	282	1,344
Antonio Serna	67	69	73	73	282	1,344
Eugene Smith	67	73	69	73	282	1,344
Greg Wells	68	68	77	69	282	1,344

Ford Culiacan Open

Country Club of Culiacan, Culiacan, Mexico
Par 71; 7,212 yards

May 3-6
purse, US$125,000

	SCORES				TOTAL	MONEY
Adam Bland	64	66	69	67	266	US$20,000
Michael Harris	66	69	68	66	269	12,000

	SCORES				TOTAL	MONEY
Stuart Anderson	70	65	71	65	271	5,750
David Faught	70	66	67	68	271	5,750
Richard Gilkey	68	68	67	68	271	5,750
Derek Gillespie	66	69	66	70	271	5,750
Marc Lawless	68	68	67	69	272	3,875
Kevin Pom Arleau	67	66	72	67	272	3,875
Tim Wood	71	65	66	70	272	3,875
George Bradford	70	67	70	67	274	2,875
Matt Daniel	71	68	69	66	274	2,875
Graham DeLaet	68	69	71	66	274	2,875
Octavio Gonzalez	68	68	66	72	274	2,875
Scott Hawley	68	69	68	69	274	2,875
Jon Abbott	66	71	69	69	275	2,125
Josh Geary	70	69	69	67	275	2,125
Mark Warman	70	68	64	73	275	2,125
Wil Collins	69	68	67	72	276	1,589
Chris Cureton	63	72	73	68	276	1,589
Steve Friesen	66	69	68	73	276	1,589
Hoyt McGarity	71	65	70	70	276	1,589
Mike Mezei	68	66	75	67	276	1,589
Paulo Pinto	65	70	70	71	276	1,589
Antonio Serna	72	65	68	71	276	1,589
Alex Quiroz	71	65	71	70	277	1,312

Riviera Nayarit Classic

Club de Golf El Tigre, Nuevo Vallarta, Mexico
Par 71; 7,230 yards

May 10-13
purse, US$125,000

	SCORES				TOTAL	MONEY
Wes Heffernan	71	62	65	68	266	US$20,000
Anthony Rodriguez	69	69	68	65	271	9,750
Adam Speirs	67	67	69	68	271	9,750
Adam Bland	69	70	65	68	272	5,500
Stephen Gangluff	69	68	68	67	272	5,500
Travis Johnson	69	70	69	67	275	4,167
Alan McLean	70	69	71	65	275	4,167
Brendan Steele	70	69	66	70	275	4,167
Graham DeLaet	67	66	72	71	276	3,500
Jose Antonio Maldonado	71	67	69	69	276	3,500
Luke Hickmott	71	69	65	72	277	3,125
Michael Harris	70	72	65	71	278	2,750
Russell Surber	74	70	67	67	278	2,750
James Lepp	70	70	76	63	279	2,312
Oscar Serna	69	72	68	70	279	2,312
Mike Grob	70	68	71	71	280	1,937
Joseph Lanza	74	67	69	70	280	1,937
Paulo Pinto	73	69	69	69	280	1,937
Danny Sahl	69	71	74	66	280	1,937
Anders Hultman	72	73	70	66	281	1,562
Calvin Kupeyan	67	76	67	71	281	1,562
Jose Trauwitz	68	76	64	73	281	1,562
Pablo Del Grosso	77	68	66	71	282	1,344
Oscar Fraustro	69	73	68	72	282	1,344
Octavio Gonzalez	71	73	71	67	282	1,344
Chad Spencer	71	68	74	69	282	1,344

Iberostar Riviera Maya Open

Iberostar Playa Paraiso Golf Club, Riviera Maya, Mexico
Par 36-36–72; 6,640 yards

May 17-20
purse, US$125,000

	SCORES				TOTAL	MONEY
Spencer Levin	67	66	69	65	267	US$20,000
Derek Gillespie	66	69	66	67	268	12,000
Anders Hultman	69	66	71	64	270	7,500
Travis Johnson	70	71	67	66	274	4,906
Joseph Lanza	70	72	67	65	274	4,906
Hoyt McGarity	75	69	65	65	274	4,906
Mike Mezei	72	64	67	71	274	4,906
Wil Collins	72	64	72	67	275	3,500
Richard Gilkey	65	65	73	72	275	3,500
Bret Guetz	70	66	68	71	275	3,500
Josh Habig	65	71	70	69	275	3,500
David Faught	74	66	67	69	276	2,750
Adam Short	68	68	70	70	276	2,750
James Lepp	69	69	69	71	278	2,312
Alan McLean	71	67	68	72	278	2,312
Graham DeLaet	70	67	69	73	279	2,062
Octavio Gonzalez	68	71	72	68	279	2,062
Liam Kendregan	67	72	73	68	280	1,875
Hidemichi Haginomori	72	70	69	70	281	1,575
Scott Hawley	69	73	67	72	281	1,575
Jose Antonio Maldonado	75	67	70	69	281	1,575
Chris Parra	71	67	74	69	281	1,575
Antonio Serna	71	72	70	68	281	1,575
Tim Wood	69	73	67	73	282	1,375
Stuart Anderson	66	72	70	75	283	1,254
Fabian Gomez	70	76	68	69	283	1,254
Dustin Risdon	70	74	68	71	283	1,254

Times Colonist Open

Gorge Vale Golf Club, Victoria, British Columbia
Par 36-36–72; 6,820 yards

June 14-17
purse, C$150,000

	SCORES				TOTAL	MONEY
Spencer Levin	70	65	71	71	277	C$24,000
Jon Abbott	69	66	72	73	280	11,700
Michael Walton	70	67	68	75	280	11,700
Mike Grob	70	73	69	69	281	7,200
Ben Hayes	70	67	74	72	283	5,250
Anders Hultman	72	74	70	67	283	5,250
Eugene Smith	70	72	70	71	283	5,250
Tom Stankowski	73	71	69	70	283	5,250
Josh Habig	70	71	71	72	284	4,200
Byron Smith	72	71	71	70	284	4,200
John Ellis	72	70	69	74	285	3,300
Steve Friesen	69	70	73	73	285	3,300
Derek Gillespie	70	67	75	73	285	3,300
Joseph Lanza	70	70	69	76	285	3,300
Stuart Anderson	70	71	71	74	286	2,203
Chris Cureton	73	68	71	74	286	2,203
Brad Heaven	72	71	74	69	286	2,203
Liam Kendregan	72	70	71	73	286	2,203
Randy Lowry	72	68	75	71	286	2,203
Anthony Rodriguez	68	72	72	74	286	2,203

	SCORES				TOTAL	MONEY
Danny Sahl	70	72	66	78	286	2,203
Russell Surber	68	72	72	74	286	2,203
Matt Bettencourt	76	69	69	73	287	1,613
Greg Machtaler	71	74	71	71	287	1,613
Kevin Pom Arleau	69	69	74	75	287	1,613
Dong Yi	73	70	69	75	287	1,613

Greater Vancouver Charity Classic

Hazelmere Golf Club, Surrey, British Columbia
Par 36-36–72; 6,806 yards

June 21-24
purse, C$100,000

	SCORES				TOTAL	MONEY
James Lepp	69	66	71	68	274	C$16,000
Anthony Rodriguez	67	72	69	70	278	7,800
Eugene Smith	73	70	66	69	278	7,800
Matt Bettencourt	69	69	68	73	279	4,133
John Ellis	68	68	72	71	279	4,133
Scott McNeil	67	70	70	72	279	4,133
Hidemichi Haginomori	74	70	69	67	280	3,200
Liam Kendregan	73	70	69	68	280	3,200
Michael Walton	71	70	69	71	281	2,900
Andres Gonzales	74	67	70	71	282	2,300
Mike Grob	74	68	69	71	282	2,300
Scott Hawley	70	71	70	71	282	2,300
Luke Hickmott	68	73	68	73	282	2,300
Joseph Lanza	68	75	67	72	282	2,300
Brad Heaven	76	68	67	72	283	1,800
Jon Abbott	70	71	71	72	284	1,600
Scott Hend	70	70	76	68	284	1,600
Rafael Lee	72	72	69	71	284	1,600
Travis Andrews	74	69	71	71	285	1,207
Scott Gibson	68	71	71	75	285	1,207
Richard Lee	71	71	70	73	285	1,207
John Lieber	73	70	67	75	285	1,207
Conner Robbins	73	68	72	72	285	1,207
Richard Scott	70	72	69	74	285	1,207
Ryan Thornberry	71	72	71	71	285	1,207

ATB Financial Classic

Calgary Elks Lodge & Golf Club, Calgary, Alberta
Par 36-36–72; 6,810 yards

June 28-July 1
purse, C$150,000

	SCORES				TOTAL	MONEY
Mike Grob	66	67	65	66	264	C$24,000
Alan McLean	66	65	66	70	267	14,400
Matt Bettencourt	69	62	71	67	269	7,400
Josh Geary	63	70	67	69	269	7,400
Joseph Lanza	69	65	68	67	269	7,400
Marc Lawless	71	67	65	69	272	5,400
Brad Heaven	72	64	66	71	273	4,800
Ryan Thornberry	70	67	67	69	273	4,800
Derek Gillespie	66	68	70	70	274	4,050
Alex Quiroz	68	68	67	71	274	4,050
Richard Scott	70	67	69	68	274	4,050
*Kris Wasylowich	69	67	68	70	274	

	SCORES				TOTAL	MONEY
Ryan Camp	70	66	69	70	275	3,038
John Ellis	68	68	69	70	275	3,038
Ben Hayes	71	69	70	65	275	3,038
Chad Spencer	67	71	70	67	275	3,038
Robert Hamilton	68	69	67	72	276	2,250
Jason Hartwick	70	67	67	72	276	2,250
Scott Hawley	69	71	69	67	276	2,250
Jens Nilsson	68	68	72	68	276	2,250
Dustin Risdon	75	66	68	67	276	2,250
Jon Abbott	70	71	69	67	277	1,688
Adam Bland	70	67	73	67	277	1,688
Chris Cureton	66	69	73	69	277	1,688
Bret Guetz	70	71	67	69	277	1,688
Russell Surber	66	72	67	72	277	1,688
Jose Trauwitz	69	69	68	71	277	1,688

Telus Edmonton Open

Glendale Golf & Country Club, Edmonton, Alberta
Par 36-35–71; 6,991 yards

July 5-8
purse, C$150,000

	SCORES				TOTAL	MONEY
Dustin Risdon	70	63	65	67	265	C$24,000
Alan McLean	66	65	70	65	266	14,400
Kevin Kim	72	63	67	66	268	9,000
Michael Harris	66	69	68	67	270	6,200
Joseph Lanza	69	67	66	68	270	6,200
Spencer Levin	66	66	72	66	270	6,200
Josh Geary	69	68	65	69	271	4,500
Mike Grob	66	66	70	69	271	4,500
Scott Hawley	68	67	69	67	271	4,500
Marc Lawless	70	67	71	63	271	4,500
Graham DeLaet	73	65	66	68	272	2,800
Derek Gillespie	67	67	67	71	272	2,800
Andres Gonzales	69	66	70	67	272	2,800
Ben Hayes	70	67	65	70	272	2,800
Wes Heffernan	68	68	69	67	272	2,800
James Lepp	67	68	73	64	272	2,800
Jim Seki	70	69	67	66	272	2,800
Pan Singhaseni	67	65	68	72	272	2,800
Ryan Thornberry	67	68	70	67	272	2,800
John Ellis	68	69	69	67	273	1,912
Rafael Lee	69	67	70	67	273	1,912
Dirk Ayers	70	64	69	71	274	1,581
Adam Bland	73	67	68	66	274	1,581
Brett Burgeson	70	70	66	68	274	1,581
Glen Dick	69	65	73	67	274	1,581
Jason Hartwick	70	67	68	69	274	1,581
Alex Quiroz	67	68	69	70	274	1,581
Eugene Smith	69	69	67	69	274	1,581

Free Press Manitoba Classic

Pine Ridge Golf Club, Winnipeg, Manitoba
Par 37-35–72; 6,622 yards

July 12-15
purse, C$150,000

	SCORES				TOTAL	MONEY
Mike Mezei	68	65	70	68	271	C$24,000
Derek Gillespie	69	69	69	65	272	14,400
Dustin Risdon	68	70	65	72	275	8,100
Craig Taylor	72	70	66	67	275	8,100
Liam Kendregan	69	69	68	71	277	6,000
Alan McLean	67	69	70	72	278	5,175
Luke Swilor	69	70	70	69	278	5,175
Andy Matthews	71	70	69	69	279	4,650
Stuart Anderson	69	72	72	67	280	3,600
Adam Bland	67	72	72	69	280	3,600
Ryan Carter	71	71	70	68	280	3,600
Matt Daniel	72	71	73	64	280	3,600
Kevin Pom Arleau	71	73	72	64	280	3,600
Brendan Steele	73	66	70	71	280	3,600
Bret Guetz	70	72	69	70	281	2,475
Josh Habig	70	70	72	69	281	2,475
Marc Lawless	71	73	68	69	281	2,475
Danny Sahl	67	70	75	69	281	2,475
Matt Bettencourt	71	70	70	71	282	1,975
Scott Gibson	74	70	71	67	282	1,975
Brandon Knight	76	66	69	71	282	1,975
Stephen Dixon	73	70	74	66	283	1,650
John Ellis	74	67	70	72	283	1,650
Scott Ford	73	71	73	66	283	1,650
Rafael Lee	71	70	75	67	283	1,650
Rob McMillan	73	71	73	66	283	1,650

Desjardins Montreal Open

Saint-Raphael Golf Club, Ile Bizard, Quebec
Par 36-36–72; 7,050 yards

August 16-19
purse, C$200,000

	SCORES				TOTAL	MONEY
Brent Schwarzrock	68	66	68	62	264	C$32,000
Byron Smith	69	66	66	63	264	19,200
(Schwarzrock defeated Smith on first playoff hole.)						
Spencer Levin	65	68	68	71	272	12,000
Jason Hartwick	71	65	70	69	275	9,600
Andres Gonzales	70	68	74	64	276	7,600
Wes Heffernan	63	67	74	72	276	7,600
Matt Bettencourt	72	69	66	70	277	6,200
Dustin Risdon	68	69	73	67	277	6,200
Justin Snelling	68	67	71	71	277	6,200
Stuart Anderson	68	72	68	70	278	4,600
Graham DeLaet	72	67	71	68	278	4,600
Brian Guetz	68	71	71	68	278	4,600
Joseph Lanza	69	67	71	71	278	4,600
Richard Scott	72	70	67	69	278	4,600
Richard Gilkey	68	69	74	69	280	3,500
Kevin Pom Arleau	67	72	77	64	280	3,500
Roberto Castro	65	73	72	71	281	2,820
Wil Collins	70	70	73	68	281	2,820
Lee Curry	68	72	73	68	281	2,820
Bret Guetz	71	69	68	73	281	2,820

	SCORES				TOTAL	MONEY
Brendan Steele	69	71	73	68	281	2,820
Mike Grob	69	72	72	69	282	2,200
Eugene Smith	70	70	74	68	282	2,200
Tom Stankowski	67	71	75	69	282	2,200
Chris Wall	72	70	73	67	282	2,200
Mark Warman	69	68	77	68	282	2,200

Jane Rogers Championship of Mississauga

Lakeview Golf Club, Mississauga, Ontario
Par 35-35–70; 6,404 yards

August 23-26
purse, C$125,000

	SCORES				TOTAL	MONEY
Byron Smith	70	65	66	63	264	C$20,000
Derek Gillespie	71	63	66	65	265	12,000
Lee Curry	66	68	67	66	267	7,500
Ryan Horn	69	72	62	68	271	6,000
Mike Grob	71	65	66	70	272	4,750
James Lepp	69	73	62	68	272	4,750
Wes Heffernan	69	64	67	73	273	4,000
Tom Stankowski	68	68	68	69	273	4,000
Graham DeLaet	70	71	65	68	274	3,375
Kevin Kisner	68	68	70	68	274	3,375
Adam Speirs	66	73	67	68	274	3,375
Travis Bertoni	69	68	70	68	275	2,531
Josh Habig	68	67	71	69	275	2,531
John Shin	66	68	72	69	275	2,531
Eugene Smith	70	72	66	67	275	2,531
Ryan Carter	70	71	64	71	276	1,823
Brian Guetz	68	68	69	71	276	1,823
Brad Heaven	64	72	67	73	276	1,823
Andrew Parr	66	68	73	69	276	1,823
Dustin Risdon	66	72	69	69	276	1,823
Ryan Yip	69	72	70	65	276	1,823
Matt Bettencourt	68	72	69	68	277	1,375
George Bradford	64	73	72	68	277	1,375
Danny King	73	67	67	70	277	1,375
Rafael Lee	69	69	70	69	277	1,375
Craig Scott	66	71	70	70	277	1,375

Canadian Tour Championship

National Pines Golf Club, Barrie, Ontario
Par 36-36–72; 7,013 yards

August 30-September 2
purse, C$200,000

	SCORES				TOTAL	MONEY
Bret Guetz	67	70	65	72	274	C$32,000
Byron Smith	71	72	70	62	275	19,200
John Ellis	70	72	64	72	278	12,000
Mike Grob	70	71	68	72	281	9,600
Joseph Lanza	68	73	70	71	282	8,000
Adam Bland	69	75	72	67	283	6,667
Graham DeLaet	70	73	69	71	283	6,667
Rob Johnson	72	69	69	73	283	6,667
Marc Lawless	71	71	71	71	284	5,600
Tom Stankowski	68	74	73	69	284	5,600
Matt Bettencourt	72	72	76	65	285	4,400

	SCORES			TOTAL	MONEY
Anders Hultman	74	74	68	69	285	4,400
Spencer Levin	74	73	64	74	285	4,400
Brendan Steele	70	73	72	70	285	4,400
George Bradford	72	73	70	71	286	3,500
Jim Lemon	70	71	69	76	286	3,500
Jorge Corral	69	78	73	67	287	2,820
Derek Gillespie	68	75	70	74	287	2,820
Scott Hawley	69	73	73	72	287	2,820
Wes Heffernan	71	70	69	77	287	2,820
Rob Oppenheim	72	74	69	72	287	2,820
Scott Gibson	75	69	73	71	288	2,153
Liam Kendregan	69	74	74	71	288	2,153
Kevin Kim	69	71	72	76	288	2,153
Ed McGlasson	73	72	69	74	288	2,153
Adam Speirs	74	71	70	73	288	2,153
Ryan Yip	70	73	72	73	288	2,153

Tour de las Americas (South America)

Colombia Masters

Country Club de Bogota, Bogota, Colombia
Par 35-36–71; 7,099 yards

February 1-4
purse, US$175,000

	SCORES				TOTAL	MONEY
Edoardo Molinari	69	69	72	69	279	US$28,000
Gustavo Mendoza	70	72	69	68	279	19,250
(Molinari defeated Mendoza on second playoff hole.)						
Camilo Benedetti	69	73	72	67	281	11,375
Michael Sims	70	67	70	74	281	11,375
Michael Lorenzo-Vera	70	75	70	68	283	6,562.50
Gary Clark	69	70	75	69	283	6,562.50
Brad Adamonis	72	69	72	70	283	6,562.50
Alvaro Salto	71	69	69	74	283	6,562.50
Ivo Giner	70	73	77	64	284	3,605
Sebastian Fernandez	67	73	75	69	284	3,605
Leif Westerberg	72	70	72	70	284	3,605
Mark Tullo	68	70	75	71	284	3,605
Antii Ahokas	72	67	71	74	284	3,605
Blaum Ryan	74	70	74	67	285	2,300.22
Gustavo Rojas	70	71	75	69	285	2,300.22
Diego Vanegas	72	72	72	69	285	2,300.22
Rodolfo Gonzalez	68	74	72	71	285	2,300.22
Hernan Rey	73	72	68	72	285	2,300.22
Juan Ignacio Gil	69	70	73	73	285	2,300.22
Miguel Carballo	72	69	71	73	285	2,300.22
Mike Capone	70	72	70	73	285	2,300.22
Kevin Harper	73	68	70	74	285	2,300.22

Kai Fieberg Costa Rica Open

Cariari Country Club, San Jose, Costa Rica
Par 35-36–71; 6,577 yards

February 8-11
purse, US$175,000

	SCORES				TOTAL	MONEY
Miguel Rodriguez	70	67	66	72	275	US$28,000
Juan Abbate	67	72	70	67	276	15,750
Gustavo Acosta	66	72	70	68	276	15,750
*Alvaro Ortiz	68	68	72	69	277	
Matthew King	70	69	70	70	279	9,625
Felipe Aguilar	73	68	66	72	279	9,625
Anthony Snobeck	72	68	71	69	280	6,300
Edoardo Molinari	73	70	68	69	280	6,300
Paulo Pinto	71	69	72	69	281	4,316.66
Fabian Gomez	66	75	70	70	281	4,316.66
Miguel Carballo	72	68	70	71	281	4,316.66
Toni Karjalainen	73	68	73	68	282	3,412.50
Rafael Gomez	73	72	67	70	282	3,412.50
Hernan Rey	71	72	71	69	283	3,150
Diego Vanegas	69	74	72	69	284	2,712.50
Clark Burroughs	73	72	70	69	284	2,712.50
Julio Zapata	71	68	73	72	284	2,712.50
Magnus A. Carlsson	72	71	69	72	284	2,712.50
Jamie Little	71	75	70	69	285	2,187.50
Manuel Merizalde	71	70	74	70	285	2,187.50

Guatemala Open

Hacienda Neuva Country Club, Guatemala City, Guatemala
Par 36-36–72; 7,043 yards

February 15-18
purse, US$150,000

	SCORES				TOTAL	MONEY
Jamie Donaldson	63	65	69	68	265	US$24,000
Emilio Dominguez	71	67	61	67	266	16,500
Ivo Giner	70	66	68	70	274	10,500
Pablo Del Grosso	69	70	69	67	275	7,500
Fabian Gomez	73	66	68	68	275	7,500
Rodolfo Gonzalez	70	68	67	70	275	7,500
Peter Kaensche	69	70	71	67	277	3,975
Fredrik Widmark	71	70	66	70	277	3,975
Cristophe Brazillier	69	71	66	71	277	3,975
Anders Hansen	70	69	65	73	277	3,975
Felipe Aguilar	71	69	67	71	278	3,000
Angel Franco	67	70	73	69	279	2,775
Jan-Are Larsen	68	69	69	73	279	2,775
Miguel Rodriguez	70	73	67	70	280	2,110.71
Rafael Gomez	69	73	67	71	280	2,110.71
Richard Treis	73	67	68	72	280	2,110.71
Manuel Merizalde	69	73	66	72	280	2,110.71
Daniel De Leon	73	66	66	75	280	2,110.71
Lasse Jensen	69	70	65	76	280	2,110.71
Julio Zapata	68	67	68	77	280	2,110.71

Abierto Visa del Centro

Cordoba Golf Club, Cordoba, Argentina
Par 35-36–71; 6,824 yards

April 12-15
purse, US$65,000

	SCORES				TOTAL	MONEY
Angel Cabrera	66	75	73	65	279	US$11,333
Raul Fretes	72	72	70	67	281	6,666
Cesar Monasterio	75	73	67	70	285	4,666
Jorge Berendt	68	71	75	72	286	3,833
Juan Abbate	74	72	69	72	287	2,391.25
Rafael Echenique	78	74	69	66	287	2,391.25
Rodolfo Gonzalez	71	69	68	79	287	2,391.25
Eduardo Romero	71	73	69	74	287	2,391.25
Pablo Del Grosso	70	68	78	72	288	1,666
Miguel Fernandez	71	77	68	73	289	1,433
Sebastian Fernandez	75	74	70	70	289	1,433
Nicolas Sedler	71	70	75	73	289	1,433
Carlos Cardeza	70	75	73	72	290	1,300
*Alan Wagner	73	72	73	72	290	
Angel Franco	73	77	71	71	292	1,233
Paulo Pinto	72	75	72	74	293	1,166
*Pablo Lozada	75	72	71	76	294	
Francisco Ojeda	70	76	74	74	294	1,083
Gustavo Rojas	78	70	76	70	294	1,083
Cesar Costilla	72	77	74	72	295	983
Rafael Gomez	72	73	76	74	295	983
Walter Miranda	72	72	77	74	295	983
Mark Tullo	79	69	78	69	295	983

Canal i Abierto de Venezuela

Valle Arriba Golf Club, Caracas, Venezuela
Par 35-35–70; 6,372 yards

May 3-6
purse, US$70,000

	SCORES				TOTAL	MONEY
Jesus Amaya	68	67	64	69	268	US$12,600
Sebastian Saavedra	68	69	67	67	271	6,790
Fabian Gomez	70	68	66	67	271	6,790
Miguel Martinez	63	64	73	73	273	4,480
Juan Berastegui	68	67	74	65	274	2,986.66
Rafael Ponce	70	69	68	67	274	2,986.66
Pablo Del Grosso	69	66	69	70	274	2,986.66
Michael Brice	71	70	70	64	275	1,750
Rafael Romero	69	69	72	65	275	1,750
Wilfredo Morales	71	67	72	65	275	1,750
Alexander Parada	66	70	71	68	275	1,750
Angel Romero	67	69	69	71	276	1,400
Alvaro Pinedo	68	67	74	68	277	1,260
Richard Rojas	69	68	71	69	277	1,260
Wolmer Murillo	67	68	71	71	277	1,260
Otto Solis	70	74	66	68	278	1,152
Jesus Osmar	70	70	70	69	279	1,100
Jesus Rivas	74	70	69	67	280	965
Juan Nutt	74	66	71	69	280	965
Miguel Fernandez	74	66	69	71	280	965
Agustin Jauretche	68	69	70	73	280	965

Torneo de Maestros

Olivos Golf Club, Buenos Aires, Argentina
Par 36-35–71; 6,740 yards

October 24-27
purse, US$135,000

	SCORES				TOTAL	MONEY
Angel Cabrera	68	73	71	65	277	US$20,000
Ricardo Gonzalez	70	68	72	67	277	12,000
(Cabrera defeated Gonzalez on first playoff hole.)						
Daniel Vancsik	72	72	71	66	281	7,000
Sebastian Saavedra	73	69	70	70	282	5,901
Rodolfo Gonzalez	72	72	69	71	284	5,000
Eduardo Argiro	71	77	70	67	285	4,501
*Federico Cabrera	71	71	72	71	285	
Christoph Guenther	69	77	68	72	286	4,000
Philippe Gasnier	73	71	71	72	287	3,501
Rafael Gomez	70	78	69	71	288	3,100
Miguel Guzman	75	72	70	71	288	3,100
Daniel Barbetti	76	71	73	69	289	2,800
*Matias O'Curry	71	72	71	75	289	
Pablo Acuna	72	77	69	72	290	2,701
Jorge Berendt	75	70	72	74	291	2,533.50
Walter Miranda	73	75	72	71	291	2,533.50
Cesar Costilla	72	72	69	79	292	2,190.50
Emilio Dominguez	79	69	73	71	292	2,190.50
Raul Fretes	75	72	72	73	292	2,190.50
Manuel Garcia	72	73	72	75	292	2,190.50
Jose Garrido	76	71	70	75	292	2,190.50
Martin Monguzzi	76	73	67	76	292	2,190.50
Julio Noguera	73	71	72	76	292	2,190.50
Paulo Pinto	73	71	74	74	292	2,190.50

Abierto de Chile

Club de Golf de Granadilla, Vina del Mar, Chile
Par 36-36–72; 6,479 yards

November 1-4
purse, US$60,000

	SCORES				TOTAL	MONEY
Angel Fernandez	68	68	73	70	279	US$10,800
Felipe Aguilar	72	70	67	72	281	6,840
Gustavo Acosta	67	72	69	75	283	4,800
Luis Berrios	72	73	68	71	284	3,840
Angel Franco	70	72	70	73	285	3,120
*Juan Cortes	74	71	69	73	287	
Luis Moreno	73	72	73	71	289	2,280
Rafael Ponce	74	72	70	73	289	2,280
Daniel Barbetti	79	69	77	65	290	1,764
Pablo Acuna	70	75	76	69	290	1,764
Francisco Ojeda	73	75	75	68	291	1,524
Francisco Cerda	72	76	73	70	291	1,524
Alejandro Villavicencio	72	75	75	70	292	1,314
Alan Wagner	67	77	76	72	292	1,314
Cristian Leon	75	75	74	69	293	1,134
Cristian Caballero	78	70	75	70	293	1,134
*Santiago Russi	72	71	76	74	293	
Christoph Guenther	67	74	77	75	293	1,134
Diego Vanegas	72	72	73	76	293	1,134
Francisco Valdes	76	73	74	71	294	924
Max Alverio	71	78	71	74	294	924
Nilson Cabrera	71	74	73	76	294	924

Abierto de San Luis

Villa Mercedes Golf Club, San Luis, Argentina
Par 71; 6,851 yards

November 22-25
purse, US$140,000

	SCORES				TOTAL	MONEY
Emilio Dominguez	72	71	69	67	279	US$22,844
Cesar Costilla	75	73	62	70	280	12,849.50
Rafael Gomez	72	69	68	71	280	12,849.50
Gustavo Acosta	69	71	68	73	281	7,852.50
Diego Vanegas	70	78	67	66	281	7,852.50
Luciano Dodda	75	73	65	71	284	5,711
Sergio Acevedo	77	72	67	69	285	3,997.33
Jesus Amaya	72	72	69	72	285	3,997.33
Roberto Coceres	73	71	68	73	285	3,997.33
Clodomiro Carranza	71	74	75	66	286	2,998
Paulo Pinto	77	71	70	68	286	2,998
Felix Cordoba	70	75	70	72	287	2,498.25
Juan Ignacio Gil	75	66	67	79	287	2,498.25
Rodolfo Gonzalez	69	77	72	69	287	2,498.25
Gustavo Rojas	74	71	71	71	287	2,498.25
Ricardo Aranda	73	74	68	73	288	2,070
Miguel Rodriguez	70	74	71	73	288	2,070
Eduardo Argiro	75	74	69	71	289	1,607.20
Ramiro Goti	68	75	74	72	289	1,607.20
Martin Monguzzi	76	73	68	72	289	1,607.20
Rafael Ponce	75	76	70	68	289	1,607.20
Jose Vega	74	72	69	74	289	1,607.20

Abierto del Litoral Personal

Rosario Golf Club, Rosario, Argentina
Par 35-35–70; 6,539 yards

November 29-December 2
purse, US$170,000

	SCORES				TOTAL	MONEY
Miguel Rodriguez	68	66	68	69	271	US$28,000
Andres Romero	63	69	71	69	272	19,250
Fabian Gomez	66	67	70	71	274	11,375
Rafael Gomez	66	72	69	67	274	11,375
Pablo Acuna	67	73	65	70	275	8,750
Sebastian Saavedra	68	74	70	66	278	7,000
Ryan Carter	65	70	76	68	279	4,637.50
Cesar Costilla	72	69	69	69	279	4,637.50
Oscar Floren	73	70	64	72	279	4,637.50
Eduardo Romero	69	69	68	73	279	4,637.50
Ignacio Sanchez-Palencia	76	70	69	65	280	3,500
Joakim Rask	75	71	68	67	281	3,325
Luciano Dodda	71	71	75	65	282	2,975
Gustavo Rojas	70	73	74	65	282	2,975
Gonzalo Ruiz	68	69	70	75	282	2,975
Diego Larrazabal	71	74	71	67	283	2,450
Elvio Ruiz	69	75	69	70	283	2,450
Mark Tullo	66	73	72	72	283	2,450
Benjamin Alvarado	74	69	71	70	284	1,954
Philippe Gasnier	71	70	71	72	284	1,954
Estanislao Goya	72	68	73	71	284	1,954

Abierto Visa de la Republica

Buenos Aires Golf Club, Buenos Aires, Argentina
Par 35-35–70; 6,902 yards

December 6-9
purse, US$200,000

	SCORES				TOTAL	MONEY
Marco Ruiz	71	69	66	69	275	US$32,000
Daniel Vancsik	70	70	68	69	277	22,000
Angel Cabrera	66	68	70	76	280	11,000
Lorenzo Gagli	75	64	72	69	280	11,000
Alexandre Rocha	69	68	73	70	280	11,000
Eduardo Romero	67	68	73	72	280	11,000
Gustavo Acosta	73	68	70	71	282	5,600
Cesar Monasterio	74	70	71	67	282	5,600
Isaac Weintraub	69	68	72	73	282	5,600
Benjamin Alvarado	71	66	77	69	283	4,066.66
Rafael Echenique	72	69	73	69	283	4,066.66
Vicente Fernandez	72	69	73	69	283	4,066.66
Mark Haastrup	70	73	73	68	284	3,300
Bruno Lecuona	69	70	74	71	284	3,300
Mark Tullo	76	67	70	71	284	3,300
Bernd Wiesberger	73	70	70	71	284	3,300
Ricardo Gonzalez	71	73	71	70	285	2,600
Anders Hansen	72	73	71	69	285	2,600
Andres Romero	68	71	75	71	285	2,600
Jesus Amaya	71	74	70	71	286	2,150
Ricardo Aranda	69	73	72	72	286	2,150

European Tours

Joburg Open
See African Tours chapter.

The Royal Trophy
See Asia/Japan Tours chapter.

Abu Dhabi Golf Championship

Abu Dhabi Golf Club, Abu Dhabi, United Arab Emirates
Par 36-36–72; 7,433 yards

January 18-21
purse, €1,556,541

	SCORES				TOTAL	MONEY
Paul Casey	71	68	67	65	271	€257,876.56
Peter Hanson	70	68	66	68	272	134,388.55
Miguel Angel Jimenez	71	65	68	68	272	134,388.55
Chris DiMarco	69	70	68	66	273	77,363.74
Retief Goosen	66	72	68	68	274	55,392.44
Padraig Harrington	68	67	68	71	274	55,392.44
Jean-Francois Lucquin	70	69	67	68	274	55,392.44
Henrik Stenson	66	72	70	67	275	38,681.87
Robert-Jan Derksen	70	69	69	68	276	32,802.23
Phillip Price	69	65	71	71	276	32,802.23
Phillip Archer	63	75	71	68	277	26,664.70
Nick Dougherty	66	72	70	69	277	26,664.70
Gary Orr	70	68	70	69	277	26,664.70
Stephen Dodd	69	70	72	67	278	21,378.18
Alastair Forsyth	71	66	69	72	278	21,378.18
Sergio Garcia	68	72	69	69	278	21,378.18
Thongchai Jaidee	68	71	67	72	278	21,378.18
Robert Karlsson	73	67	69	69	278	21,378.18
Colin Montgomerie	69	71	69	69	278	21,378.18
James Hepworth	68	71	68	72	279	16,573.03
Shiv Kapur	70	66	68	75	279	16,573.03
Paul Lawrie	67	72	69	71	279	16,573.03
Andrew McLardy	70	72	70	67	279	16,573.03
Marcel Siem	71	72	67	69	279	16,573.03
Richard Sterne	70	67	71	71	279	16,573.03
Graeme Storm	68	70	69	72	279	16,573.03
Kyron Sullivan	72	71	70	66	279	16,573.03
Steve Webster	70	73	69	67	279	16,573.03
Emanuele Canonica	70	73	68	69	280	12,864.49
Christian Cevaer	73	68	71	68	280	12,864.49
Niclas Fasth	71	69	73	67	280	12,864.49
Ian Garbutt	69	74	69	68	280	12,864.49
Richard Green	67	72	69	72	280	12,864.49
Raphael Jacquelin	70	71	68	71	280	12,864.49
Anthony Wall	68	75	66	71	280	12,864.49
Alejandro Canizares	75	68	70	68	281	10,830.92
David Carter	71	68	71	71	281	10,830.92
*Julien Guerrier	68	72	69	72	281	
Garry Houston	70	67	71	73	281	10,830.92
Gary Murphy	72	68	68	73	281	10,830.92

	SCORES				TOTAL	MONEY
Peter Hedblom	71	69	72	70	282	9,283.65
Maarten Lafeber	71	70	71	70	282	9,283.65
Graeme McDowell	71	72	69	70	282	9,283.65
Nick O'Hern	68	68	75	71	282	9,283.65
Alessandro Tadini	70	66	71	75	282	9,283.65
Oliver Wilson	70	72	73	67	282	9,283.65
Thomas Bjorn	71	71	71	70	283	7,891.10
Gregory Bourdy	70	73	72	68	283	7,891.10
Damien McGrane	72	68	71	72	283	7,891.10
Soren Hansen	73	69	69	73	284	6,962.74
James Kingston	71	68	70	75	284	6,962.74
Alvaro Quiros	70	70	75	69	284	6,962.74
Oliver Fisher	68	71	73	73	285	5,570.19
Stephen Gallacher	70	73	71	71	285	5,570.19
Andrew Marshall	73	70	73	69	285	5,570.19
Juan Parron	71	71	70	73	285	5,570.19
Brett Rumford	70	70	72	73	285	5,570.19
Miles Tunnicliff	72	71	73	69	285	5,570.19
Gary Emerson	67	70	74	75	286	4,177.64
Kenneth Ferrie	74	68	75	69	286	4,177.64
Matthew Millar	73	69	75	69	286	4,177.64
David Park	73	70	71	72	286	4,177.64
Chinarat Phadungsil	71	71	73	71	286	4,177.64
Mark Pilkington	73	70	69	74	286	4,177.64
Robert Rock	69	72	71	74	286	4,177.64
Benn Barham	75	67	72	73	287	3,404
Soren Kjeldsen	75	68	71	73	287	3,404
Francesco Molinari	69	71	74	73	287	3,404
Yasin Ali	71	70	71	76	288	2,699.43
Notah Begay	72	71	74	71	288	2,699.43
John Bickerton	74	68	72	74	288	2,699.43
Ariel Canete	68	74	74	72	288	2,699.43
Terry Price	74	69	71	74	288	2,699.43
Markus Brier	73	69	73	74	289	2,315
Lee Slattery	71	70	76	74	291	2,312

Commercialbank Qatar Masters

Doha Golf Club, Doha, Qatar
Par 36-36–72; 7,355 yards

January 25-28
purse, €1,706,653

	SCORES				TOTAL	MONEY
Retief Goosen	65	68	71	69	273	€282,743.30
Nick O'Hern	66	69	69	70	274	188,495.53
Ernie Els	69	71	68	67	275	106,200.31
Stuart Appleby	70	69	71	66	276	72,044.30
Richard Green	68	65	71	72	276	72,044.30
Graeme McDowell	73	68	68	67	276	72,044.30
Andres Romero	70	71	67	69	277	46,653.49
Henrik Stenson	68	68	70	71	277	46,653.49
Thongchai Jaidee	71	67	72	68	278	35,965.60
Liang Wen-chong	69	67	72	70	278	35,965.60
Chris DiMarco	73	66	71	69	279	27,720.66
Oliver Fisher	73	68	70	68	279	27,720.66
Soren Kjeldsen	72	69	66	72	279	27,720.66
Paul Lawrie	69	67	71	72	279	27,720.66
David Lynn	73	69	71	66	279	27,720.66
Nick Dougherty	68	71	71	70	280	22,902.62
Paul McGinley	71	68	72	69	280	22,902.62
Peter O'Malley	73	67	67	73	280	22,902.62

	SCORES				TOTAL	MONEY
Ariel Canete	69	70	72	70	281	20,357.89
Sergio Garcia	70	71	73	67	281	20,357.89
Miguel Angel Jimenez	66	70	73	72	281	20,357.89
Alejandro Canizares	70	69	70	73	282	18,152.45
Emanuele Canonica	70	68	72	72	282	18,152.45
Robert Karlsson	70	71	70	71	282	18,152.45
Edward Michaels	68	69	69	76	282	18,152.45
Jeev Milkha Singh	69	68	75	70	282	18,152.45
Michael Campbell	70	70	70	73	283	15,098.77
Robert-Jan Derksen	71	71	70	71	283	15,098.77
Stephen Dodd	72	68	73	70	283	15,098.77
Johan Edfors	73	67	74	69	283	15,098.77
Soren Hansen	72	72	68	71	283	15,098.77
Shiv Kapur	67	73	72	71	283	15,098.77
Chawalit Plaphol	73	69	70	71	283	15,098.77
Alvaro Quiros	70	70	71	73	284	12,723.68
Lee Westwood	71	70	72	71	284	12,723.68
Thaworn Wiratchant	73	70	73	68	284	12,723.68
Andrew Coltart	69	73	72	71	285	11,027.19
Peter Hanson	70	73	71	71	285	11,027.19
Simon Hurd	71	70	71	73	285	11,027.19
Jason Knutzon	73	71	70	71	285	11,027.19
Scott Strange	70	71	74	70	285	11,027.19
Suk Jong-yul	69	73	72	71	285	11,027.19
Jean Van de Velde	75	69	70	71	285	11,027.19
Phillip Archer	72	70	72	72	286	8,652.10
Anton Haig	71	70	72	73	286	8,652.10
Raphael Jacquelin	73	70	71	72	286	8,652.10
Jose Manuel Lara	73	71	71	71	286	8,652.10
Mardan Mamat	69	70	76	71	286	8,652.10
Chinarat Phadungsil	69	68	75	74	286	8,652.10
Terry Pilkadaris	71	70	72	73	286	8,652.10
Anthony Kang	72	70	71	74	287	7,125.26
Phillip Price	70	72	73	72	287	7,125.26
Marcus Both	71	73	74	70	288	5,937.72
Simon Khan	72	71	74	71	288	5,937.72
Frankie Minoza	75	69	73	71	288	5,937.72
Cesar Monasterio	73	70	74	71	288	5,937.72
Chris Rodgers	70	70	72	76	288	5,937.72
*Seve Benson	72	72	74	71	289	
Paul Broadhurst	71	69	74	75	289	5,004.65
Gary Rusnak	72	71	76	70	289	5,004.65
Steve Webster	71	72	73	74	290	4,750.17
David Bransdon	70	73	74	74	291	4,410.88
Bradley Dredge	71	72	74	74	291	4,410.88
Prom Meesawat	71	70	75	75	291	4,410.88
S.S.P. Chowrasia	72	71	75	74	292	3,986.75
Prayad Marksaeng	71	73	72	76	292	3,986.75
Juvic Pagunsan	70	71	77	75	293	3,562.63
Mahal Pearce	70	73	75	75	293	3,562.63
Thammanoon Srirot	71	72	74	76	293	3,562.63
Gonzalo Fernandez-Castano	70	73	74	77	294	3,161.64
Gary Simpson	72	69	74	79	294	3,161.64
Jarmo Sandelin	74	70	76	75	295	2,545
Kenneth Ferrie	70	74	75	77	296	2,542
Yasin Ali	69	75	78	75	297	2,539
Clay Devers	74	70	80	80	304	2,536

Dubai Desert Classic

Emirates Golf Club, Dubai, United Arab Emirates
Par 35-37–72; 7,301 yards

February 1-4
purse, €1,840,535

	SCORES				TOTAL	MONEY
Henrik Stenson	68	64	69	68	269	€309,862.23
Ernie Els	66	65	68	71	270	206,569.66
Niclas Fasth	69	69	65	68	271	104,671.46
Tiger Woods	68	67	67	69	271	104,671.46
Ross Fisher	65	65	71	71	272	78,828.95
Peter Hanson	69	65	69	71	274	65,071.07
Simon Dyson	67	69	69	70	275	47,966.67
Prom Meesawat	68	68	68	71	275	47,966.67
Jyoti Randhawa	66	68	67	74	275	47,966.67
Thomas Bjorn	70	69	66	71	276	32,349.62
Miguel Angel Jimenez	67	68	71	70	276	32,349.62
Robert Karlsson	70	67	68	71	276	32,349.62
Maarten Lafeber	70	71	69	66	276	32,349.62
Colin Montgomerie	73	66	68	69	276	32,349.62
Stuart Appleby	69	69	71	68	277	26,214.34
Andrew Coltart	69	71	67	70	277	26,214.34
Johan Edfors	72	68	69	68	277	26,214.34
Ignacio Garrido	71	67	68	72	278	23,518.54
Thongchai Jaidee	67	70	72	69	278	23,518.54
Paul Casey	70	68	68	73	279	21,045.84
Darren Clarke	68	70	68	73	279	21,045.84
Robert-Jan Derksen	70	66	71	72	279	21,045.84
David Park	70	70	70	69	279	21,045.84
Phillip Price	67	71	69	72	279	21,045.84
Paul Broadhurst	73	66	71	70	280	17,941.02
David Griffiths	71	67	69	73	280	17,941.02
Andrew Marshall	69	70	68	73	280	17,941.02
Paul McGinley	69	69	71	71	280	17,941.02
Taichi Teshima	69	69	68	74	280	17,941.02
Lee Westwood	68	69	75	68	280	17,941.02
Jean-Francois Lucquin	70	67	70	74	281	15,431.14
Marcel Siem	68	71	69	73	281	15,431.14
Oliver Wilson	73	67	71	70	281	15,431.14
Nick Dougherty	72	68	69	73	282	12,642.38
Richard Green	72	67	71	72	282	12,642.38
Joakim Haeggman	69	67	69	77	282	12,642.38
Christopher Hanell	72	69	70	71	282	12,642.38
Raphael Jacquelin	68	71	75	68	282	12,642.38
David Lynn	70	69	72	71	282	12,642.38
Damien McGrane	72	69	70	71	282	12,642.38
Andrew McLardy	75	66	70	71	282	12,642.38
Jeev Milkha Singh	70	69	67	76	282	12,642.38
Richard Sterne	69	70	70	73	282	12,642.38
Mark Foster	71	68	68	76	283	10,039.54
Stephen Gallacher	71	69	68	75	283	10,039.54
Jose Manuel Lara	66	71	70	76	283	10,039.54
Graeme McDowell	65	69	73	76	283	10,039.54
Emanuele Canonica	74	66	69	75	284	8,552.20
Gregory Havret	71	70	73	70	284	8,552.20
Francesco Molinari	70	70	70	74	284	8,552.20
Charl Schwartzel	69	72	69	74	284	8,552.20
Alastair Forsyth	70	70	70	75	285	7,622.61
*Rory McIlroy	69	69	71	76	285	
Phillip Archer	69	71	75	71	286	6,507.11
Notah Begay	71	69	73	73	286	6,507.11
Gonzalo Fernandez-Castano	73	68	71	74	286	6,507.11
Peter Hedblom	71	69	69	77	286	6,507.11

	SCORES				TOTAL	MONEY
Garry Houston	71	67	71	77	286	6,507.11
Cesar Monasterio	68	70	74	75	287	5,391.60
Hennie Otto	71	69	71	76	287	5,391.60
Alvaro Quiros	69	68	72	78	287	5,391.60
Stephen Dodd	72	68	73	75	288	5,019.77
Gregory Bourdy	71	70	73	75	289	4,833.85
Greg Norman	70	71	71	78	290	4,647.93
Bradley Dredge	69	72	79	71	291	4,462.02
Lee Slattery	70	71	76	83	300	4,276.10

Maybank Malaysian Open

See Asia/Japan Tours chapter.

Enjoy Jakarta Astro Indonesia Open

See Asia/Japan Tours chapter.

Johnnie Walker Classic

See Asia/Japan Tours chapter.

Clariden Leu Singapore Masters

See Asia/Japan Tours chapter.

TCL Classic

See Asia/Japan Tours chapter.

Madeira Islands Open BPI

Santo da Serra Golf Club, Madeira, Portugal
Par 36-36–72; 6,826 yards

March 22-25
purse, €695,980

	SCORES				TOTAL	MONEY
Daniel Vancsik	68	66	68	68	270	€116,660
David Frost	72	65	72	68	277	60,795
Santiago Luna	69	67	72	69	277	60,795
Christian Cevaer	70	65	72	72	279	29,726.67
Euan Little	73	66	69	71	279	29,726.67
Mads Vibe-Hastrup	68	70	68	73	279	29,726.67
Gregory Bourdy	74	67	68	71	280	18,060
Simon Nash	70	69	71	70	280	18,060
Alexander Noren	72	66	72	70	280	18,060
Francesco Molinari	75	70	67	69	281	14,000
Stuart Little	71	69	72	70	282	12,880
Gregory Havret	71	69	73	70	283	11,340
Iain Pyman	77	67	70	69	283	11,340
Jamie Spence	74	65	74	70	283	11,340
Johan Axgren	75	70	68	71	284	8,694
Peter Baker	67	72	72	73	284	8,694
Jamie Donaldson	71	69	70	74	284	8,694
Bradley Dredge	73	72	70	69	284	8,694
Ian Garbutt	71	69	73	71	284	8,694
Martin Kaymer	68	73	75	68	284	8,694
David Lynn	71	70	74	69	284	8,694
Miguel Rodriguez	77	68	70	69	284	8,694

	SCORES				TOTAL	MONEY
Antonio Sobrinho	74	70	71	69	284	8,694
Tom Whitehouse	74	71	70	69	284	8,694
Francois Delamontagne	74	68	70	73	285	6,650
Robert-Jan Derksen	68	72	70	75	285	6,650
Sam Little	70	69	74	72	285	6,650
Andrew Marshall	73	71	69	72	285	6,650
Wade Ormsby	76	67	72	70	285	6,650
David Park	71	68	72	74	285	6,650
Oliver Wilson	70	69	75	71	285	6,650
Steve Alker	72	71	70	73	286	5,432
Tiago Cruz	73	71	73	69	286	5,432
Pelle Edberg	74	70	72	70	286	5,432
Eirik Tage Johansen	77	67	73	69	286	5,432
Jean Van de Velde	75	67	74	70	286	5,432
Notah Begay	67	71	75	74	287	4,620
Ivo Giner	74	71	72	70	287	4,620
Jean-Baptiste Gonnet	78	67	70	72	287	4,620
Peter Gustafsson	74	70	70	73	287	4,620
Andrew Tampion	74	68	70	75	287	4,620
Simon Wakefield	74	67	73	73	287	4,620
Fredrik Andersson Hed	70	69	71	78	288	3,920
Birgir Hafthorsson	74	70	71	73	288	3,920
Gary Murphy	74	67	70	77	288	3,920
Jean-Francois Remesy	71	74	69	74	288	3,920
Benn Barham	74	69	73	73	289	3,290
David Griffiths	74	69	72	74	289	3,290
Pedro Linhart	73	71	75	70	289	3,290
Denny Lucas	72	73	73	71	289	3,290
Edoardo Molinari	71	72	74	72	289	3,290
Luis Claverie	71	70	76	73	290	2,800
Ricardo Santos	66	74	77	73	290	2,800
David Drysdale	73	72	74	72	291	2,450
David Higgins	74	70	74	73	291	2,450
Philip Talbot	73	71	77	70	291	2,450
Alvaro Salto	74	71	77	70	292	2,135
Sven Struver	70	71	73	78	292	2,135
Garry Houston	75	69	70	79	293	1,890
Steven O'Hara	71	70	76	76	293	1,890
Manuel Quiros	73	70	75	75	293	1,890
Alessandro Tadini	73	71	73	76	293	1,890
Nicolas Vanhootegem	75	70	73	75	293	1,890
Phillip Archer	71	74	79	70	294	1,680
David Bransdon	72	73	78	72	295	1,575
Kenneth Ferrie	74	70	78	73	295	1,575
Adrien Mork	73	72	78	81	304	1,470

Estoril Open de Portugal

Quinta da Marinha Oitavos Golfe, Estoril, Portugal   March 29-April 1
Par 36-35–71; 6,893 yards   purse, €1,253,747

	SCORES				TOTAL	MONEY
*Pablo Martin-Benavides	73	70	66	68	277	
Raphael Jacquelin	70	69	72	67	278	€208,330
David Griffiths	76	69	68	68	281	83,157.50
Martin Kaymer	72	69	73	67	281	83,157.50
Charl Schwartzel	74	71	67	69	281	83,157.50
Graeme Storm	72	67	70	72	281	83,157.50
Alastair Forsyth	73	69	69	71	282	35,125
Michael Jonzon	71	71	69	71	282	35,125

	SCORES				TOTAL	MONEY
Andrew Oldcorn	76	69	66	71	282	35,125
Sven Struver	70	70	72	70	282	35,125
Alejandro Canizares	71	72	71	69	283	21,187.50
Mark Foster	77	67	70	69	283	21,187.50
Stephen Gallacher	68	71	73	71	283	21,187.50
Peter Lawrie	73	70	71	69	283	21,187.50
Alexander Noren	71	68	68	76	283	21,187.50
Tom Whitehouse	74	71	68	70	283	21,187.50
Luis Claverie	72	68	73	71	284	16,531.25
Lee S. James	73	71	70	70	284	16,531.25
Ross McGowan	68	68	72	76	284	16,531.25
Gary Orr	70	73	73	68	284	16,531.25
Nick Dougherty	69	69	75	72	285	14,343.75
Simon Dyson	67	74	73	71	285	14,343.75
Pelle Edberg	71	71	71	72	285	14,343.75
Jamie Spence	72	73	66	74	285	14,343.75
Fredrik Andersson Hed	76	68	74	68	286	11,875
Benn Barham	72	67	77	70	286	11,875
Emanuele Canonica	73	70	71	72	286	11,875
Simon Khan	73	68	76	69	286	11,875
Soren Kjeldsen	72	73	72	69	286	11,875
Paul Lawrie	72	72	67	75	286	11,875
Euan Little	72	69	72	73	286	11,875
Paul McGinley	76	70	70	70	286	11,875
Van Phillips	75	70	72	69	286	11,875
Jesus Maria Arruti	75	71	69	72	287	8,510.42
Markus Brier	75	71	68	73	287	8,510.42
Robert-Jan Derksen	70	75	72	70	287	8,510.42
Oliver Fisher	73	71	73	70	287	8,510.42
Gregory Havret	72	74	68	73	287	8,510.42
Barry Lane	69	75	72	71	287	8,510.42
Sam Little	72	73	70	72	287	8,510.42
Henrik Nystrom	76	69	74	68	287	8,510.42
Carl Suneson	74	71	73	69	287	8,510.42
Alessandro Tadini	77	66	73	71	287	8,510.42
Taichi Teshima	71	69	70	77	287	8,510.42
Daniel Vancsik	72	72	75	68	287	8,510.42
Richard Bland	71	69	75	73	288	6,000
David Bransdon	71	70	74	73	288	6,000
Ian Garbutt	73	73	73	69	288	6,000
Jose Manuel Lara	72	71	73	72	288	6,000
Santiago Luna	73	71	70	74	288	6,000
Francesco Molinari	72	71	73	72	288	6,000
Adrien Mork	73	73	72	70	288	6,000
Mads Vibe-Hastrup	76	70	72	70	288	6,000
John Bickerton	74	72	71	72	289	4,178.57
Paul Broadhurst	69	71	75	74	289	4,178.57
Tiago Cruz	70	76	71	72	289	4,178.57
Brian Davis	76	70	72	71	289	4,178.57
Soren Hansen	73	72	67	77	289	4,178.57
Gary Lockerbie	71	73	73	72	289	4,178.57
Steven O'Hara	73	73	75	68	289	4,178.57
Johan Axgren	71	74	72	73	290	3,250
Gonzalo Fernandez-Castano	70	71	73	76	290	3,250
Jonathan Lomas	76	69	72	73	290	3,250
David Lynn	71	71	75	73	290	3,250
Edoardo Molinari	72	71	72	75	290	3,250
Scott Drummond	75	69	72	75	291	2,812.50
Hennie Otto	73	71	74	73	291	2,812.50
Jose-Filipe Lima	75	71	77	69	292	2,625
Marcus Higley	72	73	75	73	293	2,437.50
Gary Murphy	73	71	73	76	293	2,437.50
Mattias Eliasson	74	70	73	77	294	2,082.50

	SCORES				TOTAL	MONEY
Gary Emerson	72	72	74	76	294	2,082.50
Alvaro Quiros	74	70	76	76	296	1,872

Volvo China Open

See Asia/Japan Tours chapter.

BMW Asian Open

See Asia/Japan Tours chapter.

Open de Espana

Centro Nacional de Golf, Madrid, Spain
Par 36-36–72; 7,242 yards

April 26-29
purse, €1,984,350

	SCORES				TOTAL	MONEY
Charl Schwartzel	69	68	68	67	272	€333,330
Jyoti Randhawa	75	65	66	67	273	222,220
Carlos Rodiles	70	66	66	72	274	125,200
Simon Dyson	69	69	66	71	275	92,400
Mark Foster	68	69	70	68	275	92,400
Fredrik Andersson Hed	68	71	69	68	276	65,000
Andres Romero	70	71	69	66	276	65,000
Gregory Bourdy	67	69	71	70	277	39,700
Nick Dougherty	66	71	70	70	277	39,700
Alastair Forsyth	68	74	66	69	277	39,700
Stephen Gallacher	71	68	69	69	277	39,700
Stuart Little	67	69	70	71	277	39,700
Tom Whitehouse	71	71	67	68	277	39,700
Martin Kaymer	71	70	67	70	278	29,400
Phillip Price	73	65	70	70	278	29,400
Graeme Storm	68	72	73	65	278	29,400
Bradley Dredge	69	72	69	69	279	25,866.67
Johan Edfors	71	69	70	69	279	25,866.67
Paul McGinley	70	72	68	69	279	25,866.67
Peter Lawrie	76	65	69	70	280	23,266.67
David Lynn	72	69	69	70	280	23,266.67
Andrew Tampion	74	67	70	69	280	23,266.67
Richard Bland	68	71	71	71	281	19,900
Gareth Davies	69	70	73	69	281	19,900
Carlos Del Moral	71	73	68	69	281	19,900
Robert-Jan Derksen	67	75	72	67	281	19,900
Graeme McDowell	71	69	71	70	281	19,900
Alexander Noren	70	71	71	69	281	19,900
Jarmo Sandelin	70	71	71	69	281	19,900
Simon Wakefield	73	69	70	69	281	19,900
Notah Begay	68	70	73	71	282	15,571.43
Emanuele Canonica	72	67	69	74	282	15,571.43
Niclas Fasth	68	72	71	71	282	15,571.43
Kenneth Ferrie	69	71	71	71	282	15,571.43
Paul Lawrie	74	69	66	73	282	15,571.43
Gary Murphy	71	72	71	68	282	15,571.43
Manuel Quiros	72	68	69	73	282	15,571.43
David Carter	71	73	68	71	283	13,000
Jonathan Lomas	70	70	73	70	283	13,000
Louis Oosthuizen	73	70	69	71	283	13,000
Andrew Raitt	68	70	74	71	283	13,000

	SCORES				TOTAL	MONEY
Oliver Wilson	70	73	70	70	283	13,000
Carlos Balmaseda	70	74	69	71	284	11,800
David Drysdale	69	73	72	71	285	10,800
Gonzalo Fernandez-Castano	70	74	70	71	285	10,800
Oliver Fisher	70	74	69	72	285	10,800
David Park	70	71	70	74	285	10,800
Ariel Canete	71	73	72	70	286	9,200
Ian Garbutt	71	73	72	70	286	9,200
Damien McGrane	72	70	68	76	286	9,200
Alvaro Salto	69	73	69	75	286	9,200
Ignacio Garrido	71	72	72	72	287	8,000
Miguel Angel Jimenez	70	73	73	71	287	8,000
Andrew Coltart	70	72	74	72	288	6,800
Marcus Higley	74	70	71	73	288	6,800
Gary Orr	71	72	75	70	288	6,800
Terry Pilkadaris	69	74	73	72	288	6,800
Marcus Fraser	69	70	77	73	289	5,800
Taichi Teshima	72	71	73	73	289	5,800
Steve Webster	72	69	73	75	289	5,800
Marcel Siem	73	71	75	71	290	5,400
Alvaro Velasco	73	71	76	71	291	5,200
Francois Delamontagne	71	72	75	74	292	4,900
Terry Price	70	70	78	74	292	4,900
Nicolas Colsaerts	77	67	74	75	293	4,600
Richard McEvoy	75	69	75	75	294	4,400

Telecom Italia Open

Castello di Tolcinasco Golf & Country Club, Milan, Italy
Par 36-36–72; 7,283 yards
(Event shortened to 54 holes—rain and fog.)

May 3-6
purse, €1,700,000

	SCORES			TOTAL	MONEY
Gonzalo Fernandez-Castano	67	68	65	200	€283,330
Markus Brier	63	69	68	200	188,880
(Fernandez-Castano defeated Brier on second playoff hole.)					
Fredrik Andersson Hed	69	68	64	201	80,750
Nick Dougherty	67	64	70	201	80,750
Francesco Molinari	67	69	65	201	80,750
Henrik Nystrom	67	68	66	201	80,750
Marcus Fraser	68	66	68	202	41,395
Raphael Jacquelin	66	71	65	202	41,395
Andrew McLardy	65	65	72	202	41,395
Alexandre Rocha	70	64	68	202	41,395
Birgir Hafthorsson	67	67	69	203	29,296.67
James Heath	65	69	69	203	29,296.67
Simon Khan	68	69	66	203	29,296.67
Phillip Archer	69	68	67	204	23,047.14
Pelle Edberg	70	69	65	204	23,047.14
Oliver Fisher	69	69	66	204	23,047.14
Mark Foster	72	68	64	204	23,047.14
Martin Kaymer	69	65	70	204	23,047.14
Maarten Lafeber	69	66	69	204	23,047.14
Oliver Wilson	68	68	68	204	23,047.14
Joakim Backstrom	62	70	73	205	18,700
Alastair Forsyth	68	67	70	205	18,700
Garry Houston	66	70	69	205	18,700
Gary Lockerbie	73	65	67	205	18,700
Alvaro Quiros	65	67	73	205	18,700
Ian Garbutt	68	71	67	206	16,405

	SCORES			TOTAL	MONEY
Peter Lawrie	68	70	68	206	16,405
Mark Pilkington	71	68	67	206	16,405
Jeev Milkha Singh	69	65	72	206	16,405
Nicolas Colsaerts	66	67	74	207	13,672.86
Soren Hansen	69	70	68	207	13,672.86
Edoardo Molinari	70	69	68	207	13,672.86
Brett Rumford	66	71	70	207	13,672.86
Charl Schwartzel	67	69	71	207	13,672.86
Kyron Sullivan	70	67	70	207	13,672.86
Anthony Wall	68	72	67	207	13,672.86
Emanuele Canonica	70	69	69	208	10,540
Gareth Davies	69	71	68	208	10,540
David Drysdale	70	70	68	208	10,540
Kenneth Ferrie	68	69	71	208	10,540
Gregory Havret	67	71	70	208	10,540
Tom Lehman	70	68	70	208	10,540
Steven O'Hara	69	68	71	208	10,540
David Park	71	68	69	208	10,540
Carlos Rodiles	67	67	74	208	10,540
Sven Struver	68	70	70	208	10,540
Benn Barham	69	70	70	209	7,310
Paul Broadhurst	68	70	71	209	7,310
Bradley Dredge	71	68	70	209	7,310
Martin Erlandsson	71	66	72	209	7,310
Richard Finch	66	73	70	209	7,310
Jean-Baptiste Gonnet	72	67	70	209	7,310
Sam Little	71	69	69	209	7,310
Gary Murphy	71	68	70	209	7,310
Jyoti Randhawa	71	69	69	209	7,310
Rafael Cabrera Bello	71	69	70	210	5,227.50
Anders Hansen	66	74	70	210	5,227.50
Robert Rock	71	68	71	210	5,227.50
Andrew Tampion	68	72	70	210	5,227.50
Gregory Bourdy	73	67	71	211	4,420
Alessio Bruschi	72	68	71	211	4,420
Steven Jeppesen	74	66	71	211	4,420
Steve Jones	70	69	72	211	4,420
Duffy Waldorf	67	72	72	211	4,420
Steve Alker	70	69	73	212	3,655
Cesar Monasterio	69	70	73	212	3,655
Juan Parron	67	71	74	212	3,655
Michele Reale	71	68	73	212	3,655
Jose Manuel Carriles	70	70	73	213	3,230
Jean-Francois Remesy	70	68	78	216	3,110

Valle Romano Open de Andalucia

Aloha Golf Club, Marbella, Andalucia, Spain
Par 36-36–72; 6,881 yards

May 10-13
purse, €1,005,982

	SCORES				TOTAL	MONEY
Lee Westwood	72	64	65	67	268	€166,660
Fredrik Andersson Hed	69	71	64	66	270	86,855
Phillip Archer	69	70	66	65	270	86,855
Michael Jonzon	69	68	66	69	272	46,200
Louis Oosthuizen	67	67	69	69	272	46,200
Thomas Bjorn	71	69	66	67	273	35,000
Gonzalo Fernandez-Castano	67	68	67	72	274	27,500
Chris Gane	67	71	68	68	274	27,500
Gareth Davies	69	71	68	68	276	19,500

	SCORES				TOTAL	MONEY
David Lynn	70	71	68	67	276	19,500
Robert Rock	70	73	65	68	276	19,500
Matthew Zions	65	70	70	71	276	19,500
Francois Delamontagne	69	66	72	70	277	14,740
Jamie Donaldson	70	69	70	68	277	14,740
Soren Hansen	70	68	70	69	277	14,740
Garry Houston	71	67	72	67	277	14,740
Sam Walker	69	69	70	69	277	14,740
Paul Broadhurst	70	70	70	68	278	12,040
Alejandro Canizares	66	73	70	69	278	12,040
Joakim Haeggman	67	71	69	71	278	12,040
David Higgins	69	68	70	71	278	12,040
Richard McEvoy	69	68	73	68	278	12,040
Johan Axgren	74	68	69	68	279	11,000
Oliver Fisher	70	69	71	70	280	9,800
David Griffiths	68	72	68	72	280	9,800
Miguel Angel Jimenez	72	69	68	71	280	9,800
Steve Jones	69	67	71	73	280	9,800
Alvaro Salto	70	69	68	73	280	9,800
Carl Suneson	69	68	71	72	280	9,800
Shaun P. Webster	74	67	70	69	280	9,800
Gary Lockerbie	67	72	70	72	281	8,300
Santiago Luna	72	69	68	72	281	8,300
Sven Struver	71	71	71	68	281	8,300
Jesus Maria Arruti	73	71	68	70	282	7,200
Notah Begay	71	70	71	70	282	7,200
Andrew Butterfield	70	73	67	72	282	7,200
Birgir Hafthorsson	73	68	70	71	282	7,200
Thomas Levet	74	66	70	72	282	7,200
Scott Strange	72	71	69	70	282	7,200
Rafael Echenique	73	71	68	71	283	6,200
Ian Garbutt	72	70	71	70	283	6,200
Philip Golding	74	69	69	71	283	6,200
Sam Little	71	69	74	69	283	6,200
Carlos Aguilar	76	67	72	69	284	5,200
Sion E. Bebb	70	74	70	70	284	5,200
James Heath	75	67	72	70	284	5,200
James Hepworth	72	68	71	73	284	5,200
Paul McGinley	71	72	68	73	284	5,200
Terry Pilkadaris	71	71	71	71	284	5,200
Peter Fowler	73	71	70	71	285	4,200
Marcus Higley	70	71	69	75	285	4,200
Per-Ulrik Johansson	72	71	69	73	285	4,200
Wade Ormsby	73	70	69	73	285	4,200
Sebastian Fernandez	70	70	72	74	286	3,320
Juan Parron	72	71	70	73	286	3,320
Carlos Rodiles	72	69	72	73	286	3,320
Anthony Wall	72	72	71	71	286	3,320
Y.E. Yang	74	69	70	73	286	3,320
Peter Gustafsson	73	70	74	70	287	2,750
Pedro Linhart	72	70	71	74	287	2,750
Damien McGrane	72	70	73	72	287	2,750
Adrien Mork	71	73	72	71	287	2,750
Rafael Cabrera Bello	69	73	72	74	288	2,400
Nicolas Colsaerts	68	73	74	73	288	2,400
Eduardo De La Riva	68	73	70	77	288	2,400
Carlos Balmaseda	71	71	73	74	289	2,006
Diego Borrego	73	71	74	71	289	2,006
Martin Maritz	72	72	70	75	289	2,006
Daniel Quiros	72	72	74	71	289	2,006
Alvaro Velasco	72	72	73	72	289	2,006
Jorge Benedetti	71	73	74	72	290	1,498.50
Gary Emerson	71	72	73	74	290	1,498.50

	SCORES				TOTAL	MONEY
Matthew Millar	68	73	72	78	291	1,494
Simon Dyson	70	74	77	73	294	1,491

Irish Open

Adare Manor Hotel & Golf Resort, Co. Limerick, Ireland
Par 36-36–72; 7,453 yards

May 17-20
purse, €2,511,241

	SCORES				TOTAL	MONEY
Padraig Harrington	73	68	71	71	283	€416,660
Bradley Dredge	75	71	69	68	283	277,770
(Harrington defeated Dredge on first playoff hole.)						
Simon Wakefield	70	72	73	72	287	156,500
Richard Green	71	73	72	72	288	106,166.67
Louis Oosthuizen	69	74	73	72	288	106,166.67
Andres Romero	68	74	75	71	288	106,166.67
Simon Dyson	68	78	75	69	290	60,875
Peter Hanson	68	78	73	71	290	60,875
Raphael Jacquelin	74	72	72	72	290	60,875
Francesco Molinari	71	74	73	72	290	60,875
James Kingston	69	78	76	69	292	46,000
James Heath	74	70	77	72	293	35,611.11
David Lynn	72	75	76	70	293	35,611.11
Damien McGrane	75	72	70	76	293	35,611.11
Gary Murphy	74	72	73	74	293	35,611.11
Christian L. Nilsson	69	74	76	74	293	35,611.11
Alexander Noren	74	75	75	69	293	35,611.11
Carlos Rodiles	73	72	77	71	293	35,611.11
Jarmo Sandelin	72	78	75	68	293	35,611.11
Marc Warren	76	73	73	71	293	35,611.11
Joakim Backstrom	71	71	76	76	294	25,625
John Bickerton	75	74	75	70	294	25,625
Alastair Forsyth	72	72	74	76	294	25,625
Miguel Angel Jimenez	74	73	77	70	294	25,625
Sandy Lyle	72	74	76	72	294	25,625
Phillip Price	72	73	74	75	294	25,625
Jyoti Randhawa	76	70	73	75	294	25,625
Lee Westwood	71	77	72	74	294	25,625
Oliver Wilson	73	75	74	72	294	25,625
Y.E. Yang	72	77	71	74	294	25,625
Michael Jonzon	72	72	77	74	295	20,375
Graeme McDowell	74	74	77	70	295	20,375
David Park	72	78	74	71	295	20,375
Mark Pilkington	73	76	76	70	295	20,375
Martin Kaymer	74	77	77	68	296	18,500
Mads Vibe-Hastrup	74	74	74	74	296	18,500
Rafael Cabrera Bello	79	69	78	71	297	16,000
Christian Cevaer	75	75	73	74	297	16,000
Mark Foster	73	77	75	72	297	16,000
Stephen Gallacher	76	73	77	71	297	16,000
Ignacio Garrido	77	71	73	76	297	16,000
Soren Hansen	73	72	82	70	297	16,000
David Higgins	75	70	76	76	297	16,000
Richard Sterne	71	79	75	72	297	16,000
Fredrik Andersson Hed	76	75	74	73	298	12,250
Ariel Canete	72	75	78	73	298	12,250
Peter Gustafsson	68	75	78	77	298	12,250
Simon Khan	71	79	77	71	298	12,250
Soren Kjeldsen	74	75	77	72	298	12,250
Maarten Lafeber	75	75	72	76	298	12,250

	SCORES				TOTAL	MONEY
Edward Rush	77	73	74	74	298	12,250
Thomas Bjorn	75	73	75	76	299	9,000
Emanuele Canonica	75	76	74	74	299	9,000
Mattias Eliasson	74	74	77	74	299	9,000
Gary Lockerbie	76	75	77	71	299	9,000
Andrew Marshall	76	72	72	79	299	9,000
Brett Rumford	80	71	73	75	299	9,000
Chris Gane	76	75	75	74	300	7,250
Paul McGinley	72	76	77	75	300	7,250
Sven Struver	73	74	79	74	300	7,250
Steven Jeppesen	72	74	77	78	301	6,625
Steven O'Hara	73	76	78	74	301	6,625
Martin Erlandsson	76	72	76	79	303	5,875
Christopher Hanell	74	77	79	73	303	5,875
Thomas Levet	74	76	77	76	303	5,875
Alexandre Rocha	70	81	77	75	303	5,875
Jean-Baptiste Gonnet	75	74	74	81	304	5,125
Gary Orr	76	75	79	74	304	5,125
Kenneth Ferrie	74	75	80	76	305	4,204.25
Shiv Kapur	77	74	79	75	305	4,204.25
Matthew Richardson	79	72	79	75	305	4,204.25
Matthew Zions	71	78	80	76	305	4,204.25
*Pat Murray	76	72	79	80	307	
Peter Hedblom	75	74	82	83	314	3,744

BMW PGA Championship

Wentworth Club, Virginia Water, Surrey, England
Par 35-37–72; 7,302 yards

May 24-27
purse, €4,382,595

	SCORES				TOTAL	MONEY
Anders Hansen	74	70	67	69	280	€725,000
Justin Rose	66	70	73	71	280	483,330
(Hansen defeated Rose on first playoff hole.)						
Vijay Singh	73	72	70	66	281	244,905
Richard Sterne	68	73	66	74	281	244,905
Angel Cabrera	70	66	76	70	282	168,345
Miguel Angel Jimenez	70	68	72	72	282	168,345
Luke Donald	71	72	71	69	283	130,500
Niclas Fasth	72	73	68	71	284	93,307.50
Richard Green	73	73	67	71	284	93,307.50
Thongchai Jaidee	73	70	71	70	284	93,307.50
Henrik Stenson	70	73	72	69	284	93,307.50
Markus Brier	73	68	70	74	285	63,183.75
Paul Casey	73	67	72	73	285	63,183.75
Marcus Fraser	67	70	70	78	285	63,183.75
Mikko Ilonen	68	71	74	72	285	63,183.75
Peter Lawrie	76	69	71	69	285	63,183.75
Andres Romero	70	72	75	68	285	63,183.75
Jeev Milkha Singh	77	69	67	72	285	63,183.75
Lee Westwood	71	72	70	72	285	63,183.75
Paul Broadhurst	66	72	68	80	286	49,916.25
Alejandro Canizares	68	71	74	73	286	49,916.25
Christian Cevaer	72	72	72	70	286	49,916.25
Nick Dougherty	69	71	71	75	286	49,916.25
Fredrik Andersson Hed	69	72	72	74	287	43,935
Ernie Els	68	76	72	71	287	43,935
Padraig Harrington	69	69	75	74	287	43,935
Simon Khan	67	75	73	72	287	43,935
Brett Taylor	71	73	72	71	287	43,935

	SCORES				TOTAL	MONEY
Maarten Lafeber	73	68	75	72	288	40,020
Robert-Jan Derksen	73	71	72	73	289	33,978.33
Ignacio Garrido	71	72	73	73	289	33,978.33
Steven Jeppesen	73	72	71	73	289	33,978.33
Martin Kaymer	71	75	73	70	289	33,978.33
Francesco Molinari	67	72	78	72	289	33,978.33
Colin Montgomerie	70	76	70	73	289	33,978.33
Christian L. Nilsson	71	73	73	72	289	33,978.33
Peter O'Malley	71	72	71	75	289	33,978.33
Marc Warren	70	75	72	72	289	33,978.33
Thomas Bjorn	74	70	73	73	290	28,710
Ross Fisher	70	67	69	84	290	28,710
Martin Erlandsson	70	75	75	71	291	25,230
Peter Hedblom	72	71	75	73	291	25,230
Robert Karlsson	72	72	72	75	291	25,230
James Kingston	70	71	74	76	291	25,230
Jose Maria Olazabal	70	76	73	72	291	25,230
Jean Van de Velde	77	68	70	76	291	25,230
Garry Houston	74	71	74	73	292	21,315
Andrew Oldcorn	74	71	72	75	292	21,315
Oliver Wilson	70	71	76	75	292	21,315
Ariel Canete	72	73	73	75	293	18,270
Emanuele Canonica	72	70	77	74	293	18,270
Paul McGinley	74	69	76	74	293	18,270
Lee Slattery	69	71	76	77	293	18,270
Stephen Dodd	72	74	70	78	294	15,660
Christopher Hanell	72	72	74	76	294	15,660
Mattias Eliasson	72	72	76	75	295	13,376.25
James Hepworth	71	72	75	77	295	13,376.25
Raphael Jacquelin	72	74	73	76	295	13,376.25
Jarmo Sandelin	76	70	76	73	295	13,376.25
Gonzalo Fernandez-Castano	72	70	78	77	297	11,527.50
Matthew Millar	69	69	79	80	297	11,527.50
Jyoti Randhawa	68	75	76	78	297	11,527.50
Y.E. Yang	68	78	73	78	297	11,527.50
Richard Bland	71	71	76	80	298	10,005
Thomas Levet	70	76	79	73	298	10,005
Miles Tunnicliff	71	73	75	79	298	10,005
Shiv Kapur	67	71	81	81	300	9,135
Rafael Echenique	70	76	76	79	301	8,482.50
Ricardo Gonzalez	72	73	78	78	301	8,482.50
Peter Gustafsson	74	72	77	79	302	7,930
Louis Oosthuizen	69	77	76	81	303	6,523.50
Marcel Siem	73	72	79	79	303	6,523.50
Brett Rumford	77	69	81	77	304	6,519
Johan Axgren	75	71	77	83	306	6,514.50
Mark Foster	71	75	80	80	306	6,514.50

Celtic Manor Wales Open

Celtic Manor Resort, Newport, Wales
Par 35-34–69; 6,743 yards

May 31-June 3
purse, €2,216,194

	SCORES				TOTAL	MONEY
Richard Sterne	67	67	64	65	263	€368,812.50
Bradley Dredge	66	66	65	67	264	147,215.20
Soren Kjeldsen	65	70	64	65	264	147,215.20
Mardan Mamat	71	64	67	62	264	147,215.20
Mads Vibe-Hastrup	67	63	68	66	264	147,215.20
Mikko Ilonen	67	65	70	63	265	71,918.44

	SCORES				TOTAL	MONEY
Gary Murphy	68	65	66	66	265	71,918.44
Paul Broadhurst	65	67	67	67	266	43,925.57
Alejandro Canizares	69	67	65	65	266	43,925.57
Nick Dougherty	69	63	68	66	266	43,925.57
David Frost	68	64	67	67	266	43,925.57
Gary Orr	65	67	68	66	266	43,925.57
Tom Whitehouse	71	65	66	64	266	43,925.57
Gregory Bourdy	66	71	66	64	267	32,529.26
Andrew Coltart	69	65	67	66	267	32,529.26
Martin Kaymer	69	63	65	70	267	32,529.26
Jyoti Randhawa	69	66	68	65	268	28,619.85
Miles Tunnicliff	70	65	68	65	268	28,619.85
Oliver Wilson	66	68	68	66	268	28,619.85
Martin Erlandsson	66	69	66	68	269	25,049.75
Alastair Forsyth	66	65	70	68	269	25,049.75
Stephen Gallacher	67	66	67	69	269	25,049.75
Colin Montgomerie	70	64	72	63	269	25,049.75
Steven O'Hara	65	66	69	69	269	25,049.75
Rafael Cabrera Bello	68	68	64	70	270	22,018.11
Garry Houston	67	69	69	65	270	22,018.11
Raphael Jacquelin	68	68	69	65	270	22,018.11
Peter Lawrie	66	69	68	67	270	22,018.11
Benn Barham	70	63	69	69	271	19,030.73
Michael Campbell	66	66	69	70	271	19,030.73
Eirik Tage Johansen	69	66	66	70	271	19,030.73
Paul Lawrie	65	68	71	67	271	19,030.73
Matthew Zions	66	67	68	70	271	19,030.73
David Griffiths	68	65	71	68	272	17,039.14
Phillip Archer	68	65	70	70	273	15,047.55
Jesus Maria Arruti	69	67	69	68	273	15,047.55
Mattias Eliasson	66	69	68	70	273	15,047.55
Kenneth Ferrie	71	64	65	73	273	15,047.55
Anton Haig	68	67	74	64	273	15,047.55
Gregory Havret	69	63	71	70	273	15,047.55
Simon Khan	67	66	68	72	273	15,047.55
Thomas Levet	68	67	69	69	273	15,047.55
Rafael Echenique	72	65	65	72	274	11,949.53
Gonzalo Fernandez-Castano	67	70	68	69	274	11,949.53
Marcus Fraser	68	69	69	68	274	11,949.53
Ricardo Gonzalez	65	67	73	69	274	11,949.53
Shiv Kapur	68	69	71	66	274	11,949.53
Brett Rumford	65	66	72	71	274	11,949.53
Christian Cevaer	66	69	72	68	275	9,957.94
Ignacio Garrido	68	66	70	71	275	9,957.94
Anders Hansen	70	65	73	67	275	9,957.94
Steve Alker	65	72	69	70	276	8,408.93
Joakim Haeggman	66	71	71	68	276	8,408.93
Jose Manuel Lara	65	69	71	71	276	8,408.93
Robert Rock	67	70	69	70	276	8,408.93
David Bransdon	68	68	70	71	277	6,682.88
Mark Foster	67	68	72	70	277	6,682.88
James Kingston	66	68	72	71	277	6,682.88
Henrik Nystrom	70	67	66	74	277	6,682.88
Simon Wakefield	69	68	68	72	277	6,682.88
Liam Bond	66	68	75	70	279	5,864.12
David Carter	68	68	73	70	279	5,864.12
Emanuele Canonica	69	68	75	68	280	4,978.97
Robert-Jan Derksen	69	66	73	72	280	4,978.97
Phillip Price	67	70	70	73	280	4,978.97
Manuel Quiros	70	67	70	73	280	4,978.97
Marcel Siem	69	68	73	70	280	4,978.97
Simon Thornton	69	64	73	74	280	4,978.97
James Heath	67	69	69	76	281	4,123.32

	SCORES				TOTAL	MONEY
Kyron Sullivan	68	68	72	73	281	4,123.32
Fredrik Andersson Hed	72	64	74	76	286	3,319

BA-CA Golf Open

Fontana Golf Club, Vienna, Austria
Par 35-36–71; 7,071 yards

June 7-10
purse, €1,1,295,150

	SCORES				TOTAL	MONEY
Richard Green	66	65	67	70	268	€216,660
Jean-Francois Remesy	72	67	65	64	268	144,440
(Green defeated Remesy on first playoff hole.)						
Chris Gane	75	65	64	65	269	67,166.67
Miguel Angel Jimenez	68	65	69	67	269	67,166.67
Michael Jonzon	70	69	64	66	269	67,166.67
Stephen Gallacher	69	68	68	65	270	45,500
Steven Jeppesen	67	66	69	69	271	35,750
Graeme Storm	63	72	69	67	271	35,750
Martin Erlandsson	64	68	73	68	273	24,466
David Higgins	70	71	67	65	273	24,466
Graeme McDowell	71	69	69	64	273	24,466
Richard McEvoy	66	71	64	72	273	24,466
Tom Whitehouse	65	71	69	68	273	24,466
Pelle Edberg	67	66	73	68	274	18,720
Gary Orr	71	67	66	70	274	18,720
Jarmo Sandelin	67	68	69	70	274	18,720
Johan Skold	70	69	64	71	274	18,720
Gregory Havret	71	65	72	67	275	16,163.33
Patrik Sjoland	65	73	67	70	275	16,163.33
Taichi Teshima	69	70	70	66	275	16,163.33
Birgir Hafthorsson	70	71	68	67	276	14,105
Euan Little	68	73	66	69	276	14,105
David Park	69	66	68	73	276	14,105
Edward Rush	67	74	68	67	276	14,105
Shaun P. Webster	65	71	68	72	276	14,105
Matthew Zions	68	73	68	67	276	14,105
Francois Calmels	66	73	69	69	277	11,765
Oliver Fisher	68	72	70	67	277	11,765
David Frost	68	71	68	70	277	11,765
Garry Houston	72	63	70	72	277	11,765
Sam Little	73	67	67	70	277	11,765
Gary Lockerbie	66	72	68	71	277	11,765
Sion E. Bebb	70	68	71	69	278	10,205
David Bransdon	69	68	73	68	278	10,205
Paul Broadhurst	75	67	68	69	279	9,490
Santiago Luna	68	71	70	70	279	9,490
Bernd Wiesberger	68	71	69	71	279	9,490
Steve Alker	69	73	69	69	280	8,190
Raphael Eyraud	69	71	70	70	280	8,190
Richard Finch	66	70	73	71	280	8,190
Soren Hansen	70	70	70	70	280	8,190
Carlos Rodiles	68	70	71	71	280	8,190
Miles Tunnicliff	69	68	76	67	280	8,190
Mads Vibe-Hastrup	68	70	74	68	280	8,190
Jesus Maria Arruti	70	69	72	70	281	6,760
Nicolas Colsaerts	68	73	72	68	281	6,760
Ian Garbutt	71	67	73	70	281	6,760
Hernan Rey	69	73	69	70	281	6,760
Sebastian Fernandez	74	68	70	70	282	5,850
Terry Pilkadaris	71	70	71	70	282	5,850

	SCORES				TOTAL	MONEY
Kyron Sullivan	68	72	71	71	282	5,850
Peter Fowler	70	72	70	71	283	4,810
Roope Kakko	74	68	72	69	283	4,810
Carl Suneson	69	72	70	72	283	4,810
Alessandro Tadini	67	72	73	71	283	4,810
Lee Westwood	66	72	75	70	283	4,810
Jean Hugo	72	70	69	73	284	3,965
Simon Nash	73	68	68	75	284	3,965
Robert-Jan Derksen	70	70	69	76	285	3,770
Rafael Gomez	70	71	75	70	286	3,575
Iain Pyman	71	70	73	72	286	3,575
Richard Bland	70	71	70	76	287	3,315
Daniel Denison	66	76	73	72	287	3,315
Andrew Butterfield	72	70	73	73	288	3,120
Jose Manuel Carriles	70	71	74	75	290	2,860
Matjaz Gojcic	68	70	73	79	290	2,860
Wade Ormsby	73	69	79	69	290	2,860
Marc Cayeux	70	71	76	74	291	2,600

Open de Saint-Omer

Aa St. Omer Golf Club, Lumbres, France
Par 36-35–71; 6,845 yards

June 14-17
purse, €508,085

	SCORES				TOTAL	MONEY
Carl Suneson	67	70	70	69	276	€83,330
Francois Calmels	72	69	69	69	279	37,283.33
Peter Fowler	70	67	72	70	279	37,283.33
Marcus Higley	67	70	71	71	279	37,283.33
Mikael Lundberg	70	68	71	71	280	21,200
Michael Lorenzo-Vera	67	73	71	70	281	17,500
Stuart Davis	68	70	72	73	283	12,900
Sebastien Delagrange	72	68	73	70	283	12,900
Richard McEvoy	74	66	74	69	283	12,900
Daniel Denison	67	74	72	71	284	9,266.67
Klas Eriksson	74	70	71	69	284	9,266.67
Gareth Paddison	68	72	72	72	284	9,266.67
Liam Bond	70	73	74	68	285	7,683.33
Gary Clark	70	73	71	71	285	7,683.33
Sam Little	72	69	74	70	285	7,683.33
Raphael Eyraud	67	73	73	73	286	6,271.43
Martin Maritz	74	70	72	70	286	6,271.43
Simon Nash	66	74	73	73	286	6,271.43
Andrew Oldcorn	70	74	71	71	286	6,271.43
Wilhelm Schauman	72	70	73	71	286	6,271.43
Jerome Theunis	75	70	72	69	286	6,271.43
Julio Zapata	71	68	75	72	286	6,271.43
Mickael Dieu	74	71	68	74	287	5,350
Santiago Luna	67	71	77	72	287	5,350
Gustavo Rojas	70	75	67	75	287	5,350
Steve Alker	71	68	73	76	288	4,600
Jesus Maria Arruti	75	69	73	71	288	4,600
Sion E. Bebb	69	72	75	72	288	4,600
Birgir Hafthorsson	70	74	72	72	288	4,600
Andrew McArthur	70	73	70	75	288	4,600
Manuel Merizalde	69	72	71	76	288	4,600
Thomas Nielsen	71	74	71	72	288	4,600
Richard Finch	73	72	73	71	289	3,760
Anders Schmidt Hansen	67	75	71	76	289	3,760
David Higgins	65	76	74	74	289	3,760

	SCORES				TOTAL	MONEY
Jan-Are Larsen	74	71	71	73	289	3,760
Paul Nilbrink	73	72	71	73	289	3,760
Peter Baker	71	73	71	75	290	3,100
Robert Coles	73	70	71	76	290	3,100
Sebastian Fernandez	74	70	73	73	290	3,100
Philip Golding	71	71	74	74	290	3,100
Roope Kakko	71	73	73	73	290	3,100
Stuart Manley	73	71	73	73	290	3,100
Ross McGowan	70	73	73	74	290	3,100
Cedric Menut	73	71	73	73	290	3,100
Felipe Aguilar	72	70	77	72	291	2,500
Jean-Nicolas Billot	70	75	73	73	291	2,500
Mikko Korhonen	71	73	78	69	291	2,500
Paolo Terreni	71	68	81	71	291	2,500
Ally Mellor	69	72	78	73	292	2,100
Iain Pyman	72	72	76	72	292	2,100
Nicolas Vanhootegem	75	70	73	74	292	2,100
Alvaro Velasco	73	71	71	77	292	2,100
Jamie Donaldson	69	73	79	72	293	1,800
Adrien Mork	72	72	78	71	293	1,800
David Bransdon	65	77	78	74	294	1,405.56
Julien Clement	69	71	77	77	294	1,405.56
Carlos Del Moral	70	74	74	76	294	1,405.56
Robert Dinwiddie	71	73	75	75	294	1,405.56
Matthew King	72	68	76	78	294	1,405.56
Joost Luiten	70	75	75	74	294	1,405.56
Sven Struver	71	74	77	72	294	1,405.56
Benoit Teilleria	71	73	77	73	294	1,405.56
Niki Zitny	71	69	75	79	294	1,405.56
Luis Claverie	74	70	76	75	295	1,050
Chris Doak	73	69	78	75	295	1,050
Hernan Rey	71	72	80	72	295	1,050
Johan Skold	72	73	72	78	295	1,050
Julien Xanthopoulos	71	73	79	72	295	1,050
Rodolfo Gonzalez	70	75	76	75	296	835
Gareth Wright	71	73	74	78	296	835
Joakim Haeggman	72	72	73	80	297	742.50
Andrew Raitt	71	74	75	77	297	742.50
Scott Strange	71	74	79	73	297	742.50
Craig Williams	73	71	78	75	297	742.50
Stephen Browne	71	72	77	78	298	733.50
Phil Worthington	75	70	76	77	298	733.50
Alessio Bruschi	73	72	75	79	299	729
Kariem Baraka	73	71	81	75	300	724.50
Alvaro Salto	71	74	80	75	300	724.50
Francois Delamontagne	74	71	78	78	301	720

BMW International Open

Golfclub Munchen Nord-Eichenreid, Munich, Germany
Par 36-36–72; 6,955 yards

June 21-24
purse, €1,979,950

	SCORES				TOTAL	MONEY
Niclas Fasth	67	65	73	70	275	€333,330
Bernhard Langer	76	66	68	67	277	173,710
Jose-Filipe Lima	65	70	70	72	277	173,710
Ricardo Gonzalez	68	71	69	70	278	84,933.33
Anders Hansen	68	70	72	68	278	84,933.33
Maarten Lafeber	71	67	73	67	278	84,933.33
Ernie Els	67	71	74	67	279	55,000

	SCORES				TOTAL	MONEY
Simon Khan	70	71	72	66	279	55,000
Benn Barham	72	69	71	68	280	42,400
Thomas Levet	68	67	72	73	280	42,400
Emanuele Canonica	69	73	70	69	281	31,228.57
Simon Dyson	72	66	73	70	281	31,228.57
Alastair Forsyth	68	73	67	73	281	31,228.57
Peter Hanson	68	66	74	73	281	31,228.57
Raphael Jacquelin	65	74	73	69	281	31,228.57
Jyoti Randhawa	70	69	73	69	281	31,228.57
Anthony Wall	72	70	73	66	281	31,228.57
Miguel Angel Jimenez	69	69	74	70	282	24,450
Jeev Milkha Singh	69	72	70	71	282	24,450
Sven Struver	72	66	71	73	282	24,450
Oliver Wilson	70	68	75	69	282	24,450
Steven Jeppesen	68	74	74	67	283	21,700
Shiv Kapur	72	70	73	68	283	21,700
Sam Little	74	67	74	68	283	21,700
Andres Romero	67	68	75	73	283	21,700
Nick Dougherty	68	68	71	77	284	18,400
Ross Fisher	71	71	76	66	284	18,400
David Frost	67	70	70	77	284	18,400
Ian Garbutt	69	71	75	69	284	18,400
David Lynn	71	66	74	73	284	18,400
Steven O'Hara	69	70	73	72	284	18,400
Henrik Stenson	73	66	73	72	284	18,400
Rafael Cabrera Bello	69	70	74	72	285	14,833.33
Christian Cevaer	70	67	72	76	285	14,833.33
Peter Fowler	68	73	71	73	285	14,833.33
Philip Golding	71	69	74	71	285	14,833.33
David Griffiths	69	69	73	74	285	14,833.33
Phillip Price	73	69	68	75	285	14,833.33
Paul Casey	68	70	74	74	286	12,800
Gonzalo Fernandez-Castano	66	72	72	76	286	12,800
Peter Hedblom	71	70	75	70	286	12,800
Henrik Nystrom	71	68	75	72	286	12,800
Martin Erlandsson	68	72	75	72	287	11,600
Mads Vibe-Hastrup	74	66	78	69	287	11,600
Peter Gustafsson	73	65	75	75	288	10,600
Peter Lawrie	71	67	77	73	288	10,600
Terry Price	74	68	74	72	288	10,600
Markus Brier	71	69	74	75	289	9,200
David Higgins	73	69	74	73	289	9,200
Francesco Molinari	67	73	75	74	289	9,200
Lee Slattery	75	66	76	72	289	9,200
Paul Broadhurst	66	73	79	72	290	7,800
Alejandro Canizares	74	67	77	72	290	7,800
Tom Whitehouse	70	68	77	75	290	7,800
Edward Rush	71	70	75	75	291	7,000
Brett Rumford	70	70	77	75	292	6,600
David Park	72	70	77	74	293	6,200
Alexander Noren	72	69	74	79	294	6,000
Juan Parron	74	67	72	82	295	5,800
Marc Farry	66	76	75	80	297	5,400
Darren Fichardt	73	69	80	75	297	5,400
Jamie Spence	71	71	78	77	297	5,400
Jean-Francois Lucquin	71	71	79	77	298	5,000
Alexandre Rocha	73	67	78	81	299	4,700
Graeme Storm	71	69	78	81	299	4,700

Open de France ALSTOM

Le Golf National, Paris, France
Par 36-35–71; 7,225 yards

June 28-July 1
purse, €3,968,700

	SCORES				TOTAL	MONEY
Graeme Storm	66	74	71	66	277	€666,660
Soren Hansen	69	71	66	72	278	444,440
Thomas Bjorn	68	71	71	69	279	190,000
Simon Khan	70	67	70	72	279	190,000
Damien McGrane	68	72	74	65	279	190,000
Colin Montgomerie	68	70	71	70	279	190,000
Martin Kaymer	70	70	69	71	280	110,000
Jyoti Randhawa	68	72	72	68	280	110,000
Ian Poulter	70	74	68	69	281	89,600
Bradley Dredge	73	71	70	68	282	76,800
David Lynn	72	69	69	72	282	76,800
Robert-Jan Derksen	69	72	71	71	283	64,800
Zane Scotland	68	71	72	72	283	64,800
Jeev Milkha Singh	71	72	67	73	283	64,800
Phillip Archer	72	72	69	71	284	55,200
Mark Foster	72	72	72	68	284	55,200
Gregory Havret	69	74	71	70	284	55,200
Jose-Filipe Lima	68	72	73	71	284	55,200
Gregory Bourdy	75	71	68	71	285	48,800
Pelle Edberg	73	69	70	73	285	48,800
Soren Kjeldsen	70	75	70	71	286	45,800
Maarten Lafeber	72	73	71	70	286	45,800
Benn Barham	66	75	72	74	287	43,400
Richard Finch	71	70	75	71	287	43,400
Johan Axgren	69	76	72	71	288	37,400
Ariel Canete	70	74	76	68	288	37,400
Nick Dougherty	73	69	73	73	288	37,400
Jean-Baptiste Gonnet	73	69	75	71	288	37,400
David Griffiths	70	74	69	75	288	37,400
Paul McGinley	69	69	75	75	288	37,400
Richard Sterne	71	71	76	70	288	37,400
Kyron Sullivan	65	74	77	72	288	37,400
Markus Brier	68	76	75	70	289	28,444.44
Michael Campbell	71	74	77	67	289	28,444.44
Stephen Dodd	71	72	69	77	289	28,444.44
Stephen Gallacher	71	73	73	72	289	28,444.44
Steven Jeppesen	66	77	68	78	289	28,444.44
Paul Lawrie	71	72	75	71	289	28,444.44
Taichi Teshima	72	72	76	69	289	28,444.44
Lee Westwood	71	72	69	77	289	28,444.44
Tom Whitehouse	70	69	77	73	289	28,444.44
Christian Cevaer	71	74	72	73	290	21,600
Oliver Fisher	70	75	73	72	290	21,600
Raphael Jacquelin	68	73	76	73	290	21,600
Peter Lawrie	69	72	71	78	290	21,600
Robert Rock	71	72	71	76	290	21,600
Sven Struver	72	74	74	70	290	21,600
Alessandro Tadini	73	72	71	74	290	21,600
Oliver Wilson	73	69	73	75	290	21,600
Francois Delamontagne	72	74	76	69	291	17,600
Marcus Fraser	75	69	72	75	291	17,600
Darren Fichardt	71	71	71	79	292	16,000
Steve Webster	72	72	75	73	292	16,000
James Kamte	65	78	75	75	293	13,600
Santiago Luna	70	75	75	73	293	13,600
Miguel Angel Martin	68	77	71	77	293	13,600
Christian L. Nilsson	66	76	71	80	293	13,600

	SCORES				TOTAL	MONEY
Thomas Levet	67	73	77	77	294	12,000
Simon Dyson	75	70	76	74	295	11,600
Rafael Echenique	72	74	71	79	296	10,800
Peter O'Malley	73	73	74	76	296	10,800
Patrik Sjoland	73	71	73	79	296	10,800
Marcus Higley	70	76	74	77	297	9,800
Gary Lockerbie	74	70	75	78	297	9,800
Juan Parron	71	72	78	77	298	9,200
Marcel Siem	72	72	74	81	299	8,800

Smurfit Kappa European Open

The K Club, Straffan, Co. Kildare, Ireland
Par 36-34–70; 6,897 yards

July 5-8
purse, €3,548,214

	SCORES				TOTAL	MONEY
Colin Montgomerie	69	64	71	65	269	€593,580.01
Niclas Fasth	65	68	70	67	270	395,710.11
Pelle Edberg	67	65	73	66	271	169,170.30
Peter Hanson	68	69	66	68	271	169,170.30
Gregory Havret	65	70	68	68	271	169,170.30
Anthony Wall	68	72	66	65	271	169,170.30
Soren Hansen	69	68	63	72	272	86,722.04
Peter Hedblom	68	68	68	68	272	86,722.04
Thomas Levet	70	67	68	67	272	86,722.04
Peter O'Malley	72	68	63	69	272	86,722.04
Raphael Jacquelin	71	69	67	66	273	59,654.79
Simon Khan	67	67	71	68	273	59,654.79
Soren Kjeldsen	66	71	69	67	273	59,654.79
Robert Rock	65	71	66	71	273	59,654.79
Phillip Archer	70	69	66	69	274	50,216.87
Mikko Ilonen	67	72	69	66	274	50,216.87
Per-Ulrik Johansson	69	69	69	67	274	50,216.87
Rafael Cabrera Bello	69	71	68	67	275	41,669.32
Ariel Canete	67	71	72	65	275	41,669.32
Peter Fowler	70	71	67	67	275	41,669.32
Richard Green	69	67	71	68	275	41,669.32
Joakim Haeggman	68	70	68	69	275	41,669.32
Graeme McDowell	69	70	65	71	275	41,669.32
Alexander Noren	70	71	70	64	275	41,669.32
Markus Brier	71	68	70	67	276	32,765.62
Paul Broadhurst	72	69	67	68	276	32,765.62
Martin Erlandsson	69	66	71	70	276	32,765.62
David Frost	68	66	70	72	276	32,765.62
Ricardo Gonzalez	73	68	64	71	276	32,765.62
Thongchai Jaidee	71	67	70	68	276	32,765.62
Jyoti Randhawa	65	70	71	70	276	32,765.62
Marc Warren	69	69	70	68	276	32,765.62
Steve Webster	70	70	65	71	276	32,765.62
Christian Cevaer	71	70	70	66	277	25,286.51
Johan Edfors	69	70	68	70	277	25,286.51
Gonzalo Fernandez-Castano	70	69	70	68	277	25,286.51
David Griffiths	70	70	68	69	277	25,286.51
Andres Romero	73	67	71	66	277	25,286.51
Jeev Milkha Singh	67	73	69	68	277	25,286.51
Simon Wakefield	70	69	65	73	277	25,286.51
Jean-Baptiste Gonnet	69	68	67	74	278	21,368.88
Patrik Sjoland	66	69	72	71	278	21,368.88
Sven Struver	73	67	66	72	278	21,368.88
Mads Vibe-Hastrup	68	72	71	67	278	21,368.88

	SCORES				TOTAL	MONEY
Robert-Jan Derksen	73	66	72	68	279	17,807.40
Alastair Forsyth	72	68	69	70	279	17,807.40
David Howell	69	72	69	69	279	17,807.40
Terry Price	71	69	69	70	279	17,807.40
Marcel Siem	68	73	71	67	279	17,807.40
Graeme Storm	71	67	74	67	279	17,807.40
Michael Campbell	68	71	69	72	280	13,889.77
Stephen Dodd	66	73	71	70	280	13,889.77
Padraig Harrington	71	68	69	72	280	13,889.77
Maarten Lafeber	64	72	72	72	280	13,889.77
Paul Lawrie	70	69	72	69	280	13,889.77
Jesus Maria Arruti	68	72	74	67	281	10,951.55
Ian Garbutt	67	73	71	70	281	10,951.55
David Higgins	73	68	68	72	281	10,951.55
Gary Lockerbie	71	70	69	71	281	10,951.55
Angel Cabrera	71	69	74	68	282	9,437.92
Ignacio Garrido	69	69	66	78	282	9,437.92
Francesco Molinari	71	70	72	69	282	9,437.92
Y.E. Yang	73	68	70	71	282	9,437.92
Jose Manuel Lara	68	72	73	71	284	8,191.40
Mark Pilkington	71	70	75	68	284	8,191.40
Lee Slattery	72	68	72	72	284	8,191.40
Rafael Echenique	72	69	74	70	285	7,479.11
Thaworn Wiratchant	68	73	69	77	287	7,122.96

Barclays Scottish Open

Loch Lomond Golf Club, Glasgow, Scotland
Par 36-35–71; 7,139 yards

July 12-15
purse, €4,394,876

	SCORES				TOTAL	MONEY
Gregory Havret	68	64	70	68	270	€738,255.02
Phil Mickelson	65	68	68	69	270	492,165.09
(Havret defeated Mickelson on first playoff hole.)						
Ernie Els	69	66	71	65	271	277,288.59
Luke Donald	70	69	70	64	273	174,302.01
Pelle Edberg	67	68	72	66	273	174,302.01
Louis Oosthuizen	70	71	64	68	273	174,302.01
Richard Sterne	72	69	68	64	273	174,302.01
Mikko Ilonen	66	70	70	68	274	99,516.78
Ian Poulter	69	67	71	67	274	99,516.78
Steve Webster	68	67	69	70	274	99,516.78
Soren Kjeldsen	67	74	69	65	275	78,845.64
Graeme McDowell	70	71	67	67	275	78,845.64
Phillip Archer	68	68	69	71	276	66,664.43
Robert-Jan Derksen	69	68	73	66	276	66,664.43
Mark Foster	66	74	71	65	276	66,664.43
Peter Hanson	72	67	69	68	276	66,664.43
Shaun Micheel	67	71	70	69	277	58,469.80
Alessandro Tadini	72	68	69	68	277	58,469.80
Angel Cabrera	71	70	70	67	278	47,516.78
Alejandro Canizares	72	67	68	71	278	47,516.78
Darren Clarke	71	67	74	66	278	47,516.78
Richard Finch	68	70	72	68	278	47,516.78
Ross Fisher	69	69	69	71	278	47,516.78
Oliver Fisher	70	71	67	70	278	47,516.78
Ian Garbutt	71	69	69	69	278	47,516.78
Sergio Garcia	71	65	71	71	278	47,516.78
Soren Hansen	65	73	71	69	278	47,516.78
Jose Manuel Lara	67	65	74	72	278	47,516.78

	SCORES				TOTAL	MONEY
Lee Westwood	65	74	70	69	278	47,516.78
Bradley Dredge	68	72	72	67	279	38,758.39
Boo Weekley	68	66	74	71	279	38,758.39
Paul Broadhurst	71	70	71	68	280	34,882.55
Raphael Jacquelin	69	70	73	68	280	34,882.55
Simon Khan	67	67	75	71	280	34,882.55
Jyoti Randhawa	71	69	70	70	280	34,882.55
Peter Hedblom	69	70	70	72	281	31,449.66
Andrew McLardy	71	68	75	67	281	31,449.66
Kyron Sullivan	70	69	73	69	281	31,449.66
Thomas Levet	70	67	73	72	282	28,348.99
Andrew Marshall	70	71	70	71	282	28,348.99
Graeme Storm	65	72	72	73	282	28,348.99
Miles Tunnicliff	68	67	73	74	282	28,348.99
Gregory Bourdy	70	67	75	71	283	23,919.46
Ignacio Garrido	72	68	71	72	283	23,919.46
Peter Lawrie	68	73	71	71	283	23,919.46
Phillip Price	71	67	74	71	283	23,919.46
Jeev Milkha Singh	72	67	71	73	283	23,919.46
Patrik Sjoland	68	71	71	73	283	23,919.46
Thomas Bjorn	69	70	73	72	284	19,932.89
Garry Houston	69	71	71	73	284	19,932.89
Paul McGinley	68	70	74	72	284	19,932.89
Ariel Canete	68	68	76	73	285	17,275.17
Sam Walker	67	69	77	72	285	17,275.17
Oliver Wilson	74	67	75	69	285	17,275.17
Martin Erlandsson	72	69	72	73	286	15,060.40
Y.E. Yang	73	68	73	72	286	15,060.40
James Hepworth	71	70	73	73	287	13,288.59
Paul Lawrie	68	71	74	74	287	13,288.59
Matthew Millar	72	69	73	73	287	13,288.59
Peter O'Malley	70	70	75	73	288	11,959.73
Wade Ormsby	70	70	78	70	288	11,959.73
Lee Slattery	69	71	72	76	288	11,959.73
Joakim Backstrom	72	68	78	72	290	10,852.35
David Drysdale	70	69	75	76	290	10,852.35
Andres Romero	67	67	80	77	291	10,187.92
Mardan Mamat	69	72	75	76	292	9,744.97

The Open Championship

Carnoustie Golf Links, Carnoustie, Scotland
Par 36-35–71; 7,421 yards

July 19-22
purse, €6,162,532

	SCORES				TOTAL	MONEY
Padraig Harrington	69	73	68	67	277	€1,106,617.50
Sergio Garcia	65	71	68	73	277	663,970.50
(Harrington defeated Garcia 15-16 in four-hole playoff.)						
Andres Romero	71	70	70	67	278	427,892.10
Ernie Els	72	70	68	69	279	295,098
Richard Green	72	73	70	64	279	295,098
Stewart Cink	69	73	68	70	280	214,683.80
Hunter Mahan	73	73	69	65	280	214,683.80
K.J. Choi	69	69	72	71	281	139,802.68
Ben Curtis	72	74	70	65	281	139,802.68
Steve Stricker	71	72	64	74	281	139,802.68
Mike Weir	71	68	72	70	281	139,802.68
Markus Brier	68	75	70	69	282	86,421.56
Paul Broadhurst	71	71	68	72	282	86,421.56
Pelle Edberg	72	73	67	70	282	86,421.56

	SCORES				TOTAL	MONEY
Jim Furyk	70	70	71	71	282	86,421.56
Miguel Angel Jimenez	69	70	72	71	282	86,421.56
Justin Rose	75	70	67	70	282	86,421.56
Tiger Woods	69	74	69	70	282	86,421.56
Paul McGinley	67	75	68	73	283	67,872.54
Rich Beem	70	73	69	72	284	61,970.58
Zach Johnson	73	73	68	70	284	61,970.58
Pat Perez	73	70	71	70	284	61,970.58
Jonathan Byrd	73	72	70	70	285	52,472.11
Mark Calcavecchia	74	70	72	69	285	52,472.11
Chris DiMarco	74	70	66	75	285	52,472.11
Retief Goosen	70	71	73	71	285	52,472.11
Paul Casey	72	73	69	72	286	41,577.20
Lucas Glover	71	72	70	73	286	41,577.20
J.J. Henry	70	71	71	74	286	41,577.20
Rodney Pampling	70	72	72	72	286	41,577.20
Ian Poulter	73	73	70	70	286	41,577.20
Adam Scott	73	70	72	71	286	41,577.20
Vijay Singh	72	71	68	75	286	41,577.20
Angel Cabrera	68	73	72	74	287	35,411.76
Niclas Fasth	75	69	73	71	288	29,667.89
Mark Foster	76	70	73	69	288	29,667.89
Charley Hoffman	75	69	72	72	288	29,667.89
Shaun Micheel	70	76	70	72	288	29,667.89
Nick Watney	72	71	70	75	288	29,667.89
Boo Weekley	68	72	75	73	288	29,667.89
Lee Westwood	71	70	73	74	288	29,667.89
Nick Dougherty	71	74	69	75	289	24,161.15
*Rory McIlroy	68	76	73	72	289	
Ryan Moore	72	72	74	71	289	24,161.15
Ross Bain	73	71	72	74	290	21,394.61
Arron Oberholser	73	71	72	74	290	21,394.61
Carl Pettersson	70	75	73	72	290	21,394.61
John Senden	72	74	71	73	290	21,394.61
Jerry Kelly	74	70	71	76	291	19,181.37
Lee Won-joon	73	73	70	75	291	19,181.37
Tom Lehman	73	73	74	73	293	17,890.32
Kevin Stadler	75	71	74	73	293	17,890.32
Thomas Bjorn	70	75	74	75	294	16,783.70
Gregory Bourdy	70	72	77	75	294	16,783.70
Brian Davis	74	72	71	77	294	16,783.70
David Howell	72	74	73	75	294	16,783.70
Michael Campbell	68	78	72	77	295	15,935.29
Anders Hansen	72	73	74	76	295	15,935.29
Scott Verplank	72	73	72	78	295	15,935.29
Trevor Immelman	71	74	77	74	296	15,492.65
Mark O'Meara	74	72	76	74	296	15,492.65
Toru Taniguchi	72	72	76	76	296	15,492.65
Jon Bevan	73	73	79	72	297	15,123.77
Luke Donald	70	76	73	78	297	15,123.77
Raphael Jacquelin	74	69	76	79	298	14,828.67
Sandy Lyle	73	73	73	79	298	14,828.67
Alastair Forsyth	70	71	78	80	299	14,533.58
Sean O'Hair	71	75	74	79	299	14,533.58
Fredrik Andersson Hed	72	71	79	78	300	14,238.48
Peter Hanson	70	74	76	80	300	14,238.48

Out of Final 36 Holes

Joe Durant	77	70			147	4,721.57
Johan Edfors	72	75			147	4,721.57
Peter Fowler	74	73			147	4,721.57
Tomohiro Kondo	74	73			147	4,721.57

	SCORES		TOTAL	MONEY
Paul Lawrie	73	74	147	4,721.57
Justin Leonard	74	73	147	4,721.57
Colin Montgomerie	73	74	147	4,721.57
Tom Pernice, Jr.	74	73	147	4,721.57
Henrik Stenson	71	76	147	4,721.57
Matthew Zions	72	75	147	4,721.57
Benn Barham	75	73	148	3,910.05
Darren Clarke	72	76	148	3,910.05
Gregory Havret	72	76	148	3,910.05
Toshimitsu Izawa	75	73	148	3,910.05
Phil Mickelson	71	77	148	3,910.05
Terry Pilkadaris	74	74	148	3,910.05
Brett Quigley	72	76	148	3,910.05
John Rollins	72	76	148	3,910.05
David Toms	71	77	148	3,910.05
*Drew Weaver	76	72	148	
Steve Alker	74	75	149	3,910.05
Stuart Appleby	74	75	149	3,910.05
Peter Baker	73	76	149	3,910.05
Chad Campbell	74	75	149	3,910.05
Adilson Da Silva	74	75	149	3,910.05
Ross Fisher	74	75	149	3,910.05
David Frost	74	75	149	3,910.05
Charles Howell	73	76	149	3,910.05
Geoff Ogilvy	75	74	149	3,910.05
Nick O'Hern	71	78	149	3,910.05
Loren Roberts	74	75	149	3,910.05
Achi Sato	71	78	149	3,910.05
Hideto Tanihara	72	77	149	3,910.05
Brett Wetterich	75	74	149	3,910.05
John Daly	74	76	150	3,504.29
Bradley Dredge	76	74	150	3,504.29
Mattias Eliasson	74	76	150	3,504.29
David Higgins	79	71	150	3,504.29
Matt Kuchar	74	76	150	3,504.29
Spencer Levin	76	74	150	3,504.29
Davis Love	79	71	150	3,504.29
Graeme McDowell	77	73	150	3,504.29
Francesco Molinari	76	74	150	3,504.29
Michael Putnam	78	72	150	3,504.29
Rory Sabbatini	76	74	150	3,504.29
Charl Schwartzel	75	75	150	3,504.29
Paul Sheehan	75	75	150	3,504.29
Jeev Milkha Singh	77	73	150	3,504.29
Richard Sterne	76	74	150	3,504.29
Stephen Ames	81	70	151	3,504.29
Aaron Baddeley	78	73	151	3,504.29
John Bickerton	75	76	151	3,504.29
*Richie Ramsay	76	75	151	
Robert Allenby	73	79	152	3,504.29
Nick Faldo	79	73	152	3,504.29
Kevin Harper	77	75	152	3,504.29
Robert Karlsson	74	78	152	3,504.29
Oliver Wilson	80	72	152	3,504.29
Y.E. Yang	74	78	152	3,504.29
*David Coupland	79	74	153	
Todd Hamilton	81	72	153	3,098.53
Lam Chih Bing	76	77	153	3,098.53
Lee Dong-hwan	75	78	153	3,098.53
Lee Seung-ho	77	76	153	3,098.53
Toshinori Muto	74	79	153	3,098.53
David Shacklady	76	77	153	3,098.53
Anthony Wall	77	76	153	3,098.53

	SCORES				TOTAL	MONEY
Mark Hensby	79	75			154	3,098.53
Anders Hultman	77	77			154	3,098.53
Scott Laycock	74	80			154	3,098.53
Jose-Filipe Lima	75	79			154	3,098.53
Steven Parry	73	81			154	3,098.53
*Paul Waring	74	80			154	
Duffy Waldorf	82	73			155	3,098.53
Desvonde Botes	78	78			156	3,098.53
Vaughn Taylor	82	74			156	3,098.53
Justin Kehoe	78	79			157	3,098.53
Doug McGuigan	77	80			157	3,098.53
Ben Bunny	81	77			158	3,098.53
*Llewellyn Matthews	75	83			158	
Graeme Storm	78	80			158	3,098.53
Scott Drummond	79	81			160	3,098.53
David Gleeson	83	77			160	3,098.53
Adam Groom	79	81			160	3,098.53
Tony Jacklin	78	83			161	3,098.53
Ewan Porter	83	79			162	3,098.53

Deutsche Bank Players' Championship of Europe

Gut Kaden, Hamburg, Germany | July 26-29
Par 36-36–72; 7,290 yards | purse, €3,648,492

	SCORES				TOTAL	MONEY
Andres Romero	68	68	63	70	269	€600,000
Soren Hansen	72	70	66	64	272	312,680
Oliver Wilson	66	70	70	66	272	312,680
Peter O'Malley	69	72	68	65	274	180,000
Peter Hanson	69	70	68	68	275	139,320
Alexander Noren	67	71	65	72	275	139,320
Charley Hoffman	68	72	67	69	276	87,660
Lee Slattery	66	69	67	74	276	87,660
Steve Webster	73	67	70	66	276	87,660
Brett Wetterich	69	70	67	70	276	87,660
Johan Edfors	71	70	69	67	277	60,300
Ross Fisher	69	72	68	68	277	60,300
Rory Sabbatini	78	65	66	68	277	60,300
Zane Scotland	67	68	66	76	277	60,300
Benn Barham	69	70	68	71	278	48,672
Anton Haig	69	69	72	68	278	48,672
Miguel Angel Jimenez	69	68	71	70	278	48,672
Andrew McLardy	71	72	70	65	278	48,672
Miles Tunnicliff	73	69	66	70	278	48,672
John Bickerton	68	71	68	72	279	40,200
Peter Gustafsson	72	68	69	70	279	40,200
Robert Karlsson	69	71	66	73	279	40,200
Nick O'Hern	69	71	68	71	279	40,200
Charl Schwartzel	71	72	65	71	279	40,200
Sam Walker	70	73	67	69	279	40,200
Niclas Fasth	68	75	71	66	280	31,058.18
Ian Garbutt	71	69	71	69	280	31,058.18
Jean-Baptiste Gonnet	70	72	67	71	280	31,058.18
Retief Goosen	70	73	67	70	280	31,058.18
David Lynn	68	73	69	70	280	31,058.18
Matthew Millar	70	71	68	71	280	31,058.18
Wade Ormsby	72	69	70	69	280	31,058.18
Carlos Rodiles	67	72	71	70	280	31,058.18
Tino Schuster	69	72	66	73	280	31,058.18

	SCORES				TOTAL	MONEY
Richard Sterne	74	65	72	69	280	31,058.18
Taichi Teshima	67	74	70	69	280	31,058.18
Shiv Kapur	71	67	70	73	281	24,840
Peter Lawrie	72	69	70	70	281	24,840
Paul McGinley	72	70	69	70	281	24,840
Emanuele Canonica	71	70	69	72	282	19,800
Bradley Dredge	69	69	73	71	282	19,800
Alastair Forsyth	70	73	69	70	282	19,800
Mikko Ilonen	72	71	71	68	282	19,800
Jose-Filipe Lima	70	72	71	69	282	19,800
Christian L. Nilsson	71	72	71	68	282	19,800
Steven O'Hara	69	70	70	73	282	19,800
Rodney Pampling	71	69	70	72	282	19,800
Kyron Sullivan	71	72	67	72	282	19,800
Andrew Tampion	71	69	70	72	282	19,800
Anthony Wall	70	73	69	70	282	19,800
Ariel Canete	70	71	66	76	283	13,680
Paul Casey	68	70	68	77	283	13,680
Mark Foster	71	71	70	71	283	13,680
David Frost	68	72	69	74	283	13,680
Jean-Francois Lucquin	71	72	67	73	283	13,680
Damien McGrane	69	71	72	71	283	13,680
Oliver Fisher	71	72	68	73	284	10,980
Ricardo Gonzalez	67	76	70	71	284	10,980
Gregory Bourdy	72	69	71	73	285	9,900
David Griffiths	70	72	68	75	285	9,900
Terry Price	71	69	74	71	285	9,900
Marcel Siem	71	69	75	70	285	9,900
Gary Birch, Jr.	73	70	72	71	286	8,280
Martin Erlandsson	72	67	73	74	286	8,280
Stephen Gallacher	68	74	72	72	286	8,280
Soren Kjeldsen	70	71	74	71	286	8,280
Phillip Price	74	69	73	70	286	8,280
Garry Houston	72	70	71	74	287	6,500
Max Kramer	71	72	70	74	287	6,500
Thomas Levet	70	71	73	73	287	6,500
Brett Rumford	69	73	71	74	287	6,500
Johan Axgren	67	76	75	70	288	5,392.50
Mardan Mamat	72	71	71	74	288	5,392.50
Daniel Vancsik	70	73	74	71	288	5,392.50
Marc Warren	68	73	75	72	288	5,392.50
Jarmo Sandelin	69	74	71	75	289	5,385
Gary Murphy	70	73	73	74	290	5,380.50
Edward Rush	71	72	71	76	290	5,380.50
Sion E. Bebb	72	70	73	76	291	5,376

Russian Open Golf Championship

Le Meridien Moscow Country Club, Moscow, Russia
Par 36-36–72; 7,154 yards

August 2-5
purse, €1,469,913

	SCORES				TOTAL	MONEY
Per-Ulrik Johansson	69	62	67	67	265	€244,250.88
Robert-Jan Derksen	68	69	65	69	271	162,833.92
Alan McLean	73	64	67	68	272	91,741.55
Adam Gee	69	68	68	70	275	67,707.02
Dawie van der Walt	72	68	68	67	275	67,707.02
Christopher Hanell	73	65	69	70	277	43,965.60
Gary Murphy	67	68	70	72	277	43,965.60
Steve Webster	73	68	71	65	277	43,965.60

	SCORES				TOTAL	MONEY
Kasper Linnet Jorgensen	73	70	68	67	278	28,577.64
Sam Little	67	71	69	71	278	28,577.64
Henrik Nystrom	73	70	69	66	278	28,577.64
Sam Walker	69	71	68	70	278	28,577.64
Jesus Maria Arruti	70	68	72	69	279	20,334.09
Richard Bland	74	71	66	68	279	20,334.09
Philip Golding	70	69	70	70	279	20,334.09
Peter Gustafsson	71	69	70	69	279	20,334.09
Simon Lilly	70	71	67	71	279	20,334.09
Terry Pilkadaris	73	71	68	67	279	20,334.09
Carlos Rodiles	71	70	70	68	279	20,334.09
Kyron Sullivan	71	71	73	64	279	20,334.09
David Carter	71	67	73	69	280	16,340.55
Simon Hurd	73	70	68	69	280	16,340.55
Alexandre Rocha	68	68	72	72	280	16,340.55
Scott Strange	71	71	70	68	280	16,340.55
Gareth Davies	70	71	70	70	281	14,142.27
Joakim Haeggman	71	72	69	69	281	14,142.27
Jeppe Huldahl	69	72	69	71	281	14,142.27
Peter Lawrie	71	69	69	72	281	14,142.27
Marcel Siem	75	64	70	72	281	14,142.27
Matthew Zions	72	71	70	68	281	14,142.27
Jean-Baptiste Gonnet	66	71	71	74	282	11,410.12
Julien Guerrier	68	76	70	68	282	11,410.12
Christian L. Nilsson	65	71	72	74	282	11,410.12
Brett Rumford	72	70	67	73	282	11,410.12
Alvaro Salto	72	73	71	66	282	11,410.12
Zane Scotland	70	75	69	68	282	11,410.12
Lee Slattery	71	70	73	68	282	11,410.12
Peter Fowler	70	72	71	70	283	9,525.88
Keith Horne	73	68	72	70	283	9,525.88
Lasse Jensen	72	72	71	68	283	9,525.88
Prom Meesawat	71	70	72	70	283	9,525.88
Jean-Francois Remesy	76	68	70	69	283	9,525.88
*Chris Wood	72	68	73	70	283	
Steven Jeppesen	70	71	71	72	284	8,206.91
Euan Little	72	70	72	70	284	8,206.91
Martin Maritz	72	71	73	68	284	8,206.91
Tim Milford	75	69	70	70	284	8,206.91
Richard McEvoy	70	72	73	70	285	6,741.39
Iain Pyman	74	68	71	72	285	6,741.39
Manuel Quiros	72	73	73	67	285	6,741.39
Edward Rush	72	71	74	68	285	6,741.39
Carl Suneson	72	72	71	70	285	6,741.39
Alessandro Tadini	70	70	72	73	285	6,741.39
Marc Cayeux	71	71	75	69	286	5,007.19
Francisco Cea	72	73	71	70	286	5,007.19
Ian Garbutt	73	70	76	67	286	5,007.19
Sam Osborne	69	74	74	69	286	5,007.19
Richie Ramsay	70	72	70	74	286	5,007.19
Simon Robinson	72	70	73	71	286	5,007.19
Ignacio Garrido	73	70	72	72	287	4,030.18
Marcus Higley	70	71	74	72	287	4,030.18
Garry Houston	75	69	70	73	287	4,030.18
Pedro Linhart	73	69	74	71	287	4,030.18
Darren Fichardt	71	71	74	72	288	3,590.52
David Park	71	74	72	71	288	3,590.52
Sebastian Fernandez	75	70	72	72	289	3,297.42
Michael Jonzon	74	71	75	69	289	3,297.42
Marc Farry	70	69	73	78	290	3,077.59
Rafael Gomez	75	70	71	75	291	2,857.76
Birgir Hafthorsson	74	71	70	76	291	2,857.76
Sven Struver	72	72	76	72	292	2,674.57

	SCORES				TOTAL	MONEY
Chris Gane	73	71	76	73	293	2,198
Sion E. Bebb	74	71	76	73	294	2,195
Jean Hugo	72	71	73	79	295	2,192

Scandinavian Masters

Arlandastad Golf Club, Stockholm, Sweden
Par 34-36–70; 6,835 yards

August 16-19
purse, €1,594,030

	SCORES				TOTAL	MONEY
Mikko Ilonen	67	72	67	68	274	€266,660
Christian Cevaer	69	69	69	69	276	96,354
Nick Dougherty	68	69	69	70	276	96,354
Jean-Baptiste Gonnet	67	70	71	68	276	96,354
Peter Hedblom	68	71	68	69	276	96,354
Martin Kaymer	67	68	68	73	276	96,354
Paul Broadhurst	69	73	64	71	277	41,280
James Kingston	68	68	67	74	277	41,280
Corey Pavin	70	70	70	67	277	41,280
Mattias Eliasson	69	72	68	69	278	30,720
David Higgins	69	69	71	69	278	30,720
Steve Alker	74	69	68	68	279	23,240
Martin Erlandsson	71	72	71	65	279	23,240
Peter Hanson	70	72	67	70	279	23,240
Michael Jonzon	71	67	74	67	279	23,240
Barry Lane	70	72	69	68	279	23,240
Peter Lawrie	71	70	69	69	279	23,240
Scott Strange	64	75	69	71	279	23,240
Sam Walker	65	70	72	72	279	23,240
Garry Houston	70	73	68	69	280	18,613.33
Paul Lawrie	68	72	72	68	280	18,613.33
Edward Rush	69	68	74	69	280	18,613.33
Simon Dyson	69	71	72	69	281	16,880
Jose Manuel Lara	70	70	73	68	281	16,880
Santiago Luna	72	70	69	70	281	16,880
Alan McLean	69	74	71	67	281	16,880
Joakim Backstrom	69	69	69	75	282	14,720
Stephen Gallacher	68	72	71	71	282	14,720
Oskar Henningsson	72	71	71	68	282	14,720
Henrik Nystrom	67	68	73	74	282	14,720
Tom Whitehouse	72	69	70	71	282	14,720
Fredrik Andersson Hed	70	71	72	70	283	12,600
Luis Claverie	69	73	72	69	283	12,600
Richard McEvoy	71	67	76	69	283	12,600
Andrew Tampion	72	70	67	74	283	12,600
Phillip Archer	68	74	67	75	284	10,720
Johan Axgren	73	68	76	67	284	10,720
David Carter	73	68	71	72	284	10,720
Per-Ulrik Johansson	73	69	73	69	284	10,720
Damien McGrane	70	70	73	71	284	10,720
Brett Rumford	72	71	71	70	284	10,720
Miles Tunnicliff	72	70	72	70	284	10,720
Richard Bland	70	72	72	71	285	8,640
Ian Garbutt	67	75	70	73	285	8,640
Cesar Monasterio	71	69	70	75	285	8,640
Jesper Parnevik	70	73	74	68	285	8,640
Jeff Sluman	70	71	72	72	285	8,640
Dawie van der Walt	67	73	72	73	285	8,640
Alejandro Canizares	76	66	70	74	286	6,720
Gary Emerson	73	70	75	68	286	6,720

	SCORES				TOTAL	MONEY
Gary Lockerbie	69	74	73	70	286	6,720
Gary Murphy	68	75	71	72	286	6,720
Wade Ormsby	69	73	75	69	286	6,720
Lee Slattery	70	72	73	71	286	6,720
Rafael Cabrera Bello	67	72	72	76	287	5,280
Simon Khan	70	71	73	73	287	5,280
Terry Pilkadaris	74	69	73	71	287	5,280
*Fredrik Qvicker	65	75	73	74	287	
Jarmo Sandelin	72	71	71	74	288	4,800
*Joel Sjoholm	69	71	72	76	288	
David Bransdon	71	67	76	75	289	4,480
Lee S. James	67	73	74	75	289	4,480
Andrew Marshall	72	71	77	69	289	4,480
John Bickerton	72	70	74	74	290	4,000
Stephen Dodd	72	71	72	75	290	4,000
James Heath	71	71	71	77	290	4,000
Johan Edfors	72	71	70	78	291	3,520
Alessandro Tadini	67	74	78	72	291	3,520
Shaun P. Webster	69	72	78	72	291	3,520
Simon Wakefield	69	72	77	74	292	3,200

KLM Open

Kennemer Golf & Country Club, Zandvoort, Netherlands

August 23-26

Par 36-34–70; 6,626 yards

purse, €1,604,797

	SCORES				TOTAL	MONEY
Ross Fisher	66	67	68	67	268	€266,660
Joost Luiten	68	64	71	66	269	177,770
Steve Alker	66	66	69	71	272	70,400
Alastair Forsyth	66	71	69	66	272	70,400
Bernhard Langer	67	71	67	67	272	70,400
Thomas Levet	65	70	68	69	272	70,400
Alexander Noren	65	67	72	68	272	70,400
Markus Brier	67	68	70	68	273	34,320
Stephen Gallacher	70	68	66	69	273	34,320
Jean-Baptiste Gonnet	64	71	70	68	273	34,320
Tom Whitehouse	68	67	71	67	273	34,320
John Bickerton	68	67	69	70	274	24,768
Michael Campbell	65	71	69	69	274	24,768
Richard Finch	68	67	72	67	274	24,768
Simon Khan	67	69	69	69	274	24,768
David Lynn	65	70	70	69	274	24,768
Martin Erlandsson	69	71	71	64	275	19,653.33
David Higgins	68	67	68	72	275	19,653.33
Garry Houston	68	68	72	67	275	19,653.33
Phillip Price	68	68	67	72	275	19,653.33
Chris Riley	66	69	71	69	275	19,653.33
Brett Rumford	69	70	69	67	275	19,653.33
Alejandro Canizares	69	67	69	71	276	16,880
David Carter	65	65	71	75	276	16,880
Peter Gustafsson	70	70	69	67	276	16,880
Henrik Nystrom	66	67	72	71	276	16,880
David Bransdon	68	69	70	70	277	13,568
Simon Dyson	67	73	66	71	277	13,568
James Hepworth	70	69	66	72	277	13,568
Paul Lawrie	66	69	69	73	277	13,568
Andrew McLardy	70	70	69	68	277	13,568
Gary Murphy	67	71	70	69	277	13,568
Mark Pilkington	71	68	68	70	277	13,568

	SCORES				TOTAL	MONEY
Lee Slattery	66	73	70	68	277	13,568
Simon Wakefield	68	68	73	68	277	13,568
Sam Walker	69	64	75	69	277	13,568
Johan Axgren	67	71	69	71	278	10,080
Marc Cayeux	69	70	69	70	278	10,080
Andrew Coltart	65	73	71	69	278	10,080
Nick Dougherty	69	67	69	73	278	10,080
Marcus Higley	72	67	72	67	278	10,080
Shiv Kapur	68	71	68	71	278	10,080
Maarten Lafeber	67	69	71	71	278	10,080
Taichi Teshima	64	72	71	71	278	10,080
Steve Webster	65	71	72	70	278	10,080
Kenneth Ferrie	66	74	68	71	279	8,480
Emanuele Canonica	67	70	71	72	280	7,520
Luis Claverie	67	70	73	70	280	7,520
Nicolas Colsaerts	67	73	68	72	280	7,520
Sven Struver	66	72	68	74	280	7,520
Mads Vibe-Hastrup	69	70	70	71	280	7,520
Fredrik Andersson Hed	69	68	76	68	281	5,760
Joakim Backstrom	69	68	73	71	281	5,760
Christian Cevaer	71	66	75	69	281	5,760
James Heath	70	69	71	71	281	5,760
James Kingston	70	67	71	73	281	5,760
Steven O'Hara	68	69	69	75	281	5,760
Rafael Echenique	69	68	71	74	282	4,480
David Griffiths	71	64	72	75	282	4,480
Thongchai Jaidee	71	68	70	73	282	4,480
Martin Maritz	70	70	71	71	282	4,480
Robert Rock	69	69	72	72	282	4,480
Andrew Marshall	66	73	71	73	283	3,920
Marcel Siem	68	72	73	70	283	3,920
David Drysdale	70	68	75	72	285	3,440
Ian Garbutt	73	67	70	75	285	3,440
Anton Haig	70	69	73	73	285	3,440
Matthew Millar	68	71	72	74	285	3,440
Shaun P. Webster	71	66	74	76	287	3,040
Wade Ormsby	69	70	75	75	289	2,575.67
David Park	70	69	77	73	289	2,575.67
Anthony Wall	69	69	71	80	289	2,575.67

Johnnie Walker Championship at Gleneagles

Gleneagles Hotel, Perthshire, Scotland
Par 36-37–73; 7,320 yards

August 30-September 2
purse, €2,058,415

	SCORES				TOTAL	MONEY
Marc Warren	65	73	73	69	280	€343,692.77
Simon Wakefield	68	69	73	70	280	229,123.60
(Warren defeated Wakefield on second playoff hole.)						
Martin Erlandsson	71	72	72	66	281	116,101.07
Soren Hansen	69	72	72	68	281	116,101.07
Fredrik Andersson Hed	73	71	66	72	282	79,806.60
Graeme Storm	70	70	73	69	282	79,806.60
Ricardo Gonzalez	70	71	75	67	283	56,710.11
Steven O'Hara	71	73	71	68	283	56,710.11
Oliver Fisher	73	72	72	67	284	38,810.34
Thomas Levet	69	68	76	71	284	38,810.34
Francesco Molinari	76	70	72	66	284	38,810.34
Colin Montgomerie	69	74	71	70	284	38,810.34
Lee Westwood	74	69	69	72	284	38,810.34

	SCORES				TOTAL	MONEY
James Kingston	70	73	71	71	285	29,695.48
Barry Lane	70	71	75	69	285	29,695.48
David Lynn	72	68	74	71	285	29,695.48
Alan McLean	72	71	74	68	285	29,695.48
Jesus Maria Arruti	74	72	72	68	286	25,639.85
Alastair Forsyth	69	71	72	74	286	25,639.85
Wade Ormsby	71	69	75	71	286	25,639.85
Nicolas Colsaerts	66	75	74	72	287	22,684.05
Robert Dinwiddie	72	71	72	72	287	22,684.05
Mark Foster	74	72	72	69	287	22,684.05
Marcus Higley	69	74	72	72	287	22,684.05
Santiago Luna	73	69	75	70	287	22,684.05
Phillip Archer	68	71	73	76	288	18,972.11
Sion E. Bebb	71	72	74	71	288	18,972.11
Ariel Canete	73	72	68	75	288	18,972.11
Shiv Kapur	68	74	76	70	288	18,972.11
Joost Luiten	68	75	77	68	288	18,972.11
Carlos Rodiles	73	71	73	71	288	18,972.11
Anthony Wall	73	71	72	72	288	18,972.11
Luis Claverie	70	73	73	73	289	15,507.64
Stephen Gallacher	71	72	70	76	289	15,507.64
Soren Kjeldsen	71	72	75	71	289	15,507.64
Alexandre Rocha	71	75	73	70	289	15,507.64
Brett Rumford	72	73	75	69	289	15,507.64
Jose Manuel Carriles	74	70	75	71	290	13,404.21
Garry Houston	73	72	72	73	290	13,404.21
Paul Lawrie	69	77	73	71	290	13,404.21
Patrik Sjoland	75	71	74	70	290	13,404.21
Miles Tunnicliff	67	74	74	75	290	13,404.21
Ignacio Garrido	71	74	72	74	291	10,929.59
Mark Loftus	70	74	71	76	291	10,929.59
Mark Pilkington	68	76	73	74	291	10,929.59
Phillip Price	68	76	75	72	291	10,929.59
Jean-Francois Remesy	72	74	72	73	291	10,929.59
Dean Robertson	69	75	75	72	291	10,929.59
Mads Vibe-Hastrup	71	74	74	72	291	10,929.59
Darren Fichardt	73	71	75	73	292	8,867.40
David Griffiths	71	73	75	73	292	8,867.40
Zane Scotland	68	73	75	76	292	8,867.40
Ian Garbutt	70	74	76	73	293	7,630.09
Peter Lawrie	72	74	77	70	293	7,630.09
Jeev Milkha Singh	67	74	74	78	293	7,630.09
Gregory Bourdy	69	75	74	76	294	6,341.22
Darren Clarke	73	71	76	74	294	6,341.22
Stephen Dodd	72	74	74	74	294	6,341.22
Richard Finch	71	72	79	72	294	6,341.22
Paul Casey	71	71	73	80	295	5,567.90
Greig Hutcheon	69	75	76	75	295	5,567.90
Matthew Millar	77	67	76	75	295	5,567.90
Emanuele Canonica	69	76	77	74	296	5,155.47
Richard Bland	69	75	78	77	299	4,743.03
Peter O'Malley	73	71	81	74	299	4,743.03
Chinarat Phadungsil	73	73	77	76	299	4,743.03
James Hepworth	68	75	82	75	300	4,330.59
Terry Pilkadaris	69	76	81	78	304	4,124.37
Terry Price	71	75	80	80	306	3,918.15

Omega European Masters

Crans-sur-Sierre Golf Club, Crans Montana, Switzerland
Par 36-35–71; 6,857 yards

September 6-9
purse, €2,003,000

		SCORES			TOTAL	MONEY
Brett Rumford	68	66	66	68	268	€333,330
Phillip Archer	69	66	68	65	268	222,220
(Rumford defeated Archer on first playoff hole.)						
Bradley Dredge	66	66	68	69	269	125,200
Sion E. Bebb	71	68	63	68	270	100,000
Oliver Wilson	65	66	70	71	272	84,800
Gonzalo Fernandez-Castano	70	67	65	71	273	65,000
Lee Westwood	71	67	65	70	273	65,000
Eduardo Romero	68	69	72	65	274	44,933.33
Miles Tunnicliff	71	65	70	68	274	44,933.33
Anthony Wall	69	68	68	69	274	44,933.33
Graeme McDowell	73	69	67	66	275	36,800
Robert Karlsson	69	69	69	69	276	34,400
Richard McEvoy	71	70	71	65	277	31,400
Juan Parron	72	71	68	66	277	31,400
Joakim Backstrom	71	68	69	70	278	28,200
Richard Bland	73	68	67	70	278	28,200
David Frost	72	70	68	68	278	28,200
Mikko Ilonen	68	75	70	66	279	25,300
Steven O'Hara	74	70	70	65	279	25,300
Rafael Echenique	69	70	71	70	280	22,640
Johan Edfors	73	70	69	68	280	22,640
Manuel Quiros	74	70	70	66	280	22,640
Tino Schuster	71	65	74	70	280	22,640
Graeme Storm	69	69	71	71	280	22,640
Ariel Canete	72	69	68	72	281	19,300
Andrew Marshall	74	68	72	67	281	19,300
Jean-Francois Remesy	77	67	70	67	281	19,300
Marcel Siem	71	70	70	70	281	19,300
Alessandro Tadini	72	69	68	72	281	19,300
Daniel Vancsik	71	70	72	68	281	19,300
David Carter	73	69	70	70	282	15,800
Pelle Edberg	71	73	69	69	282	15,800
Mattias Eliasson	72	69	67	74	282	15,800
Henrik Nystrom	74	69	68	71	282	15,800
Edward Rush	72	72	64	74	282	15,800
Jeev Milkha Singh	74	68	72	68	282	15,800
Paul Casey	71	68	72	72	283	12,200
Richard Finch	70	72	64	77	283	12,200
Garry Houston	72	70	73	68	283	12,200
Barry Lane	78	65	70	70	283	12,200
Peter O'Malley	73	70	68	72	283	12,200
Alexandre Rocha	71	70	73	69	283	12,200
Zane Scotland	69	69	71	74	283	12,200
Kyron Sullivan	73	69	69	72	283	12,200
Carl Suneson	74	70	69	70	283	12,200
Simon Wakefield	74	69	73	67	283	12,200
Tom Whitehouse	73	71	68	71	283	12,200
Julien Clement	74	70	72	68	284	9,200
Soren Kjeldsen	76	68	69	71	284	9,200
Pablo Martin	71	73	71	69	284	9,200
Carlos Rodiles	69	75	66	74	284	9,200
Oscar Floren	69	67	76	73	285	8,000
Marcus Fraser	68	71	74	72	285	8,000
*Pierre Relecom	70	74	71	70	285	
Jamie Spence	70	71	72	73	286	7,400
Ian Garbutt	70	72	72	73	287	6,600

	SCORES				TOTAL	MONEY
Ricardo Gonzalez	75	69	69	74	287	6,600
Jonathan Lomas	74	70	74	69	287	6,600
Steve Alker	75	66	74	73	288	5,800
Lee Slattery	72	72	75	69	288	5,800
Sven Struver	74	68	73	73	288	5,800
Andrew Coltart	70	72	72	75	289	5,100
Francesco Molinari	74	70	70	75	289	5,100
Terry Price	75	68	74	72	289	5,100
Patrik Sjoland	70	72	72	75	289	5,100
Ignacio Garrido	74	69	71	76	290	4,400
Shiv Kapur	72	72	76	70	290	4,400
Alexander Noren	72	71	76	71	290	4,400
Sam Little	78	66	73	74	291	4,000
Jose Manuel Lara	71	71	75	75	292	3,800
Eirik Tage Johansen	75	69	68	81	293	3,650
Alessandro Napoleoni	71	69	78	77	295	3,000

Mercedes-Benz Championship

Gut Larchenhof, Cologne, Germany
Par 36-36–72; 7,289 yards

September 13-16
purse, €2,000,000

	SCORES				TOTAL	MONEY
Soren Hansen	65	68	71	67	271	€320,000
Phillip Archer	71	70	66	68	275	171,250
Alastair Forsyth	76	67	62	70	275	171,250
Thomas Bjorn	71	67	66	72	276	91,025
Bradley Dredge	68	71	70	67	276	91,025
Simon Khan	67	70	69	71	277	59,333.33
Soren Kjeldsen	73	67	72	65	277	59,333.33
Lee Westwood	61	73	72	71	277	59,333.33
Paul Lawrie	68	70	71	69	278	42,000
Richard Sterne	67	73	68	70	278	42,000
Niclas Fasth	67	71	69	72	279	35,600
Graeme McDowell	69	72	69	69	279	35,600
Johan Edfors	70	71	72	67	280	30,733.33
Mikko Ilonen	68	70	72	70	280	30,733.33
Robert Karlsson	70	71	70	69	280	30,733.33
Fredrik Andersson Hed	69	70	73	69	281	25,960
John Bickerton	71	69	71	70	281	25,960
Gonzalo Fernandez-Castano	67	73	72	69	281	25,960
Per-Ulrik Johansson	74	69	69	69	281	25,960
Jeev Milkha Singh	72	70	72	67	281	25,960
Retief Goosen	72	71	69	70	282	21,700
Richard Green	73	67	66	76	282	21,700
Thongchai Jaidee	71	72	71	68	282	21,700
Miguel Angel Jimenez	68	70	72	72	282	21,700
Andrew McLardy	70	69	70	73	282	21,700
Y.E. Yang	70	73	72	67	282	21,700
Alex Cejka	70	73	68	72	283	18,400
John Daly	67	71	76	69	283	18,400
Peter Hanson	69	74	70	70	283	18,400
Bernhard Langer	69	68	70	76	283	18,400
Ian Poulter	72	70	71	70	283	18,400
Markus Brier	74	69	72	69	284	15,520
Alejandro Canizares	70	69	73	72	284	15,520
Nick Dougherty	66	75	69	74	284	15,520
Ross Fisher	74	70	68	72	284	15,520
Martin Kaymer	70	72	71	71	284	15,520
Simon Dyson	66	71	73	75	285	13,600

	SCORES				TOTAL	MONEY
Pelle Edberg	70	72	70	73	285	13,600
Marcel Siem	71	73	70	71	285	13,600
Carl Suneson	69	72	70	74	285	13,600
Emanuele Canonica	72	68	75	71	286	11,800
Pablo Martin	70	69	72	75	286	11,800
Andres Romero	68	71	76	71	286	11,800
Simon Wakefield	70	70	74	72	286	11,800
Marc Warren	71	69	70	76	286	11,800
Mark Foster	76	70	71	70	287	9,800
Anders Hansen	72	72	70	73	287	9,800
Peter Hedblom	74	73	73	67	287	9,800
Paul McGinley	70	79	67	71	287	9,800
Colin Montgomerie	69	69	73	76	287	9,800
Raphael Jacquelin	76	73	73	66	288	8,600
Francesco Molinari	73	67	75	74	289	8,000
Sven Struver	71	72	76	70	289	8,000
Stephen Dodd	73	71	72	74	290	7,000
Scott Drummond	72	72	71	75	290	7,000
Jean-Francois Remesy	73	70	75	72	290	7,000
Ariel Canete	71	70	76	74	291	5,900
Robert-Jan Derksen	68	74	73	76	291	5,900
Peter O'Malley	70	76	72	73	291	5,900
Jyoti Randhawa	74	71	74	72	291	5,900
Ricardo Gonzalez	77	67	73	75	292	5,300
Oliver Wilson	70	76	72	74	292	5,300
Angel Cabrera	74	73	73	73	293	4,900
Gregory Havret	73	79	71	70	293	4,900
Michael Campbell	77	73	72	72	294	4,400
Kenneth Ferrie	69	73	78	74	294	4,400
Ignacio Garrido	77	71	71	75	294	4,400
Anton Haig	70	76	77	72	295	3,737.50
Phillip Price	70	71	76	78	295	3,737.50
Graeme Storm	71	78	70	76	295	3,737.50
Daniel Vancsik	73	75	72	75	295	3,737.50
David Howell	73	71	73	79	296	3,275
Mardan Mamat	70	76	73	77	296	3,275
Louis Oosthuizen	75	73	72	77	297	2,975
Jean Van de Velde	76	69	76	76	297	2,975
Darren Clarke	69	75	77	77	298	2,750
Jose Manuel Lara	72	76	77	74	299	2,600
Charl Schwartzel	73	77	74	79	303	2,450

Quinn Direct British Masters

The Belfry, Sutton Coldfield, West Midlands, England
Par 36-36–72; 7,223 yards

September 20-23
purse, €2,598,653

	SCORES				TOTAL	MONEY
Lee Westwood	68	70	70	65	273	€434,727
Ian Poulter	67	71	70	70	278	289,818
Mark Foster	71	66	69	73	279	163,283.46
Fredrik Andersson Hed	67	73	68	73	281	83,765.68
Michael Campbell	73	69	69	70	281	83,765.68
Niclas Fasth	75	66	67	73	281	83,765.68
Miguel Angel Jimenez	71	69	70	71	281	83,765.68
Soren Kjeldsen	66	72	74	69	281	83,765.68
Zane Scotland	69	73	70	69	281	83,765.68
Sam Walker	71	67	75	68	281	83,765.68
Benn Barham	70	75	67	70	282	43,690.06
Gregory Bourdy	70	73	65	74	282	43,690.06

	SCORES				TOTAL	MONEY
Nick Dougherty	72	68	75	67	282	43,690.06
Francesco Molinari	68	72	69	73	282	43,690.06
Stephen Dodd	68	79	69	67	283	35,995.40
Raphael Jacquelin	66	76	69	72	283	35,995.40
Jarmo Sandelin	65	79	67	72	283	35,995.40
Mads Vibe-Hastrup	74	71	67	71	283	35,995.40
Peter Hedblom	71	70	71	72	284	31,822.02
Colin Montgomerie	70	70	70	74	284	31,822.02
Robert Karlsson	71	75	70	69	285	29,083.24
Martin Kaymer	72	73	72	68	285	29,083.24
James Kingston	71	74	68	72	285	29,083.24
Jyoti Randhawa	70	72	73	70	285	29,083.24
Robert-Jan Derksen	69	68	74	75	286	26,344.46
David Lynn	72	70	71	73	286	26,344.46
Jean Van de Velde	69	75	70	72	286	26,344.46
Phillip Archer	68	72	73	74	287	23,214.42
Martin Erlandsson	63	75	70	79	287	23,214.42
Paul McGinley	70	75	72	70	287	23,214.42
Louis Oosthuizen	69	75	71	72	287	23,214.42
Richard Sterne	65	77	71	74	287	23,214.42
Thongchai Jaidee	70	74	73	71	288	19,888.76
Andrew Marshall	73	72	69	74	288	19,888.76
Phillip Price	71	72	72	73	288	19,888.76
Daniel Vancsik	72	71	73	72	288	19,888.76
Bradley Dredge	71	70	72	76	289	17,476.03
Marcus Fraser	70	72	72	75	289	17,476.03
Jean-Baptiste Gonnet	74	72	71	72	289	17,476.03
Carlos Rodiles	72	73	71	73	289	17,476.03
Oliver Wilson	70	74	75	70	289	17,476.03
Rory McIlroy	69	78	70	73	290	15,128.50
Simon Wakefield	71	76	69	74	290	15,128.50
Anthony Wall	73	74	72	71	290	15,128.50
Marc Warren	70	74	70	76	290	15,128.50
Kenneth Ferrie	69	74	76	72	291	12,259.30
Peter Hanson	69	75	73	74	291	12,259.30
Simon Khan	67	74	79	71	291	12,259.30
Jean-Francois Lucquin	70	74	74	73	291	12,259.30
Damien McGrane	78	69	69	75	291	12,259.30
David Park	72	74	69	76	291	12,259.30
Juan Parron	75	72	72	72	291	12,259.30
Johan Edfors	71	75	72	74	292	9,390.10
Ignacio Garrido	69	78	70	75	292	9,390.10
Peter O'Malley	73	72	73	74	292	9,390.10
Taichi Teshima	70	74	73	75	292	9,390.10
Gonzalo Fernandez-Castano	72	73	77	71	293	7,955.50
Marcel Siem	69	76	73	75	293	7,955.50
Gregory Havret	73	74	77	70	294	7,433.83
Henrik Nystrom	67	76	75	76	294	7,433.83
Marcus Higley	74	73	76	72	295	6,912.16
Garry Houston	70	76	76	73	295	6,912.16
Stephen Gallacher	69	75	79	74	297	6,260.07
Christopher Hanell	73	74	72	78	297	6,260.07
Steven O'Hara	74	73	75	75	297	6,260.07
Andrew Tampion	70	75	76	78	299	5,738.40
Carl Suneson	73	73	76	80	302	5,477.56
Darren Fichardt	71	76	79	78	304	5,216.72

The Ricoh Women's British Open, won by Lorena Ochoa, was the first for the ladies at St. Andrews.

Robert Laberge/Getty Images

Robert Laberge/Getty Images

Suzann Pettersen won six tournaments.

Morgan Pressel took the Kraft Nabisco title.

Jonathan Ernst/Getty Images

Scott Halleran/Getty Images

Cristie Kerr won the U.S. Women's Open.

Annika Sorenstam slipped to the No. 4 ranking.

Andy Lyons/Getty Images

Natalie Gulbis was the Evian Masters winner.

Harry How/Getty Images

Paula Creamer posted two victories.

Doug Benc/Getty Images

Brittany Lincicome triumphed in the Ginn Open.

Hunter Martin/Getty Images

Se Ri Pak won the Jamie Farr event.

Karrie Webb had two Australian victories.

Juli Inkster remained among the world's best.

Michelle Wie had a disastrous year.

Momoko Ueda won five times in Japan.

Mi Hyun Kim took the No. 9 ranking.

Ji-Yai Shin won 10 times on the Korea LPGA.

Seon Hwa Lee won the Match Play title.

Jeong Jang was another Korean standout.

Senior Tours

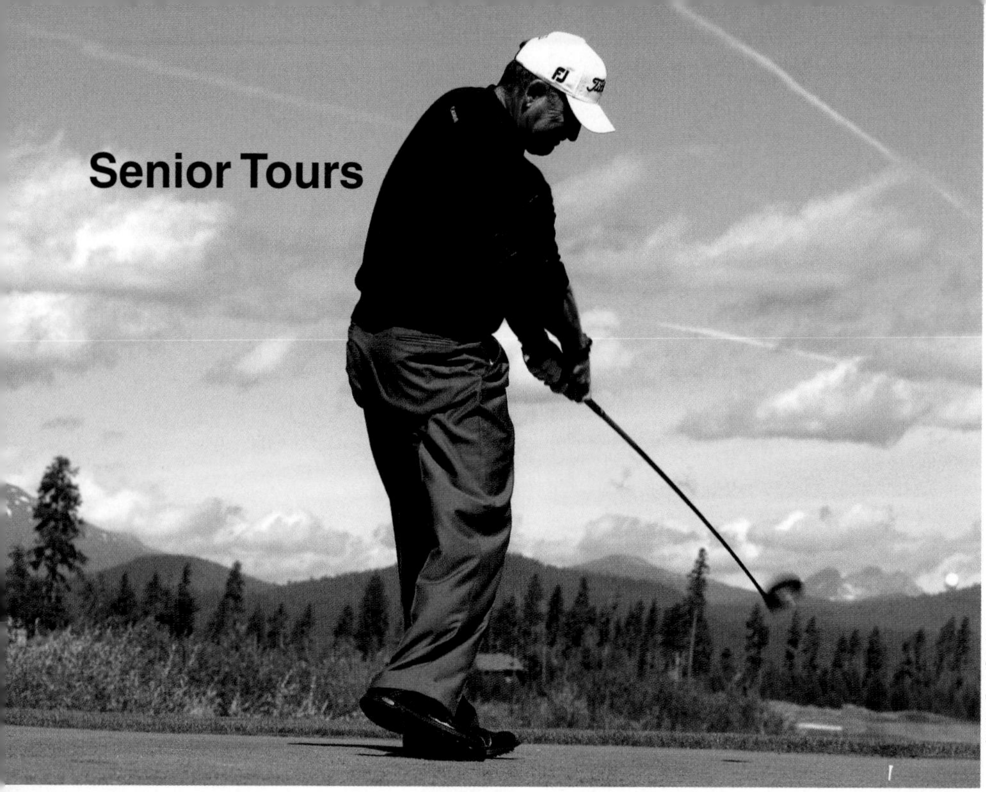

Jonathan Ferrey/Getty Images

Jay Haas posted four victories and led the Champions Tour money list.

Scott Halleran/Getty Images

Phil Inglis/Getty Images

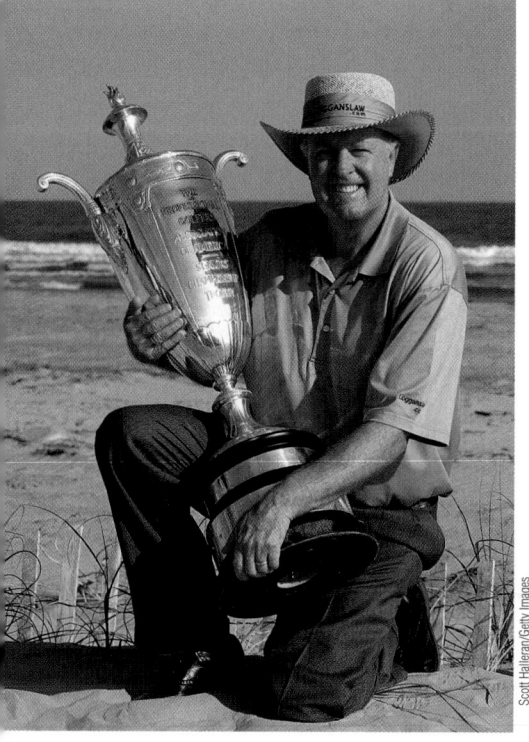

Denis Watson claimed the Senior PGA trophy.

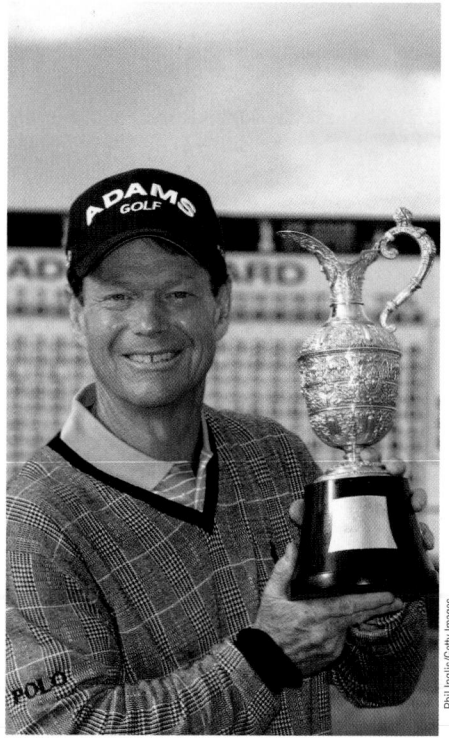

Tom Watson won another British title.

Brad Bryant took the U.S. Senior Open.

Loren Roberts was the Senior Players winner.

Fred Funk won at Turtle Bay.

Bernhard Langer had a late-year win.

Jonathan Ferrey/Getty Images

Jonathan Ernst/Getty Images

R.W. Eaks had two senior victories.

D.A. Weibring was steady.

Phil Inglis/Getty Images

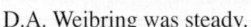

Richard Heathcote/Getty Images

Carl Mason won six times in Europe.

Tom Kite was runner-up three times.

The Seve Trophy

Heritage Golf & Spa Resort, Killenard, Co. Laois, Ireland
Par 36-36–72; 7,319 yards

September 27-30
purse, €2,000,000

FIRST DAY
Fourball

Peter Hanson and Robert Karlsson (Eur) defeated Colin Montgomerie and Marc Warren, 3 and 1.
Bradley Dredge and Phillip Archer (GB&I) defeated Miguel Angel Jimenez and Gonzalo Fernandez-Castano, 2 and 1.
Raphael Jacquelin and Gregory Havret (Eur) defeated Paul Casey and Simon Dyson, 4 and 3.
Nick Dougherty and Graeme Storm (GB&I) defeated Thomas Bjorn and Soren Hansen, 1 up.
Markus Brier and Mikko Ilonen (Eur) defeated Justin Rose and Oliver Wilson, 3 and 2.

POINTS: Great Britain & Ireland 2, Europe 3

SECOND DAY
Fourball

Dredge and Archer (GB&I) defeated Hanson and Karlsson, 5 and 4.
Jacquelin and Havret (Eur) defeated Montgomerie and Warren, 5 and 3.
Wilson and Dyson (GB&I) defeated Bjorn and Hansen, 3 and 2.
Brier and Ilonen (Eur) defeated Dougherty and Storm, 1 up.
Rose and Casey (GB&I) defeated Jimenez and Fernandez-Castano, 2 up.

POINTS: Great Britain & Ireland 5, Europe 5

THIRD DAY
Morning Greensomes

Fernandez-Castano and Karlsson (Eur) defeated Rose and Casey, 3 and 1.
Jacquelin and Havret (Eur) defeated Dougherty and Storm, 2 and 1.
Hansen and Hanson (Eur) defeated Wilson and Dyson, 1 up.
Brier and Ilonen (Eur) halved with Dredge and Archer.

POINTS: Great Britain & Ireland 5½, Europe 8½

THIRD DAY
Afternoon Foursomes

Rose and Dougherty (GB&I) defeated Jacquelin and Havret, 2 and 1.
Fernandez-Castano and Karlsson (Eur) defeated Montgomerie and Storm, 3 and 2.
Dyson and Wilson (GB&I) defeated Hanson and Hansen, 3 and 2.
Archer and Dredge (GB&I) defeated Brier and Jimenez, 2 up.

POINTS: Great Britain & Ireland 8½, Europe 9½

FINAL DAY
Singles

Montgomerie (GB&I) defeated Karlsson, 1 up.
Casey (GB&I) defeated Jacquelin, 3 and 2.
Warren (GB&I) defeated Havret, 1 up.
Dougherty (GB&I) halved with Hansen.
Storm (GB&I) defeated Bjorn, 6 and 5.
Dyson (GB&I) defeated Ilonen, 2 and 1.
Archer (GB&I) halved with Brier.
Dredge (GB&I) defeated Fernandez-Castano, 2 up.
Hanson (Eur) defeated Wilson, 1 up.
Rose (GB&I) defeated Jimenez, 2 and 1.

TOTAL POINTS: Great Britain & Ireland 16½, Europe 11½

(Each member of the Great Britain & Ireland team received €125,000; each member of the Europe team received €75,000.)

Alfred Dunhill Links Championship

St. Andrews Old Course: Par 36-36–72; 7,279 yards
Carnoustie Championship Course: Par 36-36–72; 7,412 yards
Kingsbarns Golf Links: Par 36-36–72; 7,106 yards
St. Andrews, Scotland

October 4-7
purse, €3,376,087

	SCORES				TOTAL	MONEY
Nick Dougherty	67	66	66	71	270	€562,624.90
Justin Rose	68	69	66	69	272	375,080.90
Rory McIlroy	71	67	67	68	273	211,321.90
Barry Lane	69	70	68	67	274	155,959.60
Paul Lawrie	66	73	64	71	274	155,959.60
Ernie Els	67	67	70	71	275	109,711.90
Trevor Immelman	73	65	67	70	275	109,711.90
Soren Hansen	66	70	71	69	276	80,005.27
Padraig Harrington	70	66	67	73	276	80,005.27
Paul Casey	74	68	68	67	277	58,738.04
Niclas Fasth	67	70	67	73	277	58,738.04
Anton Haig	68	66	75	68	277	58,738.04
Peter Hanson	68	68	69	72	277	58,738.04
Scott Strange	66	70	69	72	277	58,738.04
Phillip Archer	68	68	71	71	278	43,251.79
Rafael Echenique	67	67	72	72	278	43,251.79
Gonzalo Fernandez-Castano	67	67	73	71	278	43,251.79
Miguel Angel Jimenez	68	68	73	69	278	43,251.79
Martin Kaymer	69	68	70	71	278	43,251.79
Brett Rumford	70	68	72	68	278	43,251.79
Graeme Storm	74	66	68	70	278	43,251.79
Steve Webster	65	70	68	75	278	43,251.79
John Bickerton	70	70	69	70	279	33,082.35
Robert-Jan Derksen	70	71	70	68	279	33,082.35
Luke Donald	67	70	69	73	279	33,082.35
Paul McGinley	70	71	67	71	279	33,082.35
Gary Murphy	71	67	72	69	279	33,082.35
Peter O'Malley	69	64	69	77	279	33,082.35
Gary Orr	70	70	69	70	279	33,082.35
Zane Scotland	72	72	67	68	279	33,082.35
Jeev Milkha Singh	67	68	72	72	279	33,082.35
Jean-Francois Remesy	71	67	69	73	280	26,584.03
Richard Sterne	73	67	70	70	280	26,584.03
Jean Van de Velde	71	69	67	73	280	26,584.03
Anthony Wall	73	69	65	73	280	26,584.03
Alejandro Canizares	70	69	72	70	281	21,942.37
Rhys Davies	71	70	68	72	281	21,942.37
Martin Erlandsson	71	68	71	71	281	21,942.37
Kenneth Ferrie	69	65	75	72	281	21,942.37
Peter Hedblom	69	74	67	71	281	21,942.37
James Hepworth	74	70	67	70	281	21,942.37
David Lynn	67	76	68	70	281	21,942.37
Graeme McDowell	70	68	70	73	281	21,942.37
Hennie Otto	66	67	74	74	281	21,942.37
Thomas Aiken	71	66	69	76	282	17,553.90
Alexander Noren	68	73	67	74	282	17,553.90
Henrik Stenson	68	69	69	76	282	17,553.90
Alessandro Tadini	69	72	68	73	282	17,553.90
Gregory Bourdy	72	67	71	73	283	14,178.15
Scott Drummond	73	69	69	72	283	14,178.15
Ross Fisher	73	66	68	76	283	14,178.15
Nathan Green	68	74	67	74	283	14,178.15
Christopher Hanell	70	71	70	72	283	14,178.15
Mikko Ilonen	67	73	71	72	283	14,178.15
Simon Dyson	73	70	68	73	284	10,886.79

	SCORES				TOTAL	MONEY
Thomas Levet	70	65	75	74	284	10,886.79
Matthew Millar	69	74	68	73	284	10,886.79
Daniel Vancsik	70	70	71	73	284	10,886.79
Richard Finch	70	71	70	74	285	9,789.67
Steven O'Hara	70	70	69	76	285	9,789.67

HSBC World Match Play

Wentworth Club, West Course, Virginia Water, Surrey, England   October 11-14
Par 434 534 444–35; 345 434 455–37–72; 7,308 yards   purse, £2,440,000

FIRST ROUND

Paul Casey defeated Jerry Kelly, 3 and 2.
```
Paul Casey   5 3 4 4 2 3 5 4 4  34  3 4 5 3 3 4 4 4 5  35  69
Jerry Kelly  5 3 4 5 3 4 4 4 4  36  3 3 4 4 4 5 3 5 5  36  72
Casey leads, 3 up
Paul Casey   4 3 5 4 3 4 4 4 6  37  4 4 5 4 3 6 3
Jerry Kelly  4 3 5 4 3 6 4 5 4  38  3 4 5 5 2 3 4
```

Angel Cabrera defeated Retief Goosen, 6 and 5.
```
Angel Cabrera  4 3 4 5 3 4 4 3 4  34  2 3 5 4 2 4 3 4 4  31  65
Retief Goosen  4 2 4 4 3 4 4 4 4  33  2 5 4 4 3 4 4 5 4  35  68
Cabrera leads, 2 up
Angel Cabrera  4 2 4 4 3 4 4 3 4  32  3 3 6 4
Retief Goosen  4 3 4 5 2 4 4 4 4  34  3 5 6 5
```

Hunter Mahan defeated Justin Rose, 5 and 4.
```
Hunter Mahan  5 3 4 4 3 4 3 4 6  36  3 3 5 4 3 4 3 4 5  34  70
Justin Rose   6 3 5 4 3 3 4 4 4  36  2 4 5 4 2 5 4 6 4  36  72
Mahan leads, 2 up
Hunter Mahan  5 2 4 4 2 4 5 4 4  34  2 4 5 3 3
Justin Rose   4 2 5 4 3 4 5 3 4  34  3 4 5 4 4
```

Soren Hansen defeated Rory Sabbatini, 4 and 3.
```
Soren Hansen    4 3 5 4 3 4 4 4 4  35  4 4 4 5 3 4 4 4 5  37  72
Rory Sabbatini  4 3 4 4 3 3 5 4 5  35  3 4 5 4 3 4 4 4 5  36  71
Sabbatini leads, 1 up
Soren Hansen    5 2 4 4 3 4 3 4 4  33  3 3 4 4 2 3
Rory Sabbatini  4 3 5 4 3 5 5 4 4  37  3 4 4 4 2 4
```

Anders Hansen defeated Padraig Harrington, 4 and 2.
```
Anders Hansen     4 3 5 5 3 5 4 3 4  36  3 4 4 4 3 4 3 5 4  34  70
Padraig Harrington 5 3 5 4 4 4 4 4 5  38  2 4 4 4 3 5 4 4 4  34  72
Hansen leads, 2 up
Anders Hansen     4 3 5 4 3 3 5 4 3  34  2 4 4 4 3 5 4
Padraig Harrington 5 3 4 6 3 4 4 4 3  36  4 4 5 3 3 4 5
```

Henrik Stenson defeated Woody Austin, 1 up.
```
Henrik Stenson  4 3 4 4 2 4 3 4 3  31  3 4 5 3 4 5 3 5 5  37  68
Woody Austin    4 2 4 5 3 4 4 4 5  35  4 4 5 5 3 4 4 4 4  37  72
Stenson leads, 2 up
Henrik Stenson  4 4 5 4 3 4 4 4 4  36  3 3 4 4 3 4 4 6 4  35  71
Woody Austin    4 3 5 4 3 4 5 3 4  35  3 4 5 4 3 3 3 5 5  35  70
```

Andreas Romero defeated Niclas Fasth, 3 and 2.
```
Andres Romero  5 3 5 4 3 3 4 4 5  36  3 4 4 4 3 4 3 4 5  34  70
Niclas Fasth   5 2 4 4 4 3 5 3 4  34  2 4 4 4 4 4 4 4 4  34  68
Fasth leads, 2 up
Andres Romero  4 3 4 5 3 3 5 3 3  33  3 4 5 4 3 4 3
Niclas Fasth   6 2 4 6 4 4 4 4 4  38  3 4 5 4 3 4 4
```

Ernie Els defeated Colin Montgomerie, 6 and 5.

```
Ernie Els          4 3 4 4 3 3 4 4 3 32 3 5 4 4 3 3 4 4 4 34 66
Colin Montgomerie 5 2 4 5 2 4 5 4 4 35 3 3 5 4 3 C 3 5 5 X  X
Els leads, 5 up
Ernie Els         C 3 4 4 4 4 4 5 4 X 4 4 4
Colin Montgomerie W 4 5 5 3 4 4 3 4 X 4 5 4 4
```

QUARTER-FINALS

Angel Cabrera defeated Paul Casey, 4 and 3.

```
Angel Cabrera  4 4 3 3 2 5 4 5 4 34 3 3 5 4 3 4 3 4 4 33 67
Paul Casey     5 3 4 4 3 4 3 3 4 33 3 4 4 4 3 3 4 5 4 34 67
Cabrera leads, 1 up
Angel Cabrera  3 4 4 4 3 4 4 4 3 32 3 3 4 4 3 4
Paul Casey     4 3 4 4 3 4 4 5 5 36 3 4 4 3 3 4
```

Hunter Mahan defeated Soren Hansen, 6 and 4.

```
Hunter Mahan   3 3 5 4 5 3 3 4 4 34 3 4 4 3 4 4 5 5 5 37 71
Soren Hansen   5 3 4 5 5 4 3 4 5 38 3 4 6 4 4 4 3 5 4 37 75
Mahan leads, 3 up
Hunter Mahan   4 3 4 4 3 4 4 4 3 33 3 4 4 5 2
Soren Hansen   5 3 4 4 3 3 4 5 4 35 3 4 5 3 3
```

Henrik Stenson defeated Anders Hansen, 7 and 6.

```
Henrik Stenson 4 2 4 4 3 4 3 4 4 32 3 4 4 4 2 4 3 4 4 32 64
Anders Hansen  4 3 4 3 3 4 4 4 4 33 3 4 4 4 3 4 4 5 4 35 68
Stenson leads, 4 up
Henrik Stenson 4 2 4 6 2 4 4 4 4 34 2 4 4
Anders Hansen  4 3 4 4 3 5 5 4 5 37 1 4 4
```

Ernie Els defeated Andres Romero, 6 and 5.

```
Ernie Els      3 2 5 6 3 4 4 4 4 35 4 3 4 4 2 4 4 4 4 33 68
Andres Romero  4 3 4 5 4 4 4 4 5 37 2 4 4 5 4 4 4 4 4 35 72
Els leads, 4 up
Ernie Els      4 3 4 4 3 4 4 5 4 35 2 5 5 3
Andres Romero  5 3 4 6 3 4 4 3 5 37 4 4 4 4
```

SEMI-FINALS

Angel Cabrera defeated Hunter Mahan, 2 and 1.

```
Angel Cabrera  4 3 4 4 3 3 5 3 3 32 3 4 4 4 3 4 4 5 3 34 66
Hunter Mahan   4 3 5 4 3 5 4 4 4 36 2 4 5 4 3 3 4 5 5 35 71
Cabrera leads, 3 up
Angel Cabrera  3 4 3 3 4 4 4 4 32 3 3 4 4 3 4 4 4
Hunter Mahan   4 3 5 4 2 4 3 3 4 32 2 4 4 4 3 4 3 4
```

Ernie Els defeated Henrik Stenson, 3 and 2.

```
Ernie Els      4 4 4 4 3 4 4 4 4 35 3 3 3 4 3 4 5 4 5 34 69
Henrik Stenson 4 3 4 4 3 4 4 4 4 34 3 3 5 3 3 6 3 6 4 36 70
Stenson leads, 1 up
Ernie Els      3 3 4 4 3 4 4 3 3 31 3 4 4 4 3 4 4
Henrik Stenson 4 3 4 4 3 4 5 4 4 35 2 4 4 4 3 5 4
```

FINAL

Ernie Els defeated Angel Cabrera, 6 and 4.

```
Ernie Els      4 3 4 4 3 4 3 4 3 31 2 4 C 4 2 3 4 6 4 X X
Angel Cabrera  5 3 4 4 2 4 5 4 4 35 2 4 W 4 3 3 4 5 6 X X
Els leads, 3 up
Ernie Els      4 3 4 4 2 4 4 4 4 33 2 4 4 4 2
Angel Cabrera  4 3 5 4 2 3 4 4 3 32 3 4 5 5 3
```

PRIZE MONEY: Els £1,000,000; Cabrera £400,000; Mahan, Stenson £120,000 each; Casey, Anders Hansen, Soren Hansen, Romero £80,000 each; Austin, Fasth, Goosen, Harrington, Kelly, Montgomerie, Rose, Sabbatini £60,000 each.

LEGEND: C—conceded hole to opponent; W—won hole by concession without holing out; X—no total score.

Open de Madrid Valle Romano

Real Sociedad Hipica Espanola Club de Campo, Madrid, Spain October 11-14
Par 36-36–72; 7,167 yards purse, €901,350

	SCORES			TOTAL	MONEY
Mads Vibe-Hastrup	69	69	67	67	272	€150,000
Alejandro Canizares	69	66	72	68	275	100,000
Daniel Vancsik	65	70	68	73	276	56,340
Gregory Bourdy	71	69	68	69	277	41,580
Rory McIlroy	73	68	66	70	277	41,580
Emanuele Canonica	68	70	71	69	278	31,500
Benn Barham	71	71	71	67	280	19,170
Marcus Fraser	75	68	65	72	280	19,170
Christopher Hanell	70	73	66	71	280	19,170
Sam Little	72	71	68	69	280	19,170
Santiago Luna	75	67	66	72	280	19,170
Jean Van de Velde	71	66	71	72	280	19,170
Sam Walker	71	72	70	67	280	19,170
Fredrik Andersson Hed	75	70	68	68	281	12,960
Gonzalo Fernandez-Castano	71	69	69	72	281	12,960
Damien McGrane	71	74	67	69	281	12,960
Sven Struver	69	74	68	70	281	12,960
Thomas Bjorn	74	68	71	69	282	10,836
Ariel Canete	75	70	67	70	282	10,836
Shiv Kapur	72	70	69	71	282	10,836
Jose Manuel Lara	72	70	68	72	282	10,836
Henrik Nystrom	74	71	69	68	282	10,836
Manuel Quiros	72	67	69	75	283	9,765
Carlos Rodiles	71	73	66	73	283	9,765
Richard Bland	72	74	70	68	284	8,550
Martin Kaymer	67	75	68	74	284	8,550
Jose-Filipe Lima	66	76	72	70	284	8,550
Gary Lockerbie	68	68	73	75	284	8,550
Andrew Marshall	70	74	70	70	284	8,550
Robert Rock	72	74	72	66	284	8,550
Anthony Wall	75	68	72	69	284	8,550
John Bickerton	74	69	72	70	285	6,600
David Carter	71	73	69	72	285	6,600
Michael Jonzon	74	70	72	69	285	6,600
James Kingston	76	65	73	71	285	6,600
David Lynn	76	71	71	67	285	6,600
Pablo Martin	74	71	65	75	285	6,600
Graeme McDowell	74	73	68	70	285	6,600
Christian L. Nilsson	73	70	70	72	285	6,600
Francis Valera	70	67	73	75	285	6,600
Joakim Backstrom	73	70	69	74	286	5,130
Martin Erlandsson	73	74	69	70	286	5,130
Peter Gustafsson	70	70	73	73	286	5,130
Birgir Hafthorsson	75	72	68	71	286	5,130
Miguel Angel Martin	77	68	73	68	286	5,130
Matthew Millar	72	73	67	74	286	5,130
Steven O'Hara	67	79	66	74	286	5,130
Rafael Cabrera Bello	72	72	75	68	287	4,140
Rhys Davies	76	70	72	69	287	4,140
Eirik Tage Johansen	72	70	72	73	287	4,140
Marcel Siem	73	71	72	71	287	4,140
Steve Alker	72	75	69	72	288	3,510
Jean-Francois Remesy	71	69	70	78	288	3,510
Andrew Tampion	71	73	73	71	288	3,510
Johan Axgren	75	72	73	69	289	3,060
Terry Pilkadaris	74	69	73	73	289	3,060
David Park	73	71	71	76	291	2,745

	SCORES				TOTAL	MONEY
Kyron Sullivan	73	74	72	72	291	2,745
Carlos Balmaseda	79	68	76	69	292	2,385
David Drysdale	72	73	77	70	292	2,385
Stuart Little	71	76	71	74	292	2,385
Jarmo Sandelin	74	73	69	76	292	2,385
Zane Scotland	74	73	72	73	292	2,385
Lee Slattery	73	72	73	74	292	2,385
Peter Lawrie	71	75	72	75	293	2,070
Patrik Sjoland	72	75	78	69	294	1,935
Carl Suneson	75	68	76	75	294	1,935
Cesar Monasterio	73	73	70	79	295	1,800
Pedro Linhart	76	71	77	72	296	1,710
Matthew Richardson	72	72	78	75	297	1,640
Agustin Domingo	75	72	76	78	301	1,350

Portugal Masters

Oceanico Victoria Clube de Golfe, Vilamoura, Portugal
Par 35-37–72; 7,177 yards

October 18-21
purse, €3,013,491

	SCORES				TOTAL	MONEY
Steve Webster	66	66	67	64	263	€500,000
Robert Karlsson	67	68	65	65	265	333,330
Fredrik Andersson Hed	66	73	64	66	269	142,500
Peter Hanson	69	65	67	68	269	142,500
Daniel Vancsik	64	66	68	71	269	142,500
Lee Westwood	65	69	67	68	269	142,500
Ross Fisher	68	64	68	71	271	73,050
Martin Kaymer	61	72	69	69	271	73,050
Charl Schwartzel	66	67	66	72	271	73,050
Sam Walker	66	68	67	70	271	73,050
Alvaro Quiros	66	66	70	70	272	55,200
Robert-Jan Derksen	69	70	69	65	273	47,475
Bradley Dredge	68	72	67	66	273	47,475
Thongchai Jaidee	71	67	66	69	273	47,475
Alexander Noren	68	69	67	69	273	47,475
Peter Hedblom	67	71	67	69	274	38,940
James Hepworth	67	68	70	69	274	38,940
James Kingston	68	69	70	67	274	38,940
Peter Lawrie	67	71	68	68	274	38,940
Brett Rumford	67	71	66	70	274	38,940
Ariel Canete	66	70	69	70	275	30,750
Nick Dougherty	66	73	68	68	275	30,750
Mattias Eliasson	69	72	65	69	275	30,750
Retief Goosen	65	72	69	69	275	30,750
Jose-Filipe Lima	69	68	65	73	275	30,750
Pablo Martin	69	70	67	69	275	30,750
Andres Romero	69	71	69	66	275	30,750
Justin Rose	69	70	66	70	275	30,750
Anthony Wall	71	68	70	66	275	30,750
Oliver Wilson	68	70	68	69	275	30,750
Paul Broadhurst	72	66	70	68	276	24,900
Francesco Molinari	66	72	72	66	276	24,900
Gary Murphy	68	71	68	69	276	24,900
Stephen Dodd	69	71	71	66	277	21,600
Martin Erlandsson	64	68	71	74	277	21,600
Soren Hansen	72	65	70	70	277	21,600
Sam Little	67	69	70	71	277	21,600
Jean-Francois Lucquin	66	73	74	64	277	21,600
Marc Warren	71	70	69	67	277	21,600

	SCORES				TOTAL	MONEY
Rafael Echenique	67	71	72	68	278	18,000
Steven Jeppesen	70	69	72	67	278	18,000
David Lynn	70	69	71	68	278	18,000
Christian L. Nilsson	70	67	70	71	278	18,000
Jeev Milkha Singh	70	67	70	71	278	18,000
Alessandro Tadini	69	71	70	68	278	18,000
Thomas Bjorn	70	70	68	71	279	13,800
Emanuele Canonica	66	70	73	70	279	13,800
Simon Khan	71	70	71	67	279	13,800
Barry Lane	67	71	71	70	279	13,800
Santiago Luna	69	71	68	71	279	13,800
Jarmo Sandelin	67	72	73	67	279	13,800
Miles Tunnicliff	69	72	70	68	279	13,800
Mads Vibe-Hastrup	67	68	69	75	279	13,800
Gregory Havret	71	70	71	68	280	10,800
Carl Suneson	69	70	73	68	280	10,800
Richard Finch	72	68	71	70	281	9,225
Rory McIlroy	71	69	73	68	281	9,225
Terry Price	67	73	70	71	281	9,225
Lee Slattery	70	69	73	69	281	9,225
Peter Gustafsson	69	71	66	76	282	8,100
Andrew McLardy	66	72	68	76	282	8,100
Marcel Siem	70	71	70	71	282	8,100
Gregory Bourdy	65	74	71	73	283	7,500
Mark Foster	70	71	72	71	284	6,900
Shiv Kapur	67	70	70	77	284	6,900
Damien McGrane	69	72	71	72	284	6,900
Phillip Archer	67	72	73	73	285	6,150
Paul Lawrie	68	72	76	69	285	6,150
Tiago Cruz	71	70	71	74	286	5,700
David Park	71	68	73	75	287	5,470
Raphael Jacquelin	68	67	81	73	289	4,500
David Frost	67	69	76	79	291	4,497
Miguel Angel Jimenez	71	69	75	77	292	4,494

Mallorca Classic

Pula Golf Club, Mallorca, Spain
Par 35-35–70; 6,850 yards

October 25-28
purse, €2,003,000

	SCORES				TOTAL	MONEY
Gregory Bourdy	69	68	64	67	268	€333,330
Sam Little	66	69	68	67	270	222,220
Robert-Jan Derksen	66	65	70	70	271	125,200
Alastair Forsyth	68	69	70	66	273	100,000
Johan Edfors	68	71	68	67	274	77,400
Peter Lawrie	66	68	68	72	274	77,400
Richard Finch	68	69	66	72	275	48,700
Jose Manuel Lara	71	70	68	66	275	48,700
Jean-Francois Lucquin	66	65	71	73	275	48,700
Alexander Noren	71	69	64	71	275	48,700
Thomas Bjorn	71	67	68	70	276	32,680
Christian Cevaer	71	70	67	68	276	32,680
Mattias Eliasson	69	72	65	70	276	32,680
Thongchai Jaidee	71	64	75	66	276	32,680
Graeme McDowell	71	67	70	68	276	32,680
Sergio Garcia	68	67	69	73	277	27,600
Graeme Storm	67	73	67	70	277	27,600
Mark Foster	67	75	65	71	278	24,866.67
Miguel Angel Jimenez	73	69	68	68	278	24,866.67

	SCORES				TOTAL	MONEY
Carl Suneson	72	64	70	72	278	24,866.67
Rafael Cabrera Bello	68	74	72	65	279	21,700
Barry Lane	68	68	73	70	279	21,700
Paul Lawrie	69	68	72	70	279	21,700
Matthew Millar	71	67	71	70	279	21,700
Francesco Molinari	68	68	72	71	279	21,700
Y.E. Yang	68	72	72	67	279	21,700
Markus Brier	70	69	69	72	280	17,800
Niclas Fasth	65	70	79	66	280	17,800
Gonzalo Fernandez-Castano	71	69	68	72	280	17,800
Andrew McLardy	66	73	70	71	280	17,800
Jean-Francois Remesy	69	68	73	70	280	17,800
Marcel Siem	68	68	70	74	280	17,800
Anthony Wall	72	69	69	70	280	17,800
Soren Kjeldsen	69	69	73	70	281	14,600
Paul McGinley	71	72	66	72	281	14,600
Damien McGrane	71	70	70	70	281	14,600
Wade Ormsby	70	70	69	72	281	14,600
Mads Vibe-Hastrup	68	66	74	73	281	14,600
Benn Barham	70	72	71	69	282	12,600
Thomas Levet	70	71	69	72	282	12,600
Gary Orr	70	69	72	71	282	12,600
Robert Rock	69	68	70	75	282	12,600
Carlos Rodiles	74	68	69	71	282	12,600
Phillip Archer	70	72	71	70	283	10,400
Richard Bland	72	69	71	71	283	10,400
Pedro Linhart	68	74	70	71	283	10,400
Peter O'Malley	70	73	68	72	283	10,400
Francis Valera	69	73	70	71	283	10,400
Simon Wakefield	69	71	70	73	283	10,400
Peter Gustafsson	71	71	72	70	284	8,600
Jarmo Sandelin	70	73	71	70	284	8,600
Miles Tunnicliff	71	72	69	72	284	8,600
Jesus Maria Arruti	70	69	74	72	285	6,833.33
Ian Garbutt	69	69	73	74	285	6,833.33
Gary Murphy	66	74	68	77	285	6,833.33
Phillip Price	69	72	72	72	285	6,833.33
Jyoti Randhawa	68	69	75	73	285	6,833.33
Alessandro Tadini	68	73	73	71	285	6,833.33
Emanuele Canonica	69	69	73	75	286	5,600
Steven O'Hara	73	68	75	70	286	5,600
Brett Rumford	71	72	70	73	286	5,600
Luis Claverie	67	70	74	76	287	5,000
Andrew Marshall	69	74	72	72	287	5,000
Alvaro Salto	71	71	72	73	287	5,000
Joakim Backstrom	67	73	71	77	288	4,200
Andrew Coltart	69	74	70	75	288	4,200
Stephen Dodd	74	68	74	72	288	4,200
Christopher Hanell	72	71	71	74	288	4,200
Marcus Higley	73	67	76	72	288	4,200
Ariel Canete	69	71	75	74	289	3,650
James Hepworth	67	74	75	78	294	3,000

Volvo Masters

Club de Golf Valderrama, Sotegrande, Cadiz, Spain
Par 35-36–71; 6,952 yards

November 1-4
purse, €3,928,500

	SCORES				TOTAL	MONEY
Justin Rose	70	68	71	74	283	€666,660
Simon Dyson	74	70	69	70	283	347,420
Soren Kjeldsen	73	70	73	67	283	347,420
(Rose defeated Dyson and Kjeldsen on second playoff hole.)						
Padraig Harrington	71	71	71	72	285	184,800
Graeme McDowell	68	75	74	68	285	184,800
Martin Kaymer	72	78	66	72	288	140,000
Miguel Angel Jimenez	73	70	77	69	289	120,000
Ian Poulter	76	71	69	74	290	100,000
Thomas Bjorn	76	73	70	72	291	84,800
Jyoti Randhawa	73	70	74	74	291	84,800
Robert Karlsson	77	70	71	74	292	74,600
Paul McGinley	69	75	74	75	293	66,900
Anthony Wall	73	74	72	74	293	66,900
Alex Cejka	78	70	70	76	294	59,900
Ross Fisher	71	80	71	72	294	59,900
Peter Hanson	75	72	74	73	294	59,900
Markus Brier	76	72	74	73	295	52,500
Raphael Jacquelin	71	73	79	72	295	52,500
Francesco Molinari	75	71	76	73	295	52,500
Colin Montgomerie	72	73	71	79	295	52,500
Oliver Wilson	74	75	71	76	296	48,700
Niclas Fasth	75	70	76	77	298	46,100
Gonzalo Fernandez-Castano	74	75	76	73	298	46,100
Peter Hedblom	77	72	78	71	298	46,100
Paul Casey	80	73	72	75	300	38,800
Nick Dougherty	75	76	73	76	300	38,800
Soren Hansen	75	74	70	81	300	38,800
Anders Hansen	72	77	75	76	300	38,800
Peter O'Malley	70	75	75	80	300	38,800
Andres Romero	76	76	78	70	300	38,800
Brett Rumford	73	74	75	78	300	38,800
Jeev Milkha Singh	76	74	74	76	300	38,800
Simon Wakefield	75	74	77	74	300	38,800
Gregory Bourdy	75	72	77	77	301	32,250
Luke Donald	72	75	76	78	301	32,250
Sergio Garcia	77	72	73	79	301	32,250
Richard Sterne	75	70	78	78	301	32,250
Robert-Jan Derksen	73	77	81	71	302	28,650
Alastair Forsyth	75	73	77	77	302	28,650
Henrik Stenson	76	78	71	77	302	28,650
Y.E. Yang	74	74	78	76	302	28,650
Pelle Edberg	79	73	74	78	304	25,500
Mark Foster	76	78	76	74	304	25,500
Marc Warren	82	75	71	76	304	25,500
Phillip Archer	76	78	74	77	305	23,700
Steve Webster	79	74	78	75	306	22,800
Fredrik Andersson Hed	81	74	80	72	307	21,000
Simon Khan	75	79	79	74	307	21,000
Graeme Storm	81	74	77	75	307	21,000
Bradley Dredge	75	72	83	78	308	18,333.33
Mikko Ilonen	83	72	78	75	308	18,333.33
Thongchai Jaidee	73	78	80	77	308	18,333.33
Gregory Havret	83	73	76	77	309	16,800
Sandy Lyle	84	81	72	78	315	16,300
Ronan Rafferty	83	89			WD	15,800

HSBC Champions

See Asia/Japan Tours chapter.

UBS Hong Kong Open

See Asia/Japan Tours chapter.

MasterCard Masters

See Australasian Tour chapter.

Michael Hill New Zealand Open

See Australasian Tour chapter.

Alfred Dunhill Championship

See African Tours chapter.

South African Airways Open

See African Tours chapter.

Challenge Tour

Colombia Masters

See American Tours chapter.

Kai Fieberg Costa Rica Open

See American Tours chapter.

Guatemala Open

See American Tours chapter.

Tusker Kenya Open

Karen Golf Club, Nairobi, Kenya
Par 35-35–70; 6,951 yards

March 8-11
purse, €162,240

	SCORES				TOTAL	MONEY
Edoardo Molinari	68	69	67	70	274	€25,600
James Kamte	69	73	66	67	275	17,600
Mikael Lundberg	70	69	68	69	276	11,200
Andre Bossert	69	73	69	67	278	7,280
Sebastian Fernandez	70	71	66	71	278	7,280
Jacob Okello	73	69	67	69	278	7,280
Alvaro Velasco	73	67	71	67	278	7,280
Thomas Feyrsinger	71	71	68	69	279	4,160

	SCORES				TOTAL	MONEY
Rodolfo Gonzalez	70	71	68	70	279	4,160
Jamie Donaldson	71	67	72	71	281	2,902.86
Jeppe Huldahl	71	70	71	69	281	2,902.86
Lasse Jensen	69	74	71	67	281	2,902.86
Soren Juul	71	73	68	69	281	2,902.86
Toni Karjalainen	69	71	70	71	281	2,902.86
Joost Luiten	74	66	70	71	281	2,902.86
Benjamin Miarka	71	74	67	69	281	2,902.86
Tongoona Charamba	69	75	68	70	282	2,160
Tim Milford	70	70	70	72	282	2,160
Greig Hutcheon	72	72	68	71	283	1,661.33
Alec McGuinness	68	71	71	73	283	1,661.33
Eric Ramsay	70	73	71	69	283	1,661.33
Hernan Rey	69	74	72	68	283	1,661.33
Oliver Whiteley	67	75	68	73	283	1,661.33
Julien Xanthopoulos	73	70	71	69	283	1,661.33
Magnus A. Carlsson	70	72	70	72	284	1,328
Tim Dykes	70	74	71	69	284	1,328
Julien Grillon	70	67	71	76	284	1,328
Jamie Little	70	70	73	71	284	1,328
Nathan Main	70	73	68	73	284	1,328
Ally Mellor	70	75	70	69	284	1,328
Cedric Menut	73	67	74	70	284	1,328
Wilhelm Schauman	68	75	67	74	284	1,328
Paolo Terreni	74	71	67	72	284	1,328
Inder Van Weerelt	71	71	68	74	284	1,328

Tessali-Metaponto Open di Puglia e Basilicata

Riva dei Tessali: Par 35-36–71; 6,503 yards
Metaponto GC: Par 36-36–72; 6,284 yards
Puglia, Italy

April 19-22
purse, €131,820

	SCORES				TOTAL	MONEY
Michael Hoey	66	67	68	71	272	€20,800
Liam Bond	70	66	68	68	272	14,300
(Hoey defeated Bond on first playoff hole.)						
Joost Luiten	65	70	68	70	273	9,100
Marco Crespi	67	71	67	69	274	7,150
Ben Mason	70	67	69	68	274	7,150
Michael Jonzon	71	69	70	65	275	4,030
Edoardo Molinari	71	68	67	69	275	4,030
John E. Morgan	66	67	74	68	275	4,030
Wilhelm Schauman	70	71	68	66	275	4,030
Andre Bossert	68	72	70	66	276	2,730
Miguel Rodriguez	69	71	67	69	276	2,730
Magnus A. Carlsson	70	68	70	69	277	2,340
Raphael Eyraud	67	66	70	74	277	2,340
Cedric Menut	68	70	71	68	277	2,340
Felipe Aguilar	72	67	68	71	278	1,885
Anthony Snobeck	68	69	73	68	278	1,885
Nicolas Vanhootegem	66	70	71	71	278	1,885
Fredrik Widmark	69	63	71	75	278	1,885
Chris Gane	68	68	72	71	279	1,451.67
Giorgio Grillo	71	66	68	74	279	1,451.67
Van Phillips	65	74	68	72	279	1,451.67
Nicolas Colsaerts	67	70	69	74	280	1,235
Jeppe Huldahl	68	73	68	71	280	1,235
Simon Lilly	71	69	69	71	280	1,235
Martin Wiegele	69	71	71	69	280	1,235

A.G.F. Allianz Golf Open de Toulouse

Golf de Toulouse-Seilh, Seilh, France
Par 36-36–72; 6,924 yards

May 10-13
purse, €133,042

	SCORES				TOTAL	MONEY
Joost Luiten	70	71	66	64	271	€20,800
Nicolas Vanhootegem	71	65	69	67	272	14,300
Gareth Paddison	70	67	69	71	277	9,100
Jan-Are Larsen	70	70	67	71	278	6,500
Jamie Little	69	73	67	69	278	6,500
Magnus Persson	73	67	68	70	278	6,500
Michael Hoey	64	74	69	72	279	3,276
Peter Kaensche	70	70	68	71	279	3,276
George Murray	67	70	69	73	279	3,276
Van Phillips	66	72	71	70	279	3,276
Leif Westerberg	67	73	68	71	279	3,276
Kalle Edberg	68	72	67	73	280	2,340
Michael Lorenzo-Vera	69	74	67	70	280	2,340
Christian Reimbold	64	71	71	74	280	2,340
Andre Bossert	67	69	70	75	281	1,765.83
Michiel Bothma	69	66	72	74	281	1,765.83
Sebastien Delagrange	66	75	70	70	281	1,765.83
Jeppe Huldahl	72	71	66	72	281	1,765.83
Oliver Whiteley	70	73	68	70	281	1,765.83
Gareth Wright	68	70	72	71	281	1,765.83
Daniel De Leon	73	69	71	69	282	1,274
Alfredo Garcia-Heredia	71	69	72	70	282	1,274
Julien Guerrier	71	67	74	70	282	1,274
Peter Baker	70	73	68	72	283	1,196
Nicolas Joakimides	70	71	71	71	283	1,196
Iain Pyman	71	71	69	72	283	1,196

Telenet Trophy

Royal Waterloo Golf Club, Brussels, Belgium
Par 36-36–72; 6,968 yards

May 17-20
purse, €133,575

	SCORES				TOTAL	MONEY
Nicolas Vanhootegem	68	65	68	70	271	€20,800
Felipe Aguilar	66	72	69	68	275	14,300
Robert Coles	70	71	72	64	277	9,100
Didier De Vooght	65	66	72	75	278	7,800
Anthony Snobeck	71	72	67	69	279	6,500
Peter Baker	70	68	71	71	280	4,680
Inder Van Weerelt	72	68	70	70	280	4,680
Christophe Brazillier	71	72	70	68	281	2,938
Nicolas Colsaerts	65	70	72	74	281	2,938
Stuart Davis	71	69	70	71	281	2,938
Edoardo Molinari	72	70	67	72	281	2,938
Miguel Rodriguez	72	68	71	70	281	2,938
Magnus A. Carlsson	67	70	73	72	282	2,145
Mikael Lundberg	67	74	69	72	282	2,145
Thomas Nielsen	73	70	70	69	282	2,145
Anthony Tarchetti	70	69	68	75	282	2,145
Anders Schmidt Hansen	72	72	70	69	283	1,484
Toni Karjalainen	72	68	73	70	283	1,484
Iain Pyman	75	69	69	70	283	1,484
Jerome Theunis	67	72	75	69	283	1,484
Alvaro Velasco	68	70	72	73	283	1,484

	SCORES			TOTAL	MONEY
Julio Zapata	72	72	68	71	283	1,484
Niki Zitny	71	72	68	72	283	1,484
Roope Kakko	70	70	75	69	284	1,196
Ross McGowan	71	71	70	72	284	1,196
John E. Morgan	72	69	73	70	284	1,196

Open Mahou de Madrid

Casino Club de Golf Retamares, Madrid, Spain   May 24-28
Par 36-35–71; 6,575 yards   purse, €132,145
(Event shortened to 54 holes, completed on Monday—rain and fog.)

	SCORES			TOTAL	MONEY
Ben Mason	70	66	69	205	€20,800
Tim Milford	72	64	70	206	11,700
Alvaro Velasco	70	68	68	206	11,700
Jan-Are Larsen	70	67	70	207	6,500
Michael Lorenzo-Vera	69	65	73	207	6,500
Joost Luiten	72	65	70	207	6,500
Vicente Arpon	66	68	74	208	3,900
Miguel Angel Martin	71	66	71	208	3,900
Gary Clark	71	67	71	209	2,525.71
Klas Eriksson	66	69	74	209	2,525.71
Raphael Eyraud	69	69	71	209	2,525.71
Alfredo Garcia-Heredia	67	74	68	209	2,525.71
Pedro Linhart	72	68	69	209	2,525.71
Gustavo Rojas	71	65	73	209	2,525.71
Niki Zitny	71	67	71	209	2,525.71
Carlos Balmaseda	66	69	75	210	1,584.14
Marco Crespi	71	68	71	210	1,584.14
Rafael Gomez	70	67	73	210	1,584.14
Kevin Harper	70	66	74	210	1,584.14
Mikko Korhonen	71	70	69	210	1,584.14
Jamie Little	69	68	73	210	1,584.14
Martin Maritz	70	65	75	210	1,584.14
Jacques Chevalier	68	72	71	211	1,183
Eduardo De La Riva	67	70	74	211	1,183
Jamie Donaldson	72	66	73	211	1,183
Jamie McLeary	70	67	74	211	1,183
Robin Swane	68	69	74	211	1,183
Peter Whiteford	71	65	75	211	1,183

Oceanico Developments Pro-Am Challenge

Marriott Worsley Park Hotel & Country Club,   May 31-June 3
Greater Manchester, England   purse, €147,968
Par 35-35–70; 6,791 yards

	SCORES			TOTAL	MONEY
Ross McGowan	66	63	69	67	265	€23,604
Michael Lorenzo-Vera	61	66	72	66	265	16,227.75
(McGowan defeated Lorenzo-Vera on second playoff hole.)						
Stuart Davis	64	67	64	72	267	10,326.75
Tobias Dier	68	66	66	68	268	8,113.88
Ricardo Santos	67	65	69	67	268	8,113.88
Simon Robinson	71	67	66	65	269	5,310.90
Leif Westerberg	67	66	70	66	269	5,310.90

	SCORES				TOTAL	MONEY
Tim Dykes	64	72	67	68	271	3,835.65
Julio Zapata	68	62	71	70	271	3,835.65
Jean-Nicolas Billot	68	66	70	68	272	2,999.68
Zane Scotland	69	69	68	66	272	2,999.68
Alvaro Velasco	70	68	67	67	272	2,999.68
Michiel Bothma	66	70	70	67	273	2,434.16
Gabriel Canizares	70	65	66	72	273	2,434.16
David Dixon	67	68	69	69	273	2,434.16
*David Horsey	65	68	70	70	273	
Thomas Nielsen	68	67	69	69	273	2,434.16
Andrew Butterfield	67	67	69	71	274	1,728.50
Robert Coles	69	68	67	70	274	1,728.50
Eduardo De La Riva	71	67	66	70	274	1,728.50
Klas Eriksson	66	70	68	70	274	1,728.50
Martin Maritz	67	67	71	69	274	1,728.50
Van Phillips	69	67	70	68	274	1,728.50
Antti Ahokas	71	67	69	68	275	1,357.23
Peter Baker	72	65	69	69	275	1,357.23
Michael Jonzon	69	68	70	68	275	1,357.23
Ally Mellor	69	69	68	69	275	1,357.23
Bernd Wiesberger	68	66	68	73	275	1,357.23

Vodafone Challenge

Golf Club An der Elfrather Muhle, Dusseldorf, Germany
Par 36-36–72; 6,859 yards

June 7-10
purse, €133,042

	SCORES				TOTAL	MONEY
Joost Luiten	70	68	71	61	270	€20,800
Magnus A. Carlsson	69	62	75	66	272	14,300
Adam Gee	69	69	69	67	274	9,100
Juan Abbate	70	67	70	70	277	5,915
Anders Schmidt Hansen	69	72	69	67	277	5,915
James Kamte	71	71	66	69	277	5,915
John Mellor	69	72	67	69	277	5,915
Wilhelm Schauman	68	70	71	69	278	3,640
Gary Clark	71	69	72	67	279	2,762.50
Kasper Linnet Jorgensen	72	69	71	67	279	2,762.50
George Murray	71	71	68	69	279	2,762.50
Julio Zapata	70	71	68	70	279	2,762.50
Carlos Balmaseda	71	71	70	68	280	2,275
Jan-Are Larsen	72	73	64	71	280	2,275
Mark Laskey	73	69	69	70	281	1,885
Inder Van Weerelt	73	68	72	68	281	1,885
Leif Westerberg	72	65	74	70	281	1,885
Gareth Wright	69	71	74	67	281	1,885
Mickael Dieu	71	73	69	69	282	1,451.67
Jeppe Huldahl	72	68	71	71	282	1,451.67
James Morrison	72	69	71	70	282	1,451.67
Kariem Baraka	70	74	65	74	283	1,196
Marco Crespi	73	66	72	72	283	1,196
Pablo Del Grosso	69	74	71	69	283	1,196
Simon Lilly	68	71	70	74	283	1,196
Jamie Little	69	70	75	69	283	1,196
Zane Scotland	69	73	67	74	283	1,196
Anthony Tarchetti	68	69	77	69	283	1,196

Open de Saint-Omer

See European Tour section.

Credit Suisse Challenge

Wylihof Golf, Luterbach, Switzerland
Par 36-37–73; 7,202 yards

June 21-24
purse, €145,418

	SCORES				TOTAL	MONEY
Peter Baker	72	67	66	67	272	€22,400
Andrew McArthur	67	72	70	64	273	15,400
Robert Dinwiddie	67	68	71	68	274	9,800
Carlos Del Moral	65	71	69	70	275	8,400
Julio Zapata	65	74	74	63	276	7,000
Christophe Brazillier	71	70	68	68	277	4,666.67
Marco Crespi	69	70	65	73	277	4,666.67
Francis Valera	70	72	67	68	277	4,666.67
Branden Grace	70	67	72	69	278	3,220
Alvaro Velasco	71	73	68	66	278	3,220
Gareth Paddison	68	71	70	70	279	2,660
Christian Reimbold	70	69	69	71	279	2,660
Fredrik Widmark	71	71	70	67	279	2,660
Julien Clement	72	71	68	69	280	2,170
Christoffer Lange	66	70	74	70	280	2,170
Euan Little	68	68	75	69	280	2,170
Zane Scotland	72	67	71	70	280	2,170
Felipe Aguilar	68	70	71	72	281	1,750
Mikko Korhonen	71	71	72	67	281	1,750
Stuart Manley	72	72	70	68	282	1,388.33
Tim Milford	70	70	74	68	282	1,388.33
Martin Rominger	72	72	73	65	282	1,388.33
Richard Treis	68	69	73	72	282	1,388.33
Inder Van Weerelt	72	73	68	69	282	1,388.33
Peter Whiteford	70	70	70	72	282	1,388.33

Estoril Challenge de Portugal

Quinta da Marinha, Cascais, Estoril, Portugal
Par 35-36–71; 6,418 yards

June 28-July 1
purse, €132,145

	SCORES				TOTAL	MONEY
Ross McGowan	68	68	70	66	272	€20,800
Stuart Manley	65	72	70	68	275	14,300
Robert Coles	67	67	74	68	276	9,100
Jamie Donaldson	68	70	67	72	277	7,800
Peter Baker	65	66	73	74	278	5,850
Daniel Denison	70	72	66	70	278	5,850
Magnus A. Carlsson	72	67	71	69	279	4,160
Liam Bond	74	69	72	65	280	3,055
Kasper Linnet Jorgensen	67	69	73	71	280	3,055
Stephen Scahill	71	71	71	67	280	3,055
Fredrik Widmark	71	71	70	68	280	3,055
Raphael Eyraud	75	68	71	67	281	2,145
Sebastian Fernandez	69	72	73	67	281	2,145
Jan-Are Larsen	66	73	71	71	281	2,145
Ally Mellor	68	73	73	67	281	2,145
Simon Robinson	73	67	71	70	281	2,145
Antonio Sobrinho	71	68	72	70	281	2,145

	SCORES				TOTAL	MONEY
Gary Clark	68	70	78	66	282	1,373.13
Tiago Cruz	71	68	77	66	282	1,373.13
Pablo Larrazabal	72	68	69	73	282	1,373.13
David Patrick	71	72	69	70	282	1,373.13
Van Phillips	72	71	69	70	282	1,373.13
Eric Ramsay	75	69	68	70	282	1,373.13
Francis Valera	73	71	71	67	282	1,373.13
Phil Worthington	69	71	72	70	282	1,373.13

AGF-Allianz Open des Volcans - Challenge de France

Golf des Volcans, Clermont Ferrand, France
Par 36-35–71; 7,110 yards

July 5-8
purse, €132,093

	SCORES				TOTAL	MONEY
Gareth Paddison	70	69	68	66	273	€20,800
Leif Westerberg	75	68	68	68	279	14,300
Chris Gane	71	75	67	69	282	8,450
Oliver Whiteley	72	70	70	70	282	8,450
Michael Lorenzo-Vera	67	71	72	73	283	5,286.67
Stuart Manley	71	72	71	69	283	5,286.67
Benoit Teilleria	72	71	70	70	283	5,286.67
Pablo Larrazabal	77	66	69	73	285	3,380
Anthony Snobeck	71	74	72	68	285	3,380
Gustavo Acosta	70	75	69	72	286	2,643.33
Frederic Cupillard	71	74	70	71	286	2,643.33
Sebastien Delagrange	71	71	77	67	286	2,643.33
Jean-Nicolas Billot	76	70	73	68	287	2,080
Francois Delamontagne	72	71	72	72	287	2,080
Chris Doak	72	72	74	69	287	2,080
Paul Dwyer	73	74	70	70	287	2,080
Paul Nilbrink	73	75	72	67	287	2,080
*Bertrand Noel	73	72	73	69	287	
Christophe Brazillier	75	70	70	73	288	1,373.13
Stephen Browne	77	72	67	72	288	1,373.13
Andrew Butterfield	72	73	72	71	288	1,373.13
Magnus A. Carlsson	75	70	68	75	288	1,373.13
Klas Eriksson	74	73	72	69	288	1,373.13
Anthony Grenier	77	69	70	72	288	1,373.13
Julien Guerrier	72	76	71	69	288	1,373.13
Iain Pyman	75	70	73	70	288	1,373.13

MAN NO Open

Golfclub Adamstal, Ramsau, Austria
Par 36-34–70; 6,476 yards

July 19-22
purse, €132,457

	SCORES				TOTAL	MONEY
Anders Schmidt Hansen	66	68	64	71	269	€20,800
Zane Scotland	65	70	66	71	272	14,300
Stephen Browne	70	69	70	67	276	7,800
Tiago Cruz	68	71	63	74	276	7,800
Stuart Manley	69	66	72	69	276	7,800
Antti Ahokas	71	69	68	70	278	4,680
Tim Milford	69	67	71	71	278	4,680
Pontus Ericsson	68	70	68	73	279	3,380
Nicolas Vanhootegem	66	74	67	72	279	3,380

	SCORES				TOTAL	MONEY
Robert Dinwiddie	65	69	73	73	280	2,567.50
Paul Dwyer	70	70	70	70	280	2,567.50
Chris Gane	71	65	78	66	280	2,567.50
Benoit Teilleria	67	73	69	71	280	2,567.50
Florian Praegant	70	69	69	73	281	2,145
Bernd Wiesberger	71	67	69	74	281	2,145
Kalle Edberg	69	69	69	75	282	1,635.83
Thomas Feyrsinger	69	72	69	72	282	1,635.83
Roope Kakko	76	66	70	70	282	1,635.83
Toni Karjalainen	69	69	74	70	282	1,635.83
Manuel Merizalde	69	71	70	72	282	1,635.83
Martin Wiegele	69	68	70	75	282	1,635.83
Tim Dykes	69	67	76	71	283	1,261
Soren Juul	72	69	73	69	283	1,261
Klas Eriksson	73	67	72	72	284	1,170
Edoardo Molinari	68	74	70	72	284	1,170
Iain Pyman	68	70	75	71	284	1,170
Richard Treis	71	71	71	71	284	1,170
Fabrizio Zanotti	71	68	68	77	284	1,170

FirstPlus Wales Challenge

Vale Hotel Golf & Spa Resort, Cardiff, Vale of Glamorgan, Wales
Par 36-36–72; 6,436 yards

July 26-29
purse, €132,756

	SCORES			TOTAL	MONEY
Colm Moriarty	68	65	70	203	€20,800
Felipe Aguilar	70	67	69	206	14,300
Gareth Maybin	73	68	67	208	7,150
Craig Smith	69	73	66	208	7,150
Leif Westerberg	75	69	64	208	7,150
Julio Zapata	67	66	75	208	7,150
Robert Coles	72	69	68	209	3,445
Sebastien Delagrange	71	69	69	209	3,445
Stuart Manley	72	66	71	209	3,445
Andrew McArthur	68	71	70	209	3,445
Tim Dykes	70	66	74	210	2,470
Peter Fowler	74	69	67	210	2,470
Jean Hugo	72	68	70	210	2,470
Matthew King	70	73	68	211	1,763.13
Gareth Paddison	72	68	71	211	1,763.13
Stephen Scahill	72	69	70	211	1,763.13
Richard Treis	69	75	67	211	1,763.13
Fredrik Widmark	72	71	68	211	1,763.13
James H. Williams	70	72	69	211	1,763.13
Phil Worthington	73	71	67	211	1,763.13
Fabrizio Zanotti	67	73	71	211	1,763.13
Magnus A. Carlsson	74	70	68	212	1,196
Chris Gane	71	68	73	212	1,196
Branden Grace	68	71	73	212	1,196
Toni Karjalainen	75	66	71	212	1,196
Mikko Korhonen	74	71	67	212	1,196
Martin Maritz	72	69	71	212	1,196
Christian Reimbold	73	71	68	212	1,196

Challenge of Ireland

Glasson Golf Hotel & Country Club, Athlone, Ireland
Par 36-36–72; 7,159 yards

August 2-5
purse, €151,155

	SCORES				TOTAL	MONEY
Magnus A. Carlsson	69	70	69	70	278	€24,000
Michael Lorenzo-Vera	63	73	74	69	279	13,500
Julio Zapata	69	73	70	67	279	13,500
Peter Kaensche	70	73	68	72	283	9,000
Stephen Scahill	69	77	71	67	284	6,100
Leif Westerberg	71	69	71	73	284	6,100
Fredrik Widmark	67	72	73	72	284	6,100
Liam Bond	73	66	72	74	285	3,390
Matthew Cort	70	73	69	73	285	3,390
Tim Dykes	68	74	72	71	285	3,390
Magnus Persson	71	72	70	72	285	3,390
Alvaro Velasco	69	72	70	74	285	3,390
Stuart Manley	70	71	75	70	286	2,625
David Mortimer	72	71	74	69	286	2,625
Oskar Bergman	71	73	71	72	287	2,250
Gareth Maybin	69	73	72	73	287	2,250
Oliver Whiteley	72	75	68	72	287	2,250
Stuart Davis	67	77	71	73	288	1,825
Justin Kehoe	69	73	75	71	288	1,825
Mikael Lundberg	70	72	73	73	288	1,825
Juan Abbate	71	76	70	72	289	1,455
Peter Baker	72	73	71	73	289	1,455
Richard O'Hanlon	71	75	71	72	289	1,455
Martin Wiegele	70	75	73	71	289	1,455
Andrew Butterfield	74	69	74	74	291	1,335
Roope Kakko	71	75	69	76	291	1,335
Andrew McArthur	64	78	75	74	291	1,335
Colm Moriarty	72	74	72	73	291	1,335

Scottish Challenge

Macdonald Cardrona Hotel & Country Club, Cardrona, Scotland
Par 36-36–72; 6,990 yards

August 9-12
purse, €203,300

	SCORES				TOTAL	MONEY
Robert Dinwiddie	70	63	68	67	268	€32,000
Jamie McLeary	67	72	66	67	272	22,000
David Higgins	69	69	70	65	273	14,000
Carlos Del Moral	70	70	69	66	275	8,400
Jamie Donaldson	68	68	68	71	275	8,400
Joost Luiten	69	66	70	70	275	8,400
Andrew McArthur	66	69	72	68	275	8,400
*Lloyd Saltman	70	69	66	70	275	
Fabrizio Zanotti	70	66	70	69	275	8,400
Stuart Manley	64	73	69	70	276	4,600
Eric Ramsay	66	68	71	71	276	4,600
George Murray	70	68	65	74	277	3,800
Hernan Rey	66	71	72	68	277	3,800
Peter Whiteford	66	67	71	73	277	3,800
Peter Baker	70	68	69	71	278	3,200
David Dixon	72	68	67	71	278	3,200
Anders Schmidt Hansen	73	66	69	70	278	3,200
Colm Moriarty	69	72	67	71	279	2,525
David Patrick	67	69	71	72	279	2,525

	SCORES				TOTAL	MONEY
Gustavo Rojas	71	69	68	71	279	2,525
Alvaro Velasco	65	71	69	74	279	2,525
Andre Bossert	68	68	70	74	280	1,920
Francois Calmels	70	71	69	70	280	1,920
Christian Reimbold	69	68	68	75	280	1,920
Dean Robertson	70	69	70	71	280	1,920
Simon Thornton	70	71	67	72	280	1,920

Rolex Trophy

Golf Club de Geneve, Geneva, Switzerland
Par 36-36–72; 6,727 yards

August 16-19
purse, €180,250

	SCORES				TOTAL	MONEY
Robert Dinwiddie	70	68	68	64	270	€18,000
Ross McGowan	69	66	67	71	273	11,800
Michael Lorenzo-Vera	71	65	68	70	274	10,200
Magnus A. Carlsson	72	68	66	69	275	8,300
Jamie Donaldson	69	68	69	69	275	8,300
Colm Moriarty	69	68	68	70	275	8,300
Stuart Manley	67	70	72	67	276	6,600
Hernan Rey	68	69	71	68	276	6,600
Alvaro Velasco	69	68	69	70	276	6,600
Juan Abbate	67	74	67	69	277	6,000
Peter Fowler	69	71	69	68	277	6,000
James Kamte	68	71	71	68	278	5,600
Mikael Lundberg	68	74	66	70	278	5,600
Ben Mason	72	69	70	68	279	5,300
Liam Bond	67	70	72	71	280	5,100
Nicolas Vanhootegem	72	70	67	73	282	5,000
Gary Clark	68	71	72	77	288	4,850
Jan-Are Larsen	70	72	69	77	288	4,850

Lexus Open

Miklagard Golf Club, Klofta, Norway
Par 36-36–72; 7,398 yards

August 16-19
purse, €131,131

	SCORES				TOTAL	MONEY
Martin Wiegele	68	71	73	66	278	€20,800
George Murray	68	71	70	69	278	14,300
(Wiegele defeated Murray on first playoff hole.)						
Michiel Bothma	70	73	73	65	281	9,100
Francois Delamontagne	72	70	71	70	283	7,150
Gareth Maybin	72	70	68	73	283	7,150
Oskar Bergman	69	72	73	70	284	4,030
Julien Foret	72	72	68	72	284	4,030
Matthew King	71	73	70	70	284	4,030
Phil Worthington	70	71	74	69	284	4,030
Scott Henderson	73	69	70	73	285	2,643.33
Mikko Korhonen	69	73	73	70	285	2,643.33
Magnus Persson	73	71	70	71	285	2,643.33
Per Barth	73	73	72	68	286	2,080
Sam Osborne	71	74	69	72	286	2,080
Kieran Staunton	71	74	68	73	286	2,080
Robin Swane	69	73	73	71	286	2,080
Daniel Wardrop	72	73	69	72	286	2,080

	SCORES				TOTAL	MONEY
Lorenzo Gagli	69	72	75	71	287	1,427.83
Peter Kaensche	72	70	72	73	287	1,427.83
Pablo Larrazabal	74	73	70	70	287	1,427.83
Zane Scotland	73	73	74	67	287	1,427.83
Tuomas Tuovinen	72	73	73	69	287	1,427.83
Murray Urquhart	73	73	70	71	287	1,427.83
Christophe Brazillier	69	73	76	70	288	1,105
Paul Dwyer	71	72	74	71	288	1,105
Roope Kakko	71	74	73	70	288	1,105
Ally Mellor	74	71	73	70	288	1,105
Iain Pyman	70	76	71	71	288	1,105
Richie Ramsay	74	71	70	73	288	1,105
Mark Tullo	71	73	73	71	288	1,105
Paul Waring	73	73	73	69	288	1,105
Peter Whiteford	77	70	72	69	288	1,105
Craig Williams	73	73	72	70	288	1,105

Postbank Challenge

Golfclub Mulheim an der Ruhr, Mulheim, Germany
Par 35-36–71; 6,662 yards

August 23-26
purse, €142,310

	SCORES				TOTAL	MONEY
Felipe Aguilar	66	66	69	65	266	€22,400
Andrew McArthur	64	67	69	66	266	12,600
Paul Waring	68	62	68	68	266	12,600
(Aguilar defeated Waring on first and McArthur on second playoff hole.)						
Pablo Larrazabal	68	67	71	63	269	8,400
Peter Kaensche	67	68	69	66	270	6,300
Alvaro Velasco	66	68	70	66	270	6,300
Matthew Cort	69	65	69	69	272	4,200
Mark Tullo	72	66	69	65	272	4,200
Rafael Gomez	65	72	68	68	273	3,080
James Kamte	69	65	68	71	273	3,080
Zane Scotland	71	66	66	70	273	3,080
Carlos Del Moral	67	67	70	70	274	2,380
Sebastien Delagrange	66	66	71	71	274	2,380
Sebastian Fernandez	68	67	70	69	274	2,380
Chris Gane	67	66	70	71	274	2,380
Mikko Korhonen	69	69	69	67	274	2,380
Richie Ramsay	68	69	69	69	275	1,960
Raphael De Sousa	68	68	70	70	276	1,506
Adam Gee	72	66	66	72	276	1,506
Rodolfo Gonzalez	69	66	72	69	276	1,506
Soren Juul	72	64	70	70	276	1,506
Benoit Teilleria	69	68	71	68	276	1,506
Francis Valera	67	70	71	68	276	1,506
Ben Willman	66	73	69	68	276	1,506
Liam Bond	66	70	71	70	277	1,274
Benjamin Miarka	69	69	69	70	277	1,274

ECCO Tour Championship

Odense Golfklub, Odense, Denmark
Par 36-34–70; 6,583 yards

August 30-September 2
purse, €132,145

	SCORES				TOTAL	MONEY
Iain Pyman	64	67	62	67	260	€20,800
Magnus A. Carlsson	65	70	60	68	263	11,700
John E. Morgan	64	66	67	66	263	11,700
Francois Delamontagne	65	65	66	69	265	7,150
Inder Van Weerelt	65	69	68	63	265	7,150
Knud Storgaard	68	68	64	66	266	5,200
Bjorn Pettersson	73	66	61	67	267	4,160
Panu Kylliainen	67	68	66	67	268	3,380
Stuart Manley	65	72	63	68	268	3,380
John Davies	67	68	68	66	269	2,643.33
Paul Dwyer	67	71	66	65	269	2,643.33
James Kamte	69	65	64	71	269	2,643.33
Rikard Karlberg	66	69	65	70	270	2,210
Janne Martikainen	70	69	64	67	270	2,210
Bernd Wiesberger	69	67	67	67	270	2,210
Petter Bocian	66	67	70	68	271	1,635.83
Carlos Del Moral	69	67	66	69	271	1,635.83
Tobias Dier	69	68	66	68	271	1,635.83
Andreas Hogberg	69	67	65	70	271	1,635.83
Peter Kaensche	68	69	64	70	271	1,635.83
Thomas Nielsen	70	67	67	67	271	1,635.83
*Kristian Nielsen	68	67	65	71	271	
Antti Ahokas	67	70	66	69	272	1,196
Jamie Donaldson	71	63	68	70	272	1,196
Anders Schmidt Hansen	69	68	69	66	272	1,196
Pablo Larrazabal	70	65	72	65	272	1,196
Jamie Little	67	70	68	67	272	1,196
Ben Mason	68	68	66	70	272	1,196
Mark Tullo	70	68	67	67	272	1,196

Telia Challenge Waxholm

Waxholm Golf Club, Stockholm, Sweden
Par 37-36–73; 7,318 yards

September 6-9
purse, €127,547

	SCORES				TOTAL	MONEY
Iain Pyman	68	70	70	66	274	€20,028.77
Robert Coles	69	71	69	67	276	13,769.71
Benjamin Miarka	70	70	72	65	277	8,763.11
Jamie Donaldson	67	69	73	69	278	6,884.96
Ross McGowan	72	71	68	67	278	6,884.96
Gustav Adell	72	68	72	68	280	3,880.62
Oskar Bergman	67	73	71	69	280	3,880.62
Michael Lorenzo-Vera	77	67	71	65	280	3,880.62
John E. Morgan	65	78	68	69	280	3,880.62
Kariem Baraka	66	71	73	72	282	2,628.80
Richard Treis	72	71	71	68	282	2,628.80
Julien Foret	73	70	71	69	283	2,315.85
Johan Skold	69	69	77	68	283	2,315.85
Per Barth	69	72	73	70	284	1,815.13
Magnus A. Carlsson	73	70	75	66	284	1,815.13
Gary Clark	70	72	70	72	284	1,815.13
Magnus Persson	69	73	73	69	284	1,815.13
Nicolas Vanhootegem	68	73	71	72	284	1,815.13

	SCORES				TOTAL	MONEY
Paul Waring	74	71	70	69	284	1,815.13
Sebastian Fernandez	74	71	70	70	285	1,306.06
Peter Kaensche	72	70	73	70	285	1,306.06
Stuart Manley	73	64	76	72	285	1,306.06
Michael Jonzon	67	75	72	72	286	1,151.67
Roope Kakko	70	73	71	72	286	1,151.67
Daniel Lindgren	72	72	72	70	286	1,151.67
Jamie Little	73	72	71	70	286	1,151.67
Jamie McLeary	71	70	73	72	286	1,151.67

OKI Mahou Challenge de Espana

Golf Campo de Layos, Toledo, Spain
Par 36-36–72; 7,178 yards

September 13-16
purse, €131,482

	SCORES				TOTAL	MONEY
Felipe Aguilar	71	63	70	67	271	€20,800
Tobias Dier	69	64	68	70	271	14,300
(Aguilar defeated Dier on first playoff hole.)						
Francois Calmels	67	67	72	66	272	9,100
Antti Ahokas	65	72	64	73	274	7,800
Francois Delamontagne	67	70	68	70	275	5,850
Robert Dinwiddie	67	70	67	71	275	5,850
Gareth Maybin	68	70	68	70	276	4,160
Stephen Browne	69	69	68	71	277	3,640
Hernan Rey	69	66	72	71	278	3,120
Alvaro Salto	72	71	66	70	279	2,730
Fabrizio Zanotti	70	72	70	67	279	2,730
Peter Baker	69	72	69	70	280	2,340
Carlos De Corral	71	72	72	65	280	2,340
Rodolfo Gonzalez	70	73	68	69	280	2,340
Juan Abbate	69	71	73	68	281	1,820
Robert Coles	70	70	67	74	281	1,820
Santiago Luna	71	71	72	67	281	1,820
Daniel Seron	68	70	72	71	281	1,820
Ben Willman	68	70	75	68	281	1,820
Carlos Del Moral	67	70	75	70	282	1,329.25
Michael Hoey	71	71	73	67	282	1,329.25
Daniel Wardrop	70	71	72	69	282	1,329.25
Fredrik Widmark	69	71	78	64	282	1,329.25
Raymond Russell	72	68	73	70	283	1,183
Francis Valera	72	70	72	69	283	1,183
Peter Whiteford	72	68	70	73	283	1,183
Julio Zapata	64	73	74	72	283	1,183

Kazakhstan Open

Nurtau Golf Club, Almaty, Kazakhstan
Par 36-36–72; 7,301 yards

September 20-23
purse, €330,990

	SCORES				TOTAL	MONEY
Leif Westerberg	64	71	72	72	279	€52,800
Ross McGowan	68	71	67	74	280	36,300
Jamie Donaldson	70	71	71	69	281	21,450
Eric Ramsay	70	68	70	73	281	21,450
Raphael Eyraud	69	70	71	72	282	12,375
Richie Ramsay	74	69	72	67	282	12,375

	SCORES				TOTAL	MONEY
Alvaro Salto	71	73	69	69	282	12,375
Richard Treis	68	71	71	72	282	12,375
Andrew Butterfield	70	72	70	71	283	7,260
Peter Whiteford	67	71	75	70	283	7,260
Fabrizio Zanotti	68	74	73	68	283	7,260
Tim Dykes	69	71	72	72	284	5,940
Jan-Are Larsen	73	69	73	69	284	5,940
Joost Luiten	75	70	70	69	284	5,940
Pontus Ericsson	68	69	75	73	285	4,482.50
Chris Gane	72	68	70	75	285	4,482.50
Scott Henderson	73	69	73	70	285	4,482.50
Magnus Persson	74	71	69	71	285	4,482.50
Iain Pyman	72	71	74	68	285	4,482.50
Fredrik Widmark	68	73	71	73	285	4,482.50
Magnus A. Carlsson	71	71	74	70	286	3,168
Klas Eriksson	77	68	70	71	286	3,168
Jeppe Huldahl	74	71	72	69	286	3,168
Gareth Paddison	71	73	73	69	286	3,168
Martin Wiegele	72	73	68	73	286	3,168

The Dutch Futures

Golfclub Houtrak, Netherlands
Par 36-36–72; 6,996 yards

September 27-30
purse, €141,596

	SCORES				TOTAL	MONEY
Peter Whiteford	69	70	63	73	275	€22,400
Francois Delamontagne	70	70	73	64	277	15,400
Jan-Are Larsen	70	74	70	64	278	9,100
Mikael Lundberg	70	71	73	64	278	9,100
Adam Gee	74	69	68	68	279	7,000
Alessio Bruschi	73	73	69	67	282	4,088
Matthew King	71	69	73	69	282	4,088
Stuart Manley	76	68	70	68	282	4,088
Ben Mason	69	72	72	69	282	4,088
John Wade	71	70	72	69	282	4,088
Iain Pyman	73	68	73	70	284	2,730
Richie Ramsay	76	70	71	67	284	2,730
Pablo Del Grosso	74	70	70	71	285	2,240
Pablo Larrazabal	68	70	76	71	285	2,240
Hernan Rey	73	71	73	68	285	2,240
Francis Valera	70	73	70	72	285	2,240
Bernd Wiesberger	75	69	71	70	285	2,240
Tim Dykes	71	74	72	69	286	1,506
Julien Foret	71	70	74	71	286	1,506
Mikko Korhonen	75	71	73	67	286	1,506
Benjamin Miarka	75	70	72	69	286	1,506
Raymond Russell	72	72	73	69	286	1,506
Inder Van Weerelt	71	72	71	72	286	1,506
Alvaro Velasco	74	71	73	68	286	1,506
Julien Clement	75	70	71	71	287	1,246
Matthew Cort	73	72	73	69	287	1,246
Stuart Davis	70	72	74	71	287	1,246
Martin Wiegele	76	69	73	69	287	1,246

Open AGF-Allianz Cotes d'Armor Bretagne

Golf Blue Green de Pleneuf Val Andre, France
Par 35-35–70; 6,435 yards

October 4-7
purse, €141,960

		SCORES			TOTAL	MONEY
Peter Baker	64	67	65	71	267	€22,400
Ross McGowan	71	62	65	69	267	15,400
(Baker defeated McGowan on first playoff hole.)						
Jamie Donaldson	68	66	66	68	268	9,800
Francois Delamontagne	69	68	66	66	269	8,400
Andrew Oldcorn	67	66	70	67	270	7,000
Raymond Russell	68	68	70	68	274	5,040
Inder Van Weerelt	70	67	70	67	274	5,040
Richie Ramsay	70	73	65	67	275	3,920
Steve Alker	70	68	68	70	276	3,220
Gustavo Rojas	67	71	69	69	276	3,220
Frederic Cupillard	68	73	65	71	277	2,730
Jamie Little	71	66	68	72	277	2,730
Matthew Cort	70	70	68	70	278	2,310
Nicolas Joakimides	70	70	68	70	278	2,310
Paul Nilbrink	71	70	65	72	278	2,310
Daniel Wardrop	74	70	66	68	278	2,310
Stephen Browne	69	72	67	71	279	1,767.50
Emilien Chamaulte	72	69	68	70	279	1,767.50
Richard Kilpatrick	67	71	72	69	279	1,767.50
Shaun P. Webster	72	70	67	70	279	1,767.50
Paul Dwyer	69	66	71	74	280	1,316
Chris Gane	68	71	70	71	280	1,316
Jeppe Huldahl	68	70	69	73	280	1,316
Martin Maritz	67	71	72	70	280	1,316
Ben Mason	72	70	69	69	280	1,316
Eric Moreul	71	66	67	76	280	1,316
Gareth Wright	68	68	71	73	280	1,316

doc Salbe PGA European Challenge

Golf & Vital Park Bad Waldsee, New Course,
Bad Waldsee, Germany
Par 37-35–72; 7,066 yards

October 11-14
purse, €140,000

		SCORES			TOTAL	MONEY
Peter Whiteford	66	66	68	66	266	€22,400
Richie Ramsay	70	66	67	67	270	15,400
David Horsey	69	71	65	66	271	9,800
Gary Clark	69	65	67	71	272	7,000
Raphael Eyraud	72	69	69	62	272	7,000
Branden Grace	72	69	66	65	272	7,000
Joost Luiten	71	69	68	65	273	3,528
Gareth Maybin	67	70	66	70	273	3,528
Iain Pyman	70	67	71	65	273	3,528
Gustavo Rojas	73	68	69	63	273	3,528
Leif Westerberg	67	68	68	70	273	3,528
Julien Foret	67	70	67	70	274	2,520
Jeppe Huldahl	72	68	70	64	274	2,520
Mikko Korhonen	68	71	67	68	274	2,520
Andre Bossert	69	69	72	65	275	2,030
Magnus A. Carlsson	67	69	71	68	275	2,030
Martin Wiegele	64	74	69	68	275	2,030
Niki Zitny	66	72	69	68	275	2,030

	SCORES				TOTAL	MONEY
Robert Dinwiddie	72	68	69	67	276	1,563.33
Anders Schmidt Hansen	69	70	71	66	276	1,563.33
Andrew McArthur	70	71	64	71	276	1,563.33
Matthew King	66	73	71	67	277	1,344
Jamie Little	69	67	71	70	277	1,344
Stuart Manley	70	71	70	66	277	1,344
Stephen Browne	69	67	73	69	278	1,260
David Dixon	69	67	69	73	278	1,260
Hernan Rey	71	71	69	67	278	1,260

Toscana Open Italian Federation Cup

Le Pavoniere Golf & Country Club, Prato, Italy
Par 36-35–71; 7,107 yards

October 17-20
purse, €140,420

	SCORES				TOTAL	MONEY
Mikael Lundberg	66	67	62	73	268	€22,400
Stephen Browne	68	69	68	68	273	15,400
Robert Dinwiddie	68	63	72	71	274	9,100
Toni Karjalainen	67	67	68	72	274	9,100
Roope Kakko	66	68	69	72	275	6,300
Julio Zapata	72	64	67	72	275	6,300
Peter Whiteford	68	64	73	71	276	4,480
Robert Coles	67	66	70	74	277	3,164
Peter Fowler	68	69	71	69	277	3,164
Jan-Are Larsen	69	71	68	69	277	3,164
Eric Ramsay	71	67	68	71	277	3,164
Bernd Wiesberger	72	67	73	65	277	3,164
Antti Ahokas	71	66	69	72	278	2,450
Gareth Maybin	71	67	69	71	278	2,450
Juan Abbate	68	73	67	71	279	2,170
Ross McGowan	71	67	69	72	279	2,170
Klas Eriksson	71	70	72	68	281	1,960
Andrew Butterfield	71	68	67	76	282	1,703.33
Joost Luiten	68	71	71	72	282	1,703.33
Iain Pyman	71	68	68	75	282	1,703.33
Peter Kaensche	67	67	71	78	283	1,400
Liam Bond	67	71	72	74	284	1,316
Tobias Dier	67	68	73	76	284	1,316
Mikko Korhonen	71	69	69	75	284	1,316
Ben Mason	70	67	71	76	284	1,316
Martin Wiegele	70	67	71	76	284	1,316

Apulia San Domenico Grand Final

San Domenico Golf Club, Puglia, Italy
Par 34-37–71; 6,998 yards

October 24-27
purse, €250,000

	SCORES				TOTAL	MONEY
Michael Lorenzo-Vera	62	71	70	66	269	€42,800
Jamie Donaldson	66	67	68	69	270	17,095.50
Joost Luiten	69	66	68	67	270	17,095.50
Stuart Manley	69	64	69	68	270	17,095.50
Eric Ramsay	68	68	67	67	270	17,095.50
Magnus A. Carlsson	67	69	72	64	272	9,234
Francois Delamontagne	69	67	71	65	272	9,234
Hernan Rey	69	67	69	67	272	9,234

	SCORES				TOTAL	MONEY
Peter Fowler	67	70	69	67	273	7,815
Felipe Aguilar	66	69	72	67	274	6,920.50
Carlos Del Moral	68	70	65	71	274	6,920.50
Gary Clark	68	66	71	70	275	5,535.67
Mikael Lundberg	65	68	71	71	275	5,535.67
Richie Ramsay	69	70	74	62	275	5,535.67
Andrew McArthur	68	69	72	68	277	4,242
Fabrizio Zanotti	69	67	68	73	277	4,242
Stephen Browne	69	69	69	71	278	3,483
Francois Calmels	70	70	74	64	278	3,483
Miguel Rodriguez	67	71	71	70	279	3,110
Martin Wiegele	66	74	72	67	279	3,110
Peter Baker	69	70	69	72	280	2,802
Iain Pyman	71	71	71	67	280	2,802
Julio Zapata	70	70	69	71	280	2,802
Liam Bond	73	71	69	68	281	2,480.50
George Murray	71	70	69	71	281	2,480.50
Nicolas Vanhootegem	71	68	72	70	281	2,480.50
Peter Whiteford	74	68	69	70	281	2,480.50

Abierto del Litoral

See American Tours chapter.

Abierto de la Republica

See American Tours chapter.

Asian Tour

The Royal Trophy

Amata Spring Country Club, Bangkok, Thailand
Par 36-36–72; 7,322 yards

January 12-14
purse US$1,500,000

FIRST DAY
Foursomes

Darren Clarke and Lee Westwood (Europe) defeated S.K. Ho and Toru Taniguchi, 4 and 3.
Anthony Wall and Paul McGinley (Europe) halved with Jeev Milkha Singh and Y.E. Yang.
Johan Edfors and Henrik Stenson (Europe) defeated Tetsuji Hiratsuka and Prom Meesawat, 6 and 5.
Niclas Fasth and Robert Karlsson (Europe) defeated Thongchai Jaidee and Thaworn Wiratchant, 3 and 1.

POINTS: Europe 3½, Asia ½

SECOND DAY
Fourballs

Clarke and Westwood (Europe) halved with Thongchai and Prom.
Wall and McGinley (Europe) defeated Hiratsuka and Thaworn, 1 up.
Edfors and Stenson (Europe) defeated Yang and Taniguchi, 2 and 1.
Fasth and Karlsson (Europe) halved with Singh and Ho.

POINTS: Europe 3, Asia 1

THIRD DAY
Singles

Westwood (Europe) defeated Taniguchi, 4 and 3.
Clarke (Europe) halved with Prom.
McGinley (Europe) defeated Thaworn, 2 and 1.
Edfors (Europe) defeated Ho, 3 and 2.
Stenson (Europe) halved with Yang.
Wall (Europe) defeated Hiratsuka, 4 and 2.
Karlsson (Europe) defeated Singh, 3 and 2.
Thongchai (Asia) defeated Fasth, 2 and 1.

POINTS: Europe 6, Asia 2
TOTAL POINTS: Europe 12½, Asia 3½

(Each member of the European team received $125,000; each member of the Asian team received $62,500.)

Pakistan Open

Karachi Golf Club, Karachi, Pakistan
Par 36-36–72; 6,895 yards

January 18-21
purse US$300,000

	SCORES				TOTAL	MONEY
Airil Rizman Zahari	67	68	64	70	269	US$47,550
Scott Hend	70	66	66	69	271	32,550
Simon Hurd	68	65	69	72	274	18,300
Muhammad Shabbir	66	72	67	71	276	14,790

	SCORES				TOTAL	MONEY
Chris Rodgers	69	70	68	71	278	11,235
Rahil Gangjee	71	67	69	71	278	11,235
Yeh Chang-ting	69	69	72	69	279	7,620
Olle Nordberg	72	66	70	71	279	7,620
Ashok Kumar	71	66	71	71	279	7,620
Roy Moon	71	71	71	67	280	5,124
Uttam Singh Mundy	68	68	75	69	280	5,124
Gavin Flint	71	68	72	69	280	5,124
Mark Mouland	70	69	71	70	280	5,124
Barry Hume	68	68	73	71	280	5,124
Vivek Bhandari	68	72	74	67	281	3,703
Lin Chien-bing	69	70	73	69	281	3,703
Ross Bain	71	71	70	69	281	3,703
Richard Lee	68	72	72	69	281	3,703
S.S.P. Chowrasia	72	69	70	70	281	3,703
Nam Young-woo	72	70	67	72	281	3,703
Mitchell Brown	70	71	67	73	281	3,703
Digvijay Singh	71	69	66	75	281	3,703
Tony Lascuna	70	69	67	75	281	3,703
Unho Park	71	70	73	68	282	3,105
Muhammed Munir	70	71	70	71	282	3,105

Philippine Open

Wack Wack Golf & Country Club, Manila, Philippines
Par 36-36–72; 7,053 yards

February 1-4
purse, US$300,000

	SCORES				TOTAL	MONEY
Frankie Minoza	73	67	67	71	278	US$47,550
Gerald Rosales	73	70	72	65	280	32,550
Liang Wen-chong	68	69	71	75	283	18,300
Lin Keng-chi	72	72	74	66	284	14,790
Chapchai Nirat	73	73	72	67	285	12,300
Anthony Kang	68	74	76	68	286	8,257
Richard Moir	74	72	70	70	286	8,257
Neven Basic	71	67	76	72	286	8,257
Prayad Marksaeng	69	74	69	74	286	8,257
David Bransdon	69	73	73	72	287	5,910
Artemio Murakami	71	72	75	70	288	4,695
Benjie Magada	71	68	78	71	288	4,695
Tony Carolan	74	75	69	70	288	4,695
Taichiro Kiyota	70	74	72	72	288	4,695
Digvijay Singh	69	72	75	72	288	4,695
Angelo Que	75	72	68	73	288	4,695
Lu Wei-chih	71	71	75	72	289	3,790
Bryan Saltus	71	73	73	72	289	3,790
Jason Knutzon	68	72	75	74	289	3,790
Panuwat Muenlek	72	72	77	70	291	3,420
Shigemasa Higaki	72	76	72	71	291	3,420
Tony Lascuna	78	69	72	72	291	3,420
Stephen Scahill	76	73	72	71	292	3,105
*Jay Bayron	68	74	78	72	292	
Kao Bo-song	71	74	75	72	292	3,105
Park Jun-won	69	74	76	73	292	3,105
Chawalit Plaphol	76	69	73	74	292	3,105

Maybank Malaysian Open

Saujana Golf & Country Club, Kuala Lumpur, Malaysia
Par 36-36–72; 6,971 yards

February 8-11
purse, US$1,290,000

	SCORES				TOTAL	MONEY
Peter Hedblom	73	71	68	68	280	US$215,000
Jean-Francois Lucquin	72	68	74	67	281	143,330
Ignacio Garrido	76	69	68	69	282	72,627
Simon Dyson	71	68	73	70	282	72,627
Gary Lockerbie	72	71	70	70	283	49,923
Marcus Higley	72	67	70	74	283	49,923
Chinarat Phadungsil	70	67	77	70	284	31,411
Mikko Ilonen	69	70	74	71	284	31,411
Simon Yates	73	69	70	72	284	31,411
Prom Meesawat	72	69	70	73	284	31,411
Amandeep Johl	73	71	71	70	285	21,078
Graeme Storm	72	72	69	72	285	21,078
David Bransdon	70	72	70	73	285	21,078
Ricardo Gonzalez	69	71	69	76	285	21,078
Angelo Que	70	73	68	74	285	21,078
Keith Horne	73	73	71	69	286	16,180
David Drysdale	73	73	70	70	286	16,180
Gerald Rosales	70	75	70	71	286	16,180
S.S.P. Chowrasia	67	77	71	71	286	16,180
Gavin Flint	71	71	72	72	286	16,180
Andrew Coltart	74	69	70	73	286	16,180
Damien McGrane	70	73	70	73	286	16,180
Alessandro Tadini	70	72	74	71	287	13,609
Sam Walker	72	71	72	72	287	13,609
Frankie Minoza	72	70	71	74	287	13,609
Robert-Jan Derksen	70	73	70	74	287	13,609
Simon Wakefield	71	74	75	68	288	11,481
Garry Houston	75	70	74	69	288	11,481
Christian Cevaer	75	68	76	69	288	11,481
Darren Clarke	74	72	71	71	288	11,481
Gary Simpson	71	72	73	72	288	11,481
Stephen Gallacher	71	73	72	72	288	11,481
Andrew Marshall	75	69	71	73	288	11,481
Unho Park	75	71	73	70	289	9,030
Gregory Bourdy	73	72	74	70	289	9,030
Airil Rizman Zahari	71	75	72	71	289	9,030
Matthew Millar	74	72	71	72	289	9,030
Marcus Both	71	72	73	73	289	9,030
Alastair Forsyth	69	73	73	74	289	9,030
Liang Wen-chong	73	71	72	73	289	9,030
Terry Pilkadaris	72	74	68	75	289	9,030
Soren Kjeldsen	70	70	81	69	290	7,353
Shaifubari Muda	73	73	73	71	290	7,353
Jeev Milkha Singh	71	71	76	72	290	7,353
Lee Westwood	75	70	71	74	290	7,353
Kyron Sullivan	73	70	72	75	290	7,353
Robert Rock	66	78	76	71	291	6,450
Thomas Bjorn	73	72	74	72	291	6,450
Kane Webber	68	73	77	74	292	5,676
Adam Groom	73	71	75	73	292	5,676
Suk Jong-yul	71	72	74	75	292	5,676
Anton Haig	74	69	72	77	292	5,676
Steven Jeppesen	74	72	76	71	293	4,644
Yeh Wei-tze	69	75	77	72	293	4,644
Mark Foster	69	75	75	74	293	4,644
Gaurav Ghei	72	72	74	75	293	4,644
Jose-Filipe Lima	74	70	76	74	294	3,870

	SCORES				TOTAL	MONEY
Cesar Monasterio	71	71	76	76	294	3,870
Rafael Echenique	68	71	77	78	294	3,870
Gary Rusnak	74	71	75	75	295	3,483
Prayad Marksaeng	75	70	75	75	295	3,483
Chapchai Nirat	70	75	73	77	295	3,483
Mike Cunning	74	72	77	74	297	3,096
Hendrik Buhrmann	72	72	80	73	297	3,096
Edward Loar	68	71	72	86	297	3,096
S. Sivachandran	75	71	73	79	298	2,838
Emanuele Canonica	75	69	79	79	302	2,709
Rafael Cabrera Bello	73	72	75	83	303	2,580
Michael Campbell	75	70	78		WD	

Enjoy Jakarta Astro Indonesia Open

Damai Indah Golf & Country Club, Jakarta, Indonesia
Par 35-36–71; 7,121 yards

February 15-18
purse, US$1,000,000

	SCORES				TOTAL	MONEY
Mikko Ilonen	66	68	71	70	275	US$175,000
Andrew Tampion	68	66	73	69	276	78,296
Shiv Kapur	67	73	69	67	276	78,296
Frankie Minoza	71	68	66	71	276	78,296
Thammanoon Srirot	72	67	71	69	279	40,635
Suk Jong-yul	69	68	69	73	279	40,635
Alexandre Rocha	72	68	73	67	280	31,500
Chapchai Nirat	68	69	72	72	281	23,590
James Heath	70	70	70	71	281	23,590
Tony Carolan	71	71	67	72	281	23,590
Rick Gibson	72	70	72	68	282	15,703
Simon Dyson	70	71	71	70	282	15,703
Thaworn Wiratchant	75	69	72	66	282	15,703
Christian Cevaer	68	72	71	71	282	15,703
Henrik Nystrom	70	69	72	71	282	15,703
Scott Strange	69	69	72	72	282	15,703
Gareth Davies	71	67	72	72	282	15,703
Thongchai Jaidee	72	67	71	72	282	15,703
Chawalit Plaphol	65	74	70	73	282	15,703
Sam Little	72	69	71	71	283	12,215
Mark Mouland	70	70	71	72	283	12,215
Peter Gustafsson	70	73	67	73	283	12,215
Airil Rizman Zahari	70	69	74	71	284	10,132
Mike Cunning	71	72	71	70	284	10,132
Steve Alker	70	71	72	71	284	10,132
Andrew Marshall	70	71	72	71	284	10,132
Mark Brown	75	69	68	72	284	10,132
Mardan Mamat	74	67	71	72	284	10,132
David Bransdon	69	72	74	69	284	10,132
Gaurav Ghei	68	69	79	68	284	10,132
Adam Groom	69	71	77	67	284	10,132
Iain Steel	74	70	74	66	284	10,132
Prom Meesawat	71	68	74	72	285	7,573
Oliver Fisher	74	67	72	72	285	7,573
S.S.P. Chowrasia	68	72	72	73	285	7,573
Adam Blyth	73	70	69	73	285	7,573
Lam Chih Bing	72	72	72	69	285	7,573
Bryan Saltus	68	74	74	69	285	7,573
Ignacio Garrido	71	71	74	69	285	7,573
David Carter	72	72	75	66	285	7,573
Marcus Fraser	74	70	69	73	286	6,195

	SCORES				TOTAL	MONEY
Simon Yates	74	69	71	72	286	6,195
James Hepworth	71	70	74	71	286	6,195
Anthony Kang	73	69	70	74	286	6,195
Danny Chia	71	71	75	69	286	6,195
Matthew Millar	71	73	69	74	287	4,935
Emanuele Canonica	72	72	70	73	287	4,935
Francois Delamontagne	72	71	71	73	287	4,935
Ted Oh	69	74	72	72	287	4,935
Chinarat Phadungsil	70	71	72	74	287	4,935
Chris Rodgers	72	71	75	69	287	4,935
Ross Bain	73	70	67	77	287	4,935
Mads Vibe-Hastrup	67	75	71	75	288	3,587
Jose-Filipe Lima	68	76	71	73	288	3,587
Keith Horne	73	71	71	73	288	3,587
Nam Young-woo	68	69	75	76	288	3,587
Gary Emerson	71	72	73	72	288	3,587
Patrik Sjoland	69	74	73	72	288	3,587
Park Jun-won	69	75	72	73	289	2,992
Birgir Hafthorsson	71	72	74	72	289	2,992
Mark Foster	69	74	70	78	291	2,677
Alexander Noren	69	69	76	77	291	2,677
Marcus Both	70	73	73	75	291	2,677
Daniel Vancsik	74	68	74	75	291	2,677
Richard McEvoy	72	70	72	78	292	2,362
Taichiro Kiyota	74	70	78	70	292	2,362
Scott Barr	69	71	76	77	293	2,152
Kane Webber	68	72	83	70	293	2,152

Johnnie Walker Classic

Blue Canyon Country Club, Phuket, Thailand   March 1-4
Par 36-36–72; 7,179 yards   purse, £1,250,000

	SCORES				TOTAL	MONEY
Anton Haig	71	64	70	70	275	US$404,993
Richard Sterne	75	64	64	72	275	211,050
Oliver Wilson	68	66	70	71	275	211,050
(Haig defeated Sterne and Wilson on first playoff hole.)						
Retief Goosen	68	68	72	70	278	121,500
Mike Weir	66	78	68	67	279	103,032
Ernie Els	73	70	67	70	280	68,283
David Frost	69	70	72	69	280	68,283
Gaurav Ghei	69	73	74	64	280	68,283
Colin Montgomerie	69	70	70	71	280	68,283
Richard Bland	68	70	72	71	281	43,557
Simon Hurd	73	71	66	71	281	43,557
Iain Steel	69	73	70	69	281	43,557
Jean Van de Velde	72	69	71	69	281	43,557
Richard Lee	67	70	70	75	282	36,450
Marc Warren	68	72	71	71	282	36,450
Adam Bland	71	67	75	70	283	29,564
Robert-Jan Derksen	71	71	73	68	283	29,564
Alastair Forsyth	74	70	69	70	283	29,564
Garry Houston	72	68	73	70	283	29,564
Terry Pilkadaris	70	70	73	70	283	29,564
Aron Price	74	68	67	74	283	29,564
Chris Rodgers	71	70	71	71	283	29,564
Graeme Storm	66	73	70	74	283	29,564
Wang Ter-chang	68	70	71	74	283	29,564
Mark Foster	72	70	72	70	284	23,085

	SCORES				TOTAL	MONEY
Stephen Gallacher	66	76	68	74	284	23,085
Brad Kennedy	65	77	71	71	284	23,085
Matthew Millar	71	70	71	72	284	23,085
James Nitties	69	67	74	74	284	23,085
Adam Scott	74	69	70	71	284	23,085
Jeev Milkha Singh	67	72	71	74	284	23,085
Phillip Archer	74	69	67	75	285	18,856
Simon Dyson	71	70	73	71	285	18,856
David Lynn	73	69	73	70	285	18,856
Damien McGrane	71	72	69	73	285	18,856
Suk Jong-yul	70	74	70	71	285	18,856
Rahil Gangjee	72	69	71	74	286	16,281
Peter Hanson	66	72	76	72	286	16,281
Kim Kyung-tae	71	73	72	70	286	16,281
Liang Wen-chong	72	70	67	77	286	16,281
Bryan Saltus	74	69	72	71	286	16,281
Jean-Francois Lucquin	73	69	71	74	287	12,636
Edward Michaels	70	74	74	69	287	12,636
Jarrod Moseley	70	71	72	74	287	12,636
Peter O'Malley	70	73	73	71	287	12,636
Gary Orr	73	68	74	72	287	12,636
Park Jun-won	71	73	71	72	287	12,636
Jean-Francois Remesy	75	69	74	69	287	12,636
Thammanoon Srirot	71	71	74	71	287	12,636
Scott Strange	73	69	69	76	287	12,636
Zhang Lian-wei	70	71	75	71	287	12,636
Rafael Cabrera Bello	70	72	74	72	288	8,991
Keith Horne	68	71	73	76	288	8,991
Thongchai Jaidee	71	68	75	74	288	8,991
Lu Wen-teh	69	75	75	69	288	8,991
Craig Parry	69	74	77	68	288	8,991
Marcus Both	73	70	71	75	289	7,290
Kim Felton	70	68	74	77	289	7,290
Nick Flanagan	70	69	77	73	289	7,290
Peter Fowler	68	72	77	73	290	6,561
Shiv Kapur	72	70	75	73	290	6,561
Graeme McDowell	67	76	70	77	290	6,561
Andrew Coltart	72	72	74	73	291	5,953
Thaworn Wiratchant	71	71	75	74	291	5,953
Barry Hume	68	74	79	71	292	5,224
Simon Khan	70	74	72	76	292	5,224
Lin Wen-tang	70	74	75	73	292	5,224
Andrew Marshall	73	71	77	71	292	5,224
Adam Blyth	70	72	75	76	293	4,237
David Diaz	73	71	76	73	293	4,237
Ling Ken-chi	70	71	80	72	293	4,237
Unho Park	70	74	75	75	294	3,640
Markus Brier	74	68	76	77	295	3,636
Ignacio Garrido	71	71	76	78	296	3,630
Lee Sung	71	72	78	75	296	3,630
Chris Campbell	72	72	77	76	297	3,623
Scott Gardiner	67	77	79	74	297	3,623
Hendrik Buhrmann	71	73	76	88	308	3,617

Clariden Leu Singapore Masters

Laguna National Golf & Country Club, Singapore
Par 36-36—72; 7,207 yards

March 8-11
purse, US$1,100,000

		SCORES			TOTAL	MONEY
Liang Wen-chong	64	72	68	73	277	US$183,330
Iain Steel	70	65	71	71	277	122,220
(Liang defeated Steel on first playoff hole.)						
Simon Dyson	71	69	67	71	278	68,860
Anthony Wall	68	72	72	67	279	43,285
Jean Van de Velde	68	71	71	69	279	43,285
David Lynn	72	68	70	69	279	43,285
Nick Dougherty	70	72	66	71	279	43,285
Craig Smith	72	70	71	67	280	21,835
Scott Barr	70	69	71	70	280	21,835
Lin Keng-chi	73	68	69	70	280	21,835
Terry Pilkadaris	69	72	67	72	280	21,835
Peter Lawrie	66	70	70	74	280	21,835
Jyoti Randhawa	65	68	72	75	280	21,835
Peter Senior	70	70	73	68	281	15,198
Scott Strange	69	73	70	69	281	15,198
Chinarat Phadungsil	69	71	71	70	281	15,198
Francesco Molinari	69	70	70	72	281	15,198
Peter O'Malley	71	70	69	71	281	15,198
Thongchai Jaidee	69	69	69	74	281	15,198
Oliver Wilson	69	72	70	71	282	12,622
Joakim Backstrom	73	69	69	71	282	12,622
Martin Kaymer	66	73	71	72	282	12,622
Robert Rock	71	70	68	73	282	12,622
Robert-Jan Derksen	73	69	72	69	283	10,945
Marcus Both	72	69	72	70	283	10,945
Matthew Zions	68	71	73	71	283	10,945
Hendrik Buhrmann	71	69	71	72	283	10,945
Mardan Mamat	68	73	70	72	283	10,945
Andrew Coltart	69	69	72	73	283	10,945
Chawalit Plaphol	75	67	72	70	284	8,847
Graeme Storm	66	74	72	72	284	8,847
Tony Lascuna	69	72	71	72	284	8,847
Prom Meesawat	71	71	70	72	284	8,847
Shingo Katayama	65	76	70	73	284	8,847
Gary Orr	71	71	69	73	284	8,847
Gary Lockerbie	68	67	69	80	284	8,847
Gary Simpson	69	72	72	72	285	7,700
Barry Hume	65	69	76	75	285	7,700
Rahil Gangjee	72	68	77	69	286	6,710
Ariel Canete	70	72	73	71	286	6,710
Brad Kennedy	68	74	72	72	286	6,710
Gerald Rosales	72	69	72	73	286	6,710
S.M. Lee	69	72	72	73	286	6,710
Mark Foster	76	65	71	74	286	6,710
Marcus Fraser	64	73	74	75	286	6,710
Lu Wei-chih	70	72	75	70	287	5,170
Steve Webster	71	69	73	74	287	5,170
Ross Fisher	74	66	73	74	287	5,170
Mark Pilkington	72	67	73	75	287	5,170
Jeev Milkha Singh	69	73	70	75	287	5,170
Stephen Dodd	69	73	69	76	287	5,170
Suk Jong-yul	69	73	69	76	287	5,170
Scott Hend	71	70	74	73	288	4,180
Carlos Rodiles	71	70	72	75	288	4,180
Lin Wen-tang	69	70	77	73	289	3,286
Simon Khan	69	70	77	73	289	3,286

	SCORES				TOTAL	MONEY
Mark Brown	66	73	76	74	289	3,286
Jean-Francois Lucquin	69	70	76	74	289	3,286
Gaurav Ghei	68	70	77	74	289	3,286
Ross Bain	69	70	73	77	289	3,286
Richard Bland	72	67	73	77	289	3,286
Frankie Minoza	69	71	71	78	289	3,286
Brett Rumford	68	74	77	71	290	2,640
Adam Blyth	67	73	74	76	290	2,640
Adam Groom	70	72	72	76	290	2,640
Angelo Que	66	73	80	72	291	2,420
Simon Yates	68	73	75	76	292	2,255
David Griffiths	74	68	74	76	292	2,255
David Carter	74	66	72	81	293	2,090
Shaun Webster	69	73	79	73	294	2,010
Phillip Price	69	71	70	85	295	1,650

TCL Classic

Yalong Bay Golf Club, Sanya, Hainen Island, China
Par 36-36–72; 7,173 yards

March 15-18
purse, US$1,000,000

	SCORES				TOTAL	MONEY
Chapchai Nirat	61	66	68	71	266	US$166,660
Rafael Echenique	64	69	68	68	269	111,110
Prayad Marksaeng	71	68	65	67	271	62,600
Simon Nash	67	66	71	68	272	46,200
James Heath	72	63	68	69	272	46,200
David Bransdon	67	66	74	66	273	30,000
Liang Wen-chong	69	68	66	70	273	30,000
Taichi Teshima	69	65	66	73	273	30,000
Marc Warren	70	67	70	67	274	19,500
Peter Fowler	69	68	68	69	274	19,500
Pelle Edberg	71	64	69	70	274	19,500
Lee Westwood	66	70	68	70	274	19,500
Nick Dougherty	69	66	69	71	275	15,050
Kane Webber	67	71	66	71	275	15,050
Oliver Fisher	67	69	67	72	275	15,050
Miles Tunnicliff	70	65	65	75	275	15,050
Francois Delamontagne	73	62	70	71	276	12,700
Thaworn Wiratchant	69	68	68	71	276	12,700
Ashley Hall	67	69	69	71	276	12,700
Adam Blyth	67	66	70	73	276	12,700
Scott Strange	69	69	70	69	277	11,150
Scott Barr	69	68	71	69	277	11,150
Chawalit Plaphol	68	69	70	70	277	11,150
Brad Kennedy	67	67	69	74	277	11,150
Mardan Mamat	68	70	72	68	278	9,200
Stephen Scahill	71	68	71	68	278	9,200
Birgir Hafthorsson	68	70	72	68	278	9,200
Gaurav Ghei	70	69	68	71	278	9,200
Patrik Sjoland	69	69	69	71	278	9,200
Carl Suneson	66	68	72	72	278	9,200
Richard Lee	65	70	70	73	278	9,200
Iain Steel	71	68	67	72	278	9,200
Gary Rusnak	67	70	67	74	278	9,200
Paul McGinley	72	67	72	68	279	6,900
James Kingston	66	70	74	69	279	6,900
Fredrik Andersson Hed	69	69	72	69	279	6,900
Lu Wei-chih	72	66	71	70	279	6,900
Mark Pilkington	68	70	71	70	279	6,900

	SCORES				TOTAL	MONEY
Rafael Cabrera Bello	68	70	71	70	279	6,900
Wade Ormsby	66	71	70	72	279	6,900
Jean-Baptiste Gonnet	67	66	73	73	279	6,900
Lu Wen-teh	65	69	68	77	279	6,900
Gareth Paddison	69	69	72	70	280	5,700
Steve Alker	67	71	70	72	280	5,700
Mads Vibe-Hastrup	67	70	70	73	280	5,700
Unho Park	68	71	74	68	281	4,800
Francois Calmels	69	68	74	70	281	4,800
Simon Griffiths	68	70	72	71	281	4,800
Barry Lane	68	71	70	72	281	4,800
Keith Horne	65	72	70	74	281	4,800
Juvic Pagunsan	68	68	69	76	281	4,800
Alexandre Rocha	67	70	73	72	282	3,900
Sam Little	68	67	74	73	282	3,900
Neven Basic	71	67	71	73	282	3,900
Wang Ter-chang	73	66	72	72	283	3,042
Luis Claverie	68	70	73	72	283	3,042
Julien Foret	69	70	72	72	283	3,042
Adam Groom	69	70	72	72	283	3,042
Zhang Lian-wei	73	65	72	73	283	3,042
Matthew Zions	69	68	72	74	283	3,042
Carlos Rodiles	68	66	73	76	283	3,042
Scott Hend	66	73	74	71	284	2,500
Danny Chia	68	70	74	72	284	2,500
Simon Hurd	71	67	74	72	284	2,500
S.M. Lee	71	68	70	76	285	2,300
Matthew Richardson	71	67	74	75	287	2,200

Motorola International Bintan

Ria Bintan Golf Club, Bintan, Indonesia
Par 36-36–72; 7,032 yards

March 22-25
purse, US$350,000

	SCORES				TOTAL	MONEY
Jason Knutzon	69	71	68	66	274	US$55,475
Peter Fowler	68	69	71	67	275	37,975
Unho Park	71	68	69	68	276	21,350
Lu Wen-teh	71	73	64	69	277	17,255
Scott Barr	71	69	70	68	278	13,107
Rick Gibson	68	69	69	72	278	13,107
Artemio Murakami	72	68	71	68	279	9,485
Airil Rizman Zahari	69	69	71	70	279	9,485
Gareth Paddison	70	68	73	69	280	6,704
Panuwat Muenlek	69	69	72	70	280	6,704
Mo Joong-kyung	70	71	66	73	280	6,704
Adam Blyth	70	65	72	73	280	6,704
Chapchai Nirat	69	72	71	69	281	5,160
Steven Jeffress	71	72	68	70	281	5,160
Scott Strange	69	67	73	72	281	5,160
Clay Devers	68	70	70	73	281	5,160
David Gleeson	71	68	73	70	282	4,205
Ted Oh	67	69	75	71	282	4,205
Adam Groom	70	70	71	71	282	4,205
Tatsuhiko Takahashi	70	69	72	71	282	4,205
Mike Cunning	66	69	75	72	282	4,205
Park Jun-won	68	71	69	74	282	4,205
Lee Sung	73	71	69	70	283	3,727
Cameron Percy	69	73	73	68	283	3,727
Mitsuhiro Tateyama	72	72	69	71	284	3,153

	SCORES				TOTAL	MONEY
Tony Carolan	71	73	69	71	284	3,153
Corey Harris	72	67	73	72	284	3,153
Angelo Que	69	69	73	73	284	3,153
Juvic Pagunsan	72	71	72	69	284	3,153
Young Nam	71	72	74	67	284	3,153
Masaya Tomida	70	72	69	73	284	3,153
Brad Kennedy	70	68	72	74	284	3,153
Thaworn Wiratchant	70	67	73	74	284	3,153

Volvo China Open

Shanghai Silport Golf Club, Shanghai, China
Par 35-36–71; 6,792 yards

April 12-15
purse, US$2,000,000

	SCORES				TOTAL	MONEY
Markus Brier	72	68	67	67	274	US$333,330
Graeme McDowell	70	70	70	69	279	149,140
Andrew McLardy	72	70	67	70	279	149,140
Scott Hend	71	67	70	71	279	149,140
Richard Sterne	70	71	69	70	280	84,800
Peter O'Malley	74	71	67	69	281	65,000
Raphael Jacquelin	68	67	75	71	281	65,000
Prayad Marksaeng	71	74	72	65	282	47,400
Jean-Francois Lucquin	73	68	71	70	282	47,400
David Griffiths	72	71	69	71	283	40,000
Miles Tunnicliff	73	74	71	66	284	34,466
Brett Rumford	72	72	70	70	284	34,466
James Kingston	71	72	70	71	284	34,466
Steven Jeppesen	72	74	76	63	285	28,200
Unho Park	70	74	72	69	285	28,200
Peter Hanson	72	72	70	71	285	28,200
Garry Houston	71	73	70	71	285	28,200
Robert-Jan Derksen	70	72	71	72	285	28,200
Simon Wakefield	75	69	77	65	286	24,000
Simon Yates	73	66	77	70	286	24,000
Scott Strange	74	68	73	71	286	24,000
Gregory Havret	73	71	74	69	287	22,600
Mikko Ilonen	73	73	74	68	288	19,900
Jarmo Sandelin	75	71	73	69	288	19,900
Graeme Storm	73	74	70	71	288	19,900
Terry Pilkadaris	74	70	72	72	288	19,900
Tony Carolan	75	72	69	72	288	19,900
Gonzalo Fernandez-Castano	71	72	71	74	288	19,900
Prom Meesawat	72	74	68	74	288	19,900
Andres Romero	71	67	73	77	288	19,900
Benn Barham	74	71	75	69	289	15,350
Liang Wen-chong	76	71	73	69	289	15,350
Yasin Ali	70	75	74	70	289	15,350
Wang Ter-chang	73	73	71	72	289	15,350
Chris Hanell	70	70	76	73	289	15,350
Zhang Lian-wei	76	69	70	74	289	15,350
Stephen Gallacher	73	72	70	74	289	15,350
Michael Jonzon	70	72	71	76	289	15,350
Thammanoon Srirot	73	72	76	69	290	12,600
Damien McGrane	71	69	76	74	290	12,600
Gary Murphy	74	69	73	74	290	12,600
Adam Blyth	70	67	76	77	290	12,600
Peter Lawrie	72	71	70	77	290	12,600
Marcus Fraser	75	72	77	67	291	10,200
Soren Hansen	74	72	76	69	291	10,200

	SCORES				TOTAL	MONEY
Gary Emerson	72	70	79	70	291	10,200
Bryan Saltus	74	71	72	74	291	10,200
Thongchai Jaidee	71	74	71	75	291	10,200
Thomas Bjorn	70	72	73	76	291	10,200
Stephen Dodd	74	67	74	76	291	10,200
Soren Kjeldsen	72	73	76	71	292	8,000
Chapchai Nirat	76	70	74	72	292	8,000
Marcus Both	74	73	73	72	292	8,000
Adam Groom	73	72	74	73	292	8,000
Gaurav Ghei	73	73	76	71	293	7,000
Edward Loar	71	74	77	72	294	5,933
Richard Lee	70	71	81	72	294	5,933
Maarten Lafeber	71	75	76	72	294	5,933
Andrew Butterfield	77	70	75	72	294	5,933
Joakim Backstrom	74	70	74	76	294	5,933
Mahal Pearce	73	72	71	78	294	5,933
Wu Kang-chun	75	71	79	70	295	4,700
Qiu Zhi-feng	70	75	80	70	295	4,700
Liao Gui-ming	74	71	77	73	295	4,700
Lin Wen-tang	73	74	75	73	295	4,700
Gary Rusnak	69	76	76	74	295	4,700
Huang Ming-jie	68	76	72	79	295	4,700
Gareth Davies	74	73	76	73	296	3,900
Kane Webber	72	73	74	77	296	3,900
Mark Pilkington	72	75	74	76	297	3,650
Chris Rodgers	75	71	77	75	298	2,997
Tom Whitehouse	73	72	75	78	298	2,997
*Han Ren	74	72	80	73	299	
Jose-Filipe Lima	77	69	71	82	299	2,991
Shiv Kapur	72	73			WD	

BMW Asian Open

Tomson Shanghai Pudong Golf Club, Shanghai, China
Par 36-36–72; 7,326 yards

April 19-22
purse, US$2,300,000

	SCORES				TOTAL	MONEY
Raphael Jacquelin	66	69	70	73	278	US$383,330
Soren Kjeldsen	67	72	68	73	280	255,550
Scott Hend	69	70	67	75	281	129,490
Simon Yates	74	69	64	74	281	129,490
Richard Sterne	70	74	69	69	282	76,130
Lee Sung	68	70	71	73	282	76,130
Ernie Els	71	71	68	72	282	76,130
Markus Brier	71	69	68	74	282	76,130
Graeme McDowell	73	70	69	71	283	51,520
Kane Webber	71	73	69	71	284	40,020
Miguel Angel Jimenez	70	69	72	73	284	40,020
Simon Dyson	70	70	70	74	284	40,020
Andrew McLardy	72	70	67	75	284	40,020
Joakim Backstrom	70	69	68	77	284	40,020
Scott Barr	71	70	72	72	285	31,740
Retief Goosen	71	74	69	71	285	31,740
Peter O'Malley	73	72	68	72	285	31,740
Colin Montgomerie	69	70	69	77	285	31,740
Jason Knutzon	75	70	70	71	286	26,088
James Kingston	74	71	71	70	286	26,088
Tony Carolan	69	74	69	74	286	26,088
David Bransdon	76	68	68	74	286	26,088
Prayad Marksaeng	72	69	70	75	286	26,088

	SCORES				TOTAL	MONEY
Adam Blyth	71	73	67	75	286	26,088
Soren Hansen	71	70	67	78	286	26,088
Robert-Jan Derksen	74	72	69	72	287	21,160
Garry Houston	71	72	72	72	287	21,160
David Griffiths	73	69	73	72	287	21,160
Matthew Millar	73	70	71	73	287	21,160
Peter Hanson	69	71	74	73	287	21,160
Damien McGrane	70	73	69	75	287	21,160
Christian Cevaer	71	70	69	77	287	21,160
Gregory Havret	68	75	72	73	288	17,537
Shaun Webster	72	74	70	72	288	17,537
Christian L. Nilsson	71	73	73	71	288	17,537
Andres Romero	75	70	66	77	288	17,537
Liang Wen-chong	72	74	69	74	289	15,180
Mark Pilkington	71	72	70	76	289	15,180
Frankie Minoza	75	71	70	73	289	15,180
Keith Horne	73	69	70	77	289	15,180
Jarmo Sandelin	73	70	75	71	289	15,180
Brett Rumford	75	69	75	70	289	15,180
Simon Wakefield	72	70	72	76	290	13,340
Kyron Sullivan	75	66	72	77	290	13,340
Adam Le Vesconte	72	71	72	76	291	11,960
Jean-Francois Lucquin	71	74	71	75	291	11,960
Ricardo Gonzalez	72	73	72	74	291	11,960
Mardan Mamat	72	73	73	73	291	11,960
Marcel Siem	72	69	75	76	292	10,580
Juvic Pagunsan	73	71	75	73	292	10,580
Lin Keng-chi	73	71	72	77	293	9,200
Yasin Ali	74	72	71	76	293	9,200
Gary Murphy	74	72	66	81	293	9,200
Gonzalo Fernandez-Castano	73	72	77	71	293	9,200
Edward Michaels	74	72	71	77	294	7,590
Stephen Gallacher	72	73	74	75	294	7,590
Edward Loar	70	75	74	75	294	7,590
Peter Lawrie	75	71	72	77	295	6,670
Gaurav Ghei	75	70	73	77	295	6,670
Marcus Both	71	74	74	76	295	6,670
Thaworn Wiratchant	72	73	74	77	296	5,980
Chris Rodgers	73	71	75	77	296	5,980
Lin Wen-tang	73	73	73	77	296	5,980
Gavin Flint	68	73	76	80	297	5,520
Park Jun-won	69	77	72	80	298	5,060
Sven Struver	72	72	75	79	298	5,060
Simon Hurd	74	72	74	78	298	5,060
Lin Wen-hong	69	76	72	83	300	4,600
Zhang Lian-wei	73	73	78	77	301	4,370
Paul Casey	72	71	77		WD	

Pine Valley Beijing Open

Pine Valley Golf Club, Beijing, China
Par 36-36–72; 7,259 yards

April 26-29
purse, US$500,000

	SCORES				TOTAL	MONEY
Gaurav Ghei	65	72	68	69	274	US$79,250
Adam Blyth	70	68	67	71	276	54,250
Chapchai Nirat	69	67	73	68	277	27,575
Thaworn Wiratchant	72	68	67	70	277	27,575
Angelo Que	70	72	67	69	278	18,725
Scott Strange	69	68	68	73	278	18,725

	SCORES				TOTAL	MONEY
Brad Iles	69	69	72	69	279	14,550
Tony Carolan	70	72	70	68	280	11,775
David Gleeson	71	70	70	69	280	11,775
Gerald Rosales	71	67	75	68	281	8,540
Zhang Lian-wei	74	69	69	69	281	8,540
Scott Hend	72	71	68	70	281	8,540
Liang Wen-chong	70	69	69	73	281	8,540
Panuwat Muenlek	66	70	69	76	281	8,540
Ben Leong	70	72	72	68	282	6,268
Leigh McKechnie	73	69	72	68	282	6,268
Lee Won-joon	75	69	69	69	282	6,268
Craig Smith	69	72	70	71	282	6,268
Scott Barr	74	70	68	70	282	6,268
Taichiro Kiyota	70	69	71	72	282	6,268
Brad Kennedy	69	71	70	72	282	6,268
Kane Webber	71	69	70	72	282	6,268
Prom Meesawat	71	70	73	69	283	5,250
Mark Brown	71	70	71	71	283	5,250
Gavin Flint	74	69	68	72	283	5,250

GS Caltex Maekyung Open

Nam Seoul Country Club, Seoul, Korea
Par 36-36–72; 5,036 yards

May 3-6
purse, US$600,000

	SCORES				TOTAL	MONEY
Kim Kyung-tae	70	66	67	67	270	US$129,032
Liang Wen-chong	64	71	67	73	275	80,645
*Lee Jin-myung	70	73	71	65	279	
*Kim Bi-o	72	69	75	66	282	
Lee Seong-ho	72	71	71	68	282	35,483
Choi Gwang-soo	70	76	67	69	282	35,483
Yoo Jong-gu	68	73	74	69	284	17,849
Mitchell Brown	66	73	74	71	284	17,849
Kang Kyung-nam	73	67	73	71	284	17,849
Richard Lee	68	75	71	70	284	17,849
Anthony Kang	75	69	68	72	284	17,849
Kim Chang-yoon	76	70	71	68	285	10,241
Unho Park	74	69	73	69	285	10,241
Choi Sang-ho	71	73	72	69	285	10,241
Hong Soon-sang	76	72	66	71	285	10,241
Craig Smith	73	69	76	68	286	8,261
David Oh	72	71	74	69	286	8,261
Jin Park	76	71	70	69	286	8,261
Bae Sang-moon	71	72	71	72	286	8,261
Choi Joon-woo	71	73	70	72	286	8,261
Lee Won-joon	76	67	66	77	286	8,261
Mardan Mamat	70	73	75	69	287	7,204
Shin Yong-jin	70	69	74	74	287	7,204
Kim Jong-duk	75	70	68	74	287	7,204
Jang Ik-jae	76	71	71	70	288	6,586
Eddie Lee	70	73	74	71	288	6,586
Taichiro Kiyota	72	74	71	71	288	6,586
Lee Gun-hee	69	70	76	73	288	6,586

Macau Open

Macau Golf & Country Club, Macau
Par 35-36–71; 6,624 yards
(Event shortened to 54 holes—rain.)

May 17-20
purse, US$300,000

	SCORES			TOTAL	MONEY
Lu Wen-teh	65	71	65	201	US$47,550
Richard Moir	66	66	69	201	32,550
(Lu defeated Moir on third playoff hole.)					
Gaurav Ghei	65	70	67	202	18,300
Liang Wen-chong	69	68	66	203	14,790
Zhang Lian-wei	66	68	70	204	12,300
Kane Webber	68	72	65	205	8,810
Thaworn Wiratchant	69	68	68	205	8,810
Lu Wei-chih	71	70	64	205	8,810
Simon Yates	66	72	68	206	5,544
Mitchell Brown	68	72	66	206	5,544
Hur In-hoi	70	68	68	206	5,544
Gurbaaz Mann	73	63	70	206	5,544
Stephen Scahill	70	66	70	206	5,544
Brad Kennedy	70	69	68	207	3,907
Leigh McKechnie	64	74	69	207	3,907
Danny Chia	68	70	69	207	3,907
Panuwat Muenlek	69	71	67	207	3,907
Unho Park	68	69	70	207	3,907
Digvijay Singh	67	74	66	207	3,907
Scott Strange	67	69	71	207	3,907
Anthony Kang	65	69	73	207	3,907
Brad Iles	71	68	69	208	3,105
Peter Karmis	68	72	68	208	3,105
Jason Knutzon	65	72	71	208	3,105
Guido van der Valk	71	71	66	208	3,105
Chris Rodgers	68	68	72	208	3,105
Chinarat Phadungsil	70	66	72	208	3,105

SK Telecom Open

BA Vista Country Club, Seoul, Korea
Par 36-36–72; 7,147 yards

May 24-27
purse, US$600,000

	SCORES				TOTAL	MONEY
Bae Sang-moon	64	69	71	67	271	US$129,171
Aaron Baddeley	71	67	71	68	277	53,821
Kim Hyung-tae	65	71	72	69	277	53,821
Choi Hyuk-jae	71	65	73	70	279	25,026
Unho Park	67	70	73	69	279	25,026
Kang Kyung-nam	69	69	71	70	279	25,026
David Oh	70	68	70	71	279	25,026
Jun Tae-hyun	65	76	73	67	281	14,424
Young Nam	69	69	73	70	281	14,424
Simon Yates	68	72	69	72	281	14,424
Park No-seok	70	70	74	68	282	10,800
Mark Brown	72	70	71	69	282	10,800
Park Boo-won	73	67	71	71	282	10,800
S.K. Ho	71	68	74	70	283	8,546
Kang Wook-soon	74	68	71	70	283	8,546
Kane Webber	68	74	71	70	283	8,546
Bryan Saltus	70	69	73	71	283	8,546
Kim Kyung-tae	69	72	70	72	283	8,546

	SCORES				TOTAL	MONEY
Woo Chang-wan	73	70	73	68	284	7,373
Jung Ji-ho	67	71	74	72	284	7,373
Corey Harris	73	71	71	70	285	6,027
Choi Sang-ho	67	73	75	70	285	6,027
Kwanchai Tannin	72	71	72	70	285	6,027
Mo Joong-kyung	73	70	71	71	285	6,027
Kim Hye-dong	73	70	71	71	285	6,027
Kong Yong-joon	70	69	74	72	285	6,027
Han Min-kyu	72	68	72	73	285	6,027
Kang Sung-hoon	66	68	77	74	285	6,027
Park Jun-won	70	70	72	73	285	6,027

Bangkok Airways Open

Santiburi Samui Country Club, Koh Samui, Thailand
Par 35-36–71; 6,316 yards

June 7-10
purse, US$300,000

	SCORES				TOTAL	MONEY
Lee Sung	66	69	62	71	268	US$47,550
Prayad Marksaeng	69	72	64	66	271	32,550
Taichiro Kiyota	70	69	68	66	273	16,545
Prom Meesawat	72	67	66	68	273	16,545
Mardan Mamat	72	65	67	71	275	12,300
Adam Blyth	69	68	69	70	276	10,170
Lin Wen-tang	69	67	72	69	277	8,730
Lu Wen-teh	71	69	71	67	278	7,530
Rashid Ismail	72	72	69	66	279	5,370
Han Lee	71	73	67	68	279	5,370
Thaworn Wiratchant	69	69	69	72	279	5,370
Chapchai Nirat	72	64	72	71	279	5,370
Chris Rodgers	70	71	68	70	279	5,370
Chawalit Plaphol	73	67	66	73	279	5,370
Mitchell Brown	74	71	73	62	280	4,230
Thongchai Jaidee	71	70	68	71	280	4,230
Kwanchai Tannin	75	69	67	70	281	3,960
Neven Basic	71	67	75	69	282	3,705
Brad Iles	74	69	72	67	282	3,705
Olle Nordberg	72	70	71	70	283	3,465
Tony Lascuna	70	70	69	74	283	3,465
Gaurav Ghei	72	70	71	71	284	3,240
Gurbaaz Mann	73	66	72	73	284	3,240
Chen Yuan-chi	70	72	68	74	284	3,240
Gavin Flint	71	72	71	71	285	2,970
Yeh Chang-ting	69	72	74	70	285	2,970
Lu Wei-chih	75	71	69	70	285	2,970

Iskandar Johor Open

Royal Johor Country Club, Johor, Malaysia
Par 36-35–71; 6,984 yards

August 23-26
purse, US$300,000

	SCORES				TOTAL	MONEY
Artemio Murakami	70	72	69	68	279	US$47,550
Simon Yates	71	70	72	67	280	25,425
Tony Lascuna	72	71	67	70	280	25,425
Sung Mao-chang	69	75	68	69	281	13,545
Gaurav Ghei	70	69	70	72	281	13,545

	SCORES				TOTAL	MONEY
Liang Wen-chong	68	74	74	66	282	10,170
Lu Wen-teh	70	72	71	70	283	8,730
Jason Knutzon	71	67	72	74	284	7,530
Lin Wen-tang	71	71	75	68	285	6,600
Scott Barr	72	70	74	70	286	4,990
Stephen Scahill	70	72	73	71	286	4,990
Kao Bo-song	75	70	70	71	286	4,990
Gavin Flint	73	73	67	73	286	4,990
Gary Simpson	74	70	69	73	286	4,990
Adam Le Vesconte	72	69	69	76	286	4,990
Gerald Rosales	70	70	76	71	287	3,740
S. Sivachandran	74	70	72	71	287	3,740
Brad Kennedy	73	69	73	72	287	3,740
Chinarat Phadungsil	75	70	70	72	287	3,740
Atthaphon Prathummanee	72	72	70	73	287	3,740
Airil Rizman Zahari	71	69	72	75	287	3,740
Clay Devers	72	69	76	71	288	3,195
Peter Fowler	72	73	74	69	288	3,195
Lee Sung	69	69	78	72	288	3,195
Edward Michaels	72	73	70	73	288	3,195

Brunei Open

Empire Hotel & Country Club, Bandar Seri Begawan, Brunei
Par 35-36–71; 7,013 yards

August 30-September 2
purse, US$300,000

	SCORES				TOTAL	MONEY
Lin Wen-tang	65	68	71	65	269	US$47,550
Adam Le Vesconte	65	65	68	73	271	32,550
Scott Barr	71	68	67	66	272	15,130
Tony Lascuna	70	66	66	70	272	15,130
Lu Wen-teh	66	70	66	70	272	15,130
Panuwat Muenlek	67	70	70	67	274	10,170
Wang Ter-chang	70	66	71	68	275	8,130
Neven Basic	66	68	73	68	275	8,130
Scott Hend	65	74	68	69	276	6,255
Michael Wright	68	67	70	71	276	6,255
Yeh Chang-ting	69	70	70	68	277	5,070
Mark Brown	65	73	70	69	277	5,070
Gavin Flint	72	68	66	71	277	5,070
David Gleeson	72	64	72	70	278	4,410
Ashley Hall	69	71	68	70	278	4,410
Thaworn Wiratchant	70	72	70	67	279	3,877
Sung Mao-chang	67	72	71	69	279	3,877
S.S.P. Chowrasia	70	68	72	69	279	3,877
Han Lee	69	72	68	70	279	3,877
Corey Harris	68	69	75	68	280	3,330
Juvic Pagunsan	69	69	74	68	280	3,330
Jason Knutzon	72	68	69	71	280	3,330
Martin Rominger	68	70	70	72	280	3,330
Taichiro Kiyota	68	71	69	72	280	3,330
Soe Kyaw Naing	73	68	73	67	281	2,626
Brad Kennedy	70	71	71	69	281	2,626
Lin Wen-hong	72	68	72	69	281	2,626
Richard Lee	68	70	73	70	281	2,626
Mark Mouland	69	73	70	69	281	2,626
Artemio Murakami	69	70	72	70	281	2,626
Eddie Heinen	71	70	70	70	281	2,626
Anthony Kang	73	68	69	71	281	2,626

	SCORES				TOTAL	MONEY
Edward Michaels	68	74	67	72	281	2,626
Jochen Lupprian	71	69	68	73	281	2,626
Gary Rusnak	67	68	72	74	281	2,626

Midea China Classic

Royal Orchid International Golf Club, Guangzhou, China
Par 36-35–71; 6,889 yards

September 13-16
purse, US$400,000

	SCORES				TOTAL	MONEY
Thaworn Wiratchant	65	63	68	67	263	US$63,400
Simon Yates	68	64	62	69	263	33,900
Chinarat Phadungsil	68	62	64	69	263	33,900
(Thaworn defeated Yates on first and Chinarat on fourth playoff hole.)						
Scott Barr	68	66	66	66	266	19,720
Hur In-hoi	68	64	69	67	268	14,980
Mars Pucay	66	67	66	69	268	14,980
Michael Wright	67	66	69	67	269	10,840
Edward Michaels	65	64	71	69	269	10,840
Lin Wen-tang	68	67	66	69	270	8,340
Brad Iles	66	71	63	70	270	8,340
Lu Wen-teh	71	67	67	66	271	6,984
Jin Park	66	67	69	69	271	6,984
Liang Wen-chong	67	70	65	70	272	6,312
Atthaphon Prathummanee	67	69	68	69	273	5,760
Jerome Delariarte	69	69	64	71	273	5,760
S.S.P. Chowrasia	65	67	68	73	273	5,760
Stephen Scahill	68	70	68	68	274	4,960
Zhang Lian-wei	70	67	69	68	274	4,960
Chapchai Nirat	72	68	65	69	274	4,960
Choengchai Panpumpo	66	66	70	72	274	4,960
Richard Moir	72	69	68	66	275	4,440
Taichiro Kiyota	69	70	68	68	275	4,440
Rahil Gangjee	66	68	71	70	275	4,440
Lee Sung	64	72	72	68	276	3,960
Lin Keng-chi	66	68	72	70	276	3,960
S. Sivachandran	69	66	70	71	276	3,960
David Freeman	68	64	70	74	276	3,960
Troy Kennedy	69	67	66	74	276	3,960

Mercuries Taiwan Masters

Taiwan Golf & Country Club, Tamsui, Chinese Taipei
Par 36-36–72; 6,915 yards

September 20-23
purse, US$500,000

	SCORES				TOTAL	MONEY
Lu Wen-teh	72	71	69	72	284	US$100,000
Ted Oh	71	68	72	76	287	60,000
Hsu Mong-nan	70	76	69	75	290	35,000
Chen Yuan-chi	76	69	71	75	291	25,000
Jason Knutzon	75	72	76	69	292	15,000
Ashley Hall	76	71	71	74	292	15,000
Gary Simpson	72	71	75	74	292	15,000
Prayad Marksaeng	72	74	71	75	292	15,000
Wang Ter-chang	74	74	70	74	292	15,000
Terry Pilkadaris	73	73	71	76	293	8,750
Lin Wen-tang	73	75	70	75	293	8,750

	SCORES				TOTAL	MONEY
*Chiang Chen-chi	72	73	78	71	294	
Lin Wen-hong	73	75	72	74	294	7,750
Prom Meesawat	72	76	72	74	294	7,750
Gary Rusnak	73	73	76	73	295	6,583
Lin Keng-chi	72	74	74	75	295	6,583
Chapchai Nirat	72	75	73	75	295	6,583
Thaworn Wiratchant	76	73	72	75	296	5,875
Lu Wei-chih	70	76	72	78	296	5,875
Artemio Murakami	71	75	73	78	297	5,500
Scott Barr	75	76	74	73	298	4,975
Lien Lu-san	75	72	77	74	298	4,975
Panuwat Muenlek	73	74	75	76	298	4,975
Chris Rodgers	71	78	73	76	298	4,975
Brad Iles	73	73	73	79	298	4,975
Chen Tsang-te	74	73	72	79	298	4,975

Kolon-Hana Bank Korea Open

Woo Jeong Hills Country Club, Cheonan, Korea
Par 36-35–71; 7,185 yards

October 4-7
purse, US$1,000,000

	SCORES				TOTAL	MONEY
Vijay Singh	66	69	70	73	278	US$320,855
Kim Kyung-tae	67	71	75	67	280	84,491
Y.E. Yang	65	75	72	68	280	84,491
Kim Hyung-sung	67	72	73	69	281	39,572
Kang Kyung-nam	67	73	69	72	281	39,572
Bae Sang-moon	72	71	69	70	282	32,085
Anthony Kang	71	68	71	73	283	29,946
Paul Sheehan	72	76	69	68	285	23,074
Prayad Marksaeng	73	72	71	69	285	23,074
Kim Chang-yoon	71	72	72	70	285	23,074
Adam Groom	70	75	65	75	285	23,074
Scott Barr	72	75	73	66	286	14,973
Kim Sung-yoon	73	72	72	69	286	14,973
Liang Wen-chong	70	70	71	75	286	14,973
Marcus Both	70	74	72	71	287	10,962
Kim Hyung-tae	73	72	71	71	287	10,962
Kim Dae-sub	71	73	70	73	287	10,962
Lee In-woo	72	68	69	78	287	10,962
Lee Sung	69	75	71	73	288	9,732
Kim Sang-ki	69	69	76	74	288	9,732
Toshinori Muto	76	72	67	73	288	9,732
Kang Wook-soon	72	70	76	71	289	8,791
Kim Jong-duk	75	72	73	69	289	8,791
Thaworn Wiratchant	74	71	71	73	289	8,791
Suk Jong-yul	72	74	70	73	289	8,791
Simon Yates	71	71	72	75	289	8,791

Hero Honda Indian Open

Delhi Golf Club, New Delhi, India
Par 36-36–72; 7,014 yards

October 11-14
purse, US$500,000

	SCORES				TOTAL	MONEY
Jyoti Randhawa	70	69	67	69	275	US$79,250
Chang Tse-peng	68	65	77	68	278	54,250

	SCORES			TOTAL	MONEY
Rahil Gangjee	71	67	76	66	280	30,500
Mitchell Brown	74	71	69	67	281	24,650
Lu Wen-teh	68	75	67	72	282	16,137
David Gleeson	66	68	76	72	282	16,137
Chapchai Nirat	66	67	73	76	282	16,137
Mark Brown	71	72	64	75	282	16,137
Arjun Singh	73	70	71	69	283	9,958
Ashok Kumar	68	73	73	69	283	9,958
S.S.P. Chowrasia	68	71	74	70	283	9,958
Peter Senior	70	70	76	68	284	8,435
Jeev Milkha Singh	72	74	71	68	285	7,372
Ross Bain	69	72	73	71	285	7,372
Keith Horne	71	70	73	71	285	7,372
Uttam Singh Mundy	70	76	68	71	285	7,372
Chinarat Phadungsil	70	70	75	71	286	6,450
Mars Pucay	70	70	74	72	286	6,450
Bryan Saltus	69	72	75	71	287	5,866
Atthaphon Prathummanee	70	72	73	72	287	5,866
Vijay Kumar	72	71	71	73	287	5,866
Harinder Gupta	71	74	73	70	288	5,100
Hur In-hoi	66	71	79	72	288	5,100
Unho Park	70	69	77	72	288	5,100
Adam Groom	72	68	75	73	288	5,100
Gavin Flint	72	71	72	73	288	5,100
Jaiveer Virk	73	69	73	73	288	5,100
Gaurav Ghei	66	73	70	79	288	5,100

Pertamina Indonesia President Invitational

Damai Indah Golf, BSD Course, Jakarta, Indonesia
Par 36-36–72; 7,158 yards

October 25-28
purse, US$350,000

	SCORES			TOTAL	MONEY
Juvic Pagunsan	66	67	71	65	269	US$55,475
Gaganjeet Bhullar	70	64	67	69	270	37,975
Lee Westwood	67	65	70	70	272	19,302
Anthony Kang	67	65	69	71	272	19,302
Scott Barr	70	71	66	66	273	12,133
Prom Meesawat	65	70	68	70	273	12,133
Harmeet Kahlon	66	68	70	69	273	12,133
Liang Wen-chong	70	67	71	66	274	8,242
Mark Brown	70	66	71	67	274	8,242
Chapchai Nirat	72	68	71	64	275	6,372
Mo Joong-kyung	67	69	69	70	275	6,372
Neven Basic	65	67	72	71	275	6,372
Hur In-hoi	65	69	69	73	276	5,523
Adam Blyth	70	69	69	69	277	4,935
Hsu Mong-nan	68	69	70	70	277	4,935
Digvijay Singh	67	66	74	70	277	4,935
Lu Wei-chih	70	62	72	73	277	4,935
Simon Yates	69	71	69	69	278	4,246
Marcus Both	69	70	72	67	278	4,246
Olle Nordberg	69	71	68	70	278	4,246
Ashley Hall	71	68	68	72	279	3,727
Young Nam	68	72	69	70	279	3,727
Brad Kennedy	70	69	70	70	279	3,727
David Freeman	73	68	67	71	279	3,727
Atthaphon Prathummanee	69	68	73	69	279	3,727
Ben St. John	70	72	69	68	279	3,727

Barclays Singapore Open

Sentosa Golf Club, Singapore
Par 36-35–71; 7,319 yards

November 1-4
purse, US$4,000,000

	SCORES			TOTAL	MONEY
Angel Cabrera	71	63	70	72	276	US$634,000
Vijay Singh	70	70	70	67	277	434,000
Adam Scott	70	67	73	71	281	244,000
Jin Park	66	70	72	74	282	197,200
Lee Westwood	71	67	71	74	283	164,000
Prom Meesawat	72	69	72	71	284	135,600
Tetsuji Hiratsuka	68	71	73	73	285	116,400
Mark Brown	71	69	74	72	286	89,066
Kane Webber	66	76	72	72	286	89,066
Shiv Kapur	73	70	69	74	286	89,066
Azuma Yano	71	72	72	72	287	72,000
Chinarat Phadungsil	73	71	71	73	288	65,000
Gavin Flint	66	72	74	76	288	65,000
Zaw Moe	70	76	70	73	289	56,400
K.J. Choi	68	72	75	74	289	56,400
Keith Horne	70	68	74	77	289	56,400
Anthony Kang	69	70	72	78	289	56,400
Charles Howell	76	66	75	73	290	50,400
Gary Simpson	69	71	77	74	291	46,300
Guido van der Valk	71	71	74	75	291	46,300
Chapchai Nirat	70	74	71	76	291	46,300
Boonchu Ruangkit	72	71	70	78	291	46,300
S.S.P. Chowrasia	70	71	77	74	292	40,800
Bae Sang-moon	72	74	72	74	292	40,800
Darren Clarke	71	71	76	74	292	40,800
Nick O'Hern	74	70	73	75	292	40,800
Phil Mickelson	68	72	73	79	292	40,800

HSBC Champions

Sheshan International Golf Club, Shanghai, China
Par 36-36–72; 7,199 yards

November 8-11
purse, US$5,000,000

	SCORES			TOTAL	MONEY
Phil Mickelson	68	66	68	76	278	€575,445.27
Ross Fisher	68	68	68	74	278	299,893.79
Lee Westwood	70	74	67	67	278	299,893.79
(Mickelson defeated Fisher and Westwood on second playoff hole.)						
Kevin Stadler	64	69	73	73	279	172,640.49
Padraig Harrington	68	72	69	71	280	133,969.02
Vijay Singh	67	70	72	71	280	133,969.02
Steve Webster	69	70	72	70	281	103,584.29
Andrew McLardy	68	69	72	73	282	86,320.24
Paul Casey	68	71	66	78	283	73,199.57
Henrik Stenson	70	70	71	72	283	73,199.57
Louis Oosthuizen	71	68	72	73	284	63,531.70
Angel Cabrera	68	72	72	73	285	59,388.33
Nick Dougherty	71	70	74	71	286	54,209.11
Simon Yates	70	66	75	75	286	54,209.11
Mikko Ilonen	74	69	72	72	287	48,477.45
Soren Kjeldsen	71	72	73	71	287	48,477.45
Chapchai Nirat	69	73	73	72	287	48,477.45
Retief Goosen	69	74	71	74	288	42,584.65
Nathan Green	73	68	69	78	288	42,584.65

	SCORES			TOTAL	MONEY
Gregory Havret	72	75	72	69	288	42,584.65
Markus Brier	69	73	73	74	289	38,671.47
Bradley Dredge	73	73	72	71	289	38,671.47
Ernie Els	75	69	70	75	289	38,671.47
Kim Kyung-tae	71	73	74	72	290	35,563.94
Lin Wen-tang	71	72	74	73	290	35,563.94
Richard Sterne	68	72	69	81	290	35,563.94
Niclas Fasth	64	75	74	78	291	30,902.65
Scott Hend	69	74	75	73	291	30,902.65
Jose Manuel Lara	70	72	70	79	291	30,902.65
John Senden	73	72	75	71	291	30,902.65
Scott Sterling	69	73	74	75	291	30,902.65
Daniel Vancsik	70	75	74	72	291	30,902.65
Peter Hanson	72	75	71	74	292	25,723.43
Jason Knutzon	71	73	71	77	292	25,723.43
Frankie Minoza	69	70	75	78	292	25,723.43
Brett Rumford	69	71	75	77	292	25,723.43
Anders Hansen	70	72	77	74	293	23,479.11
Gonzalo Fernandez-Castano	71	75	73	75	294	20,371.58
Lee Sung	73	76	71	74	294	20,371.58
Marc Leishman	74	72	75	73	294	20,371.58
Liang Wen-chong	69	72	74	79	294	20,371.58
Michael Lorenzo-Vera	73	72	73	76	294	20,371.58
Ian Poulter	70	78	74	72	294	20,371.58
Mads Vibe-Hastrup	75	73	73	73	294	20,371.58
Zhang Lian-wei	70	74	82	68	294	20,371.58
Darren Fichardt	70	78	73	74	295	16,918.77
Sergio Garcia	73	72	76	74	295	16,918.77
Raphael Jacquelin	71	75	79	71	296	15,537.64
Charl Schwartzel	73	72	78	73	296	15,537.64
K.J. Choi	68	77	76	76	297	13,811.24
Nick O'Hern	74	74	73	76	297	13,811.24
Rodney Pampling	73	73	72	79	297	13,811.24
Thongchai Jaidee	74	74	77	73	298	12,084.83
Hennie Otto	74	71	70	83	298	12,084.83
Gregory Bourdy	77	71	77	74	299	10,703.71
Gaurav Ghei	70	75	81	73	299	10,703.71
Andres Romero	69	77	76	78	300	9,667.87
Soren Hansen	73	75	77	76	301	8,286.74
Jyoti Randhawa	70	74	78	79	301	8,286.74
Bradford Vaughan	74	72	74	81	301	8,286.74
Anton Haig	77	69	74	82	302	6,732.98
Thaworn Wiratchant	75	72	80	75	302	6,732.98
Peter Hedblom	73	75	72	85	305	5,869.78
Juvic Pagunsan	71	78	82	74	305	5,869.78
Paul Sheehan	74	75	78	78	305	5,869.78
Pablo Martin	73	76	78	83	310	5,179.21
Y.E. Yang	71	68			DQ	

UBS Hong Kong Open

Hong Kong Golf Club, Fanling, Hong Kong
Par 34-36–70; 6,703 yards

November 15-18
purse, US$2,250,000

	SCORES				TOTAL	MONEY
Miguel Angel Jimenez	65	67	66	67	265	US$375,000
Thongchai Jaidee	66	67	68	65	266	167,783
K.J. Choi	62	72	65	67	266	167,783
Robert Karlsson	64	64	66	72	266	167,783
Peter Hanson	68	66	65	68	267	95,400

	SCORES				TOTAL	MONEY
Graeme McDowell	67	66	68	68	269	78,750
Trevor Immelman	71	62	70	67	270	52,110
Jarmo Sandelin	69	64	68	69	270	52,110
Gary Simpson	69	67	65	69	270	52,110
Daniel Chopra	66	68	66	70	270	52,110
Marcus Fraser	67	68	64	71	270	52,110
Mike Weir	69	64	67	71	271	36,450
Scott Strange	66	68	66	71	271	36,450
Shiv Kapur	67	67	65	72	271	36,450
Robert-Jan Derksen	72	67	68	65	272	30,420
Garry Houston	63	71	71	67	272	30,420
Simon Dyson	68	65	70	69	272	30,420
Thaworn Wiratchant	69	68	66	69	272	30,420
Liang Wen-chong	68	66	68	70	272	30,420
Anders Hansen	67	70	68	68	273	25,125
Prom Meesawat	68	70	67	68	273	25,125
Christian Cevaer	70	65	68	70	273	25,125
Retief Goosen	69	66	68	70	273	25,125
Damien McGrane	69	66	67	71	273	25,125
Charlie Wi	67	68	67	71	273	25,125
Kang Wook-soon	65	70	71	68	274	22,050
Maarten Lafeber	68	67	68	71	274	22,050
Gary Murphy	66	70	66	72	274	22,050
Francesco Molinari	68	69	69	69	275	20,025
Markus Brier	68	68	69	70	275	20,025
Soren Kjeldsen	70	65	68	72	275	20,025
Chawalit Plaphol	67	68	71	70	276	17,718
S.S.P. Chowrasia	69	67	70	70	276	17,718
Mathias Gronberg	66	71	68	71	276	17,718
Peter Hedblom	71	67	64	74	276	17,718
Wang Ter-chang	70	68	71	68	277	15,750
Carlos Rodiles	72	67	70	68	277	15,750
Jamie Donaldson	69	68	68	72	277	15,750
Keith Horne	67	68	68	74	277	15,750
Frankie Minoza	69	69	70	70	278	13,725
Fredrik Andersson Hed	64	71	71	72	278	13,725
Gary Orr	67	68	70	73	278	13,725
Mahal Pearce	68	70	66	74	278	13,725
Michael Jonzon	70	68	67	73	278	13,725
Mardan Mamat	69	68	71	71	279	12,150
Bryan Saltus	68	65	72	74	279	12,150
Daniel Vancsik	66	71	73	70	280	11,025
Lee Sung	66	71	73	70	280	11,025
Tony Lascuna	68	69	68	75	280	11,025
Paul McGinley	68	70	72	71	281	9,225
Zhang Lian-wei	70	68	71	72	281	9,225
Juvic Pagunsan	70	67	71	73	281	9,225
Lu Wei-chih	68	71	67	75	281	9,225
Martin Erlandsson	68	65	70	78	281	9,225
Clay Devers	70	68	73	71	282	7,110
Jason Knutzon	67	69	74	72	282	7,110
Anthony Kang	66	70	74	72	282	7,110
Thomas Bjorn	68	71	71	72	282	7,110
Jean-Francois Lucquin	68	66	73	75	282	7,110
Nick Faldo	68	71	72	72	283	5,962
Rahil Gangjee	71	68	69	75	283	5,962
Ricardo Gonzalez	67	70	70	76	283	5,962
Adam Groom	70	69	67	77	283	5,962
Gregory Havret	66	73	72	73	284	5,400
Barry Hume	65	68	74	78	285	5,175
David Howell	72	66	74	74	286	4,950
Gerald Rosales	73	66	71	77	287	4,612
Bae Sang-moon	71	68	70	78	287	4,612

	SCORES				TOTAL	MONEY
Marc Warren	67	71	76	74	288	3,916
Chapchai Nirat	66	73	76	73	288	3,916
Panuwat Muenlek	68	67	72	81	288	3,916
Suk Jong-yul	71	67	72	79	289	3,370
Jose-Filipe Lima	68	69	78	75	290	3,365

Omega Mission Hills World Cup

Mission Hills GC, Olazabal Course, Shenzhen, China
Par 36-36–72; 7,251 yards

November 22-25
purse, $5,000,000

	INDIVIDUAL SCORES				TOTAL
SCOTLAND—$1,600,000 Colin Montgomerie/Marc Warren	63	68	66	66	263
UNITED STATES—$800,000 Heath Slocum/Boo Weekley	61	69	66	67	263

(Scotland defeated United States on third playoff hole.)

	INDIVIDUAL SCORES				TOTAL
FRANCE—$450,000 Gregory Havret/Raphael Jacquelin	64	71	62	67	264
ENGLAND—$240,000 Ian Poulter/Justin Rose	63	68	67	67	265
SOUTH AFRICA—$194,000 Retief Goosen/Trevor Immelman	63	69	66	69	267
GERMANY—$141,500 Alex Cejka/Martin Kaymer	62	71	66	69	268
NETHERLANDS—$141,500 Robert-Jan Derksen/Maarten Lafeber	65	69	65	69	268
ARGENTINA—$141,500 Ricardo Gonzalez/Andres Romero	65	70	64	69	268
SWEDEN—$141,500 Peter Hanson/Robert Karlsson	66	70	66	66	268
DENMARK—$101,000 Anders Hansen/Soren Hansen	65	68	68	68	269
SOUTH KOREA—$87,500 Lee Seung-ho/Lee Sung	65	69	69	68	271
CHINA—$87,500 Liang Wen-chong /Zhang Lian-wei	65	71	67	68	271
FINLAND—$72,500 Mikko Ilonen/Pasi Purhonen	63	74	65	71	273
SPAIN—$72,500 Miguel Angel Jimenez/Jose Manuel Lara	67	71	65	70	273
THAILAND—$64,000 Thongchai Jaidee/Prayad Marksaeng	63	76	63	73	275
PARAGUAY—$64,000 Carlos Franco/Fabrizio Zanotti	66	73	67	69	275

	INDIVIDUAL SCORES				TOTAL

ITALY—$58,000
Edoardo Molinari/Francesco Molinari — 65 68 69 74 — 276

CANADA—$58,000
Wes Heffernan/Mike Weir — 66 72 64 74 — 276

AUSTRIA—$58,000
Markus Brier/Claude Grenier — 64 75 69 68 — 276

INDIA—$58,000
Gaurav Ghei/Jyoti Randhawa — 65 75 65 71 — 276

AUSTRALIA—$53,000
Nathan Green/Nick O'Hern — 66 72 68 73 — 279

PHILIPPINES—$50,000
Tony Lascuna/Gerald Rosales — 67 73 68 72 — 280

WALES—$50,000
Stephen Dodd/Bradley Dredge — 63 76 67 74 — 280

IRELAND—$47,000
Michael Hoey/Gareth Maybin — 66 72 65 78 — 281

JAPAN—45,000
Tetsuji Hiratsuka/Hideto Tanihara — 67 73 69 73 — 282

COLOMBIA—$43,000
Jorge Benedetti/Gustavo Mendoza — 68 79 68 68 — 283

NEW ZEALAND—$41,000
Richard Lee/Stephen Scahill — 67 77 70 73 — 287

PUERTO RICO—$40,000
Wilfredo Morales/Miguel Suarez — 68 73 71 76 — 288

Hana Bank Vietnam Masters

Hanoi Phoenix Golf Resort, Hanoi, Vietnam
Par 34-36–70; 6,703 yards

November 22-25
purse, US$500,000

	SCORES				TOTAL	MONEY
Chapchai Nirat	68	71	70	67	276	US$79,250
Chawalit Plaphol	71	67	67	73	278	42,375
Simon Griffiths	68	70	68	72	278	42,375
Anthony Kang	73	66	70	70	279	24,650
Charlie Wi	71	70	71	69	281	16,137
Boonchu Ruangkit	68	70	73	70	281	16,137
Zaw Moe	70	72	69	70	281	16,137
Paul McGinley	74	67	68	72	281	16,137
Mo Joong-kyung	68	73	74	67	282	9,240
Ross Bain	69	72	73	68	282	9,240
David Gleeson	73	69	70	70	282	9,240
Simon Yates	70	70	70	72	282	9,240
Han Lee	69	70	70	73	282	9,240
Rahil Gangjee	69	71	74	70	284	7,200
Jason King	68	75	71	70	284	7,200
Thaworn Wiratchant	73	69	69	73	284	7,200
Kang Kyung-nam	73	71	73	68	285	6,008
Chang Tse-peng	68	74	74	69	285	6,008

	SCORES				TOTAL	MONEY
Artemio Murakami	73	70	72	70	285	6,008
Mars Pucay	72	69	73	71	285	6,008
Kang Ji-man	74	69	71	71	285	6,008
Gary Rusnak	69	70	72	74	285	6,008
S.S.P. Chowrasia	69	72	77	68	286	5,250
Lin Wen-hong	67	73	72	74	286	5,250
Martin Rominger	66	74	71	75	286	5,250

Johnnie Walker Cambodian Open

Phokeethra Country Club, Siem Reap, Cambodia
Par 36-36–72; 7,226 yards

November 29-December 2
purse, US$300,000

	SCORES				TOTAL	MONEY
Bryan Saltus	66	67	71	67	271	US$47,550
Adam Groom	65	68	70	71	274	32,550
Prom Meesawat	69	69	69	70	277	16,545
Thaworn Wiratchant	70	70	67	70	277	16,545
Danny Chia	74	68	69	67	278	11,235
Kang Ji-man	74	70	68	66	278	11,235
Anthony Kang	67	69	71	72	279	8,730
Chapchai Nirat	68	71	68	73	280	7,065
Yasin Ali	72	68	68	72	280	7,065
Harmeet Kahlon	69	69	73	70	281	5,910
Jerome Delariarte	70	72	70	70	282	5,238
Panuwat Muenlek	70	69	73	70	282	5,238
Atthaphon Prathummanee	74	72	69	68	283	4,330
Guido van der Valk	77	68	70	68	283	4,330
Michael Hoey	70	73	69	71	283	4,330
Peter Karmis	72	70	71	70	283	4,330
Boonchu Ruangkit	69	72	69	73	283	4,330
Suk Jong-yul	69	74	70	71	284	3,485
Mike Cunning	69	70	74	71	284	3,485
Arjun Singh	67	70	74	73	284	3,485
Lam Chih Bing	71	73	68	72	284	3,485
Mitchell Brown	66	77	69	72	284	3,485
Ted Oh	71	69	69	75	284	3,485
Iain Steel	76	69	72	68	285	2,970
Lien Lu-sen	75	71	70	69	285	2,970
Ben St. John	69	67	76	73	285	2,970
Jason King	73	69	72	71	285	2,970
Chris Rodgers	73	70	69	73	285	2,970

Volvo Masters of Asia

Thai Country Club, Bangkok, Thailand
Par 36-36–72; 7,082 yards

December 6-9
purse, US$750,000

	SCORES				TOTAL	MONEY
Prayad Marksaeng	67	71	68	69	275	US$135,000
Chris Rodgers	70	68	70	68	276	69,000
Juvic Pagunsan	70	65	66	75	276	69,000
Mark Brown	70	66	70	72	278	34,875
Simon Yates	69	69	67	73	278	34,875
Gerald Rosales	70	68	71	70	279	25,808
Taichiro Kiyota	72	68	70	70	280	22,208
Adam Blyth	72	69	70	70	281	17,083

	SCORES				TOTAL	MONEY
Prom Meesawat	70	67	73	71	281	17,083
Scott Hend	68	67	74	72	281	17,083
Gavin Flint	70	68	73	71	282	13,920
Lin Wen-tang	72	70	72	69	283	11,760
Simon Griffiths	68	71	75	69	283	11,760
Rahil Gangjee	70	74	70	69	283	11,760
Chapchai Nirat	71	69	71	72	283	11,760
Thaworn Wiratchant	71	70	69	73	283	11,760
Thongchai Jaidee	70	69	77	68	284	10,058
David Gleeson	72	74	65	73	284	10,058
Lee Sung	68	70	76	71	285	9,064
S.S.P. Chowrasia	69	73	71	72	285	9,064
Shiv Kapur	70	72	69	74	285	9,064
Thammanoon Srirot	69	72	69	75	285	9,064
Gary Simpson	70	73	71	72	286	8,258
Scott Strange	65	71	75	75	286	8,258
Angelo Que	70	68	72	76	286	8,258

Omega China Tour

Sofitel Golf Championship

Zhongshan International Golf Club, Nanjing
Par 36-36–72; 7,189 yards

May 10-13
purse, US$100,000

	SCORES				TOTAL	MONEY
Wu Kang-chun	73	70	67	69	279	RMB150,000
Zhang Lian-wei	72	73	69	69	283	90,000
Yuan Hao	75	67	68	75	285	50,000
*Ye Jian-feng	72	68	73	73	286	
Liu Anda	73	70	71	73	287	22,000
Fan Zhi-peng	72	70	73	73	288	17,500
Huang Ming-jie	72	72	69	76	289	15,000
Li Chao	70	73	73	74	290	14,500
Gu Cui-lin	73	70	71	77	291	14,000
Liao Gui-ming	77	69	69	77	292	13,250
Xiao Zhi-jin	74	73	70	75	292	13,250
Yuan Tian	75	74	73	71	293	12,500
Zhang Meng	74	71	74	74	293	12,500
Shang Lei	75	70	73	75	293	12,500
Deng Yong-hong	72	74	72	75	293	12,500
Ye Xiong-hui	75	70	72	77	294	11,800
Tang Jin-chang	76	74	73	71	294	11,800
Zheng Wen-gen	75	73	71	75	294	11,800
Gao Hui	74	71	75	75	295	11,400
*Su Dong	81	70	74	71	296	
Fu Xin	76	72	76	72	296	10,600
Wu Wei-huang	75	72	76	73	296	10,600
Gu Shu-tao	75	73	75	73	296	10,600
Qi Zeng-fa	72	77	74	73	296	10,600
Wang Hui-qiang	81	72	70	73	296	10,600
Gao Lei	81	69	71	75	296	10,600
Zhou Jun	71	75	74	76	296	10,600

Qingdao Leg

Huashan Golf & Resort, Qingdao
Par 36-36–72; 7,012 yards

May 31-June 3
purse, US$100,000

	SCORES			TOTAL	MONEY
Zhang Lian-wei	71	72	73	78	294	RMB150,000
Li Chao	72	74	74	76	296	54,000
Wu Wei-huang	74	73	74	75	296	54,000
Chen Xiao-ma	74	73	77	72	296	54,000
Cui Xiao-long	74	76	73	75	298	16,250
Wu Kang-chun	75	76	75	72	298	16,250
Yang Wen-zhang	71	75	79	74	299	14,500
Deng Yong-hong	74	73	74	79	300	13,325
Fu Xin	78	77	73	72	300	13,325
Tian Ye	72	82	70	76	300	13,325
Liu Jun-feng	71	78	74	77	300	13,325
Xiao Zhi-jin	77	78	74	72	301	12,300
Yang Sheng-qin	74	80	73	74	301	12,300
Huang Ming-jie	74	77	75	75	301	12,300
Zhou Xun-shu	78	76	72	75	301	12,300
Wang Lei	73	79	75	76	303	11,600
Zheng Shao-guang	75	77	72	79	303	11,600
Chen Yu	74	76	72	81	303	11,600
Qiu Zhi-feng	79	75	76	74	304	10,600
Zhang Cheng-wei	72	78	78	76	304	10,600
Liu Anda	83	75	69	77	304	10,600
Liao Gui-ming	76	73	76	79	304	10,600
Shang Lei	72	77	75	80	304	10,600
Zhou Jun	72	78	74	80	304	10,600
Liu Anlin	75	74	74	81	304	10,600

Guangzhou Leg

Dragon Lake Golf Club, Guangzhou
Par 36-36–72; 7,134 yards

June 21-24
purse, US$100,000

	SCORES			TOTAL	MONEY
Zhang Lian-wei	71	68	71	69	279	RMB150,000
Yuan Hao	68	74	71	71	284	90,000
Zheng Wen-gen	69	72	74	72	287	50,000
Huang Ming-jie	71	73	73	71	288	22,000
Li Chao	82	67	68	72	289	17,500
Kong Wei-hai	72	70	75	73	290	14,750
Liao Gui-ming	80	70	69	71	290	14,750
Wu Kang-chun	76	69	72	74	291	13,325
Zhou Xun-shu	80	72	70	69	291	13,325
Tang Wei	76	70	74	71	291	13,325
Shang Lei	69	79	72	71	291	13,325
Xiao Zhi-jin	74	71	71	76	292	12,600
Liu Jian	76	72	73	72	293	12,300
Shi Ning-jie	73	72	75	73	293	12,300
Ye Xiong-hui	75	73	75	71	294	11,700
Huang Yong-huan	73	74	73	74	294	11,700
Tuo Wen-tao	75	73	72	74	294	11,700
Yuan Zheng	78	71	70	75	294	11,700
He Shao-cai	71	76	77	71	295	11,100
Wang Lei	73	75	74	73	295	11,100

Yanji Golf Championship

Harangang Golf Resort, Mountain Course, Yanji
Par 36-36–72; 7,279 yards

July 12-15
purse, US$100,000

	SCORES				TOTAL	MONEY
Li Chao	74	72	72	71	289	RMB150,000
Zheng Wen-gen	75	78	70	70	293	70,000
Huang Ming-jie	72	72	75	74	293	70,000
Chen Xiao-ma	74	69	74	77	294	22,000
Wang Lei	73	74	75	73	295	16,250
Yuan Hao	74	74	71	76	295	16,250
Xiao Zhi-jin	73	78	71	74	296	14,250
Wu Wei-huang	72	74	73	77	296	14,250
Shang Lei	75	72	77	74	298	12,860
Zhou Jun	77	72	75	74	298	12,860
Liu Guo-jie	71	77	75	75	298	12,860
Wu Kang-chun	76	75	72	75	298	12,860
Ye Xiong-hui	77	72	73	76	298	12,860
Kong Wei-hai	80	75	74	70	299	12,000
Zhou Xun-shu	74	79	74	72	299	12,000
Qiu Zhi-feng	75	78	72	74	299	12,000
Wu Ligui	76	76	76	72	300	11,000
Huang Yong-huan	81	73	74	72	300	11,000
Fan Zhi-peng	72	75	80	73	300	11,000
Gu Cui-lin	77	70	78	75	300	11,000
Liu Jian	74	77	73	76	300	11,000
Liu Jun-feng	80	70	73	77	300	11,000
He Shao-cai	73	77	73	77	300	11,000

Shanghai Leg

Grand Shanghai International Golf & Holiday Resort, Shanghai
Par 36-36–72; 7,066 yards

August 9-12
purse, US$100,000

	SCORES				TOTAL	MONEY
Li Chao	73	72	69	68	282	RMB150,000
Tsai Chi-huang	69	77	69	68	283	90,000
Wang Ter-chang	73	74	72	68	287	50,000
Zhang Lian-wei	73	75	72	72	292	19,750
Qi Zeng-fa	74	75	74	69	292	19,750
Wu Kang-chun	73	75	74	73	295	15,000
Liao Gui-ming	73	73	74	77	297	14,500
Zheng Wen-gen	79	75	74	71	299	14,000
Xiao Zhi-jin	80	80	69	71	300	13,500
Liu Guo-jie	72	77	74	78	301	12,800
Qiu Zhi-feng	77	73	74	77	301	12,800
Liu Anda	76	81	70	74	301	12,800
Gu Shu-tao	70	79	72	81	302	12,300
Cui Xiao-long	76	75	76	75	302	12,300
Yuan Tian	76	78	74	76	304	11,900
Chen Xiao-ma	75	76	79	74	304	11,900
Wu Wei-huang	75	78	77	75	305	11,600
Yu Gen-dong	80	72	78	76	306	11,000
Yuan Hao	79	79	72	76	306	11,000
Tang Wei	75	79	79	73	306	11,000
Tan Yong-zong	77	77	79	73	306	11,000
Liu Xin	74	83	76	73	306	11,000

Kunming Leg

Lakeview Golf Club, Kunming, Yunnan
Par 36-36–72; 7,222 yards

August 23-26
purse, US$100,000

	SCORES				TOTAL	MONEY
Zheng Wen-gen	66	68	72	67	273	RMB150,000
Huang Ming-jie	69	69	74	67	279	90,000
Li Chao	72	67	71	70	280	26,125
Liao Gui-ming	71	71	68	70	280	26,125
Chen Xiao-ma	73	70	67	70	280	26,125
Ye Xiong-hui	76	67	71	66	280	26,125
Shang Lei	75	68	68	71	282	14,250
Qiu Zhi-feng	74	66	72	70	282	14,250
Yang Wen-zhang	71	69	73	71	284	12,860
Deng Yong-hong	74	71	68	71	284	12,860
Zhou Xun-shu	69	74	71	70	284	12,860
Cui Xiao-long	71	72	72	69	284	12,860
He Shao-cai	74	68	75	67	284	12,860
Cheng Hai-bao	70	72	70	73	285	12,200
Liu Guo-jie	73	66	73	75	287	11,900
Kong Wei-hai	70	71	74	72	287	11,900
Yuan Tian	71	70	73	74	288	11,300
Liu Jun-feng	75	67	73	73	288	11,300
Fan Zhi-peng	73	67	76	72	288	11,300
Liu Anlin	72	73	75	68	288	11,300

Xiamen Leg

Orient Golf & Country Club, Xiamen, China
Par 35-35–70; 6,749 yards

September 20-23
purse, US$100,000

	SCORES				TOTAL	MONEY
Li Chao	69	71	72	66	278	RMB150,000
Shang Lei	69	69	70	71	279	90,000
Wu Kang-chun	65	74	66	77	282	29,833
Fan Zhi-peng	69	67	75	71	282	29,833
Qiu Zhi-feng	71	69	73	69	282	29,833
Liao Gui-ming	71	71	70	71	283	14,750
Wu Wei-huang	67	77	71	68	283	14,750
Zheng Wen-gen	70	71	71	72	284	13,500
He Shao-cai	70	69	74	71	284	13,500
Gu Cui-lin	76	68	72	68	284	13,500
Chen Xiao-ma	67	71	75	72	285	12,800
Wang Lei	72	71	71	74	288	12,500
Liu Guo-jie	71	71	74	72	288	12,500
Ye Xiong-hui	67	75	69	78	289	12,100
Zheng Shao-guang	72	75	69	73	289	12,100
Yuan Hao	76	69	71	74	290	11,700
Ye Peng-fei	66	75	76	73	290	11,700
Huang Ming-jie	69	74	73	75	291	11,000
*Su Dong	69	75	73	74	291	
Zhou Jun	75	70	72	74	291	11,000
Kong Wei-hai	71	70	78	72	291	11,000
Xiao Zhi-jin	72	73	74	72	291	11,000
Deng Yong-hong	73	71	77	70	291	11,000

Omega Championship

Tianan Golf Club, Beijing
Par 36-36–72; 7,069 yards

October 18-21
purse, US$100,000

	SCORES				TOTAL	MONEY
Zhang Lian-wei	70	77	69	67	283	RMB150,000
Li Chao	69	77	73	71	290	90,000
Wang Ter-chang	72	78	73	68	291	50,000
Liu Guo-jie	79	70	75	70	294	22,000
Liu Anda	72	76	72	76	296	16,250
Wu Wei-huang	78	75	74	69	296	16,250
Lu Wen-teh	74	85	68	71	298	14,500
Qiu Zhi-feng	71	79	76	73	299	14,000
He Shao-cai	77	73	77	73	300	13,100
James Stewart	78	75	76	71	300	13,100
Zhang Meng	74	80	75	71	300	13,100
Deng Yong-hong	72	79	75	75	301	12,300
Zheng Wen-gen	77	73	78	73	301	12,300
Cui Xiao-long	76	78	74	73	301	12,300
Wu Kang-chun	74	84	74	69	301	12,300
Kong Wei-hai	76	78	76	72	302	11,800
*Su Dong	74	74	79	76	303	
Xiao Zhi-jin	78	73	77	75	303	11,400
Gu Shu-tao	74	78	76	75	303	11,400
Wang Lei	74	76	82	71	303	11,400

Japan Tour

Token Homemate Cup

Token Tado Country Club, Kuwana, Mie
Par 35-36–71; 7,083 yards

April 12-15
purse, ¥110,000,000

	SCORES				TOTAL	MONEY
Yui Ueda	66	65	74	71	276	¥22,000,000
Lee Dong-hwan	70	67	72	68	277	11,000,000
Steven Conran	69	72	71	66	278	6,380,000
Katsuya Nakagawa	68	67	74	69	278	6,380,000
Chang Ik-je	67	69	73	70	279	4,180,000
Kiyoshi Murota	68	71	70	70	279	4,180,000
Tadahiro Takayama	68	72	76	64	280	3,242,250
Justin Maker	71	70	70	69	280	3,242,250
Mitsuhiro Tateyama	66	71	72	71	280	3,242,250
Toshinori Muto	72	67	69	72	280	3,242,250
Hidemasa Hoshino	70	72	72	67	281	2,442,000
Toshimitsu Izawa	69	73	72	67	281	2,442,000
Hiroyuki Fujita	66	72	75	68	281	2,442,000
Naoya Takemoto	69	72	74	67	282	1,730,666
Tetsuji Hiratsuka	72	69	74	67	282	1,730,666
Brendan Jones	71	68	78	65	282	1,730,666
Yasuharu Imano	68	70	74	70	282	1,730,666
Hiroshi Iwata	70	71	70	71	282	1,730,666
Yeh Wei-tze	73	67	71	71	282	1,730,666
Azuma Yano	72	68	76	67	283	1,111,000
Toru Suzuki	74	66	76	67	283	1,111,000
Ryoken Kawagishi	72	68	75	68	283	1,111,000
Hajime Meshiai	73	69	74	67	283	1,111,000
Masashi Ozaki	69	68	77	69	283	1,111,000
Gregory Meyer	70	69	75	69	283	1,111,000
Craig Parry	70	70	72	71	283	1,111,000
Lee Seung-ho	71	67	72	73	283	1,111,000

Tsuruya Open

Yamanohara Golf Club, Kawanishi, Hyogo
Par 35-36–71; 6,778 yards

April 19-22
purse, ¥100,000,000

	SCORES				TOTAL	MONEY
Brendan Jones	67	65	68	68	268	¥20,000,000
Hirofumi Miyase	64	67	74	65	270	7,200,000
Masahiro Kuramoto	70	68	66	66	270	7,200,000
Takuya Taniguchi	68	70	65	67	270	7,200,000
Katsumasa Miyamoto	66	72	68	65	271	4,000,000
Tadahiro Takayama	69	71	66	67	273	3,450,000
Toru Taniguchi	68	69	69	67	273	3,450,000
Kiyoshi Murota	68	69	71	66	274	2,935,000
Hidemasa Hoshino	69	71	66	68	274	2,935,000
Lee Dong-hwan	68	72	69	66	275	2,620,000
Tetsuji Hiratsuka	72	66	73	65	276	2,040,000
Kaname Yokoo	69	70	70	67	276	2,040,000
Naoya Takemoto	67	68	73	68	276	2,040,000

	SCORES				TOTAL	MONEY
S.K. Ho	69	71	68	68	276	2,040,000
Naomichi Ozaki	68	69	69	70	276	2,040,000
Tadahisa Inoue	70	70	70	67	277	1,570,000
Takao Nogami	68	69	69	71	277	1,570,000
Keizo Yoshida	70	70	71	67	278	1,340,000
Tetsuya Haraguchi	70	72	67	69	278	1,340,000
Scott Laycock	66	68	71	73	278	1,340,000
Koumei Oda	72	69	71	67	279	1,060,000
Hidezumi Shirakata	71	71	69	68	279	1,060,000
Hiroyuki Fujita	66	70	71	72	279	1,060,000
Azuma Yano	70	69	68	72	279	1,060,000
Kenichi Kuboya	69	68	73	70	280	840,000
Shingo Katayama	71	70	72	67	280	840,000
Yeh Wei-tze	70	72	72	66	280	840,000
Kiyoshi Miyazato	70	68	69	73	280	840,000

The Crowns

Nagoya Golf Club, Wago Course, Togo, Aichi
Par 35-35–70; 6,514 yards

April 26-29
purse, ¥120,000,000

	SCORES				TOTAL	MONEY
Hirofumi Miyase	67	70	70	71	278	¥24,000,000
Toru Taniguchi	68	68	75	67	278	12,000,000
(Miyase defeated Taniguchi on first playoff hole.)						
Koumei Oda	69	70	74	67	280	8,160,000
Keiichiro Fukabori	67	71	69	74	281	5,760,000
Yui Ueda	73	66	76	67	282	4,360,000
David Smail	70	71	71	70	282	4,360,000
Satoru Hirota	68	73	71	70	282	4,360,000
Azuma Yano	73	72	70	68	283	3,660,000
Tomohiro Kondo	75	69	73	67	284	3,144,000
Prayad Marksaeng	72	71	72	69	284	3,144,000
Scott Laycock	74	70	69	71	284	3,144,000
Shingo Katayama	72	71	72	70	285	2,544,000
Paul Casey	73	72	69	71	285	2,544,000
S.K. Ho	72	70	77	67	286	1,888,000
Eiji Mizoguchi	70	76	70	70	286	1,888,000
Mitsuhiro Tateyama	73	69	72	72	286	1,888,000
Brendan Jones	72	72	70	72	286	1,888,000
Hiroyuki Fujita	69	70	73	74	286	1,888,000
Tadahiro Takayama	71	70	70	75	286	1,888,000
Paul Sheehan	71	71	76	69	287	1,368,000
Tateo Ozaki	72	72	70	73	287	1,368,000
Katsumasa Miyamoto	74	69	71	73	287	1,368,000
Yoshikazu Haku	72	72	70	73	287	1,368,000
Kim Jong-duk	73	71	75	69	288	1,008,000
Kenichi Kuboya	71	76	72	69	288	1,008,000
Frankie Minoza	75	71	72	70	288	1,008,000
Toru Suzuki	72	71	74	71	288	1,008,000
Sushi Ishigaki	73	74	70	71	288	1,008,000
Lee Dong-hwan	70	74	72	72	288	1,008,000

Japan PGA Championship

Kise Country Club, Nago, Okinawa
Par 36-36–72; 7,193 yards

May 10-13
purse, ¥130,000,000

	SCORES				TOTAL	MONEY
Toshimitsu Izawa	68	70	72	73	283	¥26,000,000
Satoru Hirota	72	70	71	71	284	13,000,000
Sushi Ishigaki	72	72	75	67	286	7,540,000
Kim Jong-duk	68	74	74	70	286	7,540,000
Craig Parry	72	70	77	68	287	4,940,000
Shoichi Ideguchi	71	68	73	75	287	4,940,000
Gregory Meyer	74	73	72	69	288	4,127,500
Yusaku Miyazato	70	71	72	75	288	4,127,500
Yui Ueda	70	75	74	70	289	3,666,000
Tsuneyuki Nakajima	74	73	72	71	290	2,886,000
Brendan Jones	71	72	75	72	290	2,886,000
Hiroyuki Fujita	68	75	74	73	290	2,886,000
Nobuhiro Masuda	71	75	71	73	290	2,886,000
Jun Kikuchi	70	71	72	77	290	2,886,000
Keiichiro Fukabori	73	76	72	70	291	1,868,285
Hirofumi Miyase	74	74	72	71	291	1,868,285
Kaname Yokoo	75	70	74	72	291	1,868,285
Frankie Minoza	72	75	72	72	291	1,868,285
Wayne Perske	73	71	74	73	291	1,868,285
Hiroshi Iwata	74	71	72	74	291	1,868,285
Yeh Wei-tze	69	77	70	75	291	1,868,285
Yoshi Mizumaki	79	69	75	69	292	1,192,285
Kunihiro Kamii	73	70	76	73	292	1,192,285
Shinichi Yokota	69	74	76	73	292	1,192,285
Tatsuhiko Ichihara	74	72	73	73	292	1,192,285
Hidezumi Shirakata	76	71	72	73	292	1,192,285
Katsumasa Miyamoto	70	77	72	73	292	1,192,285
Toru Taniguchi	68	75	74	75	292	1,192,285

Munsingwear Open KSB Cup

Tojigaoka Marine Hills Golf Club, Tamano, Okayama
Par 36-36–72; 7,072 yards

May 17-20
purse, ¥100,000,000

	SCORES				TOTAL	MONEY
*Ryo Ishikawa	72	69	69	66	276	
Katsumasa Miyamoto	67	73	69	68	277	¥20,000,000
Tomohiro Kondo	68	71	70	69	278	10,000,000
Yusaku Miyazato	70	70	67	72	279	4,800,000
Koumei Oda	69	70	67	73	279	4,800,000
Tadahiro Takayama	67	71	69	72	279	4,800,000
Kiyoshi Miyazato	70	66	76	67	279	4,800,000
Craig Parry	68	70	71	71	280	2,947,500
Taichiro Kiyota	68	69	72	71	280	2,947,500
Hiroyuki Fujita	67	71	73	69	280	2,947,500
Prayad Marksaeng	68	66	77	69	280	2,947,500
Lee Seung-ho	67	72	72	70	281	2,420,000
Kenichi Kuboya	72	69	71	70	282	1,945,000
Azuma Yano	66	74	70	72	282	1,945,000
Nobuhito Sato	67	72	72	71	282	1,945,000
Toru Taniguchi	64	73	71	74	282	1,945,000
Nozomi Kawahara	69	72	73	69	283	1,520,000
Kaname Yokoo	70	72	73	68	283	1,520,000
Yuudai Maeda	72	70	69	72	283	1,520,000

	SCORES				TOTAL	MONEY
Tatsuya Mitsuhashi	72	69	74	69	284	1,220,000
Yoshikazu Haku	69	72	76	67	284	1,220,000
Tatsuhiko Takahashi	68	71	71	74	284	1,220,000
Tetsuya Haraguchi	69	68	74	73	284	1,220,000
Masaya Tomida	69	71	71	74	285	980,000
Masashi Ozaki	68	71	72	74	285	980,000

Mitsubishi Diamond Cup

Oarai Golf Club, Oarai, Ibaraki
Par 36-35–71; 7,156 yards

May 24-27
purse, ¥110,000,000

	SCORES				TOTAL	MONEY
Tetsuji Hiratsuka	71	73	71	67	282	¥22,000,000
Satoru Hirota	75	71	70	67	283	9,240,000
Kiyoshi Miyazato	72	76	68	67	283	9,240,000
Daisuke Maruyama	75	73	66	70	284	5,280,000
Gregory Meyer	73	73	72	67	285	3,836,250
Toru Taniguchi	72	69	70	74	285	3,836,250
Hiroyuki Fujita	72	71	70	72	285	3,836,250
Prayad Marksaeng	72	71	70	72	285	3,836,250
Shingo Katayama	74	74	73	65	286	2,992,000
Kim Jong-duk	71	71	73	71	286	2,992,000
Kaname Yokoo	74	73	72	69	288	2,442,000
Brendan Jones	75	74	69	70	288	2,442,000
Taichiro Kiyota	76	70	70	72	288	2,442,000
Steven Conran	77	71	74	67	289	1,892,000
Azuma Yano	73	77	69	70	289	1,892,000
Keiichiro Fukabori	72	73	73	71	289	1,892,000
Chang Ik-je	77	73	71	69	290	1,569,333
Naoya Takemoto	74	76	71	69	290	1,569,333
Wayne Perske	75	74	71	70	290	1,569,333
Kiyoshi Maita	72	71	78	70	291	1,173,333
Lee Dong-hwan	74	77	71	69	291	1,173,333
Norio Shinozaki	75	75	70	71	291	1,173,333
Tadahiro Takayama	74	75	71	71	291	1,173,333
Kenichi Kuboya	73	73	72	73	291	1,173,333
Yukiharu Morita	73	76	69	73	291	1,173,333

JCB Classic

Hananomori Golf Club, Ohira, Miyagi
Par 36-35–71; 7,038 yards

May 31-June 3
purse, ¥100,000,000

	SCORES				TOTAL	MONEY
Tomohiro Kondo	68	66	68	69	271	¥20,000,000
Lee Seung-ho	68	67	71	66	272	6,400,000
Mamo Osanai	71	70	63	68	272	6,400,000
Koumei Oda	65	69	69	69	272	6,400,000
Azuma Yano	70	67	67	68	272	6,400,000
Wayne Perske	70	66	71	66	273	3,600,000
Hiroshi Iwata	70	70	65	69	274	3,056,666
Brendan Jones	67	71	69	67	274	3,056,666
Tetsuji Hiratsuka	67	67	66	74	274	3,056,666
Masaya Tomida	64	72	66	73	275	2,620,000
Shingo Katayama	67	69	73	68	277	2,040,000
Mitsuhiro Tateyama	70	67	72	68	277	2,040,000

	SCORES				TOTAL	MONEY
Kenichi Kuboya	70	70	69	68	277	2,040,000
Eiji Mizoguchi	70	70	69	68	277	2,040,000
Takao Nogami	70	67	71	69	277	2,040,000
Hisayuki Sasaki	69	72	71	66	278	1,475,000
Ryuichi Oda	70	71	70	67	278	1,475,000
Naruhito Ueda	66	70	71	71	278	1,475,000
Shigeru Nonaka	67	74	67	70	278	1,475,000
Yui Ueda	71	70	72	67	280	1,180,000
Hiroyuki Fujita	72	66	72	70	280	1,180,000
Kiyoshi Murota	69	71	70	70	280	1,180,000
Sushi Ishigaki	69	69	74	69	281	908,000
Tadahisa Inoue	67	71	74	69	281	908,000
Keiichiro Fukabori	68	70	73	70	281	908,000
Toshiyuki Hiyama	65	71	74	71	281	908,000
Fumihiro Ebine	70	67	71	73	281	908,000

Gateway to the Open Mizuno Open Yomiuri Classic

Yomiuri Country Club, Nishinomiya, Hyogo
Par 36-36–72; 7,287 yards
(Event shortened to 54 holes—rain.)

June 21-24
purse, ¥130,000,000

	SCORES			TOTAL	MONEY
Lee Dong-hwan	68	68	68	204	¥19,500,000
Hideto Tanihara	73	71	64	208	5,281,250
Toshinori Muto	69	73	66	208	5,281,250
Achi Sato	69	71	68	208	5,281,250
Lee Seung-ho	68	72	68	208	5,281,250
Lin Keng-chi	68	72	68	208	5,281,250
Masaya Tomida	71	66	71	208	5,281,250
Kim Jong-duk	70	73	66	209	2,861,625
Hiroyuki Fujita	70	72	67	209	2,861,625
Brendan Jones	65	74	71	210	2,359,500
Kouki Idoki	67	72	71	210	2,359,500
Yoshikazu Haku	67	71	72	210	2,359,500
Chang Ik-je	72	71	68	211	1,644,500
Liang Wen-chong	73	70	68	211	1,644,500
Toyokazu Fujishima	72	71	68	211	1,644,500
Steven Conran	71	72	68	211	1,644,500
Ryuji Masaoka	68	74	69	211	1,644,500
Takao Nogami	73	67	71	211	1,644,500
Tatsuaki Nakamura	68	76	68	212	1,150,500
Yoshiaki Mano	68	74	70	212	1,150,500
Lu Wen-teh	68	73	71	212	1,150,500
Tetsuji Hiratsuka	69	72	71	212	1,150,500
Scott Laycock	68	72	72	212	1,150,500
Kiyoshi Murota	72	72	69	213	838,500
Tadahiro Takayama	73	71	69	213	838,500
Tetsuya Haraguchi	71	71	71	213	838,500
Tomohiro Kondo	70	70	73	213	838,500
David Smail	66	73	74	213	838,500

UBS Japan Golf Tour Championship

Shishido Hills Country Club, Kasama, Ibaraki
Par 35-35–70; 7,214 yards

June 28-July 1
purse, ¥150,000,000

	SCORES				TOTAL	MONEY
Shingo Katayama	69	68	67	67	271	¥30,000,000
Naoya Takemoto	63	74	69	66	272	15,000,000
Lee Dong-hwan	67	74	67	66	274	10,200,000
Tetsuji Hiratsuka	72	71	69	65	277	6,600,000
Brendan Jones	70	70	70	67	277	6,600,000
Toshinori Muto	70	67	69	72	278	5,400,000
Tomohiro Kondo	72	71	69	67	279	4,585,000
Zhang Lian-wei	68	70	71	70	279	4,585,000
Kaname Yokoo	70	67	71	71	279	4,585,000
Lee Seung-ho	69	73	72	66	280	3,780,000
Hiroyuki Fujita	71	70	69	70	280	3,780,000
Koumei Oda	70	71	70	70	281	3,330,000
Toru Taniguchi	67	69	74	72	282	2,880,000
Yusaku Miyazato	74	69	68	71	282	2,880,000
David Smail	71	70	72	70	283	2,430,000
Kim Jong-duk	73	68	70	72	283	2,430,000
Frankie Minoza	69	67	73	74	283	2,430,000
Prayad Marksaeng	70	69	76	69	284	2,070,000
Tadahisa Inoue	70	71	70	73	284	2,070,000
Nobuhito Sato	68	72	73	72	285	1,770,000
Gregory Meyer	73	68	73	71	285	1,770,000
Toru Morita	71	69	71	74	285	1,770,000
Koichi Kashimura	71	71	75	69	286	1,470,000
Sushi Ishigaki	71	72	72	71	286	1,470,000
Kiyoshi Miyazato	73	73	72	69	287	1,200,000
Hideto Tanihara	73	71	72	71	287	1,200,000
Chang Ik-je	68	73	74	72	287	1,200,000
Kenichi Kuboya	71	73	71	72	287	1,200,000
Shoichi Ideguchi	72	74	67	74	287	1,200,000
Prom Meesawat	73	68	72	74	287	1,200,000

Woodone Open Hiroshima

Hiroshima Country Club, Higashihiroshima, Hiroshima
Par 35-36–71; 6,942 yards

July 5-8
purse, ¥100,000,000

	SCORES				TOTAL	MONEY
Toru Taniguchi	67	64	68	70	269	¥20,000,000
Prayad Marksaeng	67	68	68	66	269	10,000,000
(Taniguchi defeated Prayad on first playoff hole.)						
Hiroshi Iwata	66	71	68	67	272	6,800,000
Yasuharu Imano	69	69	68	68	274	4,800,000
Hiroyuki Fujita	70	68	68	69	275	3,800,000
Hideto Tanihara	67	71	67	70	275	3,800,000
Makoto Inoue	64	73	70	69	276	3,056,666
Toshimitsu Izawa	68	72	66	70	276	3,056,666
Katsumasa Miyamoto	68	72	66	70	276	3,056,666
Yusaku Miyazato	68	70	72	67	277	2,620,000
Kim Jong-duk	70	70	71	67	278	2,320,000
Toru Suzuki	68	72	70	68	278	2,320,000
Brendan Jones	72	69	72	66	279	1,686,666
Keiichiro Fukabori	71	71	70	67	279	1,686,666
Kazuhiko Hosokawa	75	68	71	65	279	1,686,666
Tatsuhiko Ichihara	72	68	69	70	279	1,686,666

	SCORES				TOTAL	MONEY
Tetsuya Haraguchi	70	70	69	70	279	1,686,666
Gregory Meyer	68	68	70	73	279	1,686,666
Kim Hyung-tae	70	73	71	66	280	1,340,000
Yoshinobu Tsukada	75	66	70	70	281	1,140,000
Yoichi Shimizu	69	66	73	73	281	1,140,000
Scott Laycock	70	69	68	74	281	1,140,000
David Smail	67	70	69	75	281	1,140,000
Prom Meesawat	67	71	75	69	282	880,000
Hisayuki Sasaki	71	69	74	68	282	880,000
Sushi Ishigaki	70	72	69	71	282	880,000
Tadahiro Takayama	68	72	71	71	282	880,000

Nagashima Shigeo Invitational Sega Sammy Cup

North Country Golf Club, Chitose, Hokkaido
Par 36-36–72; 7,127 yards

July 12-15
purse, ¥150,000,000

	SCORES			TOTAL	MONEY
Toru Taniguchi	70	70	68	68	276	¥30,000,000
Prom Meesawat	70	73	71	65	279	15,000,000
Koumei Oda	70	72	69	69	280	8,700,000
Wayne Perske	72	68	71	69	280	8,700,000
Gregory Meyer	74	71	71	68	284	6,000,000
Mamo Osanai	75	73	72	65	285	4,617,000
Yusaku Miyazato	76	70	73	66	285	4,617,000
Frankie Minoza	73	75	67	70	285	4,617,000
Tateo Ozaki	75	70	69	71	285	4,617,000
Azuma Yano	72	72	69	72	285	4,617,000
Hiroyuki Fujita	77	72	71	66	286	3,330,000
Keishiro Nakata	74	68	72	72	286	3,330,000
Toshimitsu Izawa	72	75	66	73	286	3,330,000
Chawalit Plaphol	78	71	71	67	287	2,430,000
David Smail	76	72	71	68	287	2,430,000
Steven Conran	75	71	71	70	287	2,430,000
Keiichiro Fukabori	73	74	70	70	287	2,430,000
Takao Nogami	75	71	69	72	287	2,430,000
Chang Ik-je	72	73	75	68	288	1,770,000
Tadahiro Takayama	73	74	71	70	288	1,770,000
Yuudai Maeda	72	70	73	73	288	1,770,000
Ryuichi Oda	72	72	71	73	288	1,770,000
Craig Jones	76	69	70	73	288	1,770,000
Shoichi Ideguchi	73	75	73	68	289	1,290,000
Satoshi Tomiyama	75	72	72	70	289	1,290,000
Hideki Kase	76	70	72	71	289	1,290,000
Makoto Inoue	72	73	72	72	289	1,290,000
Kiyoshi Miyazato	73	74	69	73	289	1,290,000

Sun Chlorella Classic

Otaru Country Club, Otaru, Hokkaido
Par 36-36–72; 7,535 yards

August 2-5
purse, ¥150,000,000

	SCORES			TOTAL	MONEY
Jun Kikuchi	69	73	73	68	283	¥30,000,000
Toru Suzuki	70	68	74	71	283	15,000,000
(Kikuchi defeated Suzuki on third playoff hole.)						
Hisayuki Sasaki	71	71	73	69	284	8,700,000

	SCORES				TOTAL	MONEY
Hiroshi Iwata	71	72	72	69	284	8,700,000
Hideto Tanihara	75	70	70	70	285	5,700,000
Prayad Marksaeng	75	71	69	70	285	5,700,000
Mamo Osanai	74	71	68	73	286	4,950,000
Kaname Yokoo	73	73	72	69	287	4,402,500
Toru Taniguchi	72	69	74	72	287	4,402,500
Michio Matsumura	71	72	76	69	288	3,205,000
Mitsuhiro Tateyama	74	72	74	68	288	3,205,000
Ryuichi Oda	78	69	71	70	288	3,205,000
Kenichi Kuboya	72	72	72	72	288	3,205,000
Yusaku Miyazato	73	72	71	72	288	3,205,000
Katsumasa Miyamoto	76	69	71	72	288	3,205,000
David Smail	74	69	76	70	289	1,961,250
Naruhito Ueda	73	74	73	69	289	1,961,250
Norio Shinozaki	75	69	74	71	289	1,961,250
Hidezumi Shirakata	71	73	72	73	289	1,961,250
Eddie Lee	73	70	73	73	289	1,961,250
Katsunori Kuwabara	70	75	70	74	289	1,961,250
Wayne Perske	71	71	73	74	289	1,961,250
Tetsuya Haraguchi	70	74	69	76	289	1,961,250
Frankie Minoza	74	73	72	71	290	1,230,000
Kazuhiko Hosokawa	70	70	78	72	290	1,230,000
Tateo Ozaki	73	67	80	70	290	1,230,000
Keiichiro Fukabori	74	73	73	70	290	1,230,000
Tomonori Takahashi	72	72	74	72	290	1,230,000
Nobuhiro Masuda	72	72	72	74	290	1,230,000
Masashi Shimada	74	71	69	76	290	1,230,000

KBC Augusta

Keya Golf Club, Shima, Fukuoka
Par 35-36–71; 7,142 yards

August 23-26
purse, ¥100,000,000

	SCORES				TOTAL	MONEY
Katsumasa Miyamoto	64	64	70	71	269	¥20,000,000
Koumei Oda	68	71	66	65	270	8,400,000
Steven Conran	65	67	67	71	270	8,400,000
Takashi Kanemoto	69	70	70	63	272	4,800,000
Kiyoshi Miyazato	70	66	70	67	273	3,800,000
Hiroyuki Fujita	70	69	65	69	273	3,800,000
S.K. Ho	69	70	69	66	274	3,056,666
Kaname Yokoo	69	65	71	69	274	3,056,666
Naoya Takemoto	68	66	68	72	274	3,056,666
Craig Parry	66	74	70	65	275	2,136,666
Hidemasa Hoshino	71	67	70	67	275	2,136,666
Tatsuhiko Takahashi	71	68	69	67	275	2,136,666
Shintaro Kai	68	69	74	64	275	2,136,666
Scott Laycock	69	72	67	67	275	2,136,666
Lee Dong-hwan	68	67	69	71	275	2,136,666
Fumihiro Ebine	71	68	70	67	276	1,520,000
Hiroo Kawai	67	71	71	67	276	1,520,000
Tetsuji Hiratsuka	68	71	66	71	276	1,520,000
Toru Taniguchi	71	70	69	67	277	1,140,000
Yoshikazu Haku	69	69	71	68	277	1,140,000
Sushi Ishigaki	69	66	73	69	277	1,140,000
Prayad Marksaeng	69	70	69	69	277	1,140,000
Satoru Hirota	71	70	71	65	277	1,140,000
Tatsuya Mitsuhashi	71	70	67	69	277	1,140,000
Tadahiro Takayama	71	70	69	68	278	743,333
Yusaku Miyazato	72	67	70	69	278	743,333

	SCORES			TOTAL	MONEY
Tadahisa Inoue	72	69	70	67	278	743,333
Frankie Minoza	68	72	71	67	278	743,333
Yoichi Shimizu	73	68	67	70	278	743,333
Wayne Perske	70	71	67	70	278	743,333
Tomohiro Kondo	71	69	72	66	278	743,333
Mamo Osanai	72	67	68	71	278	743,333
Paul Sheehan	70	63	73	72	278	743,333

Fujisankei Classic

Fujizakura Country Club, Fujikawaguchiko, Yamanashi
Par 35-36–71; 7,427 yards
(Event reduced to 54 holes—rain.)

August 30-September 2
purse, ¥150,000,000

	SCORES			TOTAL	MONEY
Hideto Tanihara	67	71	67	205	¥22,500,000
Prayad Marksaeng	68	70	70	208	11,250,000
Masaya Tomida	67	74	68	209	7,650,000
Mitsuhiro Tateyama	74	66	70	210	5,400,000
Lee Seung-ho	72	70	69	211	4,087,500
Nobuhito Sato	70	72	69	211	4,087,500
Tomohiro Kondo	69	69	73	211	4,087,500
Toru Taniguchi	71	73	68	212	3,183,750
David Smail	70	73	69	212	3,183,750
Yoshikazu Haku	67	76	69	212	3,183,750
Steven Conran	71	73	69	213	2,385,000
Naoya Takemoto	67	76	70	213	2,385,000
Chawalit Plaphol	70	73	70	213	2,385,000
Hiroyuki Fujita	71	68	74	213	2,385,000
Shingo Katayama	70	75	69	214	1,569,375
Keiichiro Fukabori	71	74	69	214	1,569,375
Kenichi Kuboya	72	72	70	214	1,569,375
Fumihiro Ebine	71	74	69	214	1,569,375
Brendan Jones	75	69	70	214	1,569,375
Kaname Yokoo	70	74	70	214	1,569,375
Hiroo Kawai	73	71	70	214	1,569,375
*Ryo Ishikawa	70	71	73	214	
Tadahisa Inoue	71	71	72	214	1,569,375
Hajime Meshiai	71	74	70	215	950,625
Shinichi Yokota	73	71	71	215	950,625
Prom Meesawat	75	69	71	215	950,625
Hidemasa Hoshino	75	71	69	215	950,625
Kazuhiko Hosokawa	71	72	72	215	950,625
Yui Ueda	71	72	72	215	950,625
Kim Hyung-tae	72	74	69	215	950,625
Ryuichi Oda	71	76	68	215	950,625

Suntory Open

Sobu Country Club, Inzai, Chiba
Par 35-35–70; 7,143 yards
(Second round cancelled—rain.)

September 6-9
purse, ¥100,000,000

	SCORES			TOTAL	MONEY
Hideto Tanihara	65	71	66	202	¥15,000,000
Toru Taniguchi	65	68	71	204	7,500,000
Brendan Jones	69	69	68	206	5,100,000

	SCORES			TOTAL	MONEY
Toyokazu Fujishima	71	72	64	207	2,812,500
Yasuharu Imano	71	69	67	207	2,812,500
Paul Sheehan	66	71	70	207	2,812,500
Kazuhiko Hosokawa	68	70	69	207	2,812,500
Tatsuya Mitsuhashi	68	68	71	207	2,812,500
Craig Parry	71	70	67	208	1,890,000
Kim Hyung-tae	71	71	66	208	1,890,000
Yoshiaki Mano	71	69	68	208	1,890,000
Daisuke Maruyama	71	69	68	208	1,890,000
Lee Dong-hwan	71	71	67	209	1,227,857
Frankie Minoza	67	72	70	209	1,227,857
Thammanoon Srirot	71	68	70	209	1,227,857
Cho Min-gyu	66	73	70	209	1,227,857
Hiroyuki Fujita	67	70	72	209	1,227,857
Prom Meesawat	69	68	72	209	1,227,857
Shigeki Maruyama	68	68	73	209	1,227,857
Lee Seung-ho	70	72	68	210	855,000
Nobuhito Sato	70	70	70	210	855,000
Katsuyoshi Tomori	70	69	71	210	855,000
Takao Nogami	72	72	66	210	855,000
Hidezumi Shirakata	70	72	69	211	660,000
Koumei Oda	69	73	69	211	660,000
Tatsuhiko Takahashi	73	66	72	211	660,000
Prayad Marksaeng	74	70	67	211	660,000

ANA Open

Sapporo Golf Club, Wattsu Course,
Kitahiroshima, Hokkaido
Par 36-35–71; 7,017 yards

September 13-16
purse, ¥100,000,000

	SCORES				TOTAL	MONEY
Norio Shinozaki	68	70	70	69	277	¥20,000,000
Chawalit Plaphol	69	67	72	69	277	8,400,000
Yasuharu Imano	65	71	71	70	277	8,400,000
(Shinozaki defeated Imano on second and Chawalit on fifth playoff hole.)						
Hidemasa Hoshino	70	69	72	67	278	4,400,000
Ryuichi Oda	68	68	73	69	278	4,400,000
Keiichiro Fukabori	66	69	75	69	279	3,192,500
Hiroshi Iwata	69	73	67	70	279	3,192,500
Tatsuya Mitsuhashi	69	70	70	70	279	3,192,500
Nobuhiro Masuda	72	68	68	71	279	3,192,500
Kazuhiko Hosokawa	69	72	71	68	280	2,420,000
Hideto Tanihara	70	66	73	71	280	2,420,000
Tetsuji Hiratsuka	69	67	73	71	280	2,420,000
Toshimitsu Izawa	69	67	75	70	281	1,686,666
Tatsuhiko Takahashi	67	68	75	71	281	1,686,666
Shingo Katayama	71	70	69	71	281	1,686,666
Achi Sato	72	68	69	72	281	1,686,666
Takuya Taniguchi	70	66	72	73	281	1,686,666
Katsumasa Miyamoto	70	71	68	72	281	1,686,666
Tsuneyuki Nakajima	72	69	73	68	282	1,180,000
Yoshikazu Haku	70	71	69	72	282	1,180,000
Kiyoshi Murota	68	68	73	73	282	1,180,000
Shinichi Yokota	65	74	69	74	282	1,180,000
Sushi Ishigaki	65	73	69	75	282	1,180,000
Choi Joon-woo	70	72	71	70	283	900,000
Kaname Yokoo	71	70	72	70	283	900,000
Paul Sheehan	70	69	71	73	283	900,000

Coca-Cola Tokai Classic

Miyoshi Country Club, West Course, Miyoshi, Aichi
Par 35-36–71; 7,240 yards

September 27-30
purse, ¥120,000,000

	SCORES				TOTAL	MONEY
Camilo Villegas	68	72	71	71	282	¥24,000,000
Toyokazu Fujishima	70	70	70	72	282	12,000,000
(Villegas defeated Fujishima on second playoff hole.)						
Yusaku Miyazato	70	68	74	71	283	8,160,000
Makoto Inoue	71	70	70	73	284	5,760,000
Tetsuya Haraguchi	69	71	74	72	286	4,560,000
Shingo Katayama	72	69	70	75	286	4,560,000
Katsunori Kuwabara	69	74	71	73	287	3,668,000
Eddie Lee	70	70	74	73	287	3,668,000
Kim Hyung-tae	70	74	69	74	287	3,668,000
Yasuharu Imano	70	75	71	72	288	2,904,000
Norio Shinozaki	70	70	75	73	288	2,904,000
Masaya Tomida	69	71	75	73	288	2,904,000
Kaname Yokoo	72	71	73	73	289	2,424,000
Toshimitsu Izawa	75	73	72	70	290	2,064,000
Kiyoshi Miyazato	74	73	70	73	290	2,064,000
Tatsuhiko Takahashi	69	74	72	75	290	2,064,000
Liang Wen-chong	76	68	77	70	291	1,612,800
Koumei Oda	75	72	73	71	291	1,612,800
Ryuichi Oda	73	74	73	71	291	1,612,800
Hideki Kase	74	71	75	71	291	1,612,800
Shoichi Ideguchi	72	70	76	73	291	1,612,800
Hiroshi Iwata	73	75	73	71	292	1,188,000
Shigeru Nonaka	74	74	73	71	292	1,188,000
Tadahisa Inoue	73	75	74	70	292	1,188,000
Kiyoshi Maita	71	71	75	75	292	1,188,000

Japan Open

Sagamihara Golf Club, East Course, Sagamihara, Kanagawa
Par 36-36–72; 7,259 yards

October 11-14
purse, ¥200,000,000

	SCORES				TOTAL	MONEY
Toru Taniguchi	75	70	72	66	283	¥40,000,000
Shingo Katayama	70	71	72	72	285	22,000,000
Keiichiro Fukabori	70	74	71	71	286	15,400,000
Hiroyuki Fujita	75	71	71	70	287	10,000,000
Kaname Yokoo	68	71	76	74	289	8,400,000
Prayad Marksaeng	77	72	73	68	290	6,500,000
David Smail	75	70	75	70	290	6,500,000
Koumei Oda	71	71	69	80	291	5,200,000
Takuya Taniguchi	74	69	76	74	293	4,100,000
Hideto Tanihara	71	73	75	74	293	4,100,000
Hiroshi Iwata	74	76	73	71	294	2,980,000
Tomohiro Kondo	75	76	71	72	294	2,980,000
Tetsuji Hiratsuka	74	73	72	75	294	2,980,000
Kiyoshi Miyazato	70	73	74	77	294	2,980,000
Hidemasa Hoshino	70	76	75	74	295	2,220,000
Liang Wen-chong	72	70	79	74	295	2,220,000
Michio Matsumura	72	71	75	77	295	2,220,000
Kenichi Kuboya	80	71	75	70	296	1,740,000
Wayne Perske	77	71	77	71	296	1,740,000
Azuma Yano	75	73	77	71	296	1,740,000
Yasuharu Imano	77	71	76	72	296	1,740,000

	SCORES				TOTAL	MONEY
Norio Shinozaki	75	70	78	73	296	1,740,000
*Yuta Ikeda	71	75	77	73	296	
Taichi Teshima	75	76	72	73	296	1,740,000
Lee Seung-ho	71	76	74	75	296	1,740,000
Kiyoshi Murota	72	71	74	79	296	1,740,000

Bridgestone Open

Sodegaura Country Club, Chiba
Par 36-36–72; 7,138 yards

October 18-21
purse, ¥110,000,000

	SCORES				TOTAL	MONEY
Shingo Katayama	68	67	67	68	270	¥22,000,000
Keiichiro Fukabori	67	67	70	67	271	7,920,000
Tomohiro Kondo	65	72	66	68	271	7,920,000
Steven Conran	71	68	64	68	271	7,920,000
Yasuharu Imano	69	67	66	70	272	4,400,000
David Smail	70	66	70	67	273	3,795,000
Hiroyuki Fujita	67	71	66	69	273	3,795,000
Toshimitsu Izawa	71	67	69	67	274	3,113,000
Yusaku Miyazato	68	71	68	67	274	3,113,000
Hideto Tanihara	71	68	67	68	274	3,113,000
Chris Campbell	71	66	70	68	275	2,662,000
Hidemasa Hoshino	74	68	68	66	276	2,002,000
Chawalit Plaphol	68	72	69	67	276	2,002,000
Makoto Inoue	67	70	71	68	276	2,002,000
Scott Laycock	67	72	69	68	276	2,002,000
Naoya Takemoto	74	67	66	69	276	2,002,000
Prayad Marksaeng	68	66	72	70	276	2,002,000
Lee Dong-hwan	71	72	66	68	277	1,298,000
Lin Keng-chi	71	71	67	68	277	1,298,000
Nozomi Kawahara	71	66	71	69	277	1,298,000
Yoshinobu Tsukada	70	69	69	69	277	1,298,000
Toru Taniguchi	71	70	67	69	277	1,298,000
Peter Senior	67	70	67	73	277	1,298,000
Nobuhito Sato	71	64	68	74	277	1,298,000
Hiroshi Iwata	75	66	70	67	278	858,000
Kiyoshi Miyazato	68	70	72	68	278	858,000
Masaya Tomida	71	68	72	67	278	858,000
Chang Ik-je	67	70	71	70	278	858,000
Tetsuji Hiratsuka	75	68	69	66	278	858,000
Lee Seung-ho	71	69	67	71	278	858,000
Takuya Taniguchi	68	72	66	72	278	858,000

ABC Championship

ABC Golf Club, Kato, Hyogo
Par 36-36–72; 7,217 yards

October 25-28
purse, ¥120,000,000

	SCORES				TOTAL	MONEY
Frankie Minoza	69	64	71	70	274	¥24,000,000
Lee Dong-hwan	69	65	74	66	274	12,000,000
(Minoza defeated Lee on first playoff hole.)						
Shingo Katayama	71	68	66	70	275	8,160,000
Koumei Oda	68	73	69	66	276	4,960,000
David Smail	70	68	69	69	276	4,960,000
Hiroyuki Fujita	67	66	70	73	276	4,960,000

	SCORES				TOTAL	MONEY
S.K. Ho	68	70	70	69	277	3,960,000
Tomohiro Kondo	70	70	70	68	278	3,273,000
Kouki Idoki	69	70	69	70	278	3,273,000
Kim Jong-duk	70	65	72	71	278	3,273,000
Chawalit Plaphol	72	68	68	70	278	3,273,000
Kazuhiko Hosokawa	69	73	70	67	279	2,115,428
Toru Taniguchi	67	70	74	68	279	2,115,428
Kiyoshi Maita	71	70	70	68	279	2,115,428
Takao Nogami	70	67	73	69	279	2,115,428
Prayad Marksaeng	69	69	71	70	279	2,115,428
Hideto Tanihara	70	67	70	72	279	2,115,428
Jun Kikuchi	68	70	67	74	279	2,115,428
Katsumasa Miyamoto	67	70	74	69	280	1,368,000
Masaya Tomida	70	73	68	69	280	1,368,000
Toshinori Muto	72	67	72	69	280	1,368,000
Hiroo Kawai	72	68	71	69	280	1,368,000
Nobuhito Sato	71	68	70	71	280	1,368,000
Kaname Yokoo	71	69	69	71	280	1,368,000
Takuya Taniguchi	71	69	72	69	281	913,500
Hidezumi Shirakata	69	73	70	69	281	913,500
Yoshikazu Haku	71	70	72	68	281	913,500
Michio Matsumura	71	67	73	70	281	913,500
Steven Conran	72	70	69	70	281	913,500
Brendan Jones	68	70	72	71	281	913,500
Tadahiro Takayama	72	69	69	71	281	913,500
Kenichi Kuboya	68	67	74	72	281	913,500

Mitsui Sumitomo Visa Taiheiyo Masters

Taiheiyo Golf Club, Gotemba Course, Gotemba, Shizuoka November 8-11
Par 36-36–72; 7,246 yards purse, ¥150,000,000

	SCORES				TOTAL	MONEY
Brendan Jones	67	68	69	70	274	¥30,000,000
Toru Taniguchi	67	66	74	68	275	15,000,000
Adam Scott	67	69	70	71	277	10,200,000
Geoff Ogilvy	71	68	73	66	278	6,600,000
Chris Campbell	71	68	70	69	278	6,600,000
Hiroyuki Fujita	72	68	73	67	280	4,788,750
David Smail	71	69	71	69	280	4,788,750
Steven Conran	70	69	69	72	280	4,788,750
Takuya Taniguchi	70	70	69	71	280	4,788,750
Tomohiro Kondo	73	67	72	69	281	3,480,000
Kenichi Kuboya	71	69	71	70	281	3,480,000
Daisuke Maruyama	71	67	72	71	281	3,480,000
Shingo Katayama	73	67	70	71	281	3,480,000
Hidezumi Shirakata	70	70	73	69	282	2,430,000
S.K. Ho	71	69	73	69	282	2,430,000
Hiroshi Iwata	71	70	72	69	282	2,430,000
Tetsuji Hiratsuka	68	70	73	71	282	2,430,000
Satoru Hirota	71	71	69	71	282	2,430,000
Nozomi Kawahara	72	74	67	70	283	1,491,818
Gregory Meyer	72	67	74	70	283	1,491,818
Tatsuhiko Takahashi	67	71	74	71	283	1,491,818
Yui Ueda	73	69	70	71	283	1,491,818
Hideto Tanihara	74	69	69	71	283	1,491,818
Tetsuya Haraguchi	68	71	72	72	283	1,491,818
Nobuo Serizawa	70	71	70	72	283	1,491,818
Kiyoshi Maita	69	71	71	72	283	1,491,818
Hiroo Kawai	68	69	73	73	283	1,491,818

	SCORES				TOTAL	MONEY
Koumei Oda	67	72	71	73	283	1,491,818
Toru Suzuki	70	69	70	74	283	1,491,818

Dunlop Phoenix

Phoenix Country Club, Miyazaki
Par 35-35–70; 6,919 yards

November 15-18
purse, ¥200,000,000

	SCORES				TOTAL	MONEY
Ian Poulter	65	68	67	69	269	¥40,000,000
Gonzalo Fernandez-Castano	66	69	69	68	272	20,000,000
Shingo Katayama	67	67	71	68	273	11,600,000
Luke Donald	69	66	67	71	273	11,600,000
Brandt Snedeker	70	70	68	67	275	7,600,000
Padraig Harrington	68	65	73	69	275	7,600,000
Nobuhito Sato	68	73	67	68	276	6,113,333
Jeev Milkha Singh	68	68	70	70	276	6,113,333
Daisuke Maruyama	67	67	70	72	276	6,113,333
S.K. Ho	67	70	70	70	277	4,840,000
Katsumasa Miyamoto	68	72	67	70	277	4,840,000
Shigeki Maruyama	69	69	67	72	277	4,840,000
Tomohiro Kondo	68	72	70	68	278	3,840,000
Henrik Stenson	69	69	69	71	278	3,840,000
Mamo Osanai	68	72	69	70	279	3,140,000
Craig Parry	71	66	70	72	279	3,140,000
Hideto Tanihara	68	71	68	72	279	3,140,000
Takashi Kanemoto	68	72	67	72	279	3,140,000
Lee Dong-hwan	70	69	72	69	280	2,600,000
Brendan Jones	69	67	71	73	280	2,600,000
Yusaku Miyazato	68	71	72	70	281	2,120,000
Paul Sheehan	70	69	74	68	281	2,120,000
Kim Kyung-tae	65	71	72	73	281	2,120,000
Toshinori Muto	65	71	70	75	281	2,120,000
Hiroyuki Fujita	68	71	73	70	282	1,680,000
David Smail	69	68	73	72	282	1,680,000
Yasuharu Imano	67	68	73	74	282	1,680,000
Kaname Yokoo	69	69	70	74	282	1,680,000

Casio World Open

Kochi Kuroshio Country Club, Geisei, Kochi
Par 36-36–72; 7,250 yards

November 22-25
purse, ¥140,000,000

	SCORES				TOTAL	MONEY
Taichi Teshima	69	68	73	65	275	¥28,000,000
Chris Campbell	73	70	64	69	276	14,000,000
Chang Ik-je	69	67	72	69	277	9,520,000
Yusaku Miyazato	74	66	70	69	279	6,720,000
Tomohiro Kondo	70	71	72	67	280	5,600,000
Hideki Kase	76	71	69	65	281	4,469,500
Brandt Snedeker	70	70	72	69	281	4,469,500
Tateo Ozaki	69	72	70	70	281	4,469,500
Toyokazu Fujishima	71	68	71	71	281	4,469,500
Ryuji Imada	70	70	73	69	282	3,248,000
Frankie Minoza	73	70	68	71	282	3,248,000
Hiroshi Iwata	74	68	68	72	282	3,248,000
Toru Taniguchi	69	69	70	74	282	3,248,000

	SCORES			TOTAL	MONEY
Azuma Yano	76 70 70 67			283	2,478,000
Takashi Kanemoto	75 70 70 68			283	2,478,000
Katsumune Imai	70 73 71 70			284	1,946,000
Gregory Meyer	72 74 68 70			284	1,946,000
Toshimitsu Izawa	76 70 68 70			284	1,946,000
Kenichi Kuboya	72 67 74 71			284	1,946,000
Tatsuhiko Takahashi	73 68 71 72			284	1,946,000
Dinesh Chand	71 71 70 72			284	1,946,000
Naoya Takemoto	77 69 70 69			285	1,349,600
David Smail	73 69 73 70			285	1,349,600
Hidemasa Hoshino	71 74 70 70			285	1,349,600
Kiyoshi Miyazato	75 70 70 70			285	1,349,600
Makoto Inoue	75 71 67 72			285	1,349,600

Golf Nippon Series JT Cup

Tokyo Yomiuri Country Club, Tokyo
Par 35-35–70; 7,016 yards

November 29-December 2
purse, ¥100,000,000

	SCORES			TOTAL	MONEY
Brendan Jones	70 70 68 61			269	¥30,000,000
Toru Taniguchi	69 69 67 65			270	13,700,000
David Smail	73 67 66 65			271	5,120,000
Hiroshi Iwata	69 69 65 68			271	5,120,000
Jeev Milkha Singh	69 68 66 68			271	5,120,000
Liang Wen-chong	67 73 65 66			271	5,120,000
Hideto Tanihara	69 71 68 64			272	3,200,000
Koumei Oda	70 71 65 66			272	3,200,000
Keiichiro Fukabori	70 71 65 67			273	2,700,000
Hirofumi Miyase	69 68 68 68			273	2,700,000
Prayad Marksaeng	70 67 68 68			273	2,700,000
Tetsuji Hiratsuka	69 70 72 63			274	2,100,000
Yusaku Miyazato	71 71 69 63			274	2,100,000
Tomohiro Kondo	73 69 67 65			274	2,100,000
Shingo Katayama	66 66 75 69			276	1,700,000
Hiroyuki Fujita	70 70 65 71			276	1,700,000
Satoru Hirota	69 71 71 66			277	1,500,000
Frankie Minoza	72 69 69 67			277	1,500,000
Yasuharu Imano	70 69 71 69			279	1,300,000
Steven Conran	71 72 65 71			279	1,300,000
Taichi Teshima	71 70 67 72			280	1,150,000
Norio Shinozaki	72 71 72 68			283	1,050,000
Yui Ueda	72 72 76 66			286	1,000,000
*Ryo Ishikawa	69 74 73 71			287	
Jun Kikuchi	71 74 72 70			287	960,000
Katsumasa Miyamoto	74 78 69 74			295	940,000

Australasian Tour

Jacob's Creek Open

Kooyonga Golf Club, Lockleys, South Australia
Par 36-36–72; 6,711 yards

February 15-18
purse, US$600,000

	SCORES				TOTAL	MONEY
Scott Sterling	70	69	66	71	276	A$137,862
David Lutterus	64	75	66	72	277	78,121.80
Marc Leishman	70	69	70	69	278	44,230.72
Brendan Jones	71	68	68	71	278	44,230.72
Craig Parry	71	64	73	71	279	27,572.40
Brett Rumford	66	69	73	71	279	27,572.40
Peter Senior	68	68	69	74	279	27,572.40
Nick Flanagan	70	70	71	69	280	20,679.30
Brad Ott	66	70	70	74	280	20,679.30
Peter Wilson	67	72	69	72	280	20,679.30
Greg Chalmers	67	69	71	74	281	15,318
Andrew Pitt	67	70	71	73	281	15,318
Roland Thatcher	71	69	70	71	281	15,318
Brad Fritsch	69	70	72	71	282	12,101.22
Aron Price	72	68	71	71	282	12,101.22
David Smail	70	68	72	72	282	12,101.22
Anthony Brown	67	70	71	75	283	8,800.19
Jason Caron	70	68	74	71	283	8,800.19
Gary Christian	72	69	70	72	283	8,800.19
Greg Kraft	72	70	69	72	283	8,800.19
Roger Tambellini	69	68	72	74	283	8,800.19
Gabriel Hjertstedt	71	67	69	77	284	7,429.23
Cameron Percy	69	70	70	75	284	7,429.23
Jimmy Walker	74	68	74	68	284	7,429.23
Michael Wright	72	66	75	71	284	7,429.23

HSBC New Zealand PGA Championship

Clearwater Resort, Christchurch, New Zealand
Par 36-36–72; 7,137 yards

February 22-25
purse, US$600,000

	SCORES				TOTAL	MONEY
Nicholas Thompson	69	73	70	68	280	A$137,862
David Morland	70	72	70	68	280	78,121.80
(Thompson defeated Morland on first playoff hole.)						
Michael Letzig	69	68	79	65	281	44,230.72
Lee Williamson	70	69	73	69	281	44,230.72
James Nitties	69	70	72	71	282	30,636
Mark Brown	71	75	66	71	283	23,742.90
Jason Day	73	73	68	69	283	23,742.90
Ryan Howison	65	75	70	73	283	23,742.90
Sal Spallone	69	68	75	71	283	23,742.90
Chris Downes	70	72	78	64	284	17,105.10
Peter Fowler	69	73	72	70	284	17,105.10
Marc Leishman	71	75	69	69	284	17,105.10
Greg Chalmers	73	71	73	68	285	13,020.30
Chez Reavie	67	71	76	71	285	13,020.30
Patrick Sheehan	71	70	73	71	285	13,020.30
Brad Adamonis	73	71	73	69	286	10,058.82

	SCORES				TOTAL	MONEY
Nick Flanagan	70	73	73	70	286	10,058.82
Tim Wilkinson	72	70	72	72	286	10,058.82
Craig Parry	72	71	71	73	287	8,284.48
Peter Senior	66	71	75	75	287	8,284.48
David Smail	72	71	73	71	287	8,284.48
Scott Dunlap	71	72	73	72	288	6,838.39
Hunter Haas	69	76	72	71	288	6,838.39
David Hearn	68	75	77	68	288	6,838.39
Gabriel Hjertstedt	72	73	73	70	288	6,838.39
Brendan Jones	71	70	78	69	288	6,838.39
Jon Mills	74	68	74	72	288	6,838.39
Phil Tataurangi	71	68	76	73	288	6,838.39

Johnnie Walker Classic

See Asia/Japan Tours chapter.

MasterCard Masters

Huntingdale Golf Club, Melbourne, Victoria
Par 36-36–72; 6,980 yards

November 22-25
purse, A$1,500,000

	SCORES				TOTAL	MONEY
Aaron Baddeley	70	66	69	70	275	A$270,000
Daniel Chopra	69	70	65	71	275	153,000
(Baddeley defeated Chopra on fourth playoff hole.)						
Stuart Appleby	69	71	68	69	277	101,250
Peter O'Malley	72	72	67	67	278	72,000
Dave Horsey	77	65	72	65	279	54,000
Peter Lonard	70	71	68	70	279	54,000
Rod Pampling	69	71	67	72	279	54,000
Steven Jeffress	73	72	69	66	280	42,000
Kurt Barnes	69	71	65	75	280	42,000
Andrew Tampion	70	74	68	69	281	30,600
Marcus Fraser	72	69	70	70	281	30,600
Anthony Summers	71	72	67	71	281	30,600
Robert Allenby	67	68	73	73	281	30,600
Richard Finch	70	71	67	73	281	30,600
Simon Khan	75	69	72	66	282	18,825
Martin Erlandsson	73	72	70	67	282	18,825
John Senden	73	69	71	69	282	18,825
Ross McGowan	74	71	68	69	282	18,825
Terry Pilkadaris	71	68	72	71	282	18,825
Scott Strange	70	69	72	71	282	18,825
Rory McIlroy	70	69	70	73	282	18,825
Peter Senior	72	70	71	70	283	14,700
Adam Crawford	72	69	71	71	283	14,700
Jarmo Sandelin	74	70	71	69	284	12,300
Damien McGrane	72	71	69	72	284	12,300
Rick Kulacz	70	69	72	73	284	12,300
Michael Long	69	74	68	73	284	12,300
Stephen Leaney	70	72	68	74	284	12,300
Ewan Porter	70	73	67	74	284	12,300
Edward Rush	71	73	73	68	285	9,042.85
Aaron Black	70	72	73	70	285	9,042.85
Alexander Noren	72	72	71	70	285	9,042.85
Peter Baker	68	72	74	71	285	9,042.85
Adam Bland	75	70	69	71	285	9,042.85
Robert Dinwiddie	74	71	68	72	285	9,042.85
Heath Reed	73	71	68	73	285	9,042.85

	SCORES				TOTAL	MONEY
Paul Marantz	69	75	74	68	286	7,350
Peter Wilson	72	73	72	69	286	7,350
Peter Whiteford	73	71	72	70	286	7,350
Shane Baxter	72	70	70	74	286	7,350
Ashley Hall	77	68	73	69	287	5,550
Fredrik Andersson	68	75	74	70	287	5,550
Tim Wood	71	73	73	70	287	5,550
David Bransdon	79	66	71	71	287	5,550
Paul Sheehan	72	73	71	71	287	5,550
Marcus Cain	75	70	70	72	287	5,550
Matthew Ecob	70	75	68	74	287	5,550
Matthew Zions	70	70	71	76	287	5,550
Josh Carmichael	72	70	74	72	288	3,900
Terry Price	72	72	72	72	288	3,900
Richard Green	72	73	69	74	288	3,900
Anthony Brown	74	71	73	71	289	2,906.25
Scott Laycock	75	70	72	72	289	2,906.25
Michael Wright	74	71	71	73	289	2,906.25
Chris Downes	72	72	70	75	289	2,906.25
Mahal Pearce	71	74	73	72	290	2,490
Nick Flanagan	70	73	74	73	290	2,490
Simon Furneaux	70	71	73	76	290	2,490
Peter Fowler	74	71	73	73	291	2,385
Didier De Vooght	74	70	73	74	291	2,385
Rhys Davies	70	75	72	74	291	2,385
Ryan Hammond	74	70	76	72	292	2,325
Alistair Presnell	71	70	79	73	293	2,280
Stuart Manley	71	73	76	73	293	2,280
Paul Spargo	71	72	75	76	294	2,220
Luke Hickmott	70	71	75	78	294	2,220
Jarrod Moseley	74	71	76	74	295	2,145
Michael Curtain	74	71	71	79	295	2,145

Michael Hill New Zealand Open

The Hills Golf Club, Queenstown, New Zealand
Par 36-36–72; 7,243 yards

November 29-December 2
purse, NZ$1,500,000

	SCORES				TOTAL	MONEY
Richard Finch	73	65	64	72	274	A$229,104
Paul Sheehan	68	67	73	69	277	107,869.80
Steven Bowditch	69	65	71	72	277	107,869.80
Craig Parry	68	74	70	66	278	49,639.20
Alexander Noren	76	69	67	66	278	49,639.20
Steven Jeffress	71	68	72	67	278	49,639.20
Matthew Millar	72	71	68	67	278	49,639.20
Peter Fowler	69	75	62	73	279	36,911.20
Oliver Fisher	70	69	72	69	280	33,092.80
Matthew Zions	72	73	66	69	280	33,092.80
Robert Dinwiddie	72	72	66	71	281	28,001.60
Gary Simpson	69	69	76	68	282	22,592.20
Josh Geary	75	67	70	70	282	22,592.20
Adam Bland	71	74	67	70	282	22,592.20
Michael Curtain	71	70	70	71	282	22,592.20
Anthony Brown	71	70	72	70	283	14,882.66
Gareth Paddison	70	72	71	70	283	14,882.66
Matthew Ballard	72	70	70	71	283	14,882.66
Andrew Tschudin	70	71	70	72	283	14,882.66
Scott Gardiner	72	72	67	72	283	14,882.66
Kyron Sullivan	72	68	69	74	283	14,882.66
Rick Kulacz	71	69	68	75	283	14,882.66

	SCORES				TOTAL	MONEY
Doug Holloway	72	71	74	67	284	10,691.52
Tony Christie	71	73	71	69	284	10,691.52
Bob Charles	75	68	71	70	284	10,691.52
Peter Whiteford	70	68	75	71	284	10,691.52
Michael Wright	71	69	72	72	284	10,691.52
Marc Leishman	69	70	71	74	284	10,691.52
Ewan Porter	72	66	70	76	284	10,691.52
Shane Baxter	71	73	73	68	285	7,806.50
Marcus Fraser	73	69	73	70	285	7,806.50
Anthony Summers	73	71	70	71	285	7,806.50
Dave Horsey	74	70	70	71	285	7,806.50
Terry Pilkadaris	77	68	69	71	285	7,806.50
Aaron Townsend	74	71	67	73	285	7,806.50
Paul Spargo	75	70	71	70	286	6,236.72
Matthew Woods	68	74	73	71	286	6,236.72
Didier De Vooght	73	70	72	71	286	6,236.72
Damien McGrane	72	72	69	73	286	6,236.72
Brenden Stuart	69	73	70	74	286	6,236.72
Mahal Pearce	71	70	69	76	286	6,236.72
Jamie Donaldson	70	74	77	66	287	5,218.48
Michael Long	69	67	76	75	287	5,218.48
Martin Doyle	71	72	78	67	288	4,200.24
*Danny Lee	73	71	75	69	288	
Jamie Little	72	73	71	72	288	4,200.24
Alvaro Velasco	73	70	72	73	288	4,200.24
Josh Carmichael	77	67	70	74	288	4,200.24
Kim Felton	71	73	70	74	288	4,200.24
Andrew McKenzie	71	69	72	76	288	4,200.24
Marco Soffietti	75	70	73	71	289	2,927.44
Rodney Booth	69	73	72	75	289	2,927.44
Daniel Chopra	70	71	70	78	289	2,927.44
Ben Wharton	70	74	74	72	290	2,195.58
David Bransdon	69	73	75	73	290	2,195.58
*Nick Gillespie	78	67	72	73	290	
Michael Sim	69	76	72	73	290	2,195.58
Ally Mellor	72	73	71	74	290	2,195.58
Richard Lee	70	71	78	72	291	1,998.29
Steven Jones	70	73	76	72	291	1,998.29
Peter Nolan	71	74	74	72	291	1,998.29
Scott Strange	75	70	73	73	291	1,998.29
Steven Jeppesen	72	72	73	74	291	1,998.29
Paul Marantz	69	76	72	74	291	1,998.29
Craig Scott	75	67	73	76	291	1,998.29
Luke Hickmott	70	73	75	74	292	1,883.74
Phil Tataurangi	74	71	68	79	292	1,883.74
Jarrod Moseley	73	71	75	74	293	1,820.10
Terry Price	73	71	70	79	293	1,820.10
David Hutton	75	69	76	74	294	1,743.73
Ricky Schmidt	75	70	75	74	294	1,743.73
Lucas Parsons	73	71	74	78	296	1,705.55
Lee Hunt	76	69	79	73	297	1,680.10
Henry Epstein	74	69	74	82	299	1,654.64

Cadbury Schweppes Australian PGA Championship

Hyatt Regency Resort, Coolum Beach, Queensland
Par 36-36–72; 6,851 yards

December 6-9
purse, A$1,400,000

	SCORES				TOTAL	MONEY
Peter Lonard	66	69	68	65	268	A$252,000
David Smail	67	69	67	68	271	142,800

	SCORES				TOTAL	MONEY
Greg Chalmers	72	70	66	65	273	72,566.66
Scott Laycock	69	67	71	66	273	72,566.66
Michael Sim	65	73	65	70	273	72,566.66
Adam Scott	67	67	72	68	274	47,600
Adam Bland	68	70	65	71	274	47,600
Nathan Green	71	69	71	64	275	39,200
Richard Green	66	74	66	69	275	39,200
J.B. Holmes	66	73	70	67	276	31,266.66
Michael Long	68	74	66	68	276	31,266.66
Rory Sabbatini	68	67	67	74	276	31,266.66
Brett Rumford	73	69	68	67	277	24,500
Stephen Leaney	72	70	65	70	277	24,500
Peter O'Malley	72	69	69	68	278	18,662
Brad Kennedy	70	69	70	69	278	18,662
Cameron Percy	70	66	70	72	278	18,662
Scott Gardiner	70	69	67	72	278	18,662
Jason Gore	70	69	64	75	278	18,662
David McKenzie	69	71	70	69	279	14,490
Ryan Haller	70	70	68	71	279	14,490
Nick O'Hern	70	72	65	72	279	14,490
Steven Conran	70	68	68	73	279	14,490
James Nitties	72	71	71	66	280	13,020
Wayne Grady	74	69	68	69	280	13,020

MFS Australian Open

Australian Golf Club, Sydney, New South Wales
Par 36-36–72; 7,231 yards

December 13-16
purse, A$1,750,000

	SCORES				TOTAL	MONEY
Craig Parry	74	64	70	69	277	A$315,000
Lee Won-joon	70	70	72	66	278	126,875
Brandt Snedeker	69	70	70	69	278	126,875
Nick O'Hern	70	66	72	70	278	126,875
Stuart Appleby	71	68	68	72	279	66,500
James Nitties	71	66	69	73	279	66,500
Greg Chalmers	69	72	72	67	280	49,438
Rod Pampling	73	70	69	68	280	49,438
Ewan Porter	70	71	70	69	280	49,438
Aaron Baddeley	70	71	69	70	280	49,438
Marc Leishman	72	69	71	69	281	35,000
Paul Sheehan	72	70	69	70	281	35,000
Robert Allenby	67	70	69	75	281	35,000
Paul Marantz	68	72	77	65	282	26,425
Peter O'Malley	72	71	69	70	282	26,425
Jason Gore	73	70	68	71	282	26,425
Stephen Leaney	69	75	67	71	282	26,425
Geoff Ogilvy	68	72	73	70	283	20,344
Kane Webber	70	72	69	72	283	20,344
Kevin Stadler	73	71	73	67	284	17,500
Andrew Tampion	77	67	72	68	284	17,500
Michael Sim	72	70	72	70	284	17,500
Hiroshi Iwata	71	69	73	71	284	17,500
Jarrod Lyle	70	70	73	71	284	17,500
Matthew Jones	74	68	71	71	284	17,500

African Tours

Joburg Open

Royal Johannesburg & Kensington Golf Club,
Johannesburg, South Africa
Par 36-35–71; 7,590 yards

January 11-14
purse, €1,000,000

	SCORES				TOTAL	MONEY
Ariel Canete	66	68	65	67	266	R1,451,543
Andrew McLardy	63	72	65	68	268	1,053,170
Hennie Otto	65	67	70	67	269	632,818
Alex Haindl	68	68	66	70	272	413,026
Mark Murless	64	71	69	68	272	413,026
Edward Rush	70	67	67	69	273	293,972
Adilson da Silva	71	65	69	68	273	293,972
Edoardo Molinari	64	71	69	70	274	187,510.25
Doug McGuigan	68	67	71	68	274	187,510.25
Terry Pilkadaris	67	66	74	67	274	187,510.25
James Kingston	66	66	72	70	274	187,510.25
Keith Horne	67	71	69	68	275	136,454.40
Ulrich van den Berg	68	69	70	68	275	136,454.40
Sven Struver	65	71	68	71	275	136,454.40
Jean-Baptiste Gonnet	69	67	69	70	275	136,454.40
Alastair Forsyth	67	68	69	71	275	136,454.40
Ricardo Gonzalez	68	72	71	65	276	117,680.50
Richard Sterne	69	66	71	70	276	117,680.50
Tom Whitehouse	67	73	69	68	277	104,035
Euan Little	69	71	68	69	277	104,035
Dion Fourie	71	68	70	68	277	104,035
Charl Schwartzel	69	68	69	71	277	104,035
Louis Oosthuizen	65	69	74	69	277	104,035
David Park	65	71	69	73	278	93,869.50
Matthew Zions	67	68	71	72	278	93,869.50
Lee S. James	69	71	67	72	279	87,001
Maarten Lafeber	72	66	68	73	279	87,001
Kalle Brink	69	68	72	70	279	87,001
Benn Barham	68	70	69	73	280	77,110.40
Oliver Wilson	69	68	73	70	280	77,110.40
Justin Walters	68	69	74	69	280	77,110.40
Jan-Are Larsen	70	66	74	70	280	77,110.40
Magnus A. Carlsson	69	66	72	73	280	77,110.40
Richard Bland	68	72	72	69	281	65,021.75
Antti Ahokas	73	66	71	71	281	65,021.75
Ryan Tipping	70	69	69	73	281	65,021.75
Michiel Bothma	71	68	71	71	281	65,021.75
Garth Mulroy	69	69	71	72	281	65,021.75
Shaun Norris	69	69	72	71	281	65,021.75
Brett Liddle	69	68	70	74	281	65,021.75
Jaco Van Zyl	67	68	71	75	281	65,021.75
Des Terblanche	73	67	70	72	282	53,116.40
Andrew Curlewis	70	70	71	71	282	53,116.40
Trevor Fisher, Jr.	67	72	73	70	282	53,116.40
Raphael Eyraud	70	67	72	73	282	53,116.40
Brandon Pieters	65	71	73	73	282	53,116.40
Darren Fichardt	68	72	69	74	283	41,211
Stuart Little	74	65	72	72	283	41,211
Stuart Cage	67	72	74	70	283	41,211
Robert Wiederkehr	69	70	74	70	283	41,211

	SCORES				TOTAL	MONEY
Bobby Lincoln	67	71	70	75	283	41,211
Marc Cayeux	65	73	75	70	283	41,211
David Dixon	66	71	73	73	283	41,211
Jakobus Roos	67	65	75	76	283	41,211
Peter Kaensche	69	71	73	71	284	26,329.25
Christiaan Basson	74	66	73	71	284	26,329.25
Jamie Little	66	74	72	72	284	26,329.25
Ross Wellington	69	71	71	73	284	26,329.25
Marcus Higley	71	69	72	72	284	26,329.25
Julio Zapata	70	69	71	74	284	26,329.25
Paul Nilbrink	71	68	73	72	284	26,329.25
Patrik Sjoland	66	72	71	75	284	26,329.25
Andrew Marshall	69	69	69	77	284	26,329.25
Gareth Davies	66	71	70	77	284	26,329.25
Warren Abery	64	73	73	74	284	26,329.25
Henrik Nystrom	66	69	75	74	284	26,329.25
Jaco Ahlers	72	68	72	73	285	19,232
Mike Lamb	68	71	71	75	285	19,232
David Higgins	69	69	72	75	285	19,232
Gustavo Rojas	70	70	73	74	287	16,484.33
Vaughn Groenewald	65	74	74	74	287	16,484.33
Paul Dwyer	68	71	72	76	287	16,484.33
Grant Muller	68	72	75	73	288	12,796
Hendrik Buhrmann	72	68	73	75	288	12,796
Sion E. Bebb	69	71	76	72	288	12,796
Chris Davison	68	71	74	75	288	12,796
Robert Dinwiddie	69	69	76	74	288	12,796
Dean Lambert	68	66	76	78	288	12,796
Tyrone van Aswegen	68	72	77	72	289	11,755
Simon Nash	72	68	72	78	290	11,655
Chris Gane	65	72	75	78	290	11,655
Magnus Persson	68	67	79	76	290	11,655
Omar Sandys	70	69	75	77	291	11,555

Dimension Data Pro-Am

Gary Player Country Club: Par 36-36–72; 7,831 yards
Lost City Golf Course: Par 36-36–72; 6,983 yards
Sun City, South Africa

January 25-28
purse, R1,600,000

	SCORES				TOTAL	MONEY
Louis Oosthuizen	66	71	71	69	277	R253,600
Omar Sandys	77	68	68	65	278	184,000
Michiel Bothma	69	68	70	73	280	110,560
Albert Pistorius	72	70	69	70	281	78,560
Tyrone van Aswegen	68	70	70	74	282	60,960
Vaughn Groenewald	67	72	69	74	282	60,960
Ross McGowan	67	72	70	74	283	42,560
James Kamte	71	71	67	74	283	42,560
Ryan Tipping	71	73	73	67	284	29,760
Chris Swanepoel	67	73	71	73	284	29,760
Brandon Pieters	68	69	73	74	284	29,760
Mark Murless	68	74	67	75	284	29,760
Steve van Vuuren	72	70	72	71	285	23,626.66
Charl Schwartzel	69	71	74	71	285	23,626.66
Adilson da Silva	74	71	66	74	285	23,626.66
Alex Haindl	70	69	75	72	286	21,360
Justin Walters	73	70	71	72	286	21,360
Desvonde Botes	73	72	72	70	287	18,784
Marc Cayeux	73	70	72	72	287	18,784

	SCORES				TOTAL	MONEY
Jeff Inglis	68	73	73	73	287	18,784
Grant Veenstra	70	72	72	73	287	18,784
Grant Muller	71	70	72	74	287	18,784
James Kingston	69	68	75	76	288	16,880
Bradford Vaughan	67	72	78	71	288	16,880
David Faught	72	73	72	72	289	16,160

Nashua Masters

Wild Coast Sun Country Club, Port Edward, Natal
Par 35-35–70; 6,351 yards

February 1-4
purse, R1,200,000

	SCORES				TOTAL	MONEY
Jean Hugo	64	67	68	70	269	R190,200
Titch Moore	69	66	66	68	269	138,000
(Hugo defeated Moore on first playoff hole.)						
Andre Cruse	70	64	71	67	272	82,920
Euan Little	65	68	70	70	273	54,120
Justin Walters	67	66	68	72	273	54,120
Mark Murless	74	67	69	64	274	35,320
Tyrone van Aswegen	71	68	69	66	274	35,320
Desvonde Botes	66	70	69	69	274	35,320
Steve van Vuuren	70	69	65	71	275	24,120
Hendrik Buhrmann	66	68	69	72	275	24,120
Grant Muller	70	73	66	67	276	19,920
Ross McGowan	68	69	68	71	276	19,920
Bradford Vaughan	67	68	69	72	276	19,920
Peter Karmis	77	68	66	66	277	17,220
Alan McLean	69	74	67	67	277	17,220
Marc Cayeux	73	68	68	69	278	15,720
Kevin Stone	66	69	73	70	278	15,720
Warren Abery	71	66	71	70	278	15,720
Gerlou Roux	76	68	68	67	279	13,632
Adilson da Silva	72	72	67	68	279	13,632
Gary Thain	71	68	70	70	279	13,632
Tongoona Charamba	69	68	70	72	279	13,632
Chris Williams	71	67	69	72	279	13,632
Thomas Aiken	72	70	73	65	280	11,940
Theunis Spangenberg	71	69	71	69	280	11,940
Robert Haindl	75	70	65	70	280	11,940
Chris Swanepoel	67	68	73	72	280	11,940

Vodacom Championship

Pretoria Country Club, Pretoria, South Africa
Par 36-36–72; 7,063 yards

February 15-18
purse, R2,200,000

	SCORES				TOTAL	MONEY
Richard Sterne	73	68	68	65	274	R348,700
Louis Oosthuizen	71	67	69	67	274	253,000
(Sterne defeated Oosthuizen on second playoff hole.)						
Titch Moore	68	73	67	67	275	130,020
Marc Cayeux	71	69	67	68	275	130,020
Hennie Otto	70	66	72	68	276	77,220
Euan Little	72	72	64	68	276	77,220
Neil Schietekat	69	65	73	69	276	77,220
Charl Schwartzel	68	71	70	68	277	49,720

	SCORES				TOTAL	MONEY
James Kingston	70	70	65	72	277	49,720
Mark Murless	72	69	67	70	278	42,020
Michiel Bothma	69	72	72	66	279	34,540
Vaughn Groenewald	71	72	68	68	279	34,540
Ross McGowan	68	72	68	71	279	34,540
Brandon Pieters	67	67	70	75	279	34,540
Jakobus Roos	68	70	65	76	279	34,540
Steve van Vuuren	72	71	71	66	280	27,280
Warren Abery	73	68	70	69	280	27,280
Henk Alberts	67	71	71	71	280	27,280
Doug McGuigan	72	67	70	71	280	27,280
Darren Fichardt	71	69	69	71	280	27,280
Jason Kelly	66	73	69	72	280	27,280
Wallie Coetsee	71	71	73	66	281	23,540
James Kamte	67	73	74	67	281	23,540
Tyrone van Aswegen	73	68	72	68	281	23,540
Werner Geyer	70	71	72	69	282	20,271.42
Justin Walters	72	66	74	70	282	20,271.42
Josh Cunliffe	68	73	71	70	282	20,271.42
Eugen Marugi	72	69	70	71	282	20,271.42
Bradford Vaughan	69	73	69	71	282	20,271.42
Kieran Court	71	70	69	72	282	20,271.42
Sven Struver	72	69	69	72	282	20,271.42

Telkom PGA Championship

Country Club Johannesburg, Johannesburg, South Africa
Par 36-36–72; 7,478 yards

February 22-25
purse, R2,250,000

	SCORES				TOTAL	MONEY
Louis Oosthuizen	67	65	69	65	266	R356,625
Richard Sterne	66	68	62	71	267	258,750
Charl Schwartzel	69	64	70	65	268	132,975
Marc Cayeux	66	67	65	70	268	132,975
Desvonde Botes	64	70	71	65	270	85,725
Doug McGuigan	70	68	65	67	270	85,725
Des Terblanche	70	66	67	68	271	59,850
Bradford Vaughan	70	65	65	71	271	59,850
Michiel Bothma	67	69	66	70	272	45,225
Justin Walters	68	70	64	70	272	45,225
Thomas Aiken	70	68	64	71	273	37,350
Darren Fichardt	68	66	67	72	273	37,350
Andrew McLardy	65	66	64	78	273	37,350
Hennie Otto	70	67	68	69	274	32,850
*Branden Grace	65	68	70	71	274	
Mark Murless	69	68	71	67	275	30,600
Josh Cunliffe	72	66	68	69	275	30,600
Tyrone van Aswegen	70	71	65	69	275	30,600
Nic Henning	67	68	70	71	276	27,787.50
Divan van den Heever	65	68	70	73	276	27,787.50
Ross Wellington	70	72	70	65	277	26,325
James Kamte	68	70	71	69	278	24,075
Alan McLean	72	66	69	71	278	24,075
Wallie Coetsee	68	70	69	71	278	24,075
Warren Abery	69	70	68	71	278	24,075
Neil Schietekat	67	72	68	71	278	24,075

Mount Edgecombe Trophy

Mount Edgecombe Country Club, Kwazulu Natal, South Africa
Par 36-36–72; 6,825 yards

March 8-11
purse, R500,000

	SCORES				TOTAL	MONEY
Steve van Vuuren	68	66	72	70	276	R78,500
Tjaart van der Walt	69	69	73	66	277	43,000
Des Terblanche	65	72	69	71	277	43,000
Desvonde Botes	68	71	67	71	277	43,000
Adilson da Silva	70	71	69	68	278	23,500
Chris Williams	69	68	71	71	279	17,375
Ross Wellington	68	68	69	74	279	17,375
Dale Burraston	70	67	72	71	280	13,000
Doug McGuigan	66	69	72	73	280	13,000
Bradford Vaughan	71	69	72	69	281	10,875
Grant Muller	69	69	71	72	281	10,875
Johan Etsebeth	73	69	69	71	282	9,500
Ulrich van den Berg	70	73	68	71	282	9,500
Nico van Rensburg	68	72	66	76	282	9,500
Jeff Inglis	69	68	74	72	283	8,350
Dean Lambert	71	72	68	72	283	8,350
Warren Abery	71	72	72	69	284	7,500
Henk Alberts	70	74	71	69	284	7,500
Jakobus Roos	72	70	71	71	284	7,500
Charl Coetzee	69	71	71	74	285	6,825
Mark Murless	69	67	73	76	285	6,825
Michael du Toit	71	73	72	70	286	6,200
Andrew Curlewis	72	70	71	73	286	6,200
Lindani Ndwandwe	74	69	70	73	286	6,200
Omar Sandys	70	74	75	68	287	5,550
Ian Hutchings	73	70	73	71	287	5,550
Shaun Norris	69	68	74	76	287	5,550

Finance Bank Zambia Open

Ndola Golf Club, Ndola, Zambia
Par 37-36–73; 7,079 yards

March 30-April 1
purse, R750,000

	SCORES			TOTAL	MONEY
Steve Basson	71	66	69	206	R118,875
Lindani Ndwandwe	70	69	68	207	86,250
Neil Schietekat	68	69	71	208	51,900
Chris Swanepoel	74	65	70	209	36,825
Adilson da Silva	73	70	67	210	28,762.50
George Coetzee	72	68	70	210	28,762.50
Bradford Vaughan	70	72	69	211	20,287.50
Vaughn Groenewald	71	69	71	211	20,287.50
Ulrich van den Berg	71	68	74	213	16,200
Jacob Okello	75	70	69	214	13,106.25
Charl Coetzee	73	72	69	214	13,106.25
Chris Williams	75	69	70	214	13,106.25
Theunis Spangenberg	70	73	71	214	13,106.25
Peter Karmis	69	69	77	215	11,025
Ryan Cairns	73	71	72	216	10,275
Dean Lambert	72	69	75	216	10,275
Warren Abery	73	77	66	216	10,275
Nemanja Savic	77	66	74	217	9,525
Jakobus Roos	75	72	71	218	8,475
David Hewan	75	71	72	218	8,475

	SCORES			TOTAL	MONEY
Mark Williams	74	72	72	218	8,475
Madilitso Muthiya	78	66	74	218	8,475
Darren Holder	73	77	68	218	8,475
Merrick Bremner	73	69	76	218	8,475
Deo Akope	78	71	70	219	7,312.50
Mike Curtis	74	71	74	219	7,312.50
Tyron Roelofsz	70	72	77	219	7,312.50
Tongoona Charamba	76	74	69	219	7,312.50

Eskom Power Cup

Pecanwood Golf & Country Club, Hartbeespoortdam, South Africa   April 13-15
Par 36-36–72; 7,676 yards   purse, R400,000

	SCORES			TOTAL	MONEY
Chris Swanepoel	70	63	66	199	R63,400
Warren Abery	67	72	64	203	46,000
James Kamte	69	68	67	204	32,000
Jakobus Roos	72	68	66	206	25,200
Alex Haindl	72	67	68	207	18,800
Sean Farrell	72	69	68	209	12,933.33
Wayne de Haas	69	72	68	209	12,933.33
Trevor Fisher, Jr.	70	66	73	209	12,933.33
Jean Hugo	71	71	68	210	9,066.66
Neil Schietekat	65	75	70	210	9,066.66
Divan van den Heever	69	71	70	210	9,066.66
Henk Alberts	74	71	66	211	7,600
George Coetzee	66	74	71	211	7,600
Tongoona Charamba	67	72	72	211	7,600
Brett Liddle	71	71	70	212	6,153.33
Toto Thimba	73	68	71	212	6,153.33
Omar Sandys	69	71	72	212	6,153.33
Tyrone van Aswegen	68	71	73	212	6,153.33
Grant Veenstra	72	67	73	212	6,153.33
Gary Thain	73	63	76	212	6,153.33
Dean Lambert	73	72	68	213	5,160
Dion Fourie	72	71	70	213	5,160
Shaun Norris	74	69	70	213	5,160
Alan Michell	73	72	69	214	4,600
Bradford Vaughan	70	75	69	214	4,600
Des Terblanche	73	70	71	214	4,600

Vodacom Origins of Golf Tour at Arabella

Arabella Country Club, Hermanus, South Africa   April 18-20
Par 36-36–72; 6,976 yards   purse, R400,000

	SCORES			TOTAL	MONEY
Andrew Curlewis	68	68	71	207	R63,400
Alan Michell	71	67	69	207	46,000
(Curlewis defeated Michell on third playoff hole.)					
Warren Abery	71	69	69	209	32,000
Doug McGuigan	73	65	72	210	25,200
Shaun Norris	71	73	67	211	17,000
Hennie Otto	72	67	72	211	17,000
Gerlou Roux	75	69	68	212	12,600
Desvonde Botes	73	72	69	214	10,400

	SCORES			TOTAL	MONEY
Grant Muller	72	71	71	214	10,400
Josh Cunliffe	74	75	67	216	8,466.66
Omar Sandys	71	73	72	216	8,466.66
Tongoona Charamba	70	73	73	216	8,466.66
Dean Lambert	72	75	70	217	7,040
Alex Haindl	72	75	70	217	7,040
Mark Murless	71	75	71	217	7,040
Jean Hugo	71	72	74	217	7,040
Ian Hutchings	74	71	73	218	6,120
Michael du Toit	73	72	73	218	6,120
Jaco Ahlers	72	77	70	219	5,560
Kevin Stone	74	73	72	219	5,560
Jakobus Roos	71	72	76	219	5,560
Adilson da Silva	78	70	72	220	4,870
Nic Henning	73	74	73	220	4,870
George Coetzee	72	75	73	220	4,870
Henk Alberts	68	78	74	220	4,870

Samsung Royal Swazi Sun Open

Royal Swazi Sun Country Club, Mbabane, Swaziland
Par 36-36–72; 6,715 yards

May 2-5
purse, R600,000

	POINTS				TOTAL	MONEY
Des Terblanche	14	11	13	12	50	R94,200
James Kamte	8	14	7	19	48	69,000
George Coetzee	12	11	18	5	46	48,000
Titch Moore	2	15	13	15	45	37,800
Ian Hutchings	9	15	11	9	44	25,500
Kevin Stone	13	15	10	6	44	25,500
Grant Muller	22	7	2	12	43	18,900
Wallie Coetsee	8	17	7	10	42	15,600
Warren Abery	10	5	13	14	42	15,600
Christiaan Basson	20	7	0	13	40	13,500
Adilson da Silva	14	5	8	11	38	12,000
Mark Murless	13	6	12	7	38	12,000
Steve Basson	5	13	14	6	38	12,000
Ryan Tipping	5	10	9	13	37	10,050
Gary Thain	5	10	10	12	37	10,050
Hennie Otto	8	6	5	18	37	10,050
Hendrik Buhrmann	18	6	10	3	37	10,050
Divan van den Heever	14	6	14	2	36	9,000
Ulrich van den Berg	7	8	10	10	35	8,190
Trevor Fisher, Jr.	9	4	16	6	35	8,190
Bradford Vaughan	13	13	2	7	35	8,190
Tongoona Charamba	2	12	13	8	35	8,190
Andre Cruse	7	7	10	10	34	7,290
Henk Alberts	11	15	1	7	34	7,290
Tyrone van Aswegen	5	7	8	13	33	6,900

Vodacom Origins of Golf Tour at Pretoria

Pretoria Country Club, Pretoria, South Africa
Par 36-36–72; 7,063 yards

May 9-11
purse, R400,000

	SCORES			TOTAL	MONEY
Hennie Otto	67	65	69	201	R63,400
James Kamte	68	70	66	204	46,000
Des Terblanche	68	70	68	206	32,000
Bradford Vaughan	69	68	70	207	25,200
Andrew Curlewis	69	67	72	208	18,800
Doug McGuigan	67	70	72	209	15,200
George Coetzee	69	70	71	210	11,800
Warren Abery	68	70	72	210	11,800
Shaun Norris	73	68	70	211	9,400
Titch Moore	68	72	71	211	9,400
Vaughn Groenewald	73	66	73	212	8,400
Nico van Rensburg	71	74	68	213	7,600
Albert Pistorius	71	71	71	213	7,600
Desvonde Botes	71	69	73	213	7,600
Neil Schietekat	71	75	68	214	6,272
Divan van den Heever	72	72	70	214	6,272
Brett Liddle	70	72	72	214	6,272
Kevin Stone	66	74	74	214	6,272
Tyrone van Aswegen	68	71	75	214	6,272
Andre Cruse	75	71	69	215	5,360
Steve Basson	70	70	75	215	5,360
Ulrich van den Berg	70	67	78	215	5,360
Gary Thain	72	74	70	216	4,690
Alan Michell	74	69	73	216	4,690
Ross Wellington	71	72	73	216	4,690
Ian Hutchings	71	71	74	216	4,690

Suncoast Classic

Durban Country Club, Durban, South Africa
Par 36-36–72; 6,732 yards

May 17-19
purse, R400,000

	SCORES			TOTAL	MONEY
Adilson da Silva	71	66	71	208	R63,400
Doug McGuigan	66	74	69	209	46,000
Hendrik Buhrmann	70	69	71	210	28,600
Dean Lambert	67	71	72	210	28,600
Bradley Davison	74	70	67	211	17,000
Alex Haindl	72	67	72	211	17,000
Desvonde Botes	70	72	70	212	11,133.33
Grant Muller	69	70	73	212	11,133.33
Alan Michell	67	67	78	212	11,133.33
Chris Williams	74	70	70	214	8,466.66
Warren Abery	72	71	71	214	8,466.66
Willie van der Merwe	72	69	73	214	8,466.66
Andre Cruse	76	69	70	215	7,400
Werner Geyer	69	71	75	215	7,400
Lindani Ndwandwe	72	72	72	216	6,840
Tongoona Charamba	75	72	70	217	6,380
John Bele	72	69	76	217	6,380
Rossouw Loubser	70	75	73	218	5,880
Mike Lamb	67	79	72	218	5,880
Tyrone van Aswegen	73	73	73	219	5,260
Ulrich van den Berg	72	74	73	219	5,260

	SCORES			TOTAL	MONEY
Neil Cheetham	71	72	76	219	5,260
Bradford Vaughan	71	77	71	219	5,260
Andrew Curlewis	73	74	73	220	4,520
Jbe' Kruger	74	69	77	220	4,520
Brett Liddle	74	75	71	220	4,520
Omar Sandys	72	77	71	220	4,520

Lombard Insurance Classic

Royal Swazi Sun Country Club, Mbabane, Swaziland
Par 36-36–72; 6,715 yards

June 8-10
purse, R350,000

	SCORES			TOTAL	MONEY
Peter Karmis	64	72	64	200	R55,475
Tongoona Charamba	65	69	67	201	40,250
Bradley Davison	74	66	64	204	28,000
Warren Abery	73	67	65	205	15,706.25
Bradford Vaughan	72	68	65	205	15,706.25
Alex Haindl	66	71	68	205	15,706.25
Omar Sandys	67	68	70	205	15,706.25
Desvonde Botes	74	68	64	206	8,356.25
Mawonga Nomwa	73	68	65	206	8,356.25
Ryan Cairns	70	70	66	206	8,356.25
Mark Murless	67	71	68	206	8,356.25
Jaco Ahlers	71	69	67	207	6,483.75
Adilson da Silva	70	69	68	207	6,483.75
Vaughn Groenewald	66	71	70	207	6,483.75
Wallie Coetsee	66	71	70	207	6,483.75
Titch Moore	70	72	66	208	5,582.50
Andre Cruse	68	71	69	208	5,582.50
Nic Henning	71	68	70	209	5,051.66
David Hewan	70	68	71	209	5,051.66
Nico van Rensburg	68	65	76	209	5,051.66
Grant Muller	65	74	71	210	4,690
Christiaan Basson	68	76	67	211	4,112.50
Willie van der Merwe	71	71	69	211	4,112.50
Albert Pistorius	70	71	70	211	4,112.50
John Bele	70	71	70	211	4,112.50
Eugen Marugi	69	71	71	211	4,112.50
Brett Liddle	69	69	73	211	4,112.50

Vodacom Origins of Golf Tour at Selborne

Selborne Country Club, Kwazulu Natal, South Africa
Par 36-36–72; 6,607 yards

June 13-15
purse, R400,000

	SCORES			TOTAL	MONEY
George Coetzee	70	71	66	207	R63,400
Ulrich van den Berg	72	66	71	209	46,000
Hennie Otto	70	70	70	210	28,600
Chris Williams	71	68	71	210	28,600
Grant Muller	74	70	67	211	17,000
Peter Karmis	73	69	69	211	17,000
Dale Burraston	72	73	67	212	11,800
Andrew Curlewis	71	71	70	212	11,800
Andre Cruse	71	73	69	213	9,066.66
Neil Schietekat	75	68	70	213	9,066.66

	SCORES			TOTAL	MONEY
Warren Abery	72	71	70	213	9,066.66
Werner Geyer	74	70	70	214	7,600
Brett Liddle	73	71	70	214	7,600
Adilson da Silva	73	69	72	214	7,600
Jeff Inglis	72	72	71	215	6,400
Charl Coetzee	73	71	71	215	6,400
Desvonde Botes	76	68	71	215	6,400
Alex Haindl	69	72	74	215	6,400
Ryan Cairns	74	72	70	216	5,760
David Hewan	75	73	69	217	5,160
Gerlou Roux	72	74	71	217	5,160
Josh Cunliffe	79	66	72	217	5,160
Andrew Wilson	75	70	72	217	5,160
Willie van der Merwe	72	72	73	217	5,160
Rossouw Loubser	71	76	71	218	4,440
Dean Lambert	79	68	71	218	4,440
Anil Shah	70	75	73	218	4,440

Nashua Golf Challenge

Gary Player Country Club: Par 36-36–72; 7,831 yards   June 28-30
Lost City Golf Course: Par 36-36–72; 6,983 yards   purse, R400,000
Sun City, South Africa

	SCORES			TOTAL	MONEY
Warren Abery	69	67	71	207	R63,400
Adilson da Silva	72	67	72	211	46,000
Keith Horne	72	69	71	212	32,000
Chris Williams	72	69	72	213	25,200
Hennie Otto	70	76	68	214	17,000
Jbe' Kruger	70	73	71	214	17,000
Brett Liddle	74	72	69	215	10,600
Marc Cayeux	72	75	68	215	10,600
Charl Coetzee	73	70	72	215	10,600
Bradford Vaughan	72	70	73	215	10,600
Jeff Inglis	71	72	73	216	8,400
Ross Wellington	74	71	72	217	7,800
Werner Geyer	73	68	76	217	7,800
Alex Haindl	72	75	71	218	6,853.33
Omar Sandys	72	73	73	218	6,853.33
Alan Michell	74	71	73	218	6,853.33
Ulrich van den Berg	73	72	74	219	6,120
John Bele	75	69	75	219	6,120
Des Terblanche	74	68	78	220	5,760
Andre Cruse	76	71	74	221	5,260
Christiaan Basson	75	72	74	221	5,260
Desvonde Botes	75	74	72	221	5,260
Mike Lamb	76	74	71	221	5,260
Grant Muller	75	72	75	222	4,680
Andrew Curlewis	74	74	74	222	4,680

Vodacom Origins of Golf Tour at Bloemfontein

Bloemfontein Golf Club, Bloemfontein, South Africa
Par 36-36–72; 7,302 yards

August 1-3
purse, R400,000

	SCORES			TOTAL	MONEY
Ulrich van den Berg	67	66	69	202	R63,400
Bradford Vaughan	71	66	68	205	46,000
James Kingston	70	69	67	206	32,000
Hennie Otto	69	72	66	207	19,733.33
Hendrik Buhrmann	69	69	69	207	19,733.33
Ross Wellington	67	71	69	207	19,733.33
Jeff Inglis	71	67	70	208	11,800
Vaughn Groenewald	71	66	71	208	11,800
Mark Murless	68	76	65	209	8,800
Tongoona Charamba	72	66	71	209	8,800
Nico van Rensburg	69	69	71	209	8,800
Alex Haindl	67	68	74	209	8,800
Brandon Pieters	73	70	67	210	7,040
Desvonde Botes	69	73	68	210	7,040
Adilson da Silva	71	69	70	210	7,040
Johan Etsebeth	75	64	71	210	7,040
Titch Moore	71	70	70	211	6,000
Ashley Roestoff	71	69	71	211	6,000
Trevor Fisher, Jr.	70	68	73	211	6,000
Darren Holder	74	69	69	212	5,360
Dean Lambert	67	72	73	212	5,360
Omar Sandys	70	67	75	212	5,360
James Kamte	71	72	70	213	4,690
Henk Alberts	72	70	71	213	4,690
Robert Haindl	70	72	71	213	4,690
Dion Fourie	74	65	74	213	4,690

Vodacom Origins of Golf Tour at Fancourt

The Links, Fancourt, George, South Africa
Par 36-37–73; 7,579 yards

August 22-24
purse, R400,000

	SCORES			TOTAL	MONEY
Adilson da Silva	75	72	70	217	R63,400
Warren Abery	75	69	73	217	46,000
(Da Silva defeated Abery on first playoff hole.)					
Grant Veenstra	74	73	72	219	25,333.33
Ulrich van den Berg	76	71	72	219	25,333.33
George Coetzee	75	68	76	219	25,333.33
Jbe' Kruger	73	75	72	220	13,900
Mark Murless	71	76	73	220	13,900
Hennie Otto	72	76	74	222	11,000
Chris Williams	73	73	77	223	9,800
Nic Henning	72	79	74	225	8,250
Desvonde Botes	74	78	73	225	8,250
Billy Valentyn	75	75	75	225	8,250
Titch Moore	76	77	72	225	8,250
Theunis Spangenberg	73	78	75	226	6,302.85
Ross Wellington	76	76	74	226	6,302.85
Alex Haindl	73	77	76	226	6,302.85
Thabang Simon	75	75	76	226	6,302.85
Wallie Coetsee	78	75	73	226	6,302.85
Merrick Bremner	76	78	72	226	6,302.85
Christiaan Basson	76	78	72	226	6,302.85

	SCORES			TOTAL	MONEY
Andrew Curlewis	76	76	75	227	5,260
Toto Thimba	74	77	76	227	5,260
Brett Liddle	73	78	77	228	4,860
Brandon Pieters	74	78	76	228	4,860
Patrick O'Brien	76	75	79	230	4,360
Werner Geyer	72	79	79	230	4,360
Steve van Vuuren	76	75	79	230	4,360
Neil Schietekat	75	79	76	230	4,360

Telkom PGA Pro-Am

Centurion Country Club, Pretoria, South Africa
Par 36-36–72; 7,328 yards

August 29-31
purse, R350,000

	SCORES			TOTAL	MONEY
Michiel Bothma	70	66	68	204	R55,475
Jaco Van Zyl	68	69	68	205	40,250
Hennie Otto	73	65	68	206	28,000
Tongoona Charamba	68	69	70	207	22,050
Titch Moore	69	71	69	209	13,591.66
Chris Williams	70	69	70	209	13,591.66
Ulrich van den Berg	70	67	72	209	13,591.66
Divan van den Heever	70	70	70	210	8,691.66
Gerlou Roux	71	69	70	210	8,691.66
Bradford Vaughan	69	69	72	210	8,691.66
Johan Etsebeth	70	76	65	211	6,657
Doug McGuigan	70	73	68	211	6,657
Jbe' Kruger	71	71	69	211	6,657
Teboho Sefatsa	72	70	69	211	6,657
George Coetzee	71	67	73	211	6,657
Dion Fourie	72	72	68	212	5,471.66
Adilson da Silva	72	72	68	212	5,471.66
Brandon Pieters	68	73	71	212	5,471.66
Dandre Neumeyer	70	75	68	213	4,690
Desvonde Botes	71	73	69	213	4,690
Grant Muller	72	71	70	213	4,690
Andrew Curlewis	74	68	71	213	4,690
Chris Swanepoel	70	70	73	213	4,690
Merrick Bremner	73	72	69	214	4,025
Warren Abery	71	74	69	214	4,025
Albert Pistorius	70	70	74	214	4,025

Seekers Travel Pro-Am

Dainfern Country Club, Johannesburg, South Africa
Par 36-36–72; 7,258 yards

September 6-8
purse, R400,000

	SCORES			TOTAL	MONEY
James Kamte	68	68	67	203	R63,400
Albert Pistorius	69	70	65	204	46,000
Warren Abery	71	69	65	205	28,600
Desvonde Botes	69	69	67	205	28,600
George Coetzee	67	70	69	206	18,800
Ulrich van den Berg	71	69	67	207	12,933.33
Christiaan Basson	70	69	68	207	12,933.33
Jaco Van Zyl	68	71	68	207	12,933.33
Titch Moore	71	70	67	208	8,800

	SCORES			TOTAL	MONEY
Dion Fourie	66	71	71	208	8,800
Toto Thimba	67	69	72	208	8,800
Doug McGuigan	67	68	73	208	8,800
Bradford Vaughan	70	72	67	209	7,040
Adilson da Silva	70	69	70	209	7,040
Ryan Tipping	71	66	72	209	7,040
Chris Swanepoel	64	67	78	209	7,040
Alex Haindl	70	71	69	210	6,000
Hennie Otto	66	72	72	210	6,000
Marc Cayeux	69	69	72	210	6,000
Peter Karmis	69	71	71	211	5,260
Ross Wellington	71	69	71	211	5,260
Vaughn Groenewald	66	73	72	211	5,260
Gary Thain	68	71	72	211	5,260
Tyran van Lieshout	74	69	69	212	4,600
Rossouw Loubser	68	71	73	212	4,600
Nic Henning	65	74	73	212	4,600

Vodacom Origins of Golf Tour Final

St. Francis Links, St. Francis Bay, South Africa
Par 36-36–72; 7,366 yards
(Event shortened to 54 holes—wind.)

September 26-28
purse, R400,000

	SCORES			TOTAL	MONEY
Titch Moore	68	71	70	209	R63,400
Ulrich van den Berg	77	65	70	212	46,000
Henk Alberts	71	72	74	217	32,000
Jbe' Kruger	76	72	70	218	25,200
Alan Michell	75	72	72	219	18,800
Dean Lambert	80	70	70	220	13,900
Wallie Coetsee	75	70	75	220	13,900
Gerlou Roux	73	75	73	221	10,400
Grant Muller	75	72	74	221	10,400
Desvonde Botes	74	74	74	222	9,000
Chris Williams	78	71	74	223	8,400
Peter Karmis	75	76	73	224	7,232
Warren Abery	75	75	74	224	7,232
Nic Henning	73	79	72	224	7,232
Des Terblanche	72	77	75	224	7,232
Josh Cunliffe	76	71	77	224	7,232
James Kamte	77	72	76	225	6,120
Bradford Vaughan	74	74	77	225	6,120
Theunis Spangenberg	82	69	75	226	5,360
Werner Geyer	71	78	77	226	5,360
Ryan Cairns	80	73	73	226	5,360
George Coetzee	77	76	73	226	5,360
Hennie Otto	80	75	71	226	5,360
Mark Murless	74	76	77	227	4,600
Brett Liddle	80	73	74	227	4,600
Darren Holder	77	77	73	227	4,600

Bearing Man Highveld Classic

Witbank Golf Club, Witbank, South Africa
Par 36-36–72; 6,772 yards

October 5-7
purse, R400,000

	SCORES			TOTAL	MONEY
Marc Cayeux	71	69	62	202	R79,250
Ulrich van den Berg	65	71	69	205	57,500
George Coetzee	72	68	66	206	35,750
Jbe' Kruger	68	67	71	206	35,750
Ryan Tipping	68	70	69	207	21,250
Wallie Coetsee	68	69	70	207	21,250
Grant Muller	69	72	67	208	15,750
Tongoona Charamba	71	74	64	209	13,750
Nic Henning	72	71	67	210	11,333.33
Gary Thain	69	73	68	210	11,333.33
Willie van der Merwe	71	71	68	210	11,333.33
Bradford Vaughan	72	69	70	211	9,500
Dion Fourie	69	71	71	211	9,500
Darren Fichardt	70	69	72	211	9,500
Omar Sandys	71	74	67	212	7,691.66
Ross Wellington	70	70	72	212	7,691.66
Ryan Cairns	69	70	73	212	7,691.66
Josh Cunliffe	70	69	73	212	7,691.66
Warren Abery	67	72	73	212	7,691.66
Brandon Pieters	69	70	73	212	7,691.66
Andre Cruse	72	72	69	213	6,575
Henk Alberts	72	72	69	213	6,575
Eugen Marugi	72	72	70	214	6,075
Nemanja Savic	72	71	71	214	6,075
Rossouw Loubser	72	73	70	215	5,450
Toto Thimba, Jr.	73	71	71	215	5,450
Trevor Fisher, Jr.	74	68	73	215	5,450
Lindani Ndwandwe	68	74	73	215	5,450

MTC Namibia PGA Championship

Windhoek Country Club, Windhoek, Namibia
Par 35-36–71; 7,106 yards

October 18-20
purse, R700,000

	SCORES			TOTAL	MONEY
Keith Horne	67	65	63	195	R110,950
Hennie Otto	68	66	66	200	54,436.66
Doug McGuigan	65	68	67	200	54,436.66
Ulrich van den Berg	66	66	68	200	54,436.66
Grant Muller	69	69	63	201	26,845
Tongo Charamba	65	71	65	201	26,845
Nic Henning	68	68	66	202	18,935
Adilson da Silva	65	67	70	202	18,935
Ross Wellington	67	70	66	203	13,790
Wallie Coetsee	68	68	67	203	13,790
Steve Basson	67	69	67	203	13,790
Ryan Cairns	67	72	65	204	10,727.50
Josh Cunliffe	65	73	66	204	10,727.50
Neil Cheetham	68	69	67	204	10,727.50
Andre Cruse	68	68	68	204	10,727.50
Bradford Vaughan	69	68	68	205	9,415
Chris Williams	70	66	69	205	9,415
Alex Haindl	67	73	66	206	8,166.66
Trevor Fisher, Jr.	67	73	66	206	8,166.66

	SCORES			TOTAL	MONEY
Brandon Pieters	67	72	67	206	8,166.66
Marc Cayeux	65	71	70	206	8,166.66
Desvonde Botes	66	69	71	206	8,166.66
Bradley Davison	66	68	72	206	8,166.66
Werner Geyer	69	71	67	207	6,930
Shaun Norris	69	70	68	207	6,930
Omar Sandys	70	69	68	207	6,930
George Coetzee	68	70	69	207	6,930
Andrew Curlewis	68	69	70	207	6,930

Platinum Classic

Mooinooi Golf Club, Rustenburg, South Africa
Par 36-36–72; 6,835 yards

October 25-27
purse, R705,000

	SCORES			TOTAL	MONEY
Louis Oosthuizen	64	71	70	205	R111,743
Marc Cayeux	67	74	64	205	68,737.50
Adilson da Silva	69	68	68	205	68,737.50
(Oosthuizen defeated da Silva on first and Cayeux on second playoff hole.)					
Ross Wellington	67	72	67	206	38,775
Warren Abery	67	71	68	206	38,775
Jean Hugo	69	70	68	207	26,790
Ryan Cairns	70	70	68	208	20,798
Jbe' Kruger	67	70	71	208	20,798
Gerlou Roux	68	72	69	209	15,980.33
Trevor Fisher, Jr.	70	69	70	209	15,980.33
Grant Muller	67	71	71	209	15,980.33
Grant Veenstra	69	72	69	210	13,395
Thomas Aiken	70	71	69	210	13,395
Ulrich van den Berg	70	71	69	210	13,395
James Kingston	68	76	67	211	11,774
Merrick Bremner	71	69	71	211	11,774
Tongo Charamba	71	73	68	212	9,829.85
George Coetzee	71	73	68	212	9,829.85
Andrew Curlewis	72	72	68	212	9,829.85
Brett Liddle	70	71	71	212	9,829.85
Brandon Pieters	69	72	71	212	9,829.85
Steve Basson	71	69	72	212	9,829.85
Henk Alberts	66	73	73	212	9,829.85
Dean Lambert	74	71	68	213	8,249
Lindani Ndwandwe	69	72	72	213	8,249

Hassan II Trophy

Dar-es-Salam Golf Club, Red Course, Rabat, Morocco
Par 36-37–73; 7,307 yards

October 25-28
purse, US$600,000

	SCORES				TOTAL	MONEY
Padraig Harrington	67	67	72	74	280	US$150,000
Darren Clarke	71	69	72	71	283	100,000
Simon Dyson	70	70	73	72	285	75,000
David Howell	70	75	71	71	287	55,000
Mark O'Meara	70	70	76	73	289	35,000
Sandy Lyle	73	73	71	72	289	35,000
Faycal Serghini	74	68	72	76	290	15,000
Raphael Jacquelin	71	75	73	71	290	15,000

	SCORES				TOTAL	MONEY
David Frost	74	70	74	73	291	8,000
Charles Schwartzel	73	68	79	72	292	8,000
Richard Sterne	76	74	74	69	293	8,000
Fernando Roca	72	74	75	72	293	8,000
Jaime Spence	73	72	73	76	294	8,000
Malcolm Mackenzie	75	75	71	74	295	8,000
Roger Chapman	73	72	76	74	295	8,000
Adrien Mork	73	75	75	73	296	7,500
Scott Drummond	75	71	72	78	296	7,500
Younes El Hassani	75	73	76	73	297	7,000
Mark Davis	75	73	73	77	298	7,000
Abdelhaq Sabi	78	74	73	75	300	7,000
Bobby Casper	80	72	73	78	303	7,000
Gary Evans	76	80	73	75	304	7,000
Wayne Westner	81	74	76	80	311	7,000
Jeev Milkha Singh	71	68	76	117	332	7,000

Coca-Cola Charity Championship

Arabella Golf Club, Hermanus, South Africa
Par 36-36–72; 6,976 yards

November 20-22
purse, R500,000

	SCORES			TOTAL	MONEY
Titch Moore	67	72	72	211	R81,700
Steve Basson	71	73	71	215	39,600
Louis Oosthuizen	72	72	71	215	39,600
James Kingston	69	73	73	215	39,600
Hennie Otto	66	77	73	216	21,300
Jbe' Kruger	70	76	73	219	18,200
Desvonde Botes	69	77	74	220	17,250
Des Terblanche	72	75	74	221	15,250
Neil Schietekat	74	74	73	221	15,250
George Coetzee	73	75	73	221	15,250
Steve van Vuuren	77	73	72	222	13,350
Marc Cayeux	70	74	78	222	13,350
Mark Murless	72	76	75	223	12,050
Grant Muller	72	73	78	223	12,050
Chris Williams	69	78	77	224	11,100
Brandon Pieters	72	77	76	225	10,300
Andre Cruse	72	78	75	225	10,300
Dion Fourie	72	82	71	225	10,300
Ryan Tipping	68	79	79	226	9,700
Ross Wellington	71	76	81	228	9,500
Vaughn Groenewald	73	79	77	229	9,250
Andrew Curlewis	76	80	74	230	9,050
Omar Sandys	72	77	82	231	8,850
Albert Pistorius	74	81	77	232	8,550
Tongo Charamba	80	78	74	232	8,550

Nedbank Affinity Cup

Lost City Golf Course, Sun City, South Africa
Par 36-36–72; 7,334 yards

November 26-28
purse, R500,000

	SCORES			TOTAL	MONEY
Mark Murless	71	66	65	202	R79,250
Tongo Charamba	71	64	68	203	48,750

	SCORES			TOTAL	MONEY
James Kingston	67	65	71	203	48,750
James Kamte	68	68	68	204	31,500
Ryan Tipping	68	68	70	206	23,500
George Coetzee	74	66	67	207	16,166.66
Hendrik Buhrmann	70	70	67	207	16,166.66
Darren Fichardt	69	68	70	207	16,166.66
Jean Hugo	68	69	71	208	11,750
Warren Abery	69	67	72	208	11,750
Trevor Fisher, Jr.	71	71	68	210	9,750
Marc Cayeux	68	72	70	210	9,750
Keith Horne	72	67	71	210	9,750
Dion Fourie	69	67	74	210	9,750
Titch Moore	74	70	67	211	8,350
Ross Wellington	73	70	68	211	8,350
Charl Coetzee	68	71	73	212	7,800
Thomas Aiken	74	70	69	213	7,087.50
Jbe' Kruger	75	68	70	213	7,087.50
Desvonde Botes	73	69	71	213	7,087.50
Des Terblanche	69	69	75	213	7,087.50
Eugen Marugi	69	71	74	214	6,325
Chris Williams	68	70	76	214	6,325
Teboho Sefatsa	71	72	72	215	5,850
Ulrich van den Berg	71	71	73	215	5,850

Nedbank Golf Challenge

Gary Player Country Club, Sun City, South Africa
Par 36-36–72; 7,831 yards

November 29-December 2
purse, US$4,385,000

	SCORES				TOTAL	MONEY
Trevor Immelman	67	66	67	72	272	$1,200,000
Justin Rose	68	65	67	73	273	600,000
Ernie Els	69	67	69	72	277	400,000
Henrik Stenson	72	65	72	72	281	300,000
Rory Sabbatini	76	68	67	71	282	275,000
Luke Donald	68	71	71	73	283	255,000
Geoff Ogilvy	69	73	70	71	283	255,000
Adam Scott	67	71	72	76	286	240,000
Niclas Fasth	74	72	70	72	288	230,000
Charl Schwartzel	74	74	68	74	290	220,000
Stewart Cink	72	73	75	71	291	210,000
Retief Goosen	74	71	75	78	298	200,000

Alfred Dunhill Championship

Leopard Creek Country Club, Mpumalanga, South Africa
Par 35-37–72; 7,249 yards

December 6-9
purse, €1,000,000

	SCORES				TOTAL	MONEY
John Bickerton	70	69	68	68	275	R1,607,491
Lee Slattery	73	65	67	71	276	934,069
Ernie Els	70	69	64	73	276	934,069
Joost Luiten	75	71	64	67	277	497,967
Ross McGowan	71	69	67	72	279	418,860
Pelle Edberg	74	66	73	67	280	329,104.50
David Dixon	72	72	67	69	280	329,104.50
Sion E. Bebb	67	72	74	68	281	249,491

	SCORES				TOTAL	MONEY
Michael Lorenzo-Vera	72	70	73	67	282	185,596.80
Francois Delamontagne	77	67	70	68	282	185,596.80
David Carter	72	71	70	69	282	185,596.80
Richard Bland	69	70	73	70	282	185,596.80
Hennie Otto	75	69	68	70	282	185,596.80
Robert Rock	73	72	69	69	283	141,479.50
Trevor Fisher, Jr.	74	72	68	69	283	141,479.50
Keith Horne	74	70	68	71	283	141,479.50
Omar Sandys	68	68	74	73	283	141,479.50
Martin Wiegele	74	71	73	66	284	116,631.85
George Coetzee	69	72	75	68	284	116,631.85
Andrew McLardy	72	73	71	68	284	116,631.85
Chris Swanepoel	73	73	70	68	284	116,631.85
Richard Sterne	74	70	70	70	284	116,631.85
Craig Lee	68	71	72	73	284	116,631.85
Titch Moore	71	68	72	73	284	116,631.85
Marc Cayeux	75	71	68	71	285	100,404.66
Rafael Cabrera Bello	70	75	68	72	285	100,404.66
Oliver Wilson	73	71	68	73	285	100,404.66
David Drysdale	73	72	74	67	286	88,843.20
Simon Dyson	75	68	74	69	286	88,843.20
Edoardo Molinari	75	71	71	69	286	88,843.20
Alvaro Velasco	70	74	71	71	286	88,843.20
Klas Eriksson	74	71	69	72	286	88,843.20
Ross Fisher	76	70	73	68	287	76,064.14
Stuart Manley	71	72	75	69	287	76,064.14
Chris Williams	74	69	75	69	287	76,064.14
Magnus A. Carlsson	72	71	74	70	287	76,064.14
Alan Michell	72	73	72	70	287	76,064.14
Gary Boyd	72	71	72	72	287	76,064.14
Darren Clarke	73	69	70	75	287	76,064.14
Philip Golding	72	72	73	71	288	63,894
Grant Veenstra	73	70	72	73	288	63,894
Pablo Larrazabal	70	70	74	74	288	63,894
Wallie Coetsee	72	71	71	74	288	63,894
Alessandro Tadini	72	73	69	74	288	63,894
Joachim Backstrom	77	67	77	68	289	54,766.25
Sven Struver	72	73	76	68	289	54,766.25
Benn Barham	72	71	73	73	289	54,766.25
Julio Zapata	77	69	69	74	289	54,766.25
Dion Fourie	72	71	75	72	290	47,667
Steven Jeppesen	75	69	73	73	290	47,667
Anton Haig	71	71	74	74	290	47,667
Tyrone van Aswegen	75	70	77	69	291	39,553.40
James Kingston	71	74	77	69	291	39,553.40
Michiel Bothma	78	67	76	70	291	39,553.40
Stephen Browne	70	71	77	73	291	39,553.40
Adilson da Silva	73	73	71	74	291	39,553.40
Alan McLean	75	71	73	73	292	31,440
Thomas Aiken	74	70	74	74	292	31,440
Jaco Van Zyl	75	70	72	75	292	31,440
Mikael Lundberg	76	67	73	76	292	31,440
Luis Claverie	74	70	71	77	292	31,440
Peter Whiteford	71	72	77	73	293	28,397
Gary Clark	71	72	74	78	295	27,383
Doug McGuigan	74	67	75	80	296	26,369
Kevin Stone	73	71	81	76	301	25,355
Rossouw Loubser	74	71	80	77	302	24,341

South African Airways Open

Pearl Valley Golf Estate, Paarl, Western Cape, South Africa
Par 36-36–72; 7,438 yards

December 13-16
purse, €1,000,000

	SCORES			TOTAL	MONEY
James Kingston	73	69	71 71	284	R1,554,901
Oliver Wilson	76	69	67 73	285	1,128,162
Darren Clarke	72	73	74 68	287	478,242.50
Kyron Sullivan	72	71	73 71	287	478,242.50
Louis Oosthuizen	78	72	66 71	287	478,242.50
Garth Mulroy	80	70	64 73	287	478,242.50
Craig Lile	73	73	72 70	288	233,725.50
Greg Norman	75	70	72 71	288	233,725.50
Robert Rock	70	75	71 72	288	233,725.50
Nic Henning	74	71	70 73	288	233,725.50
Simon Dyson	75	76	71 67	289	164,483
Alan Michell	76	74	68 71	289	164,483
Andrew McLardy	72	71	73 73	289	164,483
Garry Houston	76	73	68 73	290	144,208
Edoardo Molinari	75	74	72 71	292	139,303
Ernie Els	77	70	77 69	293	124,784.20
Richard Sterne	74	72	75 72	293	124,784.20
Joachim Backstrom	76	74	71 72	293	124,784.20
Charl Schwartzel	71	76	71 75	293	124,784.20
Retief Goosen	74	74	70 75	293	124,784.20
Magnus A. Carlsson	76	73	74 71	294	103,006
Hennie Otto	77	74	72 71	294	103,006
Fabrizio Zanotti	80	71	71 72	294	103,006
Francois Delamontagne	75	74	71 74	294	103,006
Peter Lawrie	74	75	71 74	294	103,006
Alan McLean	80	71	69 74	294	103,006
Miles Tunnicliff	77	74	69 74	294	103,006
Angel Cabrera	80	73	72 70	295	85,936.60
Gary Boyd	72	76	74 73	295	85,936.60
Andrew McArthur	72	74	75 74	295	85,936.60
Anton Haig	75	74	72 74	295	85,936.60
Ulrich van den Berg	71	73	71 80	295	85,936.60
David Frost	73	80	75 68	296	76,519
Joost Luiten	82	67	75 72	296	76,519
Lee S. James	76	75	73 72	296	76,519
Luis Claverie	79	74	69 74	296	76,519
Thomas Aiken	76	75	78 68	297	68,671
Peter Whiteford	81	70	76 70	297	68,671
Neil Schietekat	72	73	81 71	297	68,671
Warren Abery	76	74	71 76	297	68,671
David Dixon	76	75	73 74	298	61,804
Tim Clark	75	74	74 75	298	61,804
Paul Waring	73	76	73 76	298	61,804
Jean Hugo	78	75	75 71	299	52,974.83
Keith Horne	77	75	74 73	299	52,974.83
Michiel Bothma	85	68	73 73	299	52,974.83
George Coetzee	73	76	75 75	299	52,974.83
Adilson da Silva	77	74	73 75	299	52,974.83
Patrik Sjoland	79	71	73 76	299	52,974.83
Richard Bland	76	77	77 70	300	40,221
Birgir Hafthorsson	79	73	75 73	300	40,221
Brett Liddle	77	71	78 74	300	40,221
Alvaro Velasco	75	78	72 75	300	40,221
Euan Little	72	72	78 78	300	40,221
Alex Haindl	71	78	71 80	300	40,221
Ryan Tipping	74	75	70 81	300	40,221
Marc Cayeux	78	73	74 76	301	31,392

	SCORES				TOTAL	MONEY
Mattias Eliasson	79	73	72	77	301	31,392
Jaco Van Zyl	74	77	71	79	301	31,392
Sam Walker	80	73	76	73	302	27,958.50
Mikael Lundberg	80	73	74	75	302	27,958.50
Pablo Larrazabal	79	72	75	76	302	27,958.50
Michael Lorenzo-Vera	75	71	78	78	302	27,958.50
Chris Williams	77	74	73	79	303	25,506
Mathias Gronberg	79	74	74	77	304	24,525
Grant Muller	78	75	73	79	305	23,053.50
Ross Wellington	76	72	76	81	305	23,053.50
Lee Slattery	76	76	78	79	309	21,582
Steven Jeppesen	74	78	75	87	314	20,601

Women's Tours

Women's World Cup of Golf
See Ladies African Tour section.

SBS Open at Turtle Bay

Turtle Bay Resort, Palmer Course, Oahu, Hawaii
Par 36-36–72; 6,578 yards

February 15-17
purse, $1,100,000

	SCORES			TOTAL	MONEY
Paula Creamer	67	70	70	207	$165,000
Julieta Granada	68	71	69	208	98,269
Karrie Webb	70	70	70	210	71,286
Lorena Ochoa	71	69	71	211	45,283
Janice Moodie	69	70	72	211	45,283
Morgan Pressel	69	68	74	211	45,283
Hee-Won Han	69	69	74	212	30,397
Stacy Prammanasudh	69	74	70	213	25,285
Sherri Steinhauer	67	70	76	213	25,285
Jimin Kang	71	70	73	214	21,789
Yu Ping Lin	69	72	74	215	18,884
Alena Sharp	69	72	74	215	18,884
Pat Hurst	71	68	76	215	18,884
Aree Song	74	70	72	216	15,638
Natalie Gulbis	68	73	75	216	15,638
Seon Hwa Lee	70	70	76	216	15,638
In-Kyung Kim	73	72	72	217	12,213
Katherine Hull	71	73	73	217	12,213
Teresa Lu	71	75	71	217	12,213
Mhairi McKay	70	76	71	217	12,213
Paige Mackenzie	67	76	74	217	12,213
Na Ri Kim	71	72	74	217	12,213
Lindsey Wright	70	71	76	217	12,213
Se Ri Pak	75	73	69	217	12,213
Jee Young Lee	70	74	74	218	8,998
Hye Jung Choi	74	71	73	218	8,998
Carri Wood	73	71	74	218	8,998
Jeong Jang	73	71	74	218	8,998
Nadina Light	74	73	71	218	8,998
Heather Daly-Donofrio	71	71	76	218	8,998
Tracy Hanson	72	71	75	218	8,998
Kelli Kuehne	73	69	76	218	8,998

Fields Open in Hawaii

Ko Olina Golf Club, Kapolei, Hawaii
Par 36-36–72; 6,519 yards

February 22-24
purse, $1,200,000

	SCORES			TOTAL	MONEY
Stacy Prammanasudh	66	68	68	202	$180,000
Jee Young Lee	69	66	68	203	110,950
Ai Miyazato	71	68	66	205	64,288
Morgan Pressel	71	65	69	205	64,288
Angela Park	66	68	71	205	64,288

	SCORES			TOTAL	MONEY
Cristie Kerr	71	70	65	206	37,662
Vicki Goetze-Ackerman	70	67	69	206	37,662
Mi Hyun Kim	71	67	69	207	28,550
Wendy Doolan	70	67	70	207	28,550
Paula Creamer	72	70	67	209	22,142
Michele Redman	71	68	70	209	22,142
Aram Cho	71	68	70	209	22,142
Nicole Castrale	70	68	71	209	22,142
Nancy Scranton	73	71	66	210	16,037
Heather Daly-Donofrio	72	69	69	210	16,037
Pat Hurst	69	72	69	210	16,037
Meaghan Francella	68	73	69	210	16,037
Kyeong Bae	68	72	70	210	16,037
Se Ri Pak	67	73	70	210	16,037
Karrie Webb	70	69	71	210	16,037
Seon Hwa Lee	71	71	69	211	12,079
Lindsey Wright	70	72	69	211	12,079
Sophie Gustafson	72	69	70	211	12,079
Christina Kim	72	69	70	211	12,079
Marisa Baena	72	69	70	211	12,079
Sarah Lee	72	69	70	211	12,079
Il Mi Chung	72	68	71	211	12,079
Young Kim	70	72	70	212	9,922
Erica Blasberg	72	69	71	212	9,922
Carri Wood	70	68	74	212	9,922

MasterCard Classic Honoring Alejo Peralta

Bosque Real Country Club, Mexico City, Mexico
Par 36-36–72; 6,876 yards
(Event completed on Monday—rain & darkness.)

March 9-12
purse, $1,200,000

	SCORES			TOTAL	MONEY
Meaghan Francella	68	68	69	205	$180,000
Annika Sorenstam	69	70	66	205	109,852
(Francella defeated Sorenstam on fourth playoff hole.)					
Angela Stanford	74	67	67	208	63,652
Kyeong Bae	71	70	67	208	63,652
Stacy Prammanasudh	67	70	71	208	63,652
Shi Hyun Ahn	71	72	67	210	34,783
Hye Jung Choi	69	72	69	210	34,783
Lorena Ochoa	71	69	70	210	34,783
Sherri Steinhauer	73	69	69	211	24,559
Karin Sjodin	69	70	72	211	24,559
Seon Hwa Lee	69	69	73	211	24,559
Jimin Kang	72	71	69	212	19,767
Sophie Gustafson	70	73	69	212	19,767
Soo Young Moon	70	72	70	212	19,767
Meena Lee	73	69	71	213	16,119
Laura Davies	68	74	71	213	16,119
Beth Bader	73	68	72	213	16,119
Becky Morgan	69	70	74	213	16,119
Laura Diaz	74	72	68	214	13,352
Karine Icher	73	73	68	214	13,352
Teresa Lu	71	75	68	214	13,352
Cristie Kerr	73	71	70	214	13,352
Brittany Lang	72	72	70	214	13,352
Jin Joo Hong	73	74	68	215	9,885
Kelli Kuehne	75	71	69	215	9,885
Dorothy Delasin	72	73	70	215	9,885

	SCORES			TOTAL	MONEY
Michelle Ellis	72	71	72	215	9,885
Angela Park	71	72	72	215	9,885
Suzann Pettersen	73	69	73	215	9,885
Lindsey Wright	72	70	73	215	9,885
In-Kyung Kim	71	71	73	215	9,885
Michele Redman	68	74	73	215	9,885
Maggie Will	72	69	74	215	9,885
Giulia Sergas	70	70	75	215	9,885

Safeway International

Superstition Mountain Golf & Country Club,
Superstition Mountain, Arizona
Par 36-36–72; 6,662 yards

March 22-25
purse, $1,500,000

	SCORES				TOTAL	MONEY
Lorena Ochoa	69	64	69	68	270	$225,000
Suzann Pettersen	69	68	69	66	272	137,649
Laura Diaz	70	71	70	67	278	88,551
Jeong Jang	68	70	68	72	278	88,551
Catriona Matthew	68	68	74	69	279	56,522
Sophie Gustafson	75	66	69	69	279	56,522
Jee Young Lee	73	70	70	67	280	42,580
Rachel Hetherington	71	71	70	69	281	33,787
Annika Sorenstam	73	68	69	71	281	33,787
Shi Hyun Ahn	72	68	68	73	281	33,787
Paula Creamer	74	68	70	70	282	27,319
Hee-Won Han	70	70	71	71	282	27,319
Mi Hyun Kim	69	72	75	67	283	23,262
Morgan Pressel	72	71	72	68	283	23,262
Laura Davies	73	71	70	69	283	23,262
Brittany Lang	75	71	71	67	284	18,151
Julieta Granada	73	69	73	69	284	18,151
Young Kim	73	71	71	69	284	18,151
Sarah Lee	72	70	71	71	284	18,151
Maria Hjorth	75	70	68	71	284	18,151
Grace Park	71	76	65	72	284	18,151
Il Mi Chung	74	69	67	74	284	18,151
Irene Cho	74	68	73	70	285	14,947
Helen Alfredsson	73	70	72	70	285	14,947
Gloria Park	71	67	73	74	285	14,947
Silvia Cavalleri	74	72	70	70	286	12,586
Aree Song	74	70	70	72	286	12,586
Jamie Hullett	76	68	70	72	286	12,586
Nicole Castrale	75	70	68	73	286	12,586
Teresa Lu	76	67	69	74	286	12,586
Young Jo	68	74	69	75	286	12,586

Kraft Nabisco Championship

Mission Hills Country Club, Dinah Shore Course,
Rancho Mirage, California
Par 36-36–72; 6,673 yards

March 29-April 1
purse, $2,000,000

	SCORES				TOTAL	MONEY
Morgan Pressel	74	72	70	69	285	$300,000
Catriona Matthew	70	73	72	71	286	140,945

	SCORES			TOTAL	MONEY
Brittany Lincicome	72	71 71	72	286	140,945
Suzann Pettersen	72	69 71	74	286	140,945
*Stacy Lewis	71	73 73	70	287	
Shi Hyun Ahn	68	73 74	72	287	69,688
Stacy Prammanasudh	76	70 70	71	287	69,688
Meaghan Francella	72	72 69	74	287	69,688
Maria Hjorth	70	73 72	73	288	50,114
Angela Stanford	72	75 73	69	289	41,340
Lorena Ochoa	69	71 77	72	289	41,340
Se Ri Pak	72	70 70	77	289	41,340
Jee Young Lee	70	77 71	72	290	34,321
Sarah Lee	72	74 70	74	290	34,321
Ji-Yai Shin	76	72 71	72	291	28,651
Brittany Lang	71	73 75	72	291	28,651
Ai Miyazato	76	73 69	73	291	28,651
Paula Creamer	73	67 73	78	291	28,651
Moira Dunn	76	73 72	71	292	25,108
Karrie Webb	70	77 73	73	293	22,881
Cristie Kerr	75	73 72	73	293	22,881
Laura Davies	74	73 73	73	293	22,881
Sherri Steinhauer	71	78 70	74	293	22,881
Juli Inkster	75	75 72	72	294	20,451
Christina Kim	72	77 71	74	294	20,451
Jimin Kang	76	73 73	73	295	19,337
Angela Park	73	74 75	74	296	17,565
Julieta Granada	74	77 72	73	296	17,565
Nicole Castrale	76	71 74	75	296	17,565
Lindsey Wright	74	69 77	76	296	17,565
Laura Diaz	73	79 71	74	297	14,116
Young Jo	74	76 72	75	297	14,116
Hee Young Park	73	74 77	73	297	14,116
Annika Sorenstam	75	76 71	75	297	14,116
Heather Young	74	75 76	72	297	14,116
Leta Lindley	73	75 73	76	297	14,116
Mi Hyun Kim	74	72 74	77	297	14,116
Dorothy Delasin	73	76 74	75	298	10,782
Yuri Fudoh	73	76 75	74	298	10,782
Pat Hurst	71	76 74	77	298	10,782
Marisa Baena	73	75 73	77	298	10,782
Helen Alfredsson	78	69 74	77	298	10,782
Gwladys Nocera	72	77 72	77	298	10,782
Sakura Yokomine	76	76 71	76	299	8,943
Kim Saiki-Maloney	73	79 73	74	299	8,943
Sophie Gustafson	75	77 74	73	299	8,943
Wendy Doolan	75	78 73	74	300	7,998
Gloria Park	77	75 75	73	300	7,998
Shiho Oyama	76	75 77	72	300	7,998
Tina Barrett	74	74 77	76	301	7,011
Young Kim	76	77 74	74	301	7,011
Hee-Won Han	72	81 75	73	301	7,011
Becky Morgan	74	75 79	73	301	7,011
Veronica Zorzi	73	75 76	78	302	6,176
Karine Icher	72	73 80	77	302	6,176
Reilley Rankin	80	73 73	76	302	6,176
Jeong Jang	74	75 77	76	302	6,176
Soo Yun Kang	76	72 77	78	303	5,467
Aree Song	73	75 77	78	303	5,467
Diana D'Alessio	75	77 74	77	303	5,467
Nicole Perrot	79	74 71	80	304	4,910
Liselotte Neumann	77	74 75	78	304	4,910
Carin Koch	73	72 81	78	304	4,910
Candie Kung	75	77 78	74	304	4,910
Mi-Jeong Jeon	78	72 79	76	305	4,657

	SCORES				TOTAL	MONEY
*Taylor Leon	76	77	74	79	306	
Tracy Hanson	76	76	76	78	306	4,506
Michele Redman	76	75	77	78	306	4,506
*Esther Choe	77	76	75	79	307	
Grace Park	74	74	80	79	307	4,303
Joo Mi Kim	77	75	79	76	307	4,303
Jin Joo Hong	80	72	74	84	310	4,151
Meg Mallon	76	76	81	78	311	4,050

Ginn Open

Reunion Resort & Club, Orlando, Florida
Par 36-36–72; 6,505 yards

April 12-15
purse, $2,600,000

	SCORES				TOTAL	MONEY
Brittany Lincicome	67	72	67	72	278	$390,000
Lorena Ochoa	66	66	70	77	279	233,732
Laura Davies	66	66	70	79	281	169,557
Juli Inkster	70	71	69	72	282	118,370
Nicole Castrale	70	69	69	74	282	118,370
Birdie Kim	74	69	66	74	283	79,340
Se Ri Pak	69	70	68	76	283	79,340
Meena Lee	72	69	72	71	284	57,371
Sarah Lee	73	69	68	74	284	57,371
Hye Jung Choi	69	73	68	74	284	57,371
Carin Koch	70	71	70	75	286	44,916
Suzann Pettersen	70	69	70	77	286	44,916
Natalie Gulbis	69	66	71	80	286	44,916
Il Mi Chung	71	72	71	73	287	34,508
Karin Sjodin	74	66	74	73	287	34,508
Seon Hwa Lee	71	69	74	73	287	34,508
Grace Park	73	73	67	74	287	34,508
Karrie Webb	72	74	66	75	287	34,508
Michelle Ellis	71	72	68	76	287	34,508
Sherri Steinhauer	74	70	72	72	288	27,897
Stacy Prammanasudh	72	72	70	74	288	27,897
Jee Young Lee	73	68	70	77	288	27,897
Mi Hyun Kim	68	69	73	78	288	27,897
Ashley Hoagland	73	71	72	73	289	21,840
Ai Miyazato	72	72	72	73	289	21,840
Amy Hung	73	70	73	73	289	21,840
Paula Creamer	74	70	71	74	289	21,840
Ji-Young Oh	73	69	73	74	289	21,840
Cristie Kerr	72	72	70	75	289	21,840
Alena Sharp	74	69	70	76	289	21,840
Shi Hyun Ahn	70	73	68	78	289	21,840
Christina Kim	73	67	71	78	289	21,840

Corona Championship

Tres Marias Golf Club, Morelia, Michoacan, Mexico
Par 36-37–73; 6,600 yards

April 26-29
purse, $1,300,000

	SCORES				TOTAL	MONEY
Silvia Cavalleri	69	68	69	66	272	$195,000
Lorena Ochoa	68	74	64	68	274	101,946
Julieta Granada	71	68	67	68	274	101,946

	SCORES				TOTAL	MONEY
Pat Hurst	70	69	68	70	277	66,314
Na On Min	68	72	67	72	279	53,375
Meaghan Francella	73	70	71	66	280	37,417
Kyeong Bae	76	69	66	69	280	37,417
Stacy Prammanasudh	67	73	70	70	280	37,417
Linda Wessberg	69	74	69	69	281	25,474
Giulia Sergas	71	70	70	70	281	25,474
Teresa Lu	71	68	71	71	281	25,474
Yu Ping Lin	72	65	73	71	281	25,474
Hye Jung Choi	70	74	66	72	282	20,574
Sarah Lee	72	66	72	72	282	20,574
Beth Bader	73	68	74	68	283	17,770
Karine Icher	74	69	68	72	283	17,770
Angela Park	72	65	73	73	283	17,770
Jin Joo Hong	72	72	72	68	284	15,172
Moira Dunn	69	73	71	71	284	15,172
Erica Blasberg	73	68	72	71	284	15,172
Kate Golden	72	69	69	74	284	15,172
Kelly Cap	73	72	73	68	286	13,085
Ai Miyazato	76	72	69	69	286	13,085
Lee Ann Walker-Cooper	73	72	69	72	286	13,085
Ji-Young Oh	72	70	70	74	286	13,085
Il Mi Chung	72	78	70	67	287	10,804
Sophie Giquel	72	77	70	68	287	10,804
Soo Young Moon	74	71	72	70	287	10,804
Jane Park	77	68	71	71	287	10,804
Kris Tamulis	78	67	70	72	287	10,804
Danielle Downey	73	72	70	72	287	10,804

SemGroup Championship

Cedar Ridge Country Club, Broken Arrow, Oklahoma
Par 36-35–71; 6,602 yards

May 4-6
purse, $1,400,000

	SCORES			TOTAL	MONEY
Mi Hyun Kim	71	68	71	210	$210,000
Juli Inkster	71	70	69	210	127,258
(Kim defeated Inkster on first playoff hole.)					
Ai Miyazato	71	71	69	211	81,867
Angela Stanford	68	71	72	211	81,867
Young Kim	74	68	70	212	44,591
Lorena Ochoa	70	71	71	212	44,591
Reilley Rankin	70	68	74	212	44,591
Stephanie Louden	69	69	74	212	44,591
Paula Creamer	70	73	70	213	27,434
Aree Song	69	72	72	213	27,434
Katherine Hull	71	69	73	213	27,434
Nicole Castrale	67	71	75	213	27,434
Suzann Pettersen	74	72	68	214	19,834
Jeong Jang	75	70	69	214	19,834
Gloria Park	69	74	71	214	19,834
Meena Lee	72	69	73	214	19,834
Mikaela Parmlid	70	71	73	214	19,834
Se Ri Pak	69	71	74	214	19,834
Heather Young	73	72	70	215	16,025
Morgan Pressel	70	74	71	215	16,025
Karin Sjodin	68	70	77	215	16,025
Sherri Steinhauer	70	75	71	216	13,586
Stacy Prammanasudh	72	72	72	216	13,586
Teresa Lu	73	70	73	216	13,586

	SCORES			TOTAL	MONEY
Meredith Duncan	71	72	73	216	13,586
Angela Park	69	72	75	216	13,586
Brandie Burton	68	73	75	216	13,586
Christina Kim	75	72	70	217	9,943
Lorie Kane	74	73	70	217	9,943
Laura Diaz	74	72	71	217	9,943
Seon Hwa Lee	71	75	71	217	9,943
Shi Hyun Ahn	72	72	73	217	9,943
Dina Ammaccapane	71	73	73	217	9,943
Katie Futcher	72	71	74	217	9,943
Sarah Lee	71	72	74	217	9,943
Charlotte Mayorkas	72	70	75	217	9,943
Virada Nirapathpongporn	70	70	77	217	9,943

Michelob Ultra Open at Kingsmill

Kingsmill Resort & Spa, River Course, Williamsburg, Virginia
Par 36-35–71; 6,315 yards

May 10-13
purse, $2,200,000

	SCORES				TOTAL	MONEY
Suzann Pettersen	66	72	68	68	274	$330,000
Jee Young Lee	68	71	63	72	274	199,978
(Pettersen defeated Lee on third playoff hole.)						
Sarah Lee	63	68	72	74	277	145,070
Stacy Prammanasudh	67	70	73	68	278	101,275
Paula Creamer	70	69	67	72	278	101,275
Ai Miyazato	69	71	66	73	279	73,903
Sherri Steinhauer	70	68	70	72	280	54,926
Seon Hwa Lee	73	69	65	73	280	54,926
Becky Morgan	68	65	74	73	280	54,926
Angela Stanford	69	70	75	67	281	36,443
Se Ri Pak	70	71	70	70	281	36,443
Karrie Webb	68	73	68	72	281	36,443
Siew-Ai Lim	66	72	71	72	281	36,443
Amy Hung	67	68	74	72	281	36,443
Morgan Pressel	67	72	68	74	281	36,443
Carin Koch	67	69	70	75	281	36,443
Young Kim	73	69	68	72	282	27,226
Juli Inkster	68	73	68	73	282	27,226
Angela Park	69	70	70	73	282	27,226
Sun Young Yoo	71	71	70	71	283	24,307
Lorena Ochoa	70	69	71	73	283	24,307
Natalie Gulbis	67	70	73	73	283	24,307
Candie Kung	70	70	73	71	284	20,547
Mhairi McKay	72	67	73	72	284	20,547
Dorothy Delasin	69	68	74	73	284	20,547
Jimin Kang	71	65	75	73	284	20,547
Christina Kim	68	71	71	74	284	20,547
Mi Hyun Kim	64	75	70	75	284	20,547
Sung Ah Yim	68	75	70	72	285	15,891
Kristy McPherson	74	68	70	73	285	15,891
Johanna Head	69	72	70	74	285	15,891
Katherine Hull	68	73	70	74	285	15,891
Young-A Yang	73	67	70	75	285	15,891
Brittany Lincicome	66	71	72	76	285	15,891
Meena Lee	68	70	68	79	285	15,891

Sybase Classic

Upper Montclair Country Club, Clifton, New Jersey
Par 36-36–72; 6,433 yards

May 17-20
purse, $1,400,000

	SCORES				TOTAL	MONEY
Lorena Ochoa	68	67	67	68	270	$210,000
Sarah Lee	66	69	65	73	273	128,473
Se Ri Pak	68	72	73	66	279	93,198
Brittany Lang	70	70	73	67	280	65,063
Juli Inkster	71	68	72	69	280	65,063
Kate Golden	70	72	67	72	281	43,610
Sherri Steinhauer	70	69	70	72	281	43,610
Young Jo	72	67	70	73	282	34,817
Laura Davies	71	69	74	69	283	29,894
Suzann Pettersen	73	70	68	72	283	29,894
Brittany Lincicome	68	71	77	68	284	23,226
Karrie Webb	71	70	74	69	284	23,226
Na On Min	71	73	70	70	284	23,226
Nicole Castrale	70	72	69	73	284	23,226
Young Kim	72	71	67	74	284	23,226
In-Kyung Kim	70	72	69	74	285	19,273
Helen Alfredsson	73	73	69	71	286	17,163
Morgan Pressel	71	71	72	72	286	17,163
Jane Park	69	68	77	72	286	17,163
Natalie Gulbis	70	73	70	73	286	17,163
Stephanie Louden	71	72	72	72	287	15,334
Angela Park	68	73	71	75	287	15,334
Dorothy Delasin	72	71	75	70	288	14,209
Birdie Kim	72	73	72	71	288	14,209
Karine Icher	71	75	74	69	289	12,696
Reilley Rankin	71	71	75	72	289	12,696
Hye Jung Choi	68	73	76	72	289	12,696
Nancy Scranton	73	72	69	75	289	12,696
Beth Bader	76	72	73	69	290	11,254
Beth Daniel	73	73	75	69	290	11,254

LPGA Corning Classic

Corning Country Club, Corning, New York
Par 36-36–72; 6,188 yards

May 24-27
purse, $1,300,000

	SCORES				TOTAL	MONEY
Young Kim	68	64	68	68	268	$195,000
Mi Hyun Kim	68	67	66	70	271	102,669
Paula Creamer	66	68	66	71	271	102,669
In-Kyung Kim	67	69	68	68	272	60,269
Beth Bader	65	66	69	72	272	60,269
Diana D'Alessio	67	69	72	65	273	37,682
Seon Hwa Lee	68	71	67	67	273	37,682
Ai Miyazato	68	69	69	67	273	37,682
Pat Hurst	75	66	68	65	274	27,691
Natalie Gulbis	69	67	70	68	274	27,691
Jeong Jang	68	70	71	67	276	21,514
Laura Davies	69	69	69	69	276	21,514
Jamie Hullett	66	70	71	69	276	21,514
Grace Park	68	71	67	70	276	21,514
Becky Morgan	69	66	70	71	276	21,514
Mikaela Parmlid	71	68	72	66	277	16,984
Kyeong Bae	71	67	71	68	277	16,984

	SCORES			TOTAL	MONEY
Meg Mallon	68	70	68	71	277	16,984
Janice Moodie	69	72	67	70	278	14,725
Johanna Head	68	72	68	70	278	14,725
Maria Hjorth	70	68	70	70	278	14,725
Hye Jung Choi	67	70	70	71	278	14,725
Giulia Sergas	67	72	71	69	279	12,923
Il Mi Chung	71	69	69	70	279	12,923
Kate Golden	70	68	69	72	279	12,923
Shi Hyun Ahn	66	73	72	69	280	11,533
Laura Diaz	71	69	69	71	280	11,533
Na On Min	70	67	68	75	280	11,533
Carri Wood	69	72	72	68	281	9,643
Karin Sjodin	72	69	71	69	281	9,643
Leta Lindley	70	71	71	69	281	9,643
Meena Lee	70	69	71	71	281	9,643
Jean Bartholomew	68	68	74	71	281	9,643
Karine Icher	69	69	71	72	281	9,643

Ginn Tribute Hosted by Annika

RiverTowne Country Club, Mt. Pleasant, South Carolina
Par 36-36–72; 6,548 yards

May 31-June 3
purse, $2,600,000

	SCORES			TOTAL	MONEY
Nicole Castrale	69	71	68	71	279	$390,000
Lorena Ochoa	68	67	70	74	279	235,268
(Castrale defeated Ochoa on first playoff hole.)					
Cristie Kerr	72	70	67	73	282	170,671
Sarah Lee	70	72	70	71	283	119,147
Paula Creamer	68	71	73	71	283	119,147
Angela Park	66	72	71	76	285	86,946
Christina Kim	74	71	71	70	286	61,506
Heather Young	69	75	71	71	286	61,506
Mi Hyun Kim	74	70	69	73	286	61,506
Angela Stanford	72	68	71	75	286	61,506
Giulia Sergas	71	70	75	71	287	48,302
Charlotte Mayorkas	72	74	68	74	288	43,666
Karin Sjodin	72	70	71	75	288	43,666
Jill McGill	73	70	75	71	289	35,551
Seon Hwa Lee	71	71	73	74	289	35,551
Sherri Steinhauer	72	74	68	75	289	35,551
Meaghan Francella	73	74	66	76	289	35,551
Becky Morgan	70	75	68	76	289	35,551
Michele Redman	70	75	72	73	290	29,626
Jeong Jang	69	73	72	76	290	29,626
Pat Hurst	68	72	74	76	290	29,626
Morgan Pressel	75	73	72	71	291	24,201
Meena Lee	72	76	72	71	291	24,201
Liselotte Neumann	70	75	75	71	291	24,201
Wendy Doolan	74	74	70	73	291	24,201
Rachel Hetherington	76	70	72	73	291	24,201
Maria Hjorth	70	73	75	73	291	24,201
Laura Diaz	76	72	68	75	291	24,201
Jimin Kang	72	74	68	77	291	24,201
Shi Hyun Ahn	72	75	72	73	292	18,312
Kyeong Bae	74	73	71	74	292	18,312
Karrie Webb	71	70	77	74	292	18,312
Amy Hung	76	72	69	75	292	18,312
Stephanie Louden	73	73	71	75	292	18,312
Kimberly Hall	70	75	71	76	292	18,312

McDonald's LPGA Championship

Bulle Rock Golf Course, Havre de Grace, Maryland
Par 36-36–72; 6,596 yards

June 7-10
purse, $2,000,000

	SCORES				TOTAL	MONEY
Suzann Pettersen	69	67	71	67	274	$300,000
Karrie Webb	68	69	71	67	275	179,038
Na On Min	71	70	65	70	276	129,880
Lindsey Wright	71	70	71	66	278	100,473
Angela Park	67	73	68	71	279	80,869
Sophie Gustafson	70	71	71	68	280	53,422
Paula Creamer	71	68	73	68	280	53,422
Lorena Ochoa	71	71	69	69	280	53,422
Brittany Lincicome	69	69	73	69	280	53,422
Catriona Matthew	71	69	74	67	281	35,730
Sarah Lee	71	69	72	69	281	35,730
Jee Young Lee	71	72	68	70	281	35,730
Nicole Castrale	70	73	68	70	281	35,730
Morgan Pressel	68	71	70	73	282	30,192
Mi Hyun Kim	70	73	71	69	283	26,925
Stacy Prammanasudh	68	74	71	70	283	26,925
Annika Sorenstam	70	69	73	71	283	26,925
Cristie Kerr	75	70	73	66	284	23,396
Mhairi McKay	71	69	74	70	284	23,396
Siew-Ai Lim	72	69	70	73	284	23,396
Juli Inkster	73	73	73	66	285	20,585
Meaghan Francella	72	75	68	70	285	20,585
Shi Hyun Ahn	71	73	71	70	285	20,585
In-Kyung Kim	73	70	71	71	285	20,585
Pat Hurst	69	75	76	66	286	17,350
Wendy Doolan	76	70	70	70	286	17,350
Jeong Jang	73	71	71	71	286	17,350
Birdie Kim	67	71	73	75	286	17,350
Kim Saiki-Maloney	67	73	70	76	286	17,350
Leta Lindley	76	69	72	70	287	14,801
Laura Davies	68	75	71	73	287	14,801
Teresa Lu	70	72	72	73	287	14,801
Maria Hjorth	69	75	74	70	288	13,069
Se Ri Pak	73	70	74	71	288	13,069
Angela Stanford	73	71	72	72	288	13,069
Kate Golden	74	73	74	68	289	11,096
Nancy Scranton	73	73	74	69	289	11,096
Jimin Kang	73	72	74	70	289	11,096
Giulia Sergas	69	74	74	72	289	11,096
Seon Hwa Lee	71	74	71	73	289	11,096
Johanna Head	75	72	75	68	290	9,037
Becky Morgan	73	72	75	70	290	9,037
Irene Cho	72	72	76	70	290	9,037
Sherri Turner	71	73	74	72	290	9,037
Reilley Rankin	71	71	74	74	290	9,037
Gloria Park	72	74	76	69	291	6,862
Linda Wessberg	74	71	77	69	291	6,862
Michele Redman	74	72	75	70	291	6,862
Dorothy Delasin	74	72	75	70	291	6,862
Marcy Hart	73	69	77	72	291	6,862
Ji-Young Oh	73	72	73	73	291	6,862
Kyeong Bae	72	71	75	73	291	6,862
Joo Mi Kim	71	74	72	74	291	6,862
Kimberly Hall	74	69	73	75	291	6,862
Meena Lee	70	69	76	76	291	6,862
Charlotte Mayorkas	75	71	77	69	292	5,489
Sherri Steinhauer	74	73	75	70	292	5,489

	SCORES				TOTAL	MONEY
Christina Kim	74	69	75	74	292	5,489
Heather Young	75	70	76	72	293	4,934
Rachel Hetherington	74	71	75	73	293	4,934
Karin Sjodin	71	74	72	76	293	4,934
Lorie Kane	74	73	76	71	294	4,460
Yu Ping Lin	74	72	75	73	294	4,460
In-Bee Park	73	73	75	73	294	4,460
Silvia Cavalleri	74	73	73	74	294	4,460
Katherine Hull	71	72	77	74	294	4,460
Young-A Yang	74	72	73	75	294	4,460
Liselotte Neumann	72	74	76	73	295	4,116
Brittany Lang	75	72	77	72	296	3,882
Moira Dunn	74	73	76	73	296	3,882
Il Mi Chung	75	69	78	74	296	3,882
Jackie Gallagher-Smith	74	72	75	75	296	3,882
Marisa Baena	74	72	74	76	296	3,882
Virada Nirapathpongporn	76	71	77	73	297	3,700
Jane Park	73	70	80	74	297	3,700
Karen Davies	73	74	76	75	298	3,538
Vicki Goetze-Ackerman	73	72	78	75	298	3,538
Eva Dahllof	74	73	73	78	298	3,538
Sung Ah Yim	77	70	72	79	298	3,538
Erica Blasberg	72	72	73	81	298	3,538
Laura Diaz	76	71	78	74	299	3,360
Patricia Meunier-Lebouc	74	72	76	77	299	3,360
Meredith Duncan	71	76	74	78	299	3,360
Michelle Wie	73	74	83	79	309	3,273

Wegmans LPGA

Locust Hill Country Club, Pittsford, New York
Par 35-37–72; 6,328 yards

June 21-24
purse, $1,800,000

	SCORES				TOTAL	MONEY
Lorena Ochoa	69	71	67	73	280	$270,000
In-Kyung Kim	70	67	71	72	280	165,587
(Ochoa defeated Kim on second playoff hole.)						
Mi Hyun Kim	69	68	75	69	281	120,122
Cristie Kerr	66	75	70	71	282	92,925
Jeong Jang	71	73	71	68	283	67,994
Lindsey Wright	70	70	72	71	283	67,994
Angela Stanford	70	69	73	72	284	51,222
Jee Young Lee	71	77	69	68	285	36,233
Brittany Lincicome	69	75	73	68	285	36,233
Morgan Pressel	70	72	73	70	285	36,233
Maria Hjorth	70	71	73	71	285	36,233
Rachel Hetherington	70	71	73	71	285	36,233
Wendy Ward	74	70	69	72	285	36,233
Sophie Gustafson	70	74	75	67	286	25,656
Jin Joo Hong	71	73	69	73	286	25,656
Pat Hurst	74	69	70	73	286	25,656
A.J. Eathorne	72	71	69	74	286	25,656
Giulia Sergas	76	68	75	68	287	21,637
Mhairi McKay	72	72	74	69	287	21,637
Suzann Pettersen	68	75	72	72	287	21,637
Hye Jung Choi	74	74	71	69	288	16,755
Angela Park	76	71	72	69	288	16,755
Jimin Kang	70	75	73	70	288	16,755
Young-A Yang	76	72	69	71	288	16,755
Lorie Kane	71	74	72	71	288	16,755

	SCORES				TOTAL	MONEY
Ai Miyazato	73	71	73	71	288	16,755
Paula Creamer	70	76	70	72	288	16,755
Beth Bader	73	72	70	73	288	16,755
Leta Lindley	72	71	72	73	288	16,755
Meena Lee	71	71	73	73	288	16,755
Seon Hwa Lee	71	71	71	75	288	16,755

U.S. Women's Open

Pine Needles Lodge & Golf Club, Southern Pines, North Carolina
Par 35-36–71; 6,664 yards

June 28-July 1
purse, $3,100,000

	SCORES				TOTAL	MONEY
Cristie Kerr	71	72	66	70	279	$560,000
Angela Park	68	69	74	70	281	271,022
Lorena Ochoa	71	71	68	71	281	271,022
Se Ri Pak	74	72	68	68	282	130,549
In-Bee Park	69	73	71	69	282	130,549
Ji-Yai Shin	70	69	71	74	284	103,581
Jee Young Lee	72	71	71	71	285	93,031
Mi Hyun Kim	71	75	70	70	286	82,464
Jeong Jang	72	71	70	73	286	82,464
Ai Miyazato	73	73	72	69	287	66,177
Kyeong Bae	74	71	72	70	287	66,177
Julieta Granada	70	69	75	73	287	66,177
Morgan Pressel	71	70	69	77	287	66,177
Brittany Lincicome	71	74	71	72	288	55,032
Joo Mi Kim	70	73	70	75	288	55,032
Jimin Kang	73	73	73	70	289	44,219
Paula Creamer	72	74	71	72	289	44,219
Angela Stanford	72	71	73	73	289	44,219
Catriona Matthew	75	67	74	73	289	44,219
Birdie Kim	73	70	71	75	289	44,219
Amy Hung	70	69	75	75	289	44,219
Dina Ammaccapane	75	72	70	73	290	33,878
Sakura Yokomine	72	71	74	73	290	33,878
Shiho Oyama	69	73	73	75	290	33,878
Mi-Jeong Jeon	76	72	73	70	291	24,767
Sherri Steinhauer	75	72	72	72	291	24,767
Il Mi Chung	73	72	74	72	291	24,767
Young Kim	75	71	72	73	291	24,767
Katherine Hull	72	74	71	74	291	24,767
Seon Hwa Lee	72	73	71	75	291	24,767
Hye Jung Choi	77	68	70	76	291	24,767
Laura Davies	72	75	72	73	292	19,754
Annika Sorenstam	70	77	72	73	292	19,754
Moira Dunn	73	71	74	74	292	19,754
Charlotte Mayorkas	70	73	78	72	293	17,648
Natalie Gulbis	74	72	74	73	293	17,648
Nicole Castrale	75	73	70	75	293	17,648
Kris Tamulis	72	71	74	76	293	17,648
Janice Moodie	71	76	74	73	294	14,954
Becky Morgan	75	72	73	74	294	14,954
*Jennie Lee	71	74	75	74	294	
Laura Diaz	74	72	73	75	294	14,954
*Jennifer Song	72	73	73	76	294	
Erica Blasberg	74	69	75	76	294	14,954
Shi Hyun Ahn	70	72	76	76	294	14,954
Sherri Turner	73	74	73	75	295	12,268
Meena Lee	71	75	74	75	295	12,268

	SCORES				TOTAL	MONEY
Diana D'Alessio	73	70	77	75	295	12,268
Wendy Doolan	73	70	75	77	295	12,268
Sung Ah Yim	75	73	78	70	296	9,492
Su A. Kim	73	74	78	71	296	9,492
*Amanda Blumenherst	72	76	74	74	296	
Teresa Lu	75	72	75	74	296	9,492
Jimin Jeong	74	71	77	74	296	9,492
Song-Hee Kim	77	69	75	75	296	9,492
Leta Lindley	72	73	76	75	296	9,492
Amy Yang	74	72	74	76	296	9,492
Jane Park	73	75	76	73	297	8,240
Candie Kung	74	74	74	75	297	8,240
Katie Futcher	73	72	77	75	297	8,240
Pat Hurst	74	72	79	73	298	7,822
In-Kyung Kim	73	72	74	79	298	7,822
Allison Fouch	75	73	79	73	300	7,558
Karin Sjodin	74	74	78	74	300	7,558
Aree Song	75	73	76	77	301	7,369
Karine Icher	71	75	82	77	305	7,240
*Mina Harigae	72	75	78	80	305	

Jamie Farr Owens Corning Classic

Highland Meadows Golf Club, Sylvania, Ohio
Par 34-37–71; 6,428 yards

July 12-15
purse, $1,300,000

	SCORES				TOTAL	MONEY
Se Ri Pak	63	68	69	67	267	$195,000
Morgan Pressel	68	70	64	68	270	119,590
Wendy Ward	71	70	67	68	276	63,020
Laura Davies	71	69	67	69	276	63,020
Laura Diaz	69	70	68	69	276	63,020
Carri Wood	68	69	70	69	276	63,020
Angela Stanford	69	70	69	69	277	34,702
In-Kyung Kim	72	68	65	72	277	34,702
Stacy Prammanasudh	71	70	69	68	278	27,828
Linda Wessberg	73	68	66	71	278	27,828
Gloria Park	72	69	70	68	279	22,982
Jin Young Pak	67	69	74	69	279	22,982
Meg Mallon	72	65	70	72	279	22,982
Sherri Steinhauer	73	70	71	66	280	18,530
Mi Hyun Kim	68	73	71	68	280	18,530
Seon Hwa Lee	70	70	70	70	280	18,530
Beth Bader	69	73	66	72	280	18,530
Kristy McPherson	72	72	69	68	281	15,627
Brittany Lincicome	69	72	72	68	281	15,627
Candie Kung	70	70	69	72	281	15,627
Katherine Hull	71	72	71	68	282	13,501
Rachel Hetherington	70	71	71	70	282	13,501
Christina Kim	69	71	72	70	282	13,501
Jee Young Lee	71	71	69	71	282	13,501
Jeong Jang	69	71	69	73	282	13,501
Na Ri Kim	70	71	71	71	283	11,818
Kim Hall	73	67	72	71	283	11,818
Diana D'Alessio	72	72	71	69	284	9,167
Joo Mi Kim	74	70	70	70	284	9,167
Kristi Albers	69	73	72	70	284	9,167
Julieta Granada	71	73	69	71	284	9,167
Sophie Giquel	72	68	73	71	284	9,167
Angela Park	71	69	73	71	284	9,167

	SCORES				TOTAL	MONEY
Nicole Castrale	71	70	71	72	284	9,167
Karine Icher	71	72	68	73	284	9,167
Kelly Cap	71	70	69	74	284	9,167
Marcy Hart	72	67	71	74	284	9,167
Alena Sharp	65	74	67	78	284	9,167

HSBC Women's World Match Play

Wykagyl Country Club, New Rochelle, New York
Par 36-35–71; 6,237 yards

July 19-22
purse, $2,000,000

FIRST ROUND

Lorena Ochoa defeated Ashleigh Simon, 6 and 5.
Meaghan Francella defeated Meena Lee, 2 and 1.
Stacy Prammanasudh defeated Trish Johnson, 3 and 2.
Pat Hurst defeated Heather Young, 3 and 2.
Paula Creamer defeated Giulia Sergas, 4 and 3.
Maria Hjorth defeated Catriona Matthew, 23 holes.
Hye Jung Choi defeated Juli Inkster, 4 and 3.
Angela Stanford defeated Kyeong Bae, 19 holes.
Amy Hung defeated Cristie Kerr, 5 and 4.
Young Kim defeated In-Kyung Kim, 1 up.
Carin Koch defeated Brittany Lincicome, 4 and 3.
Reilley Rankin defeated Julieta Granada, 3 and 2.
Se Ri Pak defeated Beth Bader, 2 up.
Christina Kim defeated Natalie Gulbis, 3 and 2.
Ai Miyazato defeated Becky Morgan, 5 and 4.
Sherri Steinhauer defeated Na On Min, 5 and 4.
Charlotte Mayorkas defeated Karrie Webb, 1 up.
Laura Diaz defeated Joo Mi Kim, 2 and 1.
Jee Young Lee defeated Karin Sjodin, 1 up.
Nicole Castrale defeated Jimin Kang, 5 and 4.
Suzann Pettersen defeated In-Bee Park, 19 holes.
Rachel Hetherington defeated Shi Hyun Ahn, 2 and 1.
Mi Hyun Kim defeated Wendy Doolan, 5 and 4.
Sarah Lee defeated Il Mi Chung, 3 and 1.
Annika Sorenstam defeated Katherine Hull, 20 holes.
Lindsey Wright defeated Brittany Lang, 4 and 3.
Jeong Jang defeated Marisa Baena, 3 and 2.
Angela Park defeated Silvia Cavalleri, 1 up.
Birdie Kim defeated Morgan Pressel, 2 up.
Laura Davies defeated Michele Redman, 1 up.
Janice Moodie defeated Ji-Yai Shin, 19 holes.
Seon Hwa Lee defeated Diana D'Alessio, 1 up.

(Each losing player received $5,000.)

SECOND ROUND

Francella defeated Ochoa, 1 up.
Hurst defeated Prammanasudh, 3 and 1.
Hjorth defeated Creamer, 1 up.
Stanford defeated Choi, 5 and 4.
Hung defeated Young Kim, 1 up.
Koch defeated Rankin, 4 and 2.
Christina Kim defeated Pak, 4 and 2.
Miyazato defeated Steinhauer, 4 and 2.
Diaz defeated Mayorkas, 21 holes.
Jee Young Lee defeated Castrale, 4 and 2.
Hetherington defeated Pettersen, 1 up.
Mi Hyun Kim defeated Sarah Lee, 2 and 1.

Wright defeated Sorenstam, 3 and 2.
Jang defeated Angela Park, 2 and 1.
Davies defeated Birdie Kim, 2 and 1.
Seon Hwa Lee defeated Moodie, 5 and 4.

(Each losing player received $10,000.)

THIRD ROUND

Francella defeated Hurst, 2 and 1.
Hjorth defeated Stanford, 19 holes.
Hung defeated Koch, 19 holes.
Miyazato defeated Christina Kim, 2 and 1.
Jee Young Lee defeated Diaz, 2 up.
Mi Hyun Kim defeated Hetherington, 3 and 2.
Wright defeated Jang, 1 up.
Seon Hwa Lee defeated Davies, 2 and 1.

(Each losing player received $25,000.)

QUARTER-FINALS

Hjorth defeated Francella, 4 and 3.
Miyazato defeated Hung, 1 up.
Mi Hyun Kim defeated Jee Young Lee, 1 up.
Seon Hwa Lee defeated Wright, 3 and 2.

(Each losing player received $50,000.)

SEMI-FINALS

Miyazato defeated Hjorth, 3 and 2.
Seon Hwa Lee defeated Mi Hyun Kim, 2 up.

PLAYOFF FOR THIRD-FOURTH PLACE

Mi Hyun Kim defeated Hjorth, 2 up.

(Kim earned $200,000; Hjorth earned $150,000.)

FINAL

Seon Hwa Lee defeated Miyazato, 2 and 1.

(Lee earned $500,000; Miyazato earned $300,000.)

Evian Masters
See Ladies European Tour section.

Ricoh Women's British Open
See Ladies European Tour section.

CN Canadian Women's Open

Royal Mayfair Golf Club, Edmonton, Alberta, Canada
Par 35-36–71; 6,505 yards

August 16-19
purse, $2,250,000

	SCORES				TOTAL	MONEY
Lorena Ochoa	70	65	64	69	268	$337,500
Paula Creamer	68	69	66	68	271	204,998
Shi Hyun Ahn	67	67	74	66	274	148,711
Brittany Lang	71	67	70	67	275	103,818
Laura Diaz	65	70	68	72	275	103,818
Jeong Jang	67	71	70	68	276	64,909
Kimberly Hall	68	67	72	69	276	64,909
Ya Ni Tseng	67	71	67	71	276	64,909
Seon Hwa Lee	70	72	71	64	277	49,944
Suzann Pettersen	73	69	68	68	278	42,275
Angela Stanford	72	69	69	68	278	42,275
Alena Sharp	70	72	67	69	278	42,275
Morgan Pressel	74	69	69	67	279	32,772
Minea Blomqvist	71	70	70	68	279	32,772
Soo Young Moon	70	72	67	70	279	32,772
Meg Mallon	72	68	68	71	279	32,772
Juli Inkster	68	66	73	72	279	32,772
Diana D'Alessio	69	72	72	67	280	24,509
Heather Young	67	73	71	69	280	24,509
Mi Hyun Kim	70	72	68	70	280	24,509
Mikaela Parmlid	72	68	70	70	280	24,509
Candie Kung	72	68	70	70	280	24,509
Mhairi McKay	72	72	65	71	280	24,509
Karrie Webb	72	64	73	71	280	24,509
Julieta Granada	71	71	66	72	280	24,509
Christina Kim	74	68	72	67	281	18,041
Eva Dahllof	73	69	71	68	281	18,041
In-Bee Park	75	68	69	69	281	18,041
Kyeong Bae	66	72	74	69	281	18,041
Amy Hung	73	68	70	70	281	18,041
Jimin Kang	71	71	68	71	281	18,041
Rachel Hetherington	74	69	66	72	281	18,041
Young Jo	72	68	68	73	281	18,041

Safeway Classic

Columbia Edgewater Country Club, Portland, Oregon
Par 36-36–72; 6,397 yards

August 23-26
purse, $1,700,000

	SCORES			TOTAL	MONEY
Lorena Ochoa	67	66	71	204	$255,000
In-Bee Park	73	72	64	209	105,307
Christina Kim	69	71	69	209	105,307
Mhairi McKay	70	67	72	209	105,307
Sophie Gustafson	66	68	75	209	105,307
Ji-Young Oh	66	71	73	210	56,849
Beth Bader	70	71	70	211	44,637
Shi Hyun Ahn	73	67	71	211	44,637
Juli Inkster	75	68	69	212	34,390
Katie Futcher	72	70	70	212	34,390
Gloria Park	72	70	70	212	34,390
Paula Creamer	73	71	69	213	26,108
Sherri Turner	72	71	70	213	26,108
Sarah Lee	69	72	72	213	26,108

	SCORES			TOTAL	MONEY
Laura Diaz	71	69	73	213	26,108
Angela Stanford	68	72	73	213	26,108
Jin Joo Hong	73	72	69	214	20,179
Cristie Kerr	73	72	69	214	20,179
Stephanie Louden	73	70	71	214	20,179
Lindsey Wright	70	70	74	214	20,179
Minea Blomqvist	70	70	74	214	20,179
Song-Hee Kim	74	71	70	215	16,726
Soo-Yun Kang	75	69	71	215	16,726
*Tiffany Joh	74	70	71	215	
Kris Tamulis	72	71	72	215	16,726
Joo Mi Kim	70	72	73	215	16,726
Mi Hyun Kim	71	70	74	215	16,726
Jeong Jang	73	72	71	216	13,518
Karrie Webb	70	74	72	216	13,518
Julieta Granada	74	69	73	216	13,518
Brittany Lang	72	71	73	216	13,518
Il Mi Chung	72	71	73	216	13,518
Katherine Hull	72	69	75	216	13,518

State Farm Classic

Panther Creek Country Club, Springfield, Illinois
Par 36-36–72; 6,608 yards

August 30-September 2
purse, $1,300,000

	SCORES				TOTAL	MONEY
Sherri Steinhauer	67	66	71	67	271	$195,000
Christina Kim	69	66	71	66	272	119,296
Annika Sorenstam	71	65	71	67	274	76,744
Rachel Hetherington	69	69	67	69	274	76,744
Angela Park	69	70	69	68	276	53,884
Jeong Jang	72	69	71	65	277	44,087
Joo Mi Kim	70	70	69	69	278	34,616
Michele Redman	73	69	64	72	278	34,616
Morgan Pressel	69	73	71	66	279	25,718
Janice Moodie	69	69	74	67	279	25,718
Pat Hurst	72	71	67	69	279	25,718
Sophie Gustafson	70	69	71	69	279	25,718
Angela Stanford	72	71	70	67	280	19,072
Sung Ah Yim	73	70	69	68	280	19,072
Giulia Sergas	73	66	73	68	280	19,072
Catriona Matthew	71	69	70	70	280	19,072
Mi Hyun Kim	70	67	73	70	280	19,072
Jeanne Cho-Hunicke	72	72	71	66	281	15,588
Jin Joo Hong	70	70	70	71	281	15,588
Marcy Hart	68	69	71	73	281	15,588
Carri Wood	72	70	72	68	282	13,468
Lisa Fernandes	70	72	71	69	282	13,468
Gloria Park	70	71	70	71	282	13,468
Diana D'Alessio	73	69	68	72	282	13,468
Becky Morgan	71	67	69	75	282	13,468
Mikaela Parmlid	71	70	75	67	283	11,116
Clarissa Childs	74	68	72	69	283	11,116
Kate Golden	69	71	74	69	283	11,116
Yeon Joo Lee	72	69	72	70	283	11,116
Moira Dunn	70	70	73	70	283	11,116
*Stacy Lewis	71	71	69	72	283	

The Solheim Cup

See Ladies European Tour section.

Navistar LPGA Classic

Robert Trent Jones Golf Trail, Capitol Hill, Prattville, Alabama
Par 36-36–72; 6,632 yards

September 27-30
purse, $1,300,000

	SCORES				TOTAL	MONEY
Maria Hjorth	70	67	70	67	274	$195,000
Stacy Prammanasudh	63	68	73	71	275	116,375
Angela Park	72	68	73	63	276	74,864
Lorena Ochoa	66	68	69	73	276	74,864
Karrie Webb	70	71	69	68	278	52,563
Amy Hung	73	73	70	63	279	43,008
Hye Jung Choi	70	68	74	68	280	33,769
Angela Stanford	69	74	65	72	280	33,769
Teresa Lu	70	70	72	69	281	27,079
Nicole Castrale	73	66	70	72	281	27,079
Suzann Pettersen	71	67	74	70	282	23,096
Eva Dahllof	71	74	66	71	282	23,096
Il Mi Chung	71	71	71	70	283	18,605
Jimin Kang	70	69	73	71	283	18,605
Meaghan Francella	70	69	72	72	283	18,605
Janice Moodie	69	69	73	72	283	18,605
Lisa Fernandes	69	71	70	73	283	18,605
Dorothy Delasin	70	72	73	69	284	15,801
Lorie Kane	69	74	70	72	285	15,164
Karine Icher	71	71	70	74	286	14,399
Wendy Ward	70	69	73	74	286	14,399
Sherri Turner	73	72	74	68	287	13,125
Tracy Hanson	69	75	74	69	287	13,125
Jee Young Lee	69	72	76	70	287	13,125
Rachel Hetherington	73	71	73	71	288	11,277
Sun Young Yoo	72	69	74	73	288	11,277
Seon Hwa Lee	71	71	71	75	288	11,277
Giulia Sergas	70	73	68	77	288	11,277
Lindsey Wright	67	68	75	78	288	11,277
Na On Min	72	71	76	70	289	8,713
Linda Wessberg	72	74	69	74	289	8,713
Christina Kim	70	70	75	74	289	8,713
Ji-Young Oh	76	69	69	75	289	8,713
Minea Blomqvist	73	71	70	75	289	8,713
Jamie Hullett	70	71	72	76	289	8,713
Young Kim	71	69	72	77	289	8,713
Virada Nirapathpongporn	67	70	70	82	289	8,713

Longs Drugs Challenge

Blackhawk Country Club, Danville, California
Par 37-35–72; 6,212 yards

October 4-7
purse, $1,100,000

	SCORES				TOTAL	MONEY
Suzann Pettersen	75	65	64	73	277	$165,000
Lorena Ochoa	69	70	67	71	277	101,967
(Pettersen defeated Ochoa on second playoff hole.)						
Juli Inkster	74	66	71	70	281	73,970
Natalie Gulbis	74	71	71	66	282	51,640

	SCORES				TOTAL	MONEY
Lorie Kane	69	69	67	77	282	51,640
Nicole Castrale	71	70	73	69	283	37,683
Karrie Webb	69	69	74	72	284	31,542
Amy Hung	75	74	68	68	285	25,029
In-Kyung Kim	73	69	73	70	285	25,029
Maria Hjorth	73	69	71	72	285	25,029
Paula Creamer	77	70	70	69	286	18,434
Alena Sharp	73	70	74	69	286	18,434
Karen Stupples	71	74	70	71	286	18,434
Seon Hwa Lee	73	70	72	71	286	18,434
Se Ri Pak	69	71	73	73	286	18,434
Nancy Scranton	74	72	74	67	287	15,296
Sun Young Yoo	72	73	75	68	288	13,138
Cristie Kerr	74	71	73	70	288	13,138
Jeong Jang	74	74	67	73	288	13,138
Teresa Lu	75	70	70	73	288	13,138
Brittany Lincicome	73	68	74	73	288	13,138
Stacy Prammanasudh	69	75	69	75	288	13,138
Pat Hurst	67	76	75	71	289	11,072
Christina Kim	72	74	71	72	289	11,072
Charlotte Mayorkas	73	67	72	77	289	11,072
Gloria Park	74	72	75	69	290	9,148
Laura Diaz	73	74	73	70	290	9,148
Song-Hee Kim	74	72	73	71	290	9,148
Wendy Ward	72	71	75	72	290	9,148
Jill McGill	72	75	70	73	290	9,148
Diana D'Alessio	69	72	76	73	290	9,148
Il Mi Chung	70	78	68	74	290	9,148

Samsung World Championship

Bighorn Golf Club, Palm Desert, California
Par 36-36–72; 6,644 yards

October 11-14
purse, $1,000,000

	SCORES				TOTAL	MONEY
Lorena Ochoa	68	67	69	66	270	$250,000
Mi Hyun Kim	68	70	67	69	274	156,250
Jeong Jang	69	68	68	70	275	84,376
Angela Park	67	69	69	70	275	84,376
Suzann Pettersen	71	69	64	72	276	50,000
Jee Young Lee	70	70	70	68	278	34,375
Paula Creamer	67	69	71	71	278	34,375
Stacy Prammanasudh	72	70	70	67	279	28,751
Angela Stanford	70	66	74	71	281	26,249
Sarah Lee	72	72	69	69	282	21,667
Seon Hwa Lee	73	73	66	70	282	21,667
Se Ri Pak	69	71	70	72	282	21,667
Morgan Pressel	68	72	72	71	283	18,751
Cristie Kerr	75	66	70	73	284	17,501
Maria Hjorth	72	70	71	73	286	16,249
Nicole Castrale	73	70	75	72	290	15,000
Brittany Lincicome	74	70	72	75	291	14,375
Ai Miyazato	75	68	76	74	293	13,751
Michelle Wie	79	79	77	71	306	13,125
Bettina Hauert	76	81	74	76	307	12,499

Hana Bank-Kolon Championship

See Korea LPGA Tour section.

Honda LPGA Thailand

Siam Country Club, Pattaya Old Course, Pattaya City, Thailand
Par 36-36—72; 6,469 yards

October 25-28
purse, $1,300,000

	SCORES				TOTAL	MONEY
Suzann Pettersen	65	68	63	71	267	$195,000
Laura Davies	71	66	66	65	268	125,514
Paula Creamer	72	66	66	66	270	91,052
Rachel Hetherington	69	70	68	65	272	70,436
Stacy Prammanasudh	72	67	69	66	274	56,693
Annika Sorenstam	72	68	68	67	275	46,385
Alena Sharp	67	68	72	70	277	38,826
Laura Diaz	71	68	71	68	278	32,298
Reilley Rankin	69	70	70	69	278	32,298
Katherine Hull	68	71	68	73	280	27,831
Sophie Gustafson	71	70	72	68	281	23,381
Hee-Won Han	69	70	72	70	281	23,381
Brittany Lang	71	72	67	71	281	23,381
Seon Hwa Lee	71	69	69	72	281	23,381
*Mika Miyasato	71	73	69	69	282	
Morgan Pressel	75	68	69	70	282	19,379
Maria Hjorth	69	74	68	71	282	19,379
In-Kyung Kim	72	75	67	69	283	16,767
Lindsey Wright	74	70	69	70	283	16,767
Linda Wessberg	72	70	70	71	283	16,767
Joo Mi Kim	71	67	71	74	283	16,767
Teresa Lu	75	68	71	70	284	14,431
Virada Nirapathpongporn	72	71	70	71	284	14,431
In-Bee Park	73	68	71	72	284	14,431
Angela Park	68	70	72	74	284	14,431
Catriona Matthew	75	66	75	69	285	12,885
Jeong Jang	76	69	70	70	285	12,885
Silvia Cavalleri	74	75	68	69	286	11,242
Janice Moodie	73	70	74	69	286	11,242
Kyeong Bae	69	71	76	70	286	11,242
Onnarin Sattayabanphot	73	71	70	72	286	11,242
Gloria Park	71	73	70	72	286	11,242

Mizuno Classic

See Japan LPGA Tour section.

The Mitchell Company Tournament of Champions

Robert Trent Jones Golf Trail, Magnolia Grove,
Mobile, Alabama
Par 36-36—72; 6,253 yards

November 8-11
purse, $1,000,000

	SCORES				TOTAL	MONEY
Paula Creamer	67	65	68	68	268	$150,000
Birdie Kim	72	70	66	68	276	110,825
Natalie Gulbis	69	74	67	68	278	64,216

	SCORES				TOTAL	MONEY
Annika Sorenstam	71	67	70	70	278	64,216
Pat Hurst	69	69	68	72	278	64,216
Jimin Kang	71	76	68	65	280	35,091
Suzann Pettersen	69	71	68	72	280	35,091
Jin Joo Hong	70	67	70	73	280	35,091
Lorena Ochoa	74	69	68	70	281	27,001
Christina Kim	77	69	70	66	282	21,431
Hee-Won Han	71	74	70	67	282	21,431
Karen Stupples	72	67	74	69	282	21,431
Wendy Ward	73	69	69	71	282	21,431
Seon Hwa Lee	69	74	67	72	282	21,431
Catriona Matthew	73	73	73	65	284	17,596
Juli Inkster	74	72	71	71	288	16,201
Nicole Castrale	76	71	67	74	288	16,201
Carin Koch	72	70	76	71	289	15,048
Meg Mallon	67	82	72	69	290	14,199
Julieta Granada	74	72	68	76	290	14,199
Mi Hyun Kim	69	76	72	75	292	13,228
Liselotte Neumann	72	73	71	76	292	13,228
Moira Dunn	78	73	69	73	293	12,257
Heather Young	71	76	71	75	293	12,257
Morgan Pressel	82	72	67	74	295	11,589
Meaghan Francella	80	68	74	74	296	11,164
Heather Daly-Donofrio	75	73	75	74	297	10,740
Joo Mi Kim	72	75	76	75	298	10,315
Wendy Doolan	77	76	73	73	299	9,708
Sherri Steinhauer	75	74	77	73	299	9,708
Jennifer Rosales	75	77	73	75	300	8,980
Sung Ah Yim	77	70	75	78	300	8,980
Silvia Cavalleri	74	72	80	80	306	8,434
Kim Saiki-Maloney	71	80	77	82	310	8,070

ADT Championship

Trump International Golf Club, West Palm Beach, Florida
Par 36-36–72; 6,538 yards

November 15-18
purse, $1,550,000

	SCORES			FINAL ROUND	MONEY
Lorena Ochoa	70	70	66	68	$1,000,000
Natalie Gulbis	72	75	70	70	100,000
Paula Creamer	68	73	66	72	20,500
Cristie Kerr	69	71	69	74	19,250
Mi Hyun Kim	67	70	71	78	18,500
Sarah Lee	74	71	70	80	17,750
Christina Kim	67	71	71	81	17,000
Karrie Webb	76	70	68	84	16,250

Players who did not advance after Round 3

	SCORES			TOTAL	MONEY
Morgan Pressel	73	65	73	211	14,000
Sophie Gustafson	72	70	71	213	14,000
Nicole Castrale	71	72	71	214	14,000
Juli Inkster	68	75	72	215	14,000
Suzann Pettersen	73	68	74	215	14,000
Seon Hwa Lee	74	70	72	216	14,000
Ai Miyazato	75	72	74	221	14,000
Catriona Matthew	69	75	79	223	14,000

Players who did not advance after Round 2

	SCORES		TOTAL	MONEY
Annika Sorenstam	74	73	147	8,000
Jeong Jang	75	73	148	8,000
Shi Hyun Ahn	74	75	149	8,000
Maria Hjorth	79	70	149	8,000
Angela Park	76	73	149	8,000
Jee Young Lee	76	74	150	8,000
Angela Stanford	77	74	151	8,000
Laura Davies	79	73	152	8,000
Brittany Lincicome	77	75	152	8,000
Se Ri Pak	77	75	152	8,000
Meaghan Francella	77	76	153	8,000
In-Bee Park	79	74	153	8,000
Reilley Rankin	76	77	153	8,000
Laura Diaz	73	81	154	8,000
Stacy Prammanasudh	77	77	154	8,000
Sherri Steinhauer	76	78	154	8,000

Ladies European Tour

Women's World Cup of Golf

See Ladies African Tour section.

MFS Women's Australian Open

See Australian Ladies Tour section.

ANZ Ladies Masters

See Australian Ladies Tour section.

Tenerife Ladies Open

Golf del Sur, San Miguel de Abona, Tenerife, Spain
Par 36-36–72; 6,808 yards

May 3-6
purse, €275,000

	SCORES				TOTAL	MONEY
Nikki Garrett	69	75	71	72	287	€41,250
Trish Johnson	71	70	77	71	289	23,581.25
Tania Elosegui	71	75	71	72	289	23,581.25
Ana Larraneta	72	73	71	74	290	13,255
Becky Brewerton	71	71	73	75	290	13,255
Stefania Croce	73	71	77	70	291	8,937.50
Ana B. Sanchez	67	73	76	75	291	8,937.50

	SCORES				TOTAL	MONEY
Titiya Plucksataporn	69	76	72	75	292	6,517.50
Sophie Sandolo	70	77	68	77	292	6,517.50
Paula Marti	75	70	76	72	293	5,500
Rebecca Hudson	71	76	74	73	294	4,510
Eleanor Pilgrim	74	73	73	74	294	4,510
Amanda Moltke-Leth	72	75	73	74	294	4,510
Karen-Margrethe Juul	72	74	74	74	294	4,510
Martina Eberl	70	72	76	76	294	4,510
Danielle Masters	71	71	79	74	295	3,698.75
Nicole Gergely	73	73	74	75	295	3,698.75
Lotta Wahlin	71	75	73	76	295	3,698.75
Lisa Jean	71	71	75	78	295	3,698.75
Gwladys Nocera	71	76	70	78	295	3,698.75
Sophie Walker	71	73	72	79	295	3,698.75

Open de Espana Feminino

Mediterraneo Country Club, Castellon, Spain
Par 36-36–72; 6,337 yards

May 10-13
purse, €275,000

	SCORES				TOTAL	MONEY
Nikki Garrett	68	65	72	70	275	€41,250
Rebecca Hudson	65	69	69	73	276	27,912.50
Gwladys Nocera	66	68	71	72	277	19,250
Louise Friberg	68	71	73	66	278	14,850
Laurette Maritz	72	70	66	71	279	11,660
Kirsty Taylor	66	70	70	74	280	9,625
Cherie Byrnes	72	70	70	69	281	8,250
Iben Tinning	70	71	75	67	283	6,517.50
Sarah Kemp	70	71	73	69	283	6,517.50
*Carlota Ciganda	69	75	67	72	283	
Joanne Mills	75	71	71	67	284	4,790.50
Cassandra Kirkland	71	73	71	69	284	4,790.50
Laura Cabanillas	70	73	70	71	284	4,790.50
Veronica Zorzi	73	68	71	72	284	4,790.50
Danielle Masters	67	71	73	73	284	4,790.50
Fany Schaeffer	69	72	75	69	285	3,911.87
Elisabeth Esterl	73	73	70	69	285	3,911.87
Maria Boden	72	74	69	70	285	3,911.87
Bettina Hauert	71	74	68	72	285	3,911.87
Amy Yang	69	71	74	72	286	3,588.75
Sophie Giquel	73	72	68	73	286	3,588.75

Deutsche Bank Ladies Swiss Open

Golf Gerre Losone, Ticino, Switzerland
Par 35-37–72; 6,185 yards

May 17-20
purse, €525,000

	SCORES				TOTAL	MONEY
Bettina Hauert	68	73	72	72	285	€78,750
Paula Marti	73	73	69	70	285	45,018.75
Anna Rawson	72	72	69	72	285	45,018.75
(Hauert defeated Rawson on second and Marti on fourth playoff hole.)						
Lisa Holm Sorensen	74	71	71	70	286	28,350
Trish Johnson	74	73	71	69	287	20,317.50
Eleanor Pilgrim	68	75	70	74	287	20,317.50
Johanna Westerberg	75	70	71	72	288	15,750

	SCORES				TOTAL	MONEY
Amanda Moltke-Leth	76	73	74	66	289	10,087.50
Louise Stahle	72	75	74	68	289	10,087.50
Mianne Bagger	75	71	73	70	289	10,087.50
Sarah Kemp	71	75	73	70	289	10,087.50
Veronica Zorzi	72	75	72	70	289	10,087.50
*Katharina Schallenberg	73	72	73	71	289	
Ursula Wikstrom	70	74	73	72	289	10,087.50
Lora Fairclough	69	73	71	76	289	10,087.50
Clare Queen	73	71	76	70	290	7,577.50
Rebecca Coakley	75	74	70	71	290	7,577.50
Nikki Garrett	68	77	73	72	290	7,577.50
Gwladys Nocera	73	75	77	66	291	6,702.50
Anna Rossi	76	71	74	70	291	6,702.50
Riikka Hakkarainen	74	74	73	70	291	6,702.50
Sophie Sandolo	72	72	76	71	291	6,702.50
Lotta Wahlin	72	75	72	72	291	6,702.50
Kathryn Imrie	76	73	69	73	291	6,702.50

BMW Ladies Italian Open

Sheraton Golf Parco de Medici, Rome, Italy
Par 35-37–72; 6,269 yards

May 23-26
purse, €400,000

	SCORES				TOTAL	MONEY
Trish Johnson	68	70	69	66	273	€60,000
Bettina Hauert	70	70	72	62	274	40,600
Sarah Kemp	68	68	72	68	276	24,800
Sophie Giquel	73	69	65	69	276	24,800
Iben Tinning	69	73	70	65	277	15,480
Federica Piovano	68	72	70	67	277	15,480
Louise Friberg	67	75	70	66	278	9,740
Rebecca Coakley	67	74	70	67	278	9,740
Carmen Alonso	70	70	69	69	278	9,740
Stefania Croce	72	64	69	73	278	9,740
Mette Buus	71	71	70	67	279	6,560
Beatriz Recari	68	73	69	69	279	6,560
Natalie Claire Booth	68	73	68	70	279	6,560
Virginie Lagoutte-Clement	68	71	69	71	279	6,560
Johanna Westerberg	68	73	67	71	279	6,560
Lara Tadiotto	69	73	70	68	280	5,448
Mianne Bagger	74	68	69	69	280	5,448
Martina Eberl	73	66	69	72	280	5,448
Amy Yang	69	70	69	72	280	5,448
Anna Rossi	69	68	69	74	280	5,448

Northern Ireland Ladies Open

Hilton Templepatrick Hotel & CC, Belfast, Northern Ireland
Par 36-36–72; 6,239 yards

June 1-3
purse, €200,000

	SCORES			TOTAL	MONEY
Lisa Hall	74	69	71	214	€30,000
Gwladys Nocera	75	68	71	214	20,300
(Hall defeated Nocera on eighth playoff hole.)					
Becky Brewerton	72	74	69	215	8,546.66
Felicity Johnson	73	72	70	215	8,546.66
Laurette Maritz	73	71	71	215	8,546.66

	SCORES			TOTAL	MONEY
Sarah Kemp	71	73	71	215	8,546.66
Tania Elosegui	73	71	71	215	8,546.66
Joanne Mills	72	70	73	215	8,546.66
Kirsty S. Taylor	77	72	67	216	4,240
Samantha Head	73	71	72	216	4,240
Martina Eberl	75	71	71	217	3,560
Helena Alterby	72	73	72	217	3,560
Kris Lindstrom	73	72	73	218	2,992
Sophie Walker	75	69	74	218	2,992
Lora Fairclough	75	68	75	218	2,992
Nicole Gergely	74	68	76	218	2,992
Kiran Matharu	72	69	77	218	2,992
Leah Hart	71	76	72	219	2,680
Lynn Brooky	75	71	73	219	2,680
Asa Gottmo	77	74	69	220	2,370
Rikke Rasmussen	76	73	71	220	2,370
Virginie Lagoutte-Clement	73	76	71	220	2,370
Danielle Masters	73	74	73	220	2,370
Ashleigh Simon	71	76	73	220	2,370
Tamara Hyett	74	71	75	220	2,370
Sara Beautell	72	71	77	220	2,370
Libby Smith	71	72	77	220	2,370

KLM Ladies Open

Eindhovensche Golf Club, Valkenswaard, Holland
Par 36-36–72; 6,195 yards

June 8-10
purse, €180,000

	SCORES			TOTAL	MONEY
Gwladys Nocera	64	70	67	201	€27,000
Virginie Lagoutte-Clement	70	69	69	208	18,270
Georgina Simpson	69	67	73	209	12,600
Louise Friberg	72	72	66	210	9,720
*Benedicte Toumpsin	69	73	68	210	
Joanne Mills	70	71	70	211	6,444
Sophie Giquel	69	72	70	211	6,444
Nathalie David-Mila	70	67	74	211	6,444
Laura Terebey	66	75	71	212	4,266
Sarah Kemp	72	66	74	212	4,266
Anja Monke	69	74	70	213	3,226.50
*Christel Boeljon	67	75	71	213	
Rebecca Hudson	72	70	71	213	3,226.50
Ursula Wikstrom	70	72	71	213	3,226.50
Rebecca Stevenson	71	70	72	213	3,226.50
Eleanor Pilgrim	72	73	69	214	2,466
Lara Tadiotto	71	73	70	214	2,466
Marta Prieto	70	73	71	214	2,466
Sophie Walker	70	72	72	214	2,466
Clare Queen	71	70	73	214	2,466
Samantha Head	69	71	74	214	2,466
Ludivine Kreutz	67	72	75	214	2,466
Cassandra Kirkland	69	69	76	214	2,466
Iben Tinning	70	67	77	214	2,466

Catalonia Ladies Masters

Club de Golf Masia Bach, Barcelona, Spain
Par 36-36–72; 6,209 yards

June 15-17
purse, €200,000

	SCORES			TOTAL	MONEY
Ashleigh Simon	70	68	70	208	€58,500
Becky Brewerton	70	68	72	210	17,150
Kirsty Taylor	68	69	73	210	17,150
Trish Johnson	71	69	71	211	10,800
Paula Marti	74	67	71	212	8,480
Gwladys Nocera	75	66	72	213	7,000
Asa Gottmo	74	68	72	214	6,000
Ana B. Sanchez	76	70	70	216	4,145
Lotta Wahlin	73	73	70	216	4,145
Lora Fairclough	76	68	72	216	4,145
Iben Tinning	72	69	75	216	4,145
Marta Prieto	77	69	71	217	2,950
Rebecca Hudson	74	74	69	217	2,950
Celeste Troche	76	71	71	218	2,660
Veronica Zorzi	72	70	76	218	2,660
Anja Monke	77	73	68	218	2,660
Amanda Moltke-Leth	74	68	76	218	2,660
Tania Elosegui	76	70	73	219	2,390
Sophie Giquel	76	70	73	219	2,390
Rebecca Coakley	76	71	72	219	2,390
Lisa Hall	78	66	75	219	2,390

Vediorbis Open de France

Le Golf d'Arras, Anzin St. Aubin, Arras, France
Par 36-36–72; 6,195 yards

June 21-24
purse, €340,000

	SCORES				TOTAL	MONEY
Linda Wessberg	70	68	74	65	277	€51,000
Trish Johnson	68	70	72	68	278	34,510
Stefania Croce	72	72	67	68	279	21,080
Gwladys Nocera	70	68	71	70	279	21,080
Lotta Wahlin	68	72	72	68	280	14,416
Rebecca Hudson	67	69	72	73	281	11,900
Paula Marti	72	71	73	67	283	10,200
Asa Gottmo	72	67	76	69	284	8,500
Sophie Giquel	71	74	72	68	285	7,208
Lynn Kenny	69	74	73	69	285	7,208
Joanne Mills	70	75	74	67	286	6,052
Diana Luna	71	74	71	70	286	6,052
Cecilia Ekelundh	71	72	75	69	287	5,168
Lara Tadiotto	71	75	72	69	287	5,168
Lisa Hall	72	68	74	73	287	5,168
Becky Brewerton	71	70	72	74	287	5,168
Karen-Margrethe Juul	71	74	71	72	288	4,624
Ludivine Kreutz	75	71	69	73	288	4,624
Sarah Kemp	69	72	73	74	288	4,624
Nathalie David-Mila	75	66	77	71	289	4,386

Ladies Open de Portugal

Gramacho Pestana Golf Resort, Algarve, Portugal
Par 36-36–72; 6,153 yards

June 29-July 1
purse, €200,000

	SCORES			TOTAL	MONEY
Sophie Giquel	70	67	69	206	€30,000
Louise Stahle	70	67	71	208	20,300
Jade Schaeffer	68	69	74	211	14,000
Johanna Westerberg	69	71	73	213	9,640
Joanne Mills	69	68	76	213	9,640
Lisa Holm Sorensen	73	68	73	214	7,000
Kirsty Taylor	71	74	71	216	5,160
Laura Cabanillas	69	74	73	216	5,160
Anna Rossi	70	73	73	216	5,160
Cherie Byrnes	68	77	72	217	3,840
Melodie Bourdy	69	73	75	217	3,840
Stefania Croce	75	72	71	218	3,066.66
Rebecca Hudson	73	72	73	218	3,066.66
Antonella Cvitan	74	74	70	218	3,066.66
Titiya Plucksataporn	70	73	75	218	3,066.66
Minea Blomqvist	69	72	77	218	3,066.66
Lynn Brooky	71	70	77	218	3,066.66
Karen Lunn	74	72	73	219	2,553.33
Asa Gottmo	72	74	73	219	2,553.33
Kathryn Imrie	71	73	75	219	2,553.33
Ludivine Kreutz	76	68	75	219	2,553.33
Frederique Seeholzer	70	73	76	219	2,553.33
Eleanor Pilgrim	72	70	77	219	2,553.33

Golf Punk Ladies English Open

Chart Hills Golf Club, Biddenden, Kent, England
Par 36-36–72; 6,158 yards

July 5-7
purse, €165,000

	SCORES			TOTAL	MONEY
Becky Brewerton	67	74	68	209	€24,750
Linda Wessberg	66	78	68	212	12,402.50
Kirsty Taylor	70	73	69	212	12,402.50
Karen Stupples	71	70	71	212	12,402.50
Laura Davies	69	73	71	213	6,385.50
Gwladys Nocera	70	72	71	213	6,385.50
Martina Eberl	68	75	71	214	4,537.50
Louise Stahle	71	72	71	214	4,537.50
*Melissa Reid	70	73	72	215	
Trish Johnson	72	76	68	216	3,498
Stacy Lee Bregman	72	74	70	216	3,498
Leah Hart	73	76	68	217	2,767.87
Johanna Westerberg	71	74	72	217	2,767.87
Diana Luna	74	71	72	217	2,767.87
Cecilia Ekelundh	67	74	76	217	2,767.87
Ursula Wikstrom	72	75	71	218	2,347.12
Maria Hjorth	72	74	72	218	2,347.12
Marina Arruti	70	76	72	218	2,347.12
Danielle Masters	71	72	75	218	2,347.12
Karen Lunn	72	78	69	219	2,103.75
Eva Steinberger	74	75	70	219	2,103.75
Lill Kristin Saether	71	75	73	219	2,103.75
Eleanor Pilgrim	73	68	78	219	2,103.75

Evian Masters

Evian Masters Golf Club, Evians-les-Bains, France
Par 36-36–72; 6,286 yards

July 26-29
purse, US$3,000,000

	SCORES				TOTAL	MONEY
Natalie Gulbis	72	69	73	70	284	€341,145
Jeong Jang	69	71	72	72	284	226,544
(Gulbis defeated Jang on first playoff hole.)						
Lorena Ochoa	72	70	75	68	285	131,267
Ji-Yai Shin	73	70	70	72	285	131,267
Juli Inkster	73	68	69	75	285	131,267
Christina Kim	67	75	74	70	286	61,188.50
Sun Ju Ahn	69	73	74	70	286	61,188.50
Angela Stanford	73	74	69	70	286	61,188.50
Momoko Ueda	74	67	74	71	286	61,188.50
Annika Sorenstam	71	69	74	72	286	61,188.50
Sophie Gustafson	69	72	72	73	286	61,188.50
Morgan Pressel	73	72	73	69	287	39,566
Laura Diaz	71	71	74	71	287	39,566
Laura Davies	71	70	74	72	287	39,566
Karrie Webb	70	72	73	72	287	39,566
Eun Hee Ji	66	76	75	71	288	32,331
Shi Hyun Ahn	73	69	75	71	288	32,331
Maria Hjorth	71	71	74	72	288	32,331
Paula Creamer	75	72	73	69	289	29,023.50
Nicole Castrale	75	70	74	70	289	29,023.50
Seon Hwa Lee	72	74	71	73	290	27,536
Angela Park	70	74	75	72	291	26,046
Ai Miyazato	73	73	73	72	291	26,046
Brittany Lang	73	74	75	70	292	22,387.83
Ji-Hee Lee	73	73	75	71	292	22,387.83
Virginie Lagoutte-Clement	76	68	75	73	292	22,387.83
Ashleigh Simon	70	72	76	74	292	22,387.83
Catriona Matthew	74	70	74	74	292	22,387.83
Diana D'Alessio	69	68	76	79	292	22,387.83
Meaghan Francella	71	79	73	70	293	16,961.12
Rachel Hetherington	71	73	75	74	293	16,961.12
Joo Mi Kim	71	72	75	75	293	16,961.12
Stephanie Arricau	73	71	74	75	293	16,961.12
Michele Redman	75	69	74	75	293	16,961.12
Jin Joo Hong	67	70	80	76	293	16,961.12
Mi Hyun Kim	69	72	74	78	293	16,961.12
Il Mi Chung	73	71	70	79	293	16,961.12
Hee Young Park	72	75	76	71	294	12,924
Stacy Prammanasudh	73	77	72	72	294	12,924
Meena Lee	71	73	75	75	294	12,924
Pat Hurst	66	76	76	76	294	12,924
Young Kim	72	75	72	75	294	12,924
Suzann Pettersen	74	72	81	68	295	10,377.16
In-Kyung Kim	71	75	76	73	295	10,377.16
Jee Young Lee	77	73	71	74	295	10,377.16
Sherri Steinhauer	72	73	75	75	295	10,377.16
Helen Alfredsson	77	70	73	75	295	10,377.16
Cristie Kerr	72	73	73	77	295	10,377.16
Na On Min	75	72	76	73	296	8,589.50
Brittany Lincicome	66	74	82	74	296	8,589.50
Rebecca Hudson	72	76	73	75	296	8,589.50
Linda Wessberg	69	72	75	80	296	8,589.50
Lindsey Wright	76	72	77	72	297	7,566
Kyeong Bae	67	74	82	74	297	7,566
Lisa Hall	77	70	76	74	297	7,566
Sarah Lee	71	72	77	77	297	7,566

	SCORES				TOTAL	MONEY
Becky Brewerton	72	71	82	73	298	6,388
Candie Kung	78	68	79	73	298	6,388
Sophie Giquel	78	70	77	73	298	6,388
Lynn Brooky	75	72	75	76	298	6,388
Karin Sjodin	72	72	77	77	298	6,388
Wendy Doolan	73	76	71	78	298	6,388
Veronica Zorzi	77	73	73	76	299	5,767.50
Amy Yang	73	73	76	77	299	5,767.50
Gloria Park	73	77	76	74	300	5,519
Gwladys Nocera	80	70	73	77	300	5,519
Sung Ah Yim	76	74	82	70	302	5,271
Silvia Cavalleri	74	76	75	77	302	5,271
Michelle Wie	73	71	84	76	304	5,023
Nikki Garrett	75	71	83	75	304	5,023
Hiroko Fujishima	74	76	77	80	307	4,899
Karen-Margrethe Juul	77	73	82	83	315	4,838

Ricoh Women's British Open

The Old Course, St. Andrews, Scotland
Par 36-37–73; 6,638 yards

August 2-5
purse, €1,554,525

	SCORES				TOTAL	MONEY
Lorena Ochoa	67	73	73	74	287	€160,000
Jee Young Lee	72	73	75	71	291	85,000
Maria Hjorth	75	73	72	71	291	85,000
Reilley Rankin	73	74	74	71	292	55,000
Eun Hee Ji	73	71	77	72	293	42,000
Se Ri Pak	73	73	75	72	293	42,000
Miki Saiki	76	70	81	67	294	30,500
Paula Creamer	73	75	74	72	294	30,500
Catriona Matthew	73	68	80	73	294	30,500
Linda Wessberg	74	73	72	75	294	30,500
Mhairi McKay	75	74	79	67	295	20,300
Yuri Fudoh	74	69	81	71	295	20,300
In-Bee Park	69	79	76	71	295	20,300
Na On Min	72	75	75	73	295	20,300
Brittany Lincicome	71	76	75	73	295	20,300
Gloria Park	74	75	76	71	296	14,041.66
*Melissa Reid	73	75	76	72	296	
Virginie Lagoutte-Clement	72	73	78	73	296	14,041.66
Becky Brewerton	74	75	74	73	296	14,041.66
Stacy Prammanasudh	74	76	72	74	296	14,041.66
Annika Sorenstam	72	71	77	76	296	14,041.66
Karine Icher	72	71	77	76	296	14,041.66
Alena Sharp	77	70	79	71	297	11,060
Natalie Gulbis	73	76	76	72	297	11,060
Beth Bader	73	77	75	72	297	11,060
Sherri Steinhauer	72	71	80	74	297	11,060
Wendy Ward	71	70	80	76	297	11,060
Suzann Pettersen	74	76	78	71	299	9,100
Sarah Lee	72	76	79	72	299	9,100
Ji-Yai Shin	76	74	77	72	299	9,100
Jimin Kang	77	72	75	75	299	9,100
Karrie Webb	77	73	74	75	299	9,100
Juli Inkster	79	68	82	71	300	7,016.66
Kim Hall	74	74	79	73	300	7,016.66
Cristie Kerr	77	71	79	73	300	7,016.66
Trish Johnson	75	75	77	73	300	7,016.66
Sophie Gustafson	73	72	81	74	300	7,016.66

	SCORES				TOTAL	MONEY
Meena Lee	71	76	79	74	300	7,016.66
Louise Friberg	69	76	80	75	300	7,016.66
Candie Kung	72	74	79	75	300	7,016.66
Gwladys Nocera	78	72	75	75	300	7,016.66
*Kerry Smith	77	74	80	70	301	
Michele Redman	75	73	81	72	301	5,250
Lotta Wahlin	74	77	78	72	301	5,250
In-Kyung Kim	72	76	79	74	301	5,250
Rebecca Hudson	70	73	82	76	301	5,250
Karen Stupples	75	72	78	76	301	5,250
*Hye Yong Choi	74	76	83	70	303	
Catrin Nilsmark	72	74	86	71	303	4,500
Dina Ammaccapane	76	73	83	72	304	4,100
*Sally Watso	78	73	80	73	304	
Beth Daniel	74	75	80	75	304	4,100
*Rachel Bell	77	74	76	77	304	
Grace Park	75	74	77	78	304	4,100
Rachel Hetherington	75	72	82	76	305	3,600
*Belen Mozo	75	72	82	76	305	
Momoko Ueda	73	76	79	77	305	3,600
*Anna Nordqvist	76	75	84	71	306	
Iben Tinning	77	74	81	74	306	2,910
Jin Joo Hong	76	73	82	75	306	2,910
Lisa Hall	73	73	84	76	306	2,910
Christina Kim	75	74	79	78	306	2,910
Ai Miyazato	70	80	77	79	306	2,910
Joanne Mills	71	78	79	80	308	2,400
Diana D'Alessio	74	76	85	74	309	2,175
Martina Eberl	73	75	75	86	309	2,175
Nicole Castrale	73	78	83	76	310	2,000
Meg Mallon	74	74	83	80	311	1,900
*Naomi Edwards	74	77	86	75	312	

Scandinavian TPC Hosted by Annika

Barseback Golf & Country Club, Malmo, Sweden
Par 36-36–72; 6,500 yards

August 9-12
purse, €525,000

	SCORES				TOTAL	MONEY
Catriona Matthew	71	74	66	68	279	€78,750
Laura Diaz	69	70	75	68	282	45,018.75
Sophie Gustafson	71	73	70	68	282	45,018.75
Maria Hjorth	70	75	69	70	284	25,305
Suzann Pettersen	75	68	70	71	284	25,305
Louise Stahle	69	74	69	73	285	18,375
*Caroline Hedwal	70	72	72	72	286	
Brittany Lincicome	71	69	71	76	287	15,750
Annika Sorenstam	71	75	74	68	288	13,125
Amy Yang	75	71	72	71	289	10,640
Jade Schaeffer	70	72	74	73	289	10,640
Iben Tinning	76	70	70	73	289	10,640
Nina Reis	74	71	72	73	290	8,741.25
Laura Cabanillas	75	70	70	75	290	8,741.25
Trish Johnson	74	73	73	71	291	7,822.50
Lara Tadiotto	77	71	71	72	291	7,822.50
Veronica Zorzi	76	72	71	72	291	7,822.50
Lisa Hall	73	73	74	72	292	7,140
Paula Marti	73	69	74	76	292	7,140
Minea Blomqvist	68	76	71	77	292	7,140

S4/C Wales Ladies Championship of Europe

Machynys Peninsula Golf Club, Llanelli,
Carmarthenshire, Wales
Par 36-36–72; 6,126 yards

August 16-19
purse, €518,175

	SCORES				TOTAL	MONEY
Joanne Mills	70	68	71	73	282	€77,726
Bettina Hauert	72	71	69	71	283	44,433.50
Georgina Simpson	72	67	70	74	283	44,433.50
Iben Tinning	69	70	73	72	284	24,976
Amy Yang	73	65	72	74	284	24,976
Rebecca Hudson	70	65	74	76	285	18,136
Lisa Hall	73	69	73	71	286	14,100
Virginie Lagoutte-Clement	73	70	70	73	286	14,100
Johanna Westerberg	69	71	73	74	287	11,607
Kiran Matharu	73	70	73	72	288	9,949
Maria Verchenova	72	69	74	73	288	9,949
Lora Fairclough	72	72	73	72	289	8,239.25
Linda Wessberg	72	70	73	74	289	8,239.25
Kirsty S. Taylor	70	69	75	75	289	8,239.25
Sofia Renell	72	69	73	75	289	8,239.25
Elizabeth McKinnon	75	69	77	69	290	7,150.75
Federica Piovano	76	67	75	72	290	7,150.75
Amanda Moltke-Leth	68	72	73	77	290	7,150.75
Gwladys Nocera	70	68	74	78	290	7,150.75
Laura Terebey	74	70	76	71	291	6,451.25
Trish Johnson	74	72	73	72	291	6,451.25
Laura Cabanillas	74	70	74	73	291	6,451.25
Sophie Giquel	75	71	72	73	291	6,451.25

SAS Masters

Losby Golf Club, Oslo, Norway
Par 35-37–72; 6,203 yards

August 24-26
purse, €200,000

	SCORES			TOTAL	MONEY
Suzann Pettersen	64	72	68	204	€30,000
Nikki Garrett	69	73	71	213	20,300
Diana Luna	69	72	74	215	12,400
Anja Monke	68	73	74	215	12,400
Jade Schaeffer	69	79	69	217	8,480
Anna Tybring	72	74	72	218	6,500
Johanna Westerberg	72	73	73	218	6,500
*Sandra Gal	71	76	72	219	
Joanne Mills	72	74	73	219	4,740
Martina Eberl	75	70	74	219	4,740
Lynn Brooky	71	78	71	220	3,585
Sophie Walker	73	76	71	220	3,585
Virginie Lagoutte-Clement	75	72	73	220	3,585
Gwladys Nocera	69	75	76	220	3,585
Sara Beautell	73	78	70	221	2,811.42
Nienke Nijenhuis	75	75	71	221	2,811.42
Rebecca Hudson	74	76	71	221	2,811.42
Rebecca Coakley	71	78	72	221	2,811.42
Christine Hallstrom	71	76	74	221	2,811.42
Hanna-Leena Salonen	73	72	76	221	2,811.42
Titiya Plucksataporn	72	72	77	221	2,811.42

Finnair Masters

Helsinki Golf Club, Tali, Finland
Par 34-37–71; 5,916 yards

August 31-September 2
purse, €200,000

	SCORES			TOTAL	MONEY
Bettina Hauert	68	67	72	207	€30,000
Johanna Westerberg	68	72	70	210	20,300
Lotta Wahlin	70	71	70	211	14,000
Kiran Matharu	67	73	72	212	9,640
Asa Gottmo	66	74	72	212	9,640
Nathalie David-Mila	71	73	69	213	6,500
Kaisa Ruuttila	70	69	74	213	6,500
Joanne Mills	71	72	71	214	4,493.33
Amanda Moltke-Leth	71	70	73	214	4,493.33
Elisabeth Esterl	73	67	74	214	4,493.33
Danielle Masters	74	73	68	215	3,680
Anna Rawson	72	74	70	216	3,120
Martina Eberl	66	77	73	216	3,120
Ana Larraneta	70	72	74	216	3,120
Anja Monke	73	75	68	216	3,120
Kris Lindstrom	65	75	76	216	3,120
Stephanie Arricau	71	72	74	217	2,652
Virginie Lagoutte-Clement	66	76	75	217	2,652
Helena Alterby	77	71	69	217	2,652
Ludivine Kreutz	72	69	76	217	2,652
Lora Fairclough	71	70	76	217	2,652

Nykredit Masters

Helsingor Golf Club, Helsingor, Denmark
Par 37-34–71; 6,653 yards

September 6-9
purse, €200,000

	SCORES				TOTAL	MONEY
Lisa Hall	68	71	69	67	275	€30,000
Kiran Matharu	68	66	73	68	275	17,150
Kirsty Taylor	69	68	70	68	275	17,150
(Hall defeated Matharu and Taylor on first playoff hole.)						
Lotta Wahlin	67	68	74	69	278	10,800
Lisa Holm Sorensen	69	68	74	68	279	8,480
Virginie Lagoutte-Clement	67	73	71	69	280	6,500
Sarah Kemp	67	68	75	70	280	6,500
Lynn Brooky	72	66	72	71	281	4,740
Gwladys Nocera	70	67	72	72	281	4,740
Riikka Hakkarainen	72	68	73	69	282	3,484
Ana Larraneta	70	70	72	70	282	3,484
Diana Luna	74	65	72	71	282	3,484
Sophie Walker	70	70	71	71	282	3,484
Paula Marti	73	70	68	71	282	3,484
Anna Tybring	72	69	74	68	283	2,845
Sophie Sandolo	69	73	72	69	283	2,845
Marta Prieto	69	71	73	70	283	2,845
Hanna-Leena Salonen	72	73	65	73	283	2,845
Kris Lindstrom	71	73	71	69	284	2,520
Joanne Mills	71	74	70	69	284	2,520
Martina Eberl	70	72	71	71	284	2,520
Johanna Westerberg	69	71	72	72	284	2,520
Anna Temple	69	71	71	73	284	2,520

The Solheim Cup

Halmstad Golf Club, Halmstad, Sweden   September 14-16
Par 36-36–72; 6,615 yards

FIRST DAY
Morning Foursomes

Pat Hurst and Cristie Kerr (US) halved with Suzann Pettersen and Sophie Gustafson.
Sherri Steinhauer and Laura Diaz (US) defeated Annika Sorenstam and Catriona Matthew, 4 and 2.
Juli Inkster and Paula Creamer (US) defeated Laura Davies and Becky Brewerton, 2 and 1.
Gwladys Nocera and Maria Hjorth (Eur) defeated Natalie Gulbis and Morgan Pressel, 3 and 2.

POINTS: U.S. 2½, Europe 1½

FIRST DAY
Afternoon Fourball

Matthew and Iben Tinning (Eur) defeated Hurst and Brittany Lincicome, 4 and 2.
Angela Stanford and Stacy Prammanasudh (US) halved with Sorenstam and Hjorth.
Nicole Castrale and Kerr (US) defeated Gustafson and Nocera, 4 and 2.
Creamer and Pressel (US) halved with Trish Johnson and Davies.

POINTS: U.S. 4½, Europe 3½

SECOND DAY
Morning Foursomes

Steinhauer and Diaz (US) halved with Hjorth and Nocera.
Inkster and Creamer (US) halved with Gustafson and Pettersen.
Hurst and Stanford (US) defeated Tinning and Bettina Hauert, 4 and 2.
Sorenstam and Matthew (Eur) defeated Castrale and Kerr, 1 up.

POINTS: U.S. 6½, Europe 5½

SECOND DAY
Afternoon Fourball

Creamer and Lincicome (US) halved with Linda Wessberg and Hjorth.
Inkster and Prammanasudh (US) halved with Johnson and Tinning.
Brewerton and Davies (Eur) defeated Gulbis and Castrale, 2 up.
Sorenstam and Pettersen (Eur) defeated Kerr and Pressel, 3 and 2.

POINTS: U.S. 7½, Europe 8½

FINAL DAY
Singles

Matthew (Eur) defeated Diaz, 3 and 2.
Hurst (US) defeated Gustafson, 2 and 1.
Prammanasudh (US) defeated Pettersen, 2 up.
Inkster (US) defeated Tinning, 4 and 3.
Steinhauer (US) halved with Brewerton.
Stanford (US) defeated Johnson, 3 and 2.
Pressel (US) defeated Sorenstam, 2 and 1.
Davies (Eur) defeated Lincicome, 4 and 3.
Castrale (US) defeated Hauert, 3 and 2.
Creamer (US) defeated Hjorth, 2 and 1.
Wessberg (Eur) defeated Kerr, 1 up.
Gulbis (US) defeated Nocera, 4 and 3.

POINTS: U.S. 8½, Europe 3½
TOTAL POINTS: U.S. 16, Europe 12

De Vere Ladies Scottish Open

The Carrick at Cameron House, Loch Lomond, Scotland
Par 36-35–71; 6,141 yards

September 20-22
purse, €200,000

	SCORES			TOTAL	MONEY
Sophie Gustafson	71	68	71	210	€30,000
Danielle Masters	75	72	68	215	15,033.33
Kirsty Taylor	75	69	71	215	15,033.33
Sofia Renell	72	68	75	215	15,033.33
Lynn Kenny	72	76	69	217	6,620
Karen-Margrethe Juul	72	75	70	217	6,620
Janice Moodie	76	70	71	217	6,620
Jade Schaeffer	69	71	77	217	6,620
Sophie Walker	72	74	72	218	4,480
Rebecca Hudson	77	71	71	219	3,706.66
Johanna Westerberg	74	73	72	219	3,706.66
Elisa Serramia	71	71	77	219	3,706.66
Antonella Cvitan	73	75	72	220	2,992
Marina Arruti	74	74	72	220	2,992
*Carly Booth	74	74	72	220	
Isabella Maconi	77	73	70	220	2,992
Gwladys Nocera	74	72	74	220	2,992
Asa Gottmo	74	70	76	220	2,992
Becky Brewerton	76	74	71	221	2,553.33
Catriona Matthew	73	75	73	221	2,553.33
Ana Larraneta	75	73	73	221	2,553.33
Johanna Head	77	70	74	221	2,553.33
Mhairi McKay	73	74	74	221	2,553.33
*Sally Watson	70	75	76	221	
Anna Tybring	78	76	67	221	2,553.33

UNIQA Ladies Golf Open

Golfclub Fohrenwald, Wiener Neustadt, Austria
Par 37-35–72; 6,179 yards

September 27-30
purse, €250,000

	SCORES			TOTAL	MONEY
Laura Davies	69	65	66	200	€37,500
Sophie Gustafson	69	66	69	204	25,375
Virginie Lagoutte-Clement	71	69	69	209	15,500
Kirsty Taylor	72	68	69	209	15,500
Lora Fairclough	72	70	68	210	10,600
Clare Queen	73	68	70	211	8,750
Felicity Johnson	74	67	71	212	7,500
Stefania Croce	72	71	70	213	5,362.50
Marta Prieto	73	69	71	213	5,362.50
Trish Johnson	73	68	72	213	5,362.50
Diana Luna	68	69	76	213	5,362.50
Titiya Plucksataporn	73	70	71	214	3,771.42
Martina Eberl	74	69	71	214	3,771.42
Lisa Holm Sorensen	70	72	72	214	3,771.42
Stephanie Arricau	73	68	73	214	3,771.42
Karen-Margrethe Juul	70	70	74	214	3,771.42
Elizabeth McKinnon	70	70	74	214	3,771.42
Danielle Masters	72	68	74	214	3,771.42
Veronica Zorzi	73	74	68	215	3,075
Zuzana Kamasova	77	69	69	215	3,075
Lisa Jean	72	73	70	215	3,075
Laura Cabanillas	73	72	70	215	3,075

	SCORES			TOTAL	MONEY
Natalie Claire Booth	70	74	71	215	3,075
Georgina Simpson	72	72	71	215	3,075
Lisa Hall	71	71	73	215	3,075

Madrid Ladies Masters

Casino Club de Golf Retamares, Madrid, Spain
Par 36-37–73; 6,338 yards

October 4-6
purse, €400,000

	SCORES			TOTAL	MONEY
Martina Eberl	69	68	69	206	€100,000
Sophie Gustafson	66	66	75	207	42,440
Iben Tinning	70	68	70	208	28,000
Tania Elosegui	73	68	68	209	21,600
Marta Prieto	73	68	69	210	15,480
Laura Davies	71	69	70	210	15,480
Catriona Matthew	71	71	69	211	11,000
Becky Brewerton	72	68	71	211	11,000
Ludivine Kreutz	72	70	70	212	8,960
Rebecca Hudson	74	69	70	213	7,413.33
Lora Fairclough	71	69	73	213	7,413.33
Linda Wessberg	67	71	75	213	7,413.33
Lisa Hall	72	68	74	214	6,440
Ana B. Sanchez	70	73	72	215	6,060
Joanne Mills	69	72	74	215	6,060
Sara Beautell	73	72	71	216	5,680
Louise Friberg	71	73	72	216	5,680
Stefania Croce	76	70	71	217	5,293.33
Anja Monke	73	72	72	217	5,293.33
Sophie Giquel	73	74	70	217	5,293.33

EMAAR-MGF Ladies Masters

Eagleton Golf Resort, Bidadi, Bangalore, India
Par 36-36–72; 6,558 yards

December 5-8
purse, €200,000

	SCORES				TOTAL	MONEY
Gwladys Nocera	69	69	72	71	281	€30,000
Virginie Lagoutte-Clement	72	75	66	69	282	20,300
Lisa Hall	72	73	70	69	284	14,000
Lotta Wahlin	69	75	72	69	285	10,800
Titiya Plucksataporn	72	71	74	69	286	8,480
Karen-Margrethe Juul	73	73	70	71	287	6,000
Trish Johnson	73	70	72	72	287	6,000
Marta Prieto	73	70	72	72	287	6,000
Stephanie Arricau	72	73	76	67	288	4,053.33
Laura Davies	77	74	67	70	288	4,053.33
Martina Eberl	76	71	68	73	288	4,053.33
Maria Beautell	77	70	70	72	289	3,440
Margherita Rigon	73	72	72	73	290	3,150
Becky Brewerton	76	70	71	73	290	3,150
Bo Ri Lee	71	72	75	73	291	2,980
Stacy Lee Bregman	74	79	69	70	292	2,760
Karen Lunn	75	73	73	71	292	2,760
Chutichai Porani	73	79	69	71	292	2,760
Veronica Zorzi	75	71	72	74	292	2,760
Stefanie Michl	75	75	73	70	293	2,520

	SCORES				TOTAL	MONEY
Marjet van der Graaff	76	74	73	70	293	2,520
Johanna Head	77	71	73	72	293	2,520

Dubai Ladies Masters

Emirates Golf Club, Majlis Course,
Dubai, United Arab Emirates
Par 35-37–72; 6,406 yards

December 13-16
purse, €500,000

	SCORES				TOTAL	MONEY
Annika Sorenstam	70	70	68	70	278	€75,000
Laura Davies	67	70	71	72	280	42,875
Iben Tinning	72	68	67	73	280	42,875
Anja Monke	71	68	75	68	282	17,400
Lisa Hall	67	69	77	69	282	17,400
Gwladys Nocera	72	70	71	69	282	17,400
Catriona Matthew	70	72	70	70	282	17,400
Amy Yang	71	73	68	70	282	17,400
Veronica Zorzi	70	68	70	74	282	17,400
Paula Marti	73	72	71	67	283	8,962.50
Sophie Giquel	72	74	70	67	283	8,962.50
Lotta Wahlin	69	72	73	69	283	8,962.50
Louise Stahle	64	74	73	72	283	8,962.50
Johanna Head	71	72	70	71	284	7,700
Sophie Gustafson	68	74	72	71	285	7,325
Linda Wessberg	70	74	69	72	285	7,325
Trish Johnson	70	72	73	71	286	7,000
Laurette Maritz	73	75	73	66	287	6,616.66
Louise Friberg	72	72	74	69	287	6,616.66
*Carlota Ciganda	72	70	74	71	287	
Federica Piovano	69	75	71	72	287	6,616.66

Japan LPGA Tour

Daikin Orchid Ladies

Ryukyu Golf Club, Nanjo, Okinawa
Par 36-36–72; 6,409 yards

March 2-4
purse, ¥80,000,000

	SCORES			TOTAL	MONEY
Midori Yoneyama	72	66	72	210	¥14,400,000
Asuka Tsujimura	70	69	71	210	7,200,000
(Yoneyama defeated Tsujimura on first playoff hole.)					
Yun-Jye Wei	71	70	71	212	5,600,000
Kuniko Maeda	73	67	73	213	4,000,000
Mi-Jeong Jeon	72	70	71	213	4,000,000
Ai Miyazato	73	70	70	213	4,000,000
Mizuho Ozawa	72	72	70	214	2,065,600
Mineko Nasu	73	72	69	214	2,065,600
Ji-Yeon Han	73	71	70	214	2,065,600
Ayako Uehara	71	70	73	214	2,065,600
Michie Ohba	70	69	75	214	2,065,600
Momoko Ueda	76	68	71	215	1,408,000
Jae-Hee Bae	72	72	71	215	1,408,000
Sakura Yokomine	74	69	73	216	1,168,000
Yui Kawahara	71	71	74	216	1,168,000
Bo-Bae Song	71	72	73	216	1,168,000
Yuka Sakaguchi	72	70	74	216	1,168,000
Nobuko Kizawa	74	71	72	217	777,454
Yuko Mitsuka	72	71	74	217	777,454
Hyun-Ju Shin	70	71	76	217	777,454
Young-Me Lee	72	73	72	217	777,454
Miho Koga	76	68	73	217	777,454
Keiko Sasaki	74	68	75	217	777,454
Tamie Durdin	68	74	75	217	777,454
Yuri Fudoh	69	69	79	217	777,454
Na-Rr Lee	72	74	71	217	777,454
Nachiyo Ohtani	75	70	72	217	777,454
Akane Iijima	75	71	71	217	777,454

Accordia Golf Ladies

Aoshima Golf Club, Miyazaki
Par 36-36–72; 6,378 yards

March 9-11
purse, ¥60,000,000

	SCORES			TOTAL	MONEY
Toshimi Kimura	69	68	70	207	¥10,800,000
Shiho Oyama	73	69	71	213	5,280,000
Kuniko Maeda	72	72	71	215	4,200,000
Ji-Yeon Han	71	71	74	216	3,300,000
Mihoko Iseri	73	70	73	216	3,300,000
Ritsuko Ryu	72	71	74	217	2,250,000
Momoko Ueda	74	72	71	217	2,250,000
Yuko Mitsuka	73	74	71	218	1,800,000
Mayumi Shimomura	70	72	77	219	1,180,800
Akane Iijima	71	72	76	219	1,180,800
Yui Kawahara	73	72	74	219	1,180,800

	SCORES			TOTAL	MONEY
Yun-Jye Wei	73	73	73	219	1,180,800
Yuka Shiroto	76	74	69	219	1,180,800
Jae-Hee Bae	73	71	76	220	858,000
Tamie Durdin	74	72	74	220	858,000
Yuri Fudoh	70	76	74	220	858,000
Miho Koga	73	71	76	220	858,000
Junko Omote	76	70	75	221	565,090
Yukari Baba	72	72	77	221	565,090
Mitsuko Kawasaki	75	69	77	221	565,090
Mikiyo Nishizuka	73	74	74	221	565,090
Hiromi Mogi	73	72	76	221	565,090
Na-Rr Lee	72	72	77	221	565,090
Nikki Campbell	72	70	79	221	565,090
Ya-Huei Lu	71	74	76	221	565,090
Eun-A Lim	74	71	76	221	565,090
Maki Sasayama	74	72	75	221	565,090
Shinobu Moromizato	75	70	76	221	565,090

Studio Alice Ladies Open

Hanayashiki Golf Club, Yokawa Course, Miki, Hyogo
Par 36-36–72; 6,439 yards

April 6-8
purse, ¥60,000,000

	SCORES			TOTAL	MONEY
Jae-Hee Bae	69	69	70	208	¥10,800,000
Yui Kawahara	73	71	66	210	5,400,000
Rui Kitada	72	71	69	212	3,900,000
Hyun-Ju Shin	74	69	69	212	3,900,000
Momoko Ueda	70	71	72	213	3,000,000
Mihoko Takahashi	72	73	69	214	2,520,000
*Maiko Wakabayashi	73	69	72	214	
Nikki Campbell	73	69	73	215	1,950,000
Yun-Joo Jeong	72	72	71	215	1,950,000
Yuka Shiroto	75	73	68	216	1,195,200
Kazu Yazaki	73	72	71	216	1,195,200
Miho Koga	73	71	72	216	1,195,200
Ji-Hee Lee	72	71	73	216	1,195,200
Tomomi Hirose	70	73	73	216	1,195,200
Bo-Bae Song	75	74	68	217	730,800
Nobuko Kizawa	73	69	75	217	730,800
Miki Saiki	76	69	72	217	730,800
Michiko Hattori	71	76	70	217	730,800
Na Zhang	72	71	74	217	730,800
Mineko Nasu	74	72	71	217	730,800
Ji-Yeon Han	74	71	72	217	730,800
Akane Iijima	76	71	70	217	730,800
Mihoko Iseri	75	68	74	217	730,800
Mitsuko Kawasaki	74	71	72	217	730,800

Life Card Ladies

Kumamoto Airport Country Club, Kikuyo, Kumamoto
Par 36-36–72; 6,423 yards

April 13-15
purse, ¥60,000,000

	SCORES			TOTAL	MONEY
Momoko Ueda	70	71	70	211	¥10,800,000
Erina Hara	74	70	73	217	5,280,000

	SCORES			TOTAL	MONEY
Hyun-Ju Shin	73	70	75	218	4,200,000
Shinobu Moromizato	74	74	71	219	2,228,571
Yuri Fudoh	78	70	71	219	2,228,571
Ji-Yeon Han	77	70	72	219	2,228,571
Mie Nakata	76	74	69	219	2,228,571
Miki Saiki	79	69	71	219	2,228,571
Yukari Baba	76	74	69	219	2,228,571
Chie Arimura	73	72	74	219	2,228,571
Sakura Yokomine	77	71	72	220	1,074,000
Yuka Shiroto	73	73	74	220	1,074,000
Ayako Uehara	75	73	72	220	1,074,000
Rui Kitada	73	74	74	221	894,000
Yui Kawahara	77	75	69	221	894,000
Ji-Hee Lee	73	72	76	221	894,000
Kurumi Dohi	77	74	71	222	774,000
Eun-Hye Lee	78	71	74	223	622,800
Hiroko Yamaguchi	75	74	74	223	622,800
Mikiyo Nishizuka	76	73	74	223	622,800
Tomomi Hirose	75	74	74	223	622,800
Hiromi Takesue	75	73	75	223	622,800
Mihoko Iseri	77	76	71	224	552,000

Fujisankei Ladies Classic

Kawana Hotel Golf Club, Fuji Course, Ito, Shizuoka
Par 36-36–72; 6,464 yards

April 20-22
purse, ¥70,000,000

	SCORES			TOTAL	MONEY
Miki Saiki	70	71	69	210	¥12,600,000
Ayako Uehara	69	70	72	211	5,530,000
Midori Yoneyama	70	73	68	211	5,530,000
Akane Iijima	69	72	71	212	3,850,000
Sakura Yokomine	72	71	69	212	3,850,000
Saiki Fujita	71	70	72	213	2,800,000
Mi-Jeong Jeon	73	70	71	214	2,450,000
Yuka Shiroto	71	74	70	215	1,750,000
Shiho Oyama	74	71	70	215	1,750,000
Chie Arimura	73	69	73	215	1,750,000
Shinobu Moromizato	73	72	71	216	1,281,000
Yukari Baba	72	70	74	216	1,281,000
Erina Hara	76	72	69	217	1,001,000
Yun-Jye Wei	70	72	75	217	1,001,000
Julie Lu	73	72	72	217	1,001,000
Ji-Hee Lee	71	75	71	217	1,001,000
Mika Takushima	69	75	73	217	1,001,000
Kuniko Maeda	70	74	73	217	1,001,000
*Asako Fujimoto	73	73	71	217	
Yuka Arita	73	71	74	218	683,200
Akiko Fukushima	68	78	72	218	683,200
Aki Nakano	72	71	75	218	683,200
Yuri Fudoh	70	74	74	218	683,200
Na Zhang	70	71	77	218	683,200

Yashima Queens

Yashima Country Club, Takamatsu, Kagawa
Par 36-36–72; 6,337 yards

April 27-29
purse, ¥60,000,000

	SCORES			TOTAL	MONEY
Mi-Jeong Jeon	71	73	69	213	¥10,800,000
Chiharu Yamaguchi	73	73	68	214	5,280,000
Nikki Campbell	72	71	72	215	4,200,000
Toshimi Kimura	73	70	73	216	3,600,000
Mikiyo Nishizuka	76	72	69	217	2,160,000
Kayo Yamada	71	76	70	217	2,160,000
Yui Kawahara	70	76	71	217	2,160,000
Yun-Jye Wei	72	74	71	217	2,160,000
Mihoko Takahashi	75	71	71	217	2,160,000
Yuka Tonsho	74	76	68	218	974,250
Yukari Baba	71	76	71	218	974,250
Mineko Nasu	71	76	71	218	974,250
Mie Nakata	72	75	71	218	974,250
Julie Lu	72	74	72	218	974,250
Mihoko Iseri	72	74	72	218	974,250
Shinobu Moromizato	73	73	72	218	974,250
Yuka Shiroto	71	73	74	218	974,250
Ayako Uehara	76	73	70	219	610,800
Keiko Sasaki	74	74	71	219	610,800
Michiko Hattori	75	73	71	219	610,800
Miki Saiki	73	74	72	219	610,800
Ji-Hyun Lee	74	73	72	219	610,800

Salonpas World Ladies

Yomiuri Country Club, Tokyo
Par 36-36–72; 6,523 yards

May 3-6
purse, ¥100,000,000

	SCORES				TOTAL	MONEY
Mi-Jeong Jeon	72	70	69	71	282	¥18,000,000
Momoko Ueda	73	68	72	72	285	8,800,000
Ji-Hee Lee	70	73	73	70	286	6,500,000
Karrie Webb	76	65	70	75	286	6,500,000
Sakura Yokomine	71	70	75	71	287	5,000,000
Yun-Joo Jeong	68	74	72	74	288	4,000,000
Mihoko Takahashi	70	73	72	74	289	3,250,000
Akiko Fukushima	70	71	76	72	289	3,250,000
Michiko Hattori	75	72	72	71	290	2,500,000
Mitsuko Kawasaki	75	70	75	71	291	1,833,333
Akane Iijima	67	74	74	76	291	1,833,333
Ayako Uehara	75	69	76	71	291	1,833,333
Yuka Shiroto	71	72	75	74	292	1,500,000
Bo-Bae Song	71	72	76	73	292	1,500,000
Jeong-Eun Lee	72	73	75	72	292	1,500,000
Yasuko Satoh	70	75	74	74	293	1,200,000
Yumiko Yoshida	71	77	75	70	293	1,200,000
Yuri Fudoh	72	70	75	76	293	1,200,000
Miho Koga	75	73	74	72	294	950,000
*Kumiko Kaneda	75	72	73	74	294	
Keiko Sasaki	69	75	76	74	294	950,000

Vernal Ladies

Fukuoka Century Golf Club, Asakura, Fukuoka
Par 36-36–72; 6,541 yards

May 11-13
purse, ¥120,000,000

	SCORES			TOTAL	MONEY
Mi-Jeong Jeon	70	69	69	208	¥21,600,000
Yuri Fudoh	71	65	72	208	10,560,000
(Jeon defeated Fudoh on sixth playoff hole.)					
Erina Hara	75	69	69	213	8,400,000
Bo-Bae Song	71	72	72	215	7,200,000
Momoko Ueda	74	73	69	216	5,400,000
Yuka Irie	73	69	74	216	5,400,000
Michiko Hattori	72	72	73	217	3,900,000
Ayako Uehara	69	72	76	217	3,900,000
Jae-Hee Bae	75	73	70	218	3,000,000
Hyun-Ju Shin	73	75	72	220	2,080,000
Tamie Durdin	73	75	72	220	2,080,000
Kaori Higo	74	72	74	220	2,080,000
Miho Koga	75	71	74	220	2,080,000
Jeong-Eun Lee	74	70	76	220	2,080,000
Na Zhang	70	70	80	220	2,080,000
Hiromi Mogi	78	72	71	221	1,596,000
Shiho Oyama	73	73	75	221	1,596,000
Ji-Hee Lee	72	74	76	222	1,356,000
Akane Iijima	70	74	78	222	1,356,000
Yasuko Satoh	76	73	74	223	1,140,000
Nahoko Hirao	78	71	74	223	1,140,000
Yun-Joo Jeong	73	76	74	223	1,140,000
Young-Me Lee	75	73	75	223	1,140,000

Chukyo TV Bridgestone Ladies Open

Chukyo Golf Club, Ishino Course, Toyota, Aichi
Par 36-36–72; 6,366 yards

May 18-20
purse, ¥70,000,000

	SCORES			TOTAL	MONEY
Sakura Yokomine	70	69	70	209	¥12,600,000
Yukari Baba	69	68	73	210	5,086,666
Mie Nakata	70	68	72	210	5,086,666
Yuko Mitsuka	73	67	70	210	5,086,666
Tamie Durdin	65	73	73	211	2,712,500
Akiko Fukushima	68	73	70	211	2,712,500
Shinobu Moromizato	66	72	73	211	2,712,500
Shiho Oyama	72	69	70	211	2,712,500
Miki Saiki	69	72	71	212	1,750,000
Hiromi Takesue	68	72	73	213	1,232,000
Tomoko Kusakabe	72	72	69	213	1,232,000
Jae-Hee Bae	69	69	75	213	1,232,000
*Mai Arai	71	69	73	213	
Hyun-Ju Shin	71	68	74	213	1,232,000
Mi-Jeong Jeon	72	67	74	213	1,232,000
Mitsuko Kawasaki	73	68	73	214	910,000
Yuriko Ohtsuka	72	71	71	214	910,000
Kaori Nakamichi	73	70	71	214	910,000
Ai Ogawa	70	70	74	214	910,000
Yui Kawahara	70	72	73	215	683,666
Kaori Higo	70	73	72	215	683,666
Momoko Ueda	67	70	78	215	683,666

Kosaido Ladies Golf Cup

Chiba Kosaido Country Club, Ichihara, Chiba
Par 36-36–72; 6,333 yards

May 25-27
purse, ¥60,000,000

	SCORES			TOTAL	MONEY
Yuri Fudoh	70	68	68	206	¥10,800,000
Mi-Jeong Jeon	71	71	69	211	4,020,000
Shinobu Moromizato	73	69	69	211	4,020,000
Sakura Yokomine	69	70	72	211	4,020,000
Noriko Aso	69	69	73	211	4,020,000
Miho Koga	70	75	67	212	2,250,000
Mie Nakata	72	72	68	212	2,250,000
Yun-Jye Wei	73	72	68	213	1,650,000
Saiki Fujita	74	70	69	213	1,650,000
Chiharu Yamaguchi	75	72	67	214	1,128,000
Bo-Bae Song	69	76	69	214	1,128,000
Yun-Hee Ku	73	72	69	214	1,128,000
Mihoko Takahashi	71	73	71	215	882,000
Shiho Oyama	70	74	71	215	882,000
Kaori Aoyama	72	72	71	215	882,000
Yuko Saitoh	72	70	73	215	882,000
Akane Iijima	71	71	73	215	882,000
Yuka Shiroto	75	73	68	216	624,000
Kaori Yamamoto	78	69	69	216	624,000
Eun-Hye Lee	74	70	72	216	624,000
Ji-Hyun Lee	72	71	73	216	624,000

Resort Trust Ladies

Grande Nasushirakawa Golf Club, Nishigo, Fukushima
Par 36-36–72; 6,502 yards

June 1-3
purse, ¥70,000,000

	SCORES			TOTAL	MONEY
Momoko Ueda	69	68	68	205	¥12,600,000
Yuri Fudoh	71	69	65	205	6,300,000
(Ueda defeated Fudoh on first playoff hole.)					
Sakura Yokomine	72	67	72	211	4,900,000
Nikki Campbell	73	70	69	212	4,200,000
Miki Saiki	68	73	72	213	3,150,000
Yui Kawahara	71	71	71	213	3,150,000
Shinobu Moromizato	70	74	70	214	1,717,333
Akane Iijima	72	75	67	214	1,717,333
*Rikako Morita	75	67	72	214	
Mihoko Iseri	70	75	69	214	1,717,333
Hyun-Ju Shin	73	69	72	214	1,717,333
Shiho Oyama	75	66	73	214	1,717,333
Hiromi Mogi	78	68	68	214	1,717,333
Ritsuko Ryu	73	72	70	215	1,092,000
Mie Nakata	74	70	71	215	1,092,000
Mihoko Takahashi	73	74	68	215	1,092,000
Mayumi Shimomura	71	71	73	215	1,092,000
Kurumi Dohi	75	66	75	216	770,000
Nachiyo Ohtani	75	70	71	216	770,000
Yuka Tonsho	74	71	71	216	770,000
Hsiu-Feng Tseng	71	74	71	216	770,000
Kayo Yamada	72	72	72	216	770,000
Hiromi Takesue	72	71	73	216	770,000

We Love Kobe Suntory Ladies Open

Rokko Kokusai Golf Club, Kobe, Hyogo
Par 36-36–72; 6,457 yards

June 7-10
purse, ¥80,000,000

	SCORES				TOTAL	MONEY
Na Zhang	67	69	69	73	278	¥14,400,000
Shiho Oyama	68	77	69	67	281	7,040,000
Erina Hara	74	72	71	65	282	5,600,000
Momoko Ueda	70	75	71	67	283	3,700,000
Mikiyo Nishizuka	73	72	69	69	283	3,700,000
Shinobu Moromizato	68	70	75	70	283	3,700,000
Yuri Fudoh	68	73	72	70	283	3,700,000
Kaori Kohno	73	75	69	68	285	2,400,000
Jeong-Eun Lee	70	75	74	67	286	1,584,000
Miki Saiki	70	74	74	68	286	1,584,000
Miho Koga	69	74	72	71	286	1,584,000
Chie Arimura	74	72	69	71	286	1,584,000
Michie Ohba	72	76	72	67	287	1,048,000
Hiromi Mogi	74	74	70	69	287	1,048,000
Mi-Jeong Jeon	74	72	71	70	287	1,048,000
Ayako Uehara	72	72	72	71	287	1,048,000
Mitsuko Kawasaki	71	74	71	71	287	1,048,000
Yui Kawahara	73	76	66	72	287	1,048,000
Kuniko Maeda	68	76	72	72	288	768,000
*So-Yeon Ryu	70	72	73	73	288	

Nichirei PGM Ladies

Miho Golf Club, Miho, Ibaraki
Par 36-36–72; 6,402 yards

June 15-17
purse, ¥60,000,000

	SCORES			TOTAL	MONEY
Shiho Oyama	68	68	71	207	¥10,800,000
Kaori Aoyama	69	69	70	208	5,280,000
Mi-Jeong Jeon	67	72	70	209	3,600,000
Miki Saiki	67	68	74	209	3,600,000
Shinobu Moromizato	66	68	75	209	3,600,000
Ji-Yeon Han	74	71	65	210	1,800,000
Chiharu Yamaguchi	70	73	67	210	1,800,000
Namika Omata	69	73	68	210	1,800,000
Midori Yoneyama	72	67	71	210	1,800,000
Momoko Ueda	69	68	73	210	1,800,000
Akiko Fukushima	70	73	68	211	1,098,000
Bo-Bae Song	71	69	71	211	1,098,000
Mayumi Shimomura	72	67	73	212	978,000
Yuka Tonsho	69	69	74	212	978,000
*Kyoko Yokoyama	72	74	67	213	
Yayoi Arasaki	74	70	69	213	828,000
Ai Ogawa	73	69	71	213	828,000
Yun-Joo Jeong	70	69	74	213	828,000
Nachiyo Ohtani	73	72	69	214	596,571
Michie Ohba	70	73	71	214	596,571
Michiko Hattori	70	72	72	214	596,571
Akane Iijima	66	75	73	214	596,571
Ayako Uehara	69	71	74	214	596,571
Ji-Hee Lee	70	70	74	214	596,571
Yukari Baba	67	70	77	214	596,571

Promise Ladies

Madame J Golf Club, Kato, Hyogo
Par 36-36–72; 6,499 yards

June 22-24
purse, ¥80,000,000

	SCORES			TOTAL	MONEY
Saiki Fujita	68	69	73	210	¥14,400,000
Momoko Ueda	72	69	69	210	7,040,000
(Fujita defeated Ueda on first playoff hole.)					
Yayoi Arasaki	75	70	69	214	5,200,000
Miho Koga	75	69	70	214	5,200,000
Akiko Fukushima	73	68	74	215	4,000,000
Kuniko Maeda	74	71	71	216	3,200,000
Kaori Aoyama	76	73	69	218	2,400,000
Ritsuko Ryu	76	69	73	218	2,400,000
Miki Saiki	70	71	77	218	2,400,000
Nikki Campbell	77	71	71	219	1,468,000
Hyun-Ju Shin	78	73	68	219	1,468,000
Nachiyo Ohtani	74	72	73	219	1,468,000
Mihoko Takahashi	75	71	73	219	1,468,000
Shinobu Moromizato	76	73	71	220	1,104,000
Hiromi Mogi	81	69	70	220	1,104,000
Tamie Durdin	74	72	74	220	1,104,000
Midori Yoneyama	77	69	74	220	1,104,000
Kaori Higo	78	68	74	220	1,104,000
Chie Arimura	76	71	74	221	805,333
Mika Nakazono	76	69	76	221	805,333
Yuri Fudoh	73	71	77	221	805,333

Belluna Ladies Cup

Obatago Golf Club, Kanra, Gunma
Par 36-36–72; 6,341 yards

June 29-July 1
purse, ¥60,000,000

	SCORES			TOTAL	MONEY
Akiko Fukushima	69	66	71	206	¥10,800,000
Eun-Hye Lee	71	68	69	208	4,740,000
Michiko Hattori	69	69	70	208	4,740,000
Hyun-Ju Shin	73	69	67	209	3,000,000
Kaori Yamamoto	70	69	70	209	3,000,000
*Kumiko Kaneda	63	74	72	209	
Young-Me Lee	68	68	73	209	3,000,000
Ai Ogawa	69	74	67	210	1,650,000
Midori Yoneyama	74	68	68	210	1,650,000
Maiko Suzuki	71	69	70	210	1,650,000
Yun-Hee Ku	71	69	70	210	1,650,000
Mumi Ohkubo	71	69	71	211	1,086,000
Na Zhang	66	72	73	211	1,086,000
Yayoi Arasaki	69	72	71	212	876,000
Hiromi Mogi	70	71	71	212	876,000
Saiki Fujita	69	71	72	212	876,000
Yun-Jye Wei	71	69	72	212	876,000
So-Hee Kim	71	69	72	212	876,000
Yuko Mitsuka	70	74	69	213	604,800
Yukari Baba	71	72	70	213	604,800
Ya-Huei Lu	72	71	70	213	604,800
Keiko Sasaki	70	72	71	213	604,800
Mikiyo Nishizuka	71	71	71	213	604,800

Meiji Chocolate Cup

Sapporo Kokusai Country Club, Kitahiroshima, Hokkaido
Par 36-36–72; 6,518 yards

July 6-8
purse, ¥70,000,000

	SCORES			TOTAL	MONEY
Shiho Oyama	66	72	71	209	¥12,600,000
Shinobu Moromizato	74	70	67	211	5,530,000
Mikiyo Nishizuka	71	69	71	211	5,530,000
Chie Arimura	73	72	69	214	3,850,000
So-Hee Kim	71	73	70	214	3,850,000
Michie Ohba	74	71	70	215	2,625,000
Miho Koga	73	71	71	215	2,625,000
Hiroko Yamaguchi	76	72	68	216	1,634,500
*Maiko Wakabayashi	74	70	72	216	
Yasuko Satoh	73	70	73	216	1,634,500
Namika Omata	74	69	73	216	1,634,500
Yukari Baba	68	74	74	216	1,634,500
Momoko Ueda	75	72	70	217	1,183,000
Kasumi Fujii	72	73	72	217	1,183,000
Nobuko Kizawa	74	74	70	218	903,000
Ji-Hyun Lee	74	74	70	218	903,000
Julie Lu	73	72	73	218	903,000
Yun-Hee Ku	75	70	73	218	903,000
Kaori Yamamoto	72	72	74	218	903,000
Kayo Yamada	73	71	74	218	903,000

Stanley Ladies

Tomei Country Club, Susono, Shizuoka
Par 36-36–72; 6,454 yards
(Event shortened to 27 holes—rain.)

July 13-15
purse, ¥70,000,000

	SCORES		TOTAL	MONEY
Momoko Ueda	71	35	106	¥9,450,000
Chie Arimura	71	35	106	4,200,000
Sakura Yokomine	69	37	106	4,200,000

(Three players in three-hole stroke-play playoff; Yokomine cut. Then Ueda defeated Arimura on first sudden-death playoff hole.)

Hiromi Mori	69	38	107	3,150,000
*Kyoko Yokoyama	71	37	108	
Junko Omote	69	39	108	2,625,000
Shinobu Moromizato	74	35	109	1,404,000
Mayumi Shimomura	73	36	109	1,404,000
Bo-Bae Song	73	36	109	1,404,000
Hsiu-Feng Tseng	72	37	109	1,404,000
Nikki Campbell	72	37	109	1,404,000
Kuniko Maeda	72	37	109	1,404,000
Saiki Fujita	70	39	109	1,404,000
*Mai Arai	69	40	109	
Keiki Sasaki	75	35	110	766,500
Nachiyo Ohtani	73	37	110	766,500
Yuri Fudoh	72	38	110	766,500
Jeong-Eun Lee	71	39	110	766,500
Nobuko Kizawa	70	40	110	766,500
Aki Nakano	70	40	110	766,500

Kracie Philanthropy Japan LPGA Players Championship

Narashino Country Club, Inzai, Chiba
Par 37-36–73; 6,584 yards

July 19-22
purse, ¥130,000,000

	SCORES				TOTAL	MONEY
Na Zhang	70	73	68	75	286	¥23,400,000
Sakura Yokomine	72	72	72	70	286	11,440,000
(Zhang defeated Yokomine on first playoff hole.)						
Mi-Jeong Jeon	71	72	73	71	287	8,450,000
Chie Arimura	75	73	68	71	287	8,450,000
Momoko Ueda	71	73	73	71	288	6,500,000
Yun-Jye Wei	73	72	72	72	289	5,200,000
Hyun-Ju Shin	73	74	73	70	290	3,575,000
Yuko Mitsuka	72	71	74	73	290	3,575,000
Mizuho Ozawa	73	73	71	73	290	3,575,000
Tamie Durdin	72	75	69	74	290	3,575,000
Ji-Hyun Lee	71	71	79	70	291	2,288,000
Mie Nakata	73	75	69	74	291	2,288,000
Miho Koga	76	71	75	70	292	2,028,000
Kuniko Maeda	72	73	72	75	292	2,028,000
Eun-A Lim	73	75	75	70	293	1,703,000
Julie Lu	72	76	71	74	293	1,703,000
Yuka Irie	71	69	77	76	293	1,703,000
Jae-Hee Bae	76	72	73	73	294	1,313,000
Yasuko Satoh	74	70	76	74	294	1,313,000
Kaori Higo	75	71	74	74	294	1,313,000

AXA Ladies

Mitsui Kanto Tomakomai Golf Club, Tomakomai, Hokkaido
Par 36-36–72; 6,402 yards

July 27-29
purse, ¥80,000,000

	SCORES			TOTAL	MONEY
Na Zhang	68	70	71	209	¥14,400,000
Mayumi Shimomura	72	69	69	210	7,040,000
Yuko Saitoh	73	72	66	211	4,800,000
Nobuko Kizawa	74	67	70	211	4,800,000
Bo-Bae Song	67	72	72	211	4,800,000
Midori Yoneyama	70	72	70	212	3,200,000
Namika Omata	71	72	70	213	2,200,000
So-Hee Kim	70	72	71	213	2,200,000
Akiko Fukushima	71	71	71	213	2,200,000
Erina Hara	71	70	72	213	2,200,000
Michie Ohba	71	73	70	214	1,376,000
Yuka Shiroto	71	72	71	214	1,376,000
Kuniko Maeda	74	69	71	214	1,376,000
Mi-Jeong Jeon	69	73	72	214	1,376,000
Eun-A Lim	75	69	71	215	1,096,000
Mie Nakata	71	72	72	215	1,096,000
Mayumi Nakajima	74	69	72	215	1,096,000
Ji-Yeon Han	73	73	70	216	800,000
Nikki Campbell	73	73	70	216	800,000
Hiroko Yamaguchi	71	73	72	216	800,000
Toshimi Kimura	72	72	72	216	800,000
Ai Ogawa	69	74	73	216	800,000
Yuka Tonshu	68	73	75	216	800,000

Crystal Geyser Ladies

Keiyo Country Club, Chiba
Par 36-36–72; 6,400 yards

August 3-5
purse, ¥60,000,000

	SCORES			TOTAL	MONEY
Hiromi Mogi	71	70	65	206	¥10,800,000
Nikki Campbell	72	71	67	210	4,740,000
Mie Nakata	71	70	69	210	4,740,000
Nobuko Kizawa	70	74	68	212	2,775,000
Mikiyo Nishizuka	70	73	69	212	2,775,000
Julie Lu	70	72	70	212	2,775,000
Hiroko Yamaguchi	72	69	71	212	2,775,000
Kaori Higo	75	71	67	213	1,500,000
Mi-Jeong Jeon	71	72	70	213	1,500,000
Akiko Fukushima	71	72	70	213	1,500,000
Chiharu Tsunekawa	70	75	69	214	1,020,000
Yuka Irie	75	70	69	214	1,020,000
Ayako Uehara	71	73	70	214	1,020,000
Yuka Shiroto	71	74	70	215	750,000
Seiko Watanabe	73	71	71	215	750,000
Kaori Harada	70	73	72	215	750,000
Yukari Baba	71	71	73	215	750,000
Na Zhang	71	71	73	215	750,000
Hsiu-Feng Tseng	69	72	74	215	750,000
Mayumi Shimomura	75	73	68	216	486,000
Eun-A Lim	73	74	69	216	486,000
Iyoko Wada	74	71	71	216	486,000
Akane Iijima	67	77	72	216	486,000
Yun-Hee Ku	71	73	72	216	486,000
Saiki Fujita	71	73	72	216	486,000
Yasuko Satoh	74	70	72	216	486,000
Hyun-Ju Shin	69	74	73	216	486,000
Nachiyo Ohtani	68	74	74	216	486,000
Yuko Mitsuka	72	70	74	216	486,000

NEC Karuizawa 72

Karuizawa 72 Golf Club, Karuizawa, Nagano
Par 36-36–72; 6,571 yards

August 10-12
purse, ¥60,000,000

	SCORES			TOTAL	MONEY
Akiko Fukushima	66	66	67	199	¥10,800,000
Namika Omata	70	68	68	206	5,280,000
Yuko Mitsuka	71	67	69	207	3,900,000
Momoko Ueda	68	68	71	207	3,900,000
Paula Creamer	70	66	72	208	3,000,000
Mi-Jeong Jeon	72	68	69	209	2,400,000
Nikki Campbell	71	72	67	210	1,540,800
Michiko Hattori	72	70	68	210	1,540,800
Iyoko Wada	72	69	69	210	1,540,800
Ji-Hyun Lee	68	72	70	210	1,540,800
Akane Iijima	72	64	74	210	1,540,800
Kaori Higo	70	71	70	211	984,000
Kurumi Dohi	70	70	71	211	984,000
Yayoi Arasaki	72	68	71	211	984,000
Jeong-Eun Lee	72	71	69	212	834,000
Yuka Shiroto	70	71	71	212	834,000
Jae-Hee Bae	70	73	70	213	618,000
Shiho Oyama	70	72	71	213	618,000

	SCORES			TOTAL	MONEY
Mayumi Shimomura	73	69	71	213	618,000
Hiroko Yamaguchi	70	71	72	213	618,000
Kuniko Maeda	73	67	73	213	618,000
Miki Saiki	69	70	74	213	618,000

Shin Caterpillar Mitsubishi Ladies

Daihakone Country Club, Hakone, Kanagawa
Par 36-37–73; 6,648 yards

August 17-19
purse, ¥60,000,000

	SCORES			TOTAL	MONEY
Sakura Yokomine	67	67	72	206	¥10,800,000
Shiho Oyama	68	73	67	208	5,280,000
Akiko Fukishuma	70	71	69	210	4,200,000
Michiko Hattori	69	70	72	211	3,300,000
Miki Saiki	68	70	73	211	3,300,000
Hiroko Yamaguchi	70	71	71	212	2,250,000
Yui Kawahara	71	68	73	212	2,250,000
So-Hee Kim	71	73	69	213	1,500,000
Hyun-Jun Shin	72	70	71	213	1,500,000
Akane Iijima	67	72	74	213	1,500,000
Saiki Fujita	72	72	71	215	996,000
Miho Koga	70	73	72	215	996,000
Hiromi Mogi	71	71	73	215	996,000
Ji-Yeon Han	73	69	73	215	996,000
Yuka Irie	73	69	73	215	996,000
Yun-Joo Jeong	77	69	70	216	674,000
Chie Arimura	72	74	70	216	674,000
Yukari Baba	73	71	72	216	674,000
Yuriko Ohtsuka	68	75	73	216	674,000
Aki Ohkubo	71	72	73	216	674,000
Ji-Hyun Lee	72	71	73	216	674,000

Yonex Ladies

Yonex Country Club, Nagaoka, Niigata
Par 36-36–72; 6,346 yards

August 24-26
purse, ¥60,000,000

	SCORES			TOTAL	MONEY
Yuri Fudoh	65	70	69	204	¥10,800,000
Momoko Ueda	70	68	67	205	5,280,000
Yun-Hee Ku	70	71	66	207	4,200,000
Sakura Yokomine	71	68	69	208	3,600,000
Hyun-Ju Shin	72	69	69	210	2,500,000
*Mika Miyazato	73	70	67	210	
Miho Koga	71	68	71	210	2,500,000
Miki Saiki	70	68	72	210	2,500,000
Akane Iijima	72	72	67	211	1,399,500
Shiho Oyama	72	72	67	211	1,399,500
Yun-Jye Wei	70	70	71	211	1,399,500
Maiko Wakabayashi	71	69	71	211	1,399,500
Michiko Hattori	70	72	70	212	1,038,000
Yuko Saitoh	70	69	74	213	978,000
Kaori Higo	70	74	70	214	888,000
Ai Ogawa	71	71	72	214	888,000
Ayako Uehara	73	73	69	215	708,000
Chie Arimura	76	69	70	215	708,000

	SCORES			TOTAL	MONEY
Junko Omote	73	72	70	215	708,000
Chiharu Tsunekawa	71	71	73	215	708,000

Golf 5 Ladies

Alpen Country Club, Bibai, Hokkaido
Par 36-36–72; 6,364 yards

August 31-September 2
purse, ¥60,000,000

	SCORES			TOTAL	MONEY
Akane Iijima	72	65	69	206	¥10,800,000
Sakura Yokomine	67	70	69	206	5,280,000
(Iijima defeated Yokomine on fourth playoff hole.)					
Shinobu Moromizato	71	67	70	208	4,200,000
Hiroko Yamaguchi	68	71	70	209	3,300,000
Bo-Bae Song	69	67	73	209	3,300,000
Na Zhang	70	74	68	212	2,250,000
Mi-Jeong Jeon	69	73	70	212	2,250,000
Nobuko Kizawa	70	74	69	213	1,500,000
Miho Koga	72	70	71	213	1,500,000
Kuniko Maeda	70	70	73	213	1,500,000
*Kumiko Kaneda	72	68	73	213	
Mayumi Shimomura	70	74	70	214	1,032,000
Akiko Fukushima	71	70	73	214	1,032,000
So-Hee Kim	73	67	74	214	1,032,000
Rui Kitada	72	74	69	215	792,000
Ji-Yeon Han	71	73	71	215	792,000
Midori Yoneyama	72	70	73	215	792,000
Tomoko Kusakabe	69	72	74	215	792,000
Kasumi Fujii	70	71	74	215	792,000
Chieko Nishida	73	73	70	216	568,000
Yuko Saitoh	71	72	73	216	568,000
Ya-Huei Lu	73	70	73	216	568,000

Japan LPGA Championship Konica Minolta Cup

Regus Crest Golf Club, Grand Course, Akitakata, Hiroshima
Par 36-36–72; 6,560 yards

September 6-9
purse, ¥100,000,000

	SCORES				TOTAL	MONEY
Akane Iijima	71	68	67	68	274	¥18,000,000
Sakura Yokomine	69	70	69	70	278	8,800,000
Hyun-Ju Shin	74	69	71	67	281	7,000,000
Momoko Ueda	78	67	71	67	283	4,625,000
Hiroko Yamaguchi	71	73	70	69	283	4,625,000
Ayako Uehara	68	70	75	70	283	4,625,000
Miki Saiki	71	72	67	73	283	4,625,000
Shinobu Moromizato	71	72	71	70	284	2,500,000
Akiko Fukushima	73	74	66	71	284	2,500,000
Yuri Fudoh	76	67	67	74	284	2,500,000
Mayu Hattori	73	74	72	66	285	1,770,000
Ji-Yeon Han	71	71	74	69	285	1,770,000
Yun-Joo Jeong	76	68	72	70	286	1,520,000
Na Zhang	73	70	72	71	286	1,520,000
Jeong-Eun Lee	74	72	68	72	286	1,520,000
Kaori Nakamichi	73	71	72	71	287	1,270,000
Shiho Oyama	71	71	71	74	287	1,270,000
Tamie Durdin	73	73	72	70	288	1,020,000

	SCORES			TOTAL	MONEY
Yui Kawahara	71	71	72	74	288	1,020,000
Yuka Arita	69	75	70	74	288	1,020,000

Munsingwear Ladies Tokai Classic

Minami Aichi Country Club, South Course, Mihama, Aichi
Par 36-36—72; 6,428 yards

September 14-16
purse, ¥70,000,000

	SCORES			TOTAL	MONEY
Na Zhang	73	69	66	208	¥12,600,000
Nobuko Kizawa	65	74	71	210	5,530,000
Momoko Ueda	70	69	71	210	5,530,000
Yui Kawahara	68	73	70	211	4,200,000
Hiroko Yamaguchi	69	72	71	212	3,500,000
Ai Ogawa	68	75	70	213	2,625,000
Mi-Jeong Jeon	68	74	71	213	2,625,000
Akane Iijima	69	67	78	214	2,100,000
Shinobu Moromizato	71	73	71	215	1,484,000
Hiromi Mogi	71	72	72	215	1,484,000
Mayu Hattori	74	68	73	215	1,484,000
Jeong-Eun Lee	71	74	71	216	1,092,000
Yuka Irie	73	72	71	216	1,092,000
Yuka Arita	74	69	73	216	1,092,000
Shiho Oyama	70	72	74	216	1,092,000
Kuniko Maeda	71	70	75	216	1,092,000
Eun-Hye Lee	76	69	72	217	720,000
Kasumi Fujii	73	72	72	217	720,000
Yun-Hee Ku	72	72	73	217	720,000
Akiko Fukushima	74	70	73	217	720,000
Kaori Higo	73	71	73	217	720,000
Hyun-Ju Shin	71	72	74	217	720,000
Miki Saiki	72	69	76	217	720,000

Miyagi TV Cup Dunlop Ladies Open

Rifu Golf Club, Rifu, Miyagi
Par 36-36—72; 6,496 yards

September 21-23
purse, ¥60,000,000

	SCORES			TOTAL	MONEY
Yuko Mitsuka	71	66	71	208	¥10,800,000
Tomoko Kusakabe	70	69	70	209	5,280,000
Sakura Yokomine	68	71	72	211	4,200,000
Yun-Joo Jeong	67	75	70	212	3,600,000
Chie Arimura	72	70	71	213	3,000,000
Ji-Hee Lee	72	73	69	214	1,950,000
Kasumi Fujii	71	73	70	214	1,950,000
Jeong-Eun Lee	69	73	72	214	1,950,000
Momoko Ueda	68	70	76	214	1,950,000
Nikki Campbell	72	72	71	215	1,164,000
Erina Hara	71	71	73	215	1,164,000
Keiko Sasaki	73	72	71	216	948,000
Mayu Hattori	74	70	72	216	948,000
Miho Koga	70	73	73	216	948,000
Yun-Jye Wei	72	70	74	216	948,000
Yuka Shiroto	69	71	76	216	948,000
Natsu Nagai	74	72	71	217	738,000
Rui Kitada	74	73	70	217	738,000

	SCORES			TOTAL	MONEY
Nobuko Kizawa	74	72	72	218	570,857
Michie Ohba	73	72	73	218	570,857
Ya-Huei Lu	72	74	72	218	570,857
Yui Kawahara	72	71	75	218	570,857
Yayoi Arasaki	70	77	71	218	570,857
Yuko Saitoh	69	73	76	218	570,857
Hiromi Mogi	71	70	77	218	570,857

Japan Women's Open

Tarumae Country Club, Tomakomai, Hokkaido
Par 36-36–72; 6,522 yards

September 27-30
purse, ¥140,000,000

	SCORES				TOTAL	MONEY
Shinobu Moromizato	69	69	71	73	282	¥28,000,000
Yuri Fudoh	71	71	70	71	283	15,400,000
Nikki Campbell	70	75	71	68	284	10,780,000
Miho Koga	71	71	73	70	285	7,000,000
Jeong Jang	74	71	68	74	287	5,880,000
Sakura Yokomine	70	74	71	74	289	4,246,666
Miki Saiki	71	73	69	76	289	4,246,666
Momoko Ueda	74	71	71	73	289	4,246,666
Kurumi Dohi	76	72	70	72	290	2,730,000
Mayu Hattori	73	71	73	73	290	2,730,000
Saiki Fujita	71	74	73	72	290	2,730,000
Na Zhang	74	75	74	68	291	2,212,000
Hiromi Mogi	72	76	71	73	292	1,778,000
Namika Omata	72	73	73	74	292	1,778,000
Yuko Mitsuka	75	72	74	71	292	1,778,000
*Rikako Morita	74	75	72	72	293	
Mie Nakata	73	74	73	74	294	1,342,000
Shiho Oyama	73	72	74	75	294	1,342,000
Kuniko Maeda	69	76	76	73	294	1,342,000
Hiroko Yamaguchi	73	74	74	73	294	1,342,000
Bo-Bae Song	75	74	75	70	294	1,342,000
Yuka Shiroto	76	72	76	70	294	1,342,000
Erina Hara	74	73	72	75	294	1,342,000

Sankyo Ladies Open

Akagi Country Club, Kiryu, Gunma
Par 36-36–72; 6,474 yards

October 5-7
purse, ¥80,000,000

	SCORES			TOTAL	MONEY
So-Hee Kim	72	69	68	209	¥14,400,000
Mihoko Takahashi	71	69	69	209	6,320,000
Momoko Ueda	71	68	70	209	6,320,000
(Kim defeated Takahashi and Ueda on first playoff hole.)					
Shiho Oyama	69	70	71	210	4,800,000
Kuniko Maeda	70	71	70	211	3,100,000
Kasumi Fujii	72	69	70	211	3,100,000
Hiroko Yamaguchi	72	67	72	211	3,100,000
Mi-Jeong Jeon	69	69	73	211	3,100,000
Miho Koga	71	69	72	212	1,701,333
Mie Nakata	72	68	72	212	1,701,333
Erina Hara	70	67	75	212	1,701,333
Miki Saiki	73	71	69	213	1,184,000

	SCORES			TOTAL	MONEY
Junko Omote	73	70	70	213	1,184,000
Hyun-Ju Shin	73	70	70	213	1,184,000
Akane Iijima	70	72	71	213	1,184,000
Yukari Baba	72	70	71	213	1,184,000
Mineko Nasu	72	70	71	213	1,184,000
Yuko Saitoh	71	70	72	213	1,184,000
Yui Kawahara	73	70	71	214	805,333
Midori Yoneyama	68	74	72	214	805,333
Shinobu Moromizato	74	65	75	214	805,333

Fujitsu Ladies

Tokyu Seven Hundred Club, Chiba
Par 36-36–72; 6,591 yards

October 12-14
purse, ¥80,000,000

	SCORES			TOTAL	MONEY
Sakura Yokomine	72	66	69	207	¥14,400,000
Momoko Ueda	68	69	70	207	7,040,000
(Yokomine defeated Ueda on second playoff hole.)					
Yun-Joo Jeong	70	68	70	208	5,600,000
Hiromi Mogi	71	69	70	210	4,000,000
Mikiyo Nishizuka	70	69	71	210	4,000,000
Tamie Durdin	71	68	71	210	4,000,000
Kurumi Dohi	72	72	67	211	2,400,000
Yuko Mitsuka	71	70	70	211	2,400,000
Ayako Uehara	70	70	71	211	2,400,000
Yui Kawahara	72	72	68	212	1,401,600
Hiroko Yamaguchi	73	70	69	212	1,401,600
Shiho Oyama	71	70	71	212	1,401,600
Yukari Baba	69	71	72	212	1,401,600
Ji-Hee Lee	68	69	75	212	1,401,600
Ji-Hyun Lee	69	74	70	213	1,072,000
Namika Omata	71	72	70	213	1,072,000
Iyoko Wada	72	67	74	213	1,072,000
Tomoko Kusakabe	70	73	71	214	912,000
*Asako Fujimoto	73	69	73	215	
Seiko Watanabe	70	75	71	216	760,000
Mihoko Takahashi	75	70	71	216	760,000
Hyun-Ju Shin	75	69	72	216	760,000
Kaori Nakamichi	71	72	73	216	760,000

Masters Golf Club Ladies

Masters Golf Club, Miki, Hyogo
Par 36-36–72; 6,510 yards

October 19-21
purse, ¥123,000,000

	SCORES			TOTAL	MONEY
Miho Koga	72	69	66	207	¥22,140,000
Paula Creamer	68	73	70	211	10,824,000
Mayu Hattori	73	71	68	212	8,610,000
Sakura Yokomine	73	69	71	213	7,380,000
Mihoko Iseri	73	71	71	215	6,150,000
Chie Arimura	76	66	74	216	4,612,500
Momoko Ueda	68	72	76	216	4,612,500
Namika Omata	72	73	72	217	3,690,000
Miki Saiki	69	76	73	218	2,767,500
Ji-Yeon Han	71	72	75	218	2,767,500

	SCORES			TOTAL	MONEY
Rui Kitada	77	71	71	219	2,238,600
Ji-Hyun Lee	73	75	71	219	2,238,600
Shinobu Moromizato	73	77	70	220	1,808,100
Junko Omote	78	73	69	220	1,808,100
Aiko Yoshida	75	73	72	220	1,808,100
Michie Ohba	78	72	70	220	1,808,100
Yukari Baba	74	74	72	220	1,808,100
Ayako Uehara	75	74	72	221	1,279,200
Hiromi Mogi	77	71	73	221	1,279,200
Keiko Sasaki	75	72	74	221	1,279,200
Hiroko Yamaguchi	75	74	72	221	1,279,200

Hisako Higuchi IDC Otsuka Ladies

Musashigoaka Golf Club, Hanno, Saitama
Par 36-36–72; 6,561 yards

October 26-28
purse, ¥70,000,000

	SCORES			TOTAL	MONEY
Mi-Jeong Jeon	69	72	69	210	¥12,600,000
Miho Koga	69	70	72	211	6,300,000
Mineko Nasu	73	72	68	213	4,200,000
Kurumi Dohi	72	71	70	213	4,200,000
Akane Iijima	71	71	71	213	4,200,000
Ai Nishikawa	74	74	66	214	2,450,000
Yukari Baba	71	75	68	214	2,450,000
Ji-Yeon Han	71	74	69	214	2,450,000
Yuko Saitoh	73	74	68	215	1,575,000
Akiko Fukushima	74	72	69	215	1,575,000
*Miki Sakai	72	75	69	216	
Mihoko Iseri	73	71	72	216	1,302,000
Tamie Durdin	69	73	74	216	1,302,000
Na Zhang	75	73	69	217	1,057,000
Kaori Nakamichi	73	73	71	217	1,057,000
Ji-Hee Lee	73	73	71	217	1,057,000
Ji-Hyun Lee	68	73	76	217	1,057,000
Yun-Joo Jeong	72	69	76	217	1,057,000
Erina Hara	77	72	69	218	707,000
Sakura Yokomine	72	75	71	218	707,000
Tomoko Kusakabe	73	74	71	218	707,000
Mayu Hattori	71	75	72	218	707,000
Michiko Hattori	72	74	72	218	707,000
Rui Kitada	74	72	72	218	707,000
Chiharu Tsunekawa	74	72	72	218	707,000
Yui Kawahara	71	74	73	218	707,000

Mizuno Classic

Kinetetsu Kashikojima Country Club, Shima-Shi, Mie
Par 36-36–72; 6,506 yards

November 2-4
purse, ¥165,200,000

	SCORES			TOTAL	MONEY
Momoko Ueda	70	67	66	203	¥23,864,400
Reilley Rankin	66	72	67	205	12,447,784
Maria Hjorth	70	68	67	205	12,447,784
Shinobu Moromizato	71	70	67	208	8,097,077
Mi Hyun Kim	72	70	67	209	5,055,729
Chie Arimura	66	73	70	209	5,055,729

	SCORES			TOTAL	MONEY
Mie Nakata	68	70	71	209	5,055,729
Laura Davies	65	72	72	209	5,055,729
Angela Park	73	71	67	211	3,006,573
Hye Jung Choi	70	72	69	211	3,006,573
Yuri Fudoh	72	70	69	211	3,006,573
Bo-Bae Song	70	71	70	211	3,006,573
Jee Young Lee	70	71	70	211	3,006,573
Yui Kawahara	71	73	68	212	2,180,297
In-bee Park	71	72	69	212	2,180,297
Brittany Lang	69	73	70	212	2,180,297
Joo Mi Kim	69	72	71	212	2,180,297
Jeong Jang	69	70	73	212	2,180,297
Sophie Gustafson	73	72	68	213	1,753,692
Karin Sjodin	75	72	66	213	1,753,692
Miki Saiki	71	73	69	213	1,753,692
Hyun-Ju Shin	72	72	69	213	1,753,692
Shiho Oyama	75	68	70	213	1,753,692
Nikki Campbell	74	71	69	214	1,348,224
Hiroko Yamaguchi	74	70	70	214	1,348,224
Beth Bader	72	71	71	214	1,348,224
Sakura Yokomine	72	71	71	214	1,348,224
Carri Wood	71	72	71	214	1,348,224
Yun-Joo Jeong	70	72	72	214	1,348,224
In-Kyung Kim	69	72	73	214	1,348,224
Christina Kim	73	69	72	214	1,348,224
Erina Hara	67	72	75	214	1,348,224

Itoen Ladies

Great Island Club, Chonan, Chiba
Par 36-36–72; 6,581 yards

November 9-11
purse, ¥70,000,000

	SCORES			TOTAL	MONEY
Rui Kitada	69	70	72	211	¥12,600,000
Miki Saiki	71	71	69	211	5,530,000
Hiromi Mogi	72	68	71	211	5,530,000
(Kitada defeated Saiki and Mogi on second playoff hole.)					
Na Zhang	71	75	66	212	3,850,000
Laura Davies	68	76	68	212	3,850,000
Ji-Hee Lee	72	69	72	213	2,625,000
Tamie Durdin	67	73	73	213	2,625,000
Yui Kawahara	75	72	67	214	1,750,000
Yasuko Satoh	71	73	70	214	1,750,000
Kaori Higo	73	71	70	214	1,750,000
Akane Iijima	71	71	73	215	1,204,000
Iyoko Wada	69	75	71	215	1,204,000
Miho Koga	70	74	71	215	1,204,000
Yun-Jye Wei	71	73	71	215	1,204,000
Shiho Oyama	71	76	69	216	827,000
Nikki Campbell	71	75	70	216	827,000
Chie Arimura	73	73	70	216	827,000
Keiko Sasaki	71	74	71	216	827,000
Momoko Ueda	71	73	72	216	827,000
Mi-Jeong Jeon	72	71	73	216	827,000
Akiko Fukushima	68	73	75	216	827,000

Daioseishi Elleair Ladies Open

Elleair Golf Club, Mitoyo, Kagawa
Par 36-36–72; 6,355 yards

November 16-18
purse, ¥90,000,000

	SCORES			TOTAL	MONEY
Momoko Ueda	66	71	72	209	¥16,200,000
Yui Kawahara	69	74	69	212	6,030,000
Mikiyo Nishizuka	70	71	71	212	6,030,000
Shinobu Moromizato	71	68	73	212	6,030,000
Erina Hara	71	67	74	212	6,030,000
Shiho Oyama	70	73	70	213	2,533,500
Bo-Bae Song	75	67	71	213	2,533,500
Hyun-Ju Shin	71	70	72	213	2,533,500
Mie Nakata	70	69	74	213	2,533,500
Sakura Yokomine	72	67	74	213	2,533,500
Hiromi Mogi	69	69	75	213	2,533,500
Yasuko Satoh	69	73	72	214	1,476,000
Nobuko Kizawa	72	70	72	214	1,476,000
Yuko Saitoh	71	70	73	214	1,476,000
Chie Arimura	71	68	75	214	1,476,000
Michiko Hattori	74	71	70	215	1,161,000
Ayako Uehara	68	74	73	215	1,161,000
Na Zhang	68	73	74	215	1,161,000
Mitsuko Kawasaki	74	71	71	216	887,400
Ji-Yeon Han	71	71	74	216	887,400
Mayu Hattori	71	71	74	216	887,400
Namika Omata	72	69	75	216	887,400
Mayumi Shimomura	69	70	77	216	887,400

Japan LPGA Tour Championship Ricoh Cup

Miyazaki Country Club, Sadohara, Miyazaki
Par 36-36–72; 6,455 yards

November 22-25
purse, ¥100,000,000

	SCORES				TOTAL	MONEY
Miho Koga	74	68	66	67	275	¥25,000,000
Yuri Fudoh	65	69	69	74	277	14,500,000
Bo-Bae Song	70	73	75	65	283	10,000,000
Yuko Mitsuka	71	73	69	71	284	7,910,000
Momoko Ueda	71	69	73	72	285	6,500,000
Na Zhang	70	77	69	71	287	5,600,000
Hyun-Ju Shin	72	74	72	70	288	2,804,000
Chie Arimura	72	71	74	71	288	2,804,000
Mie Nakata	75	70	72	71	288	2,804,000
Mi-Jeong Jeon	72	73	72	71	288	2,804,000
Miki Saiki	74	68	72	74	288	2,804,000
Shinobu Moromizato	70	74	76	69	289	1,047,500
Sakura Yokomine	72	74	71	72	289	1,047,500
Shiho Oyama	69	74	73	73	289	1,047,500
Rui Kitada	74	74	68	73	289	1,047,500
Akiko Fukushima	77	71	68	74	290	670,000
Mikiyo Nishizuka	72	78	70	73	293	620,000
Nikki Campbell	71	76	75	72	294	513,333
So-Hee Kim	75	75	72	72	294	513,333
Erina Hara	71	73	75	74	294	513,333

The Kyoraku Cup

Fukuoka Century Golf Club, Asakura, Fukuoka
Par 36-36—72; 6,501 yards

December 1-2
purse, ¥61,500,000

FIRST ROUND

Yuko Mitsuka (Japan) defeated Shi Hyun Ahn, 67-74.
Erina Hara (Japan) defeated Mi-Jeong Jeon, 72-75.
Se Ri Pak (Korea) defeated Shinobu Moromizato 70-73.
Sarah Lee (Korea) halved with Miho Koga, 71-71.
Jeong Jang (Korea) defeated Miki Saiki, 72-74.
Hyun-Ju Shin (Korea) defeated Kuniko Maeda, 70-73.
Seon Hwa Lee (Korea) defeated Akane Iijima, 73-77.
Jee Young Lee (Korea) defeated Yui Kawahara, 71-74.
Chie Arimura (Japan) defeated Bo-Bae Song, 64-82.
Ayako Uehara (Japan) defeated Eun Hee Ji, 76-77.
Sakura Yokomine (Japan) defeated Sun Ju Ahn, 71-72.
Midori Yoneyama (Japan) defeated Ji-Yai Shin, 71-72.

POINTS: Japan 13, Korea 11

FINAL ROUND

Jeong Jang (Korea) defeated Yuko Mitsuka, 71-74.
Akane Iijima (Japan) defeated Shi Hyun Ahn, 76-77.
Hyun-Ju Shin (Korea) defeated Miho Koga, 72-74.
Sakura Yokomine (Japan) defeated Eun Hee Ji, 70-78.
Seon Hwa Lee (Korea) defeated Yui Kawahara, 69-73.
Mi-Jeong Jeon (Korea) halved with Erina Hara, 73-73.
Sun Ju Ahn (Korea) defeated Midori Yoneyama, 72-79.
Mi Hyun Kim (Korea) defeated Ayako Uehara, 73-76.
Kuniko Maeda (Japan) defeated Sarah Lee, 72-75.
Shinobu Moromizato (Japan) defeated Ji-Yai Shin, 68-72.
Miki Saiki (Japan) defeated Bo-Bae Song, 72-75.
Jee Young Lee (Korea) defeated Chie Arimura, 72-75.

TOTAL POINTS: Japan 24, Korea 24
Miho Koga (Japan) defeated Jeong Jang on third playoff hole.

(Each member of the Japanese team received ¥3,250,000; each member of the Korean team received ¥1,625,000.)

Korea LPGA Tour

Asia Miles Binhai Ladies Open

Binhai Golf Club, Lakes Course, Shanghai, China
Par 36-36–72; 6,341 yards

March 21-23
purse, $230,000

	SCORES			TOTAL	MONEY
Da Ye Na	74	72	76	222	KRW32,357,550
Lu Hsiao Chuan	78	72	74	224	15,639,482
Hae Jung Kim	72	77	75	224	15,639,482
Yu Pei Lin	74	75	75	224	15,639,482
Eun Hee Ji	74	74	76	224	15,639,482
Ran Hong	77	73	76	226	8,089,387
Linyan Shang	70	79	77	226	8,089,387
Young Ran Jo	75	78	74	227	4,816,116
Hsiu-Feng Tseng	78	74	75	227	4,816,116
Su-Jung Yoon	72	79	76	227	4,816,116
Wu Qunfang	75	74	78	227	4,816,116
Ha-Neul Kim	75	81	72	228	2,782,749
Ye Li Ying	75	79	74	228	2,782,749
Pornanong Phatlum	77	76	75	228	2,782,749
Porani Chutichai	78	74	76	228	2,782,749
Sun Ju Ahn	74	77	77	228	2,782,749
Mi-Hyun Cho	76	79	74	229	2,321,302
Libby Smith	74	79	76	229	2,321,302
Na Yeon Choi	74	79	76	229	2,321,302
Ye-Jin Na	72	80	77	229	2,321,302
Leah Hart	78	74	77	229	2,321,302

KB Star Tour in Busan

Busan Asiad, Pine Course, South Gyeongsang
Par 36-36–72; 6,210 yards

April 19-21
purse, KRW200,000,000

	SCORES			TOTAL	MONEY
Sun Ju Ahn	68	76	76	220	KRW36,000,000
Hyun Hee Moon	78	75	68	221	14,666,667
Ji-Yai Shin	78	74	69	221	14,666,667
Ran Hong	71	76	74	221	14,666,667
Min Sun Kim	74	75	74	223	8,000,000
Seung Hyo Sun	72	83	69	224	7,000,000
Hae Jung Kim	77	75	73	225	4,875,000
Ji-Hye Jang	71	81	73	225	4,875,000
Hye Jin Jung	77	75	73	225	4,875,000
Eun Jung Shin	72	77	76	225	4,875,000
Young Ran Jo	72	77	77	226	3,800,000
Ha-Neul Kim	71	82	74	227	3,600,000
Oh Soon Lee	77	80	71	228	2,667,500
Min Gee Song	77	79	72	228	2,667,500
Eun Jin Kim	71	84	73	228	2,667,500
Min Jung Kim	79	75	74	228	2,667,500
Kyung Hee Cho	74	78	76	228	2,667,500
Yoon Jung Won	71	80	77	228	2,667,500
Jenny Lee	73	77	78	228	2,667,500
Bo Mi Kim	75	73	80	228	2,667,500

MBC Tour MC Square Cup Ladies Open

Crown Country Club, Jeju
Par 36-36–72; 6,300 yards

April 25-27
purse, KRW200,000,000

	SCORES			TOTAL	MONEY
Ji-Yai Shin	76	73	67	216	KRW36,000,000
Jenny Lee	71	71	74	216	20,000,000
(Shin defeated Lee on first playoff hole.)					
Hyun Hee Moon	74	71	72	217	14,000,000
Ha-Neul Kim	74	74	70	218	10,000,000
Eun Hee Ji	78	71	71	220	6,500,000
Ji-Hye Jang	75	74	71	220	6,500,000
Hee Young Park	73	75	72	220	6,500,000
Sun Ju Ahn	76	72	72	220	6,500,000
Min Ji Kim	74	75	72	221	3,975,000
Ran Hong	74	74	73	221	3,975,000
Ji Na Lim	73	71	77	221	3,975,000
Jung Hwa Lee	72	71	78	221	3,975,000
Da Ye Na	78	73	71	222	3,380,000
Woo Ri Choi	73	80	70	223	2,870,000
Ye Jin Moon	74	76	73	223	2,870,000
Bo Kyung Kim	74	74	75	223	2,870,000
Bo Mi Kim	72	76	75	223	2,870,000
Mi-Hyun Cho	79	74	71	224	2,100,000
So Young Kim$_2$	78	74	72	224	2,100,000
Hae Jung Kim^2	74	72	78	224	2,100,000
Il-Hee Lee	71	73	80	224	2,100,000

Phoenix Park Classic

Phoenix Park Golf Club, Gangwon
Par 36-36–72; 6,264 yards

May 2-4
purse, KRW200,000,000

	SCORES			TOTAL	MONEY
Eun Hee Ji	64	68	72	204	KRW36,000,000
Hee Young Park	68	71	66	205	20,000,000
Ji-Yai Shin	70	70	67	207	14,000,000
Na Yeon Choi	69	71	69	209	10,000,000
Min Sun Kim	70	73	68	211	8,000,000
Eun Jin Kim	68	74	70	212	7,000,000
So Young Kim$_2$	69	73	71	213	6,000,000
Ha-Neul Kim	71	71	72	214	4,500,000
Young Ran Jo	70	70	74	214	4,500,000
Bobea Park	70	69	75	214	4,500,000
Ye-Jin Na	74	73	68	215	3,800,000
Yoon Jung Won	70	76	70	216	3,285,000
You Jin Ji	73	72	71	216	3,285,000
Kyung Hee Cho	72	70	74	216	3,285,000
Yu-Jin Choi	72	70	74	216	3,285,000
Young Ae Ham	73	74	70	217	2,352,000
Bo Mi Suh	75	71	71	217	2,352,000
Hyun Hee Moon	73	73	71	217	2,352,000
Sun Wook Lim	70	75	72	217	2,352,000
Hye In Lee	72	70	75	217	2,352,000

KB Star Tour in Hampyung

Dynasty Country Club, Majesty Course, Hampyeong
Par 36-36–72; 6,276 yards

May 10-12
purse, KRW200,000,000

	SCORES			TOTAL	MONEY
Eun Hee Ji	68	70	69	207	KRW36,000,000
Hee Young Park	70	69	68	207	20,000,000
(Ji defeated Park on second playoff hole.)					
Ji-Yai Shin	66	76	66	208	14,000,000
Ha Na Park	69	71	70	210	10,000,000
Hye Jin Jung	71	74	66	211	8,000,000
Min Sun Kim	67	74	71	212	7,000,000
Hee Kyung Seo	70	73	70	213	5,500,000
Na Yeon Choi	72	70	71	213	5,500,000
Sun Ju Ahn	73	71	70	214	4,400,000
Ran Hong	73	71	72	216	4,100,000
Min Jee Han	71	78	68	217	3,700,000
Hae Jung Kim	70	70	77	217	3,700,000
Da Ye Na	75	73	70	218	3,075,000
Sang Hee Kim	73	75	70	218	3,075,000
Chae Young Yoon	74	73	71	218	3,075,000
Kyung Hee Cho	69	73	76	218	3,075,000
Hui Jeong Kim	79	70	70	219	2,123,333
Oh Soon Lee	76	72	71	219	2,123,333
Bo Mi Kim	76	72	71	219	2,123,333
Ha-Neul Kim	73	74	72	219	2,123,333
So Young Park	75	72	72	219	2,123,333
Yu-Jin Choi	71	71	77	219	2,123,333

Taeyoung Cup Korea Women's Open

The Honors Course, Gyeongju
Par 36-36–72; 6,390 yards

May 18-20
purse, KRW400,000,000

	SCORES			TOTAL	MONEY
Sun Ju Ahn	73	69	70	212	KRW100,000,000
Cristie Kerr	71	76	69	216	30,000,000
Jae Eun Chung	72	72	72	216	30,000,000
Eun Hee Ji	70	70	76	216	30,000,000
Na Yeon Choi	78	70	69	217	10,625,000
So Young Kim₂	77	71	69	217	10,625,000
Ya Ni Tseng	71	75	71	217	10,625,000
Sophie Gustafson	71	72	74	217	10,625,000
Jeong-Eun Lee₃	72	75	71	218	8,500,000
Jin Joo Hong	77	73	70	220	7,500,000
Young Ran Jo	78	71	71	220	7,500,000
Ji-Yai Shin	76	73	71	220	7,500,000
Hye Jin Jung	73	74	74	221	6,500,000
Hye In Lee	78	73	71	222	5,700,000
Hee Young Park	73	76	73	222	5,700,000
Hee Kyung Seo	73	74	75	222	5,700,000
Sarah Nicolson	77	73	73	223	4,610,000
Ha Na Park	75	74	74	223	4,610,000
Woo Ri Choi	72	77	74	223	4,610,000
Hyun-Ji Kim	78	71	74	223	4,610,000
You Jin Ji	73	74	76	223	4,610,000

Hill State SeoKyung Ladies Open

New Seoul Golf Club, Seoul
Par 36-36–72; 6,432 yards

June 1-3
purse, KRW300,000,000

	SCORES			TOTAL	MONEY
Ji-Yai Shin	67	71	66	204	KRW60,000,000
Eun Hee Ji	69	68	68	205	27,000,000
Sun Ju Ahn	69	69	68	206	18,000,000
Yu-Jin Choi	67	70	70	207	15,000,000
Na Yeon Choi	67	72	69	208	11,250,000
Hee Young Park	68	67	73	208	11,250,000
Hae Jung Kim	70	67	72	209	9,000,000
Hye In Lee	74	68	68	210	7,050,000
Mi-Hee Jung	71	69	70	210	7,050,000
Hyun Hee Moon	71	69	71	211	6,150,000
Min-Ji Nam	71	72	69	212	5,235,000
Bobea Park	75	68	69	212	5,235,000
Jeong-Eun Lee₅	73	68	71	212	5,235,000
Sang Hee Kim	69	71	72	212	5,235,000
Jong Jin Hong	77	68	68	213	3,870,000
Ran Hong	72	72	69	213	3,870,000
Sa Lang Lim	72	71	70	213	3,870,000
Young Ae Ham	69	73	71	213	3,870,000
Hye Jin Jung	72	69	72	213	3,870,000
Jenny Lee	72	72	70	214	2,940,000
Bo Mi Kim	70	72	72	214	2,940,000

MBC Tour BC Card Classic

88 Golf Club, West Course, Seoul
Par 36-36–72; 6,133 yards

June 15-17
purse, KRW400,000,000

	SCORES			TOTAL	MONEY
Ji-Yai Shin	71	66	67	204	KRW100,000,000
Ji Yeon Woo	70	68	67	205	34,000,000
Na Yeon Choi	69	66	71	206	24,000,000
Eun-A Lim	74	68	67	209	16,666,667
Hui Jeong Kim	71	70	68	209	16,666,667
Min-Ji Nam	66	73	70	209	16,666,667
Hye Jin Jung	72	70	68	210	9,000,000
Sun Ju Ahn	72	69	69	210	9,000,000
Il-Hee Lee	67	72	71	210	9,000,000
Ha-Neul Kim	72	67	71	210	9,000,000
So Young Kim₂	71	76	64	211	4,840,000
Jin-Joo Kim	72	70	69	211	4,840,000
Da Ye Na	72	70	69	211	4,840,000
Ji-Hye Jang	68	73	70	211	4,840,000
Ran Hong	73	67	71	211	4,840,000
Hae Jung Kim	72	70	70	212	4,160,000
Ji Na Lim	72	69	71	212	4,160,000
Soo Yun Kang	68	71	73	212	4,160,000
Chang Kyung Woo	71	73	69	213	3,920,000
Bo Mi Suh	72	71	71	214	3,720,000
You Jin Ji	72	70	72	214	3,720,000
Min Ji Son	68	71	75	214	3,720,000

KB Star Tour in Pohang

Ocean Hills Golf Club, Pohang
Par 36-36–72; 6,248 yards

June 21-23
purse, KRW200,000,000

	SCORES			TOTAL	MONEY
Ji-Yai Shin	66	68	66	200	KRW36,000,000
Eun Hee Ji	64	71	67	202	20,000,000
Seul A. Yoon	69	68	67	204	12,000,000
Eun-A Lim	67	69	68	204	12,000,000
Young Ran Jo	65	73	68	206	8,000,000
Eun Hee Kim	69	69	69	207	7,000,000
Ye-Jin Na	71	67	70	208	6,000,000
Yun Hee Cho	70	71	68	209	4,500,000
Hae Jung Kim	68	73	68	209	4,500,000
So Young Kim$_2$	73	66	70	209	4,500,000
Hyun Hee Moon	71	71	68	210	3,593,333
Hee Kyung Seo	71	69	70	210	3,593,333
Bo Kyung Kim	69	71	70	210	3,593,333
Jee Hyang Park	73	70	68	211	2,973,333
Min-Ji Nam	71	70	70	211	2,973,333
Bo Mi Kim	70	68	73	211	2,973,333
Mi-Hee Jung	71	73	68	212	2,353,333
Soon Hee Kim	72	70	70	212	2,353,333
Jong Jin Hong	71	71	70	212	2,353,333
Ran Hong	70	74	69	213	1,940,000

MBC Tour Korea Golf Art Village Open

Gold Course
Par 36-36–72; 6,450 yards
(First round cancelled—rain.)

July 4-6
purse, KRW200,000,000

	SCORES		TOTAL	MONEY
Sun Ju Ahn	69	63	132	KRW36,000,000
Eun Hee Ji	66	67	133	20,000,000
Eun-A Lim	71	64	135	12,000,000
Na Yeon Choi	67	68	135	12,000,000
Jeong-Eun Lee$_5$	72	65	137	7,000,000
Young Mi Kwon	70	67	137	7,000,000
Ji-Yai Shin	69	68	137	7,000,000

KB Star Tour in Chungcheong

Silk River, Chungcheong
Par 36-36–72; 6,309 yards
(First round cancelled—rain.)

September 6-8
purse, KRW200,000,000

	SCORES		TOTAL	MONEY
Ji-Yai Shin	69	65	134	KRW36,000,000
Na Yeon Choi	66	70	136	20,000,000
Woo Ri Choi	70	67	137	14,000,000
Eun Hee Ji	71	67	138	10,000,000
Seul A. Yoon	70	70	140	7,000,000
Ran Hong	70	70	140	7,000,000
Yun Hee Cho	66	74	140	7,000,000
Young Ran Jo	70	71	141	4,700,000

	SCORES		TOTAL	MONEY
Hye Jin Jung	70	71	141	4,700,000
Chae Young Yoon	73	69	142	3,612,000
Ji Na Lim	73	69	142	3,612,000
Bo Kyung Kim	69	73	142	3,612,000
Da Ye Na	68	74	142	3,612,000
Ha-Neul Kim	65	77	142	3,612,000
Hae Young Jeon	75	68	143	2,880,000
A Reum Park	67	76	143	2,880,000
Mi-Hyun Cho	71	73	144	2,480,000
Hyun Jin Ku	71	73	144	2,480,000
Hee Young Park	74	71	145	2,033,333
Hye In Lee	72	73	145	2,033,333
Woo Gon Park	70	75	145	2,033,333

SK Energy Invitational

88 Golf Club, West Course
Par 36-36–72; 6,269 yards

September 14-16
purse, KRW400,000,000

	SCORES			TOTAL	MONEY
Ji-Yai Shin	68	66	70	204	KRW100,000,000
Hee Young Park	71	69	69	209	29,000,000
Jin Joo Hong	70	66	73	209	29,000,000
Hyun Hee Moon	73	67	70	210	18,000,000
Il-Hee Lee	68	70	72	210	18,000,000
Hee Kyung Seo	73	70	68	211	11,000,000
Eun Hee Ji	72	71	68	211	11,000,000
Bobea Park	70	70	71	211	11,000,000
Kyeong Eun Bae	72	67	72	211	11,000,000
Seul A. Yoon	71	70	71	212	5,466,667
Ha-Neul Kim	68	71	73	212	5,466,667
Eun-A Lim	72	64	76	212	5,466,667
A. Reum Park	72	72	70	214	4,320,000
Sun Ju Ahn	72	71	71	214	4,320,000
Na Yeon Choi	73	68	73	214	4,320,000
Mi-Hyun Cho	70	71	73	214	4,320,000
Yun Hee Cho	72	68	74	214	4,320,000
Bo Kyung Kim	73	67	74	214	4,320,000
Young Ran Jo	73	71	71	215	3,740,000
Da Ye Na	72	68	75	215	3,740,000
Ji-Hye Jang	74	70	72	216	3,600,000

Shinsegye Cup KLPGA Championship

Jayu Park, Incheon City, Gyeonggi
Par 36-36–72; 6,414 yards

September 19-21
purse, KRW300,000,000

	SCORES			TOTAL	MONEY
Na Yeon Choi	68	69	68	205	KRW60,000,000
Eun Hee Ji	70	70	68	208	27,000,000
Hyun Hee Moon	68	72	69	209	15,000,000
Sun Ju Ahn	70	69	70	209	15,000,000
Sun Wook Lim	73	65	71	209	15,000,000
Min Gee Song	73	67	70	210	9,000,000
Hee Young Park	68	71	71	210	9,000,000
Ji-Yai Shin	71	67	72	210	9,000,000
Ji Yae Yeo	67	70	75	212	6,600,000

	SCORES			TOTAL	MONEY
Kyung Hee Cho	71	70	72	213	5,925,000
Seul A. Yoon	69	69	75	213	5,925,000
Hee Kyung Seo	71	71	72	214	5,400,000
Ran Hong	72	72	71	215	4,458,000
Ji Na Lim	75	68	72	215	4,458,000
Ji-Hye Jang	72	71	72	215	4,458,000
Mi-Hyun Cho	71	69	75	215	4,458,000
Soo Young Moon	75	64	76	215	4,458,000
Ye-Song Lee	75	71	70	216	3,054,000
Bo Mi Kim	67	77	72	216	3,054,000
Eun-A Lim	71	71	74	216	3,054,000
Jeong-Eun Lee₅	73	69	74	216	3,054,000
So Ra Kim	70	72	74	216	3,054,000

Samsung Finance Ladies Championship

Phoenix Park, Gangwon
Par 36-36–72; 6,264 yards

October 5-7
purse, KRW300,000,000

	SCORES			TOTAL	MONEY
Ji-Yai Shin	71	67	70	208	KRW60,000,000
Hyun Hee Moon	71	74	65	210	27,000,000
Hee Kyung Seo	72	69	70	211	16,500,000
Sun Ju Ahn	70	69	72	211	16,500,000
Eun-A Lim	73	71	70	214	11,250,000
Yun Hee Cho	68	70	76	214	11,250,000
Hyun-Ji Kim	72	73	70	215	9,000,000
Sun Wook Lim	72	75	69	216	7,050,000
Ji Na Lim	67	76	73	216	7,050,000
Ji-Young Yoon	72	71	74	217	5,750,000
Ha-Neul Kim	70	73	74	217	5,750,000
Eun Hee Ji	71	71	75	217	5,750,000
Min-Ji Nam	78	71	69	218	4,350,000
Ran Hong	70	76	72	218	4,350,000
Da Ye Na	73	71	74	218	4,350,000
Bo Kyung Kim	73	70	75	218	4,350,000
Young Ran Jo	73	70	75	218	4,350,000
Min Sun Kim	70	71	77	218	4,350,000
Bo Mi Kim	78	72	69	219	3,030,000
A. Reum Park	75	73	71	219	3,030,000
Il-Hee Lee	72	75	72	219	3,030,000
Ha Na Park	71	75	73	219	3,030,000

Hite Cup Ladies Championship

Blue Heron Course, Gyeonggi
Par 36-36–72; 6,406 yards

October 11-13
purse, KRW400,000,000

	SCORES			TOTAL	MONEY
Hye Jung Choi	70	72	68	210	KRW100,000,000
Eun Hee Ji	69	72	70	211	34,000,000
In-Bee Park	72	71	69	212	24,000,000
Na Yeon Choi	72	70	71	213	20,000,000
Hyun Hee Moon	71	74	69	214	14,000,000
Ji-Yai Shin	74	70	70	214	14,000,000
Ji Na Lim	70	72	72	214	14,000,000
Hae Jung Kim	73	71	71	215	10,000,000

	SCORES			TOTAL	MONEY
Ran Hong	74	73	70	217	7,000,000
Hee Kyung Seo	77	66	74	217	7,000,000
Ji Yeon Woo	73	74	72	219	4,930,000
Bo Kyung Kim	72	75	72	219	4,930,000
Sung Ah Yim	73	74	72	219	4,930,000
Min-Ji Nam	72	71	76	219	4,930,000
Sun Wook Lim	76	76	68	220	4,213,333
Hyun-Ji Kim	74	78	68	220	4,213,333
Eun-A Lim	72	75	73	220	4,213,333
Hye Jin Jung	72	75	74	221	3,880,000
Kyung Hee Cho	71	74	76	221	3,880,000
Hee Young Park	75	79	68	222	3,560,000
Bo Mi Kim	76	73	73	222	3,560,000
Yun Hee Cho	73	73	76	222	3,560,000
Joo Mi Kim	71	75	76	222	3,560,000

Hana Bank-Kolon Championship

Mauna Ocean Golf & Resort, Kyeongbook
Par 36-36–72; 6,270 yards
(Event shortened to 36 holes — wind and cold.)

October 19-21
purse, US$1,300,000

	SCORES		TOTAL	MONEY
Suzann Pettersen	69	72	141	US$191,250
Eun Hee Ji	74	68	142	118,504
Seon Hwa Lee	72	71	143	76,234
Jeong Jang	71	72	143	76,234
Hyun Hee Moon	71	73	144	53,526
Sun Ju Ahn	72	73	145	40,226
Catriona Matthew	71	74	145	40,226
Cristie Kerr	75	71	146	27,899
Na Yeon Choi	74	72	146	27,899
Shi Hyun Ahn	73	73	146	27,899
Meena Lee	69	77	146	27,899
So Young Kim	77	70	147	19,572
Natalie Gulbis	76	71	147	19,572
Hee Young Park	75	72	147	19,572
Maria Hjorth	73	74	147	19,572
Ji-Young Oh	72	75	147	19,572
Lorena Ochoa	72	75	147	19,572
Jee Young Lee	77	71	148	14,948
Jane Park	75	73	148	14,948
Laura Davies	75	73	148	14,948
Se Ri Pak	72	76	148	14,948
Joo Mi Kim	71	77	148	14,948
Soo-Yun Kang	73	76	149	13,106
Ji-Yai Shin	73	76	149	13,106
Kyeong Bae	76	74	150	11,938
Karine Icher	75	75	150	11,938
Linda Wessberg	74	76	150	11,938
Sarah Lee	75	76	151	10,597
Mi Hyun Kim	74	77	151	10,597
Birdie Kim	73	78	151	10,597

Interburgo Masters

Interburgo Kyungsan Course, Daegu
Par 37-36–73; 6,761 yards

October 26-28
purse, KRW300,000,000

	SCORES			TOTAL	MONEY
Ji-Yai Shin	71	72	67	210	KRW60,000,000
Na Yeon Choi	70	74	71	215	27,000,000
Song Hee Kim	72	73	71	216	16,500,000
Sun Ju Ahn	72	70	74	216	16,500,000
Da Ye Na	72	72	73	217	12,000,000
Young Ae Ham	76	72	70	218	9,000,000
Seul A. Yoon	77	70	71	218	9,000,000
Hee Young Park	70	75	73	218	9,000,000
Hui Jeong Kim	74	78	68	220	5,287,500
Bo Mi Suh	75	74	71	220	5,287,500
Hee Kyung Seo	73	75	72	220	5,287,500
Bo Mi Kim	73	75	72	220	5,287,500
Yoon Jung Won	73	74	73	220	5,287,500
Sang Hee Kim	73	74	73	220	5,287,500
Eun-A Lim	72	72	76	220	5,287,500
Shin Hye Moon	72	72	76	220	5,287,500
Ye-Jin Na	75	77	69	221	3,115,714
Hey Kyung Son	75	76	70	221	3,115,714
Hyun Hee Moon	77	73	71	221	3,115,714
Eun Hee Ji	75	73	73	221	3,115,714
Ji Yeon Woo	70	77	74	221	3,115,714
Woo Ri Choi	77	69	75	221	3,115,714
Bo Bea Park	73	73	75	221	3,115,714

KB Star Tour in Seoul

Sky 72 Golf Club, West Course, Seoul
Par 36-36–72; 6,586 yards

November 1-4
purse, KRW500,000,000

	SCORES				TOTAL	MONEY
Young Ran Jo	70	68	69	74	281	KRW125,000,000
Song Hee Kim	74	71	70	67	282	42,500,000
Hye Youn Kim	73	71	71	69	284	30,000,000
Chae Young Yoon	74	74	72	68	288	19,375,000
Ran Hong	78	71	69	70	288	19,375,000
Ji-Yai Shin	70	74	73	71	288	19,375,000
Hee Kyung Seo	73	71	70	74	288	19,375,000
Eun Hee Ji	76	73	70	70	289	10,000,000
Young Jo	72	74	71	72	289	10,000,000
Na Yeon Choi	74	72	70	73	289	10,000,000
Bo Kyung Kim	75	72	75	69	291	6,162,500
Hee Young Park	77	66	75	73	291	6,162,500
Sang Hee Kim	73	72	72	74	291	6,162,500
Yun Hee Cho	72	72	73	74	291	6,162,500
Young Ae Ham	74	72	69	77	292	5,350,000
Bo Bea Park	71	70	73	78	292	5,350,000
You Jin Ji	73	77	73	70	293	5,100,000
Sun Wook Lim	74	74	75	71	294	4,950,000
Young A. Yang	74	76	73	72	295	4,562,500
Ji Young Yoon	71	73	77	74	295	4,562,500
Hyun Ji Kim	70	76	74	75	295	4,562,500
Jae Eun Chung	73	76	69	77	295	4,562,500

MBC Tour

Lord Land Club, Mountain & Lake Courses
Par 36-36–72; 6,231 yards

November 9-11
purse, KRW300,000,000

	SCORES			TOTAL	MONEY
Ji Na Lim	65	73	72	210	KRW60,000,000
Ji-Yai Shin	71	73	71	215	27,000,000
Hee Kyung Seo	69	74	73	216	18,000,000
Hee Young Park	69	74	74	217	15,000,000
Sun Ju Ahn	70	78	71	219	10,500,000
Chae Young Yoon	69	75	75	219	10,500,000
Bo-Bea Park	69	74	76	219	10,500,000
Bo Mi Suh	70	77	73	220	6,750,000
Eun Hee Ji	73	73	74	220	6,750,000
Hyun Hee Moon	68	75	77	220	6,750,000
Hye Youn Kim	70	79	72	221	5,550,000
Da Ye Na	70	74	77	221	5,550,000
Hui Jeong Kim	71	79	72	222	4,305,000
Yu-Jin Choi	70	79	73	222	4,305,000
Min Ji Kim	71	76	75	222	4,305,000
Young Ae Ham	69	76	77	222	4,305,000
Soo Yun Kang	70	74	78	222	4,305,000
Sang Hee Kim	71	73	78	222	4,305,000
Il Hee Lee	72	78	73	223	2,802,857
Hyun Ryung Kim	73	75	75	223	2,802,857
Su Jae Lee	69	78	76	223	2,802,857
Eun-A Lim	73	73	77	223	2,802,857
Soo Young Moon	70	76	77	223	2,802,857
Jung Hwa Lee	68	77	78	223	2,802,857
Bo Kyung Kim	71	73	79	223	2,802,857

ADT CAPS Championship

Sky Hill Country Club, Jeju
Par 36-36–72; 6,245 yards

November 23-25
purse, KRW300,000,000

	SCORES			TOTAL	MONEY
Ji-Yai Shin	74	69	68	211	KRW60,000,000
Sun Wook Lim	69	70	75	214	27,000,000
Hye Youn Kim	68	72	75	215	18,000,000
Joo Mi Kim	75	72	69	216	15,000,000
Ha-Neul Kim	74	74	69	217	11,250,000
Ran Hong	75	73	69	217	11,250,000
Hae Young Jeon	72	71	75	218	9,000,000
Seul A. Yoon	69	76	74	219	7,050,000
Soo Young Moon	74	71	74	219	7,050,000
Bo Mi Kim	71	78	71	220	5,925,000
Bo-Bea Park	75	73	72	220	5,925,000
Hye Jin Jung	73	71	77	221	5,400,000
Bo Kyung Kim	78	75	69	222	4,458,000
Sun Ju Ahn	76	75	71	222	4,458,000
Yun Hee Cho	71	79	72	222	4,458,000
Yoon Jung Won	70	78	74	222	4,458,000
Hyun Hee Moon	72	76	74	222	4,458,000
Yu-Jin Choi	75	76	72	223	3,127,500
Il Mi Chung	79	71	73	223	3,127,500
Hee Kyung Seo	76	73	74	223	3,127,500
Ji-Hye Jang	73	76	74	223	3,127,500

The Kyoraku Cup

See Japan LPGA Tour section.

Orient China Ladies Open

Orient Golf & Country Club, Xiamen, China
Par 36-36–72; 6,460 yards

December 14-16
purse, US$250,000

	SCORES			TOTAL	MONEY
Ji-Yai Shin	68	68	67	203	US$45,000
Ya Ni Tseng	69	70	69	208	25,000
Sun Ju Ahn	72	69	70	211	17,500
Eun Hee Ji	69	71	72	212	12,500
Hye Youn Kim	70	73	71	214	9,375
Na Zhang	71	71	72	214	9,375
Ran Hong	72	74	69	215	6,417
Feng Shanshan	74	71	70	215	6,417
Lu Hsiao Ching	73	70	72	215	6,417
Hyun Hee Moon	70	74	72	216	4,938
He Yong Choi	70	72	74	216	4,938
Woo Ri Choi	73	74	70	217	4,363
Hae Jung Kim	74	72	71	217	4,363
Yun Hee Cho	70	75	73	218	3,350
Hee Kyung Seo	75	70	73	218	3,350
Hye Jin Jung	74	71	73	218	3,350
Yang Hong Mei	72	75	71	218	3,350
Bo Kyung Kim	67	75	76	218	3,350
Eun Jung Shin	71	71	76	218	3,350
Bo-Bea Park	75	70	74	219	2,450
Yang Taoli	73	75	71	219	2,450
Ji-Hye Jang	75	74	71	220	2,300
Hyun Ji Kim	75	73	72	220	2,300
Eun-A Lim	73	69	78	220	2,300

Australian Ladies Tour

MFS Women's Australian Open

Royal Sydney Golf Club, Sydney, New South Wales
Par 36-36–72; 6,281 yards

February 1-4
purse, A$500,000

	SCORES				TOTAL	MONEY
Karrie Webb	67	71	68	72	278	A$75,000
Yun-Jye Wei	68	71	71	74	284	50,000
Minea Blomqvist	71	72	74	69	286	30,000
Paula Marti	74	69	74	69	286	30,000
Brittany Lincicome	70	73	75	69	287	18,375
Ji-Yai Shin	72	73	73	69	287	18,375
Sun Ju Ahn	70	72	74	72	288	13,375
Bettina Hauert	70	75	73	70	288	13,375
Katherine Hull	72	75	77	65	289	10,750
Hee Young Park	69	77	71	73	290	8,416.70
Marta Prieto	75	69	72	74	290	8,416.70
Virginie Lagoutte	74	70	72	74	290	8,416.70
Louise Stahle	70	75	75	71	291	6,462.50
Nadina Light	72	73	73	73	291	6,462.50
Ya Ni Tseng	75	69	75	72	291	6,462.50
Eun Hee Ji	74	77	70	70	291	6,462.50
Becky Brewerton	71	77	72	72	292	5,800
Sarah Kemp	66	78	71	77	292	5,800
Lindsey Wright	70	73	78	71	292	5,800
Ayako Uehara	71	75	77	70	293	5,287.50
*Ashleigh Simon	69	74	75	75	293	
Da Ye Na	73	71	78	71	293	5,287.50
Karen Margrethe Juul	76	67	77	73	293	5,287.50
Amy Yang	69	73	77	74	293	5,287.50

ANZ Ladies Masters

Royal Pines Resort, Ashmore, Queensland
Par 35-37–72; 6,397 yards

February 8-11
purse, A$800,000

	SCORES				TOTAL	MONEY
Karrie Webb	71	68	62	68	269	A$120,000
Ji-Yai Shin	70	66	66	69	271	79,200
Cristie Kerr	69	69	66	68	272	56,000
Sun Ju Ahn	64	68	72	70	274	40,000
Ya Ni Tseng	71	69	69	66	275	32,400
Clare Queen	69	69	70	68	276	25,400
Michelle Ellis	67	66	68	75	276	25,400
Young Jo	71	69	71	67	278	16,500
Rachel Hetherington	70	67	69	72	278	16,500
Veronica Zorzi	72	69	68	69	278	16,500
Becky Brewerton	66	73	68	71	278	16,500
Hee Young Park	70	71	69	69	279	12,400
Brittany Lincicome	72	69	66	73	280	10,400
Louise Stahle	71	70	70	69	280	10,400
Linda Wessberg	68	69	72	71	280	10,400
Lotta Wahlin	68	67	69	76	280	10,400

	SCORES				TOTAL	MONEY
Gwladys Nocera	72	70	67	72	281	9,600
Marta Prieto	69	73	69	71	282	8,940
Sakura Yokomine	67	75	68	72	282	8,940
Ana Larraneta	73	67	67	75	282	8,940
Paula Marti	71	72	67	72	282	8,940

Lexus Cup

The Vines Resort & Country Club, Perth, Western Australia
Par 36-36–72; 6,634 yards

December 7-9
purse, US$960,000

FIRST DAY
Alternate Shot

Jee Young Lee and Seon Hwa Lee (Asia) defeated Suzann Pettersen and Natalie Gulbis, 3 and 2.
Sarah Lee and Meena Lee (Asia) defeated Cristie Kerr and Nicole Castrale, 1 up.
Jeong Jang and Shi Hyun Ahn (Asia) defeated Angela Park and Nikki Campbell, 2 and 1.
Se Ri Pak and In-Kyung Kim (Asia) defeated Morgan Pressel and Stacy Prammanasudh, 2 and 1.
Amy Hung and Ji-Yai Shin (Asia) defeated Brittany Lincicome and Maria Hjorth, 4 and 2.
Candie Kung and Ayako Uehara (Asia) defeated Annika Sorenstam and Catriona Matthew, 3 and 2.

POINTS: Asia 6, International 0

SECOND DAY
Best Ball

Angela Park and Nicki Campbell (International) defeated Jeong Jang and Shi Hyun Ahn, 3 and 2.
Jee Young Lee and Seon Hwa Lee (Asia) defeated Suzann Pettersen and Natalie Gulbis, 2 up.
Cristie Kerr and Nicole Castrale (Int'l) defeated Sarah Lee and Meena Lee, 3 and 2.
Morgan Pressel and Stacy Prammanasudh (Int'l) halved with Candie Kung and Ayako Uehara.
Amy Hung and Ji-Yai Shin (Asia) defeated Brittany Lincicome and Maria Hjorth, 2 and 1.
Se Ri Pak and In-Kyung Kim (Asia) defeated Annika Sorenstam and Catriona Matthew, 1 up.

POINTS: Asia 3½, International 2½

THIRD DAY
Singles

Se Ri Pak (Asia) halved with Suzann Pettersen.
Annika Sorenstam (Int'l) defeated Candie Kung, 4 and 3.
Jee Young Lee (Asia) defeated Nicole Castrale, 2 and 1.
Angela Park (Int'l) defeated Amy Hung, 3 and 1.
In-Kyung Kim (Asia) defeated Stacy Prammanasudh, 2 and 1.
Seon Hwa Lee (Asia) defeated Cristie Kerr, 3 and 2.
Sarah Lee (Asia) defeated Nikki Campbell, 3 and 1.
Maria Hjorth (Int'l) defeated Shi Hyun Ahn, 3 and 2.
Ayako Uehara (Asia) halved with Catriona Matthew.
Morgan Pressel (Int'l) defeated Jeong Jang, 2 and 1.
Brittany Lincicome (Int'l) defeated Meena Lee, 1 up.
Ji-Yai Shin (Asia) halved with Natalie Gulbis.

POINTS: Asia 5½, International 6½
TOTAL POINTS: Asia 15, International 9

(Each member of the Asia team received $50,000; each member of the International team received $30,000.)

Ladies African Tour

Women's World Cup of Golf

Gary Player Country Club, Sun City, South Africa
Par 36-36–72; 6,466 yards

January 19-21
purse, US$1,200,000

	SCORES			TOTAL
PARAGUAY—$240,000 Julieta Granada/Celeste Troche	139	75	65	279
USA—$171,750 Pat Hurst/Juli Inkster	149	70	67	286
KOREA—$117,500 Young Kim/Ji-Yai Shin	143	77	67	287
SCOTLAND—$79,375 Janice Moodie/Mhairi McKay	145	76	68	289
ITALY—$79,375 Giulia Sergas/Veronica Zorzi	145	73	71	289
AUSTRALIA—$58,750 Nikki Garrett/Lindsey Wright	148	74	69	291
TAIWAN—$53,000 Yu Ping Lin/Amy Hung	150	77	66	293
WALES—$47,000 Becky Morgan/Becky Brewerton	148	78	68	294
ENGLAND—$41,000 Laura Davies/Trish Johnson	154	74	67	295
NEW ZEALAND—$32,375 Lynnette Brooky/Elizabeth McKinnon	146	77	73	296
FINLAND—$32,375 Riikka Hakkarainen/Jenni Kuosa	150	72	74	296
BRAZIL—$23,500 Candy Hannemann/Maria Priscila Iida	154	72	71	297
FRANCE—$21,200 Gwladys Nocera/Stephanie Arricau	157	73	69	299
JAPAN—$18,250 Shinobu Moromizato/Momoko Ueda	155	78	67	300
DENMARK—$18,250 Iben Tinning/Karen Margrethe Juul	149	83	68	300
SPAIN—$15,900 Ana B. Sanchez/Tania Elosegui	155	80	66	301
SOUTH AFRICA—$7,950 Laurette Maritz/*Ashleigh Simon	157	78	66	301

	SCORES	TOTAL
SWEDEN—$14,200		
Carin Koch/Helen Alfredsson	157 81 70	308
GERMANY—$12,400		
Denise Simon/Anja Monke	165 73 75	313
NORWAY—$12,400		
Marianne Skarpnord/Lill Kristin Saether	160 75 78	313
IRELAND—$9,000		
Hazel Kavanagh/Rebecca Coakley	160 80 75	315
KENYA—$4,250		
Rose Nialiaka/*Jane Njoroge	169 91 79	339

Pam Golding Ladies International

Dainfern Country Club, Johannesburg
Par 36-37–73; 6,223 yards

February 21-23
purse, R250,000

	SCORES	TOTAL	MONEY
Lee-Anne Pace	69 67 72	208	R37,500
Julie Tvede	70 68 71	209	27,500
Eleanor Pilgrim	72 70 69	211	20,000
Kiran Matharu	68 73 71	212	12,375
Rebecca Hudson	69 72 71	212	12,375
Stacy Bregman	66 71 75	212	12,375
Sophie Walker	73 73 68	214	8,000
Amanda Moltke-Leth	72 70 72	214	8,000
Emelie Svenningsson	70 72 73	215	6,000
Kaisa Ruuttila	76 69 70	215	6,000
Hanna-Leena Salonen	72 70 74	216	5,125
Marianne Skarpnord	71 71 75	217	4,516.67
*Ashleigh Simon	73 70 74	217	
Zuzana Kamasova	75 71 71	217	4,516.67
Anna Becker	74 73 70	217	4,516.67
*Kelli Shean	76 69 73	218	
Lisa Jean	73 72 74	219	4,062.50
Jehanne Jail	70 76 73	219	4,062.50
Emma Zackrisson	75 73 72	220	3,812.50
*Bertine Strauss	74 74 72	220	
Morgana Robbertze	71 71 78	220	3,812.50

WPGA Masters

Waterkloof Golf Club, Pretoria
Par 36-36–72

February 28-March 2
purse, R250,000

	SCORES	TOTAL	MONEY
Kaisa Ruuttila	71 69 69	209	R37,500
Julie Tvede	71 67 74	212	27,500
*Ashleigh Simon	71 73 71	215	
*Kelli Shean	72 71 72	215	
Hanna-Leena Salonen	72 72 71	215	15,666.67
Eleanor Pilgrim	72 71 72	215	15,666.67
Lee-Anne Pace	72 70 73	215	15,666.67
Johanna Westerberg	72 74 70	216	7,625

	SCORES			TOTAL	MONEY
Marianne Skarpnord	71	75	70	216	7,625
Morgana Robbertze	71	71	74	216	7,625
Amanda Moltke-Leth	73	70	73	216	7,625
Lisa Jean	75	72	69	216	7,625
Sophie Walker	72	71	74	217	4,668.75
Rebecca Hudson	71	70	76	217	4,668.75
Michelle de Vries	74	73	70	217	4,668.75
Nora Angehrn	72	74	71	217	4,668.75
Florence Luscher	76	70	72	218	4,062.50
Stacy Bregman	70	74	74	218	4,062.50
Laurette Maritz	75	73	71	219	3,875
Kirsty Fisher	75	74	71	220	3,750

Acer Women's South African Open

Durban Country Club, Durban
Par 37-36–73; 6,098 yards

March 8-10
purse, R250,000

	SCORES			TOTAL	MONEY
*Ashleigh Simon	69	64	72	205	
Stacy Bregman	72	69	69	210	R37,500
Laurette Maritz	73	70	68	211	27,500
*Kelli Shean	72	71	70	213	
Rebecca Hudson	71	69	75	215	20,000
Sophie Walker	74	70	72	216	12,375
Morgana Robbertze	68	75	73	216	12,375
Tania Elosegui	69	76	71	216	12,375
Antonella Cvitan	70	75	72	217	8,625
Johanna Westerberg	74	74	70	218	6,125
Marianne Skarpnord	76	71	71	218	6,125
Eleanor Pilgrim	76	68	74	218	6,125
Nora Angehrn	75	70	73	218	6,125
Ana Larraneta	74	74	71	219	4,750
Lena Tornevall	75	70	75	220	4,231.25
Margherita Rigon	73	71	76	220	4,231.25
Amanda Moltke-Leth	72	76	72	220	4,231.25
Lisa Jean	73	71	76	220	4,231.25
Julie Tvede	74	75	72	221	3,687.50
Clare Queen	73	71	77	221	3,687.50
Karen Margrethe Juul	74	72	75	221	3,687.50
Anna Becker	76	71	74	221	3,687.50

Telkom Women's Classic

Benoni Lakes Country Club, Johannesburg
Par 36-36–72

March 14-16
purse, R320,000

	SCORES			TOTAL	MONEY
Tania Elosegui	67	65	72	204	R48,000
Rebecca Hudson	69	71	65	205	30,400
Stacy Bregman	65	68	72	205	30,400
*Ashleigh Simon	67	70	71	208	
Nora Angehrn	70	66	73	209	19,200
Carmen Alonso	72	69	70	211	15,360
Julie Tvede	71	72	69	212	12,000
Clare Queen	71	67	74	212	12,000
Caryn Louw	69	72	72	213	8,800

	SCORES			TOTAL	MONEY
Martina Gillen	74	66	73	213	8,800
Sophie Walker	71	69	74	214	6,880
Margherita Rigon	74	69	71	214	6,880
Emma Zackrisson	70	73	72	215	5,548.80
Cecilie Lundgreen	69	73	73	215	5,548.80
Karen Margrethe Juul	75	71	69	215	5,548.80
Felicity Johnson	69	73	73	215	5,548.80
Jo Clingan	71	72	72	215	5,548.80
Lee-Anne Pace	73	69	74	216	4,800
Laurette Maritz	68	76	72	216	4,800
Maria Boden	74	72	70	216	4,800

Princess Lalla Meryem Cup

Dar-es-Salam Golf Club, Blue Course, Rabat, Morocco
Par 36-37–73; 6,785 yards

October 25-27
purse, US$120,000

	SCORES			TOTAL	MONEY
Gwladys Nocera	70	68	71	209	US$28,000
Paula Marti Zambrano	72	70	74	216	16,000
Johanna Westerberg	76	70	71	217	12,000
Anna Rawson	73	72	73	218	9,250
Lotta Wahlin	74	70	74	218	9,250
Georgina Simpson	73	75	71	219	8,000
Nikki Garrett	78	69	75	222	7,500
Patricia Meunier-Lebouc	73	76	74	223	6,750
Virginie Lagoutte-Clement	72	72	79	223	6,750
Mounya Amalou Sayeh	73	81	74	228	6,000
Bettina Hauert	74	78	80	232	5,500
Sophie Sandolo	79	76		WD	

Senior Tours

MasterCard Championship at Hualalai

Hualalai Golf Course, Ka'upulehu-Kona, Hawaii
Par 36-36–72; 7,053 yards

January 19-21
purse, $1,700,000

	SCORES			TOTAL	MONEY
Hale Irwin	66	62	65	193	$290,000
Tom Kite	67	64	67	198	150,000
Jim Thorpe	69	63	66	198	150,000
Loren Roberts	65	67	67	199	105,000
Brad Bryant	63	68	70	201	83,000
Jay Haas	69	66	66	201	83,000
Tom Jenkins	67	68	67	202	65,000
D.A. Weibring	67	68	67	202	65,000
Allen Doyle	66	67	70	203	48,000
Jerry Pate	66	67	70	203	48,000
Eduardo Romero	67	68	68	203	48,000
Tom Watson	68	67	68	203	48,000
Ben Crenshaw	65	68	71	204	35,000
Morris Hatalsky	68	66	70	204	35,000
Raymond Floyd	70	67	68	205	27,375
Mark McNulty	71	66	68	205	27,375
Gil Morgan	67	73	65	205	27,375
Ron Streck	69	68	68	205	27,375
Andy Bean	68	70	68	206	20,071.43
Peter Jacobsen	70	69	67	206	20,071.43
Tom Purtzer	69	67	70	206	20,071.43
Dana Quigley	67	70	69	206	20,071.43
Mike Reid	70	70	66	206	20,071.43
Fuzzy Zoeller	69	67	70	206	20,071.43
Bruce Lietzke	70	65	71	206	20,071.42
David Eger	70	68	69	207	15,875
Des Smyth	68	71	68	207	15,875
Fred Funk	68	69	71	208	14,750
John Harris	71	69	68	208	14,750
Stewart Ginn	72	71	67	210	13,250
Don Pooley	74	69	67	210	13,250
Scott Simpson	70	70	70	210	13,250
Craig Stadler	67	71	72	210	13,250

Turtle Bay Championship

Turtle Bay Resort, Palmer Course, Oahu, Hawaii
Par 36-36–72; 7,088 yards

January 26-28
purse, $1,600,000

	SCORES			TOTAL	MONEY
Fred Funk	65	64	64	193	$240,000
Tom Kite	67	66	71	204	98,560
Kiyoshi Murota	67	65	72	204	98,560
Tom Purtzer	70	68	66	204	98,560
Loren Roberts	69	69	66	204	98,560
Denis Watson	71	65	68	204	98,560
David Eger	67	69	69	205	51,200
Tim Simpson	70	67	68	205	51,200
D.A. Weibring	68	69	68	205	51,200

	SCORES			TOTAL	MONEY
David Edwards	72	69	65	206	38,400
Mike Reid	70	67	69	206	38,400
Scott Simpson	70	69	67	206	38,400
Chip Beck	69	69	69	207	25,008
Brad Bryant	72	68	67	207	25,008
Ben Crenshaw	72	66	69	207	25,008
Allen Doyle	69	69	69	207	25,008
Bob Gilder	72	65	70	207	25,008
Morris Hatalsky	70	69	68	207	25,008
David Ishii	68	70	69	207	25,008
Masahiro Kuramoto	70	71	66	207	25,008
Tom McKnight	67	69	71	207	25,008
Jerry Pate	68	70	69	207	25,008
Vicente Fernandez	72	64	72	208	16,800
Lonnie Nielsen	71	68	69	208	16,800
Ron Streck	72	67	69	208	16,800
John Harris	67	71	71	209	14,880
Eduardo Romero	75	66	68	209	14,880
Keith Fergus	73	68	69	210	12,672
Hale Irwin	74	67	69	210	12,672
Gil Morgan	75	70	65	210	12,672
Don Pooley	72	68	70	210	12,672
Des Smyth	69	73	68	210	12,672

Allianz Championship

Old Course at Broken Sound, Boca Raton, Florida
Par 36-36–72; 6,749 yards

February 9-11
purse, $1,600,000

	SCORES			TOTAL	MONEY
Mark James	64	69	68	201	$240,000
Jay Haas	68	65	70	203	140,800
R.W. Eaks	68	68	68	204	96,000
Morris Hatalsky	67	67	70	204	96,000
Brad Bryant	68	67	69	204	96,000
Loren Roberts	68	70	67	205	57,600
Keith Fergus	69	68	68	205	57,600
Dana Quigley	70	65	70	205	57,600
Scott Hoch	72	68	66	206	37,067
David Eger	69	70	67	206	37,067
Allen Doyle	69	70	67	206	37,067
Mike Reid	72	67	67	206	37,067
Des Smyth	71	67	68	206	37,067
Andy Bean	66	69	71	206	37,067
Vicente Fernandez	69	71	67	207	28,000
Craig Stadler	63	70	74	207	28,000
Don Pooley	70	70	69	209	24,053
Wayne Levi	68	71	70	209	24,053
John Jacobs	68	69	72	209	24,053
Nick Price	71	71	68	210	19,280
Dan Pohl	71	69	70	210	19,280
Dick Mast	72	67	71	210	19,280
Mike McCullough	69	69	72	210	19,280
Bob Gilder	75	67	69	211	14,629
Kenny Knox	72	70	69	211	14,629
Lonnie Nielsen	72	70	69	211	14,629
Tom Jenkins	68	72	71	211	14,629
John Bland	70	70	71	211	14,629
Jose Maria Canizares	68	71	72	211	14,629
Tom Kite	67	71	73	211	14,629

Outback Steakhouse Pro-Am

TPC of Tampa Bay, Lutz, Florida
Par 35-36–71; 6,638 yards

February 16-18
purse, $1,600,000

	SCORES			TOTAL	MONEY
Tom Watson	70	69	70	209	$240,000
Andy Bean	71	67	72	210	128,800
Jay Haas	69	72	69	210	128,800
R.W. Eaks	72	70	70	212	86,400
Loren Roberts	70	71	71	212	86,400
Wayne Levi	69	69	75	213	64,000
David Eger	67	72	75	214	51,200
Scott Hoch	73	71	70	214	51,200
Curtis Strange	70	71	73	214	51,200
Mark Johnson	71	71	73	215	40,000
D.A. Weibring	75	66	74	215	40,000
Keith Fergus	73	68	75	216	33,600
Tom Wargo	68	72	76	216	33,600
Brad Bryant	72	76	69	217	28,800
Tom Jenkins	71	72	74	217	28,800
Fuzzy Zoeller	72	72	73	217	28,800
David Edwards	73	73	72	218	23,320
Nick Price	74	74	70	218	23,320
Mike Reid	75	69	74	218	23,320
Denis Watson	77	70	71	218	23,320
Bob Gilder	71	76	72	219	17,760
John Harris	69	73	77	219	17,760
Mark James	72	73	74	219	17,760
Eduardo Romero	73	68	78	219	17,760
Jim Thorpe	78	70	71	219	17,760
Chip Beck	74	69	77	220	14,240
Ben Crenshaw	71	73	76	220	14,240
Tom Purtzer	76	70	74	220	14,240
Bobby Wadkins	74	72	74	220	14,240
Hugh Baiocchi	73	75	73	221	10,820
John Bland	75	75	71	221	10,820
Allen Doyle	72	72	77	221	10,820
Walter Hall	75	70	76	221	10,820
Hale Irwin	77	70	74	221	10,820
Doug LaCrosse	74	71	76	221	10,820
Andy North	74	71	76	221	10,820
Tim Simpson	77	72	72	221	10,820

ACE Group Classic

Quail West, Naples, Florida
Par 36-36–72; 7,134 yards

February 23-25
purse, $1,600,000

	SCORES			TOTAL	MONEY
Bobby Wadkins	64	69	68	201	$240,000
Allen Doyle	65	67	70	202	140,800
Mike Reid	67	67	69	203	105,600
Eduardo Romero	66	69	68	203	105,600
Mark O'Meara	65	68	71	204	70,400
Loren Roberts	68	70	66	204	70,400
Andy Bean	70	66	69	205	54,400
D.A. Weibring	67	69	69	205	54,400
Don Pooley	70	70	66	206	43,200
Fuzzy Zoeller	71	68	67	206	43,200

	SCORES			TOTAL	MONEY
Brad Bryant	67	71	70	208	32,960
Bruce Fleisher	73	67	68	208	32,960
Scott Hoch	68	69	71	208	32,960
Gil Morgan	65	73	70	208	32,960
Des Smyth	68	67	73	208	32,960
John Bland	67	71	71	209	25,600
Jay Haas	68	70	71	209	25,600
Wayne Levi	66	72	71	209	25,600
Tim Conley	70	71	69	210	20,520
Dave Eichelberger	71	71	68	210	20,520
Mark James	68	68	74	210	20,520
Curtis Strange	68	72	70	210	20,520
David Edwards	70	70	71	211	16,400
Mark Johnson	67	70	74	211	16,400
Tom Kite	72	71	68	211	16,400
Dana Quigley	69	67	75	211	16,400
Jack Ferenz	71	70	71	212	14,240
Nick Price	72	69	71	212	14,240
Masahiro Kuramoto	70	71	72	213	11,588.58
Ben Crenshaw	70	71	72	213	11,588.57
Vicente Fernandez	76	69	68	213	11,588.57
Bob Gilder	72	68	73	213	11,588.57
Morris Hatalsky	67	72	74	213	11,588.57
Bruce Lietzke	69	71	73	213	11,588.57
Graham Marsh	69	72	72	213	11,588.57

Toshiba Classic

Newport Beach Country Club, Newport Beach, California
Par 35-36–71; 6,598 yards

March 9-11
purse, $1,650,000

	SCORES			TOTAL	MONEY
Jay Haas	65	64	65	194	$247,500
R.W. Eaks	65	66	65	196	145,200
Ben Crenshaw	65	67	68	200	108,900
Naomichi Ozaki	68	64	68	200	108,900
Peter Jacobsen	66	64	71	201	64,350
Mark O'Meara	68	66	67	201	64,350
Tom Purtzer	65	68	68	201	64,350
Denis Watson	67	69	65	201	64,350
Allen Doyle	66	70	66	202	38,225
Keith Fergus	67	68	67	202	38,225
John Jacobs	70	65	67	202	38,225
Bruce Lietzke	67	66	69	202	38,225
Lonnie Nielsen	72	65	65	202	38,225
Eduardo Romero	65	69	68	202	38,225
Scott Hoch	70	65	68	203	28,875
Loren Roberts	67	69	67	203	28,875
John Bland	67	70	67	204	24,048.75
Rick Karbowski	67	66	71	204	24,048.75
Craig Stadler	69	64	71	204	24,048.75
Bruce Summerhays	68	70	66	204	24,048.75
Wayne Levi	70	65	70	205	17,875
Graham Marsh	70	67	68	205	17,875
Gil Morgan	70	66	69	205	17,875
Jerry Pate	68	68	69	205	17,875
Howard Twitty	67	69	69	205	17,875
Fuzzy Zoeller	65	69	71	205	17,875
Don Pooley	69	67	70	206	14,355
Tim Simpson	69	66	71	206	14,355

	SCORES			TOTAL	MONEY
Curtis Strange	73	68	65	206	14,355
Morris Hatalsky	66	70	71	207	11,913
Hale Irwin	69	70	68	207	11,913
Mark Johnson	68	71	68	207	11,913
Tom Kite	70	68	69	207	11,913
Mike Reid	72	69	66	207	11,913

AT&T Champions Classic

Valencia Country Club, Valencia, California
Par 36-36–72; 6,973 yards

March 16-18
purse, $1,600,000

	SCORES			TOTAL	MONEY
Tom Purtzer	69	69	68	206	$240,000
Loren Roberts	67	70	69	206	140,800
(Purtzer defeated Roberts on fourth playoff hole.)					
David Eger	71	67	69	207	115,200
Tom Jenkins	68	72	68	208	65,066.67
Naomichi Ozaki	69	72	67	208	65,066.67
Des Smyth	70	70	68	208	65,066.67
Jim Thorpe	66	71	71	208	65,066.67
Andy Bean	70	66	72	208	65,066.66
Hale Irwin	64	71	73	208	65,066.66
John Jacobs	67	71	71	209	33,371.43
Mark O'Meara	70	69	70	209	33,371.43
Tim Simpson	71	66	72	209	33,371.43
Bruce Summerhays	69	69	71	209	33,371.43
Denis Watson	70	70	69	209	33,371.43
Fuzzy Zoeller	67	71	71	209	33,371.43
Morris Hatalsky	68	69	72	209	33,371.42
Gil Morgan	69	68	73	210	23,320
Jerry Pate	70	69	71	210	23,320
Eduardo Romero	68	73	69	210	23,320
Bobby Wadkins	69	67	74	210	23,320
Keith Fergus	70	70	71	211	19,840
Tom Kite	69	73	70	212	17,653.34
Jay Haas	69	72	71	212	17,653.33
Graham Marsh	71	69	72	212	17,653.33
Bruce Fleisher	71	72	70	213	13,351.12
Ben Crenshaw	72	72	69	213	13,351.11
Jon Fiedler	72	73	68	213	13,351.11
Bob Gilder	69	72	72	213	13,351.11
John Harris	71	69	73	213	13,351.11
Wayne Levi	69	69	75	213	13,351.11
Mike McCullough	72	72	69	213	13,351.11
Scott Simpson	72	70	71	213	13,351.11
D.A. Weibring	70	73	70	213	13,351.11

Ginn Championship Hammock Beach Resort

Ocean Hammock Golf Club, Palm Coast, Florida
Par 36-36–72; 7,113 yards

March 30-April 1
purse, $2,500,000

	SCORES			TOTAL	MONEY
Keith Fergus	67	67	70	204	$375,000
Hale Irwin	69	68	68	205	200,000
Mark O'Meara	69	67	69	205	200,000

	SCORES			TOTAL	MONEY
Gil Morgan	69	68	69	206	123,333.34
Brad Bryant	67	68	71	206	123,333.33
Tom Purtzer	69	66	71	206	123,333.33
Fred Funk	71	67	70	208	90,000
David Eger	74	71	64	209	75,000
Raymond Floyd	68	69	72	209	75,000
Naomichi Ozaki	68	68	74	210	62,500
Bobby Wadkins	73	66	71	210	62,500
Ben Crenshaw	69	75	68	212	49,375
R.W. Eaks	68	69	75	212	49,375
Dana Quigley	71	70	71	212	49,375
Tim Simpson	71	72	69	212	49,375
Jay Haas	71	73	69	213	35,464.29
Scott Hoch	73	71	69	213	35,464.29
Eduardo Romero	70	72	71	213	35,464.29
D.A. Weibring	72	71	70	213	35,464.29
Andy Bean	73	74	66	213	35,464.28
Dave Eichelberger	73	68	72	213	35,464.28
Bruce Vaughan	70	71	72	213	35,464.28
David Edwards	70	71	73	214	26,875
Lonnie Nielsen	74	70	70	214	26,875
Mike McCullough	72	71	72	215	23,833.34
Wayne Levi	73	68	74	215	23,833.33
Fuzzy Zoeller	77	72	66	215	23,833.33
John Bland	72	72	72	216	18,964.29
Vicente Fernandez	73	73	70	216	18,964.29
James Mason	69	74	73	216	18,964.29
Craig Stadler	69	73	74	216	18,964.29
Bob Gilder	72	70	74	216	18,964.28
Tom Kite	74	68	74	216	18,964.28
Tom Watson	72	69	75	216	18,964.28

Liberty Mutual Legends of Golf

Savannah Harbor Golf Resort & Spa, Savannah, Georgia
Par 36-36–72; 7,087 yards

April 20-22
purse, $2,500,000

	SCORES			TOTAL	MONEY
Jay Haas	68	69	70	207	$395,000
Tom Kite	68	71	68	207	240,000
(Haas defeated Kite on first playoff hole.)					
Brad Bryant	69	69	70	208	144,500
Mark James	67	71	70	208	144,500
Wayne Levi	70	68	70	208	144,500
Gil Morgan	70	71	67	208	144,500
Hale Irwin	70	70	69	209	89,500
Nick Price	76	68	65	209	89,500
Eduardo Romero	72	73	66	211	75,000
Bobby Wadkins	74	70	67	211	75,000
Don Pooley	75	71	66	212	63,500
Curtis Strange	71	73	68	212	63,500
Keith Fergus	74	68	71	213	53,000
Mark O'Meara	73	69	71	213	53,000
Scott Simpson	70	71	72	213	53,000
Allen Doyle	74	71	69	214	38,750
Morris Hatalsky	71	72	71	214	38,750
Scott Hoch	72	70	72	214	38,750
Tom Purtzer	68	72	74	214	38,750
Loren Roberts	71	68	75	214	38,750
Craig Stadler	72	69	73	214	38,750

	SCORES			TOTAL	MONEY
Bruce Fleisher	73	71	71	215	28,400
Tom Jenkins	73	72	70	215	28,400
David Edwards	72	73	71	216	22,850
Graham Marsh	74	71	71	216	22,850
Mark McNulty	77	71	68	216	22,850
Jay Sigel	78	70	68	216	22,850
Des Smyth	71	72	73	216	22,850
John Jacobs	72	71	74	217	16,860
Dana Quigley	71	70	76	217	16,860
Jim Thorpe	77	69	71	217	16,860
D.A. Weibring	75	72	70	217	16,860
Fuzzy Zoeller	73	72	72	217	16,860

FedEx Kinko's Classic

The Hills Country Club, Austin, Texas
Par 36-36–72; 6,879 yards

May 4-6
purse, $1,600,000

	SCORES			TOTAL	MONEY
Scott Hoch	67	66	68	201	$240,000
D.A. Weibring	68	68	67	203	140,800
Loren Roberts	66	72	66	204	115,200
Hale Irwin	69	68	70	207	96,000
Tom Kite	68	73	67	208	76,800
Naomichi Ozaki	67	73	69	209	64,000
David Eger	69	75	67	211	51,200
Fred Funk	72	68	71	211	51,200
Tom Purtzer	71	67	73	211	51,200
Jay Haas	71	73	68	212	41,600
Dana Quigley	70	73	70	213	34,000
Craig Stadler	68	73	72	213	34,000
Curtis Strange	70	73	70	213	34,000
Leonard Thompson	64	73	76	213	34,000
Scott Simpson	70	71	73	214	28,800
Don Pooley	73	70	72	215	27,200
Bob Gilder	70	71	75	216	22,624
Tom Jenkins	69	73	74	216	22,624
Tim Simpson	67	73	76	216	22,624
Des Smyth	71	70	75	216	22,624
Fuzzy Zoeller	69	73	74	216	22,624
Brad Bryant	71	74	72	217	17,240
Morris Hatalsky	71	75	71	217	17,240
Gil Morgan	73	71	73	217	17,240
Bob Murphy	74	71	72	217	17,240
Ben Crenshaw	73	73	72	218	13,020
Mark Johnson	74	74	70	218	13,020
Kenny Knox	71	74	73	218	13,020
Masahiro Kuramoto	66	73	79	218	13,020
Mark Lye	72	72	74	218	13,020
Nick Price	70	77	71	218	13,020
Jack Renner	72	73	73	218	13,020
Rod Spittle	73	73	72	218	13,020

Regions Charity Classic

Robert Trent Jones Golf Trail at Ross Bridge,
Birmingham, Alabama
Par 36-36–72; 7,473 yards

May 18-20
purse, $1,600,000

	SCORES			TOTAL	MONEY
Brad Bryant	70	69	65	204	$240,000
R.W. Eaks	71	68	65	204	140,800
(Bryant defeated Eaks on third playoff hole.)					
Tom Kite	68	71	66	205	105,600
Denis Watson	72	66	67	205	105,600
Scott Hoch	65	71	70	206	76,800
Ben Crenshaw	69	70	68	207	49,600
Bob Gilder	68	66	73	207	49,600
Hale Irwin	69	68	70	207	49,600
Hajime Meshiai	73	68	66	207	49,600
Rod Spittle	68	73	66	207	49,600
Fuzzy Zoeller	68	70	69	207	49,600
Loren Roberts	72	69	67	208	32,533.34
Andy Bean	71	68	69	208	32,533.33
Curtis Strange	73	68	67	208	32,533.33
Chip Beck	72	69	68	209	25,632
Bruce Lietzke	72	70	67	209	25,632
Boonchu Ruangkit	70	70	69	209	25,632
Tim Simpson	72	67	70	209	25,632
D.A. Weibring	70	70	69	209	25,632
Mark McNulty	74	67	69	210	20,480
Jerry Pate	70	69	71	210	20,480
Jim Dent	75	67	69	211	15,740
Keith Fergus	73	70	68	211	15,740
Vicente Fernandez	71	71	69	211	15,740
Walter Hall	73	70	68	211	15,740
Tom Jenkins	70	69	72	211	15,740
Lonnie Nielsen	75	71	65	211	15,740
Naomichi Ozaki	72	70	69	211	15,740
Jim Thorpe	72	69	70	211	15,740
Dick Mast	73	71	68	212	12,320
Bobby Wadkins	69	70	73	212	12,320

Senior PGA Championship

Kiawah Island Golf Resort, Ocean Course,
Kiawah Island, South Carolina
Par 36-36–72; 7,201 yards

May 24-27
purse, $2,000,000

	SCORES				TOTAL	MONEY
Denis Watson	71	71	69	68	279	$360,000
Eduardo Romero	68	70	71	72	281	216,000
Nick Price	71	70	70	71	282	136,000
Naomichi Ozaki	69	71	72	72	284	96,000
Tim Simpson	76	71	69	70	286	76,000
Brad Bryant	71	72	73	71	287	66,000
Tom Kite	75	76	67	70	288	60,000
Craig Stadler	72	75	70	71	288	60,000
Jay Haas	72	71	75	71	289	52,000
Kong Meshiai	76	70	72	71	289	52,000
Curtis Strange	78	72	70	70	290	46,000
Masahiro Kuramoto	71	76	74	70	291	33,428.58
Doug Lacrosse	76	74	70	71	291	33,428.57

	SCORES				TOTAL	MONEY
Loren Roberts	72	74	73	72	291	33,428.57
Ben Crenshaw	73	71	74	73	291	33,428.57
Rod Spittle	75	74	70	72	291	33,428.57
D.A. Weibring	80	70	68	73	291	33,428.57
Mark O'Meara	72	73	71	75	291	33,428.57
Jeff Coston	72	75	75	70	292	20,600
Fuzzy Zoeller	74	71	75	72	292	20,600
Scott Hoch	72	75	72	73	292	20,600
Vicente Fernandez	75	70	73	74	292	20,600
Chip Beck	70	78	70	74	292	20,600
Tom Purtzer	73	73	77	70	293	16,000
R.W. Eaks	76	76	70	71	293	16,000
Bruce Vaughan	72	72	75	74	293	16,000
Jack Ferenz	74	71	77	72	294	12,750
Mike San Filippo	78	69	74	73	294	12,750
Graham Marsh	73	73	74	74	294	12,750
James Mason	72	74	73	75	294	12,750
Keith Fergus	73	75	71	75	294	12,750
Tateo Ozaki	73	74	71	76	294	12,750
John Jacobs	75	73	74	73	295	9,542.86
Kirk Hanefeld	75	72	75	73	295	9,542.86
Mike Goodes	76	71	75	73	295	9,542.86
Tom McKnight	78	72	72	73	295	9,542.86
Ron Stelten	78	71	73	73	295	9,542.86
Kiyoshi Murota	74	72	75	74	295	9,542.85
Mark James	74	71	72	78	295	9,542.85
Larry Nelson	76	76	70	74	296	7,650
Boonchu Ruangkit	72	79	70	75	296	7,650
Bob Gilder	77	74	76	70	297	6,300
Raymond Floyd	77	74	75	71	297	6,300
Bruce Fleisher	75	75	73	74	297	6,300
Bruce Summerhays	81	71	70	75	297	6,300
Andy Bean	76	70	75	76	297	6,300
Hale Irwin	78	70	73	76	297	6,300
Lonnie Nielsen	72	74	73	78	297	6,300
David Eger	74	75	75	74	298	4,833.34
Walter Hal	72	80	72	74	298	4,833.33
Gil Morgan	75	71	74	78	298	4,833.33
Ron Streck	78	72	80	69	299	4,200
Dana Quigley	72	80	76	71	299	4,200
Mitch Adcock	77	73	77	72	299	4,200
Peter Jacobsen	79	73	75	72	299	4,200
Gary Robison	78	74	73	74	299	4,200
Mitch Adams	75	76	74	74	299	4,200
Jim Thorpe	73	73	77	76	299	4,200
Tom Watson	74	75	74	76	299	4,200
Howard Twitty	77	72	74	76	299	4,200
Jay Sigel	77	74	76	73	300	3,925
John Harris	79	71	77	73	300	3,925
David Edwards	72	78	73	77	300	3,925
Scott Simpson	79	73	78	71	301	3,862.50
Katsuyoshi Tomori	76	75	73	77	301	3,862.50
Rick Karbowski	73	75	80	74	302	3,812.50
Costantino Rocca	74	74	76	78	302	3,812.50
Allen Doyle	77	73	80	73	303	3,750
Horacio Carbonetti	78	74	75	76	303	3,750
Bill Britton	75	77	73	78	303	3,750
Giuseppe Cali	75	77	76	76	304	3,675
Tim Conley	76	74	76	78	304	3,675
Bruce Lietzke	75	74	72	83	304	3,675
Bill Schumaker	80	72	75	79	306	3,612.50
Dan Pohl	77	74	71	84	306	3,612.50
Lindy Miller	75	77	77	79	308	3,575

	SCORES			TOTAL	MONEY
Mark Hayes	75	77 78	79	309	3,550
Bobby Heins	75	77 81	79	312	3,525

Boeing Championship at Sandestin

The Raven Golf Club at Sandestin, Destin, Florida
Par 35-36–71; 6,904 yards

June 1-3
purse, $1,650,000

	SCORES			TOTAL	MONEY
Loren Roberts	65	67	65	197	$247,500
Eduardo Romero	62	69	69	200	145,200
Bob Gilder	68	68	65	201	108,900
Tom Purtzer	62	68	71	201	108,900
Jay Haas	64	65	73	202	72,600
Dana Quigley	67	69	66	202	72,600
David Eger	70	64	69	203	59,400
James Mason	67	67	70	204	47,300
Tom McKnight	69	66	69	204	47,300
Denis Watson	65	67	72	204	47,300
Mark James	69	64	72	205	37,950
Masahiro Kuramoto	67	67	71	205	37,950
Jim Thorpe	64	74	68	206	33,000
David Edwards	65	73	69	207	26,470.72
Mark O'Meara	70	69	68	207	26,470.72
Tom Wargo	65	73	69	207	26,470.72
Mark McNulty	68	66	73	207	26,470.71
Lonnie Nielsen	65	72	70	207	26,470.71
Bruce Vaughan	67	71	69	207	26,470.71
Bobby Wadkins	69	69	69	207	26,470.71
Allen Doyle	68	67	73	208	18,315
Dave Eichelberger	69	70	69	208	18,315
Bruce Fleisher	69	67	72	208	18,315
Hajime Meshiai	71	68	69	208	18,315
Gil Morgan	71	69	68	208	18,315
Brad Bryant	65	67	77	209	15,015
Keith Fergus	69	68	72	209	15,015
John Harris	65	71	73	209	15,015
Vicente Fernandez	75	67	68	210	11,950.72
Nick Price	67	80	63	210	11,950.72
Bruce Summerhays	68	74	68	210	11,950.72
Ed Dougherty	68	69	73	210	11,950.71
Mike McCullough	71	70	69	210	11,950.71
Mike Reid	71	68	71	210	11,950.71
Rod Spittle	69	70	71	210	11,950.71

Principal Charity Classic

Glen Oaks Country Club, West Des Moines, Iowa
Par 35-36–71; 6,877 yards

June 8-10
purse, $1,600,000

	SCORES			TOTAL	MONEY
Jay Haas	65	67	69	201	$240,000
Brad Bryant	72	65	67	204	128,000
R.W. Eaks	72	68	64	204	128,000
Mark James	67	70	68	205	78,933.34
David Edwards	67	68	70	205	78,933.33
Jay Sigel	72	66	67	205	78,933.33

	SCORES			TOTAL	MONEY
Morris Hatalsky	70	68	69	207	51,200
Hale Irwin	73	66	68	207	51,200
Denis Watson	69	67	71	207	51,200
Andy Bean	76	69	64	209	34,400
Chip Beck	71	68	70	209	34,400
Danny Edwards	74	68	67	209	34,400
Vicente Fernandez	70	70	69	209	34,400
Dave Stockton	70	69	70	209	34,400
Bruce Summerhays	71	69	69	209	34,400
Graham Marsh	72	70	68	210	21,475.56
Tom McKnight	72	69	69	210	21,475.56
Mark McNulty	70	71	69	210	21,475.56
Dana Quigley	74	67	69	210	21,475.56
Tim Simpson	68	74	68	210	21,475.56
Donnie Hammond	72	69	69	210	21,475.55
John Jacobs	69	70	71	210	21,475.55
Tom Jenkins	72	67	71	210	21,475.55
Tom Purtzer	68	71	71	210	21,475.55
Tom Kite	69	73	69	211	14,266.67
Scott Simpson	70	73	68	211	14,266.67
Bobby Wadkins	71	71	69	211	14,266.67
Tom Wargo	68	73	70	211	14,266.67
Dave Eichelberger	66	72	73	211	14,266.66
James Mason	69	71	71	211	14,266.66

Bank of America Championship

Nashawtuc Country Club, Concord, Massachusetts — June 22-24
Par 36-36–72; 6,741 yards — purse, $1,650,000

	SCORES			TOTAL	MONEY
Jay Haas	71	66	66	203	$247,500
Brad Bryant	71	68	67	206	132,000
Leonard Thompson	69	69	68	206	132,000
Tom Purtzer	66	68	73	207	99,000
R.W. Eaks	73	64	71	208	68,200
Danny Edwards	72	66	70	208	68,200
Tom Watson	65	72	71	208	68,200
Wayne Levi	72	71	67	210	40,307.15
D.A. Weibring	71	73	66	210	40,307.15
Morris Hatalsky	71	68	71	210	40,307.14
Tom Jenkins	68	69	73	210	40,307.14
Rick Karbowski	70	69	71	210	40,307.14
Masahiro Kuramoto	68	71	71	210	40,307.14
Jay Sigel	70	70	70	210	40,307.14
Andy Bean	71	73	67	211	25,657.50
David Edwards	71	71	69	211	25,657.50
Keith Fergus	68	69	74	211	25,657.50
Bob Gilder	71	68	72	211	25,657.50
Tom McKnight	70	71	70	211	25,657.50
Dana Quigley	72	69	70	211	25,657.50
Ed Dougherty	71	73	68	212	17,466.43
Kirk Hanefeld	71	66	75	212	17,466.43
Joe Inman	69	72	71	212	17,466.43
James Mason	71	71	70	212	17,466.43
Des Smyth	74	68	70	212	17,466.43
Jim Thorpe	71	67	74	212	17,466.43
Jack Ferenz	71	66	75	212	17,466.42
Walter Hall	73	71	69	213	13,068
John Jacobs	67	72	74	213	13,068

	SCORES	TOTAL	MONEY
Mark McNulty	71 72 70	213	13,068
Larry Nelson	68 73 72	213	13,068
Craig Stadler	70 74 69	213	13,068

Commerce Bank Championship

Eisenhower Park, Red Course, East Meadow, New York
Par 35-36–71; 6,904 yards

June 29-July 1
purse, $1,500,000

	SCORES	TOTAL	MONEY
Lonnie Nielsen	66 64 69	199	$225,000
Loren Roberts	64 71 66	201	132,000
Tom McKnight	67 66 69	202	108,000
Bob Gilder	68 67 68	203	90,000
R.W. Eaks	69 66 69	204	62,000
David Edwards	68 67 69	204	62,000
Eduardo Romero	65 71 68	204	62,000
Jay Haas	67 72 66	205	48,000
John Harris	67 67 72	206	39,000
Bruce Summerhays	71 65 70	206	39,000
Tom Wargo	68 69 69	206	39,000
Allen Doyle	68 72 67	207	30,500
David Eger	71 68 68	207	30,500
Curtis Strange	68 68 71	207	30,500
Andy Bean	68 70 70	208	22,650
Ed Dougherty	70 69 69	208	22,650
Donnie Hammond	70 67 71	208	22,650
Dana Quigley	71 69 68	208	22,650
Jay Sigel	68 66 74	208	22,650
Des Smyth	67 70 71	208	22,650
Sam Torrance	71 70 67	208	22,650
Mitch Adcock	69 70 70	209	14,756.25
Brad Bryant	67 68 74	209	14,756.25
Vicente Fernandez	68 69 72	209	14,756.25
Bruce Fleisher	68 73 68	209	14,756.25
Walter Hall	70 67 72	209	14,756.25
Mike Hill	70 69 70	209	14,756.25
Naomichi Ozaki	70 68 71	209	14,756.25
Nick Price	69 68 72	209	14,756.25
Morris Hatalsky	67 71 72	210	11,062.50
Kevin King	69 68 73	210	11,062.50
Kenny Knox	71 69 70	210	11,062.50
Denis Watson	71 68 71	210	11,062.50

U.S. Senior Open

Whistling Straits, Kohler, Wisconsin
Par 36-36–72; 7,514 yards

July 5-8
purse, $2,600,000

	SCORES	TOTAL	MONEY
Brad Bryant	71 72 71 68	282	$470,000
Ben Crenshaw	72 67 76 70	285	280,000
Loren Roberts	70 69 73 74	286	176,756
Tom Watson	70 66 73 78	287	123,175
Jay Haas	73 71 73 72	289	78,415
D.A. Weibring	72 68 74 75	289	78,415

	SCORES				TOTAL	MONEY
Tom Purtzer	73	67	74	75	289	78,415
Naomichi Ozaki	72	69	73	75	289	78,415
Denis Watson	74	73	67	75	289	78,415
Sam Torrance	73	69	71	76	289	78,415
Larry Nelson	75	71	74	70	290	51,573
Lonnie Nielsen	68	71	77	74	290	51,573
Mark O'Meara	72	70	74	74	290	51,573
Jim Woodward	67	73	75	75	290	51,573
Vicente Fernandez	69	70	74	77	290	51,573
Craig Stadler	72	73	71	75	291	42,126
Bruce Vaughan	68	73	74	76	291	42,126
John Jacobs	75	69	76	72	292	35,564
Bob Gilder	74	74	70	74	292	35,564
Mark McNulty	73	71	73	75	292	35,564
John Ross	72	71	70	79	292	35,564
Donnie Hammond	72	70	80	71	293	25,612
Tom Kite	72	72	76	73	293	25,612
Jim Thorpe	72	74	74	73	293	25,612
Ron Streck	74	69	76	74	293	25,612
Des Smyth	70	69	78	76	293	25,612
David Eger	73	74	69	77	293	25,612
Eduardo Romero	66	77	71	79	293	25,612
Bobby Wadkins	73	73	74	74	294	18,500
Wayne Levi	76	72	72	74	294	18,500
Keith Fergus	72	69	77	76	294	18,500
Kirk Hanefeld	71	74	74	76	295	17,381
*George Zahringer	75	72	80	69	296	
Scott Simpson	71	74	78	73	296	15,837
Gil Morgan	69	73	80	74	296	15,837
Jeff Coston	70	70	79	77	296	15,837
Peter Jacobsen	73	73	73	77	296	15,837
*Danny Green	75	72	72	77	296	
Bruce Lietzke	71	71	74	80	296	15,837
Ron Vlosich	69	71	78	79	297	14,296
*Brady Exber	73	73	78	74	298	
Bruce Fleisher	72	73	77	76	298	13,277
Fuzzy Zoeller	73	74	75	76	298	13,277
Jerry Pate	72	72	75	79	298	13,277
Curtis Strange	72	71	79	77	299	12,002
Pete Oakley	72	74	75	78	299	12,002
Mark James	71	73	82	74	300	10,728
David Thore	71	76	79	74	300	10,728
Mike Goodes	74	73	73	80	300	10,728
*Marty West	75	73	78	75	301	
Jim Ahern	71	71	82	77	301	9,709
Mike Reid	73	74	78	77	302	8,689
Jon Fiedler	69	75	79	79	302	8,689
Jon Chaffee	72	73	78	79	302	8,689
Mike Smith	74	72	77	80	303	7,761
Mike McCullough	72	75	75	81	303	7,761
Danny Edwards	73	75	74	81	303	7,761
Masahiro Kuramoto	78	68	78	82	306	7,287
R.W. Eaks	72	74	76	84	306	7,287
Chris Dachisen	75	73	80	79	307	7,034
James Blair	72	76	81	79	308	6,874
*Jim Knoll	76	72	77	84	309	

Dick's Sporting Goods Open

En-Joie Golf Club, Endicott, New York
Par 37-35–72; 7,034 yards

July 13-15
purse, $1,600,000

	SCORES			TOTAL	MONEY
R.W. Eaks	71	62	66	199	$240,000
Bruce Vaughan	70	64	68	202	140,800
Lonnie Nielsen	73	66	67	206	115,200
Andy Bean	71	68	68	207	86,400
D.A. Weibring	74	67	66	207	86,400
John Harris	75	64	69	208	57,600
Scott Hoch	69	66	73	208	57,600
Boonchu Ruangkit	71	68	69	208	57,600
Jack Ferenz	70	71	68	209	43,200
Craig Stadler	69	67	73	209	43,200
Dave Eichelberger	74	67	69	210	31,085.72
Scott Simpson	75	67	68	210	31,085.72
Rod Spittle	69	72	69	210	31,085.72
Tim Conley	70	70	70	210	31,085.71
Gil Morgan	71	68	71	210	31,085.71
Tim Simpson	70	70	70	210	31,085.71
Jim Thorpe	72	68	70	210	31,085.71
Mark James	74	68	69	211	21,216
Dana Quigley	74	67	70	211	21,216
Steve Thomas	73	66	72	211	21,216
Howard Twitty	72	69	70	211	21,216
Denis Watson	71	70	70	211	21,216
Bruce Fleisher	70	73	69	212	16,800
Lon Hinkle	71	69	72	212	16,800
Tom Purtzer	72	70	70	212	16,800
David Eger	75	70	68	213	13,020
Walter Hall	71	73	69	213	13,020
John Jacobs	71	71	71	213	13,020
Masahiro Kuramoto	70	76	67	213	13,020
Lindy Miller	72	70	71	213	13,020
Don Pooley	71	72	70	213	13,020
Sammy Rachels	73	71	69	213	13,020
Bruce Summerhays	72	72	69	213	13,020
Danny Edwards	72	70	72	214	10,080
Vicente Fernandez	71	70	73	214	10,080

The Senior Open Championship

See European Seniors Tour section.

3M Championship

TPC of the Twin Cities, Blaine, Minnesota
Par 36-36–72; 6,909 yards

August 3-5
purse, $1,750,000

	SCORES			TOTAL	MONEY
D.A. Weibring	65	66	67	198	$262,500
Jay Haas	65	71	63	199	154,000
Mitch Adams	67	70	63	200	115,500
John Harris	65	69	66	200	115,500
Tom Jenkins	64	70	67	201	77,000
Jim Thorpe	64	68	69	201	77,000
John Jacobs	65	70	68	203	63,000

	SCORES			TOTAL	MONEY
Chip Beck	69	69	66	204	50,166.67
Bobby Wadkins	65	71	68	204	50,166.67
Craig Stadler	65	70	69	204	50,166.66
David Edwards	69	70	66	205	40,250
Tom Watson	69	65	71	205	40,250
Bob Gilder	72	66	68	206	33,250
Naomichi Ozaki	69	70	67	206	33,250
Denis Watson	68	68	70	206	33,250
David Eger	69	71	67	207	25,579.17
Gil Morgan	66	73	68	207	25,579.17
Jerry Pate	67	71	69	207	25,579.17
Jay Sigel	71	69	67	207	25,579.17
Bruce Lietzke	67	68	72	207	25,579.16
Lonnie Nielsen	67	70	70	207	25,579.16
Kenny Knox	70	70	68	208	18,856.25
Mark McNulty	73	69	66	208	18,856.25
Boonchu Ruangkit	66	73	69	208	18,856.25
Curtis Strange	68	66	74	208	18,856.25
R.W. Eaks	69	72	68	209	15,575
Keith Fergus	68	68	73	209	15,575
Jon Fiedler	69	72	68	209	15,575
Donnie Hammond	71	71	67	209	15,575
Peter Jacobsen	69	71	70	210	12,366.67
Masahiro Kuramoto	67	73	70	210	12,366.67
Mark Lye	71	73	66	210	12,366.67
Tom Purtzer	69	72	69	210	12,366.67
Ben Crenshaw	70	69	71	210	12,366.66
Fuzzy Zoeller	67	72	71	210	12,366.66

JELD-WEN Tradition

Crosswater Club, Sunriver, Oregon
Par 36-36–72; 7,683 yards

August 16-19
purse, $2,600,000

	SCORES				TOTAL	MONEY
Mark McNulty	66	68	70	68	272	$390,000
David Edwards	67	65	72	73	277	227,760
D.A. Weibring	72	66	68	72	278	187,200
Tom Kite	70	69	68	73	280	140,400
Loren Roberts	72	69	69	70	280	140,400
Keith Fergus	70	66	72	73	281	93,600
Bob Gilder	72	71	72	66	281	93,600
Tom Watson	68	72	67	74	281	93,600
R.W. Eaks	70	71	67	74	282	70,200
Denis Watson	72	70	72	68	282	70,200
Fred Funk	73	69	69	72	283	62,400
Lonnie Nielsen	69	70	73	72	284	54,600
Scott Simpson	69	68	74	73	284	54,600
Jay Haas	70	70	73	72	285	45,500
Morris Hatalsky	70	69	71	75	285	45,500
Mark O'Meara	69	76	70	70	285	45,500
Eduardo Romero	74	68	73	70	285	45,500
Chip Beck	71	71	68	76	286	36,608
Naomichi Ozaki	72	75	72	67	286	36,608
Mike Reid	66	71	76	73	286	36,608
Brad Bryant	70	74	71	72	287	28,166.67
Vicente Fernandez	72	74	70	71	287	28,166.67
John Harris	72	68	76	71	287	28,166.67
Sam Torrance	72	71	71	73	287	28,166.67
Graham Marsh	73	67	71	76	287	28,166.66

	SCORES				TOTAL	MONEY
John Ross	70	72	70	75	287	28,166.66
Andy Bean	70	73	70	75	288	22,620
Scott Hoch	71	77	67	73	288	22,620
Curtis Strange	74	73	70	71	288	22,620
Tom Jenkins	72	72	74	71	289	18,373.34
Tim Simpson	75	68	76	70	289	18,373.34
David Eger	73	70	73	73	289	18,373.33
Bruce Lietzke	70	72	74	73	289	18,373.33
Gil Morgan	74	74	68	73	289	18,373.33
Craig Stadler	72	68	73	76	289	18,373.33
Ben Crenshaw	68	77	72	73	290	14,625
Masahiro Kuramoto	74	73	72	71	290	14,625
Mike McCullough	71	74	75	70	290	14,625
Tom Purtzer	73	70	76	71	290	14,625
Larry Nelson	74	72	72	73	291	12,220
Don Pooley	72	68	74	77	291	12,220
Rod Spittle	72	72	71	76	291	12,220
Jim Thorpe	75	71	72	73	291	12,220
Fuzzy Zoeller	72	69	73	77	291	12,220
Hugh Baiocchi	69	76	72	75	292	10,140
John Jacobs	72	74	74	72	292	10,140
Dana Quigley	73	71	73	75	292	10,140
Walter Hall	74	73	74	72	293	8,840
Mark Johnson	77	73	72	71	293	8,840
Wayne Grady	76	71	71	76	294	7,800
Kenny Knox	74	74	73	73	294	7,800
Donnie Hammond	71	77	73	74	295	6,435
Hale Irwin	73	71	77	74	295	6,435
Jerry Pate	76	74	71	74	295	6,435
Bobby Wadkins	72	75	77	71	295	6,435
Tom McKnight	76	72	73	75	296	5,200
Boonchu Ruangkit	73	80	72	71	296	5,200
Jay Sigel	73	71	76	76	296	5,200
Dave Stockton	75	75	71	75	296	5,200
Bruce Vaughan	71	73	79	73	296	5,200
Bruce Summerhays	68	80	72	77	297	4,420
Wayne Levi	74	76	76	73	299	3,900
Dick Mast	79	70	76	74	299	3,900
Pete Oakley	74	73	73	79	299	3,900
Jim Colbert	75	73	75	77	300	2,880.80
Dave Eichelberger	71	73	78	78	300	2,880.80
Bruce Fleisher	72	77	74	77	300	2,880.80
James Mason	75	73	75	77	300	2,880.80
Leonard Thompson	76	72	74	78	300	2,880.80
Jim Albus	77	74	76	74	301	2,288
Isao Aoki	76	77	73	76	302	2,054
Danny Edwards	78	72	75	77	302	2,054
Allen Doyle	75	76	75	77	303	1,820
Mitch Adams	73	80	71	80	304	1,612
Ed Dougherty	77	73	73	81	304	1,612
Des Smyth	80	75	75	74	304	1,612
Bob Charles	78	73	81	81	313	1,404
Tom Wargo	77	81	84	74	316	1,300
Peter Jacobsen	72	71	76		WD	

Boeing Classic

TPC at Snoqualmie Ridge, Snoqualmie, Washington
Par 36-36–72; 7,264 yards

August 24-26
purse, $1,600,000

	SCORES			TOTAL	MONEY
Denis Watson	69	69	69	207	$240,000
Gil Morgan	68	70	69	207	91,733.34
Dana Quigley	69	70	68	207	91,733.34
R.W. Eaks	71	68	68	207	91,733.33
David Eger	72	69	66	207	91,733.33
Naomichi Ozaki	71	69	67	207	91,733.33
Craig Stadler	74	65	68	207	91,733.33
(Watson won on second playoff hole.)					
Andy Bean	69	71	68	208	45,866.67
Jerry Pate	68	71	69	208	45,866.67
Ray Stewart	66	68	74	208	45,866.66
Bob Gilder	70	71	68	209	35,200
Mark O'Meara	71	68	70	209	35,200
Eduardo Romero	69	72	68	209	35,200
Keith Fergus	70	70	70	210	28,800
Jim Thorpe	71	69	70	210	28,800
Bruce Vaughan	69	69	72	210	28,800
Scott Hoch	71	67	73	211	22,624
Tom Jenkins	72	68	71	211	22,624
Scott Simpson	74	68	69	211	22,624
Des Smyth	72	73	66	211	22,624
D.A. Weibring	71	71	69	211	22,624
Allen Doyle	73	72	67	212	16,453.34
Lonnie Nielsen	74	69	69	212	16,453.34
Jim Ahern	74	72	66	212	16,453.33
Chip Beck	73	68	71	212	16,453.33
Wayne Grady	71	73	68	212	16,453.33
Tom Purtzer	71	69	72	212	16,453.33
Kenny Knox	68	74	71	213	12,672
Dick Mast	72	73	68	213	12,672
Mark McNulty	70	70	73	213	12,672
Don Pooley	68	73	72	213	12,672
Bobby Wadkins	72	70	71	213	12,672

Wal-Mart First Tee Open at Pebble Beach

Pebble Beach Golf Links, Pebble Beach, California
Par 35-37–72; 6,822 yards
Del Monte Golf Course, Monterey, California
Par 36-36–72; 6,357 yards

August 31-September 2
purse, $2,000,000

	SCORES			TOTAL	MONEY
Gil Morgan	70	65	67	202	$300,000
Hale Irwin	70	65	69	204	176,000
Tom Watson	67	70	69	206	144,000
Don Pooley	70	71	67	208	98,666.67
Scott Simpson	72	69	67	208	98,666.67
Des Smyth	71	64	73	208	98,666.66
Jay Haas	73	65	71	209	64,000
Naomichi Ozaki	72	65	72	209	64,000
D.A. Weibring	72	67	70	209	64,000
Hugh Baiocchi	71	70	69	210	46,000
Morris Hatalsky	65	72	73	210	46,000
Peter Jacobsen	68	74	68	210	46,000

	SCORES			TOTAL	MONEY
Bernhard Langer	69	70	71	210	46,000
Andy Bean	75	65	71	211	35,000
Ben Crenshaw	70	70	71	211	35,000
Tom Purtzer	68	71	72	211	35,000
Fuzzy Zoeller	73	69	69	211	35,000
Mark McNulty	68	73	71	212	28,200
Larry Nelson	73	68	71	212	28,200
Lonnie Nielsen	68	69	75	212	28,200
Bruce Fleisher	70	71	72	213	20,700
Kirk Hanefeld	67	73	73	213	20,700
Tom Jenkins	72	70	71	213	20,700
Tom Kite	69	71	73	213	20,700
Mark O'Meara	73	68	72	213	20,700
Jerry Pate	71	72	70	213	20,700
Nick Price	71	70	72	213	20,700
Bruce Vaughan	65	76	72	213	20,700
Jim Blair	72	69	73	214	15,450
Bruce Lietzke	73	66	75	214	15,450
James Mason	72	72	70	214	15,450
Craig Stadler	68	71	75	214	15,450

Greater Hickory Classic at Rock Barn

Rock Barn Golf & Spa, Conover, North Carolina
Par 35-37–72; 7,046 yards

September 14-16
purse, $1,600,000

	SCORES			TOTAL	MONEY
R.W. Eaks	63	66	70	199	$240,000
Jay Haas	70	65	66	201	128,000
Rod Spittle	68	64	69	201	128,000
Scott Simpson	65	69	69	203	96,000
Gil Morgan	66	71	68	205	70,400
Des Smyth	67	71	67	205	70,400
Keith Fergus	69	69	69	207	51,200
Nick Price	72	67	68	207	51,200
Denis Watson	68	70	69	207	51,200
David Edwards	70	67	71	208	35,520
David Eger	71	67	70	208	35,520
Tom McKnight	67	71	70	208	35,520
Naomichi Ozaki	71	69	68	208	35,520
Dana Quigley	71	66	71	208	35,520
Brad Bryant	71	68	70	209	24,880
Tim Conley	66	71	72	209	24,880
Bruce Fleisher	72	68	69	209	24,880
John Jacobs	73	66	70	209	24,880
Jeff Sluman	67	72	70	209	24,880
D.A. Weibring	69	66	74	209	24,880
Joe Inman	69	71	70	210	18,200
Jerry Pate	71	69	70	210	18,200
Loren Roberts	72	68	70	210	18,200
Craig Stadler	72	68	70	210	18,200
Mitch Adcock	71	71	69	211	14,266.67
Allen Doyle	69	72	70	211	14,266.67
Scott Hoch	68	72	71	211	14,266.67
Tom Purtzer	70	71	70	211	14,266.67
Fred Funk	69	70	72	211	14,266.66
Tom Wargo	68	70	73	211	14,266.66

SAS Championship

Prestonwood Country Club, Cary, North Carolina September 21-23
Par 36-36–72; 7,137 yards purse, $2,000,000

	SCORES			TOTAL	MONEY
Mark Wiebe	65	66	67	198	$300,000
Dana Quigley	66	66	69	201	176,000
Keith Fergus	69	67	67	203	132,000
Bruce Lietzke	68	68	67	203	132,000
Mark McNulty	70	67	67	204	96,000
Dick Mast	67	65	73	205	72,000
Gil Morgan	69	69	67	205	72,000
Don Pooley	70	66	69	205	72,000
Jay Haas	68	67	71	206	54,000
Masahiro Kuramoto	68	67	71	206	54,000
Bernhard Langer	72	69	66	207	42,500
Des Smyth	69	67	71	207	42,500
Curtis Strange	71	68	68	207	42,500
D.A. Weibring	68	68	71	207	42,500
R.W. Eaks	69	70	69	208	32,040
David Eger	70	68	70	208	32,040
Tom Jenkins	72	66	70	208	32,040
Tom Purtzer	67	71	70	208	32,040
Tim Simpson	72	65	71	208	32,040
John Harris	69	70	70	209	23,480
Tom Kite	70	68	71	209	23,480
James Mason	69	72	68	209	23,480
Jerry Pate	69	70	70	209	23,480
Jeff Sluman	68	73	68	209	23,480
Tom McKnight	71	68	71	210	18,650
Mike Reid	71	69	70	210	18,650
Loren Roberts	74	68	68	210	18,650
Jim Thorpe	71	69	70	210	18,650
David Edwards	67	71	73	211	15,800
Boonchu Ruangkit	65	71	75	211	15,800
Bruce Vaughan	71	70	70	211	15,800

Constellation Energy Senior Players Championship

Baltimore Country Club, Timonium, Maryland October 4-7
Par 35-35–70; 7,037 yards purse, $2,600,000

	SCORES				TOTAL	MONEY
Loren Roberts	67	66	67	67	267	$390,000
Tom Watson	69	68	68	68	273	228,800
Fred Funk	68	69	66	71	274	171,600
Scott Simpson	70	69	70	65	274	171,600
Danny Edwards	68	69	71	68	276	114,400
D.A. Weibring	70	70	68	68	276	114,400
Keith Fergus	70	71	70	66	277	72,800
Scott Hoch	67	68	74	68	277	72,800
Hale Irwin	69	71	68	69	277	72,800
Eduardo Romero	73	66	70	68	277	72,800
Mark Wiebe	67	70	69	71	277	72,800
Fuzzy Zoeller	73	66	70	68	277	72,800
Andy Bean	69	71	68	70	278	48,100
Chip Beck	68	71	73	66	278	48,100
David Eger	69	67	70	72	278	48,100
Bernhard Langer	70	70	70	68	278	48,100

	SCORES				TOTAL	MONEY
Tom McKnight	74	69	72	64	279	35,663.34
Bruce Vaughan	71	71	70	67	279	35,663.34
Jay Haas	69	71	67	72	279	35,663.33
Dana Quigley	68	72	67	72	279	35,663.33
Jeff Sluman	70	70	68	71	279	35,663.33
Des Smyth	70	66	70	73	279	35,663.33
Don Pooley	74	67	67	72	280	27,950
Tom Purtzer	69	69	73	69	280	27,950
Mitch Adcock	71	70	70	70	281	23,183.34
Naomichi Ozaki	73	70	69	69	281	23,183.34
Tom Kite	70	68	72	71	281	23,183.33
Masahiro Kuramoto	72	69	67	73	281	23,183.33
Gil Morgan	69	68	70	74	281	23,183.33
Bobby Wadkins	72	70	73	66	281	23,183.33
Mitch Adams	70	73	69	70	282	17,550
Walter Hall	67	71	72	72	282	17,550
Mark McNulty	72	68	73	69	282	17,550
Mark O'Meara	74	72	71	65	282	17,550
Rod Spittle	75	73	66	68	282	17,550
Denis Watson	71	68	70	73	282	17,550
Jerry Pate	74	70	67	72	283	14,560
Craig Stadler	71	71	68	73	283	14,560
Lonnie Nielsen	70	72	70	72	284	13,520
Nick Price	68	71	75	70	284	13,520
Ed Dougherty	70	67	73	75	285	11,700
Donnie Hammond	75	69	70	71	285	11,700
Mark Johnson	73	69	70	73	285	11,700
James Mason	74	69	69	73	285	11,700
Curtis Strange	71	70	72	72	285	11,700
Brad Bryant	74	74	71	67	286	8,320
Allen Doyle	70	72	72	72	286	8,320
R.W. Eaks	67	70	73	76	286	8,320
David Edwards	73	68	72	73	286	8,320
Mark James	70	68	76	72	286	8,320
Tom Jenkins	70	72	73	71	286	8,320
Tim Simpson	71	69	74	72	286	8,320
Jim Thorpe	72	70	71	73	286	8,320
Kirk Hanefeld	69	75	72	71	287	5,720
John Harris	72	74	72	69	287	5,720
Morris Hatalsky	69	72	72	74	287	5,720
Mike McCullough	72	72	67	76	287	5,720
Boonchu Ruangkit	75	69	73	70	287	5,720
Raymond Floyd	73	69	72	74	288	4,810
Bruce Lietzke	71	75	71	71	288	4,810
Bob Gilder	73	70	68	78	289	4,420
Vicente Fernandez	74	70	74	72	290	4,030
Mike Reid	74	68	76	72	290	4,030
Hugh Baiocchi	73	74	72	72	291	3,380
Dave Eichelberger	74	72	72	73	291	3,380
Dan Pohl	73	71	75	72	291	3,380
Jim Ahern	72	72	74	74	292	2,464.80
Ben Crenshaw	74	72	78	68	292	2,464.80
Kenny Knox	74	74	74	70	292	2,464.80
Wayne Levi	72	72	73	75	292	2,464.80
Bruce Summerhays	74	68	72	78	292	2,464.80
Bruce Fleisher	79	75	69	70	293	1,898
Dick Mast	74	75	70	74	293	1,898
Wayne Grady	72	71	73	78	294	1,716
Ron Streck	77	74	75	71	297	1,612
John Jacobs	75	76	76	73	300	1,456
Tom Wargo	75	74	78	73	300	1,456
Larry Nelson	73	74	76		WD	

Administaff Small Business Classic

Augusta Pines Golf Club, Spring, Texas
Par 36-36–72; 7,006 yards

October 12-14
purse, $1,700,000

	SCORES			TOTAL	MONEY
Bernhard Langer	62	65	64	191	$255,000
Mark O'Meara	67	64	68	199	149,600
Tom Kite	66	65	69	200	122,400
Jay Haas	69	66	67	202	91,800
Lonnie Nielsen	67	67	68	202	91,800
Andy Bean	67	67	69	203	52,700
Ben Crenshaw	70	65	68	203	52,700
Mark James	68	68	67	203	52,700
Tom Jenkins	66	68	69	203	52,700
Don Pooley	68	69	66	203	52,700
Tom Purtzer	69	65	69	203	52,700
Jerry Pate	67	68	69	204	35,700
Jeff Sluman	66	68	70	204	35,700
Chip Beck	69	68	68	205	29,750
David Eger	69	67	69	205	29,750
Denis Watson	72	66	67	205	29,750
D.A. Weibring	69	68	68	205	29,750
Fred Funk	70	69	67	206	23,247.50
Mark McNulty	66	71	69	206	23,247.50
Gil Morgan	70	68	68	206	23,247.50
Fuzzy Zoeller	67	69	70	206	23,247.50
Tom McKnight	69	70	68	207	19,210
Jim Thorpe	68	66	73	207	19,210
Keith Fergus	69	69	70	208	15,193.75
Bruce Fleisher	71	65	72	208	15,193.75
Bob Gilder	67	68	73	208	15,193.75
Hale Irwin	68	72	68	208	15,193.75
John Jacobs	69	71	68	208	15,193.75
Scott Simpson	72	72	64	208	15,193.75
Tom Wargo	67	72	69	208	15,193.75
Mark Wiebe	68	70	70	208	15,193.75

AT&T Championship

Oak Hills Country Club, San Antonio, Texas
Par 35-36–71; 6,670 yards

October 19-21
purse, $1,600,000

	SCORES			TOTAL	MONEY
John Cook	65	68	65	198	$240,000
Mark O'Meara	63	68	69	200	140,800
Fred Funk	66	68	67	201	96,000
Tom Kite	66	65	70	201	96,000
Loren Roberts	68	66	67	201	96,000
Lonnie Nielsen	67	69	68	204	64,000
Mark James	67	66	72	205	51,200
Dave Stockton	69	65	71	205	51,200
Mark Wiebe	68	66	71	205	51,200
Wayne Levi	65	71	70	206	40,000
Scott Simpson	67	67	72	206	40,000
Mitch Adams	70	67	70	207	29,866.67
Phil Blackmar	70	68	69	207	29,866.67
Craig Stadler	66	71	70	207	29,866.67
D.A. Weibring	67	71	69	207	29,866.67
Tom Purtzer	66	70	71	207	29,866.66

	SCORES			TOTAL	MONEY
Bruce Vaughan	71	66	70	207	29,866.66
Brad Bryant	72	69	67	208	21,880
Jay Haas	68	68	72	208	21,880
Scott Hoch	69	68	71	208	21,880
Masahiro Kuramoto	69	70	69	208	21,880
Keith Fergus	73	69	67	209	16,453.34
Mark McNulty	69	74	66	209	16,453.34
Ben Crenshaw	70	68	71	209	16,453.33
Bob Gilder	71	67	71	209	16,453.33
Gil Morgan	67	70	72	209	16,453.33
Fuzzy Zoeller	70	66	73	209	16,453.33
Mitch Adcock	72	67	71	210	12,672
Andy Bean	71	72	67	210	12,672
Danny Edwards	69	73	68	210	12,672
Dave Eichelberger	74	67	69	210	12,672
Jerry Pate	69	69	72	210	12,672

Charles Schwab Cup Championship

Sonoma Golf Club, Sonoma, California   October 25-28
Par 36-36–72; 7,103 yards   purse, $2,500,000

	SCORES				TOTAL	MONEY
Jim Thorpe	64	69	69	66	268	$442,000
Fred Funk	70	69	66	66	271	234,500
Denis Watson	69	64	68	70	271	234,500
Mark McNulty	74	66	65	67	272	177,000
Tom Purtzer	68	67	72	66	273	129,500
Eduardo Romero	64	68	71	70	273	129,500
Tom Kite	71	67	71	65	274	94,333.34
Keith Fergus	69	68	70	67	274	94,333.33
Hale Irwin	70	73	66	65	274	94,333.33
Brad Bryant	68	67	67	73	275	74,000
Naomichi Ozaki	70	65	71	69	275	74,000
Bobby Wadkins	69	68	69	70	276	65,000
David Edwards	72	69	70	66	277	54,625
Mark James	66	70	69	72	277	54,625
Loren Roberts	71	70	69	67	277	54,625
D.A. Weibring	67	72	68	70	277	54,625
Ben Crenshaw	71	68	68	72	279	47,000
Scott Simpson	70	69	70	71	280	44,000
Scott Hoch	70	72	68	71	281	41,000
Andy Bean	70	70	75	67	282	36,000
David Eger	72	73	69	68	282	36,000
Jay Haas	68	70	71	73	282	36,000
Tom Watson	74	71	70	67	282	36,000
R.W. Eaks	73	68	71	71	283	29,000
Gil Morgan	71	70	70	72	283	29,000
Des Smyth	74	69	72	68	283	29,000
Dana Quigley	76	70	68	70	284	26,000
Bob Gilder	76	72	68	74	290	25,000
Lonnie Nielsen	77	68	77	69	291	24,500

European Seniors Tour

DGM Barbados Open

Royal Westmoreland Resort, St. James, Barbados
Par 36-36–72; 6,847 yards

February 28-March 2
purse, €189,912

	SCORES			TOTAL	MONEY
Gordon J. Brand	72	70	66	208	€29,822.82
Doug Johnson	72	70	67	209	19,881.88
Giuseppe Cali	68	69	73	210	13,917.31
Bob Cameron	70	70	73	213	9,960.82
Jose Rivero	69	74	70	213	9,960.82
Ross Drummond	72	70	72	214	7,157.47
Ian Mosey	69	73	72	214	7,157.47
Juan Quiros	73	69	72	214	7,157.47
Luis Carbonetti	69	74	72	215	5,368.11
Nick Job	67	75	73	215	5,368.11
Delroy Cambridge	71	70	75	216	4,572.83
Bruce Heuchan	75	73	68	216	4,572.83
Tony Johnstone	72	71	74	217	3,876.97
Alan Tapie	70	73	74	217	3,876.97
Martin Poxon	74	72	72	218	3,578.74
Gavan Levenson	73	74	72	219	3,181.10
Pete Oakley	71	77	71	219	3,181.10
Glenn Ralph	78	68	73	219	3,181.10
Jerry Bruner	69	77	74	220	2,631.03
Jimmy Heggarty	72	74	74	220	2,631.03
Emilio Rodriguez	80	72	68	220	2,631.03

The Gloria Classic

Gloria Golf Resort, Belek, Turkey
Par 37-35–72; 6,700 yards

May 11-13
purse, €325,309

	SCORES			TOTAL	MONEY
Nick Job	71	67	68	206	€48,750
Martin Poxon	70	66	70	206	32,500
(Job defeated Poxon on first playoff hole.)					
Delroy Cambridge	67	70	70	207	18,438.33
Luis Carbonetti	70	69	68	207	18,438.33
Stewart Ginn	67	70	70	207	18,438.33
Bob Cameron	69	71	68	208	13,000
Giuseppe Cali	71	69	69	209	10,400
Doug Johnson	70	66	73	209	10,400
Tony Johnstone	67	72	70	209	10,400
Horacio Carbonetti	68	73	69	210	7,475
Terry Gale	69	69	72	210	7,475
Juan Quiros	70	69	71	210	7,475
Jim Rhodes	73	67	70	210	7,475
Ross Drummond	71	67	73	211	5,850
Bill Longmuir	71	68	72	211	5,850
Jose Rivero	69	69	73	211	5,850
Pete Oakley	71	66	75	212	5,037.50

	SCORES			TOTAL	MONEY
Adan Sowa	69	72	71	212	5,037.50
Gordon J. Brand	70	72	71	213	4,168.13
Angel Fernandez	71	72	70	213	4,168.13
Kevin Spurgeon	75	68	70	213	4,168.13
Sam Torrance	69	69	75	213	4,168.13

Sharp Italian Seniors Open

Circolo Golf Venezia, Venice, Italy
Par 35-37–72; 6,757 yards

May 18-20
purse, €200,000

	SCORES			TOTAL	MONEY
Simon Owen	70	65	73	208	€30,000
Tony Allen	71	66	71	208	15,000
John Benda	71	63	74	208	15,000
Carl Mason	70	73	65	208	15,000
(Owen won on first playoff hole.)					
Ross Drummond	70	69	70	209	9,040
Bob Cameron	67	75	69	211	8,000
Horacio Carbonetti	70	71	71	212	5,840
Bruce Heuchan	73	69	70	212	5,840
Nick Job	70	69	73	212	5,840
Bobby Lincoln	74	70	68	212	5,840
Jose Rivero	71	69	72	212	5,840
Stewart Ginn	70	72	71	213	4,200
Sam Torrance	70	70	73	213	4,200
Gordon J. Brand	72	70	72	214	3,700
David J. Russell	72	70	72	214	3,700
Giuseppe Cali	71	72	72	215	3,300
David Merriman	71	74	70	215	3,300
John Chillas	75	70	71	216	3,000
Jerry Bruner	72	74	71	217	2,492
Doug Johnson	72	70	75	217	2,492
Gavan Levenson	72	71	74	217	2,492
John Mashego	72	73	72	217	2,492
Adan Sowa	72	73	72	217	2,492

AIB Irish Seniors Open

PGA National Ireland, Co. Kildare, Ireland
Par 36-36–72; 6,956 yards

June 1-3
purse, €450,428

	SCORES			TOTAL	MONEY
Costantino Rocca	69	71	71	211	€67,500
Juan Quiros	73	68	72	213	38,250
Kevin Spurgeon	71	70	72	213	38,250
Stewart Ginn	67	71	76	214	22,545
Doug Johnson	69	71	74	214	22,545
Tony Allen	73	72	71	216	14,580
John Bland	71	73	72	216	14,580
David Good	73	71	72	216	14,580
David Merriman	72	70	74	216	14,580
Sam Torrance	71	74	71	216	14,580
Bob Cameron	74	72	71	217	9,562.50
Horacio Carbonetti	71	73	73	217	9,562.50
Guillermo Encina	72	73	72	217	9,562.50
Glenn Ralph	73	74	70	217	9,562.50

	SCORES			TOTAL	MONEY
Ross Drummond	74	74	70	218	8,100
Delroy Cambridge	77	70	72	219	6,777
Carl Mason	73	73	73	219	6,777
Peter O'Hagan	72	71	76	219	6,777
Jose Rivero	75	72	72	219	6,777
Alan Tapie	69	75	75	219	6,777

Jersey Seniors Classic

La Moye Golf Club, Jersey, Channel Isles
Par 36-36–72; 6,581 yards

June 8-10
purse, €207,043

	SCORES			TOTAL	MONEY
Bobby Lincoln	71	67	67	205	€30,943.71
Bill Longmuir	66	72	69	207	20,629.14
Gordon J. Brand	69	72	72	213	10,157.79
Bob Cameron	70	71	72	213	10,157.79
David Good	71	72	70	213	10,157.79
Carl Mason	68	70	75	213	10,157.79
Sam Torrance	71	70	72	213	10,157.79
Tony Allen	69	72	73	214	6,601.32
Luis Carbonetti	76	69	70	215	5,157.29
Guillermo Encina	69	73	73	215	5,157.29
Pete Oakley	72	71	72	215	5,157.29
Glenn Ralph	73	72	70	215	5,157.29
Giuseppe Cali	75	69	72	216	3,816.39
Terry Gale	72	69	75	216	3,816.39
Martin Gray	73	69	74	216	3,816.39
Bob Larratt	68	74	74	216	3,816.39
Ross Drummond	72	70	75	217	2,829.63
Doug Johnson	75	68	74	217	2,829.63
Gavan Levenson	74	70	73	217	2,829.63
Martin Poxon	70	71	76	217	2,829.63
Andrew Reynolds	69	75	73	217	2,829.63
Donald Stirling	73	72	72	217	2,829.63

Ryder Cup Wales Seniors Open

Conwy Golf Club, Conwy (Caernarvonshire), Wales
Par 35-37–72; 6,935 yards

June 15-17
purse, €735,720

	SCORES			TOTAL	MONEY
Carl Mason	73	69	68	210	€110,358
Ross Drummond	73	70	69	212	62,536
Juan Quiros	75	64	73	212	62,536
Costantino Rocca	70	71	72	213	36,860
Des Smyth	71	75	67	213	36,860
Bob Cameron	75	69	70	214	29,429
Luis Carbonetti	71	73	71	215	26,486
Horacio Carbonetti	72	70	74	216	20,232
Eamonn Darcy	71	73	72	216	20,232
Guillermo Encina	69	78	69	216	20,232
Jose Rivero	75	71	70	216	20,232
Martin Gray	73	71	73	217	13,733
Tommy Horton	72	73	72	217	13,733
Tony Johnstone	74	73	70	217	13,733
Noel Ratcliffe	74	70	73	217	13,733

	SCORES			TOTAL	MONEY
Adan Sowa	79	65	73	217	13,733
Sam Torrance	74	74	69	217	13,733
Jimmy Heggarty	73	74	71	218	10,061
Emilio Rodriguez	73	74	71	218	10,061
Peter Teravainen	75	74	69	218	10,061
Denis Watson	76	69	73	218	10,061

Bendinat London Seniors Masters

London Golf Club, Ash, Kent, England
Par 36-36–72; 7,037 yards

June 22-24
purse, €221,829

	SCORES			TOTAL	MONEY
Sam Torrance	68	68	70	206	€33,274.35
Jose Rivero	69	72	66	207	22,182.90
Eamonn Darcy	70	69	69	208	13,864.31
Carl Mason	68	70	70	208	13,864.31
Jim Rhodes	70	69	71	210	10,026.67
Ross Drummond	70	68	74	212	8,873.16
Bobby Lincoln	73	66	74	213	7,985.84
John Bland	72	70	72	214	6,100.30
Gordon J. Brand	70	69	75	214	6,100.30
Tony Johnstone	71	68	75	214	6,100.30
Juan Quiros	71	71	72	214	6,100.30
Giuseppe Cali	74	69	73	216	4,658.41
John Chillas	71	70	75	216	4,658.41
Jerry Bruner	69	73	75	217	4,214.75
Mike Ferguson	70	73	75	218	3,660.18
Stewart Ginn	74	73	71	218	3,660.18
David Merriman	76	69	73	218	3,660.18
Pete Oakley	71	72	75	218	3,660.18
Tony Allen	69	72	78	219	2,623.92
Bob Cameron	73	74	72	219	2,623.92
Seiji Ebihara	75	71	73	219	2,623.92
David Good	75	70	74	219	2,623.92
Martin Poxon	72	72	75	219	2,623.92
Costantino Rocca	70	75	74	219	2,623.92
Jean Pierre Sallat	74	74	71	219	2,623.92

Open de France Senior de Divonne

Golf du Domaine de Divonne, Divonne les Bains, France
Par 37-35–72; 6,405 yards

July 12-14
purse, €325,000

	SCORES			TOTAL	MONEY
Juan Quiros	69	69	70	208	€48,750
Tony Allen	70	71	68	209	32,500
Gordon J. Brand	70	71	69	210	16,003
Bob Cameron	70	72	68	210	16,003
Seiji Ebihara	71	67	72	210	16,003
Tony Johnstone	67	70	73	210	16,003
Emilio Rodriguez	70	68	72	210	16,003
Guillermo Encina	68	69	74	211	9,750
Carl Mason	70	72	69	211	9,750
David Good	68	69	75	212	8,125
Costantino Rocca	68	73	71	212	8,125
Angel Fernandez	71	70	72	213	7,150

	SCORES				TOTAL	MONEY
Eamonn Darcy	77	67	70		214	6,012.50
John Mashego	69	72	73		214	6,012.50
David Merriman	71	72	71		214	6,012.50
Jim Rhodes	73	72	69		214	6,012.50
Giuseppe Cali	73	69	73		215	4,736.88
Nick Job	67	81	67		215	4,736.88
Denis O'Sullivan	69	72	74		215	4,736.88
Noel Ratcliffe	73	74	68		215	4,736.88

The Senior Open Championship

Muirfield, Gullane, East Lothian, Scotland
Par 36-35–71; 7,034 yards

July 26-29
purse, €1,492,690

	SCORES				TOTAL	MONEY
Tom Watson	70	71	70	73	284	€234,640.72
Stewart Ginn	71	70	69	75	285	122,301.64
Mark O'Meara	72	71	70	72	285	122,301.64
Jay Haas	70	75	73	70	288	55,392.61
Lonnie Nielsen	69	74	74	71	288	55,392.61
Loren Roberts	74	72	71	71	288	55,392.61
Eduardo Romero	70	71	73	74	288	55,392.61
John Ross	71	72	74	72	289	35,166.37
Donnie Hammond	73	71	71	75	290	31,553.08
Gordon J. Brand	68	73	74	76	291	25,174.06
Tom Kite	70	76	74	71	291	25,174.06
Des Smyth	70	70	77	74	291	25,174.06
Sam Torrance	69	75	71	76	291	25,174.06
Nick Faldo	68	74	75	75	292	21,159.30
Kiyoshi Murota	71	71	81	69	292	21,159.30
Tom McKnight	72	77	72	72	293	18,928.87
Jerry Pate	73	73	72	75	293	18,928.87
Denis Watson	69	74	73	77	293	18,928.87
Hugh Baiocchi	73	78	76	67	294	16,843.43
Jean Pierre Sallat	73	77	73	71	294	16,843.43
Tim Simpson	71	75	75	73	294	16,843.43
D.A. Weibring	72	72	74	76	294	16,843.43
John Bland	71	74	73	77	295	14,219.49
Kirk Hanefeld	72	72	76	75	295	14,219.49
Scott Hoch	69	75	78	73	295	14,219.49
Bobby Lincoln	72	74	77	72	295	14,219.49
James Mason	77	71	74	73	295	14,219.49
Katsuyoshi Tomori	71	75	72	77	295	14,219.49
Tsukasa Watanabe	71	77	71	76	295	14,219.49
Brad Bryant	72	71	78	75	296	11,802.67
Tim Conley	72	75	78	71	296	11,802.67
Ben Crenshaw	70	76	74	76	296	11,802.67
Morris Hatalsky	69	73	73	81	296	11,802.67
Bob Charles	71	77	74	75	297	10,416.09
Mark McNulty	70	76	80	71	297	10,416.09
Scott Simpson	76	72	77	72	297	10,416.09
Bruce Vaughan	74	76	75	72	297	10,416.09
Giuseppe Cali	72	76	75	75	298	8,490.48
Vicente Fernandez	75	76	73	74	298	8,490.48
John Harris	70	80	74	74	298	8,490.48
Kenny Knox	70	79	80	69	298	8,490.48
Gil Morgan	72	76	74	76	298	8,490.48
Tsuneyuki Nakajima	71	80	75	72	298	8,490.48
Simon Owen	70	75	74	79	298	8,490.48
Naomichi Ozaki	74	74	76	74	298	8,490.48

	SCORES				TOTAL	MONEY
Rod Spittle	72	74	76	76	298	8,490.48
Dave Stockton	68	76	72	82	298	8,490.48
Jon Chaffee	73	77	72	77	299	6,750.75
Dick Mast	71	80	76	72	299	6,750.75
Pete Oakley	74	75	78	72	299	6,750.75
John Benda	74	71	78	77	300	5,947.80
Guillermo Encina	70	79	74	77	300	5,947.80
Bob Gilder	70	80	76	74	300	5,947.80
David Edwards	74	75	76	76	301	4,709.38
Masahiro Kuramoto	73	78	75	75	301	4,709.38
Graham Marsh	71	71	76	83	301	4,709.38
Mike McCullough	74	73	77	77	301	4,709.38
Denis O'Sullivan	75	76	75	75	301	4,709.38
Tom Purtzer	74	77	77	73	301	4,709.38
Costantino Rocca	73	77	74	77	301	4,709.38
John Chillas	72	77	76	77	302	3,727.29
Mark James	72	75	76	79	302	3,727.29
Adan Sowa	73	77	78	74	302	3,727.29
Bob Cameron	75	74	79	75	303	3,208.09
Bob Larratt	74	73	75	81	303	3,208.09
Manuel Pinero	73	75	77	78	303	3,208.09
Jose Rivero	78	73	79	73	303	3,208.09
Bill Longmuir	71	80	80	73	304	2,802.90
Jim Rhodes	77	73	77	77	304	2,802.90
Chip Beck	71	78	79	77	305	2,535.25
Andrew Murray	72	78	77	78	305	2,535.25
Bruce Heuchan	69	78	81	78	306	2,334.51
Eamonn Darcy	77	74	79	78	308	2,133.77
Craig Stadler	76	75	81	76	308	2,133.77
Gery Watine	76	74	79	80	309	1,933.04
Gary Player	72	76	79	83	310	1,799.21
Denis Durnian	74	75	84		WD	1,665.38

Wentworth Senior Masters

Wentworth Club, Edinburgh Course, Virginia Water,
Surrey, England
Par 36-36–72; 6,873 yards

August 3-5
purse, €372,046

	SCORES			TOTAL	MONEY
Des Smyth	70	71	69	210	€55,753.88
Bob Charles	71	71	70	212	37,169.25
Eduardo Romero	71	69	73	213	26,018.48
Carl Mason	70	74	71	215	18,621.79
Katsuyoshi Tomori	67	74	74	215	18,621.79
Bruce Heuchan	72	70	74	216	14,867.70
John Chillas	70	73	74	217	13,380.93
John Bland	74	69	75	218	9,416.21
Gordon J. Brand	71	73	74	218	9,416.21
Horacio Carbonetti	73	71	74	218	9,416.21
Eamonn Darcy	71	72	75	218	9,416.21
Noel Ratcliffe	72	74	72	218	9,416.21
David J. Russell	68	76	74	218	9,416.21
Delroy Cambridge	71	77	71	219	6,504.62
Juan Quiros	72	76	71	219	6,504.62
Glenn Ralph	72	71	76	219	6,504.62
Jose Rivero	73	75	71	219	6,504.62
Bob Cameron	69	75	76	220	4,662.09
Luis Carbonetti	73	76	71	220	4,662.09
Neil Coles	74	72	74	220	4,662.09

	SCORES			TOTAL	MONEY
Seiji Ebihara	76	67	77	220	4,662.09
Terry Gale	69	75	76	220	4,662.09
Stewart Ginn	72	74	74	220	4,662.09
Andrew Murray	72	74	74	220	4,662.09

Bad Ragaz PGA Seniors Open

Golf Club Bad Ragaz, Zurich, Switzerland
Par 35-35–70; 6,183 yards

August 10-12
purse, €210,000

	SCORES			TOTAL	MONEY
Carl Mason	65	64	65	194	€31,500
Horacio Carbonetti	64	67	69	200	15,750
Costantino Rocca	68	62	70	200	15,750
David J. Russell	70	64	66	200	15,750
Steve Martin	64	67	70	201	9,492
Stewart Ginn	70	66	66	202	7,140
Jimmy Heggarty	65	72	65	202	7,140
Nick Job	69	68	65	202	7,140
Katsuyoshi Tomori	66	71	65	202	7,140
Bob Cameron	67	68	68	203	5,040
Doug Johnson	66	68	69	203	5,040
Juan Quiros	67	65	71	203	5,040
John Benda	70	66	68	204	3,675
Delroy Cambridge	68	67	69	204	3,675
Philippe Dugeny	70	65	69	204	3,675
Bobby Lincoln	69	70	65	204	3,675
Bill Longmuir	68	66	70	204	3,675
Adan Sowa	67	69	68	204	3,675
John Bland	67	72	66	205	2,693.25
Bob Lendzion	68	69	68	205	2,693.25
Glenn Ralph	70	67	68	205	2,693.25
Jose Rivero	67	67	71	205	2,693.25

The Midas English Seniors Open

St. Mellion International Hotel Golf & Country Club,
St. Mellion, Cornwall, England
Par 36-36–72; 6,854 yards

August 17-19
purse, €221,602

	SCORES			TOTAL	MONEY
Bill Longmuir	70	69	69	208	€33,240.37
Carl Mason	69	69	72	210	22,160.25
David Merriman	71	74	71	216	15,512.18
Stewart Ginn	70	75	72	217	11,102.29
Katsuyoshi Tomori	74	71	72	217	11,102.29
Philippe Dugeny	72	72	74	218	6,869.68
Martin Foster	74	72	72	218	6,869.68
Jimmy Heggarty	70	71	77	218	6,869.68
Doug Johnson	73	72	73	218	6,869.68
Ian Mosey	72	78	68	218	6,869.68
Denis O'Sullivan	72	73	73	218	6,869.68
John Bland	70	73	76	219	4,653.65
Simon Owen	71	72	76	219	4,653.65
Terry Dill	72	72	76	220	4,099.65
Martin Gray	73	75	72	220	4,099.65
Bob Cameron	74	73	74	221	3,239.09

	SCORES			TOTAL	MONEY
Angel Fernandez	73	74	74	221	3,239.09
Bruce Heuchan	74	75	72	221	3,239.09
John Mashego	74	72	75	221	3,239.09
David J. Russell	70	72	79	221	3,239.09
Gordon Townhill	72	73	76	221	3,239.09

European Senior Masters

Woburn Golf Club, Dukes Course,
Milton Keynes, England
Par 35-37–72; 6,896 yards

August 31-September 2
purse, €331,423

	SCORES			TOTAL	MONEY
Carl Mason	71	66	73	210	€49,713.41
Costantino Rocca	69	69	72	210	33,142.28
(Mason defeated Rocca on first playoff hole.)					
Bob Cameron	73	70	68	211	23,199.59
Tony Johnstone	75	69	69	213	18,228.25
Guillermo Encina	72	68	74	214	12,693.49
Simon Owen	72	71	71	214	12,693.49
Jose Rivero	74	68	72	214	12,693.49
Sam Torrance	75	71	68	214	12,693.49
Mark James	76	65	74	215	9,279.84
Gery Watine	73	70	73	216	8,616.99
Doug Johnson	75	71	71	217	7,622.72
Pete Oakley	72	70	75	217	7,622.72
Luis Carbonetti	76	71	71	218	5,965.61
Angel Fernandez	73	69	76	218	5,965.61
David Good	70	74	74	218	5,965.61
Martin Gray	78	72	68	218	5,965.61
Denis O'Sullivan	74	71	73	218	5,965.61
John Bland	74	75	70	219	4,394.67
Stewart Ginn	75	68	76	219	4,394.67
Manuel Pinero	70	75	74	219	4,394.67
Emilio Rodriguez	71	73	75	219	4,394.67
Adan Sowa	70	76	73	219	4,394.67

PGA Seniors Championship

Stoke by Nayland Golf Club, Colchester, Suffolk, England
Par 36-36–72; 6,589 yards

September 6-9
purse, €299,182

	SCORES				TOTAL	MONEY
Carl Mason	67	67	67	67	268	€49,270.41
Philippe Dugeny	75	68	68	63	274	24,731.29
Costantino Rocca	69	66	71	68	274	24,731.29
Bruce Heuchan	67	67	72	70	276	14,782.60
John Bland	70	66	69	72	277	11,456.52
Nick Job	70	69	72	66	277	11,456.52
Luis Carbonetti	69	66	73	70	278	9,313.04
Juan Quiros	69	72	68	69	278	9,313.04
Peter Teravainen	68	74	66	70	278	9,313.04
Guillermo Encina	74	68	66	71	279	6,744.56
Jim Lapsley	71	68	70	70	279	6,744.56
Jose Rivero	72	69	71	67	279	6,744.56
Gery Watine	72	70	71	66	279	6,744.56
Ross Drummond	69	67	71	73	280	4,730.43

	SCORES			TOTAL	MONEY
Bill Longmuir	71	69	69 71	280	4,730.43
Gordon J. Brand	71	71	70 69	281	3,740
Giuseppe Cali	69	73	69 70	281	3,740
Horacio Carbonetti	75	69	70 67	281	3,740
John Chillas	72	68	74 68	282	3,311.30
Terry Gale	71	69	72 72	284	3,052.61
Simon Owen	73	71	67 73	284	3,052.61
Glenn Ralph	72	70	73 69	284	3,052.61
Denis Watson	70	70	75 69	284	3,052.61

Scandinavian Senior Open

Royal Copenhagen Golf Club, Copenhagen, Denmark
Par 36-35–71; 6,414 yards

September 20-22
purse, €249,998

	SCORES			TOTAL	MONEY
John Chillas	70	67	68	205	€39,259
Glenn Ralph	72	68	65	205	26,173
(Chillas defeated Ralph on fourth playoff hole.)					
Doug Johnson	69	69	69	207	18,321
Bill Longmuir	76	67	65	208	14,395
Giuseppe Cali	70	73	66	209	11,149.50
Carl Mason	68	69	72	209	11,149.50
Luis Carbonetti	70	70	70	210	7,982.50
Ross Drummond	72	68	70	210	7,982.50
Nick Job	73	69	68	210	7,982.50
Juan Quiros	70	69	71	210	7,982.50
Bobby Lincoln	71	66	74	211	5,561.75
Simon Owen	73	68	70	211	5,561.75
Martin Poxon	73	69	69	211	5,561.75
Bertus Smit	69	71	71	211	5,561.75
Eamonn Darcy	72	70	70	212	4,192.80
Philippe Dugeny	70	66	76	212	4,192.80
David Good	71	71	70	212	4,192.80
Pete Oakley	77	66	69	212	4,192.80
David J. Russell	71	70	71	212	4,192.80
Steve Martin	70	73	70	213	3,455

Charles Church Scottish Seniors Open

Marriott Dalmahoy Hotel & Country Club, Edinburgh, Scotland
Par 35-37–72; 6,936 yards

September 28-30
purse, €323,017

	SCORES			TOTAL	MONEY
Jose Rivero	70	66	70	206	€48,452.51
Ross Drummond	69	70	68	207	32,301.67
Bob Cameron	70	71	70	211	20,188.55
Nick Job	71	69	71	211	20,188.55
Costantino Rocca	67	73	72	212	14,600.36
Angel Fernandez	73	71	69	213	12,274.64
Sam Torrance	71	73	69	213	12,274.64
Martin Poxon	74	69	71	214	9,690.50
David J. Russell	75	71	68	214	9,690.50
Bobby Lincoln	70	69	76	215	8,075.42
Andrew Murray	72	70	73	215	8,075.42
Giuseppe Cali	71	74	71	216	5,860.45
Delroy Cambridge	73	71	72	216	5,860.45

	SCORES			TOTAL	MONEY
Doug Johnson	72	72	72	216	5,860.45
Graham Marsh	73	70	73	216	5,860.45
Richard Masters	76	71	69	216	5,860.45
Denis O'Sullivan	73	74	69	216	5,860.45
Juan Quiros	73	72	71	216	5,860.45
Tony Allen	80	68	69	217	4,024.79
David Good	70	73	74	217	4,024.79
Bill Longmuir	74	72	71	217	4,024.79
Glenn Ralph	74	74	69	217	4,024.79
Alan Tapie	72	70	75	217	4,024.79

OKI Castellon Open de Espana Senior

Club de Campo del Mediterraneo, Castellon, Spain
Par 36-36–72; 6,818 yards

October 19-21
purse, €325,000

	SCORES			TOTAL	MONEY
Carl Mason	66	68	65	199	€48,750
Luis Carbonetti	69	64	70	203	32,500
David Merriman	71	66	68	205	22,750
Ross Drummond	70	70	66	206	15,188.33
Guillermo Encina	67	70	69	206	15,188.33
Sam Torrance	70	68	68	206	15,188.33
Stewart Ginn	69	68	70	207	11,050
Bill Longmuir	71	68	68	207	11,050
Bruce Heuchan	69	71	68	208	8,775
Costantino Rocca	71	67	70	208	8,775
Bob Cameron	72	66	71	209	7,800
Horacio Carbonetti	71	70	69	210	6,608.33
David Good	68	72	70	210	6,608.33
Glenn Ralph	69	69	72	210	6,608.33
Eamonn Darcy	72	68	71	211	5,362.50
Nick Job	73	68	70	211	5,362.50
Juan Quiros	68	71	72	211	5,362.50
Emilio Rodriguez	67	74	70	211	5,362.50
Gordon J. Brand	72	73	67	212	4,168.13
Tony Johnstone	72	72	68	212	4,168.13
Andrew Murray	71	71	70	212	4,168.13
Bertus Smit	73	66	73	212	4,168.13

The Kingdom of Bahrain Trophy - Seniors Tour Championship

Buckinghamshire Golf Club, Denham, England
Par 36-36–72; 6,740 yards

November 8-10
purse, €345,281

	SCORES			TOTAL	MONEY
Costantino Rocca	70	70	66	206	€55,618.72
Nick Job	70	70	67	207	37,079.14
John Chillas	67	70	71	208	21,036.23
Doug Johnson	68	73	67	208	21,036.23
Juan Quiros	70	69	69	208	21,036.23
Adan Sowa	67	69	73	209	14,090.07
Sam Torrance	68	73	68	209	14,090.07
John Bland	69	73	68	210	10,629.35
Bill Longmuir	70	69	71	210	10,629.35
Carl Mason	72	72	66	210	10,629.35
Bob Cameron	71	72	68	211	8,899

	SCORES			TOTAL	MONEY
Gordon J. Brand	72	74	66	212	8,157.41
Stewart Ginn	69	72	72	213	7,230.43
Bruce Heuchan	71	73	69	213	7,230.43
Giuseppe Cali	71	73	70	214	6,674.25
Luis Carbonetti	72	73	70	215	5,756.54
Ross Drummond	72	74	69	215	5,756.54
Angel Fernandez	71	72	72	215	5,756.54
David Merriman	69	72	74	215	5,756.54
Horacio Carbonetti	74	71	71	216	4,353.09
Philippe Dugeny	72	71	73	216	4,353.09
Guillermo Encina	71	74	71	216	4,353.09
Jose Rivero	75	68	73	216	4,353.09
Des Smyth	73	72	71	216	4,353.09

Japan Senior Tour

Aderans Wellness Open

Nakajo Golf Club, Nakajo, Niigata
Par 36-36–72; 7,034 yards

June 8-10
purse, ¥60,000,000

	SCORES			TOTAL	MONEY
Katsunari Takahashi	68	67	69	204	¥15,000,000
Kiyoshi Murota	67	68	69	204	5,700,000
(Takahashi defeated Murota on first playoff hole.)					
Noboru Fujiike	71	67	68	206	3,600,000
Tateo Ozaki	68	72	67	207	2,580,000
Tsuneyuki Nakajima	68	68	72	208	2,145,000
Seiji Ebihara	67	68	74	209	1,800,000
Takashi Miyosi	70	71	69	210	1,418,000
Takaaki Fukuzawa	70	69	71	210	1,418,000
Shinji Kuraoka	68	70	72	210	1,418,000
David Ishii	70	70	71	211	1,188,000
Minoru Hatsumi	67	73	72	212	1,128,000
Taisei Inagaki	72	71	70	213	1,038,000
Toru Nakamura	70	72	71	213	1,038,000
Hiroshi Makino	73	68	73	214	948,000
Yasunori Uehara	74	70	71	215	858,000
Tadashige Kusano	70	71	74	215	858,000
Katsuyoshi Tomori	74	69	73	216	723,000
Gohei Sato	73	73	70	216	723,000
Chen Tze-ming	75	73	68	216	723,000
Yoshinori Ichioka	72	75	69	216	723,000

Fancl Classic

Susono Country Club, Shizuoka
Par 36-36–72; 6,851 yards

August 17-19
purse, ¥60,000,000

	SCORES			TOTAL	MONEY
Kiyoshi Murota	66	70	68	204	¥15,000,000
Motomasa Aoki	70	66	69	205	6,900,000
Noboru Fujiike	70	67	69	206	3,900,000
Yoshitaka Yamamoto	72	67	69	208	2,700,000
Tsuneyuki Nakajima	70	65	74	209	2,250,000
Teruo Nakamura	69	71	69	209	2,250,000
Hajime Meshiai	70	71	69	210	1,800,000
Shinji Kuraoka	70	71	70	211	1,410,000
Takashi Miyoshi	73	68	70	211	1,410,000
Toyotake Nakao	72	71	69	212	1,230,000
Hiroshi Makino	73	71	68	212	1,230,000
Minoru Hatsumi	72	69	72	213	1,140,000
Takaaki Fukuzawa	75	66	73	214	990,000
Teruyasu Hayashi	74	68	72	214	990,000
Koji Okuno	68	75	71	214	990,000
Yoshimi Niizeki	74	70	70	214	990,000
Shuichi Sano	67	72	76	215	633,000
Takanori Sekura	67	73	75	215	633,000
Gohei Sato	68	72	75	215	633,000
Hiromi Ogino	71	71	73	215	633,000
Takeru Shibata	70	74	71	215	633,000
Tsukasa Watanabe	73	71	71	215	633,000
Dragon Taki	73	71	71	215	633,000
Hideto Shigenobu	76	69	70	215	633,000
Nobumitsu Yuhara	74	72	69	215	633,000
Yasuo Sone	76	70	69	215	633,000

Big Raisac Senior Open

Big Raisac Country Club, Miyagi
Par 36-36–72; 7,104 yards

September 6-8
purse, ¥30,000,000

	SCORES			TOTAL	MONEY
Masahiro Kuramoto	70	69	68	207	¥5,400,000
Minoru Hatsumi	73	67	71	211	2,700,000
Takashi Miyoshi	74	69	69	212	1,575,000
Yoshio Fumiyama	70	69	73	212	1,575,000
David Ishii	70	72	71	213	1,206,000
Shinji Kuraoka	76	70	68	214	960,000
Seiji Ebihara	72	73	69	214	960,000
Kinpachi Yoshimura	71	73	70	214	960,000
Kikuo Arai	73	71	71	215	744,000
Tsukasa Watanabe	73	70	73	216	634,500
Noboru Fujiike	73	73	70	216	634,500
Takaaki Fukuzawa	77	69	71	217	555,000
Katsunari Takahashi	73	71	73	217	555,000
Kazuo Kanayama	70	73	74	217	555,000
Fumio Tanaka	74	74	70	218	452,100
Yukio Noguchi	75	72	71	218	452,100
Toyotake Nakao	75	73	70	218	452,100
Katsuji Hasegawa	73	73	72	218	452,100
Nobumitsu Yuhara	76	72	70	218	452,100
Yoshitaka Yamamoto	75	72	72	219	429,000

	SCORES	TOTAL	MONEY
Toru Nakamura	75 71 73	219	429,000
Yurio Akitomi	71 73 75	219	429,000

Japan PGA Senior Championship

Shizu Hills Country Club, Hitachiomiya, Ibaraki
Par 36-36–72; 7,013 yards

September 20-23
purse, ¥50,000,000

	SCORES				TOTAL	MONEY
Tateo Ozaki	71	69	70	70	280	¥10,000,000
Seiji Ebihara	69	72	71	70	282	3,666,666
Hajime Meshiai	71	73	67	71	282	3,666,666
Katsuyoshi Tomori	72	72	67	71	282	3,666,666
Takashi Miyoshi	72	70	71	71	284	1,750,000
Yoshio Fumiyama	68	74	68	74	284	1,750,000
Yoshitaka Yamamoto	73	72	68	73	286	1,250,000
Tsuneyuki Nakajima	70	67	72	77	286	1,250,000
Kiyoshi Murota	73	68	68	77	286	1,250,000
Tsukasa Watanabe	74	75	69	70	288	1,075,000
David Ishii	73	69	72	74	288	1,075,000
Katsunari Takahashi	74	75	68	72	289	1,000,000
Masami Ito	67	73	73	77	290	950,000
Hisashi Nakase	78	69	70	74	291	900,000
Hiroshi Makino	70	78	72	73	293	728,125
Takaaki Fukuzawa	71	74	72	76	293	728,125
Gohei Sato	73	72	70	78	293	728,125
Noboru Fujiike	74	74	67	78	293	728,125
Terry Gale	73	74	74	73	294	596,250
Hikaru Emoto	72	73	72	77	294	596,250

PGA Handa Cup Philanthrophy Senior Open

Ibaraki Golf Club, West Course, Ibaraki
Par 36-36–72; 7,004 yards

September 27-29
purse, ¥100,000,000

	SCORES			TOTAL	MONEY
Katsuyoshi Tomori	67	71	66	204	¥25,000,000
Tsukasa Watanabe	66	71	70	207	11,500,000
Takaaki Fukuzawa	71	68	69	208	5,500,000
David Ishii	69	70	69	208	5,500,000
Hajime Meshiai	67	72	71	210	4,000,000
Noboru Fujiike	74	64	73	211	3,500,000
Tsunemi Nakajima	70	72	70	212	3,000,000
Nobumitsu Yuhara	74	71	68	213	2,266,666
Katsunari Takahashi	71	72	70	213	2,266,666
Tateo Ozaki	71	72	70	213	2,266,666
Kiyoshi Murota	67	75	72	214	1,950,000
Kimpachi Yoshimura	68	71	75	214	1,950,000
Seiji Ebihara	74	72	69	215	1,700,000
Dragon Taki	76	69	70	215	1,700,000
Noboru Sugai	74	70	71	215	1,700,000
Masami Ito	69	75	72	216	1,450,000
Chen Tze-ming	71	72	73	216	1,450,000
Hideto Shigenobu	72	75	70	217	1,071,428
Yasuo Sone	70	75	72	217	1,071,428
Gohei Sato	68	76	73	217	1,071,428
Renkyoku Sugiyama	72	72	73	217	1,071,428

	SCORES			TOTAL	MONEY
Somei Sudo	71	72	74	217	1,071,428
Toyotake Nakao	72	71	74	217	1,071,428
Kikuo Arai	71	71	75	217	1,071,428

Komatsu Open

Komatsu Country Club, Ishikawa
Par 36-36—72; 6,965 yards

October 5-7
purse, ¥60,000,000

	SCORES			TOTAL	MONEY
Toyotake Nakao	68	72	67	207	¥12,000,000
Kiyoshi Murota	71	70	69	210	5,700,000
Teruo Nakamura	69	72	70	211	4,020,000
Tsukasa Watanabe	72	72	69	213	2,730,000
Somei Sudo	72	72	71	215	2,175,000
David Ishii	72	71	72	215	2,175,000
Seiji Ebihara	73	76	67	216	1,457,400
Nobumitsu Yuhara	75	69	72	216	1,457,400
Katsunari Takahashi	70	73	73	216	1,457,400
Tsuneyuki Nakajima	72	71	73	216	1,457,400
Koji Okuno	72	70	74	216	1,457,400
Isao Aoki	74	72	71	217	1,100,000
Tadashige Kusano	72	74	71	217	1,100,000
Tateo Ozaki	74	69	74	217	1,100,000
Kimpachi Yoshimura	69	77	72	218	888,000
Katsuyoshi Tomori	74	72	72	218	888,000
Tsunemi Nakajima	75	71	72	218	888,000
Takaaki Fukuzawa	74	75	70	219	711,000
Hideto Shigenobu	72	75	72	219	711,000
Dragon Taki	73	74	72	219	711,000
Yoshitaka Yamamoto	71	74	74	219	711,000
Gohei Sato	73	71	75	219	711,000

Japan Senior Open

Kumamoto Chuo Country Club, Kikuchi, Kumamoto
Par 36-36—72; 6,965 yards

October 25-28
purse, ¥80,000,000

	SCORES				TOTAL	MONEY
Isao Aoki	72	69	70	65	276	¥16,000,000
Kiyoshi Murota	66	68	71	72	277	8,800,000
Tateo Ozaki	73	71	65	69	278	6,160,000
Hajime Meshiai	68	71	70	71	280	4,000,000
Katsunari Takahashi	69	69	69	74	281	3,360,000
Kimpachi Yoshimura	71	69	71	71	282	2,600,000
Tsuneyuki Nakajima	71	73	70	68	282	2,600,000
Taisei Inagaki	74	68	71	70	283	1,920,000
Nobumitsu Yuhara	73	70	70	70	283	1,920,000
Katsuyoshi Tomori	74	69	68	73	284	1,460,000
Seiji Ebihara	73	70	70	71	284	1,460,000
Minoru Hatsumi	71	71	70	74	286	1,038,400
Hikaru Emoto	75	73	66	72	286	1,038,400
Takaaki Fukuzawa	73	73	69	71	286	1,038,400
Noboru Fujiike	71	72	73	70	286	1,038,400
Yukio Noguchi	70	73	74	69	286	1,038,400
Toshihiko Otsuka	72	68	75	72	287	820,000
David Ishii	75	68	72	72	287	820,000

	SCORES			TOTAL	MONEY
Toyotake Nakao	71	71	74	72	288	681,142
Gohei Sato	72	71	73	72	288	681,142
Yoshio Fumiyama	74	71	71	72	288	681,142
Terry Gale	75	71	70	72	288	681,142
Chen Tze-ming	75	70	73	70	288	681,142
Shinji Kuraoka	76	72	70	70	288	681,142
Teruyasu Hayashi	72	72	75	69	288	681,142

Kinojyo Senior Open

Kinojyo Golf Club, Okayama
Par 36-36–72; 6,869 yards

November 9-11
purse, ¥25,000,000

	SCORES			TOTAL	MONEY
Chip Beck	72	66	69	207	¥4,500,000
Katsunari Takahashi	70	70	67	207	2,250,000
(Beck defeated Takahashi on first playoff hole.)					
Tsukasa Watanabe	66	69	73	208	1,437,500
Isao Aoki	68	69	71	208	1,437,500
Yoshitaka Yamamoto	67	71	71	209	1,125,000
Kimpachi Yoshimura	70	69	71	210	937,500
Tadami Ueno	72	68	70	210	937,500
Minoru Hatsumi	70	65	76	211	637,500
Gohei Sato	66	70	75	211	637,500
Shinji Kuraoka	69	71	71	211	637,500
Chen Tze-ming	72	69	70	211	637,500
Yoshio Fumiyama	65	74	73	212	437,500
Takashi Miyoshi	72	67	73	212	437,500
Hajime Meshiai	71	70	71	212	437,500
David Ishii	70	72	70	212	437,500
Nobumitsu Yuhara	69	67	77	213	304,285
Somei Sudo	70	70	73	213	304,285
Tateo Ozaki	68	74	71	213	304,285
Hiroshi Makino	69	73	71	213	304,285
Takeru Shibata	71	71	71	213	304,285
Seiji Ebihara	73	69	71	213	304,285
Kazuki Nagao	73	70	70	213	304,285